KU-539-923

POOLE'S INDEX

TO

PERIODICAL LITERATURE

FOURTH SUPPLEMENT

From January 1 1897 to January 1 1902

BY

WILLIAM I. FLETCHER, A. M.
LIBRARIAN OF AMHERST COLLEGE

AND

MARY POOLE
FORMERLY OF THE NEWBERRY LIBRARY CHICAGO

WITH THE COÖPERATION OF THE AMERICAN LIBRARY ASSOCIATION

UNIVERSITY OF WOLVERHAMPTON
LEARNING & INFORMATION
SERVICES
PART OF

ACC. NO. 2467732	CLASS
CONTROL NO	016
DATE 3 JUL 2009	SITE WV	POO

GLOUCESTER, MASS.
PETER SMITH
1963

Copyright, 1903,
By WILLIAM I. FLETCHER AND MARY POOLE.

REPRINTED 1938; 1958; 1963

PRINTED IN THE UNITED STATES OF AMERICA

PREFACE.

THIS fourth five-year supplement closes a period of twenty years since the publication in 1882 of the main volume. In that volume and the four supplements 427 different periodicals have been indexed, with a total of 10,881 volumes. The five volumes contain 3,677 pages, with references to about 520,000 articles.

The present supplement, it will be observed, includes 170 different periodicals out of the 427 which have been indexed from first to last. The rest have ceased to be. The following tabular statement is interesting as showing the vicissitudes of the life of periodicals : —

Sets numbered.	Started in.	Present Survivors.
1–100	1802–45	15
101–200	1845–70	25
201–300	1871–85	42
301–400	1886–95	63
401–427	1895–1901	20

The Chronological Conspectus prefixed to each volume furnishes interesting and suggestive details.

To correct misapprehensions as to the plan and method of this Index it seems advisable to reprint here the following passage from the Preface to the 1882 edition : —

The work is an index to subjects and not to writers, except when writers are treated as subjects. The contributions of Lord Macaulay to the *Edinburgh Review* do not appear under his name, but under the subjects upon which he wrote, as Bacon, Church and State, Clive, Machiavelli, etc. His name, however, appears with many references ; but they are all subject-references, which treat of him as a man, a writer, a historian, and a statesman. Critical articles on poetry, the drama, and prose fiction appear under the name of the writer whose work or works are criticised. A review of " Enoch Arden " will be found under Tennyson, and of " Ivanhoe " under Scott ; but a review of Froude's History of England will appear only under England, as England is the subject. A poem, a play, a story, or a sketch which can be said to have no subject appears under its own title. The name of writer when known is given within parentheses. Hawthorne's " Celestial Railroad " first appeared in a periodical, and is indexed " Celestial Railroad (N. Hawthorne)." A review of the same, by a writer who is known, would be indexed, " Hawthorne, Nathaniel. Celestial Railroad (J. Smith)." By this method all criticisms of Hawthorne's imaginative writings are brought together under his name ; but the review of a biographical work of his is placed under the subject of the biography.

It has always seemed very desirable that the Index should contain entries under the names of the writers of the articles. This feature is included in the Annual Literary Index, whose successive issues furnish the material from which these supplements are principally made up. But such entries added to those now included would nearly double the amount of matter and the consequent size and cost of the volumes, which consideration is simply prohibitive from a commercial point of view, as the sales but little more than cover the cost of printing as it is. If this were not so, there would be grave questions as to keeping the work, with its bulk so increased, within due limits of convenience and handiness of use.

Another paragraph from the Preface to the 1882 volume seems worth reprinting after a score of years : —

Another difficulty which required heroic treatment has grown out of the absurd practice in many periodicals of breaking the continuity in the numbering of volumes by starting *new series*. The *Eclectic Review* has seven *new series*, and these series are not numbered. The *St. James's Magazine* began with numbering consecutively twenty-one volumes ; then occurred a *new series* of fourteen volumes ; then a second *new series* of four volumes ; then consecutive numbering from the beginning was adopted, and the next volume was numbered thirty-one when it should have been forty, — leaving out nine volumes. In cases like these, what appears on the title-pages has been wholly ignored, and the volumes have been numbered consecutively from the beginning. As a general rule, series have not been regarded, and sets have been numbered consecutively ; although in a few instances, and for special reasons, the rule has been varied from.

The difficulty here referred to has not abated since these words were printed, and "modern instances" as grievous as those cited above might be given. In fact, under the present well-recognized tendency of periodical publishing, as of book-publishing too, to trim sails constantly to catch every possible fickle breeze of public favor ("raising the wind" being after all the most prominent object in view), the changes in form, style, frequency of publication, arrangement of volumes, and other important particulars, are such as to be fairly distracting to those who attempt either to make or to use such a guide as this Index aims to be.

The makers find no way to bring anything like good order out of this confusion, and the users must do the best they can, biding their time until the publishers shall catch something of the temper of steadiness and dignity which characterizes such periodicals as the *Edinburgh Review*, which has rounded out a full century of issue without a change, even the color of the cover remaining the same all the time ; or our own *Atlantic Monthly, facile princeps* among American periodicals, whose forty-five years of publication have been marked by no aberration from such a straight course as that of the *Edinburgh Review*, except the very pardonable one of having a cut of the United States flag on its front cover during the Civil War ! Honorable mention might be made of other notable exceptions to the rule of disorder, but these must suffice to point our moral.

Great as are the sins of periodical makers, it remains true that, in the language of still another citation from the Preface of 1882, —

Every question in literature, religion, politics, social science, political economy, and in many other lines of human progress, finds its latest and freshest interpretation in the current periodicals. No one can thoroughly investigate any of these questions without knowing what the periodicals have said and are saying concerning them.

In these words, which give the *raison d'être* of Poole's Index as conceived by its founder, we have a hint of its usefulness in the past, the continuance of which, depending so largely as it does on the work being kept up to date, furnishes the occasion for the present issue and at the same time the sufficient reward of its compilers and their collaborators.

W. I. F.
M. P.

AMHERST COLLEGE LIBRARY, November 26, 1902.

COLLABORATORS.

Wm. I. Fletcher, Editor . . . . Librarian Amherst College, Amherst, Mass.
Mary Poole,   "   . . . . Brookline, Mass.

Grace Ashley . . . . Assistant City Library, Springfield, Mass.
Willard Austen . . . . Assistant Librarian Cornell University, Ithaca, N. Y.
James Bain, Jr. . . . . Librarian Public Library, Toronto, Ont.
Walter S. Biscoe . . . . Librarian [Catalog Dept.] State Library, Albany, N. Y.
Caroline A. Blanchard . . . . Librarian Tufts Library, Weymouth, Mass.
Alice B. Borden . . . . . . : . . . . Assistant Public Library, Providence, R. I.
Isaac S. Bradley . . . . Librarian State Historical Society, Madison, Wis.
Arthur N. Brown . . . . Librarian U. S. Naval Academy, Annapolis, Md.
Charles H. Burr . . . . Librarian Williams College, Williamstown, Mass.
F. C. Bursch . . . . Assistant Y. M. C. A. Library, N. Y. City.
Edith M. Chase . . . . Office Associated Charities, Boston, Mass.
Mary W. Clark . . . . Assistant Harvard College Library, Cambridge, Mass.
T. Franklin Currier . . . . Assistant Harvard College Library, Cambridge, Mass.
John F. Davies . . : . . . . Librarian University of Montana, Missoula, Mont.
Raymond C. Davis . . . . Librarian University of Michigan, Ann Arbor, Mich.
May C. Essex . . . . Assistant Public Library, Providence, R. I.
Mabel A. Farr . . . . Librarian Adelphi College, Brooklyn, N. Y.
Ida F. Farrar . . . . Assistant City Library, Springfield, Mass.
Frederick W. Faxon . . . . Boston Book Co., Boston, Mass.
George L. Fox . . . . Rector Hopkins Grammar School, New Haven, Conn.
Ethel Garvin . . . . Assistant Public Library, Providence, R. I.
William D. Goddard . . . . Assistant Library of Congress, Washington, D. C.
Jessie M. Harwood . . . . Assistant City Library, Springfield, Mass.
William C. Hawks . . . . Assistant Librarian Hartford Theological Seminary, Hartford, Conn.
Caroline M. Hewins . . . . Librarian Public Library, Hartford, Conn.
William J. James . . . . Librarian Wesleyan University, Middletown, Conn.
Ellen F. Knowles . . . . Assistant Boston Athenæum, Boston, Mass.
William C. Lane . . . . Librarian Harvard College, Cambridge, Mass.
Joseph D. Layman . . . . Assistant Librarian University of California, Berkeley, Cal.
George T. Little . . . . Librarian Bowdoin College, Brunswick, Me.
Mary Medlicott . . . . Reference Librarian City Library, Springfield, Mass.
A. Louise Morton . . . . Assistant City Library, Springfield, Mass.
C. Alex. Nelson . . . . Reference Librarian Columbia University Library, N. Y. City.
Mary O. Nutting . . . . Librarian emeritus Mt. Holyoke College, South Hadley, Mass.
Helen P. Odell . . . . Assistant Y. M. C. A. Library, Brooklyn, N. Y.
Flora R. Petrie . . . . Assistant Y. M. C. A. Library, N. Y. City.
Franklin O. Poole . . . . Assistant Boston Athenæum, Boston, Mass.
Annie Prescott . . . . Librarian Public Library, Auburn, Me.
Josephine A. Rathbone . . . . Assistant Pratt Institute, Brooklyn, N. Y.
Mabel F. Reid . . . . Assistant Y. M. C. A. Library, N. Y. City.
Adelaide Richardson . . . . Assistant Amherst College Library, Amherst, Mass.
Abbie L. Sargent . . . . Assistant Public Library, Medford, Mass.
Mary E. Sargent . . . . Librarian Public Library, Medford, Mass.
Alice Shepard . . . . Assistant Librarian City Library, Springfield, Mass.
Thomas H. Smith . . . . Chief Cataloguer Public Library, New Haven, Conn.
Walter M. Smith . . . . Librarian University of Wisconsin, Madison, Wis.
Willis K. Stetson . . . . Librarian Public Library, New Haven, Conn.
Ida M. Taylor . . . . Assistant City Library, Springfield, Mass.
Mary S. Terwilliger . . . . Assistant Public Library, Worcester, Mass.
William H. Tillinghast . . . . . Assistant Librarian Harvard College Library, Cambridge, Mass.
Mary L. Titcomb . . . . Librarian Free Library, Rutland, Vt.
Percy H. Tufts . . . . Assistant Harvard College Library, Cambridge, Mass.
Agnes Van Valkenburgh . . . . Assistant Public Library, Milwaukee, Wis.
Carrie W. Whitney . . . . Librarian Public Library, Kansas City, Mo.
Solon F. Whitney . . . . Librarian Public Library, Watertown, Mass.
Harriet B. Winsor . . . . Assistant City Library, Springfield, Mass.
Eleanor B. Woodruff . . . . Assistant Pratt Institute, Brooklyn, N. Y.
Elizabeth A. Young . . . . Assistant Public Library, Chicago, Ill.

Note. The addresses given are those good at the time of collaboration. Some are since changed.

Abbreviation.	Number in Chronological Conspectus.	Title.	Published.	Dates.	Number of Volumes.
Acad.	255	ACADEMY	London	1897–1901	10
Amer. Anthropol.	422	AMERICAN ANTHROPOLOGIST	Chicago	1899–1901	3
Am. Antiq.	260	AMERICAN ANTIQUARIAN	Chicago	1897–1901	5
Am. Arch.	217	AMERICAN ARCHITECT AND BUILDING NEWS	Boston	1897–1901	20
Am. Cath. Q.	218	AMERICAN CATHOLIC QUARTERLY	Philadelphia	1897–1901	5
Am. Econ. Assoc.	304	AMERICAN ECONOMIC ASSOCIATION PUBLICATIONS	New York	1897–1901	4
Am. Hist. R.	406	AMERICAN HISTORICAL REVIEW	New York	1897–1901	5
Am. J. Archæol.	286	AMERICAN JOURNAL OF ARCHÆOLOGY	Princeton, N. J.	1897–1901	5
Am. J. Philol.	246	AMERICAN JOURNAL OF PHILOLOGY	Baltimore	1897–1901	5
Am. J. Psychol.	314	AMERICAN JOURNAL OF PSYCHOLOGY	Worcester	1897–1901	5
Am. J. Sci.	17	AMERICAN JOURNAL OF SCIENCE	New Haven	1897–1901	10
Am. J. Soc. Sci.	188	[AMERICAN] JOURNAL OF SOCIAL SCIENCE	Boston	1897–1901	5
Am. J. Sociol.	405	AMERICAN JOURNAL OF SOCIOLOGY	Chicago	1897–1901	5
Am. J. Theol.	418	AMERICAN JOURNAL OF THEOLOGY	Chicago	1897–1901	5
Am. Law R.	171	AMERICAN LAW REVIEW	St. Louis	1897–1901	5
Am. Natural.	172	AMERICAN NATURALIST	Philadelphia	1897–1901	5
Am. Statis. Assoc.	313	AMERICAN STATISTICAL ASSOCIATION PUBLICATIONS	Boston	1897–1901	3
Ann. Am. Acad. Pol. Sci.	323	ANNALS OF THE AMERICAN ACADEMY OF POLITICAL SCIENCE	Philadelphia	1897–1901	10
Anthrop. J.	202	ANTHROPOLOGICAL INSTITUTE, JOURNAL OF	London	1897–1900	4
Antiq. n. s.	208	ANTIQUARY [NEW SERIES]	London	1897–1901	5
Archæol.		ARCHÆOLOGIA	London	1883–1900	12
Archit. Rec.	367	ARCHITECTURAL RECORD	New York	1897–1900	5
Archit. R.	415	ARCHITECTURAL REVIEW	London	1897–1901	5
Arena	324	ARENA	Boston	1897–1901	10
Argosy	165	ARGOSY	London	1897–1901	14
Art J.	112	ART JOURNAL	London	1897–1901	5
Artist (N. Y.)	419	ARTIST [NEW YORK EDITION]	New York	1898–1901	10
Asia. R.	292	ASIATIC QUARTERLY REVIEW [later, IMPERIAL AND ASIATIC QUAR. REV.]	London	1897–1901	10
Ath.	261	ATHENÆUM	London	1897–1901	10
Atlan.	131	ATLANTIC MONTHLY	Boston	1897–1901	10
Bank. M. (Lond.)	85	BANKERS' MAGAZINE	London	1897–1901	10
Bank. M. (N. Y.)	104	BANKERS' MAGAZINE	New York	1897–1901	10

Abbrev.	No.	Title	Place	Dates	No.
Belgra.	174	BELGRAVIA	London	1897–1899	8
Bib. World	373	BIBLICAL WORLD	Chicago	1897–1901	10
Bib. Sac.	86	BIBLIOTHECA SACRA	Oberlin, O.	1897–1901	5
Blackw.	13	BLACKWOOD'S EDINBURGH MAGAZINE	Edinburgh	1897–1901	10
Bk. Buyer	343	BOOK BUYER	New York	1897–1901	10
Bookman	396	BOOKMAN	New York	1897–1901	10
Bk. News	340	BOOK NEWS	Philadelphia	1897–1901	5
Book R.	389	BOOK REVIEWS	New York	1897–1898	2
Brush & P.	420	BRUSH AND PENCIL	Chicago	1898–1901	8
Canad. M.	376	CANADIAN MAGAZINE	Toronto	1897–1901	10
Cassier	358	CASSIER'S MAGAZINE	London and New York	1897–1901	10
Cath. World	160	CATHOLIC WORLD	New York	1897–1901	10
Cent.	263	CENTURY	New York	1897–1901	10
Chamb. J.	89	CHAMBERS'S JOURNAL	Edinburgh	1897–1901	5
Char.	427	CHARITIES	New York	1901–	2
Char. R.	370	CHARITIES REVIEW	New York	1897–1901	5
Chaut.	307	CHAUTAUQUAN	Meadville, Pa.	1897–1901	10
Chr. Lit.	386	CHRISTIAN LITERATURE	New York	1897–	1
Church Q.	256	CHURCH QUARTERLY REVIEW	London	1897–1901	10
Citizen	404	CITIZEN	Philadelphia	1897–1898	3
Conserv. R.	421	CONSERVATIVE REVIEW	Washington	1899–1901	4
Contemp.	166	CONTEMPORARY REVIEW	London	1897–1901	10
Cornh.	138	CORNHILL MAGAZINE	London	1897–1901	10
Cosmopol.	300	COSMOPOLITAN MAGAZINE	New York	1897–1901	10
Critic	265	CRITIC	New York	1897–1901	10
Crit. R.	354	CRITICAL REVIEW	Edinburgh	1897–1901	10
Dial (Ch.)	230	DIAL	Chicago	1897–1901	5
Dub. R.	64	DUBLIN REVIEW	London	1897–1901	10
Ecl. M.	90	ECLECTIC MAGAZINE	New York	1897–1901	10
Econ. J.	329	ECONOMIC JOURNAL	London	1897–1901	5
Econ. R.	355	ECONOMIC REVIEW	London	1897–1901	5
Econ. Stud.	497	ECONOMIC STUDIES	Baltimore	1897–1899	3
Ed. R.	1	EDINBURGH REVIEW	Edinburgh	1897–1901	10
Educa.	232	EDUCATION	Boston	1897–1901	5
Educa. R.	334	EDUCATIONAL REVIEW	New York	1897–1901	10
Engin. M.	330	ENGINEERING MAGAZINE	New York	1897–1901	10
Eng. Hist. R.	290	ENGLISH HISTORICAL REVIEW	London	1897–1901	5
Eng. Illus.	279	ENGLISH ILLUSTRATED MAGAZINE	London	1897–1899	6

Abbreviation.	Number in Chronological Conspectus	Title.	Published.	Dates.	Number of Volumes.
Expos.	417	Expositor	New York	1897–1901	10
Folk-Lore	351	Folk-Lore	London	1897–1901	5
Fortn.	161	Fortnightly Review	London	1897–1901	10
Forum	291	Forum	New York	1897–1901	10
Garden & F.	362	Garden and Forest	New York	1897.	1
Gent. M. n. s.	183	Gentleman's Magazine [New Series]	London	1897–1901	10
Geog. J.	374	Geographical Journal	London	1897–1901	10
Good Words	139	Good Words	London	1897–1901	5
Green Bag	316	Green Bag	Boston	1897–1901	5
Gunton's M.	400	Gunton's Magazine	New York	1897–1901	10
Harper	116	Harper's Magazine	New York	1897–1901	10
Harv. Grad. M.	378	Harvard Graduates' Magazine	Cambridge, Mass.	1897–1901	5
Idler	363	Idler	London	1897–1901	10
Indep.	360	Independent	New York	1897–1901	5
Int. J. Ethics	326	International Journal of Ethics	Philadelphia	1897–1901	5
Internat. Mo.	423	International Monthly	Burlington, Vt.	1900–1901	4
Jew. Q.	349	Jewish Quarterly Review	London	1897–1901	5
J. H. Univ. Studies	273	Johns Hopkins University Studies in History, etc.	Baltimore	1897–1901	5
J. Am. Folk-Lore.	341	Journal of American Folk-Lore	Boston	1897–1901	5
J. Bib. Lit.	297	Journal of Biblical Literature	Boston	1897–1901	5
J. Frankl. Inst.	33	Journal of the Franklin Institute	Philadelphia	1897–1901	10
J. Hel. Stud.	296	Journal of Hellenic Studies	London	1897–1901	5
J. Mil. Serv. Inst.	408	Journal of the Military Service Institution	Governor's Island, N. Y.	1879–1901	29
J. Pol. Econ.	379	Journal of Political Economy	Chicago	1897–1901	5
J. Soc. Arts.	294	Journal of the Society of Arts	London	1897–1901	5
J. Statis. Soc.	73	Journal of the Royal Statistical Society.	London	1897–1901	5
Jurid. R.	350	Juridical Review	Edinburgh	1897–1901	5
Knowl.	268	Knowledge	London	1897–1901	5
Law Q.	344	Law Quarterly Review	London	1897–1901	5
Library	409	Library	London	1889–1901	11
Lib. J.	226	Library Journal	New York	1897–1901	5
Lippinc.	184	Lippincott's Magazine	Philadelphia	1897–1901	10
Lit. W. (Bost.)	257	Literary World	Boston	1897–1901	5
Liv. Age	91	Littell's Living Age	Boston	1897–1901	20
Lond. Q.	120	London Quarterly Review	London	1897–1901	10

Abbrev.	Page	Title	Imprint	Dates	No.
Longm.	272	Longman's Magazine	London	1897–1901	10
Luth. Q.	200	Lutheran Quarterly	Gettysburg, Pa.	1897–1901	5
McClure	387	McClure's Magazine	New York	1897–1901	10
Macmil.	140	Macmillan's Magazine	London	1897–1901	10
M. of Art	337	Magazine of Art (Cassell's)	London	1897–1901	5
Mast. in Art	425	Masters in Art	Boston	1900–1901	2
Meth. R.	78	Methodist Review	New York	1897–1901	5
Midland	414	Midland Monthly	Chicago	1897–1899	5
Mind	219	Mind	London	1897–1901	5
Monist.	331	Monist	Chicago	1897–1901	5
Month.	157	Month	London	1897–1901	10
Monthly R.	424	Monthly Review	London	1900–1901	5
Munsey	353	Munsey's Magazine	New York	1897–1901	10
Music	356	Music	Chicago	1897–1901	10
Nation	163	Nation	New York	1897–1901	10
Nat. Geog. M.	318	National Geographic Magazine	Washington	1897–1901	5
Nat'l M. (Bost.)	403	National Magazine	Boston	1897–1901	10
National	276	National Review	London	1897–1901	10
Nat. Sci.	364	Natural Science	London	1897–1898	4
Nature	194	Nature	London	1897–1901	10
N. Church R.	391	New Church Review	Boston	1897–1901	5
New Eng. M. n. s.	299	New England Magazine [New Series]	Boston	1897–1901	10
N. E. Reg.	106	New England Historical and Genealogical Register	Boston	1897–1901	5
New R.	319	New Review	London	1897–	2
New World	369	New World	Boston	1897–1900	4
19th Cent.	222	Nineteenth Century	London	1897–1901	10
No. Am.	12	North American Review	New York	1897–1901	10
Open Court	345	Open Court	Chicago	1897–1901	5
Our Day	315	Our Day	Boston	1897–	1
Outing	305	Outing	New York	1897–1901	10
Outl.	375	Outlook	New York	1897–1901	15
Overland, n. s.	186	Overland Monthly [New Series]	San Francisco	1897–1901	10
Pall Mall M.	413	Pall Mall Magazine	London	1897–1901	15
Pedagog. Sem.	332	Pedagogical Seminary	Worcester	1897–1901	5
Pennsyl. M.	223	Pennsylvania Magazine of History	Philadelphia	1897–1901	5
Philos. R.	368	Philosophical Review	Boston	1897–1901	5
Poet-Lore	328	Poet-Lore	Boston	1897–1901	5
Pol. Sci. Q.	289	Political Science Quarterly	New York	1897–1901	5

Abbreviation.	Number in Chronological Conspectus.	Title.	Published.	Dates.	Number of Volumes.
Pop. Astron.	393	POPULAR ASTRONOMY	Northfield, Minn.	1897–1901	5
Pop. Sci. Mo.	206	POPULAR SCIENCE MONTHLY	New York	1897–1901	10
Presb. and Ref. R.	327	PRESBYTERIAN AND REFORMED REVIEW	New York	1897–1901	5
Psychol. R.	392	PSYCHOLOGICAL REVIEW	New York	1897–1901	5
Pub. Lib.	411	PUBLIC LIBRARIES	Chicago	1896–1901	6
Pub. Opin.	302	PUBLIC OPINION	New York	1897.	2
Q. J. Econ.	303	QUARTERLY JOURNAL OF ECONOMICS	Boston	1897–1901	5
Quar.	6	QUARTERLY REVIEW	London	1897–1901	10
Ref. Ch. R.	228	REFORMED CHURCH REVIEW	Philadelphia	1897–1901	5
Reliquary	146	RELIQUARY	London	1897–1901	5
R. of Rs. (N. Y.)	322	REVIEW OF REVIEWS	New York	1897–1901	10
Sat. R.	252	SATURDAY REVIEW	London	1897–1901	10
School R.	377	SCHOOL REVIEW	Chicago	1897–1901	5
Science, n. s.	277	SCIENCE, n. s.	New York	1897–1901	10
Sci. Prog.	388	SCIENCE PROGRESS	London	1897–1898	2
Scot. R.	274	SCOTTISH REVIEW	Paisley, Scot.	1897–1900	8
Scrib. M.	309	SCRIBNER'S MAGAZINE	New York	1897–1901	10
Sewanee	410	SEWANEE REVIEW	Sewanee, Tenn.	1893–1901	9
Spec.	253	SPECTATOR	London	1897–1901	10
Strand	412	STRAND MAGAZINE	London	1897–1899	6
Studio (Lond.)	416	STUDIO	London	1893–1897	9
Studio (Internat.)	416	STUDIO, INTERNATIONAL	New York	1897–1901	14
Sund. M.	258	SUNDAY MAGAZINE	London	1897–1901	5
Temp. Bar	148	TEMPLE BAR	London	1897–1901	15
Theatre, n. s.	240	THEATRE	London	1897.	2
Un. Serv. (Phila.)	320	UNITED SERVICE	Philadelphia	1897.	1
Un. Serv. M.	271	UNITED SERVICE MAGAZINE	London	1897–1901	10
Westm.	28	WESTMINSTER REVIEW	London	1897–1901	10
World's Work	426	WORLD'S WORK	New York	1900–1901	2
Writer	310	WRITER	Boston	1897–1901	5
Yale R.	380	YALE REVIEW	New Haven	1897–1901	5

CHRONOLOGICAL CONSPECTUS.

SETS CONTINUED FROM PREVIOUS VOLUMES OF THE INDEX.

	1	6	12	13	17	28	33	64	73	78	85	86	89	90	91	104	106	112	116	120
	Edinburgh Review.	Quarterly Review.	North American Review.	Blackwood's Magazine.	American Journal of Science.	Westminster Review.	Journal of the Franklin Institute.	Dublin Review.	Journal of the Royal Statistical Society.	Methodist Review.	Bankers' Magazine (London).	Bibliotheca Sacra.	Chambers's Journal.	Eclectic Magazine.	Littell's Living Age.	Bankers' Magazine (N.Y.).	New England Historical and Genealogical Register.	Art Journal.	Harper's Magazine.	London Quarterly Review.
1897 .	186	186	165	162	154	148	144	121	60	57	64	54	74	129	215	55	51	49	95	88
1898 .	188	188	167	164	156	150	146	123	61	58	66	55	75	131	219	57	52	50	97	90
1899 .	190	190	169	166	158	152	148	125	62	59	68	56	76	133	223	59	53	51	99	92
1900 .	192	192	171	168	160	154	150	127	63	60	70	57	77	135	227	61	54	52	101	94
1901 .	194	194	173	170	162	156	152	129	64	61	72	58	78	137	231	63	55	53	103	96

CHRONOLOGICAL CONSPECTUS. — *Continued.*

	131	138	139	140	146	148	157	160	161	163	165	166	171	172	174	183	184	186	188	194	200
	Atlantic Monthly.	Cornhill Magazine.	Good Words.	Macmillan's Magazine.	Reliquary.	Temple Bar.	Month.	Catholic World.	Fortnightly Review.	Nation.	Argosy.	Contemporary Review.	American Law Review.	American Naturalist.	Belgravia.	Gentleman's Magazine (New Series).	Lippincott's Magazine.	Overland Monthly (New Series).	[Amer.] Journal of Social Science.	Nature.	Lutheran Quarterly.
1897 .	80	76	38	76	37	112	90	65	68	65	64	72	31	31	94	59	60	30	35	56	27
1898 .	82	78	39	78	38	115	92	67	70	67	66	74	32	32	97	61	62	32	36	58	28
1899 .	84	80	40	80	39	118	94	69	72	69	69	76	33	33	99	63	64	34	37	60	29
1900 .	86	82	41	82	40	121	96	71	74	71	72	78	34	34		65	66	36	38	62	30
1901 .	88	84	42	84	41	124	98	73	76	73	76	80	35	35		67	68	38	39	64	31

CHRONOLOGICAL CONSPECTUS. — *Continued.*

	202 Journal of the Anthropological Institute.	206 Popular Science Monthly.	208 Antiquary (New Series).	217 American Architect.	218 Amer. Catholic Quarterly.	219 Mind.	222 Nineteenth Century.	223 Pennsylvania Magazine of History.	226 Library Journal.	228 Reformed Church Review.	230 Dial (Chicago).	232 Education.	240 Theatre (New Series).	246 American Journal of Philology.	252 Saturday Review.	253 Spectator.	255 Academy.	256 Church Quarterly.	257 Literary World.	258 Sunday Magazine.	260 American Antiquarian.
1897 .	26	51	33	58	22	22	42	20	22	44	23	17	39	18	84	79	52	44	28	26	19
1898 .	27	53	34	62	23	23	44	21	23	45	25	18		19	86	81	55	46	29	27	20
1899 .	28	55	35	66	24	24	46	22	24	46	27	19		20	88	83	57	48	30	28	21
1900 .	29	57	36	70	25	25	48	23	25	47	29	20		21	90	85	59	50	31	29	22
1901 .		59	37	74	26	26	50	24	26	48	31	21		22	92	87	61	52	32	30	23

CHRONOLOGICAL CONSPECTUS. — *Continued.*

	261 Athenæum.	263 Century.	265 Critic.	268 Knowledge.	271 United Service Magazine.	272 Longman's Magazine.	273 Johns Hopkins University Studies in History, etc.	274 Scottish Review.	276 National Review.	277 Science (New Series).	279 English Illustrated Magazine.	286 American Journal of Archæology.	289 Political Science Quarterly.	290 English Historical Review.	291 Forum.	292 Asiatic Review.	294 Journal of the Society of Arts.	296 Journal of Hellenic Studies.	297 Journal of Biblical Literature.	299 New England Magazine (New Series).	300 Cosmopolitan.
1897 .	1,2	32	31	20	15	30	15	30	29	6	17	N. S. 1	12	12	23	24	45	16	16	16	23
1898 .	1,2	34	33	21	16	32	12	32	31	8	19	2	13	13	25	26	46	17	17	18	25
1899 .	1,2	36	35	22	19	34	17	34	33	10	21	3	14	14	27	28	47	18	18	20	27
1900 .	1,2	38	37	23	21	36	18	36	35	12		4	15	15	29	30	48	19	19	22	29
1901 .	1,2	40	39	24	23	38	19		37	14		5	16	16	31	32	49	20	20	24	31

CHRONOLOGICAL CONSPECTUS. — *Continued.*

	303	304	305	307	309	310	313	314	315	316	318	319	320	322	323	324	326	327	328	329	330
	Quarterly Journal of Economics.	Amer. Economic Ass'n Publications.	Outing.	Chautauquan.	Scribner's Magazine.	Writer.	Amer. Statistical Association Publications.	American Journal of Psychology.	Our Day.	Green Bag.	National Geographic Magazine.	New Review.	United Service (Phila.).	Review of Reviews.	Annals of Amer. Acad. of Polit. and Soc. Science.	Arena.	Internat. Journal of Ethics.	Presbyterian and Reformed Review.	Poet-Lore.	Economic Journal.	Engineering Magazine.
1897 .	11	13	30	25	22	10	5	8	17	9	8	17	17	16	10	18	7	8	9	7	13
1898 .	12		32	27	24	11		9	†	10	9			18	12	20	8	9	10	8	15
1899 .	13		34	29	26	12	6	10		11	10			20	14	22	9	10	11	9	17
1900 .	14	14	36	31	28	13		11		12	11			22	16	24	10	11	12	10	19
1901 .	15	15	38	33	30	14	7	12		13	12			24	18	26	11	12	13	11	21

† Continued, but not indexed.

CHRONOLOGICAL CONSPECTUS. — *Continued.*

	331	332	334	337	340	341	343	344	345	349	350	351	353	354	355	356	358	360	362	363	364	367
	Monist.	Pedagogical Seminary.	Educational Review.	Magazine of Art.	Book News.	Jour. of American Folk-Lore.	Book Buyer.	Law Quarterly Review.	Open Court.	Jewish Quarterly Review.	Juridical Review.	Folk-Lore.	Munsey's Magazine.	Critical Review.	Economic Review.	Music.	Cassier's Magazine.	Independent.	Garden and Forest.	Idler.	Natural Science.	Architectural Record.
1897 .	7	4	14	21	15	10	15	13	11	9	9	8	17	7	7	12	12	49	10	11	11	6
1898 .	8	5	16	22	16	11	17	14	12	10	10	9	19	8	8	14	14	50		13	13	7
1899 .	9	6	18	23	17	12	19	15	13	11	11	10	21	9	9	16	16	51		15		8
1900 .	10	7	20	24	18	13	21	16	14	12	12	11	23	10	10	18	18	52		17		9
1901 .	11	8	22	25	19	14	23	17	15	13	13	12	25	11	11	20	20	53		19		10

CHRONOLOGICAL CONSPECTUS. — *Continued.*

	368 Philosophical Review.	369 New World.	370 Charities Review.	373 Biblical World.	374 Geographical Journal.	375 Outlook.	376 Canadian Magazine.	377 School Review.	378 Harvard Graduates' Magazine.	379 Jour. of Political Economy.	380 Yale Review.	386 Christian Literature.	387 McClure's Magazine.	388 Science Progress.	389 Book Reviews.	391 New Church Review.	392 Psychological Review.	393 Popular Astronomy.	396 Bookman.	400 Gunton's Magazine.	403 National Magazine (Boston).	404 Citizen.	405 Amer. Journal of Sociology.	406 Amer. Historical Review.	407 Economic Studies.
1897	6	6	6	10	10	57	9	5	5	5	5	16	9	6	4	4	4	4	5	13	6	2	2	2	2
1898	7	7	7	12	12	60	11	6	6	6	6		11	7	5	5	5	5	7	15	8	4	3	3	3
1899	8	8	8	14	14	63	13	7	7	7	7		13	†	6	6	6	6	9	17	10		4	4	4
1900	9	9	9	16	16	66	15	8	8	8	8		15		7	7	7	7	11	19	12		5	5	
1901	10		10*	18	18	69	17	9	9	9	9		17		8	8	8	8	13	21	14		6	6	

* Continued in combination with "Charities," No. 427.   † Continued, but not indexed.

CHRONOLOGICAL CONSPECTUS.

SETS NOW FIRST INDEXED.

	408 Journal of the Military Service Institution.	409 The Library.	410 Sewanee Review.	411 Public Libraries.	412 Strand.	413 Pall Mall Magazine.	414 Midland Monthly.	415 Architectural Review.	416 Studio [London and International].	417 Expositor.	418 Am. Journal of Theology.	419 Artist (N. Y.).	420 Brush and Pencil.	421 Conservative Review.	422 Amer. Anthropologist.	423 International Monthly.	424 Monthly Review.	425 Masters in Art.	426 World's Work.	427 Charities.
	1879–95, Vols. I–17	1889–95, Vols. I–5	1893–95, Vols. I–3						1893–97, Vols. I–9, London ed.											Continued from Charities Review, No. 370.
1896	19	6	4	I																
1897	21	7	5	2	14*	13*	8*	4*	3	1,2	I									
1898	23	8	6	3	16	16	10	5	5	4	2	23*	1,2							
1899	25	9	7	4	18	19	11	6	8	6	3	26	4	I	I					
1900	27	N.S. I	8	5	†	22		7	11	8	4	30	6	2	2	1,2	I	I		
1901	29	2	9	6		25		8	14	10	5	32	8	4	3	4	5	2	1,2	6,7*

* Previous volumes not indexed.   † Continued, but not indexed.

POOLE'S INDEX TO PERIODICAL LITERATURE

INDEX TO PERIODICAL LITERATURE.

FOURTH SUPPLEMENT,

1897-1901.

AARON

Aaron of Lincoln. (J. Jacobs) Jew. Q. **10**: 629.

Abandoned Farm, Ideal. (A. Chamberlain) New Eng. M. n. s. **16**: 473.

Abandoned Farms. (C. S. Sargent) Garden & F. **10**: 51.

Abba Father. (K. Kohler) Jew. Q. **13**: 567.

Abbadia, Château of; Two Gifts to French Science. (H. de Parville) Pop. Sci. Mo. **54**: 81.

Abbadie, Antoine d'. (E. G. Ravenstein) Geog. J. **9**: 569. — Ath. '97, **1**: 419.

Abbas Pasha, Khedive of Egypt. (F. C. Penfield) Munsey, **18**: 917. — (F. C. Penfield) Liv. Age, **223**: 595.

Abbeville, France, Quaternary Deposits at. (G. D. Du Mesnil) Am. Antiq. **21**: 137.

Abbey, Edwin Austin. (M. H. Spielman) M. of Art, **23**: 190, 193, 247.

— The Art of. (H. Strachey) Harper, **100**: 875.

— Work of, with portrait. (Mrs. A. Bell) Artist (N. Y.) **29**: 169.

Abbot, Willis J. Lit. W. (Bost.) **32**: 110.

Abbott, Charles Conrad. (E. Ingersoll) Critic, **31**: 373.

Abbott, Jacob, Books of. Lit. W. (Bost.) **28**: 241.

Abbott, Lyman, and Evolution. (T. F. Wright) N. Church R. **4**: 183.

— Christianity and Social Problems. N. Church R. **4**: 311.

Abby and John. (N. J. Wells) New Eng. M. n. s. **17**: 505.

Abduction of Prince William Henry; Adventure of General Washington. (C. Ross) Eng. Illust. **19**: 138.

Abdul Hamid, Sultan of Turkey. (Adelaide Keen) Nat'l M. (Bost.) **9**: 49. — (E. P. Lyle) Idler, **2**: 416.

— and the Concert. (Diplomaticus) Fortn. **68**: 314.

— An Interview with. (A. W. Terrell) Cent. **33**: 133.

— Private Life of, Dorys'. (J. T. Howard) Bookman, **14**: 141.

Abdur Rahman, Ameer of Afghanistan. R. of Rs. (N. Y.) **16**: 705. — (H. B. Hanna) Fortn. **76**: 760. — Quar. **193**: 151. — Good Words, **42**: 789. — Sat. R. **91**: 113. — Liv. Age, **228**: 485. — (T. E. Gordon) National, **37**: 259.

— as Commander of the Faith. (H. Newbolt) Monthly R. **5**, no. 2: 1.

— Autobiography of. Spec. **85**: 401.

— Details in my Daily Life. Monthly R. **1**, no. 1: 35.

— Instructions to his Son on visiting England. Monthly R. **4**, no. 1: 20.

Abel, Murder of. (D. W. Amram) Green Bag, **13**: 592.

Abel's Susanna. (E. C. M. Dart) Longm. **38**: 143. Same art. Liv. Age, **230**: 437.

ABSOLUTE

Abelard and Héloise. Acad. **61**: 107.

— Letters. (J. McCabe) Critic, **39**: 119.

Aberdeen, Its Literature, Bookmaking and Circulating. Library, **6**: 238, 266.

— Public Library of. (A. W. Robertson) Library, **6**: 1. — Library, **9**: 93.

— — Ventilating and Heating System of. Library, **6**: 95.

Aberdeenshire, Macdonald's Place-names of West. Ath. '01, **1**: 41.

Aberfeldy, and its Neighborhood. (H. Macmillan) Art J. **51**: 361. **52**: 12.

Abies, A Study of. (A. V. Jennings) Knowl. **21**: 282.

Ability, Distribution of British. (H. Ellis) Monthly R. **3**, no. 1: 91.

Abnaki Rug Industry. Artist (N. Y.) **24**: 1.

Abnaki Witch-Story. (M. R. Harrington) J. Am. Folk-Lore, **14**: 160.

Abner the Humbug. (F. H. Hardy) Cornh. **82**: 224. Same art. Liv. Age, **227**: 362. Same art. Ecl. M. **136**: 61.

Abner's Whale; a story. (F. T. Bullen) Cornh. **76**: 780.

About, Edmond. King of the Mountains; introd. by Lang. Sat. R. **84**: 41.

About 'Nunziata; a story. (A. Blount) Eng. Illust. **20**: 597.

Above the Gaspereau; a poem. (B. Carman) Poet-Lore, **9**: 321.

Abraham, Patriarch, and his Mother. (C. A. Powell) Nat'l M. (Bost.) **9**: 257.

— the Heir of Yahweh. (B. W. Bacon) New World, **8**: 674.

— Pledges to. A Divine Romance. (W. F. Steele) Meth. R. **58**: 213.

Abraham a Sancta Clara; an old German divine. (W. G. Field) Macmil. **78**: 122.

Abruzzi, Duke of; portrait and sketch. Outl. **66**: 310.

Abruzzi Peasantry, Customs of. (G. M. Godden) Antiq. n. s. **33**: 83, 110.

Absalom, Story of. (A. Z. Conrad) Nat'l M. (Bost.) **9**: 57.

Absaroka Range of the Rocky Mts., Arnold on. Am. Natural. **24**: 156.

Absence; a poem. (E. Gibson) Argosy, **64**: 86.

Absent-minded Beggar, The; a poem. (R. Kipling) Outl. **64**: 86.

Absolute, The, as Ethical Postulate. (J. D. Logan) Philos. R. **8**: 484.

— Conception of. (H. Halder) Philos. R. **8**:

— of Hegelianism, The. (A. K. Rogers) Mind **25**: 332.

Absolute Power, an American Institution. (S. E. Baldwin) Am. J. Soc. Sci. **35**: 1.

Aerolite at Allegan, Mich. (H. L. Ward) Am. J. Sci. 158: 412.

Aeronaut, Modern. (Jacques Boyer) Cosmopol. 32: 13.

Aeronautical Congress, International, at Strassburg, 1898. Science, n. s. 7: 846.

Aeronautics, Military. (W. A. Glassford) J. Mil. Serv. Inst. 18: 561.

Æschylus, Agamemnon, presented at Bradfield School, 1900. Ath. '00, 1: 828. — (M. Beerbohm) Sat. R. 89: 776.

— — performed at Cambridge, 1900. (M. Beerbohm) Sat. R. 90: 644.

— Inner Life of. (H. N. Fowler) Chaut. 33: 76.

— Oresteia; Warr's edition. (J. H. McDaniels) Nation, 73: 134.

— Tragedies; ed. by Campbell. Sat. R. 85: 750.

— Translation of. Spec. 85: 973.

Æsthetic, A Dash into the. (C. L. Moore) Dial (Ch.) 30: 256.

Æsthetic Forms, Mathematical Principles of. (A. Emch) Monist, 11: 50.

Æsthetic Proportion, Idea of; Influence on the Ethics of Shaftesbury. (M. F. Libby) Am. J. Psychol. 12: 485.

Æsthetics, Criticism and. (E. D. Puffer) Atlan. 87: 839.

— Esthetology. (J. W. Powell) Am. Anthrop. 1: 1.

— Foundation of. (G. H. Joyce) Am. Cath. Q. 24, no. 4: 37.

— in our Universities. (H. R. Marshall) Scrib. M. 25: 253.

— Method of. (H. Davies) Philos. R. 10: 28.

— Santayana's. (B. I. Gilman) Philos. R. 6: 401.

— Suggestions on. (E. H. Donkin) Mind, 22: 511.

— Syllabus for Study of. (O. L. Triggs) Poet-Lore, 9: 281.

Ætna Observatory. Nature, 56: 544.

Affair at the Big Spring; a story. (M. Roberts) Eng. Illust. 17: 283.

Affair of the "Blue Coats;" a tale. (P. H. Ditchfield) Belgra. 96: 340.

Affirmative Final Clauses in Latin Historians. (R. B. Steele) Am. J. Philol. 19: 255.

Afghan Legend, An. (H. Beveridge) Asia. R. 31: 322.

Afghan War of 1880, Some Episodes of the. Chamb. J. 78: 113.

Afghanistan, Abdur Rahman, Ameer of. R. of Rs. (N. Y.) 16: 705.

— and Baluchistan, Orographic Map of. (T. H. Holdich) Geog. J. 16: 527.

— and the Indian Frontier. (Sir L. Griffin and H. B. Hanna) Fortn. 76: 748.

— Borderlands of. (A. H. McMahon) Geog. J. 9: 393.

— British Army Operations in, 1878-80. (H. Gough) Pall Mall M. 15: 36, 199. 17: 268, 389, 531.

— — Future of the Anglo-Afghan Alliance. (R. Ahmad) 19th Cent. 43: 241.

— Coming Crisis in. (D. C. Boulger) Fortn. 73: 994. Same art. Liv. Age, 226: 73.

— The Key to India. (A. R. Colquhoun) Asia. R. 30: 25.

— Present Status of. (S. M. Khan) Forum, 29: 641.

— Lord Roberts in. (S. Wilkinson) National, 28: 844.

— War in, Second, An Incident in. Eng. Illust. 20: 160.

Afoot in Quiet Places. (W. H. Hudson) Sund. M. 26: 436.

Africa, Adventure in. (A. B. Koe) 19th Cent. 44: 448.

— American Interests in. (D. A. Willey) Arena, 24: 293.

— Animals of. (R. Lydekker) Knowl. 21: 137.

— Birds of, Shelley and Stark on. (R. Lydekker) Nature, 61: 516.

Africa, Black and White Rights in. (H. R. Fox Bourne) Asia. R. 25: 72. Same art. Liv. Age, 216: 283.

— Blue and White Niles. Ed. R. 190: 267.

— Books on, 1897-98. (E. Heawood) Geog. J. 12: 300.

— Britain in. (M. Selon) Asia. R. 28: 129.

— British, Morley on. Spec. 78: 499.

— Cape-to-Cairo Railway. (J. H. Knight) Engin. M. 19: 1.

— Central, and the Sultan. (S. H. Fitzjohn) Asia. R. 30: 282.

— — British and French Spheres in, Delimitation of. Geog. J. 13: 524.

— — British, Johnston's. Ath. '97, 2: 57. — Acad. 52: 144.

— — — Native Industries in. (A. Wirner) Good Words, 59: 268.

— — East, Explorations in. Nat. Geog. M. 12: 42.

— — The French in. (Ph. Salisbury) Un. Serv. M. 16: 601.

— — German Policy in. New R. 16: 223.

— — Journey from Fort Jameson to the Kafue River. (G. P. Chesnaye) Geog. J. 17: 42.

— — Journey from Zeila to Khartum. (O. T. Crosby) Geog. J. 18: 46.

— — New Conditions in. (E. J. Glave) Cent. 31: 900.

— — Notes on the Country between Lake Chiuta and the River Luli. (F. B. Pearce) Geog. J. 15: 612.

— — Nyasa and Tanganyika Districts of. (J. E. S. Moore) Geog. J. 10: 289.

— — Priority of Gt. Britain on Middle Niger. (G. T. Goldie) New R. 16: 687.

— — since the Death of Livingstone. (W. G. Blaikie) No. Am. 165: 318.

— Darkest. (P. Augonarde) Indep. 53: 659.

— Development of. (S. P. Verner) Forum, 32: 366.

— Dutch Footprints in, Early. (A. Kinnear) Chamb. J. 77: 32.

— East, Adventures in. (F. T. Pollok) Un. Serv. M. 17: 65.

— — Along the Coast of. (R. H. Davis) Scrib. M. 29: 259.

— — and South, British Communication with. (E. Cecil) 19th Cent. 49: 630.

— — British, Journey to the Summit of Mount Kenya. (H. J. Mackinder) Geog. J. 15: 453.

— — — Road-making and Surveying in. (G. E. Smith) Geog. J. 14: 269.

— — — Trade and Administration in. (E. J. Mardon) Monthly R. 3, no. 2: 72.

— — Colonization of. (P. MacQueen) Nat'l M. (Bost.) 12: 387.

— — German, Cyprus for. Un. Serv. M. 22: 357.

— — Results of the Second Bottego Expedition into. (P. L. Sclater) Science, n. s. 10: 951.

— Equatorial, Twenty-five Years' Progress in. (H. M. Stanley) Atlan. 80: 471.

— From India to South. (S. L. Clemens) McClure, 10: 3.

— From Bulawayo to the Victoria Falls. (A. Lawley) Blackw. 164: 739.

— From the Congo to the Niger. (F. A. Edwards) Gent. M. n. s. 60: 299.

— From the Congo to the Nile. (W. S. Cherry) Idler, 20: 115.

— From the Omo to the Nile. (A. D. Smith) Indep. 52: 3093.

— Grogan's Adventures in. (C. Roberts) World's Work, 1: 304.

— in 1897. (R. N. Cust) Asia. R. 24: 312.

— Lakes of, Fauna of. (J. E. S. Moore) Sci. Prog. n. s. 1: 627.

— Largest Game Preserve in the World. (J. B. Torbert) Nat. Geog. M. 11: 445.

Agnostic's Agony, The. (F. Grierson) Westm. **156**: 385.
— — Reply. Westm. **156**: 683.
Agnostic's Side, The. (R. G. Ingersoll) No. Am. **169**: 289.
Agnosticism. (J. Reed) N. Church R. **6**: 595.
— and Disguised Materialism. (A. Llano) Philos. R. **6**: 170.
— and Naturalism, Professor Ward on. (H. Spencer) Pop. Sci. Mo. **56**: 349. — (W. R. Sorley) Crit. R. **10**: 9.
— Good and Bad. Outl. **68**: 901.
— in its Relation to Modern Unitarianism. Westm. **153**: 42.
— Theological. (A. B. Bruce) Am. J. Theol. **1**: 1.
— What is? (A. W. Benn) New World, **9**: 466.
Agra, India, Imperial. (E. A. Richings) Belgra. **93**: 404.
— in 1857; Reply to Lord Roberts. (A. Colvin) 19th Cent. **41**: 556.
Agrapha, The. (B. Pick) Open Court, **11**: 525. — (J. H. Ropes) Am. J. Theol. **1**: 758.
Agricultural Census, British, The Next. (W. E. Bear) Fortn. **73**: 591.
Agricultural Chemistry. A Corner in Nature's Laboratory. (A. E. Gibson) Westm. **147**: 439.
— Recent Progress in. (H. W. Wiley) Science, n. s. **16**: 44.
Agricultural College and Experiment Stations, Association of American. (A. C. True) Science, n. s. **14**: 883.
— — Meeting at Washington, 1898. (A. C. True) Science, n. s. **8**: 761.
Agricultural Credit. European Example for American Farmers. (A. F. Weber) No. Am. **166**: 152.
Agricultural Crisis, The. (G. M. Fiamingo) Econ. J. **8**: 259.
Agricultural Demonstration and Experiment. (Wm. Somerville) Nature, **63**: 84.
Agricultural Depression in England. (Sir E. Verney) Contemp. **73**: 346. — (J. H. Hollander) Yale R. **6**: 409.
Agricultural Depression in England. (Sir E. Verney) Contemp. **75**: 99.
— — Final Report of the Royal Commission on. (E. Canaan) Econ. R. **8**: 109.
— Natural Causes of. (J. Dowd) Gunton's M. **12**: 52.
Agricultural Discontent in the United States, An Analysis of. (C. F. Emrick) Pol. Sci. Q. **12**: 93.
Agricultural Education. (C. S. Sargent) Garden & F. **10**: 61. — (F. J. Sloyd) J. Soc. Arts, **45**: 815.
— Courses of Studies. (B. D. Bogen) Educa. **22**: 89.
— for Village Children. Ath. '00, **1**: 244.
— in Foreign Countries. (W. E. De Riemer) Pop. Sci. Mo. **51**: 218.
— in Greater Britain. (R. H. Wallace) J. Soc. Arts, **48**: 325, 665.
— — in New York. (C. S. Sargent) Garden & F. **10**: 181.
— Newer Ideas in. (L. H. Bailey) Educa. R. **20**: 377.
— of Natives. (E. M. Green) Fortn. **73**: 104.
— A Significant Factor in. (K. L. Butterfield) Educa. R. **21**: 301.
Agricultural Experiment Stations. Science, n. s. **13**: 321. — (L. B. Ellis) R. of Rs. (N. Y.) **19**: 706.
Agricultural Journalist and his Field. (DeWitt C. Wing) Writer, **14**: 129.
Agricultural Laborer, The. (J. C. Medd) Econ. R. **7**: 218. — (M. Phillimore) Econ. R. **7**: 468.
— Past and Present. (M. Phillimore) Econ. R. **7**: 13.
Agricultural Laborers, Future of. Spec. **83**: 216. Same art. Liv. Age, **222**: 910.
Agricultural Progress and the Wheat Problem. (B. W. Snow) Forum, **28**: 94.

Agricultural Progress, Motives of. (Vox Clamantis) Westm. **152**: 464.
Agricultural Machinery. (G. E. Walsh) Cassier, **19**: 137.
Agricultural Returns, English, 1878. J. Statis. Soc. **62**: 387.
Agricultural Services. (P. Vinogradoff) Econ. J. **10**: 308.
Agricultural Wage in Scotland. (A. L. Bowley) J. Statis. Soc. **62**: 140.
Agriculture, American, The Future of. (S. B. Gordon and D. A. Willey) Arena, **23**: 544.
— — Status of. (G. E. Walsh) Lippinc. **61**: 368.
— Bailey's Principles of. (E. W. Morse) Science, n. s. **9**: 328.
— British, Back to the Land! (Earl Nelson) 19th Cent. **50**: 59.
— — Economic Aspects of. (J. F. Crowell) Ann. Am. Acad. Pol. Sci. **14**: 204.
— — in 19th Century. Quar. **193**: 1, 338.
— A Centennial Stock-taking. (J. Schoenhof) Forum, **27**: 605.
— Classic Legacy of. (J. Mills) Knowl. **21**: 140.
— College Courses in, Improvement of. (A. C. True) Educa. R. **19**: 169.
— Comparative Study of Statistics of 10th and 11th Census. (N. I. Stone) Am. Statis. Assoc. **6**: 290.
— County Councils and Practical Training in. (H. E. Moore) J. Soc. Arts, **45**: 819.
— Evolution of. (R. H. Wallace) Westm. **148**: 172.
— in England, The Commission on. (F. A. Channing) Fortn. **68**: 459.
— — Depression of. Spec. **79**: 205.
— — — Williams on. Sat. R. **84**: 39.
— — during the Victorian Era. (W. E. Bear) Fortn. **67**: 850.
— in Essex during the Past Fifty Years. (F. C. Danvers) J. Statis. Soc. **60**: 251.
— in the U. S. by the 12th Census. (Le G. Powers) R. of Rs. (N. Y.) **23**: 321.
— — Statistical. (Joanna R. Nicholls) Nat'l M. (Bost.) **7**: 67.
— in the West Indies. (J. P. D'Albuquerque) Nature, **63**: 356.
— Italian. (R. de Cesare) Chaut. **25**: 290.
— Microbes in. (C. M. Aikman) Ecl. M. **131**: 204.
— Recent Legislation affecting. (C. N. Johnston) Jurid. R. **13**: 55.
— Science in. (Sir E. Verney) Contemp. **79**: 181.
— Shall it perish? (W. E. Bear) National, **30**: '31.
— Text-Book of, Development of, in North America, with bibliography. Book R. **7**: 43.
— Trend of Modern, in the U. S. (G. W. Hill) Internat. Mo. **2**: 107.
— U. S. Dept. of, Appropriations for. (E. W. Allen) Science, n. s. **13**: 572.
— — Report of Secretary, 1901. Science, **14**: 954.
— — Science as a Handmaid of National Prosperity. (B. O. Flower) Arena, **26**: 650.
— University Extension in. (A. C. True) Forum, **28**: 701.
Agrippa, Tomb of; a sketch. (N. F. Davin) Canad. M. **12**: 353.
Agrippa, Heinrich Cornelius. (H. McIlquham) Westm. **154**: 303.
Aguinaldo, Emilio; a character sketch. R. of Rs. **19**: 164.
— — and the Philippine Commission. (M. Wilcox) Forum, **31**: 259.
— At Home with. (M. Bailey) Overland, n. s. **33**: 255.
— Capital of; why Malolos was chosen. (Lt.-Col. J. D. Miley) Scrib. M. **26**: 320.

Alexandria, Library of, Destruction of the. (F. J. Teggart) Nation, 67: 11.
— Pharos of. (B. I. Wheeler) Cent. 33: 898.
Alexandrian Gospel, The. (E. P. Gould) J. Bib. Lit. 19: 5.
Alfonso of Aragon: a hero king of Naples. (Lily Wolffsohn and Bettina Woodward) Gent. M. n. s. 62: 481.
Alfonso XIII. (Hannah Lynch) Good Words, 41: 172.
Alfred the Great. (J. Bryce) Indep. 53: 1534. — (L. Dyer) Atlan. 88: 1. — (E. Myers) Cornh. 84: 1. — (F. Pollock) National, 32: 266.
— and One Thousand Years of English. (A. McIlroy) Nat'l M. (Bost.) 15: 99.
— as Man of Letters. (W. H. Draper) Antiq. n. s. 36: 102, 171, 230, 301.
— Burial Place of. (W. H. Draper) Antiq. n. s. 35: 299.
— County of. (W. Greswell) Fortn. 72: 464.
— Death of. (W. H. Stevenson) Eng. Hist. R. 13: 71.
— — and Bede's Chronology. (J. H. Ramsey and others) Ath. '00, 2: 579-827. '01, 1: 18.
— The Heritage of. (W. Besant) Outl. 67: 531.
— the Idolater. Month, 98: 425.
— Legislation and Local Government of. (W. H. Draper) Green Bag, 11: 596. 12: 48.
— Millenary of, at Winchester. (L. Dyer) Cent. 40: 396. — (H. E. Platt) Temp. Bar, 124: 257. — (M. W. Sampson) Outl. 69: 460. — (F. Y. Powell) No. Am. 173: 518. — Sat. R. 92: 357. — Church Q. 53: 139. — Antiq. n. s. 37: 310.
— — Medal for. (R. C. Jackson) Westm. 156: 673.
— Permanent Influence of. (C. W. Turner) Sewanee R. 9: 473.
— The Roman Sacring of. (H. Thurston) Month, 98: 337.
Alfred Jewel, The. Antiq. n. s. 37: 212.
Alfred Memorial, The. (L. Dyer) Nation, 66: 88.
Alfred; a story. (Ellen D. Smith) Cent. 40: 399.
Algebra and Latin, Value of, in the Eighth School Year. (N. C. Dougherty) Educa. R. 17: 178.
— Elementary, Gillet's. (H. E. Slaught) School R. 5: 479.
— — Hall and Knight's. School R. 5: 554.
— for Schools and Colleges, Text-book of, Fisher and Schwatt's. (H. E. Slaught) School R. 7: 494.
— Fundamental Principles of. (A. Macfarlane) Science, n. s. 10: 345.
— Principles of the New Education applied in. (J. V. Collins) Educa. R. 15: 183.
— vs. English. (W. D. Mackintosh) Educa. 22: 28.
— Whitehead's Treatise on Universal. (Alex. Macfarlane) Science, n. s. 9: 324.
Algeria. Ed. R. 185: 110.
— Past and Present. (Sir R. Lambert-Playfair) Chamb. J. 76: 289.
Algiers. (E. S. Risser) Overland, n. s. 36: 282.
— Exmouth's Bombardment of. (Walter Wood) Gent. M. n. s. 63: 505.
Algonkian Animal-names, Signification of Certain. (A. F. Chamberlain) Am. Anthropol. 3: 669.
Algonkian Folk-lore, Items of. (A. F. Chamberlain) J. Am. Folk-Lore, 13: 271.
Algonkin Indians, Swastika and other Marks among. (W. W. Tooker) Am. Antiq. 20: 339.
Algoma, its Industrial Development. (G. Grant) Canad. M. 15: 483.
Algraphy, a Substitute for Lithography. Studio (Internat.) 2: 243.
Alhambra, The. (W. J. Reid) Nat'l M. (Bost.) 8: 415.
Al-Hariri, The Assemblies of. Asia. R. 26: 113.
Alias "Jackson;" a story. (C. L. Clarke) Canad. M. 17: 368.

Alicante, Spain. (Arthur Symons) Sat. R. 87: 265.
Aliens, Dislike for. Spec. 80: 754.
— Legislation against, in Great Britain, and the Prerogative of the Crown. (T. N. Haycraft) Law Q. 13: 165.
Alimentation, Physiology of. (A. Dastre) Chaut. 28: 460.
Aliquid Amori; a poem. (F. B. Money-Coutts) Ecl. M. 133: 69.
Alison; a story. (M. Beaumont) Idler, 14: 155.
Alkali, Caustic, Estimation of, in Presence of Alkali Carbonate. (W. E. Ridenour) J. Frankl. Inst. 152: 119.
Alkaloids, Brühl and others on. (R. Meldola) Nature, 63: 486.
All about a Hat. (Emile Faguet) Liv. Age, 226: 723.
"All the Day Idle;" a poem. (C. Burke) Argosy, 67: 466.
All for Dolly. (J. Pratt) New Eng. M. n. s. 23: 532.
All for Naught; a story. (H. G. Sargent) Pall Mall M. 16: 111.
All I know of a Certain Star. (J. Ingersoll) Atlan. 86: 562.
All in the Moonlight; a story. (N. Garston) Temp. Bar, 111: 351.
All in One Day; a story. (Percy Fitzgerald) Gent. M. n. s. 62: 521.
All my Story. (M. Maartens) Good Words, 40: 53. Same art. Liv. Age, 220: 445.
All Souls' Day in Italy. (G. D. Vecchia) Good Words, 41: 730. — (E. C. Vansittart) Antiq. n. s. 36: 325.
— in Lower Brittany. (Anatole Le Braz) Liv. Age, 212: 419.
All Souls' Eve; a story. (M. Lyall) Temp. Bar, 124: 379.
All Souls' Eve; a story. (N. Hopper) Eng. Illust. 18: 225.
Allan Gilles, Farmer and Scholar; a story. (J. Blewett) Canad. M. 10: 433.
Allan, Robert Weir, Artist, with portrait. (Mrs. Arthur Bell) Studio (Internat.) 14: 229.
"Allee Samee;" a story. (F. A. Mathews) Atlan. 88: 704.
Alleghany Mountains, Cycling across. (J. B. Carrington) Outing, 30: 132, 240, 380.
— Folklore of. (F. A. Doughty) Pop. Sci. Mo. 55: 390.
— In the Mountains. (J. C. Cady) Outl. 69: 320.
— A Nook in the. (B. Torrey) Atlan. 81: 456, 644.
Allegheny, Pa., Carnegie Free Library, Fiction in. (W. M. Stevenson) Lib. J. 22: 133.
Allegheny Observatory, New. (J. A. Brashear) Pop. Astron. 8: 541.
Allen, Alexander V. G. Christian Institutions. Church Q. 46: 347. — (T. M. Lindsay) Crit. R. 8: 187.
Allen, Charles H., First Governor of Porto Rico, with portrait. (H. Macfarland) R. of Rs. (N. Y.) 21: 563.
Allen, Charles John, Sculptor, with portrait. (E. R. Dibdin) M. of Art, 25: 15.
Allen, Ethan. (J. W. Buckham) New Eng. M. n. s. 25: 102.
Allen, Grant. (A. M. Machar) Canad. M. 17: 13. — (C. K. Shorter) Critic. 36: 38. — Acad. 56: 317. 57: 489. — (R. Le Gallienne) Fortn. 72: 1005. — Acad. 58: 547. — (Andrew Lang) Argosy, 71: 410.
— Appreciation of. (Arch. Gibbs) Sat. R. 88: 616.
Allen, Harrison, with portrait. (B. G. Wilder) Science, n. s. 7: 253.
Allen, Sir H. H., and his Scheme for Training to Arms the Youth of the Nation. (Earl of Meath) Fortn. 67: 972.

Allen, James Lane, with portrait. (H. W. Mabie)
Outl. **56**: 357. — (E. B. Brown) Atlan. **79**: 104. —
With portrait. Bk. Buyer, **20**: 351.
— Choir Invisible. Atlan. **80**: 143. — Sat. R. **84**: 19.
— Acad. **59**: 35. Same art. Liv. Age, **226**: 585.
— Country of, with portrait. (A. B. Maurice) Book-
man, **12**: 154.
— A Note on. (J. MacArthur) Bookman, **5**: 288.
— Reign of Law. Bk. Buyer, **21**: 115. — (J. B. Gil-
der) Critic, **37**: 142.
— Stories of. (L. W. Payne, jr.) Sewanee, **8**: 45.
— Summer in Arcady. Sat. R. **83**: 204.
— Works of. (E. B. Sherman) Bk. Buyer, **20**: 374.
Allen, John Davis. Macmil. **83**: 386.
Allen, Joseph Henry. (J. W. Chadwick) New World,
7: 300.
Allen, Lewis, of Watertown Farms, and his Descend-
ants. (A. H. Bent) N. E. Reg. **54**: 396.
Allen Family. (F. O. Allen) N. E. Reg. **51**: 212.
Alliances, Dual and Triple. (F. Crispi) 19th Cent. **42**:
673. Same art. Liv. Age, **215**: 645. — (F. de Pres-
sensé) 19th Cent. **42**: 869.
— of Europe, The Natural. Spec. **78**: 196.
— — Melting of. Spec. **80**: 95.
Allie Cannon's First and Last Duel; a story. (S. Mac-
Manus) Harper, **99**: 329.
Alligator, Our Florida. (I. W. Blake) Pop. Sci. Mo.
54: 330.
Alligator Eggs, Incubation of. (A. M. Reese) Am.
Natural. **35**: 193.
Alligator Hunt, A Northern Girl's. (M. P. Quay)
Outing, **35**: 447.
Alligators; the Loathly Saurian. (J. Mackie) Chamb.
J. **76**: 411.
Allingham, Mrs., Work of. (Alfred Lys Baldry) M.
of Art, **23**: 355.
Allons! a poem. (M. MackWall) Canad. M. **8**: 506.
Allotments. (J. G. H. Crespi) Good Words, **39**: 779.
Alloys. (W. C. Roberts-Austen) J. Soc. Arts, **45**:
1151, 1163, 1176. — (W. C. Roberts-Austen; T. K.
Rose) J. Soc. Arts, **49**: 846, 858.
— Microscopic Study of. Nature, **57**: 11.
Allurement of Infants. (I. Browne) Am. Law R. **31**:
891.
Alma; a study from Spencer. (C. Hope) Month, **96**:
384.
Alma-Tadema, Lawrence. (F. Dolman) Strand, **18**:
603.
— Celebration, 1899. M. of Art, **24**: 136.
— Difficult Line. Art J. **51**: 55.
Almanac of China and Central America. (J. Wickers-
ham) Am. Antiq. **19**: 61.
Almanacs, New England. (J. Albee) New Eng. M.
n. s. **17**: 545.
— Early New England. (A. R. Marble) New Eng. M.
n. s. **19**: 548.
Almodoro's Cupid; a story. (W. W. Astor) Pall Mall
M. **13**: 517.
Alms for Oblivion: a Pagan Conventicle in the 7th
Century. (R. Garnett) Cornh. **83**: 616.
Almshouse, A Virginia County. (Emily W. Dinwid-
die) Charities, **7**: 115.
Almshouses; institutional care of destitute adults. (R.
W. Hebberd) Char. R. **10**: 509, 570.
Alna, Maine. (E. A. Sawyer) New Eng. M. n. s. **24**:
594.
Alnwick Castle. (A. H. Malan) Pall Mall M. **19**: 21.
Alone; a poem. (J. Lamb) Canad. M. **10**: 422.
Alone upon the Mountain-side; a poem. (H. Bash-
ford) Outing, **33**: 569.
Along Untrodden Ways; a story. (M. A. Bacon)
Harper, **104**: 95.
Alpaca Gown, An. Sund. M. **27**: 135.

Alpena, Mich. Notes on a Michigan Lumber Town.
(R. L. Hartt) Atlan. **85**: 100.
Alphabet, Origin of. (H. N. Hutchinson) Idler, **11**: 55.
Alphabetic Writing. Meth. R. **57**: 641.
Alphabets, Artistic. M. of Art, **22**: 156.
Alpine Climbing in America. (C. E. Fay) Munsey, **24**:
809.
Alpine Posting-inn, In an. (E. Wharton) Atlan. **85**:
794.
Alpine Prelude, An; a story. (J. Ayscough) Temp.
Bar, **123**: 358, 543.
Alpine Rose. (Mrs. J. K. Hudson) Lippinc. **65**: 627.
Alpini, The. (Perrucchetti) Un. Serv. M. **17**: 156.
Alps, Accidents of the. (F. Gribble) Outing, **36**: 602.
— Adventure in, in the Days of my Youth. (K. Little)
Sund. M. **30**: 721.
— Buried. (G. A. J. Cole) Knowl. **23**: 41.
— Climbing. (A. P. Hillier) Macmil. **78**: 416.
— — Dangers of. (Harold Spender) Sat. R. **86**: 306.
— — Joys of. (Harold Spender) Sat. R. **86**: 402.
— Cycling over the. (E. R. Pennell) Cent. **33**: 837.
— A Drive in the. (M. I. McNeal) Outing, **37**: 75.
— in 1898. (R. Hughes) 19th Cent. **45**: 145. Same
art. Ecl. M. **132**: 411.
— in literature. Ecl. M. **133**: 252. Same art. Liv.
Age, **221**: 786.
— A Journey among. (B. J. Thompson) Midland, **10**:
387.
— Mountaineering in. (F. Connell) Cornh. **82**: 196.
— Mt. Blanc Group. (S. Turner) Pall Mall M. **25**:
399.
— of Dauphine, In the. [19th Cent.] Liv. Age, **224**:
780.
— Over the, in a Balloon. (C. Herbert) Strand, **18**:
175.
— Railways in. Spec. **87**: 419.
— Silence of. (F. B. Sawvel) Educa. **17**: 594.
Alsace in 1814, Chuquet's. (A. Laugel) Nation, **70**:
495.
Alsatian Highlands, A Burning Bush in. (D. W.
Clark) Meth. R. **59**: 532.
Alsea Indians of Oregon. (L. Farrand) Am. Anthrop.
3: 239.
Alston, J. Carfrae, Art Collection of. (R. Walker)
M. of Art, **24**: 193.
Alta California, Bits of. (F. E. Winslow) Outl. **64**:
797.
Altar in the Christian Church. (W. Rupp) Ref. Ch.
R. **47**: 396.
Altar of Youth. (E. Davis) New Eng. M. n. s. **16**: 752.
17: 89.
Altars, Hebrew Rock. (H. B. Greene) Bib. World,
9: 329.
Altars of Ancient English Churches. (H. W. Brewer)
Month, **89**: 162.
Alternating-current Power Work. (T. P. Gaylord)
Cassier, **20**: 327.
Alternation of Generations in Archegoniate Plants.
(W. H. Lang) Sci. Prog. **7**: 319.
Alternative Remedies, Election between. (W. H.
Griffith) Law Q. **16**: 160, 269.
Alternators, Large. (R. S. Ball, jr.) Cassier, **21**: 22.
— Parallel Operation of. (C. F. Scott) Cassier, **20**:
468.
Althaus, Franz, Sketches by. Studio (Internat.) **13**:
255.
Altitude. Herrara and Lope's Life at High Levels.
(G. B. Halsted) Science, n. s. **9**: 255.
Altruism, Modern Education and. (J. Olden) Educa.
18: 333.
Altruism, Weak Point in. Spec. **79**: 515.
Altruria in California. (M. L. Swift) Overland, n. s.
29: 643.

Alum, A Mountain of. (E. H. Parker) Chamb. J. 74: 759. Same art. Ecl. M. 130: 223.

Alumina, Separation of, from Molten Magnas. (J. H. Pratt) Am. J. Sci. 158: 227.

Aluminium. (J. A. Steinmetz) Am. Arch. 70: 12.

— and Beryllium, Separation of, by Hydrochloric Acid. (F. S. Havens) Am. J. Sci. 154: 111.

— at Paris Exposition, 1900. (J. W. Richards) J. Frankl. Inst. 151: 107.

— Electrical Conductivity of, Recent Determinations of. (J. W. Richards and J. A. Thomson) J. Frankl. Inst. 143: 195.

— Further Separations of, by Hydrochloric Acid. (F. S. Havens) Am. J. Sci. 156: 45.

— in the Arts and Mechanics. (J. A. Steinmetz) J. Frankl. Inst. 150: 272.

— Manufacture of, in Great Britain. (E. Ristori) Cassier, 16: 647.

— A Newcomer among the Metals. R. of Rs. (N. Y.) 16: 426.

— Soldering. (J. A. Steinmetz) Cassier, 19: 409.

— a Substitute for Copper. (J. Trowbridge) Indep. 52: 2501.

— Utilization of, in the Arts. (A. E. Hunt) J. Frankl. Inst. 144: 81, 171.

Aluminium Industry, Recent Progress in. (J. W. Richards) J. Frankl. Inst. 149: 451.

Alvanley, Lord. (A. I. Shand) Cornh. 76: 161. Same art. Liv. Age, 214: 831.

Alverstone, Lord, with portrait. Green Bag, 13: 459.

Amadeo di Moïse. (D. Kaufmann) Jew. Q. 11: 662.

Amagansett and Amagansetters. (L. Cleveland) Outing, 30: 587.

Amalfi, Italy. Cath. World, 72: 340.

Amalgamated Association of Iron, Steel, and Tin Workers. (C. D. Wright) Q. J. Econ. 16: 37.

Amalgamated Bill, The. (C. Warren) Scrib. M. 24: 161.

Amalgamated Society of Engineers, History of. (F. Brocklehurst) Engin. M. 21: 423.

Aman-Jean, E., Modern Portrait Painter. (G. Mourey) Studio (Lond.) 8: 197.

"Amaranth and Asphodel;" a story. (Helen F. Hetherington) Pall Mall M. 13: 162.

Amateur Architect, An; a story. (M. Armour) Argosy, 70: 388.

Amateur Buddha, An. (J. F. Fraser) Strand, 18: 304.

Amateur Professional, An; a cricketing story. Chamb. J. 75: 524.

Amateur Spirit, The. Atlan. 88: 270.

Amateurs, A Nation of [the English]. (G. C. Broderick) 19th Cent. 48: 521. — Ecl. M. 136: 247. — (H. Maxwell) 19th Cent. 48: 1051.

Amazon, A Naturalist's Experiences on the. (A. E. Pratt) Chamb. J. 76: 716.

Ambassador, The, Hobbes'. (E. E. Hale, jr.) Dial (Ch.) 26: 269.

Ambassadors, Tales of. (G. Hill) Gent. M. n. s. 67: 462.

Ambidextry; Bi-manual Training by Blackboard Drawing. (H. B. Bare) J. Soc. Arts, 48: 125. *See* Bimanual Training.

Ambler, John. (Sallie E. M. Hardy) Green Bag, 10: 12.

Ambrose, Saint. Sat. R. 90: 78.

Ambrosius, J. (H. A. Clarke) Poet-Lore, 9: 298.

Ambulance Train, Fifth Corps, 1864. (W. F. Drum) J. Mil. Serv. Inst. 11: 566.

Amecameca. (C. Cunningham) Overland, n. s. 33: 485.

Ameghino, F., Some Remarks on the Latest Publications of. (S. Roth) Am. J. Sci. 159: 261.

Amenities of Life. (Lady Battersea) Sund. M. 28: 179.

America and the European Concert. (F. E. Anderson) Arena, 20: 433.

— and Sea Power, Mahan on. (H. E. Bourne) Citizen, 4: 8.

— and the Unity of History. (W. J. Mann) Educa. 19: 348.

— as seen from Abroad. (J. J. Keane) Cath. World, 66: 721.

— Discovery of, Buddhist. (J. Fryer) Harper, 103: 251.

— — The Hiberno-Danish Predecessors of Columbus. (Mrs. M. Mulhall) Dub. R. 122: 22.

— Finance of, Essays in, American Economic Association's. (W. P. Reeves) Econ. J. 11: 60.

— Greater. (F. Emory) World's Work, 2: 1320. 3: 1513.

— Impressions of. (F. Brunetière) McClure, 10: 67.— (F. Harrison) 19th Cent. 49: 913. — (C. W. Stubbs) Outl. 65: 446.

— In Eastern: New York; Baltimore; Bryn Mawr. (F. Brunetière) Liv. Age, 216: 1.

— Integration of. Outl. 69: 482.

— Latin, Our Trade with. (F. Emory) World's Work, 2: 1101.

— The Name, is it Native or Imported? (V. B. Denslow) Gunton's M. 21: 217.

— Naming of. (G. R. Fairbanks) Sewanee, 4: 54.

— Northwestern, Baillie Grohman's Fifteen Years in. Nature, 61: 566.

— Payne's History of. (Frank Russell) Am. Hist. R. 6: 796.

— Peopling of. (S. D. Peet) Am. Antiq. 22: 229.

— Pre-Columbian. (W. S. Merrill) Cath. World, 73: 306.

— — History of, De Roo's. (H. W. H.) Am. Hist. R. 6: 799. — (E. E. Sparks) Dial (Ch.) 30: 12.

— The Real. (G. A. Gordon) Arena, 20: 558.

— Spain and France. (E. Ollivier) Cent. 34: 776.

— Warfare in. Ath. '00, 1: 655.

America — God Save the Queen: International Patriotic Air. Outl. 59: 563.

American, The, as seen by a Melancholy Dane and a Mystical Hindoo. (M. Mykilati) Poet-Lore, 11: 237, 373.

— The Bogus. (A. G. Sedgwick) Nation, 64: 429.

American; a poem. (C. C. Bonney) Open Court, 15: 705.

American Academy of Political and Social Science, Proceedings, 1901. Ann. Am. Acad. Pol. Sci. 17: 481.

American Actors, McKay and Wingate on. (A. B. McMahan) Dial (Ch.) 22: 150.

American Admirals and a Few Other Sailors. (C. S. Clarke) Un. Serv. M. 17: 595.

American Anthology, Stedman's. (T. W. Higginson) Nation, 71: 430. — (Eleanor B. Simmons) Bookman, 12: 468.

American Archæology, Progress of, from 1890 to 1899. (H. W. Haynes) Am. J. Archæol. n. s. 4: 17.

American Art, National Expression in. (W. H. Low) Internat. Mo. 3: 231.

— Progress of. (G. Kobbé) Forum, 27: 297.

American Art Association Auction Sales. Art J. 51: 54.

American Artists' Exhibition, Chicago. (F. W. Norton) Brush & P. 7: 117.

American Artists in Paris. (Vance Thompson) Cosmopol. 29: 17.

— Society of, 23d Exhibition, 1901. Artist (N. Y.) 30: xix.

American Aspirant, An. (J. B. Waterbury) Lippinc. 61: 291.

American Association for the Advancement of Science. Science, n. s. 13: 961. — (J. Ritchie, jr.) New Eng. M. 18: 639.

— Early Presidents of. (M. Benjamin) Science, n. s. 10: 625, 705, 759.

— First Half Century of. (D. S. Martin) Pop. Sci. Mo. 53: 822.

— Proper Objects of. (E. Orton) Pop. Sci. Mo. 55: 466.

— Boston Meeting, 1898. Science, n. s. 8: 269.

— — President's Address. (W. Gibbs) Science, n. s. 8: 233.

— — Chemistry at. (C. Baskerville) Science, n. s. 8: 521.

— — Geology at. (W. Upham) Science, n. s. 8: 462, 501.

— — Physics at. (N. E. Dorsey) Science, n. s. 8: 529.

— Columbus Meeting, 1899. Science, n. s. 10: 161, 265. — (G. H. Grosvenor) Nat. Geog. M. 10: 355. — Nature, 60: 515, 562. — (D. S. Martin) Pop. Sci. Mo. 55: 828.

— — Anthropology at. (W. J. McGee) Am. Anthrop. 1: 759.

— — Geology and Geography at. (A. Hollick) Science, n. s. 10: 487.

— — Physics at. (W. Hallock) Science, n. s. 10: 438.

— — Social and Economic Science at. (C. M. Woodward) Science, n. s. 10: 442.

— — Zoölogy at. (C. L. Marlatt) Science, n. s. 10: 881.

— New York Meeting, 1900. Nature, 62: 269.

— Denver Meeting, 1901. Science, n. s. 14: 233, 345. — Pop. Sci. Mo. 59: 305.

— — Anthropology. (G. G. MacCurdy) Science, n. s. 14: 717.

— — Physics Section. (E. A. Bessey) Science, n. s. 14: 585.

— — Social and Economic Science. (R. A. Pearson) Science, n. s. 14: 912.

American Bankers' Association. Bank. M. (N. Y.) 55: 57, 368, 405.

— Cleveland, O., 1899. Bank. M. (N. Y.) 59: 509.

— Trust Company of. Bank. M. (N. Y.) 59: 705.

American Banking System. Bank. M. (N. Y.) 62: 821.

American Bar Association, Address of the President. (C. Hazen; F. Manderson) Am. Law R. 34: 641.

American Belles, V. T. Peacock's. (M. G. Humphreys) Bk. Buyer, 21: 381.

American Character, Effect of Spanish War upon. (C. J. Little) Lond. Q. 91: 1.

American Chemical Society, North Carolina Section. (C. B. Williams) Science, n. s. 13: 899.

American Christianity. Which way moving? (D. A. Godsell) Meth. R. 57: 681.

American Citizenship, Pride of. (J. E. Rankin) Indep. 52: 1610.

American Colonial Agencies in England during the 18th Century. (E. P. Tanner) Pol. Sci. Q. 16: 24.

American Colonies, Dutch and Quaker, Fiske's. (J. A. Doyle) Am. Hist. R. 5: 572.

— English Common Law in, Reinsch's. (E. D. Collins) Am. Hist. R. 6: 584.

— Executive of, Prior to the Restoration. (P. L. Kaye) J. H. Univ. Stud. 18: 261.

— Schools and Education in. (A. M. Earle) Chaut. 26: 362.

American Commerce, Europe's Peril from. (G. B. Waldron) Chaut. 34: 21.

American Competition in the World's Engineering Trades: a symposium. Cassier, 19: 374.

American Democracy. (H. Münsterberg) Internat. Mo. 4. 491, 603.

American Design, The Tendency of. (R. D. Andrews) Architec. R. 4: 64.

American Dialect Society. Nation, 72: 45.

American Diplomacy. Macmil. 77: 67.

American Eagle: First English Newspaper printed in Northampton Co., Penn. (E. A. Weaver) Pennsyl. M. 23: 69.

American Economic Association at Baltimore, 1897. (J. H. Hollander) Nation, 64: 6.

— at New Haven, 1899. (J. H. Hollander) Nation, 68: 7.

— at Ithaca, 1900. (H. R. Seager) Ann. Am. Acad. Pol. Sci. 17: 304. — (F. H. Dixon) Nation, 72: 27. — (J. H. Hollander) Nation, 70: 29.

American Education, Impressions of. (D. Salmon) Educa. R. 19: 36.

American Expansion and the Inheritance of the Race. (W. L. Clowes) Fortn. 70: 884.

— Three Years of. Bank. M. (Lond.) 68: 127.

American Evolution: Dependence, Independence, Interdependence. (J. K. Hosmer) Atlan. 82: 29.

American Federation of Labor. (M. A. Aldrich) Econ. Stud. 3: 219.

American Feeling towards England. (S. E. Moffett) 19th Cent. 50: 177.

American Fiction, A Century of. Dial (Ch.) 25: 9.

American Folk-Lore Society, Memoirs of. (W. W. Newell) J. Am. Folk-Lore, 11: 67.

— Ninth Annual Meeting of. J. Am. Folk-Lore, 11: 1.

— Southern Field of. (H. M. Wiltse) J. Am. Folk-Lore, 13: 209.

American Girl, The; her Faults and her Virtues. (R. Campbell) Arena, 20: 254.

American Historical Association, The. (W. MacDonald) Nation, 70: 7.

— Report of the Historical Manuscripts Commission. (E. E. Sparks) Dial (Ch.) 24: 350.

— New Haven Meeting of, 1898. Am. Hist. R. 4: 409.

— Boston Meeting of, 1900. Am. Hist. R. 6: 413. — (W. MacDonald) Nation, 72: 26. — Am. Hist. R. 5: 423.

American History, Can it be put into all Courses in the High School? (E. C. Warriner) School R. 6: 101.

— Civil Lists for. Am. Hist. R. 2: 758.

— College Preparatory Work in. (H. B. Learned) Educa. R. 22: 397.

— in England and America. (G. G. Groat) Educa. R. 20: 184.

— in the High School Course, Place of. (H. E. Bolton) School R. 9: 516.

— Sentimental in. (E. E. Sparks) School R. 7: 536.

— Survey of, Caldwell's. (F. W. Shepardson) School R. 7: 560.

— Text-books on; Report of Committee of New England History Teachers' Association. Educa. R. 16: 480.

American Humor, Century of. (J. L. Ford) Munsey, 25: 482.

— Essence of. (C. Johnston) Atlan. 87: 195.

— Retrospect of. (W. P. Trent) Cent. 41: 45.

— A Word concerning. (J. K. Bangs) Bk. Buyer, 20: 205.

American Industry, Invasion of Europe by. (M. P. L. Beaulieu) Indep. 53: 2207.

— E. Levasseur on. Gunton's M. 12: 407.

American Institute, and the English Institution of Electrical Engineers at Paris. Nature, 62: 415.

American Institute of Architects. Constitution. Am. Arch. 61: 94.

— 31st Annual Convention. Am. Arch. 58: 14.

— 33d Convention. Am. Arch. 66: 59.

— 34th Convention. Am. Arch. 70: 91.

American Institute of Civics. (H. R. Waite) Arena, 18: 108.

American Quality. (N. S. Shaler) Internat. Mo. 4: 48.

American Republics, Our; their true lines of progress. (A. D. Anderson) R. of Rs. (N. Y.) 16: 715.

American Revolution, The. (W. D. Green) Lond. Q. 91: 323.

— Beginning of. (J. S. Bassett) Conserv. R. 2: 84.

— Coming of Peace. (W. Wilson) Harper, 104: 104.

— French Aid in. (M. D. Conway) Ath. '00, 1: 305.

— Literary History of, Tyler's. (P. L. Ford) Nation, 66: 171. — (P. L. Ford) Am. Hist. R. 3: 375. — (E. G. Bourne) Citizen, 4: 34.

— Massachusetts Soldier in. (P. Holland) New Eng. M. n. s. 20: 315.

— Memorials of. (L. D. K. Fulton) Chaut. 31: 365.

— Plundering by the British Army. Pennsyl. M. 25: 114.

— Share of Connecticut in. (J. M. Ives) New Eng. M. n. s. 20: 263.

— Story of. (H. C. Lodge) Scrib. M. 23: 1. 24: 720. — (N. Brooks) Bk. Buyer, 19: 171.

— Trevelyan's History of. (J. W. Fortescue) Macmil. 79: 468. — (W. P. Trent) Bk. Buyer, 18: 134. — (E. M. Chapman) New Eng. M. n. s. 22: 153.

American School in Jerusalem. (J. H. Thayer) Bib. World, 16: 24.

American School of Archæology in Palestine. (J. B. Nies) J. Bib. Lit. 20: 31.

American School of Classical Studies at Athens; 16th annual report. Am. J. Archæol. 12: 91.

American School of Classical Studies at Rome; 1st annual report. Am. J. Archæol. 12: 5.

— — 2d Annual Report. Am. J. Archæol. 12: 123.

American Schoolgirl, Ideals of the. (Catherine I. Dodd) National, 37: 610. Same art. Ecl. M. 137: 474.

American Schoolgirl in England, An; a story. Temp. Bar, 116: 394.

American Shipping, Our Need of Merchant Vessels. (E. T. Chamberlain) Forum, 24: 150.

American Singing-girl in Italy. (F. H. Potter) Music, 15: 541.

American Social Forces. Spec. 80: 786. Same art. Liv. Age, 218: 123.

American Society held at Phila. for Promoting Useful Knowledge. (Mrs. W. L. Verlenden) Pennsyl. M. 14: 1.

American Society of Naturalists, Meeting, 1896. Am. Natural. 31: 174.

American Spirit, The. (H. H. Robbins) Gunton's M. 14: 376. — (F. Brunetière) Liv. Age, 230: 265-374.

— Development of. (A. D. Mayo) Educa. 20: 521.

— in Literature, The True. (C. Johnston) Atlan. 84: 29.

American Style, What is? (E. K. Broadus) Dial (Ch.) 23: 139.

American Supremacy, Two Presidents and the Limits of. Fortn. 76: 555. Same art. Liv. Age, 231: 265. Same art. Ecl. M. 137: 760.

American Swordsman, An. (Hal Harris) Overland, n. s. 34: 211.

American Temperament, The. Spec. 80: 569. Same art. Liv. Age, 217: 612.

American Toe Dancer, An; a story. (Peggy Webling) Pall Mall M. 16: 419.

American Trade Invasion of England. (C. Roberts) World's Work, 1: 606.

American Trade Relations. (J. Charlton) Canad. M. 9: 502.

American Woman, The. (H. Münsterberg) Internat. Mo. 3: 607. — (S. C. De Soissons) Artist, 23: 65.

— Progress of. (E. C. Stanton) No. Am. 171: 904.

— Retrogression of. (F. M. Thompson) No. Am. 171: 748.

Americanism and the French Clergy. Spec. 84: 406.

— The Genesis of. (J. St.C. Etheridge) No. Am. 170: 679.

— Growth of, through the Centuries. (W. E. McLennan) Meth. R. 60: 549.

— Letter to Americans on. (Leo XIII.) Am. Cath. Q. 24: 184.

— True and False. (W. Barry) No. Am. 169: 33.

Americanisms: American Use of English. (W. Archer) Pall Mall M. 19: 188. Same art. Ecl. M. 132: 60.

— Once More. (Brander Matthews) Cosmopol. 30: 274.

Americans, Abroad, Why Many Live. (B. H. Ridgly) Pall Mall M. 20: 463.

— Are they Anglo-Saxons? Spec. 80: 614. Same art. Liv. Age, 217: 681. Same art. Ecl. M. 131: 296.

— as Business Men. Sat. R. 91: 729.

— at Play. Macmil. 76: 100. Same art. Liv. Age, 214: 259.

— Dislike of, Continental. Spec. 81: 76. Same art. Liv. Age, 218: 616.

— Embryo. (E. Robins) Harper, 103: 598.

— The Making of. Outl. 67: 481.

Amerrique People, Names and Statues of. (J. Crawford) Am. Antiq. 19: 21.

Ames, Nathaniel. (A. Ames) New Eng. M. n. s. 17: 56.

Amiens, Treaty of, Secret Articles of. (J. H. Rose) Eng. Hist. R. 15: 331.

Amir, The, and the Tribes. Asia. R. 25: 271.

— When the Amir dies? (C. Lipsett) Un. Serv. M. 19: 236.

Amis and Amile. (Richard Le Gallienne) Cosmopol. 31: 261.

Amish, A Day with the Pennsylvania. (W. H. Richardson) Outl. 61: 781.

Amistad Captives. (E. S. Bartlett) New Eng. M. n. s. 22: 72.

Ammen, Daniel. (G. E. Belknap) Cassier, 14: 267.

Amminadib in the Song of Songs. (T. K. Cheyne) Expos. 5: 145.

Ammonia and Tar from Blast Furnace Gases. (A. Gillespie) Cassier, 13: 354.

— Liquid, Anhydrous, Specific Heat of. (L. A. Elleau and W. D. Ennis) J. Frankl. Inst. 145: 189, 280.

— Sources of. (B. Terne) J. Frankl. Inst. 146: 127.

Ammonium Chloride, Action upon Analcite and Leucite. (F. W. Clarke and G. Steiger) Am. J. Sci. 159: 117.

— Action upon Natrolite, Scolecite, Prehnite, and Pectolite. (F. W. Clarke and G. Steiger) Am. J. Sci. 159: 345.

Ammonium Magnesium Arseniate, Constitution of. (M. Austin) Am. J. Sci. 159: 55.

Ammonium Magnesium Phosphate of Analysis. (F. A. Gooch and M. Austin) Am. J. Sci. 157: 187.

Ammunition and Small-arms. (J. P. Farley) J. Mil. Serv. Inst. 24: 28.

— Bad, at Bisley. Un. Serv. M. 15: 296.

Ammunition Columns and Parks. (J. F. Cadell) J. Mil. Serv. Inst. 19: 567.

Ammunition Packing-boxes. (J. A. Penn) J. Mil. Serv. Inst. 17: 564.

Ammunition Service in a Sea-coast Fort. J. Mil. Serv. Inst. 12: 1189.

Ammunition Supply in Foreign Armies. (C. S. Roberts) J. Mil. Serv. Inst. 20: 547.

— in War for All Arms. J. Mil. Serv. Inst. 20: 583.

— to the Firing Line. (G. B. Duncan) J. Mil. Serv. Inst. 19: 443.

Among the Brigands; a tale. (A. Beresford) Argosy, 67: 277.

Amoor Tribes, Preliminary Notes on Explorations among. (B. Laufer) Am. Anthrop. 2: 297.

Amoris Victima, Symons's. Ath. '97, 2: 447.

Amos, the Prophet of Righteousness. (L. Abbott) Outl. 61: 971.

Amphictis, Skull of. (E. S. Riggs) Am. J. Sci. 155: 257.

Amphicyon, New American Species. (J. L. Wortman) Am. J. Sci. 161: 200.

Amsterdam, Municipal Prison of. (F. H. Wines) Char. R. 9: 282.

— Zoölog. Gardens. (C. J. Cornish) Macmil. 76: 199.

Amu-Daria, Old Beds of the. (P. Kropotkin) Geog. J. 12: 306.

Amulet, The. (Neera) Liv. Age, 214: 219–512.

Amusements, Fashions in. Liv. Age, 218: 748.

— Modern. (D. Dale) Argosy, 68: 148.

— of Girls. (H. E. Hersey) Indep. 53: 2032.

— of Old London, Boulton's. (R. Davey) Sat. R. 91: 297.

— Out-door, in the U. S. Macmil. 76: 106. Same art. Liv. Age, 214: 259.

— Popular, in New York. (F. Coates) Chaut. 24: 706.

Anachronism in Courtship, An. (A. Hodder) Harper, 102: 125.

Anacreon, Some Lyrics of. (J. Patterson) Poet-Lore, 9: 400.

Anagrams, Ancient and Modern. (A. C. Pearson) Chamb. J. 77: 200.

Analyzer, New Harmonic. (A. A. Michelson and S. W. Stratton) Am. J. Sci. 155: 1.

Anarchism. (G. J. Holyoake) 19th Cent. 50: 683. — (P. Carus) Open Court, 15: 579.

— and Atheism; a sermon. (W. C. Doane) Outl. 69: 218.

— as an Advertisement. Sat. R. 90: 166.

— in Italy. (S. Cortesi) Indep. 53: 2346.

— in Literature. (L. Strachey) Critic, 39: 530.

— Italian. (G. M. Fiamingo) Open Court, 13: 485. — (G. M. Fiamingo) Ecl. M. 135: 727.

— its Cause and Cure. Outl. 69: 252.

Anarchist, A Paradoxical. (C. Lombroso) Pop. Sci. Mo. 56: 312.

— The Real. Liv. Age, 225: 780. Same art. Ecl. M. 135: 229.

Anarchist, The; a tale. (H. Bourchier) Argosy, 63: 396.

Anarchist Blood-Feud. Spec. 79: 201.

Anarchist Conspiracies, Psychology of. (O. Malagodi) Westm. 147: 87.

Anarchistic Crimes. (G. Tosti) Pol. Sci. Q. 14: 404.

Anarchists and the Nation. (E. Wambaugh) Green Bag, 13: 461.

— and the President. (C. Johnson) No. Am. 173: 437.

— Detective Surveillance of. (R. A. Pinkerton) No. Am. 173: 609.

— How to deal with. Spec. 87: 340. — Liv. Age, 231: 128.

— in America. (F. H. Nichols) Outl. 68: 859.

— International Control of. (Duke of Arcos) No. Am. 173: 758.

— Italian. (F. S. Nitti) No. Am. 167: 598.

— National Legislation against, Need of. (J. C. Burrows) No. Am. 173: 727.

— Philosophy of. (W. Gladden) Outl. 69: 449.

— Power and Duty of the Federal Government to protect its Agents. (E. Aldrich) No. Am. 173: 746.

— Teachings of the Roman Catholic Church on. (T. L. Jouffroy) Cath. World, 74: 202.

Anarchy and Assassination. Sat. R. 92: 324.

— and Regicide in the 19th Century. (S. B. Chester) Gent. M. n. s. 67: 382.

— Can we stamp out? (G. Gunton) Gunton's M. 21: 349.

Anarchy, Causes of. (G. Gunton) Gunton's M. 21: 407.

— Congress and; a Suggestion. (S. C. T. Dodd) No. Am. 173: 433.

— Gospels of. Criticism of G. B. Shaw, M. Barrès, etc. (V. Paget) Contemp. 74: 75.

— the Gospel of Destruction. (F. L. Oswald; E. H. Roberts) Arena, 26: 449.

— Nihilism and. (C. Johnston) No. Am. 171: 302.

Anatomical Nature Casts. (H. W. Armstead) M. of Art, 23: 210.

Anatomy and Physiology, Progress in, The Century's. (H. S. Williams) Harper, 96: 621.

— Human, Morris on. Science, n. s. 9: 27.

— in Art. (W. Anderson) M. of Art, 20: 211.

— Nomenclature of, Some Misapprehensions as to the, simplified. (B. G. Wilder) Science, n. s. 9: 566.

— Peabody's Laboratory Exercises in. (F. S. Lee) Science, n. s. 9: 331.

— Present Status of. (J. P. McMurrich) Am. Natural. 33: 185.

— Teaching, Advances in. (G. S. Huntington) Science, n. s. 9: 85.

Anburey, Captain. Letters of a British Prisoner in America. (A. G. Bradley) Macmil. 76: 12.

Ancestor-worship the Origin of Religion. (G. McDermot) Cath. World, 66: 20.

Anchors, Primitive. (J. Romilly Allen) Reliquary, 38: 100.

Anc. and Hon. Artill. Co., Boston. (J. A. Torrington) Munsey, 12: 33.

Ancient Buildings, Restoration of. Reliquary, 38: 278.

And Contentment Therewith. (I. K. Friedman) Liv. Age, 227: 63.

"And the Greatest of These;" a story. (Inglis Allen) Idler, 15: 342.

And Party; a story. (H. F. Abell) Chamb. J. 74: 537–552.

And Yet — ? a story. (P. Trent) Belgra. 93: 475.

Andalusia, In, with a Bicycle. (J. Pennell) Contemp. 73: 714. Same art. Liv. Age, 218: 95.

Andaman Islands. (R. C. Temple) J. Soc. Arts, 48: 105.

— Penal System at. (R. C. Temple) J. Soc. Arts, 47: 292.

Andersen, Hans Christian, Sidelights on. (Edmund Gosse) Critic, 37: 360.

Andersen, Hendrick Christian; a new sculptor. (Mrs. S. Van Rensselaer) Cent. 39: 17.

Anderson, Ada Woodruff. Writer, 14: 168.

Anderson, Dr. John. Geog. J. 16: 481. — Ath. '00, 2: 286.

Anderson, Robert. Ath. '01, 2: 492.

Andes, Bolivian, Explorations in the. (Sir Martin Conway) Geog. J. 14: 14.

— Highest. (R. McLeod) Lond. Q. 93: 66.

— — Fitzgerald on. Ath. '99, 2: 793. — (E. Whymper) Nature, 62: 38.

— Opening the Riches of; railroad to Quito. (C. Lockhart) World's Work, 2: 1270.

— Our City in the. Chamb. J. 76: 366.

— Railway across, from Argentine to Chili. (H. Butterworth) Nat'l M. (Bost.) 10: 489.

— Volcanic, Aconcagua and the. (Sir M. Conway) Harper, 100: 109.

Andesites of the Aroostook Volcanic Area of Maine. (H. E. Gregory) Am. J. Sci. 158: 359.

Andokides. (Richard Norton) Am. J. Archæol. 11: 1.

Andorra; a hidden republic. (L. Purdy) Harper, 103: 61.

— Visit to. (H. Spender) Fortn. 67: 44. Same art. Liv. Age, 212: 601.

Andover Theological Seminary. Outl. 66: 773.

André, John, The Story of. (A. Dimock) Pall Mall M. 14: 367.

André de Valle, Cardinal, Seal of, 1517. Archæol. 50: 118.

Andrée Balloon Expedition to the North Pole. (W. Wellman) McClure, 10: 411. — (H. R. Mill) Nature, 57: 609. — (B. Baden-Powell) Sat. R. 84: 187.

Andreutsos, Odysseus, and Trelawny. (F. B. Sanborn) Scrib. M. 21: 504.

Andrews, President E. B., and Brown University. Yale R. 6: 119. — R. of Rs. (N. Y.) 16: 310. — Pub. Opin. 23: 165. — Critic, 30: 83, 118.

— and Edward W. Bemis. The New Ostracism. (C. A. Towne) Arena, 18: 433.

— and Freedom of Teaching in America. (V. S. Yarreo) Westm. 149: 8.

— Open Letter to. (J. C. Ridpath) Arena, 18: 399.

— the Public-school Politician. (A. H. Nelson) Educa. R. 19: 187.

Andrews, Henry, of Taunton. (J. H. Drummond) N. E. Reg. 51: 453.

— and the Calves' Pasture. (A. D. Hodges, jr.) N. E. Reg. 52: 16.

Andros, Gov. Edmund, Letter of Thomas Mayhew to, 1675. (C. M. Foster) N. E. Reg. 52: 203.

Androscoggin River, Canoeing down. (G. E. Browne) Outing, 32: 358.

Anecdota Oxoniensia, Semitic Series of. Asia. R. 23: 364.

Anecdotes, Duplicate. (George Eyre-Todd) Gent. M. n. s. 59: 19, Same art. Ecl. M. 129: 534.

Aneroestes, the Gaul; a tale. (E. M. Smith) Canad. M. 11: 330.

Angel, The, and the Child. (H. Pyle) Harper, 100: 831.

Angel at the Grave, The. (Edith Wharton) Scrib. M. 29: 158.

Angel, An, in a Web; a novel. (J. Ralph) Harper, 96: 546, 761, 938.

Angel O; a story. (E. L. Prescott) Temp. Bar, 111: 226.

Angel of Love, The; a poem. (E. Gibson) Argosy, 65: 506.

Angel of Murphy's Gulch; a story. (C. H. New) Cosmopol. 22: 329.

Angel of Music, The; a story. (Helena Nyblom) Music, 15: 620.

Angel of New Rochelle, An; a story. (R. B. Wilson) Indep. 53: 366.

Angel with the Flaming Sword, The. (Lady Battersea) Sund. M. 30: 43.

Angel Court; a poem. (A. Dobson) Ecl. M. 137: 256.

Angelico, Fra Giovanni. Rome. (A. McLeod) Art J. 52: 204.

— Inner Life of. (M. A. Lathbury) Chaut. 34: 170.

Angelo, Henry, Reminiscences of. (A. Dobson) Longm. 31: 503. Same art. Liv. Age, 217: 603.

Angels and Men. (C. F. Brown) Atlan. 86: 262.

— and Demons, Evolution of, in Christian Theology. (R. B. Boswell) Open Court, 14: 483.

— in Art and Poetry. Sund. M. 27: 734, 831.

Angelus, The. (H. Thurston) Month, 98: 483, 607.

Anger and Temper. (B. J. Snell) Sund. M. 26: 130.

— A Study of. (G. S. Hall) Am. J. Psychol. 10: 516, 516.

Angiosperms, Phylogeny and Taxonomy of. (C. E. Bessey) Science, n. s. 6: 398.

Angler's Summer Eve. (F. G. Walters) Longm. 30: 223. Same art. Liv. Age, 214: 464. Same art. Ecl. M. 129: 404.

Anglesey Antiquities, Some. Reliquary, 39: 260.

Anglican, How to be made an. (H. Thurston) Month, 89: 1.

Anglican Bishops and the "Vindication." Month, 91: 337.

Anglican Clergy, Quality of the. (C. H. Parkhurst) Indep. 51: 2199.

Anglican Clergyman, Obstacles to the Conversion of. (H. C. Corrance) Month, 92: 408.

Anglican Extremists. Month, 92: 579.

Anglican History. (T. Slater) Month, 90: 113.

Anglican Monk, An; a story. (T. MacDonald) Cent. 40: 873.

Anglican Orders. See Church of England.

Anglicanism, Vitality of. (R. F. Clarke) Month, 93: 263.

Angling. An Epoch on Rumbling Creek. Macmil. 75: 303.

Anglo-American Alliance. (W. C. Copeland) Westm. 150: 168. — Liv. Age, 217: 126. — (F. Greenwood) 19th Cent. 44: 1. — (C. A. Gardiner) Am. J. Soc. Sci. 36: 148.

— American Greetings and Tributes to Britain. R. of Rs. (N. Y.) 18: 71.

— and the Irish-Americans. (G. McDermot) Cath. World, 68: 75.

— Basis of. (L. Abbott) No. Am. 166: 513.

— England and America. (G. S. Clarke) 19th Cent. 44: 186.

— England as an Ally. (E. A. Ross) Arena, 23: 583.

— English-speaking Brotherhood. (C. Waldstein) No. Am. 167: 223.

— Possibilities of. (C. W. Dilke) Pall Mall M. 16: 37.

— Proposed Federation of the Anglo-Saxons. (B. O. Flower) Arena, 20: 223.

— Prospects of an. (C. S. Clark) Un. Serv. M. 17: 487.

— Silent Partner in. (J. Sohn) Gunton's M. 19: 434.

— United States and the Concert of Europe. (J. C. Ridpath) Arena, 20: 145.

— vs. a European Combination. (R. Temple) No. Am. 167: 306.

Anglo-American Commission, 1898. (E. Farrer) Forum, 25: 652. — (A Canadian Liberal) No. Am. 167: 165.

— Work of. (A Canadian Liberal) No. Am. 168: 615.

Anglo-American Diplomacy, Evolution of a Treaty in. (C. C. Hyde) Am. Law R. 34: 373.

Anglo-American Entente, The; 1898. (C. Beresford) Pall Mall M. 18: 379.

Anglo-American Friendship. (C. Schurz) Atlan. 82: 433.

Anglo-American Future. (F. Greenwood) 19th Cent. 44: 1. Same art. Ecl. M. 131: 289. Same art. Liv. Age, 218: 563.

Anglo-American Peoples, Industrial Ascendancy of. (C. L. Redfield) Engin. M. 20: 847.

Anglo-American Understanding, Is there an? Fortn. 70: 163. Same art. Liv. Age, 218: 425.

Anglo-Americanism; a Canadian appeal. (R. E. Kingsford) Canad. M. 12: 201.

Anglo-Benedictine Congregation, Rise of the. Month, 90: 581.

Anglo-French Alliance, Plea for an. (H. M. Vaughan) Westm. 156: 613.

Anglo-German Agreement. Fortn. 70: 627. Same art. Liv. Age, 219: 590.

Anglo-Indian Anecdotes. (G. D. Lynch) Argosy, 64: 763.

Anglophobia; a French warning to England. (U. Gohier) National, 34: 26.

Anglo-Russian Complication, An. (J. Mackenzie) Un. Serv. M. 15: 255.

Anglo-Saxon, Changed Significance of the Term. (F. W. Chapman) Educa. 20: 364.

Anglo-Saxon Affinities. (J. Ralph) Harper, 98: 385.

Arbor Day; National Tree-planting. (G. C. Nuttall) Gent. M. n. s. 60: 177.

Arboreal Habits, Traces of, in Man. (J. O. Quantz) Am. J. Psychol. 9: 449.

Arbuckle, James, and the Molesworth-Shaftesbury School. (W. R. Scott) Mind, 24: 194.

Arcachon, At. (W. M. Fullerton) Fortn. 68: 490.

Arcachon, France. (J. A. Cook) Pall Mall M. 17: 405.

Arcades Ambo; a story. (H. Martley) Chamb. J. 75: 680.

Arcadia, Mediæval, Village Life in. Gent. M. n. s. 65: 188.

Arcady; a poem. (J. R. Taylor) Atlan. 84: 857.
— The Elders of. (A. Jessopp) 19th Cent. 47: 776.
— More Superstitions and Some Humors of. (C. Trollope) Longm. 33: 556. Same art. Liv. Age, 221: 688.

Arch, Joseph. Lond. Q. 90: 91. — (W. T. Stead) Contemp. 73: 71. — Quar. 188: 457. — Spec. 80: 273.
— Autobiography of. Acad. 53: 113. — Sat. R. 85: 114.

Archæological Institute of America. (J. R. Wheeler) Nation, 68: 413.
— Meeting at New Haven, 1900. (T. D. Seymour) Nation, 70: 27.
— Work of. (C. E. Norton) Am. J. Archæol. n. s. 4: 1.

Archæological Progress and the Schools at Rome and Athens. (A. L. Frothingham, jr.) Internat. Mo. 2: 687.

Archæological Societies, 12th Congress of, London, 1900. Ath. '00, 2: 63.

Archæology. (Sir J. Evans) Nature, 56: 369.
— and Antiquity of Man. (Sir J. Evans) Pop. Sci. Mo. 52: 93.
— and the Bible. (T. M. Lindsay) Crit. R. 10: 27.
— and the Higher Criticism. (J. P. Peters) New World, 8: 22.
— Classical; British School in Rome. Quar. 192: 183.
— Irish. Acad. 52: 103.
— Oriental, and the Old Testament. (J. B. Fox) Luth. Q 27: 559.
— Value of. Spec. 83: 188.

Archbishop's Christmas Gift, The; a story. (R. Barr) McClure, 10: 143.

Archconfraternity for the Conversion of England. Month, 90: 449.

Archer, Frederic, Organist, Portrait of. Music, 17: 199.

Archer, William. Library, 9: 283. — (B. Matthews) Forum, 27: 375.
— and A. B. Walkley. (M. Beerbohm) Sat. R. 88: 643.

Archer in the Cherokee Hills. (M. Thompson) Atlan. 79: 468.

Archers and Archery. (F. Peacock) Antiq. n. s. 33: 139.

Archery, Woodland. (M. Thompson) Outing, 30: 22.

Arches, Early Spanish, in Mexico. (A. Butt) Cent. 38: 224.
— Masonry. (H H. Suplee) Engin. M. 13: 861.
— Triumphal. (A Fish) M. of Art, 24: 445.

Architect, The, and the Engineer. (W. H. Bryan) Am. Arch. 62: 112.
— Painter and Sculptor, Collaboration of. (W. B. Richmond) Am. Arch. 69: 21.
— True Education of an. (R. Sturgis) Atlan. 81: 246.

Architects. (R. S. Peabody) Am. Arch. 74: 11.
— as Agents. Am. Arch. 55: 70.
— British, Social Position of. Am. Arch. 74: 103.
— English Government. Am. Arch. 61: 62.
— French, Lady Dilke's. (R. Sturgis) Nation, 72: 514.
— International Congress of, 5th. (G. O. Sotten) Am. Arch. 69: 77.

Architects, Legal Position of. (L. L. Marcassey) Am. Arch. 71: 5. — Am. Arch. 71: 92.
— Legal Responsibility of. Am. Arch. 60: 46.
— Licensing of. Am. Arch. 57: 95. — (Samuel Hannaford) Am. Arch. 63: 39.
— — in Ohio. Am. Arch. 67: 101.
— — Missouri Law for. Am. Arch. 63: 12.
— N. Y. State Registration Law for. Am. Arch. 71: 14.
— Registration of. Am. Arch. 56: 91.
— Reliability of. Am. Arch. 74: 95.
— Where our Architects Work. Archit. R. 10: 77, 143.
— Younger, Work of. Brush & P. 8: 113.

Architects' Liens, Law of. Am. Arch. 56: 47.

Architectural Aberrations. Archit. R. 7: (no. 2) 219.

Architectural Books. (E. R. Smith) Archit. R. 8: 37.

Architectural Classics. (E. R. Smith) Archit. R. 7: 113, 137.

Architectural Commissions, Illicit. Am. Arch. 72: 7.

Architectural Competition Code. Am. Arch. 70: 102.

Architectural Competition. (W. M. Aiken) Am. Arch. 74: 71. — (R. Sturgis) Archit. R. 4: 43. — (W. R. Ware) Am. Arch. 66: 107. — (Barr Ferree) Am. Arch. 57: 81. 58: 55-95. — (D. MacG. Means) Nation, 65: 200.
— Principles of. (J. B. Robinson) Archit. R. 8: 1-434.
— Treasury Rules. Am. Arch. 57: 83, 103. 58: 3, 25.

Architectural Criticism. (H. D. Croly) Archit. R. 10: 398.

Architectural Design, New Method. (E. Lorch) Brush & P. 8: 253.
— Recent Progress in. (Walter Cook) Am. Arch. 71: 27.

Architectural Drawings, Liability for Defective. Am. Arch. 70: 86.
— Ownership of. Am. Arch. 55: 29.

Architectural Education. (H. P. Warren) Am. Arch. 66: 84. — (A. B. Trowbridge) Am. Arch. 68: 91. — Am. Arch. 72: 91. — Archit. R. 7: 55.

Architectural Exhibit at Royal Academy, 1897. Am. Arch. 58: 5.

Architectural Exhibition, The Boston. (H. L. Warren) Archit. R. 6: 71.
— Philadelphia. (A. M. Githens) Am. Arch. 67: 13.
— T-Square Club. (D. K. Boyd) Archit. R. 7: 1.

Architectural Exhibits at the Mechanic's Fair, Boston. Am. Arch. 62: 78.

Architectural Experiment. Archit. R. 8: 82.

Architectural Experts, Remuneration of. Am. Arch. 71: 76.

Architectural Instruction in N. Y. and Paris. (W. R. Ware) Am. Arch. 70: 3.

Architectural Freaks. Am. Arch. 61: 22.

Architectural League, N. Y., Exhibition, 12th, 1897. Am. Arch. 55: 94, 99.
— — 14th, 1899. (A. D. F. Hamlin; F. S. Lamb) Archit. R. 6: 39.
— — 15th, 1900. Am. Arch. 67: 93.

Architectural League of America. Artist (N. Y.) 25: xxvii.
— Exhibition, 1899. Artist (N. Y.) 24: xxxii, xxxvi.
— 2d Annual Convention. Am. Arch. 68: 87.

Architectural Practice, English and American. (R. C. Sturgis) Archit. R. 6: 132.
— Mutuality not Individuality. (P. B. Wright) Scrib. M. 29: 253.

Architectural School of the Berlin Technical College. (E. O. Sachs) Am. Arch. 57: 17.

Architectural Studies, Plea for. (A. D. F. Hamlin) Forum, 31: 626.

Architectural Style. (E. Grey) Brush & P. 6: 107. — (Russell Sturgis) Scrib. M. 28: 509.

Arietis 26, Occultations of, observed Photographically. (E. C. Pickering) Pop. Astron. 6: 110. Same art. Knowl. 21: 133.

Aristarchus and Sinus Iridum. (E. W. Maunder) Knowl. 20: 142.

Aristides. Apology for the Christians, Recovered. (H. M. Harmon) Meth. R. 57: 277.

Aristocracy and Evolution, Mallock on. Bk. Buyer, 17: 228. — (M. W. Patterson) Econ. R. 8: 541. — (L. L. Price) Econ. J. 8: 363. — (T. B. Veblen) J. Pol. Econ. 6: 430.

— British. (Grant Allen) Cosmopol. 30: 657.

— A Democratic ; or Voluntary Servitude. (C. Ferguson) No. Am. 166: 636.

— The New American. (H. T. Peck) Cosmopol. 25: 701.

— vs. the People. (E. Farquhar) Conserv. R. 5: 55.

Aristophanes and Agathon. (W. Rhys Roberts) J. Hel. Stud. 20: 44.

Aristotle. (F. C. S. Schiller) Mind, 25: 467.

— and the Earlier Peripatetics, Zeller on. (W. A. Hammond) Dial (Ch.) 26: 193.

— and Modern Engineering. (R. H. Thurston) Cassier, 15: 195.

— De Anima. (P. Shorey) Am. J. Philol. 22: 149.

— Political Philosophy of. (Isaac Loos) Ann. Am. Acad. Pol. Sci. 10: 313.

— Metaphysic of. (J. Watson) Philos. R. 7: 23-337.

— Politics of. (W. A. Dunning) Pol. Sci. Q. 15: 273.

— Theory of Incontinence. (W. H. Fairbrother) Mind, 22: 359.

— Theory of Poetry and Fine Art. Ed. R. 188: 60.

Aristotelian Teleology, The. (J. D. Logan) Philos. R. 6: 386.

Aristotelianism in Modern Thought. (B. Young) Meth. R. 61: 244.

Arithmetic. (W. C. Boyden) Educa. 18: 148.

— and Grammar. (J. H. Dillard) Nation, 71: 92.

— and Writing, Teaching of, in Time of the Commonwealth. (Foster Watson) Gent. M. n. s. 63: 257.

— Books on, Progress in. (F. B. Gault) Educa. 20: 295.

— Evolution of, in the U. S. (J. M. Greenwood) Educa. 20: 193.

— for Schools, Smith's. (D. E. Smith) School R. 8: 54.

— in Early New England. (W. H. Small) Educa. 22: 160.

— in Rural and Village Schools. (D. E. Smith) Educa. R. 13: 348.

— Proportion in. (R. E. Moritz) Educa. 17: 360.

— Some Historical Points. (Seth Harvey) Educa. 21: 171.

Arizona, Camel Hunt in. (L. Ballinger) Outing, 36: 656.

— Forests and Deserts of. (B. E. Fernow) Nat. Geog. M. 8: 203.

— Mineral Resources of. (T. Tonge) Engin. M. 13: 758.

Arizona Episode, An. Cosmopol. 27: 673.

Ark, Babylonian. (C. H. W. Johns) Expos. 9: 214.

Ark in the Wilderness. (A. MacGowan) Lippinc. 61: 504.

Arkansas; a typical primitive community. (C. B. Spahr) Outl. 61: 749.

Arkansas Courtship, An. (F. C. Wimberly) Overland, n. s. 34: 347.

Arks of Arktown, The. (L. B. Starr) Strand, 18: 98.

Arles, France. (E. C. Vansittart) Cath. World, 72: 577.

— Beautiful Women of. (A. Symons) Sat. R. 86: 528.

— its Churches and Antiquities. (E. Endres) Cath. World, 65: 586.

Arma Cano. (Ph. Salisbury) Un. Serv. M. 16: 156, 304.

Armada, A Medieval. Liv. Age, 218: 61.

Armaments, the World's, Growth of. (H. W. Wilson) 19th Cent. 43: 706.

Armand, Col., of the Revolutionary War. Pennsyl. M. 22: 234.

Armenia and Cuba. (T. Williams) Cent. 35: 634.

— its History and Customs, by a Refugee. Nat'l M. (Bost.) 6: 145.

— Lenz's World Tour Awheel. Outing, 29: 382.

— Massacres of 1896, by a Refugee. Nat'l M. (Bost.) 6: 3.

— — England's Hand in. (M. H. Gulesian) Arena, 17: 271.

— A Mother of Martyrs. (C. Roberts) Atlan. 83: 90.

Armenian Canons of St. Sahak Catholicos. (F. C. Conybeare) Am. J. Theol. 2: 849.

Armenian Literature, Modern. (C. Garo) Poet-Lore, 9: 122.

Armenian Question, Bryce on. (O. T. Morton) Dial (Ch.) 22: 113.

— Contribution to. (C. A. P. Rohrbach) Forum, 29: 481.

Armenian Refugees. (M. H. Gulesian) Arena, 17: 652.

Armenian Wedding, An. (L. M. J. Garnett) Argosy, 70: 347.

Armenians, Germany and the. (W. J. Stillman) Nation, 68: 351.

— Religious Customs among. (P. Terzian) Cath. World, 71: 305, 500.

— Slaughter of, in Constantinople. (Y. Troshine) Scrib. M. 21: 48.

Armies, Future of Great. (S. Low) 19th Cent. 46: 382. Same art. Liv. Age, 223: 405. Same art. Ecl. M. 134: 92.

— Great, and their Cost. (A. Griffiths) Fortn. 75: 249.

— in the Field, Supplying, during Civil War. (H. G. Sharpe) J. Mil. Serv. Inst. 18: 45.

— Large, Outposts of. (O. B. Willcox) J. Mil. Serv. Inst. 5: 337.

— of the Six European Powers compared. (M. Warren) Pall Mall M. 16: 256.

— of British Empire. Un. Serv. M. 17: 75.

— of Europe. (J. J. O'Connell) J. Mil. Serv. Inst. 15: 52.

Arminius, James, Influence on Religious Thought. (H. Hewitt) Meth. R. 59: 779.

Armor, Fire Arms and. (J. Corbett) Longm. 34: 159.

— Formulas for Penetration of. (L. G. Berry) J. Mil. Serv. Inst. 12: 1149.

— Development of. (J. Conklin) J. Mil. Serv. Inst. 11: 914.

— Trial of Iron for, 1590. (H. A. Dillon) Archæol. 51: 167.

Armored Trains. (W. Guise-Tucker) Un. Serv. M. 16: 254. — (H. G. Archer) Un. Serv. M. 15: 500.

Armorial Adversaria. (W. Bradbrook) Gent. M. n. s. 64: 572.

Armorial Bearing on Ceiling of the Monks' Choir in Abbey Church of St. Alban, England. Archæol. 51: 427.

Armor-plate, Manufacture of. (Rupert Hughes) Cosmopol. 28: 405.

— Nickel Steel, in the U. S. (T. Ulke) Cassier, 14: 34.

— Trials of, in America. J. Mil. Serv. Inst. 12: 133.

Armour, Philip D., with portrait. (F. W. Gunsaulus) R. of Rs. (N. Y.) 23: 167. — (H. I. Cleveland) World's Work, 1: 540.

— and the Leiter Wheat Deal. (P. J. O'Keefe) Nat'l M. (Bost.) 9: 25.

Arms and Armor at Westminster, the Tower, and Greenwich, 1547. Archæol. 51: 219.

Arnold, Matthew, and Thomas. (A. B. McGill) Bk. Buyer, 22: 373.
— as a Political and Social Critic. (B. N. Oakeshott) Westm. 149: 161. Same art. Ecl. M. 130: 365.
— as seen through his Letters. (C. Fisher) Gent. M. n. s. 59: 492. Same art. Liv. Age, 215: 870. Same art. Ecl. M. 129: 848.
— as Theatrical Critic. (H. Elliott) Theatre, 39: 70.
— Letters. Sewanee, 4: 181.
— Poetry of. (T. W. Hunt) Meth. R. 58: 757.
— Saintsbury's. Acad. 57: 329.
— Study of his Poetry. Sewanee, 9: 442.
Arnold, Olney. (H. B. Metcalf) N. E. Reg. 55: 189.
Arnold, Thomas, and Matthew, Influence of. Acad. 52: 517.
— — — on English Education, Fitch on. (C. H. Thurber) School R. 6: 681. — (W. M. Payne) Dial (Ch.) 24: 115. — Spec. 79: 559. — Church Q. 47: 466. Same art. Ecl. M. 132: 702. Same art. Liv. Age, 221: 99.
— Findlay on. (W. M. Payne) Dial (Ch.) 24: 113. — (C. H. Thurber) School R. 6: 272. — Sat. R. 84: 197.
Arnold Arboretum. (S. Baxter) World's Work, 2: 1182. — (W. H. Downes) New Eng. M. n. s. 19: 139.
Aronson, Maurice, Pianist, with portrait. Music, 19: 172.
Arrecifos. (Louis Becole) Chamb. J. 77: 424-553.
Arrival of the Unexpected, The. (R. Barr) Strand, 18: 648.
Arrol, Sir William, with portrait. (A. S. Biggart) Cassier, 15: 3.
Ars Domestica; story. (Bennett Col) Idler, 11: 452.
Ars longa, Vita brevis; a poem. (A. Mackay) Argosy, 65: 555.
Arrow Wounds. (J. Wilson) Am. Anthrop. 3: 513.
Arrowhead, The. (E. Elton) Overland, n. s. 37: 625.
Arrows, Antler-pointed, of Southeastern Indians. (C. C. Willoughby) Am. Anthrop. 3: 431.
Arsenal, The. J. Mil. Serv. Inst. 11: 132.
Arsenic in Beer and Food. (W. Thomson) J. Soc. Arts, 49: 198.
Arsenic Acid, Iodometric Estimation of. (F. A. Gooch and J. C. Morris) Am. J. Sci. 160: 151.
Art. (G. C. Teall) Brush & P. 4: 302.
— American, Alien Element in. (E. T. Clarke) Brush & P. 7: 35.
— — Growth and Needs of. (H. Morris) Indep. 53: 1118.
— — in Paris. Brush & P. 127.
— Ancient, and Architecture, Religious Influence on. Am. Antiq. 23: 339.
— Ancient Celtic. Reliquary, 39: 256.
— and Artists. (J. La Farge) Internat. Mo. 4: 335, 466.
— — Tolstoi on. Sat. R. 87: 680.
— and Decoration of Cities. Sat. R. 83: 645.
— and Heart on the Heights. (Joaquin Miller) Overland, n. s. 29: 33.
— and Life. (Harriet C. Towner) Midland, 8: 231.
— and Literature in the Schools. (W. T. Harris) Educa. R. 13: 324.
— and Money. (Maurice Thompson) Liv. Age, 228: 331.
— and Morality. (F. Brunetière) Ecl. M. 132: 161. Same art. Liv. Age, 220: 1.
— and other Matters. (O. Boulton) Westm. 152: 305.
— and Personality. (C. E. Laughlin) Bk. Buyer, 18: 282.
— and Philosophy, Ancient Feud between. (P. E. More) Atlan. 86: 337.
— and Socialism. (O. L. Triggs) Brush & P. 4: 20.

Art and Usefulness. (V. Paget) Contemp. 80: 362, 512. Same art. Liv. Age, 231: 696-804.
— and the Woman. Macmil. 83: 29.
— Application of, to American Industries. (C. De Kay) Artist (N. Y.) 25: xv.
— Applied, American and French, at Grafton Galleries. (H. Townsend) Studio (Internat.) 8: 39.
— Aristotelian and Christian Ideal of. (H. Lucas) Month, 97: 371.
— as the Handmaid of Literature. (W. H. Hobbs) Forum, 31: 370.
— as a Means of Expression. (W. J. Stillman) Internat. Mo. 1: 133.
— at "Home Arts and Industries Exhibition." (E. Wood) Studio (Internat.) 8: 99.
— before Giotto. (R. E. Fry) Monthly R. 1, no. 1: 126.
— A Broad View of. (L. Tolstoi) Liv. Age, 218: 489.
— Catholic. (A. Streeter) Month, 96: 13.
— Christian, Beginnings of. (M. B. Myers) Meth. R. 59: 580.
— — its Mission and Influence. (K. F. M. O'Shea) Cath. World, 71: 815.
— — its Status and Prospects in the United States. (C. De Kay) Cath. World, 74: 9.
— Church, and the Church Congress, 1899. (H. R. Haweis) M. of Art, 24: 133.
— Coincidences and Resemblances in Works of. (M. H. Spielman) M. of Art, 23: 16.
— Convention in. Brush & P. 8: 310.
— Current. M. of Art, 22: 97.
— Democratic. (O. L. Triggs) Forum, 26: 66.
— Ecclesiastical, at Nottingham. M. of Art, 22: 106.
— Education in, for Children. (C. N. Flagg) New Eng. M. n. s. 18: 321.
— English, and M. Fernand Khnopff. (W. S. Sparrow) Studio (Lond.) 2: 203.
— — at the Chicago World's Fair. Studio (Lond.) 2: 45.
— — in the Victorian Age. Quar. 187: 209.
— Ethical and Utilitarian Value of Vital. (J. W. Stimson) Arena, 26: 78.
— Evolution of. Month, 98: 44, 156, 500, 575.
— for the People. Outl. 63: 626.
— French, Modern. Quar. 185: 360.
— from Australia. (A. L. Baldry) M. of Art, 22: 378.
— Greek Tragedians and, Huddilston's. Sat. R. 85: 626.
— Important and Trivial. (L. Tolstoi) Indep. 52: 1656.
— in America. (Brooks Adams) Am. Arch. 64: 77. — (H. B. Fuller) Bookman, 10: 218.
— — Future of. (E. Aman-Jean) Brush & P. 9: 75.
— — Lesson of its History. (F. W. Coburn) Educa. 19: 222.
— in Bronze and Iron, American. (K. G. Nelson) Munsey, 25: 516.
— in the Church. (H. Sumner) Art J. 53: 52.
— in Economic Evolution. (E. E. Spencer) Gunton's M. 16: 251.
— in England; its official encouragement. Sat. R. 92: 106.
— in London, International. (E. R. Pennell) Nation, 73: 337.
— in 1901. Sketches and Studies. Artist (N. Y.) 31: 1.
— in the Public Schools. (S. W. Whitman) Atlan. 79: 617. — (S. Norse) Arena, 22: 49. — Educa. 19: 121. — (Russell Sturgis) Scrib. M. 26: 509-637.
— in Scotland. Art J. 49: 23.
— — Present Condition of. (J. L. Caw) Art J. 50: 45, 69.
— in the Tariff. Am. Arch. 59: 94.
— in the United States, Problem of. (Ada Cone) Contemp. 80: 375.

Art Treasures of America. (W. Sharp) 19th Cent. 44: 601. Same art. Liv. Age, 219: 265–601.

Artagnan d', The Real. (Ralph Nevill) Gent. M. n. s. 62: 265. — (G. Brenan) Macmil. 80: 202. — (H. Maxwell) Blackw. 161: 759.

Artemis Brauronia of Praxiteles. (J. Pickard) Am. J. Archæol. 2d s. 2: 367.

Artemisium, Excavations on the Supposed Site of. (R. P. Pullan) Archæol. 50: 58.

Arthur, King. Gent. M. n. s. 66: 101.
— Identity of Author of Morte d'Arthur. Archæol. 56: 165.
— Life and Literature in the Time of. (W. H. Babcock) Conserv. R. 3: 90.
— A New Translation of the Arthurian Epos [by W. W. Newell]. Atlan. 81: 278. — (G. L. Kittridge) Nation, 66: 150.

Arthur, Julia. (M. O'Grady) Canad. M. 11: 31.
— Portrait of. Theatre, 39: 56.

Arthur, William. (E. E. Jenkins) Lond. Q. 96: 61.

Arthur Durham; a novel. (Mrs. H. Wood) Argosy, 63: 306.

Articles of War and the Common Law Military. (G. N. Lieber) J. Mil. Serv. Inst. 1: 53.

Artillery. Sat. R. 92: 137.
— Ancient and Modern. (L. M. Hadley) Lippinc. 62: 562.
— and Ordnance. (C. F. Benjamin) J. Mil. Serv. Inst. 8: 361.
— at Battle of Omdurman. Un. Serv. M. 18: 196.
— at Colenso. (C. H. Wilson) Un. Serv. M. 20: 499.
— before the Civil War. (W. L. Haskin) J. Mil. Serv. Inst. 3: 403.
— Coast, Organization of. (S. E. Stuart) J. Mil. Serv. Inst. 12: 1224.
— — Practice for. (J. B. Richardson) J. Mil. Serv. Inst. 15: 167.
— Employment of. (J. P. Wisser) J. Mil. Serv. Inst. 7: 270.
— Field. (G. W. Van Deusen) J. Mil. Serv. Inst. 19: 336.
— — and its Critics. (C. H. Wilson) Un. Serv. M. 19: 254.
— — Carriages for. (O. E. Michaelis) J. Mil. Serv. Inst. 8: 414.
— — French. (F. A. Mahan) J. Mil. Serv. Inst 10: 357.
— — Guns for. (Galeatus) Monthly R. 3, no. 2: 26.
— — in Future Wars. (Major E. S. May) Eng. Illust. 21: 110.
— — Material for, for the United States Army. (A. O. Schenck) J. Mil. Serv. Inst. 9: 311.
— — Multiplication of Calibres in. (P. Leary) J. Mil. Serv. Inst. 15: 1157.
— — Practice Grounds. (F. S. Strong) J. Mil. Serv. Inst. 19: 239.
— — Present Status of. (H. C. Carbaugh) J. Mil. Serv. Inst. 20: 500.
— — Relative Importance of. (W. E. Birkhimer) J. Mil. Serv. Inst. 6: 191.
— — Training and Instructing Drivers for. (E. D. Hoyle) J. Mil. Serv. Inst. 15: 537.
— from an Infantry Officer's Point of View. (T. D. Pilcher) J. Mil. Serv. Inst. 20: 136.
— Future of, in U. S. (C. H. Wilson) J. Mil. Serv. Inst. 27: 381.
— Garrison. (Pack-Beresford) J. Mil. Serv. Inst. 26: 113.
— General Review of. (G. Moch) J. Mil. Serv. Inst. 15: 356, 574, 803, 1032.
— Heavy, of the Future. (A. Todd) J. Mil. Serv. Inst. 19: 260.
— — Service School for. (H. C. Carbaugh) J. Mil. Serv. Inst. 22: 323.

Artillery, Horse. Un. Serv. M. 24: 46.
— Horse and Field, Reconnaissance and Escorts for. (A. H. C. Phillpotts) Un. Serv. M. 22: 262.
— in Coast Defense. (A. C. Hansard) J. Mil. Serv. Inst. 14: 844.
— in the East; Fortifications of Japan and China. (J. P. Sanger) J. Mil. Serv. Inst. 1: 225.
— in 1870–71, from a General Army Point of View. (J. F. Maurice) J. Mil. Serv. Inst. 14: 1087.
— in the Mexican War. (G. W. Van Deusen) J. Mil. Serv. Inst. 17: 87.
— in Warfare. (J. Percy) Idler, 16: 46.
— Italian. (J. P. Sanger) J. Mil. Serv. Inst. 1: 449.
— Letters on. J. Mil. Serv. Inst. 10: 213, 376. 11: 104–452. 12: 96–1271.
— Light; its Use and Misuse. (T. McCrea) J. Mil. Serv. Inst. 22: 519.
— — Target Practice of. (H. C. Hawthorne) J. Mil. Serv. Inst. 11: 740.
— Modern. (A. J. Dawson) J. Soc. Arts, 49: 271.
— Modern French. J. Mil. Serv. Inst. 12: 138, 322.
— Mountain. (C. D. Parkhurst) J. Mil. Serv. Inst. 11: 50, 789.
— Museum of, at Paris. J. Mil. Serv. Inst. 29: 247.
— Portable. (H. C. C. D. Simpson) Un. Serv. M. 14: 625.
— Renewal of Italian Field. (C. F. Mariani) Un. Serv. M. 20: 187.
— The Royal. J. Mil. Serv. Inst. 18: 150.
— Royal Garrison, The. (G. A. Major) Un. Serv. M. 19: 639. 20: 45.
— Royal Regiment of. Un. Serv. M. 19: 513.
— Sea-coast. (H. J. Reilly) J. Mil. Serv. Inst. 17: 276.
— — Instruction of. (J. M. Califf) J. Mil. Serv. Inst. 18: 321.
— Some Thoughts on. (E. M. Weaver) J. Mil. Serv. Inst. 10: 466.
— Types of. (M. Ross) Canad. M. 14: 411.
— U. S. 2d Regt. (W. A. Simpson) J. Mil. Serv. Inst. 14: 905.
— — 3d Regt. (W. E. Birkhimer) J. Mil. Serv. Inst. 14: 458.
— — 4th Regt. (A. B. Dyer) J. Mil. Serv. Inst. 11: 843.
— — Urgent Necessity for Increase in. (G. W. Wingate) J. Mil. Serv. Inst. 21: 429.

Artillery Administration, Our Experience in. (H. J. Hunt) J. Mil. Serv. Inst. 12: 197.

Artillery Armament, Our Present. (W. E. Birkhimer) J. Mil. Serv. Inst. 17: 297.

Artillery Association, National, at Shoeburyness. (F. H. Hoskier) Un. Serv. M. 16: 219.

Artillery College, Royal, at Woolwich. J. Mil. Serv. Inst. 16: 303.

Artillery Defense, Organization of. (J. Chester) J. Mil. Serv. Inst. 12: 988.

Artillery Difficulties. (J. Chester) J. Mil. Serv. Inst. 12: 556.

Artillery Escort. (D. G. Prinsep) J. Mil. Serv. Inst. 29: 117.

Artillery Field Armament, A Proper. (W. E. Birkhimer) J. Mil. Serv. Inst. 14: 1208.

Artillery Fire, Concentration and Distribution of. (W. L. White) J. Mil. Serv. Inst. 17: 108.
— Notes on. Un. Serv. M. 22: 185, 251.

Artillery Firing Charts. (H. A. Reed) J. Mil. Serv. Inst. 20: 315.

Artillery Practice, Coast. (H. S. Jendwine) J. Mil. Serv. Inst. 21: 354.

Artillery Questions of 1890. (J. C. Bush) J. Mil. Serv. Inst. 13: 165.

Artillery Masses, Organization of. (E. N. Henriques) J. Mil. Serv. Inst. 17: 414.

Artillery Organization. Un. Serv. M. 14: 428. — (T. B. Strange) Un. Serv. M. 14: 499. — Un. Serv. M. 15: 210. — (C. L. Best) J. Mil. Serv. Inst. 17: 502. — (J. Chester) J. Mil. Serv. Inst. 29: 1.
— An Antiquated. (A. L. Wagner) J. Mil. Serv. Inst. 17: 41.
— of the Future. (G. M. Whistler) J. Mil. Serv. Inst. 5: 324.

Artillery Practice at Shoeburyness. J. Mil. Serv. Inst. 16: 48.

Artillery Reform. Un. Serv. M. 14: 504.

Artillery Reorganization. Un. Serv. M. 14: 629.

Artillery Reserve, Question of an. (W. E. Birkhimer) J. Mil. Serv. Inst. 20: 529.

Artillery School Methods, Proposed Change in. (C. H. Hunter) J. Mil. Serv. Inst. 2: 23.

Artillery Service in the U. S. Civil War. (J. C. Tidball) J. Mil. Serv. Inst. 13: 276–1085. 14: 1, 307.

Artillery Targets. (G. W. Van Deusen) J. Mil. Serv. Inst. 18: 179.

Artisan's Homes. Shattuck Prize Competition. Am. Arch. 62: 47, 115. 63: 7–79.

Artist and Business Man, The Combined. (H. R. Butler and others) Scrib. M. 24: 125.
— and his Trade. (L. F. Day) Art J. 53: 119.
— and the Man. Dial (Ch.) 28: 239.
— as Headsman, substituting a New Head. (G. S. Layard) Eng. Illust. 19: 185.
— Craftsman as an. (C. E. Norton) Archit. R. 5: 81.
— Education of the, Here and Now. (W. H. Low) Scrib. M. 25: 765.

Artist of Burning Rome. (H. Sienkiewicz) Liv. Age, 212: 145.

Artistic Impulse, The, in Man and Woman. (E. C. Randall) Arena, 24: 415.

Artistic Nemesis, An; a story. (E. T. Fowler) Pall Mall M. 17: 176. Same art. Ecl. M. 132: 718.

Artistic Success, The; a monodrame. (B. Pain) Idler, 17: 306.

Artistic Temperament, So-called. Sat. R. 89: 389.

Artist's Love Story, An. (H. Boddington) Good Words, 40: 670.

Artists, American, and Their Public. (H. Croly) Archit. R. 10: 256.
— — in Paris. (E. L. Good) Cath. World, 66: 453.
— — Lives of, in the School-room. (F. W. Coburn) Educa. 17: 490.
— and their Work. Munsey, v. 16–18.
— British, Portraits of, at National Portrait Gallery. Studio (Internat.) 1: 88.
— Foundation of a Colony of Self-supporting. Arena, 17: 642.
— Lady, in Germany. (L. Hagen) Studio (Internat.) 4: 91.
— Modern Italian. (R. Pantini) Studio (Internat.) 13: 161.
— More Noted Women Painters, with portraits. (H. Postlethwaites) M. of Art, 22: 480.
— New Books on. (Dillon) M. of Art, 25: 406, 454.
— Organization among. (C. De Kay) Internat. Mo. 1: 83.
— Pastimes of some. Art J. 50: 276.
— So-called Conceit in. (C. E. Green) Brush & P. 6: 12.
— Society of Western, 3d Annual Exhibition. Brush & P. 3: 153.
— Some Knights of the Brush. (T. H. S. Escott) Chamb. J. 76: 113.
— Women, Letter to. (A. L. Merritt) Lippinc. 65: 463.

Artists' Studios. (W. Goodman) M. of Art, 25: 357.

Artists' Types, The Quest for. (E. T. Clarke) Brush & P. 8: 51.

Arts and Crafts in 16th Century. (W. A. Baillie-Grohman) Pall Mall M. 20: 511. 21: 32, 158.
— Provincial. (G. Johnstone) Studio (Lond.) 4: 47.

Arts and Crafts Exhibition, Boston, 1897. Am. Arch. 56: 13, 21.
— London, 1896. M. of Art, 20: 63. — Studio (Lond.) 9: 50–262.
— — 1899. (Mabel Cox) Artist (N. Y.) 26: 176. — (E. F. Strange) M. of Art, 24: 86.
— — 1901. (E. Radford) Artist (N. Y.) 32: 42.
— Minneapolis, 1898. (M. A. Helmick) Artist (N. Y.) 23: 1.

Arts and Crafts Movement, The. Brush & P. 6: 110.
— in England. (L. D. Abbott) Arena, 22: 398.

Arts and Letters, National Institute of. Outl. 64: 342.

Arts Club of London, Decorations of. (A. L. Baldry) Art J. 50: 97.

Artz, Adolphe. (R. Heath) M. of Art, 20: 80.

Arun Raj. Macmil. 81: 359. Same art. Liv. Age, 225: 245.

Aryan Languages, Recent Studies in. (R. S. Conway) Contemp. 77: 266.

Aryan Migrations and Culture. Acad. 52: 5.

Aryan Question, Old and New Aspects of. (G. V. de Lapouge) Am. J. Sociol. 5: 329.

Aryans, The, and the Ancient Italians. (G. Sergi) Monist, 8: 161.
— Evolution of, Ihering's. (A. W. Stratton) Citizen, 3: 287. — (F. Starr) Dial (Ch.) 25: 45.
— New View concerning. (R. S. Conway) Contemp. 76: 74.
— Origin of. (A. J. Heller) Ref. Q. 44: 214.
— Original Home of. (C. W. Super) Am. Antiq. 20: 353.

As Bad as Truth; a story. (L. Rossi) Temp. Bar, 113: 364.

As it Fell Out; a prison story. (T. Hopkins) McClure, 14: 427.

As one having Authority. (I. Clark) New Eng. M. n. s. 24: 445.

As others See us; monologue. (G. Hibbard) Lippinc. 66: 903.

Asbestos and Asbestic. (R. H. Jones) J. Soc. Arts, 45: 544.

Asbury, Bp. F., as a Student. (F. G. Porter) Meth. R. 59: 55.

Ascension Custom, An Old-world. (D. Paton) Sund. M. 28: 326.

Ascetic Theories of Morality. (H. W. Wright) Philos. R. 10: 601.

Asceticism: its place in Christian conduct. (G. U. Wenner) Luth. Q. 30: 556.
— A Plea for. (M. Kendall) Lond. Q. 93: 124.
— Value of. Spec. 78: 539.

Asceticisms, Futile. Spec. 78: 400.

Asclepiad, Statue of an, from Gortyna. (L. Mariani) Am. J. Archæol. 12: 279.

Asclepias, Cruelty of. (M. Treat) Garden & F. 10: 641.

Ashanti. (G. K. French) Nat. Geog. M. 8: 1.

Ashanti Campaign, 1900. Un. Serv. M. 23: 135.

Ashanti Uprising, 1900. Sat. R. 89: 578.

Ashburnham Library, Sale of the. Acad. 52: 17, 35.

Ashera in the Old Testament. (K. Budde) New World, 8: 732.

Asheville, N. C. Lit. W. (Bost.) 28: 275, 292.

Ashore in a Niger Creek. Belgra. 99: 593.

Ashton, Mrs. Julian. Acad. 59: 164.

Asia, Across. (G. F. Wright) Indep. 53: 772.
— — on a Bicycle. (T. G. Allen) Outing, 33: 467.
— America's Opportunity in. (C. Denby) No. Am. 166: 32.

Asia, British Bounty to. (H. Kopsch) National, 30: 929.

— British Sphere in. (C. E. D. Black) 19th Cent. 47: 767.

— Central, Four Years' Travel in. (S. Hedin) Geog. J. 11: 240.

— — Hedin and Dutreuil de Rhins in. (Sir T. H. Holdich) Geog. J. 13: 159.

— — Hedin on. (H. M. Stanley) Dial (Ch.) 26: 44. — (E. H. Mullin) Bk. Buyer, 18: 30. — Nat. Geog. M. 12: 393. — (R. H. Sherard) McClure, 10: 180.

— — Journeys in. (H. H. P. Deasy) Geog. J. 16: 141, 501.

— — Roof of the World. (F. Younghusband) Indep. 51: 1187.

— — Russia's Advance in. (A. R. Colquhoun) Harper, 100: 636.

— — Russian; Countries and Peoples. J. Soc. Arts, 48: 555.

— The Cradle of Humanity. (W. J. McGee) Nat. Geog. M. 12: 280.

— Dislike of, for Europe. Spec. 84: 868. 85: 136.

— Eastern, Ocean Transportation to. (E. T. Chamberlin) No. Am. 171: 76.

— French Empire in. (M. P. Guieysse) Indep. 51: 1191.

— Great Britain in. (R. Temple) No. Am. 170: 897.

— — and her Rivals in. (H. Vambéry) National, 31: 191.

— — and Russia in. (A. Rustem) 19th Cent. 50: 723.

— Greece and. Ed. R. 194: 28.

— Heart of, Skrine's. Ath. '99, 2: 377.

— in the Hands of China, Russia, and England. (C. H. Clark) J. Mil. Serv. Inst. 14: 988.

— Influence of Europe on. (M. Townsend) Contemp. 79: 169. Same art. Ecl. M. 136: 616.

— Innermost, Cobbold on. (T. R. Holdich) Nature, 61: 495. — (D. B. Macdonald) Nation, 71: 174.

— International Routes of. (E. Reclus) Indep. 51: 1210.

— Journey through, Notes of my. (S. Hedin) Harper, 97: 665.

— Political and Commercial Future of. (W. C. J. Reid) Forum, 32: 341.

— Problem of. (A. T. Mahan) Harper, 100: 536-929.

— Railways in, Warfare of. (A. H. Ford) Cent. 37: 794.

— Russia's Extension in. (V. Holmstrem) Indep. 51: 1195.

— Russian Central, Visit to. (M. F. O'Dwyer) J. Soc. Arts, 45: 479.

— Russian Railway Policy in. (R. E. C. Long) Fortn. 72: 914.

— Southwestern, Link Relations of. (T. Williams) Nat. Geog. M. 12: 249, 291.

— Students of. Spec. 87: 597.

— U. S. and Politics in. (J. B. Moore) Indep. 51: 1206.

— Western, Discoveries in. (C. R. Conder) Scot. R. 34: 236.

Asia Minor. Ed. R. 189: 515.

— Archæological Field-work in. (J. R. S. Sterrett) Nation, 66: 125.

— The Archæologist Traveling in. (J. R. S. Sterrett) Indep. 51: 1477.

— Glimpses of. (J. R. S. Sterrett) Chaut. 32: 518.

— Rediscovered. Quar. 186: 64.

— Who are the People of? (J. R. S. Sterrett) Nation, 65: 371.

Asiatic Bankers. Liv. Age, 212: 222.

Asiatic Courage. Spec. 84: 916. Same art. Liv. Age, 226: 392.

Asleep on Picket; an incident of the war in Cuba. (E. F. Floyd) Overland, n. s. 33: 344.

Asmodeus in the Quarters; a devil tale. (V. F. Boyle) Harper, 100: 217.

Asnyk, Adam. (W. R. Morfill) Ath. '97, 2: 225.

Asolo, Browning in. (K. C. Bronson) Cent. 37: 920.

Aspen, The, and its Uses. Chamb. J. 74: 102.

Asphalt, Albertite-like, in the Choctaw Nation. (J. A. Taff) Am. J. Sci. 158: 219.

— Petroleum and Bitumen. (A. Jaccard) Pop. Sci. Mo. 50: 380.

— Source of Supply of. (G. Willets) Nat'l M. (Bost.) 14: 57.

Asphalt Paving. (S. F. Peckham) Pop. Sci. Mo. 58: 225.

Asphaltene. (S. F. Peckham) J. Frankl. Inst. 151: 50.

Asphalts, Laboratory Production of, from Animal and Vegetable Materials. (W. C. Day) J. Frankl. Inst. 148: 205.

Asplenium, A Study of. (A. V. Jennings) Knowl. 21: 211.

Ass, Home of the Wild. Chamb. J. 78: 135.

Assassin, The Soul of the. Liv. Age, 226: 718.

Assassination and Politics. (G. Slater) Westm. 151: 211.

— a Fruit of Socialism. (G. Langtot) Fortn. 76: 571.

Assassination Mania, The; its Social and Ethical Significance. (F. L. Oswald) No. Am. 171: 314.

Assassinations. Murdered Statesmen of the Century. (E. W. Low) Eng. Illust. 18: 595.

— of the Century. (J. Kechie) Pall Mall M. 23: 111.

— of Kings and Presidents. (J. M. Buckley) Cent. 41: 136.

— Presidential, Prevention of. (L. Wallace) No. Am. 173: 721.

Assaulting Columns. Un. Serv. M. 15: 534.

Assemblage, in Social Control. (E. A. Ross) Am. J. Sociol. 2: 823.

Assembly Ball, The: a story. (S. B. Kennedy) Harper, 94: 442.

Assessments, Confiscation by. (B. A. Rich) Am. Law R. 33: 242.

Assignats, On the Depreciation of. (C. Cuthbertson) Econ. R. 8: 482.

Assignment of Choses in Action. (E. Jenks) Law Q. 16: 241. — (W. R. Anson) Law Q. 17: 90.

Assimilation and Heredity. (J. Loeb) Monist, 8: 547.

Assisi. (E. MacMahon) Argosy, 72: 429.

Assistant Masters' Association, Meeting at Manchester, 1900. Ath. '00, 2: 379.

Associated Press; a newspaper trust. (T. W. Brown) Am. Law R. 31: 569.

Association and Experience. (W. Fite) Philos. R. 9: 268.

— Contributions to the Comparative Study of. (R. G. Kimble) Am. J. Sociol. 4: 666.

— Knowledge and. (T. L. Bolton and E. M. Haskell) Educa. R. 15: 474.

— of Ideas. (Francis A. Kellor) Pedagog. Sem. 8: 341.

Association of Amer. Agricultural Colleges and Experiment Stations. (Dr. A. C. True) Science, n. s. 10: 110.

Association of Colleges and Preparatory Schools of the Middle States and Maryland, 13th Annual Convention of. (F. H. Howard) School R. 8: 26.

Assoc. of Economic Entomologists, 11th Annual Meeting. (A. H. Kirkland) Science, n. s. 10: 333.

Assoc. of Official and Agricultural Chemists, 16th Annual Convention. (H. W. Wiley) Science, n. s. 10: 368.

Associations Law in France, The. Outl. 68: 522.

Assos, Excavations at. (W. P. P. Longfellow) Nation, 72: 9. — Am. Arch. 73: 79.

At Cross Purposes. (Th. Bentzon) Critic, **36**: 460.

At Cross Purposes; a story. (C. Burke) Argosy, **66**: 98.

At the Curve of the Road; a story. (H. C. Wood) Nat'l M. (Bost.) **6**: 224.

At the Dentist's; a play. Adapted by H. Mackenzie from the Danish of E. Höyer. Gent. M. n. s. **67**: 417.

At Diamond Price; a story. (M. Byrde) Eng. Illust. **20**: 77.

At a Dog's Grave; a poem. (A. C. Swinburne) Ecl. M. **133**: 751.

At the Door; a little comedy. (T. Jenks) Cent. **36**: 857.

At the Dovelys'; a love story. (S. Ford) McClure, **15**: 112.

At the Dropping-off Place. (W. McL. Raine) Overland, n. s. **35**: 410.

At the Eleventh Hour. (D. Lyall) Sund. M. **28**: 1–412.

At the End of the Big Curve; a story. (L. C. Senger) Bk. News, **16**: 587.

At the Fall of the Curtain; a poem. Ecl. M. **131**: 707.

At the Feet of our Lady. (L. Teeple) Overland, n. s. **36**: 263.

At the Foot of the Trail. (M. C. Graham) Cent. **40**: 220.

At the Fork of the Road. (L. B. Ellis) New Eng. M. n. s. **21**: 634.

At Four Cross-roads; a tale. (M. Q.-Couch) Argosy, **70**: 307.

At the Gate. (E. Nesbit) Longm. **36**: 26.

At the Gates of Mercy. (L. B. Edwards) Lippinc. **67**: 362.

At the Guardhouse; a story. (P. Y. Black) Canad. M. **15**: 151.

At the Half-way House; a story. (J. A. Nicklin) Gent. M. n. s. **63**: 607.

At Imlach's Crossing. (H. Bindloss) Sund. M. **30**: 36.

At the Jew's Granary; a tale of Crete. (N. W. Williams) Idler, **11**: 375.

At the Laboratory Window; a poem. (A. C. Benson) Ecl. M. **136**: 688.

At the Last; a poem. (F. Mayo) Argosy, **63**: 103.

"At Least a Martyr;" a story. (C. Cotterell) Temp. Bar, **111**: 540.

At Leisure; a song. (G. B. Stuart) Argosy, **64**: 339.

At Mat Aris Light. (J. A. Barry) Chamb. J. **74**: 394.

At McNally's Bend; a tale of the Sierras. (Marion Hill) Nat'l M. (Bost.) **5**: 427.

At the Mercy of Tiberius; a story. (G. Parker) Pall Mall M. **20**: 4.

At Nightfall. (G. Gissing) Lippinc. **65**: 705.

At Nightfall; poem. (A. Phelps) Atlan. **84**: 126.

At Ohiwa; a tale. (A. W. Bright) Argosy, **73**: 236.

At the Rising of the Waters. (J. Buchan) Chamb. J. **74**: 173.

At Seven Rivers. (W. J. Davis) Cent. **34**: 147.

At the Sign of the Ship. (A. Lang) Longm. v. 29–38.

At the Sign of the "Silver Bell." (A. W. Arnold) Chamb. J. **78**: 705–754.

At Sunset; a poem. Ecl. M. **131**: 288, 298.

At the Theatre Royal, Broadlands; a story. Macmil. **80**: 121.

At Third Hand. (W. D. Howells) Cent. **39**: 496.

At Three Thousand Yards; a story. (C. T. Jackson) Nat'l M. (Bost.) **12**: 347.

At the Time of Sheep-washing. (H. Sutcliffe) Liv. Age, **227**: 66.

At the Tunnel's End; a story. (R. S. Baker) McClure, **18**: 160.

At the Turn of the Road; a story. (B. Moses) McClure, **9**: 727.

At the Twelfth Hour; a tale of a battle. (J. A. Altsheler) Atlan. **82**: 541.

At Twilight. (G. W. Caryl) Cent. **33**: 757.

At Vulcan's Forge; a poem. (E. V. Cooke) Chaut. **30**: 380.

Athena Polias on the Acropolis of Athens. (A. S. Cooley) Am. J. Archæol. 2d s. **3**: 345.

Athenæum [Magazine], Seventieth Birthday of. Ath. '98, **1**: 9.

Athenæum Club, London. Decorations. (A. L. Baldry) Art J. **50**: 21.

Athenian Democracy in the Light of Greek Literature. (Abby Leach) Am. J. Philol. **21**: 361.

Athenian Physician to his Patient, Letter from. (J. Albee) Poet-Lore, **11**: 20.

Athens, Acropolis, Bronze-reliefs from. (Paul Wolters) Am. J. Archæol. **11**: 350.

— Ancient Paintings in Churches of. (N. H. J. Westlake) Archæol. **51**: 173.

— British School at, 1895–96. (E. Gardner) Sat. R. **83**: 693.

— A First-night at. Macmil. **76**: 407.

— History of, A Moral from. (B. Bosanquet) Int. J. Ethics, **9**: 13.

— In Modern. (S. J. Barrows) Liv. Age, **218**: 147.

— Modern. (G. Horton) Scrib. M. **29**: 1–195.

— Notes from. (S. P. Lambros) Ath. '97, **1**: 450.

— Public Spirit in Modern. (D. Bikélas) Cent. **31**: 378.

— A Religious Riot in. (D. Quinn) Nation, **73**: 469. — Indep. **53**: 3016.

— Schools of Archæology at. (J. R. S. Sterrett) Nation, **65**: 10, 67, 86, 165.

— Theseum at, Notes on. (W. Lowrie) Am. J. Archæol. 2d s. **5**: 37.

— Tragedy of. (W. B. Wallace) Un. Serv. M. **21**: 89.

— Trials in. Green Bag, **11**: 103.

— University of, Trouble in. Nation, **64**: 140.

— A Walk in. Illus. (M. Gardner) Good Words, **38**: 31.

Atherton, Mrs. Gertrude. Acad. **55**: 431.

— American Wives and English Husbands. Sat. R. **85**: 501.

— Patience Sparhawk and her Times. Sat. R. **84**: 72. Same art. Sat. R. **84**: 202.

— Senator North. Ed. R. **193**: 158. — (M. B. James) Lippinc. **68**: 351.

Athletes, Movements of, Photographic Analysis of. Nature, **64**: 377.

Athletic Championships. (M. W. Ford) Outing, **31**: 81.

Athletic Club, Chicago. (J. W. Hipwell) Outing, **33**: 145.

— New York. (M. W. Ford) Outing, **33**: 248.

Athletic Contest, A Picturesque. (H. W. Mabie) Outl. **63**: 41.

Athletic Contests, International. (W. B. Curtis) Outing, **36**: 350.

Athletic Girl, The. (A. O'Hagan) Munsey, **25**: 729.

Athletic Master in Public Schools. (H. J. Spenser) Contemp. **78**: 113.

Athletic Performances, Remarkable. (M. W. Ford) Outing, **35**: 603.

Athletics and the University Social Problem. Outing, **36**: 191.

— Abuses in. (W. Camp) Indep. **52**: 714.

— American Methods. Sat. R. **88**: 128.

— and Good Citizenship. (C. S. Loch) Int. J. Ethics, **9**: 434.

— and Health. (W. B. Thomas) Cornh. **81**: 537.

— Are the English an Athletic People? New R. **16**: 41.

— College. Outl. **67**: 896. — (A. Tyler) Lippinc. **69**: 840.

Athletics, College, for Women. (S. F. Richardson) Pop. Sci. Mo. 50: 517.
— Columbia University. (J. P. Paret) Outing, 32: 9.
— Delights of Winning. Sat. R. 91: 398.
— Directed Sport as a Factor in Education. (F. H. Tabor) Forum, 27: 320.
— Effect of Training. (Eugene A. Darling) Harv. Grad. M. 8: 26. 9: 198.
— Ethics of Ancient and Modern. (P. Collier) Forum, 32: 309.
— for Politicians. (C. W. Dilke) No. Am. 169: 237.
— Giants of the Past. (J. S. Mitchell) Outing, 38: 269.
— His First Race. (A. Ruhl) Outing, 36: 247.
— in France. (C. Whitney) Outing, 36: 178.
— in Universities. (G. W. Orton) Canad. M. 9: 396.
— Influence of Climate in International. (H. Sears) No. Am. 165: 333.
— Medical Supervision of. (E. A. Darling) Harv. Grad. M. 10: 190.
— Negative Side of Modern. (A. Bates) Forum, 31: 287.
— Notable Performances and Records. Outing, 36: 460.
— Our Gentlemanly Failures. (S. H. Jeyes) Fortn. 67: 387. Same art. Liv. Age, 213: 174.
— Physiology of Strength and Endurance. (W. L. Howard) Pop. Sci. Mo. 53: 187.
— Record Breakers. (T. I. Lee) Munsey, 25: 472.
— Rise and Fall of. (A. C. Sage) Lippinc. 60: 539.
— Specialization in. (M. W. Ford) Outing, 30: 574.
— University, English and American. (J. Corbin) Outing, 39: 31.
— — Outlook in. Outing, 36: 103, 211, 334, 452.
— Worship of. (A. H. Gilkes) National, 30: 77. Same art. Ecl. M. 129: 765.
Athos, Mount. Chamb. J. 74: 372.
Atkinson, Edward, and Freedom of Discussion. Gunton's M. 16: 409.
Atkinson, Canon J. C. Ath. '00, 1: 435.
Atlanta, Georgia, Carnegie Library. Lib. J. 25: 70.
Atlantic Cable, The Making and Laying of an. (H. Muir) McClure, 8: 255.
Atlantic Monthly, Forty Years of. Atlan. 80: 571. — Dial (Ch.) 23: 173.
Atlantic Ocean, At Sea on. (H. Hall) Chaut. 25: 393.
— North, Oceanography of. (Albert, Prince of Monaco) Geog. J. 12: 445.
— — Research in. (O. Pettersson) Geog. J. 11: 609.
Atlantic Passage, The, To-day. Chamb. J. 76: 669. — (M. E. Merington) Chaut. 30: 175.
Atlantic Speedway, The. (H. P. Whitmarsh) Cent. 36: 779.
Atlantic Union, The. (W. Besant) Forum, 30: 245.
Atlantis, a Sketch, Scott-Elliot's. Sat. R. 83: 418.
Atlas, Century. (M. B. Anderson) Dial (Ch.) 25: 97.
Atmosphere, Breathable, Waste of. (G. L. Varney) Chaut. 29: 486.
— Constituents of the. (A. Dastre) Chaut. 28: 180.
— in Astronomical Work. (A. E. Douglass) Pop. Astron. 5: 64.
— Inert Constituents of the. (W. Ramsay) Pop. Sci. Mo. 59: 581. Same art. Nature, 65: 161.
— Modern Writers on. Church Q. 51: 160.
— Sifting the. (J. M. Bacon) Contemp. 80: 231. Same art. Ecl. M. 137: 772. Same art. Liv. Age, 231: 277.
— Temperature of the, and Causes of Glacial Periods. (H. N. Dickson) Geog. J. 18: 516.
— Theory of, Reminiscences of. (G. Mooar) Bib. Sac. 58: 294.
— Upper Regions of the. (J. Trowbridge) Forum, 26: 561.

Atmosphere; U. S. Daily Astronomic Survey. (W. L. Moore) Nat. Geog. M. 8: 299.
Atmospheric Air, Separation of the Least Volatile Gases of, and their Spectra. (G. D. Liveing and J. Dewar) Am. J. Sci. 162: 207.
Atmospheric Conditions in the Central and Eastern Portions of the U. S. compared with those in the High Plateaus of the Southwest. (T. J. J. See) Pop. Astron. 6: 65.
Atmospheric Survey, U. S. Daily. (W. L. Moore) Geog. J. 12: 176.
Atnas, Who are the? (A. G. Morice) Am. Antiq. 23: 307.
Atoll Islets, Broadening of. (C. Hedley) Nat. Sci. 12: 161.
Atomic Theories in Physics, Necessity of. (L. Boltzmann) Monist, 12: 65.
Atomic Theory from the Chemical Standpoint. (H. N. Stokes) Science, n. s. 11: 601.
— Some Objections to. (F. K. Cameron) Science, n. s. 11: 608.
Atomic Weights. (F. G. Wiechmann) Science, n. s. 9: 23. — (F. P. Venable) Science, n. s. 9: 477.
Atomism, Psychological. (H. Münsterberg) Psychol. R. 7: 1.
Atoms and Energies. (W. S. Franklin) Science, n. s. 14: 295.
— On Bodies Smaller than. (J. J. Thomson) Pop. Sci. Mo. 59: 323.
"Atone," in Extra-ritual Biblical Literature. (A. B. Davidson) Expos. 6: 92.
Atonement and Government. (A. E. Thomson) Bib. Sac. 56: 689.
— and Personality. (A. Boutwood) Lond. Q. 96: 296.
— as a Factor in Divine Government. (L. R. Fiske) Meth. R. 58: 913.
— Brief Review of the History of the Doctrine of. (T. S. Laud) Ref. Ch. R. 48: 33.
— Doctrine of. (W. S. H. Hermans) Meth. R. 57: 906. — Ref. Ch. R. 47: 115.
— Elements of the Doctrine of, in the Facts of Christ's Sufferings. (J. S. Candlish) Bib. World, 9: 87.
— Hall on. (W. MacLaren) Presb. & Ref. R. 8: 813.
— in Non-Christian Religions. (G. S. Goodspeed) Bib. World, 17: 22, 96, 297.
— Moberly's Atonement and Personality. (H. R. Mackintosh) Crit. R. 11: 530. — (W. Sanday) Expos. 9: 321. — Church Q. 52: 201. — (J. Rickaby) Month, 98: 136, 253.
— Notion of Merit in the History of Theology. (W. Rupp) Ref. Q. 44: 444.
— St. Paul's Doctrine of. (W. Rupp) Ref. Q. 44: 336.
— Spiritual Principle of, Lidgett on. (D. Somerville) Crit. R. 8: 11.
— Theory of, as held by the Reformed Church in U. S. (C. Cort) Ref. Ch. R. 47: 108.
— Vicarious and Exemplary both. (H. S. Gekeler) Ref. Q. 44: 496.
— Wilson on. (E. P. Boys-Smith) Crit. R. 9: 325.
— Wilson, Simon and Robertson on. Church Q. 48: 144.
Atonement of the Vanguard's Skipper. (W. Wood) Chamb. J. 74: 264.
Attachments, Intellectual. (René Doumic) Liv. Age, 223: 574.
Attack and Counter-attack, Drill in. (S. L. Murray) Un. Serv. M. 17: 21.
— General Principles of the. Un. Serv. M. 16: 376.
— Oblique, Study of, from Battles of Kolin, Rossbach, Gravelotte, and Leuthen. J. Mil. Serv. Inst. 24: 169.
— Problem of. (E. S. May) J. Mil. Serv. Inst. 23: 83.

Attack, Thoughts on Methods of. (M. D. Hardin) J. Mil. Serv. Inst. 16: 66.

Attention, An Aspect of. (E. E. C. Jones) Monist, 8: 356.

— Dynamics of. (G. Spiller) Mind, 26: 498.

— Effect of Certain Stimuli on the Wave of. (R. W. Taylor) Am. J. Psychol. 12: 335.

— Fluctuation of the Attention to Musical Tones. (H. O. Cook) Am. J. Psychol. 11: 119.

— Fluctuations of, in some of their Psychological Relations. (J. W. Slaughter) Am. J. Psychol. 12: 313.

— Methods of Distracting. (F. E. Moyer) Am. J. Psychol. 8: 405. — (L. Darlington and E. B. Talbot) Am. J. Psychol. 9: 332.

— Psychology of. (D. H. Blanchard) Philos. R. 8: 23.

Attic Lease Inscription, An. (G. D. Lord) Am. J. Archæol. n. s. 3: 44.

Attraction and Repulsion. (L. Meadows) Argosy, 66: 339.

Attwood, F. G. (L. McK. Garrison) Cosmopol. 29: 550.

Atwater, W. W., Prof., Experiments of. Outl. 64: 646.

Aubertin, Francis, and his Decorative Work. Artist (N. Y.) 23: 90.

Aubrey, John. (H. N. Williams) Argosy, 70: 333.

Aubrey, John, F. R. S.; an odd story. (A. C. Benson) Gent. M. n. s. 58: 76.

Aucassin and Nicolete. (R. Le Gallienne) Cosmopol. 31: 145.

Auckland Islands, The. Chamb. J. 75: 459.

Audiences of London. (J. F. Nisbet) Theatre, 39: 226.

Audley End, House of Earl of Suffolk. (Elizabeth J. Saville) Pall Mall M. 12: 314.

Audrey; a poem. (T. W. H. Crosland) Ecl. M. 132: 346.

Audrey; a novel. (M. Johnston) Atlan. 87: 593-746. 88: 11-791.

Audubon, John James. Blackw. 164: 58. Same art. Ecl. M. 131: 477.

— and his Journals, Coues's. (C. H. Merriam) Science, n. s. 7: 289. — (C. H. Merriam) Nation, 66: 151.

— — M. R. Audubon on. (F. W. Halsey) Bk. Buyer, 16: 118. — Nature, 57: 386. — (S. A. Hubbard) Dial (Ch.) 24: 70. — Sat. R. 85: 577. — Spec. 80: 441.

Audubon Society, The Massachusetts. (C. S. Sargent) Garden & F. 10: 419.

Augsburg Confession and Martin Luther. (J. W. Richard) Luth. Q. 29: 497. 30: 29, 359, 463.

August Outing, An. (E. W. Sandys) Outing, 34: 489.

Augustine, St., and the Pelagian Controversy. (B. B. Warfield) Chr. Lit. 16: 248.

Augustine, St. Confessions. Acad. 58: 528. — Spec. 79: 217. — (A. F. West) Presb. & Ref. R. 12: 177.

— Landing of, in Britain. Month, 89: 449.

— J. Martin on. (G. Santayana) Philos. R. 10: 515.

— Mission to England, ed. by Mason. Sat. R. 83: 640.

Augustus as a Travelling Companion; a story. (S. J. Underwood) Nat'l M. (Bost.) 5: 434.

Aulnoy, Marie Catherine, Baroness. (A. M. Huntington) Critic, 35: 794.

Ammunition, Small-arms, Supply of. (G. S. Wilson) J. Mil. Serv. Inst. 7: 313.

Aumale, Henri d'Orléans, Duc d'. (C. G. J. Reeve) Longm. 30: 268. — (E. F. S. Dilke) Ath. '97, 1: 650. — (A. de Ternant) Westm. 153: 427. — Ed. R. 188: 122.

— and the Condé Museum. (H. Bouchot) Harper, 96: 441.

Aumonier, James, with portrait. (Mrs. A. Bell) Studio (Internat.) 11: 141.

Aunt and Orderly; a story. (A. Beresford) Argosy, 63: 728.

Aunt Eliza and her Slaves. (E. Symmes) New Eng. M. n. s. 15: 528.

Aunt Jane's Album; a story. (E. C. Hall) Cosmopol. 28: 385.

Aunt Looba's Love Philter. (G. B. Stuart) Argosy, 66: 320.

Aunt Louise; an episode. (S. E. Braine) Eng. Illust. 19: 221.

Aunt of the Savages, The; a story. (J. Barlow) Outl. 61: 306.

Aunt Sarah's Brooch. (A. Morrison) Strand, 17: 206.

Aureli, Cesare, Roman Sculptor and his Work, with portrait. (M. D. Walsh) Cath. World, 66: 731.

Aurelius Antoninus, M. Porcher's. (W. L. Brown) Nation, 66: 107, 129.

Aurevilly, Barbey d'. (C. Whibley) New R. 16: 204.

Auriferous Conglomerate of the Transvaal. (G. F. Becker) Am. J. Sci. 155: 193.

Aurora Australis, as observed from the "Belgica." (F. A. Cook) Pop. Sci. Mo. 59: 21.

— Northern and Southern Lights at the Same Time. (H. Arctowski) Pop. Astron. 9: 207.

— Observations on. (H. Arctowski) Geog. J. 16: 92.

Aurora Borealis. (W. F. Felch) Pop. Sci. Mo. 53: 467. — (Alex. McAdie) Cent. 32: 874.

— Height of the. Nature, 60: 130.

— 27-Day Auroral Period and the Moon. (H. H. Clayton) Am. J. Sci. 155: 81.

Austen, Jane. Ecl. M. 132: 725. — Acad. 53: 262. — Liv. Age, 217: 214. — (A. Repplier) Critic, 37: 514.

— The Bores of. (R. Grey) Fortn. 76: 37. Same art. Ecl. M. 137: 582. Same art. Liv. Age, 230: 694.

— More about. Temp. Bar, 122: 458.

— Novels of. Acad. 52: 96. — (Earl of Iddesleigh) 19th Cent. 47: 811. Same art. Ecl. M. 135: 206. Same art. Liv. Age, 225: 681.

— Proposed Monument to. Critic, 32: 218.

— Renascence of. (J. Harper) Westm. 153: 442.

Austerfield. (H. M. Dexter) New Eng. M. n. s. 21: 185.

Austin, Alfred. (W. Archer) Critic, 37: 145. — (W. Sharp) Good Words, 40: 406.

— as a Satirist. Acad. 58: 452.

— Conversion of Winckelmann. Acad. 51: 144.

Austin, Edward. (W. W. Vaughan) Harv. Grad. M. 7: 512.

Austin, M., Memorandum of his Journey. Am. Hist. R. 5: 518.

Australasia, Exclusion of Aliens and Undesirables from. (W. P. Reeves) National, 38: 596.

— Extensions of Democracy in. (H. De R. Walker) Atlan. 83: 577.

— Federation of. Asia. R. 29: 321.

— — and United States compared. (R. Stout) Forum, 30: 321.

— Government and Banking in. (W. H. Fitchett) R. of Rs. (N. Y.) 15: 195.

— in 1898. (G. R. Badenoch) Asia. R. 25: 344.

— Progress of, 1837-97. (J. Borthvick) J. Soc. Arts, 46: 390.

— Resources and Foreign Trade of. (Sir R. Stout) Contemp. 78: 266.

— Vegetation of. (W. B. Hemsley) Knowl. 20: 66, 118, 161, 242.

Australasian Association for Advancement of Science. (Prof. A. Liversidge) Science, n. s. 10: 143.

— Meeting of, 1898. Science, n. s. 7: 452.

— Melbourne Meeting of, 1900. Nature, 61: 494.

Australasian English. (G. L. Kittredge) Nation, 67: 169.

Australasian Poetry. (G. J. H. Northcroft) Lond. Q. 96: 119.

Australian Democracy. (E. L. Godkin) Atlan. 81: 322.

Australian Folk-Lore. (W. Dunlop) Anthrop. J. 28: 22.

Australian Horseman, The. (H. C. MacIlwaine) Harper, 99: 257.

Australian Marsupialia. (B. A. Bensley) Am. Natural. 35: 245.

Australian Memories. (F. G. Aflalo) Cornh. 83: 515.

Australian Privateering in 1804. Pall Mall M. 17: 50.

Australian Railways, Statistics of. (P. Howell) J. Statis. Soc. 62: 83.

Australian Tribes, Indian Words used by. (J. Fraser) Am. Antiq. 23: 89, 171.

Australian Verse, Some. Macmil. 85: 136.

Austria and Russia, Agreement between. Contemp. 80: 721.

— Anti-Semitism in. (L. T. Damon) Nation, 70: 453.

— Anxiety as to, 1901. (R. Blennerhassett) National, 37: 357.

— at the End of the Century. (F. Count Lutzow) 19th Cent. 46: 1008.

— Constitutional Crisis in. (M. Baumfield) Forum, 30: 55.

— Elections in. (G. P. Gooch) Westm. 154: 619.

— Future of. Outl. 67: 434.

— Home-rule Difficulties. Sat. R. 91: 166.

— Imperial Library of. (H. C. Bolton) Lib. J. 24: 247.

— Outlook in; a dream. (S. Schidrowitz) Contemp. 78: 894.

— Politics in, Crisis in. Spec. 79: 588.

— — 1899. Sat. R. 87: 773.

— Royal House of, and its Murdered Empress. (M. S. Warren) Eng. Illust. 20: 115.

— Thun's Resignation. Sat. R. 88: 413.

— Whitman's. Sat. R. 87: 434.

Austria-Hungary. Quar. 189: 266.

— and the *Ausgleich*. (E. Reich) 19th Cent. 43: 466.

— Breaking up of the Empire. (N. E. Prorok) Contemp. 73: 153. — (F. W. Hirst) Fortn. 70: 56. — Spec. 80: 852.

— The Dead-lock in. Contemp. 72: 60. Same art. Liv. Age. 214: 373.

— Finances; *Ausgleich* between Austria and Hungary. (A. Matlekovits) Econ. J. 8: 17.

— Financial Relations of. (L. S. Amery) Econ. J. 8: 314.

— Future of. R. of Rs. (N. Y.) 17: 33.

— Internal Crisis in. Ed. R. 188: 1.

— Is it Weak? Spec. 78: 790.

— National Conflict in. Quar. 194: 372.

— Parliamentary Difficulties in. (Germanicus) Fortn. 68: 948.

— Political Status of Europe. (S. Brooks) World's Work, 1: 764.

— Resumption of Specie Payments in. (W. C. Mitchell) J. Pol. Econ. 7: 106.

— Stirring Times in. (S. L. Clemens) Harper, 96: 530.

— Strike of German Students in. (S. Schidrowitz) Contemp. 73: 450.

— Taxation in, Direct, Reform of. (R. Sieghart) Econ. J. 8: 173.

— under Francis Joseph. (A. von Schäffle) Forum, 25: 574, 664. — (C. B. Roylance-Kent) Macmil. 79: 145.

Austrian, Ben, Painter. (G. Kobbé) Chaut. 33: 509.

Austro-Hungarian Bank. Bank. M. (N. Y.) 55: 695.

Author, American, Disadvantages of an. (J. R. Musick) Writer, 10: 64.

— and Publisher. Dial (Ch.) 26: 187.

— — at Peace. (Mary B. Mullett) World's Work, 1: 777.

Author, as the Printer sees him. (J. H. McFarland) World's Work, 1: 779.

— his own Press Agent. (H. Lamont) Nation, 73: 86.

— Letters to a Living. (Arthur Penn) Forum, 24: 366.

— Literary Experience of a Would-be. (Grace Whitton) Writer, 14: 164.

— Modern Cash. Sat. R. 89: 40.

— On Commencing. Quar. 186: 88.

— What is an? (A. Moffatt) Jurid. R. 12: 217.

— The Young, and the Old. (C. S. Skilton) Bk. Buyer, 18: 26.

Author-Diplomats, American. (A. I. du P. Colman) Critic, 33: 253.

Author's Reading, An, and its Consequences: a story. (Mrs. B. Harrison) Harper, 97: 729.

Author's Reading in Simpkinsville. (R. M. Stuart) Cent. 38: 612.

Author's Story, An. (M. Maartens) Scrib. M. 26: 685.

Authority and Reason. (W. Ward) Am. Cath. Q. 24: 164.

Authority as a Principle of Theology. (J. Kaftan) Am. J. Theol. 4: 673.

— Final Seat of. (C. P. Gasquoine) Westm. 153: 690.

— in Religion. Outl. 67: 435.

— the Protestant Principle. (C. F. Sanders) Luth. Q. 31: 337.

Authors and Authorship. Outl. 69: 444.

— and Publishers. (H. T. Peck) Indep. 52: 2971. — (W. Besant) Critic, 34: 546. — (W. H. Page) Writer, 13: 39.

— as Publishers. (A. C. Gunter) Writer, 14: 145.

— Disappearing. (J. M'Carthy) No. Am. 170: 395.

— Foreign, in America. (R. R. Wilson) Bookman, 12: 498, 589. 13: 58, 154, 368.

— Forgotten. Macmil. 79: 155.

— Lack of New and Noticeable. (M. Beerbohm) Sat. R. 86: 106.

— Minor. Acad. 61: 343.

— of the 18th Century, Titled. (A. Dobson) Lippinc. 68: 449.

— Old Age of New England. (H. Butterworth) R. of Rs. (N. Y.) 22: 698.

— The Profession of. (C. L. Burnham) Writer, 11: 67.

— Property of. (C. D. Warner) Writer, 13: 17.

— Publishers and Booksellers. (J. A. Steuart) Fortn. 69: 255.

— Soldier. Critic, 32: 377.

— Sorrows of Scribblers. National, 31: 63.

— Troubles of. (J. Benton) Writer, 14: 69.

— Unknown, and Publishers. World's Work, 1: 663. 2: 1211.

Authors Club. (R. W. Gilder) Critic, 30: 315.

Authorship as a Livelihood. Acad. 61: 95.

— Chronicles of an Unsuccessful Author. Lippinc. 62: 428.

— Dignity of. Spec. 79: 517. Same art. Ecl. M. 130: 430.

— Reeve on Practical. (W. H. Hills) Writer, 14: 172.

— Terrors of. (E. E. Benton) Lippinc. 61: 869.

— The Writer's Trade. Acad. 59: 15, 155, 195.

Auto-da-fé, An. (M. M. Hickson) Longm. 30: 517.

Autobiography, A Plea for. (C. B. C. Eaglesfield) Chaut. 26: 425.

Autobiography of a Child. Blackw. 164: 453, 603, 771. 165: 52-707.

Autobiography of a Curling-stone, The. (T. Dykes) Chamb. J. 75: 129.

Autobiography of a Quack. (S. W. Mitchell) Cent. 37: 109, 291, 385.

Autocrat of the Dinner Time. 19th Cent. **47**: 624. Same art. Liv. Age, **225**: 485.

Autograph Letters of Irving, Hawthorne, etc., Some Extracts from. Bookman, **13**: 152.

Autographs, Apropos of Some. (Aug. Birrell) Liv. Age, **212**: 126.

— A Chat about. Acad. **52**: 406.

— Collecting. Chamb. J. **74**: 359. Same art. Ecl. M. **129**: 710.

— Literary. (W. F. Fauley) Critic, **39**: 175.

— of Musicians, Facsimiles of. Music, **14**: 305.

Autolycus. (Evelyn Webster) Idler, **14**: 27.

Automatic Reactions. (L. M. Solomons) Psychol. R. **6**: 376.

Automatism, Interpretations of. (W. R. Newbold) Pop. Sci. Mo. **50**: 507.

— Some Mental. (E. H. Lindley and G. E. Partridge) Pedagog. Sem. **5**: 41.

Automobile, The. (H. Fournier) Indep. **53**: 2936.

— in Common Use, The. (R. S. Baker) McClure, **13**: 195.

Automobile-making in America. (J. A. Kingman) R. of Rs. (N. Y.) **24**: 297.

Automobile Race from Paris to Berlin. (W. Wellman) McClure, **18**: 21.

Automobiles. (J. G. Speed) Cosmopol. **29**: 139. — Outing, **36**: 437. — (J. G. Speed) Outl. **63**: 28. — (G. J. Varney) Lippinc. **64**: 143. — (W. W. Beaumont) J. Soc. Arts, **45**: 17.

— as a Means of Progression. (L. C. Cornford) Argosy, **73**: 342.

— Care of. (J. A. Kingman) Outing, **38**: 433.

— Development of. (M. C. Krarup) Outing, **37**: 548.

— Electric. (W. Baxter, jr.) Pop. Sci. Mo. **57**: 479.

— Evolution and Present Status of. (W. Baxter, jr.) Pop. Sci. Mo. **57**: 406.

— for the Average Man. (C. Moffett) R. of Rs. (N. Y.) **21**: 704.

— Gasoline. (W. Baxter, jr.) Pop. Sci. Mo. **57**: 593.

— Heavy, for Road Service. (F. M. Maynard) Engin. M. **19**: 733, 825.

— in France, Progress of. (R. Crawford) Pall Mall M. **25**: 59.

— in French Recreative Life. (G. W. Carryl) Outing, **37**: 376.

— in Paris. (E. Wildman) Munsey, **22**: 704.

— in Recreative Life. (R. Bruce) Outing, **36**: 81.

— Nomenclature of. (R. Bruce) Outing, **38**: 327.

— The Petroleum. (P. Daimler) Engin. M. **22**: 356.

— Place of. (R. Bruce) Outing, **37**: 65.

— Progress in Construction. (W. W. Beaumont) Engin. M. **18**: 523.

— Road Traction. (Prof. Hele-Shaw) J. Soc. Arts, **49**: 32.

— The Situation as to. (H. P. Maxim) Cassier, **16**: 599.

— Steam. (J. A. Kingman) Cassier, **19**: 117.

— Touring in. (H. R. Sutphen) Outing, **38**: 197.

— Trials of, 1000 Miles. (W. W. Beaumont) Engin. M. **20**: 81.

— Recent Progress of, in France. (Marquis de Chasseloup-Laubat) No. Am. **169**: 399.

Autonous, Story of. (W. H. Hudson) Pop. Sci. Mo. **58**: 276.

Autos da Fé and the Jews. (E. N. Adler; M. Kayserling) Jew. Q. **13**: 392. **14**: 136.

Autumn, Flowers of. (E. E. Rexford) Lippinc. **66**: 547.

— in Franconia. (B. Torrey) Atlan. **83**: 57, 207.

— Odors of. (C. C. Abbott) Lippinc. **66**: 637.

— Physical Changes of. (N. S. Shaler) Chaut. **26**: 144.

Autumn; a poem. (P. H. Savage) Atlan. **80**: 728.

Autumn; a poem. (A. Law) Ecl. M. **131**: 532.

Autumn; a poem. (P. E. Bilkey) Outing, **33**: 196.

Autumn; a poem. Outing, **35**: 18.

Autumn by the Sea. Liv. Age, **231**: 221.

Autumn Colors, in Leaf and Flower. (F. S. Mathews) Chaut. **26**: 25.

Autumn Leaves; a poem. (B. E. Howell) Outing, **31**: 80.

Autumn Retrospect. (D. R. Goodale) New Eng. M. n. s. **17**: 605.

Autumn Song. (V. W. Cloud) Atlan. **86**: 355.

Autumn Sunshine. (F. Coppée) Liv. Age, **219**: 587.

Auvergne, Churches of. (Mrs. S. Van Rensselaer) Cent. **36**: 569.

Avatars, The. (P. Carus) Open Court, **11**: 464.

Ave, Cæsar! a story. (W. B. Wallace) Gent. M. n. s. **64**: 209.

Ave Jesu; a Christmas Carol. (C. W. Stubbs) Outl. **66**: 783.

Avenarius, Richard, and his Theory of Knowledge. (F. Carstanjen) Mind, **22**: 449.

Avenger, The; a story. (M. C. Lindsay) Belgra. **93**: 37.

Avenging Angel. (Mrs. J. R. Hudson) Lippinc. **65**: 784.

Average Man, The; a poem. (H. Garland) Outl. **63**: 75.

Averted Tragedy, An; a Missouri story. (G. Norton) McClure, **15**: 217.

Avesta, Zend. Asia. R. **23**: 129.

— and the Bible. (C. F. Aiken) Chr. Lit. **17**: 477.

— not Philonian. (L. H. Mills) Asia. R. **31**: 124.

— Uncertainties of, and their Solution. (L. H. Mills) Crit. R. **9**: 329.

Awakening, The. (L. Tolstoi) Cosmopol. **27**: 34, 196.

Awakening; a poem. (C. Trembly) Outing, **30**: 159.

Awakening of Sergeant Lediard, The. (H. Child) Temp. Bar, **116**: 201.

Awakening of a Small Plover; a story. (H. T. George) Cosmopol. **32**: 75.

Awatobi, The Storming of. (G. W. James) Chaut. **33**: 497.

Awful Fluke, An. (E. P. Statham) Chamb. J. **74**: 445.

Awful Story of Heley Croft, The. (A. S. Appelbee) Chamb. J. **76**: 397.

Axe, Double, and the Labyrinth. (W. H. D. Ronse) J. Hel. Stud. **21**: 268.

Axolotls, Anatomy of a Collection from Colorado. (H. L. Osborn) Am. Natural. **35**: 887.

Axtell Family. (S. J. Axtell) N. E. Reg. **53**: 227.

Aydon, Castle, Northumberland. (W. H. Knowles) Archæol. **56**: 71.

Aye-aye: a remarkable mammal. (R. Lydekker) Knowl. **24**: 269.

Ayer Papyrus. (E. J. Goodspeed) Am. J. Philol. **19**: 25.

Aylesbury, Manor of. (J. Parker) Archæol. **50**: 81.

Aylesford, Kent, Urn-Field at. Archæol. **52**: 317.

Aylett, Patrick Henry, with portrait. (Sallie E. M. Hardy) Green Bag, **10**: 153.

Ayr, River. (W. M. Gilbert) M. of Art, **20**: 135.

Azimba and Chipitaland, A Year in. (H. C. Angus) Anthrop. J. **27**: 316.

Azores, Economics in, and the Peasantry. (P. T. Lafleur) Nation, **73**: 354.

— In the World of the. (H. Ilowizi) Harper, **104**: 85.

Aztec Calendar Stone, The. (Adelia H. Taffinder) Overland, n. s. **37**: 695.

Aztec Cities and Civilization. (S. D. Peet) Am. Antiq. **22**: 311.

B. A. and the Bells, The; a story. (A. G. Hyde) Blackw. **164**: 812. Same art. Ecl. M. **132**: 385. Same art. Liv. Age, **220**: 313.

Baalbec, A Ride to.   Liv. Age, **213**: 210.

Baba Nanak.   (W. H. Rattigan) Lond. Q. **92**: 291.

Babar's Memoirs, Was Abdur-rahim Translator of?
(H. Beveridge) Asia. R. **30**: 114, 310.

Babbage, Charles.   (J. Fyvie) Temp. Bar, **119**: 27.

Bab-el-hawiyat ; a tale.   (W. Le Queux) Belgra. **94**: 1.

Babette ; a story.   (E. Arbuthnot) Belgra. **94**: 502.

Babette's Obiter Dicta ; a child's mind.   (Florence M.
Parsons) Temp. Bar, **124**: 343.

Babies in the Bush ; a story.   (H. Lawson) Blackw.
169: 473.   Same art. Liv. Age, **230**: 233.

Babington, Charles Cardale.   (I. H. B.) Nature, **57**:
315.

Babism.   (E. D. Ross) No. Am. **172**: 606.

— and the Bab.   (J. T. Bixby) New World, **6**: 722.
— (W. H. Rattigan) Lond. Q. **92**: 291.

Babites, The.   (H. H. Jessup) Outl. **68**: 451.

Baboon-hunting on an African Farm.   Chamb. J. **74**:
191.

Babuisms.   (Cornelia Sorabji) Temp. Bar, **124**: 376.

Baby, The ; a chronicle of Putnam Place.   (G. L.
Collin) Harper, **103**: 279.

Baby Bunting ; a story.   (M. A. Low) Canad. M. **17**:
553.

Baby Corps, The ; a poem.   (Irving Bacheller) Cent.
32: 938.

Baby-farming, A Remedy for.   (F. H. Low) Fortn. **69**:
280.

" Baby Mine ; " a yachting yarn.   (G. J. Leovy) Outing, **31**: 357.

Baby Shows.   (F. Steelcroft) Strand, **14**: 378.

Babylon the Great.   (A. Bierbower) Lippinc. **62**: 837.

— Hanging Gardens of.   (B. I. Wheeler) Cent. **34**:
220.

Babylonia, American Exploration in.   Acad. **52**: 195.

— and Assyria, Rogers's History of.   Nation, **72**: 397.

— Earliest Chapter of History.   (J. A. Craig) Monist,
11: 481.

— Early History of.   (H. H. Howorth) Eng. Hist. R.
14: 625.   **16**: 1.

— Expedition in, by University of Pennsylvania, 1898.
(H. V. Hilprecht) Indep. **52**: 2717.

— History of, Radau's Early.   (J. P. Peters) Nation,
71: 369.

— Recent Discoveries in.   (A. H. Sayce) [Contemp.]
Liv. Age, **212**: 360.   Same art. Chr. Lit. **16**: 381,
484.

— Religion of.   Meth. R. **59**: 135.

— — Jastrow on.   (O. C. Whitehouse) Crit. R. **9**: 277.
— (J. P. Peters) Am. Hist. R. **4**: 502.

Babylonian and Assyrian Antiquities in the British
Museum.   Sat. R. **89**: 752.

Babylonian Discoveries.   Ed. R. **187**: 364.

Babylonian Literature, Text-book in.   (M. Jastrow, jr.)
Bib. World, **9**: 248.

Bacchante, Statue of the, and the Boston Art Commission.   (Frank Sewall) Am. Arch. **55**: 11.

Bacchylides.   (C. W. Bain) Sewanee, **6**: 349. — (L.
Dyer) Nation, **65**: 513.

— and his Native Isle.   (J. I. Manatt) Atlan. **81**: 413.

Bach, J. Sebastian.   (J. F. Runciman) Sat. R. **89**: 294,
328, 360.

— and Handel, The Importance of, in Music.   (W. S.
B. Mathews) Music, **13**: 170.

— Christmas Oratorio ; a story.   (Aimée M. Wood)
Music, **15**: 281.

— On Popularizing.   (E. Dickinson) Music, **12**: 1.

— to Beethoven, From.   (Vincent D'Indy) Music, **16**:
553.   **17**: 40.

Bach Edition, Origin of.   (H. Kretschmar) Music, **18**:
397.

Bach Society.   (H. Kretschmar) Music, **18**: 42.

Bacheller, Irving, with portrait.   Bk. News, **19**: 297.

Bacheller, Irving. Eben Holden.   (A. B. Maurice)
Bookman, **12**: 235.

— — How it was Written.   Writer, **14**: 56.

Bachelor in Fiction, The.   (P. Pollard) Bookman, **12**:
146.

Bachelor Girl, A.   (A. S. B. Rue) Chaut. **27**: 77.

Bachelor's Degree, Requirements for.   (C. W. Dabney)
School R. **7**: 154.

Bachelor's Den, A ; a poem.   (M. J. Reid) Outing, **31**:
248.

Bachelordom, Luxurious.   (J. L. Ford) Munsey, **20**:
584.

Bachelors and Spinsters, Noted.   (F. A. Doughty)
Cath. World, **67**: 650.

Bacillaria of the Occidental Sea.   (A. M. Edwards)
Am. J. Sci. **158**: 445.

Bacilli and Disease.   (C. E. Page) Am. J. Soc. Sci. **38**:
25.

Back Attic, The ; a story.   (A. Noble) Belgra. **98**: 415.

Back from the Pole.   (R. Voss) Liv. Age, **227**: 595.

Bacon, Francis, with portrait.   Acad. **52**: 53.

— the Foundation of Science.   (W. J. McGee) Forum,
27: 168.

— Idols ; a commentary.   (W. H. Hudson) Pop. Sci.
Mo. **55**: 788.

— New Atlantis, Date of.   (G. C. M. Smith) Ath. '00,
1: 146.

— Poems of.   Acad. **53**: 49. — (J. I. Manatt) R. of Rs.
(N. Y.) **17**: 445. — Quar. **187**: 422.

— — Recovery of.   (C. H. Levy) Outl. **58**: 270.

Bacon, Roger, as an Hebraist.   (S. A. Hirsch) Jew. Q.
12: 34.

— " Opus Majus " of, Bridges's.   Am. Hist. R. **3**: 526.
— Sat. R. **84**: 319.

— Unpublished Fragment by.   (F. A. Gasquet) Eng.
Hist. R. **12**: 494.

Bacon, Rev. Thos., a Pioneer in Negro Education.
(B. C. Steiner) Indep. **51**: 2287.

Bacteria and the Decomposition of Rocks.   (J. C.
Branner) Am. J. Sci. **153**: 438.

— Blood and Identification of Species of.   (A. S.
Grünbaum) Sci. Prog. n. s. **1**: 616.

— Form and Size of.   (A. Macfadyen and J. E. Barnard) Nature, **63**: 9.

— Use of, in our Food Products.   (H. W. Conn) Internat. Mo. **2**: 279.

— Useful.   (J. B. C. Kershaw) Chamb. J. **76**: 419.
See also Microbes.

Bacteria Beds of Modern Sanitation.   (Lady E. Priestley) 19th Cent. **49**: 624.   Same art. Liv. Age, **229**:
496.   Same art. Ecl. M. **137**: 85.

Bacterial Diseases of Plants.   (E. F. Smith) Am. Natural. **31**: 34, 123.

Bacterial Life, Effect of Physical Agents on.   (A.
MacFadyen) Pop. Sci. Mo. **58**: 238. — Nature, **63**:
359.

Bacterial Processes of Sewage Purification.   (R. Hering) Engin. M. **15**: 960.

Bacteriology.   (G. S. Woodhead) Nature, **55**: 517.

— American Society of Bacteriologists.   (H. W. Conn)
Science, n. s. **13**: 321.

— Chester's Manual of Determinative Bacteriology.
(H. W. Conn) Science, **14**: 967.

— Conn's Agricultural Bacteriology.   (E. W. Allen)
Science, **14**: 1001.

— Hueppe's Principles of.   (H. W. Conn) Science, n. s.
9: 513.

— in the Queen's Reign.   (G. C. Frankland) Longm.
30: 213.   Same art. Ecl. M. **129**: 266.

— Military Uses of.   (C. E. Woodruff) J. Mil. Serv.
Inst. **25**: 178.

— Origin, Scope and Significance of.   (W. T. Sedgwick) Science, n. s. **13**: 121.

Bacteriology, Systematic. (A. A. Kanthack) Nature, 58: 97.

"Baculi Cornuti." (H. W. C. Davis) Eng. Hist. R. 16: 730.

Baculites, Larval Coil of. (J. P. Smith) Am. Natural. 35: 39.

Bad-character Suit, A; a story. (Flora A. Steel) Pall Mall M. 13: 127. — Munsey, 17: 825.

Bad Hour, A; a story. (P. Vernon) Argosy, 68: 110.

Bad Lands of the Wild West. (E. H. Barbour) Outing, 36: 166.

Bad Medicine Man, The; a story. (H. Garland) Indep. 52: 2899.

Badajos, Storming of. (S. Crane) Lippinc. 65: 579.

Baden-Powell, Sir George. Geog. J. 13: 77.

Badgers and Badger-baiting. (P. A. Graham) Longm. 34: 264.

Badges used by British Army. (W. Wood) Pall Mall M. 21: 95.

Badminton, England, and its Associations. (E. Hodges) Idler, 14: 255.

Badness; a story. (J. J. à Becket) McClure, 9: 949.

Baertsoen, Albert, painter. (G. Mourcy) Studio (Internat.) 5: 227.

Baffinland, Survey in. (R. Bell) Geog. J. 18: 25.

Bagasse as Fuel, Approximate Value of. (F. N. G. Gill) J. Soc. Art, 49: 517.

Bagdad. (H. V. Geere) Chamb. J. 74: 89. Same art. Ecl. M. 128: 554.

Bagdad Railway; the focus of Asiatic policy. National, 37: 624.

Bagehot, Walter, Wit and Seer. (W. Wilson) Atlan. 82: 527. — (M. E. G. Duff) National, 34: 532. — (L. Stephen) National, 35: 936. Same art. Liv. Age, 226: 681.

Bahamas. (E. B. Worthington) Canad. M. 13: 507.
— Fishing in. (E. L. Sabin) Outing, 35: 264.

Bahawalpur, At the Court of. (R. D. Mackenzie) Cent. 35: 641.

Bahr Gazal Frontier, New Light on the. (J. T. Wills) Fortn. 70: 849.
— Why not a Buffer-state on? Spec. 81: 728.

Baikal, Lake, Hydrographic Explorations of. Geog. J. 11: 143.
— to the Yenesei. (G. F. Wright) Nation, 71: 267.

Bailey, Philip James, and his Work. (J. A. Hammerton) Sund. M. 27: 45.
— Festus. Acad. 60: 447.

Bailie's Double; a story. (J. Watson) Cosmopol. 31: 153.

Baillie, Admiral, 1756-1826. (F. P. Badham) Scot. R. 36: 81.

Baillie, Joanna, Memorial Tablet to, Hampstead, England. J. Soc. Arts, 48: 745.

Bain, James. (A. H. V. Colquhoun) Canad. M. 15: 31.

Baireuth, Wagner's Operas at. (E. P. Frissel) Music, 18: 303.

Bait, The; a story. (C. J. Cutcliffe Hyne) Pall Mall M. 16: 520.

Baker, Sir Benjamin, with portrait. Cassier, 17: 350.

Baker, Rev. Talbot H. R. Ath. '00, 1: 473.

Baker, Wm. Spohn. Bibliography of his Works. Pennsyl. M. 22: 1.

Bakrid, An Episode of the. National, 34: 749.

Baku, Persia, and its Oil Springs. (F. H. Skrine) Pall Mall M. 18: 222.
— Oil-fields of. (G. F. Wright) Nation, 72: 46. — (D. A. Louis) Engin. M. 15: 986.

Balaam, Seraphim on. (H. Hayman) Crit. R. 11: 195.

Balakirew and Borodine, Russian Musicians. (A. Pougin) Music, 12: 440.

Balance of Power, Hassall's. (H. M. Stephens) Am. Hist. R. 3: 349.

Balatka, Hans. (W. S. B. Mathews) Music, 16: 196.

Balch, William Lincoln. Writer, 14: 59.

Balcony Scene in Romantic Drama. (F. C. Drake) Cosmopol. 31: 227.

Baldassare, Galuppi, Musical Composer. (M. A. Wotquenne) Music, 16: 540.

Baldness, Secret of, according to M. Sebouraud. (G. C. Nuttall) Contemp. 73: 356. Same art. Liv. Age, 217: 172. Same art. Ecl. M. 130: 554.

Baldwin, Joseph G., and the Flush Times. (G. F. Mellen) Sewanee R. 9: 171.

Baldwin, J. M. Social Interpretations; a reply. (J. M. Baldwin) Philos. R. 7: 621.

Baldwyn, C. H. C., Birds drawn by. Artist (N. Y.) 29: 37.

Baldy; a story. (S. B. Elliott) Harper, 98: 416.

Balfour, Arthur J. The Balfour Legend. National, 33: 232.
— Failure in Literature. Sat. R. 84: 214.
— Open Letter to. Fortn. 67: 325.

Balkameh; a story. Pall Mall M. 24: 455.

Balkan Peninsula, Peoples of the. (W. Z. Ripley) Pop. Sci. Mo. 54: 614.

Balkans, Customs, Races, and Religions in. (E. M. Lynch) Cath. World, 66: 596. 67: 171.
— Disturbance in, 1899. Outl. 61: 861.
— The Dream-empire of the. Spec. 78: 538. Same art. Liv. Age, 213: 491.
— Miller on. (C. H. Cooper) Dial (Ch.) 23: 70. — (L. Heilprin) Nation, 64: 361.
— Situation in. Liv. Age, 223: 402.

Balkash Basin, The. (G. F. Wright) Nation, 71: 401.

Balkash Lake, A Trip to. (R. P. Cobbold) Contemp. 75: 248.

Ball, Wilfrid, Artist. Studio (Internat.) 7: 3.

Ball's Bluff, Battle of. (W. R. Hamilton) Un. Serv. (Phila.) 17: 8.

Ballad, Old English. (E. W. Bowen) Sewanee R. 9: 286.

Ballad of the Antiquarian. (E. P. Butler) Nat'l M. (Bost.) 12: 791.

Ballad of Bygone Days, A. (E. Gordon) Outing, 31: 377.

Ballad of Fans, A. (K. Murray) Belgra. 95: 311.

Ballad of the Harper and the King's Horse. (J. Large) Argosy, 69: 175.

Ballad of the Little Black Hound. (D. S. Shorter) Longm. 30: 45.

Ballad of Poverty Row. (H. G. Cone) Cent. 33: 230.

Ballad of Quintin Massy. (S. H. M. Byers) Midland, 8: 402.

Ballad of Reading Gaol, by C 3. 3. (A. Symons) Sat. R. 85: 365.

Ballad of Two Wheels, A. (L. A. Coonley) Outing, 29: 539.

Ballad Catalogue, Lord Crawford's. Library, 3: 1.

Ballad Literature, Old, The Ethics of. (M. Peacock) Antiq. n. s. 33: 305.

Ballade of Forgotten Names; a poem. (D. Cave) Gent. M. n. s. 64: 133.

Ballade of the Huntsman, The. (R. Taft) Outing, 33: 443.

Ballade of Tief-Blau Wasser. (A. H. Japp) Argosy, 64: 537.

Ballads, Child's English and Scottish Popular. (A. Lang) Acad. 53: 514. — Quar. 188: 66.
— A London Ballad Shop. Acad. 51: 574.
— Mitchell's "Gude and Godlie." (W. B. Warfield) Presb. & Ref. R. 10: 160.
— Old World, and Ballad Music. (F. S. Leftwich) Gent. M. n. s. 60: 224.

Ballagh, Harold. (Carrie Elizabeth Harrell) Writer, 14: 120.

Ballanafad. (J. V. Sears) Lippinc. **68**: 609.

Ballantyne, Robert Michael, as a Writer for Boys. Acad. **60**: 498.

Ballechin House, Alleged Haunting of. Acad. **59**: 595.

Ballet, Costume Designing for. M. of Art, **20**: 162.

— French, and English Masque. (H. M. Johnstone) Sewanee, **4**: 428.

— How it is Designed. M. of Art, **22**: 371.

Ballet Dancing at the Empire Theatre, London. (Selwyn Image) Sat. R. **91**: 465.

Ballet Girls in Russia, The Imperial. (F. V. Gibson) Theatre, **39**: 172.

Balliol College. (H. W. C. Davis) Argosy, **72**: 187.

Balloon and Kite in Meteorology. (A. Macivor) Gent. M. n. s. **59**: 268.

— as an Instrument of Scientific Research. (J. M. Bacon) J. Soc. Arts, **47**: 277.

— Dirigible, of M. Santos-Dumont. (S. Heilig) Cent. **41**: 66.

— First Long Voyage in a. Eng. Illust. **18**: 107.

— How to cross the Atlantic in a. (S. A. King) Cent. **40**: 855.

— in the Civil War. (W. A. Glassford) J. Mil. Serv. Inst. **18**: 255.

— in Military Operations. (A. Delmard) Pall Mall M. **17**: 161. — (H. Hergesell) Forum, **26**: 1.

— Night in a ; an Astronomer's Trip from Paris to the Sea. (D. Klumpke) Cent. **38**: 276.

— Up in a. (J. M. Bacon) Eng. Illust. **20**: 150.

Balloon Photogrammetry. (R. M. Bache) J. Mil. Serv. Inst. **15**: 372.

Balloon Racing. (W. Wellman) McClure, **17**: 203. Same art. Idler, **20**: 99.

Ballooning. Temp. Bar, **114**: 114. Same art. Ecl. M. **131**: 359.

— as a Science and a Sport. (E. S. Holden) Munsey, **25**: 761.

— John M. Bacon and. (C. Middleton) Sund. M. **29**: 748.

— Higher than the Birds. (G. W. Wood) Good Words, **42**: 52.

— How I came to bombard London. (J. M. Bacon) Good Words, **40**: 598.

— in the Civil War, Reminiscences of. (W. J. Rhees) Chaut. **27**: 257.

— Mid-air Observations. (J. M. Bacon) Knowl. **23**: 1.

— Military. (G. J. Varney) Lippinc. **62**: 568.

— — Modern. (G. E. Walsh) Chaut. **25**: 146.

— over the Alps. (C. Herbert) Strand, **17**: 664. **18**: 175.

— over London at Night. Macmil. **85**: 55.

— Scientific. (J. M. Bacon) Contemp. **74**: 851.

— Siege of Paris and the Air-ships. (K. Blind) No. Am. **166**: 474.

Balloons, Dirigible, for War Purposes. (R. Thayer) J. Mil. Serv. Inst. **7**: 177.

— Hot Air. (E. L. Zalinski) J. Mil. Serv. Inst. **14**: 32.

— in War. (A. W. Greely) Harper, **101**: 33.

— Metal. (J. W. Smith) Strand, **15**: 285.

Ballot in England, Early History of. (C. Gross) Am. Hist. R. **3**: 456.

— in the Italian Communes. (A. M. Wolfson) Am. Hist. R. **5**: 1.

— Reform of the. (O. G. Villard) Nation, **72**: 169.

Ballot Laws of New York. (J. F. Daly) No. Am. **168**: 103.

Ballot Reform, Fourth of July Celebrations and the Interests of. (A. B. Riker) No. Am. **164**: 636.

Ballot Reform in Pennsylvania. Ann. Am. Acad. Pol. Sci. **16**: 151.

Ballou, Adin, and the Hopedale Community. (G. L. Cary) New World, **7**: 670.

Ballygunge Cup, The ; a story. (W. A. Fraser) McClure, **13**: 311.

Balmoral Castle. Eng. Illust. **17**: 481.

Balnacraig. Chamb. J. **75**: 753.

Baltimore, Barons of, Religion under, C. E. Smith's. (W. H. Browne) Am. Hist. R. **5**: 577. — (W. H. Browne) Nation, **70**: 95.

Baltimore, City of. Bank. M. (N. Y.) **60**: 613.

— Municipal Art Conference. Munic. Aff. **3**: 706.

— New Charter for. (J. H. Hollander) Nation, **66**: 201.

— New England in. (W. T. Brigham) New Eng. M. n. s. **22**: 218.

— Woman's College. Meth. R. **57**: 112.

Baltimore and Ohio Railroad, Economic History of. 1827-53. (M. Reizenstein) J. H. Univ. Stud. **15**: 283.

Baltimore Orioles in Captivity, Songs of. (W. E. D. Scott) Science, n. s. **14**: 522.

Baluchistan. See Beloochistan.

Balzac, Honoré de. (L. J. Burpee) Canad. M. **9**: 347. — (G. McL. Harper) Scrib. M. **27**: 617. — (A. Symons) Fortn. **71**: 745. Same art. Liv. Age, **222**: 7.

— and his Work. (H. T. Peck) Cosmopol. **27**: 238.

— and Shakespeare ; which is the greater ? (Hiram M. Stanley) Dial (Ch.) **29**: 347.

— as he was. Pall Mall M. **19**: 423.

— Centenary of. (W. E. G. Fisher) Cornh. **79**: 603.

— Comédie Humaine. (E. S. Mapes) Critic, **39**: 159.

— "Eugénie Grandet." (W. P. Trent) Chaut. **33**: 180.

— Influence of. (E. Faguet) Fortn. **69**: 723. Same art. Liv. Age, **218**: 259.

— Intellectual Attachments. (R. Doumic) Ecl. M. **134**: 20.

— Letters of, Controversy over. Acad. **58**: 391, 423.

— Letters to Mme. Hanska. (A. S. Van Westrum) Critic, **35**: 906.

— Works ; ed. by W. P. Trent. (L. J. Block) Dial (Ch.) **29**: 417.

Balzac Literature, Some Recent. (W. P. Trent) Internat. Mo. **1**: 309.

Bamborough. (Sarah Wilson) Chamb. J. **76**: 633.

— A Royal Burgh. (S. H. Dunn) Month, **91**: 74.

Bampfield, Rev. George. Ath. '00, **1**: 178.

Banana ; how it is grown. (F. S. Lyman) Cosmopol. **24**: 365.

Banana Growing for the Markets. (R. W. Cater) Chamb. J. **74**: 421.

Banana Raising in America. (L. M. Wills) Nat'l M. (Bost.) **11**: 407.

Bananas. Spec. **80**: 400.

Banbury ; the romance in its reality. Eng. Illust. **20**: 52.

Bancroft, Frederic. Lit. W. (Bost.) **31**: 127.

Bancroft, George, Homes and Haunts of. (A. S. Roe) New Eng. M. n. s. **23**: 161.

— Letters on the Clayton-Bulwer Treaty, 1849-50. Am. Hist. R. **5**: 95.

— Teresa. (M. Beerbohm) Sat. R. **86**: 374.

Bancroft, Squire, and Mrs., Portraits of. Theatre, **38**: 7.

— Knighting of. Theatre, **39**: 53.

Bandi Miklós. Longm. **29**: 46. Same art. Liv. Age, **212**: 42.

Bandini, Manuel A., Archbishop of Lima, Peru, with portrait. (A. D. Bueno) Cath. World, **68**: 89.

Bands, Regimental. Chamb. J. **74**: 638.

Baneful Influence, A ; a story. (C. Nesbitt) Belgra. **99**: 520.

Banes, Charles Henry, 1831-97, Obituary Notice of. J. Frankl. Inst. **143**: 308.

Banff, Annals of. Quar. 186: 134.

Bangkok. (M. L. Todd) Nation, 73: 107.

Bangor, Maine. (E. M. Blanding) New Eng. M. n. s. 16: 225.

Bangs, John Kendrick. (J. Corbin) Bk. Buyer, 20: 208.

Bangweolo, Lake, Circumnavigation of. (P. Weatherly) Geog. J. 12: 241.

Bank, Abuse of the Title. Bank. M. (Lond.) 66: 18.

— Branch, Opening a. Bank. M. (Lond.) 68: 376.

— for India, State. Bank. M. (Lond.) 69: 216.

— London and River Plate. Bank. M. (Lond.) 63: 104.

— London, of Australia. Bank. M. (Lond.) 64: 323.

— of Africa, Simpson, Cullingford & Co. vs. Bank. M. (Lond.) 66: 357.

— of Belgium. Bank. M. (Lond.) 72: 221.

— — and the Bank of Holland, Variations in Rate. Bank. M. (Lond.) 70: 441.

— of England. Bank. M. (N. Y.) 54: 38, 220. — Bank. M. (N. Y.) 54: 220. — Bank. M. (Lond.) 63: 185-893. 64: 118-711. 65: 178, 361.

— — and Bimetallism. Contemp. 72: 490. — (H. R. Grenfell) Contemp. 72: 743.

— — and the Crisis of 1825. Bank. M. (Lond.) 65: 32.

— — and the Money Market. Bank. M. (Lond.) 68: 1.

— — Bankers' Balances at the. Bank. M. (Lond.) 65: 349.

— — Discount Rate of. Bank. M. (N. Y.) 54: 70.

— — from 1844 to 1899, Variations in the Rate charged by. Bank. M. (Lond.) 70: 1.

— — Reserves. (G. H. Pownall) Econ. J. 9: 394.

— — Token Money of. Bank. M. (Lond.) 69: 385, 705, 851. 70: 9, 133.

Bank of England Volunteers. Bank. M. (Lond.) 65: 402.

Bank of France. Bank M. (Lond.) 68: 165. — Bank. M. (N. Y.) 54: 509.

— — Centenary of. Bank. M. (Lond.) 69: 855. 70: 141.

— — from 1844 to 1899, Variations in Rate charged by. Bank. M. (Lond.) 70: 125.

— — Transactions for 1896. Bank. M. (Lond.) 64: 141.

— — — for 1897. Bank. M. (Lond.) 66: 165.

— — — for 1898. Bank. M. (Lond.) 68: 168.

— — — 1899. Bank. M. (Lond.) 70: 184.

— — — from 1876 to 1897. Bank. M. (Lond.) 66: 331.

Bank of Germany, Imperial. Bank. M. (Lond.) 68: 205. — Bank. M. (N. Y.) 54: 361.

— — Operations of, from 1876 to 1897. Bank. M. (Lond.) 66: 449.

— — Report for the Year 1896. Bank. M. (Lond.) 64: 169.

— — — for 1897. Bank. M. (Lond.) 66: 195.

— — — for 1898. Bank. M. (Lond.) 68: 207.

— — — for 1899. Bank. M. (Lond.) 70: 217.

— — — for 1900. Bank. M. (Lond.) 72: 189.

— — Variations in Rate. Bank. M. (Lond.) 70: 332.

Bank of Issue, Swiss, Bill for. Q. J. Econ. 12: 366.

Bank of Montreal. (J. M. Oxley) Canad. M. 16: 99.

— — and E. S. Clouston. Canad. M. 12: 424.

Bank of Russia, Imperial. Bank. M. (N. Y.) 57: 33.

Bank of Scotland. Bank. M. (N. Y.) 56: 24. — Bank. M. (Lond.) 63: 111.

Bank of Spain; is it solvent? Bank. M. (N. Y.) 57: 74.

Bank of the United States, Issues of the Second. (R. C. H. Catterall) J. Pol. Econ. 5: 421, 544.

Bank, Practical Work of a. Bank. M. (N. Y.) 63: 173-948.

— Working of a. (C. D. Lanier) Scrib. M. 21: 575.

Bank Amalgamations, Some Aspects of. Bank. M. (Lond.) 70: 325.

Bank Clearings, Interest Rates, and Politics. (C. E. Curtis) Yale R. 7: 43.

Bank Clerks and Branch Bank Managers, Dangers that beset. Bank. M. (N. Y.) 62: 402.

Bank Currency and Ideal Money. Bank. M. (N. Y.) 62: 391.

— The New, 1900. (A. D. Noyes) Nation, 70: 218.

Bank Deposits, Unclaimed. Bank. M. (Lond.) 63: 267-748.

Bank Examinations. Bank. M. (N. Y.) 62: 515.

Bank Examiners, National; do they examine? (T. L. James) No. Am. 167: 710.

Bank Fidelity Bonds. Bank. M. (N. Y.) 60: 216.

Bank Holidays. A Plea for one more. (J. Lubbock) 19th Cent. 41: 717.

— Sins of St. Lubbock. (J. E. C. Hankin) 19th Cent. 41: 467.

Bank Law, German. (S. Sherwood) Q. J. Econ. 14: 270.

Bank-note Currency, Benefits of a. Bank. M. (N. Y.) 60: 188, 354.

— Regulation of a Redeemable. Bank. M. (N. Y.) 62: 13.

Bank-note Engraving. Bank. M. (N. Y.) 54: 63.

Bank-note Forging and French Prisoners of War in Scotland. Bank. M. (Lond.) 67: 393.

Bank-note System of Switzerland. (M. Sandoz) Q. J. Econ. 12: 280.

Bank-notes and Checks, Patented. Bank. M. (N. Y.) 58: 590.

— and Legal-tender Paper. Bank. M. (N. Y.) 58: 371.

— based on Assets. Bank. M. (N. Y.) 56: 669.

— Checks and Drafts, Some Patented. Bank. M. (N. Y.) 58: 428.

— Government Notes vs. (A. I. Fonda) Arena, 20: 39.

— Making. (A. C. Campbell) Canad. M. 9: 460.

Bank Parlor, A 20th Century. (E. Bellamy) Liv. Age, 214: 141.

Bank Profits, Sources of. Bank. M. (Lond.) 69: 4.

Bank Prosecutions, Dumbell's. Bank. M. (Lond.) 70: 47.

Bank Reports, Recent, Comparative Studies of. Bank. M. (Lond.) 72: 564, 711.

Bank Reserve and Silver. Bank. M. (Lond.) 64: 429.

Bank Reserves and Gold in Germany. (F. Moos) Econ. J. 8: 556.

Bank Returns; What they Teach. (J. Hedley) Canad. M. 11: 183.

Bank Securities, Some Pitfalls of. Bank. M. (Lond.) 71: 552.

Bank Tax, Proposed, 1901. (D. MacG. Means) Nation, 72: 83.

— State, Repeal of the. (H. Justi) Sewanee, 2: 198.

Bank Taxation, Equalizing. Bank. M. (N. Y.) 60: 343.

Bank Teller, Reminiscences of a. Bank. M. (Lond.) 66: 157.

Banked Fires; a story. (A. A. Rogers) Cosmopol. 26: 295.

Banker, Education of a. Bank. M. (N. Y.) 62: 29-521.

— How to choose your. Bank. M. (Lond.) 70: 740.

— in his Public Relations. Bank. M. (N. Y.) 62: 34.

— Modern, Deplorable Moral Condition of the. Bank. M. (Lond.) 69: 911.

— of Nations, The. 1976. (A. M. Reynolds) Overland, n. s. 30: 209.

Bankers and Public Companies. Bank. M. (Lond.) 67: 1.

— as Promoters of Insurance. Bank. M. (Lond.) 64: 521.

— Company Law as it affects. Bank. M. (Lond.) 67: 73.

— A Dinner to. Bank. M. (N. Y.) 58: 602.

Bankruptcy Laws Past and Present. (W. H. Hotchkiss) No. Am. **167**: 580.

Banks, Mrs. George Linnæus. (I. F. Mayo) Argosy,
64: 21.

Banks, Sir Joseph. Journal; ed. by Hooker. Sat. R.
83: 44.

Banks, Amalgamations among. Bank. M. (Lond.)
72: 1.

— and Banking. Quar. **190**: 128.

— — A New Programme in. (R. Ewen) Westm. **148**:
611.

— and Trust Companies, Taxation of. Bank. M.
(N. Y.) **62**: 741. — (A. K. Fiske) Nation, **70**: 84.

— as Trustees of Capital and Credit. Bank. M. (N. Y.)
60: 29.

— Branch, Management of. Bank. M. (Lond.) **66**:
577, 705.

— — of Scotland. Bank. M. (Lond.) **64**: 10.

— Can they compete with the Post Office? Bank.
M. (Lond.) **63**: 357.

— Cash Holdings of. Bank. M. (N. Y.) **54**: 20.

— Competition and Touting amongst. Bank. M.
(Lond.) **68**: 573.

— Coöperative Village. (Virginia M. Crawford) Dub.
R. **121**: 269.

— Failed National, Closing of. Bank. M. (N. Y.) **62**:
811.

— General Savings and Old-age Pension Bank of Belgium. (W. F. Willoughby) J. Pol. Econ. **8**: 145.

— Government by. (G. F. Williams) Arena, **20**: 1.

— Government Deposits in. (G. E. Roberts) Forum,
29: 1.

— in Great Britain and Ireland, 1896, Capital and Reserve Funds of. Bank. M. (Lond.) **63**: 1.

— in the United Kingdom, Balance-sheets of. Bank.
M. (Lond.) **63**: 549. **65**: 505.

— Increasing the Earnings of. Bank. M. (N. Y.) **58**:
578.

— National, Government Deposits in. Bank. M. (N. Y.)
60: 200.

— — Renewal of the Charters of. Bank. M. (N. Y.)
62: 343.

— of Great Britain. Better Times Beginning. (R.
Ewen) Westm. **151**: 630.

— Penny, Competition of. Bank. M. (Lond.) **65**: 732.

— Peoples', in Italy. (G. François) J. Pol. Econ. **7**:
456.

— Saving and Lending. (R. Ewen) Westm. **147**: 188.

— Scotch, in England. Bank. M. (Lond.) **64**: 16.

— Small, in the West. (T. Cooke) Q. J. Econ. **12**: 70,
105.

— using their Credit. Bank. M. (N. Y.) **62**: 807.

Bankside, Southwark; a poem. (E. T. Jaques) Pall
Mall M. **11**: 381.

Banneker, Benjamin, the Black Astronomer. (G. M.
Jacobs) Chaut. **29**: 585.

Bannerman, Sir Henry Campbell-; will he lead?
Westm. **151**: 477.

Banquets of the Olden Time. (F. J. Ziegler) Lippinc.
60: 689.

Bantu Languages, Hymnology in the. (A. Werner)
Asia. R. **28**: 175.

Baptism and Confirmation. Church Q. **45**: 357.

— Archæology of. (H. Osgood) Bib. Sac. **55**: 1. — (A.
N. Patten) Meth. R. **61**: 440.

— for the Dead. (A. Carr) Expos. **9**: 37.

— Infant, Faith and Regeneration in. (J. D. Severing-
haus) Luth. Q. **29**: 151.

— — Review of "Baptized without Believing." (R.
H. Clark) Luth. Q. **29**: 167.

— Is it a Creative Act or merely a Declaratory Recognition of a State or Condition previously existing?
(C. Court) Ref. Ch. R. **48**: 509.

Baptismal Forms of the Evangelical Church of Prussia.
Luth. Q. **29**: 178.

Baptist Achievement, A Century of. (W. H. P.
Faunce) Outl. **69**: 190.

Baptist History, 1850-1900. (H. C. Vedder) Bib. Sac.
57: 660.

Baptistery, Florence, Restoration of. Am. Arch. **71**:
94.

Baptists of the Middle States, Vedder's. (W. H.
Whitsitt) Am. Hist. R. **4**: 553.

Bar, American; Relation, as an Order of Brotherhood,
to the State. (G. F. Hoar) Am. Law R. **32**: 641.

— English and American, Kinship of. Spec. **85**: 135.
Same art. Liv. Age, **226**: 721.

— English, Etiquette of the. Green Bag, **12**: 95.

— — under a New Light. Green Bag, **9**: 393.

— in American Colonies. Illus. Green Bag, **11**: 220.

Bar Harbor. (F. Furbush) Nat'l M. (Bost.) **8**: 395.

Barabbas and Shylock, a Character Study. (I. Davidson) Sewanee R. **9**: 337.

Baracoa, A Horseback Ride to. (G. Kennan) Outl. **61**:
627.

— The Old Town of. (G. Kennan) Outl. **61**: 813.

Baraga, Frederic, Bishop, the Apostle of the Chippe-
was, with portrait. (W. Elliott) Cath. World, **73**:
78. — (R. R. Elliott) Am. Cath. Q. **22**: 465.

— His Books in Chippewa and Ottawa Languages.
(R. R. Elliott) Am. Cath. Q. **22**: 18.

Baranof, Alexander, and the Russian Colonies of
America. (A. Inkersley) Overland, n. s. **30**: 9.

Barante, A. G. P. R. Memoirs. (A. Laugel) Nation,
70: 218.

Barasso, the Fool of San Roqué. (P. N. Beringer)
Overland, n. s. **36**: 32.

Barbara's Escapade; a story. (G. B. Millard) Midland, **9**: 440.

Barbara's Way; a story. Temp. Bar, **124**: 387.

Barbarian Codes. (G. C. Lee) Green Bag, **9**: 428.

Barbarossa. (C. T. Brady) Cent. **41**: 111, 256.

Barbecues. (J. R. Watkins) Strand, **16**: 463.

Barber, Wm. Henry, Case of; a Miscarriage of Justice.
(J. B. Atlay) Cornh. **79**: 330.

Barber's Wooing, The; a story. (K. Macquoid) Harper, **99**: 959.

Barbers, Beards and. (F. J. Ziegler) Lippinc. **60**: 852.

Barbizon School, Painters of the. (E. M. Elgin) Chaut.
30: 475.

Barb'l of Gossensass; a tale. (J. Heard, jr.) Outing,
34: 37.

Barbour, John, *vs.* John Ramsey. (G. Neilson; J. T.
T. Brown) Ath. '00, **1**: 647-760.

Barcelona, its Scenes and People. (C. Edwardes) Outing, **31**: 597.

Bards of the Gael and Gall, Sigerson's. Ath. '97, **2**:
249. — Spec. **79**: 214.

Bardsley, John Wareing, Portraits of. Strand, **13**: 550.

Barebones, Praise-God. (H. A. Gläss) Sund. M. **27**:
583.

Barefoote, Walter. (E. B. Smith) New Eng. M. n. s.
22: 157.

Barents Sea, Natural History of the Shores of. (W.
Gregory) Nature, **61**: 2.

Barère, Bertrand. Acad. **52**: 105. — Spec. **79**: 146.

— Memoirs; tr. by Payen-Payne. (A. D. Vandam)
Sat. R. **84**: 54.

Barèvau, Church at. Reliquary, **40**: 47.

Bargaining, Economics of. (J. A. Hobson) Econ. R.
9: 20.

Bargain-sales and Advertisements. Chamb. J. **78**: 61.

Barham, Richard Harris. Acad. **61**: 569.

— Ingoldsby Legends. Acad. **55**: 340.

Baring-Gould, S., or St. Paul. Church Q. **45**: 296.

Barker, Canon, A Talk with. Sund. M. **28**: 107.

Battle and a Quarrel, A. (Fred. Palmer) Scrib. M. 29: 291.

Battle of Alma Terrace; a story. (L. Quiller-Couch) Eng. Illust. 19: 13.

Battle of Slide Mountain; a story. (P. V. Mighels) Eng. Illust. 22: 41.

Battle of the Strong. (Gilbert Parker) Good Words, 39: 1-795. Same art. Atlan. 81: 29-786. 82: 78-839.

Battle under the New Conditions. (H. C. Davis) J. Mil. Serv. Inst. 23: 249.

Battle Abbey, England. (C. L. W. Cleveland) Pall Mall M. 14: 315.

Battle-call of Anti-Christ, a poem. (F. B. Crofton) Canad. M. 11: 359.

Battle Intrenchments. (J. Chester) J. Mil. Serv. Inst. 7: 298.

Battle Tactics and Mounted Infantry. (L. P. Davison) J. Mil. Serv. Inst. 20: 296.

— of Different Arms. (C. B. Mayne) J. Mil. Serv. Inst. 15: 134.

— of Infantry. (L. W. V. Kennon) J. Mil. Serv. Inst. 7: 1.

Battlefield, The Modern. (A. W. A. Pollock) Un. Serv. M. 14: 396.

Battlefields. Strand, 15: 573.

Battles, British, Stories of. (J. D. Symon) Eng. Illust. 16: 419, 625, 742.

— Proportion of Men killed in. Sat. R. 88: 319.

Battleship, Our Ideal. (P. Benjamin) Indep. 53: 2567.

— Past and Future Development of the. (H. W. Wilson) Un. Serv. M. 15: 349.

— Polity of a. (Frank T. Bullen) Spec. 83: 342.

— A Study of the Modern. (Rupert Hughes) Cosmopol. 25: 499.

— Vitals of a. (R. L. Fearn) Chaut. 27: 467.

Battleships, American. (E. W. Eberle) Cassier, 14: 167.

— and Naval Warfare. Idler, 16: 333.

— Building of, Rapid. (W. Fawcett) Pop. Sci. Mo. 58: 28.

— Greatest Fighting Machines Afloat. (F. Chester) Munsey, 24: 20.

— Nomenclature of. (J. C. D. Hay) Blackw. 163: 671.

— of the U. S. Navy. (G. H. Shepard) Cassier, 14: 179.

— The Problem of the Designs of. (E. H. Mullin) Cassier, 15: 359.

See also Warships.

Bauer, Harold, as a Musician. (J. F. Runciman) Sat. R. 91: 703.

Bauer, M., a Dutch Etcher. (A. Tomson) Studio (Internat.) 10: 38.

Baum, L. Frank. Mother Goose in Prose. Studio (Internat.) 5: 214.

Baum, Indian Village of. Nat. Geog. M. 12: 272.

Baumann, E. (L. B. Mendel) Science, 5: 51.

Baur, George. (O. P. Hay) Science, n. s. 8: 68.

— Life and Writings. (W. N. Wheeler) Am. Natural. 33: 15.

— Obituary of. Nat. Sci. 13: 140.

Bavaria, Contrasts in. (G. A. J. Cole) Knowl. 23: 121.

— Royal Palaces of, and their Builders. (Dora M. Jones) Chamb. J. 78: 199.

Bawn, An Ancient. (J. P. Mahaffy) Ath. '01, 2: 198.

Baxter, A. H., Design for a Living-room by. Artist (N. Y.) 31: 128.

Bay Psalm Book. (E. J. Carpenter) New Eng. M. n. s. 15: 575.

Bayard, Pierre du Terrail, Chevalier, Inner Life of. (V. V. M. Beede) Chaut. 32: 536.

Bayard, Samuel. Bank. M. (N. Y.) 57: 785.

Bayard, Thomas Francis. (G. F. Parker) Contemp. 74: 675. Same art. Liv. Age, 219: 739. Same art. Ecl. M. 132: 137. — Critic, 30: 375.

— and James Russell Lowell. Sat. R. 83: 308.

Bayeux Tapestry, The. Illus. (T. C. Hepworth) Artist (N. Y.) 23: 132. — Acad. 55: 468.

— Fowke on. Spec. 82: 686.

Bayle, Pierre, with portrait. (L. Lévy-Bruhl) Open Court, 12: 653.

Bayonet, The, as a Weapon. Un. Serv. M. 18: 82.

— A Plea for the. Un. Serv. M. 22: 495.

Bayreuth and its Music. (T. C. Whitmer) Music, 21: 12.

Bayreuth Performances, Decadence of. (J. F. Runciman) Sat. R. 88: 261.

— 1897. (I. Malcolm) Blackw. 162: 402. Same art. Liv. Age, 215: 328. — Sat. R. 84: 163.

— 1899. (E. I. Stevenson) Indep. 51: 2357. — Music, 16: 497.

— Some Impressions of. R. of Rs. (N. Y.) 16: 582.

Bazán, E. P. (R. Ogden) Bookman, 5: 300.

Bazar Valley, Three Expeditions to the. (H. C. Wylly) Un. Serv. M. 19: 276.

Bazin, René; an appreciation. (R. Doumic) Liv. Age, 221: 393.

— Novels of. (E. Gosse) Contemp. 79: 264. Same art. Ecl. M. 137: 36. Same art. Liv. Age, 229: 349.

Bazzini, Antonio, Violinist and Composer; with portrait. Music, 17: 643.

Beach, Mrs. H. H. A. Sonata, Opus 34. Music, 16: 208.

Beaconsfield, Benjamin Disraeli, Earl of. (R. Gottheil) Chaut. 29: 15. — (C. Whibley) Blackw. 163: 583. Same art. Liv. Age, 218: 19.

— and the Colonies. (W. Sichel) Blackw. 167: 492.

— The Man and the Minister. (A. H. V. Colquhoun) Canad. M. 11: 273.

— Pivotal Points in the Life of. (E. Hubbard) Indep. 53: 71.

— Vindication of. (F. Greenwood) Blackw. 161: 426.

Beagle, Fate of the. (V. M. Law) Pop. Sci. Mo. 57: 86.

Beagle Dogs, Use of, in Hunting. (W. H. Grenfell) Pall Mall M. 11: 333.

Bear, A, and a Panic; a hunting experience. (H. Wright) Canad. M. 17: 547.

— Celestial, in American Folk-lore. (S. Hagar) J. Am. Folk-Lore, 13: 92.

— Grizzly, Biography of a. (E. Seton-Thompson) Cent. 37: 351.

Bear-hunt in New Brunswick. (F. H. Risteen) Outing, 34: 354.

Bear-hunting. (F. L. Donohue) Outing, 29: 529.

— in the Bad Lands. (J. K. Johnson) Outing, 31: 562.

— in the Himalayas. (C. H. Powell) Blackw. 166: 362. Same art. Liv. Age, 223: 458.

— in Kashmir. (E. H. Litchfield) Outing, 38: 55.

— on Bayou Seche. (H. Ball) Outing, 31: 221.

— Smoking out a Grizzly. (J. E. Badger) Outing, 35: 115.

Bears, The Beguiling of. (F. Irland) Scrib. M. 30: 313.

— Grizzly, Adventure with. (E. Frank) Outing, 39: 147.

— of Canada. (C. A. Bramble) Canad. M. 14: 464.

— Polar, at the Zoo. (F. E. Beddard) Knowl. 20: 39.

Beards and Barbers. (F. J. Ziegler) Lippinc. 60: 852.

Beardsley, Aubrey. (L. I. Guiney) Cath. World, **69**: 201. — (F. W. Gookin) Dial (Ch.) **27**: 41. — (H. M. Strong) Westm. **154**: 86. — (Christian Brinton) Critic, **38**: 129. — (M. Beerbohm) Idler, **13**: 539. — (A. Symons) Fortn. **69**: 752. — (H. Harland) **Acad**. **55**: 437. — Idler, **11**: 189.
— Art of. Critic, **34**: 439.
— Fifty Drawings. Sat. R. **88**: 418.
— In Memoriam. Studio (Internat.) **4**: 252.
— Invention of. (A. Vallance) M. of Art, **22**: 362.
— The Memorial of. Bk. Buyer, **18**: 375.
— A New Illustrator. (J. Pennell) Studio (Lond.) **1**: 14.
— Personal Recollections of. (P. Stanlaws) Bk. Buyer, **17**: 212.
Bearer Company in the Fighting Line. (H. Stapleton) Un. Serv. M. **21**: 368.
Bearings, Roller, for Machinery. (H. A. Richmond) Cassier, **12**: 60.
Beast or Brother? (C. M. Vaile) New Eng. M. n. s. **19**: 217.
Beasts, Service of the. (H. Bindloss) Sund. M. **30**: 462.
Beasts and Birds, The Case of the. (F. G. Aflalo) Good Words, **39**: 459.
— — True Tales of. (D. S. Jordan) Pop. Sci. Mo. **54**: 352.
Beat that Failed. (A. P. Terhune) Lippinc. **66**: 756.
Beatification of a Saint, The. (C. B. Todd) Chaut. **33**: 607.
Beaton, David, Cardinal, The Murder of. (A. Lang) Blackw. **163**: 344.
— — Lang on. (D. H. Fleming) Contemp. **74**: 375.
Beatriz: a story. (M. Wilcox) Harper, **100**: 643.
Beau of, Arriette, The. (M. T. Earle) Cent. **36**: 561.
Beaufort, Margaret, Mother of Henry VII. Month, **94**: 326.
Beaulieu River, Flood-tide on. Ecl. M. **129**: 678.
Beaumarchais, Hallay's. (A. Laugel) Nation, **64**: 394, 414.
Beaumont and Fletcher. Euphrasia-Bellario; a kinswoman of Imogen. (H. Schutz Wilion) Gent. M. n. s. **62**: 203.
— Philaster. Acad. **61**: 593.
Beauties of Blood Royal. (De Fontenoy) Cosmopol. **29**: 129.
Beautiful Man of Pingalap; a story. (Lloyd Osbourne) Cosmopol. **29**: 481.
Beauty. (W. J. Stillman) Atlan. **88**: 331. — (H. T. Peck) Cosmopol. **30**: 176.
— and Immortality. Outl. **61**: 156.
— and Ugliness. (V. Paget; C. Anstruther-Thomson) Contemp. **72**: 544, 669.
— behind the Veil in Literature. Acad. **57**: 41.
— for Ashes: a poem. (E. Rhodes) Argosy, **69**: 368.
— Grades of. Month, **97**: 272.
— Health and. (C. Edson) No. Am. **165**: 509.
— Human, Varying Ideals of. (J. Collier) 19th Cent. **49**: 116.
— in Art and Nature. Sat. R. **88**: 731.
— in Common Things. (D. M. Morrell) Brush & P. **5**: 222.
— in Relation to Handicrafts. (D. Volk) Artist (N. Y.) **30**: xiii.
— Influence of, on Love. (H. T. Finck) Cosmopol. **30**: 589.
— its Relation to Use. (F. Sewall) N. Church R. **7**: 228.
— Mystery of. (E. Saltus) Cosmopol. **28**: 131.
— Novels of. (W. F. Lord) 19th Cent. **45**: 245.
— Some Types of. (I. T. Headland) Cosmopol. **26**: 65.
Beaux, Cecilia, Artist. (Mrs. A. Bell) Studio (Internat.) **8**: 215. — (W. Walton) Scrib. M. **22**: 477.
Beaver, The, in Norway. (R. Lydekker) Knowl. **20**: 293.

Beaver, Psychology of the. (W. Seton) Cath. World, **65**: 654.
— The Story of the. (W. D. Hulbert) McClure, **16**: 483.
Beaver Shooting. (F. Houghton) Outing, **33**: 471.
Because of the Judgment to Come; a story. (L. C. Morant) Belgra. **95**: 282.
Because of the Weather; a story. (A. Moore) Argosy, **71**: 30.
Beccaria and Law Reform. (U. M. Rose) Am. Law R. **34**: 524.
Bechuanaland. (J. Mackenzie) Contemp. **73**: 282.
— March Morning in. (H. A. Bryden) Sat. R. **83**: 570.
Becket, Thomas, St., of Canterbury. Church Q. **47**: 435.
— Abbott's. (A. C. McGiffert) Am. Hist. R. **5**: 117.
Beckford, Wm., "the Sultan of Lansdown Tower." Temp. Bar, **120**: 182.
Becky. (Eleanor G. Hayden) Cornh. **84**: 674.
Becky and Bithey. (M. E. Francis) Longm. **36**: 446.
Becky Sharp, Mitchell's Play. Bk. Buyer, **19**: 80.
— Portrait of Mrs. Fiske as. (P. Stanlaws) Bk. Buyer, **19**: 79.
Bede, Venerable, Alleged Error of. (A. Anscombe) Ath. '97, **1**: 744. — (E. W. B. Nicholson) **1**: 809, 841. **2**: 67.
Bedevilment of John Discombe; a story. (F. Lynde) Nat'l M. (Bost.) **7**: 227.
Bedford Jail. (L. O. Cooper) Good Words, **41**: 732.
Bedouin, In the Desert with the. (R. T. Kelly) Cent. **31**: 554.
Bedouin's Vengeance, A; a story. (E. W. Wallace) Blackw. **166**: 88–519.
Bedroom, Artistic Conversion of the. Artist (N. Y.) **23**: 36.
Beds of Fleur-de-lys; a poem. (C. P. Stetson) Atlan. **81**: 167.
Bed-warmers and Hand-warmers, Old. (R. Quick) Reliquary, **40**: 32.
Bee-keeping, Modern. (J. Kendal) Am. Cath. Q. **23**: 334.
Bee-School, A Swiss. (G. G. Thomas) Chamb. J. **76**: 20.
Bee's Brain, Optic Lobes of, in the Light of Recent Neurological Methods. (F. C. Kenyon) Am. Natural. **31**: 369.
Bees and the Development of Flowers. (F. W. Headley) Nat. Sci. **13**: 240.
— and Flowers. (G. W. Bulman) Westm. **148**: 419.
— British. (F. Enock) Knowl. **21**: 82, 97.
— Bumblebee Taverns. (C. McIlvaine) Chaut. **33**: 369.
— Daily and Seasonal Activity of a Hive of. (F. C. Kenyon) Am. Natural. **32**: 90.
— in the Hive. (M. Maeterlinck) Fortn. **75**: 465.
— Life and Battles of. (G. E. Walsh) Chaut. **25**: 648.
— Maeterlinck's Life of. (F. T. Gregg) Bk. Buyer, **23**: 115.
— Psychical Qualities of, A. Bethe on. (C. Grave) Am. Natural. **32**: 439.
— The Queen Bee and her Subjects. (H. H. Gardener) Arena, **21**: 683.
— Some Facts about. (R. W. Shufeldt) Pop. Sci. Mo. **51**: 315.
Beecher, H. W., Influence in England. (C. A. Berry) Outl. **57**: 707.
Beecher, Mrs. Henry Ward. Critic, **30**: 187.
Beechey, Sir William. (J. C. Van Dyke) Cent. **34**: 584.
Beef, Army, Verdict on. (J. B. Bishop) Nation, **68**: 347.
— Where the Beef Doth Grow. (R. Doubleday) Munsey, **23**: 45.

Beer Brewing, Modern, Influence of Science in. (F. Wyatt) J. Frankl. Inst. 150: 190, 299.

Beer-markers. (G. Dollar) Strand, 13: 75.

Beer Poisoning Epidemic. Nature, 63: 541.

" Beer Soup: " the story of an English defeat. (Maj. C. Field) Good Words, 41: 842.

Beerbohm, Max. Acad. 52: 495.

— Caricatures. (A. Lawrence) Critic, 39: 450.

— Comments on Himself. Sat. R. 85: 709.

Beers, Jan van. (M. A. Belloc) Strand, 15: 669.

Beersheba, Wells of. (G. L. Robinson) Bib. World, 17: 247. — (L. Gautier) Bib. World, 18: 49.

Beet-sugar Industry, Growth of. (R. S. Baker) R. of Rs. (N. Y.) 23: 324.

— in England. (J. Mills) Knowl. 21: 241.

Beethoven, L. van, Biography of. (A. W. Thayer) Music, 20: 143.

— Fidelio. (J. F. Runciman) Sat. R. 86: 72.

— Last Days of. (A. Quarry) Temp. Bar, 111: 564.

— Museum at Bonn. (H. E. Krehbiel) Cent. 34: 3.

— Ninth Symphony. (H. G. Daniels) Idler, 13: 127.

— Opinions of. Music, 11: 278, 342.

— Personal Appearance of. (E. Swayne) Music, 13: 139.

— A Pilgrimage to. (R. Wagner) Music, 12: 199, 318.

— Slow Movements of. (E. Swayne) Music, 18: 429.

— Sonate Characteristique, Op. 81. (F. H. Clark) Music, 15: 431.

— Sonate Pastorale, Op. 28. (F. H. Clark) Music, 15: 304.

— Works of ; their present standing. (W. S. B. Mathews) Music, 11: 428.

Beetle, Common Tiger. (F. Enock) Knowl. 20: 73.

Beetle-collector's Handbook, Hoffman's. Sat. R. 84: 20.

Before the Black Cap went on. (Flora H. Loughead) Overland, n. s. 31: 214.

Begbie, Sir Mathew, Chief Justice of British Columbia. (E. Nicolls) Canad. M. 11: 197.

" Beget " and " Begetter " in Elizabethan English. (S. Lee and others) Ath. '00, 1: 150, 315, 345.

Beggar, The ; a story. (M. Prévost) Acad. 55: 255.

Beggar of the Blue Pagoda, The. (C. Dawe) Chamb. J. 76: 741.

Beggar who chose, The. (Mary S. Boyd) Chamb. J. 78: 145-201.

Beggars, History of. (F. J. Ziegler) Lippinc. 63: 416.

Begging in Wales. Argosy, 68: 348.

Begin, Louis Nazaire, Archbishop of Quebec. (G. Stewart) Canad. M. 18: 16.

Beguiling of the Duchess Enid, The. (G. Knight) Pall Mall M. 22: 413.

Béguines Past and Present. (V. M. Crawford) Cath. World, 69: 329.

Behāri's Masterpiece ; a story. Pall Mall M. 17: 303.

Behind the Green Door ; a story. (A. T. Colcock) Nat'l M. (Bost.) 12: 356, 447, 605.

Behind Leaf Lattices. (F. S. Palmer) Outl. 65: 58.

Behind the Lines. (A. W. Burt) Lippinc. 65: 102.

Behind the Mask ; a story. (J. Friedlander) Idler, 13: 743.

Behind the Plate Glass ; a story. (L. C. Cornford) New R. 17: 587.

Behind the Purdah. (C. Sorabji) Macmil. 82: 193. Same art. Ecl. M. 135: 472. Same art. Liv. Age, 226: 380.

Behind the Veil. (T. Reynolds) New Eng. M. n. s. 23: 300.

Behn, Aphra ; the first lady novelist. (C. J. Hamilton) Cornh. 78: 522.

Behrends, A. G. F. Outl. 65: 244.

Behrens, Peter, Artist. (F. Blei) Studio (Internat.) 12: 237.

Behring Sea. See Bering Sea.

Being, Aristotelian Ideal of. (F. C. S. Schiller) Mind, 9: 457.

Being Detectives ; a story. (E. Nesbit) Pall Mall M. 18: 104.

Beira Railway, Pioneering on. (L. O. Cooper) Contemp. 78: 509.

— With Lancet and Rifle on. (L. O. Cooper) Fortn. 74: 92.

Belasco, David. Heart of Maryland. (G. B. Shaw) Sat. R. 85: 521.

Belated Boyhood, A. (M. Sherwood) New Eng. M. n. s. 15: 657.

Belden's Client. (J. B. Morgan) Green Bag, 13: 447.

Beldonald Holbein, The ; a story. (H. James) Harper, 103: 807.

Beleaguered Lady, The. (H. D. Lowry) Chamb. J. 74: 209-246.

Belfast, Notable Books printed in. (R. M. Young) Library, 7: 135.

Belfry Reminiscences. (W. H. Pollock) Sat. R. 91: 73.

Belgian Literature, 1896-97. (P. Fredericq) Ath. '97, 2: 7.

— 1897-98. (P. Fredericq) Ath. '98, 2: 10.

— 1898-99. (P. Fredericq) Ath. '99, 2: 11.

— 1899-1900. (P. Fredericq) Ath. '00, 2: 10.

— 1900-01. (P. Fredericq) Ath. '01, 2: 9.

Belgium, Art in, 1897. (E. Verhaeren) M. of Art, 20: 213.

— Current Art in. (E. Verhaeren) M. of Art, 22: 498.

— Decorative Art in. (O. Maus) M. of Art, 25: 271.

— England and. Fortn. 74: 753.

— for the Britisher. (Corbet-Seymour) Chamb. J. 74: 197-356.

— From Home to Throne in. (C. de Graffenried) Harper, 94: 722.

— Government Insurance Bank. (C. L. Roth) Ann. Am. Acad. Pol. Sci. 17: 467.

— History, Art, and Social Life of. (W. E. Griffis) Chaut. 25: 527.

— Language Difficulty in. (K. Blind) Scot. R. 31: 372.

— National Bank of. Bank. M. (N. Y.) 57: 619.

— Pirenne's Geschichte Belgiens, Band I. (W. J. Ashley) Am. Hist. R. 5: 109.

— Political Economy in. (E. Mahaim) Econ. J. 9: 129.

— Recent Politics. Sat. R. 88: 38, 157.

— The Situation in. (V. M. Crawford) Month, 90: 489.

Belief and Faith. (R. B. Steele) Meth. R. 61: 228.

— The Need to Believe. (V. Paget) Fortn. 72: 827.

— Philosophy of, Duke of Argyll's. (W. B. Greene, jr.) Presb. & Ref. R. 8: 300.

— Psychology of. (W. B. Parker) Pop. Sci. Mo. 51: 747.

— that survives Proof. Sat. R. 92: 299.

— The Will to Believe and the Duty to Doubt. (Dickinson S. Miller) Int. J. Ethics, 9: 169.

Bell, Lilian, with portrait. Bk. News, 15: 294.

Bell, Sir Lowthian, with portrait. Cassier, 12: 729.

Bell, John, of Tennessee. (J. W. Caldwell) Am. Hist. R. 4: 652.

Bell, Robert ; a Canadian geological explorer. Nature, 64: 81.

Bell, Old Flemish, at Nicholaston, Gower. Reliquary, 40: 193.

Bell that Spoke to the Soldiers, The ; a story. Acad. 55: 517.

Bell-buoy ; a ballad. (R. Kipling) McClure, 8: 364.

Bell Casting in the 17th Century. (N. H. Legge) Reliquary, 37: 193.

Bell Founder, The. (Sophus Banditz) Liv. Age, 224: 506.

Bestuzhev-Ryumin, K. N. (R. N. Bain) Ath. '97, 1: 115.

Bethany; a story. (Mrs. H. H. Penrose) Temp. Bar, 111: 427.

Bethlehem and Nazareth in Prophecy. (R. Winterbotham) Expos. 9: 14.

— as it is in 1894. (F. G. Carpenter) Nat'l M. (Bost.) 5: 390.

— Christmas at. (J. J. Tissot) Cent. 35: 176. — (C. C. Svendsen) Cath. World, 68: 459.

Bethlehem (Pa.) Ferry, 1743-94. (J. W. Jordan) Pennsyl. M. 21: 134.

Bethulah: a story. (I. Zangwill) Harper, 99: 673.

Betsy's Fulishness; a story. (A. E. Wickham) Eng. Illust. 29: 441.

Better 'an a Circus. (L. V. Lambert) Chaut. 30: 26.

Betterment Tax, The. (J. A. Webb) Am. Law R. 33: 347.

Bettina, the Redemptioner. (J. H. Walworth) Overland, n. s. 37: 685.

Betting, On. (Marcus Dods) Good Words, 38: 593.

— The Law of. (J. E. Joel) Westm. 148: 90.

— New Decision on. Spec. 78: 396.

Betting Club, Inside a. Chamb. J. 74: 49.

Betting Laws in England. Sat. R. 91: 661.

Betty and Thanksgiving; a story. (H. P. Spofford) Indep. 53: 2825.

Betty's Ancestor. (Mrs. W. P.-Gallwey) Argosy, 64: 117.

Betun, Robert de, Bishop of Hereford, and Llanthony Abbey. (A. C. Benson) Ecl. M. 128: 225.

Between the Lines; a story. Blackw. 169: 812. 170: 77.

Between the Lines at Stone River; a story. (F. A. Mitchel) Harper, 96: 283.

Between the Mountains and the Sea; a poem. (L. Morris) Acad. 53: 554.

Between the Old and the New; a tale. (R. F. Dixon) Canad. M. 9: 517.

Between Two. (J. H. Findlater) Liv. Age, 216: 493.

Between Two Shores; a story. (E. Glasgow) McClure, 12: 345.

Between Two Worlds; a story. (A. K. H. Forbes) Sund. M. 29: 631. 30: 231.

Betwixt Cup and Lip. (G. Howard Peirce) Scrib. M. 21: 632.

Betwixt the Wolf and the Door. (P. Holms) Good Words, 40: 742.

"Beware!" an episode. (T. W. Speight) Argosy, 63: 73.

Bex; a poem. (Henry Attwell) Gent. M. n. s. 62: 515.

Bexhill-on-Sea. England. (N. E. Yorke-Davies) Gent. M. n. s. 58: 269.

Beyle, Henri. (C. E. Meetkerke) Gent. M. n. s. 61: 93. — Acad. 55: 550.

Beyond Earth's Judgment. (Isabel M. Hamill) Chamb. J. 77: 396.

Beza, Baird's. (C. W. Colby) Nation, 71: 408.

Bhagavad-gita, Ethics of the. (B. C. Pal) New World, 8: 521.

Bhārata, The, and the Great Bhārata. (E. W. Hopkins) Am. J. Philol. 19: 1.

Bharti Affair; an Indian sensation. (H. C. E. Ward) Blackw. 164: 206.

Bheel Woman's Sacrifice, A; a tale. (F. A. Spencer) Argosy, 73: 219.

Bhowáni, the Cholera-goddess. (E. H. Hankin) Ecl. M. 128: 71.

Bible, The. (P. Carus) Monist, 10: 41. — (W. H. Green; P. Carus; C. H. Cornill) Monist, 10: 280.

— American Revision of. (J. M. Whiton) Outl. 58: 417.

— and Archæology (W. Rupp) Ref. Ch. R. 46: 111.

Bible, The, and the Child. (W. Rupp) Ref. Ch. R. 48: 534.

— and the London School Board. (G. B. Shaw) Sat. R. 84: 580.

— and Modern Scholarship. (H. A. Stimson) Bib. Sac. 57: 366.

— and Rationalism, Thein's. (J. J. Fox) Cath. World, 74: 380.

— and Social Ethics. Bib. World, 16: 323.

— and the Word of God. (C. S. Gerhard) Ref. Ch. R. 45: 1.

— Archæology and. (T. M. Lindsay) Crit. R. 10: 27.

— Archæology and Authority. Church Q. 49: 167.

— as Divine Revelation. (S. I. Curtiss) Bib. Sac. 58: 103.

— as Literature. (J. E. McFadyen) Bib. World, 16: 438. — (W. A. Guerry) Sewanee, 7: 83.

— as the Son of Man, or Christ. (J. Worcester) N. Church R. 4: 1.

— as the Word of God. (A. Bjorck) N. Church R. 5: 395.

— Authority of. (D. F. Estes) Bib. Sac. 55: 414. — (B. B. Warfield) Presb. & Ref. R. 10: 472.

— — as affected by the Higher Criticism. (W. D. Mackenzie) Bib. World, 13: 257.

— Criticism and. Bib. World, 11: 225.

— the Avesta, and the Inscriptions. (L. Mills) Asia. R. 31: 315.

— the Book of all Humanity. (C. Lathbury) N. Church R. 4: 27.

— The Book of God. (E. V. Gerhart) Ref. Ch. R. 47: 433.

— Children's Interest in. (G. E. Dawson) Pedagog. Sem. 7: 151.

— Claims of, as the Word of God. (J. Wagner) Luth. Q. 31: 1.

— Confirmations of the Scriptures, Some Recent. (J. Urquhart) Ecl. M. 136: 53.

— considered as a Whole. (J. Worcester) N. Church R. 4: 336.

— Defence of, Lines of. (D. S. Margoliouth) Expos. 7: 32-422. 8: 25-336.

— Deissmann's Bible Studies. (H. Hayman) Crit. R. 11: 298.

— Dictionary of; Cheyne's Encyclopædia Biblica. (B. B. Warfield) Presb. & Ref. R. 11: 516. — Am. J. Theol. 4: 364. 5: 732. — (S. D. F. Salmond) Crit. R. 11: 157. — (I. M. Price) Dial (Ch.) 31: 79. — (G. B. Gray) Jew. Q. 13: 375.

— — Davis's. (W. H. Greene) Presb. & Ref. R. 10: 333.

— — Hastings'. Bib. World, 14: 374. — (G. F. Moore and others) Am. J. Theol. 3: 84. 4: 99. — Lond. Q. 90: 225. — Presb. & Ref. R. 12: 151. — (S. D. F. Salmond) Crit. R. 8: 178. — (S. Mathews) Dial (Ch.) 24: 353. — Church Q. 46: 392. — (B. B. Warfield) Presb. & Ref. R. 9: 515.

— Difficulties in. (T. K. Cheyne) Expos. 9: 110.

— English, and English Writers. (C. M. Cady) Bib. World, 9: 185.

— — Attempts to modernize. Acad. 58: 431.

— — from Henry VIII. to James I. (H. W. Hoare) 19th Cent. 45: 646.

— — Dr. Gasquet and the Old. Church Q. 51: 138, 265.

— — Revised Version of. (A. T. Q. Couch) Ecl. M. 133: 777. Same art. Liv. Age, 222: 723.

— — Wyclif to Coverdale. (H. W. Hoare) 19th Cent. 43: 780. Same art. Ecl. M. 131: 1.

— Episcopalian Revision of. Lit. W. (Bost.) 29: 340.

— Exegesis of To-morrow. (B. W. Bacon) Outl. 67: 67.

— Fairy-tale Element in. (P. Carus) Monist, 11: 405, 500.

Bible, The; Father of English Prose Style. (J. H. Gardiner) Atlan. **85**: 684.

— fulfilled by Jesus Christ. (J. Reed) N. Church R. **4**: 41.

— German, Printed, Manuscript Copies of. (W. Kurrelmeyer) Am. J. Philol. **22**: 70.

— The Great "She." (W. Smith) Library, **2**: 1, 96, 141.

— Greatest of Books. (H. Macfarlane) Sund. M. **28**: 799.

— Gutenberg. (R. Procter) Library, n. s. **2**: 60.

— Hebrew, Ginsburg's Edition of. (L. Blau) Jew. Q. **12**: 217.

— How does it stand? (A. Brown) Lond. Q. **94**: 71.

— How it came down to us. (C. H. Levy) R. of Rs. (N. Y.) **16**: 691.

— Ignorance about the, as shown among College Students of Both Sexes. (C. F. Thwing) Cent. **38**: 123. — (N. B. Briggs) Cent. **39**: 273.

— Importance of a Correct Knowledge of. Bib. World, **14**: 227.

— in Education. (J. T. Prince) Educa. R. **16**: 353.

— in Japan, Study of. (J. L. Dearing) Bib. World, **12**: 99.

— in the Life of the People. (B. F. DeCosta) Cath. World, **71**: 751.

— in Neo-Hebraic Poetry. (A. Feldman) Jew. Q. **11**: 569.

— in Terra Cotta. (R. E. Welsh) Sund. M. **26**: 92.

— Inexact Statements in. (H. Hayman) Sund. M. **28**: 754.

— Influence of, upon the Conscience. (J. E. Rankin) Bib. Sac. **57**: 336.

— — upon Human Intellect. (J. E. Rankin) Bib. Sac. **56**: 415.

— Inspiration of. (J. C. Jacoby) Luth. Q. **37**: 217. — (B. B. Warfield) Presb. & Ref. R. **11**: 89.

— Its Spiritual Sense not known before Swedenborg. (T. F. Wright) N. Church R. **6**: 161.

— King Charles I.'s Embroidered. (C. Davenport) Library, n. s. **1**: 373.

— Language of. (J. E. Werren) N. Church R. **4**: 34.

— Literal Truth of. (T. F. Wright) N. Church R. **4**: 138.

— Making of a. (H. J. W. Dam) McClure, **8**: 331.

— Meaning and Supremacy of, Farrar's. N. Church R. **4**: 627. — Lond. Q. **89**: 112.

— Modern Faith and. (J. McIntyre) Dub. R. **120**: 38.

— Moral Evolution in. (J. F. McCurdy) Am. J. Theol. **1**: 658.

— Original Text and Swedenborg's Latin Version. (L. H. Tafel) N. Church R. **7**: 134.

— Place of, in the Roman Catholic Church. (B. F. De Costa) Cath. World, **71**: 433, 605.

— Polychrome. (C. H. Cornill) Monist, **10**: 1. — (W. H. Green) Monist, **10**: 22. — (P. Carus) Open Court, **12**: 288. — (E. L. Curtis) New World, **7**: 187. — (F. Brown) Outl. **59**: 70. — (I. M. Price) Dial (Ch.) **24**: 116. — (T. K. Cheyne) Expos. **3**: 307. — (G. P. Fisher) Bk. Buyer, **17**: 50.

— Popular Study of, in Scotland. (G. Steven) Bib. World, **11**: 239.

— Practical Use of. (P. S. Moxom) Bib. World, **15**: 424.

— Purpose of, and Faith in its Teachings. (J. W. Love) Ref. Ch. R. **48**: 182.

— Reading of, in the Worship of the New England Churches. (A. H. Coolidge) New Eng. M. n. s. **19**: 677.

— Recent Books on, 1898. (I. M. Price) Dial (Ch.) **24**: 380.

— Reference, Evolution of. (J. A. Barnes) Lond. Q. **92**: 99.

Bible, Scientific Method and its Application to the. (D. Sprague) Pop. Sci. Mo. **55**: 289.

— Stories from, in Modern English. (C. A. Powell) Nat'l M. (Bost.) **9**: 352, 463, 575.

— Strophic Forms in. (P. Ruben) Jew. Q. **11**: 431.

— Study of. (J. W. Hall) Educa. R. **14**: 348.

— — in the Home and Public School. (A. E. Goddard) N. Church R. **4**: 11.

— — Scientific, Briggs on. Church Q. **49**: 69. — (W. H. Bennett) Crit. R. **9**: 355. — (C. H. Drew) N. Church R. **6**: 580.

— — Torrey on. (B. B. Warfield) Presb. & Ref. R. **10**: 562.

— — Use of Books in. Bib. World, **16**: 3. *See also* Biblical study.

— Supernatural Revelation of. (M. Valentine) Luth. Q. **31**: 74.

— Teaching of, Importance of the Historical View in. Bib. World, **14**: 323.

— — Study Necessary for. Bib. World, **13**: 1.

— Tinkering the. Acad. **58**: 431. Same art. Liv. Age, **226**: 57. Same art. Ecl. M. **135**: 238.

— To-day in. (W. C. Elam) Lippinc. **61**: 98.

— Various Attitudes toward. (P. S. Moxom) Bib. World, **15**: 341.

— Versions of, A Century of. (B. Pick) Luth. Q. **31**: 197.

— was it all Dictated by the Lord? (T. F. Wright) N. Church R. **4**: 575.

— What is the? (D. H. Leader) Ref. Ch. R. **46**: 352.

— What it is and What it is Not. (C. M. Coburn) Bib. World, **18**: 105.

— Words in, with Obsolete Meanings. Acad. **56**: 556.

— Written by God through Men. (E. D. Daniels) N. Church R. **4**: 567.

— Woman's. (T. P. W.) Scot. R. **30**: 300.

— Old and New Testament, Criticism of. Church Q. **52**: 261.

— Old Testament. (P. Carus) Open Court, **15**: 156.

— — and Oriental Archæology. (J. B. Fox) Luth. Q. **27**: 559.

— — and Recent Assyriological Research. (M. Jastrow) Indep. **53**: 2449, 2515.

— — Books *vs.* Their Sources. (W. J. Beecher) Bib. Sac. **56**: 209.

— — Canon of, Green on. (G. C. M. Douglas) Presb. & Ref. R. **10**: 334.

— — Chief Literary Productions, from Ezra to the Maccabees. (Wildeboer, tr. J. M. P. Smith) Bib. World, **13**: 389.

— — Constructive Studies in. (W. R. Harper) Bib. World, **17**: 46-450. **18**: 56-204.

— — Criticism and, G. A. Smith on. (J. A. Selbie) Crit. R. **11**: 219.

— — Ethics of. (H. A. Stimson) Bib. World, **16**: 87.

— — Hebrew, An 11th Century Introduction to. (E. N. Adler) Jew. Q. **9**: 669.

— — Hommel on Hebrew Tradition and the Monuments. (W. L. Baxter) Presb. & Ref. R. **9**: 143.

— — Humanitarian Element in the Legislation of. (C. F. Kent) Bib. World, **18**: 338.

— — in Light of To-day. (S. R. Driver) Expos. **9**: 27.

— — Interpretation of, in the 20th Century. (W. G. Jordan) Bib. World, **17**: 420.

— — Latin Version, Old. Church Q. **52**: 130.

— — Literary Value of. Spec. **87**: 833.

— — The New. (H. G. Mitchell) Meth. R. **58**: 543.

— — Notes on Select Passages in. (F. Field) Expos. **9**: 397. **10**: 295, 395.

— — Nowack's Commentaries on. (A. H. Huizinga) Presb. & Ref. R. **12**: 465.

— — Poetical Books of, On Some Suspected Passages in. (T. K. Cheyne) Jew. Q. **10**: 13.

Bibliography and Book-collecting. (A. W. Pollard) Library, n. s. 1: 438.

— as She is Wrote. Library, 2: 449.

— Battle of. (F. Campbell) Library, 5: 120.

— Compiling a. (G. W. Cole) Lib. J. 26: 791, 859.

— of the Future. (F. Campbell) Library, 7: 33.

— Place of. (M. D. Bisbee) Lib. J. 22: 429.

— Semitic. (W. Muss-Arnolt) Bib. World, 12: 1.

— State and Local. (E. G. Swem) Lib. J. 26: 677.

Bibliomania, Concerning. Atlan. 82: 141.

Bibliomaniacs, The; a sketch. (O. Baker) Argosy, 75: 162.

Bibliotics, Frazer's. (R. S. Woodworth) Science, n. s. 14: 291.

Bicho Game, The. Chamb. J. 76: 385.

Bicycle, The American; Theory and Practice of Construction. (L. Waldo) J. Soc. Arts, 46: 46.

— and its "Wild Oats." (Eleanor Hoyt) Idler, 20: 41.

— as a Cause of Crime. (C. Lombroso) Pall Mall M. 20: 310.

— as a Military Machine. (R. G. Hill) J. Mil. Serv. Inst. 17: 312.

— Autobiography of a. (C. F. Lester) Outing, 36: 128.

— Equilibrium of the. (G. S. Hodgins) Outing, 36: 659.

— for Military Uses. (H. H. Whitney) J. Mil. Serv. Inst. 17: 542. — (E. P. Lawton) J. Mil. Serv. Inst. 21: 449. — (H. G. Wells) Fortn. 74: 914.

— Health on the. (E. B. Turner) Contemp. 73: 640. Same art. Ecl. M. 130: 835. Same art. Liv. Age, 217: 856.

— in the Bavarian Army. Chaut. 24: 567.

— in the West, The. Overland, n. s. 35: 521.

— Portable, for Mobile Infantry. (J. M. Macartney) Un. Serv. M. 14: 388.

Bicycle of Cathay, A; a story. (F. R. Stockton) Harper, 101: 109-757.

Bicycles and Tricycles, Sharp on. (C. V. Boys) Nature, 56: 217.

— as Railway Luggage. (J. A. Simon) Fortn. 72: 217.

— Cause of High Prices. Sat. R. 89: 454.

— Improvements in. (J. Pennell) Contemp. 77: 61.

— Motor, Some Experiences of. (J. Pennell) J. Soc. Arts, 49: 181.

— Water. (E. P. Bunyea) Outing, 33: 607.

Bicycle Contingency, A. (B. Atkinson) Sund. M. 29: 103.

Bicycle Factory, A. Outing, 30: 277.

Bicycle History. (G. L. Apperson) Temp. Bar, 114: 286.

Bicycle Law in the 20th Century. (H. Graves) Contemp. 77: 506.

Bicycle Pictures by A. B. Frost. Scrib. M. 23: 605.

Bicycle Regulations in Europe. (P. S. Chancellor) Am. Arch. 56: 94.

Bicycle-rider in Europe, A. (W. H. Bishop) Nation, 65: 181.

Bicycle Tax; shall we tax the human leg? (W. E. Hicks) No. Am. 165: 511.

Bicycling. (C. S. Williams) Chaut. 31: 97. — Outing, 36: 438.

— "Al'heil" — Wheeling in Tyrolean Valleys. (G. E. Waring, jr.) Cent. 31: 866.

— from Montreal to Ste. Anne. (F. Farrington) Outing, 38. 423.

— in Japan. (A. Macphail) Outing, 29: 324.

— Lenz's World Tour Awheel. Outing, 29: 382.

— through the Dolomites. (G. E. Waring) Cent. 32: 35. See Cycling.

— through Shakespeare's Land. (W. Hale) Outing, 36: 490.

Bicyclists, Rights, Duties, and Liabilities of. (W. C. Hodges) Am. Law R. 32: 221.

Bida, Alexander. The Lord's Supper, a Painting. (J. P. Lenox) Bib. World, 11: 341.

Bida and Benin. (C. F. Harford-Battersby) Asia. R. 23: 309.

Bida, Battle of. Spec. 78: 230.

Biddenden Maids, The, Born joined at Hips and Shoulders, 1100. (G. Clinch) Reliquary, 40: 42.

Biden, Sydney, singer, with portrait. Music, 19: 65.

Bidford-on-Avon as a Sketching Ground. (S. Heath) Studio (Lond.) 6: 238.

Big Basin, About the. (Josephine C. McCrackin) Overland, n. s. 36: 135.

Big Brierly. (Jos. Conrad) Liv. Age, 229: 331.

Big-Governor-Afraid. (W. R. Lighton) Atlan. 88: 409.

Big Snow, The. (H. Rogers) Chamb. J. 78: 177.

Big Yellow Stag, The. (R. B. Townsend) Overland, n. s. 37: 825.

Bigg, William Redmore. Art J. 51: 42.

"Biggest on Record." (G. Dollar) Strand, 17: 265. 18: 396.

Bigods School, Essex, England. (Countess of Warwick) 19th Cent. 50: 983.

Bill from Tiffany's, A; a story. (J. Flynt and F. Walton) McClure, 15: 473.

Bill Goldie; a pilgrim. (W. Atkinson) Chamb. J. 76: 664.

Bill's Bluff for the Church. (R. Connor) Outl. 63: 680.

Bill's Bugle; a poem. (G. E. Crump) Outing, 33: 462.

Billiards. (D. D. Pontifex) 19th Cent. 42: 965. — Quar. 193: 482.

— — and its Devotees. (W. Broadfoot) Blackw. 161: 545.

Billinghurst, P. J., Designer and Illustrator. Studio (Internat.) 5: 181.

Billings, Josh. See Shaw, Henry Wheeler.

Billotte, René, with portrait. (M. H. Spielmann) M. of Art, 22: 121.

Billy and Hans. (W. J. Stillman) Cent. 31: 619.

Billy Billson's Fire; a story. (W. Packard) Nat'l M. (Bost.) 5: 521.

Billy the Fool; a story. (H. Austin) Nat'l M. (Bost.) 7: 177.

Billy Lappin's Search for a Fortune. (S. MacManus) Cent. 37: 601.

Billy's Tearless Woe; a story. (F. Remington) McClure, 16: 455. Same art. Idler, 20: 241.

Billy-boy. (W. Caxton) Sund. M. 27: 52.

Bimanual Training. (H. B. Bare) Studio (Internat.) 5: 191. See Ambidextry.

Bimetallic Conference, International, True Reasons for the Apparent Failure of. (J. R. Challen) Arena, 19: 199.

Bimetallism Abroad. (H. White) Nation, 68: 451.

— and Democracy. (W. A. Allen) Arena, 20: 460.

— Battle of the Money Metals. (G. H. Lepper and J. C. Ridpath) Arena, 18: 168.

— British Interests and the Wolcott Commission. (T. Lloyd and others) National, 29: 660. Same art. Ecl. M. 129: 333.

— The Case against. (G. H. Smith) Arena, 18: 590.

— Darwin on. (T. N. Carver) Yale R. 8: 325. — (F. Y. Edgeworth) Econ. J. 8: 105.

— Fiasco of. (H. White) Nation, 65: 334.

— Future of. (G. G. Vest) Forum, 24: 520.

— in Europe: France. (E. d'Artois) National, 28: 797 — Germany. (O. Arendt) 803 — Great Britain. (Ld. Aldenham) 808.

— International, a Necessity. (Edward Tuck) Forum, 24: 209.

— — Negotiations for. Bank. M. (N. Y.) 56: 269.

— — Obstacles to. Bank. M. (N. Y.) 54: 194.

Bimetallism, International; Single Standard Inevitable. (W. M. Grinnell) Forum, 24: 217.

— — Wolcott Commission and its Results. (J. H. Eckels) Forum, 24: 396. — Pub. Opin. 22: 35.

— Statistical Aspects of the Recent Proposals. (F. J. Atkinson) J. Statis. Soc. 61: 83.

— Status of, in Europe. Pub. Opin. 22: 229.

Bingham, Harry, with portrait. (E. Aldrich) Green Bag, 13: 105.

Binocular Factors in Monocular Vision. (C. H. Judd) Science, n. s. 7: 269.

Binocular Vision, Some Facts of. (C. H. Judd) Psychol. R. 4: 374.

Binyon, Laurence. (R. A. Streatfield) Monthly R. 2, no. 3: 93.

— Poems. Sat. R. 85: 624. — Acad. 53: 440.

— Porphyrion; pomp in poetry. Spec. 80: 505.

Biochemistry, Scope and Present Position of. (A. Mathews) Am. Natural. 31: 271.

Biography. (H. H. Asquith) National, 38: 526.

— Aspects of. (F. J. Mather, jr.) Nation, 73: 431.

— Dictionary of National. (H. Ellis) Argosy, 72: 336. Acad. 52: 50.

— Educational Value of. (S. E. Simons) Educa. R. 17: 70.

— Limits of. (C. Whibley) 19th Cent. 41: 428. Same art. Liv. Age, 213: 311.

— New Theory of. Dial (Ch.) 24: 281.

— Popular Forms of. (A. R. Marble) Dial (Ch.) 31: 125.

— Success in Writing. Acad. 60: 167.

— Studies in, Leslie's. (E. D. Hinsdale) Dial (Ch.) 26: 46.

Biography of a Foundling; a story. (A. O'Hagan) Munsey, 25: 308.

Biological Chemistry. (P. Kropotkin) 19th Cent. 45: 404. Same art. Liv. Age, 221: 209.

Biological Determinism, Le Dantec on. (A. Binet) Psychol. R. 4: 516.

Biological Laboratory, Marine, at Pacific Grove. (A. G. Maddren) Overland, n. s. 32: 208.

Biological Problem, Hertwig on. (E. O. Jordan) Dial (Ch.) 22: 306.

Biological Problems, Statistical Study of. (C. B. Davenport) Pop. Sci. Mo. 59: 447.

Biological Research, Recent Aspects of. (E. B. Wilson) Internat. Mo. 2: 74.

Biological Science, Recent Advances in, Howe on. Nature, 63: 261.

Biological Society of Washington. (F. A. Lucas) Science, n. s. 13: 909.

Biological Stations, Fresh-water. (H. B. Ward) Science, n. s. 9: 497. — (C. A. Kofold) Am. Natural. 32: 391.

— Functions and Features of. (C. O. Whitman) Science, n. s. 7: 37.

Biological Work, Nature and Amount of, that can profitably be attempted in Secondary Schools. (H. E. Walter) School R. 8: 171.

Biologist's Quest, The. (J. M. Oskison) Overland, n. s. 38: 52.

Biology, Advance in, in 1895. (C. B. Davenport) Am. Natural. 31: 785.

— — in 1896. (C. B. Davenport) Am. Natural. 32: 867.

— and Medicine. (W. H. Welch) Am. Natural. 31: 755.

— and Metaphysics. (C. L. Morgan) Monist, 9: 538.

— as a Branch of Education. (W. M. Webb) Westm. 152: 665.

— as an Element in College Training. (W. H. Howell) Science, n. s. 13: 49.

— Educative Value of Study of. (T. B. Stowell) Science, 5: 531.

Biology, Glimpse of. (W. Seton) Cath. World, 65: 254.

— Half-century in. (J. J. Walsh) Cath. World, 70: 466.

— Marine, in Liverpool. (W. A. Herdman) Nature, 64: 115.

— Metaphysics of. Nature, 60: 458.

— Popular Ignorance of. (F. W. Chapman) Educa. 18: 414.

— Problems in, discussed by Am. Soc. of Naturalists, Ithaca, 1897. Science, n. s. 7: 145.

— Problems of, Sandeman's. (E. J. Conklin) Science, n. s. 8: 85.

— Progress in, in 19th Century. (H. S. Williams) Harper, 95: 930.

— — in Victorian Era. (R. Lydekker) Knowl. 20: 110.

— Relation to Philosophy. (J. LeConte) Arena, 17: 549.

Biondi, Ernesto, with portrait. (E. H. Brush) Brush & P. 9: 38.

Biotite-Tinguaite Dike from Manchester, Mass. (A. S. Eakle) Am. J. Sci. 156: 489.

Biotites and Amphiboles, Rock-forming. (W. F. Hillebrand; H. N. Stokes; W. Valentine) Am. J. Sci. 157: 294.

Bipolarity of Marine Faunas. (A. E. Ortmann) Am. Natural. 33: 583.

Birch, Harvey, Original of. (H. E. Miller) New Eng. M. n. s. 18: 307.

Bird, Edward. Art J. 51: 43.

Bird at the Neck, The; a story. Pall Mall M. 14: 15, 163.

Bird of Passage: an Ode to Instrumental Music. (O. Wister) Atlan. 86: 761.

Bird, Wise, Mythology of. (H. C. March) Anthrop. J. 27: 209.

Bird Anthology from Sill. (H. L. Graham) Poet-Lore, 9: 566.

Bird Architecture. (G. S.-Porter) Outing, 38: 437, 656.

Bird Artists. (F. H. Sweet) Lippinc. 60: 255.

Bird-bones from Bone Caves of Tennessee. (R. W. Shufeldt) Am. Natural. 31: 645.

Bird Catching and Bird Dealing. (R. C. Nightingale) Good Words, 39: 31. Same art. Liv. Age, 216: 616.

Bird-life from Train Windows. Spec. 82: 711. Same art. Liv. Age, 222: 462.

— Humors of. (Lady Broome) Cornh. 79: 108. Same art. Liv. Age, 220: 575.

— in Autumn in England. (H. A. Bryden) Sat. R. 84: 616.

— in the Canaries and South Africa, Harris on. (R. Lydekker) Nature, 64: 603.

— in Central America. (D. F. Randolph) Am. Natural. 31: 199.

— in the Grand River Cañon, Colo. (H. L. Graham) Midland, 8: 329.

— in Norfolk and Suffolk, England. (R. B. Lodge) Idler, 14: 823.

— Mysteries of Animal and. Quar. 187: 471.

— Winter. (F. M. Chapman) Chaut. 26: 255.

Bird-lore in Winter. (C. A. Witchell) Knowl. 24: 8.

Bird-lover, A. (H. W. Morrow) Outing, 36: 36.

Bird Message; a poem. Ecl. M. 129: 713.

Bird Pictures. (W. E. D. Scott) Scrib. M. 21: 500.

Bird-plumage for Milliners; the Little Egret. (G. A. Dewar) Idler, 13: 457.

Bird Rock. (F. M. Chapman) Cent. 36: 329.

Bird-songs in Spring. (C. A. Witchell) Knowl. 20: 81.

— in Summer. (C. A. Witchell) Knowl. 20: 157.

— in Autumn. (C. A. Witchell) Knowl. 20: 225. Same art. Ecl. M. 129: 785.

Bismarck, Otto von, as Lover and Husband. (M. A. Morrison) Ecl. M. **136**: 718. Same art. Liv. Age, **229**: 90.
— as a Maker of Empire. (W. M. Sloane) Pol. Sci. Q. **15**: 647.
— as a National Type. (K. Francke) Atlan. **82**: 560.
— as a Phrase-maker. (Munroe Smith) Bookman, **8**: 18.
— as a Student of History. (W. Miller) Gent. M. n. s. **59**: 372.
— Autobiography. (C. De Kay) Critic, **34**: 61. — Outl. **61**: 880. — (M. Smith) Am. Hist. R. **4**: 536. — (M. Smith) Nation, **68**: 113. — (E. G. Johnson) Dial (Ch.) **26**: 8. — Acad. **55**: 411.
— the Barbarian of Genius. Sat. R. **86**: 165.
— Boyhood of. (A. D. Vandam) Sat. R. **86**: 168.
— Busch's. Acad. **54**: 287. — (Munroe Smith) Nation, **67**: 314. — (E. G. Johnson) Dial (Ch.) **25**: 255. — Ath. '98, **2**: 411. — Spec. **81**: 410. — (C. H. Levermore) Am. Hist. R. **4**: 531.
— Decline and Fall of. (J. J. O'Shea) Am. Cath. Q. **23**: 836.
— An Evening with. Sat. R. **86**: 170.
— — with portrait. (J. M. Chapple) Nat'l M. (Bost.) **8**: 507.
— from 1870 till his Death. (Countess von Krockow) Indep. **51**: 1883.
— The Greatness of. (W. T. Stead) R. of Rs. (N. Y.) **18**: 309.
— his Work and its Prospects. Quar. **188**: 523. Same art. Ecl. M. **132**: 321. Same art. Liv. Age, **220**: 207.
— in his Home. (Susan W. Selfridge) Outl. **60**: 31.
— in his Writings. (Countess von Krockow) Outl. **60**: 39.
— in Retirement. (G. Valbert) Liv. Age, **215**: 67.
— the Iron Chancellor. (E. D. Keeling) Sund. M. **27**: 626.
— W. Jack's Life of. Am. Hist. R. **5**: 569.
— Lenbach, Painter of. (E. Coues) Cent. **31**: 323.
— Love-letters of. Harper, **102**: 453. — (E. L. Banks) Fortn. **76**: 307. — Sat. R. **91**: 805. — Liv. Age, **230**: 325. — Acad. **60**: 15. — (E. K. Tompkins) Critic, **39**: 62. — (E. G. Johnson) Dial (Ch.) **30**: 329.
— the Man and the Statesman. (C. T. Lewis) Harper, **98**: 329.
— The Peace of. (Diplomaticus) Fortn. **70**: 471.
— Personal Recollections of. (W. H. Dowson) Fortn. **70**: 460. Same art. Liv. Age, **219**: 97. Same art. Ecl. M. **131**: 588.
— Place in History. (T. Schwarz) Munsey, **20**: 47.
— Political Attitude. Spec. **81**: 171.
— The Real. (A. H. W. Colquhoun) Canad. M. **12**: 72.
— Work of. Quar. **188**: 523.
Bismarck Monument, Munich. Studio (Internat.) **9**: 203.
Bismarck's Apprenticeship. (W. M. Sloane) J. Mil. Serv. Inst. **25**: 396.
Bismarckiana. (Baron de Malortie) Cornh. **78**: 449.
Bisons, Fossil, of North America, Lucas'. Am. Natural. **33**: 665.
Bispham, David, Singer, Interview with. Music, **11**: 652. **14**: 32, 566. **18**: 29.
Bit of Blue China. (I. M. Hamill) Longm. **31**: 137. Same art. Liv. Age, **216**: 190.
Biter Bitten, The. (J. A. Barry) Cornh. **81**: 340.
Bites of Carnivorous Animals. Spec. **80**: 652.
Bits, Horse, Good and Bad. (W. S. Harwood) Outing, **37**: 526.
Bitter Revenge, A; a story. (R. E. Vernham) Sund. M. **28**: 750.
Bitter Root Forest Reserve. Map and Illus. (R. U. Goode) Nat. Geog. M. **9**: 387.

Bitumen, Petroleum, and Asphalt. (A. Jaccard) Pop. Sci. Mo. **50**: 380.
Bitumens of California, Technology of. (S. F. Peckham) J. Frankl. Inst. **146**: 45.
Bituminous Deposits of Cárdenas, Cuba. (H. E. Peckham) Am. J. Sci. **162**: 33.
Bivalves, Hinge Teeth of. (W. H. Dall) Am. Natural. **35**: 175.
Bixbyite, a New Mineral, and Notes on the Associated Topaz. (S. L. Penfield and H. W. Foote) Am. J. Sci. **154**: 105.
Bizet, Georges, Composer, with portrait. Music, **14**: 194.
— Carmen. (J. F. Runciman) Sat. R. **87**: 333.
Blachford, Frederic, Lord. Letters; ed. by Marindin. Sat. R. **83**: 97.
Black, A. J., Scene-painting by. M. of Art, **24**: 519.
Black, William. (J. McCarthy) Acad. **55**: 481. Same art. Liv. Age, **220**: 125. Same art. Ecl. M. **132**: 300. — Ath. '98, **2**: 866. — Lit. W. (Bost.) **30**: 8.
— Novels of. (A. Repplier) Critic, **34**: 146.
— Portrait of. Bk. Buyer, **18**: 19.
— To; a poem. (A. Campbell) Ecl. M. **133**: 914.
Black and White. (I. C. Vaughan) Good Words, **40**: 468.
Black-and-white in Nature. (T. C. Hepworth) Chamb. J. **75**: 31.
Black Billy and the Boomerang. (A. Orr) Sund. M. **29**: 254.
Black Brunswicker, Recollections of a. Macmil. **77**: 451. Same art. Liv. Age, **217**: 423.
Black Canoe, The. (V. Waite) Cornh. **79**: 675.
Black Cock Shooting. (J. Edwards Moss) Sat. R. **88**: 578, 553.
Black Death in Yorkshire in 1349. (W. H. Thompson) Antiq. n. s. **37**: 134, 182.
Black Dog, The; a tale of the Tay. Macmil. **75**: 441.
Black Dwarf, The Home of the. (A. F. Robertson) Macmil. **78**: 384. Same art. Liv. Age, **219**: 124.
Black Feather's Throw. (J. A. Altsheler) Lippinc. **63**: 127.
Black Forest, Cycling in. (A. P. Atterbury) Outing, **32**: 252.
— Stroll in. (M. E. Blake) Outing, **34**: 508.
Black Friday, Sept. 24, 1869. (G. S. Boutwell) McClure, **14**: 30.
Black Hawk, Indian Chief. (Albina M. Letts) Midland, **8**: 221.
Black Hills, In the. (Elizabeth Cumings) Music, **16**: 448.
Black Knight of Adlersdorf; a story. (H. M. Langland) Pall Mall M. **13**: 556.
Black Night, A; a story. (J. Lawson) Gent. M. n. s. **64**: 258.
Black Plague, The. (W. Wyman) No. Am. **164**: 441.
Black Rapids Love Story. (F. H. Spearman) Cosmopol. **29**: 201.
Black Rock Ledges; a poem. (A. B. De Mille) Canad. M. **9**: 467.
Black Sheep; a poem. (R. Burton) Atlan. **83**: 574.
Black Silas. (V. F. Boyle) Cent. **37**: 375.
Black Stone, The. (J. D. Bate) Asia. R. **27**: 154.
Black Will; a story. (Sir George Douglas) Gent. M. n. s. **59**: 105.
Blackbird in May, To a; a poem. (J. Truman) Macmil. **78**: 224.
Blackboard Treatment of Physical Vectors. (C. Barus) Science, **5**: 171.
Blackfeet Indians. Four Days in a Medicine Lodge. (W. McClintock) Harper, **101**: 519.
— Lodges of. (G. B. Grinnell) Am. Anthropol. **3**: 650.
Blackfriars, Church of. (J. H. Ramsey; W. F. Prideaux) Ath. '00, **2**: 33, 64.

Blackgame Shooting in Scotland. (A. J. Gordon) Belgra. **95**: 496.

Blackgum ag'in Thunder. (F. R. Stockton) Cent. **41**: 249.

Blackjack Bargainer; a story. (S. Porter) Munsey, **25**: 620.

Blacklisting: the New Slavery. (W. J. Strong) Arena, **21**: 273.

Blackmore, Richard Doddridge. Ath. '00, **1**: 114. — Lit. W. (Bost.) **31**: 42. — (S. J. Reid) Cornh. **81**: 533. — (W. L. Phelps) Indep. **52**: 296.

— Country of. (A. B. Maurice) Bookman, **14**: 29.

— in his Home. (R. W. Sawtell) R. of Rs. (N. Y.) **21**: 586.

— Maid of Sker. (E. J. Newell) Macmil. **82**: 98. — Same art. Liv. Age, **226**: 248.

— Some Letters of. (C. Shipman) Critic, **37**: 68.

— Two Glimpses of. (H. T. Bailey) Critic, **36**: 219.

Blacksmith, Mediæval, and his Work. (Wm. Fletcher) Good Words, **39**: 39.

Blackstick Papers. (Mrs. A. T. Ritchie) Cornh. v. **82**-84. Same art. Critic, v. **38**, 39.

Blackstone. (A. V. Dicey) Nation, **65**: 274, 295.

— Commentaries, Curiosities of. (A. R. Stuart) Conserv. R. **4**: 267.

Blackthorn Winter. (J. M. Bacon) Temp. Bar, **121**: 555.

Blackwood, John: a Great Editor. Chamb. J. **76**: 83.

Blackwood, William. (R. M. Lockhart) Westm. **148**: 665.

— Publishing House of. (J. H. Millar) New R. **17**: 646. — (C. Stein) Fortn. **68**: 853. — (H. Maxwell) Longm. **31**: 117. Same art. Ecl. M. **130**: 120. Same art. Liv. Age, **216**: 116. — Acad. **52**: 295. — Chamb. J. **74**: 753. — (A. M. Stoddart) Contemp. **72**: 632. Same art. Liv. Age, **215**: 727. — Ath. '97, **2**: 517. — Scot. R. **31**: 51. **33**: 83. — (L. Hutton) Bk. Buyer, **15**: 659. — Ed. R. **187**: 40. — Quar. **187**: 234.

Blades, William. Library, **2**: 205.

Blagden, Isa. Acad. **56**: 163.

Blaine, James G., and the Republican Convention of 1880. (G. S. Boutwell) McClure, **14**: 281.

— Presidential Campaign of 1884 in Augusta, Maine. (E. G. Mason) New Eng. M. n. s. **24**: 248.

Blair, James, Commissary, Life of. (D. E. Mobley) J. H. Univ. Studies, **19**: 447.

Blake, Robert, Admiral. (E. J. Blake) Un. Serv. M. **18**: 569.

— and the Dutchmen. (W. H. Fitchett) Cornh. **77**: 145.

— at Leghorn. (S. R. Gardiner) Eng. Hist. R. **14**: 109, 534.

Blake, William. (W. N. Guthrie) Sewanee, **5**: 328, 438. — With portrait. (W. B. Yeats) Acad. **51**: 634.

— Levebus's Illustrations of. (H. W. Bromhead) Art J. **52**: 237.

— Poetry of. (H. J. Smith) Cent. **38**: 284. — Acad. **61**: 15. — Poet-Lore, **11**: 25.

Blakeney, Robert. Memoirs concerning Peninsular War. Sat. R. **87**: 435.

Blanc, Marie Theresa, Autobiographical Notes. (T. Stanton) No. Am. **166**: 595.

Blanc, Mont, Geology of. (T. G. Bonney) Nature, **60**: 152.

Blanchard, Amy E., with portrait. Bk. News, **18**: 633.

Blanchard, Emile. (R. Lydekker) Nature, **61**: 473.

Bland, Richard P., Byers's Life and Times of. (A. G. Sedgwick) Nation, **71**: 352.

Blank Verse. Spec. **80**: 372.

Blankit-dole, The. (Jane Barlow) Liv. Age, **227**: 592.

Blarney Fluff. (F. R. Stockton) Liv. Age, **217**: 770.

Blaschka Flower Models of the Harvard Museum. (M. E. Hale) Pop. Sci. Mo. **50**: 663.

Blashfield, Edwin H., Decorator. (E. Knaufft) Studio (Internat.) **13**: 26.

Blasphemer, The Case of the. (D. W. Amram) Green Bag, **13**: 493.

Blass, F. Acta Apostolorum. (J. H. Moulton) Crit. R. **8**: 43.

— Evangelium secundum Lucam. (A. J. Grieve) Crit. R. **8**: 157.

Blast Furnace, By-products of, Recovery of. (A. H. Sexton) Engin. M. **14**: 987. — Chamb. J. **75**: 730.

— Waste Heat and By-products from the. (W. Whitwell) Cassier, **20**: 253.

Blast-furnace Gases for the Production of Power. (W. H. Booth) Engin. M. **15**: 420.

— Use of, in Gas Engines. Nature, **63**: 241.

Blast-furnace Practice. (J. S. Jeans) Engin. M. **13**: 34, 199.

Blavatsky, Madame, High Priestess of Isis. (H. R. Evans) Cosmopol. **28**: 241.

Blazing Hen-coop, The; a narrative. (O. Thanet) Harper, **96**: 210.

Bleckley, Logan E., Chief Justice, Wit and Wisdom of. (A. H. Russell) Green Bag, **10**: 530.

"Bleeding Bread." (G. Clarke Nuttall) Good Words, **38**: 685.

Blenheim, Marlborough at. (W. H. Fitchett) Cornh. **78**: 145.

Blenner, Carle J., Portrait Painter. Nat'l M. (Bost.) **14**: 666.

Blennerhassett, Harman, True Story of. (T. Blennerhassett-Adams) Cent. **40**: 351.

Blessed Mime, The; a story. (R. Hichens) Eng. Illust. **18**: 345.

Blessington's "Beat;" a story. (M. L. Osborne) Nat'l M. (Bost.) **14**: 251.

Blewitt, Jean, Poems of. (S. Waterloo) Canad. M. **10**: 191.

Blight in Egypt, A. (H. S. Morris) Bk. News, **15**: 491.

Blind, Karl. In Years of Storm and Stress. Ecl. M. **131**: 562.

Blind, Mathilde, as a Poet. Acad. **52**: 567.

— Poetry of. Acad. **53**: 41.

Blind, Books for. Lit. W. (Bost.) **29**: 232.

— — in Public Libraries. (H. M. Utley) Lib. J. **23**: supp. 93.

— Needed Education for. (M. Anagnos) Educa. **20**: 298.

— Roman Catholic Institutions for. (S. T. Swift) Cath. World, **67**: 507. — Month, **89**: 255.

Blind Man, The, and the Salmon. Chamb. J. **78**: 302.

Blind Mare's Warning. Longm. **34**: 414.

Blindness. My Dark World. Liv. Age, **213**: 527.

Blinman, Richard. (I. J. Greenwood) N. E. Reg. **54**: 39.

Blissus in North America. (F. M. Webster) Am. Natural. **33**: 813.

Blizzard at Imogene, The; a story. (F. B. Tracy) McClure, **14**: 263.

Blizzards. (S. B. McBeath) Strand, **14**: 228.

Bloch, Jean de, as a Prophet. (F. N. Maude) National, **37**: 102. — Reply (J. de Bloch) National, **37**: 370.

Block, Maurice. J. Statis. Soc. **64**: 292.

Block Island. (S. W. Mendum) New Eng. M. n. s. **16**: 738.

— Prehistoric Fauna of, as indicated by its Ancient Shell-heaps. (G. F. Eaton) Am. J. Sci. **156**: 137.

Block System, The. Chamb. J. **74**: 250.

Blockade of the Confederate States. (H. L. Wait) Cent. **34**: 914.

Boilers, Water-tube, Steam Appliances for. (B. H. Thwaite) Engin. M. **20**: 877.

Boiling Point Curves. (C. L. Speyers) Am. J. Sci. **159**: 341.

Bokhara, Travels in. (W. R. Rickmers) Geog. J. **14**: 593.

Bold Words at the Bridge ; a story. (S. O. Jewett) McClure, **12**: 508. Same art. Cornh. **79**: 489.

Bolingbroke and his Times, W. Sichel on. Ath. '01, **1**: 623.

— Politics of. (T. Bateson) Gent. M. n. s. **67**: 31.

Bolivia, Northern, and Pres. Pando's New Map. (G. E. Church) Geog. J. **18**: 144.

— Road to. (W. E. Curtis) Nat. Geog. M. **11**: 209.

— Undeveloped Resources of. (M. Conway) J. Soc. Arts, **48**: 234.

Bolles, Albert S., with portrait. Bk. News, **18**: 368.

Bologna. (A. Symons) Sat. R. **84**: 255.

— Art of. (H. Mereu) Am. Arch. **70**: 19, 43.

Bolometer, The. (S. P. Langley) Am. J. Sci. **155**: 241. Same art. Nature, **57**: 620.

Bolsterstone and Neighborhood, Antiquities of. (J. Kenworthy) Reliquary, **39**: 145.

Bolton, Gambier, Photographer of Animals, with portrait. (A. H. Lawrence) Idler, **14**: 147.

Bolton, Conn., Records of Rev. T. White, First Pastor. (M. K. Talcott) N. E. Reg. **52**: 307, 408.

— Records of the Church in. (M. K. Talcott) N. E. Reg. **54**: 80, 253. **55**: 34, 281.

Bomarsund, Siege of. (Marquis of Dufferin and Ava) Cornh. **78**: 595.

Bomb of an Anarchist. (A. A. Winter) New Eng. M. n. s. **22**: 90.

Bombay ; India's Threshold. (J. Ralph) Harper, **99**: 905.

— Past and Present. (G. W. Forrest) Pall Mall M. **12**: 545.

— — Town and Island of. (L. R. Windham) J. Soc. Art, **49**: 570.

— Plague in, 1897. (F. E. Clark) Lippinc. **60**: 133. — (E. W. Hopkins) Nation, **64**: 259.

— — Political Aspects of. (E. W. Hopkins) Forum, **23**: 737.

— Plague-stricken. Good Words, **40**: 842.

— — Mem Sahib in. Temp. Bar, **119**: 529. **120**: 64.

— A Voice from. Asia. R. **23**: 264.

Bonamy's Adventure. (Mrs. H. Synge) Chamb. J. **77**: 81-120.

Bonaparte, Eliza. (A. Laugel) Nation, **70**: 259.

Bonaparte, Elizabeth Patterson. (V. T. Peacock) Lippinc. **65**: 933.

Bonapartes of To-day. (F. Colonna) Cosmopol. **27**: 649.

Bonapartism. Fortn. **71**: 680.

Bonar, Horatius. [Sund. M.] Liv. Age, **214**: 100.

Bond, Sir Edward Augustus. Ath. '98, **1**: 51. — Library, **10**: 112.

Bond, Thomas. (J. W. Dean) N. E. Reg. **51**: 293.

Bond Family Records. (A. T. Bond) N. E. Reg. **52**: 464.

Bond of Blood, The ; a poem. (W. H. Thompson) Cent. **35**: 651.

Bonds of Foreign Governments as American Investments. (T. S. Woolsey) Forum, **31**: 275.

Bonds ; a Financier's story. (E. Lefevre) Idler, **19**: 192.

Bone, Henry. (G. D. Leslie and F. A. Eaton) Art J. **49**: 185.

Bone Age in Europe and America. (S. D. Peet) Am. Antiq. **19**: 314.

Bones, Human, Collections of. (Alĕs Hrdlicka) Am. Natural. **34**: 9.

Bonet-Maury, Gaston, with portrait. (T. **Stanton**) Open Court, **12**: 630.

Boneyrwals, Our Dealings with the. (H. C. **Wylly**) Un. Serv. M. **20**: 268.

Bonheur, Rosa. (S. Beale) Am. Arch. **64**: 95. — (J. Claretie) Harper, **104**: 136. — Ath. '99, **1**: 695. — (Th. Bentzon) Outl. **62**: 41.

— and her Work. (E. Knaufft) R. of Rs. (N. Y.) **20**: 34.

— Sale of her Paintings. Art J. **52**: 222.

Bonifacio, a Quaint Town of Corsica. Chamb. J. **77**: 746.

Bonnat, Leon J. F., portrait painter. (E. T. Baldwin) Outl. **61**: 543.

Book, Printed, and its Decoration. Studio (Lond.) **2**: 140.

Book of the Dead, Renouf's. (S. Y. Stevenson) Citizen, **4**: 4, 29. — Spec. **80**: 88.

"Book of Husbandry" and the "Book of Surveying," Authorship of. (R. H. C. Fitzherbert) Eng. Hist. R. **12**: 225.

"Booke of Fortune," as found in Laneham's List of Capt. Cox's Books. (C. C. Stopes) Ath. '00, **1**: 625.

Books and a Boy. (K. F. Reighard) Outl. **65**: 178.

— and Libraries. A Child's Thoughts about. (N. M. Hall) Lib. J. **26**: 731.

— and Reading. (L. Playfair) Library, **2**: 332.

— and Things Bookish. (D. Adams) Belgra. **95**: 184, 314.

— as Tools. (J. B. Anthony) Chaut. **31**: 143.

— Bad ; is it possible to tell from good ? (A. Birrell) Cornh. **81**: 305. Same art. Ecl. M. **134**: 713. Same art. Liv. Age, **225**: 73.

— Best of 1895. Pub. Lib. **1**: 92.

— — of 1896. Lib. J. **22**: 83, 136.

— — of 1897. Lib. J. **23**: 148. — Acad. **52**: 486.

— — of 1898. Outl. **60**: 811.

— — of 1899. (G. E. Wire) Pub. Lib. **5**: 50.

— — of 1900. (G. E. Wire) Pub. Lib. **6**: 6.

— Best Fifty, for a Village Library. Pub. Lib. **6**: 270.

— — of 1897. Lib. J. **23**: 148.

— — of 1898. Outl. **60**: 811.

— Booksellers and Bookselling. (J. Shaylor) 19th Cent. **45**: 775.

— Chained. Am. Arch. **60**: 93.

— Cheap, The Question of. (R. Ogden) Nation, **65**: 492.

— — Publishing. Acad. **51**: 501-636.

— Cheapening of Useful. (W. L. Clowes) Fortn. **76**: 88.

— Children's, Evaluating. (E. N. Lane ; I. F. Farrar) Lib. J. **26**: 194.

— Books that Girls have loved. (E. Graham) Lippinc. **60**: 428.

— — Some 18th-Century Children's Books. (L. A. Harper) Longm. **38**: 548.

— Colonial, The Queerest of. (J. F. Hogan) Gent. M. n. s. **64**: 562.

— Current (1899), Strength and Weakness of. (J. A. Cooper) Canad. M. **13**: 10.

— Discount on. Acad. **52**: 55, 78.

— Distribution of. Dial (Ch.) **26**: 5.

— Enemies of. (J. Macaulay) Ecl. M. **129**: 774.

— Favorite, of Statesmen. (F. G. Carpenter) Lippinc. **61**: 715.

— for Children. Acad. **54**: 13, 20.

— — Best Hundred. Acad. **58**: 107.

— for Mothers' Clubs. (L. A. Eastman) Lib. J. **22**: 436.

— for a Summer Vacation. Acad. **54**: 111-306.

— for a Village Library, A Hundred. (C. K. Shorter) Bookman, **6**: 300.

— Great. (F. W. Farrar) Sund. M. **27**: 2, 82, 195.

— Housing the. (J. L. Mauran) Pub. Lib. **6**: 603.

Book-collector, The; a story. (Mabel B. Fuller) Midland, 7: 461.

Book-cover Designing. (A. Fosdick) Writer, 10: 139.

Book-covers, Artistic. (E. Harris) Brush & P. 5: 118.

— Artistic Decoration of Cloth. (G. White) Studio (Lond.) 4: 15.

— English Embroidered. (C. Davenport) Studio (Lond.) 2: 208.

Book-hunters, The Providence of. (Anna Blackwell) Chamb. J. 74: 425.

Book-hunting. Macmil. 83: 453.

— in Rome. (W. W. Bishop) Bookman, 12: 608.

Book-keeping for Post Exchanges. (E. Anderson) J. Mil. Serv. Inst. 15: 1168.

— More Scientific Teaching of. (S. Latham) J. Soc. Arts, 45: 949.

Book-making in the West. (Delia T. Davis) Critic, 37: 222.

Bookman, The; is it misogynous? (K. Stephens) Bookman, 4: 436.

— Ten Years of the English. (W. R. Nicoll) Bookman, 14: 234.

Bookman's Dilemma, A; a story. (C. Lusted) Gent. M. n. s. 64: 1. Same art. Liv. Age, 224: 446.

Bookman's Romance, A; a story. (Chas. Lusted) Gent. M. n. s. 58: 347. Same art. Ecl. M. 129: 255.

Bookmen, American. (M. A. D. Howe) Bookman, 4: 510. 5: 14, 124, 205, 304, 383. 6: 24, 203.

Book Ornamentation by Women. Lit. W. (Bost.) 29: 340.

Book-plate Collector; an interview. (J. Milne) Eng. Illust. 19: 149.

Book Plates. (Mary Prendeville) Brush & P. 1: 53. — (W. J. Hardy) Library, 3: 47, 93.

— and the Collecting of them. (W. G. Bowdoin) Indep. 53: 2931.

— Antiquarian and Artistic, Appeal of. (C. D. Allen) Cent. 41: 238.

— Designs for, with Examples. Studio (Lond.) 1: 24-253.

— Recent. (G. White) Studio (Internat.) 1: 110. — Studio (Lond.) 4: 197. 7: 93.

— Some New York. (W. H. Shelton) Critic, 34: 342.

Book-production in France, Notes on. (A. W. Pollard) Library, 5: 102.

— Relative. (E. C. Richardson) Pub. Lib. 5: 192.

Book Publishers' Association. Lit. W. (Bost.) 31: 168.

Book Reviewing. (A. H. Morton) Critic, 39: 535. — (A. Lang) Critic, 39: 561.

— Old Order and New. (F. W. Halsey) Indep. 52: 2792.

Book Reviews, Past and Present. (J. S. Tunison) Atlan. 84: 311.

— Reply to John Cotton Dana. (J. B. and J. L. Gilder) Critic, 37: 307.

Book Sales of 1896. (T. Scott) Acad. 51: 126.

— of 1897. Acad. 53: 37.

— of 1899. (J. H. Slater) Ath. '99, 2: 899 — '00, 1: 18.

— of 1900. (J. H. Slater) Ath. '01, 1: 17.

Bookseller, The Plight of the. Dial (Ch.) 24: 173, 220.

Booksellers and Literature. (G. S. Ellis) Argosy, 65: 275.

— Authors, Publishers and. (J. A. Steuart) Fortn. 69: 255.

— Old Boston. (E. M. Bacon) Bookman, 4: 542. 5: 373. 6: 303.

Bookseller's Catalogue, Ancient. (E. N. Adler and I. Broydé) Jew. Q. 13: 52.

Bookseller's Row. (W. Roberts) Ath. '00, 1: 336.

Bookselling as a Fine Art. Acad. 51: 359.

— State of. Acad. 55: 45.

Bookshops, London. Acad. 51: 310–431. 52: 244, 284.

Book-speech and Folk-speech. Library, 3: 294.

Book-titles, Familiar. Bk. Buyer, 18: 378.

Book Trade in Canada. Acad. 51: 630.

— in the Good Old Times. (Frances H. Freshfield) Good Words, 41: 106.

Bookworms. (F. E. Beddard) Nature, 58: 435.

— in Fact and Fancy. (W. Austen) Pop. Sci. Mo. 55: 240.

— O'Conor's Facts about. Acad. 54: 54.

Boomerangs. (G. T. Walker) Nature, 64: 338.

Booms, Western Real Estate, and after. (H. J. Fletcher) Atlan. 81: 689.

Boon-services on the Estates of Ramsey Abbey. (N. Neilson) Am. Hist. R. 2: 213.

Boone Genealogy. Pennsyl. M. 21: 112.

Booster System applied to Electric Railways. (J. L. Woodbridge) J. Frankl. Inst. 145: 374.

Booth, Edwin, in London. (E. H. House) Cent. 33: 269.

— Memorial Window. Critic, 33: 61.

Booth, John Wilkes, Capture, Death, and Burial of. (R. S. Baker) McClure, 9: 574.

— Recollections of. (C. Morris) McClure, 16: 299.

Bonner, Robert, with portraits. (E. J. Edwards) R. of Rs. (N. Y.) 20: 161.

Bonnet Laird, A. (E. Anstruther) Temp. Bar, 118: 430.

Bonney, C. C., Inaugurator of the Parliament of Religions, with portrait. (P. Carus) Open Court, 14: 4.

Bonus Year, The. (A. Hewat) Bank. M. (Lond.) 65: 629.

Bonvicino, Alessandro, called Moretto. (Pompeo Momenti) Art J. 51: 73.

Borden, F. W., Canadian Minister of Militia. (C. A. Mathews) Canad. M. 14: 448.

Bordentown, New Jersey, Authors in. (T. F. Wolfe) Lippinc. 65: 129.

Border Essays. Liv. Age, 214: 684.

Border Law, The. (F. Watt) New R. 16: 281. Same art. Liv. Age, 213: 303. — Green Bag, 10: 486.

Bordighera, Past and Present. (W. Miller) Westm. 154: 48.

Bore, The; a story. (L. B. Walford) Good Words, 42: 20.

Bore of Hang-Chau, The Marvelous. (E. R. Scidmore) Cent. 37: 852.

Bores. (G. H. Darwin) Cent. 34: 898.

Borghese Villa. Am. Arch. 58: 42.

Borgia, The Real. (C. C. Starbuck) Meth. R. 58: 231.

Borgu, The Struggle for. Blackw. 165: 605.

Boric Acid, Estimation of. (F. A. Gooch and L. C. Jones) Am. J. Sci. 157: 34.

— Iodometric Method for the Estimation of. (L. C. Jones) Am. J. Sci. 158: 127.

— Volumetric Method for the Estimation of. (L. C. Jones) Am. J. Sci. 157: 147.

Born by the Sea; a poem. Ecl. M. 129: 749.

Born Farmer, A; a story. (S. O. Jewett) McClure, 17: 164.

Borneo, British North. (Sir J. Jardine) Contemp. 75: 578. — (L. H. West) Asia. R. 24: 330.

— Colonial Government in. (J. M. Hubbard) Nat. Geog. M. 11: 359.

— In the Heart of. (C. Hose) Geog. J. 16: 39.

— Tribes of, Wild Mountain. (H. M. Hiller) Harper, 102: 935.

Boro Boedor, Island of Java, Prisoners of State at. (E. R. Scidmore) Cent. 32: 655.

Borodine and Balakirew; Russian musicians. (A. Pougin) Music, 12: 440.

Borrow, George. Blackw. 165: 724. — (C. Adler) Conserv. R. 2: 22. — (A. I. du P. Coleman) Critic, 34: 430. — (A. S. Bradford) Dial (Ch.) 26: 263. — (J. H. Findlater) Cornh. 80: 596. Same art. Liv. Age, 223: 819. — (D. M. Jones) Lond. Q. 92: 18.

— and East Anglia. Illus. (W. A. Dutt) Good Words, 38: 318.

— and his Works. Quar. 189: 472.

— In the Country of. (W. A. Dutt) Macmil. 84: 145.

— Knapp's Life of. Acad. 56: 351

— a Sordid Hero. Liv. Age, 221: 594.

Borrower as a Banker sees Him. (L. Denison) World's Work, 1: 534.

Borrowing a Book; a story. (J. Kent) Gent. M. n. s. 64: 180.

Borrowing Trouble. (Fanny D. Bergen) J. Am. Folk-Lore, 11: 55.

Boscawen, Edward, Sir. (P. C. Standing) Un. Serv. M. 21: 242.

Boscawen, New Hampshire. New Eng. M. n. s. 17: 282.

Boscoreale, Italy, Newly discovered Frescoes in. (L. E. Baxter) M. of Art, 25: 318.

Bose, Jagadis Chunder; a Bengalee professor. Spec. 78: 201. Same art. Liv. Age, 212: 906.

Bosham, Ancient Church of. (H. Elrington) Reliquary, 38: 82.

Bosnia before the Turkish Conquest. (W. Miller) Eng. Hist. R. 13: 643.

— In. (P. D. Natt) Nation, 65: 28.

— Turks in. (W. Miller) Gent. M. n. s. 59: 583.

— under the Austrians. (W. Miller) Gent. M. n. s. 61: 340.

Boss, Calf, Cow, Etymology of. (C. Hempl) Nation, 72: 314.

Boss, The American. (F. C. Lowell) Atlan. 86: 289.

— in the Open, The. (R. Ogden) Nation, 72: 249.

— Political; a new form of government. (J. B. Bishop) Forum, 23: 396.

— Ward. (A. B. Poor) New Eng. M. n. s. 23: 150.

— Why the Ward Boss rules. (Jane Addams) Outl. 58: 879.

Boss Business, Light on the. (R. Ogden) Nation, 71: 45.

Boss Government, Essence of. (J. B. Bishop) Nation, 68: 308.

Boss Rule in Old English Municipalities. (E. Porritt) No. Am. 164: 125.

Bosses, Two, in St. David's Cathedral. Reliquary, 40: 191.

Bossism, Care and Cure of. Outl. 69: 525.

Bossuet, J. B., as Preacher. (A. H. Currier) Bib. Sac. 57: 585.

— Rebelliau's Life of. (A. Laugel) Nation, 70: 48.

Boston; Ancient Inns of Boston Town. (F. W. Norcross) New Eng. M. n. s. 25: 315.

— Art Commission Act, 1898. Am. Arch. 60: 62.

— at the Century's End. (S. Baxter) Harper, 99: 823.

— Children's Institutions of. (W. I. Cole) New Eng. M. n. s. 17: 327.

— Churches and Ministers of the Early Century. (E. E. Hale) Nat'l M. (Bost.) 6: 533.

— City Charities of. (F. H. Wines) Char. R. 6: 41.

— City Record, a Municipal Newspaper. Ann. Am. Acad. Pol. Sci. 11: 146.

— Colonial Theatre. (C. H. Blackall) Am. Arch. 72: 11-41.

— Common, Scenes on. Contrary Gospels. (C. Porter) Outl. 68: 633.

— Congregational House. (W. H. Cobb) New Eng. M. n. s. 21: 219.

— — Relief Tablets on. (E. G. Porter) New Eng. M. n. s. 19: 428.

Boston, Copp's Hill Burying-ground. (B. O. Flower) Arena, 19: 618.

— Criminals of. (J. Flynt) McClure, 17: 115.

— Early in the Century. (E. E. Hale) Nat'l M. (Bost.) 6: 434.

— Elevated Railway. (G. A. Kimball) New Eng. M. n. s. 24: 455.

— Faneuil Hall. (A. E. Brown) New Eng. M. n. s. 21: 519.

— Government of. (T. N. Hart) Nat'l M. (Bost.) 15: 157.

— Great Fire of 1872. (R. G. Fitch) New Eng. M. n. s. 21: 358.

— Growth of Population of. (F. A. Bushée) Am. Statis. Assoc. 6: 239.

— House at Corner of Washington and Winter Streets, 1644–1846. (S. H. Swan) New Eng. M. n. s. 17: 170.

— Historic, Facts concerning. (F. A. Waterman) Nat'l M. (Bost.) 12: 277.

— in Fiction. (L. Swift) Bk. Buyer, 23: 187. — (Frances W. Carruth) Bookman, 14: 236, 355.

— Insane Hospital. (W. I. Cole) New Eng. M. n. s. 19: 753.

— Literary, of To-day, 1900. (J. L. Wright) Nat'l M. (Bost.) 11: 368.

— Samuel Lynde's Deed of Land, 1700. (S. B. Doggett) N. E. Reg. 51: 64.

— Mental Atmosphere of. Am. Arch. 74: 87.

— Municipal Printing in. (H. S. Chase) Munic. Aff. 4: 774.

— Municipal Progress in. (J. Quincy) Indep. 52: 424.

— Municipal Service of. (F. C. Lowell) Atlan. 81: 311.

— Municipal Socialism in. (F. J. Douglas) Arena, 20: 545.

— Museum of Fine Arts; American Paintings in. (W. H. Downes) Brush & P. 6: 201.

— Old Summer Street. (H. F. Bond) New Eng. M. n. s. 19: 333.

— Park System of Greater. (C. S. Sargent) Garden & F. 10: 240.

— Parks. (Sylvester Baxter) Am. Arch. 58: 50.

— — Architectural Features of. (S. Baxter) Am. Arch. 61: 19, 51, 83.

— Pauper Institutions of. (W. I. Cole) New Eng. M. n. s. 18: 233.

— Penal Institutions of. (W. I. Cole) New Eng. M. n. s. 17: 613.

— Poor of. (A. N. Lincoln) Munic. Aff. 2: 483.

— Province House. (E. J. Carpenter) New Eng. M. n. s. 21: 428.

— Public Garden. (C. W. Stevens) New Eng. M. n. s. 24: 343.

— Public Library, Printed Catalogue for. (J. L. Whitney) Lib. J. 24: supp. 8.

— Saturday Club. (G. W. Cooke) New Eng. M. n. s. 19: 24.

— School Administration in. (S. A. Wetmore) Educa. R. 14: 105.

— Settlement Work in. (H. S. Dudley) Munic. Aff. 2: 493.

— South Terminal Railroad Station. (H. W. Weller) Am. Arch. 65: 91, 99. — (J. A. Stewart) Chaut. 29: 357. — (E. E. R. Tratman) Am. Arch. 74: 94.

— State House. (A. S. Roe) New Eng. M. n. s. 19: 659.

— Street Cries in. (A. Bates) New Eng. M. n. s. 21: 407.

— Street Railways in. (G. J. Varney) Lippinc. 63: 569.

— Subway. (G. G. Crocker) New Eng. M. n. s. 19: 523. — (G. J. Varney) Nat'l M. (Bost.) 12: 272. — (B. L. Beal) Munic. Aff. 4: 219.

Boston, Subway, Franchise of. (W. Winslow) Munic. Aff. 5: 427.
— Symphony Orchestra. (C. M. Rettock) Nat'l M. (Bost.) 10: 122.
— — and its Directors. (W. S. B. Mathews) Music, 15: 553.
— Tax List, 1687. N. E. Reg. 55: 139.
— Wooden Suburbs of. (R. C. Sturgis) New Eng. M. n. s. 18: 739.
— Writing Masters in, before the Revolution. (W. C. Bates) New Eng. M. n. s. 19: 403.
Boston Architectural Club Exhibit. Am. Arch. 64: 83. — (H. L. Warren) Archit. R. 6: 71.
Boston Merchants' Municipal Committee. (R. C. Brooks) Munic. Aff. 1: 491.
Boston Musicians. (W. S. B. Mathews) Music, 19: 505.
Boston Prisoners in the American Revolution. (V. H. Paltsits) N. E. Reg. 52: 311.
Boston, England. (S. O. Holden) New Eng. M. n. s. 21: 387.
Boston Terrier, The. (H. W. Huntington) Outing, 33: 548.
Boswell, James. Acad. 52: 213.
— in Corsica, with portrait. (M. A. Stobart) Pall Mall M. 25: 225.
— The Prince of Biographers. (P. A. Sillard) Atlan. 88: 213.
Bosworth, Battle of. (J. Gairdner) Archæol. 55: 159.
— (A. H. Diplock) Temp. Bar, 122: 108.
Botanic Gardens; Tübingen and its Botanists. (D. T. Macdougal) Pop. Sci. Mo. 50: 312.
Botanical Club, Proceedings of. (A. D. Selby) Science, n. s. 10: 364.
Botanical Laboratory, High-school, Equipment and Administration of the. (F. C. Newcombe) School R. 7: 301.
Botanical Publications, Classification of. (W. Trelease) Science, n. s. 10: 718.
Botanical Society of America. (A. Hollick) Science, n. s. 10: 288.
Botanical Terms, Structure and Significance of certain. (C. A. White) Science, 12: 62.
Botanizing in Mountains of British Columbia. (H. H. Gowen) Canad. M. 8: 513.
Botany. (H. M. Ward) Nature, 56: 455, 476.
— at the British Association, 1899. Nature, 58: 632.
— at Columbus Meeting of Amer. Assoc. for Advancement of Science. (W. A. Kellerman) Science, n. s. 10: 557.
— Barnes's. (J. M. Coulter) School R. 6: 682.
— Botanical Work wanting Workers. (E. M. Holmes) Nat. Sci. 13: 31.
— Britton's Manual of the Flora of the Northern States and Canada. (C. E. Bessey) Science, n. s. 14: 732.
— Economic. (J. R. Jackson) Knowl. 21: 28, 73, 126, 199.
— in College Entrance. (W. F. Ganong) Science, n. s. 13: 611.
— Indian, Sketch of the History of. (Sir Geo. King) Nature, 60: 581.
— The New Field. (B. D. Halsted) Pop. Sci. Mo. 56: 98.
— Northern Apetalous Flowers. (J. H. Lovell) Am. Natural. 35: 197.
— Physiological, Progress and. Problems of. (C. R. Barnes) Science, n. s. 10: 316.
— Problems and Possibilities of Systematic. (B. L. Robinson) Science, n. s. 14: 465.
— Scope of. (G. J. Peirce) Pop. Sci. Mo. 51: 662.
— Strange Practices in Plant-naming. (C. S. Pollard) Science, n. s. 14: 280.

Botany, Strasburger's Text-book of. Pop. Sci. Mo. 53: 558.
— Teaching of, Advances in. (W. F. Ganong) Science, n. s. 9: 96.
— 20th Century Problems. (W. Trelease) Science, 12: 48.
— Work at the British Museum and Kew. Science, n. s. 14: 136.
Botany Bay. (W. H. S. Aubrey) Chamb. J. 77: 778.
Botha, Louis, the New Boer Commander, with portrait. R. of Rs. (N. Y.) 21: 578.
Bottesford, Lincolnshire, Manor of. (E. Peacock) Archæol. 50: 371.
Botticelli, Sandro. Month, 96: 220. — With portrait and bibliography. Mast. in Art, 1: 145.
— The Annunciation, with illustration. McClure, 16: 220.
— Classical Pictures. (Edith Harwood) Artist (N. Y.) 30: 1.
— Madonna, Child, and St. John. (Addison McLeod) Art J. 53: 33.
— New Madonna and Child found at Pitti Palace. (Louise Lander) Art J. 52: 38.
Bottle, The, the Half Brick and the Lump of Chalk; a story. (C. B. Loomis) Indep. 53: 553.
Bottles, Floating, Drift of, in the Pacific Ocean. (J. Page) Nat. Geog. M. 12: 337.
Bottles, Voyages of. (R. P. Ryan) Outl. 58: 534.
Boucher, Frank, Medalist. (M. H. Spielmann) M. of Art, 24: 154.
Boucher, Jonathan. Letters to George Washington. N. E. Reg. 52: 57-457. 53: 303, 417. 54: 32.
Boudinot, Col. Elias, in New York City, February, 1778. (H. Jordan) Pennsyl. M. 24: 453.
— Notes of Two Conferences for the Exchange of Prisoners of War, 1778. Pennsyl. M. 14: 291.
Bough, Sam, R. S. A. Illus. (E. Pinnington) Good Words, 38: 597.
Boughton, G. H. Afternoons in Studios. Studio (Lond.) 3: 131.
— Appreciation of. (M. H. Dixon) Art J. 51: 9.
Bouguereau, W. L'Admiration. Art J. 52: 116.
Bouldin, James Wood, with portrait. (Sallie E. M. Hardy) Green Bag, 10: 110.
Boulet Process, Metallic Tubes. J. Mil. Serv. Inst. 18: 657.
Boulle-work at Buckingham Palace. (F. S. Robinson) M. of Art, 24: 119.
— at Windsor Castle. (F. S. Robinson) M. of Art, 21: 238. 22: 26.
Boulogne, France, Diary of the Expedition of 1544. (W. J. Archbold) Eng. Hist. R. 16: 503.
— An Old High Town and an Old Palace. (P. Fitzgerald) Gent. M. n. s. 66: 70.
— Our Lady of. Sat. R. 86: 267.
Boundaries of Territorial Acquisition; with map. Nat. Geog. M. 12: 373.
Boundary, Lost, of Texas. (M. Baker) Nat. Geog. M. 12: 430.
Boundary War. (W. H. Babcock) Lippinc. 61: 555.
Bounder, The; a story. (H. Wyndham) Belgra. 95: 51.
Bounties and Subsidies. Nation, 72: 389.
"Bounty," Mutiny of the. (A. Webb) Nation, 71: 90.
Bouquet, The. (C. W. Chesnutt) Atlan. 84: 648.
Bourbaki, Charles Denis Sauter. Ed. R. 187: 313.
Bourbon, Charles de. (W. B. Wallace) Un. Serv. M. 23: 161.
Bourchier, Arthur, as Play Manager. (M. Beerbohm) Sat. R. 91: 333.
Bourget, Paul. Acad. 52: 167. — (Y. Blaze de Bury) Forum, 23: 497.
— Changed Views of. Acad. 59: 483.

Brahms, Johannes. Acad. 51: 407. — (G. Kobbé) Forum, 23: 577. — Ath. '97, 1: 487. — Music, 12: 239. — With portraits. (E. Swayne) Music, 14: 155. — Music, 15: 43. — With portraits. (H. Gale) Critic, 39: 523.
— and a Young Composer. Music, 13: 373.
— and the Classical Tradition. (W. H. Hadow) Contemp. 71: 653. Same art. Ecl. M. 128: 800. Same art. Liv. Age, 213: 829. — (W. H. Hadow) Music, 12: 538.
— Charm of his Music. (G. D. Gunn) Music, 19: 246.
— Glimpses of. (E. Swayne) Music, 17: 382.
— his Place in Art. Music, 12: 59.
— his Works and Individuality. (W. S. B. Mathews) Music, 12: 67.
— Instrumental Compositions of. Music, 16: 17.
— Music of. Sat. R. 83: 468.
— Personal Recollections of. (G. Henschel) Cent. 39: 725.
— Symphony in D Minor. (W. S. B. Mathews) Music, 17: 622.
Brain, Anatomy and Psychology of. (L. Edinger) Monist, 11: 339.
— Desirability of Knowledge of, by Pre-collegiate Scholars. (B. G. Wilder) Science, 6: 902.
— Human, in Relation to Education. (N. C. McNamara) Westm. 154: 634.
— Loeb's Comparative Psychology. (H. H. Bawden) Psychol. R. 7: 74. — (J. Jastrow) Dial (Ch.) 30: 139.
— Primary Segmentation of. (C. F. W. McClure) Science, 5: 260.
— Some Byways of the. (A. Wilson) Harper, 96: 791, 928.
— Why are our Brains deteriorating? (H. Elsdale) 19th Cent. 46: 262. Same art. Ecl. M. 133: 766. Same art. Liv. Age, 222: 882.
Brain Study by the Young. (B. G. Wilder) Arena, 17: 584.
— Dangerous Tendency in. (A. C. Bowen) Arena, 24: 618.
Brain Weights and Intellectual Capacity. (J. Simms) Pop. Sci. Mo. 54: 243.
Brain-work and Health. (P. C. Mitchell) Sat. R. 86: 264.
Brainerd's Idol. (W. T. Nichols) Lippinc. 63: 396.
Brakes for High Speed Trains. (L. H. Walter) Cassier, 12: 726.
Braking a Railroad Train. (G. L. Wilkinson) Munsey, 23: 105.
Bram, T.; Why he was found Guilty. (C. E. Grinnell) Green Bag, 9: 146.
Brampton, Henry Hawkins, Baron. Strand, 17: 318.
Branch Bank at Hooroobin, The. (J. A. Barry) Chamb. J. 76: 833.
Brandes, Georg. (W. M. Payne) Bookman, 5: 106.
Brandon, Vermont. (A. W. Kellogg) New Eng. M. n. s. 17: 293.
Brandram, Rosina, with portraits. Strand, 16: 535.
Brandy-farming in Charente. Chamb. J. 74: 541.
Brangwyn, Frank, Artist, with portrait. (J. S. Little) Studio (Internat.) 3: 3.
Branscombe and its Birds. (W. H. Hudson) Longm. 32: 543.
Brantôme, Pierre de Bourdeilles, Seigneur de. Quar. 194: 435.
Brantwood Drawings, The. Ath. '00, 1: 633.
Brass Band as a Social Factor. Music, 20: 242.
— Evolution of the. (M. West) Munsey, 25: 640.
— Genesis of a. (G. Bacon) Good Words, 42: 471.
Brass Band Contests. (T. W. Wilkinson) Good Words, 42: 598.
Brasses; Brass-rubbing. (P. H. Ditchfield) Gent. M. n. s. 67: 511.

Brasses, Broadwater, Sussex. Reliquary, 40: 55.
— Some Interesting. (M. Christy; W. W. Porteous) Reliquary, 39: 9.
— — in Essex. (M. Christy; W. W. Porteous) Reliquary, 41: 73.
Brassicas, Cultivated. (L. H. Bailey) Garden & F. 10: 321.
Bray, Charles. Bank. M. (N. Y.) 56: 812.
Braybrooke's Double-event Steeplechase. (D. Gray) Cent. 33: 29.
Brazen Bells in Arcady. Liv. Age, 218: 456.
Brazil, Commerce and Resources of. (T. L. Thompson) Forum, 25: 46.
— Dutch Power in. (G. Edmundson) Eng. Hist. R. 14: 676. 15: 38.
— Financial Outlook in. Bank. M. (Lond.) 65: 377.
— Jesuit Missions in. (H. Granville) Lippinc. 59: 252.
— A Republic in the Tropics. (E. R. Hendrix) Indep. 52: 1979.
— Tertiary Sea of, Supposed. (O. A. Derby) Science, n. s. 13: 348.
Brazilian Adventure. (W. Thomson) Lippinc. 60: 694.
Brazilian Law and Judicial Organization. (T. C. Dawson) Am. Law R. 35: 31.
Breach of Promise, The Law of. (W. A. McClean) Green Bag, 10: 368.
Bread and Bread-making at the Paris Exposition. (H. W. Wiley) Forum, 30: 303.
— Rise in the Price of. (M. Ferrario) Chaut. 26: 182.
Bread and Butter; the Struggle for Existence. (W. T. James) Canad. M. 9: 74.
Bread Line. (A. B. Paine) Lippinc. 65: 3.
Breadalbane, Gavin Campbell, Lord, with portraits. Strand, 15: 410.
Breadstuffs, Duties on. (W. C. Ford) Nation, 64: 216.
— Impending Deficiency of. (C. W. Davis) Forum, 24: 173.
Break in Turpentine, The; a story of Wall Street. (E. Lefèvre) McClure, 16: 539. Same art. Idler, 19: 515.
Breakfast, Concerning. (E. V. Lucas) Cornh. 77: 208. Same art. Liv. Age, 216: 711.
Breaking in of a Cowboy, The; a story. (C. L. Andrews) Midland, 9: 3.
Breaking out of Sally Daggs; a story. (K. F. M. Sullivan) Canad. M. 8: 400.
Breakwaters, Floating, Studies among Drift-ice of Polar Seas with ref. to construct. of. (A. E. Nordenskiöld) Geog. J. 11: 492.
Breath, Second. (G. E. Partridge) Pedagog. Sem. 4: 372.
Breath of Fragrance, A; a tale. (M. B. Cross) Argosy, 72: 178.
Bred in the Bone. (T. N. Page) Cent. 40: 939.
Breeching of Sammy; a story. (H. A. Vackell) Pall Mall M. 11: 482.
Breeding. Penycuik Experiments, Ewart's. Sat. R. 87: 759.
Brehon Laws in Ireland, Supplanting of the. (J. M. Sullivan) Green Bag, 13: 299.
— Tenure under. (J. M. Sullivan) Green Bag, 13: 524.
Bremen, Germany. Town Hall. Am. Arch. 64: 71.
Brendan, St., of Clonfert. (Æ. J. G. Mackay) Blackw. 162: 135.
Brent, Mistress Margaret, Neglected Records of. (C. S. Bansemer) Harper, 97: 229.
Brentford, England, Old. (Francis Watt) Art J. 53: 83.
— in Literature. Acad. 54: 7.
Br'er Coon in Old Kentucky. (J. Fox, jr.) Cent. 33: 594.
Brest, Blockade of. (D. Hanway) Macmil. 80: 370.
Breteuil, The Laws of. (M. Bateson) Eng. Hist. 15: 73-754. 16: 92, 332.

British Association for Adv. of Science; **Meeting, 1899,** Dover, Mechanics at. Nature, **61**: 20.
— — President's Address. (M. Foster) Knowl. **22**: 219.
— — Zoölogy and Physiology at. Nature, **62**: 588.
— Meeting, 1900, Bradford. President's Address. (Sir W. Turner) Pop. Sci. Mo. **57**: 561. **58**: 34. — Nature, **62**: 300–392.
— — Anthropology at. Nature, **62**: 633.
— — Astronomy at. (A. A. Common) Science, n. s. **12**: 590.
— — Botany at. Nature, **62**: 610.
— — Conference of Delegates of Corresponding Societies. Nature, **63**: 20.
— — Geography at. Nature, **62**: 590. — Geog. J. **16**: 441. — Nat. Geog. M. **11**: 475..
— — Geology; Address of President of Section. (W. J. Sollas) Science, n. s. **12**: 745, 787. — Nature, **62**: 587.
— — Mechanics at. Nature, **62**: 609.
— Meeting, 1901, Glasgow. Nature, **64**: 470–611. — (J. G. McKendrick) Science, n. s. **14**: 517. — (J. P. McMurrich) Science, n. s. **14**: 682.
— — Chemistry. Report of Section. (W. McPherson) Science, n. s. **14**: 482.
— — Geography at. Geog. J. **18**: 508.
— — Physical Sciences at. (A. L. Rotch) Science, n. s. **14**: 757.
— — President's Address. (A. W. Rücker) Science, n. s. **14**: 425.
British Astronomical Association. (W. H. Maw) Pop. Astron. **8**: 65.
British Capital Abroad. (M. G. Mulhall) No. Am. **168**: 499.
British Cavalry, Thought on. Un. Serv. M. **18**: 273. **24**: 296.
British Colonies of North America, Industrial Experiments in, Lord's. (H. L. Osgood) Am. Hist. R. **4**: 365.
British Columbia, Archæological Researches in. (H. I. Smith) Science, n. s. **9**: 535.
— Archæology of. (H. I. Smith) Am. Antiq. **23**: 25.
— Big Game of. (J. T. Turner) Sat. R. **84**: 691.
— In the Gameland our Fathers Lost. (F. Ireland) Scrib. M. **28**: 259.
— in Summer. (J. Durham) Canad. M. **15**: 6.
— Iron Ores of. (H. M. Lamb) Engin. M. **20**: 399.
— Mineral Resources of. (A. J. McMillan) Sat. R. **84**: 690.
— Mining Centres. (C. H. Macintosh) Canad. M. **8**: 305.
— Mining Development. (C. Phillipps-Wolley) Canad. M. **8**: 299.
— Mining in. (H. M. Lamb) Engin. M. **19**: 543.
— One of our Unknown Neighbors. (A. H. Bradford) Outl. **60**: 133.
— Pastimes in. (T. L. Grahame) Canad. M. **10**: 466.
— Politics in. (T. L. Grahame) Canad. M. **15**: 330.
British Confederation. (J. W. Root) Atlan. **87**: 402.
British Consul, Duties of a. Temp. Bar, **112**: 242. Same art. Ecl. M. **130**: 215.
British Crews Abroad, Crimping. Un. Serv. M. **17**: 588.
British Economic Association, Meeting, 1899. (J. H. Hollander) Nation, **69**: 275.
British Fleet in Commission. (A. S. Hurd) Un. Serv. M. **18**: 247.
British Ideals, Mr. Bryce on. Spec. **85**: 924.
British Industries, The Position of. Bank. M. (Lond.) **72**: 337.
British Interests in the Far East. Blackw. **163**: 718.
British Islander, A: a story. (M. H. Catherwood) Harper, **96**: 345.
British Medical Assoc., Portsmouth Meeting. (F. W. Tunnicliffe) Nature, **60**: 341.

British Museum. Spec. **84**: 867.
— and its Treasures; a humorous account. (A. Golsworthy) Idler, **17**: 63.
— Book Catalogue of. Quar. **188**: 289.
— Cataloguing of, Revised Rules for. (H. B. Wheatley) Library, n. s. **1**: 263.
— Changes in the Exhibition of Books at. Library, **3**: 99, 170.
— Humorous Sketch. (Allen Upward) Idler, **10**: 799.
— Librarian of, Principal. (N. D. Davis) Nation, **65**: 314.
— Manuscript Room of. (D. C. Macdonald) Lippinc. **59**: 415.
— New Print Room Exhibition. Sat. R. **91**: 704.
— Paintings of Some Old Masters at. (J. P. Richter) Art J. **49**: 152.
— Rembrandt Exhibition at. Ath. '99, **1**: 280.
— Sliding Press at. (G. Garnett) Library, **3**: 414.
— Stuart Exhibition at. Library, **1**: 69, 137.
— The Suggestion Book in. Acad. **54**: 155.
— Tudor Book at. Library, **2**: 63.
British Museum Myth. Atlan. **84**: 718.
British Privateers. (R. B. Nicholetts) Un. Serv. M. **18**: 582.
British Radicals and Radicalism. (J. D. Miller) Arena, **23**: 254.
British Royalty and America. (F. Cunliffe Owen) Munsey, **23**: 109.
British Sailor, Traditional. (W. J. Fletcher) 19th Cent. **48**: 422.
British Scenery, Development of. (J. E. Marr) Sci. Prog. **7**: 275.
British Seamen for British Ships. (W. L. Ainslie; J. H. Voxall) 19th Cent. **45**: 39.
British Ships in Foreign Navies. (A. S. Hurd) 19th Cent. **43**: 549. — (W. H. White) 19th Cent. **43**: 866.
British Soldier, The. Un. Serv. M. **19**: 306. — J. Mil. Serv. Inst. **25**: 68.
— as a Plague Commissioner. (W. Tweedie) Blackw. **162**: 409.
— Sanitary Clothing for the. Un. Serv. M. **22**: 98.
British Soldiers. Blackw. **168**: 677.
British Statesmanship. Fortn. **76**: 635.
British Trade Methods. (A. Lambert) 19th Cent. **44**: 940.
British Workman and his Competitors. (W. Woodward) 19th Cent. **49**: 456.
Brittany. (E. W. Rinder) Argosy, **71**: 388. — (T. P. White) Scot. R. **31**: 81.
— Anthropology of. (P. Topinard) Anthrop. J. **27**: 96.
— Around. (I. P. Stevenson) Chaut. **31**: 274.
— Biological Stations of. (J. F. Gerould) Science, n. s. **9**: 165.
— Browning's Summers in. (A. M. Mosher) Cent. **32**: 755.
— Convent in, Notes in a. (Charlotte M. Mew) Temp. Bar, **124**: 238. Same art. Liv. Age, **231**: 630.
— Peoples and Customs of. (C. H. L. Emanuel) Idler, **15**: 738.
— Popular Drama in. (A. Le Braz) Internat. Mo. **4**: 403.
— Prehistoric Monuments of. (A. B. Macallum) Am. Antiq. **21**: 242.
— St. Anne d'Auray's Day. (Herbert Vivian) Sat. R. **91**: 42.
Britton, Thomas. (F. G. Walters) Temp. Bar, **115**: 429.
Broad Arrow, The; a story. (E. M. Jameson) Strand, **17**: 289.
Broader Outlook, The; a story. (E. Rickert) Argosy, **75**: 285.
Broadhurst, Henry. Autobiography. Sat. R. **91**: 709.
Broadsides, Collectors of. (W. Y. Fletcher) Library, n. s. **2**: 12.

Broadway in Worcestershire. (J. L. Gilder) Bk. Buyer, **15**: 315.

Brocades, Spitalfields. (L. Liberty) Studio (Lond.) **1**: 20.

Brockenbrough, John W., with portrait. (Sallie E. M. Hardy) Green Bag, **10**: 115.

Brockton, a Massachusetts Shoe Town. (A. F. Sanborn) Atlan. **80**: 177.

Brockville (Ont.) Rowing Club. (W. S. Buell) Outing, **34**: 69.

Broderick, George Charles. Memories and Impressions. Sat. R. **89**: 462.

Brodie, Peter B. Ath. '97, **2**: 638.

Brodie, William, *alias* Heather Jock. (R. B. C. Graham) Sat. R. **83**: 110. — (F. Brock) Gent. M. n. s. **65**: 349.

Brodrick, William St. John, Army Scheme of. (A. Griffiths) Fortn. **75**: 859.

Broken Assegai, The ; a tale. Argosy, **63**: 374.

Broken China. (F. T. Dickson) Belgra. **97**: 198.

Broken Dream, The ; a story. (G. Morley) Gent. M. n. s. **67**: 488.

Broken Gates of Death. (W. B. Yeats) Fortn. **69**: 524. Same art. Liv. Age, **217**: 383.

Broken Ideals ; a novel. (Lady M. Majendie) Argosy, **67**: 445. **68**: 85–412.

Broken Vase, The ; a poem. (R. F. A. S. Prudhomme) Argosy, **64**: 427.

Broken Wings. (K. Head) Atlan. **87**: 849.

Broken Wings. (H. James) Cent. **39**: 194.

Bromwich Castle, England. (I. Bradford) Pall Mall M. **15**: 291.

Broncho-riding. (A. Hendricks) Lippinc. **60**: 113.

Bronsart, Ingeborg von, with portrait. (E. Polko) Music, **14**: 235.

Bronson's Luck. (E. A. Vore) Overland, n. s. **30**: 550.

Brontë, Anne, At the Grave of. (P. C. Standing) Eng. Illust. **17**: 525.

Brontë, Charlotte. (Sir G. M. Smith) Critic, **38**: 51. Same art. Cornh. **82**: 778. — (W. B. Worsfold) Fortn. **71**: 74. Same art. Liv. Age, **220**: 377. — Acad. **59**: 87.

— and her Circle. (E. D'Esterre-Keeling) Dub. R. **120**: 319.

— and her Sisters. Ath. '00, **1**: 426, 453. Same art. Ecl. M. **135**: 162. Same art. Liv. Age, **225**: 626.

— and one of her Critics. (W. R. Nicoll) Bookman, **10**: 441.

— and Thackeray. (E. D. North) Bookman, **6**: 19.

— Mrs. Gaskell's Life, Haworth Edition. (C. Shipman) Critic, **36**: 415.

— Green Dwarf. (W. G. Kingsland) Poet-Lore, **9**: 479.

— her Life at Filey. (P. C. Standing) Idler, **12**: 81.

— Poems by. Bookman, **4**: 426.

— Mary Taylor and Ellen Nussey. (M. V. Terhune) Critic, **35**: 705.

Brontë, Emily, Interpretation of. (A. M. Mackay) Westm. **150**: 203. Same art. Liv. Age, **219**: 276.

— Relics of. (C. K. Shorter) Bookman, **6**: 15.

Brontë Letters, The. Lond. Q. **88**: 27.

Brontë Sisters, The. (J. B. Henneman) Sewanee R. **9**: 220.

Bronze Age, Antiquities of, found in Heathery Burn Cave. (W. Greenwell) Archæol. **54**: 87.

— Burials on Fairsnape Farm, Lancashire. Reliquary, **40**: 258.

Bronze Axes in Buxton, Discovery of. Reliquary, **40**: 125.

Bronze Bowl found at Needham Market. (J. R. Allen) Reliquary, **40**: 242.

Bronze Casting, Method. (L. Taft) Brush & P. **3**: 50.

Bronze Fragments, Two, of an Unknown Object in Royal Irish Academy, Dublin. Archæol. **47**: 473.

Bronze Instrument found on Mount Moriah, Jerusalem. Reliquary, **41**: 129.

Bronze Objects found in Wilburton Fen. (J. Evans) Archæol. **48**: 106.

Bronze Statue, Genesis of a. Artist (N. Y.) **24**: vii.

Bronzes at Windsor Castle. (F. S. Robinson) M. of Art, **21**: 295.

— French and Italian, at Windsor Castle. (F. S. Robinson) M. of Art, **22**: 318, 408.

— Greek, Roman, and Etruscan, in British Museum, Walters's. Sat. R. **87**: 616.

— Microstructure of. (A. F. Outerbridge, jr.) J. Frankl. Inst. **147**: 18. — (E. Heyn) J. Frankl. Inst. **147**: 447.

Brook and the Sea, The ; a poem. (T. C. Roney) Music, **17**: 246.

Brook Farm. (G. W. Cooke) New Eng. M. n. s. **17**: 391. — (A. M. Mitchell) Cath. World, **73**: 17.

— and its Promoters. (A. W. Tarbell) Nat'l M. (Bost.) **7**: 195.

— Experiment of. Acad. **58**: 516.

— Girl of Sixteen at. (O. G. Sedgwick) Atlan. **85**: 394.

— Swift's. (J. W. Chadwick) Nation, **70**: 152.

Brook Hospital. (W. N. Twelvetrees) Engin. M. **15**: 759.

Brooke, James, the White Rajah of Borneo ; the founding of Sarawak. (R. Wildman) Overland, n. s. **29**: 239.

— The Story of. (S. Bonsal) Outl. **64**: 550.

Brooke, Stopford A. Old Testament and Modern Life. Critic, **30**: 1.

— Religion in Literature and Life. (H. A. Clarke) Poet-Lore, **13**: 299.

Brookes, W. P., of Wenlock in Shropshire, a Typical Englishman. (Baron P. de Coubertin) R. of Rs. (N. Y.) **15**: 62.

Brookfield, Jane Octavia. Critic, **30**: 63.

Brookfield, Mass. (D. H. Chamberlain) New Eng. M. n. s. **21**: 481.

Brookline, Mass. ; a model town under the referendum. (B. O. Flower) Arena, **19**: 505.

— Public Library, School Reference Room in. (H. H. Stanley) Pub. Lib. **6**: 398.

Brooklyn, Old and New. Archit. R. **8**: 268.

Brooklyn Bridge ; poem. (C. G. D. Roberts) Atlan. **83**: 839.

Brooks, Florence. Writer, **14**: 185.

Brooks, Phillips. (C. F. Thwing) Chaut. **30**: 299.

— Allen's Life of. (C. A. L. Richards) Dial (Ch.) **30**: 133. — Atlan. **87**: 262. — (C. T. Brady) Bk. Buyer, **22**: 120. — (R. H. Newton) Critic, **38**: 245. — (L. Abbott) Outl. **67**: 717. — (J. W. Chadwick) Nation, **72**: 159. — (J. Reed) N. Church R. **8**: 225. — (J. Fox) Presb. & Ref. R. **12**: 694. — Ath. '01, **1**: 134.

— Memorials of. (H. S. Houston) Outl. **61**: 55.

Brooks, Thomas Benton. (B. Willis) Science, n. s. **13**: 460.

Brooks, William Keith, Sketch of. (E. A. Andrews) Pop. Sci. Mo. **55**: 400.

Brooks's Club, London, The Betting Book at. (G. S. Street) No. Am. **173**: 44.

Brother Boldero's Carriage ; a story. (G. B. Stuart) Argosy, **65**: 686.

Brother Felix. Liv. Age, **223**: 841.

Brother of "Chuck" McGann ; a story. (H. M. Blossom, jr.) Harper, **98**: 949.

Brother Paul's Intention ; a story. (W. S. Burton) Temp. Bar, **113**: 445. Same art. Liv. Age, **217**: 593–658.

Brother Pidgley saves the Day. (C. T. Brady) Lippinc. **68**: 232.

Brother Sims's Mistake. (H. S. Edwards) Cent. **36**: 354.

Brother to Saints; a story. (S. Bonsal) Harper, 100: 256.

Brother to St. James; a story. (W. L. Beard) Harper, 99: 303.

Brotherhood of Pity at Florence. (J. Ross) Eng. Illust. 19: 283.

Brotherhood of Railroad Trainmen. (D. L. Cease) Gunton's M. 20: 235.

Brothers; a poem. (H. M. Posnett) Gent. M. n. s. 66: 203.

Brothers, The. (H. Child) Longm. 32: 318. Same art. Liv. Age, 218: 825.

Brothers of Sincerity. (T. Davidson) Int. J. Ethics, 8: 439.

Brothers of the Wolf, The. (W. Le Queux) Chamb. J. 76: 445.

Brough, Robert. (E. Pinnington) Art J. 50: 146. — (B. Kendell) Artist (N. Y.) 31: 65.

Brown, Arnesby, Artist. Studio (Internat.) 11: 213.

Brown, Charles Brockden. (J. S. McCowan) Sewanee, 4: 174.

Brown, Ford Madox, with portrait. Bk. Buyer, 14: 39. — Acad. 51: 186.

— and Watts, G. F. (G. B. Shaw) Sat. R. 83: 266.

— Life and Work of, Hueffer's. Sat. R. 84: 41. — (K. Cox) Nation, 64: 110. — Ath. '97, 1: 284. — Spec. 78: 245.

— Paintings. Sat. R. 83: 191.

Brown, James. (E. M. Bacon) Bookman, 5: 373.

Brown, Capt. John, The Actual. (A. M. Courtenay) Chaut. 24: 446.

— and his Iowa Friends. (B. F. Gue) Midland, 7: 103, 267.

— Last Days of. (Lou V. Chapin) Overland, n. s. 33: 322.

— Last Letter of. (C. H. Small) New Eng. M. n. s. 20: 579.

— Reminiscences of. (D. B. Hadley) McClure, 10: 278.

— Trial of. Illus. (B. C. Washington) Green Bag, 11: 160.

Brown, Katharine Holland. Writer, 14: 139.

Brown, Thomas Edward. New R. 17: 632. — Acad. 52: 377, 404. (Wm. Canton) Good Words, 39: 187. — Acad. 59: 255. — (S. H. W. Hughes-Games) Fortn. 74: 765. — (J. C. Tarver) Macmil. 82: 401. — (A. T. Quiller-Couch) Monthly R. 1, no. 1: 152. — (W. E. Henley) Pall Mall M. 22: 424, 582. — (J. R. Mozley) Temp. Bar, 123: 505.

— Letters. (E. G. Johnson) Dial (Ch.) 30: 9. — Atlan. 86: 854. — Sat. R. 90: 589.

— Poems. Quar. 187: 384. Same art. Liv. Age, 218: 707.

Brown, Valentine. Poems. (J. B. Gilder) Critic, 38: 551.

Brown, Wm. Henry, the Last of the Silhouettists. (C. H. Hart) Outl. 66: 329.

Brown-Séquard, Charles Edouard. (Mrs. W. D. Cabell) Educa. 20: 431.

Brown University. (H. R. Palmer) New Eng. M. n. s. 20: 293.

— An Open Letter addressed to the Corporation of, by the Faculty. R. of Rs. (N. Y.) 16: 316.

Browne, Bradwell, and Me; a story. (Eden Phillpotts) Idler, 12: 21.

Browne, Charles F. [Artemus Ward], First Books of. (L. S. Livingston) Bookman, 8: 563.

— Recollections of. (J. F. Ryder) Cent. 41: 151.

Browne, Francis Fisher. (J. V. Cheney) Bk. Buyer, 20: 301.

Browne, Geo. F., Bishop of Stepney. Sund. M. 27: 110.

— Portraits of. Strand, 14: 416.

Browne, Gordon, as Book Illustrator. (J. W. Darton) Art J. 51: 69.

Browne, Irving, as a Poet. Green Bag, 9: 354.

Browne, Stewart. Bank. M. (N. Y.) 59: 616.

Browne, Sir Thomas. Acad. 53: 208.

Browne Charging System. Lib. J. 24: 202.

Brownell, W. C. Victorian Prose Masters. (R. Ogden) Bk. Buyer, 23: 374.

Browning, Elizabeth Barrett. (E. M. Thomas) Critic, 37: 516. — (P. Mohnenti) Liv. Age, 219: 35. — (Wm. Cameron) Good Words, 39: 43.

— as Prophetess. Acad. 61: 345.

— Aurora Leigh. (L. Hunt) Cornh. 76: 738.

— Letters. (Lucy Monroe) Book R. 5: 109. — Critic, 31: 348. — Ath. '97, 2: 627. Same art. Liv. Age, 215: 739. — Church Q. 46: 369. — (A. MacMéchan) Citizen, 4: 84.

— Other People in. Meth. R. 59: 797.

— Poetical Works; ed. by Kenyon. Sat. R. 85: 497. — Acad. 53: 117.

Browning, Robert, with portrait. (F. Thompson) Acad. 51: 499.

— and Elizabeth Barrett; a poem. (M. P. Guild) Atlan. 86: 420. — (H. W. Preston) Atlan. 83: 812.

— — First Books of. (L. S. Livingston) Bookman, 10: 76.

— — Love-Letters. (L. Abbott) Outl. 62: 485. — (E. P. Gould) Educa. 20: 214. — (H. M. Sanders) Temp. Bar, 120: 110. — Acad. 56: 235. — (V. L. Wentz) Bk. Buyer, 18: 237. — (Alice Meynell) Bookman, 9: 162. — Church Q. 49: 153. — (G. G. Buckler) Conserv. R. 1: 211. — (J. L. Gilder) Critic, 34: 246. — (A. B. McMahan) Dial (Ch.) 26: 238. — Ecl. M. 132: 736. — Same art. Liv. Age, 221: 166. — (W. Canton) Good Words, 40: 285. — (L. Stephen) National, 33: 401. — Poet-Lore, 11: 301. — Sat. R. 87: 242.

— — — and the Psychology of Love. (Hiram M. Stanley) Open Court, 13: 731. — (J. Mudge) Meth. R. 60: 694.

— — — Discretion and Publicity. Ed. R. 189: 420. Same art. Ecl. M. 133: 169. Same art. Liv. Age, 221: 807.

— and the Larger Public. R. of Rs. (N. Y.) 15: 184.

— and our Later Literature. (L. W. Smith) Midland, 7: 362.

— Bibliography of. (T. J. Wise) Ath. '97, 1: 17.

— A Blot in the 'Scutcheon; a Philistine View. (T. R. Lounsbury) Atlan. 84: 764.

— Child-critics of. Acad. 51: 573.

— Childe Roland. (T. P. Sawin) Poet-Lore, 9: 256.

— — The Mood of. (C. A. Smith) Poet-Lore, 11: 626.

— Childe Roland to the Dark Tower came. (T. W. Higginson) Poet-Lore, 13: 262.

— Chivalry, His Pictures of. (H. L. Reed) Poet-Lore, 11: 588.

— Essays in French Literature. Critic, 33: 191. — (Annie Macdonnell) Bookman, 8: 49.

— Evolution, Idea of, in his Poetry. (C. Fisher) Temp. Bar, 118: 534.

— Flight of the Duchess, Art Spirit in. (C. Moore) Poet-Lore, 11: 266.

— Folk Poems of; study program. (C. Porter and H. A. Clarke) Poet-Lore, 11: 608. 12: 105.

— in Asolo. (K. C. Bronson) Cent. 37: 920.

— in his Wife's Letters. Meth. R. 59: 450.

— Later Work, Defence of. (H. A. Clarke) Poet-Lore, 12: 284.

— Letters by. (W. G. Kingsland) Poet-Lore, 9: 83.

— the Musician. (A. Goodrich-Freer) 19th Cent. 49: 648. Same art. Ecl. M. 137: 174. Same art. Liv. Age, 229: 803.

— on Napoleon III. (C. Porter) Poet-Lore, 12: 80.

Browning, Robert, One Letter more from. (J. W. Mario) Nation, **68**: 220.

— Paracelsus. (F. L. Snow) Meth. R. **58**: 712.

— Pied Piper, Influence of. (Mrs. P. Leake) Artist (N. Y.) **26**: 131.

— — New Edition of. (H. Quilter) Artist (N. Y.) **23**: 174.

— A Plea for the Study of. (M. Connolly) Arena, **20**: 623.

— Poems of Adventure and Heroism, Study Program. (C. Porter and H. A. Clarke) Poet-Lore, **11**: 289, 403.

— Renaissance Pictures in Poetry of. (R. Burton) Poet-Lore, **10**: 66.

— George Santayana on ; a pessimist criticism. (H. D. Woodard) Poet-Lore, **13**: 97.

— Some Friends of. (J. C. Hadden) Macmil. **77**: 196.

— Soul's Tragedy. (E. G. Willcox) Poet-Lore, **13**: 411.

— Statue and the Bust, a Parable. (P. Cummings) Poet-Lore, **10**: 397.

— — The Legend of. (I. M. Bencini) Chaut. **34**: 288.

— Summers in Brittany. (A. M. Mosher) Cent. **32**: 755.

— Sun Symbolism in. (H. A. Clarke) Poet-Lore, **11**: 55.

— Theology of. (H. White) Poet-Lore, **12**: 417.

— Two Poets of Croisic, French Enthusiasms satirized in. (H. E. Cushman) Poet-Lore, **11**: 382.

— View of Love. Cornh. **75**: 226.

— Vision of Old Age. (C. W. Hodell) Meth. R. **61**: 99.

— Why Preachers should study. (J. Mudge) Meth. R. **57**: 402.

Browning Society, Boston, Programme, 1901–92. Poet-Lore, **13**: 437.

Browning Songs set to Music by C. K. Rogers. Music, **17**: 440.

Brownson, Orestes A., Brownson's. (J. W. Chadwick) Nation, **67**: 205.

— Conversion of. (W. L. Gildea) Cath. World, **69**: 14.

Bruce, Alexander Balmain. (J. E. McFadyen) Bib. World, **15**: 87.

— The Providential Order of the World. (A. Stewart) Crit. R. **8**: 3.

— Theological Work of. (J. Denney) Lond. Q. **92**: 358.

Bruce, Catherine Wolfe. (W. W. Payne) Pop. Astron. **8**: 235.

Bruce, James, in North Africa. (Sir R. Lambert-Playfair) Chamb. J. **76**: 369.

Bruce, Robert, and the Anglo-Scottish Controversy. (R. M. Lockhart) Westm. **148**: 23. — (G. Neilson) Ath. '97, **1**: 279.

— Maxwell's. Spec. **78**: 891. — Ath. '97, **1**: 572.

Bruges. Illus. (Sophia Beale) Good Words, **39**: 698.

— as a Sketching-ground. (W. Patten) Studio (Lond.) **3**: 42.

— Gables and Towers of. (M. Browne) Cath. World, **69**: 449.

— Impressions of. (E. Gosse) Indep. **52**: 1540.

Brugmann's Law and the Sanskrit Vrddhi. (C. D. Buck) Am. J. Philol. **17**: 445.

Brummell, Beau. (A. I. Shand) Cornh. **74**: 769. Same art. Ecl. M. **128**: 81.

Brunel, Isambard K. (W. M. Ackworth) Cornh. **76**: 291. Same art. Liv. Age, **215**: 201. — Same art. Ecl. M. **130**: 135.

Brunetière, F. (C. Bastide) Fortn. **72**: 500. — (T. Stanton) Nation, **64**: 239. — (A. Cohn) Bookman, **5**: 24. — (T. Bentzon) Critic, **30**: 193.

— American Tour of. Critic, **30**: 342. — R. of Rs. (N. Y.) **15**: 694.

— and his Critical Method. (I. Babbitt) Atlan. **79**: 757.

Brunetière, F., as a Critic. (A. Symons) Acad. **54**: 75. **55**: 241.

Brunissure of the Vine and Other Plants. (A. F. Woods) Science, n. s. **9**: 508.

Bruno, Camille. (D. F. Hannigan) Westm. **147**: 653.

Bruns, Karl Georg, German Jurist. (M. Smith) Pol. Sci. Q. **12**: 21.

Brunswick, Charles Wm. Ferd., Duke of, Fitzmaurice's Historical Study of. Ath. '01, **1**: 362. — Ed. R. **186**: 140.

Brushwork and Inventional Drawing. (T. J. McCormack) Open Court, **15**: 30.

Brussels, Congress of Public Art at. Artist (N. Y.) **23**: xxxiv.

— Municipal Art in. (B. Colt de Wolf) Art J. **53**: 123.

Brusson, Olivier ; a Criminal Mystery of the 17th Century. Chamb. J. **77**: 826.

Brute, The ; a poem. (W. V. Moody) Atlan. **87**: 88.

Bruyère, Elizabeth, with portrait. (F. Fitzpatrick) Cath. World, **71**: 12.

Bryan, William J. (S. J. McLean) Canad. M. **15**: 431. — (W. A. White) McClure, **15**: 232. — With portrait. (C. B. Spahr) R. of Rs. (N. Y.) **22**: 41.

— and McKinley. (J. L. Whittle) Fortn. **74**: 778.

— and the Trusts ; an anti-trust view. (F. S. Monnett) R. of Rs. (N. Y.) **22**: 439.

— as a Conjurer. (A. Carnegie) No. Am. **164**: 106.

— as Candidate for President. Sat. R. **90**: 37.

— as a Soldier. (C. F. Beck) Arena, **24**: 393.

— as a Speaker. Acad. **57**: 635.

— at Home ; with portrait. R. of Rs. (N. Y.) **22**: 179.

— The Beginnings of. (A. Watkins) Indep. **52**: 2245.

— Financial Policy of ; a Democratic view. (C. B. Spahr) R. of Rs. (N. Y.) **22**: 449.

— — a Republican View. (G. E. Roberts) R. of Rs. (N. Y.) **22**: 447.

— His Acceptance, 1900. Outl. **65**: 903.

— His Address on Imperialism ; extracts. Outl. **65**: 938.

— Jefferson, Jackson and. (J. C. Ridpath) Arena, **19**: 573.

— on the Campaign, 1900. Gunton's M. **19**: 17.

— The Passing of. (E. P. Clark) Nation, **72**: 43.

— Pedagogical Prescription of. Dial (Ch.) **22**: 299.

— Platform of. (H. White) Nation, **70**: 431.

— vs. Labor Men on Trusts. Gunton's M. **17**: 377.

Bryan, Mrs. W. J., Portrait of. Nat'l M. (Bost.) **12**: 217.

Bryanism. (S. Brooks) Contemp. **78**: 633.

— and Jeffersonian Democracy. (A. Watkins) Forum, **31**: 358.

— in Ohio. (H. White) Nation, **73**: 45.

— Socialism an Element of. (A. Watkins) Arena, **24**: 225.

Bryant, Gridley J. F. (H. T. Bailey) New Eng. M. n. s. **25**: 326.

Bryant, Joseph, MS. Record of. N. E. Reg. **54**: 101.

Bryant, Lilian True. Writer, **14**: 7.

Bryant, W. C. (M. A. D. Howe) Bookman, **5**: 124.

— First Books of. (L. S. Livingston) Bookman, **8**: 142.

— A Forgotten Chapter in his Life. (R. B. Buckham) Poet-Lore, **11**: 606.

— Home of. (T. Dreiser) Munsey, **21**: 240.

— In the Footprints of. (T. F. Wolfe) Lippinc. **66**: 765.

— Lowell's Opinion of. (W. J. Stillman) Acad. **60**: 130.

— Permanent Contribution to Literature. (H. D. Sedgwick, jr.) Atlan. **79**: 539.

Bryce, James. American Commonwealth. (E. M. Chapman) New Eng. M. n. s. **22**: 150.

— Manifesto to the Americans. (A. Hillier) Fortn. **73**: 730.

Bryce, James, Portrait of. Bk. Buyer, **15**: 639.

Brymner, Douglas, Canadian Archivist. (M. O. Scott) Canad. M. **16**: 206.

Bubble Reputation. (W. Price) New Eng. M. n. s. **20**: 285.

Bubbles; a poem. (B. McEvoy) Canad. M. **10**: 364.

Bubonic Plague. (F. G. Novy) Pop. Sci. Mo. **57**: 576. *See also* Plague.

Buccaneers, The. (J. R. Spears) Munsey, **26**: 10.

Buchan, David Stewart Erskine, Earl of. (John Buchan) Blackw. **167**: 557. Same art. Atlan. **85**: 508.

Buchan, John. John Burnet of Barns, a Romance. (C. G. D. Roberts) Bk. Buyer, **18**: 147.

Buchanan, George; the ancestor of Liberalism. Acad. **58**: 120.

Buchanan, James, Letters of, on the Clayton-Bulwer Treaty, 1849, 1850. Am. Hist. R. **5**: 95.
— Proposed Intervention in Mexico. (H. L. Wilson) Am. Hist. R. **5**: 687.

Buchanan, Robert. (Arthur Symons) Sat. R. **91**: 764.
— Acad. **60**: 504, 515. — Ath. '01, **1**: 760.
— Poetry of. Acad. **60**: 341.
— Under the Beard of. Liv. Age, **220**: 717.

Buchheim, Charles Adolphus. Ath. '00, **1**: 753. — J. Soc. Arts, **48**: 607.

Buchner, Ludwig, a Revelator of Science. (F. L. Oswald) Open Court, **13**: 465.

Bucket Shop in Speculation. (P. Thomas) Munsey, **24**: 68.

Buckhounds, Royal. Macmil. **77**: 150.

Buckingham, George Villiers, 2d Duke of. (C. Morris) Lippinc. **63**: 534. — Quar. **187**: 86.

Buckingham, J. T. (G. W. Cooke) New Eng. M. n. s. **16**: 103.

Buckingham Palace. Eng. Illust. **17**: 417.
— and its Site. (F. Rinder) Argosy, **74**: 3.
— Art Treasures at. (F. S. Robinson) M. of Art, **24**: 119-487. **25**: 9.

Buckland, Charles. Ath. '01, **1**: 370.

Buckland, Frank, Memories of. (G. C. Peachey) Temp. Bar, **122**: 79. Same art. Liv. Age, **228**: 585. Same art. Ecl. M. **136**: 500.

Buckland, Jack; "Tin Jack." (Isobel Strong) Crit. **38**: 431.

Buckle, Henry Thomas, Spencer, and Comte. (L. Gambetta) No. Am. **171**: 55.

Bucklebury, Eng. Some Hidden Histories. (G. Bacon) Eng. Illust. **19**: 447.

Buckner, Simon B., and Grant. A Blue and Gray Friendship. (J. R. Proctor) Cent. **31**: 942.

Bucks; a train-dispatcher's story. (F. H. Spearman) McClure, **14**: 147.

Buckshot War. (W. H. Egle) Pennsyl. M. **23**: 137.

Bud Leach; a sketch. (A. Miller) McClure, **16**: 171.

Bud that Blossomed, The; a story. (Louise C. Henderson) Nat'l M. (Bost.) **7**: 88.

Budapest, Electric Railways of. (A. O. Dubsky) Cassier, **16**: 91.
— Modern City of. (E. B. Terhune) Nat'l M. (Bost.) **11**: 655.

Budd, Back Number. (J. D. Barry) Lit. W. (Bost.) **29**: 73.

Buddha. (W. H. Rattigan) Lond. Q. **92**: 291.
— and Christ. (J. W. Johnston) Meth. R. **58**: 32.
— and his Doctrine. (J. S. Geisler) Am. Cath. Q. **22**: 857.
— and the Moral Order of the World, Bruce on. (J. Sandison) Open Court, **12**: 243.
— Birth of, Canonical Account of. (A. J. Edmunds) Open Court, **12**: 485.
— Birthplace of. (F. M. Müller) Blackw. **164**: 787.
— (G. Buehler) Ath. '97, **1**: 319.

Buddha, Body of, A Remnant of. (P. Landon) 19th Cent. **50**: 237.
— Discourse on the End of the World. (A. J. Edmunds) Open Court, **15**: 428.
— Tomb of. Am. Arch. **69**: 101.
— Tooth of, at Kandy, Ceylon. (W. Trant) Nat'l M. (Bost.) **6**: 424.

Buddha's Ear Precipice. (A. J. Little) Liv. Age, **231**: 65.

Buddha's Legacy to the 20th Century. (F. E. Marsden) Bank. M. (N. Y.) **62**: 824.

Buddha's most Holy Bones, Welcoming. (D. B. S. Spooner) Overland, n. s. **37**: 585.

Buddha Pictures and Statues. Illus. (P. Carus) Open Court, **12**: 337.

Buddhism. (T. W. R. Davids) No. Am. **171**: 517. — Scot. R. **33**: 286. — (J. Beames) Asia. R. **23**: 144.
— Birthplace of. (N. Stuart) Gent. M. n. s. **61**: 42.
— Breadth of. (T. Suzuki) Open Court, **14**: 51.
— Christianity and. (G. H. Palmer) Outl. **56**: 443.
— Controversy on. (F. F. Ellinwood and others) Open Court, **11**: 43.
— Davids's. (C. R. Lanman) Am. Hist. R. **2**: 330.
— Early. (D. B. Schneder) Ref. Q. **45**: 289.
— in China, and Christianity. (F. M. Müller) 19th Cent. **48**: 730.
— in India, A. D. 671-675, I-tsing's. Ath. '97, **1**: 142.
— — Revival of. (D. M. Strong) Westm. **153**: 271.
— Is there more than One? (H. Dharmapala) Open Court, **11**: 82.
— Japanese. (D. B. Schneder) Ref. Q. **45**: 483.
— Mythology of. (P. Carus) Monist, **7**: 415.
— Philosophy of. (P. Carus) Monist, **7**: 255.

Buddhist Law. (J. Jardine) Asia. R. **24**: 367.

Buddhist Legends, Chinese Rolls with. (A. W. Franks) Archæol. **53**: 239.

Buddhist Missionaries to America, Shall we Welcome? (M. L. Gordon; P. Carus) Open Court, **14**: 301.

Buddhist Monk, Travels of. A. D. 399-414. (H. H. Gowen) Am. Antiq. **21**: 3.

Buddhist Remains in India. Am. Arch. **60**: 61.

Buddhistic Funeral Rites and Ceremonies. (Mrs. W. D. Tillotson) Overland, n. s. **33**: 122.

Buds, Sir John Lubbock on. (Grant Allen) Acad. **56**: 623.

Budge Crockett of Hell Corner; a story. (J. F. Fraser) Pall Mall M. **11**: 307.

Buehler, Johann Georg. (Cecil Bensall) Ath. '98, **1**: 536.

Buelow, Hans von, Early Correspondence of. (T. F. Huntington) Dial (Ch.) **22**: 218. — (Egbert Swayne) Music, **11**: 633. **12**: 294. — Spec. **78**: 663.

Buenos Ayres, The City of. (W. E. Curtis) Chaut. **29**: 249.
— Hurlingham Club of. (H. P. Douglas) Outing, **34**: 73.

Buerger, Gottfried A., Birthplace of. (C. C. Eaglesfield) Cath. World, **72**: 82.

Buff and Blue Slipper, A. (S. A. Weiss) Chaut. **26**: 645.

Buffalo, African, Photographing a Wounded. (A. C. Humbert) Harper, **96**: 655.

Buffalo, N. Y. Ellicott Square Building. (F. L. Wilson) Am. Arch. **67**: 3.
— Pan-American Exposition, 1901. (C. Bragdon) Am. Arch. **72**: 43. — (W. H. Page) World's Work, **2**: 1015. — (M. B. Hartt) Indep. **53**: 992. — (F. E. Elwell) Arena, **25**: 53. — (J. A. Cooper) Canad. M. **18**: 99. — (J. V. Noel) Nat'l M. (Bost.) **13**: 483. — (M. Mannering) Nat'l M. (Bost.) **14**: 217. — (R. Gibson) Overland, n. s. **37**: 645. — (S. G. Blythe) Cosmopol. **29**: 507. — (A. B. McGill) Cath. World, **72**: 197.

Buffalo, Pan-American Exposition, American Art at. (K. Cox) Nation, 73: 127.

— — Architecture of. (C. Brinton) Critic, 38: 512. — Studio (Internat.) 13: 295.

— — Artistic Effects of. (E. Knaufft) R. of Rs. (N. Y.) 23: 686.

— — Artistic Exhibits. (H. S. Houston) World's Work, 2: 1125.

— — as an Educational Force. (C. E. Lloyd) Chaut. 33: 333.

— — as a Work of Art. (C. H. Caffin) World's Work, 2: 1049.

— — Aspects of. (E. R. White) Atlan. 88: 85.

— — Athletics and the Stadium. (J. E. Sullivan) Cosmopol. 31: 501.

— — The City at Night. (R. L. Hartt) Atlan. 88: 355.

— — City of Light. (D. Gray) Cent. 40: 673. — (H. Davis) Munsey, 26: 116.

— — Color Scheme. (F. M. Newton) Am. Arch. 71: 3. — (K. V. McHenry) Brush & P. 8: 151.

— — Coloring and Decorating. (Am. Arch.) 74: 52.

— — Coloring of Buildings. (H. Shearer) Nat'l M. (Bost.) 14: 390.

— — Congresses at. (T. R. Dawley, jr.) Outl. 69: 1067.

— — Decorative Sculpture at. (E. H. Brush) R. of Rs. (N. Y.) 23: 177.

— — Mr. Dooley on the Midway. (F. P. Dunne) Cosmopol. 31: 476.

— — Educational Influence of. (N. M. Butler) Cosmopol. 31: 538.

— — Fine Arts at. (K. V. McHenry) Brush & P. 7: 216.

— — Government Exhibit. (F. W. Clarke) Forum, 31: 654.

— — Human Nature at. (Lavinia Hart) Cosmopol. 31: 531.

— — Impressions of. (J. M. Chapple) Nat'l M. (Bost.) 14: 329.

— — on Dedication Day. (W. H. Hotchkiss) R. of Rs. (N. Y.) 23: 677.

— — Organization as applied to Art. (C. Y. Turner) Cosmopol. 31: 493.

— — Paintings at. Artist (N. Y.) 31: xiii. — (H. S. Granville) Brush & P. 8: 223.

— — The People at. (L. W. Betts) Outl. 69: 118.

— — Philippine Exhibit at. (D. O. N. Hoffmann) Nat. Geog. M. 12: 119.

— — Plan of. Am. Arch. 68: 7.

— — Play-side of the Fair. (Mary B. Hartt) World's Work, 2: 1097.

— — Real Value of. (Albert Shaw) Cosmopol. 31: 463.

— — Scenes at. Nat'l M. (Bost.) 14: 555.

— — — Philippine Village. Nat'l M. (Bost.) 14: 560.

— — Sculptural Scheme. (F. M. Newton) Am. Arch. 71: 35.

— — Sculpture at. Artist (N. Y.) 31: ix. — (C. H. Caffin) Studio, 14: 78. — (C. Brinton) Critic, 38: 521. — (Regina Armstrong) Bookman, 13: 348. — (W. H. Holmes) Brush & P. 8: 263.

— — Some Notes on. (Robert Grant) Cosmopol. 31: 451.

— — Some Novel Features. (H. Croly) Archit. R. 11: 591. — (Julian Hawthorne) Cosmopol. 31: 483.

— — Spirit of the New World as Interpreted by. (H. W. Mabie) Outl. 68: 529.

— — Stories of Interesting Exhibits. (A. Goodrich) World's Work, 2: 1054.

Buffalo [Reforms] Conference. (J. H. Ferriss and R. S. Thompson) Arena, 22: 71.

Buffaloes, Tracking, in Africa. (F. R. N. Findlay) Outing, 38: 249.

Buford Expedition to Kansas. (W. L. Fleming) Am. Hist. R. 6: 38.

Bugeaud, Thomas. (W. O. Morris) Un. Serv. M. 24: 75.

Bugle-calls, British. (F. J. Crowest) Sund. M. 29: 614.

Bugler in the Rear; a poem. (E. H. Crosby) Arena, 22: 536.

Bugler Boy, The; a story. (E. Dowsley) Canad. M. 17: 414.

Buhl Cabinet, The; a story. (J. Ayscough) Argosy, 69: 459.

Buhot, Felix, Etcher. Brush & P. 2: 276.

Builders, The. (H. Bindloss) Sund. M. 29: 839. Same art. Ecl. M. 136: 778. Same art. Liv. Age, 229: 314.

Building; Bills of Quantity, Estimating. (G. A. Wright) Am. Arch. 55: 27.

— How to Cheapen the Cost of. Am. Arch. 67: 47.

— How to Study. (C. H. Blackall) Archit. R. 7: 49.

Building and Loan Associations in California. (W. Corbin) Overland, n. s. 29: 671.

Building By-laws, Stupid. Spec. 86: 305.

Building Department, City, Work of. (J. H. Mayer) Munic. Aff. 4: 760.

Building Regulations in Germany. (George Sawter) Am. Arch. 58: 74.

Building Trades, Some Economic Losses in. (S. T. Wood) Am. J. Sociol. 2: 786.

— Structural Design of. (W. H. Burr) J. Frankl. Inst. 147: 417. 148: 31.

— Tall, in N. Y. City. (M. Schuyler) Archit. R. 8, no. 3: 231.

Buildings, Ancient, Treatment of. (H. H. Statham) National, 30: 96.

— and Houses, Legal Definition of. (A. Barker) Am. Arch. 68: 31.

— Engineering Plants of. (W. H. Bryan) Am. Arch. 62: 105.

— High. (R. S. Baker) Munsey, 22: 58. — (D. Adler) Cassier, 12: 193. — (O. Brainard) Chaut. 26: 131. — (J. A. Fox) Am. Arch. 62: 115.

— — Engineering Problems of. (C. O. Brown) Engin. M. 13: 406.

— — Foundation Construction for. (C. Sooysmith) Engin. M. 13: 20.

— — from an American Point of View. (A. D. F. Hamlin) Engin. M. 14: 436.

— — from a European Point of View. (S. H. Capper) Engin. M. 14: 239.

— — Insecurity of, from Fire. (H. De B. Parsons) Engin. M. 16: 767.

— — Moving of. (J. W. Smith) Strand, 13: 681.

— of the Ancients. Am. Arch. 60: 37.

— of New York. (F. Black) Chamb. J. 75: 507. — Munsey, 18: 833.

— Some Entrances to. Archit. R. 9: 363.

— Modern Business. (J. L. Steffens) Scrib. M. 22: 37.

— Steel, Dangers of. (W. L. B. Jenney) Cassier, 13: 413.

Bulawayo, South Africa, of To-day. Gent. M. n. s. 61: 324.

Bulb-farm in Ireland, A Visit to a. (Mary Gorges) Chamb. J. 78: 689.

Bulbs; how to grow them in the garden and house. (E. E. Rexford) Lippinc. 68: 477.

— Storing of. (E. O. Orpet) Garden & F. 10: 445.

Bulfinch, Charles, Interpreter of National Architecture. (H. Van Brunt) Atlan. 79: 258.

Bulgarian Cities. (C. R. Ladd) Chaut. 29: 536.

Bulkhead Doors, Watertight, on Vessels, Closing of, through a Centralized Mechanism. (W. B. Cowles) Cassier, 13: 444.

Bull, Ole, Impressions of. (G. W. Curtis) Liv. Age, 219: 396.

— in America. (George Willis Cooke) Music, 11: 296.

Bull, Ole, Life of. (Johannes Haarklow) Music, 21: 29.

Bull-dog, The. (H. W. Huntington) Outing, 31: 280.

Bull Dog Carney ; a story of Western Canada. (W. A. Fraser) Canad. M. 11: 341.

Bulldogs, Exaggerated Types of. (H. W. Huntington) Outing, 36: 198.

Bullen, Frank T. Acad. 57: 690. — (C. Middleton) Sund. M. 30: 738.

— Cruise of the Cachalot. (A. Schade van Westrum) Critic, 34: 353.

Buller. Charles. (E. Strachey) Cornh. 76: 392. Same art. Liv. Age, 215: 338.

Buller, Gen. Sir Redvers. (D. Story) Munsey, 26: 357.

— The Case of. (A. J. Butler) Nation, 73: 434.

— a Character Study. (E. Gosse) No. Am. 170: 109.

Buller-Poddington Compact, The. (F. R. Stockton) Scrib. M. 22: 217.

Bullet Wounds with Reference to the New Fire-arms. (D. Festenberg) J. Mil. Serv. Inst. 27: 56.

Bullets, Kruka-Hebler Tubular. J. Mil. Serv. Inst. 14: 1272.

Bull-fight at Valencia. (Arthur Symons) Sat. R. 36: 695.

— A Burlesque. (A. H. Broadwell) Strand, 18: 679.

— Ethics of. (L. Purdy) Harper, 97: 200.

— A Portuguese. (C. Edwardes) Macmil. 79: 202. Same art. Ecl. M. 132: 667. Same art. Liv. Age, 220: 703.

Bull-fighting in Spain and Portugal. (S. L. Bensusan) Idler, 11: 725.

— Spanish, in France. (H. A. Kennedy) Macmil. 77: 432. Same art. Ecl. M. 130: 789. Same art. Liv. Age, 217: 400. — Chamb. J. 75: 748.

Bullfinch. Sat. R. 87: 682.

Bullifant, A ; a story. (H. Fielding) Macmil. 80: 437.

Bullion Robbery, The Story of a Great. Chamb. J. 76: 109.

Bullroarers used by Australian Aborigines. Anthrop. J. 27: 52.

Bulls, Irish. Spec. 80: 177. Same art. Liv. Age, 218: 835.

Bullwinkle, Christine Wood. Writer, 14: 120.

Bully of Haiphong, The. (Guy Boothby) Chamb. J. 75: 65–104.

Bunch of Yellow Roses, The. (C. W. Chesnutt) Liv. Age, 225: 63.

Bundesrath, Seizure of the. (J. D. White) Law Q. 17: 12. — (F. J. Lippitt) Nation, 70: 30.

Bungalow, Round about a. (Sara H. Dunn) Gent. M. n. s. 59: 289.

Bungalows, English. (R. A. Briggs) Studio (Lond.) 3: 20.

Bunker Hill, Battle of. (S. Crane) Lippinc. 65: 924.

— Jabez Hamlen at. (C. W. Hall) Nat'l M. (Bost.) 14: 271.

Bunn, Charles, Adventures of, in the Barren Grounds of Canada. (A. Bridle and J. K. Macdonald) McClure, 18: 153.

Bunner, Henry Cuyler. (B. W. Wells) Sewanee, 5: 17.

Bunny's Resolution, Mission of Booklet called. (A. Lamont) Sund. M. 26: 651.

Bunsen, C. C. J. von. His Recollections of his Friends. (J. Bigelow) Cent. 36: 849.

Bunsen, Robert Wilhelm. (J. L. Howe) Science, n. s. 10: 447. — (H. E. Roscoe) Nature, 60: 424.

— and the Heidelberg Laboratory, 1863–65, Reminiscences of. (H. C. Bolton) Science, n. s. 10: 865.

Bunyan, John. Holy War, Archetype of. (R. Heath) Contemp. 72: 105.

— Pilgrim's Progress. (A. H. Bradford) Outl. 60: 622. — Acad. 54: 200.

— — Bagster's. (R. L. Stevenson) Bookman, 8: 556.

— — Local Color in. Acad. 60: 9.

Bunyan, John. Pilgrim's Progress vs. Shakespeare. (G. B. Shaw) Sat. R. 83: 11.

Burbank, Elbridge Ayer, Painter of Indians. (C. F. Browne) Brush & P. 3: 16.

Burbank, Luther, with portrait. World's Work, 2: 1209.

Burbank, Seth ; a strenuous affiant. (H. K. Darling) Green Bag, 13: 139.

Burden of Strength ; a poem. (G. Meredith) Ecl. M. 136: 758.

Burden of Time ; a poem. (F. G. Scott) Canad. M. 13: 327.

Burdock as a Vegetable. (I. Nitobe) Garden & F. 10: 143.

Burdy, Samuel ; an Irish Boswell. Blackw. 165: 884.

Bureau of the American Republics, its Past and Future. (W. W. Rockhill) Forum, 30: 21.

Bureau of Ethnology Reports, Powell's. (D. G. Brinton) Am. Hist. R. 3: 367.

Bureaucracy, Growing, and Parliamentary Decline. (A. S. Green) 19th Cent. 47: 838. Same art. Liv. Age, 225: 774.

Burgess, Ida J., Artist. (J. W. Patterson) Brush & P. 9: 87.

Burgess, John B., R. A. Ath. '97, 2: 715.

Burgess, John W. The Middle Period. (W. H. McKellar) Sewanee, 5: 349.

Burghley, Lord. Correspondence. Library, 1: 46.

— Hume's. (H. M. Stephens) Am. Hist. R. 4: 709.

Burglar and the Bank Manager ; a story. (E. Goodwin) Idler, 11: 26.

Burglar, The, the Twins, and Ernestine ; a story. (E. Jepson) Pall Mall M. 18: 212.

Burgomaster of Amsterdam ; a poem. (J. A. Macy) Green Bag, 9: 229.

Burgon, J. W. (H. W. Yule and G. H. Gwilliam) Chr. Lit. 17: 126.

Burgos ; the city of the Cid. (E. C. Vansittart) Cath. World, 68: 68.

Burgundy, Duchess of, Gagnière's. (A. Laugel) Nation, 65: 393.

Burh-geat-sett. (W. H. Stevenson) Eng. Hist. R. 12: 489.

Burial by a Friendless Post. (R. Shackleton) Scrib. M. 25: 669.

— Graveyards as to the Commonweal. (L. Windmüller) No. Am. 167: 211.

— in Assiniboia of an Indian Child. (A. H. Ball) Antiq. n. s. 36: 370.

— Living. (M. Dana) Arena, 17: 935.

— Premature. Chamb. J. 75: 491.

— Rights of. (W. A. McClean) Green Bag, 13: 88.

Burial Customs of the Fiote of the Congo Country. (R. E. Dennett) Folk-Lore, 8: 132.

Burial Service. (St.G. Mivart) 19th Cent. 41: 38.

— Christian. (G. U. Wenner) Luth. Q. 27: 331.

Buried Treasure, The. (L. Meadows) Argosy, 63: 379.

Buried Treasure, The ; a story. (A. Beresford) Argosy, 66: 518.

Burke, Edmund. Acad. 54: 64. — (W. Barry) National, 30: 762. Same art. Ecl. M. 130: 624. — (N. W. Sibley) Westm. 148: 496. — (G. McDermot) Cath. World, 65: 473. — Spec. 81: 77.

— and the French Revolution. (W. Wilson) Cent. 40: 784.

— and his Abiding Influence. (J. O'C. Power) No. Am. 165: 666.

— and the Revolution. (W. B. Morris) Dub. R. 127: 69.

— and Sir W. Scott. (T. E. Kebbel) Macmil. 76: 299.

— A Centenary Perspective. (K. H. Claghorn) Atlan. 80: 84.

— First Speeches of. (J. Cooke) Blackw. 163: 273.

Burke, Edmund. Reflections on the Centenary. (J. J. O'Shea) Am. Cath. Q. 22: 517.

Burkersdorf Heights, Battle of. (S. Crane) Lippinc. 66: 781.

Burlington, New Jersey, Authors in. (T. F. Wolfe) Lippinc. 65: 129.

— Friend's Burial Ground. (R. J. Dutton) Pennsyl. M. 14: 43, 149.

Burlington Fine Arts Club, Exhibition, 1898. Sat. R. 85: 712.

— — 1901. Ath. '01, 1: 281. — (H. H. Statham) Fortn. 75: 543.

— English Art at. (F. Wedmore) M. of Art, 25: 232.

— Silverplate at. (G. F. Laking) M. of Art, 25: 306.

Burmah and China, Trade Convention. (E. H. Parker) Asia. R. 24: 27.

— and its People. (J. F. Fraser) Pall Mall M. 16: 213.

— Chinese Frontier. (H. S. Hallett) Sat. R. 85: 709.

— — and the Kakhyen Tribes. (E. H. Parker) Fortn. 68: 86.

— Doctors in. (E. D. Cuming) Chamb. J. 75: 733.

— How the Famine came to. (H. Fielding) Blackw. 161: 536.

— Lady's Ride in. (H. Cartwright) Temp. Bar, 113: 255. Same art. Ecl. M. 130: 583.

— Loss of English Power in. (H. S. Hallett) Sat. R. 83: 344.

— A Lost People in. (H. Fielding) Temp. Bar, 118: 486.

— Lower, A Chief Court for. (J. Jardine) Asia. R. 29: 279.

— Mebya, Queen of. Acad. 57: 104.

— Pastoral. Acad. 54: 215.

— Picturesque, Hart's. Ath. '97, 1: 673.

— Railways in. (J. Nisbet) J. Soc. Arts, 47: 173.

— Temples and Archæological Treasures of. (A. Grünwedel) Open Court, 15: 464.

Burmester Reminiscences. (Wm. Armstrong) Music, 15: 495.

Burnand, Francis Cowley. Lady of Ostend. (M. Beerbohm) Sat. R. 88: 42.

Burnett, Frances Hodgson, with portrait. Bk. Buyer, 20: 270.

— First Gentleman of Europe. Critic, 30: 81.

Burnett, John; a Living Link with Scott, Hogg, and Wilson. Chamb. J. 74: 280.

Burnham, Clara Louise, with portrait. Bk. News, 17: 55.

— A Great Love. N. Church R. 6: 309.

— Miss Archer Archer. Bk. News, 17: 55.

Burnham, T. O. H. P. (E. M. Bacon) Bookman, 4: 542.

Burnham Thorpe; Nelson's Birthplace. Argosy, 69: 32.

Burning Bush, The, and the Garden of Eden. Study in Comparative Mythology. (G. H. Skipwith) Jew. Q. 10: 489.

Burns, Robert. (C. Whibley) Macmil. 77: 180. Same art. Liv. Age, 216: 528.

— and Mrs. Frances Dunlop. Acad. 53: 437. — (E. G. Johnson) Dial (Ch.) 24: 315. — (J. L. Gilder) Critic, 32: 285. — (G. McL. Harper) Bk. Buyer, 17: 18.

— and Scottish Song. (A. Lang) Eng. Illust. 17: 323.

— as a Lyric Poet. (F. Thompson) Acad. 51: 273.

— as a Social Reformer. (W. Diack) Westm. 154: 656.

— Auld Lang Syne. (H. E. Young; C. A. Ward; J. Dick) Ath. '00, 1: 721, 753, 816. 2: 250.

— R. Chambers's Estimate of. (W. E. Henley) Acad. 53: 379.

— Mr. Henley and Highland Mary. (R. M. Lockhart) Westm. 149: 332.

— Henley's Edition of. Acad. 52: 240, 254, 288. — Ath. '97, 1: 304. — Ath. '97, 2: 445.

Burns, Robert, Higher Criticism applied to. (H. Hayman) Sund. M. 28: 217. Same art. Liv. Age, 221: 445. Same art. Ecl. M. 132: 935.

— Manuscript of "Auld Lang Syne." (C. Reynolds) Cent. 33: 585.

— Monuments to. Acad. 53: 528, 613.

— New Light on. (J. Davidson) Scot. R. 29: 295. Same art. Liv. Age, 214: 335.

— Poems of. (H. E. Young) Ath. '00, 2: 153.

— Portraits of Relatives. Acad. 56: 481.

— Religion of his Poems. (A. W. Cross) Arena, 17: 177.

— Statues of. (E. Pennington) Art J. 49: 238.

— Story of a Burns Find. Chamb. J. 75: 193.

— Value of the Kilmarnock Edition of his Poems. Acad. 57: 66, 93.

Burns, Walter H. Bank..M. (N. Y.) 56: 41.

Burnt Fingers; a story. (P. Millington) Temp. Bar, 122: 210.

Burnt Offering, A: a story. (M. Brooke) Sund. M. 27: 361.

Burr, Aaron, Hamilton's Estimate of. Cent. 38: 250.

— a Romantic Wrong-doer. (Edgar Fawcett) Cosmopol. 23: 659.

Burr, Horace F. Am. Arch. 71: 69.

Burr, Theodosia. (V. T. Peacock) Lippinc. 66: 260.

Burraby; an Australian Pet. (F. J. Davey) Sund. M. 30: 344.

Burritt, Elihu. (E. S. Bartlett) New Eng. M. n. s. 16: 385.

Burro-puncher, A. (W. A. Wyckoff) Scrib. M. 30: 278.

Burroughs, John. (H. W. Mabie) Cent. 32: 560. — (C. Johnson) Outing, 37: 592.

Burs and Beggar's-ticks. (S. Trotter) Pop. Sci. Mo. 52: 68.

Burt, Charles, Engravings of. (R. Armstrong) Critic, 38: 333.

Burt, Eugene, Case of; Criminal Responsibility of the Insane. (F. E. Daniel) Arena, 20: 168.

Burton, Sir Frederick Wm., with portrait. M. of Art, 24: 330. — Ath. '00, 1: 377.

Burton, Isabel, Lady. (G. P. Curtis) Cath. World, 72: 90.

— Life of. (F. Danby) Sat. R. 83: 526.

— Wilkins's Romance of. Acad. 51: 647. — (E. G. Johnson) Dial (Ch.) 22: 354.

Burton, Richard, with portrait. Bk. Buyer, 16: 19.

Burton, Robert, and his "Anatomy of Melancholy." (J. T. Curry) Gent. M. n. s. 64: 185.

Burton, Thomas. Diary, Authorship of. (S. C. Lomas) Ath. '00, 2: 513.

Burton, William Shakespeare. (E. Rimbauldt Dibdin) M. of Art, 23: 289.

Burton Episode, A; a story. (H. C. Vernon) Midland, 10: 369.

Bury, Richard de, an Impostor. (E. C. Thomas) Library, 1: 335.

"Buryin'" of Zeb Holt. (C. H. Stanley) Chaut. 25: 372.

Bus Conductor, A; a story. (G. E. Mitton) Eng. Illust. 19: 474.

Busch, Carl, Musician, with portrait. Music, 17: 412.

Bushman's Fortune. (H. A. Bryden) Longm. 30: 229. Same art. Liv. Age, 214: 581.

Bushnell, Francis, of Guilford, and his Descendants. (R. D. Smyth) N. E. Reg. 53: 208.

Bushnell, Horace. (S. D. F. Salmond) Lond. Q. 94: 310. — (W. Allen) Atlan. 85: 414. — New Eng. M. n. s. 21: 505, 638.

— Munger's. (J. W. Chadwick) Nation, 69: 318. — (C. F. Dole) New World, 8: 699. — (T. F. Wright) N. Church R. 7: 252.

Bushnell, Horace, Preacher and Theologian. (C. Clever) Ref. Ch. R. 47: 68.
— Studio Talks with. (F. B. Carpenter) Indep. 52: 116.
— Theology of. (S. D. F. Salmond) Lond. Q. 95: 133.
Bushnells, Early. (W. T. R. Marvin) N. E. Reg. 52: 446.
Bushrangers, Boxall's Story of the Australian. Acad. 57: 304.
Bush-sleepers. The Hotel of the Beautiful Star. (W. Sharp) Harper, 103: 673.
Bushwhacker Nurse, The. (F. R. Stockton) Cosmopol. 27: 384.
Business and Speculation, Great Activity in, 1900. Bank. M. (N. Y.) 62: 657.
— at Close of 1901. Bank. M. (Lond.) 72: 681.
— The Importance of Health in. (C. W. Whitney) Chaut. 29: 545.
— in Foreign Countries, State Interference with. Bank. M. (Lond.) 71: 365.
— Political Wrecking of Business Enterprises. (B. S. Coler) Munsey, 23: 277.
— Professional Schools vs. (R. H. Thurston) Science, n. s. 9: 207.
— What shall we do for a Living? (E. Garrett) Ecl. M. 134: 753.
Business Building, The Modern. (J. L. Steffens) Scrib. M. 22: 37.
Business Education in Schools. (J. Fitch) J. Soc. Art, 49: 488.
— The True. (H. L. Biddle) Chaut. 27: 517.
Business Instinct, The. Chamb. J. 78: 577.
Business Life, Beginning a. (H. L. Biddle) Chaut. 24: 453.
Business Men, Advice to, by Lucius Tuttle. A Layman to Laymen. Outl. 67: 669.
Business Outlook; What are Normal Times? (E. V. Smalley) Forum, 23: 96.
Business Principles in the Public Service. (E. Robertson) 19th Cent. 48: 345.
— Ordinary. (J. Blyth and others) 19th Cent. 48: 184.
Business Situation in the U. S. and the Prospects for the Future, 1901. (C. R. Flint) No. Am. 172: 381.
Business Transaction, A. (Emily P. Spear) Overland, n. s. 33: 234.
Business Trip, 1827. (H. E. Mills) New Eng. M. n. s. 20: 23.
"Bussle," a story. (E. S. Grew) Pall Mall M. 21: 90.
Bustard, Great, Return of. Spec. 79: 820.
— Guitar Pouch of. (W. Pycraft) Nat. Sci. 13: 313.
But Once a Year; a story. (G. W. Carryl) Munsey, 26: 436.
Butcher-birds. (Grant Allen) Strand, 14: 401.
Bute, John, Earl of Stuart. (J. A. Lovat-Fraser) Gent. M. n. s. 67: 559.
Bute, John Patrick, Marquis of. Acad. 59: 312.
Butler, Charles, with portrait. R. of Rs. (N. Y.) 17: 54.
Butler, Lady Eleanor Charlotte. (H. M. North) Cent. 31: 424.
Butler, Frank, Case of. Green Bag, 10: 235.
— the Mountain Mystery of New South Wales. (C. McK. Smith) Chamb. J. 74: 554.
Butler, George, The Painting of. (W. C. Brownell) Scrib. M. 26: 301.
Butler, Joseph, Ethical System of. (A. Lefèvre) Philos. R. 9: 167, 395.
— Gladstone's Edition. Lond. Q. 87: 247.
Butler, Samuel, Head Master of Shrewsbury School, 1798–1836. Church Q. 45: 94. — Quar. 187: 112.
Butler, William John, Life and Letters of. Church Q. 46: 23. — Sat. R. 85: 54.
Butt, Isaac, Reminiscences of. (W. O'Brien) Cath. World, 65: 336.

Butte, Montana, Free Public Library. Lit. W. (Bost.) 28: 240.
Butter and its Adulterations. (C. B. Cochran) J. Frankl. Inst. 147: 85.
— and Bacteria. (G. C. Nuttall) Contemp. 71: 123. Same art. Ecl. M. 128: 490.
Butter-bun, The. (H. Macmillan) Sund. M. 28: 464.
Butterfield, Lindsay P., in Floral Design. (L. F. Day) Art J. 53: 369.
Butterfield & Co. (F. C. Baylor) Atlan. 80: 186, 367.
Butterflies, Classification of Day. (A. R. Grote) Nat. Sci. 12: 15, 87.
— Colors of; Mimicry and Warning. (E. B. Poulton) Nature, 60: 222.
— Evolution of, Eimer's. (M. von Linden) Science. 6: 308.
— for London Parks. Spec. 86: 383.
— of North America, Edwards's. Atlan. 80: 278.
— of Poetry; a poem. (E. Wheeler) Argosy, 72: 112.
— Protection against Extermination. (H. Hodge) Sat. R. 84: 56.
— Skinner's Catalogue of North American Phopalocera. (T. D. A. Cockerell) Science, n. s. 9: 373.
— Sleep of. Spec. 85: 267. Same art. Liv. Age, 227: 56.
— World's First. Spec. 85: 799.
— A Year of. (F. H. Sweet) Lippinc. 69: 836.
Butterfly, The Angelic. (J. A. Hamilton) Sund. M. 30: 148.
Butterfly Land, In; a new ballet. M. of Art, 25: 348.
Butterfly Lover, A. (J. W. Tompkins) Munsey, 17: 400.
Butterworth, Hezekiah, with portrait. (M. B. Thrasher) Nat'l M. (Bost.) 10: 530.
Button on Fortune's Cap. (L. G. Giltner) New Eng. M. n. s. 23: 574.
Buzzards. (D. L. Sharp) Lippinc. 60: 565.
Buying and Bargaining. Spec. 87: 509.
By Accident — Nothing more; a story. (M. Coleborn) Belgra. 95: 509.
By Courtesy of the Clown; a story. (A. F. Johnston) McClure, 13: 345.
By the Down-turned Thumb; a story. (N. H. Crowell) Midland, 10: 541.
By Faith; a story. (K. Elphinstone) Eng. Illust. 20: 153.
By June Seas. (E. Broderick) Poet-Lore, 13: 348.
By Kindness of the Curé. (J. F. Taylor) Canad. M. 16: 153.
By the Mail-balloon. (A. M. Horwood) Chamb. J. 74: 342.
By Mistake; a poem. (R. G. A. S. Prudhomme) Argosy, 65: 314.
By Mutual Consent. (Mabel Milne) Pall Mall M. 24: 85.
By Order of the Admiral; a story of the times. (Winston Churchill) Cent. 34: 323.
By a Poet's Grave; a poem. (L. G. Ackroyd) Argosy, 64: 307.
By the River; a poem. (F. B. Doveton) Gent. M. n. s. 61: 515. — Ecl. M. 131: 863.
By Sea and by Land. (Fred. T. Jane) Good Words, 38: 23.
By Sicilian Seas; a story. (C. E. C. Weigall) Argosy, 69: 233.
"By Special Interposition of Providence;" a story. (Maud Nepean) Idler, 10: 837.
By the Waters of Marah; a South African tale. (W. C. Scully) Cornh. 81: 164.
By-way to Fortune, A. Chamb. J. 74: 71.
By-way of the Boer War, A; a story. Temp. Bar, 123: 312, 466.
By Woman's Wit; a story. (L. E. Tiddeman) Belgra. 93: 341.

By the Yellow Sands. (F. Whishaw) Longm. **35**: 455.

Bygone Days. (Mrs. C. Bagot) Blackw. **165**: 461. Same art. Liv. Age, **221**: 272.

Byles, Sir John, a Forgotten Prophet. (W. S. Lilly) Fortn. **75**: 93. — Green Bag, **11**: 485.

Byles, Mather. (J. R. Gilmore) New Eng. M. n. s. **16**: 732.

Byles of Philadelphia; a story. (Hayden Carruth) Nat'l M. (Bost.) **6**: 327.

Byley. English Ancestry of the Families of Batt and Byley of Salisbury, Mass. (J. H. Lea) N. E. Reg. **51**: 181. **52**: 44, 321.

Byrde, William. Mass in D minor. (J. F. Runciman) Sat. R. **88**: 708.

Byrom, John. (I. M. Hamill) Good Words, **42**: 802.

Byron, Lord. Quar. **192**: 25. — (G. S. Street) Blackw. **170**: 761. — (J. Talman) Midland, **8**: 32.

— and the Greeks. (J. Gennadius) Eng. Illust. **17**: 289.

— and his Wife. Acad. **57**: 151.

— and Petrarch. (E. Levi) Ath. '01, **2**: 95. — (R. Edgcumbe) Ath. '01, **2**: 318.

— as a Dandy. Acad. **54**: 113.

— as a Letter Writer. Acad. **53**: 541.

— as a Man of Genius. Acad. **56**: 685.

— Childhood and School Days of. (R. E. Prothero) 19th Cent. **43**: 61.

— Did he write " Werner " ? (F. Leveson Gower) 19th Cent. **46**: 243.

— in the Greek Revolution. (F. B. Sanborn) Scrib. M. **22**: 345.

— Influence upon Goethe. (A. M. Brown) Dial (Ch.) **28**: 144.

— Lameness of. Lit. W. (Bost.) **29**: 232.

— The Man and his Work. (H. Abbey and others) Lit. W. (Bost.) **28**: 125, 163.

— Manfred, as it appeared to the Author. Acad. **59**: 113.

— Pilgrimage to the Land of. (M. Wood) Eng. Illust. **16**: 554.

— Poetry of. (L. Johnson) Acad. **53**: 489.

— Relics of. (F. M. Eddy) Munsey, **17**: 330.

— Revival of Interest in. (W. P. Trent) Forum, **26**: 242. — (S. Phillips) Cornh. **77**: 16.

— to 1816. (G. S. Street) Blackw. **166**: 620.

— The True. (F. J. Gregg) Bk. Buyer, **16**: 483.

— The Two Byrons. (W. Sichel) Fortn. **70**: 231.

— Unpublished Poem by. (P. La Rose) Atlan. **82**: 810.

— The Wholesome Revival of. (P. E. More) Atlan. **82**: 801.

— Works; ed. by Coleridge and Prothero. Sat. R. **85**: 576. — Ath. '98, **1**: 621, 781. — Ath. '01, **2**: 725. Same art. Liv. Age, **228**: 137. — (G. L. Kittredge) Nation, **71**: 154. **73**: 457. — Acad. **60**: 147, 171. — Ed. R. **192**: 358. — Acad. **55**: 413. — Sat. R. **85**: 782.

— — Ed. by Henley. (M. B. Anderson) Dial (Ch.) **23**: 113. — Ath. '97, **1**: 7. — (G. L. Kittredge) Nation, **67**: 131.

Byron, Lady, Reminiscences of. (A. Ross) 19th Cent. **45**: 821.

Byzantine Epoch; 10th cent. (Schlumberger) Ath. '97, **1**: 805.

Byzantine Silver Treasure from Cyprus preserved in the British Museum. (O. M. Dalton) Archæol. **57**: 159.

Byzantine Themes, Arabic Lists of. (E. W. Brooks) J. Hel. Stud. **21**: 67.

Byzantines and Arabs in the Time of the Early Abbasids. (E. W. Brooks) Eng. Hist. R. **15**: 728. **16**: 84.

Byzantinism. Spec. **85**: 10.

Byzantium, Rome and. Quar. **191**: 129.

Ça ira ! a tale. (W. B. Wallace) Argosy, **72**: 53.

Cabby's Jenny. (C. N. Carvalho) Sund. M. **29**: 434.

Cabell, James Lawrence. An early American Evolutionist. (C. M. Blackford) Pop. Sci. Mo. **52**: 224.

Cabell, Joseph Carrington, with portrait. (Sallie E. M. Hardy) Green Bag, **10**: 109.

Cabin Comedy, A; a farce. (H. Merrick) Idler, **16**: 642.

Cabinet Government. Spec. **80**: 471.

Cabinet Noir, The. (A. Anderson) Chamb. J. **76**: 401.

Cabinet Officers in Congress. (G. Smith) No. Am. **164**: 625.

Cable, George W. (W. M. Baskerville) Chaut. **25**: 179. — Acad. **53**: 497, 604.

— Grandissimes. (J. M. Barrie) Bookman, **7**: 401.

— Stories of. (C. A. Pratt) Critic, **34**: 250.

— Tarrywhile Edition. Bk. Buyer, **17**: 578.

Cable, Pacific. Canad. M. **13**: 180.

— — The Problems of a. (H. L. Webb) Scrib. M. **27**: 229.

Cable-way across Chilkoot Pass. (W. Hewitt) Cassier, **13**: 529.

Cable-ways. (W. T. H. Carrington) Cassier, **14**: 23.

— American, in Open-pit Mining. (S. Miller) Cassier, **13**: 204.

Cables, Submarine. (G. E. Walsh) New Eng. M. n. s. **16**: 584. — Blackw. **167**: 355.

— — All-British Trans-Pacific Cable. Blackw. **161**: 269. — (A. S. Hurd) 19th Cent. **45**: 226.

— — in Time of War. (R. J. R. Goffin) Law Q. **15**: 145.

— — Influence of, upon Military and Naval Supremacy. (G. O. Squier) Nat. Geog. M. **12**: 1.

— — Laying of. (A. P. Crouch) Strand, **16**: 163.

Cabot, Edward C. (C. A. Cummings) Am. Arch. **71**: 45.

Cabot, John. Blackw. **161**: 838. — Scrib. M. **22**: 62.

— and Sebastian, Beazley on. (F. H. Hodder) Dial (Ch.) **25**: 342.

— Celebrations of 1897. (E. G. Porter) New Eng. M. n. s. **17**: 653.

— — Outcome of. (H. Harrisse) Am. Hist. R. **4**: 38.

— Did he return from his Second Voyage ? (H. Harrisse) Am. Hist. R. **3**: 449.

— Discoverer of Canada. (J. G. Bourinot) Canad. M. **10**: 7.

— Vindication of. Acad. **52**: 7.

— Voyage of, Fourth Centenary of. (C. Markham) Geog. J. **9**: 604.

— When did he discover North America ? (H. Harrisse) Forum, **23**: 463.

Cabot, Sebastian, 1508. (G. P. Winship) Geog. J. **13**: 204.

Cabots, Home of the. (H. C. Lodge) 19th Cent. **41**: 734. Same art. Ecl. M. **129**: 58.

Cacoethes Literarum, a French Example. (Ch. Bastide) Fortn. **69**: 22.

Cactus, The Giant. (J. W. Toumey) Pop. Sci. Mo. **51**: 641.

Cadbury, Richard. (H. W. Strong) Lond. Q. **92**: 65.

— and his Work. (J. A. Hammerton) Sund. M. **28**: 376.

— " Houses of Rest " at Bournville. (W. H. Tolman) World's Work, **1**: 924.

Caddie's Tragedy, A; a story. (H. G. Hutchinson) Cornh. **75**: 400.

Cadet at the Battle of the Yalu, A; a story of the Japanese-Chinese War. (A. Kinnosuké) McClure, **15**: 99.

Cadet Corps for School Boys, of all Classes. (W. Elliot) 19th Cent. **50**: 1035.

Cadets, Increase of Number of. (P. S. Michie) J. Mil. Serv. Inst. **12**: 246.

Cadets, Naval, of the Powers. Illus. (C. D. Sigsbee) Munsey, 25: 145.

— of Other Lands. Illus. (H. H. Whitney) Munsey, 24: 536.

Cadger's Boy's Last Journey, The. (S. MacManus) Outl. 63: 46.

Cads, Prevalence of. Sat. R. 92: 170.

Cady, Daniel, with portrait. (E. F. Bullard) Green Bag, 9: 93.

Cady, Berg & See, Architects, Works of. (M. Schuyler) Archit. R. 6: 517.

Cæcilius of Calacte. (W. R. Roberts) Am. J. Philol. 18: 255.

Cædmon. (D. S. Gregory) Bib. Sac. 56: 341.

— Fall of the Angels, Translated. (J. W. Abernethy) Educa. 18: 352.

— First English Poet. Acad. 54: 275.

Cædmon Cross, Story of the. (Canon Rawnsley) Sund. M. 27: 691.

Cæn, Churches of. (Mrs. S. Van Rensselaer) Cent. 32: 421.

— to Dieppe. (S. Cross) Outing, 34: 403.

Cænogenesis, the Expression of Various Phylogenetic Energies, Mehnert on. Nature, 57: 505.

Cæsar. J. Mil. Serv. Inst. 14: 662.

— as a Text-book. (F. H. Howard) School R. 5: 561.

— Conquest of Gaul, T. R. Holmes's. Am. Hist. R. 6: 115.

— Gallic War, Greenough, D'Ooge, and Daniell's. (I. B. Burgess) School R. 7: 488.

— or Substitutes for Cæsar? (F. O. Bates) School R. 8: 324.

Cæsium and Rubidium, Certain Double Halogen Salts of. (H. L. Wells and H. W. Foote) Am. J. Sci. 153: 461.

— — as the Acid Sulphates, and Potassium and Sodium as the Pyrosulphates, Estimation of. (P. E. Browning) Am. J. Sci. 162: 301.

— and Thorium, Double Chlorides of. (H. L. Wells and J. M. Willis) Am. J. Sci. 162: 191.

— Tellurium Fluoride. (H. L. Wells and J. M. Willis) Am. J. Sci. 162: 190.

Cafés in Italy. (S. L. Bensusan) Idler, 15: 334.

— of Holland. (S. L. Bensusan) Idler, 16: 31.

— of London. (S. L. Bensusan) Idler, 15: 125.

— of Paris. (S. L. Bensusan) Idler, 15: 237.

— of Spain. (S. L. Bensusan) Idler, 15: 539.

Cagots, The. (H. Erroll) Cornh. 80: 243.

Cagliostro, Madame Seraphina, Woman Insurgent. (A. Macivor) Gent. M. n. s. 58: 461.

Cahow, Story of. (A. E. Verrill) Pop. Sci. Mo. 60: 22.

Caiaphas. (W. M. Macgregor) Expos. 7: 407.

Caien, Miss Amelia, Singer, with portrait. Music, 19: 174.

Caiman Capture in Venezuela. (W. Johnes) Outing, 33: 491.

Caine, Hall. (D. C. Murray) Canad. M. 8: 411.

— The Christian. (F. W. Farrar) Contemp. 72: 482. Same art. Ecl. M. 129: 788.

— — as Dramatized. (M. Beerbohm) Sat. R. 88: 515.

— (W. Emanuel) Idler, 16: 625.

— — and the Critics. (S. Fitz Simons) Cath. World, 68: 341.

— — "Moral" Melodrama to Order. Atlan. 81: 139.

— The Eternal City. (A. S. van Westrum) Bk. Buyer, 23: 234. — Acad. 61: 192. — (C. J. Wood) Critic, 39: 318.

— Ethical Problems raised in his Works. (T. Bradfield) Westm. 150: 194.

— Religious Novels. Ecl. M. 132: 1.

Cainguá Indians of Paraguay. (Dr. Machon) Pop. Sci. Mo. 52: 400.

Caird, John. (R. M. Wenley) New World, 7: 619.- With portrait. (R. M. Wenley) Open Court, 12: 629.—Spec. 81: 174.

— Greatest of Scotch Preachers. Liv. Age, 218: 746.

Cairo, Egypt, and its Inhabitants. (Florence Kerr-Hillhouse) Midland, 8: 291.

— and its Panorama. (H. M. Braid) Canad. M. 17: 399.

— Citadel of. Ath. '97, 1: 848.

— Fascinating. (F. C. Penfield) Cent. 36: 811.

— Folk-Lore of. (A. H. Sayce) Folk-Lore, 11: 354.

— Mosque of Sultan Hasan. Sat. R. 92: 361.

— Old, Coptic Churches of. (J. H. Middleton) Archæol. 48: 397.

— Story of Some Old Friends. (George Pangalo) Cosmopol. 23: 277.

— Where East and West meet. (C. Roberts) Harper, 100: 245.

'Cajan Bride, A ; a story. (Alice I. Jones) Midland, 7: 62.

Calabrian Sketches. Temp. Bar, 112: 275.

Calais and the Pale. (H. A. Dillon) Archæol. 53: 289.

Calamity's Girl-child ; a tale. (I. Claxton) Canad. M. 10: 234.

Calamy, Edmund, and the Education of the Early Nonconformists. (F. Watson) Gent. M. n. s. 67: 229.

Calas, Jean. (F. C. Conybeare) National, 33: 917.

Calaverite. (S. L. Penfield and W. E. Ford) Am. J. Sci. 162: 225.

Calchaqui, The ; an archæological problem. (D. G. Brinton) Am. Anthrop. 1: 41.

Calcite Crystals, On Some Interesting Developments of (S. L. Penfield and W. E. Ford) Am. J. Sci. 160: 237.

— Siliceous, from the Bad Lands, S. D. (S. L. Penfield and W. E. Ford) Am. J. Sci. 159: 352.

Calcium in the Sun. (A. M. Clerke) Knowl. 20: 232.

Calculus, Differential, Synthetical Demonstrations. (D. W. Brown) J. Frankl. Inst. 144: 348.

Calcutta. (P. E. Stevenson) Outing, 35: 353.

— High Court, Government and Judges of. (C. D. Field) Asia. R. 23: 258.

— Historical Monuments of. (K. Blechynden) Gent. M. n. s. 58: 389. Same art. Ecl. M. 128: 734.

— The Port of. (C. C. Stevens) J. Soc. Arts, 47: 628.

Calder, Sir Robert, Action of. Un. Serv. M. 23: 335.

Calderon, Philip Hermogenes, with portrait. (G. A. Storey) M. of Art, 22: 446.

Calderon School of Animal Painting, Metropolitan Schools of Art. (A. Valance) M. of Art, 22: 252.

Calderwood, Henry, The Critic of Agnosticism. (G. Campbell) Bib. Sac. 58: 580.

Caleb Gill ; a North Country Episode. (C. M. Greene) Overland, n. s. 35: 334.

Caleb West. (F. Hopkinson Smith) Atlan. 80 : 452, 653, 806. 81: 51-386.

Calendar and Rite used by the Catholics since Time of Elizabeth. (J. Morris) Archæol. 52: 113.

— Difficulties of the. (W. T. Lynn) Nature, 61: 493.

— Egyptian. Family of Seb. (G. St. Clair) Westm. 147: 156.

— The Englishman's. Cornh. 75: 1 — 76: 721.

— How to determine Easter, etc. (A. Rydzewski) Pop. Astron. 7: 416.

— On the words "O Sapientia" in the. (E. Green) Archæol. 49: 219.

— or Directory of Lincoln Use. Archæol. 51: 1.

— Proposed Reformation by Russian Astronomers. (D. O'Sullivan) Am. Cath. Q. 25: 757.

Calendar of Letters and State Papers (Spanish) relating to English Affairs, M. A. S. Hume's. (W. E. Tilton) Am. Hist. R. 5: 754.

Calendar of State Papers, Colonial Series, America and West Indies, 1677–80, Sainsbury's and Fortescue's. (P. A. Bruce) Am. Hist. R. **2**: 530.

Calendars, Maya, in Books of Chilam Balam. (C. P. Bowditch) Am. Anthrop. **3**: 129.

— Historical. (J. F. Hewitt) Westm. **155**: 45.

Calf-lymph, Bacterial Character of. (G. C. Frankland) Nature, **58**: 44.

Calhoun, John C. (C. C. Pinckney) Lippinc. **62**: 81.

— as a Lawyer and Statesman, with portrait. (W. L. Miller) Green Bag, **11**: 197, 269, 326, 371, 419.

— as Orator and Writer. (W. L. Miller) Am. Law R. **33**: 531.

— Correspondence of. (W. P. Garrison) Nation, **73**: 208, 227.

California and the Californians. (D. S. Jordan) Atlan. **82**: 793.

— and the Direct Tax of 1861. (B. Moses) Q. J. Econ. **11**: 311.

— as it was in '49. (Charles F. Lott) Overland, n. s. **36**: 225.

— Bar of, Early Native Members of, a Fireside Reverie. (Carroll Cook) Overland, n. s. **36**: 221.

— Botany. Wild Flowers of the California Alps. (Miss B. F. Herrick) Pop. Sci. Mo. **51**: 348.

— Chinese Physicians in. (W. M. Tisdale) Lippinc. **63**: 411.

— Fruit Crop in, 1897. (C. H. Shinn) Garden & F. **10**: 234.

— Gold Discoveries in. Blackw. **165**: 272.

— Gold Fields, Northern. (C. H. Shinn) Overland, n. s. **30**: 506.

— Golden Jubilee. (Mrs. E. O. Smith) Overland, n. s. **34**: 525. — (S. G. Wilson) Overland, n. s. **31**: 165.

— Greater, and the Trade of the Orient. (N. P. Chipman) Overland, n. s. **34**: 195.

— History of, Hittell's. (B. A. Hinsdale) Dial (Ch.) **24**: 292. — (C. H. Shinn) Nation, **68**: 15.

— in '49. (A. S. Marvin) Overland, n. s. **34**: 329.

— Legal Status of, 1846–49. (R. D. Hunt) Ann. Am. Acad. Pol. Sci. **12**: 63.

— Library Outlook in. (F. J. Teggart) Pub. Lib. **4**: 209.

— Material Progress of; Irrigation. (C. E. Grunsky) Overland, n. s. **29**: 516. — Dairying. (S. E. Watson) 519. — Forests. (C. H. Shinn) 522. — The Flouring Industry, 661.

— Missions; should they be preserved? (J. E. Bennett) Overland, n. s. **29**: 9–150.

— Municipal Conditions in. (J. D. Phelan) Arena, **17**: 989.

— Music in. (J. C. Fillmore) Music, **13**: 637.

— National Guard of. (F. E. Myers) Overland, n. s. **29**: 415.

— Native Sons and Daughters and the Semi-centennial. (E. D. Ward) Overland, n. s. **36**: 210.

— Naval Reserve, Training Cruise of. (D. White) Overland, n. s. **34**: 545.

— Negotiations for Cession of. (W. Bliss) Overland, n. s. **33**: 406.

— New England Influences in. (J. E. Bennett) New Eng. M. n. s. **17**: 688.

— Oddities of Climate of. (F. H. Dewey) Lippinc. **60**: 699.

— Out-of-doors in. (W. Higgs) Indep. **53**: 2819.

— Penal System of. (C. H. Shinn) Pop. Sci. Mo. **54**: 644.

— Pilotage Laws. (C. E. Naylor) Overland, n. s. **29**: 62, 409.

— The Present Political Outlook in; Republican view. (A. J. Pillsbury) Overland, n. s. **32**: 53. — Democratic View. (F. K. Lane) Overland, n. s. **32**: 145.

— Property Tax in. (C. C. Plehn) Econ. Stud. **2**: 119.

California, Races and Labor Problems in. (G. H. Fitch) Chaut. **24**: 427.

— Rainfall and Wheat in. (W. H. Fraser) Overland, n. s. **33**: 521.

— The Right Hand of the Continent. (C. F. Lummis) Harper, **100**: 171.

— Rocks and Minerals from. (H. W. Turner) Am. J. Sci. **155**: 421.

— Sea-cucumbers, Starfishes, and Sea-urchins of. (A. G. Madden) Overland, n. s. **35**: 364.

— Shipbuilding in. (I. M. Scott) Indep. **52**: 2723.

— Southern, Deserts of. (J. E. Bennett) Lippinc. **59**: 409.

— — Some Impressions of. (B. Harraden) Blackw. **161**: 172.

— State Prisons of; Folsom. (P. D. Elderkin) Overland, n. s. **34**: 257.

— State Text-book System of. (R. S. Faulkner) Educa. R. **20**: 44.

— University of, and the Legislature. (J. B. Reinstein) Nation, **68**: 46.

— — Architectural Plans for. (W. C. Jones) Science, n. s. **10**: 721.

— — The City of Education. (E. B. Payne) Overland, n. s. **34**: 353–448.

— — The College of Commerce at. (W. C. Jones) Arena, **23**: 180.

— — Concerts at. Music, **18**: 594.

— — Growth of the. (C. C. Plehn) Overland, n. s. **29**: 28.

— — Phebe Hearst Architectural Competition for. (H. S. Allen) R. of Rs. (N. Y.) **20**: 433. — Spec. **80**: 78.

— — Mark Hopkins Institute of Art. (Kate M. Hall) Overland, n. s. **30**: 539.

— — New Buildings for. (V. Henderson) World's Work, **2**: 877.

— Vines and Wines of. (A. Scarboro) Overland, n. s. **35**: 65.

California Guard, Manœuvres of the. (J. F. J. Archibald) Overland, n. s. **38**: 125.

California Indian, The. (A. V. LaMotte) Overland, n. s. **37**: 831.

California Pioneers, The Society of. (W. B. Farwell) Overland, n. s. **29**: 180–362.

California Rand, The. Mining on the Desert. (C. S. Greene) Overland, n. s. **29**: 546.

California Writers, Some Hermit Homes of. (Adeline Knapp) Overland, n. s. **35**: 3.

California's Christmas Landscape. (C. A. Keeler) Overland, n. s. **54**: 483.

California's Opportunity in the Pacific. (John Barrett) Overland, n. s. **35**: 148.

Californians, Some Primitive. (M. S. Barnes) Pop. Sci. Mo. **50**: 486.

Call, Daniel. (Sallie E. M. Hardy) Green Bag, **10**: 16.

Call from the Gorge; a story. (J. A. Dafoe) Canad. M. **18**: 65.

Call from the Sea; a poem. (J. W. Good) Ecl. M. **131**: 616.

Called to the Front; a story. (E. A. Smith) Argosy, **71**: 296.

Callender, James Thomson, Thomas Jefferson and. (W. C. Ford) N. E. Reg. **51**: 19, 153, 323.

"Calling Cañon, The;" a story. (H. Bindloss) Argosy, **75**: 94.

Calling of Cairo, The. (A. S. Winston) Cent. **38**: 759.

Calling of Jeremy, The; a story. (F. Wilkinson) Harper, **103**: 929.

Callistra's Callas, an Easter Story. (C. E. Shute) Nat'l M. (Bost.) **12**: 707.

Callot, Jacques. (Roger Ingpen) Gent. M. n. s. **59**: 553.

Callousness, Increase of. Spec. **78**: 728.

Camping. Paddle Camp and Baby. (R. K. Wing) Outing, 34: 613.
— Practical Side of. Outing, 38: 411.
— Summer, for Girls and Boys. (I. C. Barrows) New Eng. M. n. s. 18: 732.
Campion, Edmund, Journey from Rome to England. (J. H. Pollen) Month, 90: 243.
Campion, Thomas. Acad. 53: 418.
Campoamor, Ramon de. (M. T. Serrano) Critic, 39: 149. — (A. Symons) Harper, 104: 128.
"Campus." (A. Matthews) Nation, 66: 403.
Canada. Ed. R. 193: 294.
— and the American War of 1812. (J. C. Hopkins) Un. Serv. M. 21: 613.
— and Confederation. (J. A. Macdonald) Canad. M. 17: 223.
— and the Dingley Bill. (J. Charlton) No. Am. 165: 418.
— and French Canada. (E. Bouchette) Canad. M. 14: 313.
— and Imperialism. (J. Charlton) Forum, 29: 666.
— and Sir John Macdonald. Quar. 191: 337.
— and the Silver Question. (J. Davidson) Q. J. Econ. 12: 139.
— and the Tourist. (J. A. Cooper) Canad. M. 15: 3.
— and the U. S. Pub. Opin. 23: 517. — Canad. M. 9: 440.
— — our Friends the Enemy. (J. D. Spence) Arena, 19: 26.
— — Trade Relations of. (J. Charlton) Forum, 29: 471.
— and the Venezuelan Question. (J. Charlton) Canad. M. 8: 258.
— Anglo-American Joint High Commission, Claims before. (A. C. Laut) R. of Rs. (N. Y.) 19: 445.
— Archives of. (M. O. Scott) Canad. M. 16: 195.
— Are we Good Neighbors to? (E. Porritt) New Eng. M. n. s. 20: 731.
— as affected by British and American Diplomacy. (T. Hodgins) Canad. M. 10: 379.
— at the Glasgow Exhibition. (F. Yeigh) Canad. M. 17: 530.
— At the Making of. (Isabella F. Mayo) Chamb. J. 75: 49.
— Bourinot's. (V. Coffin) Am. Hist. R. 2: 565.
— British Rule in the Dominion of. (J. G. Bourinot) Forum, 31: 1.
— Capitalistic Abuses in. (J. E. Thompson) Arena, 20: 498.
— Catholic Question in. (F. C. Brown and G. Stewart) Arena, 17: 742.
— Census. (J. Davidson) Econ. J. 11: 595.
— — How it is Taken. (E. J. Toker) Canad. M. 16: 429.
— Church in, Anglican. (T. E. Champion) Canad. M. 10: 423, 515. 11: 35.
— Coal Fields of. (James Cassidy) Chamb. J. 78: 310-326.
— Commercial Policy of. (A. Shadwell) National, 30: 207. Same art. Ecl. M. 129: 730.
— Commercial Relations with the United States. (R. McConnell) Canad. M. 12: 198.
— Debts of, Public. Canad. M. 10: 539.
— Durham Road to Peace. (T. Shaw) 19th Cent. 50: 12.
— during the Seven Years' War. (J. G. Bourinot) Canad. M. 10: 302.
— Educational Bureau. (J. M. Harper) Canad. M. 14: 27.
— Elections, 1867-96. (A. H. V. Colquhoun) Canad. M. 16: 17.
— — of 1900, A Forecast. (M. E. Nichols) Canad. M. 15: 547.

Canada, Encyclopædia of, reviewed. (J. A. Cooper) Canad. M. 11: 60.
— England and the Treaties. Spec. 79: 170.
— English Principles of her Government. (J. G. Bourinot) Canad. M. 9: 93.
— Explorations in Great Bear Lake Region. (J. M. Bell) Geog. J. 18: 249.
— Fenian Raid of 1866; Adventures of a Prisoner. (W. H. Ellis) Canad. M. 13: 190.
— 1500 Miles on Fresh Water. (C. H. Williams) Blackw. 169: 49. Same art. Ecl. M. 136: 487.
— Fisheries of. (W. S. Harwood) Pall Mall M. 21: 176.
— Founders of New France. (J. G. Bourinot) Canad. M. 10: 139.
— French, and the Empire. (J. G. S. Cox) 19th Cent. 48: 777.
— — New-England Influences in. (E. Farrar) Forum, 23: 308.
— French-Canadian Liberal Party. (F. W. Fitzpatrick) Arena, 22: 151.
— French-Canadian Life and Literature. (T. O'Hagan) Cath. World, 72: 628.
— French Discoverers of. (J. G. Bourinot) Canad. M. 10: 218.
— Geological Survey of. (J. B. Tyrrell) Geog. J. 10: 623.
— Greatness of. Un. Serv. M. 17: 283.
— History; how Wolfe changed the History of the World. (A. R. Ropes) Eng. Illust. 18: 67.
— Hunting in. (C. Phillipps-Wolley) Cornh. 75: 105.
— Immigration Policy of. (J. A. Cooper) Canad. M. 13: 88.
— Imperial Defence, Canada's Share in. (C. F. Winter) Canad. M. 10: 199.
— Imperialism vs. Annexation. (J. Charlton) Canad. M. 16: 215.
— in 1896 and 1897. (J. C. Hopkins) Asia. R. 23: 328.
— in Winter. Blackw. 167: 53.
— The International Commission. (J. Charlton) Canad. M. 13: 13.
— International Status of. (C. H. Tupper) Canad. M. 11: 409.
— Isolation of. (J. D. Whelpley) Atlan. 88: 196.
— Lady's Life on a Ranche. (M. O'Neill) Blackw. 163: 1.
— Lake St. John Country. (E. T. D. Chambers) Canad. M. 15: 273.
— Legislative Power in, Lefroy's Law of. (A. G. Sedgwick) Nation, 66: 503.
— Literary Culture in. (J. G. Bourinot) Scot. R. 30: 143.
— Loss by the Treaty of Independence and since. (T. Hodgins) Asia. R. 25: 93.
— Loyalists of. (J. G. Bourinot) Canad. M. 10: 478.
— Loyalty of, to the Crown. (J. M. Oxley) Chamb. J. 77: 225. — (A. E. Ragg) Outl. 64: 235.
— Maids and Matrons of. (M. S. Pepper) Chaut. 32: 15-381.
— Makers of the Dominion of. (J. G. Bourinot) Canad. M. 11: 226, 299, 387, 505.
— Military Forces of. Sat. R. 87: 520.
— Military Geography of. (A. L. Wagner) J. Mil. Serv. Inst. 13: 429.
— Relations with U. S., and Influence in Imperial Councils. (J. G. Bourinot) Forum, 25: 329.
— Representative Institutions in, Early. (J. G. Bourinot) Canad. M. 11: 21.
— Resources of. (P. Kropotkin) 19th Cent. 43: 494. Same art. Ecl. M. 130: 645.
— Royal Military College of. (T. B. Strange) Un. Serv. M. 15: 439.
— Royal Society of. (Dr. Henry H. Ami) Science, n. s. 10: 50.

Canada, Royal Visits to; a Historical Retrospect. (J. G. Bourinot) Forum, **32**: 40.
— Social Life in. (A. Shortt) Canad. M. **11**: 3.
— Solicitors-General of. (B. Nicholson) Canad. M. **10**: 315.
— Some Light on the Canadian Enigma. (A. M. Low) Forum, **27**: 479.
— Subsidy and Bounty Legislation, in 1899. (E. Porritt) Yale R. **8**: 312.
— Summer Weather of. (J. G. Mowat) Canad. M. **12**: 3.
— Tariff of, New. (A. W. Flux) Econ. J. **7**: 427.
— Tariff Revolution in. Bank. M. (Lond.) **63**: 914.
— Thirty Years of Progress. Sat. R. **88**: 37.
— Trade of, Anti-British. Canad. M. **12**: 196.
— Trade Relations with the West Indies. (W. Thorp) Canad. M. **12**: 477.
— Trade with Great Britain. (R. Jebb) Contemp. **77**: 82.
— — with United States. (J. Charlton) Canad. M. **9**: 502.
— Two Official Languages. Sat. R. **91**: 37.
— under the Queen. Asia. R. **23**: 331.
— United States and. (L. E. Munson) Arena, **22**: 667. — Nation, **72**: 426. — (J. D. Whelpley) World's Work, **1**: 942.
— Wants and Prospects of 1898. (McLeod Stewart) Asia. R. **25**: 120.
— Wars on the Frontier of. (W. W. Knollys) Un. Serv. M. **15**: 138.
— Water-ways and Water-power of. Spec. **86**: 12.
— Wheat Lands of. (S. C. D. Roper) Pop. Sci. Mo. **55**: 766.
— Wild Fowl of. (C. W. Nash) Canad. M. **15**: 521. **16**: 42.
— Winter Pastimes. (G. W. Orton) Outing, **31**: 332.
— A Winter's Walk in. (A. Haultain) 19th Cent. **50**: 547. Same art. Liv. Age, **231**: 478.
— Women of, Patriotism among. (C. Archibald) Canad. M. **16**: 371.
— Women's Work in Western. (E. Lewthwait) Fortn. **76**: 709.
Canada Pete; a Klondike story. (A. C. Campbell) Canad. M. **15**: 541.
Canadian Art. (K. V. McHenry) Brush & P. **8**: 331.
Canadian Banking and Commerce. Bank. M. (N. Y.) **57**: 235. **63**: 229.
Canadian Boatmen, The. (P. C. Stadelman) Overland, n. s. **38**: 114.
Canadian Camping Song. (J. D. Edgar) Canad. M. **15**: 23.
Canadian Canal Policy. (E. Farrar) Canad. M. **11**: 371.
Canadian Contingent. (F. G. Stone) Un. Serv. M. **20**: 463.
Canadian Editors. (J. A. Cooper) Canad. M. **12**: 336.
Canadian Engine Works. (N. Patterson) Canad. M. **14**: 45.
Canadian Enigma. (A. Shadwell) National, **30**: 207.
Canadian Factor in Imperial Defence. (W. Wood) Un. Serv. M. **21**: 72.
Canadian Fiction, Recent. (L. J. Burpee) Forum, **27**: 752.
Canadian Folk-lore, German-; Items of. (W. J. Wintemberg) J. Am. Folk-Lore, **12**: 45.
Canadian Geography, Stanford's. (H. R. Mill) Nature, **57**: 223.
Canadian Heroes of the War of 1812-14. (J. G. Bourinot) Canad. M. **11**: 104.
Canadian Historical Publications. (N. Patterson) Canad. M. **17**: 66.
Canadian Historical Publications Review. (J. A. Coopre) Canad. M. **12**: 552.

Canadian Hymn. (C. Campbell) Canad. M. **13**: 134. — (O. A. Howland) Canad. M. **9**: 463.
Canadian Idyll, A; a sketch. (J. F. Taylor) Canad. M. **10**: 266.
Canadian Laurentian, Origin and Relations of the Grenville and Hastings Series in. (F. D. Adams; A. E. Barlow; R. W. Ells) Am. J. Sci. **153**: 173.
Canadian Literature. (R. Barr) Canad. M. **14**: 3, 130, 248. — (W. J. Brown) Canad. M. **15**: 170.
— Modern School of. (W. L. Wendell) Bookman, **11**: 515.
— Reminiscences of. (G. Stewart) Canad. M. **17**: 163.
Canadian Magazine, its Origin and History. (J. A. Cooper) Canad. M. **17**: 194.
Canadian Magazines, Century of. (A. H. V. Colquhoun) Canad. M. **17**: 141.
Canadian Military Corps. Canad. M. **14**: 232.
Canadian Military Pictures. Canad. M. **15**: 110.
Canadian Military Training. Canad. M. **9**: 529.
Canadian Militia, The. (H. J. Woodside) Un. Serv. M. **15**: 361.
— Mobilization of. J. Mil. Serv. Inst. **8**: 71, 159.
Canadian Militia System. (F. G. Stone) Un. Serv. M. **23**: 51.
Canadian Money-lending, Facetiæ of. Chamb. J. **75**: 97.
Canadian Mounted Police, The. (R. Pocock) Chamb. J. **75**: 10. — (H. C. Thompson) Outing, **32**: 75.
Canadian National Sport. Canad. M. **9**: 449.
Canadian Negro V. C. (W. D. Warner) Canad. M. **17**: 113.
Canadian Noblesse, Old French. (W. B. Munro) Canad. M. **14**: 568.
Canadian Northwest Mounted Police. (W. A. Fraser) Canad. M. **14**: 362. — (E. B. Osborn) Cornh. **81**: 774. — (C. H. Williams) Blackw. **167**: 474. — (B. J. Ramage) Sewanee, **8**: 290.
Canadian Northwest Mounted Police Commissioner. (W. Trant) Canad. M. **17**: 337.
Canadian Northwest Territories, Battlefields of. (A. S. Ronan) J. Mil. Serv. Inst. **8**: 223.
Canadian of the Mutiny. (A. MacMechan) Canad. M. **14**: 468.
Canadian Pacific Railroad, Case of. (D. MacG. Means) Nation, **67**: 196.
Canadian People; a criticism. (N. Patterson) Canad. M. **13**: 135.
Canadian Poetry. Acad. **58**: 555. — (A. B. De Mille) Canad. M. **8**: 433. — (J. A. Cooper) National, **29**: 364.
— Decade of. (D. C. Scott) Canad. M. **17**: 153.
Canadian Prose, Decade of. (L. E. Horning) Canad. M. **17**: 150.
Canadian Railroad Policy of, An Early Chapter in. (S. J. McLean) J. Pol. Econ. **6**: 323.
Canadian Railways, Strategic Value of. (T. C. Scoble) J. Mil. Serv. Inst. **15**: 161.
Canadian Red River Expedition. (J. J. Bell) Canad. M. **12**: 98.
Canadian Rocky Mountains. (C. H. Watson) Pall Mall M. **25**: 418.
— for Climbing. (W. D. Wilcox) Pall Mall M. **24**: 549.
Canadian Scenery. Canad. M. **16**: 145.
Canadian Society of Authors. (B. McEvoy) Canad. M. **12**: 561.
Canadian Soldiers, Famous. (T. E. Champion) Canad. M. **14**: 350, 499.
Canadian Troops; First Contingent to South Africa. Canad. M. **14**: 321, 417.
— Second Contingent. (N. Patterson) Canad. M. **14**: 423.
— Army Medical Service. (C. A. Mathews) Canad. M **15**: 301.

Canadian War Correspondents. (J. Lewis) Canad. M. 15: 494.

Canadians Abroad. (F. C. Brown) Canad. M. 8: 253.
— French. (M. B. Thrasher) New Eng. M. n. s. 16: 28.
— — in New England. (W. MacDonald) Q. J. Econ. 12: 245.
— Imperial Honors to. Canad. M. 8: 545.

Canal, from Atlantic to Mediterranean. Nat. Geog. M. 11: 122.
— From the Lakes to the Sea. (C. Snyder) R. of Rs. (N. Y.) 16: 563.
— The Great Drainage, of Mexico. (B. G. Hunt) Cosmopol. 24: 595.
— Inter-Oceanic. See Interoceanic Canal, also Nicaragua; Panama.
— Old Middlesex. (A. T. Hopkins) New Eng. M. n. s. 17: 519.
— Rhine-Elbe — a Feature in German Politics. (J. H. Gore) R. of Rs. (N. Y.) 21: 457. — Spec. 83: 274.

Canal-boat Episode. (A. E. P. Searing) New Eng. M. n. s. 19: 542.

Canal-dwellers, The. (J. Schayer) Cent. 34: 76.

Canal Population, Our. (E. Protheroe) Chamb. J. 75: 6.

Canals from the Great Lakes to the Sea. (T. W. Symons) Forum, 29: 203.
— in New York (State). (J. A. Fairlie) Q. J. Econ. 14: 212.
— Railroads vs. (J. A. Latcha) No. Am. 166: 207.
— Roads, and Bridges, Ancient. (S. D. Peet) Am. Antiq. 21: 151.
— Ship, Economic Effects of. (J. A. Fairlie) Ann. Am. Acad. Pol. Sci. 11: 54.
— — in Austria. Geog. J. 18: 289.

Canaries, Song-, German. (Baroness von Rotberg) Chamb. J. 75: 575.

Canary Islands, Aborigines of the. (A. C. Cook) Am. Anthrop. 2: 451.
— Plant Life of. (A. C. Cook) Pop. Sci. Mo. 53: 758.

Canavarro, Countess: her Work in Ceylon. Illus. (P. Carus) Open Court, 13: 111.

Canby, General, Assassination of. J. Mil. Serv. Inst. 9: 395.

Cancelleria, Palace of, Rome. (Alfredo Melani) Am. Arch. 63: 19, 27.

Cancer. (W. Hutchinson) Contemp. 76: 105.

Candelabra at Windsor Castle. (F. S. Robinson) M. of Art, 22: 541.
— New, for St. Paul's Cathedral. M. of Art, 23: 475.

Candidate's Wedding, The. (J. Workman) Chamb. J. 75: 689-713.

Candlestick and Modern Electric Lights. (K. C. Budd) Archit. R. 8: 118.

Canea; Among the Liars. (H. C. Lowther) 19th Cent. 41: 699.

Canes, for Self-defence. (J. Bonnafous) Outing, 31: 489.

Cannæ, Battlefield of. (E. Fry) Eng. Hist. R. 12: 748.

Cannibal Tribe, The Tonkawas, Our Last. (J. Mooney) Harper, 103: 550.

Cannibalism in Queensland, Rudder on. Science, n. s. 10: 155.

Canning, Elizabeth, Mystery of, 1753-54. (C. Kenny) Law Q. 13: 368.

Canning, George. (G. Smith) Cornh. 75: 162.
— and the Eastern Question. (L. Courtney) 19th Cent. 42: 370.
— Duel of. (A. J. Butler) Ath. '00, 2: 617.
— Unpublished Letters of. Quar. 186: 111. Same art. Liv. Age, 215: 3.

Canning Industry in the U. S. (E. S. Judge) Chaut. 28: 126.

Cannizzaro, Stanislao. (T. E. Thorpe) Nature, 56: 1.

Cannon, George Q. Outl. 67: 886.

Cannon, Story of the. (Maj. C. Field) Good Words, 42: 660.

Cannon-fire, Ordeal of. (F. S. Oswald) Open Court, 11: 150.

Canoe and Gun. (E. W. Sandys) Outing, 30: 54.

Canoe Building, Birch. (T. Adney) Outing, 36: 185.

Canoe Clubs, International Meeting, 1900. (D. J. Howell) Canad. M. 15: 513.

Canoe-craft, Samoan. (W. Churchill) Outing, 35: 75.
— Up-stream. (A. B. Chandler) Outing, 36: 358.

Canoe Sailing in the South Seas. (W. M. Clemens) Outing, 37: 568.

Canoe-trip, A. (G. F. Russel) Outing, 32: 181.

Canoeing. (G. Hyde) Outing, 34: 230. — (St.J. E. C. Hankin) Longm. 31: 359. Same art. Ecl. M. 130: 520.
— the Canoe and the Woman. (L. G. Peabody) Outing, 38: 533.
— down the Androscoggin. (G. E. Browne) Outing, 32: 358.
— down the Penobscot. (W. A. Brooks) Outing, 34: 395, 473.
— down the St. Joseph River. (K. F. Reighard) Outing, 30: 386.
— on the Iowa. (L. B. Robinson) Outing, 32: 29.
— Real. (R. B. Burchard) Outing, 37: 78.

Canoes, Champion, of To-day. (R. B. Burchard) Outing, 30: 226.

Canon Law in England. (F. W. Maitland) Eng. Hist. R. 16: 35, 625.
— Roman, in England, Maitland on. (J. Hopwood) Dub. R. 126: 67.

Canon's Inspiration, The; a tale. Argosy, 66: 200.

Cañon, Grand, Under the Spell of. (T. M. Prudden) Harper, 97: 377.

Canonization in St. Peter's, Rome, A. (J. L. Hurst) Indep. 52: 1495.
— of Two Saints. (G. M. Fiamingo) Open Court. 11: 513.

Canovas del Castillo, Antonio. (A. D. Vandam) Sat. R. 84: 157.
— Assassination of. (R. Ogden) Nation, 65: 123.
— Personal Notes on. R. of Rs. (N. Y.) 16: 559.
— Spain's Foremost Statesman. (J. L. M. Curry) R. of Rs. (N. Y.) 16: 306.

Canteen, Army. (C. A. Marshall) Arena, 25: 300. — National, 38: 436.
— Abolition of. Outl. 67: 148, 338.
— — for and Against. Outl. 67: 599.
— — from an Army Point of View. (G. Kennan) Outl. 67: 341.
— Coöperative Profit-sharing. (J. W. Fortescue) 19th Cent. 49: 874.
— Latest Argument against. (O. G. Villard) Nation, 73: 202.
— Management of. (H. A. Walsh) Un. Serv. M. 17: 661.
— Profits of. Un. Serv. M. 15: 337, 598.
— Question of. Outl. 65: 201.

Canterbury Cathedral. (M. S. Snow) Canad. M. 14: 252.
— English History in. (M. S. Snow) New Eng. M. n. s. 21: 449.
— St. Anselm's Chapel, Wall Painting in. (J. Morris) Archæol. 52: 389.

Canterbury Pilgrimage. (J. D. Symon) Temp. Bar, 114: 243.

Canton, Wm. Lit. W. (Bost.) 30: 26.

Canton. (A. Bellesort) Liv. Age, 223: 831.
— and Macao. (A. Bellesort) Ecl. M. 134: 316.
— English. (W. J. Shaw) New R. 16: 548.

Canuck and Raoul. (E. K. Carter) Lippinc. 61: 131.

Canvey Island. Spec. **85**: 234.

Canzonets; a poem. (M. A. Curtois) Gent. M. n. s. **63**: 516.

Cappadocia, Troglodyte Dwellings in. (J. R. S. Sterrett) Cent. **38**: 677.

Cappadocian Discoveries. Ed. R. **191**: 409.

Cape Breton, Iron and Steel Making in. (P. T. McGrath) Engin. M. **21**: 571.

— Past and Present. Canad. M. **17**: 435.

— Scenery of. (J. W. Longley) Canad. M. **9**: 331.

Cape Colony, Circuit Life in. (P. M. L.) Macmil. **77**: 422.

— Civil Service Pension Fund. Bank. M. (Lond.) **69**: 141.

— Future Prospects of. (R. Sykes) Month, **96**: 177.

— in Time of War. (George Ralling) Good Words, **41**: 374.

— New Governor of. (L. Dyer) Nation, **64**: 278.

— Parliament of. (G. Ralling) Good Words, **40**: 756.

— Politics of, and Colonial Policy. (H. L. W. Lawson) Fortn. **70**: 756.

— Poor Whites in. Sat. R. **91**: 101.

— Present Political Situation in. (R. Balmforth) Westm. **150**: 117.

Cape Fairweather Beds. (J. B. Hatcher) Am. J. Sci. **154**: 246.

Cape Government Railways, The. Chamb. J. **75**: 198.

Cape May, N. J., in June. (G. M. Hyde) Midland, **7**: 483.

Cape Observatory, Astronomical Results from. (W. E. Plummer) Nature, **57**: 513.

Cape to Cairo Railway. Conserv. R. **1**: 245. — (W. T. Stead) McClure, **13**: 320. — (J. T. Wills) Contemp. **75**: 161. — (H. G. Prout) Munsey, **21**: 113. — (C. de Thierry) Eng. Illust. **20**: 533.

Cape Town. (P. Bigelow) Harper, **94**: 775. — (W. B. Worsfold) Pall Mall M. **13**: 117. — (F. Dolman) Idler, **15**: 383.

— Capture of, 1795. (G. Paston) Longm. **36**: 526.

— Government House. (G. Ralling) Good Words, **42**: 36.

— to Kimberley, 1877. (Gen. Charles Warren) Good Words, **41**: 309, 412.

Capellini, Luigi, Evangelist. (G. Dalla Vecchia) Contemp. **75**: 410.

Capercallie Shooting in the Alps. (W. A. Baillie-Grohman) Pall Mall M. **25**: 186.

Capernaum, Christ's "Own City." (S. Merrill) Bib. World, **11**: 151.

Capes, Bernard. Acad. **55**: 486.

— Style of. Acad. **57**: 458.

Capital, American, Abroad. (H. P. Willis) Nation, **73**: 295.

— and Labor. (F. G. Newton) Lond. Q. **96**: 243.

— — Relations of. (G. F. Milton) Sewanee, **4**: 62. *See* Labor and Capital.

— Art of Living on. (A. J. Wilson) Contemp. **75**: 869.

— Discussion of the Concept of. (F. A. Fetter) Q. J. Econ. **15**: 1.

— Effects of a Possible Glut of. Spec. **79**: 548. Same art. Ecl. M. **130**: 212.

— in Economic Theory, Rule of. (I. Fisher) Econ. J. **7**: 511.

— Industrial Organization. (C. R. Flint) Cassier, **16**: 554.

— Labor, and the State. Gunton's M. **16**: 307.

— Large Aggregations of. (G. Gunton) Gunton's M. **12**: 334.

— Organized; its Privileges and Duties. Bank. M. (N. Y.) **55**: 600.

— Profits and the Volume of. (W. G. Sawin) Ann. Am. Acad. Pol. Sci. **18**: 420.

— Senses of the Word. (I. Fisher) Econ. J. **7**: 199.

Capital, What is? (E. Cannan) Econ. J. **7**: 278.

Capital Punishment. (Sir E. F. Du Cane) Chamb. J. **75**: 177. — (T. M. Hopkins) Westm. **155**: 144.

— Abolish the Death Penalty. (J. W. Stillman) Green Bag, **10**: 92.

— Abolition of. (M. Drayton) Westm. **155**: 424.

— as a Preventive of Crime. Ann. Am. Acad. Pol. Sci. **17**: 366.

— Failure of. (C. G. Garrison) Arena, **21**: 469.

— in Olden Times. (Florence Spooner) Green Bag, **11**: 15.

— in the U. S. Green Bag, **9**: 129.

— Judicial Killing. (Florence Spooner) Green Bag, **10**: 50.

— Modern Opposition to. Sat. R. **88**: 94.

Capitalism; the great slave power. (W. M. Stewart) Arena, **19**: 577.

— on Trial in Russia. (N. I. Stone) Pol. Sci. Q. **13**: 91.

Capitalist's Point of View. (W. J. Kerby) Am. Cath. Q. **24**, no. 3: 18.

Capitalists, Eastern, An Open Letter to. (C. C. Millard) Arena, **18**: 211.

Capitalistic Abuses in Canada. (J. E. Thompson) Arena, **20**: 498.

Capitals of Europe. Spec. **80**: 110.

Capitals, Philosophy of. Liv. Age, **217**: 885.

— Use and Misuse of. (E. Parsons) Writer, **11**: 21, 70. — (S. Merrill) Writer, **11**: 37.

Capitis deminutio in Roman Law. (H. Goudy) Jurid. R. **9**: 132.

Capitol, U. S., History of. (Glenn Brown) Am. Arch. **55**: 3, 59.

Cap'n's Cox'n, The; a story. (W. F. Shannon) Idler, **12**: 304.

Capon Springs Conference. Lit. W. (Bost.) **29**: 216.

Capri, Island of; Home of the Indolent. (F. D. Millet) Cent. **34**: 853.

— Loss of, in 1808. (A. Warren) Un. Serv. M. **23**: 525.

Caprice of the Muses; a poem. (E. M. Thomas) Dial (Ch.) **25**: 124.

Caprivi, Georg Leo, Count, Death of. Sat. R. **87**: 165.

Caps, Gowns, and Hoods, Academic. Harv. Grad. M. **7**: 540.

Captain John Adams, missing. (C. W. Doyle) Harper, **100**: 783.

Captain dreams again; a story. (Charles King) Cosmopol. **25**: 577.

Captain Nancy. (F. L. Green) Sund. M. **28**: 555.

Captain Rogers; a story. (W. W. Jacobs) Harper, **102**: 370.

Captain Tugg and the Wreck of the Brother Jonathan. (T. H. Rogers) Overland, n. s. **35**: 131.

Captain Vaurien; a story. (J. Ayscough) Macmil. **79**: 222.

Captain! my Captain! (L. G. Moberly) Sund. M. **29**: 650.

Captain of the Aphrodite, The; a story. (E. E. Peake) McClure, **14**: 339.

Captain of H. B. M. Ship Diamond Rock. (C. T. Brady) Lippinc. **68**: 721.

Captain of a Transatlantic Liner, Day's Work of. (M. Foster) World's Work, **1**: 631.

Captain's Wooing, The; a story. (E. R. Punshon) Idler, **14**: 832.

Captains Courageous; a novel. (R. Kipling) McClure, **8**: 222–521. **9**: 611.

Captiva Island, Fla. A Bit of Spain under Our Flag. (L. B. Ellis) Chaut. **33**: 578.

Captive, The; a poem. (W. P. Foster) Atlan. **81**: 837.

Captive Soul, A; a story. (Alison Buckler) Gent. M. n. s. **64**: 1.

Captivity of the Professor; a story. (A. L. Green) Blackw. **169**: 161.

Carlyle, Thomas, Homes of. (J. MacNeil) Munsey, 25: 633.
— Lecture on Literature. (R. Cade) Library, 4: 225.
— on his Contemporaries. (Elizabeth L. Smith) Bk. Buyer, 14: 409.
— Portrait of. (J. McN. Whistler) Pall Mall M. 21: 19.
— Prentice Hand of. (A. MacMechan) Citizen, 3: 200.
— A Reminiscence of. Atlan. 81: 284.
— Talk of, Recollections of. (Wm. Black) Good Words, 38: 20. Same art. Liv. Age, 212: 248.
— Unpublished Letters of. (C. T. Copeland) Atlan. 82: 289–785.
— Will of, in an Amer. Court. (O. B. Jenkins) Green Bag, 9: 452.
Carman, Bliss, and Roberts, Charles G. D. (G. White) Sewanee, 7: 48.
Carmelites, 1538. Archæol. 51: 61.
Carmelite Martyrs, French and English Benedictine Nuns. (B. De Courson) Month, 96: 461.
— of Compiègne. (C. De Courson) Month, 92: 278.
"Carmina Gadelica." (J. Britten) Month, 97: 347.
Carnarvon, Lord, and Home Rule. Fortn. 71: 363.
— A Statesman's Autobiography. (T. H. S. Escott) Fortn. 68: 583.
Carnations, a Society Tale. (C. G. Rogers) Canad. M. 11: 426.
Carnegie, Andrew. Outl. 67: 765. — (H. W. Lanier) World's Work, 1: 618. — With portrait. (J. D. Champlin) Cassier, 12: 51.
— as Economist and Social Reformer. (F. A. Cleveland) Ann. Am. Acad. Pol. Sci. 17: 474.
— Enterprises built up by. (C. M. Schwab) Engin. M. 20: 505.
— Gifts of; Example and Philosophy. Outl. 67: 668.
— — Library Movement in Light of. (M. Dewey) Am. J. Soc. Sci. 39: 139.
— Gospel of Wealth. Outl. 67: 571.
— Great Steel Makers of Pittsburg and the Frick-Carnegie Suit. (J. Moritzen) R. of Rs. (N. Y.) 21: 433.
Carnegie, David. Geog. J. 17: 202.
Carnegie Art Gallery. (D. C. Thomson) Art J. 50: 353. — Artist (N. Y.) 23: xxiv.
Carnegie Museum, Pittsburg. (W. J. Holland) Pop. Sci. Mo. 59: 1.
Carnegie Residence, N. Y. City. Archit. R. 9: 77.
Carnegie Steel Company and its President. (J. Moritzen) R. of Rs. (N. Y.) 21: 442.
Carnegie Technical University, Science, n. s. 14: 41. — (J. A. Brashear) Science, n. s. 14: 385.
Carneri, Bartholomäus Von, the Ethicist of Darwinism, with portrait. (P. Carus) Open Court, 15: 641.
Carnival Time in Russia. Liv. Age, 221: 582.
Carnotite. (W. F. Hillebrand and F. L. Ransome) Am. J. Sci. 160: 120.
Carnots, The Three. (D. C. Munro) Chaut. 25: 11.
Carolina, Feudal Laws of. (S. C. Hughson) Sewanee, 2: 471.
— Fundamental Constitutions of the Province of. (A. M. Barnes) Green Bag, 12: 312.
— Proprietary Government of. (A. M. Barnes) Green Bag, 12: 644.
Carolina Mountain Pond. (B. Torrey) Atlan. 80: 383.
Carolinas, Naming of the. (J. S. Bassett) Sewanee, 2: 343.
Caroline Matilda, Queen of Denmark, and Colonel Keith. (G. Hill) Gent. M. n. s. 66: 335.
Caroline Islands, Beach-comber in. (J. C. Wheeler) Indep. 52: 2327.
— Cyclopean Walls and Basaltic Columns in. Am. Antiq. 21: 185.
— Exploration in the. (F. W. Christian) Geog. J. 13: 105.

Caroline Islands, Spain and the. (E. E. Strong) R. of Rs. (N. Y.) 17: 706.
Caroline's Aftermath; a story. (Mrs. S. Langford) Belgra. 95: 372.
Carols, A Chat about. (F. J. Crowest) Sund. M. 26: 800.
Carolus, Joris, Discoverer of Edge Island. (M. Conway) Geog. J. 17: 623.
Carolus-Duran, M., Portrait Painter. (E. F. Baldwin) Outl. 61: 543. — Critic, 32: 320.
Carpathians, Timber Creeping in. (E. N. Buxton) 19th Cent. 41: 236. Same art. Ecl. M. 128: 495.
Carpe Diem. (A. F. Bell) Longm. 36: 541.
Carpeaux, J. B. (C. Thurwanger) New Eng. M. n. s. 19: 586.
Carpenter, Cyrus C. (J. P. Dolliver) Midland, 10: 75.
Carpenter, Edward, the Walt Whitman of England. (W. Diack) Westm. 156: 655.
Carpet-bedding of Flowers. (O. Thorne) Strand, 14: 373.
Carpet Industry, American. (F. V. Fletcher) Chaut. 29: 11.
Carpets, Designing and Making of. (F. J. Myers) Artist (N. Y.) 25: 151, 200.
Carrara, Marble Quarries of. (Ceresa Venuti) Chamb. J. 76: 212.
Carreno, Madame Teresa, Piano Playing of. (J. F. Runciman) Sat. R. 87: 748.
Carriages, Horseless. (J. Trowbridge) Chaut. 25: 37. — (J. Sachs) J. Frankl. Inst. 144: 215, 286.
— — in Paris. (C. I. Barnard) Cosmopol. 25: 479. See Automobiles.
— in Various Periods. (W. Wright) Strand, 16: 582.
— Industry in. (W. W. Beaumont) Engin. M. 13: 955.
— Sir David Solomon's Work. (Isabel Marks) Idler, 11: 477.
— Queer. Strand, 14: 457.
Carrière, Eugene. (F. Keyzer) Studio (Lond.) 8: 135. — With portrait. (M. Morhardt) M. of Art, 22: 553.
— and Some other Draughtsmen. Sat. R. 85: 742.
Carriers, Common, Right of the Public to regulate Charges of. (W. Clark) Am. Law R. 31: 685.
— in the High Mountains. (E. Platz) Chaut. 29: 37.
Carrington, Paul. (Sallie E. M. Hardy) Green Bag, 10: 16.
Carroll, Charles, of Carrollton. Am. Cath. Q. 24: 172.
— Rowland's Life and Correspondence of. (E. E. Sparks) Dial (Ch.) 25: 13.
Carroll, Lewis, pseud. See Dodgson, Charles Lutwidge.
Carroll's Promotion; a story. (F. Lynde) Nat'l M. (Bost.) 7: 417, 526.
Carruth, Howard, The Making of. (R. Barr) Strand, 18: 208.
Carson, Kit, a Missionary of the Far West. (A. I. Shand) Cornh. 79: 371. Same art. Liv. Age, 221: 378.
Cart, Country, of To-day. (C. Whitney) Outing, 36: 233.
Carter, Elizabeth. (M. Quekett) Temp. Bar, 110: 473.
Carter, Henry W. (A. N. Hall) New Eng. M. n. s. 22: 690.
Carter, Capt. John vs. Province of Mass. Bay. (L. C. Cornish) Green Bag, 12: 333.
Carter, Oberlin M. R. of Rs. (N. Y.) 16: 302.
Carter, Thomas, of Cincinnati, Ohio. (C. E. Cabot) New Eng. M. n. s. 20: 344.
Carter, Thomas Thellusson, Canon, of Clewer. Ath. '01, 2: 596.
Carthage. (J. Bryce) Nation, 64: 7. — Chamb. J. 76: 455.

Carthusians, The. Temp. Bar, 111: 92. Same art. Ecl. M. 129: 164.

Cartoons, Political. (H. T. Peck) Bookman, 12: 115.
—— in America. (M. Mannering) Nat'l M. (Bost.) 13: 12.

Carthwaite's Conversion; a story. (F. G. Tuttle) Outing, 35: 514.

Cartridge Factory, Scenes in a. (Theodore Dreiser) Cosmopol. 25: 321.

Cartwright, Richard, an Early Canadian Statesman. (A. Shortt) Canad. M. 17: 448.

Cartwright, Thomas, and Melville, Andrew, at the University of Geneva, 1569–74. Am. Hist. R. 5: 284.

Carty Carteret's Sister. (David Gray) Cent. 34: 247.

Carving, Mediæval. Acad. 51: 445.

Casa de las Brujas, La; a tale. (M. Boyd) Outing, 33: 553.

Casa Grande of Arizona. (C. Mindeleff) New Eng. M. n. s. 16: 570.
— Prehistoric Ruins of. (Alice R. Crane) Overland, n. s. 36: 295. — Am. Arch. 60: 28.

Cascael; a Portuguese Seaside Resort. Chamb. J. 76: 424.

Case, C. C., Evangelistic Singer. Music, 13: 630.

Case at the Museum, A; a story. (R. Ross) Cornh. 82: 495.

Case for Enlightenment; a story. (A. Every) Eng. Illust. 17: 267.

Case of Deflected Energy. (M. C. Smith) Eng. M. n. s. 24: 409.

Case of Eavesdropping, A; a story. (A. Blackwood) Pall Mall M. 22: 558.

Case of Faith, A; a story. (V. L. Whitechurch) Good Words, 42: 261.

Case of Friendship, A. Chamb. J. 74: 61.

Case of "Ghastly" Burke, The; a story. (W. F. Gibbons) Chaut. 31: 127.

Case of Nerves, A. (H. P. Spofford) Harper, 104: 61.

Case of Thomas Phipps; a story. (T. B. Aldrich) Harper, 103: 628.

Case of Salvage, A; a story. (W. Wood) Pall Mall M. 22: 396.

Case of the Rev. Mr. Toomey; a story. (S. B. T.) Pall Mall M. 11: 363. Same art. Ecl. M. 129: 351.

Cashiered. (Andrew Balfour) Chamb. J. 77: 542.

Cashmere Shawls, an Extinct Art. M. of Art, 25: 452.

Casilda's Mind; a story. (A. Moore) Temp. Bar, 123: 332. Same art. Liv. Age, 231: 444.

Casino Girl, The; play in London. (I. Allen) Idler, 18: 359.

Casket Letter, Second. (A. Lang) Ath. '01, 1: 19.

Caspian Sea, The. (G. F. Wright) Nation, 72: 66.

Cass, William True. Bank. M. (N. Y.) 63: 632.

Cassation, Court of, Revision Powers of. (T. Barclay) Law Q. 15: 194.

Cassatt, Alexander Johnston, with portrait. (F. N. Barksdale) World's Work, 1: 973.

Cassatt, Mary, the Artist. (A. Hoeber) Cent. 35: 740.

Cast Metal Work from Benin. Nature, 58: 224.

Castaways, and their Influence on Population. (W. Allingham) Gent. M. n. s. 67: 273.

Caste, Growth of, in the United States. 19th Cent. 42: 43. Same art. Liv. Age, 214: 433. — Spec. 79: 13.
— Pride of. Spec. 86: 561.

Castel Gandolfo, American Villa at. (P. L. Connellan) Cath. World, 71: 161.

Castelar, Emilio. (C. W. Currier) Conserv. R. 2: 97.

Castilian Amoroso; a story. (E. Nesbit) Pall Mall M. 18: 521.

Castings for Hydraulic Service. (R. P. Cunningham) Cassier, 18: 436.

Castle, Agnes and Egerton. Secret Orchard. (A. B. Maurice) Bookman, 14: 261.

Castle, Egerton, with portrait. Bk. News, 18: 553.

Castle Howard, England, Seat of Earls of Carlisle. Pall Mall M. 23: 324.

Castle in Spain, A. (F. Reddale) New Eng. M. n. s. 25: 360.

Castle Inn; a story. (S. Weyman) Cornh. 77: 116 — 78: 553. Same art. Munsey, 18: 489 — 20: 58.

Castle of Enchantment; a story. (W. Packard) Nat'l M. (Bost.) 10: 223.

Castle of the Mountains, The. Chamb. J. 78: 428.

Castles, German. (L. v. Krockow) Am. Arch. 58: 96. 59: 19.
— of England, Mackenzie's. (C. W. Colby) Nation, 64: 342.

Castlemary and Campanini, Reminiscences of. (L. G. Gottschalk) Music, 11: 593.

Castro, Cipriano, Gen., and Uribe, Rafael U., Gen.; Two men of revolutions, with portraits. (B. S. Coler) Indep. 53: 2156.

Castromediano, Sigismondo. (E. Martinengo Cesaresco) Temp. Bar, 117: 378.

Casualties. (Capt. Melville) J. Mil. Serv. Inst. 21: 376.

Casualty; a story. Outl. 61: 879.

Cat, The; a story. (M. E. Wilkins) Harper, 100: 906.

Cat, The, about Town. Spec. 80: 197. Same art. Liv. Age, 217: 47.
— in Literature. Spec. 80: 300. Same art. Liv. Age, 217: 256.
— Jayne's Skeleton of the. Am. Natural. 32: 520.
— Pedigree of the. (R. Lydekker) Knowl. 20: 181.
— Reighard's and Jennings's Anatomy of. Am. Natural. 35: 597. — (H. Jayne) Science, n. s. 14: 453.

Cat and Dog Life. Spec. 84: 594. Same art. Liv. Age, 225: 720.

Cat, The, and the King; a story. (Helen F. Huntington) Nat'l M. (Bost.) 6: 331.

Cat and the Moon, The. (G. St. Clair) Gent. M. n. s. 66: 251.

Ca . . . t Came Back, The. (J. Oxenham) Strand, 17: 546.

Cat Alley, Passing of. (J. A. Riis) Cent. 35: 166.

Cat Creek Conversion, A. (W. C. Campbell) Overland, n. s. 31: 496.

Cat Raising as a Business. (M. Cornish-Bond) Munsey, 25: 841.

Cat's Eden, A. (O. T. Miller) Liv. Age, 213: 428.

Cats, Book of, by S. W. Chance. Studio (Internat.) 6: 142.
— of Leisure and Lineage. (Harriet Martling) Overland, n. s. 36: 460.
— on Board Ship. Spec. 82: 484.
— Pictures and Studies of, Tomson's. (A. Tomson) Studio (Lond.) 2: 65.
— Saber-toothed. (S. W. Williston) Pop. Sci. Mo. 53: 348.

Catacombs of Kom-es-Shaqfeh, Egypt. (M. Brodrick) Contemp. 80: 576. Same art. Liv. Age, 231: 551.

Catacombs of Rome. (M. Campbell) Cath. World, 72: 772.
— — Legal Tenure of. (J. A. Campbell) Am. Cath. Q. 26: 147.
— — of Christian Origin. (M. Campbell) Cath. World, 72: 161.
— of Syracuse. (A. F. Spender) Dub. R. 126: 379. 127: 123.
— Wilpert's Studies in. (W. Lowrie) Presb. & Ref. R. 8: 568.

Catalogue, Coöperative, of English Literature up to 1640. (T. G. Law) Library, 5: 97.

Catalogue for the Small Library. (F. E. Smith) Pub. Lib. **6**: 147.
— Printed, Problem of, with a Possible Solution. (L. S. Jast) Library, n. s. **2**: 141.
— A State-paper, Theory of. Library, **3**: 126.
— A Universal. (R. Garnett) Library, **5**: 93.
Catalogue Cards, Printed. (M. Dewey) Library, n. s. **2**: 130. — Pub. Lib. **6**: 97. — Lib. J. **26**: 802.
Catalogues, and Indexes, Mechanical Methods of Displaying. Library, **6**: 45.
— Card Catalogue Summaries. Am. Natural. **33**: 663.
— Concerning. (E. V. Lucas) Cornh. **80**: 195. Same art. Liv. Age, **222**: 646.
See also Libraries, Catalogues of.
Cataloguing Annual Reports. (A. R. Hasse) Pub. Lib. **5**: 319.
— Author-entries, How to procure Full Names for. Library, **5**: 16.
— Curiosities of. Library, **9**: 70.
— Descriptive. (J. D. Brown) Library, n. s. **2**: 135.
— Heresies about. (G. E. Wire) Lib. J. **22**: supp. 62.
— Practical. (E. D. Bullock) Pub. Lib. **6**: 134.
— Problems in. (M. Ganley) Pub. Lib. **6**: 139.
— Some Pitfalls in. (J. J. Ogle) Library, **8**: 150.
— Suggestions to Beginners in. (L. E. W. Benedict) Pub. Lib. **1**: 266, 302.
— Symposium on. Pub. Lib. **6**: 150.
Catastrophe, The. (E. Meredith) Liv. Age, **230**: 67.
Catastrophes, Natural, The Fear of. Spec. **86**: 381. Same art. Liv. Age, **229**: 393.
Catawba Language, Grammatic Sketch of. (A. S. Gatschet) Am. Anthrop. **2**: 527.
Catbird, Coming of the. (S. Trotter) Pop. Sci. Mo. **54**: 772.
— Methods in Economic Ornithology with Special Reference to. (S. D. Judd) Am. Natural. **31**: 392.
Catboating on Jersey Inland Waters. (H. T. Brown) Outing, **34**: 345.
Catching a Tartar ; a story. (A. Paterson) Idler, **14**: 812.
Catechism in Sunday-school Instruction, Use of. Bib. World, **16**: 166.
— The New Evangelical. (W. G. Tarrant) New World, **8**: 343. — (H. P. Hughes) Contemp. **75**: 45.
— Wanted, Longer, for Church of England. Church Q. **46**: 332.
Catechumenate ; its achievements and its possibilities. (T. Chalmers) Bib. Sac. **56**: 467.
Categories, The. (J. W. Powell) Am. Anthrop. **3**: 404.
Catenæ, Greek, of the Old Testament. Church Q. **50**: 29.
Caterans, Scottish. Scot. R. **32**: 333.
Caterpillar Hunting. (C. G. Soule) Outl. **64**: 826.
Catharine. See Catherine.
Cathayans. (E. H. Parker) Asia. R. **30**: 342.
Cathcart, William Ledyard, with portrait. Cassier, **18**: 525.
Cathedral, The ; a poem. (G. M. Henton) Pall Mall M. **11**: 265.
Cathedral Architecture for the 20th Century. Sat. R. **92**: 585, 645, 650.
Cathedral Builders, The. (L. Scott) Ath. '00, **1**: 473. — (Russell Sturgis) Bk. Buyer, **19**: 286.
Cathedral Canons, English Mediæval Institutes of. (E. Bishop) Dub. R. **123**: 41.
Cathedral Planning, Changes in. (William Emerson) Am. Arch. **64**: 76.
Cathedral Reform in England. (S. A. Barnett) 19th Cent. **44**: 1031.
Cathedrals of England. Chaut. **28**: 3, 115.
— — Photographs from Models of. Sund. M. **28**: 35.
— French. (B. Ferree) Archit. R. **6**: 323, 469. **7**: 98–465. **8**: 49, 168. — New Eng. M. n. s. **18**: 162.

Cathedrals, Uses of. Sat. R. **90**: 485.
Catherine, St., in Art, Legend, and Ritual. (J. L. André) Antiq. n. s. **36**: 235.
Catherine, St., of Alexandria. (M. F. Nixon) Cath. World, **67**: 447.
Catherine, St., of Genoa. Church Q. **44**: 364.
Catherine, St., of Siena. Church Q. **43**: 344.
Catherine II. and the Comte de Ségur. (G. Hill) Gent. M. n. s. **67**: 62.
Catherine of Aragon, The True. Library, **4**: 169.
Catherine of Braganza, Side-lights upon. Longm. **33**: 434.
Catherine Carr ; a story. (M. E. Wilkins) Harper, **98**: 882.
Catherwood, Mary Hartwell, with portrait. Bk. News, **20**: 135.
— Lazarre. (M. T. Earle) Bk. Buyer, **23**: 235. — (W. S. Edwards) Bookman, **14**: 259.
Cathode Rays, On the Energy of. (W. G. Cady) Am. J. Sci. **160**: 1.
Catholic, A Strange. Month, **95**: 500.
Catholic Antiquities of Bosham. Month, **98**: 148.
Catholic Apostolic Church. (E. N. White) Presb. & Ref. R. **10**: 624.
Catholic Bible, Our English. Month, **89**: 573. **90**: 43.
Catholic Books. Pub. Lib. **4**: 110.
Catholic Church by St. Augustine, Thirteenth Centenary of Founding of. (J. Gerard) Month, **90**: 337.
Catholic Conference, 1900. (J. Britten) Month, **96**: 62.
Catholic Girl, A Plea for the. Month, **98**: 228.
Catholic Guardians' Association, Work of the. Month, **95**: 145.
Catholic Prisoners' Aid Society. (J. Cooney) Month, **95**: 290.
Catholic Progress in England. (J. Britten) Month, **94**: 69.
Catholicism, "Liberal." (G. Tyrrell) Month, **91**: 449.
— The Church and. (J. Rickaby) Month, **97**: 337.
— Roman and Anglican, Fairbairn on. (H. Rashdall) Crit. R. **9**: 211.
See Roman Catholicism.
Catiline, Conspiracy of. (W. B. Wallace) Un. Serv. M. **21**: 528.
Catskills, Up to the, Awheel. (A. H. Godfrey) Outing, **32**: 458.
Cattaneo, Carlo. (J. W. Mario) Nation, **73**: 48.
Cattle, Breeds of, recognised in the British Isles in Successive Periods. Archæol. **55**: 125.
— Concerning. (B. C. Finch) Belgra. **99**: 508.
— Insurance of. Bank. M. (Lond.) **67**: 801.
— Quarantine for. (H. H. Bowen) Lippinc. **60**: 120.
— White, in British Folktales and Customs. (R. H. Wallace) Folk-Lore, **10**: 352.
Cattle Breeding, for Amateurs. (F. S. Peer) Outing, **38**: 679.
— for Gentlemen Farmers. (F. S. Peer) Outing, **38**: 164.
Cattle Ranching in Canadian Northwest. (J. Innes) Canad. M. **16**: 8.
— in the Southwest, Economics of. (R. M. Barker) R. of Rs. (N. Y.) **24**: 305.
Cattle-trade, Revelations of the South American. Chamb. J. **75**: 68.
Catullus, C. V. Lesbia ; tr. by Tremenheere. (J. C. Collins) Sat. R. **85**: 575.
— and his Friends. Macmil. **75**: 210. Same art. Liv. Age, **212**: 460.
— and Shelley. (E. W. Bowen) Sewanee, **7**: 337.
— Ed. by Palmer. Sat. R. **84**: 203.
Catuquinarú Indians, Dr. Bach's Visit to. (G. E. Church) Geog. J. **12**: 63.
Caucasus and Tirah. (Napier of Magdala) 19th Cent. **43**: 717.
— In Frosty. (Minghi-Tau) Un. Serv. M. **20**: 371.

Celebrities, Hunting. Indep. 53: 1354.

Celestial Carp, The. (Allen Upward) Chamb. J. 78: 540. Same art. Liv. Age, 231: 171.

Celestine, Father, or the Theology of Religious Life. Month, 92: 178.

Celibacy. (C. K. Paul) Month, 91: 492.

— in the Roman Priesthood. Spec. 78: 618.

Cell, The. (J. B. Farmer) Sci. Prog. 1: 141.

— Phosphorus-containing Substances of. (T. G. Brodie) Sci. Prog. 7: 131.

— Relation between Form and Metabolism of. (M. Verworn) Sci. Prog. n. s. 1: 370.

— Zelle und Gewebe, Hertwig's. Sci. Prog. 7: xxix.

Cell-membrane, The. (J. R. Green) Sci. Prog. n. s. 1: 344.

Cell-physiology. (H. Spencer) Nat. Sci. 12: 307.

Cells, Studies on. (T. Boveri) Science, n. s. 13: 264.

Cellini, Benvenuto. Acad. 56: 319.

Cellulose, Cross and Bevan's Researches on. (F. M. Perkin) Nature, 65: 52.

— Industrial Uses of. (C. F. Cross) J. Soc. Arts, 45: 684, 703.

Celtic Beauty, A. (S. MacManus) Lippinc. 65: 586.

Celtic Church in Ireland, Heron on. (J. Herkless) Crit. R. 8: 145.

— of Wales, Bund's. Ath. '97, 1: 800.

Celtic Drama. (W. Archer) Critic, 36: 436.

Celtic Folk-lore, Welsh and Manx, Rhys on. Ath. '01, 1: 265. — (C. S. Northup) Dial (Ch.) 31: 76.

Celtic Mind, The. (S. Bryant) Contemp. 72: 533.

Celtic Race. (T. H. Graham) Gent. M. n. s. 63: 368.

Celtic Renascence. (A. Lang) Blackw. 161: 181.

Celtic Saints and Romantic Fiction. (B. W. Wells) Sewanee, 2: 17.

Celtic Stories. (A. Lang) Blackw. 164: 792.

Celtic Traces in the Glosses. (O. B. Schlutter) Am. Anthrop. 21: 188.

Celtic Traditions and Anthropology, Rhys on. (E. S. Hartland) Nature, 63: 485.

Celtic Twilight, The. (D. M. Jones) Lond. Q. 94: 61.

Celtic Writers, A Group of. (F. Macleod) Fortn. 71: 34.

"Celtic," The Steamer. (F. Macleod) Contemp. 77: 669. Same art. Liv. Age, 225: 828. — (C. Roberts) World's Work, 2: 1177.

Cement, Ancient Oil. Science, n. s. 9: 688.

— Chemical Tests of. (J. F. Wilford) Am. Arch. 65: 53.

— Effect of Salt Water upon. (A. S. Cooper) J. Frankl. Inst. 148: 291.

— for a Modern Street. (S. F. Peckham) Pop. Sci. Mo. 60: 145.

— in Constructive Work. (E. W. Dewey) Engin. M. 14: 267.

— Portland; History of the Industry in U. S. (R. W. Lesley) J. Frankl. Inst. 146: 324.

— Tests of, Manipulation of. Am. Arch. 59: 62.

Cements in Latin America. Am. Arch. 73: 22.

— Inspection and Testing of. (R. L. Humphrey) J. Frankl. Inst. 152: 441.

Cemeteries. The Garden of Sleep. (P. W. Roose) Argosy, 69: 497.

Cemetery, Christian, in a Roman Villa. (L. Scott) Reliquary, 38: 73.

— The Modern. (A. Farmer) Overland, n. s. 29: 440.

— Pre-historic, at Harlyn Bay. (S. Barber) Reliquary, 41: 189.

Cenci, Beatrice, Crime and Trial of. Illust. (H. G. Chapin) Green Bag, 12: 631.

Censorship at Manila. (H. Martin) Forum, 31: 462.

Census, British, of 1901, and the Proposed Quinquennial Census. J. Statis. Soc. 63: 107, 355.

Census, Methods of taking, American. (W. F. Willcox) Forum, 30: 109.

— U. S. (A. L. Bowley) Econ. J. 9: 428.

— — Development of. (R. P. Falkner) Ann. Am Acad. Pol. Sci. 12: 34.

— — Essays on. (R. M. Smith) Pol. Sci. Q. 14: 325.

— — Taking. (J. W. Harshberger) Educa. 20: 39.

— — 12th, 1900. (R. P. Porter) No. Am. 165: 660. — (W. R. Merriam) No. Am. 170: 99. — (F. H. Wines) Munsey, 23: 387. — (F. H. Wines) Nat. Geog. M. 11: 34. — (D. MacG. Means) Nation, 66: 473.

— — — A Bipartisan Census. (F. E. Leupp) Nation, 68: 470.

— — — Forecast of. (M. G. Mulhall) No. Am. 171: 90.

— — — Lessons of. (J. C. Rose) Nation, 71: 243.

— — — Provisions for. (C. D. Wright) Q. J. Econ. 13: 339, 351.

— — — Report of Committee on. Econ. Stud. 4: 47. — (E. P. Clark) Nation, 68: 177.

— — — Vital Statistics of. (W. A. King) Am. Statis. Assoc. 5: 209.

— of the World, Development of Plan for. (J. H. Dynes) Am. Statis. Assoc. 6: 357.

— Romance of a. (H. I. Arden) Sund. M. 30: 474.

Census Returns, Uniformity in. (J. de Körösi) Am. Statis. Assoc. 6: 20.

Census-schedule, English. (G. Bizet) Macmil. 83: 428.

Census Taking, Limitations of. (J. A. Baines) J. Statis. Soc. 63: 41. — (W. F. Willcox) Q. J. Econ. 14: 459.

Censuses of 1901. J. Statis. Soc. 64: 300.

— Notes of Recent. (J. A. Baines) J. Statis. Soc. 64: 493.

Cent Kilos, Les; fat men's club of Paris. (G. Megan) Strand, 15: 524.

Centenarian of Samos; a story. (S. L. Bensusan) Eng. Illust. 20: 43.

Centenarians. Liv. Age, 221: 530. — Spec. 82: 446.

Central America, Antiquities of. (A. H. Keane) Nature, 61: 292.

— Bird Life in. (D. F. Randolph) Am. Natural. 31: 199.

— Geological Waterways across. (J. W. Spencer) Pop. Sci. Mo. 53: 577.

— its Resources and Commerce. (W. E. Curtis) Forum, 25: 166, 354.

— Maudslay's Archæological Work in. (C. Thomas) Am. Anthrop. 1: 552.

— Ruined Cities of. (G. E. Church) Geog. J. 15: 392.

Central American Indians, Some. Chamb. J. 75: 796.

Central Technical College, Work of. (W. E. Ayrton) J. Soc. Arts, 45: 769.

Centralization, Administrative, in England. (J. T. Young) Annals Am. Acad. 10: 187.

Centres, Universal Law of. (A. Reichenbach) Educa. 19: 495.

Centrosome, The. (A. D. Mead and others) Science, 5: 230.

Century, The Change of. Liv. Age, 228: 427.

— At the Turn of the; a Literary Audit. Chamb. J. 78: 84.

— First Year of the New. (Lord Hobhouse) Contemp. 7: 397.

Century of Aunts, A; a drama. (D. Dale) Argosy, 72: 422.

Century Guild Hobby Horse. Studio (Internat.) 5: 3.

Cephalic Homologies. (C. S. Minot) Am. Natural. 31: 927.

Cephalic Index. (F. Boas) Am. Anthrop. 1: 448.

— Inheritance of. (Cicely D. Fawcett) Science, n. s. 7: 55.

— Pedagogical Significance of. (C. C. Closson) J. Pol. Econ. 6: 254.

Chamois Stalking. (W. A. Baillie-Grohman) Outing, 37: 202.

Champions of Christendom; a story. (S. Bonsal) Indep. 53: 821, 875, 934.

Champlain, S. de, Monument to. (A. G. Doughty) Canad. M. 11: 431.

Champlain, Lake. (J. W. Buckham) New Eng. M. n. s. 20: 582.

— The Battle of. (J. E. Tuttle) Outl. 69: 573.

— Naval Campaign of 1776 on. (A. T. Mahan) Scrib. M. 23: 147.

— to New York. (R. Bergengren) Outing, 30: 113.

Champlain Valley, French in. New Eng. M. n. s. 24: 322.

Champness, Thomas, Founder of a Protestant Brotherhood. (H. S. Lunn) R. of Rs. (N. Y.) 18: 432.

Champney, J. Wells, Studies by, with portrait. (S. C. De Soissons) Artist (N. Y.) 29: 159.

Champollion. (A. Laugel) Nation, 65: 514.

Chance, Mrs. W., Cat-painter. (H. Strachey) Studio (Internat.) 1: 106.

Chance. Sat. R. 88: 97. —Spec. 81: 335.

Chance Acquaintance, A; a story. (B. A. Barnett) Argosy, 66: 424.

Chance Shot, A; a story. (H. W. Phillips) McClure, 15: 380.

Chancel, An Early Christian. (L. Scott) Reliquary, 40: 220.

Change and Duration, Perception of. (G. F. Stout) Mind, 25: 1. — (S. H. Hodgson) Mind, 25: 240. — (T. Loveday) Mind, 25: 384.

— The Concept of. (A. E. Davies) Philos. R. 9: 502.

Change of Clothes, A. (C. K. Burrow) Longm. 34: 327.

Changed Man, A; a story. (T. Hardy) Cosmopol. 29: 35.

Channel Islands, Strategical Value of. (W. L. Clowes) 19th Cent. 48: 881.

— Naval Strategy and. (J. M. Macartney) Un. Serv. M. 22: 447.

Channel Passage, A, 1855; a poem. (A. C. Swinburne) No. Am. 169: 1.

Channing, Wm. Ellery, 2d, Poet. (F. B. Sanborn) Atlan. 86: 819.

Chantilly, Château. (A. Dayot) Pall Mall M. 15: 517.

— and the Duc D'Aumale. (A. de Calonne) 19th Cent. 41: 1005. Same art. Liv. Age, 214: 239.

— and the Musée Condé. (R. de la Sizeranne) M. of Art, 22: 157.

— Paintings at. (A. Laugel) Nation, 66: 46, 66, 106.

— Two Gifts to French Science. (H. de Parville) Pop. Sci. Mo. 54: 81.

Chantrey, Sir Francis. Works. (G. D. Leslie and F. A. Eaton) Art J. 51: 114.

Chanute, Octave. Cassier, 13: 448.

Chapel in the Fossil Woods [i. e. in a Coal Mine]. (W. W. Moore) Sund. M. 28: 253.

Chaperon, Decay of the. (M. Jeune) Fortn. 74: 629. Same art. Liv. Age, 227: 372. Same art. Ecl. M. 136: 19.

Chaperone, The; a story. (B. M. Hicks) Argosy, 75: 44.

Chaperone, The; an adventure. (R. Ramsay) Chamb. J. 77: 136. — Liv. Age, 224: 829.

Chaplains on the Field. (E. J. Hardy) Sund. M. 29: 171.

Chapleau, Sir J. Adolphe. Canad. M. 11: 182.

Chapman, Alvin Wentworth. (W. Trelease) Am. Natural. 33: 643.

Chapman, Dom J., as a Roman Catholic Controversialist. Church Q. 44: 21.

Chapman, George, Newly Discovered Letters and Documents. (B. Dobell) Ath. '01, 1: 369-465.

Chapman, John Jay. (M. Winsor) Critic, 34: 451.

— as an Essayist. Acad. 54: 163.

— Portrait of. Bk. Buyer, 17: 277.

Chappuis, Mary de Sales, The Miraculous Preserving of the Body of. (Father Pernin) Cath. World, 74: 234.

Chapter of Accidents, A; a story. Macmil. 76: 64-368.

Chapter of Human History, A; a story. (E. Cummings) Music, 14: 261.

Chapter's Doom, The. (B. Capes) Cornh. 81: 468.

Character and Success. (T. Roosevelt) Outl. 64: 745.

— Fixity of : its ethical interpretation. (J. D. Logan) Mind, 22: 526.

— Intricacies of. (H. M. E. Stanton) Argosy, 65: 246.

— Proof of, by Personal Knowledge or Opinion. (J. H. Wigmore) Am. Law R. 32: 713.

— What will the Boy become ? (F. D. Evans) Educa. 20: 236.

— When it is Formed. (M. V. O'Shea) Pop. Sci. Mo. 51: 648.

Characters, Congenital and Acquired. (G. A. Reid) Science, 6: 896.

Charbonnel, Victor. (T. Stanton) Open Court, 12: 293.

— Why he Failed. (P. Carus) Open Court, 12: 300.

Charcoal Drawings of Frank Mura. Studio (Lond.) 6: 153.

Chardin, Jean Baptiste Simeon, Artist, with portrait. (F. Wedmore) Pall Mall M. 22: 145.

Charge in the Dark. (H. H. Bennett) Lippinc. 62: 400.

Chariot of Fire; a poem. (J. E. Smith) Poet-Lore, 13: 1.

Charitable Foundations, Curious. (R. P. Ryan) Outl. 58: 232.

Charitable Institutions, A Study in Nativities. (B. C. Mathews) Forum, 26: 621.

Charitable Work, Sympathy and Reason in. (E. D. Jones) Char. R. 6: 289.

Charities and Corrections, National Conference of, New York, 1898. Char. R. 8: 157. — Outl. 59: 347.

— — — Cincinnati, 1899. Char. R. 9: 162.

— — — Topeka, 1900. Char. R. 10: 114, 202.

— — — Washington, 1901. Charities, 6: 463-472.

— — New York State Conference of, Nov. 20-22, 1900. Char. R. 10: 451.

— Catholic, of England. (A. W. Winthrop) Cath. World, 65: 14.

— English, The English Poor Law and. (C. H. D'E. Leppington) Chaut. 28: 452.

— in Holland. (B. B. Croffut) No. Am. 168: 251.

— Inspection of. Outl. 64: 482.

— Municipal. (H. Folks) Munic. Aff. 3: 516. — Char. R. 6: 501.

— New Orleans Conference of. (F. H. Wines) Char. R. 6: 145.

— New York City Conference of. (H. Folks) Char. R. 6: 346.

— of Kansas, County. Char. R. 10: 398.

— Organized. (N. S. Rosenau) Char. R. 6: 385. — (J. S. Menken) Char. R. 7: 751.

— — Indictment of. Gunton's M. 12: 96. — Reply. (F. W. Hamilton) Gunton's M. 12: 272. — Rejoinder. Gunton's M. 12: 397.

— Public, Duty of the Citizen in Relation to. (G. Cleveland) Charities, 7: 201.

— State Board of, Work of a. Char. R. 8: 426.

— State Organization and Supervision of. (H. A. Millis) Am. J. Sociol. 4: 178.

— Subsidizing of Private. (F. A. Fetter) Am. J. Sociol. 7: 359.

— Supervisory and Educational Movements. (J. R. Brackett) Charities, 7: 514.

Charters of the Manor of Meonstoke. (T. F. Kirby) Archæol. **57**: 285.

Chartres. Illus. (Sophia Beale) Good Words, **38**: 199.

Chartreuse, La Grande, Monastery of. Temp. Bar, **111**: 92.

Chase, Salmon P., Hart's. (W. D. Foulke) Am. Hist. R. **5**: 583. — (J. D. Cox) Nation, **70**: 207. — (F. Bancroft) Atlan. **86**: 277.

— Letters to, from the South, 1861. Am. Hist. R. **4**: 331.

Chase, William M., Painter, with portrait. (E. Knaufft) Studio (Internat.) **12**: 151.

Chase of the Tide, The; a story. (N. Duncan) Mc-Clure, **17**: 307.

Chase Overnight. A. (J. B. Connolly) Scrib. M. **29**: 496.

Chastenay, Madame de. (A. Laugel) Nation, **64**: 201, 221.

Chat, Yellow-breasted. (W. S. Kennedy) New Eng. M. n. s. **20**: 540.

Chateaubriand. (A. Laugel) Nation, **68**: 394.

— as a Statesman. (A. Laugel) Nation, **73**: 262.

— Novels of. (B. W. Wells) Sewanee, **5**: 385.

Châteaubriant, Françoise, Madame de. (A. de Calonne) 19th Cent. **41**: 96.

Chateaux of the Loire. (F. H. Briggs) Am. Arch. **63**: 11. **64**: 3.

Chatham, Lord, Colonial Policy of. (H. Hall) Am. Hist. R. **5**: 659.

Chatin, Adolphe. Nature, **63**: 351.

Chatsworth House, Seat of Duke of Devonshire, England. (A. H. Malan) Pall Mall M. **11**: 169.

— Ancient Sculptures at. (A. Furtwängler) J. Hel. Stud. **21**: 209.

Chattanooga Industrial Convention. (B. J. Ramage) Nation, **70**: 456.

Chatterton, Thomas, the Marvelous Boy. (C. E. Russell) Munsey, **24**: 666.

Chaucer, G. (F. Greenslet) Forum, **30**: 375. — (J. W. Hales) No. Am. **171**: 712.

— Canterbury Tales, Astronomy of. (E. W. Maunder) Knowl. **21**: 205.

— Cleopatra and her Pit of Serpents. (F. M. Mather, jr.) Nation, **67**: 331.

— Clerk's Tale, Story of. (C. B. Furst) Citizen, **3**: 82, 104.

— Dialectal Survivals from. (C. S. Brown) Dial (Ch.) **22**: 139.

— Early Legal History in Canterbury Tales. (Maj. Greenwood) Green Bag, **10**: 69.

— Elements of Popularity in. Acad. **53**: 303.

— In Honor of. Sat. R. **90**: 514.

— Junius's. (M. Liddell) Ath. '97, **1**: 799.

— Poetry of. Spec. **81**: 149. — Cornh. **82**: 540.

— Portraits of. (M. H. Spielmann) M. of Art, **24**: 395, 441, 494.

— Selections, Corson's. (G. M. Marshall) School R. **5**: 475.

— Sources of, One of the. (M. Liddell) Nation, **64**: 124.

— Student's, Skeat's. (G. H. Stempel) School R. **5**: 552.

Chaucer, Thomas, Son of Geoffrey. (W. W. Skeat) Ath. '00, **1**: 116.

Chaucer Garden, The. (W. H. Thompson) Gent. M. n. s. **65**: 379. Same art. Liv. Age, **227**: 379. — Same art. Ecl. M. **136**: 26.

Chautauqua Assemblies, Other. Chaut. **33**: 417.

Chautauqua Assembly Program, Is it Educative? (G. E. Vincent) Chaut. **31**: 248.

Chautauqua Boys' Club. (J. A. Babbitt) Chaut. **32**: 146.

Chautauqua Flowers and how to Know them. Chaut. **33**: 366.

Chautauqua, Lake, Geological Development of. (L. E. Allen) Chaut. **33**: 538.

— Tour round. (T. L. Flood) Chaut. **25**: 361.

Chautauqua Literary and Scientific Circle. Chaut. **33**: 337.

Chautauquan, The. Twenty Years an Editor. (T. L. Flood) Chaut. **29**: 322.

Chautauquan of Long Ago, A. (M. H. Field) Chaut. **31**: 512.

Chavannes, Puvis de. *See* Puvis de Chavannes.

Chavassa, Bishop of Liverpool. Sund. M. **29**: 485.

Cheapness; is it an evil? Gunton's M. **13**: 45.

Cheating the Devil; a story. (W. James) Temp. Bar, **113**: 585.

Che-che-puy-ew-tis, History of the. (R. Bell) J. Am. Folk-Lore, **10**: 1.

Checkmated; à Linnæus of the Hindu Kush. Blackw. **164**: 40. Same art. Liv. Age, **218**: 547.

Cheerfulness, Studies in. (M. O'Rell) No. Am. **167**: 690. **168**: 34.

Cheese, A New Light on. (G. C. Nuttall) Good Words, **40**: 554.

Cheese Makers, Swiss and German. (G. E. Walsh) Indep. **52**: 1790.

Cheese Making in Canada. (J. W. Wheaton) Canad. M. **13**: 51.

— Microbes in. (H. W. Conn) Pop. Sci. Mo. **58**: 148.

Cheever's Magic Mashie. (E. L. Sabin) Lippinc. **68**: 71.

Cheevers and the Love of Beauty; a story. (B. Pain) Eng. Illust. **20**: 325.

Cheirosophy, Manual of, Heron-Allen's. (C. B. Matheson) Bookman, **8**: 365.

Chekko and Uncle Ben; a story. (C. Warman) Canad. M. **13**: 548.

Chelan, Lake, the Leman of the West. (W. D. Lyman) Overland, n. s. **33**: 195.

— Map and Illus. (H. Garnett) Nat. Geog. M. **9**: 417.

Chelmsford Marriages. (E. W. Leavitt) N. E. Reg. **51**: 307, 447.

Chelonian Carapace and Plastron. (O. P. Hay) Am. Natural. **32**: 929.

Chelsea, England. (R. Blunt; W. F. Prideaux) Ath. '00, **2**: 124, 154, 218.

— Literary. (W. S. Harwood) Critic, **38**: 417.

Chemical Bank Forgery Case. Green Bag, **9**: 314.

Chemical Calculations, Abridgments in. (J. W. Richards) J. Frankl. Inst. **152**: 109.

Chemical Elements, New, Discovery of. (C. Winkler) Pop. Sci. Mo. **52**: 825.

Chemical Evolution. A Chapter of History. (G. C. Fry) Knowl. **23**: 139.

Chemical Formulas, Dangers of the Abuse of. (E. P. Venable) Science, n. s. **8**: 732.

Chemical Industries. (W. McMurtrie) Science, n. s. **13**: 441.

Chemical Instruction and Chemical Industries in Germany. (F. Mollwo Perkin) Nature, **65**: 176.

Chemical Reaction, Velocity of. (R. H. Bradbury) J. Frankl. Inst. **147**: 463. **148**: 65. — (W. Duane) Am. J. Sci. **161**: 349.

Chemical Science, Growth of. (L. H. Batchelder) Chaut. **28**: 25.

Chemical Societies, Early American. (H. C. Bolton) Pop. Sci. Mo. **51**: 819.

Chemical Society of Washington. (L. S. Munson) Science, n. s. **13**: 910.

Chemise Shrub. (C. Purdy) Garden & F. **10**: 72, 83.

Chemistry, Agricultural, Progress of. Nature, **61**: 116.

— Analytical. (A. Smithells) Nature, **59**: 1.

— Analytical Work in, Dignity of. (C. B. Dudley) Science, n. s. **7**: 185.

Chemistry as a Factor in Modern Civilization. (L. H. Batchelder) Chaut. **28**: 444.

— at the British Association, 1898. Nature, **58**: 556.

— — 1899. Nature, **60**: 608.

— at the Jubilee Meeting of the American Association. (C. Baskerville) Science, n. s. **8**: 521.

— Genealogy of. (M. E. Berthelot) Pop. Sci. Mo. **53**: 535.

— High School Course in. School R. **5**: 497.

— — More Profitable. (L. C. Newell) School R. **9**: 286.

— A Hundred Years of. (F. W. Clark) Pop. Sci. Mo. **56**: 673. **57**: 52.

— in Great Britain at Dawn of 20th Century; Pres. addr. Chemistry Sec. Brit. Assoc. 1901. (P. F. Frankland) Nature, **64**: 503.

— in the Kitchen. (A. G. Evans) Lippinc. **63**: 817.

— in the U. S. (F. W. Clarke) Science, **5**: 117.

— Inorganic. (W. M. Davis) Science, n. s. **13**: 349.

— — Increasing Importance of. (H. C. Jones) Science, n. s. **8**: 927.

— — Ostwald's. (J. Walker) Nature, **63**: 557.

— — Revival of. (H. N. Stokes) Science, n. s. **9**: 601.

— of High Temperatures. J. Frankl. Inst. **146**: 63.

— of To-day. (L. H. Batchelder) Chaut. **28**: 139.

— Organic. (H. Erdmann) Science, n. s. **13**: 268.

— — Cohen on. (W. T. Lawrence) Nature, **63**: 511.

— — Electric Current in. (E. F. Smith) Science, n. s. **8**: 413.

— — Loew on Energy of Living Cells. (A. F. Woods) Science, n. s. **9**: 409.

— Physical. (J. H. van't Hoff) Science, n. s. **14**: 126.

— — Progress in. (T. W. Richards) Science, n. s. **8**: 721.

— Progress of, 1837–97. (T. E. Thorpe) Knowl. **20**: 85.

— — The Century's. (H. S. Williams) Harper, **95**: 749.

— Pure and Applied, Teaching of. (O. N. Witt) J. Soc. Arts, **45**: 739.

— Recent Progress of. Sat. R. **86**: 404.

— Relation of, to Advancement of the Arts. (H. W. Wiley) J. Frankl. Inst. **148**: 327.

— Teaching of. (G. Lunge) J. Soc. Arts, **45**: 750. — (W. P. Mason) Science, n. s. **7**: 734.

— Teaching of, in Evening Schools. (J. H. Gladstone) J. Soc. Arts, **45**: 747.

— — in the Medical Schools of the U. S. (J. H. Long) Science, n. s. **14**: 360.

— — in Schools. (R. P. Williams) Science, n. s. **14**: 100.

— Technical, Fischer on. (R. Meldola) Nature, **59**: 361.

— Unsolved Problems of. (I. Remsen) McClure, **16**: 362.

Chemists, Concerning. Chamb. J. **75**: 169.

Chemotropsim of Fungi. (E. F. Smith) Am. Natural. **31**: 717.

Cheney, Anne Cleveland. Writer, **14**: 169.

Chénier, André. (J. C. Bailey) Blackw. **163**: 854.

Chepstow Castle. Acad. **57**: 139.

Cheque, Largest, in the World. Bank. M. (Lond.) **65**: 863.

— when Posted; Is it Payment? Bank. M. (Lond.) **63**: 739.

Cheques, Country, When may they be Drawn against? Bank. M. (Lond.) **66**: 353.

— Crossed, Payment of, over the Counter. Bank. M. (Lond.) **68**: 714.

Cherbuliez, Victor. (F. Brunetière) Ecl. M. **133**: 911. Same art. Liv. Age, **223**: 28. — (Othon Guerlac) Nation, **69**: 28. — Dial (Ch.) **27**: 39.

Chere, Samuel, Impeachment of. (A. P. Humphrey) Am. Law R. **33**: 827.

Chéret, Jules, with portrait. (M. H. Spielmann) M. of Art, **22**: 304.

Cherokee Indians of North Carolina. (L. T. Rightsell) Educa. **20**: 420.

Cherokee River Cult. (J. Mooney) J. Am. Folk-Lore, **13**: 1.

Cherries of Ueno. (R. A. Cram) Atlan. **85**: 479.

Cherry; a romance. (B. Tarkington) Harper, **102**: 241, 406.

Cherry; a story. (H. A. Hinkson) Idler, **15**: 453.

Cherry-bud in a Foreign Hand. (Adachi Kinnosuké) Lippinc. **67**: 506.

Cherub among the Gods, The. (C. B. Fernald) Cent. **33**: 72.

Cherubim, What were the? (A. S. Palmer) 19th Cent. **49**: 332.

Chesapeake and Ohio Canal Project, Early Development of. (G. W. Ward) J. H. Univ. Stud. **17**: 425.

"Chesapeake" and "Shannon;" a poem. (E. V. Cooke) Chaut. **31**: 352.

Cheshire Cheese Tavern, Supper at the. Temp. Bar, **120**: 238.

Cheshunt, The "Great House" at. (W. B. Gerish) Antiq. n. s. **37**: 327.

Chesnutt, Charles W. Bk. Buyer, **18**: 360. — (C. Shipman) Critic, **35**: 632.

— Stories. (W. D. Howells) Atlan. **85**: 699.

Chess and Chess Clubs. (T. H. Allbutt) Good Words, **38**: 45. Same art. Liv. Age, **212**: 341.

— as a War-game. Un. Serv. M. **23**: 646.

— Earliest Mention of, in Sanskrit Literature. (A. A. Macdonnel) Ath. '97, 2: 130.

— Muslim Legality of. (D. B. Macdonald) Nation, **71**: 170.

— Origin of. (W. Hopkins) Nation, **70**: 457. — (W. Fiske) Nation, **71**: 132.

— Some Notes on. (G. H. Ely) Macmil. **76**: 356. Same art. Liv. Age, **215**: 260.

— Tactics of the Game of. (F. K. Young) Pall Mall M. **11**: 409, 575.

Chess-playing To-day. (J. A. Green) Liv. Age, **217**: 318.

Chesson, W. H. A Great Lie. (D. F. Hannigan) Westm. **148**: 70.

Chester, George, Landscape Artist, with portrait. (A. L. Baldry) Studio (Internat.) **2**: 100.

Chester Cathedral. (J. L. Darby) Sund. M. **27**: 703, 775.

— Defence of the Liberties of, 1450. (H. D. Harrod) Archæol. **57**: 71.

— Roman Discoveries at, Recent. Reliquary, **40**: 111.

Chester, N. S. List of the First Class of Settlers. (E. W. Leavitt) N. E. Reg. **54**: 45.

Chesterfield, Philip Dormer Stanhope, Lord. (S. G. Tallentyre) Longm. **33**: 532. Same art. Ecl. M. **133**: 207. Same art. Liv. Age, **221**: 827. — (P. B. Eagle) Gent. M. n. s. **60**: 541.

Chesterfield, Fourth Earl of; an 18th-century flirtation. (C. J. Hamilton) Gent. M. n. s. **66**: 510.

Chesterfield's Creed. Spec. **78**: 840.

Chesterton, G. K., as an Essayist. Acad. **61**: 509.

Chetwode Heirloom, The. (T. W. Speight) Chamb. J. **76**: 871.

Chevalier d'Antan; a story. (N. K. Blissett) Temp. Bar, **113**: 77.

Chevalier d'Auriac. (S. L. Yeats) Longm. **29**: 205–487. **30**: 1–283.

Cheverel Manor. (G. Morley) Argosy, **68**: 272.

Cheves, Langdon, President of Bank of the United States. Bank. M. (N. Y.) **57**: 772.

Chevrillon, André, as a Descriptive Writer. Acad. **52**: 452.

Chewing Gum, Cultivation of, in Mexico. J. Soc. Arts, **45**: 383.

Cheyenne Tales. (A. L. Kroeber) J. Am. Folk-Lore, 13: 161.

Cheyennes, Experiences with the. (G. A. Woodward) Un. Serv. (Phila.) 17: 44.

Cheyne, Thos. Kelly. (W. C. Barker) Outl. 57: 466.
— in America. Critic, 31: 346.

Chicago, Administration of. (L. J. Gage) Open Court, 11: 193.
— Apollo Club. Music, 13: 511.
— Architecture in. (P. B. Wight) Pall Mall M. 18: 293. — (J. W. Pattison) Am. Arch. 65: 52.
— Armour Institute of Technology. (C. L. Snowden) New Eng. M. n. s. 16: 354.
— The Artistic Side of. (E. W. Peattie) Atlan. 84: 828.
— Athletic Club. (J. W. Hipwell) Outing, 33: 145.
— Building-trades Conflict in, 1900. (J. E. George) Q. J. Econ. 15: 348. — (E. L. Bogart) Pol. Sci. Q. 16: 114.
— Civil Service Decision. Ann. Am. Acad. Pol. Sci. 11: 140.
— Council Reform in. (E. B. Smith) Munic. Aff. 4: 347.
— Drainage Canal at. (M. N. Baker) Outl. 64: 357. — (E. O. Jordan) R. of Rs. (N. Y.) 21: 56. — (J. L. Wright) Lippinc. 60: 410.
— Educational Commission of the City of, Report of. (A. H. Nelson) School R. 9: 53. — Dial (Ch.) 26: 37. — Educa. R. 17: 261.
— Great Sanitary Waterway of. (C. S. Raddin) Overland, n. s. 34: 301.
— Greater. (J. H. Gray) Ann. Am. Acad. Pol. Sci. 17: 291.
— Housing Conditions in. (W. R. Hunter) Char. R. 10: 292.
— Mercy Hospital. (P. G. Smyth) Cath. World, 65: 776.
— Municipal Reform in. (E. P. Clark) Nation, 70: 411.
— Municipal Voters' League. (E. B. Smith) Atlan. 85: 834. — Outl. 60: 130.
— Musical Culture in, Recent Development of. (G. P. Upton) Harper, 96: 473.
— Newspapers of. (F. L. Armstrong) Chaut. 27: 538.
— Peace Jubilee, 1898. (F. Putnam) Nat'l M. (Bost.) 9: 239.
— Picturesque Aspect of. (A. Fleury) Brush & P. 6: 273.
— Post-office and Custom-house. (C. H. Blackall) Am. Arch. 68: 45.
— Public Library. (E. Parsons) Critic, 30: 177. — Dial (Ch.) 23: 207. — Pub. Lib. 2: 436.
— — New Building. Am. Arch. 58: 4. — Lib. J. 22: 692. — (F. Crissey) Outl. 57: 279.
— Public School System. (E. B. Andrews) Educa. 20: 201, 264.
— Saloon Question in. (J. E. George) Econ. Stud. 2: 57.
— Schools of. Dial (Ch.) 27: 9.
— School Situation in. (J. W. Errant) Educa. R. 18: 119.
— Stock-yards. (E. S. Hoch) Nat'l M. (Bost.) 5: 350.
— — Some Social Aspects of. (C. J. Bushnell) Am. J. Sociol. 7: 289.
— Street Railways of, and their Franchises. (M. R. Maltbie; E. F. Bard) Munic. Aff. 5: 439.
— Taxation of Banks in. (Z. S. Holbrook) Bib. Sac. 55: 526.
— Tax-reform Victory in. Outl. 69: 527.
— University of, Science at. (F. Starr) Pop. Sci. Mo. 51: 784.
— Upward Movement in. (H. B. Fuller) Atlan. 80: 534.

Chicago, Women's Work for. (J. Addams) Munic. Aff. 2: 502.
— World's Columbian Exposition, English Art at. Studio (Lond.) 2: 45.
— — Story of Some Old Friends. George Pangalo) Cosmopol. 23: 277.

Chicago Art Institute, Art Education at. (M. Key) Brush & P. 6: 237.
— Collections in. Brush & P. 1: 79-219. 2: 1-252. 3: 1.
— Modeling Class. (V. V. Dundas) Brush & P. 2: 167.
— The Munger Collection. (C. F. Browne) Brush & P. 3: 65.
— Nickerson Collection at. (A. Hewitt) Brush & P. 7: 58.
— School at. (W. M. R. French) Brush & P. 1: 35, 204. 2: 9.

Chicago Art Student's League. (M. S. Baker) Brush & P. 1: 61.

Chicago Artists and their Work. (Harriet H. Hayes) Nat'l M. (Bost.) 6: 50, 350. - - (H. W. Grey) Brush & P. 7: 373.

Chicago Historical Society. Dial (Ch.) 22: 5.

Chicago Musical College. Music, 14: 515.

Chicago Orchestra. Music, 19: 78. — Dial (Ch.) 22: 269. — (W. S. B. Mathews) Music, 16: 578.
— Concerts by. (W. S. B. Mathews) Music, 13: 369, 507. 14: 82.
— 1896-97. Music, 13: 479.

Chicago Salon, The. (W. B. Dyer) Brush & P. 6: 49.

Chicago Tongue. (E. Hubbard) Indep. 53: 545.

Chicago Women who hold Public Offices. (A. Van H. Wakeman) Chaut. 27: 300.

Chicago's Book of Days. (H. B. Fuller) Outl. 69: 288.

Chichester, England. (J. Cavis-Brown) Art J. 49: 18.
— Cathedral, Restoration of. Am. Arch. 69: 103.

Chickamauga, Battle of. (J. D. Cox) Scrib. M. 28: 326.
— Camp at, 1898. (F. Lynde) Nat'l M. (Bost.) 8: 350.

Chickens, Newly Hatched, Observations on. (H. E. Hunt) Am. J. Psychol. 9: 125.
— Pigs, and People. (B. T. Washington) Outl. 68: 291.

Chicks, Instinctive Reaction of. (E. Thorndike) Psychol. R. 6: 282.

Chicopee, Mass., City of. (C. G. Burnham) New Eng. M. n. s. 18: 361.

Chief; a story. (J. B. Hodgkin) Atlan. 83: 374.

Chief, The, as Medical Officer; a story. Eng. Illust. 18: 589.

Chief Justices of U. S., Seven. (W. E. Curtis) Chaut. 25: 339.

Chieftain's Oak, The; a tale. (C. W. Williams) Argosy, 64: 446.

Chiemsee. (D. M. Barrett) Month, 92: 625.

Chiffon; a story. (N. Syrett) Pall Mall M. 22: 70.

Child, Francis James. (A. Lang) Folk-Lore, 7: 416. — (C. E. Norton) Harv. Grad. M. 6: 161.
— Memorial Library. (W. S. Kennedy) Critic, 30: 186.

Child, Frederick S. Lit. W. (Bost.) 31: 44.

Child, George W. J. Soc. Arts, 45: 55.

Child, Lydia Maria, with portrait. Nat'l M. (Bost.) 14: 161.

Child brought up at Home, The. (F. Z. Briggs) Cosmopol. 28: 228.
— Development of. (I. and E. G. Seymour) Educa. 17: 295, 351.
— in the Library. (E. Lanigan) Atlan. 87: 122.
— in Recent English Literature. (J. Sully) Fortn. 67: 218.
— Notes on the Theological Development of a. (F. D. Bergen) Arena, 19: 254.

China, Missionary Troubles in. (Tau Sein Ko) Asia. R. 30: 278.

— a Missionary's View. (Mrs. S. L. Baldwin) Outl. 66: 107.

— Missions in. (J. S. Dennis) R. of Rs. (N. Y.) 22: 302.

— — and European Politics in. (G. M. Fiamingo) Open Court, 14: 689.

— — and Missionaries in. (P. Bigelow) No. Am. 171: 26.

— Mongolian Silhouettes. (E. Aspray) Good Words, 40: 687.

— A Monroe Doctrine for. (Diplomaticus) Fortn. 69: 321.

— New. (Tau Sein Ko) Asia. R. 26: 69.

— A New Situation in. (W. Robertson) Westm. 147: 237. Same art. Ecl. M. 128: 577.

— New Year in. (A. H. Smith) Open Court, 14: 43.

— A 19th Century Crusade. (H. B. Hulbert) Outl. 66: 926.

— North, Forces arrayed against us in. (E. H. Parker) Un. Serv. M. 21: 536.

— Notes of Progress in. Sat. R. 83: 680.

— of the Globe-trotter. (E. A. Reynolds-Ball) Chamb. J. 78: 119.

— of To-day. Church Q. 52: 50.

— Ombres Chinoises. (A. Dobson) Cornh. 84: 757.

— Open Door in. Outl. 64: 99.

— Our Consular Courts in. (M. B. Dennell) Am. Law R. 34: 826.

— Our Duty towards. (R. A. Yerburgh) National, 33: 902.

— Pagodas and Other Architecture of. (R. W. Shufeldt) Overland, n. s. 33: 293.

— Paradox of. (H. M. Watts) Nat. Geog. M. 11: 352.

— Parker's. (W. E. Griffis) Nation, 73: 229.

— Partition of. (E. L. Godkin) Nation, 65: 511. — (W. E. Gowan) Asia. R. 25: 387. — (A. Little) Asia. R. 27: 58. — (W. E. Curtis) Cosmopol. 24: 459. — (J. Foreman) National, 31: 87. Same art. Ecl. M. 130: 577. — (H. S. Hallett) 19th Cent. 43: 154. Same art. Ecl. M. 130: 322.

— — America's Share in. (D. C. Boulger) No. Am. 171: 171.

— — The Powers and. (G. Reid) No. Am. 170: 634.

— Party of Reform in. (J. Foord) Indep. 52: 1651.

— Past and Present of. (A. H. V. Colquhoun) Canad. M. 15: 445.

— Peking — and after. (D. C. Boulger) Fortn. 74: 198.

— — Fall of. (W. A. P. Martin) Indep. 52: 2419.

— Persons and Politics in Peking. (A. Michie) National, 32: 424.

— Pioneers of Commerce in. Blackw. 164: 132.

— A Plea for the Control of. (F. E. Younghusband) National, 36: 210.

— A Plea for Fair Treatment. (Wu Ting Fang) Cent. 38: 951.

— Plea for the Integrity of. (W. C. J. Reid) Forum, 31: 515.

— A Plea for Justice. (A. E. Spender) Westm. 154: 477.

— Policy of the Powers in. (H. C. Thomson) Monthly R. 3, no. 3: 41.

— Powers' Stakes in. World's Work, 1: 27.

— Present and Future of. (Sun Yat Sen) Fortn. 67: 424.

— Present-Day. (W. Muirhead) Lond. Q. 94: 105.

— Present Outlook in. (A. H. Smith) Outl. 68: 125.

— Primitive Industrial Civilization of. (G. M. Walker) Chaut. 33: 127.

— Prince Hamlet of Peking [the Emperor Teai-Tsien]. (C. Johnston) Arena, 24: 268.

China, Problem in. Ed. R. 190: 244. — (F. T. Jane) Contemp. 73: 387. Same art. Ecl. M. 130: 744. — (P. Carus) Open Court, 15: 608.

— — and its Solution. (Tau Sein Ko) Asia. R. 31: 73. Same art. Ecl. M. 136: 651. Same art. Liv. Age, 228: 793.

— — Complexity of. (A. B. Johnson) Indep. 52: 2550.

— — A German View of. (M. von Brandt) Liv. Age, 227: 320. Same art. Ecl. M. 135: 807.

— Problem of Treaty with Powers. Sat. R. 91: 228.

— Problems in. (J. M. Hubbard) Nat. Geog. M. 11: 297.

— Problems of England in. Sat. R. 86: 198.

— Punishment and Revenge in. (T. F. Millard) Scrib. M. 29: 187.

— Railroad and Mining Concessions in. (C. Denby, jr.) Forum, 28: 334.

— Railroad Enterprises in. (B. Taylor) Chamb. J. 76: 281.

— Railroads in. Cath. World, 73: 225.

— — The Squabble over. (R. Ogden) Nation, 67: 125.

— Railway Concessions in. (C. Cary) Forum, 24: 591.

— Real Difficulties in. (R. Ogden) Nation, 72: 24.

— Recent Business Tour in. (C. A. Moreing) Ecl. M. 131: 628.

— Recent Developments in. (O. P. Austin) Forum, 27: 730.

— Recent Industrial Progress in. (J. S. Fearon and E. P. Allen) Engin. M. 16: 165.

— Reconstruction in. (A. H. Smith) Outl. 69: 982.

— Reform in. (G. Reid) Forum, 28: 724. — (R. K. Douglas) Good Words, 41: 802.

— — and British Interests, 1899. Asia. R. 27: 318.

— — and the Powers. (R. Hart) Fortn. 75: 763. Same art. Liv. Age, 229: 601.

— — in Literature as an Element in. (I. T. Headland) Meth. R. 61: 581.

— — Struggle for. (C. Johnston) No. Am. 171: 13.

— Reform Movement in. (I. T. Headland) Outl. 65: 494.

— Regeneration of, The Coming. (J. H. Barrows) Gunton's M. 19: 303.

— Resentment of. (H. H. Lowry) Harper, 101: 740.

— Resources and Means of Communication of. (G. G. Chisholm) Geog. J. 12: 500.

— Revisited. (A. Michie) Blackw. 170: 523.

— Revolution in, 1898. (S. Bonsal) R. of Rs. (N. Y.) 22: 166. — (Kang Yeu Wei) Contemp. 76: 180.

— and its Causes. (R. Van Bergen) Cent. 38: 791.

— Roman Catholicism in. (B. Cothonay) Cath. World, 73: 415.

— The Root of the Chinese Trouble. (J. Foord) No. Am. 171: 401.

— Russia and. (J. D. Rees) Fortn. 75: 612.

— Russia and England in. (P. S. Reinsch) Arena, 21: 75. — (H. Norman) Contemp. 71: 153.

— Russia in, Policy of. (A. V. Markoff) National, 31: 206.

— — and Great Britain in. Spec. 80: 364-848.

— Russia in North. (S. P. Read) Indep. 53: 486.

— Russia's Interest in. (B. Adams) Atlan. 86: 309.

— Russo-Chinese Imbroglio. (Taio-ko and C. Stanford) Westm. 156: 149.

— Salisbury's Score in. (H. S. Hallett) 19th Cent. 43: 890.

— Salt Trade of. (E. H. Parker) Econ. J. 9: 116.

— The Scramble for. (D. C. Boulger) Contemp. 78: 1

— Secret Societies in. (H. Baynes) Asia. R. 26: 318. —Ecl. M. 128: 210. — (M. A. Hamm) Indep. 52: 1534. — Liv. Age, 219: 530.

— Settlement in. (T. F. Millard) Scrib. M. 29: 370.

— Shall the Open Door be closed? (G. Reid) National, 32: 491.

Chinese Civilization. (A. B. Hulbert) Gunton's M. 20: 127.

Chinese Conservatism, Philosophic Causes of. (A. K. Glover) Arena, 24: 253.

Chinese Corporations. (M. Courant) Chaut. 29: 495.

Chinese Criminal Law. (E. Alabaster) Green Bag, 12: 423.

Chinese Cue, A. (C. E. Harrell) Lippinc. 68: 88.

Chinese Daily Life. (J. K. Goodrich) Forum, 28: 197.

Chinese Defence, The. (E. H. Parker) Un. Serv. M. 22: 93.

Chinese Dinner-party. Blackw. 168: 851.

Chinese Dislike of Foreigners, Cause of. (A. H. Smith) Outl. 67: 164, 216, 400, 630.

Chinese Ethics, History and Spirit of. (K. Nakamura) Int. J. Ethics, 8: 86.

Chinese Examinations and Graduates. (W. T. Gracey) Nat'l M. (Bost.) 6: 362.

Chinese Fairy Tale. (L. Housman) Monthly R. 2 no. 2: 141.

Chinese Fiction. Illus. (G. T. Candlin) Open Court, 12: 513, 607.

Chinese Five-minute Tales Americanized by Chu Seoul Bok and V. V. M. Beede. Chaut. 32: 240.

Chinese Games of Fan-tan ; a story. (C. Dawe) Canad. M. 15: 409.

Chinese Hieroglyphics. (E. G. Tewkesbury) Chaut. 34: 130.

Chinese Humbug. (E. H. Parker) Ecl. M. 128: 362.

Chinese Imbroglio. Blackw. 163: 552.

Chinese Immigrant in Further Asia. (F. W. Williams) Am. Hist. R. 5: 503.

Chinese Ishmael, A. (Sui Sin Fah) Overland, n. s. 34: 43.

Chinese Jurisprudence. (Wu Ting Fang) Am. Law R. 35: 343.

Chinese Language. (F. Poole) Lippinc. 66: 746.

— Needed to Assist Commerce. Sat. R. 91: 363.

Chinese Literature. (I. T. Headland) Critic, 38: 440.

— Encyclopædia Maxima. (H. A. Giles) 19th Cent. 49: 659.

— Giles's History of. Ath. '01, 1: 139. — (W. E. Griffis) Nation, 73: 136.

Chinese Mandarin, The Life of a. (E. H. Parker) Ecl. M. 130: 659. Same art. Liv. Age, 217: 291.— Same art. Green Bag, 12: 93.

Chinese Mandarins, Among. (De Lancey Floyd-Jones) J. Mil. Serv. Inst. 7: 233.

Chinese Masterpieces. (C. J. Holmes) Monthly R. 1, no. 2: 137.

Chinese Misalliance, A. (A. B. Westland) Overland, n. s. 37: 611.

Chinese Monasteries, Among. (A. B. Little) Macmil. 81: 201. — Liv. Age, 224: 631.

Chinese Mother Goose Rhymes, Headland's. (E. S. Holden) Bookman, 13: 150.

Chinese Motif in Current Art. (Mary Bell) Overland, n. s. 31: 236.

Chinese Oddities, Some. (F. E. Clarke) Cosmopol. 30: 281.

Chinese Officers. (A. O. Klaussman) Chaut. 27: 262.

Chinese Peculiarities in regard to Death and Fear of Death. Sat. R. 90: 108.

Chinese Pedagogics in Practice. (F. B. Dresslar) Educa. 20: 136.

Chinese People, Future of the. (D. Z. Sheffield) Atlan. 85: 76.

Chinese Physicians in California. (W. M. Tisdale) Lippinc. 63: 411.

Chinese Poetry. (W. A. P. Martin) No. Am. 172: 853.

Chinese Prophecy. (J. Macgregor) Westm. 152: 166.

Chinese Religious Ideas, Side Lights on. (E. H. Parker) Gent. M. n. s. 58: 593.

Chinese Servants. (E. A. Irving) Blackw. 164: 617.

Chinese Slavery in America. (C. F. Holder) No. Am. 165: 288.

Chinese Snuff Bottles. (M. B. Huish) Studio (Lond.) 8: 11.

Chinese Traits and Western Blunders. (H. C. Potter) Cent. 38: 921.

— Some. (C. Denby) Forum, 31: 350.

Chino-Japanese War, The Affair of the Gaelic in the. (J. Westlake) Law Q. 15: 24.

Chinon. (E. C. Peixotto) Scrib. M. 26: 737.

Chinook Verb, Morphology of. (J. R. Swanton) Am. Anthrop. 2: 199.

Chipiez, Charles, Architect. Am. Arch. 74: 91.

Chippendale Furniture. (A. G. Nye) Archit. R. 6: 429.

Chippewa Indians, Protest of the Pillager Tribe. (F. E. Leupp) Forum, 26: 471.

Chiquita ; a story. (A. Bishard) Midland, 10: 521.

Chisholm, David. Bank. M. (Lond.) 64: 543.

Chiswick School of Arts and Crafts. (W. T. Whitley) Art J. 50: 125.

Chitral, A Day's Shoot in. (A. G. A. Durand) Contemp. 73: 84. Same art. Liv. Age, 216: 684.

— Story of a Minor Siege, Robertson's. Bk. Buyer, 18: 137.

— Story of. (Charles Lowe) Cent. 33: 89.

Chittenden, Russell H., with portrait. Pop. Sci. Mo. 53: 115.

Chitty, Lord Justice. Law Q. 15: 128.

Chivalry, Ordinances of, 15th Century, Manuscript Collection of. (H. Arthur) Archæol. 57: 29.

— The Sentiment of ; Burke and Scott. (T. E. Kebbel) Macmil. 76: 299.

Chivers, Thomas Holley, Was Poe a Plagiarist from ? (J. Benton) Forum, 23: 363.

Chlorides, Iron, Volatilization of. (F. A. Gooch and F. S. Havens) Am. J. Sci. 157: 370.

Chloroform, Deaths under. (E. A. King ; D. W. Buxton) 19th Cent. 43: 515, 668, 985. Same art. Ecl. M. 130: 620.

— Impure. (W. Ramsay) 19th Cent. 43: 676.

Choate, Rufus. (N. J. D. Kennedy) Jurid. R. 11: 113.

— (J. H. Choate) Am. Law R. 32: 831.

— Unveiling Statue of, Boston, with portrait. (J. H. Choate) Green Bag, 10: 505.

Chocolate Culture in Nicaragua and Mexico. (R. W. Cater) Chamb. J. 74: 684.

Chohan Bride, The ; a story. (A. S. K. Ghosh) Harper, 102: 772.

Choice, On. (Caroline M. Hills) Am. J. Psychol. 9: 587.

Choice of Atlas ; a poem. Ecl. M. 133: 32.

Choir Stalls and their Carvings, Phipson's. Ath. '97, 2: 70.

Cholera and Plague, Common Salt as a Preventive of. (C. G. Gümpel) Asia. R. 31: 344.

— In the Days of the Chilly Death. (H. Clifford) National, 38: 119. Same art. Liv. Age, 231: 26. Same art. Ecl. M. 137: 681.

— in Siam ; a Christmas Experience. (J. Barrett) Idler, 19: 166.

Cholmondeley, Mary, with portrait. (J. E. Hodder-Williams) Bookman, 12: 32. — Acad. 57: 689.

— Red Pottage. (E. Lyttelton) National, 35: 75.— Acad. 57: 575.

Choosing a Wall-paper ; a story. Idler, 14: 412.

Chopin, Frédéric François. (L. M. Isaacs) Bookman, 11: 526.

— and the Romantics. (J. F. Runciman) Sat. R. 89: 167.

— and Paganini. (H. Marteau) Music, 15: 57.

— as Pianist and Teacher. Music, 14: 632.

— in Scotland. (J. C. Hadden) Scot. R. 33: 94.

— Is he a Classical Composer ? Music, 14: 483.

Chopin, The Man and his Music, Huneker's. (H. T. Finck) Nation, 70: 383.
— Poet and Psychologist. (J. Huneker) Scrib. M. 27: 194.
— Remarks on Sonata Opus 35 by. (E. Liebling) Music, 12: 161.
Chopin, F. F.; a sketch. (A. Quarry) Argosy, 66: 567.
— Three Characteristic Compositions. (Marie Benedict) Music, 12: 317.
Chopin Polonaises. Music, 19: 514.
Chopin Studies; Godowsky's Arrangement. (A. Brune) Music, 17: 397.
Chorals, Old Church. (W. P. Bigelow) Music, 18: 423.
Chorister Boys and their Lives. (F. J. Crowest) Sund. M. 26: 47.
Chorister Girls. (Mabel C. Craft) Nat'l M. (Bost.) 8: 306.
Chorister's Christmas, A; a story. (H. C. Lahee) Nat'l M. (Bost.) 9: 218.
Chorus and Orchestra, Proper Balance of. (Prof. E. Prout) Music, 19: 482.
Chowder. (Phil More) Overland, n. s. 31: 403.
Christ Church, Oxford. (C. M. Blagden) Argosy, 71: 482. 72: 68.
Christ Church Cathedral, Architecture of. (J. H. Ramsay) Ath. '98, 1: 29.
Christ's College, Cambridge, Peile's History of. Ath. '01, 1: 71.
"Christe qui lux est et dies," and its Translations. (Dorothy W. Lyon) Am. J. Philol. 19: 70, 152.
Christendom, Unity and Peril of. (L. B. Halsted) Gunton's M. 19: 150.
Christening of the Muertos; a story. (E. L. Sabin) Midland, 9: 146.
Christian IX., King of Denmark. Chamb. J. 74: 254.
— Portraits of. Strand, 13: 702.
Christian, Prince, of Denmark, with portraits. Strand, 15: 666.
Christian, The; a novel. (H. Caine) Munsey, 16: 417, 595, 657. 17: 97-881. 18: 73-570.
Christian, The Name. (A. Carr) Expos. 3: 538.
Christian Apologetics, Metaphysics of. (W. B. Greene, jr.) Presb. & Ref. R. 9: 60, 261, 472, 659.
Christian Belief, Bases and Origin of, Gardner on. Church Q. 49: 305.
Christian Doctrine, History of, Fisher's. (E. K. Mitchell) Am. Hist. R. 2: 332.
— Newman on the Development of. (H. Williams) Dub. R. 128: 292.
— Principle of. (E. V. Gerhart) Ref. Q. 44: 27.
Christian Dogma and Christian Life. (A. Sabatier) Contemp. 76: 722.
Christian Endeavor Society. (J. W. Spurgeon) Sund. M. 29: 448.
— The "Sectarianism" of. (F. E. Clark) Outl. 67: 122.
— Two Decades of. (F. E. Clark) Indep. 53: 263. — (A. R. Wells) R. of Rs. (N. Y.) 23: 185.
Christian Endeavor Convention, San Francisco, 1897. (A. B. Coffey) Overland, n. s. 30: 179. — Pub. Opin. 23: 113.
Christian Endeavor Movement, Strength and Weakness of. (E. H. Delk) Luth. Q. 37: 276.
Christian Experience, Apologetic Worth of. (W. B. Greene) Meth. R. 61: 756.
— Secret of. (W. R. Nicoll) Chr. Lit. 17: 292, 350.
Christian Figures and Pagan Myths. (W. H. Jewitt) Antiq. n. s. 37: 74-264.
Christian Ideal. (C. A. Allen) New World, 9: 246. — (W. T. Davidson) Lond. Q. 95: 20.
Christian Ideas the Dominant Force in the World. (I. E. Graeft) Ref. Ch. R. 46: 368.
Christian Institutions, Allen's. (E. K. Mitchell) Am. Hist. R. 3: 523.

Christian Life; what the Church Lacks. (C. A. Eaton) Canad. M. 18: 74.
Christian Literature, Early, Harnack's History of. (C. R. Gregory) Am. J. Theol. 2: 598. — (E. C. Richardson) Presb. & Ref. R. 8: 802.
Christian Mysticism. (R. H. Starr) Sewanee R. 9: 30.
Christian Mythology. (J. Weller) Westm. 156: 577.
Christian Nurture. (J. Tomlinson) Luth. Q. 31: 364.
— Nurture of the Unconfirmed. (G. W. McSherry) Luth. Q. 28: 197.
Christian Science. Outl. 68: 524. — (J. B. Willis and A. Farlow) Arena, 25: 593. — (C. S. Mack) N. Church R. 8: 262. — (G. F. Wright) Bib. Sac. 56: 374. — Blackw. 165: 658. — (S. L. Clemens) Cosmopol. 27: 585.
— The Absurd Paradox of. (J. M. Buckley) No. Am. 173: 22.
— against Itself. (M. W. Gifford) Meth. R. 58: 281.
— and the Healing Art. (W. G. Ewing, C. B. Patterson, J. B. Leavitt, and J. W. Winkley) Arena, 25: 1.
— and its Legal Aspects. (W. A. Purrington) No. Am. 168: 345.
— and Liberty. Spec. 81: 681.
— and its Prophetess. (H. W. Dresser; J. C. Woodbury) Arena, 21: 537.
— The Case against. (W. A. Purrington) No. Am. 169: 190.
— Comedy of. (W. H. Mallock) National, 33: 74.
— Founder of. (H. H. Williams) New Eng. M. n. s. 21: 291.
— from a New-church Standpoint. (W. H. Hinkley) N. Church R. 6: 398.
— from a Physician's Point of View. (J. B. Huber) Pop. Sci. Mo. 55: 755.
— Inverted Witchcraft. Spec. 86: 760.
— Metaphysical Healing. Outl. 63: 12, 87.
— Origin of. Blackw. 165: 845.
— Phantom Fortress of. (J. M. Buckley) No. Am. 173: 387.
— Scientific and Christian View of Illness. (J. T. Bixby) New World, 8: 471.
— Simple Logic of. (W. D. McCrackan) No. Am. 173: 232.
— Strength of: a Final Word. (W. D. McCrackan) No. Am. 173: 533.
— Vagaries of. (E. Hawley) Cath. World, 69: 508. See also Mind-cure.
Christian Science View of Sin, The. (A. Farlow) Outl. 68: 745.
Christian Scientist, The. (F. Richardson) Cornh. 83: 381.
Christian Socialism, Encyclical on. (Leo XIII.) Am. Cath. Q. 26: 384.
Christian Unity, The Problem of. Lond. Q. 87: 205.
Christian Work in our Camps. (Anna N. Benjamin) Outl. 59: 566.
Christian Year; a Plea for its Wider Observance. (F. G. Gotwald) Luth. Q. 28: 519.
Christianity and Buddhism, Tiele on. (J. Sandison) Open Court, 11: 129.
— and History. (A. Harnack) Chr. Lit. 17: 425.
— and Idealism. (J. Lindsay) Bib. Sac. 56: 61.
— — Watson on. (C. W. Hodge) Presb. & Ref. R. 8: 541.
— and the Liberal Spirit. Spec. 84: 770.
— and Progress, Mackenzie on. (C. Martin) Presb. & Ref. R. 10: 377.
— and Public Life. (D. S. Cairns) Contemp. 79: 195. 80: 106.
— and Race Evolution. (J. H. Willey) Meth. R. 60: 869.
— and Sanity. (R. Dodge) Meth. R. 61: 883.

Christianity and Social Problems. (Z. S. Holbrook) Bib. Sac. 54: 348.

— and the Transformation of Paganism. (E. Martinengo-Cesaresco) Contemp. 79: 422.

— Are the Churches Christian ? Outl. 61: 720.

— as the Future Religion of India. (P. C. Mozoomdar) New World, 7: 201.

— at the Grave of the 19th Century. (F. Harrison) No. Am. 171: 817.

— Belligerency in. (P. Carus) Open Court, 12: 280.

— The Birth of. (H. Grätz) Open Court, 13: 650.

— The Cross the Final Seat of Authority. (P. T. Forsyth) Contemp. 76: 589.

— The Differentia of. (J. Robson) Contemp. 73: 547. Same art. Liv. Age, 217: 574.

— Distinctive Mark of. (C. C. Everett) New World, 8: 660.

— Early, by L. Pullan. Church Q. 47: 89.

— Elements which contributed to its Birth. Bib. World, 11: 289.

— Feminine Ideal of. (G. Matheson) Bib. World, 12: 29, 90.

— for an Age of Doubt, Van Dyke on. (T. G. Darling) Presb. & Ref. R. 8: 349.

— Foundations of, Richell's. (W. B. Greene, jr.) Presb. & Ref. R. 11: 338.

— Fundamental Ideas of, Caird on. Church Q. 51: 59. — (J. Iverach) Crit. R. 10: 146.

— Future Bias of. Spec. 87: 117.

— The Future of. (H. R. Percival) 19th Cent. 46: 514. — (W. L. Sullivan) Cath. World, 70: 146.

— Harnack's What is ? (T. L. Healy) Cath. World, 73: 377. — (W. A. Brown) Bib. World, 18: 434. — Church Q. 52: 29.

— History and Religion in, Unity of. (C. G. Shaw) Meth. R. 81: 80.

— in Relation to Buddhism, Philosophical Basis of, Eucken on. (P. Carus) Monist, 8: 273.

— in the Sphere of the Practical. (A. E. Truxal) Ref. Ch. R. 47: 182.

— In what Sense a New Creation. Ref. Ch. R. 47: 539.

— Influence of the Social Question on the Genesis of. (F. A. Christie) New World, 8: 299.

— Is it Declining ? (C. A. Briggs) Pop. Sci. Mo. 56: 423.

— Is it fitted to become the World Religion ? (J. H. Barrows) Am. J. Theol. 1: 404.

— Lines of Cleavage in. (J. H. Moulton) Lond. Q. 92: 245.

— Logic of Non-dogmatic. (W. H. Mallock) Fortn. 73: 273.

— Modern. (E. L. Godkin) Nation, 72: 190.

— Modern Evidences of. (C. F. Sanders) Luth. Q. 30: 504.

— not an Evolution. (W. Gifford) Meth. R. 61: 72.

— or Agnosticism, Picard on. Church Q. 49: 380.

— Outlook for. (W. Gladden) No. Am. 172: 919.

— Place of Prophecy in. (F. C. Conybeare) New World, 7: 68.

— Primitive, What was. (W. S. Lilly) 19th Cent. 44: 502.

— a Religion of Growth. Spec. 85: 73. Same art. Liv. Age, 226: 461.

— Root of the Evil. (L. Tolstoy) No. Am. 172: 481.

— Shall it have a Fair Trial in the 20th Century ? (R. F. Bishop) Meth. R. 61: 592.

— Social Spirit of. Spec. 87: 50.

— Spirit of Modern. (C. B. Patterson) Arena, 26: 384.

— Turton on the Truth of. (W. B. Greene, jr.) Presb. & Ref. R. 11: 690.

— Vital and Incidental Elements of. (F. A. Noble) Bib. Sac. 56: 26.

Christianity, Wernle on the Beginnings of. (D. Somerville) Crit. R. 11: 504.

— What is ? (W. Lloyd) Westm. 156: 566.

Christian's Manual of Arms, Rev. ii., iii. (G. H. Gilbert) Bib. World, 9: 269.

Christians vs. Non-Christians. (H. Macfarlane) Sund. M. 28: 775.

Christie, James, the Auctioneer. Acad. 51: 606.

— The House of. Illus. (L. W. Lillingston) Good Words, 38: 743. Same art. Liv. Age, 215: 877.

Christie, Richard Copley, Chancellor. Ath. '01, 1: 81. — Library, n. s. 1: 129.

Christina of Sweden. (A. Laugel) Nation, 68: 374.

Christmas at the Diggins. (J. T. Connor) Overland, n. s. 33: 64.

— A Chat about. (E. H. Young) Canad. M. 12: 166.

— The Fashionable. (A. O'Hagan) Munsey, 22: 344.

— The First Dream of. (J. C. Root) Outl. 69: 1022.

— History of. (F. Conybeare) Am. J. Theol. 3: 1.

— Idylls and Ideals of. (R. G. Ingersoll ; M. J. Savage ; J. W. Riley ; J. C. Ridpath) Arena, 18: 721.

— in the [British] Army. (H. Wyndham) Strand, 18: 754.

— in Clare ; a story. Temp. Bar, 115: 434.

— in Country Houses in England. Sat. R. 88: 793.

— in England, as seen by Cruikshank. (F. Wayne) Nat'l M. (Bost.) 7: 265.

— in Foreign Lands. (E. T. Nash) Chaut. 32: 242.

— in the Forest ; a poem. (A. Coll) Outing, 39: 255.

— in France. (T. Bentzon) Cent. 41: 170. — (F. M. Warren) Chaut. 30: 256.

— in London. (M. Beerbohm) Pall Mall M. 25: 563.

— in Rome. (G. V. Christmas) Cath. World, 70: 341.

— in the Tenements. (J. A. Riis) Cent. 33: 163.

— in Two Lands. (L. D. Ventura) Overland, n. s. 34: 502.

— An Unchristian. Liv. Age, 224: 318.

— under Arms. (N. Malcolm) Blackw. 168: 880.

— with the Children. (Emilie Poulsson) Outl. 60: 770.

— Woman's Sphere at. (W. Cummings) Canad. M. 18: 182.

Christmas with Trapper Lewis ; a tale. (E. W. Sandys) Outing, 29: 376.

Christmas Books of the Past. (Annie R. Marble) Critic, 35: 1122.

Christmas Carols, Ancient and Modern. (Annie R. Marble) Bookman, 14: 355.

— Poems. (N. Hopper) No. Am. 171: 949.

Christmas Customs. (N. Hopper) Eng. Illust. 20: 318.

— of Shakespeare's Greenwood. (G. Morley) Knowl. 21: 268.

Christmas Dancers, a Legend of Saxony ; poem. (E. M. Thomas) Cent. 37: 165.

Christmas Day at Sea. (W. C. Russell) Canad. M. 14: 101.

Christmas Decorations. (A. Vallance) Studio (Lond.) 2: 105.

Christmas Eve ; a poem. (B. Harlowe) Outing, 35: 406.

— at Sandifers — and Elsewhere ; a story. (John Oxenham) Idler, 12: 572.

Christmas Eve Concert ; a tale. (Grant Allen) Canad. M. 12: 140.

Christmas Festivals in Art. (E. Valise) Nat'l M. (Bost.) 13: 151.

Christmas Games in French Canada. (J. M. Oxley) Canad. M. 18: 117.

— of Yesterday. (J. Jeans) Good Words, 40: 820.

Christmas Ghost Story, A ; a poem. (T. Hardy) Outl. 64: 186.

Christmas Gold. (O. Hall) Lippinc. 61: 91.

Christmas Greenery. (C. Middleton) Sund. M. 28: 819.

Christmas Hymn, A. (R. W. Gilder) Outl. 61: 23.

Christmas Incident at Hadley's; a story. (H. Carruth) Nat'l M. (Bost.) 9: 224.

Christmas Island. (S. B. Rand) McClure, 18: 64.

— Description of. (C. W. Andrews) Geog. J. 13: 17.

— Eng. Illust. 20: 629.

Christmas Letter, A. (B. Atkinson) Good Words, 42: 835.

Christmas Loss, A. (H. van Dyke) Scrib. M. 22: 663.

Christmas Message from Ocracoke, A; a tale. (S. B. Kennedy) Outing, 35: 329.

Christmas Midnight in Mexico. (H. W. French) Lippinc. 59: 93.

Christmas Morning in Carolina, A. (F. A. Olds) Outing, 33: 383.

Christmas Music, Roman and Protestant. (J. F. Runciman) Sat. R. 90: 819.

Christmas Numbers, Old and New. Chamb. J. 74: 641.

Christmas Observances, Old German. (H. S. Saroni) Music, 11: 243.

Christmas Peacemaker. (V. Sheard) New Eng. M. n. s. 23: 438.

Christmas Play, An Alpine. (E. Martinengo-Cesaresco) Atlan. 86: 794.

Christmas Roses. (Martin Curtis) Overland, n. s. 38: 411.

Christmas Silhouette, A; a story. (Katharine P. Woods) Bookman, 8: 364.

Christmas Stories of the Saints. (A. F. Brown) Lippinc. 68: 755.

Christmas-tide in Southern India, A. (E. A. Richings) Belgra. 95: 113.

Christological Thinking. (J. I. Swander) Ref. Ch. R. 48: 170.

Christology, Need and Value of. (W. Rupp) Ref. Ch. R. 48: 394.

Christopher Colbeck's Head. (W. E. Cule) Chamb. J. 74: 561-583.

"Christus Victor," A New Cosmic Song. (C. W Hodell) Meth. R. 61: 922.

Christy, Howard Chandler. (R. Armstrong) Bk. Buyer, 19: 166.

Chromite, Occurrence, Origin, and Chemical Composition of. (J. H. Pratt) Am. J. Sci. 157: 281.

Chromo-Xylographs of Henri Rivière. (G. Mourey) Studio (Lond.) 7: 83.

Chromo-Xylography, Recent. (E. Wood) Studio (Internat.) 12: 95.

Chronicles of Aunt Minervy Ann, The. (J. C. Harris) Scrib. M. 25: 175. 26: 433.

Chronicles of Us. (J. W. Tompkins) Munsey, 25: 249. 26: 262.

Chronograph, A New Artillery. Nature, 57: 368.

Chronology, Ancient Oriental, Recent Investigations in. (L. B. Paton) Bib. World, 18: 13.

— Notes on. (R. W. McFarland) Pop. Astron. 4: 353.

— Prehistoric, History of the Week as a Guide to. (J. F. Hewitt) Westm. 148: 8.

— Schmidt's Egyptian. Nature, 63: 581.

— The Year Zero. Open Court, 14: 32.

Chronoscope, Pendulum and Apparatus. (J. A. Bergström) Psychol. R. 7: 483.

— Vernier. (E. C. Sanford) Am. J. Psychol. 9: 183.

— — Improvements in. (E. C. Sanford) Am. J. Psychol. 12: 590.

Chrysanthemum, The. Sat. R. 88: 641. Same art. Liv. Age, 223: 850.

Chrysanthemum Disease, A. (B. T. Galloway) Garden & F. 10: 293.

Chrysanthemums. Sat. R. 88: 641.

Chthonic Gods of Greek Religion. (A. Fairbanks) Am. J. Philol. 21: 214.

Chuar's Illusion; a philosophical sketch. (J. W. Powell) Open Court, 12: 577.

Chuckie; the Story of a Waif. (B. Kelly) Canad. M. 15: 78.

Chukchi Tribe of N. E. Asia. (W. Bogoras) Am. Anthrop. 3: 80.

Chummie; a Tale of Two Friends. (D. H. Nourse) Overland, n. s. 35: 77.

Chung's Baby. (Phil More) Overland, n. s. 31: 233.

Church, Richard William. Acad. 51: 274.

— Occasional Papers. (P. F. Bicknell) Dial (Ch.) 22: 360.

Church, The. (D. T. Fiske) Bib. Sac. 57: 255.

— and Educational Problems. (T. W. Dickert) Ref. Ch. R. 47: 505.

— and the Masses. Ref. Q. 44: 127. — (T. S. Lonergan) Arena, 20: 217. — Liv. Age, 218: 886.

— and Social Life. (S. Z. Beam) Ref. Ch. R. 46: 334.

— and the Social Problem. (A. W. Small) Indep. 53: 480, 537. — (E. G. Miller) Luth. Q. 31: 255, 385.

— and Social Unity. (S. Mathews) Am. J. Sociol. 5: 456.

— and Society. (J. C. Jackson) Meth. R. 61: 9.

— and State. (L. Tolstoy) Arena, 22: 541. — Am. Cath. Q. 22: 98.

— — in American Law. (P. Webster) Am. Law R. 32: 529.

— and the Workingman. Outl. 65: 432.

— as a Profession. (D. Macleane) National, 33: 945.

— as related to Outward Social Reform. (S. C. Ely) N. Church R. 4: 464.

— at Antioch. (J. M. Stifler) Bib. Sac. 57: 645.

— Attitude of the, towards Things not Seen. (J. B. Leavitt) Arena, 25: 161.

— Christian Ecclesia, by F. J. A. Hort. Church Q. 45: 312.

— The Civic. (P. Tyner) Arena, 17: 371.

— The Country. (S. G. Tallentyre) Macmil. 77: 138.

— — in America. (W. B. Bigelow) Scrib. M. 22: 601.

— Democracy, and Socialism, Hirsch on. Church Q. 52: 455.

— Expansion of. (T. F. Wright) N. Church R. 7: 439.

— Hurst's History of. (H. M. Scott) Presb. & Ref. R. 12: 153.

— in America. (S. D. McConnell) Chr. Lit. 16: 416.

— in City Politics, Power of the. (B. S. Coler) Outl. 63: 634.

— in the Large Town. (J. C. Cady) Outl. 65: 59.

— in Modern Society. (S. D. McConnell) Outl. 58: 177.

— in the Village, The. Spec. 83: 439. Same art. Ecl. M. 134: 270. Same art. Liv. Age, 224: 51.

— Institutional. (C. Clever) Ref. Ch. R. 47: 493.

— Lawlessness in the. Fortn. 71: 623.

— Mind of the. Month, 96: 125, 233.

— National, Unity of Spirit as the Basis of a. (R. A. Bray) Internat. J. Ethics, 11: 424.

— New Testament Doctrine of. (C. A. Briggs) Am. J. Theol. 4: 1.

— not an Institution, but an Organism. Ref. Ch. R. 45: 387.

— of England. (C. W. Colby) Nation, 71: 290.

— — Agnostic on the Church Question. Westm. 151: 75.

— — and the Liberal Party. (C. F. Garbett) Westm. 148: 413.

— — Anglican Compromise. (H. G. Wintersgill) Westm. 152: 194.

— — as by Law established. (E. Robertson) 19th Cent. 45: 733. — (J. H. Round) Contemp. 75: 814. — (Malcolm McColl; J. Horace Round) Contemp. 76: 220.

— — Benefices Act. (Lord Fortescue) 19th Cent. 44: 545.

Cicero, Letters of; Shuckburgh's Translation. Acad.
58: 7.

— Letters to Atticus; MS. in Brit. Museum. (S. B.
Platner) Am. J. Philol. 20: 292.

— — MSS. in Vatican. (S. B. Platner) Am. J. Philol.
21: 420.

— Select Orations of, Greenough and Kittredge's. (J.
W. Scudder) School R. 6: 49. — (J. E. Granrud)
Educa. 18: 310.

Cider Industry in France and England. (C. W. R.
Cooke) 19th Cent. 50: 276.

Cienfuegos, Cable Cutting at. (C. M. Winslow) Cent.
35: 708.

Cigar, My. (N. Amarga) Temp. Bar, 114: 589.

Cigarettes and Cigarette-making. Chamb. J. 76: 55.

Cilurnum, Roman Station at, Forum of. (J. C. Bruce)
Archæol. 46: 1.

Cincinnati, Ohio. Bank. M. (N. Y.) 60: 919.

— American Art Exhibition. Brush & P. 6: 180.

— Art Club. (E. S. Butler, jr.) Brush & P. 6: 72.

— 1802–14, Carter Family in. (C. E. Cabot) New Eng.
M. n. s. 20: 344.

Cinematograph, The. (J. Fuerst) J. Soc. Arts, 46: 255.

— Future of the. (Mrs. J. E. Whitby) Chamb. J. 77:
391.

Cinerary Urns from Stanton Moor. (J. Ward) Reliquary, 40: 25.

Cinque Ports. Blackw. 168: 711.

Cinquevalli, Paul, the Juggler. (W. G. Fitzgerald)
Strand, 13: 92.

Cipher Dispatch, A Rebel. (D. H. Bates) Harper, 97:
105.

Ciphers. (G. E. Moysey) Gent. M. n. s. 65: 365.

Circassia, The Coast of. Un. Serv. M. 21: 298.

Circero, Monte. (Alicia C. Taylor) Art J. 52: 240.

Circle, Squaring the. Temp. Bar, 120: 552.

— Traveling in a; a peculiar instinct. Chamb. J. 78:
44.

Circle of Death. (G. D. Wetherbee) Atlan. 86: 253.

Circuit Courts in England. (L. Irwell) Green Bag, 12:
593.

Circuit System, A Plea for the. (W. Grantham) 19th
Cent. 50: 964.

Circulating Medium of the United States. Bank M.
(N. Y.) 60: 545.

Circumflex, The. (Will T. Whitlock) Overland, n. s.
33: 348.

Circumpolar Variables, Northern. (J. A. Parkhurst)
Pop. Astron. 4: 369, 419.

Circumstances; a story. (A. Cahan) Cosmopol. 22: 628.

Circumstances, Victims of. (Donald N. Reid) Gent.
M. n. s. 58: 581.

Circus, The. (E. V. Lucas) Cornh. 84: 543. Same art.
Liv. Age, 231: 439.

— What the Public does not see at the. (A. T. Ring-
ling) Nat'l M. (Bost.) 12: 189.

Circus, The; a story. (E. Nesbit) Pall Mall M. 22:
324.

Circus at Sea, The. (C. T. Murray) McClure, 11: 76.

Circus Life. (C. T. Murray) Cosmopol. 29: 115.

Cited, The. (G. H. Westley) Green Bag, 13: 486.

Cited, The; a legend of Havana. (C. M. Skinner) Lippinc. 64: 149.

Cities, American, Amalgamation in Some. Ann. Am.
Acad. Pol. Sci. 16: 482.

— — and their Influence on Men's Character. (R. Bergengren) Nat'l M. (Bost.) 10: 229.

— — Development of. (J. Quincy) Arena, 17: 529.

— — Shall they Municipalize? (J. G. Agar) Munic.
Aff. 4: 13.

— — The Trend in. [Contemp.] Liv. Age, 224: 73.

— Are the Bosses Stronger than the People? (S. J. B.
Bishop) Cent. 32: 465.

Cities, Art and Architecture in. (M. M. Miller) Munic.
Aff. 1: 552.

— Beautifying. (C. H. Coffin) World's Work, 3: 1429.

— Bibliography of Conditions and Problems. (R. C.
Brooks) Munic. Aff. 5: 1.

— Finances of. (F. W. Hirst) Econ. J. 9: 384.

— Franchises of, Value and Taxation of. (L. Meriwether) Outl. 58: 920.

— Government of, American Political Ideas and Institutions relating to. (L. S. Rowe) Munic. Aff. 1: 317.

— — Borough System in. (E. Kelly) Forum, 27: 61.

— — by Taxpayers. Munic. Aff. 3: 395.

— — Council Government vs. Mayor Government.
(E. D. Durand) Pol. Sci. Q. 15: 426, 675.

— — English. (Elsie Watson) Pol. Sci. Q. 16: 262.

— — in Canada. (S. M. Wickett) Canad. M. 18: 54. —
(S. M. Wickett) Pol. Sci. Q. 15: 240.

— — in Germany. (E. J. James) Am. J. Sociol. 7: 29.

— — Lectures on the Principles of Local Government,
Gomme's. (E. Canaan) Econ. R. 8: 256.

— — Non-partisan Government in Cambridge, Mass.
(F. J. Douglas) Outl. 58: 963.

— — Non-partisanship in, Is it Feasible? (R. P.
Flower). Mayor Strong's Experiment in N. Y. (F.
D. Pavey) Forum, 23: 531, 539.

— — Party Government in the Cities of New York
State. (D. F. Wilcox) Pol. Sci. Q. 14: 681.

— — Peculiarities of American. (E. L. Godkin) Atlan. 80: 620.

— — Political Parties and. (F. J. Goodhow) Internat.
Mo. 1: 618.

— — Reform in. (W. L. Strong) Gunton's M. 13: 327.

— — — Contract by Referendum. (H. S. Pingree)
Arena, 17: 707.

— — Responsibility in. (J. H. Hyslop) Forum, 28: 469.

— Great, Growth of. (R. S. Tracy) Cent. 33: 79.

— Growth of. (E. J. James) Ann. Am. Acad. Pol. Sci.
13: 1.

— — 1890–1900. (Adna F. Weber) Munic. Aff. 5: 367.

— — in the 19th Century, Weber's. (W. F. Willcox)
Am. Hist. R. 5: 349.

— — Political Consequences of. (L. S. Rowe) Yale R.
9: 20.

— — Social Consequences of. (L. S. Rowe) Yale R.
10: 298.

— in Future, to owe much of their Importance to
Water Power. (E. H. Mullin) Cassier, 13: 27.

— A Model, for the Louisiana Purchase Exposition.
(W. S. Crandall) Munic. Aff. 5: 670.

— Municipal Coöperation vs. Municipal Consolidation.
(M. N. Baker) Munic. Aff. 3: 18.

— Municipal Corporations, Liability of, as upon Im-
plied Contracts. (S. D. Thompson) Am. Law R.
33: 707.

— Municipal Expansion. (S. M. Jones) Arena, 21: 766.

— Municipal Experiments, Recent. Gunton's M. 15:
116.

— Municipal Junketing. Nation, 67: 92.

— Municipal Reforms, Practical. Gunton's M. 16: 388.

— Municipal Statistical Offices in Europe. (E. M.
Hartwell) Munic. Aff. 1: 525.

— Municipal Trading. (W. Bond) Fortn. 72: 669.

— of the Future. (J. B. Walker) Cosmopol. 31: 473.

— of Prussia, Three-class Election System in. (R. C.
Brooks) Munic. Aff. 3: 396.

— of the World; poem. (W. P. Foster) Atlan. 87: 401.

— Overcrowding in, and the Remedy. (A. F. W. Ingraham) Cosmopol. 32: 85.

— Plans for. (J. F. Harder) Munic. Aff. 2: 25.

— Plant Decoration for. (Katharine C. Budd) Munic.
Aff. 5: 684.

— Problem of the 20th Century City. (J. Strong) No.
Am. 165: 343.

Civil Service Orders, Shall they be amended? (G. B. Rawn) No. Am. 165: 174.

Civil Service Pensions. (D. MacG. Means) Nation, 70: 452.

Civil Service Reform. (L. J. Gage) Munsey, 19: 171.

— Crisis of. (H. T. Newcomb) No. Am. 166: 196.

— Is it in Peril? (J. F. Johnson) No. Am. 169: 678.

Civil Service Reform League, A Reply to. (L. J. Gage) Indep. 51: 1919.

Civil Service Supply Association, London. (R. W. Johnston) Chamb. J. 76: 6.

Civilian-ridden Nation, A. Un. Serv. M. 22: 584.

Civilization, American, Foreign Element in. (A. H. Hyde) Pop. Sci. Mo. 52: 387.

— and Decay, Adams on Law of. (T. Roosevelt) Forum, 22: 575.

— and the Ethical Standard. (C. W. Super) Am. Antiq. 22: 358.

— and Murder. Spec. 79: 592.

— and the Social Compact. (J. Dowd) Arena, 23: 284.

— The Cradle of. (F. Legge) Acad. 55: 379. Same art. Liv. Age, 220: 200.

— Cunningham on Western. (B. Perrin) Am. Hist. R. 4: 135.

— Diffusion of. (U. A. Forbes) Lond. Q. 92: 338.

— Enemies of. (D. MacG. Means) Nation, 71: 125.

— Laying the Foundations for a Higher. (B. O. Flower) Arena, 25: 172.

— On being Civilized too much. (H. C. Merwin) Atlan. 79: 838.

— Propaganda of. (J. R. MacDonald) Internat. J. Ethics, 11: 455.

— Transit of, from England to America, in the 17th Century, Eggleston's. (B. Wendell) Am. Hist. R. 6: 802.

— Western, Cunningham's. (L. L. Price) Econ. J. 11: 48. — (E. A. Barnett) Econ. R. 11: 379.

— What is. (C. M. Beaumont) Westm. 156: 326.

— The "White Man's Burden." Ecl. M. 132: 619.

Civita Lavinia, Antiquarian Researches at. (J. S. Lumley) Archæol. 49: 367.

Clachans of Lewis. (H. W. Williams) Reliquary, 40: 73.

Cladocera, Some Manitoba. (L. S. Ross) Am. Natural. 31: 293.

Claim that took Dorlesky, The; a story. (May B. Brown) Nat'l M. (Bost.) 8: 123.

Clair de Lune; poem. (A. Ketchum) Atlan. 88: 134.

Clangs, Discrimination of, for Different Intervals of Time. (F. Angell) Am. J. Psychol. 12: 58.

Clans, Highland, in the Law of Scotland. (J. Bartholomew) Jurid. R. 13: 205, 307.

Clapp, Henry Austin. Reminiscences of a Dramatic Critic. Atlan. 88: 155–622.

Clara's Vocation. (G. F. Jones) Scrib. M. 29: 720.

Clare, St., of Rimini. (J. Winn) Argosy, 69: 186.

Clare Westwood's Brother; a story. (C. N. Carvalho) Argosy, 66: 189.

Clarendon Press, The. (A. Clifford) Sund. M. 28: 598.

— Story of. (F. J. Snell) Antiq. n. s. 37: 137.

Clark, Alvan; the American Lens Maker, with portrait. Nat'l M. (Bost.) 11: 184.

Clark, Alvan Graham. Science, 56: 158.

Clark, Capt., and the Oregon; a poem. (N. A. Hamilton) Overland, n. s. 32: 545.

Clark, George, Sr., and Clark, George, Jr., of Milford, Conn., and their Descendants. (R. D. Smyth) N. E. Reg. 54: 384.

Clark, James, Artist. (A. L. Baldry) Studio (Internat.) 5: 153.

Clark, James G., the American Laureate of Labor. (B. O. Flower) Arena, 19: 54.

Clark, John B.; an American Economist. (F. A. Fetter) Internat. Mo. 4: 127.

Clark, Walter Appleton. (J. Hambidge) Bk. Buyer, 18: 211.

Clark University, Decennial of. Outl. 64: 921.

Clarke, Charles Cowden and Mary Cowden. (Mrs. J. T. Fields) Cent. 36: 122.

Clarke, Charles W., Baritone Singer, with portrait. Music, 17: 164.

Clarke, James Greville. Ath. '01, 2: 156.

Clarke, Frank Wigglesworth, Sketch of. Pop. Sci. Mo. 54: 110.

Clarke, Fred. H., Pianist. (W. S. B. Mathews) Music, 18: 480.

Clarke, Hugh A. Elements of Vocal Harmony. Music, 18: 610.

Clarke, Richard Frederick. Month, 96: 337.

Clarke Thos. B., Collection of Pictures by American Painters. Artist (N. Y.) 24: xxx. — Outl. 61: 392.

Clarke, Thomas Shields, Artist, with portrait. (A. Holber) Brush & P. 6: 193.

Clarkson, Ralph, Artist, with portrait. (C. F. Browne) Brush & P. 1: 95.

Clarksville Conventions, 1785, 1787. (C. E. Bond) Am. Hist. R. 2: 691.

Clasen, Jacob, Spanking of. (L. M. Friedman) Green Bag, 13: 271.

Class Distinctions. Spec. 79: 819.

Class Meeting in Methodism. (J. H. Vincent) Meth. R. 61: 681.

Classic in Literature, The. Permanence of its Power to Please. (L. Johnson) Acad. 59: 574.

Classical Archæology a New Force in Classical Studies. (J. H. Huddilston) Book R. 6: 182.

Classical Culture, True Spirit of. (A. F. West) School R. 6: 630.

Classical Conference, Proceedings of, held at Ann Arbor, Michigan, 1898. (F. W. Kelsey) School R. 6: 424.

— Proceedings of, 1899. (J. H. Harris) School R. 7: 321.

— — 1900. (J. H. Harris) School R. 8: 313.

Classical Dictionary, Harper's. (C. W. Bain) Sewanee, 5: 367.

Classical Education in the Secondary Schools. (A. Fairbanks) School R. 5: 350.

Classical Languages in Education. (J. H. Stough) Luth. Q. 37: 33.

Classical Orders, How to treat the. (R. Sturgis) Archit. R. 6: 59.

Classical Programmes for Secondary Schools, Selective Bibliography for Use in Framing. (I. B. Burgess) School R. 5: 625.

Classical Studies in Germany, Recent. (C. W. Bain) Sewanee, 6: 74.

Classical Verse-writing, Decline of. (J. B. Bury) Sat. R. 83: 375.

Classicism in Literature. Acad. 57: 760.

Classics at Jimpti's Run; a story. (R. Rodgers) Nat'l M. (Bost.) 11: 35.

— Educational Value of. (E. W. Bowen) Luth. Q. 30: 18.

— How to make their Study more Interesting to College Students. (H. E. Burton) Educa. R. 18: 298.

— Ideal Method of Instruction in. (F. W. Coburn) Educa. 19: 497.

— Imagination in the Study of. (G. Lodge) Educa. R. 22: 162.

— in Education. (A. W. Ready) Macmil. 84: 218.

— Latin and Greek Conference, Ann Arbor, Mich., 1897, Report of the Proceedings of. (J. H. Harris) School R. 5: 605.

Classics, Latin and Greek *vs.* French and German. (T. M. Hopkins) Westm. **148**: 564. Same art. Ecl. M. **130**: 50.
— Rational Study of. (I. Babbett) Atlan. **79**: 355.
— Should they be required for the Degree of A. B.? (J. J. Stevenson) Science, n. s. **11**: 801.
— Study of, Blot on. Spec. **86**: 910.
— Undergraduate Interest in. (A. Z. Reed) Harv. Grad. M. **7**: 20.
— Vitality of. Harv. Grad. M. **5**: 525.
Classification, Dewey Notation and. (T. W. Lyster) Library, **8**: 482.
— of Books. (E. C. Richardson) Lib. J. **26**: 124.
— — in the Natural Sciences. (J. W. H. Trail) Library, **6**: 13.
— of the Sciences. (J. W. Powell) Am. Anthropol. **3**: 601.
Claus, Emile, Artist, with portrait. (G. Mourey) Studio (Internat.) **8**: 143.
— Painter of the Leieland. (P. De Mont) Artist (N. Y.) **25**: 169.
Clausen, George. (D. Bates) Studio (Lond.) **5**: 3.
— End of a Long Day. Art J. **50**: 149.
Clay, Henry, Portraits of, with Notes by C. H. Hart. McClure, **9**: 939.
Clays of New York, Ries's. (J. F. Kemp) Science, n. s. **13**: 946.
Clayton-Bulwer Treaty, The. (M. W. Hazeltine) No. Am. **165**: 452. — (J. W. Foster) Indep. **53**: 1167. — (E. Berwick) Arena, **23**: 464.
— and Hay-Pauncefote Treaty. (H. W. Rogers) Forum, **29**: 355.
— Dispute over. (A. G. Sedgwick) Nation, **67**: 218. Nation, **67**: 478.
— History of, I. D. Travis's. (J. B. Moore) Am. Hist. R. **6**: 150.
— Letters on, 1849, 1850. Am. Hist. R. **5**: 95.
— Proposed Abandonment of. Sat. R. **89**: 161.
— Story of. (B. Taylor) 19th Cent. **47**: 498.
— Terms and Tenor of. (L. M. Keasbey) Ann. Am. Acad. Pol. Sci. **14**: 285.
— Text of. R. of Rs. (N. Y.) **21**: 330.
Clayton Hall, Manchester. Ath. '00, **1**: 505.
Cleanliness; next to Godliness. (J. F. Fraser) Chamb. J. **76**: 305.
— Sentiment of. Sat. R. **91**: 201.
Clear Title, A. (J. W. Piercy) Atlan. **85**: 237.
Clearing-House, The. Bank. M. (N. Y.) **58**: 226, 594.
— Through the. (J. S. Metcalfe) Munsey, **16**: 672.
— Work of the. (H. White) Nation, **73**: 277.
Clearing-house Loan Certificates. (C. E. Curtis) Yale R. **6**: 251.
Clearing-houses, Cannon on. (N. D. Noyes) Nation, **71**: 354. — (F. W. Gookin) Dial (Ch.) **30**: 15.
Clearness in Thinking and Speaking. (J. M. Greenwood) Educa. **19**: 266.
Cleary, Kate M. Writer, **14**: 154.
Cleavage in Ancylus, Reversal of. (S. J. Holmes) Am. Natural. **33**: 87.
Clematis; a story from the Chinese. (R. K. Douglas) Good Words, **38**: 115, 173. Same art. Liv. Age, **212**: 899. **213**: 51.
Clemens, Samuel L. (R. Barr) McClure, **10**: 246. Same art. Idler, **13**: 23. — With portraits. (C. Smythe) Pall Mall M. **16**: 29. — Acad. **51**: 653. — (D. C. Murray) Canad. M. **9**: 498. — With portrait. R. of Rs. (N. Y.) **23**: 37.
— American Humour. (A. E. Keeling) Lond. Q. **92**: 147.
— as an Educator. (C. J. France) Educa. **21**: 265.
— as an Interpreter of American Character. With portrait. (S. E. Moffett) McClure, **13**: 523. — (C. M. Thompson) Atlan. **79**: 443.

Clemens, Samuel L., First Books of. (L. S. Livingston) Bookman, **8**: 563.
— in California. (N. Brooks) Cent. **35**: 97.
— Mark Twain: an inquiry. (W. D. Howells) No. Am. **172**: 306.
— Mark Twain and his Work. (B. Matthews) Bk. Buyer, **13**: 977.
— Mark Twain as Prospective Classic. (T. De Laguna) Overland, n. s. **31**: 364.
— Mark Twain's Place in Literature. (D. Masters) Chaut. **25**: 610.
— More than Humorist. (R. E. Phillips) Bk. Buyer, **22**: 196.
— My Debut as a Literary Person. Cent. **37**: 76.
— Portrait of. Bk. Buyer, **22**: 178.
Clement, St., of Rome, Bishops and Presbyters in the Epistle of. (J. H. Bernard) Expos. **10**: 39.
Clement XIV., Pope, Letters of. (E. L. Taunton) Cath. World, **69**: 224.
Clementina, Wife of James Stuart, the Pretender. (A. Shield) Dub. R. **122**: 291.
Cleopatra's Mummy, To; a poem. (M. G. Dickinson) Atlan. **81**: 365.
Cleopatra's Needle, Story of. (S. Esplen) Strand, **17**: 135.
Clergy and Artists' Association, Work of. (F. Miller) Art J. **50**: 110.
— and the Laity. (A. Jessopp) 19th Cent. **44**: 749.
— and Modern Life. (C. Brainerd, jr.) Bib. Sac. **55**: 730.
— and the Social Problem. (G. Tyrrell) Am. Cath. Q. **22**: 151.
— and the Teaching of Ethics. (M. G. Hering) Westm. **156**: 335.
— and the War. (N. Twycross) Westm. **154**: 256. — (E. L. Godkin) Nation, **71**: 266.
— Condition of, Gladstone on. Spec. **78**: 654.
— Deprivation of, in Elizabeth's Reign. (H. N. Birt) Dub. R. **126**: 25, 313.
— English, in Fiction. (C. F. Yonge) Gent. M. n. s. **59**: 40. Same art. Liv. Age, **214**: 600.
— — Poverty of. (H. C. Beeching) Cornh. **76**: 15.
— — Taxation of. Contemp. **75**: 323. — (A. G. Boscawen) National, **30**: 878. — (D. J. Davies) Econ. J. **8**: 127.
— in American Life and Letters, Addison's. (B. Wendell) Am. Hist. R. **6**: 576.
— Militant. (E. L. Godkin) Nation, **71**: 484.
— Notable Sons of. (W. J. Ferrar) Sund. M. **28**: 183.
— Pastoral Duties of. (P. B. Cabell) N. Church R. **6**: 380.
— Poverty of, Problem of. Spec. **80**: 815.
— Why are they Unpopular? Westm. **148**: 84.
Clergyman, Can he be a "Good Fellow"? Atlan. **81**: 575.
— True Duties of a. (T. S. Harris) N. Church R. **6**: 571.
Clergyman's Callers, A. Indep. **53**: 3068.
Clergymen, Bellicose. Liv. Age, **217**: 620.
— Jokes on. Chamb. J. **78**: 107.
— A Layman's Advice to. (Frank E. Sickels) Outl. **63**: 923.
— Pastors of the Last Century. Temp. Bar, **110**: 128.
Clerical and Lay Workers. Spec. **79**: 332.
Clerical Comedy; a story. (W. A. Gill) Cosmopol. **29**: 305.
Clerical Fixtures. (G. R. Vicars) Westm. **148**: 510.
Clerical Life, Humorous Side of. (S. F. L. Bernays) Cornh. **76**: 664, 805. **78**: 685. Same art. Ecl. M. **130**: 73, 186. **132**: 182. Same art. Liv. Age, **216**: 182.
Clerical Reaction in Europe. (G. Fiamingo) Open Court, **12**: 730.

Clerical Recollections. (A. Church) Sund. M. 29: 217, 331, 410.

Clerk, The; a study in poverty. (J. de R.) Argosy, 73: 350.

Clerkenwell, Open Lending Library. Library, 6: 344.
— — Working of. (J. D. Brown) Library, 5: 109.
— Priories of St. Mary and of St. John. (J. H. Round) Archæol. 56: 223.
— St. John's Church at. Am. Arch. 55: 54. — (H. T. Peck) Bookman, 5: 110.

Cleveland, Grover. (E. P. Clark) National, 29: 84.
— and the Senate. (J. Schouler) Forum, 23: 65.
— as President. (W. Wilson) Atlan. 79: 289.
— Last Message of. Gunton's M. 12: 1.
— Presidency of. (A. G. Sedgwick) Nation, 64: 156.
— Second Administration of. (C. Schurz) McClure, 9: 633.

Cleveland, Ohio. Bank. M. (N. Y.) 59: 473.
— Street Railway Franchises. Ann. Am. Acad. Pol. Sci. 14: 380.
— East, a Model Suburban Village. (C. E. Bolton) R. of Rs. (N. Y.) 20: 573.
— Schools of. (E. L. Harris) Educa. 20: 327.

Clever Mick Moriarty; a story. (C. K. Burrows) Macmil. 78: 274.

Clicks and Flashes, On nearly Simultaneous. (G. M. Whipple) Am. J. Psychol. 10: 280.

Cliefden Christmasse Tale, A. (W. W. Astor) Pall Mall M. 16: 466.

Cliefden Lights and Shades. (W. W. Astor) Pall Mall M. 21: 517.

Cliff Climbing and Egg Hunting. (L. S. Lewis) Strand, 13: 225.

Cliff-dwellers, Agriculture among. (S. D. Peet) Am. Antiq. 21: 209.
— and Pueblos, Age of. (S. D. Peet) Am. Antiq. 19: 100.
— — Peet's. Nation, 71: 233.
— and the Wild Tribes. (S. D. Peet) Am. Antiq. 21: 349.
— Cliff Palace of. (S. D. Peet) Am. Antiq. 20: 19.
— Great Houses and Fortresses of. (S. D. Peet) Am. Antiq. 20: 315.
— Relics of. (S. D. Peet) Am. Antiq. 21: 99.
— Religious Life and Works of. (S. D. Peet) Am. Antiq. 20: 275.
— Social and Domestic Life of. (S. D. Peet) Am. Antiq. 21: 17.

Cliff-dweller's Sandal. (O. T. Mason) Pop. Sci. Mo. 50: 676.

Cliff-dwellings and Caves compared. (S. D. Peet) Am. Antiq. 20: 193.

Cliff Fortresses. (S. D. Peet) Am. Antiq. 20: 81.

Clifford, H., East Coast Etchings. Macmil. 75: 258.

Climate and the Atmosphere. (J. M. Bacon) 19th Cent. 47: 94.
— and Character. Spec. 80: 194. Same art. Ecl. M. 130: 687.

Climate and Crops, Relations between. Nature, 64: 493.
— Recent Researches on. (H. N. Dickson) Geog. J. 10: 303.

Climatology as distinguished from Meteorology. (M. Whitney) Science, n. s. 7: 113.
— Handbook of Medical, Solly's. (E. H. Mullin) Bk. Buyer, 17: 49.

Climax, Advertising the. Atlan. 84: 142.
— in Tragedy, On. (L. Campbell) Fortn. 74: 83.

Clinohedrite. (S. L. Penfield and H. W. Foote) Am. J. Sci. 155: 289.

Clinton, Henry Laurens, with portrait. Green Bag, 10: 133.

Clinton & Russell, Architects, Work of. (R. Sturgis) Archit. R. 7: (no. 2) 1.

Clinton, New York. (E. P. Powell) New Eng. M. n. s. 23: 657.

Clitherall, Dr. James, Extracts from the Diary of, 1776. Pennsyl. M. 22: 469.

Clive, Lord Robert, and British India, Arbuthnot's. Sat. R. 87: 405.

Cliveden House, England. (Marquis of Lorne) Pall Mall M. 12: 436.

Clock, The Great Northern, London. (F. J. Crowest) Good Words, 38: 54.
— of Philadelphia City Hall. (W. S. Johnson) J. Frankl. Inst. 151: 81.

Clocks at Buckingham Palace. (F. S. Robinson) M. of Art, 24: 204.
— Carillons and Bells. (A. A. Johnston) Am. Arch. 73: 20, 28. Same art. J. Soc. Arts, 49: 359.
— Decorative, at Windsor Castle. (F. S. Robinson) M. of Art, 21: 177.
— Water, B. C. and A. D. (G. C. Nuttall) Gent. M. n. s. 59: 59.

Clogston Family of New Hampshire. (W. H. Harwood) N. E. Reg. 52: 25.

Cloister, An Abandoned. (W. H. Richardson) Outl. 63: 357.

Cloister Lily, A. Macmil. 82: 375.

Close-time Curate, The; a poem. Ecl. M. 134: 209.

Cloth Trade in North of England in 16th and 17th Centuries. (B. Hewart) Econ. J. 10: 20.

Clothes, Concerning. (E. V. Lucas) Cornh. 76: 792. Same art. Ecl. M. 130: 92.

Clothing, Psychology of Modesty and. (W. I. Thomas) Am. J. Sociol. 5: 246.

Cloud that passed. (A. H. Stirling) Longm. 30: 316.

Clouds. (F. Bate) Studio (Lond.) 3: 184. — (J. Quick) Knowl. 22: 103. — (E. M. Antoniadi; G. Mathieu) Knowl. 22: 202.
— International Cloud Work of the Weather Bureau. (F. H. Bigelow) Nat. Geog. M. 10: 351.
— — for the United States, Results of. (F. H. Bigelow) Am. J. Sci. 158: 433.
— Photographic Observation of. Nature, 55: 322.
— Photography of. (E. Antoniadi) Knowl. 23: 79, 107.
— Wave or Billow. Nature, 60: 235.

Clough, Anne Jemima, Memoir of. (M. A. Scott) Dial (Ch.) 24: 110.

Clough, Arthur Hugh. (F. R. Statham) National, 29: 200. Same art. Ecl. M. 128: 743. Same art. Liv. Age, 213: 857. — (T. Arnold) 19th Cent. 43: 105. Same art. Ecl. M. 130: 358. Same art. Liv. Age, 216: 382.
— and English Hexameters. Acad. 52: 260.
— Arnold and Newman. (R. A. Armstrong) Liv. Age, 219: 67.

Clouston, E. S., and Bank of Montreal. Canad. M. 12: 434.

Clouston, W. A. Folk-Lore, 8: 94.

Clover and Heartsease. (Mrs. B. Bosanquet) Cornh. 81: 358.

Clovers, Methods of Fertilization and Reproduction of. (Grant Allen) Strand, 14: 588.

Clowes, Rev. John, Non-separatist. (T. F. Wright) N. Church R. 8: 161.

Club, A, in being. (H. G. D. Latham) Cornh. 84: 645.

Club of Old Stories. Atlan. 81: 854.

Clubs and Club Life in New York. (R. Stewart) Munsey, 22: 105.
— London. (J. Forster) Chaut. 27: 553.
— Odd. (L. Monroe) Lippinc. 67: 110.
— Sportsmen's, of the Middle West. (L. Hubbard, jr.) Outing, 37: 446.
— A Social Want. (W. D. Kempton) Cosmopol. 24: 392.
— Village, and Mediæval Guilds. Gent. M. n. s. 58: 549.

Coccidæ of Ceylon. (T. D. A. Cockerell) Am. Natural. **31**: 701.
— Sources of Error in Recent Works on. (C. L. Marlatt) Science, n. s. **9**: 835. — Reply (T. D. A. Cockerell) **10**: 86. — (C. L. Marlatt) Science, n. s. **10**: 657.
Coccidology, Contributions to. (T. D. A. Cockerell) Am. Natural. **31**: 588.
Coccospheres and Rhabdospheres. (G. Murray and V. H. Blackman) Nature, **55**: 510.
Cochran-Patrick, R. W. Scot. R. **31**: 106.
Cochrane, Lord. *See* Dundonald, Lord.
Cochrane Redivivus. (P. Vaux) Cornh. **84**: 468.
Cockling at Morecambe Bay. (A. M. Wakefield) Pall Mall M. **16**: 130.
Cocks, Game, and Cock-fighting. Outing, **39**: 347.
Cocoa and its Adulteration. (Prof. Carmody) Chamb. J. **76**: 38.
Cocoanut, Samoan. (J. H. Mulligan) Nat. Geog. M. **9**: 12.
Cocoanut Culture in Japan. J. Soc. Arts, **45**: 476.
Cocoanut Plantation in Mosquito. (R. W. Cater) Chamb. J. **74**: 229.
Cocos-Keeling Islands. (A. Penne) Temp. Bar, **113**: 226. Same art. Ecl. M. **130**: 492. — Eng. Illust. **20**: 629. — Chamb. J. **76**: 187.
Cocos Nucifera, Anatomy of the Fruit of. (A. L. Winton) Am. J. Sci. **162**: 265.
Cod, Cape, and its People. (D. Webster) New Eng. M. n. s. **17**: 323.
Codding of Two Codgers, The; a story. (W. Packard) Nat'l M. (Bost.) **7**: 353.
Code of the Corps. (C. King) Lippinc. **67**: 337.
Coeducation. (J. Ablett) Westm. **153**: 25. — (H. Whiskin) Westm. **153**: 458.
— in Secondary Schools and Colleges. (M. W. Sewall) Arena, **17**: 767.
Coercion. (D. J. Brewer) Am. Arch. **70**: 35. — (H. Seal) Westm. **148**: 297.
— Spiritual. (J. K. Smyth) N. Church R. **4**: 112.
Coffee, How it Came to Paris. (S. Dewey) Eng. Illust. **20**: 312.
Coffee Culture in Mexico. (L. M. Terry) Overland, n. s. **37**: 703.
— in Central America. (R. W. Cater) Chamb. J. **76**: 570.
— in Our New Islands. (G. W. Caswell) Overland, n. s. **32**: 459.
Coffee-house Plan. (A. L. Sweetser) Gunton's M. **21**: 239.
Coffin, Victor, Province of Quebec. (J. G. Bourinot) Canad. M. **8**: 368.
Cogan, William, of Southchard, England, Will of. (W. Dean) N. E. Reg. **204**: 434.
Cogswell, Gen. Thomas, Wagon Master's Returns under, 1782-83. (F. E. Blake) N. E. Reg. **51**: 39.
Coherer, On the Action of the. (M. H. Lockwood and E. B. Wheeler) Science, n. s. **9**: 624.
— Quantitative Investigation of. (A. Trowbridge) Am. J. Sci. **158**: 199.
Cohn, Ferdinand. (J. B. Farner) Nature, **58**: 275.
Coils, Induction, Improved Automatic Interrupter for. (H. L. Sayen and E. G. Willyoung) J. Frankl. Inst. **143**: 231.
Coin Shilling of Massachusetts Bay. (W. G. Sumner) Yale R. **7**: 247.
Coinage, American, Curiosities of. (A. E. Outerbridge) Pop. Sci. Mo. **53**: 593.
— Bank of Montreal Token Coinage. (R. W. McLachlan) Canad. M. **16**: 113.
— Debasement of; under Edward III. (A. Hughes; C. G. Crump; C. Johnson) Econ. J. **7**: 185.
— English, in the Time of the Three Edwards. Eng. Hist. R. **12**: 754.

Coinage, History of American, D. K. Watson's. (J. L. Laughlin) Am. Hist. R. **5**: 790.
— History of the Inscription, " In God we Trust." Bank. M. (N. Y.) **54**: 391.
— in Germany; Act of 1900. (O. M. W. Sprague) Q. J. Econ. **15**: 147.
— Spanish Experiments in. (H. C. Lea) Pop. Sci. Mo. **51**: 577.
— Theory and History of. Bank. M. (N. Y.) **54**: 675, 845.
— Token, Private Issue of. (R. P. Falkner) Pol. Sci. Q. **16**: 303.
Coincidences. (F. Max Müller) Fortn. **70**: 157. Same art. Liv. Age, **218**: 544.
Coins, Curious. Chamb. J. **78**: 255.
— English, Portraiture of. (J. R. Larkby) Reliquary, **39**: 50.
Coke, John, of Coke's Rifles. Blackw. **163**: 765.
Coke and Bacon. The Conservative Lawyer and the Law Reformer. (U. M. Rose) Am. Law R. **31**: 1.
— *vs.* Bacon, Case of. Green Bag, **9**: 516.
Coke. By-product Coking Industry. (W. G. Irwin) Engin. M. **22**: 41. — Cassier, **21**: 154.
— Making in the United States. (W. G. Irwin) Cassier, **19**: 197.
— a Smokeless Fuel? (H. W. Spangler) Cassier, **13**: 409.
Coke Country, The. (H. P. Snyder) Chaut. **27**: 51.
Coke Ovens, By-product. (F. H. Crockard) Cassier, **21**: 154.
Colas, Colasse, and Colette. (Jules Simon) Liv. Age, **220**: 641.
Colchester, Duncombe, and Maynard; a Brace of Worthies. (S. M. Crawley-Boevey) Gent. M. n. s. **65**: 548.
— and the Commonwealth. (J. H. Round) Eng. Hist. R. **15**: 641.
Cold, Catching. Spec. **82**: 12.
— Coming. (A. B. MacDowall) Knowl. **20**: 241.
— Mechanical Production of. (J. A. Ewing) J. Soc. Arts, **45**: 987-1091.
Cold Storage and Our Food Supply. (E. H. Jackson) Chamb. J. **75**: 635.
Cold Water Cure; a poem. (R. Gourlay) Canad. M. **10**: 529.
Colds. Spec. **80**: 195.
Coldspring Harbor, L. I., Fauna and Flora about. (B. Davenport) Science, n. s. **8**: 685.
Coldstream Guards, The. Macmil. **75**: 312.
Coleridge, Hartley. (M. R. Hoste) Temp. Bar, **116**: 580.
Coleridge, Samuel T., with portrait. (F. Thompson) Acad. **51**: 179. — (M. Prower) Gent. M. n. s. **64**: 394.
— Ancient Mariner. (W. N. Guthrie) Sewanee, **6**: 200.
— and his Poetic Work. (T. W. Hunt) Bib. Sac. **58**: 88.
— and Swedenborg. (Chas. Higham) N. Church R. **4**: 273.
— Manuscripts in Possession of T. N. Longman. Sat. R. **83**: 665.
Coleridge-Taylor, S. Hiawatha's Wedding-feast. (E. M. Bowman) Music, **16**: 263.
Coleridge Country, The. (P. H. W. Almy) Gent. M. n. s. **67**: 66.
Coleridgeiana. Temp. Bar, **111**: 114. Same art. Ecl. M. **129**: 101.
Colette, St. (J. Winn) Argosy, **69**: 186.
Coll, Aloysius. Writer, **14**: 25.
Collaboration, Mystery of. Macmil. **85**: 70.
Collaborators, Famous. (G. A. Wade) Pall Mall M. **21**: 529.
Collar and Cuffs; a dog story. (K. F. Purdon) Argosy, **71**: 470.

Collecting Instinct, The. (C. F. Burk) Pedagog. Sem. 7: 179.

Collective Practices. (J. H. Swanton) J. Mil. Serv. Inst. 27: 409.

Collectivism, Ethical Basis of. (L. T. Hobhouse) Int. J. Ethics, 8: 137.

— Foreign Policy of. (L. T. Hobhouse) Econ. R. 9: 197.

— in the U. S. Spec. 79: 70.

— Principle of. (W. Poland) Am. Cath. Q. 26: 53.

Collector of the Porte ; a story. (R. W. Chambers) Eng. Illust. 20: 241. Same art. McClure, 11: 564.

Collectors and Collecting. Chamb. J. 76: 26.

College, Admission to, on Certificate and by Examination, Report on. (C. C. Ramsay) School R. 8: 593.

— — Our Proposed New Requirements for. (R. W. Jones) School R. 9: 105.

— — Rating of Studies in. (E. H. Hall) Educa. R. 13: 417.

— — Requirements for. (E. H. Babbitt) Sewanee R. 9: 312. — (C. H. Keyes) Educa. R. 19: 59. — (A. F. Nightingale) School R. 7: 388.

— — — Associations now engaged in Studying the Subject of. (J. R. Bishop) School R. 5: 300.

— — — Committee on. (A. F. Nightingale) School R. 5: 321.

— — — — Discussion of the Report of. (D. S. Jordan and others) School R. 7: 394.

— — — Committees Studying. School R. 5: 367.

— — — Drawing in. (H. T. Bailey) Educa. R. 13: 456.

— — — in English. (F. N. Scott) School R. 9: 365.

— — — in French and German. (H. S. White) Educa. R. 19: 143.

— — National Units. (O. L. Elliott) School R. 7: 470.

— — — Physics in. (E. H. Hall) Educa. R. 14: 140.

— — — Reform of. (A. F. Nightingale) Educa. R. 14: 34.

— — — Standards of. (W. T. Harris) Educa. 17: 579.

— — — Uniform. (C. H. Thurber) School R. 5: 231.

— — — — with a Joint Board of Examiners. (N. M. Butler) Educa. R. 19: 68.

— Age of Students Entering ; a Freshman at Nineteen. (A. Flexner) Educa. R. 18: 353.

— American, Encroachment of, upon the Field of the University. (S. E. Baldwin) Internat. Mo. 3: 634.

— Future of. (J. L. Daniels) Bib. Sac. 58: 670.

— and School, Relations of. (R. E. Jones) Educa. R. 18: 467.

— Are you Going to ? (A. L. Benedict) Lippinc. 60: 260.

— The Christian. (J. M. Ruthrauff) Luth. Q. 31: 545.

— Conspiracy against the. (E. D. Warfield) Indep. 52: 1829.

— Elements in the Choice of a. (C. F. Thwing) R. of Rs. (N. Y.) 15: 446.

— Farmers'. (Murat Halstead) Cosmopol. 22: 280.

— Freshman in, and his Parents. (L. B. R. Briggs) Atlan. 83: 29.

— in the 20th Century. (C. L. Smith) Atlan. 85: 219.

— A Labor-union. Gunton's M. 18: 548.

— Literary Drill in. (G. S. Lee) Critic, 39: 145, 218, 309.

— or not ? (H. E. Hersey) Indep. 53: 1971.

— or University — Which ? (H. Orcutt) Educa. 18: 469.

— Preparation for, and Preparation for Life. (P. H. Hanus) Educa. R. 21: 140.

— Self-support in. (L. K. Smith) Nat'l M. (Bost.) 12: 463.

— The Small, and the Large. (C. F. Thwing) Forum, 32: 319.

— — Future of. (W. MacDonald) Nation, 69: 422.

College, The Small, Mission of. (C. W. Heisler) Luth. Q. 31: 419.

— — Opportunity of. (H. W. Horwill) Atlan. 87: 763.

— Social Life in ; Girl Freshman. (Alice K. Fallows) Munsey, 25: 818.

— Training Individuality in. (H. deF. Smith) Educa. R. 19: 269.

— The Transition from School to. (L. B. R. Briggs) Atlan. 85: 354.

— What it Costs to send a Girl through College. (M. A. Frost and J. H. Caverno) Outl. 59: 82.

— Working One's Way through. (Alice K. Fallows) Cent. 40: 163.

— — in Women's College. (Alice K. Fallows) Cent. 40: 323.

College Administration, Despotism in. Nation, 70: 317.

— Thwing on. (W. H. Johnson) Nation, 71: 313.

College Architecture in America. (A. R. Willard) New Eng. M. n. s. 16: 513.

College Course, Shortened ; Graduate Opinion. (C. F. Thwing) Forum, 31: 552.

— A Shorter. (B. Perrin) Indep. 52: 1780.

— Tendency of Students to omit, that they may enter Professional Schools direct from the Secondary Schools. (A. F. Nightingale) School R. 5: 73.

— Three-year. (G. Hempl) Educa. R. 14: 433. — (J. H. Wright) School R. 5: 696. — (T. D. Seymour) School R. 5: 709. — (E. H. Hall) Harv. Grad. M. 9: 330.

— Three Years enough for. (S. E. Baldwin) Indep. 52: 1778.

College Courses, Recent Changes in. (E. G. Conklin) Indep. 53: 198.

College Curriculum, Liberalizing of. Outl. 64: 341.

College Degrees. (W. D. Mooney) School R. 7: 168.

— Unification and Equalization of, Report of the Committee on. School R. 9: 114.

College Discipline. (D. S. Jordan) No. Am. 165: 403.

College Education and Business. (J. B. Taylor) Educa. R. 19: 232.

— and Success. (J. W. Leonard) Outl. 69: 223.

— Does it Educate ? Cosmopol. 28: 471.

— Does it Pay ? (H. E. Kratz) Educa. R. 17: 297. — (J. C. Jones) Forum, 26: 354.

— from the Standpoint of the Preparatory School. (J. S. White) Overland, n. s. 33: 309.

— Ideals of. (F. S. Baldwin) New Eng. M. n. s. 17: 570.

— Modern. (J. B. Walker) Cosmopol. 22: 681. — (Timothy Dwight) Cosmopol. 23: 437. — (E. B. Andrews) Cosmopol. 23: 568. — (Grant Allen) Cosmopol. 23: 611. — (L. A. McLouth) Cosmopol. 24: 142. — (T. J. Allen) Arena, 22: 38.

— Rational. (T. J. Allen) Arena, 22: 237.

— Varied but Incomplete. (E. P. Powell) Educa. 19: 294.

— What Kind ? (T. J. Allen) Educa. 18: 377.

— What is the Student in College for ? (C. F. Thwing) Chaut. 32: 144.

College Endowments. (J. Bigham) Meth. R. 60: 941.

College Entrance Examination Board of the Middle States and Maryland. First Annual Report. Educa. R. 22: 264.

College Entrance Examinations, Curiosities of. (Harriet E. Payne) Outl. 58: 966.

College Fraternities. (P. F. Piper) Cosmopol. 22: 641. — (E. H. L. Randolph) New Eng. M. n. s. 17: 70. — (E. J. Ridgway) Munsey, 24: 729.

College Girl and the Outside World. (S. Kirk) Lippinc. 65: 596.

College Girls and Good Manners. (Mary G. Bush) Outl. 58: 676.

College Government, Alumni Representation in. (S. H. Ranck) Educa. 22: 107.

College Government, Personal Morals and. (C. F. Thwing) No. Am. 166: 297.

College Graduate, Influence of. (C. F. Thwing) Indep. 52: 704.

— Is he Impracticable ? (R. E. Jones) Forum, 30: 583.

College Graduates and Teachers. (W. MacDonald) Nation, 69: 202.

— as Teachers in the Public Schools, Certification of. (B. A. Hinsdale; C. De Garmo ; E. E. Brown) School R. 7: 331.

— Statistics of. Yale R. 8: 89, 318.

— Statistics of the Vocations of. Yale R. 7: 341.

College Honor. (L. B. R. Briggs) Atlan. 88: 483.

College Honors. (L. M. Salmon) Educa. R. 13: 370.

College Leisure Class, The. (W. MacDonald) Nation, 69: 348.

College Library, A Small, Arranging. (G. R. Colborn) Pub. Lib. 4: 450.

— Ethics of. (L. M. Duval) Pub. Lib. 4: 421.

— in Education. (A. E. Whitaker) Pub. Lib. 2: 347.

College Life. (R. Holbrook) Outing, 38: 308.

College Literature and Journalism. (C. F. Bacon) Critic, 37: 21.

College Man in Politics, The. (C. Logsdail) Arena, 22: 747.

College Music, High Standards in. Music, 18: 401.

College President, The. (C. F. Thwing) Indep. 51: 1145.

— Evolution of the. (H. A. Stimson) R. of Rs. (N. Y.) 19: 451.

— Perplexities of a. Atlan. 85: 483.

— Power of the. (L. C. Seelye) Educa. R. 20: 444.

College Professor, Confessions of a. Scrib. M. 22: 629.

— Life of a. (Bliss Perry) Scrib. M. 22: 512.

College Professors as Teachers. Wanted — a Teacher. (J. H. Canfield) Educa. R. 20: 433.

College Property, Taxation of. (C. F. Thwing) Educa. R. 17: 124.

College Rooms and their Traditions. (E. Boltwood) Munsey, 23: 447.

College Settlements in Great Cities. (A. W. Tarbell) Nat'l M. (Bost.) 7: 116.

College Slang. (E. H. Babbitt) Chaut. 31: 22.

College Student, Religion of a. (F. G. Peabody) Forum, 31: 442.

College Students, Alleged Luxury among. (A. T. Hadley and C. C. Harrison) Cent. 40: 313. — (W. R. Harper) Cent. 40: 519.

College Theatricals and Glee Clubs. (E. Carruth) Chaut. 25: 285.

College Trust, The ; a Menace to Freedom. (T. E. Well) Arena, 26: 244.

College Unit, Integrity of. (W. J. Tucker) School R. 5: 683.

College Woman and Christianity. (J. Addams) Indep. 53: 1852.

Colleges, American, Present Status of the Elective System in. (A. P. Brigham) Educa. R. 14: 360.

— and Preparatory Schools in Middle States, Convention of. (W. H. Klapp) Citizen, 2: 364.

— and Universities, Continuous Sessions for. (J. H. Raymond) School R. 7: 117.

— Degree-conferring Institutions, Report on State Supervision of. School R. 6: 350.

— Denominational, and the State Universities in the West and Northwest. (J. A. Clutz) Luth. Q. 29: 553.

— Four-year Period in, Passing of the. (G. Hempl) Forum, 28: 221.

— Ill-gotten Gifts to. (V. D. Scudder) Atlan. 86: 675.

— Military Training in. (J. Regan) J. Mil. Serv. Inst. 22: 75.

— The Older and the Newer. (C. W. Eliot) Educa. R. 16: 162.

Colleges, Problems of Our. (E. P. Clark) Nation, 69: 7.

— Problems of 20th Century. Educa. 20: 585.

— Small. See above, College, Small.

— Some Essentials of the True Academic Spirit. (C. C. Hall) Educa. R. 17: 317.

-- Southern, Needs of. (J. L. M. Curry) Forum, 28: 719.

— Three Oldest. (C. F. Thwing) Educa. 18: 1.

Colley, Sir George Pomeroy. (H. Brackenbury) Blackw. 165: 558. — (Wilfred Meynell) Eng. Illust. 22: 160.

— Butler's Life of. Acad. 56: 211. — (A. Griffiths) Fortn. 71: 306.

Collie and Sheep Dog. (H. W. Huntington) Outing, 33: 230.

Collier, The Old-fashioned. Chamb. J. 74: 585.

Colliers, Ocean, Loading of. (F. S. Snowdon) Engin. M. 20: 157.

Colliery Management and Control. (W. Blakemore) Engin. M. 21: 735.

Colliery Village, Pennsylvania. (H. E. Rood) Cent. 33: 809.

Colligo Club Theatricals, The. (C. Warren) Scrib. M. 28: 16.

Collin, Raphael. (B. Kendell) M. of Art, 25: 487.

Collins, Daniel, Deed of, to James Bird, 1696. (J. T. Hassam) N. E. Reg. 52: 167.

Collins, Geo. W., Pencil Drawings of. Artist (N. Y.) 29: 96.

Collins, J. Churton, as a Critic. Acad. 60: 203.

— A Censor of Critics. (A. Symons) Fortn. 75: 1003.

— Ephemera Critica. (L. E. Gates) Critic, 39: 23.

Collins, Wilkie, with portrait. Acad. 51: 334.

Collins, William. (C. H. Ross) Sewanee, 4: 38. — (G. D. Leslie and F. A. Eaton) Art J. 51: 139.

Collision at Sea, Fault in, and Responsibility of Shipowners. (A. Hindenburg) Law Q. 16: 355.

— Maritime Lien for. (E. T. Salvesen) Jurid. R. 9: 34.

— Remedy for. (J. H. Scott) Cassier, 12: 603.

— Where both Ships are in Fault. (L. F. Scott) Law Q. 13: 17, 241.

Colloids, Compressibility of. (C. Barus) Am. J. Sci. 156: 285.

Cologne, The City of the Rhine. (M. F. Nixon-Roulet) Cath. World, 74: 57.

Cologne ; the Rome of the Rhine. (J. C. Paget) Temp. Bar, 116: 235.

Colomb, P. H., Vice-Admiral. Un. Serv. M. 20: 214. — Cassier, 14: 175.

— Last Words of. Un. Serv. M. 20: 305.

Colombia, Aborigines of the Province of Santa Marta. (F. C. Nicholas) Am. Anthropol. 3: 606.

— Late Political Revolution. Sat. R. 92: 326. — (R. B. C. Graham) Sat. R. 92: 430. — (S. F. Massey) J. Mil. Serv. Inst. 22: 288.

— — Personal Experience of. (G. K. Chrystie) Chamb. J. 78: 649. Same art. Liv. Age, 231: 418.

Colombo, A Vision of. (Mrs. A. S. Boyd) Blackw. 166: 829. Same art. Liv. Age, 224: 251.

Colombo, Ceylon. (J. Ferguson) J. Soc. Arts, 48: 73.

Colonel Drury ; a story. (John C. Breton) Pall Mall M. 12: 332.

Colonel Fane's Secret ; a novel. (S. Hodges) Argosy, 65: 18-641. 66: 1609.

Colonel Halifax's Ghost Story. (S. Baring-Gould) Eng. Illust. 18: 209.

Colonel Joslyn, U. S. A. ; a story. (C. B. Lewis) McClure, 18: 15.

Colonel Mallory ; a story. (T. R. Mackenzie) Argosy, 65: 224.

Colonel Pargiter's Lamp ; a story. (W. B. Wallace) Gent. M. n. s. 59: 209.

Colonel Starbottle for the Plaintiff ; a story. (F. B. Harte) Harper, 102: 564.

Colonel's Christmas. (E. Robinson) Munsey, 18: 356.

Color Phenomena, Subjective. (S. Bidwell) Nature, 55: 367.
Color Printing of Textiles at Wardle's Works. (Gleeson White) Art J. 51: 14.
Color Prints. (J. H. Slater) Art J. 52: 327.
— in American Periodicals. (J. B. Carrington) Critic, 37: 222.
Color-teaching in Schools. (M. McMillan) Good Words, 42: 691.
Color-vision. (W. Le C. Stevens; E. B. Titchener; C. L. Franklin) Science, n. s. 7: 513-773. — (F. P. Whitman) Science, n. s. 8: 305.
— and the Flicker Photometer. (O. N. Rood) Am. J. Sci. 158: 258.
— Basis for a Theory of. (W. Patten) Am. Natural. 32: 833.
— Ebbinghaus's Theory. (C. L. Franklin) Science, n. s. 14: 30.
— of Approaching Sleep. (C. L. Franklin) Psychol. R. 4: 641.
— Primitive. (W. H. R. Rivers) Pop. Sci. Mo. 59: 44.
Colors, Photographic Reproduction of. (H. T. Wood) J. Soc. Arts, 45: 278.
— A Plea for the. (M. Harris) J. Mil. Serv. Inst. 13: 491.
— Representation of Tints and Shades by Rotating Discs. (A. Kirschmann) Am. J. Psychol. 9: 346.
— Subjective, and the After-image. (M. F. Washburn) Mind, 24: 25.
Colorado. Bank. M. (N. Y.) 57: 177.
— Canyon District, Notes on. (W. M. Davis) Am. J. Sci. 160: 251.
— Deer Hunting in. (H. Wright) Outing, 37: 168.
— Evolution of Mining in. (T. Tonge) Engin. M. 18: 265.
— Game Laws of. (S. W. Matteson) Outing, 38: 29.
— Gold Product of, 1899. Bank. M. (N. Y.) 59: 775.
— Mining Development of Gilpin Co. (T. Tonge) Engin. M. 22: 203.
— Out of Doors in. (H. P. Ufford) Cent. 36: 313.
Colorado Coöperative Company of Pinon. (C. E. Julihu) Nat'l M. (Bost.) 11: 29.
Colorado Desert, The. (D. P. Barrows) Nat. Geog. M. 11: 337.
Colorado Mountain Scenery. (H. A. Crafts) Midland, 7: 304.
Colorado River. (J. E. Bennett) Lippinc. 61: 495.
— Grand Cañon of. (H. Monroe) Atlan. 84: 816. — Cath. World, 70: 305.
— — and the Great Plateau. (S. D. Peet) Am. Antiq. 22: 1.
— — a New Wonder of the World. (Joaquin Miller) Overland, n. s. 37: 786.
Colorado Springs and round about Pike's Peak. (F. Walker) New Eng. M. n. s. 25: 236.
Coloration, Nocturnal Protective, of Mammals, Birds, Fishes, Insects, etc. (A. E. Verrill) Am. Natural. 31: 99.
Colored Prints, Craze for. Macmil. 76: 364.
Colossus of Rhodes. (B. I. Wheeler) Cent. 34: 661.
Colquhoun's Victory; a story. (A. Werner) Gent. M. n. s. 62: 313.
Colum-Cille, St. (M. A. O'Byrne) Cath. World, 65: 305.
Columbia, St., the Poet. Blackw. 166: 350.
Columbia; a poem. (E. W. Wilcox) Cosmopol. 26: 212.
Columbia Park Boys' Club of San Francisco. (V. L. O'Brien) Am. J. Sociol. 7: 249.
Columbia University. Architectural School. (P. C. Stuart) Archit. R. 10: 1.
— Athletics at. (J. P. Paret) Outing, 32: 9.
— The New. (C. C. Sargent, jr.) Munsey, 18: 65.

Columbia University, New Buildings, Cost of Constructing. Am. Arch. 62: 15.
— — Horizontal Curves in. (W. H. Goodyear) Archit. R. 9: 82.
— Presidency of. (O. G. Villard) Nation, 73: 317.
"Columbia" Yacht, and "Shamrock;" their design and sailing. (C. G. Davis) Outing, 35: 78. See Yacht.
— Launch of. (Capt. A. J. Kenealy) Outing, 34: 411.
— the Pride of the Ocean. (Capt. A. J. Kenealy) Outing, 35: 3.
Columbia's Motto; a poem. (E. W. Wilcox) Cosmopol. 26: 522.
Columbus, Christopher, Real Tomb of. (F. Aucaigne) Munsey, 20: 888.
— True Landing Place of. (F. MacBennett) Cath. World, 72: 784.
— Was he morally Responsible? (C. Lombroso) Forum, 27: 537.
Colville, Sir Henry E., and the Work of the Ninth Division. Sat. R. 91: 742.
Comanche Series in Oklahoma and Kansas, Outlying Areas of. (T. W. Vaughan) Am. J. Sci. 154: 43.
Combat, Method of, for Infantry on the Offensive. (W. de Heusch) J. Mil. Serv. Inst. 12: 1065.
Combination, Evolution of the. (E. Leftwich) Arena, 23: 50.
— Right of. (F. B. Thurber) Am. J. Soc. Sci. 37: 215.
Combustion, New Process of. (P. J. Schlicht) J. Frankl. Inst. 146: 357.
— of Organic Substances in the Wet Way. (I. K. Phelps) Am. J. Sci. 154: 372.
Combustion Apparatus, Shimer's. J. Frankl. Inst. 152: 469.
Comédie Française, An Episode in the History of the. (T. Hopkins) Macmil. 77: 211. Same art. Liv. Age, 216: 447.
— in London, 1879. (J. Hollingshead) Theatre, 38: 78.
— Some New Members of. (E. Friend) Cosmopol. 29: 625.
Comedy, English and American Views of. (G. B. Shaw) Sat. R. 84: 417.
— Meredith on. (G. B. Shaw) Sat. R. 83: 314.
— On. (C. L. Moore) Dial (Ch.) 24: 311.
Comedy of Conscience. (S. W. Mitchell) Cent. 39: 323.
Comedy of Crime; a story. (Maarten Maartens) Cosmopol. 30: 185.
Comedy of New Millionaires, The. (C. Ross) Munsey, 18: 218.
Comedy of Rebellion, A; a story. (C. Ross) McClure, 15: 411.
Comedy on the Moors. (W. Buchan) Chamb. J. 77: 74.
Comegys, Benjamin B. Lit. W. (Bost.) 30: 9. — Bank. M. (N. Y.) 60: 700.
Comenius, John Amos, Call of, to the Presidency of Harvard. (J. H. Blodgett) Educa. R. 16: 391.
Comet 1846, VI. (H. P. Tuttle) Pop. Astron. 6: 561.
— 1862, III., Who discovered? (Lewis Swift) Pop. Astron. 6: 562.
— Holmes's, 1889 d, Re-discovery of. (C. D. Perrine) Pop. Astron. 7: 340.
— h 1898 [Perrine]. (C. D. Perrine) Pop. Astron. 6: 513.
— i 1898 [Brooks], Orbit of. (W. J. Hussey) Pop. Astron. 6: 556.
— a 1901. (E. A. Fath) Pop. Astron. 9: 289.
— A Famous. Quar. 188: 113.
— Great Southern, 1901, I. (W. F. Denning) Knowl. 24: 201.
— Lost Periodic [Tuttle-Schuthof] III., 1858. (H. P. Tuttle) Pop. Astron. 6: 6.
— Might one Strike the Earth? (F. Campbell) Pop. Astron. 8: 253.

Commune, Life in a French. (R. Donald) Contemp. 71: 424. Same art. Liv. Age, 213: 100.

Commune, Paris, 1871, Military Chiefs of the. (A. Laugel) Nation, 73: 31.

Communication. The Shrinkage of the Planet. (J. London) Chaut. 31: 609.

Communications, Night, in Fortresses. (W. B. Spender) J. Mil. Serv. Inst. 28: 78.

Communion, Holy, on Trial. (T. F. Wright) N. Church R. 5: 441.

— of Saints. (W. F. Moulton) Lond. Q. 91: 275. — (L. A. Fox) Luth. Q. 37: 1.

— with Three Blades of Grass, of the Knights-errant. (W. Sylvester) Dub. R. 121: 80.

Communion Tables; How they were set Altar-wise. (A. H. Sayce) Contemp. 74: 270.

Community, Evolution of a. (W. L. Manson) Chamb. J. 78: 529.

— The, Monograph of. (E. Cheysson) Am. J. Sociol. 5: 110.

Community of Goods in the Apostolic Church. (S. H. Cobb) Presb. & Ref. R. 8: 17.

" Community of Interest," The. Nation, 72: 388.

Comorin Cape, The Land's End of India. Chamb. J. 74: 401.

Companies, British, in France, Status of. (T. Barclay) Law Q. 13: 426.

— Promoting of. Chamb. J. 75: 164.

— — and the Public: Spec. 81: 236. — Bank. M. (Lond.) 66: 325.

— — " Limited-Company " Craze. (S. F. Van Oss) 19th Cent. 43: 731.

— — Rascality in. (H. E. M. Stutfield) National, 31: 75.

— — Lord Russell on. Bank. M. (Lond.) 66: 763.

— — Unrevealed Profits of. (W. Z. Ripley) J. Pol. Econ. 8: 535.

— Stock-jobbing. (W. R. Lawson) National, 36: 869.

Companies Act, 1900. Law Q. 16: 414. — Bank. M. (Lond.) 71: 1, 67, 247.

Companions of the Sorrowful Way. (J. Watson) Sund. M. 26: 450–818.

Company and the Individual. Blackw. 164: 331.

Company Law, in England and Scotland, Genesis of. (R. Brown) Jurid. R. 13: 185.

— of England, Fowke's. Sat. R. 87: 406.

Company Law Reform. (R. G. Elwes) 19th Cent. 49: 638.

Company Manners; a story. (F. Converse) Atlan. 81: 130.

Company Mess, The. (V. E. Stottler) J. Mil. Serv. Inst. 15: 78.

Comparative Literature, The Science of. (H. M. Posnett) Contemp. 79: 855.

Compass Variation. (B. S. Lyman) J. Frankl. Inst. 144: 281.

Compayré, Gabriel. (W. H. Payne) Educa. R. 16: 378.

Competition and Socialism. (D. J. Lewis) Pop. Sci. Mo. 53: 701.

— Ethics of the Competitive Process. (W. W. Willoughby) Am. J. Sociol. 6: 145.

— Foreign; organisation wanted. (G. Noble) Chamb. J. 78: 97.

— in Architecture. Am. Arch. 62: 90.

— in Economics. (J. Bascom) Q. J. Econ. 14: 537.

— Limits of. (W. Gladden) Indep. 52: 540.

— Nations in, at the Close of the Century. (J. Schoenhof) Forum, 31: 89.

— Unfair, New German Law of. (J. F. Iselin) Law Q. 13: 156.

Competitive Business and its Result. (E. Brush) Outl. 64: 680.

Competitive System, What Communities lose by the. (Jack London) Cosmopol. 30: 58.

Compiègne, Visit to. (A. Hope) Cornh. 77: 606.

Complexes, Elements of Conscious. (M. W. Calkins) Psychol. R. 7: 377.

Composer's Letter, A ; a satire. (I. B. Diserens) Music, 12: 93.

Composers, American. (W. L. Hubbard) Music, 16: 303.

— Contemporaneous Italian. (A. Bazzini) Music, 17: 489.

— Relative Rank of. (E. E. Kroeger) Music, 14: 165.

— Women. (R. Hughes) Cent. 33: 768.

Composite Authorship. (S. R. Elliott) Dial (Ch.) 22: 7.

Composition, Elementary, Problem of, Spalding on. (E. H. Lewis) School R. 5: 48.

— Teaching, Five Axioms of. (S. Thurber) School R. 5: 7.

Compromise and Arbitration, Fallacy of. (C. H. Pickstone) Am. Law R. 31: 33.

Comptometer. (C. V. Boys) Nature, 64: 265.

Compton, Miss, Portrait of. Theatre, 38: 67.

Compton Wynyates. (S. Baring-Gould) M. of Art, 21: 264. — (A. Dryden) Pall Mall M. 16: 312.

Compulsory Service. Un. Serv. M. 19: 72.

— made Easy. (G. N. Bankes) Un. Serv. M. 22: 59.

Compurgation. (E. L. Godkin) Nation, 69: 368.

Comstock, Harriet T. Writer, 14: 121.

Comstock Lode, The, (E. B. Osborn) Gent. M. n. s. 66: 36.

— Awakening of the. (John Finlay) Overland, n. s. 36: 445.

— of To-day. (T. A. Rickard) Cassier, 20: 347.

Comte, Auguste, Levy-Bruhl on, with portrait. (T. J. McCormack) Open Court, 14: 364.

— Positivism of. (S. H. Mellone) Int. J. Ethics, 8: 73.

— Spencer and Buckle. (L. Gambetta) No. Am. 171: 55.

Con Heffernan's Atonement. (H. A. Hinkson) Good Words, 40: 396.

Conanicut Island, R. I., Contribution to the Geology of Newport Neck and. (W. O. Crosby) Am. J. Sci. 153: 230.

Conation, Some Remarks on. (F. H. Bradley) Mind, 26: 437.

Concarneau, Brittany, as a Sketching Ground. (F. L. Emanuel) Studio (Lond.) 4: 180.

Concealed Weapons. (M. S. Briscoe) Cent. 32: 616.

Concentration Camps. (Emily Hobhouse) Contemp. 80: 528.

Concepcion; a story. (Irene A. Wright) Nat'l M. (Bost.) 6: 180.

Concept, The. (E. Mach) Open Court, 14:'348.

Conception, Some Problems of. (L. T. Hobhouse) Mind, 22: 145.

Concerning an Indian Fort ; a story. (Rosalie Cameron) Temp. Bar, 123: 59.

Concerning People who Disappointed One. (A. K. H. Boyd) Longm. 32: 531.

Concerning Tod and Peter. (L. A. Harker) Longm. 37: 432.

Concert-giving, Art of. (J. F. Runciman) Sat. R. 88: 44.

Concerts, Mistakes of English. (J. F. Runciman) Sat. R. 88: 452.

— Promenade. (J. F. Runciman) Sat. R. 90: 296.

Conchometer, The. (H. S. Conant) Am. Natural. 35: 665.

Conciergerie, The. Green Bag, 11: 365.

Concilium Bibliographicum, Work of. (H. H. Field) Am. Natural. 92: 925.

Conclusion of a Romance ; a story. (E. L. Sabin) Chaut. 31: 515.

Conclusiveness of a Domestic Judgment as affected by the Rank of the Court which rendered it.. (A. M. Alger) Am. Law R. 33: 665.

Congregational Council, Second International, Boston, 1899. (M. L. Osborne) Nat'l M. (Bost.) 11: 193. — (A. H. Bradford) Outl. 63: 51.
— Triennial, 1901. Outl. 69: 404, 492.
Congregational House, Boston, Relief Tablets on. (E. G. Porter) New Eng. M. n. s. 19: 428.
Congregationalism, Defence of. (F. H. Foster) Bib. Sac. 58: 209.
— in America. (M. Dexter) New Eng. M. n. s. 21: 97.
— in England. (J. Brown) New Eng. M. n. s. 21: 240.
Congress of the Powers, Our Interest in the Next. (T. Beale) Forum, 26: 37.
Congress, U. S. (J. C. Ridpath) Arena, 17: 969.
— and Parliament; a contrast. (S. Brooks) No. Am. 170: 78. — (E. Cockrell) Arena, 23: 593.
— Autocrat of. (H. L. West) Forum, 23: 343.
— The Coming, 1897. Gunton's M. 13: 401.
— Decline of. (E. L. Godkin) Nation, 64: 62.
— First. (J. M. Chapple) Nat'l M. (Bost.) 8: 225.
— First American, 1774. (B. Bulkley) Nat'l M. (Bost.) 7: 257.
— 57th, 1st Session. (H. L. West) Forum, 32: 424.
— Reconquest of the House of Representatives. (J. C. Ridpath) Arena, 20: 118.
— Second. (M. Mannering) Nat'l M. (Bost.) 8: 546.
— Third and Fourth. (M. Mannering) Nat'l M. (Bost.) 9: 561.
— When should it Convene? (J. F. Shafroth) No. Am. 164: 374.
Congressional Apportionment, and Negro Disfranchisement. (F. A. Flower) Nat'l M. (Bost.) 13: 282.
— The New. (H. Gannett) Forum, 30: 568.
Congressional Extravagance, Rationale of. (R. Ogden) Yale R. 6: 37.
Congressional Library. (W. I. Fletcher) Critic, 30: 107. — Munsey, 18: 707. — (H. Putnam) Atlan. 85: 145. — (H. Putnam) Outl. 65: 122.
— and State Libraries. (H. Putnam) Lib. J. 25: 729.
— Appointment of Librarian of. (W. C. Lane) Lib. J. 24: 99.
— Document Collections of. (R. P. Falkner) Lib. J. 26: 870.
— its Work and Functions. Lib. J. 26: 851.
— Librarianship of. Nation, 68: 178.
— Mechanical Book Carriers. (B. R. Green) Library, n. s. 2: 282.
— Nation's Library. (A. R. Spofford) Cent. 31: 682.
— New Building. (N. B. Maury) Cosmopol. 23: 10. — (M. Schuyler) Scrib. M. 21: 709. — (B. R. Green) Lib. J. 21: supp. 13.
— — Decorations in. (W. A. Coffin) Cent. 31: 694.
— or National Library. Lib. J. 22: 7.
— Personal Side of the New, 1900. (I. C. Barrows) Outl. 64: 21.
— A Study in Decorative Architecture. (R. Sturgis) Archit. R. 7: 295.
Congressional Parade, The. (G. G. Bain) Munsey, 18: 585.
Congressmen and Stock Speculation; a Question of Ethics. Cosmopol. 25: 226.
Conifers, Cultivated. (C. S. Sargent) Garden & F. 10: 390-509.
Conjuring in Georgia. (R. Steiner) J. Am. Folk-Lore, 14: 173.
— Indian, Explained. (Prof. Hoffmann) Chamb. J. 78: 757.
Conjuring Deceptions, Psychology of. (N. Triplett) Am. J. Psychol. 11: 439.
Conkling-Garfield Tragedy, Secret History of. (T. B. Connery) Cosmopol. 23: 145.
Conlon. (A. Colton) Cent. 38: 294.
Connagh Worm, Superstition of. (F. J. Battersby) Knowl. 21: 256.

Connaught, The Transplantation to. (S. R. Gardiner) Eng. Hist. R. 14: 700.
Connecticut and Massachusetts, Boundary Line of. (A. Chamberlain) New Eng. M. n. s. 16: 339.
— as a Corporate Colony. (H. L. Osgood) Pol. Sci. Q. 14: 251.
— Share of, in the Revolution. (J. M. Ives) New Eng. M. n. s. 20: 263.
Connemara. Ed. R. 190: 486.
Connecticut, Land-bank of, 18th Century. (A. McF. Davis) Q. J. Econ. 13: 70.
— Old Farming in. (C. N. Hall) New Eng. M. n. s. 22: 549.
Connecticut River, Early Traffic on. (C. G. Burnham) New Eng. M. n. s. 23: 131.
Connellsville, Pa., Coke Region. (F. C. Keightley) Engin. M. 20: 17.
Connor, Ralph, pseud. See Gordon, Chas. W.
Conquest, Ethics of. Blackw. 164: 841. Same art. Liv. Age, 220: 101.
— The Spirit of. (J. Novicow) Pop. Sci. Mo. 54: 518.
— Title by, Nature and Extent of. (J. Westlake) Law Q. 17: 392.
Conquest of Charlotte; a story. Blackw. 170: 1-820.
Conquest of Radical Ted. (M. E. Francis) Longm. 29: 533.
Conquest of Mrs. Vivian; a story. (C. K. Burrow) Idler, 14: 271.
Conrad, Joseph, with portrait. Acad. 55: 82. — Bk. Buyer, 16: 389.
— Children of the Sea; Tales of Unrest. (T. R. Sullivan) Bk. Buyer, 16: 350.
— Tales of Unrest. Acad. 56: 66.
Conscience. (F. Thilly) Philos. R. 9: 18.
— in Light of the New Church. (J. Hyde) N. Church R. 7: 512.
— The Objective. (M. H. Richards) Luth. Q. 37: 71.
— Realm of. (S. Brodhurst) Macmil. 80: 23.
— Study of. (C. Caverno) Bib. Sac. 58: 556.
Conscience of Alderman McGinnis, The; a story. (A. French) McClure, 11: 287.
Conscience of a Business Man, The. (Octave Thanet) Scrib. M. 24: 310.
Conscious Amanda; a story. (F. S. Stockton) Cosmopol. 29: 185.
Consciousness, Double. (A. Wilson) Longm. 31: 151.
— Fundamental Conceptions regarding the Nature of. (J. Rehmke) Philos. R. 6: 449.
— Relation of Certain Organic Processes to. (J. R. Angell; H. B. Thompson) Psychol. R. 6: 32.
— Religious, Contents of. (J. H. Leuba) Monist, 11: 536.
— Self-consciousness and the Self. (H. R. Marshall) Mind, 26: 98.
Conscription. (W. Ley) Un. Serv. M. 22: 293.
— By a Suppliant of Nemesis. Westm. 153: 652.
— The Case against. (A. W. Livesey) Westm. 154: 260.
— for the U. S. Army. Nation, 67: 478.
— Future of. Spec. 81: 730.
— A Substitute for. (W. Hill-Climo) Un. Serv. M. 16: 259.
Consecration of Churches, its Origin, Meaning, and Rite. (M. O'Riordan) Am. Cath. Q. 23: 598.
Consecration Crosses, with Some English Examples. (J. H. Middleton) Archæol. 48: 456.
Conservation of Energy, Doctrine of. (C. H. Chase) Monist, 10: 135.
Conservative Party in England and Municipal Elections. (J. R. Diggle) 19th Cent. 43: 604.
Conservatories of Music, Advantages of Instruction in. (E. Dickinson) Music, 15: 288.
— — Public Contests in. (M. Kufferath) Music, 15: 35.

Consolation of Gamaliel. (M. M. Pope) Lippinc. 60: 843.

Consonance and Dissonance. (Bertram C. Henry) Music, 11: 525.

Conspiracy as a Fine Art. (A. Lang) Green Bag, 13: 13.

Constable, John, Artist. (F. Wedmore) Pall Mall M. 21: 437.

— Life and Letters ; ed. by Leslie. Sat. R. 84: 198.

Constable, The, of the Olden Time. (W. B. Parley) Gent. M. n. s. 64: 349.

Constabulary, Local vs. State. (W. H. Allen) Ann. Am. Acad. Pol. Sci. 17: 100.

Constance. (Th. Bentzon) Liv. Age, 219: 1-874.

Constance Weatherell and Bridget Brady ; a story. (Katrina Trask) Cosmopol. 31: 297.

Constancy of Elizabeth. (A. B. Paine) Cent. 38: 170.

Constant, Benjamin, Some Portraits by. (L. L. Phelps) Art J. 50: 126. — (B. Constant) Harper, 102: 821.

— Works of. (Emile Vedel) M. of Art, 23: 468.

Constantinople. (Peter MacQueen) Cosmopol. 23: 115. — (E. A. Grosvenor) Chaut. 32: 623.

— American College for Girls at. (E. P. Telford) New Eng. M. n. s. 18: 10. — (C. S. Baker) Outl. 67: 59.

— Byzantine, Van Milligen's. (J. P. Peters) Nation, 70: 225.

— Christian, Last Days of. (F. X. McGowan) Cath. World, 73: 153.

— a Glimpse. (O. F. Taylor) Canad. M. 14: 278.

— How the Turk came to. (B. J. Clinch) Am. Cath. Q. 22: 365.

— Mosque of the Calenders at. (E. Freshfield) Archæol. 55: 431.

— The Queen of Cities. (Frederic Whyte) Pall Mall M. 13: 450.

— The Struggle in. Spec. 78: 824.

Constants, Physical, Determination of, by the U. S. Coast Survey. (E. D. Preston) Pop. Astron. 6: 101.

Constellation-figures as Greek Coin-types. (R. Brown) Knowl. 24: 35.

Constellation Studies. (E. W. Maunder) Knowl. 24: 12-273.

"Constitution," The Frigate. (I. N. Hollis) Atlan. 80: 590. — (E. J. Carpenter) New Eng. M. n. s. 17: 263.

— as Sailors Saw her. (J. R. Spears) Chaut. 31: 377.

— Central Figure of the Navy under Sail. (H. C. Taylor) Am. Hist. R. 6: 820.

— Last Victory of. (G. Gibbs) Lippinc. 64: 736.

Constitution in the Territories, The. (J. S. Mosby) Nation, 72: 89.

— or Theory, — Which? (E. Pomeroy) Green Bag, 11: 152.

— — Reply ; an Answer that does not Confute. (B. S. Dean) Green Bag, 11: 259.
  See United States ; Constitution.

Constitutional Club of London, Decorations of. (A. L. Baldry) Art J. 50: 133.

Constitutional Construction and the Commerce Clause. (R. Mather) Am. Law R. 31: 839.

Constitutional Law, Rise of. (N. M. Rose) Am. Law R. 35: 641.

Constitutional Studies, Schouler's. (F. N. Thorpe) Am. Hist. R. 3: 379.

Constitutions, State, of American Revolution. (W. C. Webster) Annals Am. Acad. 9: 380.

Consular Service, United States. (C. Truax) Forum, 32: 488. — (G. F. Parker) Atlan. 85: 455, 669.

— The Business Man and the. (H. A. Garfield) Cent. 38: 268.

— Early History of, 1776-92. (E. H. Johnson) Pol. Sci. Q. 13: 19.

Consular Service, Evils to be Remedied in. (W. W. Rockhill) Forum, 22: 673.

— Inspection of, A Plea for. (A. H. Washburn) Forum, 30: 28.

— New Bill for. (G. Hunt) Nation, 70: 106.

— Our Inadequate. (S. M. White) Forum, 25: 546.

— Remodeling of. (H. A. Garfield) Indep. 52: 657. — Outl. 64: 245. 65: 202.

Consular Systems of Foreign Countries. (G. McAneny) Cent. 35: 604.

Consuls, U. S., and Trade. (F. Emory) World's Work, 1: 751.

Consumer's Label, The. (M. Nathan) No. Am. 166: 250.

Consumers' League, Aims and Principles of. (Florence Kelley) Am. J. Sociol. 5: 289. — (F. Kelley) Am. J. Soc. Sci. 37: 111.

— of New York. Ann. Am. Acad. Pol. Sci. 11: 135.

— Work and Problems of. (F. L. McVey) Am. J. Sociol. 6: 764.

Consumption and Consumptives. (W. L. Russell) Pop. Sci. Mo. 50: 336.

— Extirpation of. (L. Cothran) Arena, 20: 248.

— Fight against. Ed. R. 194: 438.

— Moral Aspect of. (C. S. Devas) Internat. J. Ethics, 10: 41.

— Nordrach Cure Practicable in England. (J. A. Gibson) 19th Cent. 45: 389.

— not Contagious. (R. Hunter) Canad. M. 9: 540.

— Open-air Cure of. (J. A. Gibson) 19th Cent. 45: 92. — (E. de Terrasson) Chamb. J. 76: 134.

— — at Falkenstein. Chamb. J. 77: 183.

— Prevention of. (M. Morris) Fortn. 70: 307. — (J. G. S. Coghill) 19th Cent. 45: 304. —Ann. Am. Acad. Pol. Sci. 17: 377.

— Rutland, Mass., Sanatorium. (Mrs. R. P. Williams) New Eng. M. n. s. 24: 269.

— Some Remarks on. (H. Higgs) Econ. J. 9: 505.

— War against. (J. H. Girdner) Munsey, 22: 792. — (S. Baxter) R. of Rs. (N. Y.) 23: 705.

Consumptive, The ; a story. (C. J. Cutcliffe-Hyne) Pall Mall M. 17: 473.

Consumptives, California Quarantine against. (S. A. Knopf) Forum, 28: 615.

— Cry of the. (J. A. Gibson) 19th Cent. 46: 642.

Contact Metamorphism, Interesting Case of. (H. W. Fairbanks) Am. J. Sci. 154: 36.

Contagious Diseases Acts. (E. Ethelmer) Westm. 147: 447. 152: 249-608.

— Do they Succeed ? Westm. 153: 135.

Contemporaries of our Lord. (A. Church) Sund. M. 28: 29, 90, 171.

Contempt of Court. (D. MacG. Means) Nation, 70: 412.

— and the Press. (A. E. Hughes) Law Q. 16: 292.

— Legislative. (F. W. Hackett) Green Bag, 11: 226.

Contiguity and Similarity. (W. Fite) Philos. R. 9: 613.

Continent, The Edge of a. (G. A. J. Cole) Knowl. 20: 208.

— Floor of a. (G. A. J. Cole) Knowl. 21: 25.

— Heart of a. (G. A. J. Cole) Knowl. 20: 282.

Continental Army, Uniforms of. Pennsyl. M. 22: 119, 248.

Continental Congress. (H. Friedenwald) Pennsyl. M. 21: 445.

— Journals of. (H. Friedenwald) Pennsyl. M. 21: 161, 361.

— Sessions of, in the College of Philadelphia, July, 1778. (J. W. Jordan) Pennsyl. M. 22: 114.

Continental Hospital Returns, 1777-80. (J. W. Jordan) Pennsyl. M. 23: 35, 210.

Continental System of Napoleon. (W. M. Sloane) Pol. Sci. Q. 13: 213.

Continuation School Work in Rural Districts. (H. Macan) J. Soc. Arts, 48: 355.

Continuity in the Church, Mivart on. Church Q. 50: 182.

Continuum, The Notion of a. (E. Mach) Open Court, 14: 409.

Contortionist, Bava Luchman Dass. (F. Steelcroft) Strand, 13: 176.

— A Human Alphabet. (W. G. Fitzgerald) Strand, 14: 659.

Contraband consigned to Neutral Ports. (R. C. Henderson) Jurid. R. 12: 131. — (E. L. De Hart) Law Q. 17: 193.

Contract, The Right of. (F. B. Thurber) No. Am. 165: 265.

Contracts, Building. Am. Arch. 63: 21.

— by Correspondence in Private International Law. (A. Hindenburg) Jurid. R. 9: 161, 291.

— Damages for Breach of. Am. Arch. 55: 30.

— in Restraint of Trade. (J. R. Christie) Jurid. R. 12: 283.

— Mutuality of : Promise for a Promise : Unilateral Contracts : Consideration. (A. F. Learr, jr.) Am. Law R. 32: 409.

— of Foreign Corporations. (M. S. Gunn) Am. Law R. 31: 19.

Contrasts ; verse. (C. Scollard) Chaut. 32: 248.

Contributor his Own Editor. (F. M. Bird) Lippinc. 59: 427.

Contributors, Editor's Advice to. (J. B. Walker) Writer, 12: 50.

— Editorial Talk with. (H. A. Bridgman) Writer, 12: 147.

Convalescence of the Boy ; a tale. (G.) Argosy, 75: 334.

Convent at Charlestown, Mass., Destruction of, 1834. (J. P. Munroe) New Eng. M. n. s. 23: 637.

Convent of Mar Saba. (H. Macmillan) Sund. M. 28: 248, 333.

Convent Education, Madame Marie of the Sacred Heart, on. (T. F. Willis) Dub. R. 128: 351.

Convent Enquiry Society, The. (J. Britten) Month, 93: 275.

Convent Idyll, A. (G. C. Nuttall) Argosy, 67: 62.

Convent Life in Fayal. Chamb. J. 77: 689.

Convent Library, An Old. (C. J. Willdey) Belgra. 95: 414.

Convent Man-servant, A. (M. H. Catherwood) Atlan. 79: 98.

Convention, Early Political Uses of the Word. (J. F. Jameson) Am. Hist. R. 3: 477.

Conventions and Other Gatherings of 1899. R. of Rs. (N. Y.) 19: 579.

— Four National. (G. F. Hoar) Scrib. M. 25: 152.

— National Party. (G. M. Burnham) Nat'l M. (Bost.) 12: 147.

— of 1900. R. of Rs. (N. Y.) 21: 546. — Outl. 65: 301.

— Political State. (E. McClain) Midland, 10: 535.

Conversation. (J. Payn) 19th Cent. 42: 67. Same art. Ecl. M. 129: 529. Same art. Liv. Age, 214: 576. — Chamb. J. 75: 337. — Spec. 83: 834.

— Argument in. Sat. R. 90: 453.

— The Art of. (M. E. Merington) Chaut. 30: 480.

— Qualities of American. Atlan. 81: 286.

Conversational Argument. Liv. Age, 227: 459.

Conversational Arithmetic. Un. Serv. (Phila.) 17: 199, 291.

Conversational Circle ; some Problems for the Leader. (A. H. Morton) Cent. 34: 952.

Converse, John Heman. Cassier, 20: 519.

Conversion. (J. Tomlinson) Luth. Q. 31: 364.

— Luthardt on. (C. E. Hay) Luth. Q. 30: 145.

— Normal Age for. Meth. R. 79: 943.

— A Study of. (E. D. Starbuck) Am. J. Psychol. 8: 268.

Conversion of Ah Lew Sing. (M. Austin) Overland, n. s. 30: 307.

Conversion of "Ginger Bill ; " a story. Temp. Bar, 118: 407.

Conversion of John Toms ; a story. (L. Quiller Couch) Idler, 10: 777.

Conversion of Nicolas Fothergill ; a story. (B. Marnan) Pall Mall M. 18: 256.

Conversion of Sweet-Grass ; a story. (W. A. Fraser) Canad. M. 12: 403.

Convert from Camp 2, a Nova Scotia Mining Story. (J. Blewett) Canad. M. 15: 434.

Conveyancing, Græco-Roman. Green Bag, 12: 290.

Convict of Dartmoor, A. (E. S. Bond) Sund. M. 29: 83.

— Woman, Life of a. (M. F. Johnston) Fortn. 75: 559.

Convict Labor in Massachusetts. (J. T. Codman) Arena, 19: 535.

— Problem of. (D. MacG. Means) Nation, 70: 332.

— Southwick Bill. (I. J. Wistar) Char. R. 6: 31.

— The Work at Dartmoor, England. (A. Griffiths) Pall Mall M. 22: 200.

Convict Prison, Life in a. Chamb. J. 78: 713-743.

Convict's Return. (W. N. Harben) Lippinc. 63: 549.

Convicted by a Dream. (G. H. Westley) Green Bag, 9: 356.

Convicts, What makes ? (J. D. Roth) Green Bag, 10: 513.

Convocation, Vivifying of. Spec. 79: 481.

Conway, Henry Seymour. (E. M. Chapman) New Eng. M. n. s. 19: 189.

Conway, Sir Martin. (F. Steelcroft) Strand, 13: 665.

Conyngham, Capt. Gustavus, Narrative of, while in Command of the "Surprise" and "Revenge," 1777-79. (M. B. Clark) Pennsyl. M. 22: 479.

Coogler, J. Gordon. Lit. W. (Bost.) 29: 56.

Cook, Henry Harvey. Bank. M. (N. Y.) 58: 601.

Cook, Capt. James. First Log in the Royal Navy ; a discovery. (E. E. Morris) Cornh. 80: 519.

Cook, John. Blackw. 166: 211.

Cook, John M. Geog. J. 13: 440.

Cookery, Anglo-Indian. (A. K. Herbert) Asia. R. 23: 138.

— Curiosities of. Chamb. J. 77: 327.

— A Mediæval Bill of Fare. (Mrs. A. Baldwin) Argosy, 70: 231.

— Teaching of. (M. Davies) Contemp. 73: 106.

Cookery Books, My. (E. R. Pennell) Atlan. 87: 789.

Cooking, English, Hayward on. Sat. R. 87: 554.

Cooking School, National, in 1883. (Lady Broome) Cornh. 80: 612.

Cooks and Cooking, French. (T. B. Preston) Chaut. 25: 32.

— Company, Training of. (M. L. Hersey) J. Mil. Serv. Inst. 21: 300.

— in Classical Times. (A. A. Benton) Sewanee, 2: 413.

— My. Cornh. 78: 255.

Cooling with Exhaust Steam. (A. D. Adams) Am. Arch. 69: 69.

Coomassie. See Kumassi.

Coombe, H. Bernard. Bank. M. (N. Y.) 54: 742.

'Coon Dog, The. (S. O. Jewett) Cent. 34: 498.

'Coon Hunt in Carolina. (F. A. Olds) Outing, 33: 383.

'Coon-hunting by Comet Light. (S. Waterloo) Outing, 37: 506.

Cooper, Abraham. (G. D. Leslie and F. A. Eaton) Art J. 51: 138.

Cooper, Frank, Portrait of. Theatre, 39: 187.

Cooper, Grace ; a Biography. (E. H. Cooper) Fortn. 70: 440. Same art. Liv. Age, 219: 299.

Cooper, J. Fenimore. (M. A. D. Howe) Bookman, 5: 14.

— and Mark Twain. (D. L. Maulsby) Dial (Ch.) 22: 107.

Cooper, J. Fenimore. Fenimore Cooper To-day. Outl. 69: 1037.
— Last of the Mohicans. (F. L. Pattee) Chaut. 31: 287.
— Leather-stocking Tales. (T. E. Kebbel) Macmil. 79: 191.
— Ned Myers. (G. P. Keese) Bookman, 7: 393.
— Places mentioned in Novels of. (J. N. Phillips) Midland, 9: 483.
— Spy, Original of Harvey Birch in. (H. E. Miller) New Eng. M. n. s. 18: 307.
Cooper, John Haldeman, 1828–97 ; Obituary Notice. J. Frankl. Inst. 144: 154.
Cooper, Sarah B. (G. G. DeAguirre) Arena, 17: 929.
Cooper, Rev. Samuel. Almanacs of, 1764–69. (F. Tuckerman) N. E. Reg. 55: 145.
— Diary of, 1775–76. Am. Hist. R. 6: 301.
Cooper, Dr. Thomas, Letters of, 1825–32. Am. Hist. R. 6: 725.
Cooper's Hill College. Nature, 63: 399, 568.
— Dismissal of Faculty from. Nature, 63: 378.
Co-operation, Anglo-American. (N. Barnaby) Engin. M. 16: 1.
— between Employers and Trade Unions. (H. W. Hoyt) Engin. M. 19: 173.
— by Farmers. (F. L. McVey) J. Pol. Econ. 6: 401.
— Difficulties and Limits of. (Lord Brassey) 19th Cent. 43: 915.
— A Dutch Co-operative Experiment. (A. W. Small) Am. J. Sociol. 7: 80.
— Failure of. (J. Ackland) Econ. R. 7: 338.
— — at Grimsby, England. (H. P. Willis) Nation, 73: 240.
— Freedom and Growth through. (B. O. Flower) Arena, 25: 210.
— Has it introduced a New Principle into Economics? (C. Gide) Econ. J. 8: 420.
— in Austria, Agricultural. (H. W. Wolff) Econ. R. 8: 248.
— in Business. (C. W. Whitney) Chaut. 29: 73.
— in England. (N. P. Gilman) Gunton's M. 20: 403.
— in France. (J. Cummings) Nation, 71: 342.
— — Agricultural, Rocquigny on. (H. W. Wolff) Econ. R. 10: 404.
— in Germany. (H. W. Wolff) Econ. R. 8: 246.
— in Practice. Econ. R. 8: 314.
— in Russia, Apostol's. (J. M. Ludlow) Econ. R. 9: 393.
— in the West. (W. S. Harwood) Atlan. 85: 539.
— Is it a Failure? (J. M. Ludlow and W. E. Snell) Econ. R. 7: 450.
— Labor Co-partnership. (A. Williams ; H. Vivian) Econ. R. 11: 201.
— Morality of. (L. Ross) Arena, 23: 183.
— Practical. (R. Halstead) Econ. R. 8: 446.
— Productive, in France. (C. Gide) Q. J. Econ. 14: 30.
— Sharing Prosperity. (R. E. Phillips) World's Work, 1: 761.
— Spread of. (H. W. Wolff) Econ. R. 10: 373.
— The World's. (H. W. Wolff) Econ. R. 8: 386.
Co-operative Association of America, The. (H. Vrooman) Arena, 26: 578.
"Co-operative Banking" Extraordinary. (H. W. Wolff) Econ. R. 9: 235.
Co-operative Congress, International, at Delft. (H. W. Wolff) Econ. R. 8: 30. — (W. H. Tolman) Outl. 59: 170.
— Some Impressions of. (F. Maddison) Econ. R. 10: 363. 11: 344.
Co-operative Ideals. (H. W. Wolff) Econ. R. 9: 42.
Co-operative Movement, Progress and Deterioration in. (H. W. Wolff) Econ. R. 11: 445.
Co-operative Press, The Local. (J. M. Ludlow) Econ. R. 8: 240.

Co-operative Production in England. (W. J. Ashley) Nation, 69: 203.
Co-operative Stores in the U. S. (E. Cummings) Q. J. Econ. 11: 266.
— in New England. (E. W. Bemis) Q. J. Econ. 11: 449.
Co-operative Unions not necessarily Republican. Sat. R. 88: 254.
Co-operative Workshops. (R. Shuddick) Westm. 152: 266.
Co-operators and the New Century. Westm. 156: 138.
Co-operators of Kettering. (J. Bonar) Econ. R. 9: 528.
Coote, C. H. Geog. J. 14: 99.
Copan, Honduras, Recent Discoveries in. (G. B. Gordon) Cent. 33: 407.
Cope, Edward Drinker. (J. S. Kingsley) Am. Natural. 31: 414. — (T. Gill) Am. Natural. 31: 831. — Nature, 55: 587. — (H. F. Osborn) Science, 5: 705. — (T. Gill) Science, 6: 225.
— a Great Naturalist. (H. F. Osborn) Cent. 33: 10.
— Memento of. (C. S. Minot) Science, n. s. 8: 113.
Cope, The, Origin of, as Church Vestment. (E. Bishop) Dub. R. 120: 17.
Copenhagen, Art Exhibition at, 1897. Art J. 49: 279.
— Battle of. (A. T. Mahan) Cent. 31: 525.
— Campaign of. (W. O'C. Morris) Pall Mall M. 14: 236.
— Royal Porcelain Manufactory. Illus. Artist (N. Y.) 23: 153.
Copernicus, with portrait. (C. Sterne) Open Court, 14: 385.
Copley, Sir T., Letters of ; ed. by R. C. Christie. Ath. '97, 2: 251.
Copley Boy, A. (C. Warren) Scrib. M. 26: 326.
Copper, and Bronze in Cyprus and Southeast Europe. (J. L. Myres) Anthrop. J. 27: 171.
— in Pennsylvania. (B. S. Lyman) J. Frankl. Inst. 146: 416.
— Mining of, in the U. S. (W. P. Kibbee) Cassier, 11: 215.
— Refining, by Electricity. (T. Ulke) Cassier, 12: 593.
— to Bronze, Transition from the Use of. (J. H. Gladstone) Anthrop. J. 26: 309.
— Volumetric Estimation of. (C. A. Peters) Am. J. Sci. 160: 359.
— World's Supply of. (F. H. Hatch) Engin. M. 18: 869.
Copper-mines of Ashio, Japan. (E. G. Adams, jr.) Engin. M. 22: 69.
— of Isle Royale, Lake Superior. (W. H. Holmes) Am. Anthropol. 3: 684.
Copper Mining. See Calumet.
Copper River Delta. (E. D. Preston) Nat. Geog. M. 11: 29.
Copperheads of the Civil War, The. (H. W. Wilson) National, 38: 107.
Coptic Grave-shirt, A. (E. A. W. Budge) Archæol. 53: 433.
"Copy ; " a dialogue. (Edith Wharton) Scrib. M. 27: 657.
Copying Machines, Early History of. (G. L. Apperson) Antiq. n. s. 36: 87.
Copyright. Ed. R. 191: 141.
— Anglo-American. (A. Austin) Pall Mall M. 20: 376.
— Bills of 1900. (Henry, Baron Thring) 19th Cent. 47: 1005.
— Book. (T. Solberg) Lib. J. 26: supp. 24.
— Duration of. Acad. 57: 579. — (G. B. Shaw) Acad. 58: 16.
— — Lord Monkswell's Bill. (G. H. Thring) Fortn. 73: 453.
— in News. Spec. 81: 9.
— in Speeches. Lit. W. (Bost.) 30: 280. — (R. Ogden) Nation, 69: 127. — Acad. 57: 191.

Copyright in Works of Art. (E. Bale) J. Soc. Arts, 48: 293. — Am. Arch. 60: 45. — (W. Reynolds-Stephens) Studio (Internat.) 7: 120.

— — Law of, an Exposition. (E. Bale) M. of Art, 23: 262.

— Ins and Outs of. (E. H. Spencer) Writer, 13: 65.

— International. (T. Solberg) Nation, 72: 83.

— — Possibilities of. (G. H. Thring) Fortn. 75: 894.

— Perpetual, Opinions on. Lit. W. (Bost.) 30: 360.

Copyright Act in Canada. Canad. M. 15: 475.

Copyright Law, Our Faulty. (R. Ogden) Nation, 68: 308.

— Proposed Change in. Critic, 31: 396.

Copyright Law Amendment. Nation, 72: 126.

Copyright Legislation. (W. H. Draper) Law Q. 17: 39.

— Paris Congress on. (T. Solberg) Nation, 71: 226.

— Recent Attempts at. (G. H. Thring) Fortn. 69: 461.

Copyright Reform, The Need of. (W. M. Colles) No. Am. 164: 472.

Coquelin, Bernard C., and Bernhardt. (H. Fouquier) Harper, 102: 63.

Coquette at the War. (I. K. Ritchie) Good Words, 42: 707.

Cor Cordium; a poem. (L. Thicknesse) Argosy, 70: 306.

Coral Atolls, Foundation of. (W. J. L. Wharton) Nature, 55: 390.

Coral Cactus and Rosy Cake. (A. M. Earle) New Eng. M. n. s. 23: 470.

Coral Reef at Funafuti, The. (W. J. Sollas) Nature, 55: 373.

Corals, Stramberg. (J. W. Gregory) Nature, 58: 280.

Corban. (Constance Smith) Temp. Bar, 119: 465. 120: 1–580. 121: 124.

Corbin Game Preserve. (G. T. Ferris) Cent. 32: 924.

Corcoran Gallery, Washington, Exhibition, 1900. (A. B. Bibb) Am. Arch. 68: 77.

Corday, Charlotte, the Angel of Assassination. (C. T. Clinton) Chaut. 32: 262.

Cordeaux, John. (A. Newton) Nature, 60: 398.

Cordeiro, Luciano. (E. G. Ravenstein) Geog. J. 17: 199.

Cordes. (E. C. Peixotto) Scrib. M. 29: 472.

Cordillera, Patagonian, and its Main Rivers, between 41° and 48° South Latitude. (H. Steffen) Geog. J. 16: 14, 185.

Cordite. Chamb. J. 74: 21.

Cordova, Spain. (A. Symons) Sat. R. 90: 294.

Cordova, Argentine Republic. (J. H. Kelley) Midland, 7: 291.

Corea. See Korea.

Corelli, Marie. (D. C. Murray) Canad. M. 9: 431.

— an Interview. (A. H. Lawrence) Strand, 16: 17.

— The Master-Christian. Acad. 59: 263. — Blackw. 168: 599. Same art. Liv. Age, 227: 385. Same art. Ecl. M. 136: 73.

— Religious Novels. Quar. 188: 306. Same art. Ecl. M. 132: 1.

— Theological Works of. Church Q. 51: 369. Same art. Liv. Age, 229: 201. Same art. Ecl. M. 136: 784.

Corfu and its Olive Groves. (C. E. Lloyd) Cosmopol. 22: 493.

Corinth, Agora at, Discovery of. (R. B. Richardson) Nation, 69: 147.

— — Discoveries in. (R. B. Richardson) Nation, 70: 472. — (R. B. Richardson) Indep. 52: 1855.

— American Discoveries at. (R. B. Richardson) Cent. 35: 852.

— Excavations at, in 1896. (R. B. Richardson) Am. J. Archæol. 2d s. 1: 455.

— Fountain of Glauce at. (R. B. Richardson) Am. J. Archæol. 2d s. 4: 457.

Corinth, Pre-Mycenean Graves in. (T. W. Heermance; G. D. Lord) Am. J. Archæol. 2d s. 1: 313.

— Roman Building in. (H. F. DeCou) Am. J. Archæol. 2d s. 1: 495.

— Theatre at. (F. C. Babbitt) Am. J. Archæol. 2d s. 1: 481.

Corinthian Church, Letter of, to St. Paul. (G. G. Findlay) Expos. 7: 401.

Corinthian Vase from Corinth. (R. B. Richardson) Am. J. Archæol. 2d s. 2: 195.

Cork, Siege of, in 1690. Un. Serv. M. 19: 625.

Corleone. (F. M. Crawford) Munsey, 16: 530, 707. 17: 49–849. 18: 41–738.

Corn as Fuel. (C. R. Richards) Cassier, 12: 683.

— and Oats, Cost of Production of, in Illinois in 1896. (N. A. Weston) Am. Statis. Assoc. 6: 30.

— Indian, and Cotton-seed; why the price for corn is low. (C. W. Davis) Forum, 24: 729.

— Lesson of the Maize Kitchen at Paris. (J. S. Crawford) Forum, 30: 157.

— Our Export of. (J. M. Stahl) No. Am. 166: 755.

— Varieties of. (C. E. Bessey) Science, n. s. 9: 880.

Corn-laws. How England averted a Revolution. (B. O. Flower) Arena, 24: 358.

Corn People, The; a story of Zuñi. (C. Galpin) Overland, n. s. 38: 218.

Cornaro, L., in English. (W. E. A. Axon) Library, n. s. 2: 120.

Cornell College, Mt. Vernon, Iowa. (Bessie J. Crary) Midland, 9: 129.

Cornell Glacier, Former Extension of. (T. C. Chamberlin) Science, 5: 748.

Cornely; a poem. (J. W. Howe) Nat'l M. (Bost.) 8: 357.

Cornelys, Mrs. Theresa. (E. Walford) Gent. M. n. s. 60: 451.

Corner Houses in Paris. (P. F. Marcou) Archit. R. 6: 310.

Cornered. (G. G. Farquhar) Chamb. J. 75: 236.

Cornet, The. (S. L. Jacobson) Music, 13: 622.

Cornet Player, The. (P. A. de Alarcón) Liv. Age, 212: 651.

Cornhill Magazine. Our Birth and Parentage. (G. M. Smith) Cornh. 83: 4.

Cornish Cook, The. (H. D. Lowry) Chamb. J. 77: 247.

Cornish Sketches. (Arthur Symons) Sat. R. 92: 297, 330.

Corns. A Curious Human Document. (L. Robinson) No. Am. 172: 599.

Cornu, Maxime. (W. T. Thiselton-Dyer) Natúre, 64: 211.

Cornwall, The Deep Mines of. (R. H. Sherard) McClure, 13: 184.

— Mines and Miners in. (J. H. Collins) J. Soc. Arts, 47: 359.

— Some Landscape Painters in. Illus. Artist (N. Y.) 23: 141.

— Superstition in. (W. C. Sydney) Belgra. 92: 45.

Coronado; a poem. (R. Burton) Outl. 68: 486.

Coronado Expedition, Winship's. (F. W. Hodge) Am Hist. R. 3: 370.

Coronation, The Next. (L. W. V. Harcourt) 19th Cent. 49: 975.

— of the Conqueror. (J. H. Round) Ath. '97, 1: 214.

— of an English Monarch, Some Curious Facts about. (J. De Morgan) Green Bag, 13: 287.

— of Monarchs. Illus. (A. P. Purey-Cust) Good Words, 38: 338, 416, 451.

— Omens at. (C. Benham) 19th Cent. 50: 799. Same art. Liv. Age, 231: 771.

Coronation Ceremonies. (Mrs. Belloc-Lowndes) Lippinc. 68: 710.

Coupon Clearing House, A. Bank. M. (Lond.) 67: 43.

Cour des Comptes. (G. C. d'Albi) Am. Arch. 37: 46.

Courage. (W. P. Garrison) Nation, 72: 330.

— the Chief Virtue. (W. Hutchinson) Open Court, 12: 193.

— Health and. Outl. 61: 444.

— Military. Spec. 80: 618.

— New Form of. Spec. 85: 880.

— Some Aspects of. (F. Foster) No. Am. 166: 678.

— True and Real. (W. Goddard) N. Church R. 7: 84.

Coureur de Bois ; a sketch. (W. McLennan) Canad. M. 11: 321.

Coureurs des Bois, or Coureurs de Bois. (G. Johnson) Canad. M. 13: 481.

Coursing in Kansas and Nebraska. (C. H. Morton) Outing, 38: 636.

Court of Law, In an English. Green Bag, 9: 5.

Court of Justice, In a. .(E. White) Green Bag, 10: 528.

Court of Record, What is a? (A. H. Alger) Am. Law R. 34: 70.

Court of Session in 1629. (H. P. Macmillan) Jurid. R. 12: 137.

Court Favorites, Souvenirs of Some. (Countess of Cork and Orrery) Fortn. 72: 26.

Court Presentation in England. (J. E. Wood) Canad. M. 17: 506.

Court Prisoners, A Gang of French, under Louis XIV. Macmil. 82: 432.

Court Scandal, A ; the play and its story. Eng. Illust. 21: 11.

Court Singers, A Quartette of, Four Centuries Ago. (O. Smeaton) Westm. 148: 179.

Courtenay, Miss Louisa ; notes of an Octogenarian. (Louisa Courtenay) Liv. Age, 230: 558.

Courtenay Tomb in Colyton Church, Devon. (W. H. H. Rogers) Archæol. 48: 157.

Courtesan of the French Stage. (A. De Ternant) Westm. 154: 671.

Courtesy. An Every-day Crime. (F. H. Freshfield) Westm. 153: 201.

— Has it Declined? (J. MacNeal) Munsey, 25: 590.

— in Modern Life. (E. G. Wheelwright) Westm. 153: 287.

Courting at Grizzly Spring. (J. Reimers) Overland, n. s. 32: 505.

Courting by Law ; a story. (F. Wayne) Nat'l M. (Bost.) 11: 81.

Courting of Gabriel Seabury. (M. N. Thurston) Lippinc. 68: 591.

Courtney, Leonard H., Some Characteristics of. Sat. R. 87: 454.

Courtot, Baroness Cécile de, Memoirs of. (C. D. Hazen) Am. Hist. R. 6: 130.

Courts and Politics. (B. Winchester) Green Bag, 12: 620.

— Irish Law, Humors of the. Chamb. J. 76: 539.

— — In the. (M. MacDonagh) Liv. Age, 222: 392.

— Law, Saxon and Latin. (W. S. Logan) Forum, 26: 703.

— Supreme, American System of. Green Bag, 13: 537.

— Three. (S. D. Thompson) Am. Law R. 34: 398.

— vs. Clearing Houses. (G. C. Worth) Am. Law R. 31: 213.

Courts of Love. (Edgar Saltus) Cosmopol. 28: 395.

Courtship and Marriage. (Mrs. Creighton) Sund. M. 26: 20.

— Game of, from No. Carolina. J. Am. Folk-Lore, 13: 104.

Courtship of Kezia, The. (C. Burke) Argosy, 73: 269.

Courtship of Mr. Philip Johns. (E. C. Shipman) Cent. 33: 469.

Courtship of Tambala Chalmers, The. (A. Werner) Gent. M. 64: 105. Same art. Liv. Age, 225: 28. Same art. Ecl. M. 134: 679.

Courtships, Literary. (E. A. Towle) Fortn. 72: 475. Same art. Liv. Age, 223: 220.

Courts-martial and Civilian Witnesses. (W. P. Evans) J. Mil. Serv. Inst. 12: 1004.

— Existing System of. (E. M. Cranston) No. Am. 168: 248.

— in England and America. (F. H. Jeune) No. Am. 168: 602.

— Notable American. (C. M. Rettock) Nat'l M. (Bost.) 9: 624.

Courtyer, The. (H. S. Wilson) Gent. M. n. s. 64: 461.

Cousin Flora ; a story. (E. Pugh) Pall Mall M. 16: 148.

Cousin Tom. (Blanche Atkinson) Good Words, 41: 813.

Coutts, F. B. Money, Poetry of. (S. Phillips) Acad. 54: 55.

Covenant, Book of the. (L. Abbott) Outl. 65: 351.

Covenant of Salt. (J. N. Fradenburgh) Meth. R. 58: 937.

Covent Garden, London. Pall Mall M. 24: 364. — (H. D. Lowry) Chamb. J. 78: 408.

Covent-Garden Journal, The. (A. Dobson) National, 37: 383. Same art. Liv. Age, 229: 793. Same art. Ecl. M. 137: 164.

Covent Garden Stars in Favorite Rôles. (K. Schlesinger) Strand, 18: 81.

Coventry, Eng., Notes from. (W. K. Watkins) N. E. Reg. 54: 182.

Cover, Screen, and Illusion. (M. Martin) J. Mil. Serv. Inst. 20: 365.

Coverdale Bible of 1535, The. (B. Quaritch) Ath. '00, 1: 465.

Covetousness. (W. M. Sinclair) Sund. M. 27: 793.

Covilhā, Portugal. Temp. Bar, 116: 112.

Cow-punchers on a "Round-up." (G. L. Burton) Outing, 36: 152.

Coward, A Miserable ; a story. (D. Ellis) Sund. M. 29: 299.

Cowbird, a Feathered Parasite. (L. S. Keyser) Pop. Sci. Mo. 55: 822.

Cowen, Frederic Hymen, Symphonies of. Sat. R. 85: 138.

Cowes, England, Notes on. (M. Beerbohm) Sat. R. 86: 232.

Cowles, Genevieve and Maude. (R. Armstrong) Critic, 37: 138.

Cowley, Abraham, Drag-net of. (S. T. Irwin) Monthly R. 2, no. 1 : 91.

— Letters of. (A. B. Grossart) Ath. '97, 2: 99.

Cowper, William. Acad. 58: 345, 349. — Cornh. 81: 694. Same art. Liv. Age, 225: 552. — (A. Law) Fortn. 73: 755. — (A. Birrell) Ecl. M. 135: 127. Same art. Liv. Age, 225: 391. — With portrait. Acad. 51: 381.

— and E. Gibbon ; a contrast. (C. J. Langston) Argosy, 66: 124.

— and the Ouse. (J. C. Tarver) Macmil. 82: 135. Same art. Ecl. M. 135: 364. Same art. Liv. Age, 226: 158.

— Centenary of. (A. E. Spender) Westm. 153: 532. — (E. M. Chapman) Outl. 64: 919. — (G. A. B. Dewar) Sat. R. 89: 521.

— Hymn "There is a Fountain." (A. Whyte) Sund. M. 28: 229.

— Letters of. (G. Cotterell) Argosy, 64: 152.

Cowper Centenary, The. (A. Moorhouse) Lond. Q. 93: 333.

Cowries, Colors of. (R. Lydekker) Knowl. 21: 270.

Cox, David. (Ja. Orrock) Art J. 50: 65.

Cox, George A., Canadian Senator. Canad. M. 14: 504.

Cricket in 1899. (A. C. Wootton) 19th Cent. 46: 792.
— Is it degenerating? (H. F. Abell) National, 31: 700.
— "Jubilee Cricket Book." (A. Lang) Longm. 30: 499. — Sat. R. 84: 170.
— Lost Art of Catching. (H. Macfarlane) Monthly R. 3, no. 2: 142.
— Modern Bowling. Sat. R. 92: 233, 265.
— New Light on. (J. Phillips) Blackw. 167: 780.
— Old and New. (F. Gale) Fortn. 68: 395. — Acad. 52: 175.
— The Parlous Condition of. (H. G. Hutchinson) National, 35: 789.
— Proposed Changed Rule. Sat. R. 92: 138.
— Records in. (H. Stuart) Blackw. 170: 339.
— Reform needed. Sat. R. 91: 565. — (W. G. Grace) Idler, 19: 383. — Blackw. 169: 189. — (A. Lyttelton) National, 34: 230.
— Run-getting. (G. L. Jessop) National, 30: 226.
— Sex in. (Frances A. Kelloe) Int. J. Ethics, 9: 74.
— Statistics and Comparisons. (J. H. Schooling) Pall Mall M. 15: 241, 347. 16: 101, 237.
— To bowl or to throw? (W. J. Ford) National, 36: 838.
— University. Sat. R. 89: 774.
Cricket-ball. What makes it Curl in the Air? (F. M. Gilbert) Strand, 15: 730.
Cricket Captaincy. Chamb. J. 77: 465.
Cricket Players, Recollections of Great. (E. G. Wynyard) Idler, 16: 114.
Cricket Playing, County. Sat. R. 90: 295.
— in Australia. Sat. R. 88: 228.
Cricketers, Australian, at Home. (M. R. Roberts) Strand, 18: 218.
Cricketers, Mid-century. (A. Lang) Eng. Illust. 17: 530.
Crickets, The Florentine. (S. Beale) Reliquary, 37: 65.
Crime and the Census. (R. P. Falkner) Ann. Am. Acad. Pol. Sci. 9: 42.
— and Criminal Law, A Retrospective Glance at. (J. A. Shearwood) Gent. M. n. s. 66: 500.
— and Punishment, Hegel's Conception of. (S. W. Dyde) Philos. R. 7: 62.
— — in England in the 18th Century. (G. B. Barton) Asia. R. 31: 46.
— Criminals and Prisons. (G. R. Vicars) Gent. M. n. s. 61: 575.
— Education in Respect to. (F. A. Kellar) Conserv. R. 5: 139.
— in Current Literature. Westm. 147: 429.
— in England. Quar. 185: 408.
— in Scotland, Calendar of. (H. Maxwell) Blackw. 162: 512, 657. Same art. Green Bag, 12: 278, 353.
— Increase of. Ann. Am. Acad. Pol. Sci. 13: 285.
— Influence of Weather upon. (E. G. Dexter) Pop. Sci. Mo. 55: 653.
— Juvenile Offenders, Morrison's. Sat. R. 83: 449.
— Language of. (A. F. B. Crofton) Pop. Sci. Mo. 50: 831.
— Obscure Causes of. (Thomas Holmes) Contemp. 76: 577.
— Practical Measures for promoting Manhood and preventing Crime. (B. O. Flower) Arena, 18: 673.
— Problem of. (F. H. Wines) Char. R. 7: 641.
— Professional, How to put an End to. (R. Anderson) 19th Cent. 50: 948.
— The Punishment of. (R. Anderson) 19th Cent. 50: 77.
— — an Admitted Failure. (C. J. Guthrie) Jurid. R. 13: 133.
— — Our Absurd System of. (R. Anderson) 19th Cent. 49: 268.
— Restitution to Victims of. (J. A. Stowe) Arena, 24: 102.

Crimes, New. (G. H. Westley) Green Bag, 13: 268.
— — and Penalties. (S. J. Barrows) Forum, 28: 529.
Crime of the Brigadier, The. (A. C. Doyle) Cosmopol. 28: 171.
Crimea, In the Haunted. (M. M. Norman) Contemp. 78: 38.
— Pages from a Surgeon's Journal in. (Sir G. H. B. Macleod) Good Words, 39: 46–763. Same art. Ecl. M. 130: 426.
Crimean Days, Old. (Sir Edmund Verney) Contemp. 76: 704.
Crimean Diary, Windham's. Ath. '97, 2: 119.
Crimean War, Navy in the. Un. Serv. M. 14: 652.
Criminal, The Hardened. Spec. 83: 777.
— in the Open. (J. Flynt) Forum, 22: 734.
— Insanity of the. (E. S. Yonge) Macmil. 79: 50.
— produced by Environment or Atavism? (I. Foard) Westm. 150: 90.
— Study of, in Mexico. (F. Starr) Am. J. Sociol. 3: 13.
Criminals, Betterment of. (A. R. Whiteway) Month, 91: 247.
— Condemnation of, not Punishment. (E. F. Brush) Pop. Sci. Mo. 50: 534.
— Curiously caught. Green Bag, 9: 80.
— An 18th Century Felon. (G. Paston) Longm. 39: 167.
— Felons or Misdemeanants, Best Treatment of. (Z. R. Brockway) Am. Soc. Sci. 39: 196.
— in Chicago. (J. Flynt) McClure, 16: 327.
— Making of. (C. D. Warner) Arena, 21: 15.
— Our Female. (E. Orme) Fortn. 69: 790.
— Probation of, in Massachusetts. (H. D. Ward) Indep. 52: 1437.
— Right Treatment of. (W. A. Knight) Bib. Sac. 57: 317.
— The Segregation and Permanent Isolation of. (N. Robinson) Arena, 18: 192.
— Treatment of, Prisons Bill and Progress in. (Sir E. du Cane) 19th Cent. 43: 809.
— Typical. (S. G. Smith) Pop. Sci. Mo. 56: 539.
— Women, Psychological and Environmental Study of. (Frances A. Kellor) Am. J. Sociol. 5: 527, 671.
— Young. Sat. R. 92: 550, 558.
Criminal Anthropology in Italy. (H. Zimmern) Pop. Sci. Mo. 52: 743. Same art. Green Bag, 10: 342, 382.
— in its Relation to Criminal Jurisprudence. (Frances A. Kellor) Am. J. Sociol. 4: 515, 630.
Criminal Appeal, Plea for a Court of. Sat. R. 84: 119.
Criminal Appearance, The. Liv. Age, 222: 525.
Criminal Cases, A Public Prosecutor in. (J. Johnston) Westm. 154: 692.
Criminal Classes in New York City. (J. Flynt) McClure) 16: 570.
Criminal Code of China. (A. Swindlehurst) Green Bag, 9: 297.
Criminal Jurisprudence, Decline of, in America. (G. C. Speranza) Pop. Sci. Mo. 56: 466.
Criminal Law, Reform in. (G. Pitt-Lewis) 19th Cent. 44: 591.
Criminal Legislation by Proxy. (F. Moss) Forum, 28: 46.
Criminal Procedure, French. (E. L. Gookin) Nation, 66: 162. — Quar. 191: 198.
— Margin of Error in. (W. M. Gloag) Jurid. R. 11: 87.
Criminal Proceedings in French Law, Revision of. (P. E. Weber) Jurid. R. 11: 26.
Criminal Prosecution, Needed Reform in. (S. Maxwell) Am. Law R. 32: 72.
Criminal Reform. (L. Ashburner) Westm. 156: 20.
Criminal Sociology. (E. W. McDaniel and A. Steckel) Arena, 23: 390.
— American vs. the Latin School. (Frances A. Kellor) Arena, 23: 301.

Criminal Statistics, Interpretation of. (W. D. Morrison) J. Statis. Soc. **60:** 1.

Criminal Tendencies in Boyhood. (E. J. Swift) Pedagog. Sem. **8:** 65.

— Checks to, needed. (J. L. Pickard) Educa. **17:** 389.

Criminal Trials, Early. Green Bag, **13:** 562.

Criminal Type, Lombroso's. (G. Tarde) Char. R. **6:** 109.

Criminality, Instinctive, and Social Conditions. (E. B. Rowlands) Law Q. **13:** 59.

Criminology and the University Curriculum. (F. H. Wines) Char. R. **6:** 44.

Crinoid, New, from the Hamilton of Charlestown, Indiana. (E. Wood) Am. J. Sci. **162:** 297.

Crinoids, Classification of, Wachsmuth and Springer's. Nat. Sci. **12:** 346.

Cripple Creek. (F. Lynde) Scrib. M. **27:** 603.

— Electricity in the Gold Mines at. (T. Tonge) Engin. M. **17:** 953.

Crippled Children, Day Schools for. (C. L. Brace) Char. R. **10:** 79.

Crises, Financial, and their Management. (C. A. Conant) Yale R. **9:** 374.

Crispi, Francesco. Acad. **57:** 154. — (P. d'Albàro) Contemp. **80:** 355. Same art. Liv. Age, **231:** 148. — With portrait. (S. Cortesi) Indep. **53:** 2026. — (G. M. Fiamengo) Macmil. **85:** 24. — (J. W. Mario) Nation, **73:** 165. — With portrait. Open Court, **15:** 645.

— and Italian Unity. (K. Blind) Forum, **32:** 298.

— Career of. Sat. R. **92:** 197.

— From Silvio Pellico to. (J. J. O'Shea) Am. Cath. Q. **26:** 798.

— Italy's Foremost Statesman, with portrait. (G. D. Vecchia) R. of Rs. (N. Y.) **24:** 457.

— Personal Recollections of. (Signor Raqueni) Open Court, **15:** 647.

— Political Survey of. (S. Cortesi) Internat. Mo. **4:** 622.

Crispin, Saint, and his Successors. (Edwin W. Kidd) Gent. M. n. s. **59:** 196.

Crispin, Capt. Wm., Commissioner for Settling the Colony in Pennsylvania. (O. Hough) Pennsyl. M. **22:** 34.

Crissey, Forrest. Writer, **14:** 106.

Critic, The Superfluous. (A. Gorren) Cent. **33:** 874.

Critical Dilemma; a story. (E. d'Arcy) Eng. Illust. **19:** 499.

Critical Expression, Right of. (M. Watson) Theatre, **39:** 133.

Critical Philosophy, Genesis of. (J. G. Schurman) Philos. R. **7:** 1, 135.

Criticism, American and English. (T. Cook) Acad. **52:** 451.

— Ancient and Modern. Quar. **193:** 359.

— and Æsthetics. (E. D. Puffer) Atlan. **87:** 839.

— and the Man. (J. Burroughs) Atlan. **84:** 342.

— Authority of. (W. P. Trent) Forum, **27:** 243.

— Cant in. Atlan. **87:** 142.

— Contemporary, Difficulties of. (E. Garnett) Monthly R. **5,** no. 3: 92.

— Democratic. (O. L. Triggs) Sewanee, **6:** 413.

— Development of. (H. T. Johnstone) Westm. **153:** 73.

— English, Development of. Church Q. **48:** 199.

— Ethics of. (R. Buchanan) Contemp. **77:** 221. Same art. Ecl. M. **134:** 634. Same art. Liv. Age, **224:** 729.

— French, Later Evolutions of. (E. Rod) Internat. Mo. **1:** 1.

— Function of, in the Advancement of Science. (F. H. Bigelow) Pop. Astron. **7:** 252.

— The "Gentilesse" of. (E. L. Cary) Bk. Buyer, **16:** 143.

Criticism, German. (R. M. Meyer) Internat. Mo. **3:** 526, 648.

— History of, Saintsbury's. (N. G. McCrea) Bookman, **13:** 448. — (H. O. Taylor) Internat. Mo. **4:** 295. — (Nowell Smith) Fortn. **76:** 596. — Ath. '01, **1:** 199. — (H. J. Edmiston) Nation, **73:** 113. — Outl. **68:** 689.

— Literary. (Arlo Bates) Bk. Buyer, **19:** 288.

— — in Verse. Acad. **59:** 363.

— Modern. (R. Burton) Critic, **30:** 17.

— Musical. (W. Beatty-Kingston) Theatre, **38:** 21.

— The New. Cornh. **81:** 116. Same art. Liv. Age, **224:** 432.

— On a Dictum of Matthew Arnold's. (J. Burroughs) Atlan. **79:** 713.

— The Pause in, — and After. (W. R. Thayer) Atlan. **80:** 227.

— Phraseology of Literary. Acad. **59:** 135, 157.

— Prolegomena of. (L. A. Sherman) Meth. R. **59:** 749. **60:** 361.

— Some Ideas on. (C. L. Moore) Dial (Ch.) **24:** 66.

— Two Kinds of. Spec. **84:** 870. Same art. Liv. Age, **226:** 259.

— which Helps. (C. H. Blackall) Archit. R. **5:** 67.

— which is Mere Advertising. Sat. R. **87:** 262.

Critics and Readers. (C. W. Hutson) Bookman, **14:** 280.

— Art, and the Critical Artist. (N. Garstin) Studio (Lond.) **1:** 128.

— Dramatic, Letters to. Theatre, **39:** 6-12.

— Living. (H. T. Peck) Bookman, **4:** 529.

— Living Continental. Bookman, **5:** 24, 106, 300, 487.

— Ready-made. (H. Elliott) Theatre, **38:** 25.

— Sensibility of. (S. Gwynn) Cornh. **80:** 229.

— Two Orders of. (C. L. Moore) Dial (Ch.) **26:** 360.

Crockery, Cranks in. (E. F. Spence) Eng. Illust. **20:** 584.

Crockett, Samuel Rutherford, with portrait. Bk. News, **16:** 481. — (D. C. Murray) Canad. M. **9:** 124.

Crocodile Shooting in India. (E. Stewart) Contemp. **73:** 540. Same art. Ecl. M. **130:** 716.

Croginolo; a tale. (A. Beresford) Argosy, **65:** 157.

Croker, John Wm. Temp. Bar, **117:** 327. — (P. A. Sillard) Gent. M. n. s. **61:** 145. Same art. Ecl. M. **131:** 617.

Croker, Richard. (W. A. White) McClure, **16:** 317. — With portrait. (W. A. White) Idler, **20:** 303. — (L. Seibold) Munsey, **25:** 628. — (G. Myers) National, **38:** 61.

— against Croker. Outl. **66:** 725.

— Influence of, Secret of. Gunton's M. **17:** 161.

— Rule of, A Sample of. (J. B. Bishop) Nation, **69:** 87.

— System of. (J. B. Bishop) Nation, **68:** 290.

— Testimony of, Mazet Investigation. Outl. **61:** 951.

Croll, James. Acad. **51:** 323. — Knowl. **20:** 101.

— Sketch of, with portrait. Pop. Sci. Mo. **51:** 544.

Crome, John, 1768-1821. (J. C. Van Dyke) Cent. **37:** 90.

Cromer, Lord, Biography of, Traill's. Sat. R. **83:** 559.

— in Egypt. (J. S. Horner) Un. Serv. M. **20:** 69.

Cromwell, Mary. Lady Fauconberg. (R. W. Ramsey) Gent. M. n. s. **62:** 376.

Cromwell, Oliver. (J. Telford) Lond. Q. **95:** 92. — Liv. Age, **223:** 793. — (J. Morley) Cent. **37:** 3, 257. — (A. J. Gade) Cosmopol. **26:** 565. — (W. Kirkus) New World, **7:** 430. — (J. Morley) Cent. **37:** 428-879. **38:** 226-874. — (T. Roosevelt) Scrib. M. **27:** 3-685. — (F. Harrison) Ecl. M. **134:** 214. — (S. D. White) Westm. **147:** 71. — (T. Hodgkin) Monthly R. **2,** no. 2: 82.

— Address on Unveiling of Statue of. (Earl of Rosebery) Critic, **36:** 43.

— and the Electorate. (J. H. Round) 19th Cent. **46:** 947.

Crowninshield's Brush ; a story.   (D. Gray) McClure, 17: 194.

Croxden Abbey, Staffordshire.   (G. Y. Wardle) Archæol. 49: 434.

Croxley Master, The.   (A. C. Doyle) Strand, 18: 363, 483, 615.

Cröy, Duke de, Memoirs of.   (A. Laugel) Nation, 64: 84, 141.

Crozier, John Beattie. My Inner Life. Church Q. 48: 367.

Crozier, William, Military Inventor and Expert. R. of Rs. (N. Y.) 19: 554.

Crozier's Scale.   (H. Seal) Westm. 153: 672.

Crucifix, The.   (P. Carus) Open Court, 13: 673.

Crucifixion and the War in the Creation.   (W. W. Peyton) Contemp. 78: 518, 835.

- Place of the.   (J. R. Thurston) J. Bib. Lit. 18: 203.

Cruelty, Legal. Sat. R. 84: 79.

Cruger, Mrs. Van Rensselaer. (Mrs. Clyde) Critic, 38: 370.

Cruikshank, George, Some Unpublished Sketches by. Strand, 14: 183.

Cruikshanks, The Three, Marchmont on. Ath. '98, 2: 136.

Cruise in a Cruiser, A. Chamb. J. 75: 569.

Cruise of the Catboat " Elsie ; " by the Cook. Outing, 34: 572.

Cruise of the "Catch-as-Can."   (Paul Shoup) Overland, n. s. 30: 516.

Cruise of the " Daisy," The. Spec. 81: 337. Same art. Liv. Age, 219: 454.

Cruise of the "Kodak," Missouri River. (C. F. Pearis) Outl. 59: 295.

Cruiser, The Armored. (B. W. Lees) Un. Serv. M. 22: 352.

Cruising in a Centerboard Sloop. (A. J. Kenealy) Outing, 33: 186.

— Lake Champlain to New York. (R. Bergengren) Outing, 30: 113.

Crusade, The Children's. (H. Jones) Sund. M. 26: 593.

Crusades, The. (F. F. Urquhart) Month, 92: 127.

— The Eve of the.   (S. Khuda Bukhsh) Westm. 147: 317.

— Origin of the Temporal Privileges of the Crusaders. (E. C. Bramhall) Am. J. Theol. 5: 279.

— their Influence on Economic Development of Western Europe. (H. Prutz) Internat. Mo. 4: 251.

Crushing and Pulverizing Machines. (J. Douglas) Cassier, 13: 496.

Crustacea. (T. R. R. Stebbing) Knowl. 22: 29-282.

— Curiosities about. (T. R. R. Stebbing) 19th Cent. 42: 293. Same art. Liv. Age, 215: 37.

— Current Carcinology. (T. R. R. Stebbing) Knowl. 24: 209.

— Karkinokosm, or World of. (T. R. R. Stebbing) Knowl. 23: 162.

— Prentiss's Otocyst of Decapod Crustacea. Am. Natural. 35: 857.

— Tropical, Young on. (T. R. R. Stebbing) Nature, 64: 98.

— Wonders and Blunders of. (T. R. R. Stebbing) Knowl. 23: 73, 211.

— World of. (T. R. R. Stebbing) Knowl. 21: 1-243.

Crustacean Idyl, A ; a story. (W. Cruikshank) Outing, 32: 341.

Crusty Sam's Pardner. (N. M. St. John) Sund. M. 29: 525.

Cruttenden, Abraham, of Guilford, Conn. (R. D. Smith) N. E. Reg. 52: 466.

Cry of the Child, The ; a story. (K. Tynan) Eng. Illust. 18: 411.

Cry of Fate, The ; a story. (A. E. Abbott) Idler, 12: 523.

Cry of a Soul, The. (S. L. Gerard) Overland, n. s. 33: 468.

Crypt, Saxon, at Kepton, England. Ath. '98, 2: 459.

Crystal Egg, The. (H. G. Wells) New R. 16: 556.

Crystal Gazing and Magic Mirrors. (A. Lang) Monthly R. 5, no. 3 : 115.

Crystalline Form, Significance of. (W. F. C. Morsell) J. Frankl. Inst. 150: 441.

Crystallization, Fractional, of Rocks.   (G. F. Becker) Am. J. Sci. 154: 257.

— Relation between Structural and Magneto-optic Rotation. (A. W. Wright and D. A. Kreider) Am. J. Sci. 156: 416.

Crystallography, Applications of, to Physical Chemistry. Sci. Prog. n. s. 1: 569.

Crystals, Dextro- and Lævo-rotating, Method for the Detection and Separation of. (D. A. Kreider) Am. J. Sci. 158: 133.

— Liquid. (H. A. Miers) Sci. Prog. n. s. 1: 119.

— Orthoclase, from Shinano, Japan. (C. Iwasaki) Am. J. Sci. 158: 157.

— Physical Properties of. (W. H. and G. C. Young) Nature, 58: 100.

Ctenacanthus Spines from the Keokuk Limestone of Iowa. (C. R. Eastman) Am. J. Sci. 154: 10.

Cub Reporter, The, and the King of Spain. (J. L. Williams) Scrib. M. 25: 277.

Cuba. Maps and Illus. (R. T. Hill) Nat. Geog. M. 9: 193.

— American Misgovernment of. (J. E. Runcie) No. Am. 170: 284.

— and Armenia. (T. Williams) Cent. 35: 634.

— and the Cubans. Chamb. J. 74: 153.

— and her People. (W. E. Curtis) Chaut. 27: 183.

— and her Struggle for Freedom. (F. Lee) Fortn. 69: 855. Same art. Liv. Age, 218: 155.

— and its Value as a Colony. (R. T. Hill) Forum, 25: 403.

— and the Philippines. Outl. 67: 567.

— — Indian Civil Service, A Model for. (J. Jardine) Asia. R. 27: 225.

— — the Territory with which we are Threatened. (W. Reid) Cent. 34: 788.

— and Porto Rico, Past Military and Naval Operations directed against. (C. H. Stockton) J. Mil. Serv. Inst. 28: 265.

— — Our Relation to the People of. (O. H. Platt) Ann. Am. Acad. Pol. Sci. 18: 145.

— — Spanish Population of. (C. M. Pepper) Ann. Am. Acad. Pol. Sci. 18: 163.

— and Spain. (C. H. Lincoln) Citizen, 4: 54.

— — Historical Sketch. Outl. 58: 909.

— — Neutrality of U. S. toward. (W. J. Palmer) Outl. 58: 1014.

— and the U. S. (H. Rochefort) Forum, 23: 155. — (W. H. Philips) National, 28: 598.

— Annexation of, Plea for. (A Cuban) Forum, 30: 202.

— — Why it should be Independent. (C. W. Currier) Forum, 30: 139.

— Architecture in. Our acquired Architecture. (M. Schuyler) Archit. R. 9: 277.

— as an Allied Republic of U. S. (P. Carus) Open Court, 12: 690.

— as a Field for Emigration. Chamb. J. 77: 708.

— as Seen from the Inside. (O. Welsh) Cent. 34: 586.

— Autonomy for. Outl. 58: 1012.

— — or Independence for ? (H. White) Nation, 66: 178.

— Bankruptcy Imminent in. (E. F. Atkins) No. Am. 173: 768.

— Better Days in. (R. Ogden) Nation, 68: 272.

— Blockade of, Incidents of. (W. Russell) Cent. 34: 655.

Cuba, Reciprocity with. (E. Nuñez) Indep. **53**: 2579.
— — Need for. (L. Wood) Indep. **53**: 2927.
— Reconstruction in. (R. J. Hinton) No. Am. **168**: 92.
— Red Cross in, A Ride for. (C. R. Gill) Scrib. M. **25**: 111.
— Red Cross Work and Observations in. (C. Barton) No. Am. **166**: 552.
— Regeneration of. (G. Kennan) Outl. **61**: 497 — **63**: 151–407.
— Relief in, Plan for. (W. W. Howard) Outl. **58**: 916.
— (W. W. Howard) Outl. **61**: 963.
— Relieving the Reconcentrados of. (C. Barton) Indep. **51**: 2067.
— Renovation in. (R. Ogden) Nation, **69**: 237.
— Republic of. (R. J. Hinton) Arena, **21**: 587.
— Roman Catholic Church in. (E. S. Houston) Cath. World, **68**: 794.
— School Question of. (A. G. Robinson) Indep. **53**: 385.
— Self-government of. (A. G. Robinson) Indep. **52**: 2968.
— Situation in. (O. G. Villard) Nation, **70**: 201.
— Social Conditions in. (F. L. Oswald) Open Court, **12**: 714.
— Society in. (M. C. Francis) Munsey, **23**: 489.
— Solution of the Cuban Problem. (O. H. Platt) World's Work, **1**: 729.
— Some Economic Consequences of the Liberation of. (G. K. Olmsted) Yale R. **7**: 168.
— Spain and. (J. H. Babcock) Chaut. **24**: 584. — (B. J. Clinch) Am. Cath. Q. **22**: 809.
— — and the United States. (C. Benoist) Chaut. **25**: 384.
— Spain in. (A. G. Pérez) 19th Cent. **44**: 196.
— Spain's Extortions from. (R. Cabrera) Gunton's M. **12**: 27.
— Spaniards in. (A. G. Pérez) Ecl. M. **131**: 395.
— Spanish Soldier's View. Sat. R. **85**: 611.
— Subsequent to the Ten Years' War, 1878–95. (A. G. Pérez) Un. Serv. M. **18**: 385.
— Talk with General Wood. (E. Marshall) Outl. **68**: 669.
— Tariff Bribe for. (R. Ogden) Nation, **72**: 248.
— Ten Years' War in. (A. G. Pérez) Un. Serv. M. **18**: 89.
— Terms of Autonomy of. (R. Ogden) Nation, **65**: 510.
— Trade of U. S. with. (J. Hyde) Nat. Geog. M. **9**: 247.
— under American Rule. (W. Root) Munsey, **21**: 561.
— under Spanish Rule. (F. Lee) McClure, **11**: 99.
— under Spanish vs. American Rule. Sat. R. **85**: 649.
— United States and Cuban Independence. (F. J. Matheson) Fortn. **69**: 816. Same art. Liv. Age, **217**: 505.
— United States in. (L. B. Ellis) Arena, **24**: 57.
— Wanton Destruction of American Property in. (F. A. Yznaga) Forum, **22**: 571.
— War in, 1898, The Object Lesson of the. (L. Williams) Westm. **148**: 255.
— — Some Economic Aspects of. (C. A. Harris) Econ. J. **7**: 435.
— — Why Spain has Failed in. (T. G. Alvord, jr.) Forum, **23**: 564.
— — Witnesses of. (P. Duffield) Bk. Buyer, **17**: 615.
— What is to be done with? (M. W. Hazeltine) No. Am. **167**: 318.
Cuban Diplomacy, A Century of, 1795–1895. (A. B. Hart) Harper, **96**: 127.
Cuban Educational Association of the U. S. (G. K. Harroun) R. of Rs. (N. Y.) **20**: 334.
Cuban Filibuster, A ; a story. (H. Bindloss) Macmil. **77**: 143. Same art. Liv. Age, **216**: 233.
Cuban Insurgent Newspaper. (T. W. Steep) Nat'l M. (Bost.) **8**: 147.

Cuban Insurgents, Ten Months with the. (E. W. Fenn) Cent. **34**: 302.
— their Defects and Merits. (O. O. Howard) Outl. **59**: 973.
Cuban Justice, Romantic. (G. H. Westley) Green Bag, **9**: 336.
Cuban Pictures. (H. Clergue) Temp. Bar, **115**: 535.
Cuban Reconstruction, Some Young Cuban Leaders in. (G. Reno) R. of Rs. (N. Y.) **19**: 319.
Cuban Settlers in America. (D. A. Willey) Chaut. **27**: 346.
Cuban Teachers at Cambridge. (J. Martinez) Indep. **52**: 1847. — (M. C. Francis) Nat'l M. (Bost.) **12**: 237. — (S. Baxter) Outl. **65**: 773. — (E. M. Camp) Chaut. **31**: 626. — (E. C. Hills) Harv. Grad. M. **9**: 37. — (R. Clapp) Educa. R. **20**: 217.
— Height and Weight of. (D. A. Sargent) Pop. Sci. Mo. **58**: 480.
Cubans, Character of. (F. H. Nichols) Outl. **62**: 707. — (C. Marriott) R. of Rs. (N. Y.) **19**: 176.
— Conduct of, in the Late War. (O. O. Howard) Forum, **26**: 152.
Cuckoo, The. Sat. R. **89**: 645. Same art. Liv. Age, **226**: 134.
— An English Idyll. (F. A. Fulcher) Ecl. M. **129**: 135. Same art. Liv. Age, **214**: 56.
— Habit of Newly Hatched, Sharpe on. Sat. R. **87**: 264, 305.
Cuckoo Clock, The ; a story. (E. D. Deland) Harper, **100**: 598.
Cuckoo Clock, The ; a poem. (P. Fitzgerald) Gent. M. n. s. **64**: 204.
Cuddy, Etymology of the Nautical Word. (H. Beveridge) Ath. '00, **2**: 153.
Culloden, The "No Quarter" Order at. (W. Roberts) Ath. '99, **1**: 309.
Culm in Anthracite Coal Mines. (W. Griffith) J. Frankl. Inst. **149**: 271.
Culpeper, Nicholas. (S. Peel) 19th Cent. **43**: 755.
Culross. (J. Geddie) Chamb. J. **75**: 529.
Culture and Education. (W. Rein) Forum, **26**: 693.
— European, Origin of. (W. Z. Ripley) Pop. Sci. Mo. **55**: 16.
— Fad of Imitation Culture. (J. L. Ford) Munsey, **24**: 153.
— Middle-Class, Fifty Years Ago. (J. G. Alger) Westm. **156**: 283.
— Modern. (Austin Bierbower) Educa. **19**: 543.
— Modern Hindrances. (Isabel F. Bellows) Educa. **20**: 160.
— New, for New Conditions. (M. H. Liddell) World's Work, **1**: 55.
— Short Cuts to. (Inkersley) Educa. **19**: 532.
Culture Agencies of a Typical Manufacturing Group ; South Chicago. (J. M. Gillette) Am. J. Sociol. **7**: 91, 188.
Cumæ ; Remnant of Paganism. (F. C. Dunlop-Wallace-Goodbody) Gent. M. n. s. **65**: 491.
Cumberland, Duke and Duchess of. (A. De Burgh) Eng. Illust. **20**: 183.
Cumberland, Richard, the English Terence. (G. B. Smith) Fortn. **73**: 243.
Cumberland Mountains and the Struggle for Freedom. (W. E. Burton) New Eng. M. n. s. **16**: 65.
Cumberland Valley, Pa., "Old Mother Cumberland." (G. O. Seilhamer) Pennsyl. M. **14**: 17.
Cummings, Hon. John. (W. R. Cutter) N. E. Reg. **53**: 273.
Cummings, Wm. H., Musician, with portrait. Music, **16**: 69.
Cunningham, Andrew, of Boston, and Some of his Descendants. (H. W. Cunningham) N. E. Reg. **55**: 304, 406.

Cycling, Historical and Practical. (G. L. Hillier) J. Soc. Arts, 45: 440.
— in the Black Forest. (A. P. Atterbury) Outing, 32: 252.
— in Cathay. (T. P. Terry) Outing, 38: 536.
— in Cuba. (C. P. Sweeney) Outing, 29: 424.
— in Europe. (J. Pennell) Harper, 96: 680.
— in France. (S. Cross) Outing, 34: 3-403.
— in Japan. (T. P. Terry) Outing, 33: 341. — (T. P. Terry) Outing, 30: 208.
— in Madeira. (W. J. Reid) Outing, 35: 270. — (W. J. Reid) Outing, 35: 375.
— in North Georgia. (H. F. Huntington) Outing, 31: 381.
— in Old Japan. (T. P. Terry) Outing, 37: 29.
— in Porto Rico. (L. H. Ives) Outing, 36: 45.
— in the Sandwich Islands. (T. P. Terry) Outing, 33: 585.
— Intercollegiate Cycle Championships. (D. Hines) Outing, 30: 432.
— League of American Wheelmen, Annual Meeting. (A. H. Godfrey) Outing, 31: 3.
— Military, — after H. G. Wells. (E. Balfour) Fortn. 75: 294.
— — Experiments in. (J. A. Moss) Outing, 29: 488.
— over New Jersey Highlands. (A. H. Godfrey) Outing, 33: 8.
— over an Old Virginia Pike. (G. H. Streaker) Outing, 35: 147.
— Path-building in 1900. (R. Bruce) Outing, 36: 182.
— Rewards of. (P. Pollard) Outing, 36: 299.
— Riverside, Cal., to Santa Ana. (L. W. Garland) Outing, 29: 580.
— round Old Manhattan. (A. H. Godfrey) Outing, 32: 130.
— a Royal Road to Health. Chamb. J. 74: 193.
— Sixty Years of. Eng. Illust. 17: 509.
— through France. (G. H. Leonard, jr.) Outing, 35: 598.
— through Middle England. (A. L. Moque) Outing, 29: 460.
— through San Joaquin. (C. H. Shinn) Outing, 34: 590.
— through Shenandoah Valley. (D. F. Gay) Outing, 32: 232.
— through some English Villages. Macmil. 77: 203. 78: 41.
— Twenty Years of. (J. and E. R. Pennell) Fortn. 68: 188. Same art. Ecl. M. 129: 522. Same art. Liv. Age, 214: 712.
— up the Catskills. (A. H. Godfrey) Outing, 32: 458. See also Bicycling.
Cycling Accident Risks. Bank. M. (Lond.) 65: 125.
Cycling Clubs. (A. H. Godfrey) Outing, 30: 341.
— and their Spheres of Action. Outing, 30: 488.
Cycling Courtship, A. (M. S. Greene) Belgra. 97: 86.
Cycling Epidemic. Scot. R. 29: 56.
Cycling Route, The Finest, in the World. (J. F. Fraser) Chamb. J. 75: 395. Same art. Liv. Age, 218: 605.
Cyclist, The Soldier. (H. G. Wells) Fortn. 75: 572.
Cyclist's Day, A ; a poem. (A. H. Hall) Outing, 30: 216.
Cyclones. (F. H. Bigelow) Science, n. s. 13: 589.
— and Hurricanes. (J. Madden) National, 33: 107.
— and their Habits. (H. B. Goodwin) Un. Serv. M. 20: 457.
Cylinder-boring Machines, American. (H. B. Binsse) Cassier, 14: 517.
Cylix, by Duris, Signed, in Boston. (F. B. Tarbell) Am. J. Archæol. n. s. 4: 183.
Cynthia's Wager. (A. C. Deane) Temp. Bar, 117: 351. Same art. Liv. Age, 222: 634.
Cyperaceæ, Studies in. (T. Holm) Am. J. Sci. 153: 121, 429. 154: 13, 298. 155: 47. 157: 5, 171, 435. 158: 105. 159: 355. 160: 33, 266. 161: 205.

Cyprian, St., and the Holy See. (W. Barry) Am. Cath. Q. 22: 554.
— Benson's. (T. J. Shahan) Am. Hist. R. 3: 342. — (G. McDermot) Cath. World, 66: 146. — Church Q. 45: 25. — Sat. R. 83: 386. — (F. H. Chase) Crit. R. 7: 341.
— A High-Churchman of the 3d Century. (E. W. Benson) Lond. Q. 89: 253.
Cypripediums, Notes on. (A. Herrington) Garden & F. 10: 4.
Cyprus, Actual and Possible. (P. Geddes) Contemp. 71: 892. Same art. Liv. Age, 214: 247.
— Archæology of. Nature, 61: 195.
Cyrano de Bergerac. See Bergerac ; Rostand.
Cyrus, the Lord's Anointed. (A Carr) Expos. 10: 335.
Cyrus Pincher's Threshing Bee ; a tale. (A. Bridle) Canad. M. 11: 480.
Cytological Problems, Present Aspect of Some, Wilson on. (J. B. Farmer) Nature, 63: 437.
Czarine, La. (Saidee G. Bugbee) Overland, n. s. 35: 511.
Czolgosz Trial, Lesson of the. (R. Ogden) Nation, 73: 332.

Da Costa, John. (G. White) M. of Art, 22: 345.
— and his Work. Studio (Lond.) 4: 84.
Daddy's Daughter. (R. Jacberns) Sund. M. 27: 558.
Daffodil, The. (H. Macmillan) Sund. M. 29: 167. Same art. Liv. Age, 225: 41.
Daffodils. Sat. R. 87: 521. Same art. Liv. Age, 221: 724.
Daft, Leo. Cassier, 20: 263.
Dafydd ap Gwilym. Quar. 194: 396.
Daghestan, A Trip in. (A. C. Coolidge) Nation, 67: 164.
Dagnan-Bouveret, P. A. J. In the Louvre. Art J. 49: 216.
Dahlias. Sat. R. 92: 359.
— of Mexico, Native. (J. W. Harshberger) Science, 6: 908.
Dahomey, Trouble in. (H. Bindloss) Belgra. 96: 175.
Dairy Industry in Canada. (J. W. Wheaton) Canad. M. 13: 51.
Dairy Produce and Milk Supply. (M. J. Dunstan) J. Soc. Arts, 45: 459.
Daisy, The ; a poem. (A. H. Japp) Argosy, 63: 445.
Dakota Hero, A. (Ed. S. Bond) Good Words, 38: 708.
Dale, Robert William. (R. F. Horton) Contemp. 75: 34. — Church Q. 47: 354. — (P. T. Forsyth) Lond. Q. 91: 193.
— Life of, by A. W. W. Dale. (A. H. Bradford) Outl. 63: 596.
Dalkeith Palace, Scotland. (H. Scott) Pall Mall M. 16: 4.
Dalles, The ; from Savagery to Civilization. (W. A. Tenney) Overland, n. s. 34: 141.
— of Wisconsin. (M. McNeal) Midland, 11: 207.
Dallin, Cyrus E. (W. H. Downes) New Eng. M. n. s. 21: 196. — (W. H. Downes) Brush & P. 5: 1.
Dalmatia as a Sketching Ground. (J. Pennell) Studio (Lond.) 5: 81.
— In. (T. M. Lindsay) Good Words, 39: 304, 389.
Dalmeny Experiments. (D. Young) 19th Cent. 46: 782.
Daly, Augustin. (A. I. du P. Coleman) Critic, 35: 712.
— With portrait. (M. White, jr.) Munsey, 21: 736.
— and his Life-work. (G. Kobbé) Cosmopol. 27: 405.
— Library of. (W. Roberts) Ath. '00, 1: 371. — (L. R. McCabe) Bk. Buyer, 20: 33.
— The Story of the Daly Bible, with portrait. (L. R. McCabe) Cath. World, 70: 809.
— Theatrical Portraits of. (W. Rome ; W. Roberts) Ath. '00, 1: 412, 476.
— Treasures of Library of. (C. Shipman) Critic, 36: 213.

Dante. Theory of Papal Politics. (G. McDermot) Cath. World, **65**: 356.
— Traced to India. (W. Hopkins) Nation, **73**: 277.
— Virgilio's Epitaph on. (P. H. Wicksteed) Ath. '00, **2**: 87, 124.
— Vision of Sin. (C. A. Dinsmore) Bib. Sac. **58**: 378.
— Western Precursors of. (E. Hull) Cornh. **79**: 237.
— Witte's Essays on. (E. G. Gardner) Month, **93**: 47.
Dante Literature, 1899. Ath '99, **1**: 652.
Dante's Correspondence with Guido and Messer Cino. Month, **94**: 474.
Dante's Quest of Liberty. (C. A. Dinsmore) Atlan. **87**: 515.
Dante's Vision, Date of. Quar. **194**: 149.
Danton, Georges Jacques. Acad. **56**: 375. — (I. A. Taylor) Longm. **35**: 130.
— Beesly's Life of. (H. C. Macdowall) Macmil. **80**: 184. — (H. E. Bourne) Dial (Ch.) **27**: 70. — Ath. '99, **2**: 245.
— Death of. (H. Belloc) Liv. Age, **221**: 398.
Danu, Tribes of. (W. B. Yeats) New R. **17**: 549.
Danube, Down, in a Canadian Canoe. (A. Blackwood) Macmil. **84**: 350, 418. Same art. Liv. Age, **231**: 677-747.
— Stormy Trip on. Sat. R. **90**: 485.
Danyell, John, Bell of. Ath. '00, **2**: 95.
Darby Gill and the Good People; a fairy story. (H. Templeton) McClure, **18**: 124.
Darby Township, Chester County, Penn., Names of Early Settlers. (M. Bunting) Pennsyl. M. **14**: 182.
Dardanelles, Question of the. (J. G. Whiteley) Yale R. **5**: 374.
Dargai, Frontal Attack on. Un. Serv. M. **19**: 169.
Dargai Redge; a poem. (R. Gourlay) Canad. M. **10**: 232.
Dariel; a Romance of Surrey. (R. D. Blackmore) Blackw. v. **161, 162.**
Darien, Georges. (L. de La Ramée) Fortn. **68**: 341. Same art. Liv. Age, **215**: 283.
Darien Gold-mining Region of Colombia. (E. J. Chibas) Engin. M. **16**: 49.
Daring Deeds. Ecl. M. **130**: 575.
Dark Brown Dog; a story. (Stephen Crane) Cosmopol. **30**: 480.
Dark Davie, Visions of. (F. Langbridge) Sund. M. **26**: 152.
Dark er de Moon; a Devil Tale. (V. F. Boyle) Harper, **100**: 58.
Dark Prince, The; a story. (N. Hopper) Eng. Illust. **20**: 33.
Dark Races, Minds of the. Spec. **86**: 796.
Darkest England Estate; Industrial Experiment. (W. H. Hunt) Westm. **154**: 285.
Darking, an Old Yorkshire Word. Acad. **51**: 618.
Darling, Grace, Grave of. (Mrs. E. E. Cuthell) Belgra. **98**: 253.
Darmstadt, Artist Colony in. (J. Q. Adams) R. of Rs. (N. Y.) **24**: 201. — (W. Fred) Studio (Internat.) **15**: 22, 91.
— New Palace, Furniture of. (M. B. Scott) Studio (Internat.) **7**: 107.
D'Arnalle, Vernon, Baritone Singer, with portrait. Music, **17**: 640.
Darragh, Lydia, of the Revolution. (Henry Darrach) Pennsyl. M. **23**: 88.
Dartmoor Prison, Convict Work in. (A. Griffiths) Pall Mall M. **22**: 200.
Dartmouth, Augusta, Countess of. (F. D. How) Sund. M. **30**: 690.
Dartmouth College Graduates, Statistics of Professions of. (F. H. Dixon) Yale R. **10**: 84.
Darwin, Charles, with portrait. Acad. **51**: 406.
— Americanisms of. (C. F. Smith) Indep. **53**: 2706.

Darwin, Charles. Idea of Mental Development. (M. H. Carter) Am. J. Psychol. **9**: 534.
— Ill-health of. (W. W. Johnston) Am. Anthrop. **3**: 139.
— Origin of Species, Reception of. (T. H. Huxley; The Edinburgh Reviewer; L. Agassiz; A. Gray) Pop. Sci. Mo. **60**: 177.
— Reminiscences of. (Sir J. D. Hooker) Nature, **60**: 187.
— Spencer and. (Grant Allen) Fortn. **67**: 251. Same art. Ecl. M. **128**: 463. Same art. Pop. Sci. Mo. **50**: 815.
Darwinian Botany. (A. H. Japp) Lond. Q. **96**: 193.
Darwinism and Design. (F. C. S. Schiller) Contemp. **71**: 867.
— and Lamarckism, Old and New, Hutton's Lectures on. (E. B. Poulton) Nature, **63**: 365.
— and Sir Henry Maine. Asia. R. **26**: 20.
— and the Primrose. Lond. Q. **92**: 200.
— and State Craft. (G. P. Mudge) Nature, **63**: 561.
— Dreyer on. (Tr. by F. R. Weldon) Nature, **59**: 365.
— Hutchinson on. (G. Macloskie) Presb. & Ref. R. **11**: 152.
Dash for Freedom, A; a story. (W. P. Ridge) Eng. Illust. **17**: 197.
Daskam, J. D. The Imp and the Angel. (Carolyn Wells) Bk. Buyer, **23**: 385.
Dasypeltis and the Egested Egg-shell. (G. B. Howes) Nature, **63**: 326.
Date-lines in the Pacific Ocean. (B. E. Smith) Cent. **36**: 742.
Date-palm Scale Insect. (T. D. A. Cockerell) Science, n. s. **9**: 417.
Datolite from Guanajuato. (O. C. Farrington) Am. J. Sci. **155**: 285.
Daudet, Alphonse. (A. Symons) Sat. R. **84**: 739. — (A. S. Van Westrum) Critic, **31**: 395. — Acad. **52**: 574. — Acad. **56**: 604. — (J. Viaud) Critic, **35**: 893. — (V. M. Crawford) Contemp. **73**: 182. Same art. Liv. Age, **216**: 819. — (H. Lynch) Fortn. **69**: 943. — Liv. Age, **216**: 278. — (E. Zola) Critic, **32**: 51. — Dial (Ch.) **24**: 5. — With portrait. (A. Cohn) Bookman, **6**: 502. — With portrait. (M. L. Van Vorst) Bk. Buyer, **16**: 34. — With portrait. Midland, **10**: 90. — (Jules Clarétie) Ath. '98, **1**: 53.
— and his Friends. Liv. Age, **220**: 599.
— and his Intimates. (J. F. Raffaëlli) Lippinc. **64**: 952.
— and the Making of the Novel. (A. B. Maurice) Bookman, **13**: 42.
— Chief Works and Style. (A. F. Davidson) Macmil. **78**: 175.
— Early Years of. (E. H. Barker) Temp. Bar, **116**: 82.
— Funeral of. (T. Stanton) Critic, **32**: 19.
— The Head of the Family. (F. C. Mortimer) Bk. Buyer, **16**: 523.
— — Mistranslation of. Acad. **53**: 675.
— in Private Life. (J. F. Raffaëlli) Pall Mall M. **16**: 293.
— Life, by L. Daudet. (B. W. Wells) Dial (Ch.) **26**: 242.
— Notes on. Sat. R. **83**: 43,
— Sapho. (H. T. Peck) Bookman, **11**: 158.
— Sketch of. R. of Rs. (N. Y.) **17**: 161.
Daughter, The Loyal, in Literature. (C. Porter and H. A. Clarke) Poet-Lore, **9**: 100.
Daughter of Accra Queens; a story. (A. J. Dawson) Idler, **11**: 608.
Daughter of the Aurora, A; a story. (J. London) Nat'l M. (Bost.) **13**: 223.
Daughter of the Island of Woods; a poem. (W. B. Yeats) Ecl. M. **132**: 501.

Deaconesses, Early History and Modern Revival of. Church Q. **47**: 302.

Dead, The. (P. W. Roose) Argosy, **65**: 493.

— Disposal of. (F. S. Haden) Am. Arch. **59**: 69.

— — Primitive Rites of; in India. (W. Crooke) Anthrop. J. **29**: 271.

Dead Finish, The; a story. (E. Mitchell) Temp. Bar, **117**: 261.

Dead Letters; a story. (M. T. Wright) Indep. **53**: 2102.

Dead Man's Hand, The; a story. (H. A. Hering) Temp. Bar, **111**: 389.

Dead Man's Island; a Vanishing Island. (Mrs. M. B. Williamson) Overland, n. s. **31**: 359.

Dead Sea, Water of the. (C. A. Mitchell) Knowl. **24**: 259.

Dead Sea Fruit; a story. (Lady M. Majendie) Argosy, **67**: 97, 200, 327.

Dead Selves. (J. Magruder) Lippinc. **59**: 291.

Deaf; can they Appreciate Music? (J. G. McPherson) Knowl. **20**: 135.

— and their Instruction. (A. Morton) Educa. **18**: 417.

— and their Sign-language. (W. A. Jansen) Nat'l M. (Bost.) **8**: 560.

— Education of, in U. S. Char. R. **7**: 606.

— — Higher, in America. (A. W. Greely) R. of Rs. (N. Y.) **16**: 57.

— Fay's Study of Heredity among the. Am. Natural. **24**: 146.

— Marriages of, Fay on. (S. W. Abbott) Am. Statis. Assoc. **6**: 353.

— Speech and Speech Reading for. (J. D. Wright) Cent. **31**: 331.

Deaf and Dumb, The World's. (A. Frankham) Sund. M. **30**: 197.

Deaf and Dumb World, Life in the. (G. Willets) Chaut. **29**: 40.

Deaf Colonel, The; a story. (A. H. Begbie) Belgra. **93**: 78.

Deafness. (A. W. Jackson) Liv. Age, **231**: 329.

— Inheritance of, E. A. Fay on. (M. Yearsley) Nature, **61**: 97.

Dean, Christopher, Illustrator. Studio (Internat.) **3**: 183.

Dean of St. Paul's, A; a story. (E. de Salis) Chamb. J. **76**: 353-391.

Dean's Diversion, The; a story. (D. May) Idler, **17**: 907.

Deane, William, of Southchard, Somerset, England, Will of. (W. Dean) N. E. Reg. **204**: 432.

Dear Faustina. (R. Broughton) Temp. Bar, **110**: 1-349. **111**: 1, 145.

Dear Old Barlow. (H. Corkran) Temp. Bar, **116**: 96.

Dearborn, Fort, Massacre of. (S. Pokagon) Harper, **98**: 649.

Death. (P. W. Roose) Argosy, **65**: 39.

— Beauty in. (P. W. Roose) Argosy, **64**: 500.

— Christian Conception of. (P. Carus) Open Court, **11**: 752.

— Dread of. Ecl. M. **131**: 201. — Spec. **79**: 643.

— The Dying of. (J. Jacobs) Fortn. **72**: 264.

— Fear of. (G. Ferrero) Pop. Sci. Mo. **52**: 236.

— Ghost Lights of the West Highlands. (R. C. Maclagan) Folk-Lore, **8**: 203.

— the Great Birthday. (P. W. Roose) Argosy, **68**: 220.

— in Religious Art. (P. Carus) Open Court, **11**: 678.

— The Jaws of. (A. W. Buckland) Antiq. n. s. **33**: 114.

— Modern Representations of. (P. Carus) Open Court, **12**: 101.

— Natural, Natural Right to a. (S. E. Baldwin) Am. J. Soc. Sci. **37**: 1.

— Physiology of. Spec. **84**: 442.

Death, Smyth's Place of, in Evolution. Acad. **52**: 84.

— Some Thoughts on Pain and. (H. B. Marriott-Watson) No. Am. **173**: 540.

— What should be the Fear? (P. W. Roose) Argosy, **68**: 460.

Death of Bruno, The. (S. G. Hillyer) Arena, **20**: 584.

Death of a Coward; a story. (R. Arthur) Pall Mall M. **20**: 273.

Death of Dr. Davidson; a story. (S. Johnson) Pall Mall M. **22**: 542.

Death of the Moose; a poem. (R. Gourlay) Canad. M. **13**: 250.

Death of the Red-winged Mallard; a tale. (H. S. Canfield) Outing, **37**: 427.

Death Customs of the Fiote of the Congo Country. (R. E. Dennett) Folk-Lore, **8**: 132.

Death-disk. The; a story. (Mark Twain) Harper, **104**: 19.

Death Duties, Plunder by. (C. Morgan-Richardson) National, **31**: 432.

— Three Years of the New. Chamb. J. **75**: 454.

Death-fires, The, of Les Martigues; a story. (T. A. Janvier) Harper, **100**: 136.

Death Gulch, a Natural Bear-trap. (T. A. Jaggar) Pop. Sci. Mo. **54**: 475.

Death-march of Kûlop Sûmbing. (H. Clifford) Blackw. **164**: 483. Same art. Liv. Age, **219**: 641. Same art. Ecl. M. **132**: 77.

Death-rate, The True English. (A. J. H. Crespi) Chamb. J. **76**: 727.

Death-rates in England and Wales, 1881-90. J. Statis. Soc. **60**: 33.

Death Song of the Poets. (S. G. Ayres) Meth. R. **60**: 781.

Death Vacancy; a story. (E. A. Smith) Belgra. **99**: 608.

Death Valley and the Mojave Desert. (Carmen Harcourt) Overland, n. s. **31**: 488.

Death-watch; a story. (J. Hilton) Good Words, **41**: 165.

Deathborough Mystery; a story. (A. Hurry) Eng. Illust. **18**: 531.

Death's-head Moth, Our. Chamb. J. **75**: 446.

Debat-Ponsan, E. En plein air. Art J. **53**: 243.

Debatable Land, In the; a story. (H. Bindloss) Sund. M. **29**: 239.

Debating at Harvard College. (G. P. Baker) Harv. Grad. M. **7**: 363.

— Intercollegiate. (C. F. Bacon) Forum, **26**: 222.— (R. C. Ringwalt) Forum, **22**: 633.— (G. P. Baker) Educa. R. **21**: 244.

— — How to improve. (R. C. Ringwalt) Harv. Grad. M. **9**: 337.

Debenture, Growth of. (E. Manson) Law Q. **13**: 418.

Debentures to Bearer, Negotiability of. (F. B. Palmer) Law Q. **15**: 245.

Deborah, Song of, Structure of. (D. H. Muller) Am. J. Theol. **2**: 110.

De Brosses, Charles. Letters. (A. L. Cotton) Gent. M. n. s. **64**: 443.

Debt, Imprisonment for; New York's Marshalsea. (W. J. Roe) Arena, **23**: 31.

— Old Laws concerning. (G. H. Westley) Green Bag, **11**: 445.

Debts due to Non-residents, Has the State Power to discharge? (C. Reno) Am. Law R. **32**: 34.

— World's National Indebtedness. (O. P. Austin) No. Am. **173**: 161.

— — Egypt. (C. E. Dawkins) No. Am. **173**: 487.

— — France. (J. Roche) No. Am. **173**: 632.

— — Great Britain. (H. Cox) No. Am. **173**: 355.

— — Spain. (A. Houghton) No. Am. **173**: 862.

Début of Bimbashi Joyce; a story. (A. C. Doyle) McClure, **15**: 60.

Début of Jack; a story. (E. W. Townsend) Harper, 101: 100.

Début of Patricia. (K. D. Wiggin) Atlan. 85: 599.

Decadence. (A. Lang) Critic, 37: 171.

— in Poetry. Spec. 78: 368.

Decalogue; the Third Commandment. (R. Mackintosh) Bib. World, 12: 169.

Decatur, Stephen, and the "Philadelphia." (C. T. Brady) McClure, 14: 62.

— Sea-fight off Tripoli. (G. Gibbs) Lippinc. 64: 632. — Cosmopol. 31: 400.

Decatur, Ill., Carnegie Public Library Building. Lib. J. 26: 744.

Decazes, The Duke. (A. Laugel) Nation, 68: 434.

Deccan, Ancient Monuments of the. (E. W. Hopkins) Nation, 64: 240.

Deception, A; a story. (E. R. Crosby) Outl. 68: 71.

Deception of Martha Tucker; an Automobile Extravaganza. (C. B. Loomis) Cent. 41: 291.

Decisions, Curious. (G. H. Westley) Green Bag, 11: 230.

Declaration of Independence. (H. Friedenwald) Internat. Mo. 4: 102. — (T. Jenks) Chaut. 31: 242.

— London Newspapers and. (N. D. Davis) Nation, 66: 127.

— Principles of. Outl. 62: 147.

— Signers of. (L. S. LaMance) Lippinc. 68: 118.

— Story of. (I. M. Tarbell) McClure, 17: 223.

Declaration of Paris. (J. G. Butcher) Fortn. 71: 955.

Declaration of Rights, French, 1789. (A. Lebon) Internat. Mo. 3: 672.

Decoration, Architectural; a Mural Painter's Letter to his Pupils. (Fred. Crowninshield) Scrib. M. 30: 381.

— a Bachelor's Room. (G. M. Ellwood) Studio (Internat.) 7: 243.

— Fine Art as. (R. Sturgis) Internat. Mo. 1: 463.

— Flower Studies for, Foord's. Art J. 53: 55.

— — "Elm Bank," York. Studio (Internat.) 13: 36.

— in the Home. (W. S. Morton) Art J. 49: 65, 118, 198, 257.

— Interior, of Churches. (H. R. Marshall) Archit. R. 4: 50.

— — of the City House. (R. Sturgis) Harper, 99: 208.

— Modern. (J. Schopfer) Archit. R. 6: 243.

— Novelty in, at the Trocadero. (G. E. Moira and F. L. Jenkins) M. of Art, 20: 92.

— of Cities. Munic. Aff. 5: 675.

— of Houses, Wharton and Codman on. (E. H. Blashfield) Bk. Buyer, 16: 129.

— of London Clubs. (A. L. Baldry) Art J. 50: 208. 51: 45, 204.

— of London Restaurants. (F. Miller) Art J. 52: 331.

— of Modern Steamships. (W. S. Sparrow) M. of Art, 25: 296.

— of the Page. Art J. 53: 377.

— of Public Buildings. (C. M. Shean) Munic. Aff. 5: 710.

— of School Rooms. (J. P. Haney) Munic. Aff. 3: 672.

— of Scottish Spindles and Whorls. (F. R. Coles) Reliquary, 39: 80.

— of Streets. Acad. 51: 655.

— of the Suburban House. (M. H. B. Scott) Studio (Lond.) 5: 15.

— — in England. (B. Fletcher) Archit. R. 11: 641.

— Scenes of Chase in. (L. Beatrice Thompson) Art J. 53: 278.

Decorations in Washington and Chicago. (J. W. Pattison) Am. Arch. 66: 75.

— Jubilee, in London. (H. P. Horne) Sat. R. 83: 709.

Decoration Day. (Austin Lewis) Overland, n. s. 35: 442.

Decorative Art. (E. W. Huntingford) Canad. M. 8: 390.

Decorative Art and Applied Art in Germany. (P. Schultz-Naumburg) M. of Art, 22: 669.

— and the Easel Picture. (Audley Mackworth) Art J. 53: 120.

— at the Glasgow Exhibition. (L. F. Day) Art J. 53: 215, 237, 273.

— at Her Majesty's Theatre. (A. Fish) M. of Art, 22: 110.

— at the National Competition, South Kensington. (E. Wood) Studio (Internat.) 14: 257.

— at Windsor Castle. (F. S. Robinson) M. of Art, 21: 121–295. 22: 26–541.

— British, in 1899. (A. Vallance) Studio (Internat.) 9: 37–247.

— English and French Movements in. (E. R. Pennell and R. Sturgis) Scrib. M. 23: 253.

— Frieze of Political Sketches. (F. C. Gould) Studio (Internat.) 14: 196.

— in Belgium. (Mrs. J. E. Whitby) M. of Art, 26: 41.

— in England. Sat. R. 83: 645.

— in Germany. (P. Schultze-Naumburg) M. of Art, 20: 324. 24: 231.

— in the Home. (W. S. Morton) Art J. 49: 303, 368.

— in Paris. (G. Mourey) Studio (Internat.) 4: 83.

— Italian. (A. Melani) Am. Arch. 74: 43.

— Pflanzenbilder, Mewrer's. (L. F. Day) Art J. 49: 319.

— Possibility of reviving a Taste for. (O. von Glehn) Art J. 50: 89.

— Russian. (N. Peacock) Studio (Internat.) 13: 268.

— Scandinavian. (S. Frykholm) Studio (Internat.) 12: 190.

— Wall Decoration. (A. Vallance) M. of Art, 22: 501.

Decorative Art Classes. (L. F. Day) Art J. 50: 49.

Decorative Conventions in Architecture, Use and Abuse of. (F. Crowninshield) Scrib. M. 26: 381.

Decorative Design and Color, Modern. (A. Rottmann) M. of Art, 23: 179.

Decorative Motive, Evolution of. (A. D. F. Hamlin) Am. Arch. 59: 35, 51, 91. 60: 43, 67. 61: 11. 62: 87. 63: 3, 35, 83. 68: 11, 67. 69: 83. 71: 29, 51.

Decorative Work in the Salons of 1899. (Henri Frantz) M. of Art, 23: 503.

Deed, An Indian. Green Bag, 9: 103.

— Latin, of Sale of a Slave, A. D. 166. (E. M. Thompson) Archæol. 54: 433.

Deep Dale, Ancient Remains in. (W. H. Salt) Reliquary, 37: 99.

Deepwater Politics; a story. (M. McHenry) McClure, 16: 518.

Deer, The. (W. D. Hulbert) McClure, 17: 8.

— Black-tailed, Hunting. (F. C. Crocker) Outing, 37: 145.

— British, and their Horns, Mallais on. Sat. R. 84: 146.

— The Louisiana. (G. M. Allen) Am. Natural. 35: 449.

— of Canada. (C. A. Bramble) Canad. M. 14: 382.

Deer-forest, Winter in a. (H. Fraser) Ecl. M. 131: 858.

Deer-forest Romance. Chamb. J. 74: 433.

Deer-hunt on the Coast of Georgia. (C. W. Cunningham) Outing, 35: 370.

— Thanksgiving. (B. W. Mitchell) Outing, 33: 141.

Deer-hunting, Adirondack. (G. Roberts) Outing, 31: 22.

— in Canada. (F. H. Risteen) Outing, 35: 111.

— in Colorado. (H. Wright) Outing, 37: 168.

— in La Grande Chênière. (A. Wilkinson) Outing, 29: 437.

— in Winter. ("L. C. Loct") Outing, 35: 343.

— on Sanhedrin. (N. Eames) Outing, 30: 551.

— Women at. (Mrs. S. W. Belcher) Outing, 32: 368.

Deer-stalking in Newfoundland. Argosy, 64: 538.

— in Scotland. (W. Winans) Outing, 39: 203.

Deerfield, Mass., Little Brown House on the Albany Road. (G. Sheldon) New Eng. M. n. s. 19: 36.

— Handicrafts in Old. (M. E. Allen) Outl. 69: 592.

Deerhurst, Gloucestershire, Saxon Chapel at. (J. H. Middleton) Archæol. 50: 66.

De Falbe Sale, The. Ath. '00, 1: 665.

Defalcations, Making them Difficult. Bank. M. (N. Y.) 56: 15.

Defeat of the Method; a story. (M. L. Knapp) Atlan. 88: 819.

Defective Children, Special Classes for. (W. Channing) Char. R. 10: 242.

Defective Classes, Law Relating to the Care and Treatment of. (H. A. Millis) Am. J. Sociol. 4: 51.

Defence, Armament of Outside. (E. M. Weaver) J. Mil. Serv. Inst. 9: 169.

— by Resurrection. (M. Thompson) Cent. 32: 440.

— European Systems of. (T. Turtle) J. Mil. Serv. Inst. 9: 54.

— Home. (R. F. Sorsbie) Un. Serv. M. 23: 206, 309.

— Imperial, Local Beginnings of. (H. Birchenough) 19th Cent. 47: 728.

— National. (R. Neville) Monthly R. 1, no. 2: 56.

— of a Flank. (C. Mackenzie) Un. Serv. M. 21: 181.

— of San Andres, The. (H. Bindloss) Chamb. J. 74: 378.

— Sea-coast, Personnel of. (P. S. Michie) J. Mil. Serv. Inst. 8: 1.

Defence Forces, English National. (C. S. Clark) Un. Serv. M. 24: 271.

Defences, Field, Application of. (M. H. G. Goldie) J. Mil. Serv. Inst. 21: 102.

De Feure, Georges, Artist. (O. Uzanne) Studio (Internat.) 3: 95.

Definition of Some Rhetorical Terms. (V. J. Emery) Am. J. Philol. 18: 206.

Defoe, Daniel, and Harley, Relations of. (T. Bateson) Eng. Hist. R. 15: 238.

— Apparition of Mrs. Veal. (R. H. Bretherton) Gent. M. n. s. 67: 531.

— as a Masterly Liar. Acad. 57: 256.

— in Scotland. (J. D. Cockburn) Scot. R. 36: 250.

— Robinson Crusoe. (E. E. Hale) Bk. Buyer, 14: 453.

Degeneracy, Talbot on. (G. T. W. Patrick) Science, n. s. 9: 372.

Degeneration, a Study in Anthropology. (W. W. Ireland) Internat. Mo. 1: 235.

Degradation of Kwang, The. (C. Dawe) Chamb. J. 77: 497–519.

Degrees, Concerning. Dial (Ch.) 26: 105.

— Candidates for the Doctorate at the University of Pennsylvania. Science, n. s. 14: 333.

— College, Unification of. (W. S. Sutton) School R. 8: 92. — (J. B. Henneman) Sewanee R. 9: 322.

— Dishonorary. (W. P. Garrison) Nation, 72: 308.

— Doctorates conferred by American Universities. Science, n. s. 14: 161.

— Honorary, in the U. S. (H. T. Lukens) Educa. R. 14: 8.

— — Present Status of. (C. D. Wilson) Chaut. 31: 475.

— Wanted, a Degree of Doctor of Arts. (C. F. Thwing) Outl. 65: 932.

Degrees, Doctrine of Discrete. (W. L. Worcester) N. Church R. 5: 187.

D'Heere, Lucas, Poet and Painter of Ghent. (L. Cust) Archæol. 54: 59.

D'Houdetot, Madame. (A. Laugel) Nation, 72: 450.

Deification of Kings in the Greek Cities. (E. R. Bevan) Eng. Hist. R. 16: 625.

Deigman, Osborn Warren, one of Hobson's Crew on the Merrimac. (E. M. Clark) Midland, 10: 24.

Deists and the Deistic Movement of the 18th Century. (J. M. Attenborough) Westm. 156: 620.

D'Indy, Vincent, Musician, with portrait. Music, 17: 72.

— Musical Drama "Fervaal." (M. Kufferath) Music, 12: 557.

De Kay, Charles, with portrait. Cath. World, 74: 8.

De Keyser, Sir Polydore. J. Soc. Arts, 46: 211.

De Koven, James, Rev. (T. F. Gailor) Sewanee, 1: 340.

De Koven, Reginald; Operatic Composer, with portrait. Music, 17: 408.

Delagoa Bay. (J. Geddie) Chamb. J. 74: 535. Same art. Liv. Age, 215: 56. — (R. Ogden) Nation, 70: 26.

— Arbitration on. (M. McIlwraith) Fortn. 74: 410. — Sat. R. 89: 417. 90: 38.

— British Fleet at. Blackw. 170: 699.

Delaherche, Auguste, Potter. (G. Mowrey) Studio (Internat.) 3: 112.

Deland, Margaret, with portrait. (J. M. Chapple) Nat'l M. (Bost.) 9: 522.

— at Home. (L. Purdy) Critic, 33: 33.

— Childhood of. (D. McDonald) Outl. 64: 407.

Delavan, Wisconsin, Life of Art Students at. (L. Riedel) Brush & P. 2: 115.

Delaware, Politics of; preserving a State's Honor. (W. Saulsbury) Forum, 32: 268.

— — The President's Hand in. (E. P. Clark) Nation, 72: 248.

Delaware Bill of Rights of 1776. (M. Farrand) Am. Hist. R. 3: 641.

Delaware Indians, Migrations of. (C. Thomas) Am. Antiq. 19: 73.

Delaware River, Du Coudray's Observations on the Forts on. Pennsyl. M. 14: 343.

Delcassé, M., Policy of. Spec. 83: 829.

Delft, Co-operation in. (W. H. Tolman) Outl. 59: 170.

Delft and Delft Ware. (J. P. Worden) New Eng. M. n. s. 22: 131.

Delft-ware. (J. W. L. Glaisher) J. Soc. Arts, 45: 665.

Delhi, India, Past and Present. (G. W. Forrest) Pall Mall M. 21: 233.

Delhi Zenana, A. (W. Simpson) Eng. Illust. 16: 473.

Delia; a story. (G. Roscoe) Harper, 101: 135.

Deliberation of Mr. Dunkin; a story. (P. L. Dunbar) Cosmopol. 24: 678.

Deliberativeness of Dr. Benj. Franklin Greene. (D. B. Fitzgerald) Indep. 53: 2522.

Delinquent in Art and Literature. (E. Ferri) Atlan. 80: 233.

De Lisle, Ambrose Phillipps, and the Conversion of England. Month, 95: 277.

— Purcell's Life of. Acad. 58: 139. — Church Q. 50: 307.

Delisle, Léopold. Library, n. s. 2: 1.

Deliver Us from Evil; a story. (L. G. Moberly) Argosy, 70: 329.

Deliverance Blair. (P. Wesley) New Eng. M. n. s. 16: 561.

Delles of Wisconsin, The. See Dalles.

De Lome, Madame Dupuy. Midland, 9: 212.

De Lome Letter, The. (R. Ogden and others) Nation, 66: 122, 128, 183.

Delphian Oracle. Two Famous Maxims of Greece. (P. E. More) New World, 7: 18.

Delta 15 (Star), Orbit of. Pop. Astron. 7: 306.

Delta Upsilon at Harvard College. (F. G. Cook) Harv. Grad. M. 8: 321.

Deluge, Has there been a? (A. O. Daunt) Westm. 151: 565.

— Testimony of Geology to the. (G. F. Wright) McClure, 17: 134.

Deluge Legends of American Indians. (P. Carus) Open Court, 15: 758.

Deluge Tablets. (J. N. Fradenburgh) Am. Antiq. 22: 295.

Departure of the Subaltern, The ; a story. (C. Mills) Pall Mall M. **20**: 372.

Dependencies, How they are Ruled. (D. MacG. Means) Nation, **70**: 352.

Dependent Children and Family Homes. (W. P. Letchworth) Char. R. **7**: 577.

Dependents in Iowa, County Care of. (W. R. Patterson) Charities, **7**: 523.

— Law relating to Relief and Care of. (H. A. Millis) Am. J. Sociol. **3**: 631, 777. **4**: 81, 178.

— Relief and Care of. (H. A. Millis) Am. J. Sociol. **3**: 378.

Deportation, Our Statistics of. (R. Ogden) Nation, **72**: 208.

Deppl, Piano Method of. (A. Fay) Music, **14**: 581.

Depression, the Disease of the Time. (W. T. Baylis) Westm. **156**: 14.

De Quincey, Thomas, with portrait. Acad. **51**: 47.

— Flight of a Tartar Tribe, Outline Study of. (Maud E. Kingsley) Educa. **20**: 180.

— Personality of. Acad. **56**: 478.

Derby, Edward Geoffrey Stanley, 14th Earl. (T. Raleigh) Chaut. **28**: 440.

Derby, Capt. John, Bearer of the News of Concord and Lexington to England. (R. S. Rantoul) Cent. **36**: 714.

Derbyshire, Peak of, Church in the. (R. K. Bolton) Reliquary, **40**: 80.

Derbyshire Regiment at Dargai. (A. K. Slessor) Macmil. **80**: 336.

Derelict, A. (R. H. Davis) Scrib. M. **30**: 131.

Derelict, A. (E. Mackubin) Cent. **38**: 137.

Derelict, The. (F. T. Bullen) Sund. M. **28**: 24. Same art. Liv. Age, **220**: 309.

— In Search of a. (A. P. Buller) Strand, **18**: 490.

Derelict " Neptune," The ; a story. (M. Robertson) McClure, **8**: 278.

Derry and Limerick, Sieges of. (H. Mangan) 19th Cent. **50**: 459.

Dervishes, Battle Formations against. (E. Stanton) Un. Serv. M. **17**: 209.

— Day with the. (George Grahame) Gent. M. **62**: 151. Same art. Liv. Age, **221**: 35.

— The Howling and Dancing, of Egypt. (Laura B. Starr) Nat'l M. (Bost.) **7**: 435.

— Mode of Warfare. Sat. R. **86**: 301.

Derwent Findlay, Q. C. ; a story. (W. E. Grogan) Argosy, **71**: 321. Same art. Liv. Age, **226**: 514.

Descartes, René, Biographical Sketch, with portrait. (T. J. McCormack) Open Court, **12**: 501.

— Regulæ of. (B. Gibson) Mind, **23**: 145, 332.

Descendant of King Philip. (L. Wetherell) New Eng. M. n. s. **22**: 745.

Deschanel, Paul ; a Politician with a Social Program. (J. G. Brooks) Pol. Sci. Q. **14**: 500.

Desert Campaigns, Water Supply in. (C. L. Beckurts) J. Mil. Serv. Inst. **13**: 1110.

Desert Dream, A. (E. and H. Heron) Cornh. **77**: 215.

Desert Incident, A. (W. L. Judson) Overland, n. s. **30**: 323.

Deserted House ; a poem. (F. B. Doveton) Ecl. M. **132**: 786.

Deserted Inn, The ; a poem. (B. Carman) Blackw. **162**: 132. Same art. Ecl. M. **129**: 537.

Deserter, A. (R. Horsley) Chamb. J. **74**: 695.

Deserters, Recognition of. (C. R. Greenleaf) J. Mil. Serv. Inst. **10**: 561.

Desertion in the United States Army. J. Mil. Serv. Inst. **10**: 450.

Desertion, A ; a story. (S. Crane) Harper, **101**: 938.

Deserts, American. Problems of the Arid Region. (E. Mead) Outl. **66**: 337.

Deserts and their Inhabitants. (R. Lydekker) Knowl. **21**: 101.

— Sculpture of. Geog. J. **17**: 521.

Des Genettes, Charles E. D. (M. C. Harris) Cath. World, **70**: 641.

Desiderio da Settignano *vs.* Piero della Francesca. Three Mysterious Profiles. (M. Cruttwell) Art J. **49**: 312.

Design, Argument from, Psychology and. (J. D. Logan) Philos. R. **7**: 604.

Design, Bases of. (W. Crane) Archit. R. **5**: 68.

— Good, Principles of. Archit. R. **7**: 54.

— in Painting, Element and Place of. (T. R. Spence) Artist (N. Y.) **24**: 205.

— National English Competition in 1899. (L. F. Day) Art J. **51**: 281.

— Nature Studies for. (J. I. Kay) Artist (N. Y.) **24**: 43.

— The Practical in. (L. W. Miller) Artist (N. Y.) **24**: ii.

— Some Types of, from Berlin and Vienna. Illus. Artist (N. Y.) **23**: 194.

Designing for Cottons. Quaint and Grotesque. (F. Dolman) M. of Art, **23**: 34.

Designs ; L'art Nouveau. (L. F. Day) Art J. **52**: 293.

Désirée Clary, Queen of Sweden ; the Betrothed of Napoleon. (M. Quekett) Temp. Bar, **116**: 187.

Desks, Hygienic, for School Children. (E. M. Mosher) Educa. R. **18**: 9.

Des Moines, Iowa, Architecture in. (E. E. Clark) Midland, **10**: 110, 205.

Desmoulins, Camille. (A. Laugel) Nation, **72**: 28.

Despenser, The Younger, Letter of, 21 March, 1321. (W. H. Stevenson) Eng. Illust. R. **12**: 755.

Despot on Tour, A ; a story. (G. Gissing) Strand, **15**: 25.

Dessar, Louis Paul, Artist, with portrait. (L. M. Cooper) Brush & P. **5**: 97.

Destiny ; a story. (G. King) Harper, **96**: 541.

Destiny at Drybone ; a story. (O. Wister) Harper, **96**: 60.

Destiny of Duty, The. (A. J. Pillsbury) Overland, n. s. **33**: 168.

Destroyers, The ; a war poem. (R. Kipling) McClure, **11**: 73.

Detaille, Edouard, Puvis de Chavannes and. (B. Karageorgevitch) M. of Art, **22**: 659.

— Painter of Soldiers. (A. Dayot) Cent. **34**: 803.

Detective who Detected. (P. G. Hubert, jr.) Lippinc. **61**: 64.

Detective Bureau : the Central Office. Illus. (R. C. Lewis) Munsey, **24**: 720.

Detective Novel, Germ of the. (H. L. Williams) Bk. Buyer, **21**: 268.

Detective Stories. Atlan. **81**: 573.

Detectives, The. (W. Payne) Atlan. **84**: 839.

Detmold, Maurice and Edward. (M. H. Spielmann) M. of Art, **24**: 112.

Detroit, Bicentennial Memorial. (A. Mathewson) Cent. **38**: 706.

— Municipal Electric Lighting in. (J. A. Fairlie) Munic. Aff. **4**: 606.

— Revolts at, in 18th Century. (R. R. Elliott) Am. Cath. Q. **23**: 759.

— Roman Catholicism in, Two Centuries of. (R. R. Elliott) Am. Cath. Q. **26**: 499.

— to Montreal on a Wheel. (R. Bruce) Outing, **36**: 401.

Detroit Street Railway Case. (D. MacG. Means) Nation, **69**: 25. — (F. W. Brown) Am. Law R. **33**: 853.

Deus in Machina ; a poem. (H. A. Kennedy) Temp. Bar, **111**: 69.

Development, Arrested, in Children's Minds. (N. C. Schaeffer) Educa. **22**: 202.

Development of the Powers of a Pupil. (E. L. Harris) School R. 5: 286.
— Problem of. (T. H. Morgan) Internat. Mo. 3: 274.
De Vere, Aubrey, Recollections of. (Eleanor A. Towle) Sewanee, 7: 271. — (L. J. Block) Dial (Ch.) 23: 248. — (I. A. Taylor) Cath. World, 66: 621.
Devereux, John H. (H. W. French) New Eng. M. n. s. 23: 610.
Devery, William S. (A. Ruhl) McClure, 17: 394.
Devil, The, and his Aliases. (O. Smeaton) Westm. 153: 183.
— in Britain and America, Ashton's. Ath. '97, 1: 9.
— in Folk-Lore. (R. Bruce Boswell) Gent. M. n. s. 58: 443.
— in Law. (R. V. Rogers) Ath. '01, 1: 581.
— Non-Existence of. (C. Caverno) Arena, 24: 76.
— Places Named for. Eng. Illust. 20: 370.
Devil, The ; a story. (M. Gorky) Nat'l M. (Bost.) 15: 161.
Devil-fish. (F. T. Bullen) Cornh. 78: 401. Same art. Ecl. M. 131: 831. Same art. Liv. Age, 219: 188.
Devil's Apprentice, The. (P. N. Boeringer) Overland, n. s. 29: 591.
Devil's Bothy, The ; a story. (L. Torre) Eng. Illust. 17: 13.
Devil's Bridge ; a Philippine Legend. (C. M. Skinner) Lippinc. 64: 319.
Devil's Corkscrews, The. (R. Bache) Strand, 18: 593.
Devil's Grandmother. (Isabel C. Chamberlain) J. Am. Folk-Lore, 13: 278.
Devil's Holiday ; a poem. (F. Gadsby) Canad. M. 14: 573.
Devil's Island. (A. Rossi) Chaut. 27: 409. Same art. Liv. Age, 217: 347.
— At. (A. Dreyfus) Liv. Age, 229: 589.
Devil's Little Fly ; a story. (V. F. Boyle) Harper, 101: 597.
Devil's Muskeg ; a story. (H. Whitaker) Munsey, 26: 174.
Devils, Belief in, Nevins on. Spec. 78: 664.
Devizes Castle. Acad. 57: 260.
Devonian, Southern, Formations. (H. S. Williams) Am. J. Sci. 153: 393.
Devonian Black Shale of Eastern Kentucky, Description of a Fauna found in. (G. H. Girty) Am. J. Sci. 156: 384.
Devonian Interval in Northern Arkansas. (H. S. Williams) Am. J. Sci. 158: 139.
Devonian Strata, in Colorado. (A. C. Spencer) Am. J. Sci. 159: 125.
Devonshire, Elizabeth, Duchess of, with portraits. (W. Roberts) M. of Art, 25: 368.
Devonshire, Georgiana, Duchess of, with portraits. (W. Roberts) M. of Art, 25: 368.
Devonshire, Georgiana and Elizabeth, Duchesses of, Family Correspondence. (F. W. Halsey) Bk. Buyer, 16: 319.
Devonshire, William George Spencer, 6th Duke of. (S. A. Strong) Longm. 31: 309.
Devonshire, Birds of. (W. H. Hudson) Longm. 32: 543.
Devotion of the "Three Hours." (H. Thurston) Month, 93: 249.
Devotional Life, The. (T. Allen) Meth. R. 60: 681.
Devotions, Our Popular. (H. Thurston) Month, 98: 58, 186, 264, 482.
Dewar, Prof. James. (G. G. Henderson) Good Words, 41: 765.
De Wet, Gen. Christian. (H. Robertson) Canad. M. 15: 458.
Dewey, Admiral George. Gunton's M. 18: 429. — With portraits. Strand, 16: 295. — (J. Barrett) Harper, 99: 799. — With portraits. (T. Roosevelt ; J. L. Stickney) McClure, 13: 483.

Dewey, Admiral George, Anecdotes of. (O. K. Davis) McClure, 13: 43.
— as a National Hero. (W. T. Sampson) Cent. 36: 927.
— Candidacy of, for the Presidency. Outl. 64: 857. — Nation, 70: 274.
— Character Sketch. (W. Churchill) R. of Rs. (N. Y.) 17: 676.
— Interview with, at Manila. (P. MacQueen) Nat'l M. (Bost.) 10: 431.
— Meeting, in Manila Bay. (W. Merritt) Outl. 63: 313.
— Welcome Home, Story of. (J. Barnes) Outl. 63: 299.
— Welcomes to. (J. G. Schurman and others) Indep. 51: 2505.
Dewey Arch, New York. Am. Arch. 67: 11. — Studio (Internat.) 8: xiii, supp.
Dewey Day, Decorations in New York. (E. Knaufft) R. of Rs. (N. Y.) 20: 458.
— Sculptures of. (R. Sturgis) Scrib. M. 26: 765.
Dewey Medal. Artist (N. Y.) 24: xlvi.
Dewey, Melvil, with portrait. Library, n. s. 2: 337.
De Wint, Peter. (Ja. Orrock) Art J. 50: 106.
De Wolf, Jessica, Singer, with portrait. Music, 19: 170.
Dexter, Lord Timothy. (F. E. Keay) New Eng. M. n. s. 15: 734.
Dhooly, The. (R. R. Gibson) Un. Serv. M. 21: 629.
Dia de Todos Santos, El. (L. M. Terry) Overland, n. s. 38: 199.
Diacetyl, New Derivatives of. (H. F. Keller and P. Maas) J. Frankl. Inst. 144: 379.
Diagram, Psychology of the. (F. A. Barbour) School R. 5: 240. — (G. Buck) School R. 5: 470.
"Dial," The, of 1840-45. (J. F. A. Pyre) Dial (Ch.) 26: 297.
— 1880-1900. Dial (Ch.) 28: 327.
Dialect, Abuse of. Macmil. 76: 133. Same art. Liv. Age, 214: 121.
— Day of. (T. C. De Leon) Lippinc. 60: 679.
— in Literature, Triumph of. (M. Thompson) Meth. R. 58: 426.
Dialect Poetry. Spec. 79: 679.
Dialectical Method. (E. B. McGilvary) Mind, 23: 233.
Dialects. (R. H. Bretherton) Gent. M. n. s. 65: 531. Same art. Liv. Age, 229: 24.
— English Dictionary of. Ath. '98, 2: 287.
Dials of our Timepieces, Why Twelve Divisions ? J. Mil. Serv. Inst. 26: 433.
Diamond, Discovery of the First African. Canad. M. 15: 268.
Diamond Earrings, The ; a story. Argosy, 66: 686.
Diamond Fields, So. African, to Delagoa Bay. (Gen. C. Warren) Good Words, 41: 45, 92, 198, 246.
Diamond Mines of Kimberley. Nature, 55: 519.
Diamond Mining in South Africa. (T. H. Leggett) Cassier, 14: 371.
Diamond Signet of Henrietta Maria, Queen of Charles I., and the Sapphire Signet of Mary, Queen of William III. (C. D. E. Fortnum) Archæol. 50: 104.
Diamonds, The. (R. Ramsay) Chamb. J. 77: 796. — (W. Crookes) Nature, 56: 325.
— African Supply and Price Changes. (G. W. Thornley) Art J. 52: 252.
— and other Gems, Process of Cutting. (T. C. Hepworth) Pall Mall M. 20: 182.
— as Made by Nature and by Man. (J. B. C. Kershaw) Chamb. J. 74: 633. Same art. Ecl. M. 130: 264.
— Emigrant, in America. (W. H. Hobbs) Pop. Sci. Mo. 56: 73.
— Historic. (N. Boyce) Lippinc. 61: 389.
— Origin of. Ed. R. 189: 316.
— Some Historic. Chamb. J. 76: 809.

Diamonds, South African, The Parent-rock of the. (T. G. Bonney) Nature, 60: 620.
— Tragedies of the Kohinoor. (Caroline Brown) Cosmopol. 26: 51.
— Where they come from. (R. M. Sillard) Eng. Illust. 20: 647.
Diana, Temple of, at Ephesus. (B. I. Wheeler) Cent. 34: 663.
Diane de Bragade. (M. Maartens) Fortn. 75: 378.
Diane de Poitiers, Hay's. Sat. R. 91: 396. Same art. Liv. Age, 229: 396. Same art. Ecl. M. 137: 126.
Diaphorite from Montana and Mexico. (L. J. Spencer) Am. J. Sci. 156: 316.
Diaries, Men who have kept. (W. Sichel) Blackw. 165: 70.
Diary, The Deathless. (A. Repplier) Atlan. 79: 642.
Diary of a Busaco Monk, The. (Charles Edwardes) Chamb. J. 77: 428.
Diary of a Goose Girl, The. (Kate D. Wiggin) Scrib. M. 29: 515. 30: 93.
Diary Habit, The. (Gelett Burgess) Overland, n. s. 37: 595.
Diatoms, Movement of. (F. R. Rowley) Nat. Sci. 13: 406.
— Structure and Movements of, Lauterborn's. Sci. Prog. 7: x.
Diavola; a story. (E. T. Fowler) Pall Mall M. 14: 81.
Diaz, Porfirio. (C. F. Lummis) Harper, 94: 741. — (F. L. Oswald) Chaut. 27: 157.
— and his Successor. (J. D. Whelpley) World's Work, 1: 698.
— The Man of Mexico. (C. F. Lummis) Outl. 69: 537.
Dickie, George W. (J. Richards) Cassier, 15: 245.
Dickens, Charles. (D. C. Murray) Canad. M. 8: 245. — (F. G. Kitton) Bookman, 13: 463. — (L. Hutton) Outl. 60: 318. — (A. Lang) Fortn. 70: 944. — Same art. Ecl. M. 132: 415. Same art. Liv. Age, 220: 267.
— and his Illustrators. (J. L. Gilder) Critic, 34: 240. — Bk. Buyer, 18: 112.
— and his Popularity. (E. S. Williamson) Canad. M. 14: 479.
— and Modern Humor. Macmil. 85: 31. Same art. Liv. Age, 231: 820.
— and Thackeray, W. M. Popularity as evidenced by Sale of their Works. Acad. 52: 454.
— as an Antiquary. (A. B. R. Wallis) Antiq. n. s. 37: 165.
— Dramatizations of. (P. Wilstach) Bookman, 14: 52.
— Gissing on. (E. E. Hale, jr.) Dial (Ch.) 25: 297.
— Homes and Haunts of. (A. Leach) Munsey, 17: 240.
— Memories of. (M. Q. Holyoake) Chamb. J. 74: 721.
— Memories of Gad's Hill. (Mary A. Dickens) Strand, 13: 69.
— Misquotations from. Acad. 56: 461.
— On some Illustrators of. (F. Weitenkampf) Bk. Buyer, 18: 103.
— Pickwick Papers, Writing of. (H. Hall) Bk. Buyer, 21: 189, 275.
— Pickwickian Bath. (P. Fitzgerald) Gent. M. n. s. 60: 491.
— Pseudo-Dickens Rarities. (F. G. Kitton) Ath. '97, 2: 355.
— Some Notes on. Liv. Age, 219: 133.
— What he did for Childhood. (J. L. Hughes) Cent. 35: 493.
— Works of, Gadshill edition. Pall Mall M. 18: 573.
Dickens, Charles, Jr., with portrait. Acad. 51: 573.
Dickinson, Prof. Edward, Teacher of Musical History, with portrait. Music, 17: 640.
Dickinson, John Woodbridge, Educational Services of. (H. S. Ballou) Educa. 22: 65.
Dickson, Oscar, Baron. Geog. J. 10: 106.

Dictated; a story. (A. Black) Harper, 97: 145.
Dictionary, An Hour with a. (Harold Lewis) Chamb. J. 78: 817.
— Reading a. (J. Todhunter) Cornh. 78: 207.
Dictionary of National Biography. (H. Ellis) Argosy, 72: 336.
Did he remember? Temp. Bar, 109: 481. Same art. Liv. Age, 212: 291–355.
Didascalic Inscriptions, Dating of Some. (E. Capps) Am. J. Archæol. 2d s. 4: 74.
Diderot. Acad. 55: 27.
Didier-Pouget, Landscape-painter. (W. Dewhurst) Studio (Internat.) 12: 247.
Didon, Henri, Père. (T. Bentzon) Cent. 38: 725.
Die-sinking, Artistic, of the Present Time. (R. Sturgis) Scrib. M. 24: 508.
Died for Discipline. (F. E. Myers) Overland, n. s. 29: 303.
Diefenbach, K. W., with portrait and illus. Artist (N. Y.) 24: 178.
Dieguenos, Mythology of the. (C. G. Du Bois) J. Am. Folk-Lore, 14: 181.
Dieppe, Rouen, and Chartres as Sketching Grounds. (G. H. Lenfestey) Studio (Lond.) 8: 142.
Dies Iræ, English Versions of the. (T. C. Porter) Ref. Ch. R. 48: 24. — Acad. 52: 126.
Diet, Animal, Range of. Spec. 78: 269.
Dietetics, Principles of Modern. (C. von Norden) Internat. Mo. 3: 570, 679.
Difference, A, with Distinctions; a story. (Amy Wood) Idler, 13: 121.
Differentiation, Protoplasmic Movement as a Factor of. (E. G. Conklin) Science, n. s. 9: 318.
Difficult Case, A. (W. D. Howells) Atlan. 86: 24, 205.
Difficult Minute, The. (R. E. Young) Atlan. 87: 73.
Diffusion, Note on Computing. (G. F. Becker) Am. J. Sci. 153: 280.
— Recent Work on. (H. T. Brown) Nature, 64: 171, 193.
Digby, George, Secretary of State. (E. Scott) Temp. Bar, 114: 394.
Digby, Sir Kenelm. Library, 5: 1. — (J. Hopwood) Dub. R. 121: 245. — (P. F. Bicknell) Dial (Ch.) 22: 148. — Sat. R. 83: 722.
— Unpublished Letters of. (J. G. Fotheringham) Antiq. n. s. 36: 8.
Digestion; Absorption in Vertebrate Intestinal Cells. (Howard Crawley) Science, n. s. 10: 75.
Digestive Ferments. (H. Leffmann) J. Frankl. Inst. 147: 97.
Digger Indian Burning, A. (C. H. Burnham) Outing, 35: 290.
Digger Indians, Plea for. (A. G. Morice) Am. Antiq. 21: 339.
Dijon. Temp. Bar, 110: 415. Same art. Liv. Age, 213: 49.
— A Day at. Am. Arch. 68: 45.
Dilettanti, Cust and Colvin's History of the. Spec. 81: 18. — Ath. '98, 2: 494.
Dime Novel, Degeneration of the. (R. P. Bellows) Writer, 12: 97.
Dinan, Brittany, as Sketching Ground. (A. G. Bell) Studio (Lond.) 4: 52.
Dingley Bill, Canada and the. (J. Charlton) No. Am. 165: 418.
— Tariff on Books and Art. Critic, 30: 222, 281.
Dinichthyid Osteology, Some New Points in. (C. R. Eastman) Am. Natural. 32: 747.
Dining, Art of. Quar. 190: 66. Same art. Liv. Age, 223: 75. Same art. Ecl. M. 133: 901.
Dining-clubs, Mid-air. (C. Moffett) Cent. 40: 643.
Dining-room, Scheme of Design for a. (A. H. Baxter) Artist (N. Y.) 24: 78.

Dining Societies of London. Ed. R. **188**: 102. Same art. Liv. Age, **219**: 403.

Dinkie, A Modern Egyptian. (H. Martin) Un. Serv. M. **19**: 85.

Dinner and the Duchess, The; a Study in Snobbery. Temp. Bar, **118**: 223.

Dinners and Diners. Macmil. **85**: 49.

— in Bohemia and Elsewhere. (J. P. Bocock) No. Am. **172**: 764.

Dinosaur, The Largest Known. (E. S. Riggs) Science, n. s. **13**: 549.

Dinosaurs, European, Recent Observations on. (O. C. Marsh) Am. J. Sci. **154**: 413.

— Jurassic, Footprints of. (O. C. Marsh) Am. J. Sci. **157**: 227.

— Marsh on. Nature, **55**: 463.

Diocletian, The Persecution of. (H. M. Gwatkin) Eng. Hist. R. **13**: 499.

Dionysius Cato, Proverbs of. (K. P. Harrington) Meth. R. **59**: 37.

Dionysius of Halicarnassus. Letters; ed. by W. R. Roberts. (H. Hayman) Crit. R. **11**: 408.

— Epistula II. ad Ammæum, Structure of. (W. Warren) Am. J. Philol. **20**: 316.

Dionysos, New Torso of a Youthful. (T. A. B. Spratt) Archæol. **49**: 318.

Dipeltis, a Fossil Insect? (C. J. Gahan) Nat. Sci. **12**: 42.

Diplodocus, Skeleton of. (H. F. Osborn) Science, n. s. **10**: 870.

Diplomacy, American. Macmil. **77**: 67.

— — Formative Incidents in. (E. E. Sparks) Chaut. **34**: 31, 139, 247.

— — in 1898. (A. M. Low) McClure, **15**: 255.

— and Journalism. Spec. **81**: 513.

— and Public Speaking. Spec. **78**: 655.

— as a Profession. National, **35**: 101.

— British and Russian. (A Diplomat) No. Am. **170**: 871.

— Democratic. Liv. Age, **220**: 262.

— The New. (L. Mead) No. Am. **168**: 377. — Outl. **66**: 202.

Diplomacy of Ellis Minor, The. Cornh. **79**: 96. Same art. Liv. Age, **220**: 387.

Diplomas, Fraudulent, and State Supervision. (H. W. Rogers) Educa. R. **17**: 269.

Diplomatic and Consular Service of the U. S. (H. H. D. Peirce) Arena, **17**: 909.

Diplomatic Corps, San Francisco's. (W. J. Weymouth) Overland, n. s. **38**: 272.

Diplomatic Curiosities, Some. Chamb. J. **77**: 84.

Diplomatic Etiquette in the 17th Century. (G. Hill) Gent. M. n. s. **66**: 131.

Diplomatic History, The Congress of. (J. G. Whiteley) Conserv. R. **1**: 362.

Diplomatic Service, U. S., Need of a Permanent. (G. L. Rives) Forum, **25**: 702.

Diplomatists, Literary Men as. (T. Stanton) Lippinc. **62**: 139.

Diplomats, Our Literary. Bk. Buyer, **20**: 284-440. **21**: 38-90.

Dips into a Doctor's Diary. Chamb. J. **76**: 798.

Diræ and Lydia, Further Remarks on. (R. Ellis) Am. J. Philol. **20**: 139.

Direct Legislation. (A. A. Brown and E. Pomeroy) Arena, **22**: 97.

— and Social Progress: a Conversation with Eltweed Pomeroy. Arena, **25**: 317.

— in America. (E. P. Oberholtzer) Arena, **24**: 493.

— in Switzerland and America. (J. R. Commons) Arena, **22**: 725.

    See Referendum.

Direct Primaries Demanded. Outl. **67**: 477.

Direct Primaries in Minnesota. Outl. **67**: 838.

— in Wisconsin, The. Outl. **67**: 756.

Direction, Sense of. Spec. **79**: 400. **80**: 15, 46.

Direction; a poem. (L. Mead) Chaut. **30**: 366.

Directories, Meditation on. (A. W. Pollard) Library, n. s. **2**: 82.

Directorships held by Ministers of the Crown. (J. G. S. MacNeill) Sat. R. **86**: 596.

Disabled, Transportation of the. (J. E. Pilcher) J. Mil. Serv. Inst. **9**: 222.

Disarmament of Europe. (S. Low) 19th Cent. **44**: 52. Same art. Ecl. M. **131**: 737.

— Russia and. (E. J. Dillon) Contemp. **74**: 609.

Disbandment of the Army of Northern Virginia; a sketch. (M. P. Thompson) McClure, **12**: 79.

Disbursement Sheet; a story. (W. W. Jacobs) Chamb. J. **73**: 445. Same art. Ecl. M. **128**: 612.

Discharge-current, from a Surface of Large Curvature. (J. E. Almy) Am. J. Sci. **162**: 175.

Disciple of the Old Creed, A. (M. Q. Couch) Temp. Bar, **110**: 563.

Discipline and Humanity. (Von Reichenan) J. Mil. Serv. Inst. **13**: 761.

— and Musketry. Un. Serv. M. **24**: 186.

— and Tactics. (M. Harris) J. Mil. Serv. Inst. **13**: 100.

— in the National Guard. (C. H. Hitchcock) J. Mil. Serv. Inst. **19**: 99.

— in the United States Army. (M. F. Steele) J. Mil. Serv. Inst. **17**: 1.

— — Best Means of Promoting and Maintaining. (E. M. Lewis) J. Mil. Serv. Inst. **28**: 325.

— Public Need of. Spec. **80**: 898.

— of the Home, School, and College. (H. Orcutt) Educa. **18**: 606.

— School, Child Study and. (W. S. Monroe) Educa. R. **14**: 451.

— *vs.* Dissipation in Secondary Education. (P. Shorey) School R. **5**: 217.

Disconsolate Dragoon, A; a story. Argosy, **65**: 364.

Discount Policy, Modern, History and Basis of. Bank. M. (Lond.) **72**: 351, 465.

Discount Rates in the United States. (R. M. Breckenridge) Pol. Sci. Q. **13**: 119.

Discoverer, The; a story. (I. S. Dodd) Munsey, **25**: 828.

Discoveries, The, of the 19th Century. (A. R. Wallace) Liv. Age, **219**: 63.

"Discovery," Antarctic Ship, Launch of. Geog. J. **17**: 523.

— Voyage of, to Madeira. (H. R. Mill) Geog. J. **18**: 395.

Discovery, Fortuitous. Chamb. J. **75**: 369. Same art. Ecl. M. **131**: 209.

Discriminating between Species and Subspecies. (C. H. Merriam) Science, **5**: 753.

Discussion, Belligerent, and Truth-seeking. (R. C. Cabot) Int. J. Ethics, **9**: 29.

— Free, Menace to. Dial (Ch.) **26**: 325.

Disease and Senility, Effects of, in Bones and Teeth of Mammals. (H. Allen) Science, **5**: 289.

— Cell Theory of. (W. Hutchinson) Contemp. **75**: 568.

— Defense against. (E. Duclaux) Chaut. **25**: 639.

— Genesis of. (E. Lee) Am. J. Soc. Sci. **38**: 57.

— Infectious, Causes of. (F. Hueppe) Monist, **8**: 384.

Diseases Epidemic in Armies. (C. K. Winne) J. Mil. Serv. Inst. **13**: 501.

— Preventable. (H. S. T. Harris) J. Mil. Serv. Inst. **23**: 226.

Dis-honourable, The; a story. (E. L. Prescott) Pall Mall M. **20**: 456.

Disillusioned; a story. (Maria Weed) Midland, **7**: 175, 243.

Disinfection at Quarantine. (M. E. Ward) Pop. Sci. Mo. 50: 344.

Dismal Swamp and how to go there. (H. E. Freeman and E. G. Cummings) Chaut. 33: 515.

Dispensary; Propagator of Pauperism. (G. F. Shrady) Forum, 23: 420.

Disraeli, Benjamin, Earl of Beaconsfield. See Beaconsfield.

Dissecting-room, In the. (P. Rosegger) Open Court, 11: 365.

Dissemblers, The. (T. Cobb) Lippinc. 66: 323.

Dissent in the Victorian Era. (J. G. Rogers) 19th Cent. 50: 114. Same art. Ecl. M. 137: 668. — Liv. Age, 230: 729.

— Treatment of, in English Fiction. Lond. Q. 89: 54. Same art. Liv. Age, 215: 627.

Dissenters, Society of, founded at New York, 1769. Am. Hist. R. 6: 498.

Dissociation and Association. (H. Crompton) Sci. Prog. 7: 174.

Distaff, Scottish, Decoration of a. (F. R. Coles) Reliquary, 39: 1.

Distance, The Annihilation of. (Lazare Weiller) Liv. Age, 219: 163.

— Enchantment of. Sat. R. 88: 195.

Distances, Science of. (Sir G. S. Robertson) Pop. Sci. Mo. 58: 526.

Distilling, Illicit, in Ireland. (R. E. Hodson) Gent. M. n. s. 59: 484.

Distilling Ship "Iris," U. S. Navy. (W. W. White) Cassier, 15: 75.

Distinction, The Passion for. (M. F. Egan) No. Am. 167: 573.

Distinctly a Plight; a story. (P. L. Ford) Harper, 103: 733.

Distraction by Odors. (L. G. Birch) Am. J. Psychol. 9: 45.

Distress, Study of Causes of. (W. P. Ayres) Char. R. 8: 469.

Distressed Innocents, The; a story. (G. S. Street) Pall Mall M. 19: 4.

Distribution and Exchange. (A. Marshall) Econ. J. 8: 37.

— and Variation, Locard's. (F. N. Balch) Am. Natural. 33: 440.

— Fallacies in Theory of. (A. T. Hadley) Econ. J. 7: 477.

— of Marine Mammals. (P. L. Sclater) Science, 5: 741.

— of Species, Agency of Man in. Nature, 56: 604.

District of Columbia in its Centennial Year. (H. B. F. Macfarland) Forum, 30: 545.

— Geographical Development of. (W. J. McGee) Nat. Geog. M. 9: 317.

— Hundred Years of. (A. Shaw) R. of Rs. (N. Y.) 22: 675.

— Little Kingdom of the President. (H. L. West) Forum, 25: 445.

Dittersdorf, Karl von, Coleridge's. Ath. '97, 1: 753.

Divergence, Reproductive, not a Factor in the Evolution of New Species. (K. Jordan) Nat. Sci. 12: 45.

Divers and Diving. (D. Paton) Good Words, 39: 453.

— Peculiar Danger of. Chamb. J. 76: 197.

Divided Heart, The. (G. Hibbard) Harper, 100: 474.

Divine Adventure, The. (F. Macleod) Fortn. 72: 879. 1058.

Divine Flame, A; a story. (E. and H. Heron) Cornh. 78: 510.

Divine Opulence. (J. P. Rudd) Arena, 21: 580.

Divines, Eminent, A Study of. (J. W. Webb) Meth. R. 60: 915.

Diving in a Flooded Mine. Chamb. J. 74: 412.

Divining Rod in Search for Water. (T. V. Holmes) Anthrop. J. 27: 233.

Divining Rod, Theory of Water-finding by, B. Tompkins on. (C. V. Boys) Nature, 61: 1.

Divining Rod, The; a story. (E. Nesbit) Pall Mall M. 15: 357.

Divorce and the Bible. (N. Lathrop) Bib. Sac. 56: 266.

— Banner County for; Ashtabula Co., Ohio. (A. H. Fréchette) Cent. 37: 636.

— Bibliography. Chaut. 32: 441.

— Episcopal Church on. Outl. 66: 729.

— in the United States. (G. Atherton) Contemp. 72: 410.

— Law of, in England and Germany. (J. Hirshfeld) Law Q. 13: 395.

-- Marriage and, in their Legal Aspects. (J. D. Enright) Cath. World, 70: 673.

— National Law of, Needed. (E. L. Godkin) Nation, 68: 369.

— Proposed Church Canons on. (S. W. Dike) Outl. 69: 231.

— Some Comments on. (Mrs. K. G. Wells) No Am. 173: 508.

— Some Notes on. (G. H. Westley) Green Bag, 10: 239.

Divorce Laws, Homogeneous, in all the States, are they Desirable? (E. C. Stanton) No. Am. 170: 405.

Divorce Proceedings, Physical Examination in. (B. M. Cloud) Am. Law R. 35: 698.

Divorces, Evil of. (A. E. Erchmann, H. F. Harris, and W. W. Turlay) Arena, 23: 88.

Dix, Beulah Marie, with portrait. Bk. News, 18: 1.

Dix, Dorothea Lynde. (S. M. Jackson) Char. R. 9: 176.

Dix, William Frederick. Writer, 14: 154.

Dixieland, Some Types in. (Mrs. D. B. Dyer) Cosmopol. 23: 235.

Dixon, Richard W. Ath. '00, 1: 116.

Dizzy Dave; a story. (J. L. Long) Cosmopol. 28: 295.

Djemshid or Jem. A Turkish "Young Pretender." (M. M. Currie) 19th Cent. 41: 547.

Djinns, The. (V. Hugo) Arena, 17: 966.

Dobrynia; a Russian Builina. (G. Calderon) Monthly R. 5, no. 3: 148.

Dobson, Austin, with portrait. (E. Gosse) Indep. 53: 1960.

— as an Essayist. Acad. 56: 477.

— Poetry of. (A. Symons) Bookman, 5: 195. — Acad. 52: 367.

Dock, Story of the Making of a. (James Deas) Good Words, 39: 598.

Dock Gardens. (W. H. Bell) Garden & F. 10: 252.

Docks, Floating. (S. F. Staples) Cassier, 13: 337.

— Municipal Ownership of, in N. Y. City. (B. S. Coler) Munic. Aff. 4: 207.

Doctor, The Club. (M. Byrde) Sund. M. 26: 124.

Doctor Armstrong; a story. Pall Mall M. 11: 221.

Dr. Barlow's Secret. (J. Workman) Chamb. J. 76: 17-73.

Dr. Craig and Another Woodcock Shooter; a story. (C. H. Morse) Outing, 35: 19.

Dr. Falconer's Temptation; a story. (T. Greer) Eng. Illust. 19: 341.

Dr. Felix. (F. Lynde) Lippinc. 60: 809.

Doctor Floss; a story. (A. M. Trotter) Argosy, 66: 363.

Dr. Gowdy and the Squash; a story. (H. B. Fuller) Harper, 102: 262.

Doctor Greenfield; a story. (Lady M. Howard) Argosy, 68: 407.

Dr. Johnson's Conversation; a poem. (D. Cave) Gent. M. n. s. 60: 205.

Dr. Martin's Furlough. (A. H. Norway) Chamb. J. 74: 353-408.

Doggett, Thomas. (T. A. Cook) Monthly R. 4, no. 1: 146.

Dogma and Dogmatism. Cath. World, 72: 468.

— Christian, Dörner on the History of. (J. Lindsay) Crit. R. 10: 130.

— Development of. (T. L. Healy) Cath. World, 72: 349. — (D. Moyes) Cath. World, 65: 433.

— History of, by A. Harnack. (A. T. Swing) Bib. Sac. 54: 153. — Sat. R. 84: 201.

Dogmas, Sabatier on the Vitality of. (G. Tyrrell) Month, 91: 592.

Dogmatics, Evangelical, Whence and Whither of. (O. Kirn, tr. S. G. Hefelbomer) Luth. Q. 28: 263.

"Dolce." (J. L. Long) Cent. 39: 803.

Dole, Sanford B., President of Hawaiian Republic. Midland, 9: 209.

— and the Hawaiian Question, with portrait. (L. A. Thurston) Outl. 58: 317.

Doletzki, Menahem. (H. Hapgood) Critic, 36: 254.

Dollar, Trade, Origin and History of the. Bank. M. (N. Y.) 58: 383.

Dollars, The Dignity of. (Jack London) Overland, n. s. 36: 53.

Dolls and Doll-play. (J. Sully) Contemp. 75: 58. Same art. Liv. Age, 220: 484. Same art. Ecl. M. 132: 490.

Dolls, the Gold-finder. Macmil. 85: 150.

Dolly ; a character sketch. (Frango) Belgra. 94: 223.

Dolly and Dick. (H. C. Bailey) Longm. 38: 528.

Dolly Dialogues, More. (A. H. Hawkins) McClure, 17: 3, 410.

Dolmens of Ireland, The, Borlase on. Spec. 79: 312. — Sat. R. 84: 43.

Dolmetsch, —., Concert by. (J. F. Runciman) Sat. R. 87: 717.

Dolomite Mts. (H. Spenser) Pall Mall M. 25: 109.

— Bicycling through the. (G. E. Waring) Cent. 32: 35.

— Climbing Reminiscences of the, Sinigaglia's. Ath. '97, 1: 77.

Dolores ; a story. (A. Applin) Pall Mall M. 11: 449. 12: 17.

Dolores, a Mexican Romance. (G. L. Bruce) Midland, 10: 440.

Dolson, Cora A. Matson. Writer, 14: 154.

Dome, The, and its Wanderings. (J. C. Paget) Temp. Bar, 110: 250. Same art. Liv. Age, 212: 741.

Domenico Cirillo and the Chemical Action of Light in Connection with Vegetable Irritability. (I. Giglioli) Nature, 63: 15.

Domesday Book and beyond, Maitland on. (J. Tait) Eng. Hist. R. 12: 768. — (C. M. Andrews) Am. Hist. R. 3: 130. — (J. Tait) Eng. Hist. R. 12: 768. — Sat. R. 84: 70. — (E. P. Cheyney) Citizen, 3: 118. — Spec. 78: 510. — Ath. '97, 1: 274.

— and Some 13th Century Surveys. (F. Baring) Eng. Hist. R. 12: 285.

— Breviates of. Ath. '00, 2: 346.

Domesday "Manor," The. (J. H. Round) Eng. Hist. R. 15: 293.

Domesday of Inclosures, 1517-18, Leadam's. (F. G. Davenport) Am. Hist. R. 3: 345.

Domestic Animals, Study of. (S. H. Gage) Science, n. s. 10: 305.

— Evolution of. Acad. 52: 519.

Domestic Economy ; Art of Buying Food for a Family. (Mary Graham) Cosmopol. 27: 545.

— Chautauqua Reading Course for Housewives. Chaut. 34: 70, 182, 295.

— College Women and the New Science. (C. S. Angstman) Pop. Sci. Mo. 53: 674.

— Evolution in the Kitchen. (F. A. Doughty) Chaut. 28: 386.

Domestic Economy in Girls' Secondary Schools. (A. Mitchell) J. Soc. Arts, 45: 952.

— Training Schools of, in England. (Miss Pycroft) J. Soc. Arts, 45: 967.

Domestic Helps and Hindrances. (E. D. Cuming) Chamb. J. 77: 17.

Domestic Life, Education for. (M. R. Smith) Pop. Sci. Mo. 53: 521.

Domestic Problem, The, Solved here. (E. P. Ward) Liv. Age, 229: 592.

Domestic Science in Girls' Education. (L. E. Walter) J. Soc. Arts, 45: 971.

Domestic Servant, A Plea for the. Macmil. 80: 284.

— Problem of the. (M. Major) Macmil. 82: 276. Same art. Ecl. M. 135: 610. Same art. Liv. Age, 226: 642.

— — and how to solve it. (A. Ogilvie) Westm. 152: 64.

— — Solution of, by a Grandmother. Macmil. 82: 448. Same art. Liv. Age, 227: 492. Same art. Ecl. M. 136: 47.

— Responsibility of Employers. (M. R. Smith) Forum, 27: 678.

Domestic Servants in Germany. (H. Jastrow) Econ. J. 9: 625.

Domestic Service. (L. M. Salmond) Chaut. 27: 191, 308.

— as discussed at a Woman's Club. (J. M. Parker) No. Am. 166: 639.

— in the South. (O. Langhorne) Am. J. Soc. Sci. 39: 169.

— New Views of. (L. E. Rector) Gunton's M. 14: 180.

— The Other Side of the Shield. (C. T. Herrick) No. Am. 164: 507.

Domesticity. (S. Gwynn) Macmil. 79: 56. Same art. Liv. Age, 219: 895. Same art. Ecl. M. 132: 228.

— American, Decrease of. (H. Campbell) Arena, 19: 86.

Dominant Mother, A. (A. Y. Keith) New Eng. M. n. s. 22: 712.

Dominic, Father, and the Conversion of England. (B. Camm) Dub. R. 123: 337.

Domremy, Around. (M. H. Catherwood) Atlan. 79: 816.

Domus, Domi : the House in Town. (Halsey Riccardo) M. of Art, 23: 457.

Don Quexote ; a drama. (H. Penn) Cornh. 79: 809.

Doña Dolores. (Kathryn Jarboe) Overland, n. s. 34: 265.

Donald Murray's Romance. (E. F. Benson) Lippinc. 64: 403.

Donald's Experiment ; a sketch. (C. W. Flynn) Harper, 103: 113.

Dondelet, K. (Pol de Mont) Artist (N. Y.) 29: 1.

Dongola. Ed. R. 187: 67.

— Expedition to, Knight on. Spec. 78: 890.

Donkeys, Irish, for South Africa. Spec. 79: 45.

— The Much Maligned Moke. (E. D. Cuming) Eng. Illust. 18: 171.

"Donna" in 1896. (Author of "Charles Lowder") Longm. 29: 274.

Donna Teresa. (F. M. Peard) Temp. Bar, 117: 153–457. 118: 1, 275.

Donne, John. Acad. 52: 474. — (A. Symons) Fortn. 72: 734. — (L. Stephen) National, 34: 595. — Church Q. 50: 91. — (J. W. Chadwick) New World, 9: 31. — (H. M. Sanders) Temp. Bar, 121: 614.

— and his Contemporaries. Quar. 192: 217.

— Gosse's Life of. Acad. 57: 505. Same art. Liv. Age, 223: 726. — Nation, 70: 111, 133.

— Poetry of. Acad. 59: 608.

Donne, Walter J., and the Grosvenor Life School of Art. Art J. 51: 274.

Donne, Walter J., Studio of. Studio (Lond.) **7**: 40.

Donnelly, Eleanor C., with portrait. Cath. World, **64**: 772.

Donnelly, Ignatius. Ragnarok. (I. C. Fales) Arena, **21**: 351.

Doom Castle: a romance. (N. Munro) Blackw. **168**: 449, 640. **169**: 84–764. **170**: 53.

Doom of the Air-god. Chamb. J. **74**: 730.

Doors, Artistic Front. (K. W. Clouston) Art J. **51**: 78.

— Legends of. Am. Arch. **63**: 28.

Doorways of the Bristol Renaissance. (J. W. Dow) Archit. R. **8**: 28.

Dooryards. (Alice Brown) Liv. Age, **222**: 395.

Dora's Disenchantment; a story. (I. Garvey) Argosy, **64**: 632.

Dorchester, 1st Lord, and his Descendants. (G. Johnson) Canad. M. **13**: 475.

Dorchester, Mass., Christian Names in. (W. B. Trask) N. E. Reg. **54**: 213.

— All Saints' Church. Archit. R. **7**: 101.

— British Raid on Dorchester Neck, Feb., 1776. (F. E. Blake) N. E. Reg. **53**: 177.

— Damages caused by British and American Troops in, 1776. (A. Parker) N. E. Reg. **53**: 71.

— Story of Dorchester Heights. (Lois W. Clarke) New Eng. M. n. s. **18**: 221.

Dorchester, Eng. (S. Beale) Am. Arch. **74**: 84. — (Arthur Tomson) Art J. **53**: 231. — (S. J. Barrows) New Eng. M. n. s. **22**: 420.

Dordrecht, Between Showers in. (F. H. Smith) Scrib. M. **25**: 585.

Doré, Gustav, in England, with portrait. (H. C. Daniels) Idler, **13**: 177.

Dorian Peninsula and Gulf. (T. A. B. Spratt) Archæol. **49**: 345.

Doris; a story of the Regulators. (S. B. Kennedy) Outing, **31**: 427, 573.

Dormice, Family Name of the. (T. S. Palmer) Science, n. s. **10**: 412.

Dorothea, Life of St., Fifteenth Century. (W. E. A. Axon) Antiq. n. s. **37**: 53.

Dorothy Q., O. W. Holmes's Great-grandmother. (E. P. Gould) Nat'l M. (Bost.) **10**: 642.

Dorothy Q.'s Trousseau. (F. S. Child) Liv. Age, **223**: 598.

Dorset and Devon, England. (T. P. White) Scot. R. **33**: 301.

Dorset Folk-lore. (H. C. March) Folk-Lore, **10**: 439, 478. **11**: 107.

Dorsetshire, Humor of. (R. Edgcumbe) Cornh. **82**: 238. Same art. Ecl. M. **135**: 666. Same art. Liv. Age, **226**: 648.

Dorsetshire Pastoral. (M. E. Francis) Longm. **33**: 42.

Dossi, Dosso. (E. G. Gardner) Gent. M. n. s. **60**: 373.

Dost Muhammad Khan, Amiri-kabir. (H. Pearse) Un. Serv. M. **19**: 384.

Dostèn and Shērèn; a legend. Folk-Lore, **8**: 79.

Dostoyevsky, Feodor Michailovitch. (C. Brinton) Critic, **37**: 419.

Douai, Campaign of. (Capt. Cairnes) Macmil. **81**: 227, 290, 386, 460.

Double Buggy at Lahey's Creek; a story. (H. Lawson) Blackw. **169**: 208. — Liv. Age, **229**: 567.

Double-point Threshold, The Successive. (G. A. Tawney and C. W. Hodge) Psychol. R. **4**: 591.

Double Sixes; a story. (C. Lyon) Temp. Bar, **114**: 507.

Double Stroke, A. (Wilmetta Curtis) Overland, n. s. **38**: 332.

Doubt, Fear, Apprehend, Suspect, The Verbs. (F. Hall) Nation, **70**: 90.

— Function of. (J. S. Willey) Meth. R. **57**: 554.

— Inconsistency of. (J. Cooper) Ref. Church R. **45**: 169.

— Irrationality of. (J. Cooper) Ref. Q. **44**: 409.

Doubt, Reasonable, in Law. (C. E. Grinnell) Green Bag, **9**: 97.

Doubtful Acquisition; a story. (C. G. Robertson) Blackw. **161**: 810. Same art. Ecl. M. **129**: 177. Same art. Liv. Age, **214**: 314.

Doubts: a poem. (M. A. M. Marks) Argosy, **65**: 256.

Dougherty, Daniel; with portrait. (A. O. Hall) Green Bag, **9**: 141.

Doughty, Thomas, and Sir Francis Drake. (D. Hannay) Blackw. **163**: 796.

Douglas, Amanda M., and her Books, with portrait. Bk. News, **16**: 279.

Douglas, Archibald. (A. Lang) Blackw. **170**: 94.

Douglas, Sir George, Perfidy of. (A. Lang) Macmil. **78**: 196.

Douglas, Stephen Arnold. (F. H. Hodder) Chaut. **29**: 432.

Douglas, Mrs. Stephen A. (Juliette M. Babbitt) Midland, **7**: 213.

Douglass, William, Life and Writings of. (C. J. Bullock) Econ. Stud. **2**: 265.

Doukhobors, The. (A. Maude) Outl. **60**: 913. — (H. D. Atwater) Indep. **52**: 1121.

— A Modern Exodus. (G. C. Nuttall) Good Words, **42**: 402.

Doulton, Sir Henry. J. Soc. Arts, **46**: 40.

Doumic, René. (T. Bentzon) Critic, **32**: 173. — (T. Stanton) Nation, **66**: 163.

Dove Cottage, the Home of Wordsworth and De Quincey. (W. Knight) Cent. **38**: 53.

Dove Hunting in California. (T. S. Van Dyke) Outing, **35**: 395.

Dove River, England. Temp. Bar, **119**: 121.

Dovedale, Eng. Beside the Dove. (J. Hyde) Gent. M. n. s. **61**: 291.

— The Low Peak. (J. Hyde) Gent. M. n. s. **61**: 480.

Dover, Eng., History of, Statham's. Ath. '99, **2**: 378.

— New Harbor Works at. (W. Crundall and W. Mowll) 19th Cent. **50**: 844.

Dover, New Hampshire. (C. H. Garland) New Eng. M. n. s. **17**: 97.

Dow, Lorenzo. (E. S. Gilman) New Eng. M. n. s. **20**: 411.

Dow, T. Millie, Painter, with portrait. (N. Garstin) Studio (Internat.) **1**: 145.

Dowe, Jennie E. T. Writer, **12**: 153.

Dowell, Stephen. Econ. J. **8**: 414.

Dower. A Roman Dowry. (E. C. Vansittart) Argosy, **70**: 351.

Dowie, John Alexander, and his Zions, with portrait. Indep. **53**: 1786.

Dowie, Menie Muriel. Crook of the Bough. (Frank Danby) Sat. R. **86**: 23.

Dowie Movement in Chicago. Outl. **68**: 429.

Dowlande, John. (J. S. R. Phillips) Cornh. **76**: 240.

Down in the Cimeroon; a story. (E. W. Fowler) Nat'l M. (Bost.) **6**: 522.

Down the Kentucky on a Raft. (John Fox, jr.) Scrib. M. **27**: 664.

Down Zabuloe Way; a story. (W. F. Alexander) Gent. M. n. s. **61**: 105.

Downman, John. Munsey, **19**: 98.

Downs, Across the. (G. A. J. Cole) Knowl. **23**: 89.

— Vegetation of. (W. H. Hudson) Longm. **32**: 32. Same art. Liv. Age, **217**: 879.

Downside Abbey Music. (J. F. Runciman) Sat. R. **92**: 108.

Dowson, Ernest C. (A. Symons) Fortn. **73**: 947. — Acad. **58**: 175, 328.

Doxat, Edmund Theodore. Bank. M. (Lond.) **68**: 739.

Doyle, Charles W., with portrait. (G. H. Fitch) Bookman, **10**: 117.

Doyle, Conan. (D. C. Murray) Canad. M. **9**: 499.

Doyle, Conan. Chat about Sherlock Holmes; with portrait. (H. T. Peck) Indep. 53: 2757.
— Uncle Bernac. (M. Beerbohm) Sat. R. 84: 31.
D. Q., New Minor Planet. (W. W. Payne) Pop. Astron. 7: 20. — (A. C. D. Crommelin) Knowl. 21: 250.
— Bode's Law and. (W. J. S. Lockyer) Nature, 59: 11.
Drachmann, Holger. Through the Eyes of a Great Dane. (J. H. Wisby) Arena, 24: 561.
Dragon Candlestick, The; a story. (S. M. Peck) Bk. News, 16: 271.
Dragon-flies. (E. Stenhouse) Chamb. J. 75: 385.
— British. (W. F. Kirby) Nature, 61: 418.
— Notes on. (D. S. Kellicott) Am. Natural. 31: 351.
Dragon-fly as a Beauty. Sat. R. 90: 234.
— Metamorphosis of a. (A. East) Knowl. 20: 195. Same art. Liv. Age, 214: 895.
Dragon-fly Nymphs, Respiration of. (A. East) Knowl. 23: 220.
Dragons in Art. (G. C. Williamson) Artist (N. Y.) 31: 79.
Drainage and Irrigation in Mexico. Nature, 56: 589.
Drake, Earl, Violinist, with portrait. Music, 15: 312.
Drake, Sir Francis. (L. G. C. Laughton) Un. Serv. M. 17: 453. — (A. W. Durrant) Temp. Bar, 110: 92.
— and the Tudor Navy, Corbett's. (W. F. Tilton) Am. Hist. R. 4: 516. — (J. W. Thompson) Dial (Ch.) 25: 65. — (C. H. Stockton) Nation, 66: 366.
— Corbett's Successors of. (C. H. Stockton) Nation, 72: 742. — Ed. R. 194: 1.
— Voyages of, Spanish Account of. (G. Jenner) Eng. Hist. R. 16: 46.
Drake, Joseph Rodman. (M. A. D. Howe) Bookman, 5: 304.
Drake, Samuel G. (E. M. Bacon) Bookman, 4: 542.
Drake University, Iowa. (Mary A. Carpenter) Midland, 9: 353.
Drama. About Play-acting. (S. L. Clemens) Forum, 26: 143.
— Advance of American Dramatic Art. (C. Scott) Munsey, 20: 556.
— American. (I. A. Pyle) Lippinc. 60: 130.
— and the American Library. (P. Wilstach) Bookman, 8: 134.
— and Morality. (M. Beerbohm) Sat. R. 87: 682.
— Anti-climaxes. (M. Beerbohm) Sat. R. 90: 44.
— Art for Truth's Sake in. (J. A. Herne) Arena, 17: 361.
— as Art. Dial (Ch.) 25: 333.
— as a Teacher. (W. F. Ainsworth) Argosy, 64: 368.
— Blight on the. (W. Archer) Fortn. 67: 21. Same art. Ecl. M. 128: 332. Same art. Liv. Age, 212: 643.
— Conventions of the. (Brander Matthews) Scrib. M. 23: 497.
— Criticism of, Syle's. (E. E. Hale, jr.) Dial (Ch.) 26: 119.
— Current London; a survey. (W. Archer) Pall Mall M. 23: 101.
— Educational Features of. (F. S. Root) Am. J. Soc. Sci. 35: 99.
— Evolution of the. (R. Lawson) Gent. M. n. s. 64: 362.
— Fourth Unity. (W. C. Lawton) Outl. 60: 237.
— Genesis of the New, Steiger's. (J. F. Coar) Bookman, 8: 571.
— German, Evolution of. (E. von Wildenbruch) Forum, 25: 375, 630.
— Immoral Plays. (A. Laidlaw) Westm. 154: 212.
— in England. (S. Dewey) Westm. 147: 151.
— in the English Provinces. (H. A. Jones) 19th Cent. 49: 431.
— in 1900-01. (W. D. Howells) No. Am. 172: 468.

Drama, Licensing, in London. (M. Beerbohm) Sat. R. 89: 615.
— Modern. (M. Maeterlinck) Cornh. 80: 166.
— The New Poetic. (W. D. Howells) No. Am. 172: 794.
— of Ideas, The. (N. Hapgood) Contemp. 74: 712. Same art. Ecl. M. 132: 337. Same art. Liv. Age, 220: 159.
— of the 19th Century. (H. Potter) Arena, 23: 157.
— of War. (A. B. Hyde) Meth. R. 59: 888.
— on the Downward Grade, 1868-98. (A. Laidlaw) Westm. 153: 317.
— Oriental. Lippinc. 62: 711.
— Plays of the Season. (W. Archer) Fortn. 72: 132.
— Poetic. (W. Archer) Critic, 36: 23.
— Polish. (H. Modjeska) Critic, 36: 66.
— Preface to "The Bending of the Bough." (G. Moore) Fortn. 73: 317.
— Recent English. Acad. 53: 343.
— Relation to Literature. (B. Matthews) Forum, 24: 630.
— Some Aspects of, To-day. (H. B. Tree) No. Am. 164: 66.
— Spectacular Element in. Ed. R. 194: 203. Same art. Ecl. M. 137: 748. Same art. Liv. Age, 231: 73.
— Tendency of, toward the Unintellectual. (Richard Stearns) Cosmopol. 32: 65.
— a Theory of the. (F. Greenslet) Forum, 27: 631.
— The Victorian, Filon on. (T. H. Huntington) Dial (Ch.) 23: 247.
— Wagner-Nietzsche View of. (E. Newman) Music, 14: 27.
Dramatic, Dread of the. Spec. 80: 335.
Dramatic Art in England and America. (C. Scott) Munsey, 24: 194.
— Nationality in. (H. H. Fyfe) Monthly R. 4, no. 3: 90.
Dramatic Critic; his Work and Influence. (E. A. Dithmar) Forum, 23: 237.
— Reminiscences of a. (H. A. Clapp) Atlan. 88: 155-622.
Dramatic Criticism, Theory of. (N. Hapgood) Forum, 27: 120.
Dramatic Critics and Actors. (W. H. Pollock) Theatre, 39: 281.
— Arrogance of Some Older. (M. Beerbohm) Sat. R. 90: 490.
— Letters to. Theatre, 39: 165, 238.
Dramatic Season of 1897-98 in Chicago. Dial (Ch.) 25: 11.
— 1900-01, Events of. (G. Kobbé) Forum, 31: 298.
Dramatic Style. (M. Beerbohm) Sat. R. 90: 516.
Dramatists and their Methods. (H. Wyndham) Pall Mall M. 21: 331.
— Dearth of. Theatre, 38: 205, 269.
— English, of To-day. (W. K. Tarpey) Critic, 37: 117.
Drapery Trade, The. Econ. R. 7: 42.
Draught, Fire, Mechanical. (H. B. Präther) Am. Arch. 65: 93. — (W. H. Booth) Cassier, 21: 130. — (W. B. Snow) Cassier, 15: 48.
Drawing and Nature Study. (M. V. O'Shea) Educa. 17: 369.
— a Badger. (E. Mitchell) Strand, 17: 167.
— Children's, Some Observations on. (J. S. Clark) Educa. R. 13: 76.
— Figure. (J. H. Vanderpoel) Brush & P. 3: 364. 4: 42, 128, 174, 222, 272, 321. 5: 47, 90, 138.
— — the Arm and Hand. (J. H. Vanderpoel) Brush & P. 5: 184, 274.
— for Reproduction by Process. Studio (Lond.) 1: 65. 2: 99, 132.
— — Impressionism in Black and White. Studio (Lond.) 2: 175.

Dufferin, Marquis of. *See* Blackwood, F. T.

Duffs, The Lucky. (J. M. Bulloch) Eng. Illust. 19: 235.

Duffy, Sir Charles Gavan. Acad. 53: 568.

— Life of. (E. G. Johnson) Dial (Ch.) 24: 288. — (A. Webb) Nation, 66: 280.

Dug-out Canoe, Ancient British, Discovery of an. Reliquary, 41: 54.

Dukes County, Martha's Vineyard, Seal of. (C. E. Banks) N. E. Reg. 54: 179.

Dulce sueño de Mejico, El ; The sweet dream of Mexico. (J. M. Baltimore) Overland, n. s. 36: 11.

Dull, The Dread of Being. Acad. 59: 277. Same art. Liv. Age, 227: 195.

Dull November, A. Chamb. J. 78: 824.

Duluth Tragedy ; a story. (T. A. Janvier) Harper, 99: 402.

Dumas, Alexandre, *père*. (W. S. Sparrow) Temp. Bar, 111: 365. — (E. A. Bennett) Acad. 55: 249. — (A. F. Davidson) Macmil. 79: 257. — Gent. M. n. s. 62: 100. Same art. Liv. Age, 220: 395. Same art. Ecl. M. 132: 458. — Quar. 189: 76.

— and The Three Musketeers. (B. W. Wells) Chaut. 33: 71.

— Authorship of La Boule de Neige. Acad. 57: 603, 633.

— Silver Key ; adapted by S. Grundy. (G. B. Shaw) Sat. R. 84: 59.

— Why his Novels last. (G. R. Carpenter) Forum, 27: 502.

Dumas Cycle, The. (E. H. Mullin) Bk. Buyer, 16: 50.

Dumfries and Galloway, History of, Maxwell's. Ath. '97, 1: 42.

Du Maurier, George, Artistic Position of. (L. Lusk) Art J. 52: 337.

— Trilby. (J. Fearnley) Sewanee, 3: 209.

Dumb, The. *See* Deaf and Dumb.

Dumbell's Bank, Failure of. Bank. M. (Lond.) 69: 373.

Dumbuck Crannog ; is it Neolithic ? (R. Munro) Reliquary, 41: 107.

Dumitru and Sigrid ; a story. (Abraham Cahan) Cosmopol. 30: 493.

Dummy on a Dahabeah ; a story. (E. F. Benson) Bk. News, 17: 49.

Dumont, Santos, and his Air Ship. (W. L. McAlpin) Munsey, 26: 422.

Dunbar, Charles Franklin. With portrait. (C. W. Eliot) Harv. Grad. M. 8: 469. — (F. W. Taussig) Econ. J. 10: 113. — (J. L. Laughlin) J. Pol. Econ. 8: 234.

Dunbar, Paul Laurence, Negro Poet. (C. B. Wilmar) Char. R. 7: 825.

— Poetry of. Acad. 51: 625. — (H. A. Clarke) Poet-Lore, 9: 298.

— The Uncalled. (Grace I. Colbron) Bookman, 8: 338.

Dunbar, William, Scottish Poet. (A. S. Nelson) Gent. M. n. s. 63: 35.

Dunbar's Find. (B. Paterson) Chamb. J. 76: 44.

Duncan, Adam, Admiral. Quar. 189: 137.

— and Naval Defence. Ed. R. 188: 197.

Duncan, James Allan, Designer and Illustrator. Studio (Internat.) 6: 184.

Dundas, Commander F. G. Geog. J. 13: 545.

Dundee, Lady Jean, Strange Story of. Chamb. J. 75: 253.

Dundee, Study of Old. (Edward Pinnington) Good Words, 39: 744.

Dundonald, Lord Alex. T., Trial of, before Lord Ellenborough, Atlay's. Sat. R. 85: 495. — Spec. 80: 339.

Dungarvan Whooper, The. (M. Foster) Atlan. 86: 239.

Dungeness Foreland, The. (F. P. Gulliver) Geog. J. 9: 536.

Dunkards. *See* Dunkers.

Dunkeld, Scotland. (Hugh Macmillan) Art J. 52: 232, 273.

Dunkers, Among the. (Nelson Lloyd) Scrib. M. 30: 513.

— Flowered Side in. (M. M. Miller) Outl. 60: 486.

Dunite in Western Massachusetts, Occurrence of. (G. C. Martin) Am. J. Sci. 156: 244.

Dunmow, England. (L. Viajero) Am. Arch. 74: 101.

Dunne, Finlay P., with portrait. Bk. News, 18: 262.

— With portrait. Bk. Buyer, 18: 12. — (F. A. Putnam) Nat'l M. (Bost.) 10: 207.

— as a Humorist. Acad. 56: 287.

— Casual Observations of Mr. Dooley. Critic, 37: 439.

— Mr. Dooley. (H. T. Peck) Bookman, 8: 574. — (W. I. Way) Bookman, 9: 215.

— — in Peace and War. (J. L. Ford) Bk. Buyer, 18: 60.

Dunnett Shepherdess. (S. O. Jewett) Atlan. 84: 754.

Dunning, Rev. Dr. A. E., of Boston. (F. E. Hamer) Sund. M. 30: 557.

Dunning, J. W. Ath. '97, 2: 677.

Dunning, John and Benjamin, of Stratford, Conn., Descendants of. (R. D. Smyth) N. E. Reg. 52: 38.

Dunning Devil of China and Japan. (P. Carus) Open Court, 12: 110.

Dunregan Castle, Scotland. (A. H. Malan) Pall Mall M. 24: 5.

Dunrobin Castle, Sutherland, Scotland. (R. S. Gower) Pall Mall M. 22: 292.

Dunstable, N. H., Some Ancient History of. (E. S. Stearns) N. E. Reg. 55: 186.

Dunton, Theo. Watts, with portrait. (W. Sharp) Pall Mall M. 25: 435.

— and Mr. Swinburne, at "The Pines." (W. Armstrong) Critic, 39: 512.

— Aylwin. Bk. Buyer, 17: 618. — (W. R. Nicoll) Bookman, 8: 462. — (W. R. Nicoll) Contemp. 74: 798. — Acad. 55: 150.

Dunton Family. (Z. S. Eldredge) N. E. Reg. 54: 286.

Dupuis, M. G., Designer. (G. Mourey) Studio (Internat.) 15: 100.

Dupont des Loges, Paul, Bishop of Metz. (A. Oates) Month, 95: 259.

Dupuy De Lome. *See* De Lome.

Duran, Carolus. *See* Carolus-Duran, M.

"Durbin-on-a-Log ; " a story. (E. E. Simpson) Music, 17: 617.

D'Urfey, Tom. (W. G. Hutchinson) Macmil. 85: 61.

Durham, Constance Mackenzie. Writer, 14: 72.

Durham Cathedral. (S. Glynne) Antiq. n. s. 34: 75, 139. — (H. Pope) Cath. World, 72: 17. — (Canon Fowler) Good Words, 39: 767, 835.

Durham, County Palatine of, G. T. Lapsley's. (M. M. Bigelow) Am. Hist. R. 6: 123.

Durier, John, "Reformed Librarie-keeper." Library, 4: 81.

Duris, Signed Cylix by, in Boston. (F. B. Tarbell) Am. J. Archæol. 2d s. 4: 183.

Durket Sperret, The. (S. B. Elliott) Scrib. M. 22: 372–635.

Durnford, Richard. Church Q. 50: 141.

Durno, Jeannette, Pianist, with portrait. Music, 17: 80.

Duse, Eleanora. (H. Zimmern) Fortn. 73: 980. — (A. Symons) Contemp. 78: 196.

— Acting of. (M. Beerbohm) Sat. R. 89: 648.

Dust in Office Buildings. (C. J. H. Woodbury) Cassier, 13: 225.

Dust of Defeat, The. (Lloyd Osbourne) Scrib. M. 28: 465.

Dust Explosions, Cause of. Chamb. J. 74: 613.

Dust-women. (E. Hobhouse) Econ. J. 10: 411.

Dutch and English in the Past. (A. S. Green) 19th Cent. **46**: 891. Same art. Ecl. M. **134**: 399.

— in Atjeh. (A. G. C. Van Duyl) Asia. R. **23**: 96.

Dutch and Flemish Poets, Modern. (S. Redérus) Poet-Lore, **13**: 386.

Dutch and Quaker Colonies in America, Fiske on. (B. A. Hinsdale) Dial (Ch.) **27**: 357.

Dutch Archives, The. (W. E. Griffis) Nation, **65**: 493.

Dutch Fairy Tale, A. (M. Robinson) 19th Cent. **47**: 652.

Dutch Interior, A ; a story. (J. C. E. de Vries) Cornh. **77**: 653.

Dutch Language and Literature Congress. (J. H. Gore) Nation, **73**: 220.

Dutch Literature, 1896–97. (H. S. M. van W. Crommelin) Ath. '97, **2**: 18.

— 1897–98. (H. S. M. van W. Crommelin) Ath. '98, **2**: 22.

— 1898–99. (H.S.M. van W. Crommelin) Ath. '99, **2**: 19.

— 1899–1900. Ath. '00, **2**: 20.

— 1900–01. (C. K. Elout) Ath. '01, **2**: 20.

Dutch Painters, Modern. (Mary A. Kirkup) Midland, **9**: 304.

Dutch Professors' Manifesto, The. (F. C. de Sumichrast) Nation, **70**: 416. **71**: 327. — (A. Swets) Nation, **71**: 287.

Dutch War, The First. (L. G. C. Laughton) Un. Serv. M. **19**: 233.

Dutch ; the Story of a Dog. (Maria Week) Overland, n. s. **35**: 170.

Duties, Differential, Folly of. (J. Codman) No. Am. **164**: 75.

— on Baggage, The. (R. Ogden) Nation, **73**: 430.

Duttons, Memorials of the, of Dutton-in-Cheshire. Ath. '01, **2**: 275.

Duty. (H. Sturt) Int. J. Ethics, **7**: 334.

— Sense of. Spec. **86**: 133.

— — Is it the Offspring of Self-love ? (C. C. Dove) Westm. **155**: 541.

Duty Soldier, The ; a story. (F. N. Connell) Pall Mall M. **20**: 413.

Duvernoy, Edward, Singer. (Florence Dingley) Music, **21**: 53.

Dvorak, Antonin. Critic, **30**: 241.

Dvorak, Franz. St. Laurent. Art J. **51**: 221.

Dwarf Giant, The. Atlan. **80**: 715.

Dwelling Houses Act, Dutch. (N. G. Pierson) Econ. J. **11**: 511.

Dwellings, Earliest Constructed. (S. D. Peet) Am. Antiq. **22**: 85.

— of the Saga-time in Iceland, Greenland, and Vineland. Illust. (Cornelia Horsford) Nat. Geog. M. **9**: 74.

— Prehistoric Coast and Maritime. (S. D. Peet) Am. Antiq. **22**: 157.

Dwelshauvers-Dery, Victor. (R. H. Thurston) Cassier, **11**: 222.

Dwight, John S., Editor, Critic, and Man, with portrait. (W. S. B. Mathews) Music, **15**: 525. — Lit. W. (Bost.) **30**: 85.

— Cooke's Life of. (T. W. Higginson) Nation, **68**: 189.

Dwight, Timothy, 1752–1817. (L. Hayward) New Eng. M. n. s. **23**: 256.

Dyaks of Borneo, The. Chamb. J. **74**: 438. — Spec. **78**: 145. — (J. T. van Gestel) Cosmopol. **26**: 425.

Dyck, Anthony van. Temp. Bar, **119**: 95. — With portrait. (M. F. Nixon-Roulet) Cath. World, **73**: 431. — Mast. in Art, **1**: pt. 1. — Art J. **49**: 297.

— Exhibition at Antwerp. 19th Cent. **46**: 734. Same art. Liv. Age, **223**: 799. Same art. Ecl. M. **134**: 177. — (L. Cust) M. of Art, **24**: 13. — (E. R. Pennell) Nation, **69**: 222. — (E. F. Baldwin) Outl. **63**: 317. — Art J. **52**: 25.

Dyck, Anthony van. Exhibition at Burlington House. Am. Arch. **68**: 30. — (Claude Phillips) Art J. **52**: 65.

— Exhibition at Royal Academy. (E. Law) M. of Art, **24**: 171, 199. — Am. Arch. **68**: 30.

— In Honor of. (E. R. Pennell) Atlan. **84**: 660.

— Portrait of a Lady, Study for. (E. Law) M. of Art, **24**: 322.

— Works of. Ath. '00, **1**: 25.

Dyeing of Fabrics. (F. Hargraves Smith) Artist (N. Y.) **23**: 31.

Dying Century, The ; a poem. (E. M. Rutherford) Gent. M. n. s. **65**: 617.

Dying Century, The ; a poem. (D. F. Hannigan) Westm. **152**: 653.

Dykes, John Bacchus, Life and Letters. Ath. '98, **1**: 476.

Dynamics, Groundwork of. (J. Galbraith) Science, **6**: 457.

Dynamite, Inventor of. (H. de Mosenthal) 19th Cent. **44**: 567.

Dynamite, La, au Transvaal. New R. **16**: 318.

Dynamite Factory at Ardeer. (H. J. W. Dam) McClure, **9**: 823.

Dynamite Guns Afloat and Ashore. (E. L. Zalinski) Cassier, **14**: 394.

— in Action. Un. Serv. M. **19**: 159.

Dynamo Electric Machinery, Sheldon on. (D. C. Jackson) Science, n. s. **14**: 410.

Dynamos, Compound-wound, coupled in Multiple, Equalizing Connections for. (E. R. Keller) J. Frankl. Inst. **143**: 200.

Dyson, Edward, Poetry of. Acad. **53**: 449.

Dziatzko, Karl. Library, n. s. **1**: 353.

Eagle, The Great Forest. Spec. **79**: 337.

Eagles and their Prey. (C. J. Cornish) Cornh. **80**: 759.

— on an English Lake. Spec. **80**: 724.

— Property Rights in, among the Hopi. (J. W. Fewkes) Am. Anthrop. **2**: 690.

Eames, Henry, Pianist, with portrait. Music, **14**: 627.

Eames-Story, Emma, Opera Singer, with portrait. Music, **15**: 317.

— Portraits of. Strand, **14**: 159.

Ear, Care of the Throat and. (W. Scheppegrell) Pop. Sci. Mo. **54**: 791.

— Human, Significance of Certain Features and Types of the External. (A. Keith) Nature, **65**: 16.

Ears, Human, Classification of, Miriam A. Ellis on. (A. Keith) Nature, **63**: 392.

Earl Roderick's Bride. (D. S. Shorter) Longm. **34**: 70. Same art. Critic, **35**: 1000.

Earl's Court Exhibition, London, 1899. (W. Emanuel) Idler, **16**: 122.

Earle, Alice Morse. Home Life in Colonial Days. (L. B. Lang) Longm. **35**: 323.

Earle, Pliny, Memoirs of, ed. by Sanborn. (R. Dewey) Dial (Ch.) **26**: 79.

Early Christian Romance, An. (A. Church) Sund. M. **28**: 589.

Early Rising in the East. (C. Pore) Un. Serv. M. **16**: 58.

Earning of Wages, The ; a story. (Hamilton Drummond) Eng. Illust. **21**: 167.

Earth as an Abode fitted for Life, Age of. (Lord Kelvin) Science, n. s. **9**: 665, 704.

— — Kelvin on. (T. C. Chamberlain) Science, n. s. **9**: 889. **10**: 11.

— Crust of, Secrets of. (G. A. J. Cole) Knowl. **22**: 32–268.

— Figure of. (C. A. Schott) Nature, **63**: 408.

— — Attraction and. (W. W. Payne) Pop. Astron. **8**: 177. **9**: 7, 117.

— A Flat. (T. Lindsay) Pop. Astron. **6**: 405.

Earth ; Gravitation Constant and Mean Density of. Nature, **56**: 127.

— Inside of. (C. Moffett) McClure, **14**: 363.

— The Living. (Grant Allen) Longm. **29**: 554. Same art. Ecl. M. **129**: 33. Same art. Liv. Age, **213**: 449.

— Measurement of. (A. Fowler) Knowl. **20**: 148.

— Motions of. (G. G. Hodgins) Pop. Astron. **8**: 60.

— Necessary to Heaven. (J. Worcester) N. Church R. **4**: 548.

— Plan of, and its Causes. (J. W. Gregory) Geog. J. **13**: 225.

— Shape and Size of, Our Knowledge of. (C. A. Schott) Nat. Geog. M. **12**: 36.

— Smell of. (G. C. Nuttall) Knowl. **21**: 257.

— Surface of, Configuration of, with Special Reference to the British Islands. (J. Lubbock) Geog. J. **15**: 46.

— Weight of. (J. H. Schooling) Strand, **13**: 529.

Earth's Beauty ; a poem. (C. H. Urner) Outing, **34**: 72.

Earth-crust Movements and their Causes. (J. LeConte) Science, **5**: 321.

Earthquake at Sea, 1891. (G. Hawley) Pall Mall M. **14**: 119.

— The Calcutta. (T. D. La Touche) Nature, **56**: 273. — Spec. **78**: 910.

— Charleston, S. C., 1886. (A. M. Brice) Macmil. **83**: 129.

— Great Indian, of 1897. (C. Davison) Knowl. **23**: 147, 169. — (R. D. Oldham) Nature, **62**: 305.

— in Assam, 1897. (H. Luttmann Johnson) J. Soc. Arts, **46**: 473.

— in Colima, Jan. 19, 1900. (C. W. Haines) J. Frankl. Inst. **152**: 241.

— in Giles Co., Virginia, May, 1897. (M. R. Campbell) Science, n. s. **7**: 233.

— in Hereford, 1896. (C. Davison) Knowl. **22**: 121.

— — Davison on. (J. Milne) Nature, **60**: 194.

— in Japan, Oct. 28, 1891. Geog. J. **17**: 635.

— The Recent, 1896. (J. L. Lobley) Knowl. **20**: 1.

Earthquakes. (E. S. Holden) Science, n. s. **8**: 294.

— Advances in Science of. (J. Milne) Nature, **57**: 246, 272.

— California. (F. H. Dewey) Lippinc. **63**: 527.

— Lunar and Solar Periodicities of. (A. Schuster) Nature, **56**: 321.

— Modern Studies of. (G. Geraland) Pop. Sci. Mo. **54**: 362.

— Process of Seismology during the 19th Century. (C. Davison) Knowl. **24**: 44.

— Publications of the Japanese Earthquake Investigation Committee. (O. P. Hay) Science, n. s. **14**: 178.

— Record of, by Seismograph. (L. Brownell) Idler, **20**: 195.

— Spurious. (C. Davison) Nature, **60**: 139.

Earthquake Effects, Some Remarkable. (R. D. Oldhams) Nature, **63**: 87.

Earthquake-motion, Prof. F. Omori on. Nature, **60**: 431.

Earthquake Precursors. (J. Milne) Nature, **59**: 414.

Earthquake-proof Buildings. Am. Arch. **69**: 70.

Earthquake-sounds. (C. Davison) Knowl. **23**: 83.

Earthworks, Yorkshire, On Some. (E. S. Armitage) Reliquary, **41**: 158.

Earwigs. (Grant Allen) Strand, **14**: 704.

East, Alfred, Artist, with portrait. (F. Wedmore) Studio (Lond.) **7**: 133.

East, Thomas, Printer. (H. R. Plomer) Library, n. s. **2**: 298.

East, the, American Exploration in ; a Challenge to American Scholarship. (M. Wilcox) Harper, **102**: 953.

East, the, American Interests in. (C. S. Conant) Internat. Mo. **3**: 117.

— Ancient, Maspero on. (J. H. Breasted) Dial (Ch.) **22**: 282.

— and Europe, Political Situation in. (N. A. Miles) Forum, **25**: 159.

— and West, Fusion of, Coming. (E. F. Fenollosa) Harper, **98**: 115.

— Changes in the Unchanging. Quar. **187**: 546.

— Far, America and. (W. B. Forbush) Bib. Sac. **56**: 759.

— — — Lord C. Beresford on. (C. H. Shinn) Outl. **61**: 530.

— — America and England in. (C. W. Dilke) No. Am. **169**: 558.

— — America in. (W. E. Griffis) Outl. **60**: 761-1051.

— — Antagonism of England and Russia. (D. C. Boulger) No. Am. **170**: 884.

— — British Interests in. (M. Bell) Un. Serv. M. **16**: 561.

— — British Policy in. (Sir W. Des Vœux) Contemp. **73**: 795.

— — Coming Storm in. (Ignotus) National, **34**: 494. Same art. Liv. Age, **224**: 34.

— — Crisis in. (Diplomaticus) Fortn. **74**: 143. — Fortn. **74**: 677. — (W. E. Gladstone) Liv. Age, **213**: 26. — (M. MacColl) Contemp. **72**: 497. — Quar. **186**: 268. — (A. R. Colquhoun) No. Am. **167**: 513.

— — England's Future Empire in. Contemp. **74**: 153.

— — France and. (A. Laugel) Nation, **64**: 299.

— — Question of. Asia. R. **25**: 275. — (A. V. V. Raymond) Outl. **62**: 425.

— — U. S. Relations with. (C. Denby) Munsey, **20**: 515.

— German Danger in. National, **36**: 178.

— Governing, on Western Principles. (P. S. Reinsch) Forum, **31**: 387.

— Greece and. (B. I. Wheeler) Atlan. **79**: 721.

— Japan and Russia in. (J. Murdoch) No. Am. **170**: 609.

— Pitt and. (W. B. Duffield) Fortn. **67**: 292.

— A Plot against British Interests in the Levant. (Vindex) Fortn. **67**: 811.

— The Powers and the East. (F. de Pressensé) 19th Cent. **41**: 681.

— Problem in. Contemp. **73**: 193.

— Russia on the Bosphorus. (J. W. Gambier) Fortn. **67**: 757.

— Lord Salisbury and. Fortn. **67**: 456.

— Situation in. Spec. **78**: 360.

— True Flavor of the Orient. (J. Ralph) Harper, **100**: 425.

— Vignettes from. (J. Ranken) Argosy, **71**: 233.

— What to do in. (W. M. Ramsay) Contemp. **72**: 234.

East Anglia, Highways and Byways in, W. A. Dutt on. Ath. '01, **1**: 423.

East Aurora, N. Y., Evolution, Socialism, Trusts, and the Religious Situation in. (E. Hubbard) Indep. **53**: 1473.

East India Company, First Century of. Quar. **193**: 44.

East India Company Letters. (C. W. Colby) Nation, **73**: 74.

East Indies. Administrative History of British Dependencies in the Further East. (H. M. Stephens) Am. Hist. R. **4**: 246.

East Poultney, Vermont. (R. S. Cushman) New Eng. M. n. s. **21**: 556.

Eastbourne, Antiquities of. (T. H. B. Graham) Gent. M. n. s. **64**: 551.

— Old, Annals of. (T. H. B. Graham) Gent. M. n. s. **59**: 254. **60**: 550.

Eastdale Ghost, The. (H. Martley) Temp. Bar, **121**: 406.

Easter. Sat. R. **87**: 391.
— and Easter Lore. (E. H. Young) Canad. M. **12**: 482.
— and its Significance. (W. Clark) Canad. M. **16**: 505.
— as a Festival. (Alida von Krockow) Outl. **58**: 825.
— in Paris. (E. Crawford) Canad. M. **8**: 486.
— in the Philippines. (R. R. Lala) Indep. **52**: 876.
— its Origin and its Customs. (C. E. Myles) Nat'l M. (Bost.) **6**: 90.
— Some Beliefs and Customs relating to Holy Week. (F. Peacock) Dub. R. **123**: 140.
Easter Eggs. (L. S. Lewis) Strand, **13**: 373.
Easter Flower-thought, An; a poem. (A. E. Glase) Argosy, **65**: 472.
Easter Hope, The. (W. H. Spence) Chaut. **33**: 2.
Easter Message, An. (L. Abbott) Outl. **64**: 966.
Easter Song; a poem. (J. T. Bryan) Canad. M. **8**: 536.
Eastern Question. (E. M. Bliss) Indep. **51**: 1231.— (E. Maxey) Arena, **23**: 358.
— Candia Rediviva. (Sir G. Baden-Powell) Fortn. **67**: 608.
— in 1900; World Politics of To-day. (E. A. Start) Chaut. **32**: 264.
— Kaliph and the Money-lenders. (J. W. Gambier) Fortn. **76**: 624.
— Three Years of the. (W. Miller) Gent. M. n. s. **67**: 429.
Easy Yoke, The. (A. B. Bruce) Expos. **4**: 114.
Eaton, Wyatt, the Canadian Painter. (C. Eaton) Canad. M. **10**: 241.
Ebb Tide [of Life], On the. (Mrs. Oliphant) Liv. Age, **214**: 765.
"Ebed-Yahweh Songs," So-called, and the Meaning of the Term "Servant of Yahweh" in Isaiah, chs. xl.-lv. (K. Budde) Am. J. Theol. **3**: 499.
Eberhard, Graf, der Greiner. (H. S. Wilson) Gent. M. n. s. **64**: 462.
Ebers, George. Acad. **51**: 284. — Nature, **58**: 396.
— The Art of. Acad. **54**: 152.
— at Home. (P. G. Hubert, jr.) Critic, **33**: 141.
Eca de Queiroz, J. M. d'. (W. Roberts) Ath. '00, **2**: 380.
Ecclesiastical Courts, English, Reform of. Green Bag, **11**: 187.
Ecclesiastical Development. (G. Tyrrell) Month, **90**: 380.
Ecclesiastical History, Hort's Lectures on Early. (J. P. Sheraton) Presb. & Ref. R. **9**: 766.
— Hurst's. (H. M. Scott) Presb. & Ref. R. **9**: 529.
Ecclesiastical Law. (T. J. Hacker) Ref. Ch. R. **47**: 467.
Ecclesiastical Pomp. Spec. **78**: 83.
Ecclesiasticus, British Museum Fragments of. (S. Schechter) Jew. Q. **12**: 266.
— Cambridge Fragments of. (W. Bacher) Jew. Q. **12**: 272.
— A Further Fragment of. (S. Schechter and E. N. Adler) Jew. Q. **12**: 456.
— Genizah MSS. (S. Schechter) Jew. Q. **10**: 197.
— The Hebrew. (W. T. Smith) Bib. World, **10**: 58. —(W. Bacher) Jew. Q. **9**: 543. — (H. W. Hogg) Am. J. Theol. **1**: 777. — (N. Herz) Jew. Q. **10**: 719.
— Hebrew Fragment of. (R. D. Wilson) Presb. & Ref. R. **11**: 480.
— New Fragment. (M. Gaster) Jew. Q. **12**: 688.
— The Original Hebrew of, Margoliouth on. (S. Schechter) Crit. R. **10**: 116.
— The Retranslation Hypothesis. (T. Tyler) Jew. Q. **12**: 555.
— A Romance in Scholarship. (J. Jacobs) Fortn. **72**: 696. Same art. Liv. Age, **223**: 762. Same art. Ecl. M. **134**: 158.
— Studies in Ben Sira. (C. Taylor) Jew. Q. **10**: 470.

Ecclesiasticus, ch. vii. 29-xii. 1, Notes sur. (I. Lévi) Jew. Q. **13**: 1.
— ch. xxxi. 12-31 and xxxvi. 22-xxxviii. 26, Original Hebrew of. (G. Margoliouth) Jew. Q. **12**: 1.
— — Margoliouth on. (S. Schechter) Crit. R. **9**: 387.
Echegaray, Jose, Spanish Statesman, Dramatist, Poet. (F. H. Gardiner) Poet-Lore, **12**: 405.
— Mariana. (M. Beerbohm) Sat. R. **91**: 702.
Echerolles, Mdlle. Alexandrine, Memoirs of. (J. R. Smith) Dial (Ch.) **19**: 228.
Echo; a poem. (J. R. Tabb) Atlan. **81**: 432.
Echo; a poem. (F. Rosser) Atlan. **83**: 576.
Echternach, Luxembourg, and the Dancing Pilgrims. (E. L. Taunton) Cath. World, **65**: 206.
Ecitons, Males of Some Texan. (W. M. Wheeler and W. H. Long) Am. Natural. **35**: 157.
Eckhardt, Oscar, Artist. (A. Lawrence) Idler, **16**: 832.
Eclipse of Moon, Lunar Changes during, Dec. 1899. (W. H. Pickering) Pop. Astron. **8**: 57.
Eclipse of Sun, Artificial Representation of. (R. W. Wood) Nature, **63**: 250. Same art. Science, n. s. **13**: 65.
— at Benares. (R. D. Mackenzie) Cent. **36**: 3.
— Predicted by Thales. (J. N. Stockwell) Pop. Astron. **9**: 376.
— 1896; Amherst Expedition to Japan. (D. P. Todd) Outl. **56**: 849. — (Sir R. Ball) Strand, **13**: 457. — (M. L. Todd) Atlan. **80**: 418.
— 1898. Knowl. **20**: 286. — Nature, **57**: 294, 365. — (E. W. Maunder) Knowl. **21**: 107. — (J. N. Lockyer) Nature, **56**: 154, 445. — (H. C. Wilson) Pop. Astron. **5**: 251.
— — Expedition to India for. (Norman Lockyer) Cosmopol. **26**: 135.
— — Lick Observatory Expedition. (W. W. Campbell) Pop. Astron. **6**: 231.
— — Lick Photographs of the Corona. (E. W. Maunder) Knowl. **21**: 155.
— — Prismatic Camera at. (J. Evershed) Knowl. **21**: 130.
— May, 1900. (C. P. Howard) Pop. Astron. **9**: 18. — (A. L. Cortie) Month, **95**: 464. — (G. M. Searle) Cath. World, **71**: 542. — (E. Verney) Gent. M. n. s. **65**: 303. — (C. A. Young) Indep. **52**: 2077. — J. Frankl. Inst. **150**: 133. — (E. W. Maunder) Knowl. **23**: 49, 145. — (J. McN. Wright) Lippinc. **65**: 750. — (S. Newcomb) McClure, **15**: 45. — (F. H. Bigelow) Nat. Geog. M. **11**: 33. — (E. B. Frost) Pop. Astron. **8**: 86. — Pop. Astron. **8**: 144. — (C. P. Howland) Pop. Astron. **8**: 550. — (W. H. Pickering; W. W. Payne; H. C. Wilson) Pop. Astron. **8**: 225, 240, 297, 369. — (F. H. Bigelow) Pop. Sci. Mo. **57**: 1.
— — as Observed by the Smithsonian Expedition. Nature, **62**: 246.
— — En Route to Tripoli to observe. (M. L. Todd) Nation, **70**: 455.
— — in Tripoli. (M. L. Todd) Nation, **70**: 473.
— — Result of Observations of Weather Bureau as to Probable Cloudiness. (F. H. Bigelow) Pop. Astron. **7**: 451.
— May 18, 1901. (A. Fowler) Nature, **63**: 470. — (E. W. Maunder) Knowl. **24**: 225. — (S. A. Mitchell) Science, n. s. **14**: 802.
— — Amherst Expedition. (M. L. Todd) Nation, **72**: 431, 469, 508. **73**: 29.
— — in Sumatra. (E. E. Barnard) Pop. Astron. **9**: 527.
— — Magnetic Observations during. (W. Ellis) Nature, **64**: 15.
— — Plans for Observing. (H. C. Wilson) Pop. Astron. **9**: 267.
Eclipses, Ancient, and Chronology. (R. W. McFarland) Pop. Astron. **7**: 510.

Eclipses of the Sun. (J. Morrison) Pop. Astron. 4: 502. 5: 29, 129, 368.
— — in the 20th Century. (A. C. D. Crommelin) Knowl. 24: 59.
— — New Phenomenon in Reflection Bands. (J. F. Lanneau) Pop. Astron. 9: 67.
— — Recent. (H. H. Turner) Monthly R. 1, no. 1: 98. — Ed. R. 187: 300. Same art. Liv. Age, 218: 3.
— — — and Coming, Lockyer on. Spec. 79: 899. Same art. Liv. Age, 216: 276.
— — What they teach us. (D. P. Todd) Pop. Astron. 9: 305.
Eclipse Expedition at Viziadurg. (N. Lockyer) Nature, 61: 229, 249.
Eclipse Photography. (F. E. Nipher) Science, n. s. 13: 208.
Ecole des Beaux-Arts, Paris, Architectural Section. (Arthur Cates) Am. Arch. 71: 101. 72: 4.
— French Government School from the Inside. (J. M. Howells) Cent. 40: 860.
— Influence of, upon Architecture in America. (A. L. Brockway) Am. Arch. 66: 61.
Ecole des Prévenus, L'. (E. O. Bentinck) Gent. M. n. s. 67: 1.
Ecole des Roches, A School of the 20th Century. (T. R. Croswell) Pedagog. Sem. 7: 479.
Ecole Libre in Paris. (L. Mead) Gunton's M. 20: 543.
Econometer. J. Frankl. Inst. 145: 205.
Economic Ages, The. (F. H. Giddings) Pol. Sci. Q. 16: 193.
Economic and Social Conditions Yesterday and To-day. (B. O. Flower) Arena, 20: 388.
Economic and Social Legislation of the States in 1896. (W. B. Shaw) Q. J. Econ. 11: 191.
Economic Aspects of Legislation of the Year 1898. (M. Barlow) Econ. J. 8: 563.
Economic Conceptions, New. Gunton's M. 14: 22.
Economic Development, Topography as affecting. (J. W. Redway) Gunton's M. 19: 135.
Economic Fatalism. (H. A. L. Fisher) Econ. R. 9: 289.
Economic Geography, Principles of. (L. M. Keasbey) Pol. Sci. Q. 16: 467.
Economic Harmony, Elements in. (G. Gunton) Gunton's M. 21: 207.
Economic History, Plea for the Study of. (W. Cunningham) Econ. R. 9: 67.
— Teaching of, in Relation to Teaching of Political Economy: Discussion. Econ. Stud. 3, supp. no. 1: 88.
Economic Instruction, Empirical Method of. (R. F. Hoxie) J. Pol. Econ. 9: 481.
Economic Interpretation of History. (E. R. A. Seligman) Pol. Sci. Q. 16: 612.
Economic Organization. (C. R. Flint) Cosmopol. 26: 345.
Economic Politics in U. S. (J. W. Perrin) Chaut. 27: 141.
Economic Problems, Some. Bank. M. (N. Y.) 56: 686.
Economic Reform, Christian Leadership and. (J. B. Bartlett) Arena, 26: 588.
Economic Science, Preconceptions of. (T. Veblen) Q. J. Econ. 13: 121, 396. 14: 240.
Economic Study, Old Lights and New in. (J. Bonar) Econ. J. 8: 433.
Economic Tendencies, Recent. (C. A. Conant) Atlan. 85: 737.
Economic Theory among the Greeks and Romans. (E. Simey) Econ. R. 10: 462.
— Davenport's Outlines of. (W. G. L. Taylor) J. Pol. Econ. 5: 518.
— Decade of. (R. T. Ely) Ann. Am. Acad. Pol. Sci. 15: 236.
— Future of. (J. B. Clark) Q. J. Econ. 13: 1.

Economic Theories vs. Facts. (H. Withers) Bank. M. (Lond.) 63: 32.
Economics. Address to the Economic Science and Statistics Section of the British Association. (L. Courtney) J. Statis. Soc. 59: 631.
— and Commercial Education. (L. L. Price) Econ. J. 11: 520.
— and Political Science, London School of. (W. J. Ashley) Nation, 68: 179.
— and Politics, Relation between. (A. T. Hadley) Econ. Stud. 4: 7.
— and Socialism. (J. L. Laughlin) Chaut. 30: 252.
— as an Evolutionary Science. (T. Veblen) Q. J. Econ. 12: 373.
— as a School Study. (F. R. Clow) Econ. Stud. 4: 183.
— at German Universities. (S. M. Wickett) Econ. J. 8: 146.
— Bibliography of Recent Publications. Q. J. Econ. 14: 290, 435, 562. 15: 150.
— Free Thought in College. Gunton's M. 17: 456.
— Function of the Undertaker. (S. Sherwood) Yale R. 6: 233.
— Fundamental Principle of. (C. A. Tuttle) Q. J. Econ. 15: 218.
— German, New-view Tendencies in. (A. Oncken) Econ. J. 9: 462.
— in Education. (E. J. James) Annals Am. Acad. 10: 359.
— in the High School. (J. E. Le Rossignol) Canad. M. 17: 68.
— in Italy. (A. Loria) Econ. J. 7: 450.
— in Manufactures. (R. H. Thurston) Science, n. s. 9: 583.
— in the Public Schools. (G. Gunton) Gunton's M. 21: 140.
— in Schools. (J. L. Laughlin) J. Pol. Econ. 9: 384. — Book R. 6: 275.
— in Secondary Education. (R. T. Ely) Educa. R. 20: 152.
— — Teaching of. (F. H. Dixon) School R. 6: 17.
— Kropotkin on. (E. R. A. Seligman) Pol. Sci. Q. 14: 335.
— Lessons from Ruskin. (C. S. Devas) Econ. J. 8: 28.
— Mathematical Method in, Seligman on. (F. Y. Edgeworth) Econ. J. 9: 286.
— Methods of Teaching; discussion. Econ. Stud. 3, supp. no. 1: 105.
— New Theories of. (V. Pareto) J. Pol. Econ. 5: 485.
— Newspaper, Vicious. Gunton's M. 12: 325.
— of Distribution, Hobson's. (A. W. Flux) Econ. J. 10: 380.
— Philosophical Basis of. (S. Sherwood) Ann. Am. Acad. 10: 206.
— Practical vs. Metaphysical. Gunton's M. 12: 73.
— Present Condition of. (L. L. Price) Forum, 24: 422.
— Pulpit. Gunton's M. 12: 367.
— Pure, Pantaleoni's. (A. W. Flux) Econ. J. 8: 355.
— Restoration of, to Ethics. (C. S. Devas) Int. J. Ethics, 7: 191.
— Revolt against Orthodox. Quar. 194: 345.
— Schmoller on. (T. Veblen) Q. J. Econ. 16: 69. — (H. W. Farnam) Yale R. 9: 164.
— Sociological Evolution of. (J. B. Clark) Q. J. Econ. 13: 187.
— Sociological Frontier of. (E. A. Ross) Q. J. Econ. 13: 386.
— Study of, in Schools and Colleges. (F. R. Clow) Q. J. Econ. 12: 73.
— — in Secondary Schools. (J. Haynes) Educa. 17: 338.
— Teaching of. (W. A. S. Hewins) J. Soc. Arts, 45: 42.
— — in Schools. (H. H. Robbins) Gunton's M. 16: 35.

Economics, Teaching of, Liberty in. Gunton's M. 18: 226.

— Tendencies in. (B. Moses) Q. J. Econ. 11: 372.

— — American. (S. Sherwood) J. H. Univ. Stud. 15: 573.

Economists, American, of To-day. (A. F. Weber) New Eng. M. 21: 259.

— Letters to Dead. Citizen, 3: 179.

— Old Generation and the New. (A. Marshall) Q. J. Econ. 11: 115.

Ecuador, Portrait Vases of. Am. Antiq. 23: 334.

Ecumenical Councils and Some Questions of the Day. Church Q. 51: 298.

Eddic Poems, Bugge's Home of the. (W. H. Carpenter) Nation, 71: 96.

Eddy, Clarence, Musician, Interview with. Music, 12: 143.

Eddy, Mary Baker. (H. H. Williams) New Eng. M. n. s. 21: 291.

— Christian Science and its Prophetess. (H. W. Dresser and J. C. Woodbury) Arena, 21: 537.

— What the Public wants to read. (E. Wood) Atlan. 88: 566.

Eden, Sir Robert, Life and Administration of. (B. C. Steiner) J. H. Univ. Stud. 16: nos. 7, 8, 9.

Eden, Garden of, and the Burning Bush. Study in Comparative Mythology. (G. H. Skipwith) Jew. Q. 10: 489.

— — Site of. (Gen. C. G. Gordon) Strand, 17: 314.

Edgar, King, Commendation to, in 973. (W. H. Stevenson) Eng. Hist. R. 13: 505.

Edgartown, Mass., Deaths at. (H. M. Pease) N. E. Reg. 52: 230, 368. 53: 102.

— Inscriptions at. (H. M. Pease) N. E. Reg. 51: 196.

Edgcumbe, Emma Sophia, Countess Brownlow. (F. K. E. St. George) Temp. Bar, 111: 332.

Edge, Edward, "The Dane's Man." Spec. 83: 950.

Edge, What is an? Chamb. J. 75: 534.

Edgefield, S. C., Advertiser, Gleanings from an Old Southern Newspaper. (W. P. Trent) Atlan. 86: 356.

Edgware Road, England. (J. Hawkwood) Belgra. 93: 19.

Edible Bird's-nest Island, A Day on an. (N. Annandale) Chamb. J. 78: 537.

Edict in Modern Acadia. (H. F. Day) New Eng. M. n. s. 24: 200.

Edict of Tolerance of Louis XVI., and its Amer. Promoters. (G. B. Maury) Am. J. Theol. 3: 554.

Edinburgh as a Sketching Ground. (W. B. Macdougall) Studio (Lond.) 6: 164.

— Civic Improvement. (C. M. Robinson) Munic. Aff. 3: 664.

— Frank Laing's Etchings of. (D. S. Meldrum) M. of Art, 24: 348.

— St. George's Free Church, A Sunday in. (A. W. Stewart) Sund. M. 27: 534.

— Medical School, An Anglo-Indian's Recollections of. Chamb. J. 75: 254-261.

— Memories of an Old Square in. Good Words, 41: 552.

— Romantic. Chamb. J. 77: 588.

— University Hall; the World's First Sociological Laboratory. (C. Zueblin) Am. J. Sociol. 4: 577.

Edinburgh Life Assurance Company. Bank. M. (Lond.) 63: 973.

Edinburgh Pen and Pencil Club. (T. A. Croal) Art J. 51: 232.

Edinburgh Society of Scottish Artists. Exhibition, 1900. Art J. 52: 287.

Edinburgh University. (H. W. Mabie) Outl. 62: 783.

Edison, T. A. (J. D. Cormack) Good Words, 42: 157.

Editing, Ethics of. (H. W. Massingham) National, 35: 256.

Edith; a story. (C. H. Roberts) Midland, 11: 172.

Edith Grange; a story. Argosy, 64: 590.

Editor, An, and Some Contributors. (J. Payn) Cornh. 80: 577.

— Diversions of an. (John Pendleton) Good Words, 41: 332.

— The Night. (W. M. Emery) Writer, 13: 50.

— Patriotic, in War, Duties of. (P. H. Colomb) National, 29: 253.

Editorial Carelessness. (W. S. Gidley) Writer, 10: 16.

Editorial Talks with Contributors. (A. W. Tarbell) Writer, 11: 33.

Editors and Contributors. (M. Cripps) Good Words. 42: 620.

— and Others. Blackw. 169: 597.

Editor's [C. A. Cooper's] Retrospect, An. Scot. R. 29: 128. Same art. Liv. Age, 212: 655.

Edmonton, The Witch of. Cornh. 75: 814.

Edmonton, Northwest Territories. (B. Cameron) Canad. M. 15: 99.

Edmund of Abingdon, Archbishop of Canterbury, Paravicini's. Sat. R. 87: 55.

— and the Universities. (A. Herbert) Dub. R. 123: 107.

Edmund of Langley and his Tomb. (J. Evans) Archæol. 44: 297.

Edomites in Southern Judah. (C. C. Torrey) J. Bib. Lit. 17: 16.

Educated, What it is to be. (C. W. Eliot and others) Chaut. 30: 19.

Education. (Martin Luther) Open Court, 13: 423. — (E. A. Ross) Am. J. Sociol. 5: 475.

— Adjustment of, to Contemporary Needs. (E. D. Mead) Educa. R. 19: 472.

— Affection in. (Edward Carpenter) Int. J. Ethics, 9: 482.

— Aim of. (F. H. Kasson) Educa. 18: 496.

— American, and what shall it be? (R. H. Thurston) Science, n. s. 13: 68.

— — A Distinctive. (E. P. Powell) Educa. 17: 282.

— American Ideals in. Acad. 61: 215.

— American Social Forces. Spec. 80: 786.

— among Ancient Hebrews. (C. H. Levy) Educa. 17: 457.

— and City Life. (C. De Garmo) Gunton's M. 21: 505.

— and Crime. School R. 8: 42.

— and Culture. (W. Rein) Forum, 26: 693.

— and Democracy. (G. Harris) Gunton's M. 17: 398.

— and Individuality. (H. M. Stanley) Educa. R. 18: 80.

— and Morals. (Boyd Winchester) Educa. 21: 155.

— and the National Welfare. (J. L. Tayler) Westm. 150: 129.

— and Politics. Gunton's M. 17: 98.

— and Public Morality. (C. W. Wendte) New World, 8: 417.

— and the State. (H. H. Robbins) Gunton's M. 15: 266.

— and Success. Outl. 63: 485.

— Art and; Influence of Art upon Education. (G. L. Raymond) Am. J. Soc. Sci. 36: 104.

— as a Public Peril. (F. J. Mather, jr.) Nation, 73: 488.

— as World-building. (T. Davidson) Educa. R. 20: 325.

— at the Farm. (F. Maccunn) Sund. M. 27: 770.

— Baumeister's Handbuch der. (P. H. Hanus) Educa. R. 17: 37.

— Beginning of Liberation in. (H. Campbell) Arena, 22: 350.

— Bibliography of; for 1899. (J. I. Wyer, jr., and I. E. Lord) Educa. R. 19: 334.

— — for 1900. (J. I. Wyer, jr., and I. E. Lord) Educa. R. 21: 382.

— — Recent. (J. I. Wyer) School R. 8: 475.

Education, New-fashioned, Some Old-fashioned Doubts about. (LeB. R. Briggs) Atlan. **86**: 463.

— A New Programme in. (C. H. Henderson) Atlan. **81**: 760.

— New Spirit of. (A. Henry) Munsey, **23**: 147.

— of Boys in Italy. (M. T. Mengarini) Chaut. **28**: 257.

— of Leaders of Men. Sat. R. **87**: 297.

— on the Farm. (E. K. Howell) Chaut. **32**: 28.

— Organization of. (D. MacG. Means) Nation, **71**: 106.

— Over-, The Fear of. (A. Sutherland) 19th Cent. **46**: 550. Same art. Liv. Age, **223**: 747.

— Parent and Teacher in. (A. D. Cameron) Canad. M. **15**: 536.

— Philosophy and ; Bearings of Philosophy on Education. (J. S. Mackenzie) Int. J. Ethics, **8**: 423.

— A Philosophy of. (A. C. Ellis) Pedagog. Sem. **5**: 159.

— Physical Conditions in. (C. F. Carroll) Educa. **18**: 451.

— Physical Factor in. (E. C. Willard) Forum, **25**: 311.

— A Practical. (V. M. Crawford) Month, **90**: 570.

— Preparatory and Collegiate, What is the Present Consensus of Opinion as to the most Important Problems in? (I. Sharpless ; J. Sachs) School R. **6**: 145.

— Progress due to. (F. H. Kasson) Educa. **19**: 118.

— Progressive. Nature, **59**: 235.

— Psychologic Foundations of, W. T. Harris on. (J. Dewey) Educa. R. **16**: 1.

— Recent Books on (1898). (H. M. Stanley) Dial (Ch.) **24**: 117.

— Relation to Altruistic Principles. (J. Olden) Educa. **18**: 333.

— Relation to Reform. (J. C. Guffin) Arena, **22**: 392.

— Religious, Duty of Christian Scholars to. (J. M. Gregory) Luth. Q. **28**: 490.

— Responsibility of Parents for the General Failure. (W. K. Hill) Westm. **148**: 189.

— Rise of the Christian Schools. (C. M. Graham) Am. Cath. Q. **25**: 456.

— The Road to Knowledge a Hundred Years Ago. Liv. Age, **228**: 243.

— Rural. (E. Verney) 19th Cent. **44**: 92.

— — should differ from City. Sat. R. **88**: 382.

— Science of, Scope of. (J. J. Findlay) Educa. R. **14**: 236.

— Scientific *vs.* Poetic Study of. (C. De Garmo) Educa. R. **17**: 209.

— Should Children under Ten learn to Read and Write ? (G. T. W. Patrick) Pop. Sci. Mo. **54**: 382.

— The Sins of. Blackw. **165**: 503.

— The Social Mind and, Vincent on. (J. H. Hyslop) Book R. **5**: 207.

— Social Phases of, Dutton's. (H. R. Corbett) School R. **7**: 490.

— Some Socialist and Anarchist Views of. (C. H. Matchett ; B. R. Tucker ; L. Sanial ; G. B. Kelly) Educa. R. **15**: 1.

— Spencer's Essay on. (D. S. Jordan) Cosmopol. **29**: 266.

— Spirit of the Age in. (G. H. Martin) Educa. R. **21**: 271.

— Spiritual. (R. P. St. John) Educa. **17**: 449.

— State, Types of. (L. M. Salmon) New Eng. M. n. s. **15**: 601.

— The State in Relation to. (J. C. Medd) Econ. R. **8**: 199. — (A. S. Draper) Educa. R. **15**: 105.

— The State's Obligations to. (C. B. Hubbell) Am. J. Soc. Sci. **36**: 212.

— Status of, at the Close of the Century. (N. M. Butler) Educa. R. **19**: 313.

— Study of, in American Colleges and Universities. (B. A. Hinsdale) Educa. R. **19**: 105.

Education, Study of, at the German Universities. (W. L. Hervey) Educa. R. **16**: 220.

— to follow Imperialism. (F. H. Kasson) Educa. **19**: 312.

— True Value of. (J. M. Swift) Educa. **19**: 22.

— Twentieth-century. (A. B. Woodford) Am. J. Soc. Sci. **37**: 44.

— Unification of. (W. A. Heidel) Educa. **22**: 98.

— Utilizing Boy Waste. (F. Gardiner) Cosmopol. **26**: 461.

— Walker's Discussions in. (C. H. Thurber) School R. **7**: 433.

— Waste in. (N. M. Butler) Outl. **59**: 860.

— Hezekiah Woodward on, 1640. (F. Watson) Gent. M. n. s. **64**: 35.

— Year's Progress in, 1899. (W. T. Harris) Am. J. Soc. Sci. **38**: 69.

— — 1900. (B. A. Hinsdale) Dial (Ch.) **29**: 43.

Education Exhibition, English, at South Kensington. Ath. '00, **1**: 16.

Education Society, Beginnings of an. (W. Channing) Educa. R. **14**: 354.

Education of Bob ; a story. (R. H. Davis) Harper, **94**: 934.

Education of Praed, The. (A. W. Vorse) Scrib. M. **26**: 290.

Education of Sam. (C. D. Warner) Cent. **39**: 56.

Educational Administration, State, Recent Centralizing Tendencies in. (W. C. Webster) Educa. R. **13**: 23, 134.

Educational Advance. (G. Stanley Hall) Outl. **62**: 768.

Educational and Supervisory Movements. (J. R. Brackett) Charities, **7**: 130, 213, 296, 387.

Educational Bibliography, Recent. (J. I. Wyer) School R. **6**: 615. **7**: 478. **9**: 534.

Educational Conditions and Problems. (A. D. White ; T. W. Higginson ; A. B. Hart) Educa. R. **13**: 460.

Educational Congresses at Paris Exposition. (A. T. Smith) Educa. **21**: 124.

Educational Domain, Sketch of. (J. Anderson) Am. J. Soc. Sci. **35**: 69.

Educational Experiments ; Excursions and Gardening. (A. M. Loehr) Chaut. **32**: 245.

Educational Experts. (A. H. Nelson) Educa. R. **18**: 398.

Educational Fads. Quar. **185**: 241.

Educational Forces in the Community, Correlation of. (S. T. Dutton) Educa. R. **13**: 334.

Educational Ideal, Evolution of. (F. Paulsen) Forum, **23**: 598, 672.

Educational Institutions, Federation of. (W. MacDonald) School R. **8**: 611.

Educational Journalism ; an inventory. (C. W. Bardeen) Educa. R. **18**: 281.

Educational Journals of France. (G. Compayré) Educa. R. **19**: 121.

Educational Literature, Italian. (A. F. Chamberlain) Pedagog. Sem. **8**: 424.

Educational Method, The Study of. (J. A. Reinhart) Educa. R. **14**: 71.

Educational Methods, Artistic *vs.* Scientific Conception in. (G. L. Raymond) Am. J. Soc. Sci. **38**: 92.

— Menace of Present. (L. D'Aimee) Gunton's M. **19**: 257.

Educational Movements in England. (J. Fitch) Educa. R. **14**: 313. — (W. K. Hill) School R. **6**: 514. **8**: 1, 507.

Educational Periodicals in England. (J. Russell) Educa. R. **22**: 472.

Educational Policy for the New Possessions of the U. S. (W. T. Harris) Educa. R. **18**: 105.

Educational Problems in Germany, New. (G. H. Schodde) Outl. **67**: 687.

Eight Stars, The, Constellation of. (H. Beveridge) Ath. '00, 1: 625.

Eight Years in a Rock. (Julian Hawthorne) Cosmopol. 31: 33.

1801–1901. Liv. Age, 228: 321.

1870, Some Recollections of. (G. D. Boyle) Good Words, 38: 306.

1897, Great Summer Gatherings of. R. of Rs. (N. Y.) 15: 549.

— Political New Year, The. (E. J. Dillon) Contemp. 71: 1. Same art. Liv. Age, 212: 298.

1898. "Annus Mirabilis." Spec. 81: 364. Same art. Liv. Age, 219: 324.

— Commercial History and Review of. J. Statis. Soc. 62: 159.

Eighteenth Century, In Praise of the. Atlan. 86: 716.

— Paston's Little Memoirs of. Ath. '01, 1: 561.

Eighteenth-century Convert. Month, 97: 139, 247.

Eighteenth-century Escritoire, From an. (E. M. M. McKenna) Fortn. 76: 884.

Eiskyklema in the Eretrian Theatre. (A. Fossum) Am. J. Archæol. 2d s. 2: 187.

Eland Hunting. (H. A. Bryden) Sat. R. 83: 345.

Elasticity, Theory of. (F. H. Cilley) Am. J. Sci. 161: 269.

Elba, A Month in. Illus. (I. M. Anderton) Good Words, 38: 616, 693.

El Caney, Battle of. (F. Norris) Cent. 36: 304. — (S. Bonsal) McClure, 12: 224.

— The Regulars at. (Capt. A. H. Lee) Scrib. M. 24: 403.

Elche, Bust of; an Artistic Treasure lately discovered in Spain. (C. V. R. Dearth) Cent. 34: 436. — (K. E. Phelps) Art J. 50: 281.

Elder, Sir Thomas. Geog. J. 9: 453.

El Dorado; a Kansas Recessional. (W. S. Cather) New Eng. M. n. s. 24: 357.

Elders of Aready, The. (A. Jessopp) 19th Cent. 47: 111.

Elders' Seat, The. (A. Colton) Atlan. 83: 697.

Eldredge Genealogy. (Z. S. Eldredge) N. E. Reg. 51: 46.

Eldridge, G. Morgan, 1831–98, Obituary Notice of. J. Frankl. Inst. 146: 470.

Eleanor; a novel. (Mrs. H. Ward) Harper, 100: 187–911. 101: 19–873. 102: 132.

Eleanor's Golf Ball; a story. (M. Guilds) Nat'l M. (Bost.) 10: 262.

Election and Selection. Ref. Ch. R. 47: 225.

— Doctrine of. Outl. 64: 859.

— — Paul's. (L. Abbott) Outl. 64: 866.

— Historic Purpose of, From the Standpoint of Isaiah. (W. C. Schaffer) Ref. Q. 44: 40.

Election at Cayote. (T. Gallagher) Lippinc. 61: 703.

Elections, Between. (J. J. Chapman) Atlan. 85: 26.

— Electing a Governor. (S. G. Blythe) Cosmopol. 26: 288.

— English and American. (S. Brooks) Harper, 101: 329.

— in England; Petitions and Electioneering Pledges. (S. M. Palmer) 19th Cent. 48: 551.

— — Recent and Past. (T. E. Champion) Canad. M. 16: 75.

— Police Control of Great. (A. D. Andrews) Scrib. M. 23: 131.

Election Bet, How I paid my. (R. F. Woodward) Strand, 18: 148.

Election Day in Poorer New York. (E. L. Banks) Eng. Illust. 16: 426.

Election Expenses. (J. T. Newcomb) Nation, 73: 370.

Election Law, The Black, in New York. (J. B. Bishop) Nation, 67: 47.

Election Petition Trials in England. (E. Porritt) Green Bag, 9: 231.

Election Schools, The St. Louis. (W. F. Saunders) R. of Rs. (N. Y.) 17: 326.

Electioneering, English and American. (S. Brooks) Chaut. 26: 636.

— in England. Argosy, 72: 345.

Elective Studies in Secondary Schools. (N. S. Shaler, S. Thurber, J. Tetlow, and others) Educa. R. 15: 417.

— Where? (J. H. Harris) School R. 6: 567.

Elective System of Studies in Colleges. (J. A. Burns) Cath. World, 71: 366.

— in High Schools. (C. C. Ramsay) Educa. 20: 557.

— in the Secondary School, Natural Limitations of. (J. H. Harris) Educa. R. 19: 493.

— Is it Elective? (J. Corbin) Forum, 31: 599.

— Proper Limitation of. (C. D. Schmitt; G. W. Miles) School R. 9: 92, 160. — (B. J. Ramage) Sewanee R. 9: 316.

— Some Problems of. (C. H. Thurber) School R. 9: 79.

Elective Work in the High School Courses. (W. H. Smith) School R. 7: 232.

Electives, Discussion on. School R. 7: 238.

— Galesburg Plan of, Some Results of. (F. D. Thomson) School R. 9: 13.

— in American Education. (D. E. Phillips) Pedagog. Sem. 8: 206.

— in High Schools. (J. Tetlow) Educa. R. 21: 39. — (A. F. Nightingale) School R. 9: 65.

— — Limited. (E. G. Cooley) School R. 9: 75.

— in the Secondary School. (C. H. Thurber) School R. 7: 65.

— in the Small-High School. (S. D. Brooks) School R. 9: 593.

— Problem of. (P. H. Hanus) Pop. Sci. Mo. 58: 585.

Elector of Saxony's Confession of Faith. (J. W. Richard) Luth. Q. 31: 301.

Electoral Commission of 1877. (M. H. Northrup) Cent. 40: 923.

Electoral System, American, Dangerous Defects. (J. G. Carlisle) Forum, 24: 257.

Electric Annealing of Harveyized Armor Plates on a Battleship. (C. J. Dougherty) Cassier, 11: 406.

Electric Arc, Reason for the Hissing of the. (Hertha Ayrton) Nature, 60: 282, 302.

Electric Cables for High-tension Service. (W. Maver, jr.) Cassier, 18: 467.

Electric Central-station Practice. (C. F. Scott) Engin. M. 16: 255.

Electric Central Stations vs. Isolated Plants. (R. S. Hale) Engin. M. 12: 786.

Electric Circuits, Improved Safety Device for. (L. G. Rowland) J. Frankl. Inst. 143: 357.

Electric Communication in the Field. (H. A. Giddings) J. Mil. Serv. Inst. 25: 58.

Electric Conduit Railways. (F. S. Pearson) Cassier, 16: 257.

Electric Converter, Design and Action of the Rotary. (D. B. Rushmore) Engin. M. 22: 414.

Electric Current in Organic Chemistry. (E. F. Smith) Science, n. s. 8: 413.

Electric Currents, Large, Rapid Break for. (A. G. Webster) Am. J. Sci. 153: 383.

Electric Distribution for Street Railways. (C. F. Bancroft) Cassier, 20: 75.

Electric Fish of the Nile. (F. Gotch) Science, n. s. 10: 968.

Electric Furnace, The. (J. Trowbridge) Chaut. 27: 162.

Electric Haulage in Belgium. (L. Gérard) Cassier, 19: 215.

Electric Lady; a story. (Hamlin Garland) Cosmopol. 29: 73.

Electric Lamps, Incandescent, Photometry of. (A. J. Rowland) J. Frankl. Inst. 148: 376.

Electric Light from City Refuse in Shoreditch. (N. W. Perry) Cassier, 13: 99.

— Nernst's. (J. Swinburne) J. Soc. Arts, 47: 253.

Electric Light Fittings, W. H. Cooper's Designs for. Artist (N. Y.) 29: 105.

Electric Light Plants, Municipal, in Massachusetts Cities. (A. D. Adams) Yale R. 10: 205.

— — in Massachusetts Towns. (A. D. Adams) Yale R. 10: 320.

Electric Light Projectors. (T. J. Hardy) J. Mil. Serv. Inst. 16: 110.

Electric Lighting and Traction Plants, Union of. (A. D. Adams) Cassier, 17: 221.

— Crocker on. (E. Thompson) Science, n. s. 13: 943.

— from Central Stations, (H. C. Hall) Engin. M. 17: 206.

— in Gt. Britain, Cost of. (R. Hammond) Engin. M. 16: 624.

— in N. Y. State Capitol. Archit. R. 9: 211.

— of Railway Trains in Great Britain. (H. Scholey) Cassier, 16: 121.

— of Ships. (E. G. Bernard) Cassier, 11: 298.

Electric Lighting Fixtures, Ornamental. Art J. 52: 23.

Electric Locomotives. (G. R. Mair) Cassier, 16: 461.

Electric Mining Machinery in the British Collieries. (S. F. Walker) Engin. M. 19: 847.

Electric Motor for Speed Regulation. (S. S. Wheeler) Cassier, 19: 505.

Electric Motor Driving, Direct. (R. T. E. Lozier) Cassier, 17: 158.

Electric Motors applied to Printing-press Machinery. (W. H. Tapley) J. Frankl. Inst. 148: 259.

— for Small Industrial Purposes. (A. H. Gibbings) Cassier, 15: 237.

— for Street Railways, Development of. (C. T. Hutchinson) Cassier, 16: 337.

— Gearing for. (A. H. Gibbings) Cassier, 18: 503.

Electric Plant of the Modern Tall Building. (F. A. Pattison) Engin. M. 13: 782.

Electric Plants, Isolated, vs. Central Stations. (P. R. Moses) Engin. M. 13: 750, 896.

— Objections to Municipal Ownership of. (T. C. Smith) Engin. M. 14: 780.

Electric Power, Application of, to Pumping Machinery. (S. H. Bunnell) Engin. M. 16: 429.

— at High Altitudes. (A. B. Blainey) Cassier, 12: 145.

— at Jajce in Bosnia. (J. B. C. Fershaw) Cassier, 20: 443.

— at Rheinfelden, Germany. (E. Rathenan) Cassier, 12: 98.

— Distribution of. (W. E. Ayrton) Nature, 62: 296. — J. Frankl. Inst. 151: 1. — (C. F. Scott) J. Frankl. Inst. 151: 282.

— Expansion in the Use of. (L. Bell) Engin. M. 12: 630.

— for Engineering Workshops. Cassier, 19: 349.

— for Factories. (W. S. Aldrich) Cassier, 18: 194.

— for Trunk-line Railways. (G. Forbes) Engin. M. 14: 1.

— from High Water Heads. (J. E. Bennett) Cassier, 12: 3.

— in Engineering Works. (L. Bell) Engin. M. 18: 69.

— in Factories. (P. R. Moses) Engin. M. 21: 883.

— in Gt. Britain. (W. H. Booth) Engin. M. 20: 41.

— in the Machine Shop. (E. H. Mullin) Cassier, 13: 240.

— in a Railway Shop. Cassier, 12: 687.

— in Steel Making. (E. B. Clark) Cassier, 15: 441.

— Transmission of, from Niagara. (O. E. Dunlap) Cassier, 11: 197.

— — Difficulties of. (I. R. Edmands) Cassier, 19: 299.

Electric Power, Transmission of, Long Distance. (G. Forbes) J. Soc. Arts, 47: 25.

— — Modern Methods of. (L. Duncan) Cassier, 11: 505. — (W. B. Esson) J. Soc. Arts, 45: 399.

— — Short Distance. (J. Swinburne) Engin. M. 17: 827. See Electric Transmission.

— Transition to. (A. D. Adams) Cassier, 18: 485.

Electric Power Distribution and the Small Consumer. (L. Bell) Engin. M. 18: 240.

Electric Power Machinery in Iron and Steel Works. (S. F. Walker) Engin. M. 20: 858.

Electric Power Stations, Modern. (P. Dawson) Cassier, 19: 211.

Electric Power Supply in Great Britain. (C. S. V. Brown) Cassier, 21: 162.

Electric Progress, Official Obstruction of. (J. A. Fleming) 19th Cent. 49: 348.

— during the Last Decade. (M. I. Pupin) Cosmopol. 31: 523.

Electric Railroad, The Coming. (S. H. Short) Cosmopol. 26: 269.

— Memorial, between Liverpool and Manchester. (F. B. Behr) J. Soc. Arts, 49: 305.

Electric Railways. (P. Cardew) J. Soc. Arts, 49: 641–665.

— Building of. (L. W. Serrell) Cassier, 16: 303.

— Country. (S. Baxter) Harper, 97: 60.

— Ground Current of. (A. B. Herrick) Engin. M. 15: 451.

— in America from a Business Standpoint. (W. J. Clark) Cassier, 16: 518.

— in Great Britain. (R. W. Blackwell) Cassier, 16: 283.

— Light. (L. Bell) Cassier, 16: 433.

— Making Long Trolley Lines. (W. F. McClure) World's Work, 3: 1511.

— Multiple Unit System for. (F. J. Sprague) Cassier, 16: 439.

— on City Streets. (N. W. Perry) Cassier, 11: 419.

— Operation of, Comparative Economy in. (C. H. Davis) Engin. M. 12: 942.

— Overhead Construction for. (J. G. White) Cassier, 16: 319.

— Overhead Line and Ground Return Circuit of. (D. Pepper, jr.) J. Frankl. Inst. 146: 55.

— Polyphase Alternating Currents for. (D. C. Jackson) Cassier, 16: 487.

— Selection of Rolling-stock for. (C. F. Uebelacker) Cassier, 16: 502.

— Some Early Traction History. (T. Reid) Cassier, 16: 357.

— Transportation Problems in Large Cities. (E. E. Higgins) J. Frankl. Inst. 147: 315, 344.

— Trolley Road Construction, Modern Overhead. (B. Willard) Cassier, 11: 367.

— What Makes the Trolley-car Go? (W. Baxter, jr.) Pop. Sci. Mo. 56: 316, 408, 564.

— with Overhead Trolley Wires, What Pressure is Dangerous on. (W. Rung) Nature, 62: 399.

Electric Railway Features in Sicily, Some. (E. Bignami) Cassier, 20: 464.

Electric Railway Finance. Bank. M. (Lond.) 65: 895.

Electric Signalling, Recent Developments in. Nature, 64: 6.

Electric Stations, Development of. (A. D. Adams) Cassier, 17: 91.

Electric Street Traction in England. (E. F. V. Knox) Engin. M. 16: 25.

Electric Telegraph in Warfare. (F. C. Grugan) J. Mil. Serv. Inst. 3: 376.

Electric Traction. (C. H. Davis and H. C. Forbes) Engin. M. 15: 811. — (C. A. Carus-Wilson) J. Soc. Arts, 46: 833, 857, 873. — (E. G. Craven) Chamb. J. 78: 440.

Elevators, Office Building. (C. C. Darrach) Am. Arch. 74: 4.

Eleventh Hour, The. (B. King) Atlan. 87: 253.

Elgin, James Bruce, Lord. Rule in India. Sat. R. 87: 8.

— — Features and Events of. Asia. R. 27: 1.

Elgood, G. S., Garden of, and its Art with Especial Reference to his Paintings. Studio (Lond.) 5: 51.

Elias, Ney. Nature, 56: 228. — With portrait. (S. Wheeler) Geog. J. 10: 101.

Eliduc, The Lay of. (Tr. Alice Kemp-Welsh) Monthly R. 4, no. 1: 128.

Elijah; the Country in which he Lived. (S. Mathews) Bib. World, 12: 162.

Eliot, Charles W. Address at Tremont Temple, with portrait. (G. McDermot) Cath. World, 72: 56.

— American Contributions to Civilization. (E. Cary) Bk. Buyer, 16: 514.

— as an Educational Reformer. (W. De W. Hyde) Atlan. 83: 348.

Eliot, George. Acad. 61: 175. — (E. P. Dargan) Conserv. R. 5: 36. — (A. Fields) Cent. 36: 442. — (W. C. Brownell) Scrib. M. 28: 711. — (J. B. Kenyon) Meth. R. 57: 563.

— Adam Bede, Notes from the Country of. (J. Hyde) Gent. M. n. s. 61: 15. Same art. Ecl. M. 131: 336. Same art. Liv. Age, 218: 508.

— and George Sand. (Mary E. Ponsonby) 19th Cent. 50: 607.

— Home and Haunts of. (G. Morley) Art J. 49: 233. — (A. Leach) Munsey, 12: 753.

— Literary Reputation of. Acad. 52: 551, 573.

— Reminiscences of. (F. Harrison) Harper, 103: 577.

— Romola; a study. (S. R. Tarr) Canad. M. 10: 295.

— — Suggestions for Study. Poet-Lore, 13: 281.

Eliot, John. (J. T. Prince) Educa. 17: 342.

Elise; a story. (A. Lauston) Harper, 102: 829.

Elixir, The; a story. (G. Gissing) Idler, 15: 430.

Eliza Hepburn's Deliverance. (H. B. Fuller) Cent. 37: 533, 698.

Elizabeth, Queen, and the Earl of Essex's Book. (W. J. Hardy) Library, 2: 65.

— Courtships of, Hume on. (R. Poole) Eng. Hist. R. 12: 168.

— Creighton's. (W. F. Tilton) Am. Hist. R. 2: 346.

— Death of. (S. Lee) Cornh. 75: 291.

— Did she starve her Seamen? (Sir C. Bridge) 19th Cent. 56: 774.

— Last Years of, Hume on. Ath. '01, 1: 683.

— On a Portrait of, from Boughton House. (G. Scharf) Archæol. 51: 213.

— Treason and Plot for Catholic Supremacy. Sat. R. 92: 145.

— A Wardrobe Book of. (H. G. Hewlett) Library, 3: 314.

Elizabeth, Empress of Austria. Acad. 57: 34. — Sat. R. 88: iii. — (J. L. Gilder) Critic, 34: 321.

— and Queen of Hungary. (A. Hegedius, jr.) R. of Rs. (N. Y.) 18: 658. — (M. S. Warren) Eng. Illust. 20: 115. — (A. De Burgh) Idler, 14: 429.

— Assassin of. (B. H. Ridgely) Strand, 18: 298.

— Assassination of. Sat. R. 86: 368.

— Memorial Chapel, Geneva. Am. Arch. 70: 31.

— Reminiscences of. (D. S. Béni) Cath. World, 68: 168.

Elizabeth of Bavaria. Acad. 59: 176. Same art. Liv. Age, 226: 847.

Elizabeth, Queen of Bohemia. (C. W. Wood) Argosy, 68: 411. 69: 61.

Elizabeth, "Carmen Sylva," Queen of Roumania, Portraits of. Strand, 13: 389.

— Doll Show of. (A. B. Henn) Strand, 16: 682.

Elizabeth Leslie, Spinster; a story. (E. Moreton) Pall Mall M. 14: 377.

Elizabeth and her German Garden, Authorship of. Critic, 37: 99.

"Elizabeth," the Ship. Passenger List, 1819. Pennsyl. M. 25: 254.

Elizabethan Adventure in Elizabethan Literature. (G. Wyndham) Fortn. 70: 793. Same art. Ecl. M. 131: 846.

Elizabethan Days, Adventures of Church Students in. (B. Camm) Month, 91: 375.

Elizabethan Gleanings. (F. W. Maitland) Eng. Hist. R. 15: 120-757.

Elizabethan Literature, Beginnings of. (G. White) Sewanee, 4: 478. 5: 210.

Elizabethan Rejoicings. (E. V. Heward) 19th Cent. 42: 245.

Elizabethan Religion. (J. H. Round) 19th Cent. 41: 191. — Reply. (G. W. E. Russell) 19th Cent. 41: 418. — Rejoinder. (J. H. Round) 19th Cent. 41: 837.

Elizabethan Revivals. (A. Dillon) M. of Art, 21: 302.

Elizabethan Stage Society. (S. Urban) Gent. M. n. s. 61: 310.

Elk and Camera; a Photographing Adventure. (B. J. Bretherton) Overland, n. s. 35: 112.

— Dream of. (F. Whishaw) Longm. 30: 145.

Elk-chase, An. (F. Whishaw) Longm. 34: 451.

Elk-hunting in Norway. Blackw. 164: 403.

— in the Rockies. (J. B. Doe) Outing, 32: 589.

Elks, Diving. (E. James) Strand, 16: 699.

Elks Mineral Spring, Nevada. (S. Davis) Nat'l M. (Bost.) 9: 67.

Ellenborough, Lord. (S. Walpole) 19th Cent. 46: 123. — Reply. (Lord Colchester) 19th Cent. 46: 238.

Elleneen; a story. (S. O. Jewett) McClure, 16: 335. Same art. Idler, 20: 177.

Ellice, Jane H., Recollections by. Cornh. 77: 340. Same art. Ecl. M. 130: 608.

Ellie. (A. L. Seligsberg) New Eng. M. n. s. 24: 554.

Elliot, Hugh; the Soldier Diplomatist. (G. Hill) Gent. M. n. s. 66: 576.

Elliott, Flower. Writer, 14: 7.

Elliott, Sarah Barnwell, with portrait. Bk. News, 16: 53.

Ellis, Frederick S. Ath. '01, 1: 275.

Ellis, Leonora Beck. Writer, 14: 73.

Ellis, Mrs. Viner. Ath. '01, 2: 632.

Ellsworth, Oliver, with portrait. (F. R. Jones) Green Bag, 13: 503.

Elmira Reformatory, Character Building at. (R. C. Bates) Am. J. Sociol. 3: 577.

Elocutionists, Women. (J. D. Miller) Nat'l M. (Bost.) 13: 55.

Eloquence, Old-time, at the Bar. (J. De Morgan) Green Bag, 13: 120.

Elopement, An; a monologue. (P. Hart) Pall Mall M. 18: 550.

Elrick Walks. Blackw. 161: 823. Same art. Ecl. M. 129: 604.

Elsie's Dance for her Life; a story. (S. R. Crockett) Cosmopol. 32: 33.

Elson, Louis C. Lit. W. (Bost.) 30: 362.

Elswick Works and Lord Armstrong. (B. Taylor) Engin. M. 20: 491.

Elton, Charles I. Ath. '00, 1: 528.

Elton, Sir Edmund, and Elton Ware. (C. Quentin) Art J. 53: 375.

Elton Slade's Auction Habit; a story. (A. H. Donnell) Cosmopol. 127: 559.

Elwell, Frank Edwin; the American Sculptor. (Emeline G. Crommelin) Overland, n. s. 32: 201.

Elwell Family in America. (R. Elwell) N. E. Reg. 53: 25.

Elwin, Whitwell. Quar. 191: 291. — Ath. '00, 1: 48.

Elwood, Thomas. Acad. 58: 161.

England; Gifts to the West.   Chamb. J. **75**: 276.
— The Government and the Newspaper Press in.   (E. Porritt) Pol. Sci. Q. **12**: 666.
— The Handwriting on the Wall.   Fortn. **67**: 161.
— History, Civil War; Leslie, Alexander, and Prince Rupert.   Ed. R. **191**: 429.
— — Gardiner's History of the Commonwealth and Protectorate.   Acad. **52**: 441. — (A. V. Dicey) Nation, **66**: 13, 32. — (G. Smith) Am. Hist. R. **3**: 529. — Quar. **187**: 446. — (B. Terry) Dial (Ch.) **25**: 222. — (W. O. Morris) Scot. R. **31**: 267.
— — Gross's Sources and Literature of.   (W. J. Ashley) Nation, **72**: 261.
— — in American School Text-books.   (C. Welsh) Educa. R. **19**: 23.
— — Recent Writing on.   (E. P. Cheyney) Internat. Mo. **1**: 399.
— — The Rising of 1381, from a Contemporary Manuscript.   (G. M. Trevelyan) Eng. Hist. R. **13**: 509.
— Imperialism in, Causes of.   (A. V. Dicey) Nation, **73**: 203.
— in the age of Wycliffe, Trevelyan's.   (G. Kriehn) Am. Hist. R. **5**: 120.
— in the 19th Century, McCarthy's.   (A. I. du P. Coleman) Critic, **34**: 328.
— in 1897.   (G. T. Denison) 19th Cent. **42**: 1009.
— in 1899.   (R. B. Johnson) Atlan. **85**: 66.
— in 1900.   Difficulties of Mr. Bull.   (A. D. Godley) Cornh. **81**: 635.
— in 1901, Prospects in.   (J. McCarthy) Indep. **53**: 2621.
— — What should she do to be Saved?   (W. J. Corbet) Westm. **155**: 604.
— in the Night-watches.   (C. W. Wood) Argosy, **65**: 65, 191, 315, 434, 567, 694.
— Industrial Position of, Dominant.   (C. Zueblin) J. Pol. Econ. **5**: 216.
— Industrial Situation of; an American View.   (J. P. Young) Forum, **31**: 472.
— — Why it is beaten.   Chamb. J. **78**: 167.
— Industrial Supremacy of.   Is it a Myth?   (S. N. D. North) Forum, **23**: 101.
— Insecurity of, The Volunteers and.   (J. G. B. Stopford) 19th Cent. **47**: 734.
— Ireland, and the Century.   (T. W. Russell) Fortn. **75**: 391.
— An Invasion of.   Spec. **78**: 653. — (H. W. Wilson) National, **33**: 653.
— Judicial Customs in.   (J. F. Walker) Green Bag, **12**: 614.
— Long Credit.   Blackw. **163**: 123.
— Mediæval, Village Life in.   (E. P. Cheyney) Lippinc. **68**: 365.
— Middle, Cycling through.   (A. L. Moque) Outing, **29**: 460.
— Military Situation and the Transvaal.   Spec. **83**: 240.
— — in 1899.   Spec. **83**: 904.
— Military Weakness of, and the Militia Ballot.   (S. Low) 19th Cent. **47**: 14.
— Monarchs of; Accession and Coronation.   Ath. '01, **1**: 211.
— Municipal History of, Gross's Bibliography of.   (G. E. Howard) Am. Hist. R. **3**: 528.
— my England; a poem.   (W. E. Henley) Ecl. M. **134**: 416.
— "My Own!" a story.   (S. Pickering) Pall Mall M. **22**: 21.
— "Nation of Shopkeepers," How we became a.   (A. Law) Econ. R. **10**: 498.
— National Home Interests.   (N. M. Taylor) Westm. **149**: 73.   Same art. Ecl. M. **130**: 410.
— A New National Gallery for.   (E. R. Pennell) Nation, **71**: 48.

England, North and South of.   (W. A. Atkinson) Macmil. **83**: 376.
— of the Westminster Assembly.   (E. D. Warfield) Presb. & Ref. R. **9**: 44.
— Paramountcy of, Rational Basis of.   (G. S. Bowles) Monthly R. **4**, no. **1**: 68.
— Parlous Position of.   (W. S. Lilly) 19th Cent. **47**: 580.
— Partition of.   Spec. **79**: 394.
— Peasantry of, Formerly and Now.   (A. Jessopp) 19th Cent. **49**: 16.
— Peasants' Rising of 1381.   Ed. R. **191**: 76.
— Perilous Position of.   (W. T. Stead) R. of Rs. (N. Y.) **21**: 195.
— A Place in the Country.   Quar. **190**: 316.   Same art. Ecl. M. **134**: 218.
— Places and Things of Interest and Beauty in.   (R. Hunter) 19th Cent. **43**: 570.
— Political House Parties in.   ("Ignota") Lippinc. **65**: 121.
— Politics in, and the [Boer] War.   (R. Ogden) Nation, **70**: 453.
— Popular Dislike of.   Sewanee, **4**: 252.
— A Possible Continental Alliance against.   (D. C. Boulger) No. Am. **169**: 805.
— Premiership of, Succession to the.   (C. A. Whitmore) National, **38**: 197.
— Present Mood of.   (W. Clarke) New Eng. M. n. s. **16**: 690.
— Present Situation of, a Canadian Impression.   (G. T. Denison) 19th Cent. **42**: 1009.   Same art. Ecl. M. **130**: 97.
— Problem of the North.   (G. T. Lapsley) Am. Hist. R. **5**: 643.
— Progress in Sixty Years of Victoria.   (J. Holt Schooling) Pall Mall M. **12**: 297.
— Rebellion in, The Last, 1817.   (J. Hyde) Gent. M. n. s. **64**: 323.
— Religious Condition of.   (H. C. Corrance) Dub. R. **128**: 95.
— Religious Situation in.   (J. Watson) No. Am. **168**: 539.
— Representation of, Due.   (A. V. Dicey) National, **38**: 359.
— Resources of.   (D. MacG. Means) Nation, **70**: 238.
— The Road to.   (T. W. Higginson) Atlan. **84**: 521.
— Roman.   Ed. R. **189**: 369.
— Royal Family of.   Entertaining English Royalty.   (Ignota) Lippinc. **64**: 394.
— Royal Standard of.   (J. Leighton) Chamb. J. **74**: 321.
— Rural Streams of Somersetshire.   (W. Raymond) Idler, **13**: 425.
— Rural Village in.   Pall Mall M. **15**: 461.
— Rural Work and Workers in.   (C. Johnson) Canad. M. **13**: 215.   Same art. New Eng. M. n. s. **20**: 325.
— Russia, and China, Asia in the Hands of.   (C. H. Clark) J. Mil. Serv. Inst. **14**: 988.
— Settling with.   (A. G. Sedgwick) Nation, **67**: 123.
— Social Life, Changes in, during the Queen's Reign.   (A. West) 19th Cent. **41**: 639.   Same art. Ecl. M. **128**: 695.
— Social Transformation in.   (E. L. Godkin) Nation, **67**: 182.
— Society in.   (G. W. Smalley) Harper, **94**: 274.
— Scotland, and Ireland, Financial Relations of.   Bank. M. (Lond.) **65**: 381.
— South Coast.   (R. D. Ward) Science, n. s. **13**: 1033.
— Sovereignty in.   Spec. **80**: 700.
— "Splendid Isolation" or What?   (H. M. Stanley) 19th Cent. **43**: 869.   Same art. Liv. Age, **218**: 67.   Same art. Ecl. M. **131**: 234.
— A Summer in, for Two Hundred Dollars.   (R. L. Hartt) Outl. **65**: 294.

England, Towns and Roads in, in the 13th Century. (A. Law) Econ. R. 7: 289.

— — Distribution of. (G. G. Chisholm) Geog. J. 9: 76. 10: 511.

— Trade of; Cry for New Markets. (F. Greenwood) 19th Cent. 45: 538.

— — Falling. (A. G. Herzfeld) Westm. 150: 618.

— Travels through, by C. P. Moritz; a Forgotten Book. (A. Dobson) Library, 1: 1.

— Turkey, and India. (T. G. Bowles) Forum, 24: 129.

— Under the Charlies. (W. Andrews) Argosy, 74: 73.

— Understandings with. (A. G. Sedgwick) Nation, 67: 4.

— War with Europe in the 20th Century, Effects of. (J. Foreman) Westm. 151: 146.

— West; a Week in the West Country. (F. H. Candy) Gent. M. n. s. 65: 372.

— Will it Last the Century? Fortn. 75: 20. Same art. Liv. Age, 228: 529. Same art. Ecl. M. 136: 421.

— Working Classes, in English Villages. (A. Jessopp) 19th Cent. 45: 865. Same art. Ecl. M. 133: 532.

England's Allies; a poem. (R. Gourlay) Canad. M. 9: 227.

Englemann, Gruel, Parisian Bookbinder. (M. Van Vorst) Bookman, 11: 534.

English, Thomas Dunn; author of "Ben Bolt." (A. H. Noll) Midland, 7: 3.

English, The, at Home. [Spec.] Ecl. M. 130: 480.

— and Dutch in the Past. (A. S. Green) 19th Cent. 46: 891. Same art. Liv. Age, 224: 278.

— and French, Concerning. (A. Bréal) Contemp. 79: 117. Same art. Ecl. M. 136: 534.

— at Home. (M. H. Krout) Chaut. 29: 234.

— a Nation of Amateurs. (G. C. Brodrick) 19th Cent. 48: 521. Same art. Ecl. M. 136: 247.

English and Scottish Banking. Bank. M. (Lond.) 69: 552.

English Archives, Gleanings from. (J. H. Lea) N. E. Reg. 54: 188, 325. 55: 95, 432.

English Art, R. de La Sizeranne on. Artist (N. Y.) 23: 72.

English Attitude, The. (A. Flexner) Nation, 67: 184.

English Bards and Scotch Reviewers. (G. R. Redgrave) Library, n. s. 1: 18.

English Cases as Scot's Authorities. (J. H. Henderson) Jurid. R. 12: 304.

English Channel, Across the, at Railway Speed. Chamb. J. 78: 219.

English Character, Has it Changed? Spec. 84: 733.

English Characteristics. (J. Ralph) Harper, 98: 562.

English Composition and Literature, Webster's. (A. Abbott) School R. 9: 54.

— Final Report of the Harvard Committee. Harv. Grad. M. 6: 200.

— in Elementary Schools. (Ja. S. Snoddy) Educa. 20: 353, 423.

— in the High School. (F. A. Barbour) School R. 6: 500.

— — Professor Barbour's Paper on. (C. H. Horn) School R. 7: 309.

— in Secondary Schools, Plea for More. (M. L. Warner) Educa. 21: 163.

— Recent Tendencies in Teaching of. (G. Buck) Educa. R. 22: 371.

English Country Banks in 1900. Bank. M. (Lond.) 69: 886.

English Country Inn, A Typical. (S. G. Tallentyre) Macmil. 78: 131.

English Country Life. Quar. 190: 316. — (W. J. Stillman) Nation, 71: 286.

English Country Shop, a Typical. (S. G. Tallentyre) Macmil. 77: 447.

English Culture, Proper Basis of. (S. Lanier) Atlan. 82: 165.

English Dialect Dictionary, Wright's. (C. P. G. Scott) Nation, 64: 183.

English Dictionaries, Evolution of. (J. A. H. Murray) Sat. R. 90: 557.

English Dictionary, Pedigree of the. Acad. 58: 556.

English Drama, Raleigh on. (M. Beerbohm) Sat. R. 92: 13.

— Victorian. Acad. 51: 605. — (C. Scott) Eng. Illust. 17: 451. — (H. H. Fyfe) Theatre, 38: 319.

— Ward's History of. (R. Burton) Dial (Ch.) 27: 120. — Sat. R. 87: 307.

English Essayists, Modern, The Social Passion in. (V. D. Scudder) Chaut. 27: 593.

English Girl, Modern. (S. Grand) Canad. M. 10: 297.

English Grammar in Elementary Schools. (J. S. Snoddy) Educa. 19: 522.

— Lax Use in Speech. (Gertrude Darling) Educa. 19: 555.

— Teaching of. (O. F. Emerson) School R. 5: 129.

— — in the Elementary Schools. (L. Owen) Educa. 21: 585.

English Historical Grammar. (M. H. Liddell) Atlan. 82: 62.

English History, Early, Recent Historical Development in. (E. King) Month, 98: 371, 598.

English Husbandman, in 17th Century. (S. E. Cartwright) Belgra. 95: 429.

English Industries, German Peril to. Blackw. 163: 107.

English Inn, Life at. (C. Johnson) Outl. 59: 61.

English Judicature, A Century of. Green Bag, 13: 573.

English Language. (J. W. Sewell) School R. 8: 80.

— Accurate, Plea for. (J. N. Phillips) Writer, 13: 33.

— America and the. Liv. Age, 219: 514.

— and Latin in the Illinois High Schools. (D. K. Dodge) Educa. R. 14: 370.

— as affected by U. S. New Political Relations. (F. W. Chapman) Educa. 21: 357.

— as the International Language. (R. W. Leftwich) Westm. 148: 283.

— as it is Taught. (C. H. Thurber) School R. 6: 328.

— as a Vehicle of Expression. (E. D. Warfield) Educa. 21: 579.

— Brief History of, Emerson's. (E. E. Hale) School R. 5: 406.

— Can it be Preserved? (R. J. Lloyd) Westm. 147: 286.

— College. (E. L. Godkin) Nation, 65: 351. — (C. F. Adams) Nation, 65: 453. — Critic, 30: 115. — (W. H. McKellar) Sewanee, 5: 479.

— — Deterioration of. (W. H. Johnson) Dial (Ch.) 22: 271.

— — Illiteracy of American Boys. (E. L. Godkin) Educa. R. 13: 1.

— — Why College Graduates are Deficient in English. (A. E. P. Searing) Educa. R. 16: 244.

— Conference on. (C. W. French) School R. 5: 343.

— Cultivating The, Plea for. (A. Ayres) Harper, 103: 265.

— Debt to King Alfred. (B. Matthews) Harper, 103: 141.

— Dictionary of, Murray's. (L. W. Lillingston) Good Words, 40: 159. Same art. Ecl. M. 132: 762. Same art. Liv. Age, 221: 189. — Acad. 56: 361. Same art. Liv. Age, 221: 730. — (N. D. Davis) Nation, 66: 144. — Library, 2: 220.

— First Book in Writing, Lewis's. (F. I. Carpenter) School R. 5: 477.

— Future of. (B. Matthews) Munsey, 20: 100.

— Good, What is? (H. T. Peck) Bookman, 7: 125.

— Harvard Report on. Critic, 31: 277, 289.

English Poetry. Some Minor Poets. Quar. **186**: 323.

English Political Philosophy, Graham on. (A. M. Wergeland) Dial (Ch.) **30**: 336.

English Politics, Robertson's. (J. L. Stewart) Nation, **72**: 161.

English Prose-writers. Quar. **186**: 453.

English Race, A Common Citizenship for the. (A. V. Dicey) Contemp. **71**: 457. Same art. Liv. Age, **213**: 691. Same art. Ecl. M. **128**: 721.

English Royalty, Home Life of. (A. H. Beavan) Cosmopol. **26**: 185.

English Schoolboys on the " Trek." R. of Rs. (N. Y.) **16**: 445.

English Schools, Lay and Clerical Head Masters in. Acad. **56**: 53.

English Shires, Story of Some. Lond. Q. **89**: 302.

English Solicitor's Note Book, Leaves from. (B. Borret) Green Bag, **12**: 86–512. **13**: 141, 539.

English-speaking Brotherhood, The. (C. Waldstein) No. Am. **167**: 223.

English-speaking Folk, Rule of the. (World's Work) **1**: 479.

English Stage, Filon on. (T. F. Huntington) Dial (Ch.) **23**: 217.

English Studies, Advancement of. (W. W. Skeat) Ath. '00, **2**: 123.

English Style in the Victorian Period. (W. R. Nicoll) Bookman, **10**: 144.

English Thought, Development of, Patten's. (S. Ball) Econ. R. **10**: 114. — (C. M. Andrews) Am. Hist. R. **5**: 330. — (M. Smith) Pol. Sci. Q. **15**: 112. — (C. M. Hill) J. Pol. Econ. **7**: 554. — (W. J. Ashley) Econ. J. **9**: 417. — (A. Hodder) Nation, **69**: 12. — (R. M. Wenley) Science, n. s. **9**: 713. — (J. R. Angell; Sadie E. Simons) Am. J. Sociol. **4**: 823.

English Towns in the 14th Century. (C. Bonnier) Eng. Hist. R. **16**: 501.

English Township, The. (T. H. B. Graham) Gent. M. n. s. **60**: 252.

English Verse, Rhyme and Reason in. (H. G. Hewlett) Library, **3**: 37, 84.

English Villages, Destruction of. (A. Marshall) Macmil. **81**: 374.

English Wills, Abstracts of. (L. Withington) N. E. Reg. **52**: 65.

English Words, Anderson on. (M. C. McGiffert) Dial (Ch.) **23**: 217.

Englishman, Evolution of the. (H. Hutchinson) Monthly R. **3**, no. 1: 136.

— Insularity of the. (T. S. Knowlson) World's Work, **1**: 603.

— The Mean. (J. Jacobs) Fortn. **72**: 53. Same art. Ecl. M. **133**: 596. Same art. Liv. Age, **222**: 608.

— Prospects of an, in the U. S. Chamb. J. **74**: 500.

Englishmen in the United States. (F. Cunliffe-Owen) Forum, **29**: 38.

— Historic, on the Amer. Stage. (Louise C. Hale) Bookman, **13**: 535.

— Selfishness of. Spec. **80**: 231. Same art. Ecl. M. **131**: 231.

" Englishwoman's Love Letters, An." Acad. **59**: 510–629. — Acad. **60**: 18–149. Same art. Liv. Age, **228**: 453 — **229**: 37. — (F. T. Cooper) Bookman, **12**: 559. — (M. C. Jones) Critic, **38**: 149.

Englishwomen and Agriculture. (V. M. Crawford) Contemp. **74**: 426.

— Modesty of. (Mrs. W. Mahood) 19th Cent. **49**: 588.

Engraving and Etching, Recent. (F. Wedmore) Studio (Internat.) **14**: 14.

— Color, Modern. (Marie Jacounchikoff) Studio (Lond.) **6**: 148.

— Copperplate, Early American. (W. L. Andrews) Bk. Buyer, **15**: 653.

Engraving ; Fine Prints of 1898. (F. Wedmore) M. of Art, **22**: 603.

— Line, 1780–1830. (G. Clulow) J. Soc. Arts, **45**: 604.

— Mezzotint ; Discovery and Process. (Fred Miller) Idler, **11**: 455.

— Steel, Evolution of, in America. (F. Weitenkampf) Bk. Buyer, **23**: 93.

Engravings, Exhibition of J. P. Morgan's Collection. Artist (N. Y.) **31**: xxiii.

Engurirra, The, or Fire Ceremony. (B. Spencer and F. J. Gillen) Nature, **56**: 136.

Enim, Use of, in Plautus and Terence. (W. K. Clement) Am. J. Philol. **18**: 402.

Enlistment, Fraudulent, How to prevent it. (W. T. Dooner) Un. Serv. M. **14**: 599.

— Oath of, in Germany. (S. W. Crawford) J. Mil. Serv. Inst. **12**: 266.

— Voluntary, The Breakdown of. (S. Low) 19th Cent. **47**: 365.

Enna, Emil, Pianist, with portrait. Music, **18**: 466.

Ennodius, Saint, and the Papal Supremacy. (E. Maguire) Am. Cath. Q. **26**: 317, 523.

Enoch, Book of, and the New Testament. (H. Hayman) Bib. World, **12**: 35.

Enoch — a Born Naturalist. (E. C. M. Dart) Longm. **38**: 334. Same art. Liv. Age, **230**: 774. Same art. Ecl. M. **137**: 658.

Enoch Arden, Music to. (R. Stauss) Music, **20**: 396.

Enshrinement of an Idol, The ; a story. (M. J. Charlton) Temp. Bar, **110**: 100. Same art. Liv. Age, **212**: 669.

Ensign Knightley's Home Coming ; a story. (A. E. W. Mason) Pall Mall M. **17**: 1.

Ensigns, The Three. (L. G. C. Laughton) Un. Serv. M. **18**: 493.

Enstatite from North Carolina. (J. H. Pratt) Am. J. Sci. **155**: 429.

Entasis in Mediæval Italian Architecture. (W. H. Goodyear) Archit. R. **7**: 63, 180.

Enter a Dragoon ; a story. (T. Hardy) Harper, **102**: 25.

Enterprise of Flora. (F. Gribble) Lippinc. **67**: 499.

Entertaining, Art of. (Lady Jeune) Cosmopol. **31**: 75.

Entertainment, Sheer. Liv. Age, **223**: 394.

Enthusiasms and Human Change. Sat. R. **90**: 718. Same art. Liv. Age, **228**: 395. Same art. Ecl. M. **136**: 543.

— Literary Value of. (Clara L. Burnham) Writer, **14**: 180.

Entomologist, The. (Geo. W. Cable) Scrib. M. **25**: 50–315.

Entomology, Packard's Text-book of. Am. Natural. **32**: 592.

Entrenchments. Sat. R. **92**: 167.

Environment, Influence of, on Bacilli. (A. W. Peckham) Science, **5**: 981.

— Man and the. (P. Geddes) Internat. Mo. **2**: 169.

— *vs.* Heredity. (Sarah M. Crawford) Char. R. **9**: 174.

Envoy Extraordinary ; a story. (H. S. Brooks) Cosmopol. **25**: 292.

Envoys at Washington. (Waldon Fawcett) Cosmopol. **31**: 3.

Envy. Nemesis ; or, The Divine Envy. (P. E. More) New World, **8**: 625.

Enzymes, Chemical Nature of. (O. Loew) Science, n. s. **10**: 955. — (E. O. Jordan) Pop. Sci. Mo. **59**: 497.

Eocene Mammalia, in the Marsh Collection, Peabody Museum. (J. S. Wortman) Am. J. Sci. **161**: 333, 437. **162**: 143–421.

Epaphroditus, Scribe and Courier. (J. R. Harris) Expos. **4**: 455.

Ephemerid, Air Viviparous. (M. Causard) Am. Natural. **31**: 165.

Ephemeris of Comet or Planet, Computation of. (Mary C. Traylor) Pop. Astron. 9: 311.

Ephesus. (W. M. Ramsay) Bib. World, 17: 167.

— Council of, Dr. Rivington on the. Month, 93: 469.

Ephraim, Tribe of, Genealogy of. (H. W. Hogg) Jew. Q. 13: 147.

Ephraim's Breite ; a drama. (C. Hauptmann) Poet-Lore, 12: 465.

Epic and Romance, Ker on. (W. M. Payne) Dial (Ch.) 23: 45.

Epicurus and his Sayings. Quar. 185: 68.

Epidemics, Nervous. (W. Seton) Cath. World, 68: 98.

— Sanitary Methods of Dealing with. (J. L. Notter) J. Mil. Serv. Inst. 25: 111.

— Suppression of. (W. Wyman) Am. J. Soc. Sci. 38: 50.

Epidote and Garnet from Idaho. (C. Palache) Am. J. Sci. 158: 299.

Epigram, The Systematic. (F. M. Colby) Bookman, 10: 31.

— Use and Abuse of. Spec. 83: 654. Same art. Ecl. M. 134: 411.

Epigrams, Some. Chamb. J. 75: 539.

Epilepsy, Debate concerning. Am. J. Soc. Sci. 35: 138.

Epileptic Children, Home Care of. (E. Flood) Am. J. Soc. Sci. 35: 132.

Epileptic Colony, Craig, at Sonyea. (H. M. Plunkett) Indep. 52: 1501.

— A New York "Colony of Mercy." (S. Brooks) R. of Rs. (N. Y.) 21: 313.

Epileptics, Colony Care of. (H. C. Rutter) Char. R. 6: 469.

Epilogue ; a poem. (W. E. Henley) Ecl. M. 132: 444.

Epilogue to Fleet Street Eclogues. (J. Davidson) Sat. R. 86: 696.

Epinay, Louise Florence Pétronille d'Esclavelles, Madame d'. (S. G. Tallentyre) Longm. 36: 141. Same art. Liv. Age, 226: 237.

Epirus, The Thirty Days in. (H. W. Nevinson) Contemp. 72: 319.

Episcopacy in Massachusetts. Spec. 80: 272.

— Our Disjointed. (J. H. Potts) Meth. R. 57: 899.

Episcopate, Lightfoot on the. (J. L. Parks) Sewanee, 2: 425.

Episode, An. (D. L. Johnstone) Chamb. J. 75: 14.

Episode at Slaters, The ; a story. (I. Allen) Idler, 17: 861.

Episode in the Life of a New Woman, An. (A. T. Oppenheim) Belgra. 92: 312.

Episode of Vera and the Overcoat. (I. Allen) Idler, 17: 417.

Epistemology and Experience. (A. K. Rogers) Philos. R. 7: 466.

— and Mental States. (J. E. Russell) Philos. R. 7: 394.

— and Physical Science. (A. H. Lloyd) Philos. R. 7: 374.

— Can it be based on Mental States ? (J. H. Tufts) Philos. R. 6: 577.
    See Knowledge.

Epitaph ; a poem. (W. K. Johnson) Ecl. M. 132: 110.

Epitaphs, A Bundle of. (H. A. Lincoln) Acad. 52: 74.

— History and Humor of. (J. R. Fryar) Gent. M. n. s. 63: 12.

Epping Forest. (P. A. Graham) Longm. 32: 63. Same art. Ecl. M. 131: 19.

Epoch-makers, World's. (J. R. Smith) Dial (Ch.) 31: 235.

Equador as a Health Resort. Spec. 82: 676.

— Portrait Vases of. Am. Antiq. 23: 334.

Equality. (James Bryce) Cent. 34: 459.

— American Notion of. (H. C. Merwin) Atlan. 80: 354.

— Human, The Principle of. (C. W. Berry) Arena, 24: 629.

Equality, Social, Bellamy's. (N. P. Gilman) Q. J. Econ. 12: 76.

Equations, Partial Differential, of Mathematical Physics, Weber on. (G. H. Bryan) Nature, 63: 390.

Equatorial Telescope, Adjustment of. (K. Laves) Pop. Astron. 8: 424, 535. 9: 13.

Equilibrium, Maintenance of, as a Function of the Central Nervous System. (Heinrich Obersteiner) Am. Natural. 33: 313.

Equinoxes, Precession of the, before Hipparchus. (G. St. Clair) Westm. 150: 647.

Equity. (W. W. Towle) N. Church R. 7: 177.

— Jurisdiction of, for the Rescission of Contracts. (F. M. Hudson) Am. Law R. 33: 702.

— Will a Court of, compel a Purchaser to accept a Title resting solely on Adverse Possession ? (F. B. Patten) Am. Law R. 33: 357.

Equity Courts, Falstaff and, Phelps on. (F. Head) Bk. Buyer, 23: 42.

Equivocation and Lying. (H. Garnet) Month, 92: 7.

Erasmus, Desiderius, Emerton's. Am. Hist. R. 5: 751.

— in Italy. (J. G. Rosengarten) Citizen, 2: 369.

Erastianism. (J. L. Davies) 19th Cent. 45: 1014.

Erdeswick Family. Some Historical Notes from the Margins of a MS. (H. N. Birt) Dub. R. 124: 291.

Eretria, Gymnasium at, Inscriptions from. (R. B. Richardson and T. W. Heermance) Am. J. Archæol. 11: 152, 173.

— — Sculpture from. (R. B. Richardson) Am. J. Archæol. 11: 165.

— Theatre at, Excavation of. (T. W. Heermance) Am. J. Archæol. 11: 317.

Erhardt, Jakob. Geog. J. 18: 543.

Eric Hermannson's Soul ; a story. (W. S. Cather) Cosmopol. 28: 633.

Erickson, Louis ; a Remarkable Counterfeiter of Indian Implements. (A. E. Jenks) Am. Anthrop. 2: 292.

Ericsson, Capt. John, Personal Recollections of. (E. P. Watson) Engin. M. 21: 361.

— First Monitor and the Later Turret Ships. (G. L. Fowler) Engin. M. 14: 110.

Erie, Lake, Abnormal Wave in. (H. S. Reed) Am. Natural. 33: 653.

— Biological Study of. Science, n. s. 8: 13.

— Climatic Influence of, on Vegetation. (E. L. Moseley) Am. Natural. 31: 60.

— Yachting Circuit of. (G. F. Flannery) Outing, 30: 355.

Erie Canal, The, and Transportation. (E. P. North) No. Am. 170: 121.

— Our Policy with. (H. White) Nation, 70: 85.

Erigenia Bulbosa, Nutt. (T. Holm) Am. J. Sci. 161: 63.

Erionite, a New Zeolite. (A. S. Eakle) Am. J. Sci. 156: 66.

Erler, Fritz, Decorator. (B. Bibb) Studio (Internat.) 8: 25.

Ermak, The ; Ice-breaking Ship. (E. T. Meyer) Chaut. 29: 284.

Eros, New Planet. (E. Ledger) 19th Cent. 45: 612. — (E. C. Pickering) Pop. Astron. 7: 66. — (W. W. Payne) Pop. Astron. 8: 445. — (S. I. Bailey) Pop. Sci. Mo. 58: 641.

— and the Astrographic Conference. Knowl. 23: 207.

— Observations of. (M. Loewy) Pop. Astron. 8: 488.

— — Tables for. Pop. Astron. 8: 437.

— Opposition of, Coming. (M. C. Traylor) Pop. Astron. 9: 496.

— Variability in Light of. (E. C. Pickering) Pop. Astron. 9: 290.

Erroll, Elizabeth Jemima, Countess of. (G. Festing) Longm. 30: 121.

Ethical Instruction in School and Church, Need of. (E. M. Fairchild) Am. J. Sociol. 4: 433.

Ethical Legislation by the Church. (B. P. Bowne) Meth. R. 58: 370.

Ethical Motive, The. (F. H. Giddings) Int. J. Ethics, 8: 316.

"Ethical" Philosophy, The New. (John Watson) Int. J. Ethics, 9: 414.

Ethical Postulates in Theology. (W. Rupp) Am. J. Theol. 3: 654.

Ethical Progress through Experience. (C. W. Super) Am. Antiq. 23: 384.

Ethical Revival, The. Outl. 61: 723.

Ethical Self, Genesis of the. (J. M. Baldwin) Philos. R. 6: 225.

Ethics and Literature. (Julia Wedgwood) Contemp. 71: 63. Same art. Liv. Age, 212: 537.

— Bigge's British Moralists. (J. Gibb) Crit. R. 8: 22.

— Christian. (B. P. Raymond) Meth. R. 60: 513.

— — Gretillat on. (A. H. Douglas) Crit. R. 9: 19. 10: 307.

— — Recent Books on. (G. D. B. Pepper) Am. J. Theol. 4: 386.

— — T. B. Strong on. (A. S. Wilkins) Crit. R. 7: 3.

— Developmental. (A. Llano) Open Court, 11: 162, 280.

— English. (W. J. Corbet) Arena, 22: 429.

— Evolution of. (C. W. Super) Am. Antiq. 22: 69.

— Evolutionary, A. Sutherland on. Outl. 61: 828.

— for Children. (B. L. Putnam) Educa. 19: 314.

— from a Practical Standpoint; a reply. (B. Bain) Mind, 22: 371.

— Gay's Ethical System. (E. Albee) Philos. R. 6: 132.

— Hume's Ethical System. (E. Albee) Philos. R. 6: 337.

— Influence of Evolution on the Theory of. (M. H. Valentine) Luth. Q. 28: 208.

— Is it Possible? (P. Carus) Open Court, 11: 295.

— Kantian Doctrine of, Futility of the. (F. A. Henry) Internat. J. Ethics, 10: 73.

— Modern. (H. Thomas) Westm. 152: 142.

— Natural vs. Spiritual. (N. M. Steffens) Presb. & Ref. R. 11: 461.

— The Normal Self. (R. R. Marett) Mind, 25: 496.

— of Advocacy. (S. Rogers) Law Q. 15: 259.

— of Intellectual Life and Work. (T. Fowler) Int. J. Ethics, 9: 296.

— Paulsen's System of. (G. S. Patton) Presb. & Ref. R. 11: 326. — (J. Iverach) Crit. R. 10: 201. — Ath. '99, 2: 887.

— Practical, Aims and Illustrations in. (B. Bain) Internat. J. Ethics, 10: 330.

— Relation to Religion. N. Church R. 6: 434.

— Relation to Sociology. (H. Sidgwick) Internat. J. Ethics. 10: 1.

— Science and. (J. Wedgwood) Contemp. 72: 218. Same art. Liv. Age, 214: 843.

— Scientific and Christian. Bib. World, 18: 83.

— Scottish. (J. Seth) Philos. R. 7: 561.

— Sidgwick and Schopenhauer on the Foundation of Morality. (M. Macmillan) Int. J. Ethics, 8: 490.

— Standpoint and Method of. (J. Seth) Philos. R. 6: 275.

— Study of, among the Lower Races. (W. Matthews) J. Am. Folk-Lore, 12: 1.

— System of Henry More. (G. N. Dolson) Philos. R. 6: 593.

— Wundt on. (E. H Griggs) Dial (Ch.) 25: 300.

Ethnographical Collections in Germany. Nature, 60: 461.

Ethnology at the British Museum. (R. Lydekker) Knowl. 21: 223.

— Keane's Man, Past and Present. (O. T. Mason) Science, n. s. 10: 147.

Ethnology of Tribes, Notes on. (J. R. L. MacDonald) Anthrop. J. 29: 226.

— Ratzel's History of Mankind; v. 3. (O. T. Mason) Science, n. s. 10: 21.

— Romance of Race. (Grant Allen) Pop. Sci. Mo. 53: 511.

— Was Middle America peopled from Asia? (E. S. Morse) Pop. Sci. Mo. 54: 1.

Etiam, in Plautus and Terence. (W. H. Kirk) Am. J. Philol. 18: 26.

Etiquette, Ethics and. (G. Meyrick) No. Am. 167: 756.

— Hawkins's Youth's Behaviour. (F. M. Parsons) Longm. 33: 175.

— Rational, in Social Life. (A. H. Morton) Chaut. 30: 149.

— Summer Hotel Manners. (Mary Mayne) Outl. 60: 236.

— Use and Abuse of. (Countess of Cork and Orrey) Pall Mall M. 24: 67.

Eton College. (H. W. Mabie) Outl. 59: 851.

— Old, and Modern Public Schools. Ed. R. 185: 355.

— Provost's Lodge at; a historic house. (W. Durnford) Pall Mall M. 14: 269.

Etretat, France, and its Environs. (A. T. Gibert) Art J. 52: 277.

Etruscan Ware of Wales. (W. Turner) Reliquary, 37: 77.

Ettinger, Rose; singer, with portrait. Music, 13: 750.

Etude, Piano-forte, Evolution of the. (W. S. B. Mathews) Music, 15: 258.

Eucharist. See Lord's Supper.

Εὐδόκησα, Aorist, Supplementary Note on. (B. W. Bacon) J. Bib. Lit. 20: 28.

Eudora Drake's Rummaging. (P. Wesley) New Eng. M. n. s. 24: 280.

Eugen, Prince, of Sweden; landscape painter. (T. Hedberg) Studio (Internat.) 3: 162.

Eugénie, Empress of France. (R. G. Michel) Eng. Illust. 20: 251.

— Flight of. (B. G. Taylor) Cosmopol. 24: 537.

Eulalie; a story. (M. Arnold) Argosy, 70: 39.

Euphrates Valley Railway, The. Spec. 83: 371. — (H. L. Washington) Am. Arch. 58: 6.

Euphues, Lyly's. (L. H. Vincent) Poet-Lore, 9: 47.

Eurasian Problem in India. (A. Nundy) Asia. R. 28: 56.

Eureka Stockade, The. Chamb. J. 74: 124.

Euripides. Alcestis, as a Foreshadowing of the Christian Doctrine of Redemption. (M. O'Connor) Dub. R. 124: 119.

— Browning's Interpretation of. (M. S. Daniels) Meth. R. 58: 55.

— Cyclops. (John Patterson) Scot. R. 31: 349.

— Iphigenia as a Heroine. (W. S. Scarborough) Educa. 19: 213, 285.

— — in Athens. (D. Quinn) Nation, 73: 450.

— Medea of, and of Grillparzer. (C. C. Ferrell) Sewanee, 9: 337.

— Way's Verse Translation of. Acad. 53: 597.

Europe. (Henry James) Scrib. M. 25: 753.

— American Impressions of. (P. A. Bruce) 19th Cent. 49: 472.

— and America. (S. Brooks) Atlan. 88: 577. Same art. Ecl. M. 137: 120.

— and the "American Peril." (A. D. Noyes) Nation, 73: 4.

— and the East, Political Situation in. (N. A. Miles) Forum, 25: 159.

— and India, My Ways and Days in. (Gaekwar Maharajah) 19th Cent. 49: 215.

— and the Ottoman Power before the 19th Century. (W. Miller) Eng. Hist. R. 16: 452.

— Armies of. (J. J. O'Connell) J. Mil. Serv. Inst. 14: 765.

Evil, Problem of, and the Material Basis of Inheritance. (R. C. Schiedt) Ref. Q. **44:** 101, 269.
Evolution and the Amateur Naturalist. (L. Robinson)
Blackw. **161:** 561. Same art. Ecl. M. **129:** 25.
— and Authority, the Life of Catholic Dogma. (G.
Tyrrell) Month, **93:** 493.
— and Christian Doctrine. (W. D. Mackenzie) Bib.
Sac. **54:** 542.
— and Consciousness. (O. H. P. Smith) Monist, **9:** 219.
— and Creative Development. (J. W. Dawson) Expos.
3: 43, 211, 356.
— and Ethics. (J. Dewey) Monist, **8:** 321. — (A. W.
Benn) Internat. J. Ethics, **11:** 60.
— and the Fall, Gore on. Spec. **78:** 298.
— and Immortality. (W. Spence) Arena, **23:** 315, 432.
— (Lyman Abbott) Liv. Age, **216:** 487.
— and the Problem of Evil. (R. C. Schiedt) Ref. Q.
44: 101, 269.
— and Religion, Marshall on. Church Q. **50:** 157.
— and Teleology. (J. A. Zahm) Pop. Sci. Mo. **52:** 815.
— and Theology. (O. Pfleiderer) New World, **7:** 413.
— (W. Spence) Arena, **26:** 612.
— and War. (C. O. Ovington) Westm. **153:** 411.
— Appeal to, for Human Guidance, Mackintosh on.
(J. Iverach) Crit. R. **10:** 544.
— An Argument against; Separation and Creation.
(W. T. Freeman) Gent. M. n. s. **58:** 292.
— as taught in Scripture. (A. E. Deitz) Luth. Q. **37:**
210.
— Biology and Human Guidance. Church Q. **50:** 343.
— by Means of Natural Selection, Rise and Fall of.
(S. Fitzsimons) Am. Cath. Q. **26:** 87.
— Christian, Griffith-Jones on. (H. C. Minton) Presb.
& Ref. R. **11:** 721.
— Creation of Plants and Animals. (G. Hawkes) N.
Church R. **8:** 75.
— Determinate. (J. M. Baldwin) Psychol. R. **4:** 393.
— Evolved. (A. H. Lloyd) Monist, **9:** 197.
— Extra-organic. (A. Allin) Science, n. s. **7:** 267.
— Half Century of, with Special Reference to the
Effects of Geological Changes on Animal Life. (A.
S. Packard) Am. Natural. **32:** 623. Same art.
Science, n. s. **8:** 243, 285, 316.
— Headley on Neo-Darwinian. (F. A. D.) Nature, **63:**
341.
— Historical, American Expansion considered as. (S.
L. Parrish) Am. J. Soc. Sci. **37:** 99.
— Hypothesis of. (W. Seton) Cath. World, **66:** 198.
— in Light of New Church. (G. Hawkes) N. Church
R. **7:** 24-565. **8:** 194, 366. **16:** 546.
— Individuality in. (A. C. Lane) Outl. **58:** 479.
— Influence of, on the Theory of Ethics. (M. H.
Valentine) Luth. Q. **28:** 208.
— Inorganic, Methods of. (N. Lockyer) Nature, **61:**
129, 296.
— in Intellectual Development, Crozier on. (L. M.
Keasbey) Citizen, **4:** 58.
— A Kinetic Theory. (O. F. Cook) Science, n. s. **13:**
969.
— Limits of, Howison on. Nature, **64:** 323.
— Love as a Factor in. (W. Hutchinson) Monist, **8:**
205.
— Lucretius and. (W. L. Poteat) Pop. Sci. Mo. **60:** 166.
— of a Citizen. (A. E. P. Searing) New Eng. M. n. s.
22: 310.
— of the Civic Idea. (G. H. Fall) Meth. R. **58:** 899.
— of Evolution. (M. D. Conway) Open Court, **11:** 498.
— of Plants, Campbell's Lectures on. (C. E. Bessey)
Science, n. s. **9:** 618.
— Organic, Cope's Primary Factors of. (J. M. Tyler)
Monist, **7:** 301.
— — Duke of Argyll on. (R. Meldola) Nature, **59:** 217.
— — Elements of. (D. S. Jordan) Arena, **19:** 752.

Evolution, Organic, Isolation in. (G. J. Romanes)
Monist, **8:** 19.
— Pearson on. (F. Starr) Dial (Ch.) **23:** 218.
— Philosophy of. (C. L. Morgan) Monist, **8:** 481.
— Physiological, of the Warm-blooded Animal. (H.
M. Vernon) Sci. Prog. **7:** 378.
— Principle of Economy in. (E. Noble) Pop. Sci. Mo.
51: 324.
— Questions it does not Answer. (H. W. Conn) Meth.
R. **61:** 31.
— Regressive. (P. Mantegazza) Liv. Age, **217:** 155.
— Regressive Phenomena in. (C. Lombroso) Monist,
8: 377.
— Remarkable Anticipation of Modern Views on. (E.
B. Poulton) Sci. Prog. n. s. **1:** 278.
— Social, and Individual. (H. Jones) New World, **7:**
453.
— — What is? (H. Spencer) 19th Cent. **44:** 339.
— Spencer and Darwin. (Grant Allen) Pop. Sci. Mo.
50: 815.
— Spencer and Lord Salisbury on. (Duke of Argyll)
19th Cent. **41:** 387, 569. — Reply. (H. Spencer)
19th Cent. **41:** 850.
— Theistic. (G. Macloskie) Presb. & Ref. R. **9:** 1.
— The True. (J. C. Ridpath) Arena, **17:** 1097.
— What it is and What it is not. (D. S. Jordan) Arena,
18: 145.
— without Selection, Piepers on. Nature, **60:** 97.
Evolution of a Nihilist; a story. (Fred Whishaw)
Idler, **12:** 288.
Evolution Theory and New-Church Philosophy. (H.
C. Hay) N. Church R. **8:** 481.
— Present Aspect of the. (J. A. Thompson) Lond. Q.
95: 324.
Evolutionary Ethics. (H. Spencer) Pop. Sci. Mo. **52:**
497.
Evolutionary Fad. (G. F. Wright) Bib. Sac. **57:** 303.
Evolutionist's View of Nature and Religion. (L. H.
Bailey) Indep. **51:** 335.
Examinations. (F. Paulsen) Educa. R. **16:** 166.
— An Apology. (A. C. Chapin) Educa. R. **20:** 519.
— Blunders in. Spec. **87:** 347. Same art. Liv. Age,
231: 842.
— Competitive, for Woolwich and Sandhurst. (H. H.
Almond) Fortn. **71:** 85.
— Dangers of. (C. F. Wheelock) School R. **5:** 43.
— Entrance, Conflicting Views regarding. (A. T.
Hadley) School R. **8:** 583.
— Humors of. (G. S. Ellis) Cornh. **79:** 519.
— Influence of. (E. H. Nichols) Educa. R. **19:** 443.
— R. H. Quick on. (H. Sabin) Educa. **21:** 210.
— School. (M. H. Leonard) Educa. **21:** 282. — (H. L.
Clapp) Educa. **21:** 387.
— Use and Control of. (A. T. Hadley) Educa. R. **21:**
286.
Ewing, Ephraim B., with portrait. (C. W. Sloan)
Green Bag, **11:** 441.
Examination Answers, Sample Mistakes. Sat. R. **90:**
143.
Examination System, Use and Abuse of. Month, **94:**
16.
Example, Education of. (E. L. Godkin) Nation, **70:** 86.
— Influence of. (E. L. Godkin) Nation, **72:** 44.
Excalibur, Derivation of. (W. W. Skeat and others)
Acad. **51:** 49, 85.
Excavations at Cærwent, Monmouthshire. (A. T. Mar-
tin) Archæol. **57:** 295.
— in a Cemetery of South Saxons, Sussex. (C. H.
Read) Archæol. **55:** 203.
— on Site of Roman City at Silchester in 1900. Ar-
chæol. **57:** 229. — Antiq. n. s. **34:** 246.
Excelente Balade of Charitie. (T. Rowley) Poet-Lore,
9: 181.

Exceptional Girl, An; a story. (M. Raylton) Eng. Illust. **19**: 427.

Exchange, German; Act of 1896. (E. Loeb) Q. J. Econ. **11**: 388.

Exchange-value, General, Measurement of, Walsh's. (F. Y. Edgeworth) Econ. J. **11**: 404.

Excommunication. (L. Tolstoy) Indep. **53**: 1662.

Execution, A Novel. Chamb. J. **77**: 605.

Executions and Executioners. (J. De Morgan) Green Bag, **12**: 125.

Executive Power and Constitutional Amendment. (C. R. Woodruff) Ann. Am. Acad. Pol. Sci. **14**: 344.

— in Democracy, Weakness of. (H. L. Nelson) Harper, **98**: 210.

Executive Regulations. (G. N. Lieber) Am. Law R. **31**: 876.

Executors, in Scotland and England, Liability of. (W. F. Trotter) Jurid. R. **13**: 320.

Exegesis and Preaching. (W. Rupp) Ref. Ch. R. **48**: 99.

— as an Historical Study. Bib. World, **17**: 178.

— Biblical. (B. Jacob) Jew. Q. **12**: 434.

Exercise and Longevity. (D. A. Sargent) No. Am. **164**: 556.

— Value of. (H. Campbell) Nature, **59**: 150.

Exeter Cathedral. (W. J. Edmonds) Sund. M. **26**: 758, 820.

Exeter College, Oxford. (W. K. Stride) Argosy, **74**: 148.

Exhibition. (D. S. MacColl) Studio (Lond.) **1**: 49.

Exhibitions. Ath. '00, **1**: 472.

— at Royal Academy and New Gallery. Am. Arch. **67**: 36.

— International, Promise of. (F. G. Aflalo) Fortn. **73**: 830.

— London, 1899. Studio (Internat.) **7**: 221.

— Winter Art, English. Belgra. **98**: 129.

Exmoor Railway; Utility and Natural Beauty. Spec. **80**: 686.

Exmouth, Edward Pellew, Viscount. (F. H. Pellew) Un. Serv. M. **17**: 333.

— Bombardment of Algiers by. (Walter Wood) Gent. M. n. s. **63**: 505.

"Exmouth," The Training-ship. (C. H. Leibrand) Strand, **17**: 88.

Exner, Therese, Blind Deaf-mute. (B. M. Ward) Good Words, **38**: 272.

Exodus, Route of. (G. L. Robinson) Bib. World, **18**: 410.

Exodus Material and the Use made of it in the Scriptures. (I. M. Price) Bib. World, **18**: 451.

Expansion, An Academic Discussion of. (J. H. Hollander) Nation, **68**: 292.

— America in Far East. (W. E. Griffis) Outl. **61**: 110.

— American, and the Inheritance of the Race. (W. L. Clowes) Fortn. **70**: 884. Same art. Liv. Age, **220**: 31.

— — considered as an Historical Evolution. (S. L. Parrish) Am. J. Soc. Sci. **37**: 99.

— American Debate on. Spec. **82**: 43.

— American Policy of. (C. Clark) Conserv. R. **1**: 78.

— American Protestantism and. (J. P. Brushingham) Meth. R. **59**: 585.

— Americanism and. (P. Carus) Open Court, **13**: 215.

— and the Constitution. (H. Zeichmueller) Am. Law R. **33**: 202.

— and Foreign Trade. (J. Schoenhof) Pop. Sci. Mo. **55**: 62.

— and Protection. (H. H. Powers) Q. J. Econ. **13**: 361.

— Anti-, Movement. Gunton's M. **16**: 5.

— Are Our Hands Clean? (S. D. McConnell) Outl. **61**: 216. — Reply. (H. B. Woods; J. E. R.; J. T. Bell) Outl. **61**: 421.

Expansion; Justice Brewer's Warning. (D. MacG. Means) Nation, **67**: 64.

— but not Imperialism. Outl. **64**: 662. — (P. Carus) Open Court, **14**: 87.

— Doom of Protection. Gunton's M. **18**: 411.

— The Dread of. (J. B. McMaster) Outl. **61**: 161.

— Ethical and Political Principles of. (T. Williams) Ann. Am. Acad. Pol. Sci. **16**: 227.

— Ethics of. (H. H. Powers) Internat. J. Ethics, **10**: 288.

— Growth of Our Foreign Policy. (R. Olney) Atlan. **85**: 289.

— Literature of. (C. A. Conant) Internat. Mo. **3**: 719.

— Louisiana and Texas Precedents. (J. S. Mosby) Nation, **68**: 44.

— National Bigness or Greatness — Which? (H. C. Potter) No. Am. **168**: 433.

— of the American People. (E. S. Sparks) Chaut. **30**: 49-593. **31**: 39-250.

— Opportunity for the Best Americans. (J. Hawthorne) Forum, **27**: 441.

— Our Right to Acquire and Hold Foreign Territory. (C. A. Gardiner) Am. Law R. **33**: 161.

— Past and Prospective. (H. D. Money and J. M. Scanland) Arena, **23**: 337.

— The Philippines — The Oriental Problem. (N. P. Chipman) Overland, n. s. **34**: 491.

— A Political and Moral Opportunity. (H. K. Carroll) Meth. R. **60**: 9.

— Problem of. (J. G. Schurman) R. of Rs. (N. Y.) **20**: 567.

— The Real Issue. Outl. **65**: 335.

— Two Opinions of. Overland, n. s. **32**: 364.

— Types of Anti-expansionists. Gunton's M. **19**: 216.

— Whigs as Anti-expansionists. (A. Watkins) Sewanee, **8**: 56.

Expedient of John Chinaman, The. (Emma M. Wise) Nat'l M. (Bost.) **8**: 250.

Expenditure. (B. F. Dunelm) Econ. R. **10**: 75.

— Personal Budgets of Unmarried Persons. (W. B. Bailey) Yale R. **10**: 70.

Expenditures, Personal Equation in. Sat. R. **87**: 583. Same art. Liv. Age, **221**: 848.

— Public, Growth of. (C. A. Conant) Atlan. **87**: 45.

Expensive Living, the Blight on America. (J. Lee) New Eng. M. n. s. **18**: 53.

Experience. (J. Rehmke) Philos. R. **6**: 608.

— Actual. (E. Montgomery) Monist, **9**: 359.

— Epistemology and. (A. K. Rogers) Philos. R. **7**: 466.

Experiment, An; a story. (Mrs. E. Cartwright) Belgra. **92**: 418.

Experiment in Burglary, An; a story. (H. H. Nichols) McClure, **10**: 404.

Experiment in Time. Atlan. **81**: 717.

Experimental Life, The. (C. H. Henderson) Atlan. **85**: 640.

— Realities of. (C. L. Morgan) Monist, **8**: 1.

Experimental Research, The Field in. (E. Thomson) Science, n. s. **10**: 236.

Experimental Station Publications, Card Index of. (A. C. True) Science, n. s. **10**: 650.

Experiments, Evidence of, Admissibility, Weight, and Effect of. (A. R. Watson) Am. Law R. **34**: 28.

Expert Testimony. (W. P. Mason) Science, **6**: 243.

— Medical; Obstacles to Radical Change in Present System. (W. Bartlett) Am. Law R. **34**: 1.

— Medical and other. (St. Clair McKelway) Am. J. Soc. Sci. **36**: 222.

"Expertizing," Morality of. Spec. **85**: 521. — Liv. Age, **227**: 523. Same art. Ecl. M. **136**: 104.

Experts. (Mrs. H. I. Munro) Westm. **156**: 466.

— Scientific, and Patent Cases. Nature, **57**: 562.

Fact and the Poet; a poem. (L. I. Guiney) Cosmopol. 22: 640.

Factories, Economy of Heating and Ventilating. (L. Allen) Engin. M. 21: 75.

— New England, in 1827. (C. Holbrook) New Eng. M. n. s. 20: 23.

Factory, The, as an Element in the Improvement of Society. (J. H. Patterson) Char. R. 8: 473.

— The Business of a. (P. G. Hubert, jr.) Scrib. M. 21: 306.

Factory Acts and State Employees. (S. W. Belderson) Westm. 154: 177.

— and Women Compositors. (L. B. Bradby; A. Black) Econ. J. 9: 261.

— Consolidation Bill, 1901. (J. Shirley) Westm. 156: 318.

— Effect of Exemption of Fish-curing and Fruit-preserving. Sat. R. 85: 454.

Factory Bill of 1900, English. (G. M. Tuckwell) Fortn. 73: 972.

Factory Communities, Beautifying of Operatives' Homes in. (C. B. Going) Engin. M. 21: 59.

— Measures taken for Comfort of Workmen. (J. H. Patterson) Engin. M. 20: 577.

Factory Expense. Apportionment of Office and Selling Expense. (A. H. Church) Engin. M. 22: 367.

— Classification of Charges. (A. H. Church) Engin. M. 22: 31.

— Factory and Mass Production and the New Machine Rate. (A. H. Church) Engin. M. 22: 231.

— Proper Distribution of. (A. H. Church) Engin. M. 21: 508.

Factory Girl, The London. Liv. Age, 229: 369. Same art. Ecl. M. 137: 96.

Factory Girl's Day, A. (B. S. Knollys) Belgra. 93: 437.

Factory Homes, Landscape Gardening for. (W. H. Tolman) R. of Rs. (N. Y.) 19: 441.

Factory Inspection in London. (M. S. Grew) Sat. R. 84: 617.

Factory Labor in the South. Gunton's M. 14: 217.

Factory Laws of Europe, Richards on. Ath. '98, 2: 351.

Factory Legislation, The Courts and. (G. W. Alger) Am. J. Sociol. 6: 396.

— for Women in Canada. (Annie M. MacLean) Am. J. Sociol. 5: 172.

— in Victoria. (J. Hoatson) Westm. 154: 398.

— Inspection of Women's Workshops in London. (A. Harrison) Econ. R. 11: 32.

Factory Life and Legislation in England. (A. M. Anderson) Chaut. 28: 243.

— in New England, Old Time. (A. K. Fiske) New Eng. M. n. s. 18: 249.

Factory Sales Dept., Organization of the. (O. D. Hogue) Engin. M. 20: 853.

Factory Town, A Model. (L. B. Ellis) Forum, 32: 60.

Factory Towns in New England, The Old. (C. B. Spahr) Outl. 61: 285.

Facts and History. (C. G. D. Roberts) Bk. Buyer, 18: 355.

Fads. (Agnes Grove) Cornh. 81: 515.

Faed, Thomas. Ath. '00, 2: 256.

— In Memoriam, with portrait. M. of Art, 24: 564.

Faelten's Music School, Boston. (W. S. B. Mathews) Music, 15: 564.

Faenza, On the Maiolica of. (C. D. E. Fortnum) 19th Cent. 45: 273.

Faguet, Emile. (O. Guerlac) Nation, 70: 160.

Fa-hien, Travels of, A. D. 399-414. (H. H. Gowen) Am. Antiq. 21: 3.

Failure, The Literature of. Acad. 60: 427. Same art. Ecl. M. 137: 194. Same art. Liv. Age, 229: 788.

Failure of Justice, A; a story. (F. Remington) Harper, 100: 267.

Failure of Martha Morris; a story. (J. F. Fraser) Idler, 13: 31.

Failure of Penelope Price; a story. (E. H. Stooke) Belgra. 98: 1.

Failure of Success, The; a story. (A. B. Paine) Bk. News, 16: 179.

Failures. Spec. 78: 693. Same art. Ecl. M. 129: 286.

— in the United States and Canada. Ann. Am. Acad. Pol. Sci. 17: 391.

Fair and Dark Persons, Comparative Abilities of. (H. Ellis) Monthly R. 4, no. 2: 84.

Fair England; a poem. (H. G. Cone) Atlan. 80: 604.

Fair Episode, A; a story. (E. M. Acreff) Midland, 8: 349.

Fair Frondeuse, A; a story. (E. H. Gifford) Argosy, 75: 323.

Fair Head, Ireland. (G. A. J. Cole) Knowl. 24: 198.

"Fair Ines." (E. W. Brodhead) Cent. 39: 913.

Fairfax-Muckley, Louis, Artist. Studio (Lond.) 4: 146.

Fairfield; a Peakland Township. (J. Hyde) Gent. M. n. s. 66: 238.

Fairhaven, Mass., H. H. Rogers's Gift of Water-works to. (S. Baxter) R. of Rs. (N. Y.) 23: 441.

Fairies in Board Schools. (Lady Magnus) Good Words, 41: 181.

— West-country Pixies. (A. Ballantyne) Argosy, 64: 410.

Fairs, Country. (H. G. Archer) Good Words, 40: 301.

Fairy on Horseback, A; a story. (J. S. Winter) Belgra. 92: 407.

Fairy Blacksmith, The; from the Gaelic. (Marquis of Lorne) Pall Mall M. 12: 289.

Fairy Funeral, The; a poem. (L. M. Whelan) Argosy, 71: 351.

Fairy Gold; a story. (A. J. Colcock) Nat'l M. (Bost.) 11: 73.

Fairy Land, Invention of. (K. Grahame) Acad. 52: 542.

Fairy Mythology of English Literature. (A. Nutt) Folk-Lore, 8: 29.

Fairy Rings. (A. B. Steele) Knowl. 22: 197.

Fairy Tale "Morals." (F. MacCunn) Sund. M. 28: 289.

Fairy Tales as Literature. Ed. R. 188: 37.

Fairmount Park, Phila., Extension of. Am. Arch. 69: 79.

Faith. Spec. 86: 725. Same art. Liv. Age, 230: 132.

— and Belief. (R. B. Steele) Meth. R. 61: 228.

— and Folly. Month, 98: 100.

— as an Effort of the Soul. (A. T. Burbridge) Bib. World, 18: 185.

— Author of Our. (J. Clifford) Outl. 60: 381.

— Doctrine of, in Hebrews, James, and Clement. (B. W. Bacon) J. Bib. Lit. 19: 12.

— An Epoch for. Outl. 67: 478.

— Genesis of. (A. Gehring) New World, 8: 460.

— of the Millions, The. Month, 98: 432.

— Physiological Effect of. (G. E. Gorham) Outl. 62: 888.

— Quest of, Saunders on. Ath. '99, 2: 119.

— Religion To-day abandoning the "Faith Alone" Theory. (H. C. Hay) N. Church R. 4: 380.

— Reorganization of the. (W. DeW. Hyde) New World, 8: 43.

— Rule of, Kunze on. (R. A. Lendrum) Crit. R. 11: 52.

— Scientific. (C. C. Bonney) Open Court, 15: 257.

— The Spiritual Foundations of; a sermon. (L. Abbott) Outl. 61: 221.

— Supremacy of. (G. W. Richards) Ref. Ch. R. 47: 518.

— Symbolism of. (A. C. Zenos) Presb. & Ref. R. 11: 397.

— The Venture of. (Emma Marie Caillard) Contemp. 76: 889. Same art. Ecl. M. 134: 329. Same art. Liv. Age, 224: 158.

Faith Healing, Effects of Mind on Body as evidenced by. (H. H. Goddard) Am. J. Psychol. 10: 431. — (W. E. Hull) Luth. Q. 37: 263.

Faithful ; a story. (E. Dowsley) Canad. M. 8: 356.

Faithful Failure, A ; a story. Pall Mall M. 21: 445.

Faithful Wife of Duck Peter. (A. E. P. Searing) New Eng. M. n. s. 21: 211.

Faithless Faith ; a poem. (H. Johnstone) Outl. 67: 520.

"Fakes," An Exhibition of. (A. Lang) Indep. 53: 2453.

Fakir, Aghori, History of. (H. Balfour) Anthrop. J. 26: 340.

Fakirs, Indian, Voluntary Trance of. (R. Garbe) Monist, 10: 481.

— Story of. (R. S. Spears) Munsey, 23: 136.

Falcon, the Migrant, Haunt of. Spec. 78: 729.

Falconry in France. (V. Thompson) Outing, 39: 296.

— Revival of. (C. W. Hall) Nat'l M. (Bost.) 10: 155. — Spec. 83: 911. — (C. Q. Turner) Outing, 31: 473.

Falize, Lucien ; a great Goldsmith. (H. Frantz) M. of Art, 22: 414.

Falkland Islands, The. (K. A. Patmore) Temp. Bar, 111: 59. Same art. Liv. Age, 214: 30.

Falkner, Harold, Work of. (G. C. Williamson) Artist (N. Y.) 32: 149.

Fall, The ; a poem. (P. F. Camp) Outing, 31: 50.

Fall, The ; a poem. (E. H. Thorold) Argosy, 72: 323.

Fall from Grace ; a story. (M. Robertson) Cosmopol. 30: 17.

Fall of a God ; a poem. (F. Gadsby) Canad. M. 12: 484.

Fall of the House of Robbinson. (A. S. Winston) Cent. 31: 916.

Fall of Man, and Anthropology. (C. J. Wood) Outl. 69: 134.

— and Evolution. (D. W. Simon) Bib. Sac. 54: 1.

— and its Consequences according to Genesis. (H. G. Mitchell) Am. J. Theol. 1: 913.

— Economic Interpretation of. (T. N. Carver) Bib. Sac. 57: 483.

Fall River, Mass. (P. W. Lyman) New Eng. M. n. s. 24: 291.

Fallacies, Some Consecrated. (A. K. Fiske) No. Am. 169: 821.

Falling Bodies, Deviation of, from Vertical. (H. C. Wilson) Pop. Astron. 5: 186.

Falmouth Harbor, Day in. (H. S. Tuke) Studio (Lond.) 3: 76.

False Colors. (W. W. Jacobs) Strand, 17: 97.

False Confession, A ; a story. (G. S. Godkin) Argosy, 66: 469.

False Gods of Doc Weaver. (E. P. Butler) Cent. 40: 691.

Falsetto, True Nature of. (E. D. Palmer) 19th Cent. 41: 216. Same art. Liv. Age, 213: 249.

Falstaff, Don Quixote, and My Uncle Toby. (J. B. Hadley) Gent. M. n. s. 62: 470.

— Original of. Month, 93: 606.

Fame ; a poem. (J. J. Bell) Spec. 80: 339.

— Genius and. (C. H. Cooley) Ann. Am. Acad. Pol. Sci. 9: 317.

— Guesses at. (T. W. Higginson) Indep. 52: 1964.

Fame's Recognition ; an allegory. (Samuel Freedman) Cosmopol. 24: 102.

Familiar of Megat Pendîa, The ; a story. (H. Clifford) Macmil. 77: 385. Same art. Liv. Age, 217: 273.

Families, Breaking up of. (E. T. Devine) Char. R. 10: 461.

— Founding of. Spec. 81: 353.

— Small vs. Large. (Ida H. Harper) Indep. 53: 3055.

Family, The, the Primary Social Settlement. (K. K. Ide) Pop. Sci. Mo. 52: 534.

Family Budgets. (A. Morrison) Cornh. 83: 446 — 84: 184.

Family Buffer, The. (Anna A. Rogers) Overland, n. s. 32: 329.

Family Heirloom, A ; a story of 1715. (L. Hardy) Ecl. M. 136: 56. — Same art. Liv. Age, 227: 501.

Family Home, Glasgow. (F. W. Moore) Econ. R. 10: 333.

Family Living, A. (A. Marshall) Longm. 34: 510. Same art. Liv. Age, 223: 655. Same art. Ecl. M. 134: 201.

Family Scandal, A ; a tale. (E. E. Kitton) Argosy, 67: 153.

Family Skeleton, The. (A. Eyre) Chamb. J. 78: 6-58.

Famine in the Diamond Jubilee Year. Cath. World, 66: 205.

— After the. Contemp. 71: 547. Same art. Liv. Age, 213: 388.

Famine in my Garden, The. (P. Robinson) Contemp. 71: 394. Same art. Liv. Age, 212: 884.

Famine-camp in Burmah, On a. (H. Fielding) Macmil. 76: 242.

Famine Month, The. Spec. 86: 419.

Famines in India and their Remedy. (R. C. Dutt) Fortn. 68: 198.

— Science of Relieving. Sat. R. 87: 583.

Famous Adventure of the Leading Hands ; a story. (W. F. Shannon) Idler, 11: 513.

Fancy, Humors of the. Spec. 85: 331.

— Limitations of. Spec. 85: 741.

Fancy and I ; a poem. (J. V. Cheney) Outl. 67: 546.

Fancy-dress Balls. (Edgar Saltus) Cosmopol. 28: 253.

Fans, Ancient and Modern. Art J. 49: 253.

Fantin-Latour, Henri ; with examples of his Lithographs on Musical Motives. (F. Keppel) Cent. 38: 63.

Far Islands, The. (J. Buchan) Blackw. 166: 604.

Far-seeing. Chamb. J. 77: 814.

Faraday and Schonbein. (R. Meldola) Nature, 61: 337.

Farce for England. (M. Beerbohm) Sat. R. 90: 359.

Fargo, N. Dakota. (W. A. Edwards) Nat'l M. (Bost.) 15: 237.

Farina, Salvatore, an Italian Goldsmith. (F. Spear) Fortn. 70: 550. Same art. Liv. Age, 219: 715. Same art. Ecl. M. 132: 130.

Farinelli ; a biographical romance. (Irma Hadzsits) Music, 13: 177.

Farm, The, and the City. (W. Besant) Contemp. 79: 792. Same art. Liv. Age, 216: 304.

— Boy's Life on a. (C. C. Munn) Nat'l M. (Bost.) 12: 77.

— Future Value of the New England. (H. Butterworth) R. of Rs. (N. Y.) 20: 330.

— The Northern. (C. B. Spahr) Outl. 63: 558.

— Old, Revisited. (H. W. Gleason) New Eng. M. n. s. 22: 668.

— Solidarity of Town and. (A. C. True) Arena, 17: 538.

— Two Months on a. (T. L. Flood) Chaut. 26: 59.

Farm Colony, Gen. Booth's. (W. Besant) Contemp. 72: 792.

Farm Hand, The, from the Standpoint of the Farmer. (G. R. Henderson) Arena, 20: 105.

Farm Laborers' Earnings in England. Sat. R. 90: 262.

Farm Life, Expansion of. (K. L. Butterfield) Arena, 24: 188.

Farmer, Education of the Young. (W. M. Beardshear) Educa. 22: 209.

— English Tenant. (H. A. Bryden) Sat. R. 86: 495.

Farmer-preacher, A. (S. Currie) Nation, 71: 188.

Farmer's Balance Sheet for 1898, An American. (F. H. Spearman) R. of Rs. (N. Y.) 19: 325.

Farmer's Railroad, The ; a story. (F. B. Tracy) Mc-Clure, 13: 35.

Father's Knife. (L. G. Moberly) Sund. M. **27**: 598.

Fathers, Church, Work of the. (A. A. Benton) Sewanee, **3**: 477.

— Greek, Literary Significance of. (J. Reinhard) Sewanee, **6**: 29.

— Harnack's Chronology of Early Christian Literature. (E. C. Butler) Dub. R. **124**: 1.

Fatigue, Æsthesiometric Method as a Measure of, Invalidity of. (G. B. Germann) Psychol. R. **6**: 599.

— Griesbach Method of Determining, Validity of. (J. H. Leuba) Psychol. R. **6**: 573.

— Mental. (Edward Thorndike) Science, n. s. **9**: 665.

— — Binet and Henri on. (J. Jastrow) Science, n. s. **8**: 132.

— of Metals. (H. F. J. Porter) J. Frankl. Inst. **145**: 241, 321.

Fauley, Wilbur Finley. Writer, **14**: 140.

Fauna, European, Origin of the. (R. F. Scharf) Nature, **56**: 625.

— of Central Borneo. (G. R. Stetson) Science, **5**: 640.

Faunal and Geological Relations of Europe and America during the Tertiary Period. (H. F. Osborn) Science, n. s. **11**: 561.

Faunistic Work in Europe, Some Recent. (C. A. Kofoid) Am. Natural. **32**: 789.

Faure, Auguste, Reminiscence of. Music, **13**: 734.

Faure, Felix ; a sketch. R. of Rs. (N. Y.) **19**: 293.

— Visit to Russia. Spec. **79**: 265.

Faust in Music. (Ernest Newman) Music, **20**: 209.

— of the Marionettes. (H. C. Macdowall) Macmil. **83**: 198. Same art. Liv. Age, **228**: 390. Same art. Ecl. M. **136**: 452.

Faust Legend, Shakespeare and the. (R. A. Redford) Gent. M. n. s. **61**: 547.

Favrile Glass and its Beauty Source. (J. L. Harvey) Brush & P. **9**: 167.

— Designs by L. C. Tiffany. (G. C. Teall) Brush & P. **4**: 302. — Artist (N. Y.) **24**: iv.

Fawcett, Waldon. Writer, **14**: 41.

Fay Halifax ; a tale. (A. Rede) Canad. M. **9**: 168.

Fear as an Ethic Force. (E. Ethelmer) Westm. **151**: 300.

— The Conquest of. (T. B. Reed) Cosmopol. **24**: 628.

— What do I ? Cosmopol. **26**: 217.

— Words for, in Certain Languages. (Alex. F. Chamberlain) Am. J. Psychol. **10**: 302.

Fearing, Miss Blanche. (Bessie L. Putnam) Educa. **21**: 565.

Fears, A Study of. (G. S. Hall) Am. J. Psychol. **8**: 147.

Feasts in Fiction. (W. E. G. Fisher) Cornh. **82**: 377. Same art. Liv. Age, **227**: 85. Same art. Ecl. M. **135**: 791.

Feathers, Hair and. (J. S. Kingsley) Am. Natural. **31**: 767.

— Fine. (W. C. Mackenzie) Chamb. J. **77**: 772.

Feature Articles, Illustrated. (A. Coll) Writer, **48**: 181.

"February's Day ; " a story. (M. Bower) Argosy, **71**: 180.

Federal Convention of 1787, Notes of Major William Pierce on. Am. Hist. R. **3**: 310.

Federal Courts, Aggressions of. (J. W. Allen) Am. Law R. **32**: 669.

— Should they ignore State Laws ? (H. E. Mills) Am. Law R. **34**: 51.

Federal Question, When a, is raised on the Record. (W. D. Hines) Am. Law R. **35**: 536.

Federal Receiver ; Is it a Federal Question ? (F. Bausman) Am. Law R. **34**: 856.

Federalist, Authorship of. (E. G. Bourne) Am. Hist. R. **2**: 443. — (P. L. Ford ; E. G. Bourne) Am. Hist. R. **2**: 675.

Federalist ; Ford's Edition. (E. G. Bourne) Am. Hist. R. **4**: 172.

Federation of Labor, American. *See* American.

Fee, John G., a Southern Abolitionist. Outl. **67**: 200.

Fée. (E. S. Phelps Ward) Cent. **39**: 671.

Fee Simple, Evolution of the American. (M. A. Greene) Am. Law R. **31**: 227.

Fee System, American Colonial ; its Relation to Political Liberty. (T. K. Urdahl) Ann. Am. Acad. Pol. Sci. **12**: 58.

Feeble-minded, Care of. (F. M. Powell) Char. R. **7**: 674.

— Education and Care of. (A. Johnson) Am. J. Sociol. **4**: 463.

— Education of. (K. G. Wells) New Eng. M. n. s. **22**: 6.

— Condition and Increase of. (A. Johnson) Am. J. Sociol. **4**: 326.

— A Notable Factor in Social Degeneration. (A. W. Butler) Science, n. s. **14**: 444.

Feeble-minded Children. (J. C. Carson) Am. J. Soc. Sci. **35**: 142.

— Special Schools for. (H. L. Clapp) Educa. **19**: 195.

Feeble-minded Women, New York State Custodial Asylum for. Char. R. **8**: 289.

Feeling and Thought. (A. F. Shand) Mind, **23**: 477.

Feeling of being Stared at. (E. B. Titchener) Science, n. s. **8**: 893.

Fees, Gossip about. (G. H. Westley) Green Bag, **13**: 535.

Feet and Hands. (M. Bernard) Pop. Sci. Mo. **52**: 333, 522.

Feet, Baring the, at Worship. (G. Birdwood) Ath. '01, **2**: 632.

Feet of the Young Men, The ; poem. (R. Kipling) Scrib. M. **22**: 679.

Feldspars of Pennsylvania. (T. C. Hopkins) J. Frankl. Inst. **148**: 1.

Félibre, The. (A. Brisson) Liv. Age, **213**: 395.

Felidæ, Extinct. (G. I. Adams) Am. J. Sci. **154**: 145.

Felix, Saint, of Cautalice. Month, **92**: 489.

Fell, Herbert Granville, New Decorative Artist. Studio (Lond.) **2**: 164.

Fellaheen, An Artist among the. Cent. **33**: 878.

Fellow-feeling as a Political Factor. (T. Roosevelt) Cent. **37**: 466.

Fellow-servant Doctrine. (S. Mosley) Am. Law R. **30**: 840.

— — Why are the Decisions under, so Vacillating and Contradictory ? (N. M. Thygeson) Am. Law R. **31**: 93.

Fells, Walking the, Records in. (W. T. Palmer) Cornh. **79**: 507.

Felon, An 18th Century. (G. Paston) Longm. **39**: 167.

Felons of Ireland in Poetry. (Augusta Gregory) Cornh. **81**: 622.

Felsophyre, Dikes of, and of Basalt in Paleozoic Rocks in Central Appalachian Virginia. (N. H. Darton and A. Keith)·Am. J. Sci. **156**: 305.

Feltre, Vittorino da. (C. H. Thurber) School R. **7**: 295.

Feminine, The Eternal. (Agnes Repplier) Liv. Age, **215**: 144.

Feminism. (E. Ethelmer) Westm. **149**: 50.

— in France. Fortn. **61**: 524. Same art. Liv. Age, **213**: 435.

— Psychology of. Blackw. **161**: 104. Same art. Liv. Age, **212**: 707.

— Reaction against, in Germany. (E. Saillier) Liv. Age, **225**: 265-358.

— The Reverses of Britomart. (E. Gosse) No. Am. **168**: 720.

Femme Dispose. (E. F. Benson) Lippinc. **66**: 313.

Fen Flowers, Some Curious. (Wm. A. Dutt) Good Words, **41**: 631.

Fences, Curious. (T. E. Curtis) Strand, 16: 281.

Fencing for Women. (J. C. Bull) Munsey, 17: 491.

— in Modern Fiction. (A. R. Marble) Dial (Ch.) 28: 269.

Fénelon, François de. Acad. 52: 277. 61: 401.

— Inner Life of. (C. M. Stuart) Chaut. 32: 77.

Fenian Memory, A ; a story. (S. L. MacIntosh) Belgra. 95: 489.

Fenian Raid into Canada, 1866. (J. A. Cooper) Canad. M. 10: 41, 121. — (R. Larmour) Canad. M. 10: 228. — (J. W. Dafoe) Canad. M. 10: 348.

— on the St. Croix. (J. Vroom) Canad. M. 10: 411.

Fenians and Fenianism, O'Leary on. Spec. 78: 479.

Fenland, A Floating Church in. (A Fenlander) Sund. M. 26: 487.

Fennan Moss. (Wm. Buchan) Chamb. J. 76: 774.

Fenno Family. (A. H. Bent) N. E. Reg. 52: 448.

Fenswood and the Great Air Lens. (R. T. Ross) Overland, n. s. 35: 250.

Fenton, W. T. Bank. M. (N. Y.) 57: 917.

Ferd's Luck, — a Character Sketch. (Clara H. Holmes) Midland, 9: 154.

Ferdinand, Prince, Policy of. Spec. 79: 235.

Ferdinand of Aragon, Letter of, to Diego Columbus, 1510. Am. Hist. R. 3: 83.

Ferguson, Richard S. Ath. '00, 1: 312.

Fergusson, Robert, Grosart's Life of. Acad. 53: 87. — Ath. '98, 1: 687.

Fermartine, Scotland. Scot. R. 34: 342.

Ferme à Marie, La ; a story of 1870. (L. H. Yates) Good Words, 38: 818.

Fermentation, Chemistry of, Geometry and. (W. J. Pope) J. Soc. Arts, 49: 677-713.

— Early Theories on. (W. S. Smith) Knowl. 23: 154.

— Enzymes, Green on. Nature, 60: 361.

— without Living Cells and Synthetic Protein. (H. W. Wiley) Science, n. s. 8: 893.

Ferments, Inorganic. (H. C. Jones) Science, n. s. 13: 940.

Fernald, C. B. Moonlight Blossom. (M. Beerbohm) Sat. R. 88: 421.

Ferranti, Sebastian Ziani de. (H. Scholey) Cassier, 11: 315.

Ferrara, Francesco. (A. Loria) Econ. J. 10: 114.

Ferraris, Galileo. J. Soc. Arts, 45: 287.

Ferrier, Susan. (S. Gwynn) Macmil. 79: 419. Same art. Liv. Age, 221: 603. Same art. Ecl. M. 133: 53.

— Doyle's Memoir and Correspondence of. Acad. 56: 152. — Sat. R. 87: 214. — Church Q. 52: 157.

— Novels of. Scot. R. 34: 70.

Ferries, Car-. (J. C. Hodson) Strand, 15: 443.

— — on American Lakes. (A. S. Chapman) Cassier, 13: 519.

Ferry, A Connecticut River. (M. B. Thrasher) New Eng. M. n. s. 22: 659.

Fertilization, Experimental Study of. (J. A. Thomson) Nature, 61: 551.

— of Cycas, Ikeno's. Am. Natural. 33: 751.

— Salvia Cœcinea, an Ornithophilous Plant. (R. C. McGregor) Am. Natural. 33: 953.

Fertilizers, Soils and. (C. M. Blackford) Pop. Sci. Mo. 54: 392.

— Soluble, or Enzymes. (E. O. Jordan) Pop. Sci. Mo. 59: 497.

Fessenden, Wm. Pitt. (R. Webb) New Eng. M. n. s. 18: 116.

Festina Lente ; a story. (P. Millington) Temp. Bar, 122: 469. Same art. Liv. Age, 229: 449.

Festing, John Wogan, Portraits of. Strand, 14: 158.

Fetch, The. (D. S. Shorter) Longm. 31: 318.

Fetish, West African. Nature, 60: 243. Same art. Ecl. M. 133: 785. Same art. Liv. Age, 222: 790.

Fetish View of the Human Soul. (Mary H. Kingsley) Folk-Lore, 8: 138.

Feudalism, Anglo-Saxon. (G. B. Adams) Am. Hist. R. 7: 11.

— Belated, in America. (H. G. Chapman) Atlan. 80: 745, 81: 41.

— Brentano on. (E. Schuster) Econ. J. 9: 248.

Feuillâtre, E., Metal Enamel Work of. Artist (N. Y.) 31: 39.

Feuilletons. Chamb. J. 76: 509.

Fever Panics. (F. L. Oswald) Chaut. 26: 201.

Fez, Morocco. (G. Montbard) Art J. 53: 12, 107, 264, 347.

Fiat Justitia. (Ph. Salisbury) Un. Serv. M. 17: 93.

Fiber Industries, Possible, of the United States. (C. R. Dodge) Pop. Sci. Mo. 54: 15.

Fibulæ, Two, of Celtic Fabric from Æsica. (A. J. Evans) Archæol. 55: 179.

Fichte, J. G., Philosophy of ; Relation of its Two Periods. (Ellen B. Talbot) Mind, 26: 336.

Ficquet, Etienne. (W. L. Andrews) Bk. Buyer, 18: 115.

Fiction, America as a Field for. (A. S. Winston) Arena, 23: 654.

— American, a Century of. Dial (Ch.) 25: 9. — (W. C. Blakeman) Meth. R. 60: 270.

— — Life Element in. (Kate Corkhill) Midland, 9: 328.

— — A New Ideal in. (M. S. Anderson) Dial (Ch.) 23: 269.

— — Two Principles in Recent. (J. L. Allen) Atlan. 80: 433.

— and Politics. Ed. R. 193: 158. Same art. Liv. Age, 228: 729. Same art. Ecl. M. 136: 584.

— Art of. (G. Parker) Critic, 33: 467. — (W. Besant) Writer, 12: 113. — (H. James) Writer, 12: 130.

— — Made easy. Macmil. 84: 31. Same art. Ecl. M. 137: 108. Same art. Liv. Age, 229: 561.

— Classification of. (J. D. Brown) Library, 8: 22.

— Compressed. (H. E. Belin) Writer, 10: 48.

— Contemporary, Some Tendencies of. Spec. 83: 602.

— Democracy of. (A. S. Winston) Lippinc. 62: 293.

— Difference of Masculine and Feminine Taste in Choice of. Acad. 55: 553.

— Dixon's Comprehensive Subject-index to Universal Prose Fiction. (W. M. Griswold) Nation, 66: 288.

— Dread of being Dull. Acad. 59: 277. Same art. Ecl. M. 135: 769.

— Dreamland in. (F. Foster) Arena, 20: 112.

— English and American, A Possible Difference. (W. D. Howells) No. Am. 173: 134.

— — Some Characteristics of. (G. Moore) No. Am. 170: 504.

— English Clergy in. (C. Fortescue Yonge) Gent. M. n. s. 59: 40.

— Examinations in. (A. Lang) Cornh. 83: 80. Same art. Ecl. M. 136: 433.

— The Fallow Fields of. Acad. 60: 517. 61: 57.

— Fundamentals of. (R. Burton) Forum, 28: 451.

— Grey Eyes in. (N. R. Allen) Lippinc. 62: 578.

— Heroines of, Howells on. (R. Burton) Dial (Ch.) 31: 506.

— Historical, Craze for, in America. Acad. 58: 275. Same art. Ecl. M. 135: 37. Same art. Liv. Age, 225: 523.

— — The New. (W. D. Howells) No. Am. 171: 935.

— — Recent, 1898. (W. M. Payne) Dial (Ch.) 24: 293.

— in Free Libraries. (T. Mason) Library, 2: 178. — (J. C. Dana) Lib. J. 24: 670.

— — Selection of. Lit. W. (Bost.) 30: 296.

— Language used in. (Ruth Hall) Writer, 14: 81.

— Low, Protest against. (T. M. Hopkins) Westm. 149: 82.

— Modern, Disease in. (J. J. Morrissey) Cath. World, 66: 240.

Fiction, Moral Purpose in. (L. R. Ramsdell) Writer, 13: 1.
— Morality in. Outl. 67: 11.
— The Newest; Brief Reviews of Current Novels. Acad. 52: Fiction supplement, 1–130.
— 19th Century, Spirit in. (S. B. Elliott) Outl. 67: 153.
— of 1901. (T. Williams) R. of Rs. (N. Y.) 24: 586. — Acad. 61: 429. — (W. M. Payne) Dial (Ch.) 31: 365. — Liv. Age, 231: 648.
— of Popular Magazines, The. Acad. 58: 167.
— Old. Liv. Age, 214: 743.
— On the Theory and Practice of Local Color. (W. P. James) Macmil. 76: 16.
— Penny. Blackw. 164: 801. Same art. Liv. Age, 220: 177. Same art. Ecl. M. 132: 351.
— Popular, Library Editions of. (C. R. Dudley) Lib. J. 21: supp. 41.
— Recent, 1898. (W. M. Payne) Dial (Ch.) 24: 354. 25: 20.
— — 1899. (W. M. Payne) Dial (Ch.) 27: 490.
— — A Psychological Counter-current in. (W. D. Howells) No. Am. 173: 872.
— Recent Foreign, 1898. (W. M. Payne) Dial (Ch.) 24: 184.
— Religion of Modern. Sat. R. 89: 581. Same art. Ecl. M. 135: 266.
— Sex-conscious School in. (G. S. Lee) New World, 9: 77.
— Slum Movement in. (J. H. Findlater) National, 35: 447. Same art. Ecl. M. 135: 174.
— Some Hard Facts about. (J. Gilbert) Library, 10: 170.
— Some Tendencies of Contemporary. Liv. Age, 223: 587.
— Study of. (Brander Matthews) Cosmopol. 27: 537.
— Tales of Terror. (C. F. Fiske) Conserv. R. 3: 37.
— The Talk of. (Ruth Hall) Writer, 10: 77.
— Technical Element in. (M. Roberts) Ecl. M. 137: 263. Same art. Liv. Age, 229: 723.
— Theology in. Acad. 51: 405.
— Truth in, An Appeal for. Writer, 14: 178.
— Weeding out, in Public Libraries. (W. M. Stevenson) Lib. J. 22: 133. — (J. W. Harbourne) Lib. J. 22: 251.
— Writing of. (F. M. Bird) Lippinc. 60: 533.
Fiction-fiends. (R. Ogden) Nation, 64: 258.
Fiction-reading and the Minister. (L. Gilbert) Meth. R. 60: 715.
Fiddle and Jimmie. (M. McHenry) New Eng. M: n. s. 19: 423.
Fiddle in the Desert. (C. M. Skinner) Lippinc. 60: 399.
Fiddler Green. (J. Patey) Chamb. J. 76: 9.
Fiddler of Dooney; a poem. (W. B. Yeats) Ecl. M. 133: 369.
Fiddlin' on Heartstrings; a story. (Anna Farquhar) Nat'l M. (Bost.) 8: 482.
Fiduciary Fec, The, in Feudal Conveyancing. (T. Lindsay Clark) Jurid. R. 12: 25.
Field, Eugene. (B. W. Wells) Sewanee, 5: 153.
— Lullaby-land. Sat. R. 85: 499.
Field, George W. A typical life. (G. A. Gordon) Outl. 64: 554.
Field, Kate, Lilian Whiting on. (J. L. Gilder) Critic, 36: 163.
Field, Stephen J., Justice, with portrait. (A. Hopkins) Green Bag, 11: 245.
— A Great Judicial Career. (E. P. Clark) Nation, 65: 313.
Field Columbian Museum, Department of Anthropology; a review of six years. (G. A. Dorsey) Am. Anthrop. 2: 247.
— Recent Progress in Anthropology. (G. A. Dorsey) Am. Anthropol. 3: 737.

Field Engineering for Home Defence. (R. F. Sorsbie) Un. Serv. M. 22: 21, 202, 266.
Field Exercises. (J. B. Babcock) J. Mil. Serv. Inst. 12: 938.
Field Flowers; a poem. (E. T. Hoffman) Outing, 36: 623.
Field Intrenchments for Infantry. (S. M. Foote) J. Mil. Serv. Inst. 25: 71.
Field Manœuvres, On. (E. Nash) J. Mil. Serv. Inst. 10: 84.
Field Outfit of an Infantryman. (J. Ronayne) J. Mil. Serv. Inst. 20: 321.
Field Service Instruction. (A. Milinowski) J. Mil. Serv. Inst. 29: 216.
Fielding, Henry. Acad. 53: 127.
— Amelia, Note on. (C. Thomson) Westm. 152: 579.
Fielding, Robert. (F. Norman) Lippinc. 62: 415.
Fielding had an Orderly; a story. (G. Parker) Pall Mall M. 18: 450.
Fields, Annie T. Authors and Friends. (J. L. Gilder) Critic, 30: 123.
— at Home. (L. I. Guiney) Critic, 32: 367.
Fife, Earls of; the lucky Duffs. (J. M. Bulloch) Eng. Illust. 19: 235.
'15, Last of the. (K. D. Preston) Good Words, 42: 203.
Fig Industry brought by an Insect. (L. O. Howard) Forum, 30: 605.
— of Smyrna. (L. P. Mainetty) Nat'l M. (Bost.) 6: 559.
Fight for a Soul, A; a story. (A. Forbes) Idler, 15: 729.
Fighting and Fox-hunting. (T. E. Kebbel) Macmil. 82: 36.
— Words applied to. (F. B. Crofton) Canad. M. 17: 52.
Fighting Cardinal, The, or the Conquest of Oran. (C. E. de La Poer Beresford) Un. Serv. M. 17: 28.
Fighting Drill. (J. B. Babcock) J. Mil. Serv. Inst. 7: 167.
Fighting Manager, The; a story of the St. Louis Railroad Strike. (C. Warman) McClure, 13: 475.
Figuier, Guillaume Louis, with portrait. (I. M. Tarbell) Pop. Sci. Mo. 51: 834.
Figureheads of the Navy. (A. S. Hurd) Eng. Illust. 19: 125.
Figurines, Terra-cotta from Corinth. (R. B. Richardson) Am. J. Archæol. 2d s. 2: 206.
Fijian Fiery Ordeal, The. Chamb. J. 76: 287.
Fiji Islands and Coral Reefs. (A. Agassiz) Am. J. Sci. 155: 113.
Filia Pulchrior. (W. E. Norris) Longm. 35: 437.
Filial Impulse, A. (W. N. Harben) Cent. 37: 363.
Filipino in Sport. (E. Wildman) Outing, 36: 122.
Filipino Characteristics, Some. (A. N. Benjamin) Outl. 68: 1003.
Filipinos' War Contribution. (C. J. Crane) J. Mil. Serv. Inst. 29: 20.
Filling in the Blank; a story. (H. Flowerden) Argosy, 63: 518.
Fillmore, John Comfort, Teacher of Music. Music, 14: 472.
Filtering of Feed Water on Board Ship. (N. Sinclair) Cassier, 12: 698.
— of Water in the U. S. (A. R. Leeds) Cassier, 11: 304.
Fin-de-siècle; a story. Temp. Bar, 122: 249. Same art. Ecl. M. 136: 509. Same art. Liv. Age, 228: 607.
Final Clauses, Affirmative, in Latin Historians. (R. B. Steele) Am. J. Philol. 19: 255.
Final Quest, The. (A. Brown) Atlan. 87: 126.
Finance and Currency. (H. Haupt) Arena, 17: 217.
— and Disarmament. Bank. M. (Lond.) 66: 468.
— as affected by War with Spain. Sat. R. 85: 587.
— Federal, Seven Years of. Bank. M. (N. Y.) 56: 399.
— of the Australian Commonwealth. Bank. M. (Lond.) 71: 862.

Finance, Public, Some Problems of Classification in. (C. C. Plehn) Pol. Sci. Q. 12: 82.
— Rascality in. (H. E. M. Stutfield) National, 31: 75. Same art. Ecl. M. 130: 601.
— Reconstruction of. Outl. 63: 865.
— Science of, Adams's. (C. F. Bastable) Econ. J. 9: 432. — (A. C. Miller) J. Pol. Econ. 7: 269. — (E. R. A. Seligman) Pol. Sci. Q. 14: 128. — (M. West) Dial (Ch.) 26: 153. — (E. Cannan) Econ. R. 10: 118.
— Sectionalism in. (W. P. G. Harding) Sewanee, 2: 56.
— Some Practical Suggestions from Students of. R. of Rs. (N. Y.) 15: 45.
Financial Development, A Decade of. Bank. M. (N. Y.) 63: 621.
Financial Frauds, Punishment of. Spec. 85: 739.
Financial Law, New, Defects in. Bank. M. (N. Y.) 62: 93.
Financial Opinion, Growth of Sound. Gunton's M. 12: 159.
Financial Resolution of the Democrats, 1900. (G. E. Roberts) Forum, 30: 13.
Financial Situation in 1899, The Remarkable. (A. D. Noyes) Nation, 68: 61.
— Why the People are "Short." (H. S. Pingree) Arena, 17: 868.
Financial Year in America, 1900. Bank. M. (Lond.) 71: 218.
Finch, The. (Marie von Ebner-Eschenbach) Liv. Age, 217: 829.
Finches, Among the. [Sund. M.] Liv. Age, 213: 612.
Findlay, Ellen Boyd. Writer, 14: 26.
Fine Art as Decoration. (R. Sturgis) Internat. Mo. 1: 463.
— in Canada, Decade of. (M. L. Fairbairn) Canad. M. 17: 159.
Fine Arts in England. Exodus of Pictures from England. Ed. R. 185: 327.
— — Painters behind the Scenes. Ed. R. 185: 487.
— Influence of. (C. M. Fairbanks) Chaut. 25: 614.
— Practical Art among Club-women. (A. S. Hall) Chaut. 31: 621.
— vs. Arts and Crafts. (L. C. Phillips) Brush & P. 7: 172.
Fines, The Earliest. (J. H. Round) Eng. Hist. R. 12: 293.
Fingalian Legends, Source and Historic Value of. (W. G. Mackenzie) Gent. M. n. s. 65: 168.
Finger of the Devil's Hand; a story. (L. Wyndham) Canad. M. 10: 32.
Finger-prints as Evidences of Personal Identity. (R. Lydekker) Knowl. 24: 66.
— of Crime, The. Liv. Age, 226: 788.
Finger-ring Lore. Antiq. n. s. 35: 54.
Finland and the Czar. (E. Westermarck) Contemp. 75: 652. Same art. Liv. Age, 221: 597. — (R. N. Bain) Fortn. 71: 735.
— and her Soldiers. (C. E. de La Poer Beresford) Un. Serv. M. 16: 522.
— and its Lakes. (M. A. Stobart) Pall Mall M. 12: 467.
— and its People. (H. R. Mill) Geog. J. 15: 145.
— and Russia. (A. Birrell) Contemp. 78: 16.
— and the Tsars. (J. R. Fisher) Spec. 84: 141.
— Artistic Movement in. Studio (Lond.) 6: 227.
— Case of. (J. Westlake) National, 35: 111. Same art. Ecl. M. 134: 734. Same art. Liv. Age, 225: 159.
— Collieries in. Chamb. J. 76: 831.
— Constitutional Conflict in. (A member of the Finnish Diet) No. Am. 169: 180.
— Downfall of; an object lesson in Russian aggression. Blackw. 166: 1.
— The Finnish Question. (R. Eucken) Forum, 28: 274.
— Plea for. (D. F. Hannigan) Westm. 153: 7.

Finland, Plight of. (E. Limedorfer) Forum, 32: 85. (J. Moritzen) Gunton's M. 17: 258.
— Russia and. Spec. 82: 741. — (J. N. Reuter) 19th Cent. 45: 699.
Finlaystone, Residence of G. J. Kidston. (Edward Pinnington) Good Words, 39: 823.
Finn, Herbert, Architectural Water Color Paintings. (F. Wedmore) Art J. 52: 33.
Finn Poacher, A. (F. Whishaw) Longm. 31: 322.
Finnan Haddie. (B. Macgregor) Eng. Illust. 20: 221.
Finney, C. G., and Oberlin Theology. (A. T. Swing) Bib. Sac. 57: 465.
Finns, Traditional Poetry of, Comparetti on. (A. H. Tolman) Dial (Ch.) 27: 94. — (W. H. Carpenter) Nation, 69: 319.
Finsbury Technical College, Some Work from. Art J. 52: 90.
Finsen Institute, The, in Copenhagen. (Edith Sellers) Chamb. J. 77: 517.
Firdusi an Accurate Historian. (J. P. Kapadia) Asia. R. 27: 390.
Fire. (W. Payne) Liv. Age, 230: 328.
— Philosophy of. (W. H. Buss) N. Church R. 5: 161.
— Precautions against, in America. Bank. M. (Lond.) 66: 550.
— Sacred, among the Slavic Races of the Balkan. (Vl. Titelbach) Open Court, 15: 143.
Fire and Water Resistance. (Howard Constable) Am. Arch. 59: 59.
Fire-appliances. Cosmopol. 27: 94.
Firearms and Armor. (J. Corbett) Longm. 34: 159.
Fireball, Great, of Dec. 7, 1900. (L. L. Stingley) Pop. Astron. 9: 426.
Firebrand, The; a story. (S. R. Crockett) Temp. Bar, 122: 1-433. 123: 1-433. 124: 1-417.
Fire Control, A System of. (W. C. Rafferty) J. Mil. Serv. Inst. 21: 76.
Fire Department, Equipment and Organization of a City. (H. Bonner) Engin. M. 14: 789.
Fire Department Stories, Chicago. (W. P. Cornell) Nat'l M. (Bost.) 14: 69.
Fire-festivals, British. (T. H. B. Graham) Gent. M. 62: 172.
Fire Hazards. (H. de B. Parsons) J. Frankl. Inst. 150: 172. — (H. de B. Parsons) Am. Arch. 69: 85.
Firelight. Spec. 79: 367.
Fire Losses, Advice about the Adjustment of. (T. Hale) Am. Law R. 31: 104.
"Fire Out" in Literary English. (S. Lee) Ath. '01, 1: 80.
Firemen, Heroic. (J. A. Riis) Cent. 33: 483.
— of N. Y. City. (J. R. Sheffield) Outl. 58: 579.
Fireplace of the Suburban House. (M. H. B. Scott) Studio (Lond.) 6: 101.
Fireplaces, Smoky. (W. W. Jackson) Am. Arch. 72: 30.
Fire-prevention and Fire-protection, International Exhibition. Berlin, 1901. (W. P. Gerhard) Am. Arch. 71: 53.
Fireproof Building, Unscientific Enquiry into. (R. Sturgis) Archit. R. 9: 229.
Fireproof Buildings. (Edward Atkinson) Am. Arch. 59: 36.
Fireproof Construction. (Henry Maurer & Son) Am. Arch. 56: 79. — (W. M. Scanlan) Engin. M. 12: 1001.
— in Philadelphia. (E. F. Bertolett) Am. Arch. 73: 78, 83.
— in the Pittsburg Fire, 1897. Am. Arch. 56: 70. — (H. H. Fernald) 56: 86, 103.
— of Domestic Buildings. (Thomas Potter) Am. Arch. 59: 76. — Same art. J. Soc. Arts, 46: 213.
Fireproof Doors. (Edward Atkinson) Am. Arch. 64: 22.

Fireproof Dwellings. (J. W. Pattison) Am. Arch. 65: 78.

Fireproof Floors. (A. W. Woodman) Am. Arch. 32: 35.

Fireproof Structures of U. S. Government. (J. E. P.) Am. Arch. 72: 102.

Fireproofing of Wood. (J. L. Ferrell) J. Frankl. Inst. 151: 161. — (C. J. Hexamer) J. Frankl. Inst. 147: 65.

Fireproofing Tests. Am. Arch. 56: 45.

Fire-resisting Construction. (G. A. T. Middleton) Engin. M. 15: 780.

Fire Risks, Electric. (H. S. Winkoop) Cassier, 19: 225.

Fire Temple at Surakhani, near Baku. (W. Simpson) M. of Art, 20: 196.

Fire-walking; Curious Religious Rite of Hawaii. (Ernestine Coughran) Cosmopol. 32: 30.

— in Tahiti. (S. P. Langley) Nature, 64: 397.

Fireworks of the Past. (A. Whitman) Strand, 14: 530.

Fire Worship. The New-fire Ceremony at Walpi. (J. W. Fewkes) Am. Anthrop. 2: 80.

Fires due to Leakage of Electricity, Prevention of. (F. Bathurst) J. Soc. Arts, 45: 331.

— in Coal Mines. Am. Arch. 63: 93.

— in London in 1898. J. Statis. Soc. 62: 194.

— — Three Years with the Metropolitan Fire Brigade. (G. Nugent-Bankes) Blackw. 170: 165.

— Lessons of the $175,000,000 Ash-heap. (W. J. Boies) Forum, 29: 566.

— Prevention of, 1899. Am. Arch. 67: 5.

— Subterranean, in the Black Country. (H. G. Archer) Good Words, 42: 231.

— World's Great. (M. C. Crosby) Am. Arch. 69: 38.

Firing, Experimental, Results of. (W. M. Black) J. Mil. Serv. Inst. 16: 513.

First Aid, Instruction in. (J. E. Pilcher) J. Mil. Serv. Inst. 19: 416. — (R. Fletcher) J. Mil. Serv. Inst. 22: 255.

First Books of Some English Authors. (L. S. Livingston) Bookman, 10: 437. 11: 26, 131.

First Bride at Barend's. (L. H. Yates) Sund. M. 30: 624.

First Impulse, The. (J. Lemaitre) Liv. Age, 223: 321.

First Judas, The; a story. (F. M. Kingsley) Outl. 65: 571.

First Lord and the Last Lady. (W. E. Norris) Longm. 33: 349.

First Men in the Moon; a story. (H. G. Wells) Cosmopol. 30: 65-643. 31: 84, 196.

First-night, A, at Athens. Macmil. 76: 407.

First Nights at Theatre. (M. Beerbohm) Sat. R. 89: 12.

First or Second Class. (R. Grant) Liv. Age, 223: 66.

First Performance in Shakespeare's Time. (H. W. Fisher) Atlan. 81: 379.

First Step of a Mighty Fall, The. (Q. M. Anderton) Good Words, 38: 821.

First Violin in Amana Colony, The; a story. (M. V. Ebersole) Midland, 9: 446.

Firth of Kirkby Lonsdale, Gardener and Potter. Chamb. J. 74: 540.

Fiscal Friction, Hicks-Beach on. Spec. 79: 73.

Fish and Fishing in Australia. Chamb. J. 74: 463.

— — in Florida Waters. (W. C. Harris) Outing, 35: 391.

— Artificially Hatched, Identification of. (H. C. Bumpus) Am. Natural. 32: 407.

— Blind, Causes of Degeneration in. (C. H. Eigenmann) Pop. Sci. Mo. 57: 397.

— — of the Caves, Eigenmann's. Am. Natural. 33: 895.

— — of North America. (C. H. Eigenmann) Pop. Sci. Mo. 56: 473.

— — Structure of. (C. H. Eigenmann) Pop. Sci. Mo. 57: 48.

Fish, Blind: Troghlichtys Rosæ. (C. H. Eigenmann) Science, n. s. 9: 280.

— Breeding Habits of Ameiurus Nebulosus. (A. C. Eycleshymer) Am. Natural. 35: 911.

— Can the Sea be Fished Out? (R. B. Marston) 19th Cent. 50: 812.

— Curious Deep-sea. (C. F. Holder) Midland, 7: 298.

— Edible, English Neglect of. (F. G. Aflalo) Sat. R. 83: 601.

— Food of. (F. G. Alflalo) Cornh. 82: 397. Same art. Liv. Age, 227: 245. Same art. Ecl. M. 135: 738.

— Foreign, for English Rivers. Spec. 84: 735.

— Fossil, Names of Certain. (O. P. Hay) Am. Natural. 33: 787.

— Game, in the Thames. Blackw. 165: 621.

— Halibut from Pacific for N. E. (E. H. Miller) Nat'l M. (Bost.) 6: 217.

— How to dress Fish — after Walton. (C. Deming) Outing, 38: 415.

— In the Little Brook. (D. S. Jordan) Pop. Sci. Mo. 55: 355.

— Movements of. (E. F. T. Bennett) Art J. 51: 289.

— of Our Boyhood. (E. W. Sandys) Outing, 30: 433.

— of South Shore of Long Island. (T. H. Bean) Science, n. s. 9: 52-55.

— Photographing, under Water. (R. W. Shufeldt) Outing, 38: 543.

— Propagation of, in California. (A. V. La Motte) Overland, n. s. 30: 559.

— Sea-trout. (W. R. Kerr) Sat. R. 84: 337.

— Strange, in English Seas. Spec. 87: 511.

— Tropical, Photographs of. (A. R. Dugmore) World's Work, 1: 929.

— Viviparous. (C. H. Eigenmann) Overland, n. s. 30: 217.

Fishes and their Ways. (J. Isabell) Longm. 37: 347.

— Breathing Valves of. (Ulric Dahlgren) Science, n. s. 9: 313.

— Changes in Colors of Certain. (A. E. Verrill) Nature, 55: 451.

— Classification of the Amioid and Lepisosteoid. (O. P. Hay) Am. Natural. 32: 341.

— Deep-sea, of the Northern Atlantic. Nature, 55: 559.

— Fossil, New American. (C. R. Eastman) Science, n. s. 9: 642.

— Game, of Florida. (H. G. Carleton) Outing, 29: 329.

— Note on the Psychology of. (E. Thorndike) Am. Natural. 33: 923.

— of Japan. (D. S. Jordan) Pop. Sci. Mo. 60: 76.

— of the Nile. (J. Anderson) Nature, 59: 399.

— Photographing. (R. W. Shufeldt) Overland, n. s. 33: 550.

— Poisonous, West Indian. (J. M. Rogers) Pop. Sci. Mo. 55: 680.

— Seven Senses of. (Matthias Dunn) Contemp. 76: 199.

Fish Fauna of the Woods Holl Region, 1899. (H. M. Smith) Science, n. s. 10: 878.

Fish Jam on Kelsey Creek. (W. L. Rideout) Overland, n. s. 34: 333.

Fish Lore. (B. C. Finch) Gent. M. n. s. 66: 558.

Fish Propagation in California. (A. V. La Motte) Overland, n. s. 32: 237.

Fish Supply, Our, and its Deficiencies. (A. H. Gouraud) No. Am. 168: 254.

Fish-warden of Madrid, The; a story. (B. Perry) Harper, 97: 423.

Fisher, Alexander, Enameller. (F. Miller) Art J. 50: 263.

— and his Work. (F. Miller) Studio (Lond.) 8: 149.

Fisher, A. Hugh, Exhibition of Works by, 1901. Artist (N. Y.) 30: 22.

Fisher, Joshua, of Dedham, Mass., Next of Kin to. (A. Ames) New Eng. M. n. s. **17**: 56.

Fisher, Sydney George, with portrait. Bk. News, **15**: 500.

Fisher, S. Melton, and his Work. (A. C. R. Carter) Art J. **51**: 235.

Fisher Folk, Dutch. (W. E. Carlin) Outing, **38**: 526.

Fisher Life, Scotch, as it was and is. Chamb. J. **76**: 541.

"Fisher's Ghost," The Truth about. (A. Lang) Blackw. **162**: 78.

Fisheries, Atlantic, Question of. (P. D. M'Grath) No. Am. **167**: 729.

— Decay of our Sea-. Quar. **194**: 83.

— Deep-sea, New England, Decadence of. (J. W. Collins) Harper, **94**: 608.

— English. (M. Dunn) Contemp. **80**: 58.

— Reciprocity and the British North American. (D. W. Prowse) Nation, **72**: 29.

— Stockholm Conference on, Proposals of. (H. M. Kyle) Nature, **61**: 151.

Fisherman's Luck. (H. van Dyke) Cent. **36**: 171.

Fishery Legislation, International. (O. Pettersson) 19th Cent. **45**: 295.

Fishin' for Fiddlers. (G. V. Triplett) Outing, **34**: 596.

Fishing. Outing, **36**: 448.

— Amateur Rod-making. (H. C. Daniels) Outing, **33**: 610.

— and Hunting. (F. H. Risteen) Outing, **36**: 507.

— and Trapping. (C. C. Mann) Nat'l M. (Bost.) **12**: 132.

— April Fishing Camp in Missouri. (E. B. Quisenberry) Outing, **34**: 35.

— as a School of Virtues. (W. H. Johnson) Outing, **38**: 215.

— Baits and Still-fishing. (H. C. Daniels) Outing, **34**: 33.

— Below the Great Lakes. (L. Hubbard, jr.) Outing, **38**: 315.

— Evolution of the "Kentucky Reel." (Dr. J. A. Henshall) Outing, **37**: 288.

— Fly. (S. Buxton) 19th Cent. **45**: 113. — Liv. Age, **220**: 613. Same art. Ecl. M. **132**: 605. — (H. Gove) Outing, **36**: 242.

— Fly-casting. (G. E. Goodwin) Outing, **34**: 157.

— — Practical. (J. H. Keene) Outing, **36**: 367.

— for Tuna in the Pacific. (H. A. Vachell) Pall Mall M. **16**: 353.

— Greatest Game. (M. Foster) Munsey, **24**: 473.

— in Florida Waters. (W. W. De Hart) Outing, **33**: 604.

— in Hawaiian Waters. ("Buck Waterhouse") Outing, **33**: 515.

— in the Middle West. (E. Hough) Outing, **38**: 495.

— in the Solway Firth. (A. J. Gordon) Belgra. **96**: 426.

— in West Africa. (M. H. Kingsley) National, **29**: 213. Same art. Ecl. M. **128**: 773.

— Leaves from a Test Angler's Diary. (G. A. B. Dewar) Longm. **35**: 149.

— Making of the Artificial Fly. (J. H. Keene) Outing, **37**: 634.

— Night, in Mountain Tarns. (W. T. Palmer) Spec. **85**: 299.

— of Japan and Geographical Distribution of Fishes. (D. S. Jordan) Science, n. s. **14**: 545.

— on the Spleuchan. (R. C. Drummond) Argosy, **65**: 533.

— Rare Books on. (J. N. Hilliard) Bk. Buyer, **17**: 36.

— Sea Angling and Legislation. (F. G. Aflalo) J. Soc. Arts, **48**: 95.

— Sea-, A bit of. (E. W. Sandys) Outing, **32**: 511.

— — The Devil-fish. (M. Dunn) Pall Mall M. **24**: 528.

Fishing, Sea-, in Californian Waters. (H. A. Vachell) Overland, n. s. **30**: 483.

— — in France. (F. G. Aflalo) Eng. Illust. **20**: 365.

— — off San Clemente. (S.-M. Beard) Outing, **30**: 257.

— The September Grayling. Temp. Bar, **111**: 548.

— Trolling in Norway. (P. A. W. Henderson) Blackw. **164**: 629. Same art. Ecl. M. **131**: 838.

— Trout, in England. (T. W. Lech) Pall Mall M. **11**: 507.

— Where the Big Fish feed. Macmil. **83**: 266.

— Woman's Outing on the Nepigon. (Bergthora) Outing, **30**: 583.

Fishing Club, Oldest in the World. (L. Hubbard, jr.) Outing, **37**: 520.

Fishing Convert, A; a tale. (O. Kemp) Outing, **34**: 190.

Fishing Industry of U.S. (G. A. Copeland) Chaut. **26**: 387.

Fishing Schooner, Evolution of. (J. W. Collins) New Eng. M. n. s. **18**: 336.

Fishing Sketches, Florida. (M. T. Townsend) Outing, **33**: 390.

Fisk, Mary Isabel. Writer, **14**: 41.

Fiske, John. Atlan. **88**: 282. — (G. L. Beer) Critic, **39**: 117. — Ath. '01, **2**: 95. — Dial (Ch.) **31**: 47. — Outl. **68**: 619. — With portrait. (G. Gunton) Gunton's M. **21**: 161. — With portrait. (J. G. Brooks) R. of Rs. (N. Y.) **24**: 175. — With portrait. (E. Cary) Bk. Buyer, **23**: 15.

— American Revolution. Atlan. **79**: 269.

— and the History of New York. (Mrs. S. Van Rensselaer) No. Am. **173**: 171.

— and the New Thought. (R. O. Mason) Arena, **25**: 365.

— as a School Boy. (F. W. Osborn) Educa. **22**: 206.

— as a Thinker. (J. Royce) Harv. Grad. M. **10**: 23.

— Historical Service of. (A. B. Hart) Internat. Mo. **4**: 558.

— Histories of. (L. Abbott) Outl. **69**: 709.

— Popularizer. (R. Ogden) Nation, **73**: 26.

— Simplicity of. Atlan. **88**: 717.

— Sketch of his Life, with portrait. (W. R. Thayer) Harv. Grad. M. **10**: 33.

— Through Nature to God. (W. N. Guthrie) Sewanee, **8**: 12. — Poet-Lore, **11**: 309.

Fiske, Mrs. Minnie M., as Becky Sharp. (J. L. Gilder) Critic, **35**: 897.

Fitch, W. Clyde. (J. Ranken Towse) Critic, **38**: 225. — (E. F. Coward) Bk. Buyer, **17**: 118.

— Cowboy and the Lady. (M. Beerbohm) Sat. R. **87**: 718.

Fitch, Zachary, of Reading, Mass., Descendants of. (E. S. Stearns) N. E. Reg. **55**: 288, 400.

Fitchett, Rev. W. H. Deeds that won the Empire. (J. R. Spears) Bk. Buyer, **17**: 52.

Fithian, Philip Vickers. Journal and Letters. (A. A. Woodhull) Nation, **73**: 114. — (P. F. Bicknell) Dial (Ch.) **30**: 301. — Am. Hist. R. **5**: 290.

Fitton, Michael. (W. J. Fletcher) Temp. Bar, **114**: 350.

Fitzgerald, Lord Edward. (I. A. Taylor) 19th Cent. **43**: 214. — (B. Torrey) Atlan. **86**: 617. — Acad. **59**: 75.

— and T. E. Brown. Macmil. **83**: 212.

— as a Letter-writer. Acad. **61**: 583, 619.

— Glyde's Life of. Acad. **58**: 327.

— Last Days of. (K. F. Purdon) Cornh. **78**: 453.

— Letters to Fanny Kemble. Sewanee, **4**: 73.

— Omar Khayyám at the Caxton Club, Chicago. (W. I. Way) Bookman, **8**: 446.

Fitzgerald, George Francis. (R. Lydekker) Nature, **63**: 445.

FitzGerald, Mrs. Lucy Barton. Acad. **55**: 380.

Fitzgerald, Lady Pamela. (I. A. Taylor) Eng. Illust. **19**: 331.

Fitzgibbon, John, Earl of Clare. Ed. R. **190**: 70.

Florida, Mammals of, O. Bangs on. Am. Natural. 32: 433.

— Purchase of, by the United States. (F. S. Barton) Lippinc. 64: 787.

— Raising Winter Vegetables in. (R. G. Robinson) Lippinc. 61: 246.

— Sea-monster of. (A. E. Verrill) Am. Natural. 31: 304.

— South. (R. G. Robinson) Lippinc. 59: 101, 229.

— Storms in. (R. G. Robinson) Lippinc. 61: 551.

— A Tourist in. (F. Furbish) Nat'l M. (Bost.) 8: 40.

— The Tourist Land. (A. W. Tarbell) Nat'l M. (Bost.) 5: 491.

— West, and its Relation to the Historical Cartography of the United States. J. H. Univ. Stud. 16: no. 5. See West Florida.

— Winter Trip in. Outing, 31: 585.

Florida Farm, A. (F. Whitmore) Atlan. 81: 498.

"Florida," Confederate Steamer, Eventful Cruise of. (G. T. Sinclair) Cent. 34: 417.

Flotilla Craft. (J. H. Burton) Un. Serv. M. 18: 367.

Flotsam ; a story. (H. Vandervell) Idler, 14: 637.

Flotsam and Jetsam. (Mrs. A. Baldwin) Good Words, 42: 406.

Flour and Flour Milling. (B. C. Church and F. W. Fitzpatrick) Cosmopol. 26: 495.

— Whole-wheat Flour the Perfect Food. (Lucy Hall-Brown) Outl. 59: 177.

Flournoy, M. From India to the Planet Mars. (J. H. Hyslop) No. Am. 171: 734.

Flower, Sir William. Spec. 83: 47.

Flower, William Henry. (E. Ray Lankester) Nature, 60: 252. — Knowl. 22: 178. — Geog. J. 14: 217.

Flower o' the Clove ; a tale. (G. Festing) Argosy, 72: 269.

Flower of the Flock ; a story. (W. E. Norris) Temp. Bar, 119: 1–587. 120: 127–457.

Flower of the Flock ; a story. (G. Parker) Pall Mall M. 22: 500.

Flower of the Prairie Land ; a poem. (J. Duff) Canad. M. 13: 437.

Flower of Sleep. (F. German) Good Words, 42: 776.

Flower Arrangement, Japanese. (T. Wores) Scrib. M. 26: 205.

Flower Garden at Longleat, England. (R. S. Nichols) Archit. R. 8: 1.

— Hardy. (W. McK. Twombley) Garden & F. 10: 193.

— Renaissance of the. Spec. 82: 907.

Flower Observatory. (C. L. Doolittle) Pop. Astron. 5: 122.

Flower-wizard, The. (E. M. Thomas) New Eng. M. n. s. 24: 469.

Flower-work, Mrs. Delaney's. Strand, 18: 472.

Flowered Tea-set, The. (S. Swett) New Eng. M. n. s. 15: 631.

Flowering Plants. (R. L. Praeger) Knowl. 24: 281.

— English. (E. Phillpotts) Pall Mall M. 25: 99.

Flowers, Animated. Argosy, 68: 402.

— Arrangement of. (D. Root) Garden & F. 10: 83, 93, 103.

— Autumn, in the Pines. (M. Treat) Garden & F. 10: 411.

— Beauty of Early Wild. (F. S. Mathews) Chaut. 27: 238.

— Colors of. (H. Coupin) Pop. Sci. Mo. 55: 386.

— — Experiments on. (P. Q. Keegan) Nature, 61: 105.

— — Williams on. Am. Natural. 33: 905.

— Early. (C. S. Sargent) Garden & F. 10: 131.

— English, in an Egyptian Garden. (E. L. Butcher) Longm. 38: 465.

— Fashions in. (Lady A. Amherst) Longm. 30: 528. Same art. Ecl. M. 130: 25.

— German Wayside. (M. Todhunter) Westm. 155: 136.

Flowers, Impersonation of, on the Stage. Illus. (C. Wilhelm) M. of Art, 23: 1.

— in London — Natural and Artificial. (G. H. Pike) Good Words, 38: 607.

— in the Pave. (C. M. Skinner) Cent. 23: 310, 452, 619.'

— Language of. Sat. R. 92: 644.

— Monocotyledonous. (J. H. Lovell) Am. Natural. 33: 493.

— of the Grassfields. Liv. Age, 222: 788.

— of San Juan, The. (Katharine Lansing) Overland, n. s. 33: 418.

— Personified. (C. Wilhelm) M. of Art, 23: 187.

— Rare, Our Duty toward. Sat. R. 91: 731.

— Red and Blue Colorings of. (P. Q. Keegan) Nat. Sci. 12: 194.

— The Spring Revival among the. (F. S. Mathews) Chaut. 27: 127.

— Why we Love. (W. H. Hudson) Sat. R. 87: 296.

— Wild. (F. French) Outing, 38: 485.

— — for Cultivation. (Bessie L. Putnam) Educa. 19: 632.

— — in California : Redwood Blooms. (V. L. Boardman) Overland, n. s. 33: 427.

— — Romance of, Step's. (W. Canton) Good Words, 40: 717.

Floyd Obelisk, The. Nation, 72: 471.

Fluids, Compressible, Motion of. (J. W. Davis) Am. J. Sci. 162: 107.

Flunkeyism. Sat. R. 92: 203.

Fluorides, Cæsium-antimonious, and some other Double Halides of Antimony. (H. L. Wells and F. J. Metzger) Am. J. Sci. 161: 451.

Fluorine, Liquid. (C. F. Townsend) Knowl. 21: 31. — Nature, 56: 126. 57: 82.

— Moissan's Researches on. (H. F. Keller) J. Frankl. Inst. 152: 123.

Fly, The, "Syritta Pipiens." (W. Wesché) Knowl. 23: 33.

Flycatchers, Our Northern. (W. E. Cram) New Eng. M. n. s. 20: 417.

Fly-fisher's Aftermath, The. (H. T. Sheringham) Macmil. 84: 264.

Fly Leaf Rhymes and Decorations. (F. D. Bergen) New Eng. M. n. s. 23: 505.

Fly-wheels, Development of. (C. H. Benjamin) Cassier, 18: 248.

— Rolling Mill. (J. Fritz) Cassier, 16: 129.

Flying, Art of. (W. E. G. Fisher) Fortn. 72: 746.

— Experiments in. (O. Chanute) McClure, 15: 127.

Flying Bishops, The. Macmil. 75: 298.

Flying Dutchman, The. (S. Bauditz) Liv. Age, 221: 420.

— a poem. (L. M. Sill) Cent. 36: 133.

Flying Horse, The ; Burmese Fairy Tale. Eng. Illust. 17: 39.

Flying Machine, The. (S. P. Langley) McClure, 9: 647.

— Danilewsky's. (H. C. Fyfe) Strand, 17: 596.

— The Long-sought. (A. P. Teros) Eng. Illust. 19: 3.

— of S. P. Langley. Strand, 13: 707.

Flying Machines. (O. Chanute) Indep. 52: 1058.

— Aerial Navigation. (O. Chanute) Cassier, 20: 111.

— Birds as. (F. A. Lucas) Pop. Sci. Mo. 57: 473.

— in 1896–97. Sat. R. 83: 672.

— The Newest. Eng. Illust. 20: 39.

— Possible. (G. L. O. Davidson) Sat. R. 84: 37. See Aerial Navigation.

Flying Squadron, The ; a story. (K. and H. Prichard) Cornh. 79: 201.

Flynt, Henry. (D. M. Wilson) New Eng. M. n. s. 23: 284.

Flynt, Josiah, pseud. See Willard, Josiah F.

Foa, Edouard. Geog. J. 18: 223.

Foam-fringe and the Winds. Spec. 86: 51. Same art. Ecl. M. 137: 522. Same art. Liv. Age, 230: 587.

Fodor, Joseph von. Nature, 63: 544.

Foerster, Ad. M., Music Composer and Teacher, with portrait. Music, 15: 460.

Foes in Law. (R. Broughton) Temp. Bar, 121: 1–473.

Fog, Can we do away with? (A. McAdie) No. Am. 164: 119.

— Possibilities of. (A. McAdie) Harper, 94: 263.

Fog and Dew Ponds. Spec. 87: 755.

Fog-sea, A, by Moonlight. Overland, n. s. 35: 333.

Fog-signalling on Our Railways. (V. L. Whitechurch) Good Words, 39: 173.

Fog Studies on Mount Tarnalpais. (A. McAdie) Pop. Sci. Mo. 59: 535.

Fogs and their Teaching. (J. M. Bacon) Contemp. 77: 533. Same art. Ecl. M. 135: 80. Same art. Liv. Age, 225: 407.

— Sea, of San Francisco, with photographs. (A. McAdie) Nat. Geog. M. 12: 108.

Fogazzaro, Antonio. (F. Aranjo) Liv. Age, 221: 645.

Foiled by a Violin; a story. (H. J. T. Hill) Canad. M. 17: 320.

Foix, Gaston de La Chasse. (W. A. Baillie-Grohman) Monthly R. 5, no. 3: 140.

Folk-life, African. (H. Chatelain) J. Am. Folk-Lore, 10: 21.

Folk-lore, Armenian, Items of, Collected in Boston. (G. D. Edwards) J. Am. Folk-Lore, 12: 97.

— Dorset. (H. C. Marsh) Folk-Lore, 10: 478, 489. 11: 107.

— Ethnological Data in. (G. L. Gomme) Folk-Lore, 10: 129. — A reply. (A. Nutt) Folk-Lore, 10: 143.

— Greek. (W. Metcalfe) Scot. R. 29: 276.

— Icelandic. (Olaf Davidson) Scot. R. 36: 312.

— in the Legends of the Punjab. (R. C. Temple) Folk-Lore, 10: 384.

— in Schools, German Discussions on. (A. F. Chamberlain) Pedagog. Sem. 7: 347.

— Lessons of. (J. W. Powell) Am. Anthrop. 2: 1.

— Malay. (R. C. Ford) Pop. Sci. Mo. 51: 239.

— Maryland, Collection of. (Mrs. W. R. Bullock) J. Am. Folk-Lore, 11: 7.

— North American. Nature, 64: 425.

— of the Alleghanies. (F. A. Doughty) Pop. Sci. Mo. 55: 390.

— of Great Britain. (A. Nutt) Folk-Lore, 10: 71.

— of Staffordshire. (C. S. Burne) Folk-Lore, 7: 366.

— Persian. (E. C. Sykes) Folk-Lore, 12: 261.

— Relating to Women, Bibliography of. (I. C. Chamberlain) J. Am. Folk-Lore, 12: 32.

— Some Entertaining. (G. M. Hyde) Bk. Buyer, 17: 232.

Folk-lore Parallels and Coincidences. (M. J. Walhouse) Folk-Lore, 8: 196.

Folk-Lore Society, Amer., Memoirs of. J. Am. Folk-Lore, 12: 55.

Folk-Lore Theories, Rival. Acad. 52: 124.

Folk-melody. (H. F. Gilbert) Music, 11: 268.

Folk-rhymes of Places. (A. L. Salmon) Gent. M. n. s. 65: 67. 66: 614.

Folk-song, The Sponsor of. (T. Nunns) Temp. Bar, 111: 527.

Folk-songs, Forms spontaneously Assumed by. (J. C. Fillmore) Music, 12: 289.

— from Modern Greece. Poet-Lore, 9: 353.

— of White Russia. (Ludvik Kuba) Music, 15: 162.

Folk-tales, English, in America. (E. J. Cooke) J. Am. Folk-Lore, 12: 126.

— from the Ægean. (W. R. Paton) Folk-Lore, 10: 502. 11: 113, 333. 12: 317.

Folk-tales from Georgia. (Emma M. Backus) J. Am. Folk-Lore, 13: 19.

— from Lesbos. (W. R. Paton) Folk-Lore, 10: 495.

— The Green Lady. Folk-Lore, 7: 411.

— Korean. (E. B. Landis) J. Am. Folk-Lore, 10: 282.

— The Quicken Tree of Dubhros. (L. L. Duncan) Folk-Lore, 7: 321.

Folkestone, Excavations at Cæsar's Camp near. (Pitt-Rivers) Archæol. 47: 429.

Folkschauspiel at Brixlegg. Month, 90: 71.

Folly of Albertina; a story. (A. Merry) Idler, 13: 367.

Folly of Women; a tale. (C. Smith) Argosy, 66: 239.

Font, The, at Zedelghem, near Bruges. Reliquary, 38: 259.

Fontainebleau, Forest of, A Tramp through. (Hannah Lynch) Good Words, 41: 464. Same art. Liv. Age, 226: 661.

— Palace of; Notes by Russell Sturgis. Archit. R. 10: 129.

Fontane, Theodor. Acad. 55: 555.

— Child-life. (L. Wolffsohn) Temp. Bar, 112: 173.

Fontenelle, with portrait. (L. Levy-Bruhl) Open Court, 12: 705.

Fontenoy, Battle of, Despatches relative to. (E. M. Lloyd) Eng. Hist. R. 12: 523.

Fonthill, Caliph of. (C. Whibley) New R. 16: 59.

Fonts, Some Derbyshire. (G. Le Blanc Smith) Reliquary, 41: 267.

Food and its Preparation in Modern Palestine. (E. W. G. Masterman) Bib. World, 17: 407.

— Artificial. (S. Williamson) Nature, 58: 368.

— Beans, Peas, and other Legumes as. (M. H. Abel) J. Mil. Serv. Inst. 28: 96.

— Comparative Amounts used by Different Nations. (G. B. Waldron) McClure, 12: 16.

— for Powder. (J. H. Burton) Un. Serv. M. 20: 490.

— for Troops, Inspection of. (J. J. Miller) J. Mil. Serv. Inst. 18: 128.

— Frozen. (L. W. Lillingston) Good Words, 39: 237. Same art. Ecl. M. 131: 382. Same art. Liv. Age, 217: 598.

— How it is used in the Body. (W. O. Atwater) Cent. 32: 246.

— Physiology of Alimentation. (A. Dastre) Chaut. 28: 460.

— Pure, Development of Legislation for. (W. D. Bigelow) Science, n. s. 7: 505.

— — Urgent Need of. (H. B. Mason) Outl. 65: 400.

— — Vital Question of. (H. B. Mason) R. of Rs. (N. Y.) 21: 67.

— The Story of the Scales. (I. Bevier) Chaut. 30: 375.

— which Fails to Feed. (L. Windmüller) No. Am. 169: 694.

— World's Food Supply. (E. S. Holden) Munsey, 21: 828.

Food Poisoning. (V. C. Vaughan) Pop. Sci. Mo. 56: 47. See Adulteration.

Food Preservatives, Use and Abuse of. (S. Rideal) J. Soc. Arts, 48: 384.

Food-stuffs as Contraband of War. (T. Barclay) Contemp. 77: 243. — (E. Maxey) Am. Law R. 34: 205.

Food Substances, Reserve, in the Stems of certain Deciduous Trees, Winter Condition of. (E. M. Wilcox) Am. J. Sci. 156: 69.

Food Supplies of the Prairies and the Orient. (W. R. Lighton) World's Work, 1: 655.

Food Supply, Foreign Competition in. (E. E. Williams) New R. 16: 13–645. — Reply. (R. H. Rew) New R. 17: 183.

— in Time of War. (S. L. Murray) J. Mil. Serv. Inst. 29: 254.

Food Supply of England, in Time of War. (T. A. Le Mesurier) Westm. 147: 658. — (A. D. Noyes) Nation, 64: 277. — (E. E. Williams) Sat. R. 85: 738–839. — (W. Crookes) Science, n. s. 8: 561, 601.
See also Breadstuffs.

Fool and his Wife. (W. R. A. Wilson) New Eng. M. n. s. 17: 374.

Fool or Angel? a story. (M. Diver) Temp. Bar, 110: 384.

Foolish Doings of Amy Finch, The; a story. (F. Langbridge) Ecl. M. 134: 49. Same art. Liv. Age, 223: 505.

Fool's Gold; a sketch. (P. Pastnor) Outing, 34: 151.

Fools' Paradise. (Wolf von Schierbrand) Cosmopol. 22: 406.

Fool's Wisdom. (L. H. Yates) Good Words, 42: 317.

Football. (G. H. Brooke) Outing, 35: 12. — (H. C. Pierson) Outing, 31: 185.

— Army and Navy. (H. S. Graves) Outing, 37: 453.

— Canadian and United States Rugby. (G. W. Orton) Canad. M. 10: 57.

— Cherokee Indian. (A. G. Robinson) Outing, 31: 278.

— Coach's Relation to the Players. (W. C. Forbes) Outing, 37: 336.

— College, 25 Years ago. (W. J. Henderson) Outing, 37: 15.

— Development in 1901. (W. Camp) Outing, 39: 217.

— English, in 1896–97. New R. 16: 572.

— English and American Rugby. (J. Corbin) Outing, 39: 101.

— Ethical Functions of. (C. F. Thwing) No. Am. 173: 627.

— in Armor. (C. E. Cook) Strand, 13: 285.

— in England. Sat. R. 89: 261.

— Incidents of the Present College Game. (Freeman Furbush) Nat'l M. (Bost.) 7: 161.

— Making of a Rugby Player. (G. W. Ross) Canad. M. 12: 302.

— Middle Western. (H. L. Williams) Outing, 39: 206.

— Need of Different Rules for Professionals and Amateurs. Sat. R. 91: 232.

— of 1896. (W. Camp) Outing, 31: 26.

— of 1897. (W. Camp) Outing, 31: 133. 33: 40.

— of 1898. (W. Camp) Outing, 33: 189. 35: 69.

— of '99, Forecast of. (W. Camp) Outing, 35: 173.

— Present Condition of. (W. Camp) Indep. 53: 2394.

— Story of. (E. B. Bloss) Outing, 39: 178.

— Symposium on. (W. Camp and others) Outing, 37: 171.

Football Madness, The. (E. Ensor) Contemp. 74: 751. Same art. Liv. Age, 219: 681. Same art. Ecl. M. 132: 93.

Football Nations. (H. Stuart) Blackw. 169: 489.

Foot-binding. Social Revolution in China. Spec. 80: 406.

Footprints; a Christmas story. (O. B. Hoblit) Outl. 69: 1026.

Foote, Arthur, Pianist and Composer. Music, 13: 528.

Foote, Mary Hallock, as Illustrator. (R. Armstrong) Critic, 37: 131.

For Better, for Worse; a story. (M. Elliston) Pall Mall M. 21: 77.

"For Better, for Worse." (Amelia E. Barr) Good Words, 40: 339.

For the Cause; a story. (H. Elliot) Temp. Bar, 116: 227.

For Conscience' Sake; a story. (E. E. Taylor) Sund. M. 25: 165.

For a Consideration. (C. Mullett) Temp. Bar, 116: 365.

For the Credit of his Color; a story. (H. Bindloss) Gent. M. n. s. 64: 417. Same art. Liv. Age, 226: 50.

For Cuba Libre; a story. (Elizabeth Harman) Midland, 8: 447.

For Ever; a story. (R. A. J. Walling) Ecl. M. 134: 115. Same art. Liv. Age, 223: 524.

Forever and a Day; a song. (T. B. Aldrich) Atlan. 80: 471.

Forever if Need be; a story. (E. E. Rexford) Nat'l M. (Bost.) 8: 3, 134.

For the French Lilies. (I. N. Whiteley) Lippinc. 63: 147.

For the Good of his Soul. (A. French) New Eng. M. n. s. 17: 418.

For the Hand of Haleem. (N. Duncan) Atlan. 86: 347.

For his Own People. (A. Knapp) Lippinc. 60: 708.

For his Sake; a story. (D. H. Talmadge) Munsey, 26: 246.

"For Love;" a story. (James Cassidy) Gent. M. n. s. 62: 350.

For Love of the King; a story. Idler, 17: 260.

For Love of Tony; a story. (E. M. Moon) Argosy, 68: 280.

For my Sake; a poem. (T. F. Mayo) Argosy, 65: 512.

"For the Nonce," "Purposely," and the like. (F. Hall) Nation, 64: 104.

"For the Nones" in Chaucer. (R. M. Allen) Nation, 64: 203.

For One Night only, a Psychological Study. (C. R. Kennedy) Idler, 13: 169.

For the Sake of Appearances; a story. (L. Wilbar) Nat'l M. (Bost.) 6: 370.

For the Sake of Humanity; a story. (Emma S. Jones) Midland, 11: 41.

For the Sake of a Kiss. (A. W. Arnold) Chamb. J. 77: Extr. no. p. 1.

For the Señora. (Mrs. S. Crowninshield) Lippinc. 66: 589.

For the Third Time of Asking; a story. (N. M. Marris) Temp. Bar, 122: 92.

Forbes, Archibald. Ath. '00, 1: 433.

Forbes, Elizabeth Stanhope, Paintings and Etchings of. Studio (Lond.) 4: 186.

Forbes, John Murray. (E. W. Emerson) Atlan. 84: 382. — Lit. W. (Bost.) 30: 433.

Forbes, Stanhope A., Artist, with portrait. (N. Garstin) Studio (Internat.) 14: 81.

Force. (Emma M. Caillard) Good Words, 38: 314.

— Reign of. (M. Twycross) Westm. 154: 609.

— The Use of. Outl. 64: 386.

Forces of the Universe; the dynamics of silence. (H. Frank) Arena, 22: 211.

Ford, Daniel Sharp, pub. of "Youth's Companion," with portrait. (M. Mannering) Nat'l M. (Bost.) 11: 476.

Ford, Edward Onslow. (M. H. Dixon) Art J. 50: 294.

— Bust of Queen Victoria. M. of Art, 22: 618.

Ford, John. Acad. 60: 429.

— Plays. (H. M. Sanders) Gent. M. 66: 169.

Ford, Paul Leicester, with portrait. Bk. News, 15: 237.

— at Home. (L. Swift) Critic, 33: 343.

— Janice Meredith. Critic, 36: 27.

Foreground Studies, Photographic. (C. F. Townsend) Studio (Lond.) 4: 155.

Foreign Competition. (G. Gibbon) Westm. 147: 311.

Foreign Exchange Bank Clerk, his Training and Duties. Bank. M. (N. Y.) 63: 707.

Foreign News and the Press. (R. Ogden) Atlan. 86: 390.

Foreign Relations, The Key to Good. (A. G. Sedgwick) Nation, 65: 161.

Foreign Words, On Naturalization of. (B. Matthews) Bookman, 4: 443.

Foreigner, The. (S. O. Jewett) Atlan. 86: 152.

Foreigner in the Farmyard, The; a story. (W. F. Shannon) Idler, **12**: 824.

Fore-names, Contractions of. Library, **1**: 302.

Forenoon and Afternoon. (C. F. Dowd) Pop. Sci. Mo. **56**: 492.

Forerunners of Empire; a story. (M. O. Wilcox) McClure, **12**: 189.

Forest, Fascination of the. (H. Clifford) Macmil. **81**: 90. Same art. Liv. Age, **224**: 188.

— The Submerged, at Leasowe. Chamb. J. **74**: 382.

— Summer in the. (W. H. Hudson) Longm. **35**: 263. Same art. Ecl. M. **135**: 110.

Forest Culture of To-day. (G. E. Walsh) New Eng. M. n. s. **16**: 408.

Forest Fables. (A. Coll) Outing, **37**: 651. **38**: 74, 400.

Forest Fires. (H. Gannett) Forum, **26**: 406.

— Relation of Forests and. (Gifford Pinchot) Nat. Geog. M. **10**: 393.

Forest Leaves; a poem. (W. H. Taylor) Canad. M. **12**: 24.

Forest Management in the Adirondacks. (V. M. Spalding) Science, n. s. **13**: 542.

— in Maine. (Austin Cary) Am. Arch. **66**: 4, 12.

Forest Park Farm. (E. B. Abercrombie) Outing, **30**: 81.

Forest Pleasures. Sat. R. **92**: 235.

Forest Policy for the U. S. (C. S. Sargent and others) Science, **5**: 893.

— in Suspense. Atlan. **80**: 268.

Forest Preservation. (T. Roosevelt) Am. Arch. **74**: 85.

— in the State of New York. (C. Reynolds) New Eng. M. n. s. **19**: 203.

Forest Problems in the U. S. (H. S. Graves) Yale R. **10**: 236.

Forest Reservations, Our. (J. W. Toumey) Pop. Sci. Mo. **59**: 115. — Critic, **30**: 240.

— Camping in; the Woodlands of Southern California. (J. H. Barber) Overland, n. s. **33**: 449.

— U. S. National. (C. S. Sargent) Garden & F. **10**: 221. — (F. H. Newell) Nat. Geog. M. **8**: 177. — Nat. Geog. M. **11**: 369. — (C. D. Walcott) Pop. Sci. Mo. **52**: 456.

— — Administration of. (C. S. Sargent) Garden & F. **10**: 291.

— — Congress and the. (C. S. Sargent) Garden & F. **10**: 101, 141.

— — New. (C. S. Sargent) Garden & F. **10**: 81.

— — Peril to. (J. B. Bishop) Nation, **66**: 358.

— — Policy of. (B. E. Fernow) Science, **5**: 489.

— — A Year in. (W. C. Bartlett) Overland, n. s. **35**: 243.

Forest Reserve, N. Y. State. Am. Arch. **70**: 22.

Forest Reserve, Appalachian, Proposed. (W. J. McGee) World's Work, **3**: 1374.

Forest Runner, The; a story. (S. E. White) McClure, **18**: 113.

Forest Schoolmaster. (P. Rosegger) Critic, **37**: 453. — Critic, **38**: 61-400.

Forestalled; a story. (G. G. Farquhar) Chamb. J. **74**: 622.

Forestation, Relations to Water-supply. (H. M. Wilson) Engin. M. **14**: 807.

Forester, The, and his Work. (P. W. Ayres) Outl. **68**: 301.

Forestry and Geology in New Jersey. (A. Hollick) Am. Natural. **33**: 1, 110.

— the Anticipated Scarcity of Timber. (A. Ransom) Gent. M. n. s. **67**: 56.

— British, and its Improvement. Sat. R. **92**: 394.

— — The Sad Plight of. (Sir H. Maxwell) 19th Cent. **50**: 564.

— Bureau of. Science, n. s. **14**: 115.

— Deforestation in China, Effects of. (F. L. Garrison) J. Frankl. Inst. **152**: 141.

Forestry for Beauty and Use. Chamb. J. **77**: 677.

— Future of Cut-over Timber Lands. (M. Mannering) Nat'l M. (Bost.) **14**: 402.

— in Great Britain. Nature, **63**: 565.

— in Pennsylvania. Garden & F. **10**: 261.

— in relation to Physical Geography and Engineering. (J. Gifford) J. Frankl. Inst. **146**: 1.

— Indian. (D. Brandis) Nature, **63**: 597.

— its Place in High School Instruction. (J. Gifford) School R. **9**: 560.

— National. (D. E. Hutchins) J. Soc. Arts, **48**: 22.

— N. Y. State College of. (B. E. Fernow) Science, n. s. **8**: 494. — Am. Natural. **32**: 875.

— Private and State. (C. A. Schenck) Garden & F. **10**: 232, 252, 262.

— Roth's Forestry Conditions and Interests of Wisconsin. Am. Natural. **32**: 603.

Forestry Idyl. (M. S. Paden) Lippinc. **59**: 262.

Forestry Problems of the San Joaquin. (C. H. Shinn) Overland, n. s. **34**: 152.

Forests, Administration of, European. (A. B. Bibb) Am. Arch. v. **67**-70.

— American. (J. Muir) Atlan. **80**: 145.

— and Sheep. (E. V. Wilcox) Forum, **31**: 311.

— and Water Supply of White Mts. (C. S. Sargent) Garden & F. **10**: 450.

— Canadian, in Winter. (F. Remington) Harper, **98**: 62.

— The Church as a Protector of. (R. B. Richardson) Nation, **73**: 183.

— Destruction of. Spec. **86**: 343.

— Devastation of. (E. A. Fruhr) Chamb. J. **77**: 70.

— Distribution of. (Bittinger) Science, n. s. **9**: 690.

— English. (S. H. Dunn) Month, **94**: 488.

— from an Economic Standpoint. (A. Chamberlain) New Eng. M. n. s. **17**: 766.

— How India has saved her. (E. K. Robinson) Cent. **34**: 628.

— Replanting of. (E. S. Hammatt) Am. Arch. **62**: 81.

— Royal, of England. (F. Reddall) Overland, n. s. **34**: 416.

Forfeit to the Gods; a story. (T. A. Janvier) Cosmopol. **31**: 593. **32**: 89, 211.

Forgery and Kindred Frauds. Bank. M. (Lond.) **66**: 150.

— Literary, Ethics of. (E. Lawless) 19th Cent. **41**: 84. Same art. Liv. Age, **212**: 613.

Forget me, Death; a poem. (J. L. Allen) Acad. **52**: 448.

Forgiveness, Ethics of. (H. Rashdall) Internat. J. Ethics, **10**: 193.

Forgiveness of Creegan; a story. (C. T. Brady) Harper, **101**: 845.

Forgotten Millions, The. II. John Gilley. (C. W. Eliot) Cent. **37**: 120.

Forgotten Pilgrimage, A. (E. C. Peixotto) Scrib. M. **30**: 691.

Forgotten Trail; a story. (Phoebe Lyde) Cosmopol. **31**: 422.

Form, Mould of. (J. Hawkwood) Belgra. **92**: 413.

Form-design in Applied Art. (H. Stannus) J. Soc. Arts, **46**: 885.

Formania Perforating the Cranial Region of a Permian Reptile, On. (E. C. Case) Am. J. Sci. **153**: 321.

Formosus, Pope, and Reordination. (H. Davis) Am. Cath. Q. **24**, no. 3: 1.

Forrest, Alexander. Geog. J. **18**: 223.

Forrest, Edwin, McCullough, and Myself. (Alice Kingsbury-Cooley) Overland, n. s. **29**: 604.

Forrest, Nathan Bedford, Gen. (T. F. Gailor) Sewanee, **9**: 1.

— at Brice's Cross-roads. (J. A. Wyeth) Harper, **98**: 530.

France, Army of, Independent Position of. Spec. 80: 535.

— — Military Terror in France. Spec. 81: 39, 140.

— — of To-day, 1900. Un. Serv. M. 21: 349.

— — Officers in. (A. D. Vandam) No. Am. 165: 722.

— — — and Navy. (H. W. Raymond) Chaut. 24: 524.

— — under the Empire. (F. H. Tyrrell) Un. Serv. M. 20: 581.

— — under the Bourbon Restoration. (F. H. Tyrrell) Un. Serv. M. 21: 265.

— — under the Consulate. (F. H. Tyrrell) Un. Serv. M. 20: 476.

— — under the Empire. (F. H. Tyrrell) Un. Serv. M. 21: 26.

— A Year's Service in. (C. Regnier) Cornh. 79: 472.

— Army Manœuvres in. (H. S. Somerset) 19th Cent. 48: 807. — (Fritz Morris) Cosmopol. 30: 339. — (J. M. Schofield) J. Mil. Serv. Inst. 3: 151. — (W. J. Volkmar) J. Mil. Serv. Inst. 5: 121.

— as it is To-day (1898). Lond. Q. 90: 102.

— A Bit of Old. (H. Monroe) Atlan. 86: 58.

— Bodley's. (B. W. Wells) Sewanee, 6: 443. — (M. Betham-Edwards) National, 31: 422. — (E. G. Johnson) Dial (Ch.) 24: 222. — Book R. 5: 399. — (M. J. Darmesteter) Contemp. 74: 60. — Ed. R. 187: 522. — Quar. 188: 160. — (G. Valbert) Liv. Age, 218: 817. — (J. W. Jenks) Yale R. 7: 220. — (J. B. Perkins) Bk. Buyer, 16: 516. — Church Q. 46: 265. — (C. W. Colby) Nation, 66: 267. — Atlan. 81: 845. — (J. H. Robinson) Pol. Sci. Q. 13: 687. — Acad. 53: 221. — (W. J. Ashley) Am. Hist. R. 4: 353.

— — Why it is not Right. (N. C. Frederiksen) Westm. 152: 277.

— British Companies in, Status of. (T. Barclay) Law Q. 13: 426.

— Cahiers of 1789 as an Evidence of a Compromise Spirit. (C. H. Lincoln) Am. Hist. R. 2: 225.

— Catholic, To-day (1897). (V. M. Crawford) Month, 89: 142.

— Cavalry Manœuvres, 1883. (W. J. Volkmar) J. Mil. Serv. Inst. 5: 72.

— A Century of Civilization in. (P. Farrally) Cath. World, 68: 819.

— Chamber of Deputies, Composition of. (A. D. Vandam) Sat. R. 86: 138.

— Church and State since the Concordat. (J. Legrand) Contemp. 79: 682.

— Civil War in. (F. A. Maxse) National, 33: 734.

— Clergy of, Evangelical Movement among. (A. Bourrier) Contemp. 75: 677.

— Colonial Craze in. (G. Dounet) Fortn. 70: 864.

— Colonial Expansion of. (J. C. Bracq) Nat. Geog. M. 11: 225. — (C. Guy) Internat. Mo. 4: 511.

— Colonial Policy of. (A. Laugel) Nation, 69: 463.

— Colonial Weakness of. (J. Adye) 19th Cent. 45: 56.

— Colonies in the Far East. (H. E. Bourne) Yale R. 8: 8.

— Coming Revolution in. Contemp. 75: 106.

— Commerce and Manufactures of. (Y. Guyot) Chaut. 25: 480.

— Commerce of, Women and. (A. Cone) Contemp. 75: 710.

— Contradictions of Modern. (P. de Coubertin) Fortn. 69: 341, 977.

— Constitution of. (J. Kirkpatrick) Jurid. R. 9: 69.

— — Points in, compared with the American. (N. Grön) Arena, 18: 49.

— Country Life in. (G. W. Carryl) Outing, 38: 141.

— Cycling in. (S. Cross) Outing, 34: 3, 170, 253.

— Cycling thro'. (P. E. Jenks) Outing, 30: 457, 591. 31: 65, 145.

— Cycling Trip in. (E. R. Pennell) Lippinc. 65 : 777.

France, Cycling Trip in, Easter. (G. H. Leonard) Outing, 35: 598.

— Demoralization of. Contemp. 73: 305.

— Depopulation of. (J. Bertillon) Pop. Sci. Mo. 55: 676.

— Economic Life of. (E. D. Jones) Pop. Sci. Mo. 58: 287.

— Education in. (J. C. Bracq) New Eng. M. n. s. 22: 588.

— — Crisis in, 1900. (O. Guerlac) Nation, 70: 69.

— Elections of 1898. Spec. 80: 684-751.

— Elements of Stability in. Outl. 61: 807.

— England's Debt to. Temp. Bar, 119: 492.

— English Services in. (C. Middleton) Sund. M. 26: 620.

— English View of. (E. M. de Vogüe) Ecl. M. 137: 455. Same art. Liv. Age, 230: 613.

— "Entente" with. Fortn. 67: 311.

— A Few French Facts. (R. Davey) Fortn. 74: 268. Same art. Liv. Age, 227: 1.

— — A Few More. (R. Davey) Fortn. 76: 995.

— Financial Anxiety of. (W. R. Lawson) National, 38: 206.

— Financial Strain on. (W. R. Lawson) National, 32: 411.

— Finances; Budget of 1899. (A. Laugel) Nation, 69: 106.

— Gallia Devota. Macmil. 84: 200.

— Germany and England; Two French Views. (D. F. Hannigan) Westm. 147: 1.

— Glimpses of Life in. (C. Johnson) Outl. 61: 47.

— Gorce's Histoire du Second Empire. (C. M. Andrews) Am. Hist. R. 5: 131.

— Greene's Plains and Uplands of Old. (H. T. Porter) Poet-Lore, 11: 436.

— History, Bibliography and Classification of. (H. R. Tedder) Library, 1: 15.

— — Directory, Consulate, Empire. (H. M. Stephens) Chaut. 25: 252.

— Impressions in; the Provincial Wife. (Mrs. V. R. Cruger) Cosmopol. 31: 403.

— in 1572-1899. (C. J. Langston) Argosy, 69: 269.

— in 1899. Blackw. 166: 543.

— — New Cabinet. (A. Laugel) Nation, 69: 66.

— — A Regenerated? Fortn. 72: 140.

— in 1901, Past Events and Coming Problems. (H. G. de Blowitz) No. Am. 172: 23.

— in International Commerce. (A. Lebon) Internat. Mo. 3: 252.

— Judicial System in. (A. de Calonne) 19th Cent. 45: 378. Same art. Liv. Age, 221: 150. Same art. Ecl. M. 132: 767.

— A Letter from. (A. F. Sanborn) Atlan. 85: 798.

— Liberation of, Doniol on. (C. W. Colby) Nation, 65: 521.

— Liberty of the Press in. (J. P. Wallis) 19th Cent. 45: 315.

— Life in a French Commune. (R. Donald) Contemp. 71: 424. Same art. Liv. Age, 213: 100. Same art. Ecl. M. 128: 649.

— Lycées of. (E. L. Hardy) School R. 7: 549. 8: 18.

— Military Espionage in. Quar. 187: 521.

— Military Justice in. (E. L. Godkin) Nation, 69: 349.

— Military Situation in, 1884. (J. A. Lockwood) J. Mil. Serv. Inst. 11: 428.

— Military Terror in. (L. J. Maxse) National, 31: 745.

— Ministerial Crisis in, 1876. Am. Hist. R. 6: 765.

— Ministerial Instability. Sat. R. 87: 774.

— Modern. (H. G. Keene) Westm. 150: 390.

— Modern Government. (H. de Balzac) No. Am. 171: 769.

— Modern History and Historians in. (P. de Coubertin) R. of Rs. (N. Y.) 20: 43.

— National Debt of. (J. Roche) No. Am. 173: 632.

Francis Joseph, Emperor. (E. I. Prime-Stevenson) Outl. 66: 567. — (S. Brooks) Chaut. 28: 153. — Liv. Age, 220: 288.

— the Beloved Monarch. (C. F. Dewey) Cosmopol. 25: 377.

— Fifty Years of. (S. Brooks) Harper, 98: 310.

— Franz Josef's Dream. (C. Johnston) Arena, 21: 228.

Francis, M. E. [Mrs. Francis Blundell]. The Duenna of a Genius. Bk. Buyer, 16: 525.

Francis of Assisi. (K. Little) Good Words, 38: 377, 478. — Acad. 52: 318. — Acad. 56: 237. — Quar. 189: 1.

— and the Mazarinus MS. (F. Andrew) Dub. R. 125: 144.

— and the Religious Revival in the 13th Century. (Father Cuthbert) Am. Cath. Q. 25: 657.

— and Spiritual Heroism. Spec. 85: 798.

— Last Days of. (K. Little) Sund. M. 26: 754.

— Sabatier's Life of. (H. D. Rawnsley) Contemp. 74: 505. — (C. A. Scott) Crit. R. 8: 434.

Francis Gordon ; a study. (G. S. Street) Monthly R. 5, no. 3: 130.

Francis Letters ; ed. by Beata Francis and Eliza Keary. Sat. R. 91: 740.

Franciscans, Decrees of. (A. G. Little) Eng. Hist. R. 13: 703.

Francisco and Francisca. (Grace E. Channing) Scrib. M. 26: 277.

Francisco the Filipino. (H. C. Rowland) Outl. 67: 359.

Franco-Prussian War, 1870-71. Un. Serv. M. 14: 658.

— Battlefields of. (W. T. Sherman) Cent. 36: 278.

— Extracts from History between 1870-71. (G. Weitzel) J. Mil. Serv. Inst. 3: 1, 195, 417.

— Lessons of. (F. Maurice) J. Mil. Serv. Inst. 16: 581.

— Rousset's History of. (A. Laugel) Nation, 69: 443.

— von Moltke on, 1892. J. Mil. Serv. Inst. 13: 189.

François Lebœuf, the Old Voyageur ; a sketch. (G. Fisk) Canad. M. 13: 160.

Franconia, Autumn in. (B. Torrey) Atlan. 83: 57, 207.

— A Day in. (B. Torrey) Indep. 52: 1423.

— May in. (B. Torrey) Atlan. 85: 628.

Frangipani Ring, The. Ecl. M. 129: 467.

— Thode on. (E. K. Dunton) Dial (Ch.) 30: 227.

Frankie's Wooing ; a story. (L. D. Mitchell) Outing, 30: 266.

Frankland, Sir Edward. Nature, 60: 372.

Franklin, Benjamin, with portraits. (W. P. Trent) McClure, 8: 273.

— and Rattlesnakes. (P. L. Ford) Nation, 67: 165.

— and the Royal Society. (N. D. Davis) Nation, 66: 222.

— as Genealogist. (J. W. Jordan) Pennsyl. M. 23: 1.

— Autobiographies of, Two Rival. (R. M. Bache) Pennsyl. M. 14: 195.

— Ballads of. (E. E. Hale) New Eng. M. n. s. 18: 505.

— J. J. Boyle's Statue of. Artist (N. Y.) 24: 56.

— Ceremonial Coat. (R. M. Bache) Pennsyl. M. 23: 444.

— Fictitious Address of King to Parliament, 1774. (P. L. Ford) Nation, 68: 108.

— Kite Experiment with Modern Apparatus. (A. McAdie) Pop. Sci. Mo. 51: 739.

— The Many-sided Franklin. (P. L. Ford) Cent. 35: 30-803. 36: 144-881.

— — Ford on. (F. N. Thorpe) Am. Hist. R. 5: 579.

— "Note for." Pennsyl. M. 22: 458.

— Prayer-book amended by. Pennsyl. M. 21: 502. — (R. M. Bache) Pennsyl. M. 21: 225.

— True, Fisher's. Sat. R. 90: 273.

— Unpublished Portrait of. (C. H. Hart) McClure, 8: 459.

Franklin, Sir John, and the Arctic. Blackw. 161: 238.

Franklin, S. R. Memories of a Rear-Admiral. (G. E. Belknap) Am. Hist. R. 4: 378.

Franklin, Mass. (J. C. Gallison) New Eng. M. n. s. 21: 321.

Franklin, Tennessee, Battle of, Cox on. (A. A. Woodhull) Nation, 66: 92.

Franklin Institute, The. (J. Birkinbine) Cassier, 15: 315.

— 75th Anniversary of. (J. Birkinbine) J. Frankl. Inst. 147: 81.

Franks, Sir A. W. J. Soc. Arts, 45: 698. — Ath. '97, 1: 720.

— Medallion Portrait in Bronze of. Reliquary, 39: 46.

Franks, Rebecca. Letter, Aug., 1781. Pennsyl. M. 23: 303.

Franz Josef I., King of Bohemia. (I. P. Stevenson) Indep. 53: 2036.

Franz Josef Land, Revised Map of. (R. Copeland) Geog. J. 10: 180.

— Thousand Days in the Arctic, by F. G. Jackson. Pop. Sci. Mo. 55: 705.

— Three Years' Exploration in. (F. G. Jackson and others) Geog. J. 11: 113.

Franz, Robert, with portrait. (A. M. Foerster) Music, 15: 19. — (M. Aronson) Music 13: 455. — (Anne K. Whitney) Music, 11: 370.

— Songs of. (S. P. Biden) Music, 19: 249.

Fraser, Allan, Art College of. (M. H. Spielmann) M. of Art, 25: 507.

Fraser, John Foster. (J. P. Blair) Strand, 16: 642.

Fraser, Sir William. Blackw. 163: 841.

Fraternalism vs. Paternalism in Government. (R. T. Ely) Cent. 33: 780.

Fratricide, A Famous. (M. A. S. Hume) Eng. Illust. 29: 499.

Fraud and Illegality, Setting up, under the General Denial. (S. D. Thompson) Am. Law R. 31: 535.

— and the Marriage Contract. (L. M. Friedman) Am. Law R. 32: 568.

— Proof of, under Denial. (A. F. Sears, jr.) Am. Law R. 31: 865.

Fräulein Dorothy, The ; a story. (H. S. Canby) Outl. 66: 272.

Frazer, James George. Acad. 53: 376.

— Golden Bough. Church Q. 52: 171. — (A. Lang) Fortn. 75: 235.

Freak of Cupid, A. Temp. Bar, 109: 427. Same art. Liv. Age, 212: 11.

Freak of Memory, A ; a story. (D. H. Talmadge) Munsey, 25: 284.

Freak of Memory, A ; a story. (C. Burke) Pall Mall M. 19: 413.

Freaks of Nature in Olden Times. (H. S. C. Everard) Eng. Illust. 18: 660.

Frechette, Louis. (F. C. Smith) Canad. M. 16: 443. — With portrait. (J. G. Menard) Nat'l M. (Bost.) 12: 61.

Freckled Fool, The ; a story. (H. Whitaker) Munsey, 26: 96.

Freckles ; a story. (W. Pett Ridge) Eng. Illust. 20: 409.

Freddy Elwyn's Wife. (E. Harling) Belgra. 94: 209.

Frederick the Great. (W. O. Morris) Un. Serv. M. 21: 602. 22: 28-601. 23: 33-149.

— and Marshal de Grumbkow. (G. Valbert) Liv. Age, 222: 114.

— Religion of, with portrait. (W. H. Carruth) Open Court, 13: 580.

Frederick III., the Noble, Emperor of Germany. (H. Oakley) Macmil. 79: 441.

Frederick, Empress. See Victoria, Empress.

Frederick Lewis of Hanover. (Alison Buckler) Gent. M. n. s. 58: 166.

Frederic, Harold. (R. H. Sherard) Idler, 12: 531. — (M. E. Wardwell) Citizen, 3: 152. — (Frank Harris) Sat. R. 86: 526. — Dial (Ch.) 25: 289.

— Death of. Acad. 55: 103.

Frederic, Harold, Death of, Cause of. (Frank Harris) Sat. R. **86**: 629.
— A Half-length Sketch from the Life. (L. I. Guiney) Bk. Buyer, **17**: 600.
— Market Place. Sat. R. **88**: 107.
Free Church in England. (R. F. Horton) Fortn. **67**: 597.
Free Church Simultaneous Mission. (A. Harper) Sund. M. **30**: 104.
Free Thought, History of. (J. M. Robertson) Internat. J. Ethics, **10**: 509.
— Robertson on. (R. S. Rait) Crit. R. **10**: 22.
Free Trade and the Empire. Spec. **82**: 125.
— and Cheap Sugar. (C. S. Parker) Fortn. **70**: 44.
— and Foreign Policy in England. (J. A. Hobson) Contemp. **74**: 167.
— and Imperial Commerce. Lond. Q. **88**: 84.
— and Protection in Practice. Gunton's M. **16**: 66.
— between Canada and Great Britain. (C. A. Boulton) Canad. M. **13**: 107.
— Cobden Club against. Westm. **156**: 531.
— Domestic. (W. A. Linn) Nation, **70**: 65.
— Gladstone on. Gunton's M. **14**: 166.
— Imperial. (G. Baden-Powell) Fortn. **67**: 935.
— Rosebery on. Spec. **79**: 639.
— Tory Origin of. (W. J. Ashley) Q. J. Econ. **11**: 335.
— with the Colonies. (H. White) Nation, **70**: 64.
Free Trader, The. (A. J. Brown) Overland, n. s. **38**: 184.
Freear, Louie, with portraits. Strand, **16**: 296.
Freedman's Bureau. (W. E. B. DuBois) Atlan. **87**: 354.
Freedom and Free-will. (G. S. Fullerton) Pop. Sci. Mo. **58**: 183.
— and its Opportunities. (J. R. Rogers) Arena, **18**: 577. **19**: 1.
— Failure of. (J. H. Batten) Arena, **26**: 459.
— Kent's Doctrine of. (G. E. Moore) Mind, **23**: 179.
— of Speech. Italian Republican Prisoners. (M. C. Smith) Outl. **61**: 919.
— of Thought, Germans and. Spec. **80**: 157.
— Personal and Institutional. Outl. **64**: 664.
— Relation of Choice to. (E. M. Caillard) Contemp. **73**: 439.
— Theological, Limits of. (F. H. Foster) Bib. Sac. **58**: 209.
— Universal. (H. W. Dresser) Arena, **20**: 568.
Freeman, Edward A., Historical Method of. (F. Harrison) 19th Cent. **44**: 791.
Freeman, The ; a poem. (E. Glasgow) Atlan. **80**: 796.
Free-masonry and the Roman Church. (F. J. W. Crowe) Cornh. **75**: 826.
— An Anti-masonic Mystification. (H. C. Lea) Lippinc. **66**: 948.
— in Iowa ; First Lodge, 1840. (T. S. Parvin) Midland, **8**: 367.
— in Latin America. (R. Parsons) Am. Cath. Q. **23**: 802.
— Origin of. (G. S.) Westm. **151**: 671.
Freemasons, Noblest Guild of. Antiq. n. s. **36**: 306.
Freer, Frederick W., Painter. (F. W. Morton) Brush & P. **8**: 289.
Free-soil Party in the Northwest, Smith on. (J. D. Cox) Nation, **66**: 384.
Freeze, Spoor, and allied Families, Family Record of. (F. H. Curtiss) N. E. Reg. **51**: 344.
Freeze, The ; a story. Argosy, **63**: 778.
Freezing up ; a Canadian sketch. Spec. **87**: 1022.
Frei, Hans, Swiss Medallist, with portrait. M. of Art, **26**: 7.
Freiberg Expert, a Tale of British Columbia Gold Fields. (R. Pocock) Chamb. J. **74**: 744.
Freight-rates ; The Nebraska Decision. (A. G. Sedgwick) Nation, **66**: 260.

Freight Tariffs, Our Interstate Protective. (J. J. Wait) Arena, **19**: 18.
Frejus, Provence, Grateful. Folk-Lore, **12**: 307.
Fremantle, W. H. Lit. W. (Bost.) **32**: 110.
Fremont, Jessie Benton, a Woman who has lived History. (Margaret C. Kendall) Overland, n. s. **37**: 640.
French, Alice, and her Theories. (Mary J. Reid) Midland, **9**: 99.
French, Daniel Chester, Sculptor, with portrait. (N. R. Abbott) Brush & P. **8**: 43. — (J. P. Coughlan) M. of Art, **25**: 311. — Munsey, **19**: 234. — (H. B. Emerson) New Eng. M. n. s. **16**: 259. — (W. A. Coffin) Cent. **37**: 871. — With portrait. Brush & P. **5**: 145.
French, George Arthur. Outl. **64**: 542.
French and English, Concerning. (A. Bréal) Contemp. **79**: 117. Same art. Ecl. M. **136**: 534. — Liv. Age, **228**: 374. — (G. H. Ely) Macmil. **83**: 257.
— — in Africa. Blackw. **162**: 557.
— As Others See us. (A. Fouillé) Liv. Age, **212**: 67.
— in Central Africa. (Ph. Salisbury) Un. Serv. M. **16**: 601.
— of To-day, Demolins on. (A. Laugel) Nation, **67**: 222.
French Art at the Court of Berlin. (C. Brinton) Critic, **37**: 531.
— at the Guildhall. (M. H. Spielmann) M. of Art, **22**: 597.
— Brownell's. (K. Cox) Nation, **73**: 400.
— Recent. Archit. R. **8**: 275. — (J. L. Caw) Scot. R. **31**: 241.
— Two Centuries of. Ed. R. **188**: 175.
French Art Industry, Decline of. (H. C. Morris) Am. Arch. **60**: 6.
French Associations Law. (W. Hubbard) 19th Cent. **50**: 818.
— and its Authors. Month, **98**: 449, 561.
French-Canadian Decisions. (R. V. Rogers) Green Bag, **10**: 387.
French Churches, Gleanings from. (S. Beale) Antiq. n. s. **33**: 50, 310.
French Classicists, The. (B. W. Wells) Sewanee, **3**: 10.
French Courtship, A ; a story. (H. Lavedan) Liv. Age, **221**: 203–286. Same art. Ecl. M. **132**: 838.
French Criticism, Evolution of. (B. W. Wells) Sewanee, **3**: 385.
French Declaration of the Rights of Man, 1789. (J. H. Robinson) Pol. Sci. Q. **14**: 653.
French Drama at the End of the Century. (B. Matthews) Internat. Mo. **1**: 420.
— Modern. (A. Filon) Fortn. **67**: 871. **68**: 42, 368, 692. **69**: 119, 486. **70**: 98.
French Emigrant Army of the Prince de Condé ; 1792–1802. (F. H. Tyrrell) Un. Serv. M. **20**: 360.
French " Evidence." (E. L. Godkin) Nation, **66**: 180.
French Fiction and Fact, Eros in. (A. D. Vandam) Fortn. **75**: 1045.
— Social Psychology in Contemporary. (L. Marillier) Fortn. **76**: 520.
— The Social Novel. (M. J. Darmesteter) Contemp. **75**: 800. Same art. Ecl. M. **133**: 394.
French Fleet at Brest, Plan to burn, 1804. (J. Leyland) Macmil. **84**: 185.
French Genius in Criticism. (G. L. Swiggett) Dial (Ch.) **24**: 136.
French Girls in Domestic Life. (Th. Bentzon) Outl. **58**: 629.
French Grand Manœuvres of 1891. (J. Chester) J. Mil. Serv. Inst. **13**: 716.
French Historical Monuments, Preservation of. Am. Arch. **60**: 68.
French Idealism, The New. (Count de Soissons) Contemp. **78**: 502.

French Invasion of 1797, The. (C. Edwardes) Chamb. J. **75**: 187. Same art. Liv. Age, **216**: 886.

French Language and Literature, Teaching of, in France. (J. Texte) Educa. R. **13**: 121.

— Development of Study of, in American Colleges. (C. W. E. Chapin) Chaut. **32**: 581.

— Learning, by International Correspondence. (Gaston Mouchet) Educa. **19**: 603.

— *vs.* English as a Suggestive Language. Sat. R. **88**: 287.

French Law, Modern, Droit Administratif in. (A. V. Dicey) Law Q. **17**: 302.

— Specific Performance in. Law Q. **17**: 372.

French Literary Circle, A. (Aline Gorren) Scrib. M. **23**: 102.

French Literature. (J. Reinach) Ath. '97, **2**: 10.

— Brunetière's Manual of History of. Poet-Lore, **11**: 138.

— Cacoethes Literarum. (Ch. Bastide) Fortn. **69**: 22.

— Critical Essays in. (P. Bourget) Longm. **34**: 316.

— Critical Studies in. (F. M. Warren and others) Chaut. **32**: 71-636. **33**: 71, 180.

— Current. (E. Gosse) Liv. Age, **214**: 67. — (H. Houssaye) Chaut. **24**: 410. — Fortn. **68**: 543.

— Dilettanteism in. (Count de Soissons) Contemp. **80**: 77. Same art. Ecl. M. **137**: 432. Same art. Liv. Age, **230**: 540.

— An Elysian Conversation. (Ch. Bastide) Fortn. **69**: 401.

— English as against. (H. D. Sedgwick, jr.) Atlan. **81**: 289.

— Evil Tendencies in Recent. (H. Lynch and others) Acad. **61**: 137-347.

— in 1896-97. (J. Reinach) Ath. '97, **2**: 10.

— in 1897-98. (F. Brunetière) Ath. '98, **2**: 12.

— in 1898-99. (G. J. Pravieux) Ath. '99, **2**: 13.

— in 1899-1900. (G. J. Pravieux) Ath. '00, **2**: 12.

— in 1900-01. (G. J. Pravieux) Ath. '01, **2**: 12.

— Making of. (W. H. Kent) Dub. R. **125**: 402.

— Masters of, Harper on. (S. C. Earle) Dial (Ch.) **31**: 104.

— of 1900. Sat. R. **90**: 184.

— Pellissier's Literary Movement in France. (E. E. Hale, jr.) Dial (Ch.) **24**: 375. — (R. Doumic) Fortn. **75**: 918. Same art. Ecl. M. **137**: 182. Same art. Liv. Age, **229**: 729.

— The Place of. (G. McL. Harper) Atlan. **85**: 360.

— Present Situation in. (H. James) No. Am. **169**: 488.

— Reaction in. (A. D. Malley) Cath. World, **70**: 70.

— Recent. (E. Gosse) Contemp. **74**: 890. Same art. Liv. Age, **220**: 236. Same art. Ecl. M. **132**: 376.

— Style in. (F. Brunetière) Atlan. **80**: 442.

— Tendencies in. (P. Edgar) Pop. Sci. Mo. **55**: 207.

French Marriage Law, New Departure in. (O. E. Bodington) Am. Law R. **31**: 28.

French Nation, The, as seen through New-Church Teaching. (W. L. Gladish) N. Church R. **4**: 193.

French Novel, The, and the Young Girl. (Th. Bentzon) Outl. **67**: 80.

French Novelists, Contemporary. (A. Schade van Westrum) Critic, **34**: 513.

— — Doumic's. (E. G. Martin) Bk. Buyer, **18**: 235.

— Poet-Lore, **11**: 431.

— Modern. (F. Brunetière and others) Pub. Opin. **22**: 595.

French Officialism. (Alphonse de Calonne) 19th Cent. **43**: 230.

French Open-mindedness. (A. F. Sanborn) Atlan. **84**: 843.

French Painting, Idealism in. (C. Mauclair) M. of Art, **25**: 529.

French People, The. (H. E. H. Jerningham) 19th Cent. **44**: 554.

French Poetry in the 19th Century. (F. Brunetière) Gent. M. n. s. **63**: 430. Same art. Ecl. M. **134**: 386. Same art. Liv. Age, **224**: 265.

— Lyrists and Lyrics of Old France. (J. A. Harrison) Chaut. **32**: 421.

— The New. (G. Lanson) Internat. Mo. **4**: 433.

— of To-day. (E. Verhaeren) Fortn. **75**: 723.

— Recent. (G. Mourey) Fortn. **68**: 650.

French Poets, Contemporary. (B. W. Wells) Sewanee, **3**: 355.

French Press, The. Cornh. **84**: 239. Same art. Liv. Age, **231**: 178.

— Troubles of the. (R. Ogden) Nation, **66**: 24.

French Primary School, A. (W. Burnet) Ecl. M. **133**: 761. Same art. Liv. Age, **222**: 711.

French Prisoners at Portchester. (J. Vaughan) Cornh. **76**: 217.

French Revolution. (F. N. Maude) Un. Serv. M. **22**: 107.

— and Edmund Burke. (W. Wilson) Cent. **40**: 784.

— and English Literature, Dowden's. Sat. R. **84**: 16.

— Aulard's Political History of. (C. W. Colby) Nation, **73**: 399.

— A Feminist of. (A. Laugel) Nation, **70**: 434.

— Greppi on. Ath. '01, **1**: 591.

— Masterpieces of. Chaut. **32**: 22.

— Political Clubs during. (J. W. Perrin) Chaut. **32**: 24.

French Society, Superstition and Sorcery in. (E. von Jagow) Chaut. **24**: 424.

French Speech Sounds, A Few. (E. B. Davis) Nation, **72**: 87.

French Syntax, State Simplification of. Educa. **21**: 244. — Acad. **59**: 425.

French Trooper, A. (L. Decle) Liv. Age, **223**: 61.

French Universities, The New. (G. Compayré) Educa. R. **13**: 379.

French Wit in the 18th Century. (S. G. Tallentyre) Cornh. **82**: 688. Same art. Ecl. M. **136**: 155.

French Wives and Mothers. (A. L. Bicknell) Cent. **33**: 339.

French Women in French Industry. (Y. Blaze de Bury) Fortn. **70**: 127.

— in Industry. (A. Cone) Contemp. **77**: 250.

Frenchy's Last Job. (L. Osbourne) Cosmopol. **28**: 55.

Freneau, Philip. (F. L. Pattee) Chaut. **31**: 467.

Frere, Sir Bartle, South African Policy of. (W. B. Worsfold) Cornh. **82**: 51.

Frere, John Hookham. (G. Festing) Longm. **30**: 121.

— Selections from Papers of. Temp. Bar, **113**: 373.

Frescoes in Little Kimble Church. Antiq. n. s. **36**: 279.

— of Runkelstein. (W. D. McCrackan) Harper, **96**: 222.

Fresenius, C. R. Nature, **56**: 202. — Ath. '97, **1**: 813. — J. Soc. Arts, **45**: 838.

Fresh-air Work, Advertising. (F. Almy) Char. R. **9**: 280.

Fret or Key Ornamentation in Mexico and Peru. (R. P. Greg) Archæol. **47**: 157.

Fretwork, its Possibilities. (F. Miller) Art J. **50**: 141.

Friar, The ; a Philippine sketch. (P. Whitmarsh) Outl. **64**: 834.

Fribourg in Switzerland, University of. (W. J. Ashley) Nation, **67**: 238.

Frick, Henry Clay. Cassier, **16**: 706.

Frick-Carnegie Suit, Great Steel Makers of Pittsburg and the. (J. Moritzen) R. of Rs. (N. Y.) **21**: 433.

Frid Stool in Hexham Abbey. Reliquary, **40**: 59.

Frida Petersen's Lover. (C. Edwardes) Chamb. J. **75**: 392-408.

Friday ; Catholic Devotion and the Nine First Fridays. (T. V. Moore) Cath. World, **73**: 137.

Friday's Church ; a story. Temp. Bar, **111**: 189.

Fuel, Liquid. (E. L. Orde) Cassier, **20**: 61. — (Sir M. Samuel) J. Soc. Arts, **47**: 384.

— — for Locomotives. (A. M. Bell) Cassier, **13**: 371.

Fugue, The. (W. S. B. Mathews) Music, **15**: 374.

Fulfilling of the Law; a story. (R. H. Russell) Harper, **102**: 38.

Fulford, Wm. Ath. '97, **1**: 416.

Fulgurite, Spiral, from Wisconsin. (W. H. Hobbs) Am. J. Sci. **158**: 17.

Fulgurites, What are? Liv. Age, **212**: 702.

Fulham Palace. (Beatrice Creighton) Art J. **52**: 297.

"Fulish Jan;" a story. (Henry Wilson) Gent. M. n. s. **63**: 587.

Fuller, Henry B. (R. Riordan) Critic, **30**: 211.

Fuller, Horace Williams, First Editor of "The Green Bag;" with portrait. (C. C. Soule) Green Bag, **13**: 551.

Fuller, John, of Ipswich, Mass. (E. P. Everett) N. E. Reg. **53**: 335.

Fuller, Margaret. (Kenyon West) Lit. W. (Bost.) **28**: 224.

Fuller, Thomas; a broad-chested soul. (Tom Russell) Gent. M. n. s. **58**: 403.

Fuller Family; early New England Fullers. (F. H. Fuller) N. E. Reg. **55**: 192.

— of Redenhall, Eng. (F. H. Fuller) N. E. Reg. **55**: 410.

Fuller's Earth, Occurrence of, in the U.S. (D. T. Day) J. Frankl. Inst. **150**: 214.

Fullerton, Lord, Lawyer and Judge. (A. Ure) Jurid. R. **13**: 379.

Fulleylove, John, Artist, Greek Drawing of. Studio (Lond.) **7**: 77.

Fully-qualified Assistant, A; a story. (I. Smith) Sund. M. **28**: 629.

Fulton, Robert. New Eng. M. n. s. **23**: 124.

Funafuti Coral-boring Expedition. Geog. J. **11**: 50.

— Legendary History of. (W. J. Sollas) Nature, **55**: 353.

Functions, Harkness and Morley's Analytic. (James Pierpont) Science, n. s. **9**: 586.

Funds, Patriotic, Administration of. (Earl Nelson) Monthly R. **3**, no. **1**: 51.

Fundy, Bay of, Seiches on. (A. W. Duff) Am. J. Sci. **153**: 406.

— — Wonderful Tides of. (G. F. Foster) Overland, n. s. **33**: 239. — Nature, **60**: 461. Same art. Liv. Age, **223**: 463.

Funeral at Sea. (J. H. Barker) Strand, **17**: 114.

Funeral Masks in Europe. (J. Abercromby) Folk-Lore, **7**: 351.

Funeral Music: "With Military Honors." (F. J. Crowest) Sund. M. **29**: 251.

Funeral Processions, Two, in the Mall: 2d Feb. 1901, 30th Jan. 1649. (H. W. Lucy) Chamb. J. **78**: 257.

Funeral Reforms. (S. L. Krebs) Ref. Church R. **45**: 33.

Funerals, West Pyrenean. (A. R. Whiteway) Gent. M. n. s. **65**: 559.

Fungi, Chemotropism of. (E. F. Smith) Am. Natural. **31**: 717.

— Conception of Species as affected by, Investigations on. (W. G. Farlow) Am. Natural. **32**: 675.

— Interesting Facts about. (A. J. H, Crespi) Chamb. J. **78**: 513.

— New Species. (J. B. Ellis; B. M. Everhardt) Am. Natural. **31**: 339, 426.

Funston, Brig.-Gen. Frederick. (J. H. Canfield) R. of Rs. (N. Y.) **23**: 577. — With portraits. (C. F. Scott) Indep. **53**: 817. — World's Work, **1**: 696. — (C. S. Gleed) Cosmopol. **27**: 321.

Fur Coats, The. (A. E. Allen) New Eng. M. n. s. **25**: 469.

Fur-pullers of South London. (E. F. Hogg) 19th Cent. **42**: 734.

Fur-trade, Romance of the. (E. B. Osborn) Macmil. **81**: 269. — (W. S. Harwood and F. Crissey) World's Work, **3**: 1526.

— — The Companies. Blackw. **164**: 495. Same art. Ecl. M. **131**: 637.

— — The Mountain Men. Blackw. **165**: 37.

Furs, London's Store of. (C. J. Cornish) Cornh. **78**: 783.

Furmans of South Carolina; a Family of Educators. (McD. Furman) Educa. **17**: 435.

Furnaceman, The. (A. M'Q. Cleland) Chamb. J. **74**: 417–472.

Furness, Horace Howard. (A. H. Smyth) Lippinc. **65**: 267.

Furness, Ancient Settlements, Cemeteries, and Earthworks of. Archæol. **53**: 389.

Furniss, Harry. (M. H. Spielmann) M. of Art, **23**: 345.

— Confessions of. (I. A. Pyle) Dial (Ch.) **31**: 504.

— Work of, with portrait. Bk. Buyer, **13**: 941.

Furniture, Antique; English Chairs. (K. W. Clouston) Archit. R. **8**: 150.

— — in Modern Houses. (A. C. Nye) Archit. R. **7**, no. 2: 156.

— — Singleton on. Bk. Buyer, **22**: 27.

— at Glasgow Exhibition, 1901. Studio (Internat.) **14**: 165.

— at Paris Exposition, 1900. Am. Arch. **71**: 6.

— Chippendale, Sheraton, and Hepplewhite Designs, edited by J. M. Bell. Ath. '01, **1**: 87.

— — Clouston on. Ath. '98, **2**: 135.

— Designs for. Illus. Artist (N. Y.) **23**: 164, 214.

— Designs of A. W. Jarvis. Studio (Internat.) **5**: 50.

— English. (L. Liberty) J. Soc. Arts, **48**: 370. — (L. Liberty) Am. Arch. **68**: 14, 23, 28.

— — and Carved Woodwork. Quar. **189**: 384.

— Evolution of. (A. C. Nye) Archit. R. **7**: 426.

— Examples of Modern French. Archit. R. **10**: 244.

— for New Palace, Darmstadt. (M. H. Baillie-Scott) Studio (Internat.) **5**: 91.

— History of, Litchfield's. Studio (Lond.) **1**: 30.

— in Home of Arthur Sanderson. (C. Monkhouse) Art J. **49**: 134.

— Inlaid Wood, at Windsor Castle. (F. S. Robinson) M. of Art, **22**: 149.

— Later Wooden, at Windsor Castle. (F. S. Robinson) M. of Art, **22**: 349.

— Old and New. (Mrs. W. Chance) Artist (N. Y.) **31**: 197.

— — Beautiful Examples of. Artist (N. Y.) **24**: 187.

— — Old and New Style. Art J. **50**: Oct. supp., 1.

— Some Old. (Mrs. Scott-Moncrief) Chamb. J. **77**: 305.

— Wooden, at Windsor Castle. (F. S. Robinson) M. of Art, **22**: 245.

Further Adventures of a Guinea Pig. (C. J. Langston) Argosy, **63**: 624.

Fustel de Coulanges as an Historian. (E. Jenks) Eng. Hist. R. **12**: 209.

Futuna, or Horn Island, Fiji Group. (F. T. Bullen) Cornh. **77**: 496.

Future, Provision of the. (C. Flammarion) Arena, **17**: 590.

Future Life. (P. W. Roose) Argosy, **64**: 619. **66**: 635. — Argosy, **65**: 147. — (S. C. Burnett) Nat'l M. (Bost.) **9**: 143.

— Athenian Conceptions of a. (D. Quinn) Harper, **103**: 923.

— Carlyle, Tennyson, and Browning on. (R. S. Ingraham) Meth. R. **59**: 360.

— Change and Progression Assured. (J. S. Bogg) N. Church R. **6**: 16.

— Conception of, in Homer. (A. Fairbanks) Am. J. Theol. **1**: 741.

— Psychical Research concerning. N. Church R. **7**: 598.

Future Life ; Testimony of Genius. (P. W. Roose) Argosy, 64: 669.

— vs. Occultism ; reply to A. Besant's Eschatology. N. Church R. 4: 122.

Future Probation or Absolute Predestination. Ref. Church R. 45: 119.

Future Punishment. (E. Sutherland) Luth. Q. 31: 94.

Future State, The. Spec. 85: 330.

— Babylonian and Hebrew Views of Man's Fate after Death. (P. Carus) Open Court, 15: 346.

Futures, Business in. (H. Stokes) Econ. R. 8: 304.

Fyander's Widow. (M. E. Francis) Longm. 38: 64-193.

Fylfot and Swastika, Meaning and Origin of the. (R. P. Greg) Archæol. 48: 293.

Fytton, Mary, and Shakespeare. (F. J. Furnivall) Theatre, 39: 293.

"G., H., and I. ; " a story. (E. Nesbit) Pall Mall M. 16: 534.

Gabriel, Archangel. Month, 97: 598.

Gabrilovitch, Ossip, Musician, with portrait. (W. S. B. Mathews) Music, 19: 168.

Gade, Niels W. Letters. (T. L. Krebs) Sewanee, 3: 48.

Gad's Hill, Memories of. (Mary A. Dickens) Strand, 13: 69.

Gadsden, Christopher, Letters of, 1778. Am. Hist. R. 3: 83.

Gadski, Johanna, Opera Singer, with portraits. (Emma D. Nuckols) Music, 16: 525.

Gael, The, and his Heritage. (F. Macleod) 19th Cent. 48: 825.

Gaelic Beliefs. (J. Macleay) Good Words, 42: 92.

Gaelic Church and Presbyterial Ordination. (C. C. Starbuck) Meth. R. 59: 365.

Gaelic Revival in Ireland. (T. O'Donnell) R. of Rs. (N. Y.) 24: 188.

Gage, Lyman J., with portrait. World's Work, 1: 735. — Bank. M. (N. Y.) 58: 408.

— Ancestry of. (A. E. Gage) N. E. Reg. 53: 201.

— Character Sketch. (M. P. Handy) R. of Rs. (N. Y.) 15: 289.

— on the Monetary Situation. Bank. M. (N. Y.) 59: 779.

— to the Amer. Bankers' Association at Milwaukee. (H. White) Nation, 73: 314.

Gage and Kingsbury, Families of. (A. E. Gage) N. E. Reg. 54: 260.

Gainsborough, Thos. (M. Madison) Munsey, 12: 217, 386. — With portrait. Mast. in Art, 2: pt. 23.

— and his Place in English Art, Armstrong's. Sat. R. 87: 234.

— Bell's Life of. M. of Art, 22: 613. — Studio (Internat.) 3: 280.

— The Blue Boy. Acad. 59: 582-630. 60: 193.

— Cole's Old English Masters. (J. C. Van Dyke) Cent. 33: 202.

— Musidora Bathing her Feet. (M. Beerbohm) Sat. R. 86: 199.

— New Paintings at National Gallery. (C. Phillips) Art J. 49: 207.

Gainsborough, England, as Scene of "Mill on the Floss." (P. C. Standing) Idler, 11: 789.

Galapagos Archipelago ; Criticism of R. Ridgway's Paper. (G. Baur) Am. Natural. 31: 777.

— King of. (Thomas Leander) Chamb. J. 77: 463.

— New Observations on the Origin of. (G. Baur) Am. Natural. 31: 661, 864.

Galdós, B. Perez. (A. M. Huntington) Bookman, 5: 220. — (H. Ellis) Critic, 39: 213.

— and Pereda in the Spanish Academy. (E. G. Baquero) Liv. Age, 214: 330.

— Novels of. (W. Miller) Gent. M. n. s. 67: 217. Same art. Liv. Age, 231: 509.

Galicia, Spain. (H. Lynch) Blackw. 162: 109. Same art. Liv. Age, 214: 644. — (L. Lorimer) Blackw. 165: 669. Same art. Ecl. M. 133: 70. Same art. Liv. Age, 221: 628.

— Mining Industry in. J. Soc. Arts, 46: 197.

— Peasantry of, Most Miserable in Europe. Good Words, 39: 162. Same art. Liv. Age, 217: 162.

Galician Wedding ; a Canadian Incident. (B. C. D'Easum) Canad. M. 13: 83.

Galileo, Dialogue of. (F. R. Wegg-Prosser) Am. Cath. Q. 26: 266, 453.

— Struggle regarding the Position of the Earth, with portrait. (C. Sterne) Open Court, 14: 449.

— Tribuna di, in Florence. (W. A. Parr) Knowl. 23: 103.

Galileo's Tower at Florence. (A. W. Parr) Knowl. 22: 157.

Gallé, Emile, with portrait. (H. Frantz) M. of Art, 20: 249.

Galleon Gold ; a tale. (F. Reddale) Outing, 37: 440.

Galleries, National and Provincial. (C. T. J. Hiatt) Studio (Lond.) 1: 227.

Gallery of Great Masters ; a story. (L. Housman) Idler, 14: 127.

Gallery of Pictures, A ; a story. (Catherine Pullein) Temp. Bar, 124: 199.

Gallican Church, and the French Nation. (C. T. Odhner) N. Church R. 4: 522.

Gallifet, General the Marquis de. Outl. 63: 45.

Gallop, John, of Taunton, Mass. (A. D. Hodges) N. E. Reg. 54: 89.

Gallops. (D. Gray) Cent. 33: 24-698. 34: 132, 247.

Galloway, Joseph, Some Letters of, 1774-75. Pennsyl. M. 21: 477.

Galton, Sir Douglas. Am. Arch. 64: 20. — J. Soc. Arts, 47: 395.

Galton, Francis, Portraits of. Strand, 14: 518.

Galvanizing, Improvement in. (G. C. Reese) J. Frankl. Inst. 144: 312.

Galvanometers of High Sensibility. (C. E. Mendenhall and C. W. Waidner) Am. J. Sci. 162: 249.

Galveston, Texas, Destruction by Hurricane, Sept. 8, 1900. (C. Ousley) Nat'l M. (Bost.) 13: 533. — Outl. 66: 252. — (J. Fay) Cosmopol. 30: 33. — (W. B. Stevens) Munsey, 24: 334.

— — Lessons of. (W. J. McGee) Nat. Geog. M. 11: 377.

Gama, Vasco da. Spec. 80: 723.

— 4th Centenary of his Voyage to India. (C. R. Markham) Geog. J. 12: 10. — Nat. Sci. 12: 379.

Gambetta, Leon. Critic, 37: 72.

— Methods of Study. (J. Reinach) No. Am. 171: 55.

Gambia, Judging in. (H. L. Stephen) 19th Cent. 44: 783.

Gambling and Aids to Gambling. (C. E. B. Russell ; E. T. Campagnac) Econ. R. 10: 482.

— and Betting ; Why are they Wrong ? (A. T. Barnett) Econ. R. 7: 168.

— Ethics of. (E. Lyttelton) Econ. R. 7: 1.

— in England, Ashton on. Ath. '98, 2: 745. — Spec. 81: 806.

— Licensed, in Belgium. (G. F. Babbitt) Forum, 32: 481.

— Ocean. Chamb. J. 76: 438.

See Gaming,

Gambling Mania, The. Nation, 69: 373.

Gambling Resorts in Germany in Earlier Years. Sat. R. 90: 389.

Gambold, John, Poet and Moravian Bishop. Church Q. 53: 65.

Game, Awakening concerning. (J. S. Wise) R. of Rs. (N. Y.) 24: 567.

— Big. Spec. 80: 301.

— — Books on. (T. Roosevelt) Fortn. 69: 604.

Game, Big; Distribution in America, 1900. (G. B. Grinnell) Outing, 37: 251.

— — in the Rockies. (J. N. Ostrom) Outing, 34: 457.

— — in South Africa. (W. W. Van Ness) Outing, 35: 545.

— by Hedge, Stream, and Spinney. (Y. Stewart) Eng. Illust. 18: 41.

— in New Brunswick; Wild Geese. (A. P. Silver) Canad. M. 17: 524.

— of Canada; Wapiti and Antelope. (C. A. Bramble) Canad. M. 14: 285.

Game and the Candle, The. (R. Broughton) Temp. Bar, 116: 1-465. 117: 1.

Game, and the Nation, The; a story. (O. Wister) Harper, 100: 884.

Game of Chess. (L. B. Walford) Longm. 30: 426.

Game of Cottabos, A; a story. (J. F. Rowbotham) Argosy, 68: 334.

Game of Death, The; a story. (W. O. Stout) Midland, 11: 284.

Game of Nă-wá-tă-pĭ, Shoshonean. (G. A. Dorsey) J. Am. Folk-Lore, 14: 24.

Game of Solitaire. (M. Y. Wynne) Atlan. 80: 685.

Game of Wei-ch'i, A. (Julian Croskey) Chamb. J. 76: 561-617.

Game-bird Shooting in So. Africa. (H. A. Bryden) Outing, 37: 139.

— Wildfowl-shooting in the Outer Hebrides. (G. W. Hartley) Blackw. 165: 413.

Game Books, Our. (C. Stein) Fortn. 73: 399.

Game-law, New, for Norway. (J. Forrest) Blackw. 164: 558.

Game-law Problem. (J. S. Wise) Outing, 38: 46.

Game-laws of Indian Territory. (R. Bruce) Outing, 38: 451.

— of Ontario and Quebec. (A. C. Shaw) Canad. M. 17: 520.

Game Preservation in U. S. Spec. 80: 572. 82: 11.

Game Preserves. (C. J. Cornish) Cornh. 75: 37.

— American. (M. Foster) Munsey, 25: 376. — (G. E. Walsh) Outing, 37: 539.

Game Preserving, Growth of. (W. A. B. Grohman) Outing, 39: 79.

Game-shops in London. (C. J. Cornish) Cornh. 76: 171.

Game Wardens, Benefits of. (S. E. Connor) Outing, 36: 632.

Games and Pastimes. Liv. Age, 224: 126. Same art. Ecl. M. 134: 301.

— in Old and Modern France. (A. Lang) Blackw. 170: 484.

— Musical, of Antiquity. (J. E. Rowbotham) Good Words, 40: 411. Same art. Ecl. M. 133: 441. Same art. Liv. Age, 222: 188.

— of Klasmath Indians. (G. A. Dorsey) Am. Anthropol. 3: 14.

— of the Red-men of Guiana. (E. F. im Thurn) Folk-Lore, 12: 132.

— on Paper, and Elsewhere. (W. B. Thomas) Macmil. 81: 129. Same art. Liv. Age, 224: 389.

— Pelota, in Madrid. (Poultney Bigelow) Cosmopol. 26: 578.

— Psychological, Pedagogical, and Religious Aspects of Group. (L. Gulick) Pedagog. Sem. 6: 135.

— Queer. (F. Steelcroft) Strand, 14: 55.

— Social Recapitulation expressed in. (A. Allen) Educa. R. 18: 344.

Gamin, The Paris. (M. T. Blanc) McClure, 9: 890.

Gaming Instinct, The. (W. I. Thomas) Am. Sociol. 6: 750.

Gandia, Duke of, Murder of. (A. H. Norway) Macmil. 77: 46. Same art. Liv. Age, 215: 812.

Gang, Genesis of the. (J. A. Riis) Atlan. 84: 302.

Gano, John A. (C. Abbe) Science, n. s. 7: 123.

Ganodonta, The. Science, 5: 611.

Ganomalite, Note concerning the Chemical Composition of. (S. L. Penfield and C. H. Warren) Am. J. Sci. 158: 339.

Ganz, Rudolph, Pianist, with portrait. Music, 18: 468.

Garbage, City, Utilization of. (G. E. Waring, jr.) Cosmopol. 24: 405.

Garbage Disposal. (R. Hering) Eng. M. 13: 392.

Garcés, Francisco, Diary of, Coues's Ed. (C. F. Lummis) Dial (Ch.) 29: 172. — (C. F. Lummis) Nation. 71: 388.

Garcia, Gen. Calixto. (G. Reno) R. of Rs. (N. Y.) 19: 52.

Garden, Alexander, Letter from, 1743. (G. A. Gordon) N. E. Reg. 54: 390.

Garden, An American. (J. Horace McFarland) Outl. 63: 327.

— and its Art. (G. S. Elgood) Studio (Lond.) 5: 51.

— and its Development. (Paul Falkenburg) Am. Arch. 72: 100. 73: 2.

— Animal Life in the. (P. Robinson) Contemp. 75: 843. Same art. Liv. Age, 222: 276. Same art. Ecl. M. 133: 332.

— as an Adjunct to Architecture. (R. C. Sturgis) Archit. R. 5: 21.

— Content in a. (C. Wheeler) Atlan. 85: 779. 86: 99, 232.

— The, in Literature. Acad. 57: 765.

— in relation to the House. (B. Jones) Garden & F. 10: 132.

— Making a. (A. L. Merritt) Lippinc. 67: 353.

— My; a Hamlet in Old Hampshire. (A. L. Merritt) Cent. 40: 342.

— My Midwinter. (M. Thompson) Cent. 39: 3.

— On the Edge of a Parson's. Church Q. 50: 63.

— Wild. Quar. 19: 100. Same art. Ecl. M. 134: 722. Same art. Liv. Age, 225: 137.

Garden of Attalus, The; a story. (C. L. Antrobus) Temp. Bar, 123: 243.

Garden of Childhood, A. (S. S. Stilwell) Harper, 102: 73.

Garden of Climes. (H. Beveridge) Asia. R. 29: 145.

Garden of Proserpine, The. (E. E. Dickinson) Temp. Bar, 117: 369. Same art. Liv. Age, 222: 772.

Garden of Seven Fruits, The; a story. (H. Compton) Pall Mall M. 22: 462.

Garden of Swords, The; a story. (M. Pemberton) Munsey, 20: 178 — 21: 450.

Garden Architecture. Spec. 84: 770.

Garden Books, Vogue of. (H. M. Batson) 19th Cent. 47: 974. Same art. Liv. Age, 226: 210. Same art. Ecl. M. 135: 292.

Garden Design, Thomas on. (C. S. Sargent) Garden & F. 10: 121.

Garden Friends and Enemies, Our. (G. E. Walsh) Cosmopol. 22: 571.

Garden-making. (E. S. Prior) Studio (Internat.) 12: 28, 86.

— Conditions of Material. (E. S. Prior) Studio (Internat.) 12: 176.

Garden Spirit. (M. B. Brown) Cosmopol. 30: 579.

Gardener's Daughter, The. Temp. Bar, 121: 81.

Gardening. (R. V. Rogers) Green Bag, 13: 293.

— Amateur. (R. Blight) Outing, 38: 428.

— Can it be made to Pay? (S. W. Fitzherbert) National, 34: 73.

— Egyptian, Ancient. (P. E. Newberry) J. Soc. Arts, 48: 145-173.

— Fashion in. Spec. 81: 336.

— Formal Scotch Gardens. (J. J. Joass) Studio (Internat.) 2: 165.

— Home, Some Hints on. (E. E. Rexford) Lippinc. 65: 633.

Gas Works in Philadelphia, Lease of. (W. D. Lewis) Q. J. Econ. **12**: 209. — Munic. Aff. **1**: 718.

— Management of, and Consumers' Interests. Chamb. J. **75**: 189.

— Municipal, Some Recent History. (E. W. Bemis) Forum, **25**: 72.

— of Paris. (A. Shaw) Munic. Aff. **1**: 549.

Gascoigne, Geo., Soldier and Poet. (G. Serrell) Temp. Bar, **119**: 263.

Gascony, The Sons of. (M. L. Van Vorst) Bk. Buyer, **17**: 204. — (T. Stanton) Critic, **33**: 349.

Gaseous Celestial Bodies, Fundamental Law of Temperature for. (T. J. J. See) Pop. Astron. **7**: 129.

Gaseous Mixtures. (Leduc and Sacerdote) J. Frankl. Inst. **148**: 303.

Gaseous Sphere Contracting from Loss of Heat, Lane's Law of Increase of Temperature in. (C. A. Young) Pop. Astron. **7**: 225.

Gases, Absorption of, in a High Vacuum. (C. C. Hutchins) Am. J. Sci. **157**: 61.

— and Gaseous Mixtures, Explosive. (W. G. Mixter) Am. J. Sci. **157**: 327.

— Endothermic, Experiments with. (W. G. Mixter) Am. J. Sci. **157**: 323.

— Kinetic Theory of. (W. Ramsay) Contemp. **74**: 681. Same art. Science, n. s. **8**: 768. Same art. Ecl. M. **132**: 242. Same art. Liv. Age, **220**: 23.

— Multiple Spectra of. (J. Trowbridge and W. Richards) Am. J. Sci. **153**: 117.

— Temperature and Ohmic Resistance of, during the Oscillatory-electric Discharge. (J. Trowbridge and T. W. Richards) Am. J. Sci. **153**: 327.

Gaskell, Mrs. E. C., Short Tales of. (F. H. Low) Fortn. **72**: 633.

Gaspar of the Black Le Marchands. (C. G. D. Roberts) Atlan. **83**: 246.

Gaspard l'Imbecile. Temp. Bar, **113**: 537. Same art. Liv. Age, **217**: 336.

Gaspé Sketches. (M. MacMurchy) Canad. M. **16**: 335.

Gasquet, Francis Aidan. Eve of the Reformation. Critic, **36**: 449.

Gastaldi, J. Maps of Asia, Influence of "Travels of M. Polo" on. (A. E. Nordenskjöld) Geog. J. **13**: 396.

Gaston, Edward Page. Writer, **14**: 73.

Gaston de Latour, Pater's. (E. E. Hale, jr.) Dial (Ch.) **22**: 85.

Gates, Lewis E. Three Studies in Literature. (H. Knorr) Poet-Lore, **11**: 435.

Gates, Our Town and City. (Sarah Wilson) Chamb. J. **77**: 470.

Gates of Paradise, The ; a story. (E. O. Peterson) Music, **15**: 174.

Gâthas, The. (L. H. Mills) Crit. R. **10**: 411.

— as Consecutive Words. (L. H. Mills) Am. J. Philol. **20**: 65.

Gathmann Gun, Experiments with. (Hudson Maxim) Indep. **53**: 663.

Gaul, Gilbert, with portrait. (Jeannette L. Gilder) Outl. **59**: 570.

Gaul, Roman Conquest of. Ed. R. **192**: 427.

Gault Sea, Depths of, as indicated by its Rhizopodal Fauna. (F. Chapman) Nat. Sci. **13**: 305.

Gauss, Carl Friedrich, and his Children. (F. Cajori) Science, n. s. **9**: 697.

Gautier, Théophile. Concerning a Red Waistcoat. (L. H. Vincent) Atlan. **80**: 427.

Gavarni, the Artist. (T. Hopkins) Macmil. **77**: 378. Same art. Liv. Age, **217**: 176.

Gavelkind and the Family House. (S. O. Addy) Ath. '99, **1**: 468.

Gaver, James. (W. H. Allnutt) Library, n. s. **2**: 384.

Gaveston, Piers. Acad. **56**: 580.

Gay, Rev. Mr., 1731, Ethical System of. (E. Albee) Philos. R. **6**: 132.

Gay Tragedy, A. Liv. Age, **223**: 53.

Gayangos, P. de. Ath. '97, **2**: 529.

Gayley, James. (J. Birkinbine) Cassier, **19**: 511.

Gayley's Mountain Trip ; a story. (J. Lee) Outl. **65**: 740.

Gaylord Family. (H. E. Keep) N. E. Reg. **53**: 450.

Gaynor, Mrs. Jessie L., Music Composer and Teacher. Music, **16**: 297.

Gear-teeth, Fellows' Machine and Cutter for Generating. J. Frankl. Inst. **150**: 81.

Gebhardt, Eduard von. The Sermon on the Mount, a Painting. (J. P. Lenox) Bib. World, **11**: 126.

Geddes, William Duguid. Ath. '00, **1**: 208.

Geese, After Wild, in Manitoba. Blackw. **168**: 350. Same art. Liv. Age, **227**: 486. — Same art. Ecl. M. **136**: 32. — (G. Baird) Outing, **37**: 436.

— Wild, in the Northwest. (Z. M. Hamilton) Outing, **39**: 187.

— — Shooting, in New Brunswick. (A. P. Silver) Canad. M. **17**: 524.

— — Shooting, on the Gulf Coast. (E. Hough) Outing, **37**: 702.

Gegenschein, The. (I. E. Christian) Pop. Astron. **20**: 145. — (E. E. Barnard) Pop. Astron. **7**: 169.

— Observations of, 1895-96. (A. E. Douglass) Pop. Astron. **5**: 178.

— Parallax of the. (J. Evershed) Pop. Astron. **7**: 289, 352.

— Possible Explanation of the. (W. H. Pickering) Pop. Astron. **8**: 2.

Geisha Girls. (Alice Nielsen) Cosmopol. **26**: 145.

Geissler Tubes, Theory to explain the Stratification of the Electric Discharge in. (H. V. Gill) Am. J. Sci. **155**: 399.

Gems, Ancient. (M. A. Curl) Am. Antiq. **22**: 284. — Quar. **194**: 416.

— Cutting of. (T. C. Hepworth) Pall Mall M. **20**: 182.

— Furtwängler on Ancient. Nation, **72**: 359.

— Marlborough. (C. Newton-Robinson) 19th Cent. **46**: 251.

Gender in Language, A Suggestion as to the Origin of. (J. G. Fraser) Fortn. **73**: 79.

Genealogical Gleanings in England. (H. F. Waters) N. E. Reg. **51**: 105, 249, 389. **52**: 105, 234. **53**: 9.

Genealogical Index of Newberry Library. (A. J. Rudolph) Lib. J. **24**: 53.

Genealogical Nomenclature. (B. P. Mann) N. E. Reg. **51**: 305.

Genealogy. The Great and Small of Family Trees. (A. L. Benedict) Cosmopol. **24**: 277.

— Pitfalls of. (W. H. Whitmore) Nation, **69**: 13.

Genera, Subdivision of. (E. W. Hilgard) Science, n. s. **10**: 649.

General Green and Admiral Brown. Chamb. J. **77**: 572.

Generals, Great Irish. (G. A. Wade) Idler, **15**: 365.

Genet, Edmond Charles, Proposed Attack on Louisiana and the Floridas, Origin of. (F. J. Turner) Am. Hist. R. **3**: 650.

Geneva, Famous Escalade in. (T. L. L. Teeling) Gent. M. n. s. **59**: 125.

— Higher Life of. (L. Wuarin) Outl. **56**: 541.

Genevra ; a story. (A. Farquhar) Nat'l M. (Bost.) **11**: 168.

Genius and Character. (H. W. Mabie) Outl. **60**: 131.

— and Regeneration. (H. Maxim) Arena, **23**: 425.

— and Stature. (H. Ellis) 19th Cent. **42**: 87.

— British, Study of. (H. Ellis) Pop. Sci. Mo. **58**: 372, 595. **59**: 59-441.

— Economics of. (J. M. Robertson) Forum, **25**: 178.

— Fame, and Comparison of Races. (C. H. Cooley) Ann. Am. Acad. **9**: 317.

Geological Congress, Excursions of. (D. S. Martin) Pop. Sci. Mo. 52: 228.

Geological Formations, Nomenclature of N. Y. Series of. (J. M. Clark; C. Schuchert) Science, n. s. 10: 874.

Geological Nomenclature; Duplication of Names. (F. B. Weeks) Science, n. s. 9: 490.

Geological Progress of the Century. (H. S. Williams) Harper, 94: 907.

Geological Record, Imperfection of the. (A. S. Woodward) Nat. Sci. 13: 327.

Geological Society of America. (J. J. Stevenson) Science, n. s. 9: 41.

Geological Survey of Great Britain and Ireland. Nature, 63: 33.

Geological Time, Some New Data for Converting into Years. (W. C. Knight) Science, n. s. 10: 607.

Geologist awheel. (W. H. Hobbs) Pop. Sci. Mo. 58: 515.

Geology and Physical Geography, Field Work in. (R. S. Tarr) School R. 5: 519.

— and Revelation. (O. Scott) Bib. World, 9: 112.

— and Sanitary Science. (W. Whitaker) Nature, 57: 319.

— Arctic, Some Problems of. (J. W. Gregory) Nature, 56: 301, 351.

— Elementary, Tarr's. (A. P. Brigham) School R. 5: 553.

— Explorations near Pikermi. Science, n. s. 14: 268.

— Govt. Explorations. (S. F. Emmons) Science, n. s. 5: 1, 42.

— History of, Influence of Oxford on. (W. J. Sollas) Sci. Prog. 7: 23.

— — Zittel's. Nature, 61: 145.

— in the Secondary Schools. (R. S. Tarr) School R. 8: 11.

— in the 19th Century. (J. Le Conte) Pop. Sci. Mo. 56: 431, 541.

— in the 20th Century. (C. R. Keyes) Arena, 26: 21.

— Is it a Science? (G. C. H. Pollen) Am. Cath. Q. 23: 399.

— Italian. (H. J. Johnston-Lavis) Nature, 64: 640.

— North American. Nature, 61: 600.

— of China. (G. F. Wright) Science, n. s. 13: 1029.

— of Igneous Rocks, Recent Advances in. Nature, 63: 276.

— of Scotland, Recent Advances in; Pres. addr. Geol. Sec. Brit. Assoc. 1901. (J. Horne) Nature, 64: 509.

— of Switzerland, Recent. Nature, 63: 443.

— Recent Advances in General. (H. B. Woodward) Nature, 63: 233.

— Recent Progress in. (A. C. Lawson) Internat. Mo. 2: 403.

— Sixty Years of Geological Research. (G. A. J. Cole) Knowl. 20: 112.

— Teaching, New Method of. (Lillian B. Sage) Educa. 21: 463.

Geometrical Theorems and Problems with their History, Famous. (J. H. McDonald) School R. 9: 125.

Geometry, Analytical, Elements of, Briot and Bouquet's. (A. S. Hathaway) School R. 5: 480.

— Ancient and Modern. (E. S. Crawley) Pop. Sci. Mo. 58: 257.

— Elementary and Constructive, Nichols on. (E. P. Brown) School R. 5: 52.

— Euclid and his Modern Rivals. (K. Miller) Educa. 21: 398.

— Foundations of. (H. Poincaré) Monist, 9: 1.

— Mathematics in Secondary Schools. (B. F. Brown) School R. 8: 292.

— Methods of Attack of Originals in. (H. B. Loomis) School R. 6: 89.

Geometry, Non-Euclidean. (G. B. Halsted) Pop. Astron. 9: 187. — (G. B. Halsted; W. H. S. Monck) Pop. Astron. 8: 189, 267, 333.

— — and Astronomy. (W. H. S. Monck) Pop. Astron. 9: 370.

— — Lobachévski on. (G. B. Halsted) Science, n. s. 9: 813.

— — Report of Progress in. (G. B. Halsted) Pop. Astron. 7: 482, 519. 8: 8. Same art. Science, n. s. 10: 545.

— — Supplementary Report on. (G. B. Halsted) Pop. Astron. 9: 555. Same art. Science, n. s. 14: 705.

— Related Theorems in. (G. W. Evans) School R. 7: 517.

— Russell on. (D. A. Murray) Philos. R. 8: 49.

— Teaching, Modern Methods of. (S. M. Barton) Sewanee, 4: 278.

— vs. Euclid. (G. M. Minchin) Nature, 59: 369.

Geordie Blair's Luck; a story. (B. Vye and S. Phelps) Belgra. 92: 388.

George, St. (E. Sellers) Argosy, 70: 468.

— and the Dragon. (H. A. Heaton) Antiq. n. s. 35: 113.

— — Votive Painting of. Archæol. 49: 243.

George II. at Dettingen. (W. H. Fitchett) Cornh. 77: 577.

George III., Jubilee of. (A. D. Vandam) Eng. Illust. 17: 579.

George IV., Coronation of. (E. O. Robertson) Blackw. 162: 691. Same art. Liv. Age, 215: 676.

— Marriage to Mrs. Fitzherbert. (J. Fyvie) 19th Cent. 50: 127.

George Frederick, Prince of Wales, at Home. (C. Bryan) Canad. M. 17: 502.

— Character Sketch. (J. T. Clark) Canad. M. 18: 3.

— in Australia. (J. A. Cooper) Canad. M. 17: 575.

— The Royal Imperial Tour. (E. Salmon) Fortn. 76: 780.

— Visit to Canada. (N. Patterson) Canad. M. 17: 537. 18: 133. — (N. Patterson) Canad. M. 18: 7.

— — Significance of. (A. H. V. Colquhoun) Canad. M. 17: 495.

George I., King of Greece. (W. E. Waters) Chaut. 25: 52.

George, Grand Duke of Russia, with portraits. (E. Glenton) R. of Rs. (N. Y.) 20: 321.

George, Alfred, with portraits. Strand, 16: 194.

George, Ernest, Work of. Studio (Lond.) 7: 147. 8: 27, 204.

George, Henry. (H. M. Hyndman) Sat. R. 84: 485. — Econ. J. 7: 639.

— and Charles A. Dana. (J. B. Walker) Cosmopol. 24: 199.

— and his Economic System. (W. A. Scott) New World, 7: 87.

— Apostle of Reform. (F. L. Oswald) Chaut. 26: 416.

— Biography of. (T. Scanlon) Westm. 156: 197. — (D. MacG. Means) Nation, 72: 95.

— Candidacy for Mayor of N. Y. Gunton's M. 13: 333.

— Character Sketch of. (A. McEwen) R. of Rs. (N. Y.) 16: 547.

— Doctrine of. (L. Tolstoi) R. of Rs. (N. Y.) 17: 73.

— Influence of, in England. (J. A. Hobson) Fortn. 68: 835.

— Last Book of. (H. Garland) McClure, 10: 386. — Atlan. 81: 852.

— Poetical Tributes to. (M. M. Miller, W. J. Armstrong, W. H. Venable, and J. A. Edgerton) Arena, 19: 104.

— A Study from Life. (C. F. McLean) Arena, 20: 296.

Giants in Brussels, A Procession of. (E. Dessaix) Strand, 15: 343.
— Some Famous. (W. Gordon Smythies) Eng. Illust. 12: 715.
Gibb, E. J. W. (E. C. Browne) Ath. '01, 2: 814.
Gibb, Robert. (W. M. Gilbert) Art J. 49: 25.
— Portraits of. Strand, 13: 552.
Gibbon, Edward. Ed. R. 185: 275. — Quar. 185: 1.
— and W. Cowper ; a Contrast. (C. J. Langston) Argosy, 66: 124.
— at Lausanne. Quar. 187: 177.
— Autobiography. (L. Stephen) National, 28: 51. Same art. Ecl. M. 128: 595. Same art. Liv. Age, 213: 162.
— Decline and Fall of the Roman Empire. (H. M. Stephens) Book R. 5: 260.
— Evolution of an Historian. Chamb. J. 74: 257.
— From the New. Blackw. 165: 241. Same art. Liv. Age, 220: 563.
— Library of. (W. F. Rae) Ath. '97, 1: 744.
— Life and Letters. (H. Paul) 19th Cent. 41: 293.
— The Man. (J. C. Bailey) Fortn. 67: 441.
— New Memoirs of. (F. Harrison) Forum, 22: 749.
— Sequel to his Love Letters. (Mrs. E. Lyttelton) National, 29: 904. Same art. Liv. Age, 214: 824.
Gibbons, J. S., Author of War-song " 300,000 More." (E. G. Cohen) Overland n. s. 34: 341.
Gibbs, Frederick S., Collector of Oil Paintings. (K. D. Henry) Brush & P. 8: 207.
Gibson, Charles Dana. (J. M. Bullock) Studio (Lond.) 8: 75. — (C. B. Davis) Critic, 34: 48.
— and his Work. (J. A. Reid) Art J. 52: 39.
— as an Artist of Love and Life. (A. Hope Hawkins) McClure, 9: 869.
— Drawings. Artist (N. Y.) 23: xxxii.
— Illustrator. (F. W. Morton) Brush & P. 7: 277.
— in London with. (Sara Crowquill) Nat'l M. (Bost.) 8: 99.
— London as seen by ; People of Dickens. Studio (Internat.) 4: 131.
Gibson, Wm. Hamilton. (J. C. Adams) New Eng. M. n. s. 15: 643.
Gibson, Wm. J., Removal of, as Counsel of the Treasury Department. (E. P. Clark) Nation, 72: 506.
Gibson Girl, The Original ; Jobina Howland, with portrait. (F. Furbush) Nat'l M. (Bost.) 10: 120.
Gibraltar. (H. Wyndham) Argosy, 70: 259.
— as a Winter Resort. (J. L. Whittle) Fortn. 68: 386.
— Bay of. Un. Serv. M. 22: 377.
— Civil Government of. (L. Williams) Westm. 147: 398.
— Day in. (T. J. Houston) Cath. World, 67: 669.
— Our Offers to Surrender. (W. F. Lord) 19th Cent. 49: 1012.
— Taking of. (D. Hannay) Macmil. 80: 217.
Gidel and Veron. (W. Roberts) Ath. '00, 2: 616.
Gideon, Story of. (D. Bronson) Nat'l M. (Bost.) 8: 345.
Giéra, Jules. Critic, 32: 348.
Gifford, Electa, Singer, with portraits. (E. Swayne) Music, 20: 3.
Gifford Lectures, Recent, and the Philosophy of Theism. (J. Seth) New World, 9: 401.
Gifford Lectureships, The. (R. M. Wenley) Open Court, 13: 72.
Gift of Abner Grice, The ; a story. (R. Barr) McClure, 11: 433.
Gift of Fulfilment ; an allegory. (B. Harraden) Blackw. 165: 283.
Gift of Life, The ; a story. (V. Fenton) Belgra. 96: 441.
Gift of Mahatma. (H. G. Hutchinson) Cornh. 83: 457. Same art. Ecl. M. 137: 246. Same art. Liv. Age, 230: 14.
Gift Horse, A ; a story. (Y. Stewart) Eng. Illust. 18: 138.

Gifts of Money. Spec. 81: 206.
— Oppression of. (A. Repplier) Lippinc. 68: 732.
Gilbert, St., of Sempringham and the Gilbertines, Rose Graham on. Ath. '01, 2: 178.
Gilbert, Mrs. Anne Hartley, Stage Reminiscences of. (Charlotte M. Martin) Scrib. M. 29: 166, 460.
Gilbert, Miss Elizabeth. (F. D. How) Sund. M. 30: 771.
Gilbert, Franklin, Curate. (F. W. Grey) Month, 89: 76-627. 90: 78-407.
Gilbert, Prof. G. H., Case of. Outl. 63: 955. 65: 155.
Gilbert, Sir John. Ath. '97, 2: 494. — With portrait. (M. H. Spielman) M. of Art, 22: 53.
— and Illustration in the Victorian Era. (E. Knaufft) R. of Rs. (N. Y.) 16: 673.
— Pictures by. Sat. R. 85: 169. — Am. Cath. Q. 23: 639.
Gilbert, William. Gilbert of Colchester. (Brother Potamian) Pop. Sci. Mo. 59: 337.
Gilbert, William Schwenk. (R. M. Bruns) Conserv. R. 2: 390. — (W. Archer) Pall Mall M. 25: 88.
— as a Dramatist. Acad. 52: 265.
— The Bab Ballads. Acad. 53: 26.
— Conversation with. (W. Archer) Critic, 39: 240.
— Lucky Star. (J. F. Runciman) Sat. R. 87: 45.
— Pygmalion. (M. Beerbohm) Sat. R. 89: 744.
— The Work of, with portrait. (J. M. Bullock) Bk. Buyer, 17: 565.
Gilbert Islands, Life on. (A. Inkersley) Overland, n. s. 37: 1008.
Gilchrist, R. Murray. Acad. 57: 689.
Gilder, Richard Watson, Religion of the, Poetry of. Meth. R. 60: 791.
— a Singer of Sunrise. (G. D. Goodwin) Poet-Lore, 9: 407.
Gilds, Ancient and Modern Hindu. (E. W. Hopkins) Yale R. 7: 24, 197.
— Craft, in the 15th Century. (T. B. Snow) Dub. R. 122: 275.
— Scottish. Scot. R. 32: 61.
— Mediæval, and Village Clubs. Gent. M. n. s. 58: 549.
Gilead and Bashan. (H. Hayman) Bib. Sac. 55: 29.
Giles, Ernest. Geog. J. 11: 78.
Gilgit, Life in. (G. H. Brotherton) Contemp. 74: 872.
Gillespie, Mrs. E. D. Book of Remembrance. (J. L. Gilder) Critic, 38: 543.
Gillespie ; a poem. (H. Newbolt) Atlan. 81: 696.
Gillette, William, with portraits. (R. Burton) Bk. Buyer, 16: 26.
Gilley, John. (C. W. Eliot) Cent. 37: 120.
Gillicus. (O. P. Hay) Am. J. Sci. 156: 230.
Gillman, Henry. Hassan ; a Fellah. N. Church R. 5: 639.
Gillray, James, with portrait. (J. Grego) M. of Art, 21: 257.
Gilman, Daniel Coit, with portrait. Bk. Buyer, 22: 7. — (G. S. Hall) Outl. 68: 818.
— Administration at Johns Hopkins University. (N. M. Butler) R. of Rs. (N. Y.) 23: 49.
Giorgione and Veronese ; Magician and Conjuror. (R. C. Witt) Temp. Bar, 123: 116.
Giotto. (R. E. Fry) Monthly R. 2, no. 2: 96.
— The Church of S. Francesco at Assisi. (R. E. Fry) Monthly R. 1, no. 3: 139.
— Inner Life of. (M. A. Lathbury) Chaut. 34: 60.
Giotto of the Coteswolds, A. (L. A. Harker) Longm. 36: 40. Same art. Liv. Age, 225: 632.
Giovanni's Revenge ; a story. (F. W. Haselfoot) Eng. Illust. 17: 145.
Gippsland, A Winter's Camp in. (C. B. Luffmann) National, 34: 576.
Girard, Stephen, and his College. (J. M. Beck) Cosmopol. 24: 247.

Girardin, Emile de, the King of the Journalists. (A. D. Vandam) Fortn. 68: 259.

Girl, A, and a Game of Golf; a story. (C. Mullett) Idler, 14: 17.

Girl, The, and the Game; a football story. (J. L. Williams) Harper, 98: 78.

Girl at Glaser's, The; a story. (E. M. Ludlum) Harper, 100: 456.

Girl from Noumea, The. (J. F. Rose-Soley) Overland, n. s. 37: 809.

Girl-graduate of Spain, A. Macmil. 82: 362. Same art. Liv. Age, 227: 168.

Girl in the Garden Hat, The; a story. (I. Allen) Idler, 16: 314.

Girl in the Long Tan Ulster, The; a story. (A. W. Tarbell) Nat'l M. (Bost.) 11: 49.

Girl in Red. (S. E. White) Lippinc. 65: 313.

Girl of Modern Tyre. (H. Garland) Cent. 31: 401.

Girl-ranchers of California. (W. F. Wade) Cosmopol. 28: 613.

Girl Widow, The; a story. (C. Smith) Belgra. 66: 299.

Girl who got Rattled. (S. E. White) Cent. 40: 464.

Girl who was the Ring, The; Indian folk-tale. (G. B. Grinnell) Harper, 102: 425.

Girl's Life in the 18th Century. (M. W. Goodwin) Cosmopol. 30: 502.

Girls, All Sorts and Conditions of. (L. W. Betts) Outl. 64: 737.

— Education of. (E. Hadwen) Chamb. J. 78: 269.

Girls' Lodging-house, A. (D. M. Leake) 19th Cent. 44: 1015.

Girls' Private School, Opportunity of the. (C. W. Porter) No. Am. 165: 252.

Girlhood and its Chances. (J. P. Faunthorpe) Sund. M. 27: 156.

— Renaissance, Art and Romance of. (L. Scott) M. of Art, 22: 647.

Girolamo da Cremona, Altar-piece by. (B. Berenson) Am. J. Archæol. n. s. 3: 161.

Gismondo; a story of to-day. (L. Gurnell) Gent. M. n. s. 60: 105.

Gissing, George. Acad. 52: 489. 53: 258. 57: 724. — With portrait. (J. N. Hilliard) Bk. Buyer, 16: 40. — (G. White) Sewanee, 6: 360.

— as a Traveller. Acad. 60: 535.

— Novels of. (F. Dolman) National, 30: 258. — (H. G. Wells) Contemp. 72: 192. Same art. Liv. Age, 215: 22.

— The Whirlpool. Acad. 51: 516.

Giving, Art of Large. (G. Iles) Cent. 31: 767.

— Measure of. (W. Hull) Luth. Q. 29: 491.

Glacial Geology in America. (D. S. Martin) Pop. Sci. Mo. 54: 356.

Glacial Lakes Newberry, Warren and Dana, in Central New York. (H. L. Fairchild) Am. J. Sci. 157: 249.

Glacial Pot-hole in the Hudson River Shales. (H. F. Osborne) Am. Natural. 35: 33.

Glaciation of Central Idaho, Notes on. (G. H. Stone) Am. J. Sci. 159: 9.

Glaciers of No. America. (I. C. Russell) Geog. J. 12: 553.

— of Russia in 1896. Geog. J. 12: 184.

— Recent Papers on. Nature, 57: 571.

— Size of the Ice Grain in. (J. Y. Buchanan) Nature, 64: 400.

Gladden, W. The Christian Pastor and the Working Church. (J. C. Grant) Crit. R. 8: 323.

Glade in the Forest, The. (S. Gwynn) Cornh. 82: 698, 839.

Gladstone, Samuel Steuart. Bank. M. (Lond.) 67: 881.

Gladstone, William Ewart. (J. J. O'Shea) Am. Cath. Q. 23: 618. — Atlan. 82: 1. — Blackw. 164: 146. — Bk. Buyer, 16: 479. — (T. E. Champion) Canad. M. 11: 139. — (C. J. Little) Chaut. 27: 403. — Church Q. 46: 456. — (N. Hapgood) Contemp. 74: 34. — (H. Hale) Critic, 32: 85, 339. — Dial (Ch.) 24: 343. — (W. H. Kent) Dub. R. 123: 1. — (M. MacColl) Fortn. 69: 1008. Same art. Liv. Age, 218: 80. Same art. Ecl. M. 131: 261. — (Lord Stanmore) Fortn. 70: 1. — (F. W. Hirst) Econ. J. 8: 395. — (J. McCarthy) Forum, 25: 513. — (J. Bryce) Nation, 66: 399. — (R. A. Armstrong) New World, 7: 401. — (W. T. Stead) R. of Rs. (N. Y.) 18: 61. — Spec. 80: 716. Same art. Liv. Age, 217: 748. — (W. Boyd Carpenter) Sund. M. 27: 466. — (F. W. Hirst) Econ. J. 8: 533. — (J. McCarthy) Indep. 49: 673. — Liv. Age, 231: 593. — (J. L. M. Curry) Conserv. R. 2: 216.

— and his Critics, with portrait. (G. McDermot) Cath. World, 67: 622.

— and his Missionary Heroes. (G. Smith) Sund. M. 28: 21.

— and the Nonconformists. (J. G. Rogers) 19th Cent. 44: 30.

— and his Party. (W. Reid) 19th Cent. 44: 169.

— and the Roman Catholic Church. (W. Meynell) 19th Cent. 44: 21.

— Another Side of. Spec. 80: 785.

— as a Book Collector. Liv. Age, 212: 415.

— as Chancellor of the Exchequer. (S. Buxton) Fortn. 75: 590, 785.

— as a Contributor to the Nineteenth Century. (J. Knowles) 19th Cent. 43: 1043.

— as a Financier. Bank. M. (Lond.) 65: 890.

— as a Parliamentarian. (E. Beckett) Sat. R. 85: 705.

— as Reader and Critic. Acad. 53: 582-645. 54: 45.

— as a Religious Teacher. Lond. Q. 90: 315.

— as seen near at Hand. (E. C. Wickham) Good Words, 39: 480.

— as viewed by W. E. H. Lecky. Acad. 56: 121. — Spec. 82: 81.

— Aspects of his Life and Mind. Spec. 81: 683.

— An Autumn Morning with, with portrait. (J. M. Chapple) Nat'l M. (Bost.) 8: 301.

— Bagehot's Forecast (1860), with portrait. (W. Bagehot) Bk. Buyer, 16: 379.

— Bibliography of. Lit. W. (Bost.) 29: 168.

— Burying Cæsar, and after; by a True Liberal. Westm. 150: 237.

— A Chat with. (Mrs. E. Cotes) Liv. Age, 218: 484.

— Equipment of. (T. C. Crawford) Cosmopol. 25: 559.

— First Campaign of, The Field of. (M. Wood) Eng. Illust. 19: 107.

— Foreign Policy of. (J. Bryce) Liv. Age, 218: 768. — (M. D. O'Brien) Westm. 156: 253.

— Fragments of Conversation. (Mrs. R. E. Goodhart) 19th Cent. 50: 590.

— Fragments of Personal Reminiscences. (E. Ashley) National, 31: 536.

— Funeral of. Spec. 80: 753.

— Glimpses of. (H. Furness) Cent. 32: 716.

— in Hawarden. (C. Morley) Strand, 16: 494.

— Influence on English Life. Spec. 80: 748.

— Last Months of. (J. McCarthy) Outl. 59: 221.

— Life of. (J. McCarthy) Outl. 55: 59-891. 56: 1-860. 57: 39-847.

— — McCarthy's. (A. Shaw) Book R. 5: 145. — (J. Cooper) Presb. & Ref. R. 9: 555. — (J. A. Cooper) Canad. M. 10: 443. — (W. C. Murray) Citizen, 4: 10.

— the Man, Williamson's. (G. M. Hyde) Bk. Buyer, 17: 45.

— Memorial for, Best. Spec. 80: 853.

— Morley on. (R. Ogden) Nation, 73: 373.

Gladstone, William Ewart, A Note on, with last portrait. (H. T. Peck) Bookman, **7**: 388.

— Portrait of, J. E. Millais'. (Benjamin-Constant) M. of Art, **24**: 152.

— Public Career of. Gunton's M. **14**: 425.

— Recollections of. (F. Lawley) Sat. R. **85**: 673.

— Reid's Life of. Ath. '98, **1**: 820.

— Reminiscences, Anecdotes, and an Estimate. (G. W. Smalley) Harper, **97**: 476, 796.

— Reminiscences of. (W. Sidebotham) Chamb. J. **77**: 56.

— Reminiscences of a Few Days spent at a Country House with. (S. H. Oldfield) Longm. **32**: 229.

— Some Stray Letters of. (H. St. J. Raikes) Fortn. **70**: 11.

— Talks with, Tollemache's. (C. K. Shorter) Bookman, **8**: 146.— (G. M. Hyde) Bk. Buyer, **17**: 45.

— Theology of. (G. W. E. Russell) Contemp. **73**: 778. Same art. Liv. Age, **218**: 188.

— Thoughts on the Passing of. Westm. **150**: 1.

— True Secret of his Greatness and Influence. (R. Didden) Westm. **150**: 153.

— Undoing of his Policy after his Death. Sat. R. **89**: 608.

— Versatility of. (Sir E. W. Hamilton) Liv. Age, **220**: 68.

— Visit to. (Susan W. Selfridge) Outl. **59**: 425.

Gladstone, Mrs., as seen from near at Hand. (Dean of Lincoln) Good Words, **41**: 534. Same art. Ecl. M. **135**: 494. Same art. Liv. Age, **226**: 573.

Gladwin, Henry, and the Siege of Pontiac. (C. Moore) Harper, **95**: 77.

Glamis Castle, Scotland. (Lady Cecelia Glamis) Pall Mall M. **11**: 292.

Glamour; a poem. (E. Wilder) Atlan. **82**: 540.

Glasgow, Ellen, with portrait. Bk. News, **19**: 1.

Glasgow, Scotland. Pall Mall M. **24**: 289.

— and its Records. Scot. R. **32**: 249.

— Art Gallery Decorations by G. Frampton. Studio (Internat.) **13**: 14.

— District Subway. (B. Taylor) Cassier, **14**: 459.

— International Exhibition, 1901. (A. Mudie) M. of Art, **25**: 409, 457.— Studio (Internat.) **14**: 165, 237.— (P. Geddes) Contemp. **80**: 703.— Studio (Internat.) **14**: 44.— (E. R. Pennell) Nation, **73**: 67.— (Alex. M'Gibbon) Art J. **53**: 129, 187, 219.— (W. D. Wansbrough) Cassier, **20**: 358.

— — Applied Art at. M. of Art, **26**: 60.

— — Arts and Crafts at. (W. Fred) Artist (N. Y.) **32**: 26.

— — Decorative and Industrial Art. (L. F. Day) Art J. **53**: 299, 327.

— — Pictures at. (D. C. Thomson) Art J. **53**: 294, 321.— Sat. R. **92**: 427.

— — Power Plant and Electric Equipment. (B. Taylor) Engin. M. **21**: 207.

— Mitchell Library, A Day's Reading in. Library, **1**: 281.

— Municipal Tramways. (M. R. Malthie) Munic. Aff. **4**: 40.

— Underground Cable Railroad. (P. F. Slater) Good Words, **40**: 389.

— University of. Addison's Roll of Graduates. Ath. '98, **2**: 126.

— — Library. Library, **8**: 381.

— — Ninth Jubilee of. (T. D. Seymour) Nation, **73**: 8. — Ath. '01, **1**: 789.

— Water Works of. (B. Taylor) Engin. M. **17**: 937.

Glasgow Designers and their Work. (G. White) Studio (Internat.) **2**: 86, 227. **3**: 47.

Glasgow Institute of the Fine Arts. Art J. **49**: 91.

Glasgow School of Art. Studio (Internat.) **10**: 232.

Glass, Artistic American, at the Paris Expositions. (G. Teall) Brush & P. **6**: 176.

— Decay in, and History of its Manufacture. (J. Fowler) Archæol. **46**: 65.

— for Optical Uses, Manufacture of. (J. A. Brashaer) Pop. Astron. **6**: 104.

— A House of. (J. Henrivaux) Chaut. **28**: 389.

— Hydrated, Thermodynamic Relations of. (C. Barus) Am. J. Sci. **157**: 1.

— in American Architecture. (G. R. Dean) Brush & P. **6**: 31.

— Painted, in Ibberton Church, Dorsetshire. (F. J. Baigent) Archæol. **48**: 347.

— Soluble, in House Construction. (C. Colné) Am. Arch. **59**: 51.

— Stained. (E. R. Suffling) Sund. M. **30**: 579.

— — and Leaded. Archit. R. **5**: vii.

— — by G. Moira. Studio (Internat.) **9**: 18.

— — Curiosities of. Chamb. J. **75**: 590.

— — Designs for. (F. Brangwyn) Studio (Internat.) **7**: 252.

— — Domestic, in France. (R. de Cuers) Archit. R. **9**: 115.

— — Making of. (T. Dreiser) Cosmopol. **26**: 243.

— — Making of a Window of. (L. F. Day) J. Soc. Arts, **46**: 421.

— Tiffany Favrile. (C. Warren) Studio (Internat.) **2**: 156. **5**: 16.

Glass Decoration, Notes on. (A. Fields) Atlan. **83**: 807.

Glass Houses; a psychological comedy. (G. Burgess) Cent. **37**: 308.

Glass Industry and Ceramics in Sweden. Illus. (S. Frykholm) Artist (N. Y.) **23**: 198.

Glass-makers, French, in England in 1567. Antiq. n. s. **34**: 142.

Glass Manufacture at Jena, Germany. (R. S. Baker) Idler, **19**: 95.

Glass Painting, Technique in. (H. A. Kennedy) Studio (Lond.) **1**: 245.

Glassware, Tiffany's. Sat. R. **87**: 716.

Glasses, English Drinking. (P. Bate) Studio (Internat.) **15**: 45, 106. — Antiq. n. s. **34**: 112.

Glasses, Eye, and their Uses. (J. S. Stewart) Lippinc. **63**: 690. *See also* Eyeglasses.

Glastonbury Abbey, Lady Chapel of, Sculptured Doorways of. (W. H. St. John Hope) Archæol. **52**: 85.

Glastonbury Tor, From. (J. S. Simon) Sund. M. **26**: 583.

Glaucophane Schists, Chemical Study of. (H. S. Washington) Am. J. Sci. **161**: 35.

Glazes, Leadless. (W. P. Rix) J. Soc. Arts, **47**: 324.

Gleam in the Darkness; drama. (H. Aidé) Fortn. **72**: 905.

Gleason, Fred. G., an American Musician and Composer, with portrait. (W. S. B. Mathews) Music, **13**: 331.

Gleek; a Forgotten Old Game. (J. S. McTear) Gent. M. n. s. **63**: 358.

Glen, Captain Johannes Sanderse. (Z. S. Eldredge) N. E. Reg. **52**: 475.

Glen Affaric, Scotland. (W. Sinclair) Art J. **49**: 73.

Glen Eila; a poem. (W. W. Campbell) Canad. M. **16**: 136.

Glendalough, Seven Churches of. (H. W. Ashby) Midland, **10**: 17.

Glenfestey, Giffard H. (G. C. Williamson) Artist (N.Y.) **32**: 1.

Glenn, D. G., Pianist and Teacher. Music, **16**: 413.

Glennie, George F. Bank. M. (Lond.) **66**: 615.

Glenure, Who Shot? (A. Lang) Macmil. **79**: 136.

Glinka, Michel Ivanovitch, Russian Musician. (A. Pougin) Music, **14**: 245.

— Father of Russian Opera. (A. E. Keeton) Contemp. **76**: 413. Same art. Liv. Age, **223**: 432.

Globe, A Great. (E. Reclus) Geog. J. **12**: 401.

Gloria in Excelsis; a poem. (Christian Burke) Pall Mall M. **13**: 433.

Gloria Mundi; a story. (Harold Frederic) Cosmopol. **24**: 259 — **26**: 33.

Gloriana; a story. (H. A. Vachell) Pall Mall M. **13**: 529.

Glorious Privilege, A. (H. H. Bennett) Nat'l M. (Bost.) **13**: 30.

Glory, Paths of. (J. Jacobs) Fortn. **73**: 59. Same art. Ecl. M. **134**: 442.

Glory of his Shame. (A. McKenzie) New Eng. M. n. s. **16**: 245.

Glossopteris Flora, The. (A. C. Seward) Sci. Prog. n. s. **1**: 178.

Gloucester, Mass.; the Fishing City. (L. W. Betts) Outl. **68**: 61.

Glove, The; a story. (M. A. M. Marks) Argosy, **65**: 670.

Gloversville Plunger, The; a story. (C. B. Davis) Munsey, **24**: 846.

Gloves. (E. F. Seat) Lippinc. **59**: 270.

Gluck, Christoph Willibald von, The Founder of German Opera. (B. O. Flower) Arena, **18**: 802.

— Iphigénie en Tauride. (J. F. Runciman) Sat. R. **89**: 457, 487.

Gnats. (R. K. Dents) Library, **3**: 408.

Gneist, Rudolf von. (Munroe Smith) Pol. Sci. Q. **16**: 641. — (M. Smith) Pol. Sci. Q. **12**: 21.

"Gnome," Yacht. Un. Serv. (Phila.) **17**: 183, 279.

Gnosticism in Relation to Christianity. (P. Carus) Monist, **8**: 502.

Gnosticismus, Band XV., Heft 4. (C. A. Scott) Crit. R. **8**: 215.

Goat, The; his Useful Qualities and how he came by them. (L. Robinson) Blackw. **161**: 398.

— Wild, Hunting on Santa Catalina. (D. C. Lockwood) Outing, **32**: 187.

— — Stalking. Chamb. J. **76**: 641.

— — Winter Hunting in the Rockies. (J. W. Schultz) Outing, **37**: 437.

Goatherd, The. (Jean Rameau) Liv. Age, **216**: 809.

— Moorish. (W. B. Harris) Sat. R. **83**: 312.

Goats at the Dairy Show. Spec. **79**: 593.

Go-away Child, The; a story. (F. A. Mathews) Harper, **102**: 945.

Gobelins Tapestry Manufactory of the French Govt. (L. Turgan) J. Soc. Arts, **47**: 744.

Gobi to Urga, Through. (J. H. Roberts) Indep. **52**: 2545.

Gobineau, Count, with portrait. Open Court, **15**: 440.

Goblets and Drinking Cups. (P. Gordon) Gent. M. n. s. **63**: 284.

— — Antique. Chamb. J. **76**: 654.

God, Afraid of. (A. G. Gekeler) Ref. Ch. R. **46**: 487.

— and his Divine Care of Man. (B. Worcester) N. Church R. **6**: 9.

— and the Lord in Relation to Men. (J. Worcester) N. Church R. **6**: 346.

— and the Soul, Armstrong on. Spec. **78**: 18.

— as manifested to Men in the Lord. (J. Worcester) N. Church R. **5**: 321.

— Christian Idea of, Rocholl on. (J. Macpherson) Crit. R. **11**: 437.

— Conception of. (P. Carus) Monist, **9**: 106.

— — Royce on. (A. Stewart) Crit. R. **8**: 266. — (J. Bascom) Dial (Ch.) **24**: 46.

— — — Real Issue in. (G. H. Howison) Philos. R. **7**: 518.

— Creator and Lord of all, Harris's. (E. D. Morris) Presb. & Ref. R. **8**: 346. — (S. D. F. Salmond) Crit. R. **7**: 336.

— Evolution of the Idea of. (A. Lang) Contemp. **72**: 768. Same art. Liv. Age, **216**: 260.

God, Evolution of the Idea of, Allen on. (F. Starr) Dial (Ch.) **24**: 45. — (H. G. Wells) Sat. R. **85**: 211.

— — Andrew Lang on. Acad. **56**: 555.

— Existence of. (C. Walker) Bib. Sac. **55**: 459.

— Fatherhood of. (L. Abbott) Outl. **59**: 681. — (A. H. Bradford) Bib. World, **12**: 230. — (R. W. Dale) Expos. **3**: 56, 166. — (J. M. King) Presb. & Ref. R. **10**: 589. — (J. F. Wright) N. Church R. **6**: 116. — (G. W. Northrup) Am. J. Theol. **5**: 473. — (C. M. Mead) Am. J. Theol. **1**: 577. — (A. S. Weber) Ref. Ch. R. **47**: 453.

— — a Pentecostal Climax. (H. King) Luth. Q. **30**: 211.

— Goodness in the Severity of. (H. M. Tenney) Bib. Sac. **55**: 485.

— His Relation to the World. (J. T. Gladhill) Luth. Q. **31**: 177.

— How to think of. (G. L. Allbutt) N. Church. R. **7**: 73.

— Human Life of. (H. van Dyke) Chaut. **28**: 235.

— Immanence of, Illingworth on. Church Q. **46**: 318. — (J. Iverach) Crit. R. **8**: 259. — (H. C. Minton) Presb. & Ref. R. **10**: 331.

— in Science and in Religion. (G. J. Low) Monist, **8**: 596. — (P. Carus) Monist, **8**: 610.

— in Trifles. (T. F. Manning) Good Words, **40**: 683.

— The Indwelling. Lond. Q. **90**: 256.

— Indwelling of, in Man. (C. B. Hulbert) Bib. Sac. **56**: 78.

— Is He Silent? (Richard Heath) Contemp. **76**: 437. Same art. Liv. Age, **223**: 341. — (Robert Anderson) Contemp. **76**: 683. Same art. Liv. Age, **223**: 540.

— Justice of. Spec. **87**: 9.

— Kingdom of. (E. M. Chapman) Bib. Sac. **54**: 525.

— — and the Church. (W. Rupp) Ref. Ch. R. **46**: 528.

— — Lütgert's. (G. Yos) Presb. & Ref. R. **11**: 171.

— Love of, Bradley on. (G. Hopkins) Presb. & Ref. R. **12**: 171.

— not to be Feared, but Lovable. (H. G. Drummond) N. Church R. **7**: 51.

— Old Testament Teaching concerning. (G. R. Berry) Am. J. Theol. **5**: 254.

— Personality of. (F. A. Shoup) Sewanee, **4**: 87. — (H. Loyson and P. Carus) Open Court, **11**: 618.

— Sovereignty of, Consistent with Human Freedom. (J. Cooper) Ref. Ch. R. **48**: 433.

— The Suffering; a Study in St. Paul. (Emma M. Caillard) Contemp. **79**: 69. Same art. Liv. Age, **228**: 577. Same art. Ecl. M. **136**: 467.

— Supreme, of the Lowest Races. (J. H. Woods) New World, **9**: 441.

— Use of Divine Name Lord, Jehovah, etc., in the Bible. (G. Hawkes) N. Church R. **6**: 226.

God and the Pagan; a story. (W. A. Fraser) McClure, **11**: 225.

God of his Fathers, The; a story. (J. London) McClure, **17**: 44. Same art. Idler, **20**: 137.

God of Iron; a hymn, with music. (P. Carus) Open Court, **12**: 188.

"God of Our Fathers," or Barty's Lamp. (E. Marryat) Pall Mall M. **22**: 569.

God of the Red Man. (R. M. Potter) J. Mil. Serv. Inst. **7**: 61.

"God Rest Ye, Merry Gentlemen;" a story. (S. Crane) Cornh. **79**: 578.

"God Save the Queen" Myths. (J. E. Hadden) Argosy, **72**: 93.

Goddard and Frost Families, Records relating to. (A. Holden) N. E. Reg. **53**: 242.

Goddess on a Pedestal. (M. A. Hartwell) Lippinc. **68**: 218.

Godfrey, Sir Edmondbury. An Unsolved Mystery. (M. Hume) Eng. Illust. **20**: 3.

Godfrey de Bouillon. (J. M. Ludlow) Cosmopol. 23: 411.

Godkin, Edwin Lawrence. Outl. 64: 285.

— and the New Political Economy. (H. S. Green) Arena, 20: 27.

— in New York. (J. B. Gilder) Critic, 32: 293.

— Political Writings. Atlan. 79: 116.

Godliness ; an address. (L. Abbott) Outl. 64: 217.

Godowsky, Leopold, Pianist. (W. S. B. Mathews) Music, 18: 474.

— Arrangement of Chopin's Studies. (W. S. B. Mathews) Music, 20: 108.

— Compositions and Arrangements for Piano. Music, 17: 111.

— Concerts in Berlin. Music, 19: 402.

— Musical Compositions of. (W. S. B. Mathews) Music, 12: 603.

— Recitals of. Music, 19: 595.

— Selected Studies by Chopin. Music, 16: 331

— Works for Piano. Music, 16: 628.

God's Changeling ; a story. (A. A. Martin) Idler, 12: 671.

Gods, Ailing, Treatment of. (W. Matthews) J. Am. Folk-Lore, 14: 20.

Gods, Contemporary Human. (F. Boyle) New R. 16: 195.

— How made in India. (E. W. Hopkins) New World, 8: 75.

— of Savages ; are they Borrowed from Missionaries ? (A. Lang) 19th Cent. 45: 132.

Gods Arrive, The ; a story. (A. E. Holdsworth) Sund. M. 26: 38-807.

Godwin, Parke. Dial (Ch.) 28: 37.

Goethe, Johann Wolfgang v. Sat. R. 88: 287. — (J. T. Hatfield) Meth. R. 59: 767.

— and Germany. Spec. 83: 278.

— and Kant. (F. Jodl) Monist, 11: 258.

— and the 19th Century. Quar. 191: 56.

— and Victor Hugo ; a comparison. National, 34: 901.

— and Weimar. (H. Schutz Wilson) Gent. M. n. s. 58: 369. Same art. Ecl. M. 129: 89.

— Anniversary of. (K. Francke) Outl. 63: 39.

— as a Stage Manager. (W. S. Sparrow) 19th Cent. 41: 628.

— Byron's Influence upon. (A. M. Bowen) Dial (Ch.) 28: 144.

— Faust. (B. W. Wells) Sewanee, 2: 385.

— — pt. 1 ; tr. by McLintock. Sat. R. 84: 228.

— — Job and. Quar. 186: 213.

— — What was the Homunculus ? (M. Earll) Poet-Lore, 13: 269.

— in Practical Politics. (F. P. Stearns) Lippinc. 59: 561.

— in Strassburg. (J. T. Hatfield) Dial (Ch.) 27: 113.

— Iphigenie, at Harvard. (K. Francke) Nation, 70: 239.

— — Original of. (E. J. Allen) Music, 14: 441.

— Life and Work of. (R. W. Moore) Chaut. 26: 139.

— Loves of. (E. H. Nason) Cosmopol. 24: 172.

— Man and Poet. (G. B. Rose) Sewanee, 9: 398 .

— Message to America. (K. Francke) Atlan. 84: 609.

— Religion of. (J. C. Bay) Arena, 22: 383.

— E. Rod's Estimate of. Acad. 53: 157.

— Swedenborg's Influence upon. N. Church R. 7: 541.

— The Two Sides of. Spec. 84: 201.

— Youth of. (Ja. A. Harrison) Conserv. R. 3: 299.

Goethe Society, Publications of. (C. H. Genung) Nation, 65: 301.

Goettingen, American Doctorates at. (J. D. Butler) N. E. Reg. 54: 439.

— and Harvard Fifty Years Ago. Letters from Cogswell, Ticknor, and Everett. (T. W. Higginson) Harv. Grad. M. 6: 6.

Goff, Colonel, Etchings by. Studio (Lond.) 2: 41.

Goff, J. W., with portrait. Green Bag, 9: 465.

Gogol, Nicholas Vassilievitch. (C. Brinton) Critic, 37: 418.

Going down to Jericho. (P. H. Coggins) Atlan. 88: 166.

"Going Fantee." Spec. 85: 797.

Going to School ; a poem. (Edward Carpenter) Gent. M. n. s. 58: 616. Same art. Ecl. M. 129: 285.

Gokteik Viaduct in Burma. (J. C. Turk) World's Work, 2: 1148.

Gold and other Resources of the Far West. (J. A. Latcha) Forum, 26: 97.

— and Silver, Mining of. (C. C. Goodwin) Chaut. 24: 670.

— — Relative Stability of. (E. S. Meade) Ann. Am. Acad. Pol. Sci. 14: 38.

— Appreciation of, A Texas View of. Gunton's M. 13: 436.

— Discovery of, in California. (M. Bellamy) Overland, n. s. 31: 161.

— Dredging for. (A. W. Robinson) Cassier, 16: 33.

— Effect of the New, on Prices. (C. A. Conant) No. Am. 165: 540.

— Experiment with. (M. C. Lea) Am. J. Sci. 153: 64.

— Exports of. (A. D. Noyes) Nation, 69: 463.

— Extraction by the Cyanide Process. (T. K. Rose) Sci. Prog. 7: 306. See Gold Ores.

— Have we Sufficient in Circulation ? (R. P. Falkner) Forum, 27: 740.

— History of Endeavors to make. (L. Bell) Nat'l M. (Bost.) 9: 551.

— in Australasia, Production of. Bank. M. (Lond.) 71: 878.

— in Ireland. Chamb. J. 76: 237.

— in the Philippines. (H. G. Hanks) Overland, n. s. 32: 141.

— Increasing the Circulation of. Bank. M. (N. Y.) 57: 66.

— Increasing Supply of. (G. E. Roberts) Forum, 26: 656. — (H. M. Chance) Engin. M. 17: 562. — (A. F. Outerbridge, jr.) Pop. Sci. Mo. 54: 635.

— Iodometric Determination of. (F. A. Gooch and F. H. Morley) Am. J. Sci. 158: 261.

— is Where you Find it. (F. M. Stocking) Overland, n. s. 32: 30.

— Lumps of Luck. (H. Preskin) Chamb. J. 76: 123.

— Melting Point of. (L. Holborn and A. L. Day) Am. J. Sci. 161: 145.

— Mining and Minting of. (A. E. Outerbridge, jr.) J. Frankl. Inst. 146: 401.

— New Supplies of, Influence of. (G. E. Roberts) No. Am. 173: 254.

— Placer, and how it is Secured. (J. E. Bennett) Cosmopol. 26: 23.

— Production of, since 1830. (E. S. Meade) J. Pol. Econ. 6: 1.

— — Recent, of the World. (W. Hooper) J. Statis. Soc. 64: 415.

— Scramble for, at Six Per Cent. Bank. M. (Lond.) 69: 1.

— Stock of, in the U. S. (M. L. Muhleman) Pol. Sci. Q. 16: 96. — (F. P. Powers) Q. J. Econ. 14: 552.

— Supply of, Future of. (N. S. Shaler) Internat. Mo. 4: 676. — (H. White) Nation, 73: 361.

— — Our. Chamb. J. 78: 149.

— The Transition to, in England and in India. (W. W. Carlile) J. Pol. Econ. 7: 99.

— Tyranny of. (H. White) Nation, 66: 82.

— World's Quest for. Bank. M. (Lond.) 64: 746.

Gold of Vincosta, The ; a story. (R. Copplestone) Cornh. 79: 39. Same art. Liv. Age, 220: 707.

Gold Assaying as a Profession. (P. G. Holms) Chamb. J. 75: 712.

Gold Beads; a story. (M. A. Taylor) Liv. Age, 212: 312. Same art. Ecl. M. 128: 390.

Gold Bricks, Studies in. Green Bag, 13: 448.

Gold Certificates, Resumption of the Issue of. Bank. M. (N. Y.) 57: 751.

Gold Coast, The, Ashanti, and Kumassi. (G. K. French) Nat. Geog. M. 8: 1.

— Glimpse at. (H. Bindloss) Asia. R. 30: 300.

— Interior of. (R. A. Freeman) Macmil. 80: 105.

Gold Contracts; Can Contracts to pay in Specific Coin be enforced? (N. M. Thygeson) Am. Law R. 30: 716.

Gold Country, Exploring a. (A. Williams) Engin. M. 14: 70.

Gold Currency, A. (H. White) Nation, 68: 411.

— in the U. S., Possibility of. (C. F. Dunbar) Q. J. Econ. 13: 314.

Gold Democrats, Position of the. (D. MacG. Means) Nation, 71: 84.

Gold Dredging, How to make it Pay. (A. W. Robinson) Cassier, 18: 480.

Gold Economics. Bank. M. (Lond.) 69: 222.

Gold Field of Transvaal, Richest in World. (S. C. Norris) Macmil. 82: 294.

Gold Fields of Alaska and the Yukon. (C. C. Adams) Chaut. 26: 54. — (D. MacG. Means) Nation, 65: 83. — (C. H. Macintosh) Canad. M. 8: 305. See Klondike.

— of British Columbia and the Klondike. (W. H. Merritt) J. Soc. Arts, 46: 649.

— of the Porce River, Colombia. (J. D. Garrison) Eng. Illust. 12: 983.

— of Siberia. Chamb. J. 76: 549.

Gold Fish, The. Liv. Age, 221: 133.

— and the Ornamental Fish of Japan. Illus. (K. Kishinouye) Nat. Sci. 13: 39.

Gold Mines, Lost. (C. Michelson) Munsey, 26: 367.

— Mine-salting. (C. M. Dobson) Cosmopol. 24: 575.

— of British Columbia. Chamb. J. 77: 421.

— of West Africa. (J. Irvine) J. Soc. Arts, 47: 305.

— of the Witwatersrand. (J. H. Hammond) Engin. M. 14: 733, 911.

Gold-mining in British Columbia. (C. Phillipps-Wolley) Canad. M. 8: 299.

— in Canada. (W. H. Merritt) Canad. M. 8: 319.

— in Georgia. (W. Tatham) J. Frankl. Inst. 146: 19.

— in North America. (G. E. Walsh) Lippinc. 60: 801.

— on the Rand. (H. White) Nation, 71: 400.

Gold Monometallism in Japan. (J. Soyeda) Pol. Sci. Q. 13: 60.

Gold Myth, Origin of the. (A. G. C. Van Duyl) Asia. R. 23: 68.

Gold Nobles found at Bremeridge Farm, Westbury, Wilts. (J. Baron) Archæol. 47: 137.

Gold Nuggets, Fortunes in. (G. E. Walsh) Cassier, 13: 428.

Gold Objects, Votive Deposit of, found in Ireland. (A. J. Evans) Archæol. 55: 391.

Gold Ores, Cyanid Process for, in Western America. (T. Tonge) Engin. M. 14: 652. — (J. W. Richards) Cassier, 14: 413. — (J. W. Richards) J. Frankl. Inst. 143: 96.

— of the Witwatersrand, Mining of. (H. H. Webb and P. Yeatman) Engin. M. 15: 39, 261, 401.

Gold Ornaments of the Time of Theodoric in the Museum at Ravenna. Archæol. 46: 237.

Gold Palace of Out-of-doors, The; a poem. (J. H. La Roche) Outing, 32: 259.

Gold Reserve of the Banks. Bank. M. (Lond.) 68: 117

— of Great Britain. Bank. M. (N. Y.) 63: 998.

— Our [English] National, How to Strengthen and Maintain. (G. L. Ayre) Bank. M. (Lond.) 72: 589.

Gold Resources of India. (W. King and T. W. H. Hughes) Engin. M. 15: 797.

Gold-seeker in the West. (S. Davis) Chaut. 25: 631.

Gold-seekers. Trampers on the Trail. (Hamlin Garland) Cosmopol. 26: 515.

Gold Standard, Adoption of, in Japan. (J. Soyeda) Econ. J. 9: 469.

— The Greenback and the. (H. M. Brosius) No. Am. 165: 11.

— in Austria, Adoption of the. Bank. M. (N. Y.) 55: 561.

— Maintaining the. Gunton's M. 17: 286.

— Securing it by Law. (J. Dalzell) No. Am. 169: 912.

— Stability of the. (E. S. Meade) Am. J. Soc. Sci. 38: 206.

Gold Standard Act, The New. (H. White) Nation, 71: 418.

Gold Standard Defence Association, Pamphlets of. (L. Darwin) Econ. J. 8: 349.

Gold-stealers. (E. Dyson) Longm. v. 38-39.

Golden Arrow; a poem. (J. V. Cheney) Cosmopol. 23: 556.

Golden Bars, The. (John Stafford) Chamb. J. 75: 625-666.

Golden-crown Sparrow of Alaska; a poem. (J. Burroughs) Cent. 37: 106.

Golden-eye or Lace-wing Fly. (C. M. Weed) Am. Natural. 31: 500.

Golden Fleece, Knights of the. (Edgar Saltus) Cosmopol. 30: 324.

Golden Fleet, The; a Day-dream. Temp. Bar, 113: 581.

Golden Gate Park. (R. M. Gibson) Overland, n. s. 37: 735.

Golden Glory; a tale. (M. M. Halliwell) Canad. M. 11: 250.

Golden Lily, The. (P. L. M'Dermott) Chamb. J. 75: 721-820.

Golden Messias, The; a story. (L. C. Cornford) Pall Mall M. 19: 505.

Golden Morning, A. (S. R. Crockett) Sund. M. 28: 721.

Golden River, Prairie Route to the. (H. Garland) Indep. 51: 245.

Golden Sally. (M. E. Francis) Longm. 35: 244.

Golden Sepulchre, A. (W. C. Morrow) Overland, n. s. 36: 501.

Golden Silence; a tale. Argosy, 66: 333.

Golden Spurs, The; a story. (Tresham Gwaines) Idler, 12: 601.

Golden Tiger, The. (F. N. Connell) Strand, 17: 588.

Golden Venture, A; a story. (W. W. Jacobs) Harper, 101: 775.

Golden Wedding, A. (E. Rod) Poet-Lore, 10: 483.

Golden Wedding, A; a story. Idler, 17: 124.

Goldschmidtite, a New Mineral. (W. H. Hobbs) Am. J. Sci. 157: 357.

Goldsmith, Oliver, Country of. (J. A. Leeper) Temp. Bar, 110: 280. Same art. Ecl. M. 128: 682.

— Deserted Village. (L. S. Livingston) Ath. '00, 1: 499.

— — 1770 Editions of. (L. S. Livingston) Bookman, 12: 563.

— Grave of. (C. Hiatt) Ath. '00, 1: 592.

— A New Letter of. (J. H. Lobban) Ath. '00, 1: 628.

— She Stoops to Conquer; is it a Comedy? Acad. 58: 109.

— Vicar of Wakefield. Ecl. M. 132: 721.

Goldsmithery. (A. Fisher) M. of Art, 20: 184.

Goldsmiths' Institute, The, London. M. of Art, 20: 192.

Goldsmith's Mould, Greek, in the Ashmolean Museum. (H. S. Jones) J. Hel. Stud. 16: 323.

Goldsmith's Trade and its Relation to Wealth. (P. Gaultier) Chaut. 24: 541.

Goldsmith's Work, Mediæval, at Conques. Scrib. M. 25: 637.

Goldsmiths, Some, and their Work. Artist (N. Y.) 24: 154.

Golf. Blackw. 164: 52. — (A. Haultain) Contemp. 80: 195. Same art. Liv. Age, 230: 739. — (M. Hardie) Macmil. 85: 45. — (H. J. Whigham) Scrib. M. 21: 566. — Liv. Age, 215: 134. — (F. S. Douglas) Outing, 34: 219.

— Advent and Status of. Outing, 30: 249.
— Advice to Beginners. (H. H. Hilton) Outing, 36: 653.
— and the American Girl. (H. L. Fitzpatrick) Outing, 33: 294.
— and its Attractions. (J. G. McPherson) Gent. M. n. s. 64: 123. Same art. Ecl. M. 134: 793. Same art. Liv. Age, 225: 226.
— and its Literature. (William Wallace) Scot. R. 34: 22. Same art. Ecl. M. 133: 694. Same art. Liv. Age, 222: 865.
— Canadian. (J. P. Roche) Outing, 32: 260.
— Chicago Clubs. (A. J. Colman) Outing, 34: 354.
— Development of, in the West. (H. C. C.-Taylor) Outing, 36: 531.
— for 1896. (P. Collier) Outing, 31: 271.
— Form in. (H. Vardon) Outing, 36: 86.
— from a St. Andrew's Point of View. (A. Lang) No. Am. 169: 138.
— Golfers in Action. (P. Collier) Outing, 30: 419.
— How to play. (W. Tucker) Outing, 32: 437.
— Horace Hutchinson on. Spec. 83: 190.
— Whigham on. (W. T. van Tassel Sutphen) Bk. Buyer, 16: 349.
— in America, Rise of. (P. Collier) R. of Rs. (N. Y.) 22: 459.
— in California. (A. Inkersley) Overland, n. s. 35: 387.
— in Canada. (W. A. R. Kerr) Canad. M. 17: 340.
— in Colorado. (S. H. Thompson, jr.) Outing, 38: 552.
— in England, Early. (E. J. L. Scott) Ath. '01, 1: 434.
— in the Far West. (T. H. Arnold) Outing, 35: 559.
— in New York. (C. Turner) Outing, 34: 443.
— Instructions in. (H. Vardon) Outing, 36: 146.
— Isle of Wight Links. (C. W. Barnes) Outing, 32: 621.
— its Present and its Future. Blackw. 162: 102. Same art. Liv. Age, 214: 613. Same art. Ecl. M. 129: 649.
— Knickerbocker, and Other Forbidden Sport of New Netherlands. (L. M. Friedman) Green Bag, 13: 67.
— Medal Day at St. Andrew's, 1899. (T. M. Parrott) Outing, 35: 611.
— Modern Clubs and Modern Methods. (H. Hutchinson) Outing, 37: 264.
— Moral Side of. (S. D. McConnell) Outl. 65: 299.
— Most Difficult and Best Holes. (H. Hutchinson) Outing, 38: 393.
— New School. (H. Hutchinson) Outing, 36: 478.
— The Old and the New. Blackw. 168: 385. Same art. Liv. Age, 227: 237. Same art. Ecl. M. 135: 730.
— on the Seaboard. (H. L. Fitzpatrick) Outing, 32: 498.
— Open Championship, 1899. (C. Turner) Outing, 35: 117.
— Popularity of. (T. W. Legh) Pall Mall M. 12: 189.
— Psychology of. (L. Robinson) No. Am. 165: 649.
— Round and about the Quaker City. (H. Hiss) Outing, 34: 260.
— Special Attraction of. Ecl. M. 131: 346. — Liv. Age, 218: 680.
— Strokes of: Approaching. (H. M. Harriman) Outing, 36: 421.
— — Driving. (C. B. Macdonald) Outing, 36: 419.
— — Putting. (W. J. Travis) Outing, 36: 416.

Golf, Theory and Practice in. (J. A. Tyng) Outing, 38: 213.
— — of Teaching. (A. D. Cochrane) Outing, 37: 537.
— Winter, in the South. (J. D. Dunn) Outing, 35: 486.
— Women's Championship, 1899. (C. Turner) Outing, 35: 233.
Golf Alphabet, A New; a poem. (C. F. Weeks) Outing, 36: 387.
Golf Bonnet, The; a poem. (J. B. Hartswick) Cent. 37: 131.
Golf Championships, Amateur. (H. L. Fitzpatrick) Outing, 33: 132.
— Future of. (A. Pottow) Outing, 39: 54.
Golf Club, St. Andrew's, of America. (J. Reid) Outing, 32: 399.
Golf Clubs of Long Island. (C. Turner) Outing, 34: 602.
Golf Course, Laying out and Care of. (W. Tucker) Outing, 36: 286.
Golf Lullaby, A; a poem. (M. Barbour) Outing, 36: 133.
Golf Rules, Why and Wherefore of. (C. B. Macdonald) Outing, 36: 255.
Golfer's Conquest of America, The. (C. Whitney) Harper, 95: 695.
Golfing about Boston. (G. H. Sargent) Outing, 34: 129.
Golgotha, The Cross of. (P. Carus) Open Court, 13: 472.
Golly and the Christian; a story. (Bret Harte) Cosmopol. 31: 644.
Goluchowski, Count. Spec. 79: 724.
Gomez, General, at Santa Clara. (G. Kennan) Outl. 63: 151.
— In the Field with. (G. Flint) McClure, 11: 193.
— True Story of. (T. R. Dawley, jr.) Munsey, 22: 210.
Gommeuse, La; a story. (C. B. Davis) Harper, 94: 572.
Goncourt, E. de. (A. F. Davidson) Macmil. 76: 413.
— and J. de, The Academy of. Acad. 51: 635. — Critic, 30: 92.
Gondomar, Count. (G. Hill) Gent. M. n. s. 66: 258.
Gongora. (J. Mew) 19th Cent. 41: 821.
Good, T. S. No News. Art J. 53: 293.
Good, An Analysis of the. (H. M. Stanley) Philos. R. 6: 257.
— and Evil, Royce on. (H. C. Minton) Presb. & Ref. R. 9: 730.
— Concept of. (W. G. Everett) Philos. R. 7: 505.
— G. Lowes Dickinson on the Meaning of. Ath. '01, 1: 270.
Good that came of it, The. (A. O. Tibbits) Strand, 17: 736.
Good Americans. (Mrs. Burton Harrison) Cent. 33: 56-912.
Good Baronet, The; a story. (G. S. Street) Pall Mall M. 25: 14.
Good Fellow's Wife. (H. Garland) Cent. 33: 937.
Good-for-nothing, A; a story. (A. O. Brazier) Eng. Illust. 20: 24.
Good Friday Night; a poem. (W. V. Moody) Atlan. 81: 700.
Good Government Clubs, Junior. Experiment in Citizen Training. (W. Buck) Pop. Sci. Mo. 52: 111.
Good Hope, Cape of, Capture of, 1806. Un. Serv. M. 16: 551.
— French East-Indian Expedition at, in 1803. (J. H. Rose) Eng. Hist. R. 15: 129.
— A Run to. (D. Macleod) Good Words, 40: 131, 167.
— — Transport Cruise to, 1795. (E. M. O. Marshall) Longm. 37: 147.
Good Hunter, The, and the Iroquois Medicine. (W. M. Beauchamp) J. Am. Folk-Lore, 14: 153.
Good Hunting; a story. (E. Nesbit) Pall Mall M. 14: 536.
Good Investment, A; a story. (E. S. Grew) Idler, 13: 757.

Good News from Scovia; a poem. (J. M. Neale) 19th Cent. 44: 747.

Good-night; a poem. (A. Austin) Ecl. M. 132: 626.

Good Shepherd Convent and their Accusers. Month, 95: 608.

Good Time; a story. (B. C. D'Easum) Canad. M. 16: 3.

Good Turn, A; a story. (S. C. Grier) Blackw. 164: 393. Same art. Liv. Age, 217: 179.

Goode, George Brown, with portrait. Pop. Sci. Mo. 50: 400. — (S. P. Langley) Science, 5: 369.

Goodenough, Wm. A., Lieut.-Gen. (C. R. Markham) Geog. J. 12: 620.

Goodman, A. J. (F. M. Crawford) Munsey, 17: 40.

Goodness, Instinctive. Spec. 78: 865.

Goodrich House, Cleveland, O. Ann. Am. Acad. Pol. Sci. 11: 134.

Gooseherd, The. (H. Ludermann) Liv. Age, 216: 78.

Goodwin, Alfred, Notes on. Sat. R. 87: 109.

Goodwin, Ernest. (H. W. Bromhead) Art J. 50: 305.

Goodwin, W. W., Greek Grammar. (B. L. Wiggins) Sewanee, 1: 225.

Goodwin Sands, The. (E. A. Du Plat) Idler, 14: 737.

Goodyear, Charles, Sketch of. (C. Dooley) Pop. Sci. Mo. 53: 690.

Googan's Christmas; a story. (W. H. Crowell) Midland, 10: 532.

Gooseberry and the Goblin, The; a story. (M. L. Pendered) Argosy, 74: 271.

Goose-shooting. (E. W. Sandys) Outing, 31: 34.

— on Cascumpec Bay. (R. R. Fitzgerald) Outing, 30: 49.

Gopher, Pocket or Pouched. (C. L. Webster) Am. Natural. 31: 114.

Gordon, A. J. Address on "Absence of Theology" criticised. (J. K. Smyth) N. Church R. 5: 107.

Gordon, Adam Lindsay. (C. R. Haines) Temp. Bar, 112: 222.

Gordon, Sir Charles Alexander. Recollections of 39 Years in the Army. Sat. R. 85: 531.

Gordon, Gen. Chas. Gordon. (Ellen M. Clerke) Dub. R. 121: 294.

— Campaign in China, by Himself. Fortn. 74: 372, 601.

— Myth of, in China. (R. K. Douglas) 19th Cent. 44: 256.

— Statue of. J. Mil. Serv. Inst. 11: 812.

— Sun Yat Sun and Li Hung-Chang. Asia. R. 23: 51.

Gordon, Charles W. [Ralph Connor], with portrait. Bk. News, 19: 355. — Critic, 37: 310.

Gordon, Jane Maxwell, the Daring Duchess of. (J. M. Bulloch) Eng. Illust. 17: 275. — (F. F. Armytage) Pall Mall M. 14: 409.

Gordon, Robert. Bank. M. (Lond.) 69: 901.

Gordon's Daughter. (F. Wilson) New Eng. M. n. s. 25: 57.

Gordon's Reprieve. (G. P. Greble) Cent. 37: 559.

Gordon Highlanders, The. (J. M. Bulloch) Blackw. 163: 254. Same art. Liv. Age, 216: 889.

— Raising of the. (F. F. Armytage) Pall Mall M. 14: 409.

— Stories of the. (C. Lowe) McClure, 10: 485.

Gore, Canon, A Sunday with. Sund. M. 27: 177.

Gore-Booth, Henry William. Geog. J. 15: 290.

Goree; a Lost Possession of England. (W. F. Lord) 19th Cent. 41: 759.

Gorgon's Head, The. (G. Bacon) Strand, 18: 635.

Gorham, Col. John. "Wast Book" Facsimiles. (F. W. Sprague) N. E. Reg. 52: 186.

Gorham Desire, Petition of. (F. W. Sprague) N. E. Reg. 52: 229.

Gorham Families of Yarmouth, Mass. (W. P. Davis) N. E. Reg. 52: 357, 445.

Gorham Family, Notes on the Providence Line of. (G. Guild) N. E. Reg. 54: 167.

Goring, George. (E. Scott) Cornh. 77: 195.

Gorky, Maxim, the new Russian Novelist, with portrait. (J. W. Clarkson) Indep. 53: 2213. — (R. N. Bain) Monthly R. 5, no. 2: 159. — (E. Garnett) Acad. 60: 497. — (E. D. North) Outl. 69: 417. — (Count S. C. de Soissons) Contemp. 80: 845. — (Christian Brinton) Critic, 39: 45. — Bk. Buyer, 23: 186.

— Foma Gordyeff. (A. M. Logan) Nation, 73: 209. — (C. A. Pratt) Critic, 39: 354. — (C. Brinton) Bk. Buyer, 23: 205.

— Russia's Tramp Novelist. (A. Hornblow) Bookman, 13: 50.

Gormley's Scoop. (E. A. Walcott) Scrib. M. 24: 187.

Goro: the Story of his Harakiri. (A. Kinnosuké) Lippinc. 66: 628.

Gorse. (Grant Allen) Strand, 15: 626.

Gorton, Samuel. (L. G. Janes) New Eng. M. n. s. 18: 287.

Gortyna, Epigraphical Researches in. (F. Halbherr) Am. J. Archæol. 2d s. 1: 159.

— Statue of an Asclepiad from. (L. Mariani) Am. J. Archæol. 2d s. 1: 279.

Gosha, Journey in. (C. H. Craufurd) Geog. J. 9: 54.

Gospel for a World of Sin. (S. A. Ort) Luth. Q. 29: 528.

— A New, and Some New Apocalypses. (J. Rendel Harris) Contemp. 76: 802.

Gospel of Action. (L. F. Ward) Indep. 51: 1865.

Gospel of the Air-ball, The. (P. Millington) Temp. Bar, 117: 235. Same art. Ecl. M. 133: 405. Same art. Liv. Age, 222: 298.

Gospel of the Reformation, Has it become Antiquated? (F. Loofs) Am. J. Theol. 3: 433.

Goss, Charles Fred., with portrait. Bk. News, 19: 115.

Gossamer Threads; a poem. Ecl. M. 131: 335.

Gossip of the Switch-shanty. (C. De L. Hine) Cent. 40: 685.

Gossips of Killymard. (S. MacManus) Cent. 36: 245.

Gota Canal in Sweden. (E. W. Foster) Outing, 32: 329.

Gotch, T. C., Artist. (A. L. Baldry) Studio (Internat.) 4: 73.

Gotham, Stampleton's Merry Tales of. Ath. '01, 1: 104.

Gothenburg Movement. (W. W. Carlile) Econ. R. 11: 322.

Gothenburg System; How it Works. (F. C. Bray) Chaut. 24: 443.

Gothic Architecture in Cyprus, Enlart's. (C. H. Moore) Nation, 69: 265.

— in Tyrol. (W. A. Baillie-Grohman) M. of Art, 23: 299.

Gothic Art, Place of, in Civilization. (W. R. Lethaby) Archit. R. 7: 17.

Gothic Descent of American People. (M. Emery) Gunton's M. 18: 534. 19: 50, 142, 242.

Gottschalk, L. G., with portrait. Music, 13: 496.

Gottschalk, Louis M., Pianist. (W. S. B. Mathews) Music, 13: 351. — Music, 18: 519.

Gould, Benjamin Apthorp. (S. C. Chandler) Harv. Grad. M. 5: 373. — (A. Hall) Pop. Astron. 4: 337.

— Life and Work of. (S. C. Chandler) Pop. Astron. 4: 341.

Gould, F. Carruthers, Artist. Studio (Internat.) 14: 196.

Gould, Geo. Home at Lakewood. (K. Hoffman) Munsey, 23: 301.

Gould, Helen Miller. (J. P. Coughlan) Munsey, 25: 387.

— Fresh Air Home, Woody Crest. (C. B. Todd) Gunton's M. 20: 71.

Goulding, Frederick. Lithographs (Interview). Studio (Lond.) **6**: 86.

Gounod, Charles. (C. Saint-Saens) Music, **13**: 1–267.
— Conversations with. (E. Martinengo-Cesaresco) Macmil. **82**: 181. Same art. Ecl. M. **135**: 432. Same art. Liv. Age, **226**: 410.

Governess, The, in Fiction. Acad. **57**: 163. Same art. Liv. Age, **222**: 851.

Governess, The, and the Hat-band ; a story. (I. Allen) Idler, **17**: 152.

Governesses, On. (Mary Maxse) National, **37**: 397.

Government and Liberty. (H. E. S. Fremantle) Internat. J. Ethics, **10**: 439.
— Basis of. Outl. **66**: 297.
— by "Gentlemen." (F. P. Powers) Lippinc. **60**: 670.
— by Injunction. (B. S. Dean) Green Bag, **9**: 540.
— Cabinet, or Departmentalism ? (J. A. R. Marriott) 19th Cent. **48**: 685.
— Capture of, by Commercialism. (J. J. Chapman) Atlan. **81**: 145.
— Civil, Practical Problems of. Book R. **5**: 81.
— Cost of, in City and State. (M. R. Maltbie) Munic. Aff. **4**: 685.
— Fraternalism *vs.* Paternalism in. (R. T. Ely) Cent. **33**: 780.
— Honest. The Smelting of the Hon. Jerry Webb. (C. Lesbald) Arena, **19**: 108.
— in War Time. (René Bache) Cosmopol. **25**: 255.
— Local Self-, Early Days of. (W. H. Frere) Econ. R. **11**: 231.
— A Moral from Athenian History. (B. Bosanquet) Int. J. Ethics, **9**: 13.
— or Human Evolution, Kelly's. (D. C. Wells) Yale R. **9**: 337.
— Present Scope of. (E. Wambaugh) Atlan. **81**: 120.
— Province of. (C. C. Bonney) Open Court, **15**: 130.
— Self-, The Natural Right of. (A. Steckel) Arena, **23**: 449.
— Some Consecrated Fallacies. (A. K. Fiske) No. Am. **169**: 821.

Government Buildings, Suggestion for Grouping. (G. Brown) Archit. R. **7**: 89.

Government Deposits in Banks. (G. E. Roberts) Forum, **29**: 1.

Government Loans to Farmers. (C. F. Emerick) Pol. Sci. Q. **14**: 444.

Government Ownership of Quasi-public Corporations. (E. R. A. Seligman) Gunton's M. **20**: 305.

Government Purchases and Funds, Price of the. Bank. M. (Lond.) **67**: 352.

Government Rat, A. (Z. A. Norris) Arena, **19**: 273.

Government Service in the U. S. ; does it pay ? (A. M. Low) Forum, **29**: 623.

Governments and Parties in Continental Europe, Lowell's. (C. H. Lincoln) Citizen, **3**: 15. — (J. Macy) Am. Hist. R. **2**: 729.

Governor, Judicial Functions of the. (D. MacG. Means) Nation, **71**: 5.

Governor of St. Kitts, The ; a story. (A. C. Doyle) McClure, **9**: 565.

Governor's Rehearsal, The ; a story. (C. Warren) McClure, **15**: 76.

Governor-general, his Functions. (W. A. Weir) Canad. M. **8**: 269.
— His Function and Duties. Canad. M. **15**: 167.

Governor-general, The ; a story. (F. R. Stockton) Cosmopol. **25**: 677.

Governors elected Nov., 1896, with portraits. Outl. **55**: 35.

Gower, John. Acad. **58**: 181.
— Macaulay's. (G. L. Kittredge) Nation, **71**: 254.

Gowrie Conspiracy. (A. Lang) Critic, **37**: 338.

Goya y Lucientes, Francisco ; Spanish Artist. (P. G. Konody) Idler, **15**: 746.

Grace, Doctrines of. (J. Watson) Expos. **5**: 161–321. **7**: 53–347. **8**: 37, 180.
— Paul's Doctrine of, Scope of. (G. H. Gilbert) Am. J. Theol. **1**: 692.

Grace of Chance ; a tale. (W. A. Fraser) Canad. M. **12**: 216.

Grade in Schools a Fiction. (W. S. Jackman) Educa. R. **15**: 456.

Grading of Schools inside of Class Lines. (J. T. Bergen) Educa. R. **16**: 81.

Græco-Turkish War. J. Mil. Serv. Inst. **21**: 167.

Graf, Arturo, Poetry of. Acad. **52**: 564.

Grafly, Charles. (V. C. Dallin) New Eng. M. n. s. **25**: 228. — With portrait. (L. Taft) Brush & P. **3**: 343.

Grafton, Augustine Henry, 3d Duke of. Autobiography. (J. A. Woodburn) Am. Hist. R. **4**: 715. — Ed. R. **189**: 489. — Quar. **189**: 219. — Ath. '98, **2**: 599. — Spec. **81**: 692.

Grafton Galleries, The. Ath. '00, **1**: 663.
— Second Romney Exhibition. Ath. '00, **2**: 763.

Graftonite, and its Intergrowth with Tryphylite. (S. L. Penfield) Am. J. Sci. **159**: 20.

Graham, Sir Gerald, Vetch's. Blackw. **170**: 623.

Graham, Henry Grey, as an Historian. Acad. **58**: 64.

Graham, Peter. Evening. Art J. **50**: 309.

Graham, Col. T., Despatches of. (J. H. Rose) Eng. Hist. R. **14**: 111, 321.

Graham, William ; a Famous Scotch Song-writer. Chamb. J. **78**: 31.

Grahame, Kenneth. Acad. **52**: 493.

Grain and Flour Traffic, Diversion of, from the Great Lakes to the Railroads. (G. G. Tunell) J. Pol. Econ. **5**: 340, 413.
— Discharging and Storage of, at British Ports. (W. G. Wales) Cassier, **13**: 11.

Grain Elevators and Conveyors, Pneumatic. (F. E. Duckham) Cassier, **15**: 31.

Grain Market, Futures in. (H. C. Emery) Econ. J. **9**: 45.

Grain Trade from Manitoba. (E. Farrar) Canad. M. **11**: 371.
— of the Northwest, Abuses in. (L. Walker, jr.) Ann. Am. Acad. Pol. Sci. **18**: 488.

Grammar of the Great, The. Scrib. M. **27**: 633.
— Modern Teaching of. (S. E. Lang) Educa. R. **20**: 294.
— Psychological Significance of the Parts of Speech. (G. Buck) Educa. **18**: 269.
— Teaching of, by the Sentence-diagram. (G. Buck) Educa. R. **13**: 250.

"Grammar of Science," The Psychology of. (I. M. Bentley) Philos. R. **6**: 521.

Grammar Schools, Mediæval. (J. B. Milburn) Dub. R. **125**: 153.
— Rational Grading of. (C. H. Gordon) Educa. **21**: 16.

Grammarians, Compliments to the. (F. Sarcey) Liv. Age, **221**: 794.

Gramme, Zenobe Théophile. Nature, **63**: 327.

Grana, The : an Old Country-house in Spain. (G. C. Cunninghame Graham) Chamb. J. **77**: 297.

Granada, By Diligencia to. (T. R. Dawley) Outl. **67**: 802.
— A Yankee in, after our War with Spain. (T. R. Dawley, jr.) Outl. **68**: 343.

Granby, Marchioness of. Portraits. Critic, **39**: 128.

Grand, Sarah. (J. J. Cotton) Macmil. **82**: 381.
— and Mere Man. Sat. R. **91**: 733.
— as a Novelist. Acad. **60**: 347.

Grand Army of the Republic. (G. Morgan) Lippinc. **64**: 437.

Great Britain, Politics in. Trade, and the Outlook. (R. Giffen) Econ. J. 10: 295.
— — Recreant Leaders. Fortn. 71: 1.
— — Settling Day. (G. C. Noel) Fortn. 71: 326.
— — Tyranny of the Party Whip. (J. D. Holms) Westm. 150: 477.
— — Wanted — a Man. Contemp. 75: 145.
— — Will the Liberals repent? Westm. 151: 606.
— Position of, in the World. Spec. 80: 331. Same art. Liv. Age, 217: 123.
— Postal Pettifogging. (J. H. Heaton) 19th Cent. 50: 315.
— Problems and Policies for 1898. (W. T. Stead) R. of Rs. (N. Y.) 17: 189.
— Prosperity and Government Waste. (A. J. Wilson) Contemp. 75: 470.
— Ptolemy's Geography of. (H. Bradley) Archæol. 48: 379.
— Republic of the United States of. (J. B. Walker) Cosmopol. 29: 401.
— Sale of Goods Act, 1893. Has Section 4 made any Change in the Law? (L. F. Cussen) Law Q. 13: 298.
— Scenic Geology of. (J. E. Marr) Sci. Prog. 7: 275.
— Sea-power of, Dangers to, under the Present Rules of Naval Warfare. (N. Synnott) Fortn. 67: 568.
— Shrinkage of. (H. Macfarlane) Good Words, 41: 763. Same art. Liv. Age, 227: 784. Same art. Ecl. M. 136: 163.
— Social Future of. (W. Clarke) Contemp. 78: 858.
— Statesmanship in. Fortn. 76: 635.
— Strong Men of. (D. Story) Munsey, 26: 396.
— Tariff Tendencies in. (T. G. Bowles) Forum, 27: 641.
— Trade and Imperialism. Contemp. 76: 132, 282.
— — and Foreign with British Subjects. Spec. 79: 364.
— — and German Competition. (A. W. Flux) Econ. J. 7: 34.
— — British and Foreign. Spec. 79: 364.
— — Danger to, Lord Rosebery on. (H. Birchenough) 19th Cent. 48: 1064.
— — Do Foreign Annexations injure? (H. Birchenough) 19th Cent. 41: 993.
— — 1860–1900. (M. G. Mulhall) Contemp. 77: 383.
— — Foreign. (D. MacG. Means) Nation, 69: 106.
— — Future of. (J. B. C. Kershaw) Fortn. 68: 732.
— — Geographical Conditions affecting. (G. C. Chisholm) Geog. J. 18: 424.
— — in 1898. (J. W. Cross) 19th Cent. 45: 850.
— — in 1900. Sat. R. 91: 70.
— — with Germany and Belgium. (M. G. Mulhall) Contemp. 72: 333.
— — within the Empire. (J. A. Baines) J. Statis. Soc. 61: 1.
— An Unarmed People. (W. A. Baillie-Grohman) Fortn. 75: 527.
— United Kingdom, Smith's. Ed. R. 192: 1. — (C. M. Andrews) Am. Hist. R. 5: 738. — (J. Bryce) Nation, 70: 94.
— vs. France and Russia. (J. N. Hampson) National, 31: 502. Same art. Ecl. M. 131: 159.
— Victorian, and its Future. (T. Davidson) Forum, 23: 629.
— War Office. (A. Griffiths) Fortn. 73: 214. — Blackw. 170: 146.
— — Admiralty, and Coaling Stations. (J. C. R. Colomb) Monthly R. 3, no. 3: 15.
— — A Business. (Sir R. Giffen) 19th Cent. 50: 1.
— — Conflicting Responsibility of Secretary and Commander-in-chief. Sat. R. 91: 292.
— — Insufficient Proposals of. (H. O. Arnold-Forster) 19th Cent. 47: 554.
— — Its Duties. Pall Mall M. 21: 225.
— — Organization of. Contemp. 79: 38.

Great Britain; War Office, Reform in, A Future for (H. Gordon) Westm. 155: 244.
— — Report of, 1901, Danger of the. (S. Low) 19th Cent. 50: 227.
— Why is Britain hated? (F. E. S. Scholes) Westm. 153: 643.
Great Catch, A. (P. A. de Alarcón) Liv. Age, 213: 404.
Great Central Railway of England. (C. G. Harper) Fortn. 71: 586.
Great Circle on the Celestial Sphere. (O. E. Harmon) Pop. Astron. 4: 555.
Great Electric Trust; a story. (Francis Lynde) Cosmopol. 14: 395.
Great Game of Checkers, A; a story. (G. W. Rose) McClure, 9: 664.
Great God Ram, The. (W. L. Armstrong) Atlan. 81: 430.
Great Gold Robbery, A; a story. (B. Copplestone) Green Bag, 12: 397. Same art. Cornh. 77: 518. Same art. Liv. Age, 217: 535.
Great Good Place, The. (H. James) Scrib. M. 27: 99.
Great-great-grandmother's Adventure, a Kentucky Sketch. (Ella H. Johnson) Midland, 7: 543.
Great Grey Heron and the Two Little Peewits. (J. S. Thomson) Good Words, 40: 775.
Great Heresy Trial of the Rev. Epaphroditus Plummer. (C. A. Stanley) Cent. 39: 882.
Great Invitation, The; a story. (A. Macdonell) Macmil. 84: 284.
Great Man Theory of Progress. Liv. Age, 219: 306.
Great Men and Evolution, Mallock on. (F. H. Giddings) Book R. 5: 391.
— Present Dearth of. Sat. R. 92: 264.
— Their Simplicity and Ignorance. (M. MacDonagh) Cornh. 78: 498. Same art. Ecl. M. 131: 683. Same art. Liv. Age, 219: 378.
Great Middleville Cyclone; a story. (W. L. Alden) Pall Mall M. 11: 274.
Great Salt Lake Trail, Inman and Cody's. Bk. Buyer, 18: 409.
Great Secretary-of-State Interview, The. (J. L. Williams) Scrib. M. 24: 540.
Great Stone of Sardis; a novel. (F. R. Stockton) Harper, 95: 19–899.
Great Woodchuck Race at Stubbs Farm. (J. O. Whittemore) Outing, 39: 214.
Greater Game, The. (C. D. Haskins) Liv. Age, 226: 589.
Greater Love hath no Man. (I. M. Strobridge) Arena, 21: 335.
Greatest of these, The. (H. B. Fuller) Atlan. 80: 762.
Greatness, True. (A. Maclaren) Chaut. 28: 135.
Greece; American Excavations in Sparta and Corinth. (J. Gennadius) Forum, 24: 619.
— — Our Learned Philhellenes. (H. D. Traill) Fortn. 67: 504. Same art. Liv. Age, 213: 367.
— — Peasant of. (E. M. Cesaresco) Contemp. 72: 887.
— and Asia. Ed. R. 194: 28.
— and Crete. (W. J. Stillman) Nation, 64: 433. — Spec. 78: 260, 496.
— — a poem. (A. C. Swinburne) 19th Cent. 41: 337.
— — Perris's. Sat. R. 83: 647.
— and the Eastern Question. (B. I. Wheeler) Atlan. 79: 721.
— and Europe. (F. A. Maxse) National, 29: 352.
— and Ireland. (E. M. Lynch) Gent. M. n. s. 65: 43.
— and the Powers. Spec. 78: 224.
— — Government by Possession. Spec. 79: 360.
— and Roumania. (C. W. Super) Nation, 65: 128.
— Archæology in, 1900–01. (R. C. Bosanquet) J. Hel. Stud. 21: 334.
— Athens, Bœotia, and Corinth. (R. B. Richardson) Chaut. 33: 164.

Greece, The Bicycle in. (R. B. Richardson) Nation, 68: 198.

— The Case against. Fortn. 67: 772.

— Dawn of. Quar. 194: 218.

— Excavations in, American. (J. Gennadius) Forum, 22: 607. 23: 50, 432. 24: 372.

— — The Spade before the Sword. (J. R. S. Sterrett) Nation, 64: 318, 354.

— Fate of. (E. J. Dillon) Contemp. 72: 1.

— Holm's History of. (J. R. Smith) Dial (Ch.) 22: 216. 25: 468. — Ath. '98, 1: 266. — Sat. R. 83: 583.

— Ignominy of Europe. (T. Davidson) Forum, 23: 282.

— in 1897. (W. B. Harris) Blackw. 162: 286.

— Intervention in Crete, Motive of. (W. J. Stillman) Nation, 64: 200.

— Lawsuits in Athens. (A. H. Nelson) Green Bag, 12: 479.

— Modern. Acad. 61: 127. — (C. E. Lloyd) Cosmopol. 22: 587. — (J. S. Blackie) Forum, 23: 113.

— — Social Life in. (E. Capps) Chaut. 24: 545.

— My Sixty Days in. (B. L. Gildersleeve) Atlan. 79: 199, 301, 630.

— Mycenæan Age in, Recent Discoveries in. (C. Waldstein) No. Am. 172: 431.

— A New Archæological Law for. (Edward Capps) Nation, 69: 88.

— Older Civilization of. Nature, 64: 11.

— Patriot Songs of. (I. F. Mayo) Good Words, 38: 275. Same art. Liv. Age, 213: 484.

— Prehistoric. Quar. 188: 90.

— Ridgeway's Early Age of. (T. D. Seymour) Nation, 73: 494.

— Royal Family of. (B. I. Wheeler) Cent. 32: 139.

— Soldiers of. (E. Gardner) Sat. R. 83: 435.

— Some Things we owe to. (C. C. Taylor) Chaut. 31: 613.

— Uprising of. (C. W. Dilke ; D. N. Botassi) No. Am. 164: 453.

— War of Independence, 1821-33. (R. P. Keep) Nation, 65: 522.

— War of 1897. (C. Williams) Fortn. 67: 959. — With map. Pub. Opin. 22: 522. — (G. Eastman) Chaut. 25: 348.

— — as I saw it. (B. Burleigh) Fortn. 68: 134.

— — Catastrophe of. (W. J. Stillman) Nation, 64: 374.

— — Defeat of Greece. Spec. 78: 612.

— — Downfall of Greece. (H. W. Wilson) National, 29: 525. Same art. Ecl. M. 129: 119. — (H. Norman) Scrib. M. 22: 399.

— — Expenses of. Spec. 78: 586.

— — Glimpse of. (C. E. Callwell) Blackw. 162: 165.

— — The Greek Resolve. Spec. 78: 648.

— — The Greeks and their Lesson. (A. Gaye) Macmil. 76: 334.

— — How the Greeks were defeated. (Frederick Palmer) Forum, 24: 350.

— — In the Wake of. (J. Ralph) Harper, 96: 548.

— — Mistakes of. Sat. R. 84: 333.

— — Nevinson's. (W. Huysche) Sat. R. 85: 723.

— — The Powers and. (T. S. Woolsey) Forum, 23: 513.

— — With the Greek Soldiers. (R. H. Davis) Harper, 95: 813.

— — Year of Shame for England. Westm. 149: 117.

Greek, and Turk. Spec. 78: 364.

— Modern, as a Fighting Man. (B. I. Wheeler) No. Am. 164: 609.

Greeks, Modern, Cowardice of. Sat. R. 84: 456.

Greek and Latin Proper Names, English Pronunciation of. (G. Hempl) School R. 6: 412.

Greek Art in Asia. (C. R. Conder) Scot. R. 30: 340.

Greek Boys, Education of. (F. E. Whitaker) Pop. Sci. Mo. 53: 809.

Greek Church, Hore's Orthodox. Church Q. 51: 413.

Greek Drama, Prof. Murray on. (H. S. Edwards) Theatre, 38: 322.

— Rise of. (W. C. Lawton) Sewanee, 9: 156.

Greek Dramatists, Husbandry in the. (E. M. Cesaresco) Contemp. 72: 119.

Greek Elegy, The. (W. P. Trent) Sewanee, 6: 1.

Greek Folk as revealed in their Poetry. (J. S. Stuart-Glennie) Scot. R. 32: 113.

Greek Games. (W. McK. Bryant) New World, 9: 301.

Greek History and Greek Monuments. (P. Gardner) Atlan. 84: 183.

Greek Idealism in Common Things of Life. (S. H. Butcher) Educa. R. 22: 240.

Greek Independence, War of, Phillips's. (J. I. Manatt) Am. Hist. R. 3: 537.

Greek Landscape and Architecture. (A. Higgins) M. of Art, 22: 33.

Greek Language, College Entrance Requirements in, Report of the Committee of Twelve on. (J. H. Harris) School R. 9: 183.

— Development of Study of, in American Colleges. (C. W. E. Chapin) Chaut. 32: 581.

— Elementary, for College Freshmen. (J. I. D. Hinds) Educa. R. 14: 169.

— High School Programme without. (W. H. Butts) School R. 5: 292.

— in the Curriculum. (J. A. Baber) Educa. 20: 641.

— in Modern Education. (J. H. T. Main) Educa. 17: 474.

— Jeopardy of. (H. W. Auden) Blackw. 169: 529.

— Modern, Study of. (H. de F. Smith) Educa. 19: 65.

— A Pinch of Attic Salt. (M. E. Merington) Chaut. 32: 369.

— Preparatory, in the University. (J. H. Harris) School R. 8: 38.

— Pronunciation of, in England. (J. Gennadius) Contemp. 71: 373.

— Shall it be taught in High Schools. (W. F. Webster) Forum, 28: 459.

— Study of. (H. A. Scomp) Bib. Sac. 54: 501.

— A Substitute for. (W. C. Lawton) Atlan. 85: 807.

— written Phonetically in the Early Service Books of Church of England. Archæol. 46: 389.

Greek-letter Societies. (M. Hutton) Canad. M. 17: 55.

Greek Literature, Campbell on Religion in. (J. L. Salmond) Crit. R. 9: 421.

— 1896-97. (S. P. Lambros) Ath. '97, 2: 18.

— 1897-98. (S. P. Lambros) Ath. '98, 2: 20.

— 1898-99. (S. P. Lambros) Ath. '99, 2: 20.

— 1899-1900. (S. P. Lambros) Ath. '00, 2: 20.

— 1900-01. (S. P. Lambros) Ath. '01, 2: 19.

— Murray on. (M. L. D'Ooge) Dial (Ch.) 23: 89.

— Religion in. Ed. R. 191: 334. — (J. Iverach) Lond. J. 93: 85. — Month, 93: 17.

Greek MSS. on Mount Athos, Lambros Catalogue of. V. 2. Ath. '01, 1: 204.

Greek Matrons and Maids. (L. M. J. Garnett) Good Words, 40: 461.

Greek Maxims, Two Famous. (P. E. More) New World, 7: 18.

Greek Monachism. (Z. T. Sweeney) Cosmopol. 23: 297.

Greek Music from the Modern Point of View. (C. W. Seidenadel) School R. 6: 541.

Greek Mysteries and the Gospel. (A. S. Carman) Bib. World, 10: 104.

— Farnell's Cults of. (P. Shorey) Nation, 65: 189.

Greek Myths. (W. A. Leonard) Westm. 155: 432.

Greek Philosophers, Early. Church Q. 52: 387.

Greek Philosophy and Modern Culture, Gomperz on. Nature, 64: 345. — (H. Sturt) Crit. R. 11: 291. — (P. Shorey) Dial (Ch.) 31: 100.

Greek Poetry, The Last Peasant in. (E. M. Cesaresco) Contemp. **74**: 576. Same art. Liv. Age, **219**: 488. Same art. Ecl. M. **132**: 70.

Greek Religion. (G. Santayana) New World, **8**: 401.

— and Mythology. (P. Carus) Open Court, **14**: 513, 705. **15**: 1.

— Literary Influence in the Development of. (A. Fairbanks) Bib. World, **11**: 294.

Greek Retreat from India. (T. Hungerford) J. Soc. Arts, **49**: 417.

Greek Temples, Orientation of. (F. C. Penrose) Nature, **63**: 492.

Greek Terra-cotta Head found at Rome. Archæol. **49**: 453.

Greek Theatre, Dörpfeld and. (T. D. Goodell) Am. J. Philol. **18**: 1.

— Dörpfeld and Reisch's. (J. H. McDaniels) Nation, **65**: 153.

— Setting of a Greek Play. Quar. **188**: 360.

Greek Tragedy, Shall we still read? (T. D. Goodell) Atlan. **81**: 474.

Greek Tragic and Comic Poets, Chronological Studies in. (E. Capps) Am. J. Philol. **21**: 38.

Greek Tragic Drama, Haigh on. (J. H. McDaniels) Nation, **66**: 286.

Greek View of Life. (J. A. Nicklin) Internat. J. Ethics, **11**: 227.

Greiffenhagen, Maurice, Painter. (B. Kendell) Artist (N. Y.) **32**: 57. — With portrait. (E. R. Pennell) Bk. Buyer, **14**: 84.

— and his Work. (J. S. Little) Studio (Lond.) **9**: 235.

Greiner, Otto, Lithographer. (H. W. Singer) Studio (Internat.) **6**: 260.

Gregor, Walter. Folk-Lore, **8**: 188.

Gregorian Melodies, On the MSS. and Printed Editions of. (W. Corney) Dub. R. **121**: 332.

Gregory, Edward John, with portraits. Strand, **16**: 60.

Gregory, Francis Hoyt, Rear Admiral U. S. N. (J. A. Smith) Midland, **10**: 156.

Greeley, Horace, Early Home of. (R. S. Cushman) New Eng. M. n. s. **21**: 556.

— Personal Reminiscences of. Bookman, **13**: 126.

Green, Guy W. Writer, **14**: 170.

Green, John Richard. Letters. Acad. **61**: 423. — (W. M. Payne) Dial (Ch.) **31**: 430.

Green, Thomas Hill. Metaphysics. (S. S. Laurie) Philos. R. **6**: 113.

— Philosophy of. (H. Sidgwick) Mind, **26**: 18.

— Reputation of Empiricism. (H. V. Knox) Mind, **25**: 62.

Green, William, Judge. (Sallie E. M. Hardy) Green Bag, **10**: 111.

Green, William Henry. (J. D. Davis) Bib. World, **15**: 406. — (J. D. Davis) Presb. & Ref. R. **11**: 377.

Green Family. Hasey-Green. (D. P. Corey) N. E. Reg. **54**: 211.

Green, The Color, in Literature. Acad. **56**: 535, 565.

Green Dwarf, The; an Early Romance of C. Brontë. (W. G. Kingsland) Poet-Lore, **9**: 479.

Green Grasshopper. (A. W. Colton) New Eng. M. n. s. **16**: 667.

Green Lady, The; a folk-tale. Folk-Lore, **7**: 411.

Green Mountains of Oman, Across the. (S. B. Miles) Geog. J. **18**: 465.

Green Pigs, The. (S. H. Preston) Scrib. M. **28**: 190.

Green River, Origin of. (S. F. Emmons) Science, **6**: 19.

Green Withes. (J. H. Walworth) Lippinc. **63**: 723.

Greene, Nathanael, General. J. Mil. Serv. Inst. **14**: 1321. — (M. A. Greene) New Eng. M. n. s. **17**: 558.

— and Family, Recollections of. (M. L. Phillip) Cent. **33**: 363.

— Letters to Col. Jeremiah Wadsworth. Pennsyl. M. **22**: 211.

Greenaway, Kate. Ath. '01, 2: 669. — (E. V. Lucas) Acad. **61**: 466.

Greenbacks and the Gold Standard. (H. M. Brosius) No. Am. **165**: 11.

— and the Cost of the Civil War. (W. C. Mitchell) J. Pol. Econ. **5**: 117.

— Imprisoning the. Bank. M. (N. Y.) **54**: 191.

— Mr. Turpie's Speech for. (H. White) Nation, **66**: 416.

— Value of, during the Civil War. (W. C. Mitchell) J. Pol. Econ. **6**: 139, 285.

— Were they a War Necessity? Bank. M. (N. Y.) **54**: 505.

Greenfield. (H. C. Parsons) New Eng. M. n. s. **15**: 609.

Greenhorn's Luck, A. (Alice J. Stevens) Overland, n. s. **38**: 205.

Greenland, Artist in. (R. W. Porter) New Eng. M. n. s. **16**: 289.

— Expedition to, Berlin Geographical Society's, 1891. (J. Geikie) Nature, **58**: 413.

— North, Journeys in. (R. E. Peary) Geog. J. **11**: 213.

— — Hunting Trip to. (F. Merrill) Nat. Geog. M. **11**: 118.

— — Capt. Sverdrup's Expedition to. Geog. J. **13**: 136.

— Northeastern, Map of King Oscar Fjord and Kaiser Franz Josef Fjord. (A. G. Nathorst) Geog. J. **17**: 48.

— Peary's 1896 Expedition to. (G. H. Barton) Nat'l M. (Bost.) **8**: 312.

— Swedish Expedition to East. (A. G. Nathorst) Geog. J. **14**: 534.

Greenough, James Bradstreet, Sketch of Life of, with portrait. (G. L. Kittredge) Harv. Grad. M. **10**: 196.

Greenwood, Customs of Shakespeare's. (G. Morley) Knowl. **22**: 90.

Grenadiers, King William I. of Prussia and his Giant. (J. R. Hutchinson) Pall Mall M. **13**: 375.

Grenville, Sir Richard, in the Azores. (D. Hannay) New R. **16**: 491. Same art. Liv. Age, **213**: 872.

Grettis Saga, edited by R. C. Boer. Folk-Lore, **11**: 406.

Greuze, Jean Baptiste. (H. Armitage) Temp. Bar, **112**: 30.

Grey, Lady Katherine, and Edward Seymour, Earl of Hertford. (W. L. Rutton) Eng. Hist. R. **13**: 302.

— Carved Oaken Chest of. (W. L. Rutton) Reliquary, **40**: 120.

Grey, Sir George. (J. Robinson) 19th Cent. **44**: 754. — Sat. R. **86**: 396.

— and the China Expedition of 1857. (R. Garnett) Eng. Hist. R. **16**: 739.

— and the Poetry of the Maoris. (R. Hodder) Gent. M. n. s. **63**: 382.

— and South Africa. (J. Milne) Fortn. **73**: 933.

— a Builder of the Empire. (L. Becke and W. Jeffery) Fortn. **70**: 620.

— Memoirs of, Milne's. (W. Canton) Good Words, **40**: 501.

Grey Day and a Golden; a prairie sketch. (J. Blewett) Canad. M. **17**: 548.

Grey Glove, The. (Helen Boddington) Good Words, **42**: 126.

"Grey Men" of Kunharva, The; a story. (A. M. Judd) Belgra. **97**: 1.

Grey Mullet Fishery in Japan. Illus. (K. Kishinouye) Nat. Sci. **13**: 253.

Grey Wig, The; a story. (I. Zangwill) Pall Mall M. **25**: 450.

Grey Wolf, The. (J. A. T. Lloyd) Cornh. **81**: 57.

Gribble, Francis. Sunlight and Limelight. Sat. R. **85**: 532.

Gridirons, Art in. (F. A. Jones) Studio (Internat.) **4**: 99.

Grief and God ; a poem. (S. Phillips) Cornh. **77**: 675. Same art. Ecl. M. **131**: 136.

— Golden. (P. W. Roose) Argosy, **66**: 442.

Grieg, Edward Hagerup. (A. E. Keeton) Temp. Bar, **113**: 275.

— an Evening with. (W. S. B. Mathews) Music, **13**: 254.

— Music of. Sat. R. **83**: 506.

Grievance, Luxury of. Spec. **84**: 337.

Griffelkunst of Max Klinger. Sat. R. **85**: 459.

Griffin, Lieutenant, on the Volunteer Force. (E. Balfour) Un. Serv. M. **15**: 267.

Griffin, Bradney B. Sience, n. s. **7**: 523.

Griffin. See Gryphon.

Griffis, Wm. Elliott, with portrait. Bk. News, **18**: 707.

Griggs, Edward Howard, with portrait. Bk. News, **18**: 434.

Griggs, John William, with portrait. Green Bag, **10**: 89.

Grignion, Thomas, Clockmaker. J. Soc. Arts, **48**: 478.

Grigoresco, Niculæ Ion ; Roumanian painter. (W. Ritter) Studio (Internat.) **6**: 115.

Grimaldi, Joseph, King of Clownland. (C. Scott) Eng. Illust. **20**: 271.

Grimaux, Edouard. Ath. '**00**, **1**: 595.

Grimm, Herman. (K. Francke) Nation, **72**: 507.

Grindelwald, Growth of. (F. Gribble) Outing, **36**: 362.

Grindstone Question, The ; a story. (R. Barr) McClure, **9**: 748.

Grinnell, G. B., Work of. (A. B. Scoville) Char. R. **6**: 141.

Grinnell, Iowa. (J. I. Manatt) New Eng. M. n. s. **18**: 457.

Grip of the Sun ; a story. (A. Villiers) Eng. Illust. **19**: 145.

Griselda of the Cabins, A. (A. S. Winston) Outl. **66**: 177.

Griswold, R. W., Correspondence of. (G. E. Woodberry) Nation, **67**: 372.

Grit of Women ; a story. (J. London) McClure, **15**: 324.

Grizzly, Biography of a. (E. Seton-Thompson) Cent. **37**: 27, 201.

Grolier Club Bindery, The. Bookman, **11**: 159.

Groom's Story, The ; a poem. (A. C. Doyle) Cornh. **77**: 452.

Grön, Niels, Explanation and Amende to. (J. C. Ridpath) Arena, **19**: 575.

— How to get an Article into a Magazine. (J. C. Ridpath) Arena, **18**: 853.

Gronow, Captain, Reminiscences of. Pall Mall M. **20**: 297.

Grosart, Alexander Balloch. (O. Smeaton) Westm. **151**: 527. — Acad. **56**: 347.

Grosbeak, Black-headed, of California. (A. Knapp) Lippinc. **62**: 538.

Grosseteste, Robert, Bishop of Lincoln. Acad. **58**: 251. — Church Q. **49**: 412.

— Stevenson's. (C. L. Peirce) Nation, **70**: 302.

Grosvenor Hotel, Case of. Spec. **80**: 296.

Grote, Mrs. George, a Radical Lady of the Last Generation. (J. Fyrie) Temp. Bar, **121**: 527.

Grotius, Hugo. New Eng. M. n. s. **22**: 121.

Groton (Mass.) Genealogy, Contribution to. (E. Stone) N. E. Reg. **51**: 199.

— Local Scandal. (S. A. Green) N. E. Reg. **51**: 68.

Grounds, Private, Planting of. (C. S. Sargent) Garden & F. **10**: 329.

Groups, Theory of, Burnside's. (H. Burkhardt) Nature, **59**: 122.

Grouse and Quail, Clark's Relationships of North American. Amer. Natural. **33**: 259.

— Ruffed, Shooting. (E. Sandys) Outing, **39**: 3. — (R. Gourlay) Canad. M. **13**: 539.

Grouse, Sport with. (H. A. Scott) Outing, **34**: 351.

Grouse-hunting. (J. R. Benton) Outing, **35**: 144.

Grouse Shooting and Dinners. Sat. R. **90**: 170.

— in Morocco. (A. I. Shand) Sat. R. **92**: 202.

— in the Snow. (R. B. Buckham) Outing, **29**: 426.

— in Tropical Weather. Sat. R. **86**: 236.

Grout, John William. (H. L. Jillson) New Eng. M. n. s. **16**: 131.

Grove, Sir George. Ath. '**00**, **1**: 698. — Spec. **84**: 808. — J. Soc. Arts, **48**: 587.

Growers of Haarlem, The ; a story. Liv. Age, **218**: 114.

Grown Baby ; a story. (J. Blewitt) Canad. M. **17**: 116.

Grub Street of To-day, The. Bookman, **11**: 225.

— An American Impression of the New. (E. Fawcett) Bookman, **12**: 129.

— Origin of the Phrase. Acad. **60**: 38.

Grubhofer, Tony, Drawings by. Studio (Lond.) **5**: 8. — Studio (Internat.) **6**: 23.

Grueby Faience. Artist (N. Y.) **23**: xxxix.

Grul's Hour. (C. G. D. Roberts) Liv. Age, **212**: 781.

Grundy, Sydney. Debt of Honor. (M. Beerbohm) Sat. R. **90**: 296.

— Degenerates. (M. Beerbohm) Sat. R. **88**: 325.

Gryphon, Heraldic and Mythological. (R. Brown) Archæol. **48**: 355.

Guadaloupe, the Sacred City. (G. C. Cunningham) Overland, n. s. **35**: 483.

Guadalquivir, Two Months on the. (H. F. Witherby) Knowl. **22**: 6, 51, 183, 222, 272.

Guam and its Governor. (E. C. Rost) Munsey, **23**: 15.

— Capture of the Island of ; the true story. (D. White) Overland, n. s. **35**: 225.

Guanaco Hunt with the Fuegians. (F. A. Cook) Outing, **37**: 576.

Guanajuato, Ancient City of. (Vera Granville) Overland, n. s. **33**: 99.

— Picturesque. (Clara S. Brown) Overland, n. s. **37**: 617.

Guano Islands, African. Chamb. J. **75**: 356. Same art. Ecl. M. **131**: 493.

Guantanamo, A Few Days in. (G. Kennan) Outl. **61**: 957.

— Marines signaling under Fire at. (S. Crane) McClure, **12**: 332.

Guardian Angel, A ; a story. (H. P. Spofford) Harper, **94**: 941.

Guards, The, under Queen Anne. (J. W. Fortescue) Macmil. **76**: 248.

Guasimas, Rough Riders' Fight at. (R. H. Davis) Scrib. M. **24**: 259.

Guatemala, In. (N. H. Castle) Overland, n. s. **35**: 99-265.

Gudgeon-fishing. Spec. **87**: 183.

Guerdon from the Grave, A. (H. Hervey) Chamb. J. **78**: 497-535.

Guérin, Eugénie de. Temp. Bar, **119**: 576. — Liv. Age, **225**: 451.

— and Maurice de. (H. Barton Baker) Gent. M. n. s. **62**: 563.

Guérin, Jules, surrenders Fort Chabrol. Sat. R. **88**: 383.

Guérin, Maurice de. (L. E. Tiddeman) Westm. **152**: 199.

Guérin's School of Art. (H. Frantz) M. of Art, **22**: 485.

Guernsey Island, Government of. Sat. R. **83**: 463.

— Sarnia Felix. (G. Pringle) Westm. **152**: 451.

Guerrilla Warfare. Outl. **67**: 10. — (T. M. Maguire) Un. Serv. M. **23**: 187-583. **24**: 52. **29**: 86.

— and Counter-guerrilla. (Sir C. W. Dilke) Fortn. **76**: 927.

— in History. (J. B. Firth) Fortn. **76**: 803.

Guns, Machine, Uses of. (J. H. Parker) J. Mil. Serv. Inst. **24**: 1.

— Naval, and how Manufactured. (A. M. Laise) Nat'l M. (Bost.) **8**: 569. — (E. J. Prindle) Engin. M. **15**: 371.

— Old, and their Owners. Fortn. **67**: 139. Same art. Ecl. M. **128**: 676. Same art. Liv. Age, **212**: 735.

— Pointing Sea Coast. (J. Chester) J. Mil. Serv. Inst. **1**: 356.

— Precision in Aim of, with Reference to Special Vessels to be attacked. (S. W. Barnaby) Cassier, **14**: 321.

— Rapid Fire. (G. W. Van Deusen) J. Mil. Serv. Inst. **13**: 75.

— Story of the Sporting Gun. (W. Gerrare) Outing, **37**: 510.

Guri Witch. (Johannes Reimers) Overland, n. s. **31**: 32.

Gurkha Scouts. Blackw. **165**: 802.

Gurkhas, Records of the Regiments of. (F. P. Gibbon) Pall Mall M. **14**: 416, 527.

Gurnard Rock, The. (J. Patey) Chamb. J. **75**: 7-57.

Gurteen, Stephen Humphreys. (T. G. Smith) Char. R. **8**: 364.

Gustavus Adolphus. J. Mil. Serv. Inst. **18**: 695.

— Campaign of, in Germany. (S. Crane) Lippinc. **66**: 299.

Gutenberg. (J. E. Scripps) Pub. Lib. **6**: 3.

— and the "Yellow" Editor. Blackw. **168**: 399. Same art. Ecl. M. **136**: 126.

Gutenberg Anniversary. (T. L. De Vinne) Outl. **65**: 31. — Spec. **84**: 917.

Guthrie, James J. (S. C. de Soissons) Artist (N. Y.) **29**: 197.

Guthrie, J. L., "The Elf," and Bookplates by. Artist (N. Y.) **25**: 125.

Gutta Percha. (E. F. A. Obach) Nature, **58**: 136. — (E. F. A. Obach) J. Soc. Arts, **46**: 97-169.

— and India Rubber. (C. Dooley) Pop. Sci. Mo. **50**: 679.

Gutter Merchant; a story. (H. Hesford) Temp. Bar, **115**: 120. Same art. Ecl. M. **131**: 625. Same art. Liv. Age, **219**: 106.

Guyon, Mme. Autobiography of a Mystic. Church Q. **47**: 180.

— The Inner Life. (J. L. Hurlbut) Chaut. **32**: 302.

— Mysticism of. (J. R. Harris) Lond. Q. **92**: 313.

Gwynn, Stephen. Highways and Byways in Donegal. (F. J. Gregg) Bk. Buyer, **18**: 383.

Gwynne, Nell. (Clara B. Colby) Overland, n. s. **38**: 323.

Gycia, Story of. (R. Garnett) Eng. Hist. R. **12**: 100.

Gymnasium, German. (F. Horn) Educa. R. **17**: 479.

— — from a Pupil's Standpoint. (E. Bruncken) Educa. R. **21**: 163.

Gymnastics, Non-hygienic. (J. Buckham) Harper, **101**: 207.

— Use of Weights in. (G. E. Flint) Outing, **35**: 292.

Gymnosperms, Origin of. (J. M. Coulter) Science, n. s. **8**: 377.

Gypsies, About. (A. J. Gordon) Gent. M. n. s. **63**: 409.

— Humor of the Romany "Chi." (T. Watts-Dunton) Bookman, **9**: 260.

— of Granada. (C. S. Pelham-Clinton) Eng. Illust. **17**: 44.

— of Turkey. (Lucy M. J. Garnett) Good Words, **41**: 807.

— The Surrey. Spec. **79**: 894.

— The Tent-dwellers. (B. Marsh) Argosy, **63**: 679.

Gypsum, Growth of Plants in. (J. D. A. Cockerell; F. Garcia) Science, n. s. **8**: 119.

Gypsy Folk-tales, Groome's. Acad. **55**: 366.

Gypsy Moth and Economic Entomology. Am. Natural. **33**: 419.

Gypsy Moth and its Introduction into America. (W. F. Kirby) Nature, **60**: 80.

— in Massachusetts. (F. Osgood) New Eng. M. n. s. **21**: 677.

Gyroscope and "Drift." (E. T. C. Richmond) J. Mil. Serv. Inst. **12**: 54.

H's, A Basketful of dropped. (K. A. A. Biggs) Gent. M. n. s. **61**: 382.

Ha Hin, Chinaman; a story. (G. R. Pattullo, jr.) Canad. M. **16**: 361.

Haberfeldtreiben, The; a Strange Tribunal of Bavaria. (G. H. Westley) Green Bag, **10**: 352.

Habibullah, Amir of Afghanistan. (D. C. Boulger) Contemp. **80**: 634.

Habington, William. (E. G. Gardner) Month, **90**: 16.

Habiri, The, in the El Amarna Tablets. J. Bib. Lit. **16**: 143.

Habit and Instinct, Morgan on. (E. B. Poulton) Nature, **57**: 553. — (C. A. Kofoid) Dial (Ch.) **22**: 333.

— its Nature and Substance. (S. E. Day) Canad. M. **8**: 430.

Habit of the Fraile; a story. (C. F. Lummis) Cosmopol. **23**: 561.

Habits, Transmission of Newly Acquired. (R. C. Schiedt) Ref. Ch. R. **46**: 310.

Hacienda de Ramona. (E. A. Wiseman) Overland, n. s. **33**: 112.

Hacker, Arthur. Annunciation. (Rose G. Kingsley) Art J. **53**: 8.

Hackett, James K. A Representative Young American Actor. (B. O. Flower) Arena, **25**: 220.

Hackley, Charles H., What he has done for Muskegon, Mich. (A. Hadden) R. of Rs. (N. Y.) **22**: 195.

Hadassah, Story of. (D. L. Sharp) Nat'l M. (Bost.) **14**: 63.

Haddon Aylmer and — Things. (A. J. Dawson) Pall Mall M. **11**: 185.

Hades. (H. King) Luth. Q. **29**: 401.

— and Gehenna explained. (J. F. Buss) N. Church R. **7**: 275.

Hadleigh, England, Interesting Industrial Experiment at. (W. H. Hunt) Westm. **154**: 285.

Hadley, Arthur T., President of Yale. Cent. **40**: 868.

— With portrait. (A. R. Kimball) Bk. Buyer, **14**: 274.

Hadley vs. Baxendale, The Rule in. Law Q. **16**: 275.

Hadrian and his Time, Gregorovius's. Sat. R. **87**: 19.

— (W. C. Lawton) Dial (Ch.) **26**: 306.

Haeckel, E., and his Critics. (C. E. Stowe) Nation, **72**: 356.

— and his Work. (R. S. Baker) McClure, **17**: 328.

— and the New Zoölogy. (H. S. Williams) Harper, **101**: 297.

Hæmon to Antigone. (A. Mackay) Argosy, **66**: 679.

Haendel, Georg Friedrich. (B. O. Flower) Arena, **18**: 386.

— and the Haendel Festivals. (H. H. Statham) Fortn. **68**: 244.

— Genius of. (H. H. Statham) 19th Cent. **47**: 10, 20.

— the Man. (J. C. Hadden) Argosy, **71**: 141.

— Messiah; at the Festival of 1900. (J. F. Runciman) Sat. R. **89**: 775.

— — Inspired or Sacred? Music, **11**: 469.

— Music of, Overestimation of. (J. C. Hadden) Music, **18**: 361.

— Saul, performed at Hamburg. (J. F. Runciman) Sat. R. **87**: 492.

— Williams's. (J. F. Runciman) Sat. R. **91**: 467.

Haendel Festival at London, 1897. Sat. R. **83**: 712.

— at Bonn, 1900. Ath. '00, **1**: 697.

Haendel Revival in Germany. (B. Schrader) Forum, **25**: 191.

Haffner, Johann Fried. Wilhelm. Geog. J. 17: 313.

Hafiz, Mohammed. Visions; tr. by Leaf. Sat. R. 85: 598.

Hagar, The Two Accounts of. (H. Gunkel) Monist, 10: 321.

Hagar of the Farm; a story. Temp. Bar, 112: 209.

Haggada, Passover, Egyptian Fragments of. (I. Abrahams) Jew. Q. 10: 41.

Haggard, H. R., Educational Views of. (R. R. C. Gregory) Longm. 38: 155.

— The Evolution of an Artist. (Katharine P. Woods) Bookman, 9: 350.

Hagiology, Study in. (J. M. Gillis) Cath. World, 72: 758.

Hague, George. Bank. M. (N. Y.) 55: 344.

Haidah and Tlingit Villages about Dixon's Entrance. (G. A. Dorsey) Pop. Sci. Mo. 53: 160.

Haidah Indians. (M. W. Leighton) Overland, n. s. 37: 1083.

Haig, Axel Hermann. Buckingham Palace. (A. Yockney) Art J. 53: 326.

Haige, William. (M. White) Pennsyl. M. 14: 81.

Hail, Formation of. (C. Abbe) Nature, 63: 337.

Hail the Queen; a Jubilee Ode. (W. T. James) Canad. M. 9: 137.

Hailstorms obviated by Artillery. (W. N. Shaw) Nature, 64: 159. — Nat. Geog. M. 11: 239.

Haimberger's Appetite Cure. (Mark Twain) Liv. Age, 227: 330.

Hair and Feathers. (J. S. Kingsley) Am. Natural. 21: 767.

— Plant-bearing. (R. Lydekker) Knowl. 24: 223.

Hair-cut, A. (Jeannette Lee) Liv. Age, 230: 659.

Haité, George C., The Art of. (W. S. Sparrow) M. of Art, 23: 324, 416, 447.

— Sketches by. Artist (N. Y.) 26: 163.

Haiti, Through. (H. Prichard) Geog. J. 16: 306.

Hajis and the Hajj. (J. D. Batte) Asia. R. 28: 163.

Hakluyt Society, Jubilee of. Geog. J. 9: 169.

Halbe, Max. Mother Earth. (K. Francke) Bookman, 7: 136.

Halcyon Days; a story. Blackw. 161: 37. Same art. Liv. Age, 212: 397.

Half-brothers. (M. Hewlett) Fortn. 75: 939.

Half-caste, The; a story. (A. Linden) Pall Mall M. 16: 19.

Half-crown Fortune, A. (Mary S. Boyd) Chamb. J. 78: 353–410. Same art. Liv. Age, 231: 557–622.

Half-hearted; a story. (John Buchan) Good Words, 41: 793.

Half Time Boy and a Goat. (A. L. Merritt) Cent. 40: 590.

Half-tone Process of Picture Reproduction. (W. C. Whittan) Brush & P. 7: 92.

Hale, Edward Everett. (G. S. Lee) Critic, 39: 40. — Outl. 69: 411. — With portrait. (G. P. Morris) R. of Rs. (N. Y.) 23: 549.

— at the Aldine Club. Critic, 31: 385.

— Memories of 100 Years. (E. E. Hale) Outl. 69: 547, 918.

— Portrait of. Bk. Buyer, 14: 453.

— Recollections of the Century. Nat'l M. (Bost.) 6: 30, 124, 240, 341, 434, 533.

— A Word from. Outl. 65: 983.

Hale, Horatio, with portrait. Pop. Sci. Mo. 51: 401.
— (A. F. Chamberlain) J. Am. Folk-Lore, 10: 60.
— (J. A. Cooper) Canad. M. 8: 449. — (F. Boas) Critic, 30: 40. — Ath. '97, 1: 152. — (D. G. Brinton) Science, 5: 216.

Haliburton, Robert Grant. (G. T. Denison) Canad. M. 17: 126.

Halicarnassus, Mausoleum at; a New Restoration. (E. Oldfield) Archæol. 54: 273. 55: 343.

Halifax Charles L. W., Lord, on the Joint Pastoral. Month, 97: 616.

Halifax, George Savile, 1st Marquis. Life and Letters. (E. Porritt) Am. Hist. R. 4: 519. —Spec. 81: 804. — Acad. 55: 109.

— and Neo-Anglicanism. (J. Moyes) Dub. R. 124: 241.

— A Character of the "Trimmer." (H. C. Foxcroft) Fortn. 71: 789.

— the Great Tractarian. (H. Paul) 19th Cent. 45: 447. Same art. Liv. Age, 221: 425.

Halifax, Nova Scotia, and its Attractions. (E. S. Tupper) Canad. M. 13: 347.

— The Open Door of Canada. (J. Taylor Wood) Canad. M. 12: 521.

Halifax; a poem. (C. Fairbanks) Canad. M. 8: 231.

Halifax Commission, The. (A. G. Sedgwick) Nation, 65: 217.

Halkett, Anne Murray, Lady. (M. M. Verney) Longm. 29: 419.

Hall, Fitzedward. (H. Bradley) Ath. '01, 1: 210. — (W. P. Garrison) Nation, 72: 127.

Hall, G. Stanley. Confessions of a Psychologist. Pedagog. Sem. 8: 92.

Hall, James. Nat. Sci. 13: 262.

— Relation of, to American Geology. (L. P. Gratacap) Am. Natural. 32: 891.

Hall, Newman. Come to Jesus; how a Little Book was blessed. (N. Hall) Sund. M. 28: 145.

Hall, Oliver, as a Follower of Turner. Sat. R. 86: 634.

Hall, Sharlot M. Writer, 14: 106.

Hall of Fame. (H. M. MacCracken) R. of Rs. (N. Y.) 22: 563.

Hallamshire, Antiquities of. Ed. R. 187: 434.

Halle a S., Government of; a Typical Prussian City. (E. J. James) Ann. Am. Acad. Pol. Sci. 15: 313.

Hallé, C., Life and Letters of. Spec. 78: 92.

Halleck, F. G. (M. A. D. Howe) Bookman, 5: 304.

Hallowe'en Adventure; a story. (E. R. McDonald) Canad. M. 12: 61.

Hallowing of the Fleet, The; a poem. (W. Cory) Argosy, 73: 317.

Hallucinations. (A. Wilson) Harper, 102: 929.

Haloid Salts, Determination of Tellurous Acid in Presence of. (F. A. Gooch and C. A. Peters) Am. J. Sci. 158: 122.

Hals, Franz. (A. French) New Eng. M. n. s. 18: 267.

— With portrait and bibliography. Mast. in Art, 1: pt. 11.

Halt on the King's Highway, A. Blackw. 170: 115. Same art. Liv. Age, 230: 453.

Halvorsen, Jens Braage. (E. Gosse) Ath. '00, 1: 275.

Hamadryad, The, and her Kinsfolk. (W. C. Lawton) Sewanee, 8: 399.

Hambourg, Mark, Pianist, Interview with, with portrait. Music, 17: 391.

Hamburg, Siege of, 1813. Un. Serv. (Phila.) 17: 157.

— Warehouses. (E. O. Sachs) Am. Arch. 62: 29.

Hamerton, P. G., with portrait. (R. Sturgis) Bk. Buyer, 13: 960.

— Life and Works of. Ed. R. 186: 432.

Hamilton, Alexander, with portraits. (H. C. Lodge) McClure, 8: 502.

— the Lawyer. (H. D. Esterbrook) Am. Law R. 35: 841.

— What we owe to, with portrait. Gunton's M. 14: 364.

Hamilton, Anthony. Mémoires de Grammont. (S. Gwynn) Macmil. 78: 23.

Hamilton, Lady Emma, True Story of. Belgra. 96: 369.

Hamilton, Gavin. Letters to Charles Townley. (A. H. Smith) J. Hel. Stud. 21: 306.

Hamilton, John McLure, Paintings of. (H. S. Morris) Scrib. M. 27: 733.

Hamilton, Mrs. Vereker, Medals of. M. of Art, 25: 424.

Hamilton College, Clinton, N. Y. (E. P. Powell) New Eng. M. n. s. 20: 449.

Hamilton Honeymoon; a story. (C. D. Leslie) Eng. Illust. 19: 321.

Hamilton, Mount, as it appears to the Tourist. (Alice Kirke) Overland, n. s. 34: 35.

Hamlet, An Argument for. (Mary E. Cardwill) Green Bag, 12: 227.

— as a Fool. Atlan. 84: 285.

— Character Sketch. (W. F. Whitlock) Meth. R. 58: 881.

— in Iceland, Gollancz's. (G. L. Kittredge) Nation, 67: 188.

Hamlet's Castle. (J. A. Riis) Cent. 39: 388.

Hamlin, Cyrus. Outl. 65: 904.

Hamlin, Hannibal, C. E. Hamlin's Life of. Am. Hist. R. 5: 588.

Hamlinite, Chemical Composition of, and its Occurrence with Bertrandite at Oxford County, Maine. (S. L. Penfield) Am. J. Sci. 154: 313.

Hammerstein, Oscar; the Romance of an Emigrant Boy. (O. Hammerstein) Cosmopol. 25: 571.

Hammond, Chris: In Memoriam. (A. Forman) Argosy, 71: 343.

Hammond, John, of Lavenham, Eng. (F. S. Hammond) N. E. Reg. 54: 288.

Hammurabi, King's Letters and Inscriptions of. Ath. '01, 1: 42.

Hampshire, Eng., A Hamlet in. (A. E. Merritt) Cent. 40: 3, 251, 342, 590.

Hampshire Common. (G. A. B. Dewar) Longm. 30: 440.

Hampstead, Literary. Acad. 52: 166.

— — and Artistic. (C. K. Burrow) Idler, 14: 49, 189.

— Literary Landmarks of a Northern Height. (W. C. Sydney) Gent. M. n. s. 63: 139.

— Sweet. Antiq. n. s. 36: 267.

Hampton, N. H., Church Records of. (S. E. Cram) New Eng. M. n. s. 16: 309.

Hampton Court Palace. (H. W. Brewer) Pall Mall M. 21: 17. — (A. Leach) Munsey, 18: 528.

— in By-gone Years. (Mrs. R. C. Boyle) National, 28: 668. Same art. Liv. Age, 212: 431. Same art. Ecl. M. 128: 341.

— Iron Work at. (J. S. Gardner) M. of Art, 22: 300.

Hampton Folk-lore Society, Work and Methods of. (Alice M. Bacon) J. Am. Folk-Lore, 11: 17.

Hampton Institute, Va., Learning by doing at. (A. Shaw) R. of Rs. (N. Y.) 21: 417.

Hampton Roads Conference, 1865. (J. Goode) Forum, 29: 92.

Hamza's Adventure. (H. Iliowizi) Harper, 102: 872.

Hand, Joseph, of East Guilford (now Madison), Conn., and his Descendants. (R. D. Smyth) N. E. Reg. 55: 145.

Hand, Symbol of the. (L. W. Gunckel) Am. Antiq. 19: 260.

Hand of a Boy, The; a story. (E. M. Moon) Idler, 17: 279.

Hands All Round; a story. (S. B. Elliott) Bk. News, 17: 1.

Hands and Feet. (M. Bernard) Pop. Sci. Mo. 52: 333, 522. — (F. G. Aflalo) Good Words, 38: 537.

Handel, Geo. F. See Haendel.

Handful of Perils, A. Chamb. J. 75: 28.

Handicraft and the Life of the Craftsman. (E. F. Strange) Art J. 51: 332.

Handicrafts, England's Oldest. (J. S. Robson) Antiq. n. s. v. 34-37.

Handkerchiefs, Lace. (Effie B. Clarke) Art J. 52: 361.

Handwriting and Handwriting Experts. (J. D. Miller) Nat'l M. (Bost.) 11: 411.

Hanging of a Mexican. (R. B. C. Graham) Sat. R. 83: 535.

Hanging of Talton Hall, The; a tale. (J. Fox, jr.) Outing, 39: 39.

Hanging-on of "By Jocks." (E. P. Butler) Cent. 38: 944.

Hanna, Hugh H. Bank. M. (N. Y.) 60: 558.

Hanna, Marcus A. (W. A. White) McClure, 16: 56. — With portrait. (W. A. White) Idler, 19: 172.

— and his Family. (Mrs. C. F. McLean) Midland, 7: 19.

Hanna, Mrs. Marcus A., Portrait of. Nat'l M. (Bost.) 12: 105.

Hannibal. Acad. 52: 234.

— and Rome. (C. H. Wilson) Un. Serv. M. 20: 349.

— W. O'Connor Morris's History of. Ath. '98, 1: 112.

Hanotaux, Gabriel. Fortn. 69: 173.

— Chancellor of the French Republic. (Baron P. de Coubertin) R. of Rs. (N. Y.) 15: 545.

Hanoverian Letters of 1746. (A. H. Millar) Scot. R. 31: 149.

Hansen Genealogy. (G. D. Miller) N. E. Reg. 53: 118.

Hapgood, Norman, as a Critic. Acad. 53: 52.

Happen and Chance; a tale. (M. B. Hardie) Belgra. 95: 527.

Happiness. Sat. R. 90: 324.

— and Material Progress. Sat. R. 88: 258.

— Hamerton's Quest of. Acad. 53: 170.

— The Problem of. (A. F. Palmer) Chaut. 30: 259.

— Pursuit of. (C. D. Warner) Cent. 39: 271.

— Unearned, Quest for. (D. S. Jordan) Indep. 52: 925.

Happiness; a poem. (J. P. Peabody) Atlan. 82: 855.

Hapsburgs, The, and the Germans. Spec. 79: 812.

— Misfortunes of. (A. De Burgh) Idler, 14: 599.

Harben, Will N., with portrait. Bk. News, 16: 529.

Harbor Feud, A. (M. Foster) Atlan. 84: 667.

Harbor Partners, The. (C. K. Burrow) Temp. Bar, 120: 93.

Harbors, Great, on our Seaboard. (C. C. Adams) Chaut. 27: 67.

Harcourt, George, with portrait. (M. H. Spielmann) M. of Art, 20: 233.

Harcourt, Sir William, and Canning, George. Blackw. 161: 877.

— and the Church. Spec. 81: 5.

— Career of. Sat. R. 86: 806.

— Parliamentary Anecdotes of. (W. Sidebotham) Chamb. J. 77: 753.

Hardenberg, F. Novalis' Schriften edited by E. Heilborn. Ath. '01, 1: 685.

Hardenbergh, Henry J., Architectural Works of. (M. Schuyler) Archit. R. 6: 335.

Hardie, R. G. (W. H. Downes) New Eng. M. n. s. 19: 3.

Harding, J. D., Reminiscences of, with portrait. (W. Collingwood) M. of Art, 22: 80.

Harding & Gooch, Architects, Work of. Arch. R. 7: 104.

Hardware Trade in the United States. (W. G. Smythe) Chaut. 29: 114.

Hardwicke, Lord, and the Stock Exchange. Spec. 85: 922.

Hardy, Dudley, with portrait. (M. H. Spielmann) M. of Art, 21: 206. — (A. H. Lawrence) Art J. 49: 353.

— Leaves from Sketch-book. (E. F. Spence) Studio (Lond.) 8: 33.

Hardy, E. J. Mr. Thomas Atkins. (W. E. Henley) Pall Mall M. 21: 280.

Hardy, Thomas, with portrait. (W. Archer) Pall Mall M. 23: 527. — (D. C. Murray) Canad. M. 9: 38. — (L. Johnson) Acad. 55: 251.

— and Meredith, George, Historic Place of. (E. Gosse) Internat. Mo. 4: 299.

— An Appreciation of. (V. Brown) Acad. 58: 208.

Hardy, Thomas, Art of. Sewanee, **3**: 447.
— as a Poet. Acad. **56**: 43.
— Country of. (C. Holland) Bookman, **9**: 328-519.
— Novels. (W. P. Trent) Sewanee, **1**: 1.
— Pessimism in the Poems of. (M. Kendall) Lond. Q. **91**: 223.
— Poems of. (W. B. Columbine) Westm. **152**: 180. — Sat. R. **87**: 19.
— Real Conversation. (W. Archer) Critic, **38**: 309.
— Tess, dramatized. Sat. R. **89**: 264.
— The Well-beloved. Acad. **51**: 345, 381.
Hare, Augustus J. C., American Stories in his Life. (C. H. Dall) Nation, **73**: 109.
— Story of my Life. (C. J. Wood) Critic, **39**: 250. — Lond. Q. **87**: 285. — (T. F. Huntington) Dial (Ch.) **22**: 51.
Hare, St. George. (A. L. Baldry) M. of Art, **24**: 370.
Hare and Tortoise ; a story. (G. M. Martin) McClure, **17**: 297.
Hare Chasing. (H. A. Bryden) Sat. R. **85**: 135.
Hare Hunting. Sat. R. **87**: 104. **89**: 74.
Hare in the Snow, A. (H. A. Bryden) Chamb. J. **78**, supp. 1.
Hare Electoral System in Tasmania. (W. J. Brown) Law Q. **15**: 51.
Harem, An Egyptian. Good Words, **40**: 594.
— of the Sultan, Women of. (L. M. J. Garnett) Gent. M. n. s. **64**: 355.
Harem Hospitality. Chamb. J. **76**: 469.
Hargrove, John, Statement on withdrawing from Methodist Church. N. Church R. **5**: 244.
Harland, Henry. The Story-teller at large. (H. James) Fortn. **69**: 650.
Harley, Robert, Earl of Oxford. The Harley Papers. Ed. R. **187**: 151. **193**: 457.
Harmony, Chadwick on. Music, **13**: 671.
— Different Systems of. (H. J. Wrightson) Music, **14**: 406.
— Modern. (C. W. Grimm) Music, **20**: 283.
— Modern Chromatic. (H. A. Norris) Music, **11**: 688.
Harmony in Small Country Places. (C. S. Sargent) Garden & F. **10**: 339.
Harnack, Adolf, as a Theological Teacher. (W. A. Brown) Outl. **68**: 882.
— in his Seminar. (D. S. Muzzey) Bib. World, **13**: 110.
— vs. Harnack. (W. B. Smith) New World, **7**: 648.
Harney, George Julian. Open Court, **12**: 116.
Harold Bradley, Playwright. (E. S. Van Zile) Lippinc. **62**: 3.
Harp, The. (Theodore Dreiser) Cosmopol. **24**: 637. — (F. Crissey) Chaut. **27**: 370.
— New Chromatic. Music, **13**: 783.
Harp of Israfel ; a poem. (Minna Irving) Midland, **8**: 106.
Harp's Song, The ; a poem. (Ella W. Wilcox) Nat'l M. (Bost.) **9**: 305.
Harper, George McL. Masters of French Literature. (L. E. Gates) Critic, **39**: 21.
Harper, Robert Goodloe. (C. W. Sommerville) Conserv. R. **1**: 370.
Harper's Magazine, Fifty Years of. (H. M. Alden) Harper, **100**: 947.
Harpignies, Henri, Artist. (F. Lees) Studio (Internat.) **4**: 143.
Harraden, Beatrice. Ships that Pass in the Night. (Beatrice Harraden) Bookman, **13**: 222.
Harriman Alaska Expedition. (H. Gannett) Nat. Geog. M. **10**: 507.
Harrington, Nathan Russell. (F. H. Herrick) Science, n. s. **10**: 529.
Harrington, Nathaniel, jr., Letter of, to his Father, in 1781. (E. M. Gill) N. E. Reg. **51**: 322.

Harris, Frank. Mr. and Mrs. Daventry. (M. Beerbohm) Sat. R. **90**: 551.
Harris, William T., and his Methods as Commissioner. (F. H. Kasson) Educa. **19**: 377.
— Psychologic Foundations of Education. (J. Dewey) Educa. R. **16**: 1.
Harrisburg Capitol Competition. Am. Arch. **58**: 32, 79.
Harrison, Alexander, Painter. (C. F. Browne) Brush & P. **4**: 133.
Harrison, Benjamin. (R. Ogden) Nation, **72**: 228. — Outl. **67**: 664. — World's Work, **1**: 695. — With portraits. (J. W. Noble) Indep. **53**: 644. — With portrait. (J. M. Chapple) Nat'l M. (Bost.) **14**: 4. — (T. J. Morgan) R. of Rs. (N. Y.) **23**: 430.
— Views of an Ex-President. (C. H. Cooper) Dial (Ch.) **31**: 280.
Harrison, Clifford, Drawings of. M. of Art, **24**: 304.
Harrison, Frederic, as a Critic. Acad. **58**: 27.
— in America. R. of Rs. (N. Y.) **23**: 558.
— New Essays. (W. P. Trent) Forum, **30**: 119.
Harrison, Mrs. Mary St. Leger. (J. L. Ford) Bookman, **14**: 232.
— Sir Richard Calmady. (F. Bell) Fortn. **76**: 894.
Harrison, Robert. Ath. '97, **1**: 50.
Harrow Art School. (M. H. Spielmann) M. of Art, **22**: 19.
Harrow School. Quar. **189**: 58.
— Howson on. Ath. '98, **2**: 525. — Spec. **81**: 606.
Harrower, John, Diary of, 1773-76. Am. Hist. R. **6**: 65.
Hart, Ernest. Nature, **57**: 251.
Hart, Sir Robert. Outl. **65**: 715. — (H. C. Whittlesey) Atlan. **86**: 699.
Harte, Bret. (D. C. Murray) Canad. M. **9**: 495.
— Country of. (W. M. Clemens) Bookman, **13**: 223.
— First Books of. (L. S. Livingston) Bookman, **8**: 564.
— in California. (N. Brooks) Cent. **36**: 447.
— Portrait of. Bk. Buyer, **22**: 278.
Harte, Walter Blackburn, with portrait. (F. Putnam) Nat'l M. (Bost.) **11**: 198.
Harter Act, The. Recent Legislation in the U. S. respecting Bills of Lading. (E. P. Wheeler) Am. Law R. **33**: 801.
Hartford, Conn., American Fountain at. (C. D. Warner) Munsey, **23**: 40.
Hartig, Ernst. (R. H. Thurston) Science, n. s. **12**: 66.
Hartley, Col. Thomas, of the Pennsylvania Line. Pennsyl. M. **25**: 303.
Harvard, John, and the Early College. (W. R. Thayer) New Eng. M. n. s. **25**: 131.
— A New Autograph of. Harv. Grad. M. **9**: 473.
Harvard Astrophysical Conference. (M. B. Snyder) Science, n. s. **8**: 449.
Harvard College and University. (W. R. Thayer) New Eng. M. n. s. **25**: 131.
— Actualities of the Three-year A. B. Degree. (A. B. Hart) Harv. Grad. M. **10**: 201.
— and the Charles River. (F. L. Olmsted) Harv. Grad. M. **7**: 173.
— and the Radcliffe Spectre. (W. E. Byerly) Harv. Grad. M. **8**: 161.
— Archives of. (W. G. Brown) Harv. Grad. M. **6**: 314.
— "Athalie" given at. (F. C. de Sumichrast) Harv. Grad. M. **6**: 320.
— Benefactions to, located in Chelsea, Mass. (W. K. Watkin) N. E. Reg. **52**: 64.
— Choice of Overseers. (J. Noble) Harv. Grad. M. **5**: 491.
— Comenius and the Presidency of. (J. H. Blodgett) Educa. R. **16**: 391.
— Comparisons, 1869-99. (W. R. Thayer) Harv. Grad. M. **7**: 527.

Harvard College and University, Degrees in Science at. (J. M. Cattell) Science, n. s. 9: 522.

— Dudleian Lecture for 1899. (J. J. Fox) Cath. World, 71: 245.

— Entrance Requirements of, New. (A. B. Hart) Educa. R. 14: 217.

— Examination in 1757. (John Adams) Harv. Grad. M. 9: 348.

— — in 1821 and 1837. (S. K. Lothrop ; T. W. Higginson) Harv. Grad. M. 9: 491.

— Fifty-eight Years ago. (G. F. Hoar) Scrib. M. 28: 57.

— Franchise in, Extension of ; Reasons for and against, by Alumni Committees. Harv. Grad. M. 7: 210.

— Franchise Movement, Sketch of the. (G. B. Shattuck) Harv. Grad. M. 6: 465.

— A Freshman in 1845. Harv. Grad. M. 9: 203.

— Growth of the Graduate School. (W. W. Goodwin) Harv. Grad. M. 9: 169.

— Gymnastics at, Required. (H. W. Putnam) Harv. Grad. M. 6: 309.

— E. E. Hale's Recollections of, in the Thirties. Nat'l M. (Bost.) 6: 241.

— in the Seventies. (R. Grant) Scrib. M. 21: 554.

— in the Sixties. (M. Storey) Harv. Grad. M. 5: 327.

— in the Spanish-American War, Roll of. (W. G. Brown) Harv. Grad. M. 7: 309.

— in the West. (F. W. Taussig) Harv. Grad. M. 9: 321.

— its Unsymmetrical Organization. (C. S. Minot) Harv. Grad. M. 5: 485.

— Library. (E. Emerton) Harv. Grad. M. 7: 509.

— — Plain Facts about. (Wm. C. Lane) Harv. Grad. M. 8: 168.

— Literary Output of. (F. W. Coburn) Writer, 11: 81.

— Memorial Gates. (W. D. Swan) Archit. R. 8: 61.

— Observatory and Astronomical Work. (M. L. Todd) Cent. 32: 290.

— — Conference of Astrophysicists. (H. R. Donaghe) Pop. Astron. 6: 481.

— — Growth of, in Twenty Years. (E. C. Pickering) Pop. Astron. 8: 89.

— Opportunity of, in Medicine. (W. T. Councilman) Harv. Grad. M. 9: 339.

— Past and Present Government of. (W. A. Richardson) N. E. Reg. 51: 26.

— Philosophy at. (H. Münsterberg) Harv. Grad. M. 9: 474.

— Playgrounds of. (I. N. Hollis) Harv. Grad. M. 8: 164.

— Professors in, Undue Multiplication of. (T. Dwight) Harv. Grad. M. 6: 485.

— Proposed Reduction of the Course. (J. W. Brannan) Harv. Grad. M. 6: 1.

— Prospect Union at. (Louis F. Berry) Outl. 63: 691.

— Recent Buildings at. (H. D. Hale) Archit. R. 8: 65.

— Reform in Entrance Requirements. (A. B. Hart) Educa. R. 18: 263.

— Religious Situation at. (D. Drake) Outl. 65: 555.

— The Rowing Question at. (H. Richards) Harv. Grad. M. 7: 183.

— Senior Alumni, 1800–1900. Harv. Grad. M. 9: 504.

— Strength Tests at. (D. A. Sargent) Harv. Grad. M. 5: 513.

— Undergraduate Life at. (E. S. Martin) Scrib. M. 21: 531.

Harvard [Daily] Crimson, The. (Henry James, 2d) Harv. Grad. M. 8: 181.

Harvard Divinity School. (C. C. Everett) Harv. Grad. M. 5: 503.

Harvard Graduates as College Presidents. Harv. Grad. M. 5: 347.

— in the Public Service. Harv. Grad. M. 6: 40.

Harvard Lampoon, History of the. (W. B. Wheelwright) Harv. Grad. M. 9: 324.

Harvard Law School. (A. V. Dicey) Contemp. 76: 742.

— Professor Dicey on. (L. Dyer) Nation, 68: 433.

Harvard Lay Brother, A ; a story. (Mabel S. Clarke) Nat'l M. (Bost.) 8: 327.

Harvard Museum, Blaschka Flower Models of. (M. E. Hale) Pop. Sci. Mo. 50: 663.

Harvard Teachers' Association, Papers prepared for the Sixth Annual Meeting. Educa. R. 13: 417.

— Seventh Annual Meeting. Educa. R. 15: 417.

Harvard Union, Opening of. Harv. Grad. M. 10: 214.

Harvard Verse, Recent. Harv. Grad. M. 9: 495.

Harvard-Yale Regatta, The First, 1852. (J. M. Whiton) Outl. 68: 286.

Harvest of the Snow, The ; a poem. (A. C. Waldron) Outing, 31: 572.

Harvest on the Prairie ; a story. (H. Bindloss) Gent. M. n. s. 67: 521.

Harvest Home, The. (D. Dale) Belgra. 97: 82.

Harvest Home in Thrums. (M. E. Leicester Addis) Lippinc. 66: 553.

Harvest Tea in a Country Schoolhouse in England. (S. G. Tallentyre) Macmil. 78: 355.

Harvesting Great Crops in Western U. S. (N. C. Young) Nat'l M. (Bost.) 9: 19.

Harvey, A. S. Bank. M. (Lond.) 65: 401.

Harvey, Francis. Ath. '00, 1: 209.

Harvey, Martin, Don Juan's Wager. (M. Beerbohm) Sat. R. 89: 295.

Harvey, William, Power on. Nature, 57: 481.

— Was he " W. H. "? (C. C. Stopes) Ath. '00, 2: 154.

Hasey Family. Hasey-Green. (D. P. Corey) N. E. Reg. 54: 211.

Haslemere ; as a literary centre. Acad. 54: 35

הִקְטַ־ע־יִם, 1 Kings xviii. 21. (M. Jastrow, jr.) J. Bib. Lit. 17: 108.

Haskell, Ernest. (R. Riordan) Critic, 35: 801.

Hassam, Childe, Impressionist. Brush & P. 8: 141.

Hasting, The Sea-king. (W. C. Abbott) Eng. Hist. R. 13: 439.

Hastings, Eng., Reminiscences of. Temp. Bar, 118: 262.

— Battle of. (J. H. Round) National, 28: 687.

— Spatz's. (J. H. Round) Am. Hist. R. 2: 512.

Hastings Family Records. (W. H. Davis) N. E. Reg. 54: 406.

Haswell, Charles H., with portrait. Cassier, 17: 438.

— Reminiscences. (W. L. Andrews) Bk. Buyer, 13: 957.

Hat, The Conferring of the. (Luis Coloma) Liv. Age, 226: 594.

Hats and Hat-worship. Macmil. 76: 342.

— Evolution of the Top Hat. (C. Johnston) Cosmopol. 29: 427.

Hatch, Edwin. (A. M. Fairbairn) Contemp. 71: 342.

Hatch, Col. Jabez, his Ancestry and Descendants. (A. H. Bent) N. E. Reg. 51: 34.

Hatfield, Massachusetts. (G. B. Stebbins) New Eng. M. n. s. 19: 167.

Hatred, Holy. (J. W. Diggle) Expos. 5: 434.

Hatry, Col. A. G. Midland, 9: 315.

Hatto, the Hermit ; a legend. (S. Lagerlof) Poet-Lore, 11: 348.

Hatzfeld, M. Adolphe. (W. Roberts) Ath. '00, 2: 481.

— and the German Embassy. Eng. Illust. 20: 89.

Haud, Latin, and Greek ou. (L. Horton-Smith) Am. J. Philol. 18: 43.

Haughton, Sam. Nature, 57: 55. — Ath. '97, 2: 637.

Haunted Burglar. (W. C. Morrow) Lippinc. 60: 116.

Haunted Chamber at Glamis Castle. Chamb. J. 75: 627.

Haunted Houses. (A. Goodrich-Freer) Scot. R. 35: 1.

Haunted Island, A ; a story. (A. Blackwood) Pall Mall M. 17: 445.

Haunted Pulpit, The ; a story. (Louise C. Henderson) Nat'l M. (Bost.) 7: 336.

Haunted Quack. (N. Hawthorne) New Eng. M. n. s. 17: 688.

Haunted Schooner, The. (H. Clifford) Macmil. 76: 207.

Haunted Spring, The ; a poem. (E. Nesbit) Argosy, 63: 400.

Haupt, Lewis Muhlenburg. (H. W. Lanier) R. of Rs. (N. Y.) 16: 292.

Haupt, Ottomar. Bank. M. (Lond.) 65: 915.

Hauptmann, Gerhart. (J. F. Coar) Atlan. 81: 71. — (T. S. Baker) Critic, 34: 231. — (W. N. Guthrie) Sewanee, 3: 278. — (B. Marshall) Fortn. 76: 459. — (M. Müller) Atlan. 86: 368. — With portrait. Bk. Buyer, 20: 276.

— and Sudermann. Two German Dramatists. (E. A. Steïner) Outl. 67: 74.

— Dramas of. (Gustav Kobbé) Forum, 24: 432. — (E. E. Hale, jr.) Dial (Ch.) 28: 430. — Quar. 191: 317.

— Return to Naturalism. (K. Francke) Nation, 72: 151.

— Tragi-comedy. (C. Harris) Nation, 73: 490.

— Versunkene Glocke. Acad. 53: 400. — (K. Francke) Nation, 67: 462.

Hauran, Ruins of the. (Gertrude L. Bell) Monthly R. 3, no. 1 : 105.

Hauslick, Edouard, Musical Professor, with portrait. Music, 15: 452.

Havana. Munsey, 19: 430. — (A. Ashton) Midland, 9: 458. — (T. R. Dawley) Outl. 67: 253.

— after Three Years. (T. R. Dawley, jr.) Outl. 69: 728.

— and the Havanese. (R. Davey) Fortn. 69: 705. Same art. Ecl. M. 130: 823. Same art. Liv. Age, 217: 691.

— before and after the War of 1898. (G. Willets) Midland, 10: 291.

— Capture of, by England, 1762. (J. Adye) 19th Cent. 44: 116. Same art. Ecl. M. 131: 271.

— City Government, Organization of. (A. Govin) Ann. Am. Acad. Pol. Sci. 18: 363.

— Holy Week in. (M. E. Henry-Ruffin) Cath. World, 69: 34.

— in 1870. (F. T. Bullen) Cornh. 78: 53.

— In, Just before the War. (F. C. Baylor) Cosmopol. 25: 127.

— Post-office Scandal in. (R. Ogden) Nation, 70: 372.

— Sanitary Regeneration of. (G. M. Sternberg) Cent. 34: 578.

— Sanitation of. (G. E. Waring) Forum, 26: 529.

— Since the Occupation. (J. F. J. Archibald) Scrib. M. 26: 86.

— Social Life of. (T. B. Mott) Scrib. M. 27: 172.

— Transition in. (G. W. Ludlow) Indep. 52: 866.

Haven, A ; a poem. (S. R. Lysaght) Ecl. M. 137: 268.

Haven of Dead Ships ; a story. (S. Baxter) Cosmopol. 26: 451.

Hawaiian Islands. Bank. M. (N. Y.) 57: 238. — (P. E. Nylander) Cath. World, 68: 489. — (G. H. Barton) Nat'l M. (Bost.) 7: 359. — (C. H. Austin) Midland, 8: 195.

— Agriculture in. (H. W. Wiley) J. Frankl. Inst. 147: 31.

— America in, E. J. Carpenter's. Am. Hist. R. 5: 786.

— American and " Malay " in. (W. L. Marvin) R. of Rs. (N. Y.) 19: 457.

— and the Changing Front of the World. (J. R. Procter) Forum, 24: 34.

— and Porto Rico as Colonies. (G. L. Bolen) Gunton's M. 18: 26.

Hawaiian Islands, Annexation of. (J. R. Musick) Arena, 17: 461. — Pub. Opin. 22: 771. — (S. M. White) Forum, 23: 723. — (R. Ogden) Nation, 64: 332. 65: 272. — Spec. 78: 859.

— — The Administration and. (L. Gorman) No. Am. 165: 379.

— — Advantages of. (A. C. James) No. Am. 165: 758.

— — Duty of. (J. T. Morgan) Forum, 25: 11.

— — Folly of. (F. Bausman) Nation, 66: 107.

— — from a Japanese Point of View. (K. Nakamura) Arena, 18: 834. — Pub. Opin. 23: 138.

— Climate of. (C. F. Nichols) R. of Rs. (N. Y.) 16: 180.

— Cycling in. (T. P. Terry) Outing, 33: 585.

— Education in. (C. D. Martin) Educa. 19: 36. — (F. B. Dresslar) Educa. R. 15: 50. — (H. S. Townsend) Forum, 24: 612.

— First Impressions of. (A. C. Coolidge) Nation, 65: 259.

— A Glimpse of. (Carrie W. Banks) Midland, 9: 44.

— Government of. (D. MacG. Means) Nation, 70: 178.

— Home Market of. (W. C. Ford) Nation, 65: 5.

— How are we to Govern ? (R. Ogden) Nation, 65: 432.

— How Honolulu cared for the American Troops. (E. Van C. Hall) Overland, n. s. 32: 463.

— Importation of Gnats into. (C. R. Osten Sacken) Nation, 69: 409.

— Impressions of. (H. C. Potter) Cent. 40: 762.

— In Dreamy. (G. W. Merrill) Cosmopol. 26: 263.

— Language of. (E. D. Preston) Science, n. s. 11: 841, 894.

— The Latest Phase. (E. L. Godkin) Nation, 66: 42.

— Leprosy and the Hawaiian Annexation. (B. Foster) No. Am. 167: 300. — Cosmopol. 24: 557.

— Liliuokalani on. (C. A. Kofoid) Dial (Ch.) 24: 228.

— Making of, W. F. Blackman's. Am. Hist. R. 5: 786.

— Natives of. (T. M. Coan) Ann. Am. Acad. Pol. Sci. 18: 9.

— Our New Fellow-citizens. (W. E. Griffis) Outl. 59: 722.

— Our New Possessions, Musick on. (J. K. Goodrich) Bk. Buyer, 16: 149.

— Our Pacific Paradise. (K. Jarboe) Munsey, 19: 837.

— Passages from a Diary in the Pacific. (John La Farge) Scrib. M. 29: 537.

— The People of. (H. S. Townsend) Forum, 25: 585.

— — Plea for. (F. L. Coombs) Overland, n. s. 30: 273.

— Political Situation in, 1900. (H. P. Williams) Outl. 64: 863.

— Problems after Annexation. (A. Allen) Overland, n. s. 32: 432.

— Public Lands in. (S. B. Dole) Indep. 52: 225.

— Real, L. Young's. Am. Hist. R. 5: 786.

— Real Story of. (F. L. Clarke) Forum, 29: 555.

— Reasons for Annexing. (F. H. Kasson) Educa. 18: 308.

— Since Annexation. (S. E. Bishop) Indep. 52: 588.

— Situation in. (P. Whitmarsh) Outl. 63: 489.

— Sugar Growing in. (F. H. Seagrave) Overland, n. s. 32: 455.

— The Territory of. (H. White) Nation, 67: 254.

— Thirty Years after ; supplemental notes. (Geo. B. Merrill) Overland, n. s. 32: 64.

— — Unconstitutionality of the Treaty. (Daniel Agnew) Forum, 24: 461.

— United States and. (M. H. Krout) Chaut. 27: 176, 265.

— Why not annex, to England ? (D. Archibald) Eng. Illust. 17: 93.

Hawaiian Architecture. Our acquired architecture. (M. Schuyler) Archit. R. 9: 277.

Hawaiian Expedient, An. (Jessie Kaufman) Overland, n. s. 35: 10.

Hercules, A Bronze Statuette of. (A. S. Murray) Archæol. 55: 199.

Hercynian Forest, Cæsar's Account of the Animals in. (G. G. Begle) School R. 8: 457.

Herd-widdie-flow, The. Temp. Bar, 119: 348.

Herder, Gottfried. (T. Nunns) Temp. Bar, 111: 527.

Heredea, José Maria da, the Elder, with portrait. (Minna C. Smith) Bookman, 9: 515.

— Sonnets of. (J. C. Bailey) Fortn. 70: 369.

Hereditary Influences and Medical Progress. (J. J. Morrissey) Arena, 17: 283.

Heredity and Environment; a rejoinder. (C. C. Closson) Q. J. Econ. 15: 143. — (C. W. Super) Conserv. R. 4: 246.

— and Human Progress, McKim's. (A. A. Woodhull) Nation, 71: 349.

— and Newly Acquired Habits. (R. C. Schiedt) Ref. Ch. R. 46: 310.

— as a Social Force. (T. H. S. Escott) Fortn. 70: 115.

— Assimilation and. (J. Loeb) Monist, 8: 547.

— Biological, Some Ideas concerning. (G. Sergi) Monist, 12: 1.

— Environment vs. (L. P. Alden) Char. R. 9: 85. — (F. H. Nibecker; T. F. Chapin; F. H. Briggs; Elizabeth Kerr) Char. R. 9: 118.

— Fay's Study of Heredity among the Deaf. Am. Natural. 35: 146.

— in Man. (W. Seton) Cath. World, 74: 67.

— Israel's Idea of. (J. E. Hartman) Ref. Ch. R. 48: 317.

— Law of Ancestral. (K. Pearson) Science, n. s. 7: 337.

— New Law of, Galton's. Nature, 56: 235.

— of Acquired Characteristics. (C. Lombroso) Forum, 24: 200.

— of Observation, Memory, and Intelligence. (A. B. Morton) Educa. 18; 562, 624.

— of Richard Roe. (D. S. Jordan) Arena, 17: 1082.

— The Power of. (I. Foard) Westm. 151: 538.

— Variation vs. (H. S. Williams) Am. Natural. 32: 821.

Hereford Cathedral. (J. W. Leigh) Good Words, 42: 749, 844.

Heresies, Some Moral, of the Present Day. (C. C. Dove) Lond. Q. 95: 313.

Heresy, The Unconscious Spirit of. (J. F. Seebach) Luth. Q. 27: 548.

Heretic, The; a poem. (W. J. Long) Outl. 64: 356.

Heretics, Just Punishment of. (W. Wood) 19th Cent. 44: 46.

Herefordshire, Superstitions and Humors of. (H. C. Trollope) Longm. 33: 556.

— Untrodden Ways in. (H. C. Trollope) Longm. 31: 535.

Hereward, In the Land of. (H. F. Abell) Gent. M. n. s. 66: 604.

Herkomer, Hubert von, with portrait. (M. E. Abbott) Brush & P. 9: 176. — (E. F. Baldwin) Outl. 69: 715.

— as a Painter in Enamels. (M. H. Spielmann) M. of Art, 23: 105, 163.

— as Portrait Painter. (E. F. Baldwin) Outl. 61: 545.

Herkomer School. (A. L. Baldry) Studio (Lond.) 6: 3.

Hermengarde. (Jules Lemaitre) Liv. Age, 216: 882.

"Hermione," Mutiny in the. (H. W. Wilson) Cornh. 80: 387.

Hermit of Accona, The; a tale. (G. G. Godkin) Argosy, 64: 290.

— of Antrim Caves. (J. H. Bernard) Sund. M. 26: 456.

Hermite, Charles. (G. H. Bryan) Nature, 63: 350. — (J. J. Durán-Loriga) Science, n. s. 13: 883.

Hermits of the Wissahickon, Hymn-book of the. (S. W. Pennypacker) Pennsyl. M. 25: 336.

Herne, James A., Actor, Dramatist, and Man. (H. Garland, J. J. Enneking, and B. O. Flower) Arena, 26: 282.

— and his New Play Sag Harbor, with portrait. (F. Wayne) Nat'l M. (Bost.) 11: 393.

— in "Griffith Davenport." (M. Tiempo) Arena, 22: 375.

Hero, A; a story. (A. Blount) Eng. Illust. 17: 563.

Hero and his Wife, A; a story. (Clara H. Holmes) Midland, 11: 143.

Hero and the Burglars, The; a story. (G. S. Street) Pall Mall M. 17: 98.

Hero of Fiction, The Model. (J. B. Perry) Bk. Buyer, 19: 100.

Hero of Fiction; a story. (M. Sinclair) Temp. Bar, 115: 135.

Hero of the Pantheon, A; a story. Macmil. 80: 138. Same art. Liv. Age, 222: 242.

Hero of the Plague; a story. (W. C. Morrow) Eng. Illust. 19: 36.

Hero of the Regiment; a story. (H. D. Ward) Cosmopol. 27: 269.

Hero, The Two Stages of a. Atlan. 82: 856.

Hero-hunting on the Wanks. (R. W. Cater) Chamb. J. 74: 44.

Hero Worship. Dial (Ch.) 23: 105.

Herod Antipas, The Leaven of Herod. (A. Black) Expos. 5: 173.

Heroes. (M. Creighton) Cornh. 78: 729.

— and Heroines in Fiction. Sat. R. 87: 519. Same art. Liv. Age, 222: 134. Same art. Ecl. M. 133: 306.

— Need for. Spec. 81: 430.

— of 1899. (A. T. Story) Strand, 18: 696.

Heroic Resistance, A. (H. Bindloss) Macmil. 76: 423. Same art. Liv. Age, 215: 664.

Heroic Revivalists. (W. E. Norris) Longm. 37: 226.

Heroine and Foil in Modern Fiction. (A. R. Marble) Dial (Ch.) 28: 269.

Heroine of Destiny, A; a story. (E. E. Peake) Nat'l M. (Bost.) 9: 359.

Heroine of the Future. Atlan. 82: 139.

Heroine of Lydenberg, The. (W. W. Dixon) Chamb. J. 76: 801.

Heroine of Romance, Autobiography of; a sketch. (K. W. Yeigh) Canad. M. 12: 67.

Heroines. (D. J. Murdock) Strand, 14: 665.

— and Beauties. [Longm.] Liv. Age, 229: 391. Same art. Ecl. M. 137: 123.

— in Fiction. (H. A. Spurr) Argosy, 72: 265.

— The Other Grace. (J. H. Findlater) National, 29: 130.

Heroism, Deeds of. (R. S. Baker) McClure, 17: 401.

— Every-day. (G. Kobbé) Cent. 33: 400.

— on the Battlefield. (Sara C. Burnett) Nat'l M. (Bost.) 8: 217.

Heroism of Helen Carrothers; a story of the Minnesota Massacre of 1862. (F. W. Calkins) Midland, 9: 533.

Heroism of Youth; a story. (I. Allen) Idler, 14: 671.

Herons in England. Sat. R. 88: 130.

Herpetology of North America, Cope's. (G. A. Boulenger) Nature, 63: 415.

Herrick, Robert. Temp. Bar, 111: 26. Same art. Ecl. M. 128: 841. — Acad. 53: 257.

— The Gospel of Freedom. (G. R. Carpenter) Book R. 5: 396.

— The Man and the Poet. (T. B. Aldrich) Cent. 37: 680.

— Some Thoughts on. (H. A. Spurr) Gent. M. n. s. 66: 270.

Herrick; a poem. (C. Lusted) Gent. M. n. s. 63: 413.

Herring Fishing by Torchlight. (R. W. Sise) Outing, 35: 60.

High School Extension. (D. S. Sanford) Atlan. **81**: 780. — (F. A. Manny) School R. **5**: 171.

High School Management. (S. B. Laird) School R. **7**: 221.

High-school Paper: its Status and its Possibilities. (A. P. Hollis) School R. **9**: 174.

High-school Principal, Equipment of the. (S. O. Hartwell) School R. **9**: 160.

— Rights, Duties, and Opportunities of. (J. Tetlow) Educa. R. **17**: 227.

High School Problems at opening of 20th Century. (R. G. Huling; H. L. Boltwood; C. C. Ramsay; A. W. Bacheler) Educa. **21**: 129.

High School Programme without Greek. (W. H. Butts) School R. **5**: 292.

High School Pupils in some Cities in Indiana, Habits of Work and Methods of Study of. (N. C. Johnson) School R. **7**: 257.

— Study of. (M. T. Scudder) School R. **7**: 197.

High School Reform. (C. M. Clay) Educa. **21**: 144, 217.

High School Visitor, Work of a. (S. D. Brooks) School R. **9**: 26.

High School Work, Greater Flexibility in. (W. J. Shearer) School R. **9**: 137, 232.

High Schools and Academies in the State of New York. Approved Course of Study for. School R. **7**: 58.

Higher Criticism, As to. Liv. Age, **217**: 466.

— at High-water Mark. (S. C. Bartlett) Bib. Sac. **55**: 656.

— When it has done its Work. (T. Davidson) Int. J. Ethics, **7**: 435.

See Biblical Criticism.

Higher Education in Paris. (A. T. Simmons) Nature, **60**: 10.

Higher Rascality. (H. E. M. Stutfield) National, **31**: 75.

Higher than Heaven. (E. A. Steiner) Outl. **66**: 887.

Highland Clan System. (W. C. Mackenzie) Gent. M. n. s. **62**: 601. Same art. Liv. Age, **222**: 844.

Highland River, A West-. Chamb. J. **74**: 289.

Highlanders, Passing of the. (E. L. Godkin) Nation, **65**: 449.

Highlands, Scottish, and Islands under Commissioners. (S. M. Penney) Jurid. R. **13**: 423.

— Summer Life in. (J. Macleay) Argosy, **75**: 111.

Highlaws. Chamb. J. **76**: 284.

Highwayman, The Modern. (A. R. Kimball) Indep. **52**: 307.

Highwaymen. (C. B. Angier) Argosy, **64**: 281.

— and Pirates, Some Famous. (E. Saltus) Cosmopol. **29**: 44.

Highways, Ancient and Modern. (C. L. Whittle) New Eng. M. n. s. **17**: 749.

— and Hedges, In the. (A. Sherwell) Sund. M. **26**: 623.

— of the People. (H. H. Lusk) No. Am. **169**: 873.

See Roads.

Hilary, Bishop of Chichester. (J. H. Round) Ath. '97, **1**: 115.

Hilda Wade. (Grant Allen) Strand, **17**: 327–693. **18**: 65–684.

Hildegarde; a story. (E. Durand) Canad. M. **17**: 323.

Hilder, Frank Frederick, with portrait. Nat. Geog. M. **12**: 85.

Hiles, Bartram, Artist without Arms, with portrait. M. of Art, **20**: 141.

Hilger, Adam. (A. F.) Nature, **56**: 34.

Hill, David. (S. R. Hodge) Lond. Q. **91**: 62.

Hill, James J., with portrait. (M. C. Blossom) World's Work, **1**: 721.

Character Sketch of. (M. H. Severance) R. of Rs. (N. Y.) **21**: 669.

Hill Prayer, A; a poem. (M. W. Wildman) Cent. **37**: 221.

Hill Town Problem. (E. A. Wright) New Eng. M. n. s. **24**: 622.

Hillis, Newell Dwight. (F. Crissey) Outl. **61**: 270.

— a New Evangelism. Outl. **64**: 860.

— Sketch of. (Z. S. Holbrook) Bib. Sac. **55**: 540.

Hills, Margaret Mary. Writer, **14**: 186.

Hills of Habersham, The; a story. (M. A. Bacon) Harper, **103**: 688.

Hillyer, William Hurd. Writer, **48**: 10.

Hilton, Walter. The Scale of Perfection. (J. McSorley) Cath. World, **74**: 33.

Hilton, William. (G. D. Leslie and F. A. Eaton) Art J. **51**: 118.

Himalayas, Among the, Waddell's. (Sir T. H. Holdick) Geog. J. **13**: 422. — Ath. '99, **1**: 202.

— Climbing in, Workman on. (T. G. Bonney) Nature, **63**: 254.

— in Midwinter. Blackw. **170**: 206. Same art. Liv. Age, **231**: 424.

— Sikhim. Nature, **59**: 443.

— Tent Life in. (W. H. Workman) Outing, **38**: 68.

Hinckaert, Philip, 15th Century Diptych of. (E. Green) Archæol. **50**: 72.

Hindman, Capt. James, Roll of Company, 1776. Pennsyl. M. **21**: 503.

Hindu and Mussulman Law, Privy Council as Judges of. (Lord Stanley of Alderley) Asia. R. **23**: 1.

Hindu Astronomer, A. (W. E. Plummer) Pop. Astron. **7**: 244.

Hindu Home, A. (J. D. Rees) 19th Cent. **46**: 996.

Hindu Law and English Judges. (W. C. Petheram) Law Q. **15**: 173. **16**: 77, 392.

Hindu Manners and Customs, Dubois on. (M. Winternitz) Nature, **59**: 145.

Hindu Society, Women in. (Abhedananda Swami) Arena, **22**: 757.

Hinduism and Christianity. (J. P. Jones) Bib. Sac. **55**: 591.

Hindus, Religion of Early. (H. W. Magoun) Bib. Sac. **54**: 603. **55**: 92, 296.

Hinkson, Mrs. Katharine Tynan. Acad. **52**: 527.

— The Wind in the Trees. Acad. **53**: 597.

Hinsdale, Burke Aaron, with Bibliography. Educa. R. **21**: 185.

— Work of, for Rural Schools. (H. Sabin) Educa. R. **21**: 307.

Hippalus and its Surroundings. (E. W. Maunder) Knowl. **22**: 275.

Hippeastrums, The. (H. Nehrling) Garden & F. **10**: 166, 174, 186, 194.

Hiprah Hunt's Journey through the Inferno; drawings by Arthur Young. Cosmopol. **29**: 84, 159, 332, 442.

Hiram's Majority. (H. A. Nash) New Eng. M. n. s. **20**: 245.

Hired Girl, A. (E. A. Dix) Cent. **39**: 236.

Hirsch, Dr. Adolph. Nature, **64**: 18.

Hirsch, Joseph. (R. H. Thurston) Science, n. s. **14**: 927.

Hirschgasse in Heidelberg. (E. Kleinschmidt) Chaut. **28**: 478.

Hirschl, Adolf Hirémy. Paintings. (Helen Zimmern) Art J. **52**: 353.

Hirsute Adornments and their Law. (W. S. Sparrow) M. of Art, **26**: 77.

His Baptism of Fire. Macmil. **84**: 456.

His Birthright; a story. (E. E. Peake) Nat'l M. (Bost.) **11**: 431.

His Debt of Honor. (D. H. Talmadge) New Eng. M. n. s. **25**: 120.

His Enemy. (A. Brown) Atlan. **88**: 320.

His First Client; a story. (D. H. Talmadge) Green Bag, **12**: 450.

History, Rescue Work in. (D. S. Jordan) Pop. Sci. Mo. 58: 81.

— Sifted Grain and the Grain Sifters. (C. F. Adams) Am. Hist. R. 6: 197.

— Study of; Ideal Course for Secondary Schools. (E. Van D. Robinson) School R. 6: 672.

— Study of, in Schools. (G. E. Howard) Educa. R. 19: 257.

— — — Committee of Seven's Report on. (N. M. Butler) Am. Hist. R. 5: 320. — (A. C. McLaughlin) School R. 5: 346.

— — Original Documents in. (Rosa V. Winterburn) Educa. 19: 436.

— a Teacher of Liberal Religion. (S. M. Crothers) New World, 8: 215.

— Teaching of. (W. Cook) School R. 7: 227. — (T. G. Tibbey) Westm. 151: 516. — (Lucy M. Seymour) Educa. 17: 624.

— — and Study of, Methods in, Mace's. (H. B. Learned) Am. Hist. R. 4: 133.

— — Concreteness an Essential in. (H. E. Bolton) School R. 8: 528.

— — in Public Schools. (A. L. Smith) Acad. 51: 106.

— — in a Small High School, Some Difficulties in. (J. T. McManis) School R. 8: 535.

— — Modern Methods for. (M. A. Tucker) Educa. 20: 220.

— — Practical Methods of. Educa. R. 15: 313.

— — Sources in England for. (E. and M. Barnes) Educa. R. 15: 331.

— — to Children for Character Building. (Rosa V. Winterburn) Educa. 21: 37.

— Value of, in the Formation of Character. (C. Hazard) School R. 9: 634.

History Studies, Ethnological Consideration of. (Rosa V. Winterburn) Educa. 22: 212.

History of the Lady Betty Stair; a story. (M. E. Seawell) Cosmopol. 22: 649. 23: 57.

History of Wong Toke and Ah Ho; a tale. (A. Brebner) Argosy, 72: 80.

Hitchcock, Charles Henry, Sketch of. Pop. Sci. Mo. 54: 260.

Hitchcock, George, with portrait. (A. Fish) M. of Art, 22: 577.

Hito-Kitsune; a story. (E. W. Mumford) Cosmopol. 26: 571.

Hittite Discoveries, Recent. (C. R. Conder) Scot. R. 36: 62.

Hittite Gods in Hittite Art. (W. H. Ward) Am. J. Archæol. 2d s. 3: 1.

Hittite Inscription, A New. (J. G. C. Anderson) J. Hel. Stud. 21: 322.

Hittite Research, Decade of. (C. W. Super) Am. Antiq. 21: 175.

Hittites and their Language, Conder's. (J. R. S. Sterrett) Nation, 68: 134.

— Who were the? (C. W. Super) Meth. R. 59: 260.

Hoar, George F., Speech of, Apr., 1900. Outl. 64: 947.

Hoar, Leonard, Descendants of. (F. P. Wheeler) N. E. Reg. 54: 149.

Hoar Family in America, Ancestry of. (H. S. Nourse) N. E. Reg. 53: 92, 186, 289.

Hoarseness of Vocalists, Causes of, and Treatment for. (E. Pynchon) Music, 16: 40.

Hoban, James, the First Government Architect. (F. D. Owen) Archit. R. 11: 581.

Hobbes, Thomas, Psychology of, and its Sources. (V. F. Moore) Am. J. Psychol. 11: 49.

Hobby-Goblins as Easter Angels; a story. (W. Packard) Nat'l M. (Bost.) 8: 59.

Hoboken Catastrophe. (A. Sullivan) Cath. World, 71: 664. — (R. L. Foster) Munsey, 23: 769.

Hobgoblins in Literature, Some. (Rebecca Harding Davis) Bk. Buyer, 14: 229.

Hobson, Richard Pearson. (J. B. Gilder) Critic, 33: 159. — (W. H. Ward) R. of Rs. (N. Y.) 18: 36. — (M. Young) Chaut. 27: 561. — With portraits. Strand, 16: 430. — Nat'l M. (Bost.) 8: 534.

— Sinking of the "Merrimac." Nat'l M. (Bost.) 8: 377.

Hobson, Thomas, of Cambridge, Eng., Will of, 1630. (H. F. Waters) N. E. Reg. 52: 487.

Hockey, Ice. (J. P. Paret) Outing, 31: 371.

— in Canada. (A. H. Beaton) Canad. M. 10: 555.

— with Rajputs. (A. G. Thompson) Un. Serv. M. 17: 556.

Hockey Match, A. (M. G. Cundill) Outing, 33: 334.

Hocking, Joseph, A Letter from. Month, 95: 207.

Hocking, Silas Kitto. Early Recollections. (S. K. Hocking) Sund. M. 30: 217.

— Popularity as a Novelist. Acad. 57: 17.

Hodgson, Brian H., Hunter on. Spec. 78: 339.

Hodgson, Shadworth. Metaphysic of Experience. (H. W. Carr) Mind, 24: 383.

Hodson, Samuel J., as Painter of Romantic Cities. (Lewis Lusk) Art J. 53: 270.

Hodson, William S. R. Blackw. 165: 522.

Hoff, J. H. van t', 25th Anniv. Celebration at Rotterdam. (H. M. Dawson) Nature, 61: 321.

Hoffman, Walter James. (A. F. Chamberlain) J. Am. Folk-Lore, 13: 44.

Hoffmann, Josef, Architect and Decorator. (F. Khnopff) Studio (Internat.) 13: 261.

Hofmann, Johann Michael Heinrich, Artist. (Harriet C. Connor) Midland, 7: 12. — (S. C. Eby) Nat'l M. (Bost.) 11: 630.

Hofmann, Josef, Pianist, with portraits. Music, 13: 499. — (Amy Fay) Music, 19: 565.

Hogan, Michael. Acad. 56: 487.

Hogarth, William. (J. C. Van Dyke) Cent. 32: 323.

— as Topographer. Acad. 53: 171.

— Drawings in British Museum. (A. Dobson) M. of Art, 25: 104.

— Portrait of Mrs. Salter. (C. Phillips) Art J. 51: 149.

— Suppressed Plates by. (G. S. Layard) Pall Mall M. 19: 46.

Hogs and their Habits. (Martha M. Williams) Idler, 19: 274. Same art. McClure, 16: 282.

Hoisting Engines. (J. Horner) Cassier, 19: 492.

Hokusai and the Biggest Picture on Record. Strand, 15: 558.

Holarek, E. Bohemian Painter. (W. Fred) Artist (N. Y.) 32: 196.

Holbein, Hans, and House Decoration in Lucerne. (R. H. E. Starr) Nat'l M. (Bost.) 5: 372.

— Picture "The Ambassadors." (W. F. Dicks) M. of Art, 26: 21.

Holbein, Hans, the Younger, Painter, with portrait and bibliography. Mast. in Art, 1: pt. 4.

Holbein's Porch. (G. Fidler) Art J. 49: 45.

Holberg, Ludvig. (W. M. Payne) Sewanee, 7: 257, 383.

Holbrook, Chandler, Journal of. New Eng. M. n. s. 20: 23.

Hold-up at La Ciudad, The. (C. T. Jackson) Overland, n. s. 36: 57.

Holden, Sir Isaac. (Mrs. E. Crawford) R. of Rs. (N. Y.) 16: 419.

Holden, James. Cassier, 13: 178.

Holden, Oliver. (A. E. Brown) New Eng. M. n. s. 16: 708.

Holden Family of Cranbrook, Kent, England. (E. S. Holden) N. E. Reg. 51: 214.

Holder, John, Some Passages in the Life of. (E. G. Henham) Macmil. 80: 469.

Hole, William, with portraits. Strand, 15: 411.

Hole in the Ground, A. (G. S. Dowell) Overland, n. s. 35: 307.

Holiday Episode, A ; a story. (J. C. Ochiltree) Harper, 96: 311.

Holiday Evening, The. (H. L. Bradley) Atlan. 81: 488.

Holiday Making, Art of. (Lady Battersea) Sund. M. 27: 21.

Holiness, Hebrew Idea of. (J. P. Peters) Bib. World, 14: 344.

— Nature of. (J. W. Diggle) Expos. 7: 366.

— Rabbinical Conception of. (S. Schechter) Jew. Q. 10: 1.

Holland, Mary Sibylla, Letters of. (E. Sichel) Fortn. 72: 780. — Spec. 80: 909.

Holland, Park, Reminiscences of. New Eng. M. n. s. 20: 315.

Holland. Liv. Age, 212: 99.

— and the Boer War. (P. McQueen) Nat'l M. (Bost.) 12: 54.

— and the Dutch Country Life. (P. G. Konody) Pall Mall M. 18: 483.

— Art Village in. (E. L. Good) Cath. World, 70: 514.

— Cafés of. (Idler, 16: 31.

— Charities in. (B. B. Croffut) No. Am. 168: 251.

— Dikes of. (G. H. Matthes) Nat. Geog. M. 12: 219.

— Flying Visit to. (F. L. M. Davidson) Argosy, 73: 209.

— from a Canadian Canoe. (F. L. Emanuel) Studio (Lond.) 2: 166.

— Influence of, on American Institutions. (S. G. Fisher) Lippinc. 59: 79.

— On the Waterways of. (C. Turner) Outing, 30: 166.

— Outdoor Life in. (C. J. Cornish) Contemp. 71: 858. Same art. Liv. Age, 214: 113. Same art. Ecl. M. 129: 171.

— Past and Future Politically. Sat. R. 91: 165.

— Principal Cities of. (H. H. Ragan) Chaut. 27: 227.

— Recent Scientific Work in. (J. P. Kuenen) Nature, 64: 208.

— Sketching Grounds of. (A. G. Bell) Studio (Lond.) 1: 116.

— South, as Sketching Ground. (G. Horton) Studio (Internat.) 2: 26.

— Taxation in, Progressive. (A. J. C. Stuart) Econ. J. 8: 325.

"Holland," Submarine Torpedo-boat. (F. Matthews) McClure, 12: 291.

Holland House. (E. Ayrton) Lippinc. 68: 752. — (C. Roche) Pall Mall M. 16: 191.

Holland House, Little. Cornh. 79: 181. Same art. Ecl. M. 132: 740. Same art. Liv. Age, 221: 42.

Hollister, Harvey J. Bank. M. (N. Y.) 59: 921.

Holloway, Charles Edward. Obituary Note. Art J. 49: viii.

Holloway College Collection of Paintings. (C. W. Carey) Art J. 49: 129-334.

Holls, Frederick W., Lawyer and Political Scientist. R. of Rs. (N. Y.) 19: 555.

Holly ; a story. (J. Ingersoll) Outing, 31: 321.

Hollyer, Frederick. Art in Photography ; Interview. (H. Townsend) Studio (Lond.) 1: 193.

Holm, Prof. Adolf. Ath. '00, 1: 786.

Holm Lea, Brookline, Mass., a Suburban Home. (Mrs. S. Van Rensselaer) Cent. 32: 3.

Holman, David Shepherd, 1826–1901, Obituary of. J. Frankl. Inst. 152: 72.

Holme, Frank, Illustrator, with portrait. (I. McDougall) Brush & P. 2: 107.

Holmes, John, Brother of O. W. Holmes. (T. W. Higginson) Atlan. 84: 175.

Holmes, Obadiah. (W. A. Slade) New Eng. M. n. s. 17: 342.

Holmes, Oliver Wendell, with portraits. (M. A. DeW. Howe) Bookman, 7: 217.

Holmes, Oliver Wendell, First Books of. (L. S. Livingston) Bookman, 8: 141.

— Letters to a Classmate, Isaac E. Morse. (M. B. Morse) Cent. 32: 946.

Holmes vs. Walton. (A. Scott) Am. Hist. R. 4: 456.

Holophane Globes. J. Frankl. Inst. 145: 262.

Holothurian, A Viviparous. (J. H. Gerould) Am. Natural. 32: 273.

Holothurians ; Mortensen's Anatomy and Embryology of Cucumaria Glacialis. Am. Natural. 32: 273.

Holroyd, Maria Josepha, Girlhood of. (M. L. Woods) Fortn. 67: 269.

— Letters of. Citizen, 3: 31.

Holstein, Charles L., with portrait. Green Bag, 10: 365.

Holtzapffel, John Jacob. J. Soc. Arts, 45: 1189.

Holy Club. (R. T. Stevenson) Bib. Sac. 54: 66.

Holy Communion ; a poem. (W. E. Gladstone) McClure, 11: 342.

Holy Ghost, The, in Spiritual Perception. (J. R. T. Lathrop) Meth. R. 58: 781.

Holy Grail, The. (E. G. Crommelin) Overland, n. s. 31: 155.

— The High History of the. (E. G. Gardner) Month, 92: 241.

— Legend of. (W. W. Newell) J. Am. Folk-Lore, 10: 117, 217, 299. 11: 39. 12: 189.

— Vision of ; a poem. Month, 89: 621.

Holy Island. (Sarah Wilson) Chamb. J. 75: 305.

Holy Medal, The. (F. Coppée) Outl. 65: 874.

Holy Picture, The ; a story. (H. L. Bradley) Atlan. 80: 217.

Holy Saint Claus ; a tale. (K. B. Coleman) Canad. M. 12: 157.

Holy Spirit and the Unity of the Church. (A. E. Truxal) Ref. Ch. R. 48: 161.

— in the Early Apostolic Age. (R. A. Falconer) Presb. & Ref. R. 11: 438.

— Kuyper on. (T. G. Darling) Presb. & Ref. R. 12: 499.

— Operations of. (J. H. Weaver) Luth. Q. 31: 80.

— Paul's Conception of, as Pledge. (H. A. A. Kennedy) Expos. 10: 274.

— Weinel on the Operations of, in the Post-apostolic Age. (J. Macpherson) Crit. R. 11: 152.

Holyoke, Massachusetts. (E. L. Kirtland) New Eng. M. n. s. 17: 715.

Holz, Arno. A German Poet of Revolt. (L. Magnus) Fortn. 67: 492.

Homburg. Sat. R. 88: 225.

Home and Friendship. (B. J. M. Donne) Ecl. M. 131: 432.

— How it may help the Teacher. (F. H. Palmer) Educa. 21: 292.

— Ideal and Practical Organization of. (E. E. Wood) Cosmopol. 26: 659. — (Van Buren Denslow) Cosmopol. 27: 49. — (C. W. Eastman) Cosmopol. 27: 297. — (50 Young Women) Cosmopol. 27: 167.

Homes. Homewood — a Model Suburban Settlement. (E. R. L. Gould) R. of Rs. (N. Y.) 16: 43.

— Improved, for Wage-earners. (J. C. Johnson) Bib. Sac. 54: 513.

Home Army, The. (H. Pritchard) Cornh. 81: 679.

Home Arts and Industries Association. (G. White) Studio (Lond.) 8: 91.

— — Exhibition 1897. Art J. 49: 219.

— — 1900. (E. Wood) Studio (Internat.) 11: 78.

— — 1901. (E. W. Gregory) Artist (N. Y.) 31: 135.

Home Coming, The ; a story. (M. M. Fitzgerald) Belgra. 98: 236.

Home-coming of the Nakannies ; a story. (W. A. Fraser) Canad. M. 14: 207.

Home Congress : The New Education. (W. T. Harris) Arena, 17: 353.

Hood, Robin. Argosy, 67: 472.

Hood, Vice Admiral Samuel. (R. V. Hamilton) Un. Serv. M. 18: 117.

Hood, Thomas. Temp. Bar, 110: 186. Same art. Ecl. M. 128: 408.

— and "Punch." (M. H. Spielmann) Bookman, 10: 151.

— Centenary of. (H. C. Shelley) Fortn. 71: 987. Same art. Liv. Age, 222: 160. Same art. Ecl. M. 133: 380. — (H. C. Shelley) Indep. 51: 1414.

Hood, Mt., to the Summit of. (M. K. Locke) Cosmopol. 25: 369.

Hood Game at Haxey, Lincolnshire. (Mabel Peacock) Folk-Lore, 7: 330. 8: 72.

Hoodoo M'Figgin's Christmas ; a sketch. (S. Leacock) Canad. M. 12: 285.

Hook, Private Henry ; Bravery in So. Africa. (A. E. Bonser) Macmil. 78: 452. Same art. Liv. Age, 219: 581.

Hook, Theodore. (A. Quarry) Argosy, 64: 751.

Hooke, Humphrey, of Bristol, Eng., Will of. (H. W. Lloyd) N. E. Reg. 54: 410.

Hooke, William, An Early Governor of New Somersetshire. (F. W. Todd) N. E. Reg. 52: 441.

Hooker, Richard, and the Puritans, Paget on. Church Q. 49: 116.

Hoole, Charles, and Elementary Education. (F. Watson) School R. 9: 526.

— a Schoolmaster of the Commonwealth. (F. Watson) School R. 9: 433.

Hooley, Ernest Terah, and his Guinea-pigs. (T. C. Crawford) Cosmopol. 26: 97.

— Company Promoting "a la mode." (W. R. Lawson) National, 32: 103.

— Company Scandal. (H. E. M. Stutfield) National, 32: 574.

— A Millionaire at Work. (E. Legge) Eng. Illust. 18: 368.

Hooligan, Making of the. (T. Holmes) Contemp. 80: 562.

— Voice of the. (R. Buchanan) Contemp. 76: 774. Same art. Liv. Age, 224: 1.

Hooliganism. (A. Morrison) Ecl. M. 136: 611. Same art. Liv. Age, 228: 640. — (J. Trevarthen) 19th Cent. 49: 84.

— and Juvenile Crime. (A. A. W. Drew) 19th Cent. 48: 89.

— and Working-boys' Clubs. (E. Morley) Westm. 155: 560.

Hooligans at Home and Abroad. (R. M. Barrett) Good Words, 42: 388.

— Use for. Sat. R. 86: 574.

Hoosier Youngster, The ; poems. (J. W. Riley) Cent. 37: 608.

Hop-fields, Washington, Some Aspects of. (Susan L. J. Currier) Overland, n. s. 32: 541.

Hop-trade, German. J. Soc. Arts, 45: 837.

Hope, Anthony. See Hawkins, Anthony Hope.

Hope, James Barron. (J. H. Marr) Conserv. R. 3: 142.

Hope and Memory. (H. Pyle) Cent. 41: 108.

Hope Deferred. (J. D. Daskam) Cent. 40: 420.

Hope is Green ; a story. (H. Kielland) Music, 19: 131.

Hopefulness. (L. Abbott) Outl. 64: 298.

Hopi Expedition. (G. A. Dorsey) Science, n. s. 13: 219.

Hopi Indians of Arizona. (G. A. Dorsey) Pop. Sci. Mo. 55: 732.

— Alosaka Cult of. (J. W. Fewkes) Am. Anthrop. 1: 522.

— Basket Dances of. (J. W. Fewkes) J. Am. Folk-Lore, 12: 81.

— Property in Eagles among. (J. W. Fewkes) Am. Anthrop. 2: 690.

Hopi Indians, Ritual of. (J. W. Fewkes) J. Am. Folk-Lore, 11: 173.

— — Sacrificial Element in. (J. W. Fewkes) J. Am. Folk-Lore, 10: 187.

Hopkins, Arthur. (J. A. Reid) Art J. 51: 193.

Hopkins, Esek. (R. Grieve) New Eng. M. n. s. 17: 346.

Hopkins, E. J., Organist of Temple Church, London. Music, 14: 210.

Hopkins Seaside Laboratory. (V. L. Kellogg) Am. Natural. 33: 629.

Hopkinson, John. Nature, 58: 419.

Hoppe-Seyler, Felix, Life and Work of. (A. P. Mathews) Pop. Sci. Mo. 53: 542.

Hopper, Nora. Songs of the Morning. Acad. 58: 250.

Hoppner, John. (J. C. Van Dyke) Cent. 34: 686.

Horace and Pope. (W. H. Williams) Temp. Bar, 15: 87.

— and Virgil, The Meeting of. (W. M. Ramsay) Macmil. 77: 11.

— Childhood of. (W. M. Ramsay) Macmil. 76: 450.

— First Ode of. (A. E. Thiselton) Acad. 53: 506.

— Letters of ; are they Satires ? (G. L. Hendrickson) Am. J. Philol. 18: 313.

— Notes on. (C. Knapp) Am. J. Philol. 18: 325.

— Odes and Epodes of. Ed. R. 190: 119.

— Satires, I., 4 ; a Protest and a Programme. (G. L. Hendrickson) Am. Anthrop. 21: 121.

— Some Translations from. (W. P. Trent) Sewanee, 3: 111.

Horizontal Curves, Discovery of, in Mediæval Italian Architecture. (W. H. Goodyear) Archit. R. 6: 447.

Horn, Andrew, as Author of "Mirror of Justices." (I. S. Leadam) Law Q. 13: 85.

Horn, Geo. Henry. Science, n. s. 7: 73.

Horn Relics in Ontario. (G. E. Laidlaw) Am. Antiq. 20: 65.

Horne, Richard Hengist, Recollections of. (E. Gosse) No. Am. 168: 490.

Horner, Ann Susan. Ath. '00, 2: 793.

"Hornet," Brig. (P. S. P. Conner) New Eng. M. n. s. 23: 268.

Horns of the Altar ; a story. (A. Ashmore) Canad. M. 16: 244.

Hornung, Ernest William, with portrait. Bk. Buyer, 22: 90.

Horrocks, Jeremiah, and the Transit of Venus. Nature, 62: 257.

Horror, Psychology of. (G. F. Milton) Sewanee, 3: 421.

Horse, Ancestry of the. (F. A. Lucas) McClure, 15: 512.

— Education of. (L. W. Lillingston) Good Words, 41: 204.

— Equine Toilet. (Treacy) J. Mil. Serv. Inst. 17: 572.

— How to Judge a. (E. A. A. Grange) Cosmopol. 30: 229.

— in Ancient Babylonia. (W. H. Ward) Am. J. Archæol. 2d s. 2: 159.

— in Folk-lore. (J. F. O'Donnell) Lippinc. 62: 702.

— in relation to Water-lore. (Mabel Peacock) Antiq. n. s. 33: 72.

— Present and Future of. (J. G. Speed) R. of Rs. (N. Y.) 20: 197.

— Return of. (H. T. Peck) Bookman, 13: 425.

— Shire, in England. Sat. R. 91: 265.

— Thoroughbred. (T. A. Cook) Monthly R. 5, no. 2: 122.

— The Wild. Spec. 87: 835.

Horse Artillery and Cavalry. (E. S. May) J. Mil. Serv. Inst. 20: 596.

Horseback Riding ; should Woman ride Astride ? (E. Y. Miller) Munsey, 25: 553.

Horse-breaking. (A. H. Broadwell) Strand, 16: 386.

Horse-breeding. Forest Park Farm, Vt. (E. B. Abercrombie) Outing, 30: 81.

Horse-dealing, True Stories about. (A. S. Appelbee) Eng. Illust. 20: 431.

Horse-fair Pilgrimage, A. (E. S. Nadal) Scrib. M. 30: 387.

Horse-racing, English. (W. H. Rowe) Outing, 38: 281.
— Ethics of. (R. F. M. Thompson) National, 33: 595.
— Grand Prix de Paris. (G. W. Carryl) Outing, 38: 643.
— Passing of Jerome Park. (W. S. Vosburgh) Outing, 38: 513.

Horse-shoeing, Developments in. (M. W. Rowell) J. Mil. Serv. Inst. 20: 524.
— Few Words on. (G. B. Rodney) J. Mil. Serv. Inst. 10: 165, 395.

Horse-swapping Convention; a story. (W. W. Brewer) Cosmopol. 27: 581.

Horse-thief, The; a story. (E. Hough) McClure, 15: 555. Same art. Idler, 19: 222.

Horse-thief, The; a story. (W. L. Beard) Eng. Illust. 17: 303.

Horse-training, Old and New. (G. Tompkins) Outing, 37: 402.

Horse Transport from India to China. (B. Vincent) J. Mil. Serv. Inst. 28: 395.

Horseless Carriages, 400 Years Ago. (A. R. Sennett) Cassier, 15: 458.

Horses, American, and Jockeys abroad. (E. W. Kelly) Munsey, 24: 353.
— American Heavy Harness. (F. M. Ware) Outing, 37: 127.
— and Mules, Army. (C. D. Rhodes) Lippinc. 60: 837.
— Arab, in England. Sat. R. 88: 68.
— Army, Ancient and Modern, Shoeing of. (G. Fleming) J. Mil. Serv. Inst. 13: 983.
— at Sea. Spec. 83: 778.
— Blind, and False Tails. (J. Bainbridge) Chamb. J. 78: 660.
— Breeding Thoroughbred Ponies. (T. C. Patterson) Outing, 37: 270.
— Development of the American Trotter. (N. A. Cole) Outing, 37: 6.
— Hereditary Color in. (W. de Fonvielle) Nature, 56: 598.
— His Majesty the Thoroughbred. (H. P. Mawson) Munsey, 23: 579.
— Homes of Fine. (F. Morris) Munsey, 23: 233.
— How to Breed, for War. (W. S. Blunt) 19th Cent. 48: 198.
— in the Spanish-American War of 1898. (G. Willets) Nat'l M. (Bost.) 8: 555.
— Kentucky Thoroughbred. (R. W. Woolley) Outing, 36: 642.
— Light, Exhibit of. Sat. R. 87: 298.
— Light Artillery. (W. E. Birkhimer) J. Mil. Serv. Inst. 18: 532.
— Military. (H. Thomson) J. Mil. Serv. Inst. 18: 375.
— Private Stables of Manhattan. (R. W. Woolley) Outing, 38: 169.
— Race-, English. Sat. R. 87: 744.
— Rearing a Derby-winner. Strand, 17: 706.
— Shire or Draft, Improvement of. Sat. R. 87: 231.
— Thoroughbred. (W. H. Rowe) Outing, 36: 446.
— Thoroughbreds of Edward VII. (E. Spencer) Outing, 39: 127.
— Trotting, Heredity of. Am. Natural. 32: 55.
— Two-year-olds. (W. H. Rowe) Outing, 36: 671.
— Types of. (A. H. Godfrey) Outing, 33: 111.
— Vice in, and its Correction. (F. M. Ware) Outing, 39: 284.
— War, Famous American. (J. G. Wilson) Outl. 55: 51.
— Zebras and Hybrids. Quar. 190: 404.

Horses' Heads. (N. W. Thomas) Folk-Lore, 11: 322.

Horsfall, Bruce, Artist. (B. Ostertag) Brush & P. 2: 193.

Hort, Fenton John Anthony. (A. M. Fairbairn) Contemp. 71: 342.
— Christian Ecclesia. Church Q. 45: 312.
— Life and Letters. (W. Sanday) Am. J. Theol. 1: 118.
— (B. B. Warfield) Presb. & Ref. R. 9: 348.

Hortensius. Green Bag, 12: 486.

Horticultural Education. (L. H. Bailey) Garden & F. 10: 168.

Horticulture as a Profession. (A. G. Freer) 19th Cent. 46: 769.
— Course in, Outline of. (W. M. Munson) Garden & F. 10: 2.
— in Colleges. (W. E. Britton) Garden & F. 10: 107.
— Trend of. (G. E. Walsh) Lippinc. 60: 370.

Horton, R. F. Early Recollections. (R. F. Horton) Sund. M. 30: 338.

Hoskins, A. H., Admiral. Geog. J. 18: 222.

Hospital, Day in a Paris. Contemp. 79: 524.
— London, An American in. (B. Galpin) Nat'l M. (Bost.) 11: 508.
— Model. (K. Hoffman) Munsey, 22: 487.
— Post, Management of a. (J. R. Hoff) J. Mil. Serv. Inst. 15: 296.
— Sick Children's, at Toronto. (A. Wood) Canad. M. 12: 314.

Hospital Construction, Axioms and Principles of. (H. M. Junghaendel) Am. Arch. 67: 76.

Hospital Life, Humors of. Cornh. 78: 549. Same art. Ecl. M. 131: 719.
— in a Canadian City. (J. McCrae) Canad. M. 13: 320.

Hospital Receiving Room, In a. (Lucian Sorrel) Good Words, 38: 188.

Hospital Returns, Continental, 1777–80. (J. W. Jordan) Pennsyl. M. 23: 35, 210.

Hospital Sketch, A. (E. B. Thelberg) Outl. 64: 509.

Hospital Yarns. (J. de Renzy) Argosy, 74: 343. 75: 34.

Hospitals, Chaos in English. (H. Morten) National, 34: 734.
— Charity vs. Governmental. Sat. R. 91: 762.
— Construction of Isolation. (G. A. T. Middleton) Engin. M. 16: 269.
— Dispensaries, and Nursing. (H. M. Hurd) Char. R. 10: 298, 317, 408.
— Evolution of. (C. K. Winne) J. Mil. Serv. Inst. 12: 734.
— in London. Sat. R. 85: 799–802.
— Relationship of, to Medical Schools. (S. Wilks) 19th Cent. 49: 781.
— Scientific Use of. (Sir M. Foster) 19th Cent. 49: 57.
— Small. (G. W. Shinn) New Eng. M. n.,s. 22: 255.

"Hospodar." (H. S. Brooks) Overland, n. s. 32: 17.

Hosts and Hostesses, Concerning. (T. H. S. Escott) Fortn. 74: 74. Same art. Liv. Age, 226: 506.

Hosts, Divided, at Treaty Communions. (W. Sylvester) Dub. R. 124: 342.

Hosts of the Lord, The; a story. (F. A. Steel) Pall Mall M. 19: 197–520. 20: 100–521. 21: 103–550.

Hot-foot Hannibal. (C. W. Chesnutt) Atlan. 83: 49.

Hot-houses. (G. E. Walsh) Lippinc. 59: 386.

Hotel, The American. (E. J. Edwards) Chaut. 28: 330.
— Behind the Scenes in a Large. Chamb. J. 78: 161.
— A Great. (J. L. Williams) Scrib. M. 21: 135.

Hotel at Pescadores, The. (A. Colton) Scrib. M. 24: 756.

Hotel Management in California, A Study in. (F. W. Parks) Overland. n. s. 29: 396.
— on New Lines. (F. J. Gardiner) Chamb. J. 77: 29.

Hotel Mudie, The; a story. (H. Penn) Cornh. 80: 103. Same art. Liv. Age, 222: 490.

Hotel Porter's Day, A. Liv. Age, 215: 132.

Hotel Problem, The. (F. J. Mather, jr.) Nation, 73: 26.

House Party, A. Ecl. M. 132: 519. Same art. Liv. Age, 220: 458.

House Party at Christmas Cross-Roads; a story. (F. Furbish) Nat'l M. (Bost.) 9: 275.

House Visitation, Reaching the Masses by. (H. Cork) Chaut. 31: 130.

Household Crusader, A. (F. T. Cox) New Eng. M. n. s. 22: 435.

Household Gods. Good Words, 41: 397.

Household Industries, Colonial. (A. M. Earle) Chaut. 26: 473.

Household Management, Practical Hints on. Chamb. J. 77: 188.

Housekeeper's Stone. (A. W. Quimby) Forum, 31: 453.

Housekeepers, Born. (Mrs. Scott-Moncrief) Chamb. J. 78: 625. Same art. Ecl. M. 137: 742. Same art. Liv. Age, 231: 284.

Housekeeping, European. (F. C. Baylor) Lippinc. 60: 415.
— Study of, in Boston. (M. E. Trueblood) New Eng. M. n. s. 23: 243.

Houses, Artistic. (J. S. Gibson) Studio (Lond.) 1: 215.
— Country, Designs for. (C. F. A. Voysey) Studio (Internat.) 7: 157. — (E. Newton) Studio (Internat.) 8: 157.
— People and. (H. Bosanquet) Econ. J. 10: 47.

Houses, Glass. Spec. 86: 833.

Housewives, Training of. (A. Strachey) Cornh. 77: 530.

Housing, Graded Factors of. (E. T. Potter) Am. Arch. 74: 100.
— Half a Century of Improved. (W. H. Tolman) Yale R. 5: 389.
— of Educated Working Women. (A. Zimmern) Contemp. 77: 96.
— of the English Poor. (Monkswell) No. Am. 165: 52.
— of the Poor. (R. Donald) Contemp. 77: 323. — (H. Newbolt) Monthly R. 2, no. 2: 11.
— — Improved. (E. H. Cooper) Gunton's M. 12: 416.
— — in Chicago. (F. B. Embree) J. Pol. Econ. 8: 354.
— — in London. (A. Lewis) Econ. R. 10: 164. — Ann. Am. Acad. Pol. Sci. 16: 160.
— — Progress in. (C. H. Denyer) Econ. J. 7: 487.
— of a Provincial City. (A. J. Carlyle) Econ. R. 11: 460.
— of the Working-classes. (E. Wilson) J. Soc. Arts, 48: 253.
— — in France, Modern Movement for. (W. F. Willoughby) Yale R. 8: 233.
— — in Germany. (W. H. Dawson) Econ. J. 9: 445.
— — in Yonkers, N. Y. (E. L. Bogart) Econ. Stud. 3: 273.
— — Laborers' Dwellings. (L. Fisher) Econ. J. 9: 605.
— — Results of State, Municipal and Organized Private Action on. (J. F. J. Sykes) J. Statis. Soc. 64: 189.

Housing Committee, National. (E. R. Pease) Econ. R. 10: 246.

Housing Conditions in the Principal Cities of New York. (E. T. Devine) Charities, 7: 491.

Housing Question. Quar. 193: 432. — (S. A. Barnett) 19th Cent. 49: 794. — (L. Fisher) Econ. R. 10: 434. — (E. R. L. Gould) Munic. Aff. 3: 108.
— and the L. C. C. (D. S. Waterlow) Fortn. 75: 187. — (C. S. Jones) Fortn. 74: 967. 75: 387.
— and the Savings Banks. (H. W. Wolff) Westm. 155: 631.
— and Scientific Reform. (W. Caldwell) Bib. Sac. 54: 366.
— Co-operators, the State, and the. (G. Slater) Contemp. 79: 254.
— in Great Cities. (E. R. L. Gould) Q. J. Econ. 14: 378.
— in London. (E. Cannan) Econ. R. 11: 383.

Housing Question, Mr. Ritchie on. Spec. 84: 200.
— Pioneers in, Liverpool. (L. Ilbert) Econ. R. 9: 450.
— Shattuck Competition for Artisans' Homes. (G. M. Huss) Munic. Aff. 3: 141.
— Working-men's Conference on. (R. Feetham) Econ. R. 10: 526.

Housman, Alfred Edward. A Shropshire poet. (W. Archer) Fortn. 70: 263. — Acad. 55: 23.

Housman, Laurence. Acad. 52: 496.
— Work of. (Gleeson White) M. of Art, 23: 199.

Houston, Sam, and Texan Independence. (B. J. Ramage) Sewanee, 2: 309.
— Elliott's. Critic, 38: 123.

Houzeau, Jean Charles, Great Belgian Astronomer (J. E. Gore) Gent. M. n. s. 67: 445.

"Hovelling." (F. T. Bullen) Cornh. 79: 89.

Hovey, Alvah, Notice of. (J. M. English) Bib. Sac. 56: 579.

Hovey, Richard, with portrait. Bk. News, 15: 238. — Acad. 58: 335.
— Along the Trail; lyrics. Poet-Lore, 11: 129.
— Launcelot and Guenevere. (E. E. Hale, jr.) Dial (Ch.) 26: 17.
— Plays and Poems of. (C. H. Page) Bookman, 8: 360, 449. — (C. G. D. Roberts) Bk. Buyer, 17: 616.
— Promise and Work of. (H. Knorr) Poet-Lore, 12: 436.

How, Walsham. Crit. R. 9: 88.
— Note-books. (F. D. How, ed.) Sund. M. 29: 50, 99, 186. Same art. Ecl. M. 134: 760. Same art. Liv. Age, 225: 168.

How Aunt Polly prevented a Jail Delivery. (E. A. Brinnistool) Overland, n. s. 30: 82.

How Betty spoke the Governor. (A. E. Herrick) New Eng. M. n. s. 21: 353.

How Bois-Rosé and I captured the King. (E. W. Jennings) Pall Mall M. 13: 331.

How Browne-Martyn and I nearly made Ourselves Ridiculous. (O. Deane) Temp. Bar, 119: 254.

How the Buzzards worked a Spell. (E. W. Kemble) Cosmopol. 31: 664.

How Clytemnestra saved a Kingdom; a story. (M. J. H. Skrine) Temp. Bar, 113: 243. Same art. Liv. Age, 217: 32.

How Constantinople fell; a poem. (F. Coppee) Belgra. 93: 250.

How Dead Injun did its Duty; a story. (O. Agnus) Eng. Illust. 18: 115.

How Donald Roy got a White Head. (J. A. Steuart) Temp. Bar, 119: 227.

How an Editor tests a Story. (F. Bellamy) Bookman, 10: 343.

How the French Army crossed the Channel. Cosmopol. 26: 626. 27: 89.

How the Gods fought for Baron Krilof; a story. (F. Whishaw) Idler, 11: 702.

How he found the Name and Address. (J. E. Anderson) Good Words, 40: 109.

How I Did n't become an Author. (N. Chester) Temp. Bar, 120: 565. Same art. Liv. Age, 226: 712.

How I drove a Hansom; by a girl. Eng. Illust. 17: 191.

How I drove an Omnibus; by a girl. Eng. Illust. 18: 155.

How I mobilized my Company. (H. D. Sichel) Contemp. 79: 558.

How I reared the Aylesburys; a tale. (M. G. Wightwick) Argosy, 65: 756.

How I saved Ben. (L. Wallace) Cent. 40: 758.

How Jean Bossy missed his Chance. (Mrs. Orpen) Good Words, 40: 549.

How Kelly came to Billabong. (Carlton Dawe) Chamb. J. 77: extr. no. 46.

Hudson, Hendrick, Voyage of, to Spitzbergen, 1607. (M. Conway) Geog. J. 15: 121.

Hudson, John Elbridge. (G. V. Leverett) N. E. Reg. 55: 135.

Hudson's Bay; Early Days at York Factory. (B. Willson) Canad. M. 13: 18, 117.

— Explorations South of. (R. Bell) Geog. J. 10: 1.

— French Capture of Fort Nelson. (B. Willson) Canad. M. 13: 210.

Hudson's Bay Company. Ed. R. 192: 161. — (B. Willson) Cornh. 82: 660. — Scot. R. 35: 226.

— at Edmonton. (B. Cameron) Canad. M. 15: 99.

— Bryce on. (R. G. MacBeth) Canad. M. 15: 449.

— Chronicle of. (A. G. Bradley) Macmil. 83: 231.

— a Review. (J. A. Cooper) Canad. M. 13: 576. 14: 170.

Hudson's Bay Trading Post. (R. W. Porter) New Eng. M. n. s. 20: 715.

— New Year's Day at. (W. B. Cameron) Outing, 33: 328.

Hudson River, Canal-boat Voyage on. (C. Johnson) Outl. 60: 309.

— The Lordly. (Clarence Cook) Cent. 32: 483.

— Palisades of, Preserving the. R. of Rs. (N. Y.) 24: 49.

— Summer Homes on. (J. W. Harrington) Munsey, 21: 721.

Huerfano Bill, the Bandit; a story. (C. Warman) McClure, 8: 443.

Huggins, William. (H. Kayser) Nature, 64: 225.

Hugh Wynne, Free Quaker. (S. Weir Mitchell) Cent. 31: 362 — 32: 861.

Hughes, Arthur, Landscapes of. Ath. '00, 2: 64.

Hughes, David Edward. Nature, 61: 325.

Hughes, Rev. Griffith, Letters of. (B. F. Owen) Pennsyl. M. 14: 139.

Hughes, Talbot, with portrait. M. of Art, 26: 1.

Hughes, Thomas, Rugby School Memorial to. School R. 5: 409.

Hughie McGlanachie's Courtin'; a story. (J. MacManus) Idler, 13: 341.

Hugo, Victor. (P. Bourget) Critic, 39: 257.

— as an Artist. (B. Constant) Harper, 102: 100. — (P. Meurice) Harper, 102: 444.

— as Draftsman and Decorator. (Le Cocq de Lautreppe) Cent. 36: 428.

— as a Poet. (A. Fortier) Chaut. 25: 122.

— at his House. (G. Larroumet) Chaut. 25: 141.

— Characteristics of his Work and Career. (F. C. de Sumichrast) Chaut. 25: 132.

— Correspondence, 1836–82. Sat. R. 85: 527.

— Goethe and; a comparison. National, 34: 901.

— The Great Poet of Childhood. (W. Canton) Sund. M. 28: 383.

— Home at Guernsey. (G. Jeanniot) Scrib. M. 21: 108.

— in Exile. Liv. Age, 216: 765.

— in France. (G. McDermot) Cath. World, 67: 37.

— Les Misérables. (L. O. Kuhns) Chaut. 25: 126.

— — Jean Valjean. (W. A. Quayle) Meth. R. 59: 692.

— Letters. (R. G. Valentine) Nat'l M. (Bost.) 11: 9.

— — 1815, 1835. Ath. '98, 2: 92.

— Love-letters. Harper, 101: 924. 102: 47. — (E. K. Tompkins) Critic, 39: 65. — (E. L. Banks) Fortn. 76: 307. — Harper, 102: 304.

— Lyric Poetry of. (C. E. Meetkerke) Gent. M. n. s. 67: 400.

— Memoirs. (E. G. Johnson) Dial (Ch.) 27: 355. — (A. S. Van Westrum) Critic, 35: 1046. — Acad. 57: 487.

— Ninety-three. (F. M. Warren) Chaut. 32: 532.

— Novels. (J. Reinhard) Sewanee, 7: 29.

— Story of. (J. A. Harrison) Chaut. 25: 115.

— Things seen. (A. Laugel) Nation, 69: 407, 425.

Hugo, Victor; Was he Color-blind? (C. E. Meetkerke) Gent. M. n. s. 66: 376.

Huguenots, History of, Two Phases of. (E. Böhl) Presb. and Ref. R. 9: 83.

Hull House, Chicago. (F. Kelley) New Eng. M. n. s. 18: 550.

— Day at. (Dorothea Moore) Am. J. Sociol. 2: 629.

— and the Ward Boss. (R. S. Baker) Outl. 58: 769.

Hulst, Comte Maurice d', with portrait. Cath. World, 65: 620.

Human, On being. (W. Wilson) Atlan. 80: 320.

Human Body as an Engine. (E. B. Rosa) Pop. Sci. Mo. 57: 491.

Human Breed, Possible Improvements of, under the Existing Conditions of Law and Sentiment. (F. Galton) Nature, 64: 659.

Human Bundle, A; a story. (E. G. Henham) Temp. Bar, 111: 42.

Human Development, Course of. (W. J. McGee) Forum, 26: 56.

Human Energy, Problem of Increasing. (N. Tesla) Cent. 38: 175.

Human Nature. (C. W. Whitney) Chaut. 29: 171.

— Knowledge of, is Half the Science of War. (J. P. Finley) Un. Serv. (Phila.) 17: 79.

— Significance of Butler's View of. (A. Lefevre) Philos. R. 8: 128.

— Unity of. (J. J. Chapman) Internat. J. Ethics, 11: 158.

Human Perfectibility in the Light of Evolution. (A. Forel) Internat. Mo. 4: 179.

Human Race, Has it Degenerated? (W. S. Sparrow) Idler, 12: 678.

Human Sacrifices, Alleged, in Italy. (J. Britten) Month, 92: 390.

Human Soul, A; a poem. (F. Peacock) [Chamb. J.] Ecl. M. 129: 519.

Humanism in Germany, Beginnings of. (R. C. Ford) Meth. R. 58: 41.

— New, Griggs'. (J. McSorley) Cath. World, 70: 752.

— under Francis I. (A. Tilley) Eng. Hist. R. 15: 456.

Humanitarianism, The New. Blackw. 163: 98. Same art. Ecl. M. 130: 338. Same art. Liv. Age, 216: 720. — (T. Stanley) Westm. 155: 414.

Humanity, Science of. (W. J. McGee) Science, 6: 413.

Humbert, King of Italy. Outl. 65: 768.

— Character Sketch, with portrait. R. of Rs. (N. Y.) 22: 316.

— Death of. Sat. R. 90: 137.

Hume, David, Ethical System of. (E. Albee) Philos. R. 6: 337.

Humming-bird of the Lantee, a story. (A. T. Colcock) Nat'l M. (Bost.) 14: 448.

Humming-birds. (W. S. Kennedy) New Eng. M. n. s. 20: 540.

— of Ontario. (C. W. Nash) Canad. M. 17: 443.

Humor, British. Scot. R. 31: 329.

— Genial, and Aggressive Wit. (J. L. Ford) Munsey, 24: 624.

— German. (C. B. C. Eaglesfield) Cath. World, 69: 319.

— in Black and White. (E. T. Reed) M. of Art, 25: 116.

— in the Law Courts. Strand, 17: 746.

— Intercivic. (T. Jenks) Cent. 36: 154.

— An Italian View of. (W. D. Howells) No. Am. 173: 567, 709.

— The Mission of. (S. M. Crothers) Atlan. 84: 372.

— of the Primary School. Month, 89: 615.

— Sense of. Sat. R. 87: 489.

— — in Men. (Edith Slater; F. H. Freshfield) Cornh. 79: 347.

— — in Women. (R. Y. Tyrrell) Cornh. 79: 627.

— Uses of. (J. Sully) National, 29: 852. Same art. Ecl. M. 129: 441.

Humorists, Some American. (M. A. DeW. Howe) Bookman, 6: 24.

Humors of an Irish Country Town. Cornh. 81: 238. Same art. Liv. Age, 225: 53.

— of Speech and Pen. (E. G. Henham) Cornh. 78: 821. Same art. Liv. Age, 220: 249. Same art. Ecl. M. 132: 404.

Humorous Writing. (W. J. Lampton) Writer, 11: 65.

Hun Kiang Gorges, Manchuria, Through the. (R. T. Turley) Geog. J. 14: 292.

Hundred Days, The First of the. [Longm.] Liv. Age, 229: 104.

Hundredth Princess, The ; a story. (E. Sharp) Pall Mall M. 16: 509.

Huneker, James. Chopin and his Works. (E. Swayne) Music, 18: 33.

— Mezzotints in Modern Music. (J. F. Runciman) Sat. R. 88: 292. — (E. Swayne) Music, 16: 17.

Hungarian Cattle. (R. H. Wallace) Good Words, 40: 838.

Hungarian Gipsy Minstrels. (J. F. Rowbotham) Good Words, 39: 690.

Hungarian Literature, 1896–97. (L. Katscher) Ath. '97, 2: 20.

— 1897–98. (L. Katscher) Ath. '98, 2: 22.

— 1898–99. (L. Katscher) Ath. '99, 2: 20.

— 1899–1900. (L. Katscher) Ath. '00, 2: 21.

— 1900–01. (L. Katscher) Ath. '01, 2: 21.

— Reich on. Ath. '98, 2: 785.

Hungary, The Banderium of. (R. H. Davis) Scrib. M. 21: 267.

— Strike against Taxes in. Spec. 80: 8.

Hunger. (W. J. Youmans) Cosmopol. 25: 434.

Hungerford, Anthony. "Memorial." (L. M. Roberts) Eng. Hist. R. 16: 292.

Hungerford, Margaret. (E. B. Sherman) Critic, 30: 94.

Hunnewell Family. (J. F. Hunnewell) N. E. Reg. 54: 140.

Hunnewell, Hollis H., Estate of, Wellesley, Mass. (W. M. Thompson) New Eng. M. n. s. 25: 157.

Hunnis, William, Dramatist. (C. C. Stopes) Ath. '00, 1: 410.

— Interlude ; or Comedie of Jacob and Esau. (C. C. Stopes) Ath. '00, 1: 538.

Hunt, Albert Sanford. (H. Welch) Meth. R. 60: 177.

Hunt, Alfred, English Painter. Sat. R. 83: 138.

Hunt, Charles Wallace. Cassier, 13: 361.

Hunt, Leigh. (Sir G. M. Smith) Critic, 38: 48. — With portrait. Acad. 51: 79. — (W. Lewin) Acad. 51: 161, (A. Stone) 190.

— and Stevenson, Some New Letters by. (E. A. Ireland) Atlan. 82: 122.

Hunt, Sandford. (A. B. Sandford) Meth. R. 57: 9.

Hunt, Walter, Animal Painter. (M. H. Dixon) M. of Art, 25: 433.

Hunt, W. Holman. (W. Bayliss) Good Words, 40: 331.

— Triumph of the Innocents, a Painting. (J. P. Lenox) Bib. World, 11: 45.

Hunt, William, Reminiscences of, with portrait. (W. Collingwood) M. of Art, 22: 503.

Hunt, William Morris, Art Life of, Knowlton's. (R. Sturgis) Bk. Buyer, 19: 382.

Hunt-club, Green Spring Valley. (H. Hiss) Outing, 33: 226.

Hunt-supper, A, in Old Virginia. (Mrs. B. Harrison) Liv. Age, 214: 485.

Hunter, Robert M. T. (M. T. Hunter) Conserv. R. 5: 169.

Hunter, William Wilson. Ath. '00, 1: 179. — Geog. J. 15: 289.

— A Great Anglo-American. (J. A. R. Marriott) Fortn. 73: 1033.

Huntercombe House, England. (E. V. Boyle) Pall Mall M. 15: 551.

Hunting ; After Big Game in Africa and India. (H. W. Seton-Karr) Cent. 32: 370.

— After Big Game with Packs. (J. C. Ayres) Cent. 36: 221

— and Hunting Men. Sat. R. 87: 168.

— and its Future. (H. A. Bryden) Fortn. 69: 448.

— Christmas Week in Lower Louisiana. (A. Wilkinson) Outing, 31: 211.

— Covert Owners, Keepers. (A. G. Bagot) Pall Mall M. 23: 88.

— Curious Methods of the Ghauts. (H. Hudson) Outing, 36: 394.

— The Field-riders. Pall Mall M. 22: 553.

— in Indian Territory. (E. H. Hudson) Outing, 34: 566.

— in Oregon. (R. L. Warner) Outing, 35: 35.

— in South Africa. (H. A. Bryden) Sat. R. 84: 311.

— Master, Servants, and Hounds. (A. G. Bagot) Pall Mall M. 22: 391.

— Mediæval. Spec. 86: 235.

— Need of Trained Observation in. (T. Roosevelt) Outing, 37: 631.

— A Novice on the Trail. (E. W. Sandys) Outing, 35: 284.

— Riding to Hounds. (R. Newton, jr.) Munsey, 22: 73.

— Singular Shots. (R. Gourlay) Outing, 39: 93.

— Three Centuries Ago. (W. A. Baillie-Grohman) Pall Mall M. 16: 159.

— Where the Big Game runs. (M. Foster) Munsey, 24: 426.

— The Wilderness Hunter. (O. Wister) Outing, 39: 251.

Hunting Knife and Rifle Pit. (J. P. Sanger) J. Mil. Serv. Inst. 19: 409.

Hunting Methods of Russia. (W. Gerrare) Outing, 37: 34.

Hunting Regions. Spec. 80: 301.

Hunting Song. (W. T. Olcott) Outing, 35: 188.

Hunting Songs, Old. (Laura A. Smith) Idler, 15: 847.

Hunting Trials. (M. P. Turnbull) Sat. R. 91: 497.

Huntingdon, David, Earl of. (R. Aitken) Scot. R. 31: 127.

Huntingham Club of Buenos Ayres. (H. P. Douglas) Outing, 34: 73.

Huntington, Collis P., with portrait. R. of Rs. (N. Y.) 22: 325.

— on Education. (E. B. Payne) Arena, 22: 257.

Huntington, Ebenezer, Letters of, 1774–81. Am. Hist. R. 5: 702.

Hunton, Eppa, with portrait. (Sallie E. M. Hardy) Green Bag, 10: 159.

Huret, Jules. Sara Bernhardt. (A. S. Van Westrum) Critic, 35: 806.

Huron Missions, Last of the. (R. R. Elliott) Am. Cath. Q. 23: 526.

Hurricane, West Indian, of Sept., 1900. (E. B. Garriott) Nat. Geog. M. 11: 384.

Hurricane in Mauritius, A ; a story. Temp. Bar, 110: 274. Same art. Liv. Age, 212: 842.

Hurricanes on Coast of Texas. (A. W. Greely) Nat. Geog. M. 11: 442.

Hurry, Nation in a. (E. Gregory) Atlan. 85: 609.

Hurst, Charles Herbert, Obituary of. Nat. Sci. 13: 62.

Hurst, Hal, and his Work. (A. H. Lawrence) Art J. 50: 198.

— Pictures by. Artist (N. Y.) 26: 146.

Hus, John, and Home Rule in Bohemia. (W. H. Crawford) Meth. R. 58: 681.

Husband and Wife. (M. Hart) Eng. Illust. 16: 523.

— — as Partners. (W. A. Coutts) Am. Law R. 33: 215.

— Ideal. (Lavinia Hart) Cosmopol. 31: 444.

Hymns, Tinkering of. (J. C. Hadden) 19th Cent. 47: 139. Same art. Ecl. M. 134: 489. Same art. Liv. Age, 224: 490.

— to the Heavens, the Sea, the Earth, and to Heroes. (G. d'Annunzio) Critic, 37: 165.

Hymnology, Catholic. (C. T. Gatty) Dub. R. 120: 70.

— Mediæval Latin. (A. R. Kremer) Ref. Church R. 45: 212.

Hyoid in Birds, Nomenclature of. (F. A. Lucas) Science, n. s. 9: 323.

Hypnotic Suggestion, Moral Value of. (J. D. Quackenbos) Harper, 100: 466.

Hypnotism. Sat. R. 90: 235. — (A. MacDonald) Chaut. 29: 574.

— Alcoholic. (A. MacDonald) Am. J. Sociol. 5: 383.

— Educational Use of. (J. D. Quackenbos) Harper, 101: 264.

— in its Scientific and Forensic Aspects. (M. L. Dawson) Arena, 18: 544.

— Physiological Aspects of. (F. Gotch) Sci. Prog. n. s. 1: 511.

— Reciprocal Influence in. (J. D. Quackenbos) Harper, 103: 110.

Hypothetics. (E. R. Hull) Am. Cath. Q. 22: 124.

Hysteresio, Yoke with Intercepted Magnetic Circuit for Measuring. (Z. Crook) Am. J. Sci. 161: 365.

I nunc and *i* with another Imperative. (E. B. Lease) Am. J. Philol. 19: 59.

" I require and charge you both ; " a story. (W. Richards) Belgra. 96: 197.

I shall arise ; a poem. (J. P. Peabody) Atlan. 86: 710.

" I Sing of Honor and the Faithful Heart ; " a story. (G. M. Martin) McClure, 17: 558.

Iatro-chemistry in 1897. (H. Carrington Bolton) Science, n. s. 7: 397.

Ibn Al-Hiti. Arabic Chronicle of Karaite Doctors. (G. Margoliouth) Jew Q. 9: 429.

Ibn Chiquitilla, nebst der Fragmenten seiner Schriften von S. Poznanski. (G. G. Cameron) Crit. R. 8: 86.

Ibn Hanbal, Ahmed, and the Mihna. (G. G. Cameron) Crit. R. 8: 444.

Ibn Iyas, Egyptian Chronicle of. (K. Vollers) Asia. R. 23: 356.

Ibsen, Henrik. Acad. 57: 79. — (A. I. du P. Colman) Critic, 34: 33.

— and the Ethical Drama of the Nineteenth Century. (Helena Knorr) Poet-Lore, 10: 49.

— John Gabriel Borkman. (V. Thompson) Nat'l M. (Bost.) 8: 120. — (G. B. Shaw) Sat. R. 83: 114. — (W. M. Payne) Dial (Ch.) 22: 37. — (C. Porter) Poet-Lore, 9: 302.

— — as performed in London. (G. B. Shaw) Sat. R. 83: 507.

— — Fatherhood in. (C. Porter and H. A. Clarke) Poet-Lore, 11: 116.

— Brand, New Light on. (M. A. Stobart) Fortn. 72: 227.

— Brandes on. (M. Beerbohm) Sat. R. 88: 101. — Sat. R. 85: 821. — (W. M. Payne) Dial (Ch.) 27: 314.

— Doll's House, as played in 1897. (G. B. Shaw) Sat. R. 83: 539.

— Ghosts. (G. B. Shaw) Sat. R. 84: 12.

— Language of. (D. K. Dodge) Critic, 30: 69.

— Little Eyolf ; a plea for reticence. (A. S. Spender) Dub. R. 120: 112.

— Love's Comedy. Acad. 58: 527.

— — Scene from. (C. H. Herford) Fortn. 73: 191.

— Masterbuilder, played in New York. (H. Knorr) Poet-Lore, 12: 95.

— Norwegian of. (S. Sondresen) Critic, 31: 308.

— Passing of. (Baron de Stampenbourg) Indep. 53: 2630.

Ibsen, Henrik, Personal Impressions of Björnson and. (W. H. Schofield) Atlan. 81: 567.

— Pillars of Society. (M. Beerbohm) Sat. R. 91: 631.

— Plays of, in England. Acad. 60: 244. — Liv. Age, 230: 789.

— Portrait of. (V. Greene) Bk. Buyer, 19: 90.

— The Real. (P. Maxwell) Bk. Buyer, 19: 91. — (W. Archer) Internat. Mo. 3: 182.

— Russell and Standing on. (W. S. W. McLay) Citizen, 3: 230.

— Seventieth Birthday. Acad. 53: 352.

— — Honors on. (G. B. Shaw) Sat. R. 85: 428.

— Solness. (T. R. Price) Sewanee, 2: 257.

— When we Dead Awaken. (J. Joyce) Fortn. 73: 575. — Acad. 58: 307.

Ibsenism. (H. D. Traill and R. McNeill) National, 28: 641. Same art. Liv. Age, 212: 317.

Ice. Ecl. M. 129: 719.

— Arctic Sea, as a Geological Agent. (R. S. Tarr) Am. J. Sci. 153: 223.

— Glacial, Plasticity of. (I. C. Russell) Am. J. Sci. 153: 344.

Ice-boating on Beaver Dam Lake. (E. Elliott) Outing, 29: 341.

Icebound ; a tale of Three Mariners. (H. Russell) Ecl. M. 128: 45.

Ice-breaker " Yermak." (Admiral Makaroff) Geog. J. 15: 32. — (E. Mayo) McClure, 14: 537.

Ice-breaking Steamers. Fighting the Ice. (G. E. Walsh) Cassier, 16: 115.

— in Polar Exploration. (E. S. Balch) J. Frankl. Inst. 149: 141.

Ice Carnival, Passing of the. (E. Wildman) Outing, 33: 360.

Ice Caves and Causes of Subterranean Ice. (E. S. Balch) J. Frankl. Inst. 143: 161.

— and Frozen Wells. (W. J. McGee) Nat. Geog. M. 12: 433.

Ice Company, The Case of the. (D. MacG. Means) Nation, 71: 421.

Ice Deposits, Subterranean, in America. (E. S. Balch) J. Frankl. Inst. 147: 286.

Ice-houses. Amer. Arch. 58: 71.

Ice-seals, Habits of. (R. L.) Nature, 57: 346.

Ice Trust Outrage. Gunton's M. 18: 515.

Ice-yacht ; how to build for $60. (H. P. Ashley) Outing, 35: 244.

Ice-yachting up to Date. (H. P. Ashley) Outing, 31: 384.

— Orange Lake Ice-yacht Club and its Rivals. (H. P. Ashley) Outing, 33: 408.

Ice-yachting Adventures, Some. (N. Wright) Outing, 33: 502.

Ice-yachts, Modern. (H. P. Ashley) Outing, 31: 453.

Iceland and the Faröe Islands. (A. C. Little) Dub. R. 125: 385.

— Explorations in, during 1881-98. (Th. Thoroddsen) Geog. J. 13: 251, 480.

— Thoroddsen's Exploration in. Geog. J. 12: 496.

Icelandic Poetry, Characteristics of. (W. C. Green) Antiq. n. s. 36: 262.

Ichabod. (M. Beerbohm) Cornh. 82: 636. Same art. Liv. Age, 227: 633. Same art. Ecl. M. 136: 106.

Ichthyodectes, Notes on Species of. (O. P. Hay) Am. J. Sci. 156: 225.

Icknield Way in Norfolk and Suffolk, Eng. (W. G. Clarke) Knowl. 22: 43.

Iconoclast, An ; a drama. (Mrs. A. Dean) Eng. Illust. 20: 178.

Idaho and Montana, Boundary Line. (R. U. Goode) Nat. Geog. M. 11: 23.

— University of. (W. K. Clement) Overland, n. s. 29: 146.

Ide, Albert L. Cassier, 14: 544.
Idea, Hegel's Treatment of the Categories of the. (J. E. McTaggart) Mind, 25: 145.
Ideal, The; a poem. (C. Scollard) Chaut. 31: 82.
Ideal in the Actual, The. Outl. 61: 494.
— Power of, over Individual and National Life. (B. O. Flower) Arena, 26: 417.
— Value of an. (H. A. Dallas) Econ. R. 7: 480.
Idealism and Christianity, Watson on. (C. W. Hodge) Presb. & Ref. R. 8: 541.
— and Theology, D'Arcy on. (J. B. Gibson) Crit. R. 10: 313.
— Ethical vs. Intellectual. (J. Lindsay) Internat. J. Ethics, 10: 235.
— Fallacy of Extreme. (S. S. Colvin) Am. J. Psychol. 11: 511.
— German. Spec. 80: 903.
— in America. Outl. 63: 439.
— Naturalism and. (C. S. Myers) Philos. R. 10: 463.
— Practicable. (A. Boutwood) Lond. Q. 94: 327.
Idealist Movement and Positive Science. Liv. Age, 215: 306.
— British, in the 19th Century. (R. M. Wenley) Am. J. Theol. 5: 445.
Idealistic Philosophy: Reality of the External World. (W. R. Carson) Dub. R. 125: 97.
Idealists, Olive Branches offered to. (J. Rickaby) Month, 98: 354.
Ideals, Ancient, Taylor on. (G. S. Goodspeed) Dial (Ch.) 22: 359.
— Dead. Belgra. 94: 421.
— of Schoolgirls. Spec. 86: 870.
Ideas, General; their Genesis from Group Perception. (H. M. Stanley) Psychol. R. 7: 58.
Identification Offices in India and Egypt. (F. Galton) 19th Cent. 48: 118.
Identity, Disputed, An Interesting Case of. (B. Borret) Green Bag, 13: 464.
Idiocy; Mental Defectives and the Social Welfare. (M. W. Barr) Pop. Sci. Mo. 54: 746.
— Pretended. (M. Carmichael) Sat. R. 88: 129.
Idiots, Training of. (C. Bernstein) Am. J. Soc. Sci. 35: 149.
— Training of Mentally Deficient Children. (M. W. Barr) Pop. Sci. Mo. 53: 531.
Idleness, Profession of. (J. L. Ford) Munsey, 26: 100.
Idler's Idyll, An; a story. (A. Beresford) Argosy, 66: 400.
Idol Cup, The. (N. W. Driscoll) Overland, n. s. 30: 276.
Idol Temple, An; a poem. (E. Rhodes) Argosy, 66: 534.
Idols, Two, from Syria. (W. H. Ward) Am. J. Archæol. 2d s. 4: 289.
Idyl in Delft, An; a story. (H. T. George) Nat'l M. (Bost.) 13: 327.
Idyl of a Chicken Ranch. (Blanche M. Boring) Overland, n. s. 29: 482.
Idyl of the Fourth Estate; a story. (E. T. Royle) Munsey, 25: 392.
Idyl of the "Gass." (M. Wolfenstein) Lippinc. 66: 918.
Idyl of a Pariah, The; a story. (J. M. M'Govern) Nat'l M. (Bost.) 12: 241.
Idylls of the Sea. (F. T. Bullen) Spec. 81: 241-649.
"If he'd only Come to Me." (H. C. Baker) Overland, n. s. 31: 483.
"If I should die To-night," Disputed Authorship of. (W. W. Gist) Midland, 7: 250.
"If 'twere done when 'tis done;" a story. (M. S. Hancock) Gent. M. n. s. 63: 1.
Ightham Mote. Artist (N. Y.) 26: 86. — (S. Baring Gould) M. of Art, 24: 537.

Ignatius, St., of Antioch, by E. Bruston. (T. M. Lindsay) Crit. R. 8: 400.
— Christianity of. (A. C. Giffert) New World, 7: 470.
— A Study of. (J. Rickaby) Month, 98: 1.
Igneous Rocks, Causes of Variation in the Composition of. (T. L. Walker) Am. J. Sci. 156: 410.
— from Smyrna and Pergamon. (H. S. Washington) Am. J. Sci. 153: 41.
— Intrusive, Phenocrysts of. (L. V. Pirsson) Am. J. Sci. 157: 271.
— of the Leucite Hills and Pilot Butte, Wyoming. (W. Cross) Am. J. Sci. 154: 115.
Ignorance, Our, tested with a Tape-line; it is Millions of Miles Long. (R. P. Lovell) Overland, n. s. 34: 337.
Igorrote Runners of Luzon. (W. Dinwiddie) Outing, 36: 536.
Igorrotes, Land of the. (P. Whitmarsh) Outl. 64: 960.
Ilario's Temptation. (E. B. Mabury) Overland, n. s. 31: 50.
Ilkley, Archæological Museum at. (W. Cudworth) Reliquary, 38: 217.
Illimani, Ascent of. (Sir M. Conway) Harper, 99: 657.
Illinois, Mason on. (E. E. Sparks) Dial (Ch.) 30: 266.
— Picturesque. (L. Taft) Brush & P. 2: 179.
— Sport in. (L. Hubbard, jr.) Outing, 39: 343.
— State University Library, Mural Decorations for. (N. A. Wells) Brush & P. 6: 228.
— University of, Astronomical Observatory. (G. W. Myers) Pop. Astron. 6: 319.
— — Library Building. (P. F. Bicknell) Lib. J. 22: 303.
"Illinois," Battleship, launched. (D. O. Fletcher) Nat'l M. (Bost.) 14: 619.
Illinois Central Railroad, Charter Tax of. (W. H. Allen) J. Pol. Econ. 6: 353.
Illinois County. (C. E. Boyd) Am. Hist. R. 4: 623.
Illinois Gulch Meteorite. (H. L. Preston) Am. J. Sci. 159: 201.
Illinois Indians to Captain Abner Prior, 1794. Am. Hist. R. 4: 107.
Illinois State Library Association. Pub. Lib. 2: 278.
— Fourth Annual Meeting of. Pub. Lib. 5: 119.
Illinois Theatre, Chicago. Am. Arch. 71: 59.
Illiteracy and Citizenship. (F. H. Casson) Educa. 18: 438.
— in the South. (A. Sledd) Indep. 53: 2471.
— in the U. S., Significance of. (A. D. Mayo) Educa. 19: 30.
Illness, Scientific and Christian View of. (J. T. Bixby) New World, 8: 471.
— Some Aspects of. Spec. 84: 45.
Illuminated MSS., English Art in. (E. M. Thompson) J. Soc, Arts, 46: 461.
Illuminating Globes, Photometric Comparison of. (R. B. Williamson and J. H. Klinck) J. Frankl. Inst. 149: 66.
Illumination, Art of. (G. C. Teall) Brush & P. 5: 71.
— (H. A. Heaton) Artist (N. Y.) 23: 79.
— History of. (H. Crew) Am. Arch. 62: 3.
— Methods of, in other Days. (F. R. Coles) Reliquary, 41: 170.
Illumination of Lee Moy. (C. W. Doyle) Lippinc. 64: 263.
Illusion of the Deflected Threads, Prof. Judd on. (A. H. Pierce) Psychol. R. 7: 490.
— of Length. (C. E. Seashore and M. C. Williams) Psychol. R. 7: 592.
Illusion of a Sacrifice, The; a story. (K. F. Hills) Pall Mall M. 18: 471.
Illusions, Contribution to Study of. (F. E. Bolton) Am. J. Psychol. 9: 167.
— Geometrical. (C. H. Judd) Psychol. R. 6: 241.

Immortality, Do Men desire? (F. C. S. Schiller) Fortn. **76**: 430.

— Evidence of Life after Death. (T. J. Hudson) Harper, **101**: 432.

— Genetic Study of. (J. R. Street) Pedagog. Sem. **6**: 267.

— a Hymn, with Music. Open Court, **12**: 58.

— in the Light of Scripture and Nature. (W. F. Eyster) Luth. Q. **27**: 441.

— in the Old Testament. (T. McK. Stuart) Meth. R. **60**: 21.

— its Place in the Thought of To-day. (W. H. Johnson) Arena, **19**: 583.

— Jewish Doctrine of. (S. D. F. Salmond) Crit. R. **10**: 167.

— of the Lower Animals. (P. W. Roose) Temp. Bar, **113**: 64.

— of Man. (C. E. Locke) Meth. R. **61**: 604.

— Place of, in Religious Belief. (J. E. Carpenter) New World, **6**: 601.

— Presages of. (P. W. Roose) Argosy, **65**: 614.

— Problem of ; Some recent Mediumistic Phenomena. (J. H. Hyslop) Forum, **25**: 736.

— Psychical Research and. (J. H. Hyslop) Indep. **52**: 868.

— Scripture View of. (J. C. Jacoby) Luth. Q. **28**: 406.

— Spinozistic, G. S. Fullerton on. (J. E. Creighton) Philos. R. **9**: 423.

— J. E. C. Welldon on. Church Q. **47**: 202. — Spec. **81**: 150.

— Wish for. Spec. **87**: 309. Same art. Liv. Age, **231**: 784.

Immunity. Toxicity of Eel-serum. (G. C. Frankland) Nature, **58**: 369.

Imp, The, and the Author. (J. D. Daskam) Harper, **101**: 202.

Impact Testing Machine, Photographic. (B. W. Dunn) J. Frankl. Inst. **144**: 321. **145**: 36.

Imperative, Moral, Psycho-physiology of. (J. H. Leuba) Am. J. Psychol. **8**: 528.

Imperial Civil Service ; Suggestion from Australia. (E. E. Morris) 19th Cent. **49**: 445.

Imperial Democracy. (D. S. Jordan) New World, **7**: 601.

— Jordan on. (J. J. Halsey) Dial (Ch.) **27**: 45.

Imperial Federation in Politics. (Goldwin Smith) Sat. R. **83**: 187.

Imperial Idea, Some Economic Aspects of the. (E. R. Faraday) Fortn. **70**: 961.

Imperial Inquisitor, An. (M. I. Taylor) Chamb. J. **216**: 141.

Imperial Policy, The. (E. L. Godkin) Nation, **66**: 396.

Imperial Republicanism Historically considered. (H. Bonis) Arena, **23**: 321.

Imperial Responsibilities a National Gain. (G. S. Clarke) No. Am. **168**: 129.

Imperialism. (S. C. Parks) Arena, **25**: 577. — Yale R. **7**: 121. — (F. H. Giddings) Pol. Sci. Q. **13**: 585. — (C. de Thierry) New R. **17**: 716. — (W. Baird) Conserv. R. **4**: 135. — (W. P. Trent and others) Sewanee, **6**: 461. — (O. Hall) Lippinc. **63**: 389. — 19th Cent. **44**: 487.

— American. (S. Brooks) Fortn. **76**: 226. — (B. Martin) 19th Cent. **48**: 393. — (P. de Rousiers) Chaut. **29**: 364.

— Americanism vs. (A. Carnegie) No. Am. **168**: 1, 362.

— America's Historic Policy. (W. A. Peffer) No. Am. **171**: 246.

— and Christianity. (F. W. Farrar) No. Am. **171**: 289.

— and the Coming Crisis for Democracy. (T. E. Ellam) Westm. **156**: 237.

— and Liberty. Westm. **155**: 126.

— and Militarism. Monthly R. **1**, no. **2**: **1**.

Imperialism and Protection. (D. MacG. Means) Nation, **67**: 217.

— Anti-imperialist League. (E. Winslow) Indep. **51**: 1347.

— Anti-imperialist Position. [Address with Signatures] Outl. **61**: 698.

— The Antithesis of True Expansion. (E. V. Long) Arena, **24**: 337.

— as a Policy for America. (B. J. Clinch) Am. Cath. Q. **24**: 150.

— Basis of English. Sat. R. **90**: 105.

— British. (Goldwin Smith) Nation, **73**: 200.

— — and the Reform of the Civil Service. (G. Howard) Pol. Sci. Q. **14**: 240.

— Canadian, in England. Canad. M. **17**: 331.

— Christianity and. (F. Stewart) Arena, **23**: 565.

— Danger of. Outl. **65**: 857. — (E. D. Mead) Outl. **66**: 184.

— Danger of Empire. (F. A. A. Rowland) Westm. **153**: 605.

— Dangers of. (W. MacDonald) Forum, **26**: 177.

— Economic Basis of. (C. A. Conant) No. Am. **167**: 326.

— English. (W. Cunningham) Atlan. **84**: 1.

— Evolution vs. (J. C. Griffin) Arena, **23**: 141.

— for Great Britain, Changes Required. Sat. R. **91**: 730.

— Future of British. (J. Lewis) Canad. M. **15**: 252.

— Giant Issue of 1900. (F. Parsons) Arena, **23**: 561.

— in England. (J. L. Walton) Contemp. **75**: 305.

— — Radicalism and. (A. R. Carman) Contemp. **77**: 18.

— in extremis, alias Shabby Imperialism. (J. M. K.) Westm. **154**: 495.

— in the United States. (Goldwin Smith) Contemp. **75**: 620. — (W. Archer) Pall Mall M. **19**: 95.

— Industrial. (T. Hitchcock) Cassier, **15**: 455.

— Is the Republic Overthrown? (G. H. Shibley) Arena, **22**: 443.

— The Issue of. (E. P. Clark) Nation, **70**: 158.

— its Place in Historic Evolution. (G. W. Kenney) Arena, **24**: 357.

— its Strength and Weakness. (A. H. Coggins) Arena, **24**: 345.

— Literary Inspiration of. Scot. R. **35**: 262. Same art. Liv. Age, **225**: 801. Same art. Ecl. M. **135**: 151.

— Mission of Empire. (E. D. Bell) Westm. **154**: 446.

— New American. (E. Dicey) 19th Cent. **44**: 487. Same art. Ecl. M. **131**: 577. Same art. Liv. Age, **219**: 329.

— An Official Disclaimer of. Outl. **61**: 207.

— Paradox of. Monthly R. **1**, no. **1**: 1.

— The Passing of the Declaration. (L. C. Prince) Arena, **25**: 353.

— The Predominant Issue. (W. G. Sumner) Internat. Mo. **2**: 496.

— The Republic and the Empire. (J. C. Ridpath) Arena, **20**: 344.

— Seamy Side of. (R. Wallace) Contemp. **75**: 782.

— Spectre of, in the United States. (S. Solis-Cohen and E. D. Weed) Arena, **20**: 445.

— vs. the Constitution. (W. MacDonald) Nation, **68**: 25.

— Washington's Farewell Address and its Applications. (R. E. Jones) Forum, **28**: 13.

— What it means. (J. H. Muirhead) Fortn. **74**: 177.

— Which is? Outl. **66**: 248.

— Whig. (B. King) Contemp. **77**: 564.

— The World's True Heirs. (F. A. White) Westm. **155**: 491.

— Year One of the Empire. (R. Ogden) Nation, **70**: 105.

Important Members of the Family, The ; a story. (Alice L. Anderson) Nat'l M. (Bost.) **5**: 341.

In the Name of a Woman. (A. W. Marchmont) Longm. 35: 541. 36: 56 — 37: 155.

In Nature's Waggish Mood. (Paul Heyse) Liv. Age, 214: 627 — 215: 85.

In the Nick of Time. (E. S. Bond) Sund. M. 29: 493.

In the North; poem. (T. Sherman) Atlan. 81: 473.

In the Northwest; a story. (H. Bindloss) Ecl. M. 134: 614.

In Nubibus. (G. J. Low) Open Court, 11: 116, 155, 424.

In the Old Sugar Factory. (R. M. Steele) Overland, n. s. 31: 433.

In on the Ground Floor. (C. Lockhart) Lippinc. 68: 472.

In One Fellowship. (L. H. Wall) Cent. 38: 348.

In an Orchard; a story. (J. A. Bridges) Cornh. 76: 90.

In a Palace; a poem. (E. Gibson) Argosy, 64: 256.

In the Palace of the King; a story. (F. M. Crawford) Munsey, 23: 26 — 24: 589.

In the Panic. (W. Payne) Cent. 38: 527.

In Paradise; a poem. (C. G. Alexander) Atlan. 86: 711.

In Penumbra; a poem. (E. M. Thomas) Outl. 61: 509.

In Perils in the Wilderness. (L. Jervis) Cornh. 84: 102. Same art. Liv. Age, 231: 116.

In the Prince's Shoes. (E. Sharp) Lippinc. 65: 138.

In the Public Eye. Eng. Illust. 19: 71-572. 20: 71-348.

In the Queen's Name; a story. (M. M. Helliwell) Canad. M. 16: 364.

In Quest of Ravens. (B. Torrey) Atlan. 79: 792.

In Reflected Glory; a story. (M. Reed) Outing, 33: 596.

In Remembrance; a story. (Ellen A. Smith) Good Words, 41: 387.

In the Secret Service; a series of stories. (R. Buckley) Canad. M. 18: 19.

In the Security Trust Building; a story. (W. R. Lighton) Cosmopol. 28: 539.

In the Service of Love. (Jo Hathaway) Overland, n. s. 35: 60.

In the Shadow of a Cathedral; a story. (G. W. Williams) Gent. M. n. s. 58: 509.

In the Shadow of Ely; a story. (M. L. Luther) Nat'l M. (Bost.) 7: 34.

In the Shadow of the Live-oak. (Flora H. Loughead) Overland, n. s. 34: 14.

In the Shadow of the Pines. (H. M. Sayres) Outing, 36: 634.

In the Shadow of the Sphinx. (A. M. Horwood) Chamb. J. 74: 30.

In the Shelter of the Cross; a story of Chinese Life. (Gak-Tsok-Sin) Sund. M. 26: 462, 547.

In Shimmer of Satin; a story. (A. Beresford) Argosy, 66: 277.

In Siberia; a poem. Ecl. M. 133: 232.

In the Small Hours. (B. Matthews) Scrib. M. 26: 502.

In Sour Misfortune's Book; a story. ("A.") Belgra. 95: 65.

"In the Spring, the Violets;" a story. (W. B. Foster) Nat'l M. (Bost.) 7: 534.

In Strawberry Time. (H. Hesford) Eng. Illust. 17: 327.

In the Strong Young Spring; a poem. (A. Furber) Outing, 33: 606.

"In Terra Pax;" a poem. (G. L. Gower) No. Am. 171: 663.

In the Third House; a political story. (W. Barr) McClure, 12: 362.

In a Tight Fix. Strand, 17, 658.

In Tight Places; Adventures of an Amateur Detective. (A. Griffiths) Eng. Illust. 18: 89-617. 19: 63-249.

In Time of Sickness. (H. Bindloss) Good Words, 40: 175. Same art. Liv. Age, 221: 355.

In the Track of the Forty-pounders. (W. Wood) Chamb. J. 74: 571.

In the Trenches; a poem. (F. Whitmore) Atlan. 83: 162.

In the Twilight; a poem. (I. F. Mayo) Argosy, 65: 566.

In Virginia; a story. (Mary M. Hall) Nat'l M. (Bost.) 7: 141.

In a Visible Form; a story. Temp. Bar, 111: 271.

In War-time. Chamb. J. 77: 318.

In War-time; a story. (May Bateman) Temp. Bar, 123: 183.

In the Watches of the Night; a story. (B. Matthews) Harper, 94: 267.

In the Way of Strategy; a story. (W. T. Nichols) Nat'l M. (Bost.) 8: 537.

In a Welsh Garden; a story. Temp. Bar, 112: 61.

In a Woodsman's Way; a story. (R. Thomas) Outl. 66: 983.

In Years of Storm and Stress. (K. Blind) Cornh. 81: 788. Same art. Liv. Age, 219: 442.

Incandescent Lamps. (F. W. Willcox) J. Frankl. Inst. 149: 282, 353, 419.

— Selection of. (A. D. Adams) Cassier, 15: 42.

Incandescent Lights [in nature]. (J. Parkinson) Good Words, 40: 415.

Incandescent Oil Lamp, Ritson. Bank. M. (N. Y.) 60: 930.

Incarnation, The, and Culture. (G. A. Derby) Expos. 3: 337.

— and Dogma. (G. A. Derby) Expos. 3: 242.

— and Judgment. (G. A. Derby) Expos. 3: 124.

— as Proof of Doctrine of Kenosis. (F. C. H. Wendel) Bib. Sac. 54: 729.

— Doctrine of, R. L. Ottley on. (W. L. Gildea) Dub. R. 120: 126.

— Mystery of. Lond. Q. 89: 38.

— a Normal Sequence. (E. D. Daniels) N. Church R. 5: 25.

Incense and Lights, the Decision on, 1899. Church Q. 49: 210. — Month, 94: 225.

— Concerning. (J. Wells) Sund. M. 30: 55.

— The Hearing at Lambeth on, 1899. Church Q. 48: 261.

— Lambeth Opinion on Use of. (W. J. Knox Little) Contemp. 76: 648.

Inch Buil. (H. Macmillan) Good Words, 40: 448.

Inchbald, Elizabeth. (E. Manson) Westm. 148: 336. Same art. Ecl. M. 129: 671.

Incident, An; a story. (S. B. Elliott) Harper, 96: 458.

Incident in the Bishop's Career; a story. (A. O'Hagan) Munsey, 26: 285.

Incident in Excise Life, An. Chamb. J. 74: 142.

Incident of the Boom; a story. (J. Mausergh) Pall Mall M. 14: 246.

Incident of the British Ambassador, The; a story. (B. Perry) McClure, 10: 165.

Incident of 1870, An. Chamb. J. 75: 652.

Incident of the Niger Trade; a story. (H. Bindloss) Chamb. J. 76: 154. Same art. Ecl. M. 132: 729. Same art. Liv. Age, 221: 159.

Incognito, An. (K. Silvester) Good Words, 40: 197.

Income, Distribution of, Smart's. (J. Bonar) Econ. J. 10: 67. — (S. Ball) Econ. R. 10: 255.

— That Tyrant. (E. Anstruther) Cornh. 84: 355.

Income Tax and the National Revenues. (M. West) J. Pol. Econ. 8: 433.

— — English. (J. A. Hill) Econ. Stud. 4: 247.

— — Hill's. (J. Cummings) Nation, 71: 197. — (G. H. Blunden) Econ. J. 10: 387.

— Future of. (G. H. Blunden) Econ. J. 11: 157.

— Shall it be Re-established? (G. S. Boutwell) No. Am. 166: 673.

Incubation, Mysteries of Artificial. (H. Russell) Chamb. J. 78: 715.

Incubator Baby and Niagara Falls. (Arthur Brisbane) Cosmopol. 31: 509.

India, Rivers of, Great, Value of the Water of. Blackw. **167**: 658.

— Romantic, Chevrillon's. Sat. R. **84**: 93.

— Round about a Bungalow. Ecl. M. **129**: 654.

— Russia in. (C. Beresford) Un. Serv. M. **16**: 655.

— — Could Russia take British India? (Rogalla von Bieberstein) No. Am. **166**: 324.

— Russian Advance on. (E. C. R. Thomson) National, **30**: 844. Same art. Ecl. M. **130**: 482.

— Sanitary and Administrative Reform in. (C. W. MacRury) Asia. R. **27**: 277.

— Scotsmen in. (J. Jardine) Asia. R. **31**: 255.

— Secretariats in. (F. L. Petre) Asia. R. **31**: 243.

— Sedition Law of, The New. (R. C. Dutt) Asia. R. **25**: 248.

— Seditious Unrest in. (L. Griffin) Sat. R. **84**: 26. — Spec. **79**: 5, 37.

— Short Route to, Pioneer of the. (A. E. Waghorn) Asia. R. **26**: 386.

— Silver in, Government and. Cath. World, **66**: 510.

— The Silver Situation in. (J. C. Harrison) Pol. Sci. Q. **12**: 603.

— Sketches in Black and White in. (S. H. Dunn) Month, **89**: 53–607.

— Some Reminiscences of. (Mrs. Montague Turnbull) Chamb. J. **78**: 334.

— South, Famine Relief in. (W. H. Campbell) Westm. **151**: 259.

— State of. (D. MacG. Means) Nation, **71**: 126.

— State Trial in. (G. H. Trevor) Gent. M. n. s. **66**: 461.

— Statistics of. (F. C. Danvers) J. Statis. Soc. **64**: 31.

— Sugar Duties of. (R. Lethbridge) Asia. R. **28**: 255.

— The Supernatural in. (S. Eardley-Wilmot) Temp. Bar, **123**: 348.

— Survey Report, 1895–96. Geog. J. **11**: 58.

— Technical Education in. (J. Wallace) Cassier, **12**: 614.

— Theological Situation in. (V. Shastri) Fortn. **70**: 686.

— Tirah Campaign. (An Eye-Witness) Fortn. **69**: 390.

— to South Africa; the Diary of a Voyage. (S. L. Clemens) McClure, **10**: 3.

— Trade in. Scot. R. **34**: 1.

— Trade of, Growth and Trend of; a Forty Years' Survey. (H. J. Tozer) J. Soc. Arts, **49**: 333.

— The Transport Service and the Health of the Army in India. (R. Wallace) Blackw. **163**: 262.

— Treaties connected with. (E. B. Osborn) Gent. M. n. s. **64**: 506.

— Troops of. (H. H. Howorth) 19th Cent. **47**: 36.

— under Queen Victoria. (A. C. Lyall) 19th Cent. **41**: 865. Same art. Ecl. M. **129**: 187.

— University in, Proposed Muslim. (R. Ahmad) 19th Cent. **44**: 915.

— up to the Hills in. (P. E. Stevenson) Outing, **34**: 117, 289.

— Viceroy's Life and Duties in. Idler, **15**: 349.

— Viceroyalty of, Tenure of. Spec. **82**: 6.

— Victims of Circumstances. Gent. M. n. s. **58**: 581. Same art. Liv. Age, **214**: 203.

— Water-supply in Mitigation of Drought in. (W. Sowerby) Asia. R. **31**: 35.

— Western, and Gujarat, Political Tenures and Landlord of. (B. H. Baden-Powell) Asia. R. **25**: 126. **27**: 165, 400.

— Wild Tribes of. (R. Lydekker) Knowl. **23**: 67.

— Women of. (F. A. Steel) No. Am. **169**: 846.

— — Legal Status of. (C. Sorabji) 19th Cent. **44**: 854.

India Rubber and Gutta-percha. (C. Dooley) Pop. Sci. Mo. **50**: 679. — (J. R. Jackson) Nature, **55**: 610.

— The Home of; across the Head-waters of the Amazon. Chamb. J. **76**: 628.

— Sources of Commercial. (D. Morris) J. Soc. Arts, **46**: 745, 773, 785.

India Rubber, Stress-strain Relations of. (R. H. Thurston) Science, **6**: 758.

— Value of. Ecl. M. **129**: 718.

India Rubber Plants. (J. N. Gerard) Garden & F. **10**: 26.

Indian Afoot. (W. T. Larned) Lippinc. **61**: 691.

— from Artist Point of View. (J. H. Sharp) Brush & P. **4**: 1.

— in Transition. (M. A. Harriman) Overland, n. s. **35**: 33.

— of Commerce, The. (C. F. Lummis) Nation, **72**: 319.

— Origin of the Name. (F. F. Hilder) Am. Anthrop. **1**: 545.

— The Representative. (J. W. Cook) Outl. **65**: 80.

Indian Agencies, The Spoilsmen and the. (F. E. Leupp) Nation, **65**: 333.

Indian Burial-place, A Curious. (Jennie Lown) Cosmopol. **26**: 314.

Indian Chiefs, Portraits of. (E. A. Burbank) Brush & P. **3**: 16.

Indian Childhood, Impressions of an. (Zitkala-Ša) Atlan. **85**: 37.

Indian Clergy Impossible. (F. Eberschweiler) Cath. World, **65**: 815.

Indian Contract Schools. (M. P. Casey) Cath. World, **71**: 629.

Indian Corn. (C. F. Millspaugh) Chaut. **31**: 338.

— in Colonial Times. (A. M. Earle) Chaut. **26**: 586.

Indian Corn Stories and Customs. (W. M. Beauchamp) J. Am. Folk-Lore, **11**: 195.

Indian Dances of the Southwest. (W. H. Draper) Outing, **37**: 659.

Indian Dialects. (J. W. Wilkinson) Educa. **18**: 395.

Indian Epigrams, A Century of. Atlan. **84**: 573.

Indian Garden, My. (G. A. Levett-Yeats) Macmil. **79**: 70. Same art. Liv. Age, **219**: 744.

Indian Ghost Dancer, Rising Wolf; an autobiographical sketch. (H. Garland) McClure, **12**: 241.

Indian Girl, The School Days of an. (Zitkala-Ša) Atlan. **85**: 185.

Indian Giver; a comedy. (W. D. Howells) Harper, **94**: 235.

Indian Grave, Triple, in Western New York. (A. L. Benedict) Am. Natural. **31**: 826.

"Indian Harvest." (A. Matthews) Nation, **70**: 183.

Indian Languages, Number of, in Washington. (J. Wickersham) Am. Antiq. **20**: 253.

— "Real," "True," or "Genuine" in. (A. S. Gatschet) Am. Anthrop. **1**: 155.

Indian Legends in Music. (Wm. Armstrong) Music, **16**: 119.

Indian Life, Glimpses of, at Omaha Exposition. R. of Rs. (N. Y.) **18**: 436.

Indian Music, Harmonic Structure of. (J. C. Fillmore) Music, **16**: 453.

Indian Orchard, Mass., Industrial Experiment at. (S. A. Underwood) New Eng. M. n. s. **18**: 537.

Indian Paintings, Old, at Los Angeles. (E. T. Mills) Overland, n. s. **37**: 766.

Indian Pipe, A Remarkable. Reliquary, **40**: 119.

Indian Place-names in the Adirondacks. (J. D. Prince) J. Am. Folk-Lore, **13**: 123.

Indian Plague Story, An. (C. Sorabji) 19th Cent. **46**: 410. Same art. Liv. Age, **223**: 155–231.

Indian Poetry, English Neglect of. (K. Blind) Forum, **32**: 53.

Indian Policy of Colonial Pennsylvania, Walton's Conrad Weiser and. Nation, **72**: 416.

Indian Prince, At the Court of an. (R. D. Mackenzie) Cent. **35**: 641.

Indian Reservations. (P. B. Eagle) Gent. M. n. s. **60**: 51. Same art. Ecl. M. **130**: 303.

Insect, A Bubble-blowing. (E. S. Morse) Pop. Sci. Mo. 57: 23.

Insect Augury. (F. G. Walters) Gent. M. n. s. 63: 73. Same art. Liv. Age, 222: 375.

Insect Communities. (A. B. Comstock) Chaut. 26: 479.

Insect Domestic Economy. (A. B. Comstock) Chaut. 27: 294.

Insect Jewels, The ; a story. (E. Mitchell) Argosy, 68: 352.

Insect Larders, Some. (T. Wood) Sund. M. 26: 452.

Insect Musicians. (A. B. Comstock) Chaut. 27: 652.

Insect Weapons and Tools. (J. J. Ward) Pall Mall M. 25: 387.

Insects. (M. M. Williams) McClure, 17: 489.

— and Birds, Songs of. (J. N. Huyette) Music, 13: 564.

— and Reptiles ; unbidden Guests. Ecl. M. 132: 939.

— and Yeasts. (I. Giglioli) Nature, 56: 575.

— as Carriers of Disease. (S. E. Jelliffe) Munsey, 25: 707. See Mosquitoes.

— Classification of. (J. B. Smith) Science, 5: 671.

— Common, of Autumn. (B. S. Cragin) Lippinc. 64: 626.

— Economic Status of. (L. O. Howard) Science, n. s. 9: 233.

— Enemies in the House. (E. Step) Good Words, 42: 168.

— A Game of Hide and Seek. (C. M. Weed) Pop. Sci. Mo. 53: 661.

— How they Recognize their Friends and Warn their Enemies. (A. S. Packard) Chamb. J. 77: 356.

— Hydrocyanic Acid for exterminating Household. (W. R. Beattie) Science, n. s. 14: 285.

— in Fruits International Relations disturbed by. (L. O. Howard) Forum, 25: 569.

— Injurious, in 1897, Eleanor Ormerod on. (W. F. H. B.) Nature, 57: 558.

— Living, Camera Studies of. (C. M. Weed) Outing, 38: 148.

— Migration of. Spec. 86: 796.

— Mining. (F. Enock) Knowl. 21: 178, 209.

— of a London Back-garden. (F. Enock) Knowl. 20: 105, 153.

— of the Sea. (G. H. Carpenter) Knowl. 24: 19-245.

— of the Thames. Spec. 86: 871.

— On Describing and Drawing. (F. Enock) Knowl. 20: 5.

— Plateau's Rôle of Vexillary Organs. Am. Natural. 33: 736.

— Securing them from Birds. (S. D. Judd) Am. Natural. 33: 461.

— Social Habits of. (A. B. Comstock) Chaut. 26: 366.

— Some Remarkable Habits of. (P. H. Grimshaw) Chamb. J. 74: 365.

— Spread of, by Agency of Man. (L. O. Howard) Science, 6: 382.

— Stinging. Spec. 87: 475.

— Strength of. (J. Scott) Strand, 15: 104.

— Studies with the Camera. (C. M. Weed) Outing, 37: 163.

— Wings of. (J. H. Comstock and J. G. Needham) Am. Natural. 32: 43-903. 33: 117, 573, 845.

Insecurity, Uses of. (L. B. Halsted) Gunton's M. 20: 449.

Insight of the Christian, The. (W. P. Allis) Outl. 66: 609.

Insolvency, Appointment of Liquidators by Creditors as a Method of Settling up Affairs in Cases of. (F. H. Maugham) Law Q. 13: 104.

Insomnia, Moral Aspect of. (A. H. Morton) Chaut. 32: 364.

Inspector of Private Nuisances, The. Liv. Age, 230: 710.

Inspiration. (C. L. Moore) Dial (Ch.) 25: 215. — (A. E. Truxal) Ref. Ch. R. 48: 457.

— Lutheran Doctrine of. (A. Stump) Luth. Q. 30: 88.

— not Invalidated by Criticism. (G. H. Bennett) Meth. R. 61: 934.

— Scripture, and Authority. (S. D. McConnell) Outl. 64: 360.

Instinct and Intelligence in Animals. (C. L. Morgan) Nature, 57: 326.

— and Reason, Marshall on. (G. A. Tawney) Psychol. R. 6: 517. — (W. B. Pillsbury) Philos. R. 8: 632. — Sat. R. 87: 371.

— Curiosities of. Liv. Age, 223: 56.

— Human Mind and Animal Intelligence. Quar. 185: 477.

— in the Animal and Vegetable Kingdoms. Ed. R. 186: 173.

— or Reason. Liv. Age, 231: 503.

— Psychology of. (A. J. Hamlin) Mind, 22: 59.

Institute of Infectious Diseases at Tokio. (A. Nakagawa) Science, 6: 313.

Institute of Painters in Water Colors. Ath. '00, 1: 407, 569, 633. 2: 553.

Institutional Christianity. (R. Ogden) Nation, 67: 346.

Institutional Church, The. (A. Holden Byles) Good Words, 38: 665.

Institutions, Charitable, Buildings of, Sanitation of. (C. F. Wingate) Char. R. 8: 63.

— Some Vanished Victorian. (W. J. Kechie) Gent. M. n. s. 60: 391.

Instruction, Principles in. (F. P. Bachman) Educa. 20: 613.

Instrumentation, Modern. (A. Weld) Music, 13: 553.

Instruments, Astronomical and Optical. Nature, 61: 241.

Insufficient Explanation, An ; a story. (Elizabeth Cumings) Music, 11: 249.

Insular Cases before the Supreme Court. (G. F. Edmunds) No. Am. 173: 145. — (G. S. Boutwell) No. Am. 173: 154.

— — Conquered Territory and the Constitution. (H. Taylor) No. Am. 173: 577.

Insurance and the War, 1898. Sat. R. 85: 586.

— as an Investment. Sat. R. 91: 501.

— Curiosities of Early. Chamb. J. 75: 430.

— Fire and Life, in Canada. Canad. M. 18: 88.

— — The Craft of. (F. H. Kitchin) National, 38: 97.

— — in New England. (C. W. Burpee) New Eng. M. n. s. 19: 101.

— — Municipal. Bank. M. (Lond.) 63: 333. 64: 290.

— — Practical Notes on. (A. Watt) Jurid. R. 9: 195.

— — Wasteful Methods of. (L. Windmüller) R. of Rs. (N. Y.) 21: 464.

— for the Unemployed in Basel. Yale R. 9: 86.

— Fraternal. (A. C. Stevens) R. of Rs. (N. Y.) 21: 59. — Sat. R. 92: 204.

— — in the United States. (B. H. Meyer) Ann. Am. Acad. Pol. Sci. 17: 260.

— German Workmen's Compensation for Accidents. (H. W. Wolff) Econ. R. 8: 236.

— in the West, at Des Moines. Midland, 10: 353.

— Industrial. (H. Fiske and others) Char. R. 8: 26, 68, 138. — (W. E. Snell) Econ. R. 10: 370.

— Labor, in Germany. Gunton's M. 13: 207.

— Life, Developments of. Sat. R. 85: 322-741.

— — in 1895. Bank. M. (Lond.) 63: 817.

— — in relation to Military and Naval Risks. Un. Serv. M. 18: 657.

— — Interest Problem in. Bank. M. (Lond.) 66: 657.

— — Is it a Good Investment ? (F. H. Kitchin) National, 36: 692.

— — Latest Phases of. (S. Homans) Gunton's M. 17: 358.

"International Library," Editorship of. (A. Lang)
Ath. '00, 1: 564.

International Meteorological Committee, Meeting of.
Nature, 60: 591.

International Politics; the International Ferment.
Quar. 188: 242.

International Society of Painters, Sculptors, and
Gravers. (G. Sauter) Studio (Internat.) 5: 109. —
(A. L. Baldry) M. of Art, 23: 391.
— Third Exhibition, 1901. (B. Kendell) Artist (N. Y.)
32: 119. — (O. Sickert) Studio (Internat.) 15: 117.

International Sympathy. (E. D. Warfield) Educa. 19:
391.

International Trade, Bastable's Theory of. (F. Y.
Edgeworth) Econ. J. 7: 397.

International Wheat Corner, An; a sketch. (J. D.
Whelpley) McClure, 15: 363.

Interoceanic Canal. (R. Ogden) Nation, 70: 104. —
(E. R. Johnson) Nat. Geog. M. 10: 311. — (C. B.
Levita) J. Mil. Serv. Inst. 24: 479. — Bank. M.
(N. Y.) 57: 30.
— Attitude of the American Government toward. (I.
D. Travis) Yale R. 9: 419.
— Central American. (H. C. Hawthorne) J. Mil. Serv.
Inst. 10: 576.
— Diplomacy of U. S. in Regard to. (J. G. Whiteley)
No. Am. 165: 364.
— The Dream of Navigators. (A. S. Crowninshield)
No. Am. 165: 695.
— from a Military Point of View. (P. C. Hains) J. Mil.
Serv. Inst. 28: 371. Same art. Ann. Am. Acad.
Pol. Sci. 17: 397.
— The Hay-Pauncefote Treaty. (H. W. Rogers) Forum,
29: 355.
— Outlook for. (R. Ogden) Nation, 73: 64.
— Population and. (L. M. Haupt) Lippinc. 67: 740.
— Preliminary Report of the Commission. (A. F.
Walker) Forum, 31: 131.
— Problems of. Pol. Sci. Q. 14: 189. — (G. L. Rives)
Pol. Sci. Q. 14: 189.
— Projects for. (D. Turpie) Harper, 96: 351.
— Proposed, in its Commercial Aspects. (J. Nimmo,
jr.) Nat. Geog. M. 10: 297.
— Prospects and Routes. Nat'l M. (Bost.) 15: 285.
— Questions as to. (H. White) Nation, 72: 270.
— Report on. (R. Ogden) Nation, 71: 458.
— United Kingdom, United States and the. (C. W.
Dilke) Forum, 29: 449.
— West Indian and Pacific Islands in relation to. (E.
V. Robinson) Indep. 52: 523.
    See Nicaragua; Panama.

Interoceanic Canals; the Clayton-Bulwer Treaty. (M.
W. Hazeltine) No. Am. 165: 452.

Interoceanic Communication, The Urgent Need of.
(L. M. Keasbey) Pol. Sci. Q. 14: 594.

Interparliamentary Conference, The. (S. J. Barrows)
Indep. 51: 2432.

Interpleader Doctrine of Independent Liability. (R.
J. Maclennan) Am. Law R. 32· 331.

Interpolation. (R. T. A. Innes) Pop. Astron. 9: 389.

Interposition, An. (M. A. Kimball) Overland, n. s. 35:
373.

Interpretation, Function of, in relation to Theology.
(E. DeW. Burton) Am. J. Theol. 2: 52.

Interpretation; a poem. (B. G. Davis) Cosmopol. 24:
561.

Interpretation; a poem. (A. Lamont) Argosy, 63: 286.

Interrupted Journey, An. (M. B. Peck) New Eng. M.
n. s. 20: 699.

Interstate Commerce, Federal Taxation of. (H. C.
Adams) R. of Rs. (N. Y.) 19: 193.
— Some Phases of. (M. A. Spoonts) Am. Law R. 33:
188.

Interstate Commerce Commission and the Public. (S.
M. Davis) Outl. 64: 626.
— and Ratemaking. (J. Nimmo, jr.) Forum, 24: 92.
— Dangerous Demands of. (M. H. Smith) Forum, 25:
129.
— Inordinate Demands of. (M. H. Smith) Forum, 27:
551.
— Powers of. (C. A. Prouty) Forum, 27: 223. — (C. A.
Prouty) No. Am. 167: 543. — (M. H. Smith) No.
Am. 168: 62. — Pub. Opin. 22: 711.

Interstate Robbery; a poem. (J. A. Macy) Green Bag,
9: 433.

Intervention in Europe, Doctrine and Practice of. (W.
E. Lingelbach) Ann. Am. Acad. Pol. Sci. 16: 1.

Intervention of Gran'pap. (E. M. Tybout) Lippinc. 68:
243.

Interventions in the Federal Courts. (E. C. Eliot) Am.
Law R. 31: 377.

Interview, The, as Literature. (R. Ogden) Nation, 65:
124.

Interviews. (Lady Broome) Cornh. 83: 473.
— Some First. Chamb. J. 78: 841.

Intestinal Cells, Absorption in Vertebrate. (Howard
Crawley) Science, n. s. 10: 75.

Intolerance in Protestantism, Wane of. (W. Rupp)
Ref. Ch. R. 48: 109.

Intracranial Physics. (J. Chappie) Monist, 7: 358.

Intrenching, Portable Tools for. (W. C. Wren) J. Mil.
Serv. Inst. 15: 726.

Intrenchments for Infantry, Hasty. (W. A. Shenck)
J. Mil. Serv. Inst. 10: 421. — (A. L. Wagner) J.
Mil. Serv. Inst. 22: 221.

Intrigue at the Yildiz Kiosk. (H. A. Hering) Idler,
17: 359.

Intrinsicate, Intrinsecate. (F. Hall) Nation, 71: 11, 113.

Introduction, The. (V. Mapes) Munsey, 17: 26.

Invalid, Revolt of the. (Madge MacGeorge) National,
37: 69.

Inventing for a Living. (G. E. Walsh) Cassier, 13: 525.
— Practical. (W. H. Smyth) Cassier, 18: 117.

Invention, Age of. (A. P. Greeley) Munsey, 21: 706.
— as a Factor of American National Wealth. (W. C.
Dodge) Cassier, 18: 198.
— Effect of, upon Labor and Morals. (E. C. Williams)
Chaut. 28: 557.
— Faculty of. (W. K. Palmer) Educa. 19: 372.
— Forecasting the Progress of. (W. Baxter, jr.) Pop.
Sci. Mo. 51: 307.
— Mythology and Folk-lore of. (A. F. Chamberlain)
J. Am. Folk-Lore, 10: 89.

Inventions, American. (A. H. Ford) New Eng. M. n. s.
25: 3.
— — Century of. (L. Mead) Gunton's M. 21: 151.
— and Invention. (A. Daniell) Jurid. R. 11: 151.
— Great, since the World's Fair, 1893. (J. B. Walker)
Cosmopol. 31: 556.
— Modern, Anticipated. (H. G. Archer) Good Words,
41: 775. Same art. Liv. Age, 228: 12. Same art.
Ecl. M. 136: 208.
— Unfinished. (C. W. Scribner) Cassier, 21: 150.

Inventive Faculty. Is it a Myth? (W. H. Smyth)
Cassier, 12: 676.

Inventories, Early 18th Century. (W. J. Kayl) Antiq.
n. s. 36: 50.
— made for Sir W. and Sir T. Fairfax, Knights, in the
16th and 17th Centuries. (E. Peacock) Archæol.
48: 121.
— of Plate and Vestments belonging to the Cathedral
of Blessed Mary, Lincoln. Archæol. 53: 1.

Inventory and Sale of Goods in Time of Henry VIII.
and Edward VI. Antiq. n. s. 33: 278, 312, 331.
— of the Goods of James Cockerell, Prior of Gins-
borough, 1519. Antiq. n. s. 35: 52.

Inventory of the Parish Church of St. Mary, 1434. Archæol. **51**: 61.

Inverary and its Castle. (A. H. Malan) Pall Mall M. **22**: 43.

Inverary Castle. (H. C. Shelley) New Eng. M. n. s. **17**: 683.

Invertebrate Fossils, from Patagonia. (A. E. Ortmann) Am. J. Sci. **160**: 368.

Invertebrates, North American. (M. J. Rathbun; H. L. Clark; C. W. Hargitt) Am. Natural. **35**: 131-725. — (C. B. Davenport and others) Am. Natural. **33**: 593-872.

Invest, How to. (H. Withers) Contemp. **72**: 126.

Investigation, Position that Universities should take in Regard to. Nature, **61**: 417.

Investment and Speculation. (G. Yard) Cornh. **84**: 25.
— Can New Openings be found for? (C. A. Conant) Atlan. **84**: 600.
— Trade and Gambling. (H. Newbolt) Monthly R. **3**, no. 2: 1.

Investor's Opportunity, The. (W. R. Lawson) National, **36**: 261.

Invitation, An; a tale. (R. Barr) Belgra. **93**: 114.

Invocation, An; a poem. (A. M. F.) Argosy, **66**: 540.

Involuntary Movements. (M. A. Tucker) Am. J. Psychol. **8**: 394.

Involuntary Murderer, An; a story. (Y. Korolenko) Gent. M. n. s. **61**: 417.

Involuntary President, An; a story. (W. L. Alden) Cornh. **77**: 165.

Iodic Acid in the Analysis of Iodides. (F. A. Gooch and C. F. Walker) Am. J. Sci. **153**: 293.
— Titration of Sodium Thiosulphate with. (C. F. Walker) Am. J. Sci. **154**: 235.

Iodine, Application of, in the Analysis of Alkalies and Acids. (C. F. Walker and D. H. M. Gillespie) Am. J. Sci. **156**: 455.

Iolanthe. (C. L. Clarke) New Eng. M. n. s. **23**: 499. Same art. Canad. M. **16**: 257.

Iona, the Isle of Columba's Cell. (A. C. Storer) Cath. World, **73**: 746. — (F. Macleod) Fortn. **73**: 507, 692.

Ionian Islands, British Evacuation of. Cath. World, **64**: 790.

Ionian Sea, By the. (G. Gissing) Fortn. **73**: 884. **74**: 161-701.

Ionians, Prehistoric. (J. B. Bury) Eng. Hist. R. **15**: 288.

Ions, Dissociation into. (S. Pickering) Nature, **55**: 223.

Iostephanos. (A. B. Cook) J. Hel. Stud. **20**: 1.

Iowa and Currency Reform. (E. P. Clark) Nation, **67**: 178.
— Constitution and Admission into the Union. (J. A. James) J. H. Univ. Stud. **18**: 345.
— The Iowans. (R. L. Hartt) Atlan. **86**: 195.
— Political History. (Mrs. J. S. Clarkson) Midland, **8**: 61.
— Rural, Regeneration of. (N. A. Weeks) Outl. **65**: 357.

"Iowa," U. S. Steamer. (Minna Irving) Midland, **8**: 99.

Iowa College, Grinnell, Iowa. (J. I. Manatt) New Eng. M. n. s. **18**: 457.
— History of. (J. H. T. Main) Educa. **18**: 570.
— Social Life at. Midland, **9**: 449.

Iowa Farmers, With. (W. A. Wyckoff) Scrib. M. **29**: 525.

Iowa Girls, Four Famous, in Chicago. (Ethel M. Colson) Midland, **8**: 107.

Iowa River, Canoeing on. (L. B. Robinson) Outing, **32**: 29.

Iowa Soldiers at Jacksonville, 1898. (J. V. Cantwell) Midland, **10**: 70.

Iowa Soldiers; 50th Regiment. Midland, **9**: 558.
— 51st Regiment at San Francisco, 1898. (J. Snure) Midland, **10**: 99.
— 52d Regiment at Chickamauga, 1898. (E. S. McCulloch) Midland, **10**: 214.

Iredell, James, with portrait. (J. Davis) Green Bag, **12**: 165.

Ireland, John, Archbishop. (M. C. Blossom) World's Work, **1**: 646.

Ireland. (H. Methven) Belgra. **93**: 313.
— Agricultural and Industrial Resources. (H. Plunkett) J. Soc. Arts, **45**: 179.
— Agricultural Coöperation in. (E. E. Williams) Sat. R. **84**: 280.
— Agricultural Organization Society of. (S. Gwynn) Blackw. **168**: 573.
— Agriculture in. (H. Plunkett) Econ. J. **7**: 131.
— Alleged Repeopling of. (E. Byrne) No. Am. **165**: 383.
— and American Tourists. (J. Murphy) Cath. World, **70**: 39.
— and Bimetallism. (E. F. V. Knox) National, **29**: 577.
— and the Budget. (Earl of Mayo and N. Synnott) Fortn. **76**: 672.
— and the Empire. (A. Webb) Nation, **73**: 373.
— and the Government, 1901. Monthly R. **5**, no. 2: 53.
— and Greece. (E. M. Lynch) Gent. M. n. s. **65**: 43.
— and Irish Land once more. (T. W. Russell) Fortn. **75**: 1.
— and the Liberal Party. (J. A. M. Macdonald) Contemp. **80**: 50.
— and the Next Session, 1897. (J. E. Redmond) 19th Cent. **41**: 104.
— and the Queen. Spec. **84**: 336.
— and the Royal Visit, 1900. (M. O'Brien) Nation, **70**: 276.
— Antiquities of. (H. Methven) Belgra. **95**: 170.
— Art in, Early Christian. (M. Stokes) Reliquary, **39**: 110.
— Balfour's Irish Policy. Spec. **78**: 758.
— Balfour's Promise to. (A. Webb) Nation, **64**: 431.
— "Balfourian Amelioration" in. (H. Plunkett) 19th Cent. **48**: 891.
— Ballycastle. Sorley Boy's Town. (W. J. Hardy) Blackw. **168**: 189.
— Bankers and Farmers in. Bank. M. (Lond.) **68**: 748.
— Banking System. (R. Ewen) Westm. **147**: 534.
— Bards of Gael and Gall. (E. D'E. Keeling) Dub. R. **123**: 262.
— Bench and Bar of, Absent-mindedness in. Green Bag, **12**: 69.
— Bewitched; Biddy Early the Wise Woman. (W. B. Yeats) Contemp. **76**: 388.
— Boyne Valley. (J. R. Eyre) Idler, **20**: 88.
— Catholic University for, Refusal to Grant a. Spec. **84**: 437.
— Centenary of '98. (J. E. Redmond) 19th Cent. **43**: 612. Same art. Liv. Age, **217**: 440.
— Charms of an Irish Holiday. Spec. **83**: 247.
— Church of, from the Danish to the Anglo-Norman Invasion. (E. A. D'Alton) Dub. R. **127**: 301.
— Common-sense in. Spec. **79**: 508.
— Congested Districts Board. (S. Gwynn) Blackw **166**: 484.
— Contemporary. (W. O'C. Morris) Fortn. **74**: 314.
— Dublin to Cork and Killarney. Idler, **19**: 462.
— Economic Movement in, 1880-1900, Some Features of. (C. F. Bastable) Econ. J. **11**: 31.
— Education in. (M. Dalton) Westm. **148**: 306.
— — "Council of Ten" System in. (J. J. O'Shea) Am. Cath. Q. **25**: 565.

Ireland, Royalty in. Spec. **79**: 236.

— Rural, In the Bye-ways of. (M. MacDonagh) 19th Cent. **48**: 75, 298. Same art. Liv. Age, **226**: 529. Same art. Ecl. M. **135**: 511.

— Secret of. (S. Gwynn) Macmil. **83**: 410.

— since '98. (J. E. Redmond) No. Am. **166**: 385.

— Social and Intellectual Revolution in. (S. Mac-Manus) Cath. World, **69**: 522.

— A Stride in Irish Civilization. (G. H. Bassett) No. Am. **167**: 123.

— Structure of. (G. A. J. Cole) Knowl. **21**: 74.

— Taxation in. (Sir J. Lubbock) 19th Cent. **42**: 791. — Spec. **78**: 7. — (M. Frewen) Sat. R. **83**: 263. — Spec. **78**: 113. — Blackw. **161**: 118.

— — Balfour *vs.* Asquith. Spec. **78**: 78.

— — Clarke on. Spec. **78**: 41.

— — Incidence of. (B. Holland) Econ. J. **7**: 214.

— — Ireland's Financial Grievance. Spec. **81**: 38.

— — Over-. (O'C. Don) National, **28**: 739. — (J. J. O'Shea) Am. Cath. Q. **22**: 280.

— Things Irish. (E. M. Lynch) Gent. M. n. s. **66**: 280.

— Through the Emerald Isle. (Adelaide S. Hall) Overland, n. s. **35**: 159–257.

— Tourist in. (Earl Mayo) 19th Cent. **42**: 173.

— under Queen Victoria. (J. A. R. Marriott) Fortn. **75**: 446.

— University Commission for. (W. O'C. Morris) Fortn. **76**: 445.

— University Education for Catholics in. (E. O'Dwyer) 19th Cent. **45**: 67.

— University for. Ed. R. **187**: 101. — Quar. **187**: 567. — (G. Salmon) Contemp. **75**: 588. — (F. St. J. Morrow) Westm. **151**: 492.

— — Mr. Balfour on. (E. J. Dillon) Contemp. **75**: 445. — Sat. R. **87**: 100.

— — Need of a State Supported Catholic. Sat. R. **91**: 529.

— — A Proposed Catholic. Contemp. **75**: 263. — Church Q. **52**: 320. — (D. S. A. Cosby) Westm. **155**: 293. — (F. St. J. Morrow) Macmil. **77**: 101. — (W. Nicholas) Lond. Q. **91**: 250.

— *vs.* England. House of Commons Representation Unjust to England. (J. H. Schooling) Pall Mall M. **22**: 77.

— Victoria's Third Visit, Significance of. Sat. R. **89**: 416.

— What Ireland has done for America. (F. S. Baldwin) New Eng. M. n. s. **24**: 68.

— What the Unionists have done for. (T. W. Russell) No. Am. **167**: 129.

— Winter by the Atlantic. (M. Seton) Temp. Bar, **114**: 433.

Irish, The London. Blackw. **170**: 124.

— Origin and Traditional History of. (C. S. Wake) Am. Antiq. **20**: 73.

Irish Bards, Ancient. (N. M. Holland) Canad. M. **11**: 203, 326.

Irish Bench and Bar, Choice Anecdotes of. Green Bag, **11**: 160.

Irish Brogue, The. Acad. **61**: 291.

Irish Cemetery, An Ancient. (H. Macmillan) Lond. Q. **96**: 313.

Irish Channel, Tunnel under. (J. F. Walker) Contemp. **71**: 406.

Irish Elegies, Some Notable. (A. L. Milligan) Westm. **155**: 150.

Irish Experiment, An. (Rosa M. Barrett) Good Words, **41**: 526.

Irish Guards, The. (F. Manners) 19th Cent. **47**: 1030.

Irish History, Some, and a Moral. (B. Holland) National, **28**: 630.

Irish Home Industries — Point Lace. Chamb. J. **75**: 564. Same art. Liv. Age, **218**: 744.

Irish Home Industries — Poplin Manufacture. (M. Gorges) Chamb. J. **75**: 651.

Irish Humors, Country Town. (E. Ensor) Cornh. **81**: 238. Same art. Ecl. M. **134**: 802.

Irish Immigration, A Century of. (H. J. Desmond) Am. Cath. Q. **25**: 518.

— to Pennsylvania, 1736, Obstructions to. **21**: 485.

Irish Language and Literature, Revival of. (J. McCarthy) Ecl. M. **136**: 350. — Liv. Age, **230**: 190.

— in Elementary Schools. Ath. '00, **2**: 186. Same art. Liv. Age, **127**: 447.

— Recent Fuss about the. (J. P. Mahaffy) 19th Cent. **46**: 213. Same art. Liv. Age, **223**: 110. Same art. Ecl. M. **133**: 880.

Irish-Latin Charm, An. (O. B. Schluter) Am. J. Philol. **20**: 71.

Irish Leaders in Many Nations. (J. P. Bocock) Cosmopol. **26**: 305.

Irish Leaven in American Progress. (J. J. O'Shea) Forum, **27**: 285.

Irish Legal Repartees. Green Bag, **10**: 468.

Irish Legislation. Lond. Q. **90**: 336.

Irish Life and Character. Liv. Age, **221**: 263.

Irish Literary Movement, The. Acad. **58**: 235.

Irish Literary Theatre, The. (M. W. Sampson) Nation, **73**: 395.

— and its Affinities. (S. Gwynn) Fortn. **76**: 1050.

Irish Literature. Acad. **56**: 625.

— Hull's Cuchullin Saga in. (W. H. Carpenter) Nation, **69**: 17.

— Hyde's History of. Sat. R. **87**: 689, 785. — (J. Malone) Bk. Buyer, **19**: 103. — (G. McDermot) Cath. World, **69**: 480. — (W. Canton) Good Words, **40**: 645.

Irish Members of Parliament, What shall we do with? (R. Lucas) National, **37**: 466.

Irish Movement, New. Spec. **81**: 267.

Irish National Reunion. (J. E. Redmond) Arena, **23**: 353.

Irish Nuisance and how to Abate it. (E. Dicey) 19th Cent. **50**: 353.

Irish People, Impolitic Outbursts of. Sat. R. **91**: 293.

— Plea for the. (G. Moore) 19th Cent. **49**: 285.

Irish Poetry, A Specimen of Mediæval. (S. Gwynn) Fortn. **75**: 520.

Irish Problem, An. (E. Æ. Somerville and M. Ross) National, **38**: 407.

Irish Protestants, Downtrodden. (J. F. Taylor) 19th Cent. **50**: 222.

Irish Race, Convention of. Cath. World, **64**: 511.

Irish Records, Truthfulness of. (J. Watson) Ath. '00, **2**: 218.

Irish School of Oratory. (J. F. Taylor) Ecl. M. **128**: 664.

Irish Surnames. (R. R. Elliott) Am. Cath. Q. **24**: 101.

— Indigenous and Exotic. (J. Beddoe) Anthrop. J. **27**: 164.

Irish Tunnel, The. Spec. **79**: 72.

Irish Volunteers, Why not? (T. E. Naughten) Westm. **155**: 515.

Irish Wit and Humor. Spec. **86**: 234.

Irish Witch Doctors. (W. B. Yeats) Fortn. **74**: 440.

Irenæus on the Fourth Gospel. (H. M. Gwatkin) Contemp. **71**: 221.

Ireson, Nathaniel; a West Country Potter. (G. Sweetman) Gent. M. n. s. **64**: 277.

Ireson, Skipper. (J. Codman) McClure, **8**: 458.

"Iris," Distilling Ship, U. S. Navy. (W. W. White) Cassier, **15**: 75.

Iron and Steel, British and American Methods in Making. (E. Phillips) Engin. M. **21**: 173.

— — Great Britain and her Competitors in. (E. Phillips) Engin. M. **21**: 333.

Irrigation in Colorado. (H. A. Crafts) Midland, **11**: 330.
— in Southern California. (W. E. Smythe) World's Work, **2**: 1261.
— Prehistoric. (S. D. Peet) Am. Antiq. **21**: 285.
— Self, in Plants. (A. S. Wilson) Knowl. **21**: 160, 173, 245.
— Tank, in Central India. (G. Palmer) Engin. M. **15**: 59, 289.
— Types of, in the West. (C. E. Walsh) Gunton's M. **21**: 339.
— Water Rights in the Arid West. (R. P. Teele) J. Pol. Econ. **8**: 524.
Irrigation Engineering in Colorado. (H. A. Crafts) Engin. M. **14**: 829.
Irritability and Movement. (W. Haacke) Chaut. **28**: 276.
Irtish River, Up the. (G. F. Wright) Nation, **71**: 383.
Irving, Sir Henry. (H. J. W. Dam) McClure, **14**: 47.
— (C. Scott) Internat. Mo. **1**: 323. — With portrait. (F. Wayne) Nat'l M. (Bost.) **11**: 495. — With caricature portrait. Idler, **17**: 305.
— as Coriolanus. (M. Beerbohm) Sat. R. **91**: 536.
— as Richard III. (Sir E. Russell) Theatre, **38**: 249.
— Reading of Tennyson's "Becket" by, in Canterbury Cathedral. (H. H. Fyfe) Theatre, **39**: 14.
— seen from the Stage. Music, **17**: 644.
Irving, Laurence. Peter the Great. (G. B. Shaw) Sat. R. **85**: 42.
Irving, Washington. (M. A. DeW. Howe) Bookman, **4**: 516.
— Country of. (H. E. Miller) New Eng. M. n. s. **23**: 449.
— First Books of. (L. S. Livingston) Bookman, **8**: 230.
— Services to American History. (R. Burton) New Eng. M. n. s. **16**: 641.
Is this Love? (I. F. Mayo) Argosy, **66**: 214.
Isabella, Queen, her Landing in 1326. (J. H. Round) Eng. Hist. R. **14**: 104.
Isabella, Queen, Wife of Edward II., Inventory of Jewels and Wardrobe of. (W. E. Rhodes) Eng. Hist. R. **12**: 517.
Isabelle d'Este, Camerino of. (C. Yriarte) Art J. **50**: 41, 102.
Isabey, Eugene Gabriel, Note on. Argosy, **74**: 350.
Isaiah, Martyrdom of. (W. E. A. Axon) Antiq. n. s. **37**: 145.
— The Myth and Isaiah the Prophet. (H. Osgood) Bib. Sac. **58**: 68.
— to Ezra, From. (T. K. Cheyne) Am. J. Theol. **5**: 433.
— The Work of. (W. R. Harper) Bib. World, **10**: 48.
Isam's Spectacles. (H. S. Edwards) Cent. **40**: 741.
Isban, Ahmed. Khaver, a Turkish Story. (C. L. Crisfield) Conserv. R. **1**: 173.
Ishan's Martyrdom, The. (C. Johnston) Contemp. **77**: 366.
Isherwood, Benjamin F. (R. H. Thurston) Cassier, **18**: 344.
Ishmael; a story. (R. Pocock) Idler, **15**: 24.
Ishtar, Descent of. (Diana White) New R. **16**: 405.
Isis and Nephthys, Festival Songs of. Archæol. **52**: 457.
— Mysteries of, De Jong on. Ath. '01, **1**: 493.
Islam, De Castries on. (C. H. Toy) New World, **7**: 180.
— Islamic Revival. (Rafiüddin Ahmad) 19th Cent. **42**: 517.
— Philosophical Disintegration of. (H. W. Hulbert) Bib. Sac. **56**: 44.
— Religion of. (H. Loyson) Open Court, **11**: 449.
— — Reply. (Rafiüddin Ahmad) 19th Cent. **49**: 77.
— The Sources of, and Moulvie Rafiüddin Ahmad. (W. St. Clair-Tisdall) 19th Cent. **49**: 364.
See Mohammedanism.

Island Number Ten, Captain Walke Passing. Chaut. **31**: 527.
Island of the Current, The. (C. Edwards) Macmil. **83**: 445.
Island of Love, The; a tale. (G. Smith) Argosy, **70**: 460.
Island Valley of Avilion, The; a poem. (E. M. Rutherford) Gent. M. n. s. **66**: 307.
Islander's Love, An. (M. E. Starbuck) New Eng. M. n. s. **17**: 147.
Islands, The Empire of. (J. Sohn) Forum, **32**: 434.
— Our Seaboard, on the Pacific. (J. E. Bennett) Harper, **97**: 852.
Islay, Autumn Days in. Temp. Bar, **111**: 511. Same art. Ecl. M. **129**: 499.
Isle of Unrest, The. (H. S. Merriman) Cornh. **81**: 125-837. **82**: 1-460. Same art. Munsey, **22**: 361 — **23**: 400.
Isles of Shoals, Story of. (A. W. Moore) New Eng. M. **18**: 519.
Isomorphous Salts and Atomic Weight of Metals contained. (A. E. Tutton) Nature, **57**: 36.
Isopel Berners. (G. Borrow) Temp. Bar, **110**: 128.
Isopods, Relation of Nuclei and Cyptoplasm in the Intestinal Cells of. (E. G. Conklin) Am. Natural. **31**: 66.
Israel in Palestine, Physical Preparation for. (G. F. Wright) Bib. Sac. **58**: 360.
— "Lost Ten Tribes," Historic Relics of. Cath. World, **65**: 535.
Israels, Jozef, Artist, with portrait. (M. Liebermann) Pall Mall M. **25**: 25. — (Mary A. Kirkup) Midland, **9**: 304.
"It;" a story. (S. Lagerlof) Poet-Lore, **11**: 321.
Italian Anarchism. (G. M. Fiamingo) Contemp. **78**: 339. Same art. Liv. Age, **227**: 234.
Italian Art, Modern, Trend of. (Helen Zimmerman) M. of Art, **26**: 55.
— Unfamiliar Masterpieces of. (E. Halsey) J. Soc. Arts, **48**: 490.
Italian Artists, Early. (F. M. Crawford) Book R. **5**: 255.
— Modern. (R. Pantini) Studio (Internat.) **13**: 161.
Italian Castle, Old, Summering in. (J. P. Rudd) Outing, **32**: 63.
Italian Cities, Blashfield on. (Edith Wharton) Bookman, **13**: 563. — (J. S. Fiske) Nation, **73**: 13.
Italian Educational Literature, Recent. (A. F. Chamberlain) Educa. R. **20**: 278.
Italian Expansion and Colonies. (A. G. Keller) Yale R. **9**: 175.
Italian Fiction. (H. B. Fuller) Critic, **30**: 365.
— Last Year's (1897) Crop of. (J. S. Fiske) Nation, **66**: 242.
Italian Folk-song, Specimens of. (L. Wolffsohn) 19th Cent. **42**: 602.
Italian Garden, The. (J. S. Pray) Am. Arch. **67**: 43, 51, 83, 91. — (A. D. F. Hamlin) Am. Arch. **71**: 43.
Italian Immigrants in Boston. (F. A. Bushée) Arena, **17**: 722.
Italian Journalism as seen in Fiction. Blackw. **162**: 207.
Italian Landlord, An. (C. and L. Tod-Mercer) Longm. **34**: 552.
Italian Language, Pronunciation of. (G. D. Kellogg) Chaut. **34**: 182.
Italian Literature, 1896-97. (G. Giacosa) Ath. '97, **2**: 20.
— 1897-98. (G. Biagi) Ath. '98, **2**: 20.
— 1898-99. (G. Biagi) Ath. '99, **2**: 21.
— 1899-1900. (G. Biagi) Ath. '00, **2**: 21.
— 1900-01. (G. Biagi) Ath. '01, **2**: 22.
— Garnett's. (W. K. Thayer) Nation, **67**: 33. — (F. Thompson) Acad. **53**: 513.

Italian Literature; Novels of the Renaissance. Ed. R. **185**: 306.

Italian Novel, Birth of the. (F. Aranjo) Liv. Age, **225**: 526.

Italian Novelists in 1897. (D. Olina) Liv. Age, **216**: 843.

Italian Politics. (H. R. Whitehouse) Forum, **31**: 175.

Italian Republican Prisoners, 1899. (M. C. Smith) Outl. **61**: 919.

Italian Revolution, History of the. (D. Sampson) Month, **95**: 225, 337, 449.

Italian Unity, King's History of. (C. W. Colby) Nation, **70**: 400. — (W. R. Thayer) Am. Hist. R. **5**: 567.

Italian Wine Making. (L. Housman) Argosy, **71**: 261.

Italians and Homicide. (N. Colajanni) Forum, **31**: 62.

— Anti-Italianism of the. (C. Lombroso) Liv. Age, **230**: 126.

— in America. (L. Franklin) Cath. World, **71**: 67.

— in Africa. (F. A. Edwards) Westm. **148**: 477.

Italics in Fiction. (W. Le Queux) Bookman, **11**: 57.

Italy, Anarchy and. Outl. **65**: 853.

— and the Alliances. (R. Ogden) Nation, **72**: 290.

— and France. (S. Cortesi) Internat. Mo. **4**: 530.

— and her Invaders, Hodgkins's. Am. Hist. R. **5**: 734. — Acad. **57**: 473, 565.

— and her Makers. (W. Littlefield) Munsey, **24**: 137.

— and the House of Savoy. (S. Cortesi) Indep. **52**: 2198.

— and the Triple Alliance. (W. B. Duffield) Monthly R. **4**, no. **3**: 63.

— — after 18 Years. (F. Crispi) Ecl. M. **136**: 214.

— and the Vatican. Spec. **79**: 889.

— Art in. (H. Zimmern) M. of Art, **21**: 37.

— as a "Great Power." (F. P. Nash) Nation, **65**: 146.

— Can the Italian Monarchy endure? (A. Diarista) Cath. World, **71**: 721.

— Church and State in. Spec. **80**: 721.

— Churches on the Eastern Coast of. (E. Freshfield) Archæol. **50**: 407.

— Completion of Unity, 1861–71. Ed. R. **192**: 322.

— Conservative Party in. (F. Novili-Vitelleschi) Liv. Age, **218**: 219.

— Crime and Misery in. (J. W. Mario) Nation, **64**: 470.

— Crisis in, and the New Ministry. (F. Novili-Vitelleschi) Liv. Age, **216**: 627.

— Customs and Traditions, Ancient. (E. C. Vansittart) Antiq. n. s. **36**: 198.

— Dawn of a Reign in. (G. Dalla Vecchia) Fortn. **75**: 72. Same art. Liv. Age, **227**: 601–700.

— Disillusionment of. (W. Miller) Gent. M. n. s. **62**: 613.

— Famine in, and its Causes. (E. C. Strutt) Monthly R. **4**, no. **2**: 62.

— Foreign Policy of. (G. Dalla Vecchia) Westm. **152**: 271.

— Historical Monuments of, Conservation of. (Alfredo Melani) Am. Arch. **59**: 67. **60**: 51.

— Hunger and Poverty in. (F. D. Papa) No. Am. **167**: 126.

— in 1898, Present Condition of. (Ercole Vidari) Liv. Age, **219**: 201.

— — Revolt in. (G. Dalla Vecchia) Contemp. **74**: 113. Same art. Ecl. M. **131**: 341. Same art. Liv. Age, **218**: 369. — Spec. **80**: 682. — (De Viti de Marco) National, **31**: 902.

— in 1899. (L. de La Ramée) Fortn. **71**: 475.

— in 1900, Position in. (B. King) Contemp. **78**: 738.

— The King and Queen of. (G. Dalla Vecchia) Good Words, **41**: 302.

— Lake Region of. (E. R. Pennell) Cent. **40**: 836.

— A Letter from. (H. D. Sedgwick, jr.) Atlan. **88**: 27.

— Love and Marriage in. (L. L. Pepper) Chaut. **34**: 290.

Italy, Misery in. Liv. Age, **218**: 89.

— Misgovernment of. (L. de La Ramée) Fortn. **69**: 957.

— Modern, An Impeachment of. (L. de La Ramée) R. of Rs. (N. Y.) **18**: 547. — Reply. (G. Dalla Vecchia) R. of Rs. (N. Y.) **18**: 561.

— — King and Okey on. Ath. '01, **1**: 715.

— Monarchy and Republic in. (R. Garibaldi) No. Am. **171**: 811.

— Municipal Art in. (A. French) New Eng. M. n. s. **18**: 33.

— The New. (S. Cortesi) Internat. Mo. **2**: 388.

— The New Reign in. (B. King) Contemp. **80**: 806.

— The Niobe of Nations. (E. S. Morgan) Westm. **150**: 514.

— Northern, In the Chestnut Groves of. (Susan N. Carter) Scrib. M. **23**: 53.

— Parliament, Twentieth. (L. de La Ramée) Fortn. **67**: 679. Same art. Liv. Age, **213**: 817.

— — Undignified Proceedings. Sat. R. **89**: 641.

— Parliamentary Government in. Nation, **69**: 29.

— Political Outlook in. Sat. R. **87**: 582.

— Political Status of Europe. (Sidney Brooks) World's Work, **1**: 648.

— Politics in: Shall Catholics keep out of? (P. Molmenti) Liv. Age, **223**: 616.

— — Situation in August, 1898. Spec. **81**: 172.

— — in 1899. Garibaldians and the Vatican. (B. Odescalchi) Contemp. **75**: 563.

— Present Day Problems in. (P. Villari) Liv. Age, **224**: 410.

— Present Needs of. (J. J. Mather, jr.) Nation, **71**: 106.

— Problems of. (H. R. Whitehouse) Forum, **29**: 657.

— Prosperity and Politics in. Ed. R. **186**: 1.

— Revolt in, 1899. (F. D. Papa) Arena, **21**: 646.

— Riots in. (E. L. Godkin) Nation, **66**: 378. — (J. W. Mario) Nation, **66**: 402.

— Silk and Cotton Industries of. J. Soc. Arts, **46**: 93.

— The Situation in, 1898. (W. J. Stillman) Nation, **66**: 458. — (G. Dalla Vecchia) 19th Cent. **48**: 385. — Spec. **79**: 266.

— Social Life in. Macmil. **82**: 454. Same art. Liv. Age, **227**: 835.

— Socialism in. (D. W. Fisher) Presb. & Ref. R. **8**: 198.

— Southern, Crawford on. (J. R. Smith) Dial (Ch.) **29**: 352.

— The State of. (W. J. Stillman) Nation, **71**: 169.

— Struggle for Independence, 1815–49. Ed. R. **191**: 380.

— Sunset or Dawn? (J. W. Mario) Nation, **71**: 305.

— The Third Life of. (G. D'Annunzio) No. Am. **171**: 627.

— To-day. Month, **98**: 104.

— — King on. (L. L. Price) Econ. J. **11**: 384.

— Tour in, 1791 and 1793, by Four Ladies. Antiq. n. s. **33**: 273, 296.

— Union of; a retrospect. (D. Sampson) Am. Cath. Q. **24**: 20.

— — Stillman on. Nation, **67**: 488.

— Unknown. (W. H. Goodyear) Archit. R. **8**: 125.

— Water Powers of. (E. Bignami) Engin. M. **17**: 778.

— Wealth, Poverty, and Socialism in. (L. Villari) Monthly R. **5**, no. **2**: 105.

Itambe, Peak of. Nat. Geog. M. **9**: 476.

Itchen, Summer's End on. (W. H. Hudson) Longm. **38**: 17.

Item of Fashionable Intelligence; a story. (J. K. Jerome) Idler, **10**: 722.

Ithacan Days. (J. I. Manatt) Atlan. **88**: 808.

Ito, Marquis, the Great Man of Japan. (Fred. Palmer) Scrib. M. **30**: 613. — Outl. **68**: 77.

Its Own Reward; a story. (K. Murray) Belgra. **96**: 432.

Its Walls were as of Jasper. (K. Grahame) Scrib. M. 22: 157.

Ivanka the Wolf-slayer. (M. Eastwood) Strand, 17: 144.

Ivory, Faces in. Eng. Illust. 19: 401.

— its Sources and Uses. (N. B. Nelson) Pop. Sci. Mo. 51: 534.

Izumo, Notes of a Trip to. (L. Hearn) Atlan. 79: 678.

Jachin and Boaz. (G. St. Clair) Westm. 154: 421.

Jack, George. (F. Miller) Artist (N. Y.) 24: 14.

Jack. (A. C. Goodloe) Cent. 35: 834.

Jack; a story. (G. L. Drew) Canad. M. 8: 349.

Jack, For; a story. Sund. M. 27: 192.

"Jack and the Beanstalk," the Play, Review of. (W. Emanuel) Idler, 17: 928.

Jack and Jill. Macmil. 76: 126.

Jack and Jill of the Sierras, A; a story. (B. Harte) McClure, 15: 219.

Jack Dean's Whistle; a story. (Kate W. Patch) Nat'l M. (Bost.) 5: 439.

Jack Farley's Flying Switch. (C. Warman) Lippinc. 66: 454.

Jack Snipe, Shooting the. (R. H. Johnson) Outing, 39: 333.

Jack Starbuck of Nantucket; a story. (C. N. Williamson) Eng. Illust. 19: 387.

Jack's Mother. Macmil. 83: 217. Same art. Liv. Age, 228: 656.

Jackson, Andrew. (S. D. Thompson) Am. Law R. 31: 641, 801.

— and the National Bank. (R. S. Long) Eng. Hist. R. 12: 85.

— and Nullification. (M. L. Osborne) Nat'l M. (Bost.) 12: 713.

— Parton's Life of. J. Mil. Serv. Inst. 14: 889.

— Petticoat Politics. (A. H. Wharton) Lippinc. 68: 494.

— Reminiscences of, with portraits. (R. J. Lawrence) McClure, 9: 792.

Jackson, F. Stanley, with portraits. Strand, 16: 195.

Jackson, Helen Hunt. (A. W. Armstrong) Meth. R. 57: 444. — (E. P. Gould) Educa. 21: 182.

— How Ramona was written. Atlan. 86: 712. — (H. H. Jackson) Writer, 14: 13.

Jackson, John. Art J. 51: 67.

Jackson, Leonora, Violinist. Music, 19: 302.

Jackson, Thomas. Bank. M. (Lond.) 68: 499.

Jackson, Gen. Thomas J. [Stonewall]. (H. Brackenbury) Blackw. 164: 721. — Acad. 54: 317. Same art. Liv. Age, 219: 428. — (J. D. Cox) Nation, 67: 395, 412. — J. Mil. Serv. Inst. 24: 157. — Ed. R. 189: 48. — (R. Barton) Conserv. R. 1: 41. — (J. W. Jones) Chaut. 30: 84.

— and the American Civil War, Henderson's. (H. K. Douglas) Am. Hist. R. 4: 371. — (F. W. Shepardson) Dial (Ch.) 26: 302. — (S. S. P. Patterson) Sewanee, 7: 88.

Jackson, Me., First Settlers of. (J. Williamson) N. E. Reg. 55: 367.

Jacksonian Epoch, Peck's. (E. M. Shepard) Am. Hist. R. 5: 148.

Jacob and Esau. Meth. R. 59: 961.

— — Comedie of, Was W. Hunnis Author of? (C. C. Stopes) Ath. '00, 1: 538.

— Wrestling by the Brook Jabbok. (P. C. Simpson) Expos. 4: 435.

Jacob's Well, Present Appearance of. Bib. World, 11: 263.

Jacob, John, Shand's. Blackw. 168: 237.

Jacob Leffle; a story. (K. O. Halitvock) Idler, 18: 105.

Jacobean Manor House, A. (B. Hall) Archit. R. 11: 667.

Jacobs, Joseph. (R. Gottheil) Critic, 30: 53.

Jacobs, William Wymark, with portraits. Strand, 16: 676. — Acad. 52: 496. — With portrait. Bk. News, 19: 55.

— as a Writer. Acad. 59: 305.

Jacopone da Todi. Church Q. 50: 443.

Jacounchikoff, Marie, Some Work of. (O. Uzanne) Studio (Lond.) 6: 148.

Jacqueminots. (E. M. Smith) Lippinc. 63: 683.

Jacques Grue's Reformation. (M. Madison) Munsey, 17: 227.

Jade. (Ed. Pennington) Good Words, 39: 166.

— Etymology of. (J. A. H. Murray; J. Platt) Ath. '00, 2: 513, 549.

Jagor, Dr. Friedrich. Geog. J. 15: 430.

Jaguar Hunting in Venezuela. (W. W. Howard) Cent. 32: 382.

Jahn, Friedrich Ludwig, Father of Gymnastics. (W. G. Field) Gent. M. n. s. 63: 155.

Jainism. (E. M. Bowden) 19th Cent. 45: 981.

— Contribution of, to Philosophy. (V. R. Gandhi) Asia. R. 30: 140.

Jalaguier, P. F., Introduction à la Dogmatique. (W. P. Paterson) Crit. R. 8: 64.

Jamaica. (A. Eric) Midland, 7: 128. — (S. E. Saville) Westm. 155: 315.

— and Jamaicans. (T. H. MacDermot) Canad. M. 13: 502.

— Botanical Aspects of. (D. H. Campbell) Am. Natural. 32: 34.

— Dress Rehearsal of Rebellion in. (P. Robinson) Contemp. 74: 746. Same art. Liv. Age, 219: 652.

— From Sea to Summit. (P. Robinson) Good Words, 40: 733. Same art. Liv. Age, 223: 751.

— Has it solved the Color Problem? (J. Moritzen) Gunton's M. 20: 31.

— An Impression. (I. Malcolm) Blackw. 165: 304.

— In a Mangrove Swamp. (Mrs. Woods) Cornh. 84: 162.

— Legend of. (F. M. Alleyne) Longm. 32: 460.

— A Lesson in Colonial Government? (J. Moritzen) R. of Rs. (N. Y.) 22: 451.

— Maroons of. (E. Blake) No. Am. 167: 558.

— One Day's Sport in. (L. C. Shirley) Outing, 31: 361.

— Past and Present. (N. S. Rankin) Canad. M. 11: 419.

— Phases in Natural History of. (R. T. Hill) Science, 5: 15.

— Summer at Christmas-tide. (J. Hawthorne) Cent. 31: 428.

— A Tropic Climb. (J. Hawthorne) Cent. 31: 593.

— Zoölogical. (H. L. Clark) Nat. Sci. 13: 161.

James I. and VI. (O. Smeaton) [Westm.] Ecl. M. 128: 124.

James, Edmund J., Appreciation of. (R. P. Falkner) Ann. Am. Acad. Pol. Sci. 17: 287.

James, Francis E., Watercolor Artist. (F. Wedmore) Studio (Internat.) 3: 259. — (M. H. Dixon) Art J. 53: 249.

James, Gilbert, Artist, and his Work. (A. Lawrence) Idler, 16: 577.

James, Henry. (D. C. Murray) Canad. M. 9: 496. — (H. Harland) Acad. 55: 339.

— The Awkward Age. Acad. 56: 532.

— Evolution of. (C. A. Pratt) Critic, 34: 338.

— The Henry James Myth. (R. Burton) Writer, 14: 5.

— In the Cage. Sat. R. 86: 319.

— Sacred Fount. (C. A. Pratt) Critic, 38: 368.

— The Spoils of Poynton. Acad. 51: 256.

James, William. The Need to Believe, an Agnostic's Notes on. (V. Paget) Fortn. 72: 827.

— on Philosophy. (B. L. Hobson) Presb. & Ref. R. 9: 726.

— Talks on Psychology. (C. A. Pratt) Critic, 36: 119.

James Barrett's Will.   (Victor L. Whitechurch) Good
    Words, 41: 320.
Jameson's Raid.   (J. C. Willoughby) 19th Cent. 42: 9.
    — Spec. 78: 8. — Sat. R. 89: 225.
— The Inquiry Fiasco.   Spec. 78: 788.
— Some Causes of.   Sat. R. 83: 212, 237, 261, 285, 294.
— The Suppressed Telegrams.   Spec. 78: 722.
Jan, the Unrepentant ; a tale.   (J. London) Outing,
    36: 474.
Jan Hunkum's Money.   (M. Maartens) Temp. Bar,
    121: 291, 450, 629.
Jane, St., of Valois.   (J. Winn) Argosy, 69: 186.
Jane Anne, — Lump.   (M. D. Evans) Longm. 35: 143.
Jane Simmons, Trustee.   (A. G. Spencer) New Eng.
    M. n. s. 21: 307.
Janesville, N. Y., Geologic Fault at.   (P. F. Schneider)
    Am. J. Sci. 153: 458.
Janet, Paul.   (A. Cohn) Educa. R. 18: 503.
Janet ; a study.   (H. R. Haweis) Gent. M. n. s. 60: 64.
Janice Meredith ; a story of the Revolution.   (P. L.
    Ford) Bookman, 9: 26-540. 10: 58-385.
January ; a poem.   (E. Stein) Bk. Buyer, 15: 667.
Japan after the War.   Bank. M. (Lond.) 71: 55.
— among Nations, Future of.   (C. Pfoundes) Un. Serv.
    M. 17: 423.
— and America.   (M. Shinoda) Indep. 52: 1048.
— and China.   (M. G. M. Innes) Contemp. 73: 403.
    Same art. Ecl. M. 130: 557. — (H. Webster) Nat.
    Geog. M. 12: 69.
— — Policy of Japan.   Spec. 80: 5.
— and the Gold Standard.   Yale R. 6: 3, 84.
— and Korea.   Outl. 65: 156.
— and the New Far East.   (Ignotus) National, 36: 25.
    Same art. Ecl. M. 135: 703. Same art. Liv. Age,
    227: 201.
— and the U. S.   (M. Komatz) World's Work, 3: 1388.
— — Relations of, Japanese View of Certain. (Hiro-
    kichi Mutsu) Overland, n. s. 32: 406.
— Artistic Gardens in.   (C. Holme) Studio (Lond.) 1:
    129.
— as a Continental Power.   (Count S. Okuma) Indep.
    51: 1215.
— as " Nouveau Riche."   Spec. 78: 434.
— as a Power in the Pacific.   (C. Pfoundes) Arena, 20:
    647.
— Bank of.   Bank. M. (N. Y.) 54: 587. 58: 536.
— — Annual Report of, 1899.   Bank. M. (N. Y.) 60:
    819.
— Banking in.   Bank. M. (Lond.) 70: 52. 72: 239.
— Between the Sea and Fuji San.   (S. Ballard) Sund.
    M. 30: 310.
— Bicycling in.   (A. Macphail) Outing, 29: 324.
— The Britain of the East.   (I. T. Headland) Munsey,
    24: 321.
— Children in.   (A. Edmonds) Canad. M. 16: 119.
— China's Secret Mission to.   (W. N. Brewster) R. of
    Rs. (N. Y.) 20: 710.
— Christian Missions in.   (F. Penman) Cath. World,
    71: 460.
— Christian Unity in. (J. H. De Forest) Indep. 52: 2994.
— Colonial Experience of.   (F. E. Leupp) Nation,
    69: 4.
— The Coming Sea-power.   (C. H. Cramp) No. Am.
    165: 444.
— Commercial.   (O. P. Austin) Forum, 28: 146.
— Commercial Development of.   (O. P. Austin) Nat.
    Geog. M. 10: 329.
— Commercial Rivalry of, as Studied on the Ground.
    (M. L. W. Curtis) Overland, n. s. 30: 227.
— Constitutional Outlook in.   (T. Yokoi) Contemp.
    74: 446. Same art. Ecl. M. 131: 540.
— Constitutional Struggle in.   (N. E. Walz) Am. Law
    R. 32: 31.

Japan, Currency in, Brief History of.   (F. K. Abe)
    Overland, n. s. 30: 173.
— Cycling in.   (T. P. Terry) Outing, 30: 208. 33: 341.
— Dolmens and Burial Mounds in.   (W. Gowland)
    Archæol. 55: 439.
— Dramatic Art in.   (D. E. Amsden) Overland, n. s.
    36: 99.
— during the China-Japan War, Visit to.   (R. J. B.
    Mair) Un. Serv. M. 14: 418.
— Early Architecture of.   (R. A. Cram) Archit. R. 5:
    54.
— Early Metallurgy in.   Archæol. 56: 267.
— Earthquakes in, 1885-92.   (C. Davison) Geog. J. 10:
    531.
— Economic Situation in.   (B. Moses) J. Pol. Econ. 6:
    168.
— Economic Transition in.   (G. Droppers) Nation, 66:
    379.
— Elections in, 1898.   (G. Droppers) Nation, 66: 298.
— Elementary Schools in.   (W. Burnet) Gent. M. n. s.
    67: 282.
— England and.   (H. W. Wilson) Fortn. 69: 503.
    Same art. Ecl. M. 130: 613. Same art. Liv. Age,
    217: 188.
— English Artist in.   Studio (Lond.) 8: 162.
— Entry of, into the Family of Nations.   (T. R. Jar-
    nigan) No. Am. 169: 218.
— — into the World's Politics.   (G. Droppers) Inter-
    nat. Mo. 1: 162.
— Farming in.   (H. H. Guy) Midland, 7: 196.
— Feudal and Modern, Knapp's.   (W. E. Griffis) Na-
    tion, 64: 73.
— Finance of.   Bank. M. (Lond.) 70: 161.
— — Adoption of Gold Standard.   (E. Foxwell) Econ.
    J. 10: 232.
— Finance and Economy in.   (J. Soyeda) Econ. J. 11:
    435.
— Financial Condition of.   (R. Machray) Monthly R.
    5, no, 1: 73.
— A Forecast.   (J. Morris) Asia. R. 25: 309.
— Foreign Relations.   (D. W. Stevens) Forum, 26: 427.
— Foreign Residents in.   (R. Young) 19th Cent. 42:
    305.
— Future of.   (P. Alden) Outl. 60: 482.
— Gold Standard in.   (J. L. Laughlin) J. Pol. Econ. 5:
    378. — Bank. M. (N. Y.) 60: 552.
— A Grave in.   (S. Ballard) Sund. M. 30: 477.
— Home Life in.   (A. H. Ford) Outl. 69: 579.
— — contrasted with American.   (C. Kochi) Arena,
    20: 239.
— Imperialism in.   (G. T. Ladd) Nation, 71: 283.
— Impressions of.   (H. C. Potter) Cent. 39: 663.
— In Aino-land.   (M. L. Todd) Cent. 34: 342.
— in America, A Bit of.   (V. V. M. Beede) Chaut. 31:
    569.
— in 1888 ; Fall of the Cabinet.   (G. Droppers) Nation,
    67: 407.
— — The New Cabinet.   (G. Droppers) Nation, 67:
    256.
— — Political Crisis.   (G. Droppers) Nation, 67: 91.
— in the Sisterhood of Nations.   (K. Takahira) Indep.
    53: 1547.
— Industrial Revolution in.   (Count S. Okuma) No. Am.
    171: 677.
— Intellectual Future of.   Liv. Age, 224: 558.
— Journalism in.   (T. J. Nakagawa) Forum, 29: 370.
— Labor in.   (F. Takano) Gunton's M. 12: 236.
— Labor Troubles in.   Gunton's M. 14: 173.
— Ladies of.   Cornh. 79: 794.
— Lafarge's Artist's Letters from.   Ath. '98, 1: 124.
— Later Architecture of.   (R. A. Cram) Archit. R. 5:
    77.
— Letter from.   (J. Soyeda) Econ. J. 9: 651.

Jesus Christ, Ethical Method of. (J. H. Thayer) J. Bib. Lit. 19: 146.
— Ethics of ; are they Practicable? (L. Abbott) Bib. World, 17: 256.
— Face of, in Art. (K. P. Hampton) Outl. 61: 735.
— First Miracle of, and the Exaltation of his Human Nature. (N. J. D. White) Expos. 7: 177.
— Forrest, D. W., on the Christ of History and of Experience. (T. B. Kilpatrick) Crit. R. 8: 24. — (H. C. Minton) Presb. & Ref. R. 11: 192.
— The Forty Days of the Risen Life. (W. B. Carpenter) Sund. M. 26: 433, 739.
— Glorification of. (L. P. Mercer) N. Church R. 5: 527.
— God's Glory in the Face of. (L. Abbott) Outl. 60: 1063.
— Growth of. (M. J. Cramer) Meth. R. 57: 229.
— His Foreknowledge of his Sufferings and Death. (O. Pfleiderer) New World, 8: 431.
— Historical and Spiritual. (R. M. Pope) Lond. Q. 91: 15.
— Historical Christology. (G. White) Sewanee, 5: 33.
— How he became the Saviour. (H. G. Bilbie) Meth. R. 58: 454.
— How he gathered his First Disciples. (E. I. Bosworth) Bib. World, 15: 112.
— How we Know. (W. C. Schaeffer) Ref. Ch. R. 48: 289.
— Human Life of God. (H. van Dyke) Chaut. 28: 235.
— If Christ were here? (L. Abbott) Outl. 59: 127.
— in Art. (E. A. Starr) Cath. World, 66: 795. — (C. M. Fairbank) Chaut. 26: 243.
— in Modern Thought. (C. J. Little) Meth. R. 59: 190.
— in the Old Testament. (W. Rupp) Ref. Ch. R. 48: 382.
— in Paul's Epistles. (R. R. Lloyd) Bib. Sac. 58: 270.
— in the 20th Century. (J. I. Buell) Meth. R. 57: 595.
— Incarnation of, Simon on. (H. C. Minton) Presb. & Ref. R. 11: 367.
— — Works on. (B. B. Warfield) Presb. & Ref. R. 10: 701.
— Infallibility of, H. MacIntosh on. (J. Macpherson) Crit. R. 11: 353.
— Influence of, in Civilization. (N. D. Hillis) Bib. Sac. 56: 327.
— — on the Doctrine of God. (G. B. Foster) Bib. World, 11: 306.
— — on Social Institutions. (C. R. Henderson) Bib. World, 11: 167.
— Irony of. (W. R. Paterson) Monist, 9: 345.
— Judges of, Three. (W. M. Macgregor) Expos. 8: 59, 119.
— Knowledge of, as Man. Lond. Q. 90: 1.
— Last Passover and the Day of Crucifixion. (J. C. Kunzman) Luth. Q. 29: 251.
— Law of Sacrifice obeyed by. (J. H. Bethards) Meth. R. 57: 861.
— Light of Galilee. (A. B. Bruce) Expos. 3: 505.
— Likeness of. (F. W. Farrar) Contemp. 74: 215. Same art. Liv. Age, 218: 658. — (W. Bayliss) Contemp. 74: 354. Same art. Liv. Age, 219: 157.
— — from the Time of the Apostles to the Present Day. (W. Bayliss) M. of Art, 22: 173.
— — Have we an Authentic Likeness? (C. Middleton) Sund. M. 27: 685.
— — in Art. (J. P. Lenox) Bib. World, 12: 380.
— Life of. Cath. World, 70: 290. — (E. I. Bosworth) Bib. Sac. 57: 445. — (J. Watson) McClure, 14: 99 — 16: 116.
— — Constructive Studies in. (E. D. Burton and S. Mathews) Bib. World, 15: 36–433. 16: 26–451.
— — Present Knowledge of. (J. Stalker) Contemp. 76: 124. Same art. Liv. Age, 224: 572.
— — Sources of, outside of the Gospels. (E. D. Burton) Bib. World, 15: 26.

Jesus Christ, Logia of. (Adolf Harnack) Expos. 2: 481.
— (M. R. James) Contemp. 72: 153. Same art. Liv. Age, 214: 675. Same art. Ecl. M. 129: 505. Same art. Chr. Lit. 17: 360. — Liv. Age, 214: 467. — (G. F. Wright) Bib. Sac. 54: 759. — Acad. 52: 83.
— — How we Found. (B. P. Grenfell) McClure, 9: 1022.
— — Resch on. (J. H. Ropes; C. C. Torrey) Am. J. Theol. 3: 695.
— Medley on Christ, the Truth. (J. Traill) Crit. R. 11: 117.
— Moral Character of. (J. Tomlinson) Luth. Q. 30: 254.
— The Name of Jesus. (J. Watson) Expos. 3: 97.
— Nativity of. (W. Canton) Expos. 5: 123.
— Thomas on. (G. Milligan) Crit. R. 10: 397.
— Nature of, Marshall's. (J. W. Dawson) Expos. 7: 398.
— of History and Faith. (C. H. J. Ropes) Am. J. Theol. 2: 80.
— of St. Paul. (M. D. Conway) Open Court, 13: 517.
— Our Redeemer ; Encyclical, Latin, and English. (Leo XIII.) Am. Cath. Q. 26: 163.
— Our Saviour and Companion. (O. Dyer) N. Church R. 5: 328.
— Outline of the Life of. (S. Mathews) Bib. World, 11: 328.
— Paulinism of. Bib. World, 12: 49.
— St. Paul's Conception of, Somerville on. (H. C. Minton) Presb. & Ref. R. 10: 362.
— Peace of, Secret of. (L. Abbott) Outl. 59: 333.
— Person and Work of, in the Letters of Paul. (A. S. Weber) Ref. Ch. R. 46: 51.
— Personal Religion of. (E. D. Burton) Bib. World, 14: 394.
— Personality of, and his Historical Relation to Christianity. (P. Carus) Monist, 10: 573.
— Phelps-Ward's Life of. (S. Mathews) Dial (Ch.) 24: 17.
— Political Effects of his Teaching. (H. P. Judson) Bib. World, 11: 229.
— Preëxistence of: Argument from John xvii. (G. H. Gilbert) Bib. World, 13: 308.
— Presence of, and Eschatology. (W. Rupp) Ref. Ch. R. 46: 241.
— Protestantism of. (Author of Pro Christo et Ecclesia) Monthly R. 3, no. 2: 98.
— Reality and Simplicity of. Bib. World, 16: 83.
— Really the Last of the Buddhas. (J. H. Wilson) N. Church R. 4: 44.
— Recent Studies in the Life and Teaching of. (R. M. Pope) Lond. Q. 94: 46.
— Recovery of, from Christianity. (G. D. Herron) Arena, 26: 225.
— Resurrection of. (W. Weber) Monist, 11: 361.
— — Appearances of the Risen Lord to Individuals. (N. J. D. White) Expos. 6: 66.
— — Belief in, and its Permanent Significance. (P. Schwartzkopff) Monist, 11: 1.
— — the Central Fact in Christianity. (H. G. Weston) Bib. Sac. 57: 696.
— — Harnack on. (S. McComb) Expos. 10: 350.
— — Power of. (W. H. Wynn) Luth. Q. 30: 173.
— — Stapfer on. (A. Hovey) Am. J. Theol. 4: 536.
— Revelation of, and Example of. (A. Carr) Expos. 9: 118.
— Sacred Manhood of. Church Q. 45: 163.
— Sanctified by the Offering of the Body of. Ref. Ch. R. 47: 238.
— Sayings of. The Oxyrhynchus Fragment. (J. A. Cross) Crit. R. 8: 135.
— — Danger of False. Spec. 79: 107.
— — not in the Gospels. (G. H. Schodde) Indep. 53: 2877.

John the Baptist, Place of, in Gospel History. (A. C. Zenos) Bib. World, 15: 11.

— Sudermann's. (K. Francke) Nation, 66: 105.

John, St., and Philo Judæus. (W. E. Ball) Contemp. 73: 219.

— Gospel of, and the Quartodecimans. (J. Drummond) Am. J. Theol. 1: 601.

— Martyrdom of. (F. P. Badham) Am. J. Theol. 3: 729.

John, Father, the Russian Priest. Acad. 56: 229. — (J. Y. Simpson) Expos. 6: 261.

John. (M. Maartens) Temp. Bar, 119: 206.

John and the Ghosts; a story. (A. T. Couch) Pall Mall M. 25: 498.

John Barrington, jr.; a story. (E. L. Atherton) 11: 443 — 13: 709.

John Bull in 1712 and Now. (O. Smeaton) Westm. 147: 260.

John Burnet of Barns. (J. Buchan) Chamb. J. 75: 1–547.

John Carew's Christmas Eve; a story. (C. G. Rogers) Canad. M. 10: 110.

John Crerar Library. Pub. Lib. 5: 343.

John Day Fossil Beds, The. (J. C. Merriam) Harper, 102: 581.

John Durham; a story. Temp. Bar, 122: 399. Same art. Liv. Age, 230: 314.

John England's Outgoing. Liv. Age, 225: 82-414.

John Foster. (H. W. Mabie) Bookman, 13: 584.

John Gayther and the Galleon; a story. (F. R. Stockton) Cosmopol. 27: 183.

John Hammel, Railroad Conductor; a story. (C. W. Reamer) Nat'l M. (Bost.) 10: 310.

John Jardine; a story. (S. Clarke) Temp. Bar, 111: 554.

John Nolan's Inheritance. (J. William Breslin) Longm. 39: 144.

John of London and George of Castelfranco. Sat. R. 90: 821.

John Olmstead's Nephew. (H. W. French) Lippinc. 61: 3.

John P. Kelly's Daughter; a story. (A. B. Lees) Argosy, 74: 321.

John Rutland's Christmas. (H. A. Parker) Lippinc. 63: 116.

John Splendid; the tale of a Poor Gentleman, and the Little Wars of Lorn. (N. Munro) Blackw. 162: 587, 721. 163: 17-743. 164: 70-186. Same art. Liv. Age, 217: 563-863. 218: 14-861.

John Thomson of Duddingston. Chamb. J. 74: 107.

John Tyson's Friend; a story. (A. Waite) Sund. M. 28: 795.

John, W. Gascombe, Artist. (A. L. Baldry) Studio (Internat.) 7: 115.

John Wilson's Dream. (B. Atkinson) Sund. M. 30: 815.

Johneen; a poem. (M. O'Neill) Ecl. M. 133: 240.

Johnny. (A. Morrison) Liv. Age, 223: 62.

Johnny Bear. (E. Seton-Thompson) Scrib. M. 28: 658.

Johnny's Job. (Octave Thanet) Scrib. M. 24: 439.

Johnson, Andrew, Pres. Controversies in the War Department. (J. M. Schofield) Cent. 32: 576.

— Early Love Affair of. (G. Rouquie) Nat'l M. (Bost.) 6: 63.

— Impeachment of. (F. A. Burr) Lippinc. 63: 512. — (G. S. Boutwell) McClure, 14: 171.

— Recollections of. (E. V. Smalley) Indep. 52: 2152.

Johnson, Clifton, and his Pictures of New England Life. (M. B. Hartt) New Eng. M. n. s. 24: 661.

Johnson, C. E., Landscape-painter, with portrait. (A. L. Baldry) M. of Art, 21: 306.

Johnson, E. Borough, Artist. (A. L. Baldry) Studio (Internat.) 4: 3.

— Sketches by. Studio (Internat.) 8: 245.

Johnson, Ellen Cheney. (I. C. Barrows) New Eng. M. n. s. 21: 614.

Johnson, Lionel, Poetry of. Acad. 52: 544.

Johnson, Samuel, Dr. (A. Birrell) Outl. 63: 542.

— among the Poets. (H. C. Minchin) Macmil. 85: 98.

— and his Friends at the Society of Arts. J. Soc. Arts, 48: 829.

— as Lover and Husband. (C. C. Molyneux) Temp. Bar, 120: 532.

— at Church. Acad. 54: 132.

— Catholic Tendencies of. (P. Fitzgerald) Month, 93: 64.

— Do we really know Dr. Johnson? (A. Birrell) Outl. 69: 907.

— Memorials of. Church Q. 50: 355.

— Monument of. (E. E. Morris) Longm. 36: 32.

— on Law and Lawyers. Green Bag, 9: 403. 12: 501.

— Politics of. (J. Sargeaunt) Bookman, 6: 420.

— Transmitted Personality of. (A. Birrell) Critic, 36: 140.

Johnson, William, Eton Master. (B. Holland) National, 30: 867.

— Reminiscences of, as Eton Tutor. Macmil. 78: 102.

Johnson, W. T.; Twelve Years of a Soldier's Life. Ath. '97, 2: 519.

Johnson Family. Wallingford (Conn.) Johnsons. (F. C. Johnson) N. E. Reg. 55: 369.

Johnson's Regeneration. (R. V. Carr) Overland, n. s. 38: 147.

Johnsoniana. (L. Stephen) National, 30: 61.

Johnston, Annie Fellows. Writer, 12: 154.

Johnston, Charles, Travels in Ohio, 1790. (E. W. Lahnier) Lippinc. 62: 242.

Johnston, Joseph F. Bank. M. (N. Y.) 54: 743.

Johnston, Mary, with portrait. Bk. News, 18: 7. — With portrait. (M. Mannering) Nat'l M. (Bost.) 10: 533.

— Virginia of. (T. Dixon, jr.) Bookman, 12: 237.

Johnston, Richard Malcolm. (B. M. Steiner) Conserv. R. 1: 74. — Dial (Ch.) 25: 213. — With portrait. (R. Armstrong) Cath. World, 68: 261. — Conserv. R. 3: 229. 4: 5, 203.

Johnston, Thos. Brumby. Geog. J. 10: 446.

Johnstone, G. W., Landscape Paintings of. (W. M. Gilbert) Art J. 51: 146.

Joint-Stock Companies, Liquidation of. Bank. M. (Lond.) 67: 359.

Joint-stock Nuisance, The. Spec. 78: 794.

Joinville, Jean de. Chronicles. Scot. R. 33: 115.

Joinville Tunnel, The; a story. (F. M. White) Cornh. 78: 671. Same art. Liv. Age, 219: 773.

Jokai, Maurus. (N. Blanchan) Critic, 33: 167. — Critic, 31: 261. — (R. N. Bain) Monthly R. 4, no. 2: 137. Same art. Ecl. M. 137: 720. Same art. Liv. Age, 231: 185.

— at Home. (A. Hegedüs, jr.) Bk. Buyer, 17: 588.

Joke of the Season; a story. (Clara Morris) Cosmopol. 31: 614.

Jokes, Practical. (I. Browne) Green Bag, 10: 378.

Joliet Township High School. (J. S. Brown) School R. 9: 417.

Jolly; a story. (J. J. á Becket) Cosmopol. 23: 273.

"Jolly Boy" Jago. (J. L. Hornibrook) Argosy, 72: 324.

Jolo, Our Friend the Sultan of. (C. B. Hagadorn) Cent. 38: 26.

Joly, Alex. (J. L. Howe) Science, n. s. 7: 230.

Jonah, Purpose of his Mission to Nineveh. (A. W. Ackerman) Bib. World, 12: 190.

— Story of. (Ed. G. J. Varney) N. Church R. 4: 478.

Jonah-monument in New York. (W. Lowrie) Am. J. Archæol. 2d ser. 5: 51.

Jones, Agnes. (F. D. How) Sund. M. **30**: 618.

Jones, Sir Edward Burne. (G. White) Conserv. R. **5**: 212. — (S. Beale) Am. Arch. **61**: 13. — (W. Sharp) Atlan. **82**: 375. — Critic, **32**: 409. **33**: 53. — (W. Sharp) Fortn. **70**: 289. — (Julia Cartwright) Art J. **50**: 247. — (F. M. Hueffer) Contemp. **74**: 181. Same art. Liv. Age, **219**: 110. — Quar.**188**: 338. — (E. R. Pennell) Nation, **67**: 8. — Spec. **80**: 908. Same art. Liv. Age, **218**: 275. — Sat. R. **85**: 837. — Acad. **53**: 687. **54**: 19. — (M. Bell) Studio (Internat.) **7**: 175.

— and Rembrandt. (R. A. M. Stevenson) Art J. **51**: 57.

— Art, Life, and Bibliography, with portrait. Mast. in Art, **2**: pt. 19.

— Art of. (A. Streeter) Month, **93**: 25.

— Collected Works of. (E. R. Pennell) Nation, **68**: 65.

— Cupid and Psyche Frieze. Studio (Internat.) **6**: 3.

— Decorative Art of, Vallance's. Art J. **52**: 115.

— Drawings at the British Museum. (W. Roberts) M. of Art, **24**: 453.

— Ethics and Art of. Ed. R. **189**: 24.

— Exhibition of Works at the New Gallery. Sat. R. **87**: 11. — Ath. '99, **1**: 23.

— Garden of the Hesperides. (Julia Cartwright) Art J. **52**: 94.

— In Memoriam. (R. de La Sizeranne ; F. Khnopff ; M. H. Spielmann) M. of Art, **22**: 513.

— Letters to a Child. Strand, **17**: 375.

— The Painter of the Golden Age. (W. Bayliss) Good Words, **40**: 189.

— Recollections of. (J. Jacobs) 19th Cent. **45**: 126.

— Studies by. Studio (Internat.) **5**: 38. — Studio (Lond.) **7**: 199.

— Unfinished Works by. (P. Burne Jones) M. of Art, **24**: 159.

Jones, Hannah, Opera-singer, with portrait. Music, **17**: 78.

Jones, Henry Arthur. (W. K. Tarpey) Critic, **37**: 123.

— Lackey's Carnival. (M. Beerbohm) Sat. R. **90**: 423.

— The Liars. Acad. **52**: 306.

— Physician. (G. B. Shaw) Sat. R. **83**: 348.

— Popular Success of. (M. Beerbohm) Sat. R. **90**: 458.

— with Bibliography of his Plays. (J. M. Bulloch) Bk. Buyer, **16**: 225.

Jones, Dr. John, of Hollis, N. H. (C. E. Ellis) New Eng. M. n. s. **24**: 28.

Jones, John Paul, Buell's Life of. Critic, **38**: 122. — (C. H. Stockton) Nation, **72**: 180. — (M. E. Seawell) Bk. Buyer, **21**: 557.

— Daring of. (G. Gibbs) Cosmopol. **31**: 639.

— Effrontery of. (G. Gibbs) Lippinc. **64**: 376.

— Founder of the American Navy. Sewanee R. **9**: 296.

— His Fight with the "Serapis." (C. T. Brady) McClure, **13**: 142.

— in the Revolution. (A. T. Mahan) Scrib. M. **24**: 22–204.

Jones, Rev. Morgan, and the Welsh Indians of Virginia. (I. J. Greenwood) N. E. Reg. **52**: 28.

Jones, Paul, the Globe-trotter. (G. Dollar) Strand, **13**: 678.

Jones, Reginald, Water-colors by. Artist (N. Y.) **25**: 30.

Jones, Samuel M., Mayor of Toledo. (W. Gladden) Outl. **62**: 17.

Jones, Viriamu. (W. E. Ayrton) Nature, **64**: 161.

Jones of the 49th ; a poem. (B. Kelly) Canad. M. **12**: 47.

Jones of Pannmaen ; a story. Blackw. **170**: 749.

Jonson, Ben, Newly-discovered Letters and Documents of. (B. Dobell) Ath. '01, **1**: 403, 465.

— Poems of. (H. N. Sanders) Temp. Bar, **121**: 213.

Jonsson, Bo. A Great Chancellor of Sweden. (F. Bayford Harrison) Gent. M. n. s. **62**: 573.

Joopiter Ploovius, Private. (W. P. Drury) Un. Serv. M. **18**: 440.

Jopling, Mrs. Louise, with portrait. Strand, **16**: 196.

— Studio of. Studio (Lond.) **7**: 40.

Joppa ; a story. (W. L. Alden) Idler, **15**: 784.

Jordan, Sources of the. (J. L. Leeper) Bib. World, **16**: 326.

— Upper. (J. L. Leeper) Bib. World, **17**: 86.

Jordan "Fault," The Great. (G. F. Wright) Nation, **72**: 250.

Jordan Pictures. (G. R. Lees) Good Words, **42**: 828.

Josaphat, Holy Saint, of India. (A. D. White) Open Court, **15**: 284.

Joseph, as Statesman. (J. Monroe) Bib. Sac. **54**: 484.

— An Ethical and Biblical Study. (A. Black) Expos. **7**: 63 — **8**: 445.

— Story of. (D. L. Sharp) Nat'l M. (Bost.) **13**: 250.

Joseph's Dream ; a story. (Grant Allen) Cosmopol. **26**: 277.

Josephine at the Malmaison. (A. Laugel) Nation, **68**: 199.

— Masson's. (A. Laugel) Nation, **67**: 386.

— The Pre-imperial. (A. Laugel) Nation, **68**: 142, 160.

Josephus, Flavius ; a Soldier Historian. (George Martin) Gent. M. n. s. **62**: 162.

— History of the Jews ; a book of the past. (W. L. Andrews) Bookman, **10**: 571.

— Sources of, for History of Syria. (A. Büchler) Jew. Q. **9**: 311.

Josephus, Pseudo-. Joseph Ben Gorion. (A. Neubauer) Jew.Q. **11**: 355.

Joseppa ; Sweetest of Tagalog Children. (P. N. Beringer) Overland, n. s. **35**: 360.

Joshua Goodenough's Old Letter ; a story. (F. Remington) Harper, **95**: 878.

Joshua Quemby's Daughter ; a story. (E. F. Strange) Pall Mall M. **23**: 78.

Josiah, King of Judah, and the Law-book, told for Children. (W. F. Adeney) Bib. World, **13**: 106.

Joubert, Joseph. (R. Arthur) Westm. **148**: 524.

Joubert, General P. J., with portrait. R. of Rs. (N. Y.) **21**: 573.

Jouett, James Edward, Rear-Admiral. Un. Serv. (Phila.) **17**: 17.

Jouett, Matthew Harris ; Kentucky's Master-painter. (C. H. Hart) Harper, **98**: 914.

Joullin, Amédée, The Work of. (A. L. Street) Overland, n. s. **33**: 1.

— Kentucky Children painted by. (C. H. Hart) Harper, **101**: 51.

Journalism, Amateur. (G. Burgess) Acad. **57**: 212, 258, 290.

— American, Decay of. Dial (Ch.) **22**: 237.

— and Diplomacy. Spec. **81**: 513.

— as a Basis for Literature. (G. S. Lee) Atlan. **85**: 231.

— as a Career. National, **32**: 211.

— as a Profession. (W. Avenel) Forum, **25**: 366. — (A. Shadwell) National, **31**: 845. — (W. N. Shansfield) Westm. **146**: 686. Same art. Ecl. M. **128**: 169.

— Bye-ways of. (M. Macdonagh) Cornh. **79**: 395. Same art. Ecl. M. **132**: 820. Same art. Liv. Age, **221**: 171.

— Collection of News. (T. B. Connery) Cosmopol. **23**: 21.

— Disreputable. Gunton's M. **15**: 321.

— English. (M. H. Krout) Chaut. **28**: 445.

— — Reminiscences of. (W. Reid) 19th Cent. **42**: 55. Same art. Liv. Age, **214**: 653. Same art. Ecl. M. **129**: 408.

— Fifty Years of. Scot. R. **29**: 128.

— for University Men. (F. S. A. Lowndes) Contemp. **80**: 814.

Judgment of Peter and Paul on Olympus, a Poem in Prose. (H. Sienkiewicz) Cent. **37**: 316.

Judgment of Solomon, A. (M. Wolfenstein) Lippinc. **68**: 48.

Judgment of Venus. (D. Osborne) Atlan. **88**: 262.

Judicature, English, Century of, with portraits. (V. V. Veeder) Green Bag, **13**: 23–527.

Judicature Acts at Work. (R. F. G.-Campbell) National, **35**: 989.

Judiciary, Elective. Am. Law R. **32**: 237. — (W. B. Cochran) Am. Law R. **32**: 868.

— Federal, Usurpations of, in the Interest of the Money Power. (D. J. Russell) Arena, **19**: 721.

— Growing Power of. (B. Winchester) Am. Law R. **32**: 801.

— Politics and the. (F. G. Cook) Atlan. **83**: 743.

Judiciary Act of 1801. (M. Farrand) Am. Hist. R. **5**: 682.

Judith of 1864, A. (C. F. Cavanagh) Munsey, **16**: 434.

Judith Dauntry; a story. (H. P. Spofford) Cosmopol. **25**: 643.

Juergens, Alfred, Painter. (E. E. Howard) Brush & P. **7**: 355.

"Jugend," German Periodical, Decorative Work in. (G. White) M. of Art, **22**: 40.

"Juggernaut;" a story. (H. F. Hetherington) Pall Mall M. **21**: 127.

Juggler, The. (C. E. Craddock) Atlan. **79**: 73–825. **80**: 106, 241.

Juggler of Notre Dame, The; a story. (A. France) Acad. **55**: 84.

Jugglers of the Sect of Isawiyah. (R. E. Fry) Cornh. **79**: 353.

— Indian. Are they Humbugs? Strand, **18**: 657.

Juggling, Paul Cinquevalli and. (W. G. Fitzgerald) Strand, **13**: 92.

Jullien's Promenade Concerts. Music, **18**: 284.

July in England. Sat. R. **90**: 79.

Jumping of Mr. John Higgins. (O. North) Strand, **14**: 507.

Jumping Procession in Echternach, The. (Baroness Rotberg) Good Words, **41**: 420.

June, In Praise of. (B. P. Galdos) Liv. Age, **225**: 741.

June Night on the Kama, A; a story. (R. Bowman) Temp. Bar, **124**: 351.

June Roses; a poem. (I. F. Mayo) Argosy, **65**: 663.

Juneau, Alaska's Metropolis. (Mrs. F. Schwatka) Midland, **8**: 353.

Jung, Sir Salar, Visit to Europe in 1876. (G. H. Trevor) Macmil. **79**: 390.

Jungermannia. (A. V. Jennings) Knowl. **21**: 115.

Jungfrau, Early Ascents of the. (F. Gribble) Outing, **36**: 362.

— Electric Railway on. (E. K. Scott) Engin. M. **19**: 33. — (E. R. Dawson) Scrib. M. **24**: 371. — Chamb. J. **75**: 449.

— To the Summit of, by Rail. (F. E. Hamer) Liv. Age, **214**: 211.

Jungle, The; a story. (E. Nesbit) Pall Mall M. **21**: 473.

Jungle Courtship, A. (E. D. Cuming) Chamb. J. **77**: extr. no. 38.

Jungle Folk. (J. Wells) Sund. M. **30**: 510.

Jungmann, Nico, Artist. Studio (Internat.) **4**: 25.

— Pictures by. Artist (N. Y.) **31**: 144. — Studio (Internat.) **12**: 37.

Junior Sub, The; a story. (Sophie Hart) Idler, **12**: 787.

Juniper Street Episode. (E. P. Butler) Lippinc. **67**: 252.

Junius and the Epistle to the Hebrews. (I. W. Riley) Bib. Sac. **58**: 607.

— Mr. Lecky on. (W. N. Sibley) Westm. **147**: 57.

Junius, Letters of. Sir Philip Francis as Author. Sat. R. **91**: 740.

— Sir Philip Francis not the Author of. (W. F. Rae) Ath. '98, **1**: 51, 87.

— New Light on. (W. F. Rae) Ath. '99, **1**: 434–563. '00, **1**: 17.

— A Theory of. (N. W. Sibley) Westm. **152**: 50, 261.

Junot, The Wife of. (A. Laugel) Nation, **73**: 451, 470.

Jupiter and his Markings. (W. F. Denning) Nature, **63**: 355. — (W. F. Denning) Knowl. **23**: 200.

— — Hypothesis regarding. (A. E. Douglass) Pop. Astron. **8**: 473.

— Fifth Satellite of. (A. A. Common) Pop. Astron. **5**: 1.

— Motion of Markings on. (W. F. Denning) Pop. Astron. **9**: 488.

— Present Appearance of. (W. F. Denning) Nature, **57**: 586.

— Red Spot on. (W. F. Denning) Nature, **60**: 210.

— Rotation of. (G. W. Hough) Pop. Astron. **7**: 62.

— Satellites of, Visible to the Naked Eye. (T. J. J. See) Pop. Astron. **6**: 257.

— Third Satellite, Drawings of. (A. E. Douglass) Pop. Astron. **5**: 308.

Jupiter Capitolinus, From the Temple of, in Rome. (A. Marquand) Am. J. Archæol. 2d s. **2**: 19.

Jura and Neocomian of Arkansas, Kansas, Oklahoma, New Mexico, and Texas. (J. Marcou) Am. J. Sci. **154**: 197.

— Reply to J. Marcou. (R. T. Hill) Am. J. Sci. **154**: 449.

Jurassic Formation on the Atlantic Coast. (O. C. Marsh) Am. J. Sci. **156**: 105.

Jurassic Vertebrates. (W. C. Knight) Am. J. Sci. **160**: 115.

— from Wyoming. (W. C. Knight) Am. J. Sci. **155**: 186, 378.

Jurisdiction, Cession by States to U. S. (G. Norman Lieber) Am. Law R. **32**: 78.

Jurisdictions, Heritable. (W. K. Dickson) Jurid. R. **9**: 428.

Jurisprudence, American. (H. Teichmueller) Am. Law R. **32**: 701.

— Department of. Am. J. Soc. Sci. **38**: 218.

— Ethnological. (A. H. Post) Open Court, **11**: 641, 718.

— Scope of. (C. Thorne) Am. Law R. **35**: 546.

Jury, Charging the. (Edward S. Doolittle) Am. Law R. **35**: 546.

— Trial by, at *nisi prius*. (S. L. Holland) Law Q. **17**: 171.

— — in France. (U. M. Rose) Am. Law R. **35**: 17.

— — The Perfection of. (A. G. Sedgwick) Nation, **67**: 163.

— Trial by Judge and. (H. C. Caldwell) Am. Law R. **33**: 321.

— Trial by, in Civil Cases. (J. E. R. Stephens) Gent. M. n. s. **62**: 189.

Jury Bribing, The Beginning of. (E. P. Prentice) Arena, **22**: 312.

Jury Challenge. Green Bag, **10**: 28.

Jury-room Sentiments and Diversions. (A. H. Walker) Green Bag, **13**: 196.

Jury Stories. (H. Macfarlane) Argosy, **67**: 113.

Jury System, The. Spec. **78**: 690.

— English and Scotch, in Criminal Trials. (J. Johnston) Westm. **148**: 700.

Jus Gentium of the Ancient Aryans. (W. H. Rattigann) Law Q. R. **15**: 303.

Jus Primæ Noctis. (N. Munro) New R. **16**: 662.

Just be Glad; a poem. (J. W. Riley) Outl. **67**: 358.

"Just Break the News to Mother;" the English War Ballad. Acad. **60**: 329.

Kantara to El Arish, Itinerary from. (A. R. Guest; A. McKillop) Geog. M. 13: 281.

Kanthack, Alfredo Antunes. Nature, 59: 252.

Kaolins of Pennsylvania. (T. C. Hopkins) J. Frankl. Inst. 148: 1.

Karaginski Island, Kamtchatka, A Visit to. (H. O. Jones) Geog. J. 12: 280.

Karain; a memory. (J. Conrad) Blackw. 162: 630. Same art. Liv. Age, 215: 796-852.

Karaitica. (E. N. Adler) Jew Q. 12: 674.

Karia, East, and South Lydia, Sites in. (W. R. Paton) J. Hel. Stud. 20: 57.

— Researches in. (W. R. Paton and J. L. Myres) Geog. J. 9: 38.

Karian Sites and Inscriptions. (W. R. Paton and J. L. Myres) J. Hel. Stud. 16: 237.

Karim; a Model Shikari. Blackw. 164: 89.

" Karl Sandèze ; " a literary episode. (Mrs. Campbell-Praed) Lippinc. 64: 794.

Karlsbad, An American at. (C. Warman) McClure, 10: 205.

Karnak, Egypt, Restorations at. Am. Arch. 72: 103.

Karst, Borders of the. (G. A. J. Cole) Knowl. 23: 218.

Kashmir and East Punjab, Travels in. (C. Bolitho) Cornh. 78: 353.

Kaskaskia; a vanished capital. (A. G. Culver) Chaut. 30: 472.

Kassala. (H. Martin) J. Mil. Serv. Inst. 24: 449. — Un. Serv. M. 18: 55.

" Katahdin," U. S. Ram, A Cruise on. (J. A. Guthrie) Strand, 16: 61.

Katcina Worship, Interpretation of. (J. W. Fewkes) J. Am. Folk-Lore, 14: 81.

Katharine de Valois, Remains of. Archæol. 46: 281.

Katherine, St. See Catherine.

Kate. (G. William) Lippinc. 63: 705.

Kate Everley's Pen; a story. (S. Doudney) Argosy, 64: 159.

Kate Keith. (Janie M. Clerk) Good Words, 38: 625.

Kate Petrie. (Mrs. W. H. Smith) Good Words, 39: 684.

Kate the Queen; a story. (A. Eyre) Eng. Illust. 17: 318.

Kathode Rays, Experiments with. (A. A. C. Swinton) Nature, 55: 568.

Katmu-Dogbahk War, The. (W. P. Drury) Un. Serv. M. 17: 665.

Katwijk, Holland. (W. E. Carlin) Outing, 38: 526.

Kaufmann, Angelica. (F. Miller) Eng. Illust. 19: 20.

Kaun, Hugo, with portrait. Music, 13: 748.

Kauri Gum. (C. Waterston) Longm. 35: 220.

Kavirondo. (C. W. Hobley) Geog. J. 12: 361.

Kean, Mr. and Mrs. Charles. (C. Morris) McClure, 17: 53.

" Kearsarge " and " Alabama," Naval Battle of. Idler, 13: 138.

Keary, Charles F. Acad. 57: 688.

Keats, Gwendoline, Author of " Life is Life." Acad. 55: 520.

— On Trial. Acad. 58: 63.

Keats, John. (A. Symons) Monthly R. 5, no. 1: 139.

— and his Editor. Acad. 60: 307.

— and Charles Lamb. (F. Harrison) Contemp. 76: 62. Same art. Ecl. M. 133: 494.

— First Books of. (L. S. Livingston) Bookman, 11: 131.

— Ode to the Memory of. (L. Mifflin) Bk. Buyer, 16: 301.

— Poetry of. (T. W. Hunt) Meth. R. 60: 432.

— — Forman's Edition. Ath. '98, 2: 351.

— Portrait of, from a Drawing by Joseph Severn. Bk. Buyer, 16: 296.

Kebeth the Aleut, Story of. (F. A. Vanderlip and H. Bolce) McClure, 17: 172.

Kedleston Hall. (G. Curzon) M. of Art, 21: 20.

Keeler, James Edward. (G. E. Hale) Science, n. s. 12: 353. — (W. W. Campbell) Pop. Sci. Mo. 68: 85. — (C. D. Perrine; J. A. Brashear) Pop. Astron. 8: 409, 476.

Keely, John W., Extraordinary Story of. Illus. (J. Moritzen) Cosmopol. 26: 633.

Keene, Charles, and Pretty Women. (Lewis Lusk) Art J. 53: 24.

— The Art of. (J. Pennell) Cent. 32: 823.

— Sketches by. Studio (Internat.) 15: 125.

— Social Pictorial Satire by. (G. Du Maurier) Harper, 96: 505.

— Work of. Spec. 80: 20.

— — Pennell's. Art J. 50: 39.

Keene, James P., with portrait. World's Work, 1: 997.

Keene, New Hampshire. (F. S. Fiske) New Eng. M. n. s. 17: 225.

Keeper of the Records, The Deputy. (N. D. Davis) Nation, 66: 299.

Keepers of the Lamp; a story. (A. T. Q. Couch) Pall Mall M. 21: 205.

Keeping up Appearances. Month, 89: 132.

Keewatin in Minnesota, Distribution of. (C. W. Hall) Science, n. s. 10: 107.

Keightley, S. R., with portrait. Bk. News, 15: 496.

Keith, James, Judge, with portrait. (Sallie E. M. Hardy) Green Bag, 10: 156.

Keith, James Francis Edward. Scot. R. 32: 316.

Kekulé, Friedrich August, Sketch of. Pop. Sci. Mo. 54: 401.

Kell, John McIntosh, Naval Career of. (J. R. Eggleston) Conserv. R. 4: 113.

Keller, Arthur L. (W. Patten) Bk. Buyer, 20: 450.

Keller, Helen, Endowment for. Critic, 30: 276.

Kelley, Ellsworth. Writer, 14: 59.

Kelmscott Manor, Holiday Visit to. Illus. Artist (N. Y.) 23: 94.

Kelmscott Press. Scot. R. 36: 19.

— and the New Printing. (A. L. Cotton) Contemp. 74: 221.

— Publications of, Bibliography of. (E. D. North) Bk. Buyer, 16: 423.

Kelvin, Lord. (A. Gray) Good Words, 41: 27. — With portrait. (J. D. Cormack) Cassier, 16: 3, 133. — — With portrait. (H. C. Marillier) Pall Mall M. 25: 237.

Kelvin's Laboratory in Univ. of Glasgow. (A. Gray) Nature, 55: 486.

Kemble, Frances Anne. (C. C. Harrison) Critic, 37: 520.

Kemp-Welch, Lucy, a Rising Artist. (Marion Hapworth Dixon) M. of Art, 23: 481.

Kempis, Thos. à. Imitation of Christ. (F. W. Farrar) Sund. M. 27: 802.

Kempley, near Ross, Paintings in the Church of. (J. T. Micklethwaite) Archæol. 46: 187.

Kendal, Mrs. Madge Robertson. Acad. 54: 334.

Keng-Hung Convention. (E. H. Parker) Asia. R. 25: 39.

Kenilworth, A Chapter from. (C. F. Yonge) Temp. Bar, 116: 272.

Kenilworth Castle, A Legend of. Argosy, 67: 291.

Kenmore and Taymouth Castle. (Hu. Macmillan) Art J. 51: 326.

Kennan, George, with portrait. (W. W. Ellsworth) Outl. 59: 275.

— Apprenticeship in Courage. (K. West) Atlan. 79: 717.

Kennedy, Sarah Beaumont, with portrait. Bk. News, 19: 784.

Kenosis, The. (W. Major) Meth. R. 59: 763. — (E. McChesney) Meth. R. 58: 96.

Kilmacolm, Scotland, and the Glencairns. Scot. R. 33: 52.

Kim; a novel. (R. Kipling) McClure, 16: 122 — 17: 567.

Kimball, Alonzo S. Science, n. s. 7: 54.

Kimball, Conrad B., Baritone Singer. Music, 16: 496.

Kimball, Francis H., Works of. (S. Montgomery) Archit. R. 7: 479.

Kimberley, Lord. Spec. 78: 115.

Kimberley, Cronje's Capture and the Relief of. (J. Barnes) Outl. 64: 953.

— In, during the Siege. Chamb. J. 77: 385.

— The March to. (J. Barnes) Outl. 65: 343.

— Siege of. Good Words, 41: 468, 539.

Kind Gray Day, The; a poem. (H. P. Kimball) Poet-Lore, 11: 356.

Kindergarten, The, and Higher Education. (N. C. Vandewalker) Educa. R. 16: 342.

— from a New-Church Standpoint. N. Church R. 4: 144.

— History of, in the U. S. (S. E. Blow) Outl. 55: 932.

— in America. Outl. 61: 954.

— — Some Defects of. (G. S. Hall) Forum, 28: 579.

— in Tokio, The Peeresses'. (N. A. Smith) Outl. 61: 329.

— Mistakes of. (F. H. Kasson) Educa. 19: 179.

— Musical Methods in. (C. Faelten) Music, 13: 435.

— Nature's. (F. Maccunn) Sund. M. 29: 756.

— New Gifts of. (M. M. Glidden) Educa. R. 14: 1.

— Reconstruction of. (F. Eby) Pedagog. Sem. 7: 229.

— Sociology of. (M. West) Outl. 65: 452.

— Some Criticisms of. (N. M. Butler) Educa. R. 18: 285.

Kindergarten Child, after the Kindergarten. (M. H. Carter) Atlan. 83: 358.

Kindergarten Story, Art in the. (A. K. Benedict) Outl. 66: 275.

Kindergarten Work in the Chicago Ghetto. (R. G. Frost) Outl. 66: 212.

Kindest-hearted of the Great, The. Liv. Age, 216: 633.

Kindliness as an Element of Faith. (Emily S. Hamblen) Poet-Lore, 10: 85.

Kindly Fruits of the Earth; a story. (E. Hope) Temp. Bar, 114: 571.

Kindness of Mrs. Rutherford; a story. (C. Angus) Eng. Illust. 20: 55.

Kindness to Animals; an Incident of '49. (J. H. Holmes) McClure, 10: 251.

Kinds that Cured. (W. L. Sawyer) Cent. 32: 722.

Kinetic Theory, Old and New. (G. H. Bryan) Nature, 61: 289.

Kinetography. (H. S. Ward) Knowl. 20: 216.

King, Basil. Writer, 14: 41.

King, Capt. Charles, the Novelist. (H. Austin) Nat'l M. (Bost.) 7: 157. — Lit. W. (Bost.) 29: 184.

King, Mrs. Hamilton. Acad. 52: 94.

King, James M. Facing the 20th Century. (J. F. Loughlin) Am. Cath. Q. 24, no. 4: 184.

King, Richard, of Scarborough, Maine. (L. L. Hight) New Eng. M. n. s. 20: 501.

King, William, Abp. of Dublin. Autobiography. Eng. Hist. R. 13: 309.

King, Yeend, Artist, with portrait. (F. Miller) Idler, 15: 287.

King, The; a poem. (R. Kipling) McClure, 14: 80.

King a-begging, The; a story. (R. Barr) McClure, 16: 305.

King against Trevor, The; a tale. (W. Richards) Argosy, 67: 212.

King Baulah, Story of. (C. C. Torrey) Open Court, 13: 559.

King Custom; a story. (M. S. Rawson) Harper, 103: 718.

King Fishing. (J. D. Peabody) Outing, 33: 497.

King Florus and the Fair Jehane. (R. Le Gallienne) Cosmopol. 31: 388.

King for a Day; a story. (W. A. Fraser) McClure, 10: 505.

King in the Golden Mask, The; a story. (M. Schwab) Indep. 53: 257.

King, The, in Jewish Post-exilian Writings. (C. H. Toy) J. Bib. Lit. 18: 156.

King McDougal's Kitten. (A. M. Roundy) Lippinc. 63: 843.

King Neptune's Toll. (J. Le Breton) Longm. 29: 372.

King of Bath, The; a story. Idler, 18: 424.

King of the Beasts. (E. P. Weaver) Good Words, 42: 475.

King of Beaver, The. (M. H. Catherwood) Harper, 96: 185.

King of the Sedangs, The. (H. Clifford) Macmil. 84: 230.

King Philip, Lobster; a story. (R. K. Munkittrick) Cosmopol. 31: 308.

King William; a story. (H. Godfrey) Pall Mall M. 14: 475.

King's Flagon, The; a poem. (F. Gadsby) Canad. M. 13: 70.

King's Friend, A; a story. (F. H. Melville) Eng. Illust. 20: 353.

King's Gambit, A. (E. E. Kellett) Chamb. J. 78: 746–761.

King's Gold, The; a story. (R. Barr) McClure, 17: 122. Same art. Idler, 19: 414.

King's Jackal, The. (R. H. Davis) Scrib. M. 23: 413 — 24: 80.

King's Love-letters, The. (R. Le Gallienne) Liv. Age, 229: 325.

King's Mirror; a story. (A. H. Hawkins) Munsey, 20: 563 — 22: 268.

King's Taster, The; a story. (P. Hart) Pall Mall M. 17: 498.

King's Test Declaration. (Sir G. S. Baker) 19th Cent. 49: 698.

King's Tintoretto, The. (A. R. Thomson) Chamb. J. 77: extr. no. 16.

King's Visit, The; a story. (R. Barr) McClure, 17: 534.

"Kingdom for Micajah, A;" a story. (V. F. Boyle) Harper, 100: 527.

Kingdom of God: a symposium. Bib. World, 12: 12.

— Future of. (R. A. Falconer) Expos. 6: 339.

— Weiss on. (L. A. Muirhead) Crit. R. 11: 243.

Kingdom of Matter. (M. Maeterlinck) Fortn. 74: 567.

Kingfisher, Photographing the. (G. S. Porter) Outing, 39: 198.

"Kingis Quair," Scribe of the. (G. Neilson) Ath. '99, 2: 835.

Kings and their Capitals. Spec. 87: 473.

— Divine Right of. (W. J. Brown) Westm. 147: 211.

— Insane. (F. L. Oswald) Lippinc. 67: 493.

Kings' River Cañon. (T. Magee) Overland, n. s. 29: 121.

Kingsbury, and Gage. (A. E. Gage) N. E. Reg. 54: 260.

Kingsford, William, Canadian Historian. (R. W. Shannon) Canad. M. 12: 191.

Kingship in the 19th Century. (C. B. Roylance Kent) Longm. 36: 436.

Kingsley, Charles. (R. R. Suffield) Library, 3: 77.

— as a Novelist. Acad. 57: 213.

— Recollections of. (F. Max Muller) Liv. Age, 212: 385.

Kingsley, Henry. Acad. 60: 309.

Kingsley, Mary H. (D. Kemp) Lond. Q. 94: 137. —
Ath. '00, 1: 750, 784. — Spec. 84: 836. — Geog. J.
16: 114. Same art. Liv. Age, 226: 198. — (L. T.
Smith and Mrs. Humphry Ward) Folk-Lore, 11:
348. — (L. T. Smith) Good Words, 42: 120.
— in West Africa. Lond. Q. 88: 296.
Kingston, Capital of Jamaica. (W. Thorp) Pall Mall
M. 20: 443.
— An Electric Tramway in. (H. Holgate) Cassier, 17:
74.
Kingsville Plan of Education. (E. Erf) Arena, 22: 61.
Kinney, Troy S., and Margaret West, Illustrators. (H.
Hyde) Brush & P. 9: 24.
Kinsmen. (M. Jokai) Liv. Age, 221: 66.
Kiōsai, Kawanabé; Japanese Artist. (W. Anderson)
Studio (Internat.) 6: 29.
Kipling, Rudyard. (C. D. Lanier) R. of Rs. (N. Y.)
15: 173. — (D. C. Murray) Canad. M. 8: 475. — (L.
R. Cautley) Conserv. R. 5: 78. — (R. Bridges) Outl.
61: 281, 490. — (C. E. Norton) McClure, 13: 282. —
(N. Munro) Bookman, 9: 258. — (N. Munro) Good
Words, 40: 261. — Liv. Age, 220: 786. — With
portrait. (W. Packard) Nat'l M. (Bost.) 10: 77.
— The Absent-minded Beggar. (R. Le Gallienne) Idler,
17: 77.
— and Chaucer. Atlan. 84: 714.
— and his Writings. (C. E. Russell) Cosmopol. 31:
653.
— and the Racial Instinct. (H. R. Marshall) Cent. 36:
375.
— as Artist. Critic, 33: 473.
— as Moralist. Critic, 33: 360.
— as a Poet. (F. G. Gilman) Arena, 20: 312.
— as a Poet of Patriotism. Outl. 64: 18.
— Blind Bug. Acad. 54: 156.
— Books of, in Sunday Schools. Lit. W. (Bost.) 30:
298.
— The Case of. Sat. R. 87: 776. Same art. Liv. Age,
222: 322. Same art. Ecl. M. 133: 447.
— Comparative Psychologist. Atlan. 81: 858.
— Contributions to a Critique of. (F. Gratz) Ecl. M.
132: 641. Same art. Liv. Age, 221: 139.
— The Cult of. Month, 95: 28.
— Day's Work. (F. C. Mortimer) Bk. Buyer, 17: 298.
— (H. T. Peck) Bookman, 8: 350. — Acad. 55: 76. —
Macmil. 79: 131. — Spec. 81: 526.
— Early Poems of. Acad. 51: 476.
— First Books of. (L. S. Livingston) Bookman, 10:
329.
— From Sea to Sea. (L. S. Livingston) Bookman, 9:
429.
— from a Soldier's Point of View. (P. C. W. Trever)
Idler, 14: 136.
— The God of. Outl. 64: 372.
— his View of Americans. (G. H. McKnight) Book-
man, 7: 131.
— Hysteria over. (H. Austin) Dial (Ch.) 26: 327.
— in America. R. of Rs. (N. Y.) 19: 419.
— A Japanese View of. (A. Kinnosuké) Arena, 21:
699.
— Kim. Acad. 61: 289. — (J. D. Adams) Bk. Buyer,
23: 232.
— Madness of. Macmil. Same art. Liv. Age, 220: 91.
Same art. Ecl. M. 132: 253.
— Men of. (A. B. Maurice) Bookman, 8: 348.
— Poetry of. (E. Dowden) Critic, 38: 219. — Lond. Q.
89: 325. — (C. E. Norton) Atlan. 79: 111.
— Prose Writings. Scot. R. 34: 291.
— Recessional. (A. W. Rollins) Critic, 30: 115. — Mc-
Clure, 9: 1104. — Spec. 79: 106.
— Religion of. (H. F. Ward) Meth. R. 60: 262. — (W.
B. Parker) New World, 7: 662. — (J. T. Sunder-
land) New Eng. M. n. s. 20: 604.

Kipling, Rudyard. "Rudyard," a Humorous Poem on
Kipling's Verse. (W. A. Gorham) Midland, 11:
223.
— The Seven Seas. (W. D. Howells) McClure, 8: 453.
— (J. O. Miller) Canad. M. 8: 456.
— — and the Rubáiyát. (P. E. More) Atlan. 84: 800.
— — an Atavism. (C. Porter) Poet-Lore, 9: 291.
— Stalky & Co. (R. Le Gallienne) Idler, 16: 545. —
Acad. 57: 421.
— Suppressed Works of. (L. S. Livingston) Bookman,
9: 62.
— Theology of. Outl. 64: 692.
— Truce of the Bear. Critic, 33: 502. — (R. Ogden)
Nation, 67: 292.
— Verse-people of. (A. B. Maurice) Bookman, 9: 57.
— Voice of "The Hooligan." (R. Buchanan) Con-
temp. 76: 774.
— — Is it the Voice of the Hooligan ? (Sir W. Besant)
Contemp. 76: 27. Same art. Liv. Age, 224: 401.
— Women of. (A. B. Maurice) Bookman, 8: 479.
— Works. (E. E. Hale, jr.) Dial (Ch.) 23: 42. —
Ed. R. 187: 203. Same art. Liv. Age, 216: 691. —
Blackw. 164: 470. Same art. Ecl. M. 131: 673.
Kipling Family, Reminiscences of. (M. Benson) Sund.
M. 28: 822.
Kips ; a story. (Parma Gentry) Nat'l M. (Bost.) 9: 37.
Kirby Gate. Spec. 87: 694.
"Kirishima-san." (Onoto Watanna) Idler, 20: 315.
Kirkpatrick, Richard Trench. Geog. M. 13: 204.
Kirtland vs. Hotchkiss, Case of. (D. A. Wells) Pop.
Sci. Mo. 52: 798.
Kismet ; a story. (L. M. Montgomery) Canad. M. 13:
228.
Kissane, William. McClure, 8: 236.
Kisses ; a poem. (C. H. Page) Cosmopol. 22: 675.
Kissing, Causes of the Hobson. (C. Lombroso) Pall
Mall M. 18: 544.
"Kissing Bugs," Spider Bites and. (L. O. Howard)
Pop. Sci. Mo. 56: 31.
Kissing Kitty ; a story. Argosy, 64: 735.
Kissingen. (C. W. Wood) Argosy, 67: 67, 173, 209, 411.
Kistoæns found in Stewartry of Kirkcudbright. (F.
R. Coles) Reliquary, 37: 1.
Kitchen, Model Science in the. (Anna Leach) Cosmo-
pol. 27: 95.
Kitchen-garden, The. (L. Winnington) Outl. 68: 52.
Kitchener, Lord, of Khartoum. Outl. 61: 273.
— and Khartoum. (A. Griffiths) Fortn. 70: 450.
— the Man with a Task. (J. Barnes) World's Work,
1: 404.
— Methods of. (R. H. Davis) Indep. 53: 326.
— A Story of. (C. L. Shaw) Canad. M. 12: 392.
Kitchi-Gami, Around. (E. Cumings) Music, 18: 530.
Kite as an Instrument of Meteorological Research. (C.
F. Marvin) J. Frankl. Inst. 148: 241.
Kite-flying in 1897. (G. J. Varney) Pop. Sci. Mo. 53:
48.
— Scientific, Woglom on. Spec. 78: 576.
Kites at Sea, Meteorological Observations with. (A. L.
Rotch) Science, n. s. 14: 896.
— Experiments with. (H. D. Wise) Cent. 32: 78.
— Franklin's Kite Experiment with Modern Appara-
tus. (A. McAdie) Pop. Sci. Mo. 51: 739.
— in Meteorology. (A. L. Rotch) Science, n. s. 14: 412.
— in War and Peace. (G. E. Walsh) Chaut. 29: 582.
— Modern Kite and the Government Experiments. (H.
C. Hunter) Outing, 30: 43.
— Photographing from. (W. A. Eddy) Cent. 32: 86.
— Scientific Kite-flying. (J. B. Millet) Cent. 32: 66.
— Tailless, How made. (M. N. Briggs) Outl. 58: 1026.
— their Theory and Practice. (B. F. S. Baden-Powell)
J. Soc. Arts, 46: 359.
— War-. (B. F. S. Baden-Powell) McClure, 12: 543.

Kites, Work with, of the United States Weather Bureau. (H. C. Frankenfield) Nature, 63: 108. — (H. C. Frankenfield) Nat. Geog. M. 11: 55.

Kittery, Remonstrance of Freeholders of, to the General Court, 1784. N. E. Reg. 54: 444.
— Tax Lists, 1756, 1758, and 1770. N. E. Reg. 55: 249.

Kitton, Frederic G., Author and Artist. (A. H. Garland) Bk. Buyer, 18: 109.

Kittredge, Walter. (G. H. Gerould) New Eng. M. n. s. 20: 723.

Kitty: Duchess and Madcap. (Sheila E. Braine) Good Words, 41: 350.

Kleinenberg, Nicolaus, Obituary of. (A. Willey) Nat. Sci. 12: 133.

Klepplestone Collection of Pictures, The. Illus. Good Words, 38: 166, 254.

Klindworth, Karl, Musician, with portrait. Music, 15: 88.

Klinger, Max. (H. W. Singer) Studio (Lond.) 5: 43.
— and Griffelkunst. Sat. R. 85: 459.

Klinglets of Alaska. (E. Odlum) Chaut. 25: 627.

Klondike, The. Lond. Q. 90: 79. — (J. G. Smith) Canad. M. 10: 322. — (A. A. Hill) Munsey, 20: 704.
— Adventures at. (T. C. Down) Fortn. 70: 745. Same art. Ecl. M. 131: 806.
— Alaska and the. (A. Heilprin) Pop. Sci. Mo. 55: 1, 163. — (W. H. Dall) Forum, 24: 16.
— All-American Route to. (E. Gillette) Cent. 38: 149.
— and Climatic Reflections. (F. L. Oswald) Lippinc. 61: 846.
— and the Cost of Production of Gold. Bank. M. (Lond.) 66: 583.
— and its Gold Mines. (Katherine Sleeper) Nat'l M. (Bost.) 6: 551.
— and Some Experiences in the Chilkoot Pass. (T. S. Scott) Canad. M. 10: 329.
— and the Yukon Valley. (H. B. Goodrich) Engin. M. 13: 941.
— Building a Railroad into. (C. Warman) McClure, 14: 419.
— Dawson City as it is. (H. J. Woodside) Canad. M. 17: 403.
— Economics of. (J. London) R. of Rs. (N. Y.) 21: 70.
— Exploring a Gold Country. (A. Williams) Engin. M. 14: 70.
— Fourth of July in. (L. R. Clements) Nat'l M. (Bost.) 10: 339.
— From the Coast to. (E. Spurr) Outing, 30: 521.
— Gate of. (A. A. Hill) Munsey, 22: 401.
— Geology of. (A. Heilprin) Pop. Sci. Mo. 55: 300.
— Gold Fields of. (W. H. Merritt) J. Soc. Arts, 46: 649. — (M. S. Wade) Fortn. 68: 464. — (H. De Windt) Contemp. 72: 305. — (Robert Oglesby) Cosmopol. 23: 523. — Spec. 79: 134. — (C. C. Adams) Chaut. 26: 54.
— — and Routes to them. (H. Garland) Idler, 13: 529, 766.
— — Best Route to. Overland, n. s. 31: 577.
— Gold-mining at. (T. C. Down) Cornh. 77: 347. Same art. Ecl. M. 130: 537.
— Government and Society in. (F. Palmer) Forum, 26: 603.
— How to Reach. (W. A. Baillie-Grohman) Eng. Illust. 18: 483.
— Impressions of. (C. C. Osborne) Macmil. 82: 347, 442. 83: 43, 143.
— Life in. (J. L. Steffens) McClure, 9: 956.
— Mining in. (G. Chapman) Overland, n. s. 30: 262.
— The New Arctic El Dorado. (H. W. Lanier) Chaut. 27: 168. — (W. G. Fitzgerald) Strand, 14: 419. — Liv. Age, 214: 620.
— Outfitting for. (L. W. Buckley) Overland, n. s. 31: 171.

Klondike, The, Overland Route to. Illus. (H. Garland) Nat. Geog. M. 9: 113.
— Pilgrimage to the Gold-fields and its Outcome. (F. Palmer) Forum, 26: 45.
— Pioneering in. (A. Macdonald) Blackw. 165: 781, 986. 166: 71.
— Placers of. (T. K. Rose) Nature, 56: 615.
— Railroads in. (H. Emerson) Engin. M. 17: 750. — (W. M. Sheffield) Cosmopol. 27: 76.
— The Real. (J. S. Easby-Smith) Cosmopol. 24: 227.
— Reindeer for. Spec. 80: 113.
— River Trip to. (J. S. Webb) Cent. 33: 672.
— Romance of. (C. Pullen) Cosmopol. 25: 417.
— Routes to. (H. Garland) McClure, 10: 443.
— The Rush to. (T. C. Down) Cornh. 77: 31. Same art. Ecl. M. 130: 267. — (S. S. Bush) R. of Rs. (N. Y.) 17: 289. — (E. S. Curtis) Cent. 33: 692. Same art. Ecl. M. 130: 114. — (A. C. Coolidge) Nation, 65: 125.
— Stampedes on. (Joaquin Miller) Overland, n. s. 30: 519.
— A Study in Booms. (E. E. Williams) National, 33: 934. Same art. Liv. Age, 222: 823.
— To. (T. C. Down) Cornh. 76: 769.
— — by River and Lake. (T. Magee) Overland, n. s. 31: 66.
— Travel in. (R. Pocock) Idler, 14: 766.
— Two Women in. Critic, 34: 424.
— A Winter Journey to, with a Glimpse of the Mines. (F. Palmer) Scrib. M. 25: 465.
— Woman's Trip to. (E. L. Kelly) Lippinc. 68: 625.
— A Year's Progress in. (A. Heilprin) Pop. Sci. Mo. 56: 455.
    See Yukon.

Klondike Assay Office. (G. E. Adams) Cosmopol. 28: 425.

Klopstock, Frederic Gottlieb. (A. J. Gordon) Belgra. 98: 486.

Klum, Hermann, Pianist, with portrait. Music, 18: 469.

Klumpke, Anna and Dorothea. (B. Van Vorst) Critic, 37: 224.

Knapsack, The. (W. Quinton) J. Mil. Serv. Inst. 14: 57.
— and the Army Shoe. (W. E. Dougherty) J. Mil. Serv. Inst. 14: 494.

Knaresborough, Yorkshire, England. (J. S. Fletcher) Idler, 13: 317.

Knave of Conscience; a story. (F. Lynde) Nat'l M. (Bost.) 11: 378–735. 12: 17–547. 13: 37–124.

Kneisel String Quartet, of Boston. Music, 13: 64.

Kneller, Sir Godfrey. Munsey, 17: 542.

Knies, Karl. (G. Cohn) Econ. J. 9: 489.

"Knife, Big," "Great," and "Long." (Albert Matthews) Nation, 72: 213.
— How it is made. (G. R. Fleming) Good Words, 38: 557.

Knight, Buxton. Paintings. Sat. R. 88: 99.

Knight, Chas. Parsons. Ath. '97, 1: 156.

Knight, Daniel Ridgway, Painter, with portrait. (H. T. Lawrence) Brush & P. 7: 193.

Knight, George. A Son of Austerity. Acad. 59: 283.

Knight, A; a story. (J. Sinjohn) Argosy, 73: 195, 332. 74: 81.

Knight of the Golden Spur, A; a story. (Lillian M. Baugh) Music, 16: 349.

Knight of the Highway. (C. Scollard) Lippinc. 68: 259.

Knight of Philadelphia. (J. A. Altsheler) Lippinc. 30: 435.

Knight of the Wheel; a story. (W. Bates) Nat'l M. (Bost.) 6: 131.

Knight-Darwin Law. (F. Darwin) Nature, 58: 630.

Knight Errant, A; a story. (J. W. Weigal) Idler, 15: 191.

Knighted, How I was. (R. Tangye) Chamb. J. 54: 305.

Knighthood, Cheapness of Modern. (M. Beerbohm) Sat. R. 83: 683.

Knighthood of Tony, The; a story. (Myrtle Reed) Nat'l. M. (Bost.) 6: 336.

Knights Hospitallers Past and Present. Chamb. J. 76: 782.

Knights of Eldorado. (D. L. Johnstone) Chamb. J. 78: supp. 6.

Knights of the Garter, Early Stall-plates of the. (W. H. St. John Hope) Archæol. 51: 399.

Knights of St. John. Temp. Bar, 117: 270.

Knights Templars in Scotland. (R. Aitken) Scot. R. 32: 1.

— Soldiers, Monks, Heretics. Ed. R. 192: 45.

Knights Templars' Chapel at Garway. Reliquary, 39: 193.

Knightsbridge International Art Exhibition, 1898. (T. Dartmouth) Art J. 50: 249.

— 1899. (R. A. M. Stevenson) Art J. 51: 201.

Knoblauch, Edward G. Club Baby. (G. B. Shaw) Sat. R. 85: 616.

Knocking at the Door, The; a story. (C. K. Burrow) Pall Mall M. 21: 65.

Knots and Threads. Chamb. J. 74: 298.

Knower, The, in Psychology. (G. S. Fullerton) Psychol. R. 4: 1.

Knowledge and Practice. (C. S. Minot) Science, n. s. 10: 1.

— and Theism, Theory of. (G. A. Coe) Meth. R. 58: 68.

— Belief and Certitude. (F. S. Turner) Science, n. s. 13: 422.

— — F. S. Turner on. (J. Iverach) Crit. R. 11: 104.

— Foundations of. (T. O. McCosh) Science, n. s. 13: 182.

— — Ormond on. (H. C. Minton) Presb. & Ref. R. 12: 338.

— from the Standpoint of Association. (T. L. Bolton and E. M. Haskell) Educa. R. 15: 474.

— The Goal of. (J. H. Muirhead) Mind, 22: 476.

— Hobhouse on. (F. C. Sharp) Dial (Ch.) 23: 215.

— Mivart's Ground-work of Science. (J. E. Creighton) Science, n. s. 9: 147.

— A Plea for. (M. Creighton) Contemp. 79: 502. Same art. Liv. Age, 229: 529.

— Philosophy of, Ladd's. (H. Grenfell) Citizen, 3: 211. — (H. C. Minton) Presb. & Ref. R. 9: 721.

— Psycho-physiological Theory of, Ziehen on. (E. F. Buchner) Psychol. R. 6: 432.

— Sense-, and Spirit-. (W. E. Fischer) Luth. Q. 29: 390.

— Sorrow of. Outl. 61: 347.

— Stages of. (A. H. Lloyd) Psychol. R. 4: 164.

— The Utilitarian Estimate. (J. Seth) Philos. R. 10: 341.

Knowledge-making, Utility of, as a Means of Liberal Training. (J. G. Macgregor) Nature, 61: 159.

Knowles, Frederic Lawrence. Writer, 14: 8.

Know-nothing Party in Maryland, History of. (L. F. Schmeckebier) J. H. Univ. Stud. 17: 147.

— Success of, in Massachusetts, Causes of. (G. H. Haynes) Am. Hist. R. 3: 67.

Know-nothing Legislature, 1854. (G. H. Haynes) New Eng. M. n. s. 16: 21.

Knox, Frank. Bank. M. (N. Y.) 63: 757.

Knox, Henry M. Bank. M. (N. Y.) 56: 569.

Knox, John, Services to Education. (M. S. Kistler) Educa. 19: 105.

Knox, Philander C., Attorney-General, with portrait. Green Bag, 13: 281.

Koch, Robert, and his Work, with portrait. (H. M. Biggs) R. of Rs. (N. Y.) 24: 324.

Koehler, Robert, Painter, with portrait. (C. Whitcomb) Brush & P. 9: 144.

Koelliker, Albert von. (W. F. R. Weldon) Nature, 58: 1.

Koenenia, Texan. (A. Rucker) Am. Natural. 35: 615.

Koenig, Rudolph. (S. P. Thompson) Nature, 64: 630. — (W. L. Stevens) Science, n. s. 14: 724.

Königsmark Question, Present Status of. (E. F. Henderson) Am. Hist. R. 3: 464.

Koerner, Theodor, Romance of. (E. H. Nason) Cosmopol. 24: 602.

Kohinoor, The; Was it Babar's Diamond? (H. Beveridge) Asia. R. 27: 370.

— Tragedies of the. (Caroline Brown) Cosmopol. 26: 51.

Kohlsaat, Hermann H., of Chicago, his Part in the Political History-making of 1896. (W. Wellman) R. of Rs. (N. Y.) 15: 41.

Koiné, Source of the So-called Achæan-Doric. (C. D. Buck) Am. Anthrop. 21: 193.

Kooswap; a tale. (F. Leather) Outing, 38: 40.

Kootenay Group-drawings. (A. F. Chamberlain) Am. Anthrop. 3: 248.

Kootenays, The Golden, in 1898. Chamb. J. 75: 419.

Koran, Rhyme and Rhythm in the. (D. J. Rankin) Open Court, 14: 355. — (W. F. Warren) Open Court, 13: 641.

Korea. (E. H. Parker) Fortn. 69: 224. — (E. Cazalet) Econ. J. 11: 431. — (H. B. Hulbert) Indep. 51: 1220.

— and her Neighbors, Mrs. Bishop on. Bk. Buyer, 16: 461. — (H. R. Mill) Nature, 57: 512. — Ath. '98, 1: 77.

— and its People. (R. B. Peery) Midland, 11: 224. — (H. B. Hulbert) Forum, 27: 217.

— and the Koreans. Scot. R. 31: 217.

— Capping Ceremony of. (E. B. Landis) Anthrop. J. 27: 525.

— Changes in the Unchanging East. Quar. 187: 546.

— Clan Organization in. (W. Hough) Am. Anthrop. 1: 150.

— Enfranchisement of. (H. B. Hulbert) No. Am. 166: 708.

— An Eye Witness on. Lond. Q. 90: 157.

— from the Japanese Standpoint. (H. N. G. Bushby) 19th Cent. 49: 834.

— Hermit Nation. (H. Webster) Nat. Geog. M. 11: 144.

— Independence of, A Pioneer of. (E. B. Landis) Asia. R. 26: 396.

— Nursery Rhymes of. (A. T. Smith) Am. J. Folk-Lore, 10: 181.

— The Pearl of the Orient. (C. M. Salwey) Asia. R. 30: 154.

— Queen of, Funeral of. (J. W. Hardwick) Chaut. 27: 633.

— Rhymes of the Children of. (E. B. Landis) J. Am. Folk-Lore, 11: 203.

— Russia in. Sat. R. 85: 548.

— Trolley Road in. (H. B. Smith) Outl. 68: 215.

— Unconscious. (J. S. Gale) Outl. 68: 494.

— under the Russians. (C. S. Addis) Un. Serv. M. 15: 232.

— Visit to, in 1899. (H. F. M. Lewis) Canad. M. 16: 491.

— War-cloud in the Farthest East. (H. S. Hallett) 19th Cent. 46: 988.

Korean Beliefs. (J. S. Gale) Folk-Lore, 11: 325.

Korean Interviews. (E. S. Morse) Pop. Sci. Mo. 51: 1.

Korean Inventions. (H. B. Hulbert) Harper, 99: 102.

Korean Question, The. (R. J. Byford Mair) Un. Serv. M. 21: 280.

הרייזידהו and קיישי. (R. J. H. Gottheil) J. Bib. Lit. 17: 199.

Korolenko, Vladimir Galaktionovitch. (J. Mackenzie) Gent. M. n. s. 64: 340.

Lace-making among the Indians. (J. W. Guthrie) Outl. **66**: 59.
— in Belgium. (E. F. Johnson-Browne) Cath. World, **71**: 443.
Laces, Italian, Old and New. (A. Sterling) Chaut. **34**: 16.
— Nottingham, W. S. Elliott's Designs. Artist (N. Y.) **26**: 99.
— Venice, Making of. (A. Sterling) Chaut. **34**: 243.
Lacedæmon, In Low-lying. (J. I. Manatt) Indep. **52**: 1373.
Lacey, Brig.-Gen. John, Memoirs of. Pennsyl. M. **25**: 1, 191, 341.
La Chalmelle, France, Municipal Agricultural Colony at. Ann. Am. Acad. Pol. Sci. **16**: 165.
La Chapelle, France. (C. Johnson) New Eng. M. **23**: 37.
Lacock Abbey. (A. H. Diplock) Gent. M. n. s. **65**: 434.
— (H. Brakspear) Archæol. **57**: 125.
Lacordaire and Lamennais. (R. Parsons) Am. Cath. Q. **22**: 256.
Lacquered Furniture at Buckingham Palace. (F. S. Robinson) M. of Art, **25**: 9.
Lad in Homespun, A; a story. (E. C. McCants) Nat'l M. (Bost.) **12**: 46.
Lad of Mettle, A; a story. (T. McEwen) Sund. M. **29**: 455.
Ladd, G. T., Dualism of. (J. W. Powell) Monist, **10**: 383.
— Philosophy of Knowledge. (J. Lindsay) Crit. R. **8**: 83.
"Ladies and Gentlemen." (B. Bosanquet) Internat. J. Ethics, **10**: 317.
Ladies, Poor, How are they to Live? Spec. **78**: 333.
Lady and the Highwayman, The. (B. Ellis) Pall Mall M. **21**: 187.
Lady and the Parson. (S. N. Robins) Atlan. **79**: 502.
Lady Asenath in the Witness-box. (B. Thomson) New R. **16**: 513.
Lady Barbarity; a romantic comedy. (J. C. Snaith) Eng. Illust. **20**: 227, 653. **21**: 89, 193, 617.
Lady Brockden's Niece; a story. (A. G. Hopkins) Belgra. **92**: 97.
"Lady Fast" Wheel. (H. J. Feasey) Antiq. n. s. **33**: 248.
Lady General, A; a story. (E. Stuart) Sund. M. **26**: 726.
Lady Griselda's Dream. (M. Morris) Longm. **32**: 145.
Lady Gwendolen's Episode; a story. (R. Barr) Canad. M. **14**: 513.
Lady Haversham's Butler; a story. (P. B. Jones) Belgra. **93**: 320.
Lady in the Box, The; a story. (C. Ross) McClure, **8**: 431.
Lady in the Box; a story. (F. R. Stockton) Cosmopol. **27**: 625.
Lady-killer, The; a story. (H. M. Robins) Argosy, **69**: 215.
"Lady Macquarie," The; a story. (J. A. Barry) Cornh. **79**: 522.
Lady Mary's Mistake; a story. (M. Maartens) Cosmopol. **27**: 595.
Lady of the Barge, The; a story. (W. W. Jacobs) Harper, **101**: 424.
Lady of the Garden, The; a story. (A. Duer) Harper, **99**: 341.
Lady of La Jeunesse. (O'N. Latham) Cosmopol. **29**: 313.
Lady of Lisle, The; a tale. (A. Dawson) Argosy, **71**: 111.
Lady of the Pistols, The; a story. (H. A. Hinkson) Idler, **15**: 808.
Lady of Quality, A. (H. B. Fuller) Liv. Age, **228**: 328.

Lady of the Ship; a story. (A. T. Quiller-Couch) Cosmopol. **28**: 331.
Lady of Tantivy, The; a story. (R. M. Gilbert) Temp. Bar, **113**: 119.
Lady on the Hillside; a story. (M. E. Coleridge) Cornh. **77**: 769.
Lady Patentee, A; a story. (D. W. Smith) Belgra. **98**: 63.
Lady Stalland's Diamond. (W. E. Cule) Chamb. J. **75**: 769–825. Same art. Liv. Age, **220**: 38–302.
Lady Sylvia; a story. (H. B. M. Watson) Pall Mall M. **24**: 515.
Lady Tantivy, The; a story. (R. M. Gilbert) Temp. Bar, **113**: 119.
Lady with the Waterfall, The; a story. (A. Fitch) McClure, **15**: 526.
Lady Wivenhoe's Diamonds; a story. (E. Noble) Idler, **14**: 537.
Lady's Magazine, 1813. (Mary Geoghegan) Idler, **13**: 142.
Ladysmith after the Siege. (H. B. Smith) National, **35**: 416. Same art. Ecl. M. **135**: 94. Same art. Liv. Age, **225**: 537.
— Diary of a Boer before. Blackw. **167**: 700. Same art. Liv. Age, **225**: 688.
— In, during the Siege. (G. W. Steevens) Liv. Age, **225**: 61.
— Relief of. (R. H. Davis) Scrib. M. **28**: 39.
— Siege of. (W. T. Maud) J. Soc. Arts, **49**: 57. — (H. H. Balfour) Temp. Bar, **122**: 26.
Ladysmith Relief Column. Un. Serv. M. **21**: 257.
LaFarge, John. (Russell Sturgis) Scrib. M. **26**: 1.
LaFarge, Mme. Marie F. C., Strange Story of. (A. H. Millar) Cornh. **77**: 95. Same art. Ecl. M. **130**: 682.
— Trial of. (S. J. James) Argosy, **64**: 624.
Lafayette, Adrienne, Wife of the Marquis. (L. W. Reilly) Cath. World, **68**: 608.
LaFayette, Marie Louise de. Month, **98**: 285, 364, 590.
Lafayette, Marquis de, and President Monroe. (Murat Halstead) Cosmopol. **23**: 681.
— Charavay's. (A. Laugel) Nation, **66**: 203, 221, 261.
Lafayette Monument, Paris, 1900. (J. M. Chapple) Nat'l M. (Bost.) **9**: 195.
Lafayette Monument Scandal, The. Bookman, **10**: 150.
Lafayettes, Household of the, E. Sichel on. (E. I. Stevenson) Bk. Buyer, **17**: 140.
La Ferronays, Count de. (A. Laugel) Nation, **70**: 474.
La Ferronays, Mme. de, Memoirs of. (A. Laugel) Nation, **69**: 149, 167, 186.
La Forgue, Jules. Works. (Arthur Symons) Sat. R. **86**: 305.
LaFontaine, Jean. (J. A. Harrison) Sewanee, **2**: 282.
Lagoon, The; a story. (J. Conrad) Cornh. **75**: 59.
Laguna, Daniel Israel Lopez. (M. Kayserling) Jew. Q. **12**: 708.
Lahmids, Dynasty of, in Hira. (G. G. Cameron) Crit. R. **11**: 237.
Laing, Frank, Etchings of Edinburgh. (D. S. Meldrum) M. of Art, **24**: 348.
Laird, William, with portrait. Cassier, **12**: 234.
Laird's Luck, The; a story. (A. T. Quiller-Couch) Pall Mall M. **23**: 373, 475.
Laisikawai; a Hawaiian Legend. (J. Rae) J. Am. Folk-Lore, **13**: 241.
Lake, Dr., at Balliol. (L. A. Tollmache) Spec. **80**: 14.
Lake of Gaube, The; a poem. (A. C. Swinburne) Bookman, **10**: 248.
Lake of the Mournful Cry, The. (A. G. Bradley) Macmil. **80**: 259.

Lake of the Woods, Macmillan's Observations on Distribution of Plants along Shore of. (R. Pound; F. E. Clements) Am. Natural. **31**: 980.

Lake District, English, Mountains of. (C. Edwards) Gent. M. n. s. **60**: 30. Same art. Liv. Age, **216**: 672.

— Old-fashioned Contrivances in. Reliquary, **38**: 15.

Lake-dwellers. (A. Jessopp) 19th Cent. **48**: 743. Same art. Liv. Age, **228**: 567.

Lake Dwellings on the Banks of the Costa, near Pickering, Yorkshire. (C. Duncombe) Anthrop. J. **28**: 150.

Lakes and Inland Seas, Undulations in, due to Wind and Atmospheric Pressure. (W. H. Wheeler) Nature, **57**: 321.

— Classification of, according to Temperature. (G. C. Whipple) Am. Natural. **32**: 25.

— English. (J. Shaylor) Idler, **13**: 793.

— — Literary Associations of. (J. C. Hadden) Argosy, **70**: 379.

— — Minor. Spec. **87**: 655.

— — Nights in Lakeland. (W. T. Palmer) Gent. M. n. s. **65**: 357.

— — Stories of. (L. W. Smith) Dial (Ch.) **31**: 440.

— Forel on Limnology. (H. R. Mill) Geog. J. **17**: 296.

— Great, of America. (E. S. Roscoe; H. Clergue) Temp. Bar, **121**: 92.

— — and the Modern Navy. (J. H. Gibbons) No. Am. **166**: 437.

— — and our Commercial Supremacy. (J. Foord) No. Am. **167**: 155.

— — Art-gallery of. Illus. (C. W. Stoddard) Cosmopol. **27**: 489.

— — Carrying Trade of. (A. Hendricks) No. Am. **166**: 716.

— — Changes in Level of. Am. Arch. **66**: 46. **69**: 36.

— — Commerce on. (J. Birkinbine) Cassier, **11**: 487.

— — Control of the Levels of. (W. A. Jones) Engin. M. **13**: 217.

— — Empire by the. (F. C. Howe) World's Work, **1**: 408.

— — Marine Mail Service on. (E. J. Peck) Nat'l M. (Bost.) **5**: 328.

— — Neutrality of, and Anglo-American Relations. (J. M. Callahan) J. H. Univ. Stud. **16**: 1–4.

— — On the. (F. W. Fitzpatrick) Cosmopol. **25**: 3.

— — Origin of. (J. E. Marr) Sci. Prog. n. s. **1**: 218.

— — Shipbuilding and Transportation on. (J. R. Oldham) Cassier, **12**: 499.

— — Shipping and Casualties on. (G. E. Walsh) Cassier, **15**: 499.

— — Shipping on. (F. W. Fitzpatrick) Midland, **8**: 48.

— — A Trip on. (C. H. Williams) Blackw. **169**: 49.

— of New England, Natural History of. (C. L. Whittle) New Eng. M. n. s. **16**: 605.

Lakeview Shooting and Fishing Association, Kansas. (C. H. Morton) Outing, **38**: 447.

Lalique, Rene, and his Goldsmith's Work. (H. Frantz) M. of Art, **21**: 270.

Lally Tollendal, Thomas Arthur, Comte de. (F. Dixon) Temp. Bar, **113**: 25.

Lalo, Edouard. Le Roi d'Ys. (J. F. Runciman) Sat. R. **92**: 74.

Lamarck, J. B., and Neo-Lamarckianism. (A. S. Packard) Open Court, **11**: 70.

— Views of, on the Evolution of Man, Morals, and Relation of Science to Religion. (A. S. Packard) Monist, **11**: 30.

Lamb, Charles. Quar. **192**: 312. — With portrait. Acad. **51**: 208.

Lamb, Charles, and John Keats. (F. Harrison) Contemp. **76**: 62. Same art. Ecl. M. **133**: 494. Same art. Liv. Age, **222**: 478.

— and the Law. Green Bag, **11**: 156.

— and Lloyd, R., Unpublished Letters. (E. V. Lucas) Cornh. **77**: 595, 734. Same art. Lippinc. **61**: 721, 873.

— and the Lloyds, Lucas's. (E. M. Colie) Bookman, **9**: 251.

— A Literary Curiosity from his Library. (L. S. Livingston) Bookman, **8**: 453.

— of the India House. Macmil. **75**: 192. Same art. Liv. Age, **212**: 333.

— Two Notes on. (E. V. Lucas) Fortn. **75**: 643.

— An Unpublished Letter of. Acad. **57**: 373.

— Where he still Lives. (A. Leach) Munsey, **17**: 569.

Lamb, The. Temp. Bar, **122**: 328. Same art. Ecl. M. **136**: 742. Same art. Liv. Age, **229**: 112.

Lamballe, Princesse de. Church Q. **46**: 409.

Lambeth Conference, 1897. Church Q. **45**: 190. — Spec. **79**: 41.

— and the Historic Episcopate. (V. Bartlet) Contemp. **72**: 68.

— Encyclical of. Spec. **79**: 173.

Lambeth Decisions, Canon MacColl on the. Church Q. **51**: 398.

Lambeth Encyclical, The. Month, **90**: 265.

Lambeth Palace. (F. Watt) Art J. **52**: 373.

Lame Boy, The. (W. Payne) Atlan. **84**: 121.

Lame Coyote's Lone War; a story. (C. Michelson) Cosmopol. **30**: 631.

Lame Lizbeth; a story. (T. W. Speight) Argosy, **65**: 345.

Lame Priest, The. (S. Carleton) Atlan. **88**: 760.

Lamennais, H. F. R. de. Quar. **185**: 447. — (J. J. O'Shea) Cath. World, **64**: 634. — (G. Tyrrell) Month, **89**: 19. — (W. S. Lilly) Fortn. **72**: 73. Same art. Liv. Age, **222**: 702.

— Lacordaire and. (R. Parsons) Am. Cath. Q. **22**: 256.

Lament; a poem. (L. Binyon) Ecl. M. **133**: 105.

Lamentation; a poem. (W. Watson) Ecl. M. **137**: 69.

Lamond, Frederic. Sat. R. **83**: 86.

La Motthe, Jacques de, Petition of. (L. M. Friedman) Green Bag, **13**: 396.

Lamoureux, Charles, Musical Conductor. Music, **17**: 535.

— as Orchestra Leader. Sat. R. **85**: 250.

Lamp of Liberty, The; a story. (N. Duncan) Atlan. **85**: 649.

Lamparagua, The; a Chilean Legend. (May Cromelin) Pall Mall M. **12**: 502.

Lamprey. Macrophthalmia Chilensis. (Bashford Dean) Science, n. s. **9**: 740.

Lamsdorff, Count, First Failure of. Fortn. **74**: 694.

Lancaster, England. (H. Pope) Cath. World, **70**: 632.

Lancaster, Pa., St. James P. E. Church, 1790. Pennsyl. M. **22**: 251.

Lance, Resurrection of the. (G. J. Younghusband) J. Mil. Serv. Inst. **12**: 316.

Land, Prof. J. P. N. Ath. '97, **1**: 165.

Land, An Ancient Conveyance of. (D. W. Amram) Green Bag, **10**: 77.

— and the Laborers. (C. R. Earl Carrington) 19th Cent. **45**: 368.

— and Lodging-houses. (G. W. E. Russell) 19th Cent. **42**: 383.

— Back to the; a sequel. (Earl Nelson) 19th Cent. **50**: 59, 977.

— Credit. (O. Taft, jr.) J. Pol. Econ. **6**: 476.

— for Public Purposes, Expropriation of. (A. H. B. Constable) Jurid. R. **13**: 164.

— How to lower the Rates. (W. C. Wright) Westm. **153**: 261.

Land, Law of the. (W. A. McClean) Green Bag, 12:
135, 523, 570, 653.
— Monopoly in, Keystone of. (G. F. Saunders) Westm.
152: 510.
— Nationalization of. (F. Thomasson) Westm. 154:
162.
— On which Side art thou? Westm. 152: 369.
— Question of, Ethics of the. (J. B. Bartlett) Arena,
26: 490.
— Tenure of, Curiosities of. Chamb. J. 74: 734.
— — Food and. (E. Atkinson) Pop. Sci. Mo. 59: 568.
— Transfer of, by Registration of Title in Germany
and Austria-Hungary. (C. F. Brickdall) Am.
Law R. 31: 827.
— — in Germany and Austria. (J. Burns) Jurid. R.
9: 155.
— — Torrens Land Transfer Act, Constitutionality of.
(S. D. Thompson) Am. Law R. 31: 254.
Land o' Dreams; a poem. (L. Harris) Canad. M. 8:
355.
Land o' the Leal; a story. (D. Dale) Argosy, 64: 757.
Land of the Maple; a Patriotic Song with Music. (H.
H. Godfrey) Canad. M. 10: 264.
Land of Suspense; a story of the Seen and Unseen.
Blackw. 161: 131. Same art. Liv. Age, 212: 466–
515. — Spec. 78: 11.
Land Allotments in England. (Caro Lloyd) Outl. 59:
430.
Land Forces, Organization and Training of Our. (N.
D. Hamilton) Un. Serv. M. 15: 193.
Land-forms, Origin of, Through Crust-torsion. (M.
M. O. Gordon) Geog. J. 16: 457.
Land Grant College Funds, Perversion of. (D. G.
Porter) Am. J. Soc. Sci. 35: 77.
Land Ownership. (F. Thomasson) Westm. 155: 523.
— and Home-building. (F. B. Sanborn) Am. J. Soc.
Sci. 39: 158.
Land Question. Westm. 153: 664.
— and Economic Progress. (B. Hall) Arena, 24: 645.
— A Manufactured. (C. Morgan Richardson) Na-
tional, 28: 654.
Land Tenure, Ideal, and the Best Make-shift. (W. E.
Bear) Fortn. 69: 68.
— in Ancient India. (E. W. Hopkins) Pol. Sci. Q. 13:
669.
Land-title Registration in Massachusetts. (W. D.
Turner) Am. Law R. 33: 42.
Land Titles, A Double System of. (A. G. Sedgwick)
Nation, 67: 46.
— State Insurance of. Outl. 61: 392.
Land Transfer Registries. (W. Strachan) Law Q. 15:
15.
Land Values: Anticipating the Unearned Increment.
(I. W. Hart) Arena, 18: 339.
— Taxation of. (G. M'Crae) Chamb. J. 78: 33.
Lands, Public, Utilization of the. (E. F. Best) Nat.
Geog. M. 8: 49.
Landen, Battle of. (F. Dixon) Temp. Bar, 117: 174.
Landlocked Sailor, A. (S. O. Jewett) Lippinc. 64: 753.
Lando, Ortensio. (J. B. Fletcher) Sewanee, 2: 484.
Landor, A. Henry Savage, in Tibet. Acad. 55: 71,
130.
— Portrait of. Bk. Buyer, 22: 363.
Landor, Walter Savage. (G. M. Adam) Canad. M. 18:
128. — With portrait. Acad. 51: 258.
— and Llanthony Abbey. (A. C. Benson) National,
28: 519. Same art. Ecl. M. 128: 225.
— Bibliography of. (S. Wheeler) Ath. '00, 1: 335.
2: 28, 88.
— Last Writings of. (Maltus Q. Holyoake) Gent. M.
n. s. 62: 6.
— Letters of. Acad. 56: 209. — Sat. R. 87: 215. —
Ath. '97, 2: 557.

Landor, Walter Savage, Unpublished Letter of. (B.
Dobell) Ath. '01, 2: 285.
Landrail, or Corncrake. (H. A. Bryden) Sat. R. 86:
373.
Landscape and Literature. Spec. 80: 855. Same art.
Liv. Age, 218: 402.
— as a Means of Culture. (N. S. Shaler) Atlan. 82:
777.
— Imaginative Element in. (Sylvester Baxter) Am.
Arch. 59: 11.
— in Connection with Washington Public Buildings.
(F. L. Olmsted, jr.) Am. Arch. 71: 19.
— in Poetry. (R. Y. Tyrrell) Macmil. 76: 153. Same
art. Liv. Age, 214: 180.
— — Palgrave on. Church Q. 46: 186.
— Modern Study of. (W. W. Fenn) M. of Art, 21:
196.
— — Palgrave's. (J. C. Collins) Sat. R. 83: 694.
— Sixty Years' Change in. Spec. 78: 865. Same art.
Ecl. M. 129: 800.
— Symbolic, Imaginative, and Actual. Ed. R. 193: 28.
Landscape Architecture, Renaissance of. (G. F. Pen-
tecost, jr.) Scrib. M. 27: 337.
Landscape Art, Field of. (C. S. Sargent) Garden & F.
10: 161.
Landscape Exhibition, Dudley Gallery, 1900. M. of
Art, 24: 167.
Landscape Gardener and his Work. Garden & F. 10:
282.
Landscape Gardening. (C. S. Sargent) Garden & F.
10: 499. — (F. I. Thomas) Am. Arch. 55: 52, 60.
78, 85.
— Art and Nature in. (C. S. Sargent) Garden & F. 10:
191.
— Doing too Much. (C. S. Sargent) Garden & F. 10:
231.
— Mediterranean. (W. H. Kilham) Am. Arch. 56: 11,
35, 53.
Landscape Painter, Apology of. (F. Miller) Art J. 51:
272.
Landscape Painters, The, and the Summer. (F. Crown-
inshield and R. Sturgis) Scrib. M. 23: 765.
— A Society of. (Arthur Fish) M. of Art, 23: 218.
Landscape Paintings, Some English. (C. Monkhouse)
Art J. 49: 78.
Landseer, Sir Edwin, the Animal Painter. (Charlotte
R. Jones) Nat'l M. (Bost.) 5: 397.
Lane, George Martin. (M. H. Morgan) Harv. Grad. M.
6: 44. — (M. H. Morgan) Nation, 65: 28.
— Latin Grammar. (C. C. Smith) Harv. Grad. M. 7:
374.
Lane, James H.; Career of a Kansas Politician. (L.
W. Spring) Am. Hist. R. 4: 80.
Lane, Mrs. Sara, and her Theatre. (G. B. Shaw) Sat.
R. 85: 487.
Lanesborough, Mass. (E. P. Thompson) New Eng. M.
n. s. 19: 696.
Lanfranc and the Anti-pope. (F. Liebermann) Eng.
Hist. R. 16: 328.
Lang, Andrew, Making of Religion. (Joseph V. Tracy)
Am. Cath. Q. 24, no. 4: 172.
— on the Origin of Religion, with Reply. (J. M. Rob-
ertson) Fortn. 70: 726.
— Pickle, the Spy. (A. B. Millar) Scot. R. 29: 201.
— Quiller-Couch on. (M. Beerbohm) Sat. R. 84: 109.
Langdon, John. (C. R. Corning) New Eng. M. n. s.
16: 616.
Langham Artist's Club, London. (A. Lawrence) Idler,
14: 577.
Langley, Samuel Pierpont, Portraits of. Strand, 13:
705.
Langley, of Newport, R. I. (I. J. Greenwood) N. E.
Reg. 51: 168.

Language and Image. (H. M. Stanley) Psychol. R. 4: 67.

— and Style. (C. Whibley) Fortn. 71: 100.

— Animal and Human. (E. Mach) Open Court, 14: 171.

— Art in. (B. I. Wheeler) Atlan. 86: 810.

— as Interpreter of Life. (B. I. Wheeler) Atlan. 84: 459.

— as a Test of Race. (C. S. Wake) Am. Antiq. 23: 379.

— Common Origin of. (J. B. Wilkinson) Educa. 18: 205.

— How abolish Bad English ? (T. J. Allen) Educa. 20: 638.

— Influence of Christianity on ; Love and Righteousness. (A. Carr) Expos. 6: 321.

— An International. Cosmopol. 24: 569.

— Modern Corruption of. Gent. M. 67: 309. Same art. Liv. Age, 231: 131.

— Origin of. (J. Donovan) Westm. 151: 197.

— The Primæval. (C. Johnston) Contemp. 76: 694.

— Psychology of Learning a Foreign. (B. D. Bagen) Educa. 20: 152.

— Significance of. (M. Bréal) Pop. Sci. Mo. 52: 832.

— Speech of Children. (S. S. Buckman) 19th Cent. 41: 793.

— Symbolic, A Plea for. (C. Lofengluh) National, 34: 545.

— Universal ; " Lingua Franca " for Mankind. Spec. 83: 45. Same art. Ecl. M. 133: 742. Same art. Liv. Age, 222: 718.

Language Arts, Teaching the, Hinsdale on. (M. V. O'Shea) School R. 5: 178.

Language Standard in Modern Greece. (B. I. Wheeler) Am. J. Philol. 18: 19.

Language Study. (J. M. Baldwin) Science, n. s. 8: 94.

Language Teaching, A Study in. (J. R. Street) Pedagog. Sem. 4: 269.

Languages and their Monuments, Necessity of Studying. (C. De Harlez) Cath. World, 64: 467.

— Correlation of, in the High School. (O. L. Manchester) School R. 7: 462.

— Diversity of. (R. T. Colburn) Science, 6: 682.

— Foreign, History of Teaching. (B. D. Bogen) Educa. 20: 340.

— How to Learn. (L. Charvet) Educa. R. 15: 74.

— Latin and Greek vs. French and German. (T. M. Hopkins) Westm. 148: 564.

— Modern, in Colleges. (J. P. Carroll) Cath. World, 71: 622.

— — Neglect of. Blackw. 169: 263. Same art. Ecl. M. 136: 645.

— — Teaching of. (E. Lecky) Longm. 32: 158.

— of Shakespeare's Greenwood. (G. Morley) Knowl. 20: 146, 172, 265.

— Parent, Character of Inferred. (H. Oertel) Am. J. Philol. 18: 416.

— Sacred, in Primitive Art. (S. Dewey) Westm. 148: 622.

— The Science of Meaning. (J. P. Postgate) Fortn. 68: 418.

— The Series Method ; a Comparison. (C. Taylor) Pop. Sci. Mo. 54: 537.

— The Study of. Acad. 60: 67.

Languet, Hubert, Sir Philip Sidney and. (G. Serrell) Temp. Bar, 110: 47. Same art. Ecl. M. 128: 248.

Lanier, Sidney. (F. A. King) Sewanee, 3: 216. — (Mme. Blanc) Liv. Age, 217: 411–517. — (G. L. Swiggett) Conserv. R. 5: 187. — (R. Le Gallienne) Acad. 58: 147. Same art. Liv. Age, 224: 840. Same art. Ecl. M. 134: 631.

— and Bayard Taylor, Correspondence of. (H. W. Lanier) Atlan. 83: 791. 84: 127.

— as revealed in his Letters. (W. P. Woolf) Sewanee, 8: 346.

Lanier, Sidney, Color and Motion in. (J. S. Snoddy) Poet-Lore, 12: 558.

— Essays. (R. Burton) Bk. Buyer, 18: 144.

— Poet and Musician. (E. Swayne) Music, 16: 125.

— Poet Laureate of the South. (M. S. Kaufman) Meth. R. 60: 94.

— A Poet's Musical Impressions ; from his Letters. Scrib. M. 25: 622–745.

— a Singer of Sunrise. (G. D. Goodwin) Poet-Lore, 9: 407.

Lanigan, Edith. Writer, 14: 26.

Lannigan System with Girls. (C. B. Fernald) Cent. 39: 569.

Lansdowne, Lord, A Year of his Administration. (H. Whates) Fortn. 76: 581.

Lante, Villa. (E. S. Gale) Archit. R. 8: 117.

— Garden of. (H. V. Magonigle) Am. Arch. 58: 103.

Lanty Foster's Mistake. (B. Harte) New Eng. M. n. s. 25: 413. Same art. Overland, n. s. 38: 399.

Lanuvium, Excavations at. (Lord Savile) Archæol. 53: 147.

Lao Ren ; a Chinese story. Argosy, 70: 471.

Lao-Tze, with portrait. Open Court, 12: 306.

— and his System. (G. H. Trever) Meth. R. 59: 230.

— and the Tao-Teh-King. (P. Carus ; T. Suzuki) Monist, 11: 574, 612.

Laon and Liesse. Temp. Bar, 115: 228.

Laplace, Pierre Simon de, with portrait. Open Court, 12: 54.

Lapland, Girls' Home in. (J. Beveridge) Sund. M. 29: 845.

— Modern. (G. H. Nall) Pall Mall M. 15: 492.

— the People of the Reindeer. (J. Stadling) Cent. 36: 582.

— Swedish, Iron Mining in. (D. A. Louis) Engin. M. 17: 632.

Lapp Prayer, A ; a poem. (N. Hopper) Ecl. M. 132: 414.

Lapse of Brother Antonio and Sister Bethlehem. (May Turner) Overland, n. s. 34: 529.

Lara, —— de. Messaline. (J. F. Runciman) Sat. R. 88: 100.

La Ramée, Louisa de. See Ouida.

Large Skating-rink, A ; a tale. (P. Vernon) Argosy, 66: 228.

Largest Life, The ; a poem. (A. Lampman) Atlan. 83: 416.

Lark, Meadow, of Western U. S. (Ida A. Baker) Midland, 8: 129.

— Song of the. Outl. 63: 394.

"Lark, The," an Amateur Journal. (G. Burgess) Acad. 57: 212.

Larkspur ; a story. (M. A. Bacon) Harper, 103: 52.

La Rouërie, Marquis de. (A. Laugel) Nation, 73: 357.

Larry McNoogan's Cow ; a story. (Walter Barr) Cosmopol. 27: 81.

Larynx as an Instrument of Music. (E. W. Scripture) Science, n. s. 13: 913.

Las Casas, Bartholomew. (Bryan J. Clinch) Am. Cath. Q. 24, no. 3: 102.

La Salle, Jean Baptiste de. (C. M. Graham) Cath. World, 71: 672.

La Salle, R. C. de, Connection of, with the Jesuits. (J. W. Wilstach) Cath. World, 65: 82.

La Scala and Giuseppe Verdi. (E. B. Perry) Music, 13: 277.

Lasko, John a, and the Reformation in Poland, 1499–1560. (G. B. Maury) Am. J. Theol. 4: 314.

Last Assembling. (A. Brown) New Eng. M. n. s. 19: 120.

Last Aztec, The ; a tale. (T. G. Randall) Outing, 32: 41.

Last Chance Cabin. (M. Sherwood) Overland, n. s. 30: 152.

Last Chapter, The. Atlan. 82: 856.

Last Chapter, The; an Episode of the Frontier. (A. M. Reynolds) Overland, n. s. 30: 56.

Last Crossing. (H. Child) Longm. 31: 228.

Last Dance of Mademoiselle Fan-Tan; a story. (C. Holland) Idler, 13: 447.

Last Dance of the Leaves; a poem. (J. V. Cheney) Dial (Ch.) 25: 162.

Last Dinner. (L. E. MacBrayne) New Eng. M. n. s. 17: 710.

Last Encore, The; a story. (A. L. Mearkle) Poet-Lore, 12: 334.

Last Experience of Adam Skirving; a story. (M. W. M. Falconer) Pall Mall M. 14: 264.

Last Fight; a poem. (L. F. Tooker) Cent. 32: 174.

Last Hunt of Dorax. (O. Huck) Cent. 39: 748.

Last Jump, The; a story. (C. Shelley) Outing, 34: 279.

Last Laugh, The; more Adventures of the Amateur Cracksman. (E. W. Hornung) Scrib. M. 29: 483.

Last Letter of Ernest Arnold, The; a story. (C. Maynard) Harper, 103: 888.

Last Lynching, The, in Cimarron; a story. (C. T. Brady) Harper, 102: 233.

Last of the Fairy Wands, The. (W. H. Bishop) Scrib. M. 30: 697.

Last of the Mulberry-street Barons. (J. A. Riis) Cent. 36: 119.

Last of the Neoliths; a tale. (H. Gilbert) Argosy, 73: 168.

Last of the Smugglers; a story. (S. R. Crockett) Cosmopol. 30: 93.

Last Rebel. (J. A. Altsheler) Lippinc. 62: 155.

Last Throw; a story. (Wingrove Bathon) Cosmopol. 25: 201.

Last Voyage of Boat-steerer Nicholson; a story. (H. Bindloss) Gent. M. n. s. 62: 28. Same art. Liv. Age, 220: 506. Same art. Ecl. M. 132: 502.

Last Voyage of Martin Vallance. (J. A. Barry) Chamb. J. 74: Xmas no.

Laszlo, Filip E., Hungarian Painter. (A. Tahi) Studio (Internat.) 15: 3.

Late Love; poem. (M. E. Martyn) Ecl. M. 130: 288.

Late Relaxing, The. (Addie E. Scott) Overland, n. s. 31: 506.

Late Supper, After; a sketch. (H. M. Henne) Cornh. 75: 652.

Lateral Support of Land. (L. A. Jones) Am. Law R. 31: 247.

Latest Love Affair at San Marcos; a story. (L. Balliet) Midland, 8: 242.

Latham, John C. Bank. M. (N. Y.) 59: 629.

La Thangue, Henry Herbert, with portraits. Strand, 16: 536.

— and his Work. (G. Thomson) Studio (Lond.) 9: 163.

Lathbury, Mary Artemisia. (V. V. M. Beede) Chaut. 30: 35.

Lathes, Ideal Engine. (W. D. Forbes) Cassier, 11: 502.

— Some American Turret. (P. J. Connor) Cassier, 20: 243.

Latimer, Hugh. Liv. Age, 225: 458.

Latimer, Ralph R. Writer, 14: 27.

Latin-American Constitutions and Revolutions. (J. W. Foster) Nat. Geog. M. 12: 169. Same art. Am. J. Soc. Sci. 39: 39.

Latin Composition, Bennett's. (J. H. Harris) School R. 6: 273.

— in Preparatory Schools. (H. Preble) School R. 6: 261.

— Preparatory, Moulton's. (F. A. Gallup) School R. 5: 473.

Latin-English Dictionary, Nall's. (H. W. Johnston) School R. 6: 136.

Latin Grammar, Gildersleeve's. (F. A. Gallup) School R. 8: 46.

Latin Inscriptions, Lindsay's. (G. M. Jackson) School R. 6: 618.

Latin Language and Algebra, Value of, in the Eighth School Year. (N. C. Dougherty) Educa. R. 17: 178.

— and English in the Illinois High Schools. (D. K. Dodge) Educa. R. 14: 370.

— and Greek. (J. H. Kirkland) School R. 8: 86.

— — for Secondary Schools, Courses in. (F. W. Kelsey) School R. 5: 360.

— A Brief for. (W. T. Harris) Educa. R. 17: 313.

— Elementary, Suggestions for Teachers of. (H. L. Wilbur) School R. 8: 280.

— Grammar of, Lane's. (M. Warren) Nation, 68: 14.

— in French Schools. (S. Dewey) Educa. R. 16: 460.

— in Secondary Schools. (R. C. Bentley) Pedagog. Sem. 8: 395.

— in 7th and 8th Grades; Chicago Experiment. (A. F. Nightingale) School R. 6: 379.

— Influence of, upon English. (W. C. Lawton) Chaut. 27: 243.

— Junior Book in, Rolfe and Dennison's. (F. A. Gallup) School R. 7: 432.

— Preparatory Course in. (F. J. Miller) School R. 5: 588.

— Roman Pronunciation of, Notes on the. (W. G. Hale) School R. 6: 394.

— Syntax of, Schmalz's Corrections of. (E. B. Lease) Am. J. Philol. 20: 59.

— Teaching of: Changes in, in Germany. (F. Paulsen) Educa. R. 18: 332.

— — Difficulties in. (F. W. Coburn) Educa. 18: 264.

Latin Lexicon, The New German. (J. C. Rolfe) Bookman, 6: 216.

Latin Literature. A Study of Literature in Rome. (W. C. Lawton) Chaut. 27: 121.

Latin Manuscripts, Johnson's. (W. M. Aber) School R. 5: 730.

Latin Monetary Union, Willis's. (H. White) Nation, 72: 278.

Latin Nations, Plight of. (E. L. Godkin) Nation, 67: 328.

Latin Poets, Nature in the Last. (E. Martinengo-Cesaresco) Contemp. 76: 239.

Latin Programmes of the Committee of Twelve, Four-year. (C. E. Bennett) School R. 6: 239. — (J. E. Barss) School R. 6: 482.

Latin Prohibitives in the Silver Age. (W. K. Clement) Am. Anthrop. 21: 154.

Latin Races; are they Doomed? (R. Ogden) Nation, 69: 481.

— Decadence of, and Slav Advance. Outl. 63: 711.

— Decline of. (G. Sergi) Liv. Age, 223: 203. Same art. Ecl. M. 133: 850.

Latin Subjunctive, Cicero's Use of the Imperfect and Pluperfect in Si-Clauses. (H. C. Nutting) Am. J. Philol. 21: 260.

Latin Verses, Reasons for composing. Acad. 52: 452.

Latitude, Variation of, at New York. (J. K. Rees) Pop. Astron. 8: 169.

La Touche, Gaston, Artist. (G. Mousey) Studio (Internat.) 7: 77.

La Trappe de Notre Dame du Lac. (P. T. Lafleur) Nation, 69: 68.

Latude in the Bastille. (C. Whibley) Macmil. 78: 350.

Lauder, Robert Scott, and his Pupils. (E. Pinnington) Art J. 50: 339, 367.

Lauder, William, the Literary Forger. (A. H. Millar) Blackw. 166: 381.

Laugh, A, and a Laugh. (E. W. Parker) Overland, n. s. 32: 109.

Laugh of Fate, The. (L. Macnab) Overland, n. s. 38: 445.

Laughing Aspen. (G. L. Calderon) Cornh. 76: 759.

Laughter, Disuse of. (Lewis Morris) Forum, 24: 319.

— of Savages. (J. Sully) Internat. Mo. 4: 379.

— Philosophy of. (P. Carus) Monist, 8: 250.

— Prolegomena to a Theory of. (J. Sully) Philos. R. 9: 365.

— Psychological Cause of. (C. Méllinand) Pop. Sci. Mo. 53: 398.

— Psychology of. (G. S. Hall; A. Allin) Am. J. Psychol. 9: 1.

— Tickling and. (Hiram M. Stanley) Am. J. Psychol. 9: 235.

Launching of Larry; a story. (C. L. Field) Cosmopol. 27: 212.

Launching of a Ship. (R. Caird) Cassier, 12: 341.

Laundries, Commercial. (H. Bosanquet) 19th Cent. 41: 224.

— in Religious Houses. (L. C. F. Cavendish) 19th Cent. 41: 232.

— Small. (M. Greenwood) Westm. 147: 698.

Laundry Machinery. (J. L. Couper) Cassier, 20: 507.

— Steam. (S. Tebbutt) Cassier, 15: 291.

Laura. (B. Marnan) Strand, 17: 672.

Laureateship, English. (W. Archer) Critic, 37: 145.

Laurel Walk, The. (Mrs. Molesworth) Sund. M. 27: 9–614.

Laurels, Withered; a reverie among the tombs. Macmil. 79: 155. Same art. Liv. Age, 220: 372.

Laurens, Col. John. (James Barnes) McClure, 14: 109.

Laurentian Mountains. The Home of the Windigo. (C. A. Bramble) Chaut. 33: 518.

Laurier, Wilfrid, Canada's Premier. (B. Willson) Eng. Illust. 17: 257. — (J. W. Russell) Arena, 17: 615.

— and Manitoba. (J. G. S. Cox) 19th Cent. 41: 656.

— at Washington. (J. W. Longley) National, 30: 837. Same art. Ecl. M. 130: 421.

Lava Flows of the Western Slope of the Sierra Nevada, Cal. (F. L. Ransome) Am. J. Sci. 155: 355.

Laval University, Quebec. (A. D. DeCelles) Canad. M. 8: 207.

Lavedan, Henri. Les Jeunes. Acad. 52: 95.

La Verna, A Pilgrimage to. (H. D. Rawnsley) Blackw. 164: 410. Same art. Liv. Age, 219: 519.

Lavender; a story. (F. P. Warren) Gent. M. n. s. 66: 105.

Lavender, Sweet. (L. W. Lillingston) Good Words, 40: 527.

Lavigerie, Cardinal. (W. C. Robinson) Am. Cath. Q. 22: 1.

Lavoisier Monument, The. Nature, 62: 390.

Law, Arthur. Sea Flower. (G. B. Shaw) Sat. R. 85: 355.

Law, David. Etching of St. Michael's Mount. (R. G. Kingsley) Art J. 50: 60.

— On the Thames, near Cookham; etching. Art J. 52: 59.

Law, William. His "Serious Call." Church Q. 47: 453.

Law, Ancient, in Modern Life. (F. P. Walton) Green Bag, 13: 384. Same art. Jurid. R. 13: 70.

— Analogues and Differences of the Civil and the Common. (H. Denis) Am. Law R. 33: 28.

— and Equity, Blending of. (W. L. Prather; G. W. Davis; L. R. Bryan) Am. Law R. 30: 813.

— and Lawyers, Proverbs about. (J. DeMorgan) Green Bag, 10: 484.

— and Liberty. The Rights of Man. (L. Abbott) Outl. 68: 41.

Law and Medicine, Better Training for. (C. F. Thwing) Educa. R. 16: 49.

— and Nature in Greek Ethics. (J. Burnet) Int. J. Ethics, 7: 328.

— and Politics in the Middle Ages, Jenks's. (A. V. Dicey) Nation, 66: 345.

— and Responsibility. (T. W. Taylor, jr.) Philos. R. 7: 276.

— and the Study of Law. (O. W. Holmes) Jurid. R. 9: 105.

— as a Profession for Young Men. (F. S. Stratton) Am. Law R. 31: 99.

— Bench and Bar in the Middle Ages. Green Bag, 11: 283.

— Constitutional, Limits of. (T. Thacher) Yale R. 6: 7.

— Correction of. (C. Thorn) Am. Law R. 33: 522.

— Costs in, Complicated and Cumbersome. (S. T. Wood) Canad. M. 13: 499.

— Delay of the. (D. MacG. Means) Nation, 72: 486.

— Delays and Uncertainties of the. (C. C. Bonney) Open Court, 13: 705.

— Due Process of. (T. W. Brown) Am. Law R. 32: 14.

— English, Influence of Roman Law on. (H. W. Rogers) Chaut. 26: 496.

— Fashions in. (S. D. Thompson) Green Bag, 11: 487.

— Golden Age of the. Green Bag, 11: 557.

— Hebrew, Development of. (E. Peck) Bib. World, 16: 351.

— Is it for the People or for the Lawyers? (A. Emden) 19th Cent. 49: 858.

— Judge-made, Evil Tendencies of. Sat. R. 92: 101.

— Lawful Pleasures. (G. M. Smith) Cornh. 83: 188.

— Literature and. (G. R. Hawes) Green Bag, 11: 234.

— Lumber-room of the. Green Bag, 10: 257.

— Names and Nature of the. (J. W. Salmond) Law Q. 15: 367.

— Origin and Nature of. (G. H. Bennett) Meth. R. 59: 382.

— Philosophy of. (R. W. Joslyn) Green Bag, 12: 142.

— Present State of. (U. M. Rose) Am. Law R. 31: 161.

— Profession of, in the South. (Walter L. Miller) Am. Law R. 33: 84.

— Progress of. (W. Clark) Am. Law R. 31: 410. — Reply. (J. S. Barton) Am. Law R. 31: 548.

— — and Law Study; a reply. (J. W. Whalley) Am. Law R. 31: 553.

— Respect for. (J. Addams) Indep. 53: 18.

— Rewards of. (W. O. Inglis) Munsey, 25: 425.

— Roman, Spirit of. (G. Ravene) Green Bag, 12: 598.

— Science modifying Principles of. Green Bag, 12: 597.

— Statute, Improvement of. Quar. 189: 172.

— Study of. (W. E. Glanville) Green Bag, 9: 301.

— Traditional Misconceptions of. (R. P. Bolton) J. Am. Folk-Lore, 14: 113.

— Written, Domain of. (I. F. Russell) Am. J. Soc. Sci. 38: 219.

Law of Life, The; a story. (J. London) McClure, 16: 435.

Law of the Medes and Persians. (C. B. Taylor) Overland, n. s. 38: 45.

Law of the Prophecy, The. (Mary H. Rose) Overland, n. s. 36: 108.

"Law of the Road, The." Nation, 68: 222, 239.

Law-abiding Citizens. (W. R. Lighton) Atlan. 87: 783.

Law Books in the Reign of Elizabeth. Green Bag, 10: 460.

— Some Old. Green Bag, 9: 426.

Law Libraries in Colonial Virginia. (B. C. Steiner) Green Bag, 9: 351.

Lawmaking. (J. W. Griggs) Am. Law R. 31: 701.
— Our Process of. (R. P. Reeder) Arena, 23: 480.

Law Merchant and Transferable Debentures. (F. A. Bosanquet) Law Q. 15: 130.
— in England, Early History of the. (A. T. Carter) Law Q. 17: 232.

Law Practice in New York City. (H. E. Howland) Cent. 40: 803.

Law Reform, Century of. Sat. R. 92: 83.
— in England, Need of. Sat. R. 88: 192.
— Near Future of. Law Q. 16: 129. — (T. Snow) Law Q. 16: 229.

Law Reporting, Good and Bad. (S. D. Thompson) Green Bag, 11: 105.

Law Reports, Abridgment of, by Commission. (E. P. Payson) Am. Law R. 34: 392.
— Humor of English. (I. Browne) Am. Law R. 32: 814.
— Study of. (S. Rogers) Law Q. 13: 250.

Law School, An Antebellum. (A. M. Barnes) Green Bag, 10: 262.

Law Schools, Why they are Crowded. (F. Russell) Am. J. Soc. Sci. 37: 164.

Laws, Early Jewish and Christian. (J. Silversmith) Bib. World, 13: 170.
— Road, Curious Old. Green Bag, 12: 445.
— State, Uniformity of. (L. N. Dembitz) No. Am. 168: 84.

"Laws of Nature," Some Unrecognized. (C. H. Henderson) Pop. Sci. Mo. 51: 776.

Lawes, Sir John Bennet. J. Statis. Soc. 63: 498. — Spec. 85: 296. — J. Soc. Arts, 48: 78.

Lawlessness and Law Enforcement. (C. B. Wilcox) Bib. Sac. 55: 158.
— the Real Peril. Outl. 66: 10.

Lawn-tennis, Honors of the Season. (J. P. Paret) Outing, 31: 153.

Lawn-tennis Courts, Building of. Outing, 32: 50.

Lawrance, Sir John Compton, Portraits of. Strand, 13: 553.

Lawrence, Sir Thomas. Munsey, 16: 686. 17: 88. — (J. C. Van Dyke) Cent. 37: 372.

Lawrence-Eckert, Ida. Writer, 14: 155.

Lawrence, Massachusetts. (G. H. Young) New Eng. M. n. s. 17: 581.

Lawson, Henry. Acad. 56: 409.
— as Poet. (A. Maquarie) Argosy, 71: 436.
— as Prose Author. (A. Maquarie) Argosy, 72: 81.
— Poetry of. Acad. 53: 424.

Lawson, Sir John, Notes on Documents belonging to. (C. S. Perceval) Archæol. 47: 179.

Lawson, Thomas W., of Boston. (R. G. Anderson) Nat'l M. (Bost.) 14: 394.

Lawton, George K., with portrait. (T. J. J. See) Pop. Astron. 9: 374. — (T. J. J. See) Science, n. s. 14: 215.

Lawton, Gen. Henry W., with portrait. (W. G. Brown) Harv. Grad. M. 8: 337. — With portrait. (O. O. Howard) R. of Rs. (N. Y.) 21: 184. — With portrait. (P. McQueen) Nat'l M. (Bost.) 11: 536. — Outl. 64: 55.
— in the Philippines. (D. C. Worcester) McClure, 15: 19.

Lawyer, The, and Catholic Philosophy. Month, 97: 493.
— in Literature. (M. D. Post) Green Bag, 11: 553.
— The State's Duty to the. (A. G. Sedgwick) Nation, 67: 24.

Lawyer's Lullaby, A; a poem. (J. A. Macy) Green Bag, 9: 300.

Lawyers, American, and their Making. (C. N. Gregory) Am. Law R. 31: 177.

Lawyers among the Poets. (E. V. B. Christian) Green Bag, 12: 175, 221.
— and Law Practice in England and the U. S. Green Bag, 9: 223, 255.
— and Scholarship. (W. L. Miller) Am. Law R. 34: 876.
— as Citizens, The Responsibility of. (D. MacG. Means) Nation, 69: 45.
— English Military. (J. E. R. Stephens) Gent. M. n. s. 63: 398.
— Government by. (S. D. Thompson) Am. Law R. 30: 672.
— in England. Sat. R. 91: 531.
— Kentucky, of the Past and Present. (S. E. M. Hardy) Green Bag, 9: 260, 305, 341.
— Presidential. Green Bag, 9: 104.
— Responsibilities of. (J. B. Warner) Int. J. Ethics, 7: 204.
— Who became Authors. (G. H. Westley) Green Bag, 12: 446.

Laycock, Samuel, Poetry of. Acad. 58: 269.

Laying up the Boat. (A. T. Quiller-Couch) Cornh. 84: 447.

Lays of the True North; a review. (E. McManus) Canad. M. 14: 175.

Lazarus, Resurrection of. (Arturo Graf) Liv. Age, 230: 753.

Lazy Man, in Indian Lore. (Alice C. Fletcher) J. Am. Folk-Lore, 14: 100.

Lea, Mathew Carey, 1823–97, Obituary Notice of. J. Frankl. Inst. 145: 143.

Lead, Native, Occurrence of, with Roeblingite, etc., Franklin Furnace, N. J. (W. M. Foote) Am. J. Sci. 156: 187.

Lead Compounds in Pottery Glazes, Thorpe's Report on. (W. Burton) Nature, 60: 18.

Lead-poisoning in the Potteries, Prendergast's. Sat. R. 86: 114, 176. — (Harold Hodge) Sat. R. 86: 200. — (F. L. Farrington; B. Wilson) Econ. R. 8: 521.

Lead-tin and Lead-antimony Alloys, Quick Testing of. (J. Richards) J. Frankl. Inst. 147: 398.

Lead Work. (W. R. Lethaby) J. Soc. Arts, 45: 452.
— in Northumberland Alley. Reliquary, 39: 48.

Lead-working. Revival of Handicrafts. (J. S. Gardner) M. of Art, 23: 488.

Leader-writer, Lament of a. Westm. 152: 656.

Leading Article, The. Cornh. 80: 797.

Leading Motive in Music Discussed. Music, 19: 226.

Leaf from an Unopened Volume, C. Brontë's. (W. G. Kingsland) Poet-Lore, 9: 169.

Leaf from our Imperial Diary. (C. de Thierry) Un. Serv. M. 21: 311.

League of American Municipalities, 3d Annual Convention. Ann. Am. Acad. Pol. Sci. 14: 378.

Leamington, Round and about. (F. Dolman) Eng. Illust. 22: 50.

Lear, Edward: a Leaf from the Journals of a Landscape Painter. Macmil. 75: 410.

Lear, Mrs. Sidney. (F. D. How) Sund. M. 30: 99.

Learning, The New. 19th Cent. 42: 928. Same art. Liv. Age, 216: 330.

Lease of Life; a tale. (H. M. Bonter) Canad. M. 15: 262.

Leaseholds, Renewals of Settled. (W. Strachan) Law Q. 15: 378.

Leasowe; Submerged Forest at. Chamb. J. 74: 382. Same art. Ecl. M. 129: 573.

Least Action, The Principle of, as a Psychological Principle. (W. R. B. Gibson) Mind, 25: 469.

Leather, Embossing. (F. Kruekl) Studio (Lond.) 3: 51.
— Manufacture of. (H. R. Procter) J. Soc. Arts, 47: 827–863.
— Methods of Ornamenting. (F. Miller) Art J. 50: 213.

Leather Work, Incised and Embossed. Studio (Lond.) 6: 108.

Leathley, Mary Elisabeth Southwell. Acad. 57: 756.

Leaves, Forest, Chemistry of. (P. Q. Keegan) Nat. Sci. 13: 177.

— Ministry of. (A. S. Wilson) Knowl. 20: 197.

Leaves from an English Solicitor's Note-book. III. (B. Borret) Green Bag, 11: 581.

Leaves from a Note-book. (T. B. Aldrich) Cent. 38: 50.

Leavitt, Dudley, and his New Hampshire Almanac. (J. Albee) New Eng. M. n. s. 17: 545.

Lebanon, Connecticut. (W. E. Griffis) New Eng. M. n. s. 17: 3.

Lebarge, Mike ; a Yukon Pioneer, with portrait. (W. H. Dall) Nat. Geog. M. 9: 137.

Le Brun, M. E. Vigée. Munsey, 18: 104.

Lecky, W. E. H. (H. Walker) Good Words, 40: 114.

— England in the 18th Century. (E. M. Chapman) New Eng. M. n. s. 22: 148.

— Liberty and Democracy. (F. P. Powers) Lippinc. 60: 670.

— Map of Life. (A. V. Dicey) Nation, 70: 186. — Church Q. 51: 101.

Leclerq, Rose, Portrait of. Theatre, 38: 310.

Le Conte, Joseph. (J. Royce) Internat. Mo. 4: 324. — With portrait. (A. C. Lawson) Harv. Grad. M. 10: 211. — With portrait. Nat. Geog. M. 12: 310. — (A. C. Lawson) Science, n. s. 14: 273.

Lecture, Popular, as an Educator. (B. Ferree) Educa. 18: 527.

Lecture System, Free. (S. T. Willis) Cosmopol. 25: 661. — — in New York City. (H. M. Leipziger) Munic. Aff. 3: 462. — (S. D. McCormick) Outl. 64: 121. — (S. T. Willis) Forum, 29: 332.

— — in Connection with Free Public Libraries. Library, 6: 354.

Lecturers, Eminent, Reminiscences of. (J. Benton) Harper, 96: 603.

Ledidæ and Nuculidæ of the Atlantic Coast of the United States, Revision of the Genera of. (A. E. Verrill and K. J. Bush) Am. J. Sci. 153: 51.

Ledscha, the Model for Arachne. (G. Ebers) Liv. Age, 218: 765.

Lee, Edward and John, of Guilford, Conn., Descendants of. (R. D. Smyth) N. E. Reg. 53: 53.

Lee, Fitzhugh, Life and Public Services of. (E. L. McCrary) Midland, 10: 42.

Lee, Franklyn Warner, Author. (J. Talman) Midland, 10: 139.

Lee, Colonel Henry, of Brookline, Mass. (D. G. Mason) New Eng. M. n. s. 20: 339. — (C. W. Eliot) Harv. Grad. M. 7: 348.

Lee, Nat, the Plays of. (H. M. Sanders) Temp. Bar, 124: 497.

Lee, Richard Henry, of Virginia, Letters of. Pennsyl. M. 22: 489.

Lee, Robert E., as a College President. (S. D. McCormick) Outl. 56: 684.

— at Defence of Richmond, 1862. (H. Tyrrell) Pall Mall M. 12: 345.

— at Antietam. (H. Tyrrell) Pall Mall M. 12: 511.

— at Fredericksburg and Chancellorsville. (H. Tyrrell) Pall Mall M. 13: 19.

— at Gettysburg. (H. Tyrrell) Pall Mall M. 13: 181.

— Inner Life of. (J. W. Jones) Chaut. 31: 187.

— Lee's Life of. (S. S. P. Patteson) Sewanee, 3: 468.

— Johnston, and Davis, White on. (J. D. Cox) Nation, 65: 502.

— Surrender of. (E. F. Andrews) Chaut. 31: 522.

— Virginia, and the Union. (C. W. Turner) Sewanee, 9: 302.

— White's Life of. (J. J. Halsey) Dial (Ch.) 24: 11.

Lee, Sidney. Dictionary of National Biography. (H. Ellis) Critic, 37: 434.

Lee, Wm. (E. M. Bacon) Bookman, 6: 305.

Lee-Mitford Rifle. (W. Broadfoot) Blackw. 163: 831.

Leech, Edward Owen. Bank. M. (N. Y.) 60: 698.

Leech, John, and Social Pictorial Satire. (G. Du Maurier) Harper, 96: 331.

Leetham, Sidney ; Interior Decoration of his House "Elm Banc," York. Studio (Internat.) 13: 36.

Leeuwenhoek, Antoon van, Malpighi, and Swammerdam. (W. A. Locy) Pop. Sci. Mo. 58: 561.

Lefort des Ylouses, M., Embossed Paper-work by. (H. Frantz) M. of Art, 21: 332.

Legacy Tax, the United States. (J. M. Gray) Am. Law R. 34: 869.

Legal Aid Society of New York City. Ann. Am. Acad. Pol. Sci. 17: 164.

— Past and Future of. (F. W. Holls) Char. R. 8: 15.

Legal Documents, Two, of the 11th Century. (D. W. Amram) Green Bag, 13: 115.

Legal Education. (F. M. Finch) Am. Law R. 35: 481.

— and its relation to General Education. (C. D. Ashley) Am. J. Soc. Sci. 37: 229.

— and Law Practice. (A. Swindlehurst) Am. Law R. 34: 214.

— of Women. (I. M. Pettas) Am. J. Soc. Sci. 38: 234.

— State of, in the World. (C. N. Gregory) Am. Law R. 34: 841.

Legal Maxims, Concerning. (C. Morse) Am. Law R. 35: 529.

Legal Menu ; poetry. (R. P. Clapp) Green Bag, 13: 10.

Legal Profession, Some Delights of the. (W. B. Dowd) Green Bag, 13: 417.

Legal Puzzles, Historic. Green Bag, 11: 353.

Legal Reform, Recent. (Sir A. T. Watson) Jurid. R. 13: 1.

Legal Relations between Bench and Bar. (A. E. Pillsbury) Am. Law R. 32: 161.

Legal Shreds and Patches. Chamb. J. 77: 721.

Legal-tender Laws, Are our, ex post facto? (B. T. De Witt) Pol. Sci. Q. 15: 96.

Legal-tender Note, History of the. Bank. M. (N. Y.) 56: 20.

Le Gallienne, Richard, as an Essayist. Acad. 59: 605.

— as a Literary Man. (C. G. D. Roberts) Cosmopol. 25: 459.

Legend of Blood Pool, The. (A. F. Mockler-Ferryman) Chamb. J. 76: 65.

Legend of the Bloodroot, A ; poem. (E. S. Thompson) Outing, 36: 177.

Legend of Little Panther, The. (E. Kemeys) Outing, 37: 458.

Legend of Nelly Legrave, A. (D. C. Scott) Scrib. M. 23: 470.

Legend of Spirit Lake, A. (W. W. Wiatt) Overland, n. s. 34: 334.

Legend of the White Reindeer. (E. T. Seton) Cent. 41: 79.

Legerdemain ; Robert-Houdin. (H. R. Evans) Cosmopol. 28: 645.

Legerwood of Legerwood ; a story. (G. Douglas) Gent. M. n. s. 59: 473.

Legge, James. Ath. '97, 2: 788.

— Life and Labors of. Asia. R. 25: 187.

Leghorn, Italy. (M. Carmichael) Pall Mall M. 16: 391.

Legion D'Honneur de France. (B. Landreth) Un. Serv. (Phila.) 17: 89.

Legion of Honour, A. (N. K. Blisset) Temp. Bar, 118: 574.

— Our. (J. F. J. Archibald) Overland, n. s. 38: 19.

Legislation, Cumbrousness of. Spec. 83: 112.

— Liberty through. (J. Lee) New Eng. M. n. s. 20: 434.

— The Menace of. (J. H. Eckels) No. Am. 165: 240.

Legislation, Political and Municipal, in 1896. (E. D. Durand) Ann. Am. Acad. 9: 231.
— — in 1897. (E. D. Durand) Ann. Am. Acad. Pol. Sci. 11: 174.
— — in 1898. (E. D. Durand) Ann. Am. Acad. Pol. Sci. 13: 212.
— — in 1899. (R. H. Whitten) Ann. Am. Acad. Pol. Sci. 15: 160.
— — in 1900. (R. H. Whitten) Ann. Am. Acad. Pol. Sci. 17: 244.
— Private Bill. Ed. R. 189: 76.
— Special, Tendency of the Courts to sustain. (J. Woodward) Am. J. Soc. Sci. 37: 193.
— State, Tendencies in. (D. MacG. Means) Nation, 72: 125.
— The Trend of. (D. MacG. Means) Nation, 71: 44.
— We are too much Governed. (D. B. Hill) No. Am. 170: 367.
Legislative Upper Chambers, Rehabilitated. (E. Porritt) No. Am. 166: 752.
Legislator, The Complete; Socratic Dialogue. (E. Manson) Law Q. 16: 196.
Legislatures, Decline of. (E. L. Godkin) Atlan. 80: 35.
— Follies of. (E. Pomeroy) Green Bag, 12: 14.
— Heads of Departments before. (R. L. Bridgman) New Eng. M. n. s. 17: 738.
Legitimism in England. (Marquis of Ruvigny) 19th Cent. 42: 362.
Legros, Alphonse. (A. Alexandre) Art J. 49: 105, 214.
— (C. Ricketts) Sat. R. 83: 406.
Leguminosæ, Zinsser on Root Tubercles of. (E. F. Smith) Am. Natural. 32: 365.
Lehmann, Liza, and other Song-writers. Music, 15: 139.
Leibl, Wilhelm, Artist. (G. Gronau) Studio (Internat.) 9: 163.
Leibnitz and Spinoza, Philosophy of. (R. Latta) Mind, 24: 333.
— Russell's Critical Exposition of Philosophy of. (G. M. Duncan) Philos. R. 10: 288.
— Space and Time Doctrine, Kant's Conception of. (M. W. Calkins) Philos. R. 6: 356.
Leicester, Massachusetts. (J. W. Chadwick) New Eng. M. n. s. 22: 349.
Leicester Square, A Fight in, Oct., 1698. (M. Hume) Eng. Illust. 20: 205.
Leicester Vellum Book, Legal Texts in. (M. Bateson) Eng. Hist. R. 14: 502.
Leigh, Benjamin Watkins. (Sallie E. M. Hardy) Green Bag, 10: 66.
Leigh, W. R. (J. B. Carrington) Bk. Buyer, 17: 596.
Leighton, E. Blair, Work of. (Fred. Miller) Art J. 52: 133.
Leighton, Frederick, Lord. (Lewis F. Day) M. of Art, 23: 167.
— and Academicism. Sat. R. 83: 241.
— and Watts. (H. H. Statham) Fortn. 67: 303. — (E. R. Pennell) Nation, 64: 44.
— Art of. (G. White) Sewanee, 7: 469.
— as a Modeller in Clay. Studio (Lond.) 1: 3.
— Captive Andromache. (F. B. Sawvel) Educa. 21: 32.
— Drawings and Studies of. Studio (Internat.) 4: 277. — Ath. '98, 1: 27.
— Jessica. Art J. 50: 202.
— Notes on. (G. Costa) Cornh. 75: 373.
— the Painter of the Gods. (W. Bayliss) Good Words, 40: 42.
— Paintings of. Acad. 51: 52.
— Parable of the Wise and Foolish Virgins, a Painting. (J. P. Lenox) Bib. World, 11: 256.
— Sketches by. (A. L. Baldry) M. of Art, 20: 69. — (Mrs. R. Barrington) National, 28: 505. Same art. Ecl. M. 128: 180.
— Studies by. Studio (Lond.) 9: 106.

Leighton, Frederick, Lord, Works of, at the Royal Academy Winter Exhibition. — (S. Beale) Am. Arch. 55: 43. — Art J. 49: 58.
Leipzig as a Student Centre. (L. Campbell-Tipton) Music, 16: 437.
— Decisive Days before. (W. V. Bremen) J. Mil. Serv. Inst. 12: 620.
— Laboratory for Physical Chemistry at, Opening of New. (H. C. Jones) Science, n. s. 7: 786. Nature, 64: 127.
— Music in. Music, 12: 117.
— Music Students in. (M. H. Chamberlain) Music, 14: 147.
— The Retreat from. Blackw. 165: 704.
Leisure, Genius, Books, and Reading. (A. Birrell) Chamb. J. 75: 81. Same art. Liv. Age, 216: 557.
Leisure Class and its Critics. (W. H. Mallock) Indep. 52: 2725.
— Theory of, Veblen's. (D. C. Wells) Yale R. 8: 213.
— (J. Cummings) J. Pol. Econ. 7: 425.
— — — Cummings's Strictures on. (T. Veblen) J. Pol. Econ. 8: 106.
Leiter Corner in Wheat. Spec. 80: 854. — (J. M. C. Hampson) Nat'l M. (Bost.) 8: 572. — (P. J. O'Keefe) Nat'l M. (Bost.) 9: 25.
Leitner, Dr. Gottlieb Wm. Geog. J. 13: 545. — J. Soc. Arts, 47: 441. — Asia. R. 27: 224.
Lejeune, L. F. Memoirs; ed. by Mrs. Bell. (E. G. Johnson) Dial (Ch.) 22: 302.
Leland Stanford University. See Stanford University.
Lely, Sir Peter. Munsey, 17: 542.
Lemaire, Madeleine, Pictures by. Artist (N. Y.) 26: 146.
Lemaitre, Jules. (B. W. Wells) Bookman, 5: 487.
Lemon-ranching on the Pacific Slope. (D. Wingate) Chamb. J. 78: 719.
Le Moyne, Mr. and Mrs. William T. Critic, 33: 57.
Lenbach, Franz von, Painter of Bismarck. (E. Coues) Cent. 31: 323. — (S. Whitman) Harper, 102: 398. — (C. Brinton) Critic, 39: 503. — (J. Anderson) Pall Mall M. 17: 483.
L'Enfant, Pierre Charles, the First Government Architect. (F. D. Owen) Archit. R. 11: 581.
Length, Notes on Mental Standards of. (F. W. Colegrove) Am. J. Psychol. 10: 292.
— Visual and Tactuo-muscular Estimation of. (E. J. Swift) Am. J. Psychol. 11: 527.
Lennox, Margaret Douglas, Countess of. (Mrs. A. M. Smith) Lippinc. 65: 430.
Lennox, Lady Sarah, Life and Letters of, edited by Countess of Ilchester and Lord Stavordale. Ath. '01, 2: 691.
— Romance of. (J. Mowbray) Cornh. 79: 68. Same art. Ecl. M. 132: 547.
Lenox, Massachusetts. (F. Lynch) New Eng. M. n. s. 23: 192.
— Summer Colony at. (C. M. Lincoln) Munsey, 17: 674.
Lenox Library and its Founder. (W. Eames) Lib. J. 24: 199.
Lens-making. (R. S. Baker) McClure, 15: 544.
— Modern, Lummer on. (R. T. Glazebrook) Nature, 63: 227.
Lent, Fashionable. (K. Hoffman) Munsey, 22: 825.
Lenten Season, The. Outl. 64: 481.
Lenz, — von, Piano Virtuoso. (A. J. Jeroloman) Music, 16: 247.
Leo XIII., Pope. (E. M. de Vogüé) Forum, 22: 513. — (F. M. Crawford) Outl. 61: 773. — (Giovanni D. Vecchio) Good Words, 41: 695. — Month, 94: 324. — (E. M. de Vogüé) Pall Mall M. 23: 290. Same art. Ecl. M. 136: 711. Same art. Liv. Age, 229: 83.

Leo XIII. and the Next Pope. (E. Meynier) Outl. 66: 53.
— Bull on Anglican Orders. Church Q. 43: 365.
  See Church of England.
— Busy Holiday of. (A. Diarista) Cath. World, 74: 17.
— Encyclical on the Unity of the Church. Church Q. 43: 289.
— Encyclicals of, Recent. Am. Cath. Q. 23: 852.
— Intellectual Activity of. (J. Murphy) Cath. World, 73: 238.
— Jubilee of. (J. L. Hurst) Indep. 52: 243. — (H. Thurston) Month, 94: 561. 95: 48.
— on Americanism. Cath. World, 69: 133. — Outl. 61: 491.
— — and the "Outlook." Cath. World, 69: 1.
— Poetry of. (A. B. McGill) Cath. World, 71: 685.
— Prince of Diplomats. (W. Burt) Meth. R. 60: 57.
Leon, Spain. (Mrs. M. L. Woods) Cornh. 80: 299.
Leoncavallo's Story, told by Himself. Music, 16: 444.
Leonids. See Meteors, Leonid.
Leopard Hunt in Northern Bengal. (J. W. Parry) Outing, 33: 385.
Leopard Hunting in India. (C. E. Clay) Outing, 37: 706.
Leopardi, Giacomo. (W. K. Johnson) Fortn. 70: 17.
— and Evolutional Pessimism. (W. N. Guthrie) Sewanee, 4: 129.
— Carducci's. (J. W. Mario) Nation, 67: 201.
— The Home of. (Sir G. Douglas) Bookman, 7: 470.
— Poems; Morrison's ed. (F. Greenslet) Nation, 72: 241.
— Poet and Philosopher. (W. B. Wallace) Idler, 17: 221.
Lepage, Jules Bastien, in London. (D. Stanley) Art J. 49: 53.
Lepère, Auguste; a French Wood-engraver. (G. Mourey) Studio (Internat.) 3: 143.
Lepers, The; a tale of South Africa. (W. C. Scully) Scrib. M. 25: 208.
Lepidoptera of British Isles: genus Dianthœcia, Barrett on. (W. F. Kirby) Nature, 57: 460.
Le Play Method of Social Observation. Am. J. Sociol. 2: 662.
Leprosy and Hawaiian Annexation. (P. A. Morrow) No. Am. 165: 582. — (B. Foster) No. Am. 167: 300.
— in India. (H. A. Acworth) J. Soc. Arts, 47: 415.
— of the Bible, Nature of. (J. F. Schamberg) Bib. World, 13: 161.
— Shall we Annex? Cosmopol. 24: 557.
Le Puy, Cathedral of. (Mrs. S. Van Rensselaer) Cent. 36: 723.
Lerberghe, Charles van. Entrevisions. (Arthur Symons) Sat. R. 86: 243.
Le Sage, A. R. Don Quixote, Alleged 1604 Edition of. (J. Fitzmaurice-Kelly) Ath. '97, 2: 99.
— — Shelton's. Ath. '97, 1: 143.
Lesbos, Folktales from. (W. R. Paton) Folk-Lore, 10: 495.
Lescarbot, Marc, of Vervins, the French Hakluyt. (H. P. Biggar) Am. Hist. R. 6: 671.
Leschetizky, the Greatest Music Master in Europe. (J. F. Rowbotham) Good Words, 41: 599.
Lèse Majeste. Indep. 53: 1836.
Le Sidaner, Artist. (G. Mourey) Studio (Internat.) 15: 30.
Leslie, Alexander, 1st Earl of Leven, C. T. Terry's Life of. (T. A. Dodge) Am. Hist. R. 5: 756. — Acad. 57: 424.
Leslie, Charles Robert. (J. C. Van Dyke) Cent. 39: 235.
Leslie, David: a Comrade of the Napiers. (S. Gwynn) Cornh. 77: 645.
Leslie, Mrs. Frank. (J. M. McGovern) Writer, 6: 178.
Le Sœur, Herbert. Equestrian Statue of King Charles I. (C. Monkhouse) Art J. 53: 35.

Les Pennes to St. Chamas. (B. Harrison) Outing, 29: 430.
Lespinasse, Julie Jeanne Elenore de, 1732-75. (S. G. Tallentyre) Longm. 36: 425. Same art. Liv. Age, 227: 121. Same art. Ecl. M. 135: 783. — Temp. Bar, 116: 436.
— Some Real Love Letters. (Mrs. T. Chapman) 19th Cent. 49: 1038.
— A Spinster's Salon in the 18th Century. (C. Jebb) Westm. 151: 417.
Lessi, Tito. Art J. 49: 41.
Lessing, Gotthold Ephraim. (J. Forster) Chaut. 26: 378.
— as a Librarian. (A. Clarke) Library, n. s. 2: 376.
— Minna von Barnhelm, Cutting's. (C. B. Wilson) School R. 7: 562.
Lessing, Madge, Actress, Interview with. (Caroline A. Morton) Idler, 20: 413.
Lesson in Acting; a farce. (H. Aïde) 19th Cent. 44: 760.
Lesson in Heraldry, A; a story. (J. London) Nat'l M. (Bost.) 11: 635.
Lesson in Manners, A. Liv. Age, 231: 758.
Lesson Books, Our Ancestors'. (S. E. Braine) Good Words, 40: 403.
Lesson Plans; an experiment. (C. A. Scott) Educa. R. 21: 153.
Lessor's Covenant to Repair, A Curious Point as to Rights of the Lessee. (A. E. Hughes) Law Q. 17: 26.
Let us Follow Him. (H. Sienkiewicz) Outl. 56: 997.
Lethe; a poem. (C. E. Meetkerke) Argosy, 65: 85.
Lethean Apocalypse, A. Open Court, 12: 357.
Letreïs, Brittany. (Cecilia Warren) Scrib. M. 23: 460.
Letter from the 'Hio, A; a story. (R. E. Robinson) McClure, 11: 393. Same art. Idler, 20: 77.
Letter-box, The; a story. (R. Bazin) Outl. 64: 543.
Letter-writer, An Ideal. (R. E. S. Hart) Temp. Bar, 110: 526.
Letter-writers, Complete. (F. M. Parsons) Longm. 31: 526. 32: 331.
— Roman, of To-day. (L. Oxenden) Temp. Bar, 115: 454. Same art. Liv. Age, 219: 864.
Letter-writing and a Modern Writer. Month, 96: 272.
— Art of. (H. Paul) 19th Cent. 44: 132. — Acad. 55: 322.
— Survival of. (R. Ogden) Nation, 70: 5.
Lettering. (E. F. Strange) Am. Arch. 69: 52.
— Design in. (L. F. Day) J. Soc. Arts, 45: 1103, 1115.
— in Ornament. (L. F. Day) Archit. R. 8: 25, 37.
— Office. (F. C. Brown) Archit. R. 8: 87, 123.
— Practice of. (E. F. Strange) Art J. 52: 313. Same art. J. Soc. Arts, 48: 611.
Letterman, Jonathan. J. Mil. Serv. Inst. 4: 250.
Letters and Politics. Spec. 83: 949. Same art. Liv. Age, 224: 322.
— and Public Life. Nation, 67: 442.
Letters and Letter-writing. (R. Gee) Ecl. M. 128: 850.
— A Bundle of Early Virginia. Pall Mall M. 15: 397.
— A Child's. (H. W. Moody) McClure, 14: 55.
— of Elizabeth. Macmil. 84: 298.
— of a Staff-officer in 1794. (E. M. Lloyd) Un. Serv. M. 15: 506.
— Some Writers of Good. (R. Cortissoz) Cent. 31: 780.
— to Clorinda. (J. K. Jerome) Idler, 11: 131, 684. 12: 275.
Letters to Sadie; a story. (E. Broderick) Poet-Lore, 12: 347.
Lettice; a story. (A. Gissing) Eng. Illust. 17: 69.
Lettie. (B. N. Roy) Overland, n. s. 35: 19.
Lettres Closes. (N. W. Sibley) Westm. 148: 159.
Leuckart, Rudolf. Nature, 57: 542.
Leuthen, Battle of. (F. Dixon) Temp. Bar, 115: 58.

Levasseur, Emile, on the American Workman. (S. N. D. North) Pol. Sci. Q. 13: 321.

Levebus, Celia, as Illustrator of Blake. (H. W. Bromhead) Art J. 52: 237.

Levee System, Success of. (R. S. Taylor) Forum, 24: 325.

Levees, Dredging vs. (Gustave Dyes) Forum, 24: 334.

Levens Hall, North of England. (Dosia Bagot) Pall Mall M. 11: 436.

Lever, Charles. Spec. 80: 91. — Acad. 51: 404.

Levi, Genealogies of the Tribe of. (M. Berlin) Jew. Q. 12: 291.

— Testament of, Aramaic Text of. (H. L. Pass and J. Arendzen) Jew. Q. 12: 651.

Levi, David, Poet and Patriot. (Helen Zimmern) Jew. Q. 9: 363.

Levitical Code, The. (L. Abbott) Outl. 65: 441.

Levitical Ritual, Babylonian Influence in. (P. Haupt) J. Bib. Lit. 19: 55.

Levy, Amy, Poetry of. (A. Wallas) Acad. 57: 162.

Levy, M. Paul Calmann. Ath. '00, 1: 208.

Levy, Uriah P., an American Forerunner of Dreyfus. (J. M. Morgan) Cent. 36: 796.

Lévy-Dhurmer, M. L., Painter. (G. Mourey) Studio (Internat.) 1: 3.

Lewes, Campaign of. (H. E. Malden) Un. Serv. M. 20: 37.

Lewis, Cora Amanda. Writer, 14: 60.

Lewis, Francis Owen. Acad. 57: 637.

Lewis, Henry, Obituary of. Nat. Sci. 12: 420.

Lewis vs. Clay. Bank. M. (Lond.) 65: 220.

Lexicography, Dr. Murray on. (L. Dyer) Nation, 71: 28.

Lexington and Concord, News of, carried to the King. (R. S. Rantoul) Cent. 36: 714.

Leyden, Pilgrim Press in. (W. E. Griffis) New Eng. M. n. s. 19: 559.

Leyendecker, Joseph C., Illustrator. (F. B. Rae, jr.) Brush & P. 1: 15.

Lhasa, City of. (T. H. Holdich) Geog. J. 18: 602.

— in 1811, A Visit to. (H. Pearse) Un. Serv. M. 16: 183.

Lhermitte, Léon, Work of. Illus. (F. Lees) Artist, (N. Y.) 23: 84.

Liar, The; a story. (A. R. Brown) Bk. News, 16: 465.

Libel Actions, Newspapers and. Spec. 85: 796.

Libel, Newspapers and. (J. B. Bishop) Nation, 66: 64.

Liberal Congress of Religion. R. of Rs. (N. Y.) 18: 434.

Liberal Movements of the Last Half-century. (L. Campbell) Fortn. 73: 427.

Liberal Party and Free Soil Party in the Northwest, Smith's. (J. D. Cox) Nation, 66: 384.

Liberal Party in England. Forum, 30: 513. — Nation, 72: 409.

— and the Church. (C. F. Garbett) Westm. 148: 413.

— and its Failures in 1898. Spec. 81: 105.

— and the Liberal Clergy. Spec. 78: 77.

— and the Peers. (F. G. Thomas) Westm. 151: 20.

— Churchmen in. (H. C. Garrod) Westm. 154: 519.

— Collapse of. (J. G. Rogers; S. Low; J. K. Hardie; J. R. MacDonald) 19th Cent. 45: 1.

— Dilke on. Spec. 79: 586.

— Educating the. Fortn. 71: 175.

— Future of the. Fortn. 74: 929.

— Future of Liberalism. Spec. 81: 170.

— Hope of. (R. T. Lang) Westm. 155: 370.

— How to re-unite. (D. S. A. Cosby) Westm. 151: 332.

— "in extremis." (E. Dicey) Fortn. 76: 204.

— in 1900. Wanted a Leader. (J. G. Rogers) 19th Cent. 48: 149.

— Is it in Collapse? (J. G. Rogers) 19th Cent. 43: 135.

— Main Stream of. (H. Newbolt) Monthly R. 4, no. 2: 1.

Liberal Party in England, a Menace to English Democracy. (H. E. Mahood) Forum, 31: 587.

— The New. (G. F. Millin) Fortn. 75: 634.

— Next Liberal Leader. Spec. 80: 782.

— Present State of. Fortn. 69: 910.

— Rallying-point and the Touchstone. Westm. 152: 237.

— Rallying-points for. Fortn. 72: 17.

— What should be the Policy of? Westm. 152: 26.

Liberalism and its Cross-currents. (J. G. Rogers) 19th Cent. 46: 527.

— and Intransigeance. (W. Ward) 19th Cent. 47: 960.

— Decline of. (H. W. Massingham) National, 35: 560. — (W. Clarke) Pol. Sci. Q. 16: 450.

— Downfall of. (E. Dicey) Fortn. 74: 803.

— Eclipse of. (D. MacG. Means) Nation, 71: 105.

— Future of. (A. B. C. and Expertus) Fortn. 69: 1. — Spec. 78: 4.

— Harcourt and Bryce on. Spec. 78: 393.

— A Lead for. Fortn. 74: 457.

Liberals, Forward! March!! Westm. 156: 370.

— The Leaderless, and Lord Rosebery. (W. L. Stobart) Fortn. 69: 920.

Liberati, Alessandro, Cornet Player. (S. L. Jacobson) Music, 15: 60.

Liberty, A. Lasenby, and his Influence on Artistic Textiles. (A. L. Baldry) Art J. 52: 45.

Liberty. (F. L. Oswald) Lippinc. 63: 122.

— and Government. (H. E. S. Fremantle) Internat. J. Ethics, 10: 439.

— Christian. (J. M. Hark) Outl. 63: 334.

— Christian Ideal of. (E. M. Caillard) Contemp. 73: 838.

— Delusions about. (J. C. Ridpath) Arena, 19: 281.

— Law and. (F. Exline) Arena, 26: 298.

— The Law of. (E. M. Caillard) Contemp. 71: 531.

— Lawful, and Reasonable Service. (M. D. Petre) Am. Cath. Q. 24, no. 3: 90.

— Of; a poem. (W. P. Foster) Atlan. 86: 424.

— of God's Children. (L. Abbott) Outl. 65: 125.

— of the Individual. (J. P. Poole) Westm. 149: 611. Same art. Ecl. M. 131: 312.

— through Sovereignty. (J. Lee) New Eng. M. n. s. 23: 294.

Librarian, A. Library, 4: 233.

— The, and the Importer. (E. Lemcke) Pub. Lib. 2: 443, 487. Same art. Lib. J. 22: supp. 12.

— and the Patriotic Societies. (A. Scott) Lib. J. 22: 80.

— and Staff, Personal Relations of. (T. Hitchler) Lib. J. 23: 49.

— Being a. (H. J. Carr) Lib. J. 26: supp. 1.

— His Helps and Hindrances. (S. Smith) Library, 8: 157.

— in relation to Readers, Duties of a. (H. Midworth) Library, 5: 130.

— Trained, in a Small Library. (J. A. Hopkins) Pub. Lib. 2: 490.

— Trials of a. (C. H. Garland) Lib. J. 22: 129.

— A University, 250 Years Ago. (A. W. Robertson) Library, 2: 154.

Librarian-made Books and Titles. (J. Gilburt) Library, 4: 8.

Librariana, or, Literature of Libraries. (F. J. Teggart) Lib. J. 25: 223, 577, 625.

Librarians at Montreal, The. Nation, 70: 492.

— Children's, Special Training for. Lib. J. 23: supp. 80. — Pub. Lib. 4: 99.

— College, Special Training for. (G. T. Little) Lib. J. 23: supp. 79.

— Congress at Paris. (W. Roberts) Ath. '00, 1: 751. 2: 283. — (M. W. Plummer) Lib. J. 25: 580.

Libraries, Public, Laws for Management of Small. (M. W. Freeman) Lib. J. 24: supp. 76.
— — Medical Departments in Rate supported. (G. E. Wire) Pub. Lib. 6: 267.
— — of the Future. (M. W. Plummer) Lib. J. 26: 63.
— — of Manchester, Eng. Library, 4: 288.
— — Open Access in. (H. K. Moore) Library, n. s. 1: 49. — (J. Thomson) Lib. J. 23: supp. 40.
— — — and Public Morals. (I. E. Lord) Lib. J. 26: 65.
— — — Women Readers and Juvenile Departments in. Library, 4: 105.
— — Opportunities of. (G. Countrymen) Lib. J. 26: supp. 52.
— — Organization of. (G. E. Wire) Lib. J. 24: supp. 70.
— — Paternalism in. (L. Swift) Lib. J. 24: 609. — (B. W. Pennock) Lib. J. 25: 61.
— — Photographs and Photoprints in. (C. A. Cutter) Lib. J. 25: 619.
— — Picture Bulletins in. (E. W. Gaillard) Lib. J. 26: 192.
— — Picture Work in Children's Room. (C. W. Hunt; E. L. Moore) Lib. J. 25: supp. 66.
— — Pictures for Children. (A. C. Moore) Lib. J. 25: 159.
— — Proposals made nearly Two Centuries ago to Found. (W. Blades) Library, 1: 9.
— — Provision for Children in. (K. L. Smith) R. of Rs. (N. Y.) 22: 48.
— — Public Documents in Small. (E. D. Fuller) Lib. J. 23: 564.
— — Reading Room and Periodicals. (H. P. James) Lib. J. 21: supp. 49.
— — Reference Work. (E. B. Woodruff) Lib. J. 22: supp. 65.
— — Relation of, to Literature. (L. Swift) Lib. J. 25: 323.
— — Rhode Island. (H. R. Palmer) New Eng. M. n. s. 22: 478.
— — Selection of Books for. (A. Schinz) Lib. J. 24: 661.
— — Staff of, Organization and Management of. (F. P. Hill) Lib. J. 22: 381.
— — State Supervision of. (C. A. Torrey) Pub. Lib. 6: 271.
— — Statistics of. Library, n. s. 2: 164.
— — — and Reports of. (E. C. Doren) Lib. J. 24: supp. 57.
— — — Science of. (F. J. Teggart) Lib. J. 26: 796.
— — Trustees of. (T. L. Montgomery) Lib. J. 25: supp. 42.
— — — Functions of. (F. M. Crunden) Lib. J. 21: supp. 32.
— — Two-book System. (E. A. Birge) Lib. J. 23: 93. — Pub. Lib. 2: 173.
— — Use of, by Artisans. (W. E. Foster) Lib. J. 23: 188.
— — Ventilation, Heating, and Lighting of. (W. H. Greenhough) Library, 2: 421.
— — What may be done by the City. (T. L. Montgomery) Lib. J. 26: supp. 5.
— — What may be done by the Nation. (H. Putnam) Lib. J. 26: supp. 9.
— — What may be done by the State. (E. A. Birge) Lib. J. 26: supp. 7.
— — Work for Children in. (M. W. Plummer) Lib. J. 22: 679. — (L. A. Eastman) Lib. J. 22: 686.
— — Work in. (L. A. Eastman) Lib. J. 22: supp. 80.
— — Workingmen's Clubs and. (A. L. Peck) Lib. J. 23: 612.
— Public Library Movement in Organized Form. (W. I. Fletcher) Citizen, 3: 157.

Libraries, Prussian, Central Catalogue of the. Library, n. s. 2: 274.
— Railroad Travelling. (S. H. Ranck) Lib. J. 22: 10.
— Reference-books and, Instruction in Use of. Lib. J. 23: supp. 84.
— — Report on, 1898. (F. A. Hutchins) Lib. J. 23: supp. 56.
— Reference Work in Small Circulating. (A. E. Bostwick) Pub. Lib. 5: 419.
— Rural Public. (E. A. Baker) Library, 8: 298
— School. (E. C. Doren) Lib. J. 22: 190.
— — and Public Libraries. Pub. Lib. 1: 94.
— State, and the Library of Congress. (H. Putnam) Lib. J. 25: 729. Same art. Pub. Lib. 6: 23.
— — Collection, Distribution, and Exchange of Public Documents. (W. E. Henry) Lib. J. 24: supp. 85.
— — Newspapers in. (L. D. Carver) Pub. Lib. 6: 19.
— Traveling. (J. Thomson) Lib. J. 21: supp. 29. — Lit. W. (Bost.) 30: 378. — Sat. R. 92: 269. — Pub. Lib. 2: 47.
— — a Boon for American Country Readers. (W. B. Shaw) R. of Rs. (N. Y.) 17: 165.
— — Department of Brooklyn Public Library. Pub. Lib. 5: 329.
— — for Country Schools in the South. Pub. Lib. 5: 427.
— — Forgotten; Itinerating Libraries, 1817-34. (S. H. Ranck) Lib. J. 26: 261.
— — in Alabama. (Kate H. Morrissette) Sewanee, 6: 345.
— — in England. Acad. 52: 329.
— — in Farming Communities. (A. B. Hostetter) Pub. Lib. 6: 223.
— — in Lumbering Camps. (A. Fitzpatrick) Canad. M. 17: 49.
— — in Nebraska. Pub. Lib. 1: 269.
— — in Wisconsin. (J. W. White) Outl. 58: 219. — Liv. Age, 216: 470.
— — Local Supervision of. (F. A. Hutchins) Lib. J. 22: supp. 17.
— — Management of. (J. Brigham) Lib. J. 24: supp. 81.
— — of Illustrations. (H. J. Carter) Lib. J. 22: 293.
— — Railroad. (K. L. Smith) Outl. 67: 961.
— Service in. Lit. W. (Bost.) 29: 265.
— Small, Organization of. (Virginia Dodge) Midland, 9: 373, 472, 568.
— Sunday-school. (B. C. Steiner) Lib. J. 23: 276.
— University, and Department Libraries. (G. H. Baker) Lib. J. 23: supp. 103. — (W. W. Bishop) Lib. J. 26: 14.
— Village, Problem of. (J. D. Brown) Library, 6: 99.
— — Work of. (G. Iles) World's Work, 1: 443.
— Workmen's, in Glamorganshire and Monmouthshire. (E. Owen) Library, 8: 1.
— Yorkshire Village. (B. Wood) Library, 6: 37.
Libraries Acts, and Parish Councils. Library, 6: 307.
Library as an Aid to School Work. (W. H. Bates) School R. 7: 179.
— Branch, Functions of a. Pub. Lib. 6: 275.
— Business Men and the. (J. C. Dana) Pub. Lib. 5: 202.
— Cathedral, A Thousand Years of a. (J. K. Floyer) Reliquary, 41: 11.
— Clippings for the. (E. C. Lyon) Pub. Lib. 6: 329.
— An East End Free. (G. F. Hilcken) Library, 2: 174.
— for Children, A Selected. (M. Temple) Pub. Lib. 6: 406.
— Function of the. (S. C. Fairchild) Pub. Lib. 6: 527.
— How to interest Schools in the. (M. E. Sargent) Pub. Lib. 6: 9.
— in relation to Literature. (L. Swift) Pub. Lib. 5: 196.

Library, Iowa State Loaning. Midland, 11: 84.
— Lawyer's. Library, 1: 161.
— of the Average Young Man. (J. H. Canfield) Cosmopol. 30: 609.
— of the Cathedral Church of Wells, England. Archæol. 57: 201.
— of Congress. *See* Congressional Library.
— of a Political Club. (A. W. Hutton) Library, 2: 77.
— of a Scottish Bank Forger. Bank. M. (Lond.) 65: 223.
— Old Convent. (C. J. Willdey) Belgra. 95: 414.
— Open Shelves in the Toledo, O., Public. (F. D. Jermain) Pub. Lib. 5: 53.
— A Perfect. Belgra. 98: 119.
— Public, at Auckland, N. Z. (W. L. F. Covert) Library, 2: 328.
— — The Child in the. (G. T. Clark) Pub. Lib. 1: 310.
— — in a Small Town. (W. R. Harshaw) Outl. 68: 492.
— — in the 20th Century. (W. I. Fletcher) Pub. Lib. 6: 379.
— — Place of, in Popular Education. (J. J. Ogle) Library, 3: 401.
— — Small; What it needs. Pub. Lib. 5: 187.
— Reference, Books for a. (F. T. Barrett) Library, 8: 473. — (B. Wood) Library, 8: 522.
— Reference Work in a Small. (A. C. Granger) Pub. Lib. 6: 548.
— Relation of the State to. (W. Ford) Pub. Lib. 5: 251.
— The Romance of a Famous. (H. Putnam) Atlan. 81: 538.
— Small, Distribution of Labor in. (E. L. Moore) Pub. Lib. 6: 229.
— Some Books in my. Chamb. J. 77: 785.
— Some Hints towards the Formation of a. Chamb. J. 74: 149.
— State, Classification and Cataloging of a. (C. B. Galbreath) Pub. Lib. 4: 437.
— — Lending Books from. (M. Dewey) Pub. Lib. 6: 34.
— Subscription, in Connection with a Public Library. Library, 5: 40.
— Traveling, of Pictures. (M. E. Tanner) Pub. Lib. 2: 263.
— Village, Aspirations of. (E. Peck) Lib. J. 23: 522.
— What can it best do for Children? Pub. Lib. 4: 317.
Library Accessions; Checking of the Processes. (L. S. Jast) Library, n. s. 1: 152.
Library Apprentice, Experience of a. Pub. Lib. 6: 155.
Library Architecture. Lit. W. (Bost.) 28: 274. — (N. S. Patton) Pub. Lib. 6: 200. — (G. Warner) Pub. Lib. 6: 607.
— from the Architect's Standpoint. (E. B. Green) Pub. Lib. 6: 599.
Library Assistant, Education of the. (H. D. Roberts) Library, 9: 103.
Library Assistant's Associations and Training Classes in England. Pub. Lib. 4: 107.
Library Assistant's Opportunity. (H. L. Elmendorf) Library, 9: 137.
Library Assistants, Training of. (M. London) Library, 10: 101.
Library Association, Ohio, Annual Meeting of. Pub. Lib. 3: 389.
Library Association of the U. K., 1877-97. (W. H. K. Wright) Library, 10: 197, 245.
— 13th Annual Meeting of. Library, 2: 365.
— 14th Annual Meeting of, Nottingham. Library, 3: 353.
— Meeting at Bristol, 1900. Ath. '00, 2: 413, 442.
— Work and Aims of. (C. Christie) Library, 1: 353.

Library Association Summer School. (W. E. Doubleday) Library, 8: 207.
Library Building, How to plan a Small. (H. M. Utley) Lib. J. 24: supp. 21.
Library Buildings, New Ideas in. (W. E. Foster) Am. Arch. 61: 38.
— Planning of. (O. Bluemner) Pub. Lib. 3: 3, 39, 75, 92, 115, 201, 239, 283, 335, 375.
— Preliminaries. (F. P. Hill) Lib. J. 24: 563.
— Report on, 1898. (W. E. Foster) Lib. J. 23: supp. 13.
— Suggestions on. (E. N. Lamm) Pub. Lib. 6: 610.
Library Bureau, The London. Acad. 51: 406.
Library Call Numbers, Simplicity in. (H. P. James) Pub. Lib. 1: 189.
Library Catalogues, Acceptable. (H. E. Curran) Library, 7: 21.
— and Reference Books, Instruction of Children in Use of. Pub. Lib. 4: 311.
Library Clubs, State and Local. (W. H. Tillinghast) Lib. J. 23: 519.
Library Commissions, State. (A. H. Chase) Pub. Lib. 6: 38.
— — and State Librarians. (C. B. Galbreath) Lib. J. 25: supp. 54.
— — How to organize. (L. E. Stearns) Lib. J. 24: supp. 16.
— — Work of. (G. A. Countryman) Lib. J. 25: supp. 51.
Library Committee, Public, and other Educational Bodies. (J. J. Ogle) Library, 7: 129.
Library Conference, Second International, 1897. Library, 9: 285. — Lib. J. 22: 391, 690. — Pub. Lib. 2: 193, 410.
Library Congress, Trans-Mississippi, 1898. Pub. Lib. 3: 349. — (H. J. Carr) Lib. J. 23: 571.
Library Coöperation. (L. Ambrose) Dial (Ch.) 31: 49.
Library Development, Latest Stage of; Brumback County Library. (E. I. Antrim) Forum, 31: 336.
Library Economy, Instruction in. (K. L. Sharp) Lib. J. 23: supp. 75.
Library Exhibits. Pub. Lib. 4: 148.
Library Fund Entertainment, The; a story. (F. W. Lee) Midland, 9: 427.
Library History, Literature of. (F. J. Teggart) Lib. J. 22: supp. 35.
Library Hospital. (D. Tylor) Library, 7: 347.
Library Indicators, with Special Reference to the "Duplex Indicator." (A. W. Robertson) Library, 2: 21.
Library Law, Good. (W. R. Eastman) Lib. J. 25: supp. 49.
Library Legislation. (H. W. Fovargue) Library, n. s. 1: 89.
— in New York. Lib. J. 25: 9.
— in Wisconsin. (F. A. Hutchins) Lib. J. 22: 255.
Library Literature of the 19th Century. (F. J. Teggart) Lib. J. 26: 257.
Library Movement, Educational Value of. (E. Foskett) Library, 7: 110.
— How Women's Clubs may help. (E. G. Browning) Lib. J. 24: supp. 18.
— in America. (S. C. Fairchild) Lib. J. 26: 73.
— in Bristol, Eng., History of the. Library, 8: 198.
— in the Far West. (J. C. Dana) Library, 8: 446.
— in Greater London. (W. E. Doubleday) Library, 4: 141.
— in Kent. (H. R. Plomer) Library, 4: 329.
— in London. (C. Welch) Library, 7: 97.
— in the United States. (J. L. Harrison) Library, 8: 110, 141.
Library Primer, A. L. A. Pub. Lib. 1: 5, 79.

Li Hung Chang's Furs. Spec. 80: 405.

Like Old Times; a story. (G. Fosbery) Argosy, 66: 721.

Like to Like; a trivial romance. (G.S. Street) Blackw. 165: 682, 816.

Likeness, The; a story. (A. Ponsonby) Pall Mall M. 22: 58.

Likuku; a Congoland love story. (M. D. Hatch) Outing, 30: 28, 146.

Lilford, Lord Thomas. Acad. 60: 160.

Liliencron, Detley von. (R. C. Ford) Meth. R. 61: 264.

Lilies. (Bessie L. Putnam) Educa. 17: 545.
— and Lilies. (B. Jones) Sund. M. 27: 239.
— and Men. (E. B. Payne) Overland, n. s. 35: 349.
— Lilium Humboldtii and Allied Species. (C. Purdy) Garden & F. 10: 43.
— Lilium Parvum and L. Parviflorum. (C. Purdy) Garden & F. 10: 502.

"Lilliput," Letters from. Chaut. 33: 492.

Lily of London Bridge. (V. Sheard) New Eng. M. n. s. 20: 737. 21: 52. Same art. Canad. M. 13: 310, 407.

Lima, Peru, "City of the Kings." (M. MacMahon) Cath. World, 73: 54.

Lime-juice Cure, The. Chamb. J. 77: 670.

Limerick, Ireland, Old and New. (F. J. Austin) Belgra. 96: 314.

Limerick Tigers; a story. (H. S. Edwards) Cent. 35: 467.

Limestone at Bethany, Mo. (H. F. Bain) Am. J. Sci. 155: 433.

Limestone Reefs, Tertiary Elevated, of Fiji. (A. Agassiz) Am. J. Sci. 156: 165.

Limestones, St. Joseph and Potosi, of St. François County, Mo., Geological Relations and Age of. (F. S. Nason) Am. J. Sci. 162: 358.

Limit of Wealth, A. (F. H. Sweet) Lippinc. 62: 116.

Limitations; a poem. (E. K. Herron) Poet-Lore, 11: 477.

Limitations; a character sketch. (E. Wyatt) McClure, 16: 551.

Limited vs. Unlimited Liability. (S. Brodhurst) Macmil. 79: 20.

Limnological Commission of the American Microscopical Society. Science, n. s. 13: 897.

Limoges Enamels. (S. Baring-Gould) Sund. M. 30: 223. — (S. Baring-Gould) M. of Art, 23: 394, 440.

Lincoln, Abraham; a study from life. (H. C. Whitney) Arena, 19: 464.
— and the Matson Negroes. (J. W. Weik) Arena, 17: 752.
— and Seward, Recollections of. (J. M. Scovel) Overland, n. s. 38: 265.
— and Temperance. (D. D. Thompson) Meth. R. 59: 9.
— as an Antagonist. (C. P. Button) Lippinc. 67: 209.
— as a Literary Man, with portrait. (H. W. Mabie) Outl. 58: 321.
— Assassination of. (L. B. Fletcher) Chaut. 31: 243.
— Birthday of; a poem. (R. H. Stoddard) Outl. 61: 294.
— Death of. (E. C. Brown) Chaut. 31: 5⋈.
— Entering Richmond, 1865. (L. Leslie) Midland, 7: 410.
— Hapgood's Life of. Am. Hist. R. 5: 778.
— Home Life in Washington. (L. J. Perry) Harper, 94: 353.
— How he Righted a Wrong. (H. S. Burrage) Indep. 53: 379.
— in Caricature. (R. R. Wilson) Bk. Buyer, 15: 209.
— in Contemporary Caricature. R. of Rs. (N. Y.) 23: 156.
— Inner Life of. (N. Hapgood) Chaut. 31: 79.
— Lamon and Field's Life of. (H. W. Fischer) Bookman, 7: 200.

Lincoln, Abraham, Later Life of. (I. M. Tarbell) McClure, 12: 161, 259. 13: 448.
— Mother of. (H. M. Jenkins) Pennsyl. M. 14: 129.
— Origin of his Phrase "Government of the People," etc. (G. F. Parker) R. of Rs. (N. Y.) 23: 196, 335.
— Origin of the Lincoln Rail, as related by Gov. Oglesby. (J. M. Davis) Cent. 38: 271.
— Portraits of. McClure, 10: 339.
— Power of Expression of. (R. W. Gilder) Meth. R. 61: 694.
— Recollections of. (L. A. Nash) Green Bag, 9: 479.
— (J. M. Scovel) Lippinc. 63: 277.
— Side-lights on. (J. M. Scovel) Overland, n. s. 38: 204.
— Skill as a Lawyer. (J. L. King) No. Am. 166: 186.
— A Correction. (P. Selby) No. Am. 166: 507.
— Tarbell's Life of. Am. Hist. R. 5: 778.
— Visiting Card; story of the Parole of a Confederate Officer. (J. M. Bullock) Cent. 33: 565.
— War Policy of. Quar. 185: 214.
— Washington and. (L. P. Powell) R. of Rs. (N. Y.) 23: 191.

Lincoln, Mrs. Emily Todd. (E. T. Helm) McClure, 11: 476.

Lincoln, Mrs. Jeanie Gould. (F. L. Benedict) Writer, 11: 24.

Lincoln, Levi, Gov. (J. W. Dean) N. E. Reg. 51: 425.

Lincoln, Hon. Levi, Sr. (S. May) N. E. Reg. 52: 193.

Lincoln, Thomas. (H. B. Glassco) Indep. 53: 135.

Lincoln, England, Diocese of. Church Q. 45: 174.
— Episcopal Visitations in the 15th, 16th, and 17th Centuries. (E. Peacock) Archæol. 48: 249.

Lincoln Cathedral, Library of. Library, 4: 306.
— St. Hugh's Choir, Architectural History of. Archæol. 47: 41.
— Statutes of, by Henry Bradshaw. Ath. '98, 1: 813.

Lincoln Loquitur; a poem. (E. Fawcett) Poet-Lore, 11: 528.

Lincoln (Maine) Bar. (R. K. Sewall) Green Bag, 12: 71.

Lincoln of Coyote. (J. T. McKay) Lippinc. 62: 819.

Lincoln University. (C. D. Smith) Outl. 65: 604.

Lincoln's Inn, Black Books of. Cornh. 82: 258.
— Round about. Green Bag, 10: 122.

Lincolnshire, Folklore of. (Mabel Peacock) Folk-Lore, 12: 161.

Lind, Jenny, Characteristics of. (H. Appy) Cent. 32: 554.
— in St. Louis, with portrait. (T. Papin) Music, 19: 20.
— What she did for America. (F. M. Smith) Cent. 32: 558.

Lind, Letty, Portrait of. Theatre, 39: 158.

Linda; a story of the Gippsland Bush. (B. Marnan) Strand, 18: 419.

'Linda; a tale of the Klondyke goldfields. (W. C. Platts) Chamb. J. 75: 145-200.

Lindemann, Eduard. Nature, 57: 299.

Liner and the Iceberg, The; a story. (C. Hyne) McClure, 11: 333.

Lindisfarne, Miles's Bishops of. Acad. 54: 217.

Line and Form, Crane on. Art J. 53: 119.
— Magic of a. (W. H. Hillyer) Writer, 10: 111.

Line of Least Resistance. (E. Wharton) Lippinc. 66: 559.

Line-fishing in the Solway Firth. (A. J. Gordon) Belgra. 96: 426.
— Steam. Chamb. J. 75: 699.

Linen Industry of Langdale. (B. Russell) Art J. 49: 329.

Linen Smoother, Glass, Old English, from Wilts. Reliquary, 39: 125.

Lines at Sea; a poem. (Robert Loveman) Cosmopol. 26: 252.

Lines to a Portrait by a Superior Person. (Bret Harte) Cent. 33: 71.

Linguists, Some Noted, of the Century. Chamb. J. 77: 253.

Lingulepis, Genus, Note on. (C. D. Walcott) Am. J. Sci. 153: 404.

Link with the Past, A. (H. G. Hutchinson) Longm. 37: 61. — Liv. Age, 227: 659.

Links with the Past. Spec. 86: 10-170.

Linoleum, How it is Made. (G. R. Fleming) Good Words, 38: 748.

Linotype, Story of the. Chamb. J. 74: 69. Same art. Ecl. M. 129: 54.

Linotype Work at the Carnegie Library of Pittsburgh. (E. H. Anderson) Lib. J. 23: 273.

Linton, James D., Painter. Studio (Internat.) 11: 243.

Linton, Mrs. Lynn. Acad. 54: 107. 60: 439. — With portrait. (Beatrice Harraden) Bookman, 8: 16.

— A Censor of Modern Womanhood. (G. Paston) Fortn. 76: 505.

Linton, Wm. Jas. (B. J. Hendrick) Dial (Ch.) 24: 313. — With portrait. Bk. Buyer, 16: 17. — Ath. '98, 1: 59, 94. — (B. J. Hendrick) New Eng. M. n. s. 18: 139. — (R. H. Stoddard) Critic, 32: 29.

Linuparus. New Species of Palinurid-Genus Linuparus found in the Upper Cretaceous of Dakota. (A. E. Ortmann) Am. J. Sci. 154: 290.

Linyanti Region, Journeys in the. (P. C. Reid) Geog. J. 17: 573.

Liolah. (C. S. Chase) Overland, n. s. 38: 138.

Lion, The, as Game. (F. H. Major) Overland, n. s. 37: 719.

— Habits and Nature of. (G. Bolton and A. Lawrence) Idler, 14: 520.

— in Sculpture and Painting. (L. Beatrice Thompson) Art J. 51: 371.

Lion among Ladies. (A. D. Sedgwick) Cent. 40: 381.

Lion and the Ass, Luther's Fable of. (W. H. Carruth, trans.) Open Court, 11: 221.

Lion and the Unicorn, The. (R. H. Davis) Scrib. M. 26: 129.

Lion in the Way, A; a story. (G. Hibbard) Harper, 103: 175.

"Lion," The, an Old East Indiaman. (F. T. Bullen) Spec. 82: 604.

Lion Hunt in Somaliland. (M. Wright) Outing, 35: 441.

Lion-tamer, The; a story. (H. G. Paine) Harper, 94: 963.

Lion's Mouth, The. (Alice Duer and H. W. Miller) Scrib. M. 28: 685.

Lioness, Battle with a. (A. S. Jennings) Outing, 36: 608.

Lions, Man-eating. (J. H. Porter) Outing, 34: 15.

— Training of. (S. H. Adams) McClure, 15: 387.

Lipa Gidorovna; a story. Temp. Bar, 113: 269.

Lippe-Detmold Incident. Spec. 81: 731.

Lippi, Fra Lippo. (E. Hutton) Idler, 13: 595.

— A Florentine Monk's Romance. (E. M. Elgin) Chaut. 33: 585.

Lipton, Sir T. (Lavinia Hart) Cosmopol. 31: 673.

— at Home. (D. Stewart) Outing, 38: 647.

Liquefied Air. (G. F. Barker) Chaut. 27: 526.

Liquefied Gases and Air in the Industries. (F. Mancini) Chaut. 28: 500.

Liquid Air. See Air, Liquid.

Liquids, Color of. (R. H. Bradbury) J. Frankl. Inst. 152: 321.

Liquor. Alcoholism in France. (J. C. Bracq) Outl. 62: 387.

Liquor Interests in English Politics. (E. Porritt) Chaut. 28: 554.

Liquor Laws, Our, as seen by the Committee of Fifty. (F. A. Fernald) Pop. Sci. Mo. 52: 216.

Liquor Legislation in Norway. (F. G. Peabody) Forum, 26: 551.

— New England Colonial. (E. H. Baldwin) New Eng. M. n. s. 20: 567.

Liquor Licensing, Two Reports on. (A. West) 19th Cent. 47: 260.

— Temperance Reply to Sir A. West. (T. P. Whittaker) 19th Cent. 47: 510.

Liquor Problem, Some Economic Aspects of the. (H. W. Farnam) Atlan. 83: 644.

Liquor Question in New York City. Outl. 69: 480.

Liquor Traffic, The Committee of Fifty and their Investigation. (E. T. Devine) Ann. Am. Acad. Pol. Sci. 11: 89. 12: 225.

— Dispensary, in North Carolina. (A. I. McKelway) Outl. 61: 820.

— Economic Aspects of. (C. Osborn) Econ. J. 8: 572.

— in New York. Ann. Am. Acad. Pol. Sci. 11: 157.

— in West Africa. Sat. R. 87: 485.

— Law and. (F. H. Wines) Char. R. 7: 721, 838.

— Licensing Commission. (T. C. Fry) Econ. R. 9: 476.

— Licensing Laws, Great Britain. (C. H. Denyer) Econ. J. 10: 264.

— Norwegian System of Regulating. (A. T. Kiaer) Econ. J. 9: 101.

— Public-house Reform. (O. Mordaunt) Econ. R. 11: 99.

— State Monopoly of Spirits in Russia. (A. Raffalovich) J. Statis. Soc. 64: 1.

— with West Africa. (M. H. Kingsley) Fortn. 69: 537.

Liquors, Alcoholic, Consumption of. (H. Bence-Jones) J. Statis. Soc. 63: 272.

— Injurious Constituents in. Nature, 63: 491.

— Intoxicating, Some Statistics of their National Use. Sat. R. 85: 6.

— Old English Strong Waters. Sat. R. 91: 533.

Lisbon, Notes on. (C. Edwardes) Chamb. J. 74: 717.

Lisette; a poem. (F. E. Weatherly) Temp. Bar. 113: 107.

Listemann, Bernhard, Violinist, with portrait. Music, 15: 319.

Lister, Lord. (H. C. Cameron) Good Words, 41: 516.

Lister, Sir Joseph, with portrait. Pop. Sci. Mo. 52: 693.

Liszt, Franz, as a Conductor. Music, 12: 383.

— Letters to Two Women. (H. T. Finck) Nation, 73: 248.

— Recollections of. (Karl Reinicke) Liv. Age, 217: 742.

Litany; a poem. (E. Gibson) Argosy, 63: 528.

Litchfield, Connecticut. (W. L. Adam) New Eng. M. n. s. 15: 705.

Literary Allusion, The Decay of. (W. MacDonald) Nation, 69: 369.

Literary Aspirant, The. Indep. 52: 997. — Writer, 13: 71.

Literary Aspirants and Magazine Editors. Indep. 53: 2337.

Literary Centre of the English Language, The Future. (B. Matthews) Bookman, 12: 238.

Literary Courtships. (E. A. Towle) Fortn. 72: 475. Same art. Ecl. M. 133: 824.

Literary Criticism, American, and the Doctrine of Evolution. (W. M. Payne) Internat. Mo. 2: 26, 127.

— its Scope and Effect. (I. C. Doull) Canad. M. 11: 255.

— Recent Phases of. (J. Burroughs) No. Am. 168: 42.

Literary Decency, The Evolution of. (A. Lang) Blackw. 167: 363. Same art. Ecl. M. 134: 692. Same art. Liv. Age, 225: 46.

Literary Evolution, Phenomena of. (J. London) Bookman, 12: 148.

Literary Fame and Criticism. Acad. 54: 251.

London Bridge, Old, Rebuilding of. (H. B. Philpott) Pall Mall M. **25**: 549.

London Dock, A Ramble round a. (E. R. Suffling) Chamb. J. **77**: 221.

London Libraries, and London Government Act, 1899. (T. Mason) Library, n. s. **1**: 25.

London Library, The. Acad. **54**: 88.

London Mendicity Society; inside a Beggars' Museum. (A. H. Mann) Eng. Illust. **19**: 33.

London Museums and Collections, Old. (G. L. Apperson) Antiq. n. s. **35**: 118-368.

London Quarterly Review. Lond. Q. **89**: 108.

London Sights, Some Photographs of. (H. S. Ward) Art J. **50**: 90.

London Times. Its Valuable Newspaper Characteristics. Sat. R. **91**: 39.

— Lessening Influence of. Sat. R. **84**: 434.

London, Canada. (B. Willson) Eng. Illust. **17**: 622.

Londonderry, Relief of, 1689. (A. Leeper; M. Oppenheim) Ath. '00, **1**: 689, 721.

Londonderry, N. H., Contributions to the History of. (E. S. Stearns) N. E. Reg. **204**: 460.

Londoner's Log-book. Cornh. **83**: 258. **84**: 804. Same art. Liv. Age, **229**: 618 — **231**: 637. Same art. Ecl. M. **137**: 199-733.

Lone Charge of William B. Perkins; a war story. (S. Crane) McClure, **13**: 279.

Lone Hand, A; a story. (Mrs. Geppert) Music, **12**: 429.

Long, Lily A. Writer, **14**: 42.

Long Arm of Coincidence, The; a story of Circumstantial Evidence. Green Bag, **11**: 398.

Long Duel; a comedy. (Mrs. W. K. Clifford) Fortn. **76**: 555.

Long Island, Ancient Burial-grounds of. (E. D. Harris) N. E. Reg. **53**: 74-412. **54**: 53, 427. **55**: 84, 200, 278.

— Country Homes on. (L. Hubbard, jr.) Outing, **37**: 340.

— Snipe Shooting on. (F. A. Partridge) Outing, **36**: 661.

Long Ladder, The; a story. (R. Barr) McClure, **10**: 226.

Longespee, Nicholas, Bp. of Salisbury, Will of. (A. R. Malden) Eng. Hist. R. **15**: 523.

Longevity. (M. G. Watkins) Gent. M. n. s. **67**: 253. Same art. Liv. Age, **231**: 56.

Longevity and Degeneration. (W. R. Thayer) Forum, **28**: 741.

— Exercise and. (D. A. Sargent) No. Am. **164**: 566.

— in Man, Inheritance of. (Mary Beeton; K. Pearson) Nature, **60**: 356.

— Increasing Duration of Life. (A. Glenesk) 19th Cent. **42**: 393.

— A Man's Chance of Life. (J. H. Schooling) Eng. Illust. **18**: 290.

— A Woman's Chance of Life. (J. H. Schooling) Eng. Illust. **19**: 411.

Longfellow, H. W. New Eng. M. n. s. **23**: 707. — With portrait. Acad. **51**: 455. — With portraits. (M. A. DeW. Howe) Bookman, **7**: 217.

— Evangeline. (F. L. Pattee) Chaut. **30**: 415.

— — Superior to Goethe's Hermann and Dorothea. (Della Courson) Educa. **20**: 362.

— First Books of. (L. S. Livingston) Bookman, **8**: 138.

— Giles Corey. New Eng. M. n. s. **23**: 586.

— Portland Home of. (F. K. Earl) Midland, **9**: 402.

— A Special Study of. (W. C. Lawton) Chaut. **30**: 466.

— Spiritual Messages from Poetry of. (P. H. Swift) Meth. R. **59**: 538.

— To the Memory of; a poem. (E. Gibson) Argosy, **65**: 146.

— with his Children. (Alice Longfellow) Strand, **14**: 250.

Longford Castle Collection of Paintings. (C. Phillips) Art J. **49**: 97-363.

Longhi, Pietro. Sat. R. **83**: 630.

Longinus and the Treatise on the Sublime. Quar. **192**: 401.

Longleat, Country Manor of Sir John Thynne. (A. H. Malan) Pall Mall M. **13**: 292..

Longmead Golf Cup; a story. (Mary Guild) Nat'l M. (Bost.) **8**: 238.

Longmeadow, Mass., Two Centuries and a Half in. (J. M. Bliss) New Eng. M. n. s. **18**: 582.

Longmore's Reward; a story. (M. Marstyn) Canad. M. **8**: 502.

Longprè, Paul de; Le roi des fleurs. (P. N. Beringer) Overland, n. s. **35**: 234.

Longstreet, James. Memoirs. (S. S. P. Patteson) Sewanee, **4**: 326.

Loo; a story. (B. Marnan) Strand, **15**: 41.

Look Backwards, A. (P. Kent) Gent. M. n. s. **61**: 24.

Looker-on, The. Spec. **86**: 797.

Looking for a Wife. (O. Fowler) Chaut. **27**: 303.

Looking-glass for the Mind: a Resurrected Juvenile. (C. B. Loomis) Bk. Buyer, **21**: 102.

Looking Round. (A. K. H. Boyd) Longm. **30**: 49.

Loomis, Mahlon, Inventor of Wireless Telegraphy. (G. Loomis) New Eng. M. n. s. **24**: 145.

Looms of Time, The. (Mrs. Hugh Frazer) Good Words, **38**: Xmas app.

Loon, The. (W. D. Hulbert) McClure, **17**: 262.

Loos, Herman Andreas. (M. C. Whitaker) Science, n. s. **12**: 403.

Loot, Ethics of. (G. Reid) Forum, **31**: 581.

Looting in China, An Answer to Charges of. (A. Favier) Cath. World, **74**: 387.

Looting of the Ly-Chee, The. (J. A. Barry) Chamb. J. **75**: 344.

Loras, Rev. Mathias. (J. Ireland) Cath. World, **67**: 721. **68**: 1.

Lord, John, Literary Rank of. (W. J. Armstrong) Meth. R. **59**: 911.

Lord Bateman, Mystery of. (A. Lang) Cornh. **81**: 185.

Lord Chief Justice, The; a story. (H. B. M. Watson) Harper, **97**: 393.

Lord Gilberthorpe's Proposal; a story. (H. Rawdon) Cornh. **76**: 365.

Lord Jim; a story. (J. Conrad) Blackw. **166**: 441-807. **167**: 60-803. **168**: 251-688.

Lord Marlowe's Dilemma; a story. (R. Neish) Pall Mall M. **25**: 160.

Lord of Creation, A. (C. Mand) Temp. Bar, **118**: 33.

Lord of Powder, The; a story. (H. Carruth) Nat'l M. (Bost.) **9**: 571.

Lord Tottenham; a story. (E. Nesbit) Pall Mall M. **15**: 51.

Lord Venetia; a story. (J. M. W. van der P. Schwartz) Cosmopol. **25**: 709.

Lords of the Night and the Tonalamatl of the Codex Borbonicus. (C. P. Bowditch) Am. Anthrop. **2**: 145.

Lord's Prayer. (P. Carus) Open Court, **12**: 491.

— Divine Name in the. (J. Bigelow) N. Church R. **8**: 498.

Lord's Remnant, The; a story. (C. F. Cunninghame) Pall Mall M. **22**: 345.

Lord's Supper. (F. P. Manhart) Luth. Q. **27**: 457.

— and Christ's Glorified Humanity. (S. L. Keyser) Luth. Q. **37**: 62.

— and the Food of Life. (P. Carus) Monist, **12**: 246, 343.

— and the Passover. (T. G. Selby) Expos. **5**: 210.

— Archbishop of Canterbury on. Spec. **81**: 518. — (J. Orr) Contemp. **74**: 779.

— Doctrine of the Eucharist in the Eastern Church. Dub. R. **122**: 174.

Louise, Queen of Prussia. (H. Tuttle) Open Court, 12: 129.

— and her Posthumous Portrait, with portraits. (Countess de Montaigu) Midland, 11: 111.

— Girlhood of. (A. W. Ward) Cornh. 82: 509.

Louise-Ulrique, Queen of Sweden. (F. M. F. Skene) Blackw. 164: 383.

Louisbourg, Colonial Fighters at. (C. T. Brady) McClure, 17: 457.

— Rolls of Artificers and Laborers at. N. E. Reg. 55: 65.

Louisiana and the Floridas, Origin of Genet's Proposed Attack on. (F. J. Turner) Am. Hist. R. 3: 650.

— Carondelet on the Defence of, 1794. Am. Hist. R. 2: 474.

— Documents on the Relations of France to, 1792-95. (F. J. Turner) Am. Hist. R. 3: 490.

— The Wilderness we bought from France. (C. F. Manderson) Cosmopol. 25: 69.

Louisiana Expansion in its World Aspect. (C. M. Harvey) Atlan. 84: 549.

Louisiana Purchase, and Napoleon I. (A. D. Anderson) Indep. 52: 1967. — (C. W. Hall) Nat'l M. (Bost.) 11: 381.

Louisiana Territory. The Record of a Lost Empire in America. (E. E. Sparks) Chaut. 33: 478.

Louisville, Ky. Bank. M. (N. Y.) 60: 925.

— St. Xavier's College, Sons of. (L. S. Flintham) Cath. World, 67: 732.

Lounsbury, Thomas R., an American Scholar. (B. Matthews) Cent. 33: 561.

Lourdan, Monat. Portraits of Children. (H. Armitage) Artist (N. Y.) 24: 57.

Lourdes. (A. F. Robertson) Temp. Bar, 14: 582. Same art. Ecl. M. 131: 572.

— and Pilgrimages. (C. P. Whiteway) Month, 94: 154.

— Nôtre Dame de. (S. E. Saville) Belgra. 98: 58.

— The Superstition of. Sat. R. 86: 230.

Louvain, Belgium, Picturesque. (M. P. Seter) Cath. World, 69: 595.

L'Ouverture, Toussaint. (I. A. Taylor) Temp. Bar, 113: 404.

— The Greatest Black Man known to History. (J. H. Batten) Arena, 24: 573.

Louvre, The New. (F. Rinder) M. of Art, 25: 107.

— New Rooms in the. (E. R. Pennell) Nation, 71: 306.

Louys, Pierre. Acad. 53: 100.

— Works of. (A. G. Des Voisines) Sat. R. 86: 572.

Lovat, Lord, Life and Execution of. Eng. Illust. 18: 282.

Love, Mabel, with portrait. Strand, 15: 55.

Love and the Brownings. (J. Mudge) Meth. R. 60: 694.

— Hugo's Praise of. (J. McSorley) Cath. World, 72: 727.

— Let it be Controlled. (I. H. Harper) Indep. 53: 1477.

— The Master Passion. (W. I. Fletcher) Bib. Sac. 54: 86.

— Modern, Scope of. (H. T. Finck) Harper, 103: 277.

— Primitive Love and Love Stories, H. T. Finck on. (W. G. Everett) Am. Hist. R. 6: 108.

— Swedenborg's Doctrine of. (L. F. Hite) N. Church R. 7: 241.

Love; a poem. (P. L. Dunbar) Cosmopol. 25: 89.

Love; a poem. (E. W. Watson) Bk. Buyer, 16: 139.

Love across the Lines. (H. S. Edwards) Lippinc. 64: 483.

Love among the Lions; a story. (A. S. Forrest) Idler, 14: 31, 163.

Love and the Capello. (W. A. Fraser) Canad. M. 11: 11.

Love and Change; a poem. (R. Hovey) Cent. 33: 572.

Love and a Coward; a story. (William James) Eng. Illust. 22: 126.

Love and the Dai Butsu. (M. L. W. Curtis) Overland, n. s. 31: 14.

Love and Photography; a story. (Margaret Westrupp) Temp. Bar, 124: 365.

Love and Sport. (M. M. Hickson) Longm. 30: 173.

Love and Suicide; a poem. Ecl. M. 129: 764.

Love and a Wooden Leg. (W. R. Lighton) Atlan. 83: 550.

Love at the Point of the Sword. (A. Powell) Overland, n. s. 36: 230.

Love the Conqueror came to Me; a poem. (R. U. Johnson) Atlan. 87: 390.

"Love, the Idler;" a story. (P. Trent) Argosy, 72: 201.

Love in a Fog; a London story. (H. C. Oakley) McClure, 11: 325.

Love in a Mask; a story. (H. A. Hinkson) Idler, 16: 445.

Love in the Winds; a poem. (R. Hovey) Atlan. 81: 464.

"Love Knows no Caste;" a story. (L. A. Harker) Argosy, 69: 111.

Love of Darby Macartney; a story. (A. Merry) Belgra. 97: 415.

Love of a Fool. (I. H. Ballard) Cent. 34: 254.

Love of Hester Ricketts, The; a story. (B. Marnan) Pall Mall M. 20: 300.

Love of an Ideal; a story. (L. S. Porter) Harper, 95: 304.

Love of Parson Lord, The; a story. (M. E. Wilkins) Harper, 98: 219.

Love that Glorifies, The; a sketch. (L. T. Bryant) McClure, 16: 50.

Love will have its Way; a story. (C. E. Ogden) Outl. 61: 166.

Love Affairs of the Comte de Fauras. (L. M. Eassie) Idler, 17: 311, 535.

Love Affairs of Julius Standen. (G. Stanhope) Chamb. J. 78: 481-675.

Love-apple, The; a story. Temp. Bar, 15: 79.

Love-child, The; a story. (L. Housman) Idler, 14: 713.

Love laughs at Blacksmiths; a story. (O'Neill Latham) Cosmopol. 27: 515.

Love-letters, A Batch of Famous. (A. Turner) Temp. Bar, 121: 65.

— Eighteenth-century. (G. Paston) Fortn. 75: 364.

— Should they be Published? Outl. 68: 620.

— Unimaginary. Ed. R. 193: 511. Same art. Liv. Age, 230: 1. Same art. Ecl. M. 137: 141.

Love-letters of an Englishwoman. (M. D. Petre) Month, 97: 116.

Love Lyric, A. (A. G. Hopkins) Argosy, 68: 391.

Love-making in the Cevennes. (Z. de Ladevèze) Cornh. 80: 779.

Love Poems of Greece. Acad. 53: 476.

Love Story, A. (A. Webster) McClure, 15: 573.

Love Story, A. (A. J. Dawson) Pall Mall M. 12: 165.

Love Story of an Old Marquise, The; a tale. (J. Garry) Gent. M. n. s. 67: 180.

Love Story of a Selfish Woman. (E. Mackubin) Atlan. 83: 691.

Loveliness; a story. (E. S. Phelps) Atlan. 84: 216.

Lovely Sentiment, A; a story. Macmil. 83: 59.

Love's Apologie; a poem. (M. A. M. Marks) Argosy, 66: 110.

Love's Counter spell; a tale. (C. W. Williams) Gent. M. n. s. 64: 455.

Love's Delay; poem. (E. W. Peattie) Atlan. 79: 257.

Love's Gift; a poem. (J. V. Cheney) Cosmopol. 27: 220.

Love's Flower; a story. (M. Beaumont) Sund. M. 29: 619.

Lugh, Africa. (Lily Wolffsohn) Gent. M. n. s. 58: 140.

Luigi and the Salvationist; a story. (Grant Allen) Pall Mall M. 19: 489.

Luigi's Sacrifice. (M. B. Whiting) Sund. M. 30: 605.

Luksch, Josef, Prof. Geog. J. 18: 544.

Lulea in Norbotten. (J. L. Robertson) Chamb. J. 74: 39.

Lullaby; a poem. Outl. 61: 196.

Lullaby Mullen; a story. (P. V. Michels) Outing, 31: 51, 173.

Lully, Raymond. (H. C. McDowall) Macmil. 76: 23.

Lumber, American. (B. E. Fernow) Chaut. 28: 436.

Lumber-camps and Logging in America. (M. Mannering) Nat'l M. (Bost.) 7: 483.

Lumber Town, Notes on a. (R. L. Hartt) Atlan. 85: 100.

Lumbering in Canada. (C. Fairbairn) Chamb. J. 74: 58.

Luminous Creatures; Natural Incandescent Lights. (C. Parkinson) Good Words, 40: 415.

Luminous Objects, Projection of, in Space. (E. L. Bruce) J. Soc. Arts, 46: 201.

Lumley vs. Wagner, Doctrine of. (E. C. C. Firth) Law Q. 13: 306.

Lumsden, Sir Harry Burnett. Blackw. 165: 1003.

Lunacy Commissions. (F. B. Sanborn) Char. R. 6: 36.

Lunatics, Contracts by. (H. Gondy) Law Q. 17: 147.

— Illustrious. (W. J. Corbet) Arena, 21: 571.

Lunch for the General, A; a story. (D. Dallas) Belgra. 95: 225.

Luncheon for a Million. (G. Sudley) Munsey, 24: 834.

Lung of Desmognathus. (H. H. Wilder) Am. Natural. 35: 182.

Lungs and Swimming-bladder, Secretion and Absorption of Gas in. (J. S. Haldane) Sci. Prog. n. s. 2: 120, 237.

Lura; Story of a Smuggler's Life. (P. B. Elderkin) Overland, n. s. 29: 636.

Lurilla Ann's Day; a story. (F. R. Sterrett) Midland, 10: 554.

Lustre Ware, Making Paints for. Artist (N. Y.) 26: 156.

Lute, The, in France. (Brenet) Music, 16: 140.

Luther, Dr. C. T. R., and Dr. G. Rumker. Nature, 61: 473.

Luther, Martin. Quar. 186: 1.

— and the Augsburg Confession. (J. W. Richard) Luth. Q. 29: 497. 30: 463.

— and Free Will. (L. A. Fox) Luth. Q. 29: 453.

— and Tetzel. Month, 92: 588.

— as a Preacher. (J. Yutzy) Luth. Q. 28: 579.

— Attitude at the Marburg Colloquy. (J. J. Young) Luth. Q. 27: 488.

— Gayety of. (W. Cowan) Good Words, 40: 49.

— his Idea of the Real Presence. (C. F. Fleming) Crit. R. 11: 249.

— Influence on Literature. (D. C. Munro) Chaut. 26: 11.

— Protestant Biographers of. (H. G. Ganss) Am. Cath. Q. 26: 582.

— Relation to Dogmatic Tradition. (R. Seeberg) Luth. Q. 31: 186.

— Side-light on. (R. C. Ford) Bib. Sac. 56: 114.

Lutheran Book of Worship, New. (O. H. Gruver) Luth. Q. 29: 381.

Lutheran Church, Evangelical, Meaning of Fundamental Doctrines in Augsburg Confession. (L. S. Keyser) Luth. Q. 27: 501.

— in Georgia, Early History of. (D. M. Gilbert) Luth. Q. 37: 155.

— in New Jersey, History of. (A. Hiller) Luth. Q. 28: 98, 165.

— in the United States, Doctrinal Standpoint of, Development of. (J. L. Neve) Luth. Q. 31: 413.

— The Press in. (V. L. Conrad) Luth. Q. 28: 532.

Lutheran Quarterly. Luth. Q. 28: 153.

Lutherans of America, Education among the Early. (B. C. Steiner) Luth. Q. 29: 273.

Lutiger, François, and his Silver Work. (G. C. Williamson) Artist (N. Y.) 25: 72.

Lutkin, P. C., Organist and Musician, with portrait. Music, 13: 343.

Lutzen, Battle of. (S. Crane) Lippinc. 66: 462.

Lux ex Tenebris; a poem. (E. Gibson) Argosy, 64: 384.

Lux Hominum; a poem. Pall Mall M. 11: 1.

Luxembourg, Marshal de. (A. Laugel) Nation, 70: 375.

Luxembourg, Musée de. (L. Bénédite) M. of Art, 24: 433.

Luxuries; are they Wasted Wealth? (G. Gunton) Gunton's M. 12: 151.

Luxury and Extravagance. (J. Davidson) Int. J. Ethics, 9: 54.

— Evolution of. (G. Ferrero) Internat. J. Ethics, 11: 346.

— in America. Spec. 82: 482. Same art. Liv. Age, 221: 585. Same art. Ecl. M. 133: 109.

— Some Aspects of. (F. S. Baldwin) No. Am. 168: 154.

Luzon, Civilization and Barbarism in. (M. L. Todd) Nation, 73: 221.

— Northward through. (P. Whitmarsh) Outl. 64: 913.

— Southern, and Northern Mindanao, In. (H. M. Reeve) Indep. 52: 2035.

— A Taste of War in. (P. Whitmarsh) Outl. 64: 493.

Lycées of France. (E. L. Hardy) School R. 9: 459.

Lyceum, American. (H. D. Jenkins) Presb. & Ref. R. 8: 46.

— at Fort Agawam. (E. Swift) J. Mil. Serv. Inst. 20: 229.

— The Bygone. (M. L. Luther) Dial (Ch.) 25: 291.

Lyddite — the New Explosive. Chamb. J. 76: 72.

— in Action. Chamb. J. 77: 269.

Lydia; a poem. (M. Cawein) Bk. Buyer, 16: 314.

Lyell, Mount, Trip to. (C. E. Townsend) Overland, n. s. 34: 1.

Lying, Art of. (L. H. Bugg) Cath. World, 66: 109.

— Equivocation and. Spec. 81: 110.

Lyke-wake, The; a story. (C. L. Antrobus) Gent. M. n. s. 60: 385.

Lyke-wake Fight, A; a story. (H. Sutcliffe) Pall Mall M. 19: 343.

Lyme House, Cheshire, England. (E. Newton) Pall Mall M. 12: 149.

Lyme Regis, At; a poem. (M. Prower) Gent. M. n. s. 67: 307.

Lynch, Charles, the Real Judge Lynch. (T. W. Page) Atlan. 88: 731.

Lynch, Hannah. Autobiography of a Child. Critic, 36: 30.

Lynch-law. (M. Thompson) Lippinc. 64: 254. — (D. MacG. Means) Nation, 65: 6. — (O. F. Hershey) Green Bag, 12: 466.

— Epidemics of. (F. L. Oswald) No. Am. 165: 119.

— — Prevention of. (E. L. Pell) R. of Rs. (N. Y.) 17: 321.

— in America. (I. B. Wells-Barnett) Arena, 23: 15.

— Origin and History of. (H. C. Featherstone) Green Bag, 12: 150.

— Remedies for. Sewanee, 8: 1.

Lynching and the Excuse for it. (I. W. Barnett) Indep. 53: 1133.

— and the Franchise Rights of the Negro. Ann. Am. Acad. Pol. Sci. 15: 493.

— in the South. (W. H. Levell) Outl. 69: 731.

— — Causes of. Sat. R. 85: 717.

— — How can it be checked? (Q. Ewing) Outl. 69: 359.

— Quintuple, in Indiana. Pub. Opin. 23: 389.

— Southern Sentiment on. Outl. 62: 200.

— Urban, O. June, 1897. Pub. Opin. 22: 741.

Lynching Horror, The. Nation, **73**: 162.

Lynde, Samuel, Deed of Land by, 1700. (S. B. Doggett) N. E. Reg. **51**: 64.

Lynn, Mass., a City by the Sea. (L. W. Betts) Outl. **68**: 207.

Lynx that Triumphed. (F. Whishaw) Longm. **33**: 241.

Lynxes, Pair of. (F. Whishaw) Longm. **31**: 519.

Lyon, Mary. (Mrs. M. Smith) Educa. **17**: 471.

— Inner Life of. (A. E. Dunning) Chaut. **30**: 420.

Lyon, Gen. Nathaniel; his Missouri Campaign of 1861. (J. S. Clark) Midland, **8**: 111.

Lyons, Vice-admiral Sir Edmund, S. E. Wilmot's Life of. (F. A. Maxse) National, **33**: 655. — Blackw. **165**: 120.

Lyons, France. Nôtre Dame de Fourvières. (E. Endres) Cath. World, **64**: 623.

Lyre, Legends of the. (C. Feeney) Music, **14**: 379.

Lyric, A; a poem. (S. Phillips) Bk. Buyer, **16**: 145.

Lyric Poetry, American, Knowles's. (H. M. Belden) Citizen, **4**: 8.

— Intensive Study of. (B. A. Heydrick) Chaut. **31**: 617.

— Irish. Acad. **52**: 143.

Lyrists, Lesser Elizabethan. (S. Gwynn) Macmil. **76**: 181 — Liv. Age, **214**: 544.

Lyttelton, Lucy, Letters of. (Maude Lyttelton) National, **37**: 87.

Lyttelton, Sir Thomas, an 18th Century Soldier. (Maude Lyttelton) National, **38**: 241.

Lytton, E. L. E. B., Lord, Novels. (W. F. Lord) 19th Cent. **50**: 449. — Liv. Age, **231**: 562.

— A Sketch from Memory. Macmil. **83**: 360.

Lytton, Edward Robert, Lord, Indian Administration of. Blackw. **166**: 852.

Ma Blonde; a romance. (M. G. Cundill) Outing, **33**: 448.

Maas-Tapper, Bertha, Pianist, with portrait. Music, **13**: 340.

Mabel's Lover; a story. Gent. M. n. s. **61**: 583.

Mabie, Hamilton Wright, with portrait. Bk. News, **17**: 8. — (H. van Dyke) Bk. Buyer, **18**: 279.

Mac, the Divil an' his Dip'ties. Temp. Bar, **118**: 505.

Macao. (A. Bellesort) Liv. Age, **223**: 831.

— and Canton. (A. Bellesort) Ecl. M. **134**: 316.

Macaroni. (M. C. Perry) Cent. **38**: 323.

Macartney, James, Macalister's Memoir of. Ath. '01, **1**: 55.

Macaulay, Thos. Babington, Lord, with portrait. (F. Thompson) Acad. **51**: 121.

— Ancestors of. (W. C. Mackenzie) Gent. M. n. s. **61**: 128.

— A Day with. (G. L. Apperson) Chamb. J. **75**: 113.

— Vitality of. (H. D. Sedgwick, jr.) Atlan. **84**: 163.

Macaulay, Zachary, Life and Letters of, Knutsford's. (E. C. Wilson) Econ. R. **11**: 386. — (F. M. Bird) Nation, **72**: 299.

McAuley, Jerry, and his Prayer-meeting. (G. Kennan) Outl. **67**: 306.

Macbeth and Saul. (H. W. Blanc) Sewanee, **1**: 273.

Macbeth, R. W. Art Works. (A. L. Baldry) Art J. **52**: 289.

McCarthy, D'Alton. Canad. M. **11**: 92.

McCarthy, Justin, Historian of the Queen's Reign. Eng. Illust. **17**: 398.

— Reminiscences. (J. L. Gilder) Critic, **35**: 720. — (W. P. Trent) Forum, **28**: 374. — (E. G. Johnson) Dial (Ch.) **27**: 42.

McCauley, James A. (T. S. Thomas) Meth. R. **57**: 849.

McClellan, Gen. Geo. B., Michie's Life of. (I. R. Pennypacker) Dial (Ch.) **31**: 318. — (G. A. Thayer) Nation, **73**: 323.

McClure, S. S. (J. D. Barry) Lit. W. (Bost.) **28**: 88.

MacColl, Malcolm. His "New Convocation." (F. W. Maitland) Fortn. **72**: 926.

McComas, Francis, Artist, with portrait. Brush & P. **6**: 92.

MacConglinne, Legend of. Cornh. **81**: 829.

MacCormac, William. Nature, **65**: 131.

McCoy, Sir Frederick; obituary. Nature, **60**: 83.

McCribben sues the City; a story. (H. S. Edwards) Cent. **37**: 302.

McCulloch, George. Collection of Paintings. (A. L. Baldry) Art J. **49**: 1–373.

M'Culloch, J. R., and J. S. Mill, with portraits. Gunton's M. **15**: 341.

Maccunn, Hamish, Composer, with portrait. Music, **15**: 86.

McCurdy, J. F. History, Prophecy, and the Monuments. Vol. 3. (A. B. Davidson) Crit. R. **11**: 387.

McCutcheon, Geo. Barr, with portrait. Bk. News, **19**: 603.

Macdonald, Flora. (B. J. Ramage) Sewanee, **2**: 212.

— Portraits of. (J. Penderel-Brodhurst) Art J. **51**: 111.

Macdonald, George. (D. C. Murray) Canad. M. **9**: 240.

— a Great Teacher. Spec. **86**: 382.

— Pedagogics of. (F. W. Lewis) Educa. **19**: 357.

Macdonald, Sir John A. Quar. **191**: 337. — Canad. M. **17**: 206. — (Baroness Macdonald of Earnscliffe) Pall Mall M. **13**: 347.

Macdonell, Colonel John. (A. Lang) Macmil. **78**: 113.

Macdonnell, Alastair, a Jacobite Arch-traitor. (A. Lang) Lond. Q. **88**: 229.

MacDowell, Edward A. Music, **13**: 656.

— an American Composer. (H. T. Finck) Cent. **31**: 448.

— Criticism on. (P. Woolf) Music, **16**: 100.

— Third Sonata for Piano. (W. S. B. Mathews) Music, **19**: 410.

— Woodland Sketches, Musical Compositions by. Music, **13**: 400.

McDuffie, George, with portrait. (W. L. Miller) Green Bag, **11**: 1.

Macedonia and Southern Albania, Cvijic's Researches in. Geog. J. **16**: 215.

— Anticipated Revolt in. (H. C. Thomson) Sat. R. **83**: 215.

— The Danger in the Near East. Liv. Age, **220**: 587.

— Unwise Desire for Autonomy. Sat. R. **87**: 133.

"Macedonian" and "United States." (G. A. Stockwell) Canad. M. **15**: 68.

Maceo. (E. Castelar) Liv. Age, **213**: 120.

— Death of; a poem. (A. E. Ball) Arena, **17**: 641.

Macfadyen, Dugald. Alfred, the West Saxon King of the English. (W. Canton) Good Words, **42**: 357.

McFarland, Walter Martin. (G. W. Melville) Cassier, **20**: 85.

McFarland Girls, The; a story. (Anna Farquhar) Nat'l M. (Bost.) **9**: 478.

McGiffert, A. C., Apostolic Age. (M. S. Terry) Meth. R. **60**: 196.

— Case of. Outl. **64**: 19, 343.

— Personal Influence of. Outl. **64**: 345.

— Position of. Outl. **63**: 531.

McGranahan, James, Evangelistic Singer, with portrait. Music, **13**: 630.

MacGrath, Harold, with portrait. Bk. News, **19**: 764.

Machiavelli. Acad. **52**: 63.

— and the English Reformation. (W. A. Phillips) 19th Cent. **40**: 907. Same art. Liv. Age, **212**: 84.

— in Modern Politics. Liv. Age, **214**: 876.

— "The Law of the Beasts." (F. Greenwood) 19th Cent. **42**: 532.

— The Modern. (F. Harrison) 19th Cent. **42**: 462. Same art. Ecl. M. **129**: 659. Same art. Liv. Age, **215**: 236.

Madame Geoffrin. Liv. Age, **228**: 189.

Madame J——; a sketch. Argosy, **73**: 232.

Madame Maman; a story. (J. Madeleine) Acad. **57**: 234.

Madame Mills; a story. (A. Beresford) Argosy, **66**: 35.

Madame Noel, an Acadian Idyl. (G. H. Picard) Lippinc. **66**: 643.

Madame Poulard's Day Dream; a story. Macmil. **79**: 216. Same art. Liv. Age, **220**: 570.

Madeira, Cycling in. (W. J. Reid) Outing, **35**: 270, 375.

— Winter Solstice at. Garden & F. **10**: 33.

Madeira Waterways. (R. Owen) Blackw. **164**: 550. Same art. Ecl. M. **131**: 731.

Mademoiselle Angéle. (R. R. Gilson) Atlan. **87**: 398.

Mademoiselle de Castelfranc; a story. (Adolphe Ribaux) Cosmopol. **30**: 371.

Mademoiselle Parchesi; a story. (G. Burgess) McClure, **15**: 495.

Mademoiselle's Romance; a story. (A. H. Begbie) Temp. Bar, **122**: 345, 523. Same art. Liv. Age, **230**: 686 — **231**: 20.

Madison, James. (G. Hunt) Conserv. R. **2**: 296.

— Debate with Parson Leland. (M. N. Marshall) Green Bag, **12**: 339.

— Letters from Presidents of the U. S. and Ladies of the White House. Pennsyl. M. **25**: 355.

Madness of Mercy Newdigate; a story. (Martin A. S. Hume) Gent. M. n. s. **58**: 1. Same art. Ecl. M. **128**: 269.

Madness of Philip, The; a story. (Josephine D. Daskam) McClure, **16**: 183. Same art. Idler, **19**: 4.

Madness of Sur Birbel Sahad; a story. (Helen F. Huntington) Nat'l M. (Bost.) **6**: 36.

Madonna, The, in Art. (P. W. Dykema) Brush & P. **2**: 97.

Madonna, The, of the Ermine Mantle. (E. W. Champney) Harper, **103**: 775.

Madonna of the Peach-tree; a story. (M. Hewlett) Blackw. **165**: 317.

Madonna that is Childless, The. (T. R. Sullivan) Scrib. M. **23**: 351.

Madonna's Robe, The; a story. (E. Andrews) Outl. **63**: 570.

Madonnas, Famous, in California. (Eva V. Carlin) Overland, n. s. **36**: 517.

Madras, Etymology of. (G. Birdwood) Ath. '00, **2**: 412.

— Landholders' Grievances, The. (P. P. Pillai) Asia. R. **23**: 277.

— The Southern Satrapy. (J. D. Rees) J. Soc. Art, **49**: 469.

Madrazo, Raimundo de; Spanish Painter in America. (L. Cooper) Munsey, **20**: 561.

— Departure from the Masquerade. Art J. **51**: 92.

Madreporaria, Classification of. (M. M. Ogilvie) Nature, **55**: 280.

Madrid. (E. Hübner) Chaut. **27**: 545.

— Carnival at. (Mrs. M. L. Woods) Cornh. **80**: 174.

— El Prado. (Mrs. M. L. Woods) Cornh. **80**: 754.

— In the National Library at. (A. P. Valdes) Ecl. M. **133**: 774. Same art. Liv. Age, **222**: 720.

— Life in. (C. Edwardes) Chamb. J. **75**: 468.

— Royal Functions at. (J. R. Lowell) Critic, **33**: 171.

— Scenes in the Spanish Capital. (A. Houghton) Cent. **35**: 779.

Madroña at Ukiah, The. (C. Purdy) Garden & F. **10**: 283.

Maedchen, Das. (A. E. Herrick) New Eng. M. n. s. **22**: 399.

Maeterlinck, Maurice. (D. M. J.) Westm. **151**: 409. — (A. R. Ropes) Contemp. **76**: 422. — Acad. **52**: 45, 113. — (V. M. Crawford) Fortn. **68**: 176. Same art. Liv. Age, **215**: 185.

— and Music. (E. Newman) Atlan. **88**: 769.

Maeterlinck, Maurice, and Mystery. (W. Archer) Critic, **37**: 220.

— as Artist. (C. Weekes) Argosy, **75**: 77.

— as an Essayist. Acad. **51**: 465.

— as a Mystic. (A. Symons) Contemp. **72**: 349.

— as a Realist. Acad. **56**: 285.

— as Thinker. (T. Fortebus) Argosy, **75**: 86.

— Bluebeard and Aryan. (S. C. de Soissons) Fortn. **74**: 994. Same art. Ecl. M. **136**: 390. Same art. Liv. Age, **228**: 130.

— Later Work of. (A. Phelps) Poet-Lore, **11**: 357.

— The Life of the Bee. Acad. **60**: 459.

— Moralist and Artist. Ed. R. **193**: 350. — Liv. Age, **230**: 201. Same art. Ecl. M. **137**: 281.

— Pelleas and Melisande. (M. Beerbohm) Sat. R. **85**: 843.

— Treasure of the Humble. Study of Death. (W. N. Guthrie) Sewanee, **6**: 276.

— A Visit to. (E. A. Steiner) Outl. **69**: 701.

— Wisdom and Destiny. Acad. **55**: 147.

Maeterlinck of the Midlands, A; a tale. (Ethel Wheeler) Argosy, **71**: 203.

Mafeking, With Plumer to the Relief of. Blackw. **168**: 804.

Mafia, The. (G. C. Speranza) Green Bag, **12**: 302.

— and Omerta. (R. Bagot) National, **36**: 856.

— Observations by a Non-member. Nation, **73**: 7, 27.

Mag's Limitation. (Addie E. Scott) Overland, n. s. **34**: 172.

Magazine, Making a. Cosmopol. **23**: 465.

Magazine of Art, The, its Majority; a Retrospect. M. of Art, **23**: 316.

Magazine Day. (M. E. Hazeltine) Pub. Lib. **1**: 51.

Magazine Editors, Notes on Some American. (Flora M. Holly) Bookman, **12**: 357.

Magazine Literature, Decade of. (C. H. Eaton) Forum, **26**: 211.

Magazines, American, Conduct of. Atlan. **86**: 425.

— Half-forgotten. (G. N. Lovejoy) Chaut. **33**: 28.

— Purposes of National. (J. G. Mowat) Canad. M. **17**: 166.

— Writing for. (F. M. Bird) Lippinc. **61**: 572.

Magdala, Back from; Cholera and Mutiny upon the High Seas. (H. Hervey) Chamb. J. **77**: 381.

Magee, William Connor, Archbishop of York. Church Q. **43**: 400. Same art. Liv. Age, **212**: 589. — (A. K. H. Boyd) Longm. **29**: 358. — Lond. Q. **88**: 20.

Magellan Straits, Winter Voyage through. (R. W. Meade) Nat. Geog. M. **8**: 129.

Magellanian Beds of Punta Arenas, Chile, Fauna of. (A. E. Ortmann) Am. J. Sci. **158**: 427.

Magersfontein, The Fight at. (J. Barnes) Outl. **64**: 249.

— A Visit to the Battlefield. (W. S. Fletcher) Chamb. J. **77**: 433.

Magic. (W. B. Yeats) Monthly R. **4**, no. 3: 144.

— and Astrology, Modern. Chamb. J. **74**: 742.

— and Primitive Man. Westm. **148**: 439.

— and Religion, Lang on. Ed. R. **194**: 343.

— An Experiment in. (F. Legge) Pall Mall M. **15**: 73.

— Old and New. Illus. (P. Carus) Open Court, **14**: 333, 422.

Magic of a Voice. (W. D. Howells) Lippinc. **64**: 901.

Magic Flute, The. (A. Theuriet) Outl. **63**: 798.

Magic-lantern, Evolution of the. (T. C. Hepworth) Chamb. J. **75**: 213.

Magic Lines. (S. R. Elliott) Dial (Ch.) **23**: 239.

Magic Organ, The; a story. (Mrs. Pfirshing) Music, **12**: 79.

Magic Word, The. (C. Smith) Good Words, **40**: Xmas no.

Maginnis, Charles D., with portrait. Cath. World, **74**: 246.

Magna Charta, with Text. Gunton's M. **12**: 380.

Magnanimity, The New. (C. De Thierry) J. Mil. Serv. Inst. 28: 231.

Magnanimity of the Man of Pleasure; a story of the days to come. (H. G. Wells) Pall Mall M. 19: 122.

Magnetic Circuit, The, Du Bois on. (A. Gray) Nature, 57: 385.

Magnetic Concentrating Process, Wetherill. (H. B. C. Nitze) J. Frankl. Inst. 143: 279.

Magnetic Curves. (J. Pawling) J. Frankl. Inst. 152: 269.

Magnetic Elements, Recent Values of. (C. Chree) Sci. Prog. n. s. 1: 424.

Magnetic Increment of Rigidity in Strong Fields. (H. D. Day) Am. J. Sci. 153: 449.

Magnetic Survey of the U. S. Science, n. s. 13: 353.
— Progress of. Nature, 63: 398.

Magnetism, Action of Light on. (J. H. Hart) Am. J. Sci. 160: 66.
— and Morals. (F. R. Statham) Westm. 150: 561.
— Magnetic Observations of Peary Exped. to Greenland, 1896. Nature, 57: 347.
— Solar and Terrestrial, Bigelow's Comments on. (F. H. Bigelow) Am. J. Sci. 155: 455.
— Terrestrial. (A. W. Rücker) Geog. J. 11: 522.
— — and Atmospheric Electricity. (C. Chree) Nature, 64: 151.
— — Trowbridge's Theory of. (L. A. Bauer; J. Trowbridge) Science, n. s. 9: 264.

Magnetization, Circular, and Magnetic Permeability. (J. Trowbridge and E. P. Adams) Am. J. Sci. 161: 175.

Magneto-optic Rotation, and Explanation by a Gyrostatic System. (A. Gray) Nature, 60: 379, 404.

Magnets. Properties of Seasoned Magnets made of Self-hardening Steel. (B. O. Peirce) Am. J. Sci. 155: 334.
— Temperature Coefficients of Certain Seasoned Hard Steel. (A. Durward) Am. J. Sci. 155: 245.

Magnitude, Judgments of, by Comparison with a Mental Standard. (R. S. Woodworth and E. Thorndike) Psychol. R. 7: 344.

Magnolia Glauca. (M. L. Dock) Garden & F. 10: 402.

"Magpie and Stump," The New. Studio (Lond.) 5: 67.

Magruder, Julia, with portrait. Bk. News, 15: 343.

Mahabharata, the Iliad of Ancient India. (R. C. Dutt) Asia. R. 6: 368.

Mahaffy, John Pentland, on International Jealousy. Sewanee, 4: 361.

Mahan, Alfred T., with portrait. Bk. News, 15: 429.
— With portrait. Bk. Buyer, 16: 200.
— Counsels to the United States. (G. S. Clarke) 19th Cent. 43: 292. Same art. Liv. Age, 216: 833.
— in New York. (C. De Kay) Critic, 32: 353.
— Interpreter of Naval History. R. of Rs. (N. Y.) 19: 553.

Maharaja's Entry for the Maripoor Cup; a story. (D. G. Wood) Belgra. 95: 501.

Maharaja's Justice; a story. (C. Carnegie) Temp. Bar, 114: 131.

Maharaja's Stratagem; a story. (Helen F. Huntington) Nat'l M. (Bost.) 7: 425.

Maharaja's Water Carnival. (R. D. Mackenzie) Cent. 38: 112.

Mahat, J. P., as an Englishman. (W. Roberts) Gent. M. n. s. 64: 426.

Mahdi, Remains of the, Lord Kitchener and. Spec. 82: 813.

Mahdiism; What its Crushing signifies. (F. C. Penfield) Forum, 28: 708.

Mahmoud II. (G. F. White) Un. Serv. M. 16: 62.

Mahnet; a story. (W. A. Fraser) Harper, 103: 268.

Mahogany, In Quest of. (R. W. Cater) Chamb. J. 74: 549.

Mahomet's Paradise; a Russian story. (A. N. Begetsky) Idler, 14: 378.
See Mohammed.

Mahrattas, In the Land of. (E. A. Richings) Belgra. 93: 293.

Maid and Two Swords, A. (C. G. D. Roberts) Chamb. J. 77: 125. Same art. Canad. M. 15: 74. Same art. Liv. Age, 224: 713.

Maid Mattie. (E. H. Bell) Sund. M. 28: 318.

Maid of Athens; Theresa Macri. (E. Singleton) Bookman, 5: 121.

Maid of Many Moods; a story. (V. Sheard) Canad. M. 17: 28.

Maiden Effort, A; a cycle story. (K. F. M. Sullivan) Outing, 32: 276.

Maiden Land, Hawkins's, Can it be Identified as the Falkland Islands? (B. M. Chambers) Geog. J. 17: 414.

Maiden of Tretallow, The; a poem. (H. Overy) Argosy, 72: 171.

Maidstone, The Lesson of. Spec. 79: 479.

Mail Service, Foreign, at New York. (E. G. Chat) Scrib. M. 26: 61.

Mails in England. Chamb. J. 77: 13.
— Rural Free Delivery. (P. S. Heath) Nat'l M. (Bost.) 12: 383.

Maimon, Solomon. Temp. Bar, 120: 413.

Maimonides, Moses, Treatise on Eternal Bliss by. (W. Bacher) Jew Q. 9: 270.
— Apostasy of. (D. S. Margoliouth) Jew. Q. 13: 539.
— Mishneh Torah, A Muhammadan Commentary on. (G. Margoliouth) Jew. Q. 13: 488.
— Responses of, in the Original Arabic. (G. Margoliouth) Jew. Q. 11: 533.

Maine, Sir Henry, and Darwinism. Asia. R. 26: 20.
— and India. (C. L. Tupper) J. Soc. Arts, 46: 390.
— His Work for India. J. Soc. Arts, 46: 390.
— A Lawyer with a Style. (W. Wilson) Atlan. 82: 363.

Maine de Biran, F. P. G., with portrait. (L. Levy-Brühl) Open Court, 13: 458.

Maine, Defences of Houses in. (J. S. H. Fogg) N. E. Reg. 54: 408.
— in Literature. (W. I. Cole) New Eng. M. n. s. 22: 726.
— Musical Festival. Music, 13: 89.
— — Preliminary Preparations. (B. H. Dingley) Music, 11: 449.
— National Guard of. (C. B. Hall) Outing, 29: 388, 493, 597. 30: 77, 182, 281.
— The Plight of, 1901. (W. MacDonald) Nation, 72: 271.

Maine Woods, Hunting in. (S. H. Nealy) New Eng. M. n. s. 19: 373.

"Maine" The, Explosion of. (Minna Irving) Midland, 9: 387.
— — and after. (F. T. Jane) Fortn. 69: 640.
— — Personal Narrative of. (C. D. Sigsbee) Cent. 35: 74-373.
— — Truth about. (H. W. Wilson) National, 31: 671.

Maintenon, Madame de. (Mlle. d'Aubigné) Temp. Bar, 110: 393.
— as an Educator. (A. Laugel) Nation, 73: 147.
— Portrait of. Bk. Buyer, 18: 84.

Maisonneuve Monument, Montreal. Canad. M. 17: 98.

Maitland, Edward. Acad. 52: 301.

Maitland, Sir Thomas, Lord on. (C. W. Colby) Nation, 67: 133.

Majesty of the Law; a story. (B. W. Howard) Eng. Illust. 16: 537.

Major, Charles, with portrait. Bk. News, 17: 609.

Major, The, and a Peg Leg; a story. (H. S. Canby) Outl. 67: 538.

Major John; a story. (F. H. Spearman) Outl. 66: 849.

Major Marr's Yarn. Chamb. J. **76**: 190.

Major's Mistake, a French-Canadian Tale. (M. A. Low) Canad. M. **15**: 439.

Major's Wife's Maiden Aunt, The. (D. Dallas) Belgra. **96**: 472.

Major-domo of Hezekiah, Isaiah's Prophecy concerning. (A. Kamphaussen) Am. J. Theol. **5**: 43.

Majority, The; must it always rule? (E. D. Mead) Outl. **64**: 644.

Majuda, From, to Omdurman. (T. B. Townshend) Chamb. J. **76**: 407.

Makar Chudra. (M. Gorky) Monthly R. **5**, no. **2**: 173.

Makart, Hans. (P. G. Konody) Idler, **16**: 530.

Make and Break, New Form of. (C. T. Knipp) Am. J. Sci. **155**: 283.

Making Money ; a story. (B. Copplestone) Cornh. **78**: 230. Same art. Liv. Age, **218**: 720.

Making of a Jockey, The. (C. E. Newell) Overland, n. s. **36**: 291.

Making of a Man, The. (Ann Scott) Chamb. J. **76**: 273-342.

Making of a Marchioness. (F. H. Burnett) Cent. **40**: 178, 358, 521. Same art. Cornh. **83**: 730 — **84**: 146.

Making of a Pilot, The. (A. W. Vorse) Scrib. M. **30**: 661.

Making Progress ; a story. (G. King) Harper, **102**: 423.

Makovsky, Vladimir. Come unto me ; a painting. (J. P. Lenox) Bib. World, **11**: 199.

"Malahack." (R. Garnett) Nation, **73**: 377.

Malakand Field Force, Story of, Churchill's. Sat. R. **85**: 561.

Malan, Solomon Cæsar, Life of, by A. N. Malan. Church Q. **46**: 73. — Ath. '98, **1**: 207.

Malaria. (G. M. Sternberg) Pop. Sci. Mo. **58**: 360.

— and Certain Mosquitos. (L. O. Howard) Cent. **39**: 941. — Quar. **192**: 291.

— and its Prevention. (R. Fielding-Ould) Nature, **63**: 494. Same art. Liv. Age, **229**: 251. Same art. Ecl. M. **136**: 754.

— Cause and Prevention of. (R. Ross) Nature, **60**: 357.

— Life-history of the Parasites of. (R. Ross) Nature, **60**: 322.

— Mosquito Theory of. (R. Ross) Pop. Sci. Mo. **56**: 42.

— New Discoveries in, 1900. (G. B. Grassi) Indep. **52**: 2975.

Malaria Expedition to Sierra Leone, Report of. Nature, **61**: 614. — (R. Fielding-Ould) Nature, **63**: 32.

Malaria Germ and Allied Forms of Sporozoa. (G. N. Calkins) Pop. Sci. Mo. **59**: 189.

Malarial Fever, Causation and Prevention of. (H. M. Biggs) Science, n. s. **14**: 266.

Malarial Parasite. Science, n. s. **14**: 297.

— and Other Pathogenic Protozoa. (G. M. Sternberg) Pop. Sci. Mo. **50**: 628.

Malay Language. (R. C. Ford) Pop. Sci. Mo. **54**: 813.

Malay Literature. (R. C. Ford) Pop. Sci. Mo. **55**: 379.

Malay Magic, Skeat on. (J. Abercromby) Folk-Lore, **11**: 305.

Malay Peninsula. (H. Clifford) Blackw. **166**: 160. Same art. Ecl. M. **133**: 860.

— Bushwhacking in. (H. Clifford) Blackw. **167**: 1-194.

— East Coast Etchings. Macmil. **75**: 258. Same art. Liv. Age, **212**: 689.

— Fascination of the Forest in the. (H. Clifford) Macmil. **81**: 90. Same art. Liv. Age, **224**: 188. Same art. Ecl. M. **134**: 367.

— Primitive Socialists. (E. A. Irving) Blackw. **168**: 42.

Malay States, A Lesson from the. (H. Clifford) Atlan. **84**: 587.

— Trengganu and Kelantan. (H. Clifford) Geog. J. **9**: 1.

Malcolm, Sir John, Unpublished Manuscript by. (G. Paston) Longm. **36**: 526.

Malden, Massachusetts, Two Centuries and a Half in. (D. P. Corey) New Eng. M. n. s. **20**: 357.

Maldon as a Sketching Ground. (E. W. Charlton) Studio (Lond.) **8**: 215.

Malebranche, Nicholas, with portrait. (L. Lévy-Bruhl) Open Court, **12**: 543.

Malet, Lucas, *pseud. See* Harrison, Mrs. M. S.

Maletesta, Temple of, at Rimini. Am. Arch. **55**: 62.

Malicious Fortune ; a novel. (S. M. Düring) Argosy, **75**: 3, 122, 242.

Malicious Motive as a Ground of Action. (J. H. Henderson) Jurid. R. **13**: 452.

Mallard Shooting in the Timber. (F. E. Kellogg) Outing, **32**: 54.

Mallarmé, Stéphane. (Edmund Gosse) Sat. R. **86**: 372. — Acad. **54**: 304. — (H. T. Peck) Bookman, **8**: 227. — (M. L. Van Vorst) Bk. Buyer, **17**: 306. — (A. Symons) Fortn. **70**: 677. Same art. Liv. Age, **219**: 766. — Sat. R. **86**: 372. Same art. Liv. Age, **219**: 261. — Blackw. **164**: 692.

— Divagations. (A. Symons) Sat. R. **83**: 109.

Mallock, W. H. (D. C. Murray) Canad. M. **9**: 280.

— Aristocracy and Evolution. (F. H. Giddings) Book R. **5**: 391.

— as Political Economist. (J. A. Hobson) Contemp. **73**: 528.

— Works of. Acad. **53**: 388, 453.

Mallomonas, Vertical Distribution of. (G. C. Whipple ; H. N. Parker) Am. Natural. **33**: 485.

Mallory, Peter, of New Haven, Conn. (J. Shepard) N. E. Reg. **54**: 320.

Malmaison, Chateau of. Am. Arch. **62**: 37.

Malmesbury, James Harris, 1st Earl of. (G. Hill) Gent. M. n. s. **66**: 453.

Malmesbury as a Village Community, History of. (G. L. Gomme) Archæol. **50**: 421.

Malmesbury Abbey. (S. Beale) Am. Arch. **73**: 92.

Malory, Sir Thomas. (A. T. Martin) Ath. '97, **2**: 353.

Malpighi, Marcello, and his Works. (M. Foster) Nature, **57**: 529.

— Swammerdam, and Leeuwenhock. (W. A. Locy) Pop. Sci. Mo. **58**: 561.

Malta and the Question of Language. (J. W. Mario) Nation, **71**: 484.

— Grievances of. (O. Eltzbacher) Contemp. **80**: 239.

Malthus, Thomas R., with portrait. Gunton's M. **15**: 188.

— Centenary of. (J. Bonar) Econ. J. **8**: 206.

— Letter to. (W. M. D.) Citizen, **3**: 225.

— Letters of, to Macvey Napier. Econ. J. **7**: 265.

— on Population. (F. A. Fetter) Yale R. **7**: 153.

Mammal, Newly discovered. Spec. **86**: 691. Same art. Liv. Age, **230**: 198.

Mammals, Evolution of. (W. B. Scott) Internat. Mo. **4**: 21, 224.

— Eyes of. Spec. **87**: 1023.

— from the Liu Kiu Islands. (O. Bangs) Am. Natural. **35**: 561.

— Geography of. (W. L. Sclater) Geog. J. **9**: 67. **10**: 84.

— in Europe and North America. (A. S. Woodward) Nat. Sci. **12**: 328.

— in San Miguel Island, Panama. (O. Bangs) Am. Natural. **35**: 631.

— in the Water. Spec. **78**: 370.

— North American. (V. Bailey) Am. Natural. **35**: 221.

— of North America and the Adjacent Seas, Elliot's. (G. S. Miller) Science, n. s. **14**: 25.

— Origin of. (H. F. Osborn) Am. Natural. **32**: 309. — (O. C. Marsh) Am. J. Sci. **156**: 406. — (H. F. Osborn) Am. J. Sci. **157**: 92.

— Physical Geography of the West Indies. (F. L. Oswald) Pop. Sci. Mo. **54**: 802.

Man who could work Miracles; a tale. (H. G. Wells) Canad. M. 11: 348.

Man who Died, The. (H. A. Vachell) Cornh. 81: 640. Same art. Ecl. M. 135: 184. Same art. Liv. Age, 225: 765.

Man who gave no Tip, The; a story. (B. H. Ridgely) McClure, 17: 423.

Man who hung on. (W. B. Foster) Lippinc. 61: 865.

Man who Intervened, The; a story. (Robert Hichens) Pall Mall M. 12: 383.

Man who played the Cymbals; a story. Music, 18: 279.

Man who stole the Castle, The. (T. Gallon) Strand, 18: 704.

Man who wanted the Earth, The. (W. O. McGeehan) Overland, n. s. 35: 345.

Man who went with the Place, The. (M. L. Knapp) Cent. 39: 399.

Man who Won, The; a story. (E. Lefêvre) McClure, 17: 360.

Man who worked for Collister. (M. T. Earle) Cent. 31: 728.

Man with a Bacon Rind. (W. H. Shelton) Scrib. M. 22: 467.

Man with the Cap, The. (Sol. N. Sheridan) Overland, n. s. 38: 278.

Man with the Empty Sleeve. (F. H. Smith) Atlan. 84: 206.

Man with the Gash, The; a story. (J. London) McClure, 15: 459. Same art. Idler, 20: 232.

Man with the Hoe, The; a poem. (E. Markham) Arena, 22: 15. Same art. McClure, 13: 15. Same art., with the picture. Outl. 62: 38.

Man with No Character; a story. (A. Merry) Idler, 12: 807.

Man with One Talent; a story. (R. H. Davis) Cosmopol. 24: 510.

Man without a Country, with a New Introduction. (E. E. Hale) Outl. 59: 116.

Man without a Past. (J. D. Ruff) Cent. 33: 758.

Man-eater, The; a story. (J. H. Rosny) Nat'l M. (Bost.) 9: 139.

Man-eater of Avaghoe, The. (A. Merry) Belgra. 97: 165.

Man-hunting in India. (Charles Johnston) Cosmopol. 24: 656.

Man-hunting in the Pound; a story. (J. Fox, jr.) Outing, 36: 346.

Mankind, History of, Ratzel's. (F. Russell) Am. Hist. R. 5: 323. — (D. G. Brinton) Am. Hist. R. 2: 322. — (F. Starr) Dial (Ch.) 23: 86. 24: 143.

Man-trap from Monmouthshire. (E. Hartland) Reliquary, 41: 126.

Man's Death, A. (M. Roberts) Eng. Illust. 18: 241.

Man's Dependence on the Earth. (L. Gallouédec) Pop. Sci. Mo. 53: 99.

Man's Message, A; a story. (C. Lyon) Belgra. 98: 218.

Man's Place in the Cosmos, Seth on. (R. A. Armstrong) New World, 7: 149.

Man, Isle of. (N. Webb) Nation, 69: 90.

— Anthropology of. (A. W. Moore and J. Beddoe) Anthrop. J. 27: 104.

— as a Sketching Ground. (A. Knox) Studio (Lond.) 7: 142.

— Manx Life, Undercurrents of. Chamb. J. 77: 618.

— Manxland in Winter. Chamb. J. 77: 207.

— Old Ionan Church. (A. Knox) Antiq. n. s. 34: 75.

Man-o'-war's Last Berth. (L. W. Lillingston) Good Words, 42: 396.

Manacled; a story. (S. Crane) Argosy, 71: 364.

Manatees. Sat. R. 83: 36.

Manchester, Eng. (E. A. Davies) Chaut. 28: 531.

— Ancient Name of. (H. Bradley) Eng. Hist. R. 15: 495.

Manchester, Eng.; Arts and Crafts Exhibition, 1895. Studio (Lond.) 5: 128.

— — Sept. 1898. (E. Wood) Studio (Internat.) 6: 121.

— Free Library, "Weeding out" at the. (E. Axon) Library, 8: 264.

— Gifts of Mrs. Rylands, Mr. Darbishire, and Mr. Christie to. Nature, 60: 578.

— John Rylands Library. Lib. J. 24: 621.

— Population of; Essay in Statistics. (E. T. Campagnac; C. E. B. Russell) Econ. R. 11: 73.

— School of Art. (A. L. Baldry) Studio (Lond.) 5: 104.

— Technical Education in. (A. T. Simmons) Nature, 63: 336.

Manchester, New Hampshire. (J. W. Fellows) New Eng. M. n. s. 16: 33.

Manchester School and To-day. (A. Carnegie) 19th Cent. 43: 277.

— End of the. Spec. 81: 681.

Manchu Dynasty, Legend of the Origin of the. (R. Morrison) Open Court, 15: 624.

Manchu Imperial Family. (E. H. Parker) Cornh. 82: 458.

Manchuria, The Future of. (F. Younghusband) 19th Cent. 43: 481. Same art. Liv. Age, 217: 49. Same art. Ecl. M. 130: 592.

— in Transformation. (A. R. Colquhoun) Monthly R. 5, no. 1: 58.

— Micawberism in. (E. J. Dillon) Contemp. 79: 649.

— Russian Exploration in. (P. Kropotkin) Geog. J. 11: 63.

— Russian Problem in. (G. F. Wright) R. of Rs. (N. Y.) 24: 60.

— Russians in. (P. Kropotkin) Forum, 31: 267. — (G. F. Wright) Nation, 71: 207.

'Manda. (J. Pemberton) New Eng. M. n. s. 25: 349.

Mandalay, Burmah. (Marie A. Millie) Idler, 12: 160.

— From Canton to. (W. A. Johnstone) Fortn. 69: 264.

Mandarin, Life of a Chinese. (E. H. Parker) Cornh. 77: 375.

Mandarins, Our Own. (T. M. Maguire) Un. Serv. M. 22: 138.

Mandeville, Bernard de, his Place in English Thought. (N. Wilde) Mind, 23: 219.

Mandrake, The; a poem. (G. F. Northall) Gent. M. n. s. 62: 91.

Mandrake, Notes upon. (F. Starr) Am. Antiq. 23: 259.

"Manerius." (W. W. Skeat) Ath. '01, 1: 696.

Manet, Edouard, Artist, with portrait. (A. Proust) Studio (Internat.) 12: 227. — (A. J. Eddy) Brush & P. 1: 137.

Mangan, James Clarence. (F. Thompson) Acad. 52: 241. — (A. P. Graves) Cornh. 77: 328.

— and his Poetry. (P. A. Gillard) Westm. 149: 648.

— Genius of. Cath. World, 65: 528.

— O'Donoghue's Life of. Acad. 53: 142.

Manganese as the Pyrophosphate, Determination of. (F. A. Gooch and M. Austin) Am. J. Sci. 156: 233.

— as the Sulphate and as the Oxide, Estimation of. (F. A. Gooch and M. Austin) Am. J. Sci. 155: 209.

— Estimation of, separated as the Carbonate. (M. Austin) Am. J. Sci. 155: 382.

Manganese Ore Deposits of the Queluz (Lafayette) District, Minas Geraes, Brazil. (O. A. Derby) Am. J. Sci. 162: 18.

Manhattan Company, The, 1799-1899; a Historic Institution. (J. K. Bangs) Harper, 98: 971.

Manicheans, Italian, Unpublished Treatise against. (F. C. Conybeare) Am. J. Theol. 3: 704.

Manifest Destiny, A Fresh View of. (J. H. Bridge) Overland, n. s. 31: 115.

Manila. (L. M. J. Garnett) Nation, 66: 475.

— An American in. (J. E. Stevens) McClure, 11: 186.

Manuscripts of Amer. Authors, McKelly Collection of. (S. A. Cunes) Bookman, **7**: 289.

— Market for. (Alice M. Douglas) Writer, **14**: 138, 152.

— Whereabouts of the Lost. (Z. A. Norris) Writer, **12**: 36.

Manx. *See* Man, Isle of.

Manzanillo's Conscience; a story. (W. Pain) Idler, **16**: 649.

Manzoni, Alessandro. (W. D. McCrackan) Am. J. Soc. Sci. **35**: 112.

Maori Houses. (C. J. Prætorius) Studio (Internat.) **13**: 18.

Maori Wood Carving. (C. J. Prætorius) Studio (Internat.) **12**: 15.

Maoris, Poetry of the. (R. Holder) Gent. M. n. s. **63**: 382.

Map, Transformation of the, 1825–1900. (J. Sohn) Scrib. M. **29**: 349.

Map Making and Graphic Representation. (W. Z. Ripley) Am. Statis. Assoc. **6**: 313.

Maps and Charts in a Library. (R. S. Fletcher) Pub. Lib. **4**: 444.

— Care of. (T. Letts) Lib. J. **26**: 688.

— Mediæval, New Light on Some. (C. R. Beazley) Geog. J. **14**: 620. **15**: 130, 378. **16**: 319.

— Preservation of, in the Library of Congress. (P. L. Phillips) Lib. J. **25**: 15.

— Weston Tapestry. (W. K. R. Bedford) Geog. J. **9**: 210.

Mapes, Victor. Writer, **14**: 107.

Maple Sugar and Syrup Industry of Canada. Chamb. J. **76**: 335.

Maple Sugar, Making. (M. B. Thrasher) Cosmopol. **30**: 623. — (E. P. Powell) Indep. **53**: 781.

Mapleson, Col. J. H., Operatic Manager. Music, **21**: 75.

Mappemonde, Crawford Reproductions of. (C. R. Beazley) Geog. J. **12**: 569.

Maranos. *See* Marranos.

Marat, Jean Paul, Bax's Life of. (E. D. Adams) Dial (Ch.) **30**: 229.

Marble. (William Brindley) Am. Arch. **66**: 86, 92.

— Greek. Chamb. J. **77**: 171.

— Moulding, by Pressure. Chamb. J. **75**: 523.

— used in Greek Sculpture, Identification of. (H. S. Washington) Am. J. Archæol. 2d s. **2**: 1.

Marbles, Lore of. (J. L. Steele) Outing, **38**: 203.

Marcelle, the Blanchisseuse; a story. Idler, **14**: 391.

Marcet, Dr. William. (F. W. Tunnicliffe) Nature, **61**: 497.

March of Progress. (C. W. Chesnutt) Cent. **39**: 422.

March Genealogy. (E. G. March) N. E. Reg. **53**: 121.

March Hare, A. (C. Strachey) Longm. **32**: 42. Same art. Ecl. M. **131**: 45.

March Weather, In. (E. Ingersoll) Outl. **61**: 537.

— in the United States, Types of. (O. L. Fassig) Am. J. Sci. **158**: 319.

March Wind, A. (A. Brown) Atlan. **83**: 537.

Marches. (T. L. Crittenden) J. Mil. Serv. Inst. **1**: 33.

Marches, The. (G. Law) Jurid. R. **11**: 226.

Marchesi, Matilda. (Florence Dingley) Music, **13**: 606, 676.

— her Methods of Work. Interview with Mrs. S. H. Eddy. Music, **12**: 677.

— Marvellous Memory of. (J. G. Huneker) Bk. Buyer, **16**: 61.

— Reminiscences. Music, **17**: 91.

Marching, "Flexion." (Sir E. Verney) Contemp. **75**: 702.

Marconi, William, and Wireless Telegraphy, with portrait. (J. S. Ames) R. of Rs. (N. Y.) **23**: 700.

Marcus Aurelius Antoninus, Porcher's. (W. L. Brown) Nation, **66**: 107, 129.

See Antoninus.

Marcy, Mt., A Winter Ascent of. (C. G. La Farge) Outing, **36**: 69.

Mare Island, Social Life at. (Ella M. Hammond) Overland, n. s. **38**: 485.

Mare's Nest, A; a story. (M. P. Williams) Pall Mall M. **13**: 307.

Mare's Nest, A; a story. (C. Rook) Idler, **15**: 699.

Maréchal, François, Etcher. (F. Khnopff) Studio (Internat.) **11**: 102. — (Pol de Mont) Artist (N. Y.) **29**: 1.

Mareuil, Col. De Villebois. (J. E. C. Bodley) Ath. '00, **1**: 465.

Marg. (Alma M. Estabrook) Overland, n. s. **37**: 775.

Margaret; a poem. (R. Bourne) Argosy, **65**: 764.

Margaret; a poem. (R. Le Gallienne) Ecl. M. **132**: 92.

Margaret Emma Henley; a poem. (W. E. Henley) Ecl. M. **132**: 361.

Margaret of Anjou, Shakespeare's "Life beyond Life" of. (L. W. Spring) Educa. **17**: 617.

Margaret of Denmark, Hill's. (J. E. Olson) Am. Hist. R. **5**: 122.

Margaret of Scotland; a poet-princess. (A. Shield) Gent. M. n. s. **63**: 559.

Margaret Perris; a story. (A. Radford) Eng. Illust. **17**: 291.

Margaret Sinclair; a story. (Lady M. Howard) Argosy, **65**: 557.

Margherita, Queen. History of a Prayer. (G. Dalla Vecchia) Good Words, **42**: 164.

Margot; a story. (F. H. Sweet) Nat'l M. (Bost.) **5**: 333.

Margrave, Bachelor; a story. (C. M. Parker) Harper, **96**: 229.

Marguerite of Navarre as Princess and Poetess. (Katherine W. Elwes) Gent. M. n. s. **65**: 33.

Marguerite's Carnival; a story. (L. Zangwill) Eng. Illust. **16**: 592.

Marguerite's Husband; a story. (J. W. Tompkins) Munsey, **21**: 819.

Marholm, Laura. Six Modern Women. (L. C. Bull) Critic, **30**: 35.

Maria Theresa and Joseph II., Bright's. (C. H. Lincoln) Citizen, **3**: 140.

Maria d'Arquien, Queen of Poland. Acad. **56**: 184.

Maria de la Luz. (Mary H. Rose) Overland, n. s. **35**: 181.

Maria Gaetana Agnese. (V. M. Crawford) Month, **97**: 575.

Maria Theresa, Sketch of. Argosy, **67**: 343.

Marianson; a story. (M. H. Catherwood) Harper, **96**: 92.

Marie-Antoinette and Louis XVI., Last Days of. (A. L. Bicknell) Cent. **33**: 33.

— as Dauphine. (A. L. Bicknell) Cent. **32**: 841.

— Last Attempt at Rescue of. (C. E. Meetkerke) Argosy, **63**: 422. Same art. Liv. Age, **213**: 552.

— Lenôtre on. (H. M. Stevens) Citizen, **3**: 257.

— Nolhac's. (A. Laugel) Nation, **65**: 434.

Marie Antoinette Houses of the United States. (J. M. Parker) New Eng. M. n. s. **22**: 53.

Marie Duplan's Child; a story. (Imogen Clark) Cosmopol. **25**: 77.

Marienberg. (C. De Kay) Archit. R. **9**: 1.

Marie's Story; a tale of Prussia's Invasion of France, 1870. (John le Breton) Pall Mall M. **11**: 416.

Marigold-Michel. (B. W. Howard) Atlan. **79**: 313.

Mariki; a story. Macmil. **82**: 419.

Marine, Mercantile, as a Feeder to the Royal Naval Reserve. Un. Serv. M. **16**: 233.

Marine Animals and Plants. Preparation as Lanternslides. (H. C. Sorby) Nature, **57**: 520.

Marine Biological Laboratories. (H. S. Williams) Harper, 100: 335.

Marine Carrying-trade. (J. Codman) Engin. M. 13: 497.

Marine Engineering, Development of, and Untrammeled Shipbuilding. (J. R. Oldham) Cassier, 16: 559.

— The Outlook in. (G. W. Melville) Cassier, 15: 251, 401.

— Progress in British Cargo Boat Machinery. (J. F. Walliker) Cassier, 21: 26.

Marine Engines, 1807–50, in the U. S. (C. H. Haswell) Cassier, 15: 160.

— Modern. (C. E. Hyde) Cassier, 12: 441.

Marine Garrisons for Naval Bases. (F. C. Ormsby-Johnson) Fortn. 67: 98.

Marine Insurance, Intricacies of. (W. Allingham) Chamb. J. 78: 684.

Marine Station, A Scottish, and its Development. (W. Sinclair) Good Words, 42: 629.

Mariner, William, Adventures of, 1805–06. (E. S. Holden) Outing, 39: 308.

Marines, The, and the Navy, British. Un. Serv. M. 15: 87.

— Antiquity of. (R. F. Collum) J. Mil. Serv. Inst. 9: 243.

Marinus, a Jewish Philosopher. (S. Krauss) Jew. Q. 9: 515.

Marinus of Reijmerswale, Paintings of. (A. R. Evans) M. of Art, 21: 246.

Mariology, Highland, A Study in. (R. M. Lockhart) Westm. 147: 128.

Marion; a story. (Violet Needham) Temp. Bar, 124: 335.

Marion, Massachusetts. (M. H. Leonard) New Eng. M. n. s. 20: 613.

Marionettes as Actors. (A. Symons) Sat. R. 84: 55.

Maris, James. (R. A. M. Stevenson) M. of Art, 24: 481.

— With portrait. (P. Zilcken) Studio (Internat.) 9: 231.

— Art Work of. Art J. 52: 107.

Marischal, George Keith, 10th Earl of. Scot. R. 32: 316.

Maritime Capture; Enemy's Property at Sea. (A. G. Sedgwick) Nation, 67: 24.

Maritime Expeditions in relation to Sea-power. (T. C. Ormsby-Johnson) Fortn. 72: 815.

Marivaux, P. C. de C. de, Deschamps's. Sat. R. 84: 66.

— Novels of. (B. W. Wells) Sewanee, 7: 287.

Mark and his Lantern. (G. F. Scott) Good Words, 42: 176.

Mark on the Shack; a story. (M. Roberts) Eng. Illust. 17: 115.

Marked Cards; a tale of justice. (C. Ross) Canad. M. 12: 545.

Marken, A Visit to. (E. Robinson) Outing, 35: 475.

Market-gardens, World's Largest. (J. E. Bennett) Cosmopol. 28: 495.

Market Wrecking. (W. E. Bear) Fortn. 67: 546.

Markets, Open, and Foreign Policy. (D. MacG. Means) Nation, 67: 124.

Markham, Edwin; with portrait. (J. M.) Bookman, 9: 441.

— and Cora Chase. (G. L. Farnell) Critic, 35: 1031.

— Man with the Hoe. (E. B. Sherman) Critic, 35: 1033.

— (E. B. Payne) Arena, 22: 17.

— Mission of, as Poet, with portrait. (F. Putnam) Nat'l M. (Bost.) 11: 54.

— a Pessimist. (G. McDermot) Cath. World, 69: 688.

Markham, Gervase. (E. V. Lucas) Cornh. 76: 537.

Marks, Gilbert, Artist in Silver. M. of Art, 21: 158.

— Silver Work of. M. of Art, 22: 564.

Marks, Henry Stacy, with portrait. (G. D. Leslie) M. of Art, 22: 237. — Acad. 53: 76. — Ath. '98, 1: 93.

Marksmanship, Old and New. (W. A. Baillie-Grohman) 19th Cent. 47: 753.

— Needful in Soldiers. (A. P. Hillier; W. Murray) Sat. R. 85: 748, 818, 848.

Marlborough, John Churchill, Duke of, with portrait. (W. F. Fauley) Bookman, 13: 318. — (W. O. Morris) Un. Serv. M. 19: 474, 609. 20: 24, 543. 21: 1.

— Unconscious Treason of. (A. Lang) Blackw. 161: 798.

Marlborough, Sarah, Duchess of, Molloy's Life of. (E. K. Dunton) Dial (Ch.) 31: 435.

Marlborough House, London. (A. H. Beavan) Cosmopol. 23: 135.

Marlowe, Christopher, and Shakespeare, Joint Authorship of. (J. T. Foard) Gent. M. n. s. 64: 134.

— New Light on. (F. S. Boas) Fortn. 71: 212.

Marlowe, Julia, An Appreciation. (E. N. Bagg) Nat'l M. (Bost.) 12: 704.

Marlowe's Assignment. (J. R. MacMahon) Outl. 64: 74.

Marmosets; the Dulce-Piji Family. (J. Ingersoll) Cent. 37: 809.

Marni, Jeanne. (F. Loliée) Bookman, 11: 316.

Maroons of Jamaica. (E. Blake) No. Am. 167: 558.

— A Dress Rehearsal of Rebellion. (P. Robinson) Contemp. 74: 746. Same art. Ecl. M. 132: 88.

— Story of the. Chamb. J. 74: 711.

Marotse and Mashikolumbwe Countries, Journey in. (A. St.H. Gibbons) Geog. J. 9: 122.

Marotseland, Explorations in, and Neighboring Regions. (A. St.H. Gibbons; F. C. Quicke) Geog. J. 17: 106.

Marquand, Henry G. (E. A. Alexander) Harper, 94: 560.

Marquette Iron Range, Petrography of, Van Hise and Bayley on. Am. Natural. 31: 1050.

Marranos, Expulsion from Venice in 1550. (D. Kaufmann) Jew. Q. 13: 520.

Marriage, Alleged Decline of. Ecl. M. 133: 466.

— and Chastity. (W. H. Mayhew) N. Church R. 4: 70.

— and Divorce. (C. Cort) Ref. Ch. R. 48: 221.

— — in their Legal Aspects. (J. D. Enright) Cath. World, 70: 673.

— — U. S. Cases before Canadian Courts. (E. Lafleur) Am. J. Soc. Sci. 36: 196.

— and Modern Civilization. (W. S. Lilly) 19th Cent. 50: 905.

— and Morality. (A. G. Lewis) Westm. 156: 184.

— and Motherhood Spiritually Considered. (Lydia F. Dickinson) N. Church R. 4: 346.

— and Unselfishness. Sat. R. 90: 544.

— The Artist and. Atlan. 83: 142.

— the Choice Matrimonial. Chamb. J. 75: 497.

— Contract of, Fraud and. (L. M. Friedman) Am. Law R. 32: 568.

— Early. (E. J. Hardy) Argosy, 69: 52.

— Education and. (A. L. Mearkle) Arena, 23: 661.

— English and French Views of. Sat. R. 89: 133.

— in the 15th Century. (E. B. Stone) Lippinc. 59: 107.

— in Modern Fiction, Chapman on. Spec. 79: 246.

— Morality of, Caird's. (F. Danby) Sat. R. 85: 257.

— National Views of. Sat. R. 89: 133. Same art. Liv. Age, 224: 722.

— The "New" in the Old. (A. Lang) No. Am. 164: 415.

— or Free Love. (E. Johnson) Westm. 152: 91.

— Scouring Shakespeare's Dictum. Atlan. 82: 860.

— Vacarius on. (F. W. Maitland) Law Q. 13: 133, 270.

— Why More Men do not Marry. (K. G. Wells) No. Am. 165: 123.

— A Woman's Chance of. (J. H. Schooling) Strand, 15: 266.

Marriage of Convenience, A; a story. (L. W. Betts) Outl. 66: 221.

Marriage of a Rajput Prince. Macmil. 80: 212.

Marriage of Thomasina; a Queensland story. (F. Campbell) Pall Mall M. 20: 318.

Marriage, A, without a Wooing. Chamb. J. 78: 349.

Marriage Ceremonies, Quaint. Belgra. 97: 62.

Marriage Ceremony, The. Outl. 68: 663.

Marriage Customs, Hutchinson on. (M. L. Miller) Dial (Ch.) 24: 181.

— Oraibi. (H. R. Voth) Am. Anthrop. 2: 238.

Marriage Laws and Customs of the Cymri. (R. B. Holt) Anthrop. J. 28: 155.

— Mediæval, and Anglican Bishops. Month, 92: 113.

— Suggestion of a Substitute for the. (H. Flowerden) Westm. 152: 293.

Marriage Market, The. Spec. 78: 588. Same art. Liv. Age, 213: 622.

Marriage Questions .in Fiction, Miss Chapman on. (Sarah Grand) Fortn. 69: 378. Same art. Liv. Age, 217: 67. Same art. Ecl. M. 130: 667.

Marriage-rate, Correlation of, with Trade. (R. H. Hooker) J. Statis. Soc. 64: 485.

— English. (J. H. Schooling) Fortn. 75: 959.

Marriage Returns; Ignoring the Law. (R. W. Brokaw) Outl. 66: 1007.

Marriages at Sea. (J. D. White) Law Q. 17: 283.

— Foreign; Americans who have married Titles. (Frances De Forest) Cosmopol. 27: 227.

— Happy, of Noted Persons. (F. A. Doughty) Cath. World, 66: 587.

— Scotch. (R. V. Rogers) Green Bag, 11: 426.

— Unhappy, of Noted Persons. (F. A. Doughty) Cath. World, 67: 526.

— Validity of, Performed in a Jurisdiction other than that of the Domicile of the Parties. (W. C. Rodgers) Am. Law R. 31: 524.

— West-Pyrenean. (A..R. Whiteway) Gent. M. n. s. 65: 404.

Married Women in England, Legal Capacity of. (E. Stocquart) Am. Law R. 32: 562.

Marriott, C. The Column. Macmil. 84: 120. Same art. Ecl. M. 137: 387.

Marrying of Kat, The. (R. Ashton) Temp. Bar, 119: 44.

Mars, The Planet. (S. F. Breckenridge) Luth. Q. 27: 520.

— as a World. (R. A. Gregory) National, 34: 914. Same art. Liv. Age, 225: 21.

— Calendar for. (D. A. Drew) Pop. Astron. 4: 417.

— Canals on. (M. A. Orr) Knowl. 24: 38.

— Hourglass Sea on. (E. M. Antoniadi) Knowl. 20: 169.

— in Jan., 1899. (A. E. Douglass) Pop. Astron. 7: 113.

— An Invasion from. Spec. 79: 398.

— Is Aqueous Vapor Present on? (E. I. Yowell) Pop. Astron. 7: 237.

— Is it Possibly Inhabited? (G. S. Jones) Pop. Astron. 9: 234.

— Lowell's Observations of. (G. Schiaparelli) Science, n. s. 9: 633.

— Signalling to. (R. Ball) Pall Mall M. 23: 365. Same art. Ecl. M. 136: 770. Same art. Liv. Age, 229: 277.

— What we know about. (E. S. Holden) McClure, 16: 439. Same art. Idler, 20: 218.

— Where did it get its Moons? (E. Miller) Pop. Astron. 4: 424, 499.

Mars-La-Tour, Battle of. Un. Serv. M. 23: 24.

Marseillaise, Strange Origin of the. (K. Blind) 19th Cent. 50: 93.

Marseilles to Les Pennes. (B. Harrison) Outing, 29: 370.

Marsh, Othniel Charles. (C. E. Beecher) Am. J. Sci. 157: 403. — (J. L. Wortman) Science, n. s. 9: 561. — Nature, 59: 513.

Marsh, Othniel Charles, Bequests of. Science, n. s. 9: 494.

— Bibliography of. Am. J. Sci. 157: 420.

Marsh, Richard, as a Novelist. Acad. 59: 423.

Marsh Gas. (T. L. Phipson) Chamb. J. 74: 123.

Marshall, Charles, with portrait. (Sallie E. M. Hardy) Green Bag, 10: 160.

Marshall, Mrs. Emma. Acad. 56: 497. 59: 487.

Marshall, John. (Sallie E. M. Hardy) Green Bag, 10: 22. — (J. B. Thayer) Atlan. 87: 328. — (A. Russell) Am. Law R. 35: 1. — (J. F. Dillon) Am. Law R. 35: 161. — (H. C. Lodge) No. Am. 172: 191. — (D. MacG. Means) Nation, 72: 104. — (R. Olney) Outl. 67: 573. — With portraits. (F. R. Jones) Green Bag, 13: 53. — With portraits. Green Bag, 13: 158, 213. — (W. Goddard) N. Church R. 8: 330. — (R. Olney) Am. Law R. 34: 550.

— and John Scott. (J. B. Cassody) Am. Law R. 33: 1.

— and Joseph Story, Friendship between. (A. Moses) Am. Law R. 35: 321.

— Anecdotes of. World's Work, 1: 394.

— A Great American Judge. Spec. 86: 198.

— Jefferson's Opinion of. Am. Law R. 35: 63.

— Letter to R. Smith, July 27, 1812. Pennsyl. M. 25: 263.

— Letters of, when Envoy to France, 1797, 1798. Am. Hist. R. 2: 294.

— Southern Federalist. (B. J. Ramage) Sewanee, 9: 129.

— Voyage of, 1795. (E. M. O. Marshall) Longm. 37: 147.

Marshall, R. His Excellency the Governor; a farce. (M. Beerbohm) Sat. R. 85: 815.

Marshall, William. (B. Chew) Bk. Buyer, 19: 265, 572.

Marshfield, Mass., and its Historic Houses. (R. A. Bradford) New Eng. M. n. s. 24: 422.

Marsiglio of Padua and William of Ockam. (J. Sullivan) Am. Hist. R. 2: 409, 593.

Marston Friars; a novel. (M. C. Rowsell) Belgra. 99: 676.

Marston Moor. (C. H. Firth) Cornh. 76: 3. Same art. Ecl. M. 129: 345.

Marston St. Lawrence, Excavation of an Ancient Burial Ground at. (H. Dryden) Archæol. 48: 327.

Marsupials and their Skins. Spec. 78: 169.

— Australian. (B. A. Bensley) Am. Natural. 35: 245.

Marta's Inheritance. (Mrs. S. Crowninshield) Lippinc. 64: 444.

Marteau, Henri, Violinist, Interview with, with portrait. Music, 13: 740.

Marten, German Officer; a German Dreyfus. (O. G. Villard) Nation, 73: 260.

Martha and Mary; a character study. (J. D. Walsh) Meth. R. 59: 421.

Martha Ellen at the Chicago Exposition. (E. E. Wood) Cent. 38: 46.

Martha Middleton's Version of the Business. (A. Beresford) Argosy, 66: 643.

"Martha Washington," Case of the. (L. R. McCabe) Eng. Illust. 12: 695. Same art. McClure, 8: 236.

Martha's Lady. (S. O. Jewett) Atlan. 80: 523.

Martha's Vineyard. (W. A. Mowry) New Eng. M. n. s. 16: 543.

— Genealogical Notes from. (C. E. Banks) N. E. Reg. 52: 27.

— Is Capowack the Correct Indian Name of? (C. E. Banks) N. E. Reg. 52: 176.

Marthy's Dress. (C. B. Morgan) Lippinc. 69: 677.

Martial, Literary Influence of, upon Juvenal. (H. L. Wilson) Am. J. Philol. 19: 193.

Martial Law and Social Order. (J. Chester) J. Mil. Serv. Inst. 17: 57.

Martial Law in Insurrection. (R. N. Scott) J. Mil. Serv. Inst. **4**: 408.
— Proper. (H. C. Carbaugh) J. Mil. Serv. Inst. **15**: 1176.
Martian, The; a novel. (G. Du Maurier) Harper, **94**: 186-839. **95**: 129, 182.
Martin, Helena Faucit, Lady. Blackw. **168**: 906. Same art. Ecl. M. **136**: 372. Same art. Liv. Age, **228**: 303.
Martin, Henri, French Painter. Artist (N. Y.) **29**: 113.
Martin, John, Painter, Works of. (E. Wakecook) Artist (N. Y.) **30**: 189.
Martin, John Biddulph. Econ. J. **7**: 300.
Martin, Hon. Joseph. (J. R. Robinson) Canad. M. **13**: 424.
Martin, Samuel, Baron, with portrait. Green Bag, **12**: 105.
Martin, T. Byam, Admiral. (R. B. Martin; R. V. Hamilton) Un. Serv. M. **19**: 437.
Martin, William. (E. P. Payson) N. E. Reg. **54**: 27.
Martin, Dr. W. A. P., with portrait. Bk. Buyer, **21**: 8. — Outl. **65**: 783.
Martin Farroner; a story. (M. Merington) Harper, **96**: 358.
Martin Keary's Dago Partner; a story. (A. J. Dawson) Idler, **10**: 741.
Martineau, James. (P. T. Forsyth) Lond. Q. **93**: 214. — Acad. **51**: 455. — (F. H. Foster) Presb. & Ref. R. **12**: 579. — (A. W. Jackson) No. Am. **171**: 543. — (A. W. Jackson) New World, **9**: 1. — (C. C. Everett) Atlan. **86**: 317. — (P. H. Wicksteed) Contemp. **77**: 187. — Acad. **58**: 65. — (J. Jacobs) Ath. '00, **1**: 83. — Outl. **64**: 153. — (E. E. Hale) Outl. **64**: 259. — (J. W. Chadwick) Outl. **64**: 421. — With portrait. (M. D. Conway) Open Court, **14**: 257. — Spec. **84**: 82. Same art. Liv. Age, **224**: 523.
— and Harriet. (A. W. Jackson) Liv. Age, **228**: 325.
— and the Term Unitarian. (J. Morrow) Outl. **64**: 694.
— as an Ethical Teacher. (S. H. Mellone) Internat. J. Ethics, **10**: 380.
— An Hour with. (W. C. Wilkinson) Bookman, **13**: 427.
— Jackson's Life of. (H. C. Minton) Presb. & Ref. R. **12**: 312. — (J. W. Chadwick) Nation, **71**: 312. — (J. W. Chadwick) Critic, **37**: 445. — (E. G. Johnson) Dial (Ch.) **19**: 222.
— on the Four Notes of the Church. Dub. R. **127**: 261.
— Recollections of. (F. P. Cobbe) Contemp. **77**: 174. Same art. Liv. Age, **224**: 793. — Macmil. **81**: 342.
— Some Letters of. Atlan. **86**: 489.
Martini, Ferdinando, with portrait. (F. T. Cooper) Bookman, **7**: 25.
Martyn, Edwin. Heather Field. (M. Beerbohm) Sat. R. **87**: 106.
Martyrdom of Fame, The. (C. E. Laughlin) Scrib. M. **22**: 777.
Martyrdom of "Mealy" Jones; a story. (W. A. White) McClure, **9**: 968.
Martyrs, English, Relics of. (D. B. Camm) Dub. R. **129**: 320.
— in the Valladolid Manuscript. (D. B. Camm) Month, **96**: 345.
— of Sebaste, The Forty. (H. Dalehaye) Am. Cath. Q. **24**: 161.
Martyrs' Idyl, The; a poem. (L. I. Guiney) Harper, **98**: 130.
Maruska; an Incident in Modern Life. Blackw. **162**: 778. Same art. Liv. Age, **216**: 418.
Marvell, Andrew, with portrait. Acad. **51**: 478.
— Home in Highgate. (Alex. Ramsay) Art J. **51**: 250.
— Lyrical Poems of. (H. C. Beeching) National, **37**: 747. Same art. Liv. Age, **230**: 637.
— Pamphlet against the Members of Parliament of Charles II. (F. G. Walters) Gent. M. n. s. **65**: 57.

Marvellous, Propensity toward the. (E. Mach) Open Court, **14**: 539.
Marvels of Science, The; a play. (George Hibbard) Scrib. M. **29**: 476.
Marvin, Matthew, and his Second Wife, Widow Alice Bouton. (W. T. R. Marvin) N. E. Reg. **51**: 330.
Mary, Virgin, Dedication of the Month of May to. (H. Thurston) Month, **97**: 470.
Mary Magdalene, St., and the Early Saints of Provence. (H. Thurston) Month, **93**: 75.
Mary, Queen of Scots. Acad. **61**: 207, 381.
— and the Grand Papal League. (J. H. Pollen) Month, **97**: 258.
— and Opinions of her Catholic Contemporaries. (J. H. Pollen) Month, **91**: 575.
— and Recent Research. (J. H. Pollen) Month, **91**: 342.
— Casket Letters. (A. Lang) Blackw. **168**: 890.
— Did she love Bothwell? (A. Tasker) Gent. M. n. s. **67**: 570.
— Letter to. Archæol. **47**: 242.
— Mystery of, A. Lang on. Ath. '01, **2**: 653.
— Portrait of, at Osborne House, Isle of Wight. (G. Scharf) Archæol. **51**: 469.
— Silver Casket at Hamilton Palace, connected with. (Mary A. Baillie-Hamilton) Macmil. **80**: 131.
— Studies on the History of. (J. H. Pollen) Month, **96**: 167, 241, 392.
Mary Tudor, Personal Character of. (J. M. Stone) Month, **94**: 128.
Mary of Guise, Alleged Treachery of. (A. Lang; E. G. Atkinson) Ath. '00, **1**: 657, 690, 720, 753, 784, 815.
Mary Amelia Spot; a story. (G. Keats) Blackw. **165**: 616. Same art. Ecl. M. **137**: 154. Same art. Liv. Age, **229**: 772.
Mary and Martha. Few Things Needful. (T. K. Cheyne) Expos. **9**: 256.
Mary Connor's Release; a story. Temp. Bar, **113**: 566. Same art. Liv. Age, **217**: 374.
Mary Ellen; a story. (Mary Hartier) Gent. M. n. s. **58**: 88.
Mary Ellen's Auction. (P. Leonard) New Eng. M. n. s. **21**: 605.
"Mary had a Little Lamb," True Story of. (E. A. Warren) Nat'l M. (Bost.) **6**: 251.
Mary's "Past;" a story. (R. Wood) Idler, **18**: 555.
Maryland, Adoption of the Federal Constitution by. (B. C. Steiner) Am. Hist. R. **5**: 22.
— Bar of, Early. (E. S. Riley) Green Bag, **12**: 577.
— Browne's Archives of. (J. W. Black) Am. Hist. R. **3**: 377.
— Constitution of, 1864. (W. S. Myers) J. H. Univ. Stud. **19**: 347.
— Eastern Shore of. (C. D. Wilson) Lippinc. **61**: 57.
— Governors before made a Royal Province. (B. C. Steiner) Pennsyl. M. **22**: 98.
— Harford County. (C. D. Wilson) New Eng. M. n. s. **20**: 161.
— Memories of. (J. Edgeworth) Chaut. **25**: 161.
— Taxation in. (T. S. Adams) J. H. Univ. Stud. **18**: 1.
Marysienská, Queen of Poland, Waliszewski's. Sat. R. **87**: 340.
Marx, Karl, and the close of his System, Boehm-Bawerk's. Sat. R. **85**: 754.
— Boehm-Bawerk on. Gunton's M. **16**: 56.
Masaniello; a nine days' king. Macmil. **76**: 279.
Masawa or Elgon, Mt., Journey round. (C. W. Hobley) Geog. J. **9**: 179.
Mascagni and his New Opera. (Alma Dalma) Cosmopol. **22**: 316.
Mashonaland Railway Survey. Geog. J. **15**: 144.

Mask of Life; a story. (V. W. Cloud) Cosmopol. 29: 326.

Masks. (E. A. B. Hodgetts) Strand, 15: 169.

— Curious, among Greeks and Barbarians. (C. de Kay) M. of Art, 22: 583, 651.

Mason, Alfred Edward Woodley. Acad. 57: 690.

Mason, Eugene, Poetry of. Acad. 56: 626.

Mason, George, Painter, 1818-72. (A. L. Coghill) Longm. 30: 301.

Mason, James Mason, with portrait. (Sallie E. M. Hardy) Green Bag, 10: 114.

Mason, Hon. Jeremiah, with portrait. Green Bag, 12: 497.

Mason, J. R., with portraits. Strand, 15: 668.

Mason, John Y., with portrait. (Sallie E. M. Hardy) Green Bag, 10: 111.

Mason, William, American Pianist and Composer. (W. S. B. Mathews) Music, 13: 351.

— Memories of a Musical Life. (W. Mason) Cent. 38: 438-848.

— Musical Memories. (W. Mason) Music, 18: 561.

— Piano Method. (L. A. Nelson) Music, 18: 597.

— 70th Birthday of. Music, 15: 516.

— System of Technics. (W. S. B. Mathews) Music, 16: 621.

Masonry, Face Bonding in. (C. A. Martin) Am. Arch. 63: 45.

Masque, The English. (E. Dowden) 19th Cent. 46: 102.

— — and French Ballet. (H. M. Johnstone) Sewanee, 4: 428.

— A Modern. (E. R. Pennell) Nation, 69: 47.

Masquerade, The. (P. Lee) Atlan. 81: 255.

Mass, The. (G. W. E. Russell; J. A. Round) 19th Cent. 41: 418, 837.

— Fresh Light on the Early History of the. Month, 95: 129.

— Genuflexion at. (H. Thurston) Month, 90: 391.

— Lessons from the. (J. Foxley) Contemp. 75: 178.

— Low, The Vestments of. (H. Thurston) Month, 92: 265-615.

— Primitive and Protestant. (G. W. E. Russell) 19th Cent. 41: 418.

Masses, The Sacrifices of. (J. F. Besant) Am. Cath. Q. 25: 548.

Massachusetts and Connecticut, Boundary Line of. (A. Chamberlain) New Eng. M. n. s. 16: 339.

— and New Hampshire, Boundary Line of. (G. J. Varney) New Eng. M. n. s. 16: 347.

— Birth-rate in. (F. S. Crum) Q. J. Econ. 11: 248.

— Coat of Arms and Great Seal of. (E. H. Garrett) New Eng. M. n. s. 23: 623.

— Farmer in, and Taxation. (C. S. Walker) Yale R. 6: 63.

— Gas Commission of. (J. H. Gray) Q. J. Econ. 14: 509.

— Hill Towns of. (E. P. Pressey) New Eng. M. n. s. 22: 695.

— — Are they Degenerating? (A. E. Winship) New Eng. M. n. s. 22: 654.

— Manufactures in, Annual Statistics of. (G. H. Wadlin; S. N. D. North) Am. Statis. Assoc. 6: 77.

— Political Development of. (R. L. Bridgman) New Eng. M. n. s. 23: 116.

— Provincial to Commonwealth Government in, Transition of, Cushing's. (A. M. Davis) Am. Hist. R. 2: 740.

— Public Charities in. Ann. Am. Acad. Pol. Sci. 12: 128.

— Public School System of. (A. W. Edson) Educa. R. 16: 435.

— Recent Legislation in. (A. N. Lincoln) Char. R. 6: 404.

— Slave Trade in. (L. Brandt) New Eng. M. n. s. 21: 83.

Massachusetts, Tax Report, 1896. (A. C. Miller) J. Pol. Econ. 6: 225.

— Western, Record of Marriages in, 1795 to 1823. (G. Sheldon) N. E. Reg. 52: 340.

— Woodward's and Saffery's Map of 1642. (L. B. Chase) N. E. Reg. 55: 155.

Massachusetts Archives, Gleanings from. (F. E. Blake) N. E. Reg. 55: 388.

Massachusetts Bay, Courts of Justice in the Province of, under the First Charter, 1630-84. (T. L. Phillips) Am. Law R. 34: 566.

— Davis's Currency and Banking in. (W. C. Ford) Nation, 73: 250.

Massacre, Oriental, The Motive of. Spec. 85: 72.

Massacres, A Tale of Two. Chamb. J. 74: 529.

Massai's Crooked Trail; a story. (F. Remington) Harper, 96: 240.

Massasoit, Sowams the Home of; where was it? (V. Baker) N. E. Reg. 53: 317.

Massean, Fix, Art Work of. Artist (N. Y.) 30: 93.

Massena's Lines of March in Portugal and French Routes in Northern Spain. (T. J. Andrews) Eng. Hist. R. 16: 472.

Massenet, J., Debut of. (Victorin Joncieres) Music, 15: 268.

— Grisélidis. (J. F. Runcimann) Sat. R. 92: 776.

— Mary Magdalen; oratorio. (W. S. B. Mathews) Music, 18: 150.

Massinger, P. The Fatal Dowry. (H. S. Wilson) Gent. M. n. s. 63: 180, 294.

— Note on. (A. L. Casserley) Westm. 152: 444.

Massingham, H. W., a Gifted Editor. (C. K. Shorter) Eng. Illust. 17: 243.

Masson, David, with portrait. (W. Archer) Pall Mall M. 25: 378.

— Conversation with. (W. Archer) Critic, 39: 457.

Massorah, The, A Contribution to the Study of. Asia. R. 26: 110.

Massoretic Studies. (L. Blau) Jew. Q. 9: 471.

Master, The, and the Bees. (Isabel M. Hamill) Chamb. J. 76: 631-650. Same art. Liv. Age, 224: 562.

Master Builder, The; a poem. (E. N. Lyon) Outl. 68: 456.

Master Casimir; a story. (G. Hesekiel) Argosy, 68: 225.

Master-key of Newgate, The; a prison story. (T. Hopkins) McClure, 14: 329.

Master Mathematician, The. (D. B. Vare) Temp. Bar, 123: 480.

Master Maynard; a tale. (H. A. Hering) Argosy, 73: 97.

Master Mind of Hollydene; a story. (G. W. Ross) Canad. M. 12: 160.

Master of Craft, A. (W. W. Jacobs) Strand, 17: 532, 638. 18: 88-775.

Master of Finance, A; a story. (A. St. J. Adcock) Good Words, 39: 829.

Master of Palmyra; a dramatic poem. (A. Wilbrandt) Poet-Lore, 13: 161.

Master Peaceful; a story. (H. A. Hinkson) Idler, 16: 88.

Master sold by a Slave, A; a story. (J. S. Bonner) McClure, 9: 709.

Masterpiece of God; a sketch. (F. Baird) Canad. M. 18: 148.

Mastodon, Early Discoveries of the. (T. J. Freeman) Am. Antiq. 23: 320.

Masut, the New Substitute for Coal. Chamb. J. 74: 293.

Mataafa, Catholic Hero of Samoa. (J. G. Leigh) Month, 95: 163.

Matabele Campaign, 1896, Baden-Powell's. Sat. R. 84: 201.

Matabele Outbreak, What I saw of the. (D. Kearns) Good Words, 38: 774.

Matabele Revolt, History of, Selous on. Spec. **78**: 513.

Match Factory, An English. (James Cassidy) Gent. M. n. s. **58**: 149. Same art. Ecl. M. **128**: 448.

Match Game, The; a story. (W. A. Walker) Outing, **30**: 464.

Matches, Manufacture of, How can it be made Healthful? (E. Magitot) Chaut. **25**: 273.

Mate for Melinda, A; a story. (E. B. Tiffany) Harper, **102**: 923.

Materfamilias; a story. (J. Mansergh) Cornh. **76**: 801. Same art. Ecl. M. **130**: 142.

Materia Medica, Folk. (R. H. True) J. Am. Folk-Lore, **14**: 105.

Materialism. (C. Thomas) Luth. Q. **30**: 297.

— and Socialism *vs.* Spiritual Development. (M. M. Sheedy) Cath. World, **66**: 577.

— and the Unknowable. (A. E. Maddock) Westm. **155**: 163.

— Modern, Idealist's Prescription for. (J. J. Tigert) Meth. R. **59**: 219.

— of the Age. (J. W. Longley) Canad. M. **12**: 93.

— will it be the Religion of the Future? (H. C. Corrance) Dub. R. **125**: 86.

Materials, The Cost of Raw. (H. M. Chance) Gunton's M. **18**: 19.

Maternal Associations, Early History of. (M. L. Butler) Chaut. **31**: 138.

Maternal Solicitude. (Geo. Courteline) Liv. Age, **216**: 681.

Maternity, An Educated. (A. L. Moqué) Westm. **153**: 53.

— Mexican Superstitions of. (V. A. Lucier) J. Am. Folk-Lore, **10**: 108.

Mathematical Economics, Cournot's. (I. Fisher) Q. J. Econ. **12**: 119, 238.

Mathematical Tripos, The. Ath. '00, **1**: 149.

Mathematicians, International Congress of, 1897. (C. A. Scott) Nation, **65**: 183.

— — Paris, 1900. (C. A. Scott) Nation, **71**: 186. — Nature, **62**: 418. — Ath. '00, **2**: 253.

Mathematics. (A. Hume) School R. **8**: 75.

— and Biology. (K. Pearson) Nature, **63**: 274.

— and Physics in Public Schools. (G. H. J. Hurst) Nature, **63**: 370.

— Beginning of. (W. J. McGee) Am. Anthrop. **1**: 646.

— Elementary, Cajori's History of. (D. E. Smith) School R. **5**: 184.

— for Children. (M. Laisant) Pop. Sci. Mo. **55**: 800.

— History of. (W. W. Beman) Science, **6**: 297.

— in the Higher Schools of Prussia, Teaching of, Young on. (G. W. Myers) School R. **9**: 262.

— The Limitations of. (J. H. Gore) Educa. R. **17**: 164. — (W. H. Maltbie and J. L. Coolidge) Educa. R. **17**: 390.

— Preparation of High School Teacher of. (P. H. Hanus) School R. **5**: 504.

— Recent Work on the Principles of. (B. Russell) Internat. Mo. **4**: 83.

— Routine Work in. (H. L. Coar) School R. **8**: 271.

— Teaching of. (J. Perry) Nature, **62**: 317.

— — Different Methods Contrasted. (J. V. Collins) School R. **7**: 97.

— — in High Schools. (E. S. Loomis) Educa. **20**: 102.

— — Smith's Rational. (J. Perry) Nature, **63**: 367.

— What ought the Study of, to contribute to the Education of the High-school Pupil? (F. Milner) School R. **6**: 105.

Mather, Cotton, and the Witch-maid. (Pauline B. Mackie) Liv. Age, **218**: 771.

— Witch-finder. (K. L. Montgomery) Gent. M. n. s. **66**: 150.

Mather, Nathaniel; a Colonial Boyhood. (K. M. Cone) Atlan. **88**: 651.

Mather, Richard, Parents of. (W. F. Irvine) N. E. Reg. **54**: 348.

Mather, Samuel, Will of. (L. Withington) N. E. Reg. **52**: 366.

Matheson, Dr. George. (A. W. Stewart) Sund. M. **30**: 238.

Mathews, Albert. (A. O. Hall) Green Bag, **9**: 1.

Mathews, W. S. B. Songs of all Lands. Music, **17**: 343.

Mathurin; a story. (G. Parker) Liv. Age, **212**: 112.

Matin Song. (J. B. Tabb) Atlan. **88**: 538.

Matinée Girl, The. Munsey, **18**: 34.

Matinicus Rock, Maine, Lighthouse Service. (G. Kobbé) Cent. **32**: 219.

Matrimonial Campaign, A; a story. (M. R. French) Nat'l M. (Bost.) **12**: 455.

Matrimonial Confidence Club; a story. (Marie E. Beynon) Midland, **7**: 156.

Matrimonial Opportunities of Maria Pratt. (V. W. Cloud) Cent. **37**: 217.

Matrimony, How Miss Miggs fitted herself for. (F. C. Baylor) Cosmopol. **26**: 505.

Matsys, Quentin. (M. Van Even) Scot. R. **36**: 230.

Mattapoisett, Massachusetts. (M. H. Leonard) New Eng. M. n. s. **20**: 613.

Mattawa Valley, Ontario, Scoured Bowlders of. (F. B. Taylor) Am. J. Sci. **153**: 208.

Matteo Falcone; a story. (P. Mérimée) Gent. M. n. s. **60**: 480.

Matter and Spirit. (W. E. Krebs) Ref. Church R. **45**: 311.

— Lord Armstrong's Theory of. Spec. **78**: 863.

— Modern Views of. (O. J. Lodge) Internat. Mo. **1**: 493.

Matter of Authority, A; a story. (H. W. Phillips) McClure, **16**: 444.

Matter of Interest; a story. (R. W. Chambers) Cosmopol. **23**: 315, 421.

Matter of a Mashie. (D. Gray) Cent. **36**: 18.

Matter of Opinion, A. (Geo. Hibbard) Scrib. M. **28**: 233.

Matter of Prosody; a story. (F. Gadsby) Canad. M. **16**: 66.

Matter of Taste, A; a story. (E. Wyatt) McClure, **16**: 236.

Matterhorn, Ascent of the. (C. W. Hodell) Outing, **36**: 290.

— The Spirit of the. Acad. **52**: 215.

— Up the. (S. Turner) Canad. M. **17**: 309.

Matthew the Apostle and Zacchæus, were they the Same Person? (J. H. Wilkinson) Expos. **4**: 37.

Matthews, Brander, as a Critic. (W. P. Trent) Sewanee, **3**: 373.

— as a Dramatic Critic. (W. P. Trent) Internat. Mo. **4**: 289.

Matthias, Election of, to the Apostolate. (A. Carr) Expos. **7**: 388.

Maturing, Lines of Growth in. (R. G. Boone) Educa. R. **14**: 118.

Maud-Evelyn. (H. James) Atlan. **85**: 439.

Maude, Cyril, Portraits of. Strand, **15**: 53.

Mauna Loa, On the Summit of, Guppy's. Nature, **57**: 20.

Maundy-Daly Affair, The; a story. (I. Allen) Idler, **16**: 3.

Maupassant, Guy de. Boule de Suif. Acad. **57**: 107.

— Love-letters of. (H. Lynch) Fortn. **68**: 571. Same art. Liv. Age, **215**: 648.

Maurice, Frederick Denison. (W. P. Roberts) Good Words, **40**: 250.

— Recollections of. (E. Strachey) Cornh. **75**: 536. Same art. Liv. Age, **213**: 730.

Mauritius, the Island of "Paul and Virginia." (C. Smythe) Chamb. J. 76: 29.

— Memories of. (Lady Broome) Cornh. 81: 486. Same art. Ecl. M. 135: 168.

Mauser Self-loading Pistol. (F. S. Foltz) J. Mil. Serv. Inst. 21: 515.

Mausoleum of Maussolus. (B. I. Wheeler) Cent. 34: 495.

Mausoleums. How the Rich are Buried. Archit. R. 10: 23.

Max, Gabriel, the Painting of, with portrait. (M. F. Nixon-Roulet) Cath. World, 74: 157.

Max — or his Picture. (Alice French) Scrib. M. 26: 739.

Max Beverley's Model; a tale. (C. Young) Belgra. 92: 271.

Max Tegelstein's Duel; a story. (F. Whishaw) Idler, 11: 112.

Maximilian I. of Mexico. (S. Y. Stevenson) Cent. 33: 420.

— and Iturbide. (R. M. Potter) J. Mil. Serv. Inst. 5: 404.

— Fall of. (S. Y. Stevenson) Cent. 33: 853.

— Footprints of. (A. Inkersley) Overland, n. s. 32: 395.

— his Allies and Enemies, Reminiscences of. (S. Y. Stevenson) Cent. 33: 113.

— How an Austrian Archduke ruled an American Empire. (S. Y. Stevenson) Cent. 33: 602.

Maximite, the United States Government's New Explosive. (Hudson Maxim) New Eng. M. n. s. 25: 36.

Maxims and Ideas, Pernicious. (A. H. Holmes) Arena, 24: 99.

— Two Famous Greek. (P. E. More) New World, 7: 18.

Maximus; a story. (A. Williams) Outing, 29: 568.

Maxwell, James Clerk, Influence on Modern Physics. (A. Gray) Nature, 58: 221.

May, Phil. (R. Riordan) Critic, 34: 55. — With portrait. Bk. Buyer, 14: 13.

— The Children of Velendam. (P. May) M. of Art, 24: 299.

May, Samuel, of Leicester, Mass. (J. W. Chadwick) New Eng. M. n. s. 20: 201.

May Carols. (A. M. Wakefield) 19th Cent. 41: 722. Same art. Ecl. M. 128: 793.

May Day in Olden Times. (A. W. Jarvis) Pall Mall M. 12: 32.

May it Please Your Highness. (B. Copplestone) Temp. Bar, 120: 496. Same art. Liv. Age, 227: 31.

May Meetings, The, 1898. Month, 92: 52.

May Queen, A Cheshire. (A. G. Skinner) Sund. M. 28: 294.

May Queens in Wales. (M. D. Griffith) Strand, 15: 583.

May Week Melodrama, A. (V. L. Whitechurch) Good Words, 41: 21.

Maya Indians, Among. (F. Starr) Indep. 53: 2164.

— Architecture of. (S. D. Peet) Am. Antiq. 23: 113.

— Superstitions and Customs of. (Thomas Gann) Chamb. J. 77: 167.

Maya Inscriptions, Archaic. (A. P. Maudslay) Nature, 56: 224.

Maya Ruins, On the Age of. (C. P. Bowditch) Am. Anthrop. 3: 697.

Maya Time System and Time Symbols. (C. Thomas) Am. Anthrop. 2: 53.

Maybrick, Mrs. F. E., Trial of; the English Dreyfus Case. (H. Densmore) Arena, 22: 598.

— — Legal Aspect of. (C. Bell) Green Bag, 9: 185.

Mayer, Alfred M., with portrait. (W. LeC. Stevens) Science, n. s. 6: 261.

Mayer, Henry, Humorous Caricaturist. Brush & P. 8: 161.

Maynooth, Second Plenary Synod of. (M. O'Riordan) Am. Cath. Q. 26: 136.

Mayor, Fred., Pictures by. Artist (N. Y.) 26: 92.

Mayor, Office of, in the U. S. (E. A. Greenlaw) Munic. Aff. 3: 33.

Mayor of Five Rivers. (H. A. Nash) New Eng. M. n. s. 23: 19.

Mazahua Hieroglyphic Catechism. (N. León) Am. Anthrop. 2: 724.

Mazamas, The. (J. S. Diller) Nat. Geog. M. 8: 58.

Mazarinus MS. and St. Francis of Assisi. (F. Andrew) Dub. R. 125: 144.

Mazdaism. (P. Carus) Open Court, 11: 141.

Mazers, English Mediæval Drinking Bowls called. Archæol. 50: 129.

Mazzini, Giuseppe. (F. Moscheles) Liv. Age, 214: 191.

— Early Letters, 1834-40. (J. W. Mario) Nation, 66: 146.

— Idealist. (S. M. Burnett) Am. Anthrop. 2: 502.

Mazzucato, Giannandrea, Musical Critic, with portrait. Music, 18: 513.

Meacci, Ricciardo. (Helen Zimmern) M. of Art, 23: 149.

Meade, Gen. George G., Bache's Life of. (F. W. Shepardson) Dial (Ch.) 26: 304. — Nation, 66: 444.

— Pennypacker's Life of. (T. L. Livermore) Nation, 73: 35. — (C. L. Moore) Dial (Ch.) 30: 394.

Meade, Mrs. L. T. Writer, 14: 28.

Meade, Sir Richard, Thornton's Life of. Spec. 81: 152. — Ath. '98, 2: 213. — Acad. 54: 318.

Meade, Admiral R. W., with portrait. Nat. Geog. M. 8: 142.

Meadow Frogs; poem. (J. B. Tabb) Atlan. 83: 720.

Meakin, L. H., Artist. Brush & P. 3: 224.

Meaning, Science of. (J. P. Postgate) Fortn. 68: 418.

Meanings, Science of. (A. J. Bell) School R. 9: 379.

Meason, George S. Ath. '01, 1: 313.

Measure of Eyes, The; a poem. (E. V. Cooke) Chaut. 32: 21.

Measurement, Evolution of Standards of. (J. A. Brashear) Cassier, 20: 410.

Measuring Machine, The, in the Workshop. (J. E. Sweet) Cassier, 20: 388.

Meat Extracts, Preparation of. (C. R. Valentine) J. Soc. Arts, 46: 430.

Mechanical Arts, Progress of, 1824-99. (C. Sellers) J. Frankl. Inst. 149: 5.

Mechanical Devices in Warfare, Importance of. (J. B. Walker) Cosmopol. 25: 343.

Mechanical Engineering, Progress and Tendency of, during the Nineteenth Century. (R. H. Thurston) Pop. Sci. Mo. 59: 34, 141.

— — Pres. Addr. Mech. Sec. Brit. Assoc. 1901. (R. E. Crompton) Nature, 64: 517.

— Influence of the Machine upon the Worker. (M. P. Higgins) Engin. M. 20: 568.

Mechanical Engineers in China, Openings for. (C. Beresford) Cassier, 18: 290.

Mechanical Science, Progress in, 1837-97. (R. G. Blaine) Knowl. 20: 132.

Mechanical World, Revival in the; symposium. Engin. M. 12: 684.

Mechanics, Applied, Perry on. (J. A. Ewing) Nature, 57: 313. — Sci. Prog. 7: vii.

— Developmental, Roux on. Nature, 57: 531.

— Theoretical, Love's. Sci. Prog. 7: ix.

Mechanism and Biology. Hertwig's. Nature, 56: 98.

Mecklenburg and Pomerania, Architecture and Ecclesiology of Towns in. (A. G. Hill) Archæol. 49: 301.

— Around an Ancient Duchy. (M. Todhunter) Westm. 150: 68.

Medallist's Art in France during the 19th Century, Evolution of. (Henri Frantz) M. of Art, 23: 373.

Medals at the Paris Exhibition. (R. Marx) Studio (Internat.) 13: 221.

Medals awarded to Artists, Alma Tadema Collection. (W. Roberts) M. of Art, 24: 342.
— A Cabinet of. (A. Laugel) Nation, 73: 244.
— English. (G. F. Hill) Knowl. 20: 82, 184.
— — and their Strange Story. (R. S. Loveday) Eng. Illust. 18: 624.
— French, The Renaissance in. (R. Marx) Studio (Internat.) 6: 14.
Medaska's Lost Cup, The ; a yarn. (R. Slye) Outing, 35: 180.
Mediæval Mechanicians, Some. (S. H. Hollands) Antiq. n. s. 33: 234.
Mediæval Students, Life of, as Illustrated by their Letters. (C. H. Haskins) Am. Hist. R. 3: 203.
Medical Charities. (S. Smith) Char. R. 8: 9.
Medical Department in the U. S. Army. (J. R. Williams) J. Mil. Serv. Inst. 14: 81. — (C. Smart) J. Mil. Serv. Inst. 14: 692.
Medical Education at the Univ. of Pennsylvania. Educa. 21: 631.
— A Forgotten Factor in. (A. L. Benedict) Educa. R. 15: 79.
— Knowledge and Practice. (C. S. Minot) Science, n. s. 10: 1.
— Research Work in. Nature, 60: 569.
Medical Ethics. (R. B. Carter) Internat. J. Ethics, 11: 22.
Medical Expert and the Legal Examiner. (J. C. Patterson) Green Bag, 11: 356.
— as a Witness. (F. S. Rice) Green Bag, 10: 464.
Medical Jurisprudence, New Questions in. (T. D. Crothers) Pop. Sci. Mo. 51: 454.
Medical Practice and the Law. (C. S. Andrews) Forum, 31: 542.
— Legal Restriction of. (W. R. Fisher) Arena, 19: 527.
— — and the Public Weal. (B. O. Flower) Arena, 19: 781.
Medical Profession, Organization of the. (P. M. Foshay) Forum, 32: 166.
Medical School of the Future. (H. P. Bowditch) Science, n. s. 11: 681.
Medical Schools, Opening of. (F. W. Tunnicliffe) Nature, 62: 572.
Medical Science, Need of State Endowment for Advancement of. (D. B. St. J. Roosa) Internat. Mo. 1: 531.
— Recent Advance in. (R. W. Wilcox) Internat. Mo. 1: 632.
Medical Services in Time of War. (F. P. Nichols) J. Mil. Serv. Inst. 14: 622.
Medical Students, Preparatory Education of. (A. L. Benedict) School R. 7: 18.
Medical Teaching. (M. A. Crockett) Educa. R. 14: 160.
Medical Trust, The. (T. A. Bland) Arena, 19: 520.
Medical Woman in Fiction, The. Blackw. 164: 94. Same art. Liv. Age, 218: 570.
Medici, Catherine de. (Eleanor Lewis) Cosmopol. 23: 483. — Argosy, 66: 24.
Medici, Cosimo de', Constitutional Position of. (K. D. Vernon) Eng. Hist. R. 15: 319.
Medicine, Amateur, Fallacies of. (R. W. Leftwich) Westm. 151: 70.
— and Law, Better Training for. (C. F. Thwing) Educa. R. 16: 49.
— and Surgery, A Court of : a symposium. Arena, 17: 211, 494.
— — Recent Triumphs in. (G. F. Shrady) Forum, 23: 28.
— as a Science and as an Art. (P. H. Pye-Smith) Nature, 62: 356.
— Biology and. (W. H. Welch) Am. Natural. 31: 755.
— The Fallible Physician. (W. T. Larned) Arena, 24: 150.

Medicine, Family Doctor's Relation to Recent Progress in. (A. Caillé) R. of Rs. (N. Y.) 23: 459.
— Folk, in Ancient India. (M. Winternitz) Nature, 58: 233.
— Hindu, Sinh Jee on. Nature, 55: 221.
— in relation to Life Insurance. Bank. M. (Lond.) 66: 525.
— Masters of, ed. by Hart. (H. M. Lyman) Dial (Ch.) 24: 231.
— Physics and Chemistry in relation to. (J. Crichton-Browne) Nature, 56: 556.
— Practice of, Freedom in ; a conversation with Alexander Wilder. Arena, 26: 631.
— Preventive, True Aim of. (A. Shadwell) Contemp. 78: 579.
— Progress of, in Victoria's Reign. (M. Morris) 19th Cent. 41: 739. Same art. Liv. Age, 213: 843. Same art. Ecl. M. 129: 75. — (H. B. Crofts) Westm. 148: 568.
— Science and, Relation between. (J. Burdon-Sanderson) Nature, 61: 254.
— Science and Pseudo-science in. (G. M. Sternberg) Science, 5: 199.
— Scientific, Century's Progress in. (H. S. Williams) Harper, 99: 38.
Medicine Bags. Chamb. J. 74: 367.
Medicine-men, Kootenay. (A. F. Chamberlain) J. Am. Folk-Lore, 14: 95.
— of the North American Indians. (W. T. Parker) Open Court, 15: 290.
Medicines, Patent, Some Facts about Making. (A. C. Cantley) Chaut. 27: 387.
Medico-legal Conflict over Mental Responsibility. (G. C. Speranza) Green Bag, 13: 123.
Mediterranean Race, Sergi on. . (F. Starr) Dial (Ch.) 31: 360.
Mediterranean Scare, 1903. (A. S. Hurd ; E. Robertson) 19th Cent. 50: 293.
Mediterranean Sea. Gibraltar to Alexandria. (M. Jadwin) Chaut. 32: 59.
— Great Britain's Position in ; a Fool's Paradise. (W. Verner) Fortn. 75: 951.
Médoc, France. (P. C. Mitchell) Sat. R. 84: 309.
Medusa. Regeneration in the Hydromedusa. (T. H. Morgan) Am. Natural. 33: 939.
Meehan, Thomas. (S. A. Skan) Nature, 65: 132.
Meek, Alexander Beaufort. (C. H. Ross) Sewanee, 4: 411.
Mees, Arthur, Musician, with portrait. (E. Swayne) Music, 14: 45.
Meess. (M. Maartens) Temp. Bar, 118: 190.
Meeting Cousin Agatha ; a story. (A. H. Donnell) Canad. M. 11: 124.
Meetings, Annual, Too Many. Sat. R. 88: 414.
Mega Spelæon ; or, the Monastery of the Great Cave. (D. Quinn) Am. Cath. Q. 26: 70.
Megascolides, Undescribed Species of, from the United States. (F. Smith) Am. Natural. 31: 202.
Meier, Edward Daniel. (R. W. Hunt) Cassier, 18: 174.
Meilhac, Henri. Ath. '97, 2: 76.
Meir Ben Ephraim of Padua. (D. Kaufmann) Jew. Q. 11: 266.
Meissen Porcelain. (Paul Schultze-Naumberg) M. of Art, 23: 278.
Meissonier, J. L. Ernest, Life and Art, Greard's. Sat. R. 84: 170. — Ath. '98, 1: 90.
— Personal Recollections and Anecdotes. (C. Yriarte) 19th Cent. 43: 822. Same art. Ecl. M. 131: 104. Same art. Liv. Age, 217: 843. — (V. Verestchagin) Contemp. 75: 660. Same art. Ecl. M. 133: 118. Same art. Liv. Age, 221: 706.
Melancthon, Philip. (W. Kelly) Luth. Q. 37: 12. — (E. D. Warfield) Presb. & Ref. R. 8: 1.

Melancthon, Philip, and the Augsburg Confession. (J. W. Richard) Luth. Q. **27**: 299. **28**: 355, 545.
— as a Theologian. (H. E. Jacobs) Chr. Lit. **16**: 512.
— (G. F. Behringer) Luth. Q. **37**: 254.
— Boyhood of. (E. D. Warfield) Educa. **17**: 383.
— Doctrine of the Will. (J. F. Seebach) Luth. Q. **30**: 190.
— Greek Letter to Camerarius, June 16, 1525. (W. A. Lambert) Luth. Q. **30**: 415.
— the Teacher of all the Churches. Ref. Q. **44**: 243.
Melanesian Mission, Tragedy in. (A. R. Bush) Sund. M. **29**: 543.
Melanesians, Intellectual Life of, Expression of. (G. v. Pfeil) Anthrop. J. **27**: 181.
Melann, Ernst, Designer in Wrought-iron. (W. Seegmiller) Brush & P. **5**: 60.
Melba, Madame, with portraits. (P. C. Standing) Strand, **17**: 12. — Music, **18**: 278.
— Melba Talks. Eng. Illust. **19**: 315.
Melbourne, William Lamb, 2d Viscount. (T. Raleigh) Chaut. **28**: 333.
Melbourne, Australia. (C. Short) Pall Mall M. **15**: 4. — (F. Dolman) Idler, **15**: 15.
Melbourne, Golden. Chamb. J. **78**: 337.
Melchers, Frantz M., Artist. (Pole de Mont) Studio (Internat.) **8**: 85.
Melchers, Gasi, and his Work, with portrait. (J. Brenchley) M. of Art, **24**: 145.
Melchisedech, Priest and King. (W. H. Johnson) Cath. World, **73**: 179.
Meldrum, Charles. (A. Buchan) Nature, **65**: 9.
Meleager, The Harvard, with Plate. (R. Norton) Harv. Grad. M. **8**: 485.
Meliador; the romance of a song-book. (H. Newbolt) Monthly R. **3**, no. 3: 135.
Méline, M. Spec. **83**: 79.
Meliorism, Philosophy of. (J. H. Browne) Forum, **22**: 624.
Mellone, S. H., Studies in Philosophical Criticism and Construction. (J. Iverach) Crit. R. **8**: 317.
Melodrama, A Plea for. Theatre, **39**: 176.
— Public educated above the Common. (M. Beerbohm) Sat. R. **91**: 368.
Melody, Dr. Meyer's Elements of a Psychological Theory of. (C. K. Wead) Psychol. R. **7**: 377.
— Theory of. (M. Meyer) Psychol. R. **7**: 241.
Melos, Report on Archæology in, 1896. (Cecil Smith) J. Hel. Stud. **16**: 347.
Melrose Abbey. (D. Y. Cameron) Artist (N. Y.) **24**: 113.
Melville, Andrew, and the Revolt against Aristotle in Scotland. (R. S. Rait) Eng. Hist. R. **14**: 250.
Melville, George Wallace. (W. L. Cathcart) Cassier, **11**: 459. — With portrait. Nat. Geog. M. **8**: 187.
Member from the Ninth, The; a story. (J. G. Sanderson) McClure, **15**: 150.
"Member of Parliament." (J. Gairdner) Eng. Hist. R. **13**: 708.
Members of Parliament and their Fads. (A. Mackintosh) Eng. Illust. **20**: 416.
Memoir, Decline of the. Spec. **84**: 546. Same art. Liv. Age, **225**: 651.
Memoirs and Biographies. (Agnes Repplier) Liv. Age, **227**: 328.
Memoirs of a Pair of Stays. (E. Bergerat and M. Leloir) Overland, n. s. **31**: 61.
Memoranda, Reason for keeping. (Clara M. White) Educa. **19**: 379.
Memorial of Two Lady Margarets. (H. Thurston) Month, **95**: 596.
Memorial Tablets, Bronze. Archit. R. **5**: vii.
Memories, Early. (G. Stanley Hall) Pedagog. Sem. **6**: 485.
— — Study of. (Eliz. B. Potwin) Psychol. R. **8**: 596.

Memories, Phenomenal. (E. S. Holden) Harper, **103**: 906.
— Propagation of. (C. L. Herrick) Psychol. R. **4**: 294.
Memories; a poem. (M. Cawein) Bk. Buyer, **16**: 318.
Memories; a poem. (A. E. Ragg) Canad. M. **17**: 253.
Memorizing Music, Method of. Music, **19**: 272.
Memory. (P. W. Roose) Argosy, **63**: 497.
— and Individuality. Spec. **86**: 909.
— and Inference. (F. H. Bradley) Mind, **24**: 145.
— and its Cultivation. (F. B. Denio) Educa. **18**: 217.
— Education of. (F. A. Shoup) Sewanee, **1**: 63.
— Experiments on Discrimination of Clangs. (F. Angell; Henry Harwood) Am. J. Psychol. **11**: 67.
— in Old Age. Spec. **86**: 614.
— Individual Memories. (F. W. Colegrove) Am. J. Psychol. **10**: 228.
— An Inductive Study, Colegrove on. (C. A. Scott) School R. **9**: 127.
— Interpolation in. (M. Hartog) Contemp. **78**: 532.
— Logic of Emotions, and. (W. M. Urban) Psychol. R. **8**: 262, 360.
— A Mystery of. (I. F. Mayo) Argosy, **66**: 537.
— Notes on the Experimental Study of. (A. Binet) Am. Natural. **31**: 912.
— Nursery Mnemonics. (C. Wells) Bk. Buyer, **18**: 37.
— Training of. (F. B. Denio) Educa. **20**: 399.
Memory, A; a poem. (E. Gibson) Argosy, **64**: 597.
Memory, A; a story. (O. M. Crawford) Sund. M. **30**: 551.
Memory Image, Analytical Study of. (G. M. Whipple) Am. J. Psychol. **12**: 409.
— and its Qualitative Fidelity. (I. M. Bentley) Am. J. Psychol. **11**: 1.
Memory-saver, The; a story. (F. C. Younger) Strand, **17**: 228.
Memory Tests of Whites and Blacks. (G. R. Stetson) Psychol. R. **4**: 285.
Memory Types, Experiments on. (C. J. Hawkins) Psychol. R. **4**: 289.
Memphis, Ancient, and the Necropolis of Sakkara. (L. W. Gunckel) Am. Antiq. **23**: 323.
Memphis Packet, The. (Willis Gibson) Scrib. M. **30**: 228.
Memphremagog, Lake. (I. C. Barrows) New Eng. M. n. s. **24**: 626.
Men and Machinery. (M. Carey) Un. Serv. M. **23**: 395.
— and Microbes. (E. Stenhouse) Knowl. **24**: 187.
— What Women like in. (H. T. Peck) Cosmopol. **31**: 303.
Men of Blood; a story. (J. McCrae) Canad. M. **14**: 61.
Men of Forty-mile, The. (Jack London) Overland, n. s. **33**: 401.
Men-of-War, Misnamed. (W. G. F. Hunt) Un. Serv. M. **19**: 136.
Men who would be Kings. (A. de St. André and G. G. Thomas) Eng. Illust. **19**: 129.
Men, a Woman, and the World, as Bob saw them; a story. (A. L. Provost) Nat'l M. (Bost.) **10**: 480.
Menageries, Travelling. Spec. **79**: 733.
Menalcas. Idyl viii. 63–66. (E. C. Lefroy) Ecl. M. **132**: 580.
Ménard, René, a Precursor of Marquette. (H. C. Campbell) Am. Cath. Q. **23**: 248.
Menasha, Wis., Public Library. Lib. J. **22**: 748.
Menasseh Ben Israel's Mission to Oliver Cromwell. (L. Abrahams) Jew. Q. **14**: 1.
Mendelssohn, and his Violin Concerto. (J. N. Huyette) Music, **16**: 179.
— in Scotland. (J. C. Hadden) Scot. R. **33**: 94.
— Rondo Capriccioso; explanatory remarks. (E. Liebling) Music, **12**: 362.
— Visit to Queen Victoria. Music, **12**: 494.

Mendicant, A; a story. (A. Kinnosuke) McClure, 18: 180.

Mendocino, Northern, Less Known Resorts of. (C. S. Greene) Overland, n. s. 30: 61.

Mends, Sir W. Blackw. 165: 853.

Ménégoz, E., and *Fidéisme*. (A. H. Douglas) Crit. R. 11: 232.

Menelek, King, and his People. (C. Moffett) McClure, 13: 466.

— and Morocco. Ecl. M. 135: 268.

— The Mission to. Spec. 78: 295.

— Myth of. (E. de Poncins) 19th Cent. 45: 424. Same art. Liv. Age, 221: 498.

Menpes, Mortimer. (A. L. Baldry) National, 31: 96.

— and his Mexican Memories. Studio (Lond.) 6: 161.

— an Artist of Many Methods. (A. L. Baldry) National, 31: 96.

— as Portraitist. (M. H. Spielmann) M. of Art, 23: 184.

— Japanese Drawings by. Studio (Internat.) 1: 165.

— The Man and his Methods. (C. Roberts) Harper, 101: 703.

— Sketches by. Studio (Internat.) 8: 91.

Mental Activity, Theories of. (T. Loveday) Mind, 26: 455.

Mental and Motor Ability, Correlation of, in School Children. (W. C. Bagley) Am. J. Psychol. 12: 193.

Mental Attitudes, Positive, Efficacy of. (H. Frank) Arena, 21: 326.

Mental Development, Baldwin on. (A. T. Ormond) Presb. & Ref. R. 10: 177. — (J. Dewey) Philos. R. 7: 398.

— Culture-epoch Theory of, from an Anthropological Standpoint. (N. C. Vandewalker) Educa. R. 15: 374.

— Romanes' Idea of. (M. H. Carter) Am. J. Psychol. 11: 101.

— Social and Ethical Interpretations of. (W. Caldwell) Am. J. Sociol. 5: 182.

Mental Diseases, Prevention of. (J. Morel) Am. J. Sociol. 5: 72.

Mental En-rgy. (E. Atkinson) Pop. Sci. Mo. 57: 632.

Mental Fatigue. (E. Thorndike) Psychol. R. 7: 466, 547. — (M. V. O'Shea) Pop. Sci. Mo. 55: 511.

— due to School Work. (E. Thorndike) Science, n. s. 9: 862.

Mental Functions, Effect of Improvement in One, upon Others. (E. L. Thorndike; R. S. Woodworth) Psychol. R. 8: 247, 384, 553.

Mental Growth in Childhood, Highways of. (M. V. O'Shea) Indep. 53: 87.

Mental Stimuli, Double Effect of. (S. Bryant) Mind, 25: 305.

Mental Variety, Biologic Origin of. (H. Nichols) Am. Natural. 31: 3.

Mental Work, Physiological Effects of. (H. C. Warren) Am. Natural. 31: 732.

Menus, Royal. (J. J. Moran) Strand, 15: 132.

Menzel, Adolf Friedrich Erdmann. (W. H. Winslow) New Eng. M. n. s. 19: 457.

— Latest Works and Studies of. (J. Jessen) M. of Art, 26: 49.

Meonstoke, Charters of the Manor of. (T. F. Kirby) Archæol. 57: 285.

Mephistopheles, Goethe's. (J. Reinhard) Sewanee, 5: 80.

Meran, Austria, Open-air Folks-play at. Cath. World, 67: 780.

Mercantile Training-ships or Barracks. (R. B. Nicholetts) Un. Serv. M. 20: 234.

Mercer, Hugh. Orders of Mercer, Sullivan, and Stirling, 1776. Am. Hist. R. 3: 302.

Merchant-marine, American. (W. L. Marvin) R. of Rs. (N. Y.) 21: 319. — (S. E. Payne) No. Am. 168: 240.

Merchant-marine and the Subsidy Bill. (C. H. Cramp) Indep. 53: 130.

Merchant Service, English. (P. E. LeConteur) Un. Serv. M. 14: 508.

Merchants of the Staple. (S. Brodhurst) Law Q. 17: 56.

Mercurius Caledonius; the earliest Scottish newspaper. Good Words, 42: 58.

Mercury, as Mercurous Oxalate, Separation and Determination of. (C. A. Peters) Am. J. Sci. 159: 401.

— Motion of a Submerged Index Thread of. (C. Barus) Am. J. Sci. 159: 139.

— Titration of, by Sodium Thiosulphate. (J. T. Norton) Am. J. Sci. 160: 48.

Mercury Resistance, Pressure Coefficient of. (A. deF. Palmer, jr.) Am. J. Sci. 154: 1.

Mercury, Planet. (W. W. Payne) Pop. Astron. 7: 466. — (P. Lowell) Pop. Astron. 4: 360.

— as a Naked-eye Object. (W. F. Denning) Nature, 61: 430. Same art. Pop. Astron. 8: 202.

— in the Light of Recent Discoveries. (P. Lowell) Atlan. 79: 493.

— Visibility of. (G. S. Jones) Pop. Astron. 9: 367.

Mercury of the Foothills; a story. (Bret Harte) Cosmopol. 31: 271.

Mercy. (P. W. Roose) Argosy, 66: 269.

— The Prerogative of. (A. R. Whiteway) Month, 94: 271.

Mercy of Death, The. (W. A. White) Scrib. M. 27: 237.

Mercy of Lord Hungerford; a story. Pall Mall M. 21: 342.

Mere Folly. (M. L. Pool) Lippinc. 61: 731.

Mère Susanne; a story. (A. Smith) Belgra. 94: 285.

Meredith, Ellis. Writer, 48: 11.

Meredith, George. (W. Sharp) Good Words, 40: 477. — Acad. 53: 187, (F. Thompson) 293. — (J. W. Young; W. N. Guthrie) Sewanee, 7: 129. — (D. C. Murray) Canad. M. 8: 411.

— and his Critics. Acad. 58: 393.

— and Thomas Hardy. Bookman, 9: 146.

— Diana of the Crossways, The Real. (J. Fyvie) Temp. Bar, 121: 391.

— Early Poetry of. Acad. 55: 121, 204.

— Egoist, Dramatization of. Acad. 54: 178.

— Historic Place of. (F. Grosse) Internat. Mo. 4: 299.

— Note on. (A. Symons) Fortn. 68: 673.

— Novels of. Quar. 186: 159. — Spec. 79: 342. — (P. E. More) Atlan. 84: 484. — (C. A. Pratt) Critic, 33: 156.

— Obscurity of. Acad. 60: 211.

— on the Source of Destiny. (E. G. Hooker) Poet-Lore, 12: 238.

— Poetry of. Church Q. 44: 386. Same art. Liv. Age, 214: 634. — Acad. 52: 253.

— A Reading of Life. Acad. 60: 547.

Mérejkowski, Dmitri. (H. Trench) Critic, 39: 264. — (E. D. North) Outl. 69: 417.

— Death of the Gods. (C. A. Pratt) Critic, 39: 353. — Sat. R. 91: 209.

Merely a Matter of Business. (G. McF. Galt) New Eng. M. n. s. 24: 615.

Meridian Line, Establishing a. (G. C. Comstock) Pop. Astron. 9: 246.

Meriel. (A. Rives) Lippinc. 61: 435.

Mérimée, Prosper. (C. E. Meetkerke) Gent. M. n. s. 60: 19.

— Fiction of. (B. W. Wells) Sewanee, 6: 167.

Merit System in the British Colonies. (W. MacDonald) Nation, 68: 414.

Merivale, Charles, Dean. Ath. '98, 2: 379.

— Autobiography of. (J. W. Chadwick) Nation, 71: 73. — Sat. R. 89: 206.

Mermillod, Gaspard, Cardinal. (T. L. L. Teeling) Am. Cath. Q. 26: 757.

Merrimac, Original Significance of. (W. W. Tooker) Am. Antiq. 21: 14.

"Merrimac," Heroes of the. Outl. 59: 374.

— Sinking of the. (R. P. Hobson) Cent. 35: 265, 427, 580, 752. — (R. P. Hobson) Strand, 17: 628.

Merriman, Henry Seton (pseud.). See Scott, Hugh S.

Merritt, Anna Lea. Writer, 14: 60.

Merritt, Darwin R., lost on the "Maine," with portrait. Midland, 9: 273.

Merritt, Henry, and the Conservation of Pictures. (M. Q. Holyoake) M. of Art, 24: 310.

Merryweather vs. Nixan, The Rule in. (J. F. Williams) Law Q. 17: 293.

Merycochœrus in Montana, New Species of. (E. Douglas) Am. J. Sci. 160: 428. 161: 73.

Méryon, Charles, French Etcher. (F. Wedmore) Pall Mall M. 16: 456.

Mesa, The Enchanted. (F. W. Hodge) Nat. Geog. M. 8: 273.

— — Ascent of. (F. W. Hodge) Cent. 34: 15.

Mesa Verde. (F. H. Newell) Nat. Geog. M. 9: 431.

Mesa Life, Old. (Fernand Lundgren) Cent. 34: 26.

Mescal Intoxication. (H. Ellis) Contemp. 73: 130. Same art. Ecl. M. 130: 280.

Mesdag, H. W. Modern Dutch Master. (M. H. Spielmann) M. of Art, 22: 73.

Mesopotamia, Oppenheim's Journeys in. (C. W. Wilson) Geog. J. 17: 183.

— Petroleum Field of. (F. R. Maunsell) Geog. J. 9: 528.

Mesozoic Flora of the U. S., Ward's. (D. P. Penhallow) Science, n. s. 13: 904.

Message-sticks and Prayer-sticks. (A. W. Buckland) Antiq. n. s. 33: 299.

Messages from the Sea. (W. Allingham) Chamb. J. 74: 715.

Messenger, The; a story. (R. W. Chambers) Scrib. M. 21: 194.

Messenger, Adventures of a Royal. (P. H. Litchfield) Chamb. J. 78: 385.

Messenger from the Dead, A. (A. Oscar) Chamb. J. 75: 284.

Messer Cino and the Live Coal; a story. (M. Hewlett) Macmil. 78: 296. Same art. Liv. Age, 219: 240.

Messiah. Foreshadowings of the Christ. (G. S. Goodspeed) Bib. World, 9: 34-457.

— Jews' Expectation of, in the Time of Jesus. (S. Mathews) Bib. World, 12: 437.

— The Ordination of. (R. McC. Edgar) Presb. & Ref. R. 10: 599.

Messiahs, False. (A. M. Hyamson) Gent. M. n. s. 66: 79.

Messiahship as conceived by Jesus. (A. B. Bruce) Bib. World, 12: 6.

Messianic Movement among Jews of Germany and the Byzantine Empire, about 1096. (D. Kaufmann) Jew. Q. 10: 139.

Messianic Prophecy, Arrangement of Passages containing. (G. S. Goodspeed) Bib. World, 12: 400.

— Some Books on. (G. S. Goodspeed) Bib. World, 12: 444.

Messmates; poem. (H. Newbolt) Atlan. 82: 616.

Meta; a story of the burnt woods of Oregon. (Clara A. Nash) Midland, 9: 165, 251, 346.

Metabolism in Human Body, Experiments upon. Science, 5: 493.

— of the Salmon. (W. D. Halliburton) Sci. Prog. 7: 371.

Metal, Expanded. (W. M. Bailey) Am. Arch. 72: 20.

— — and its Uses. (J. S. Merritt) J. Frankl. Inst. 150: 431.

Metal, Expansion of, at High Temperatures. (L. Holborn and A. L. Day) Am. J. Sci. 161: 374.

— Flow of. (H. V. Loss) J. Frankl. Inst. 151: 456.

Metal Bowls of the Late-Celtic and Anglo-Saxon Periods. (J. R. Allen) Archæol. 56: 39.

Metal Decoration Exhibition. (W. T. Whitley) Art J. 50: 254.

Metal Rolling, Early. (W. F. Durfee) Cassier, 15: 478.

Metal Squirting Machine. (J. W. Meyjes) Cassier, 13: 257.

Metal Stamping, Machinery for. (O. Smith) Engin. M. 14: 973.

Metal Work and Leaded Glass, Design for. (Walter S. Sparrow) M. of Art, 23: 324.

— Art. (N. Dawson) J. Soc. Arts, 48: 517. — (A. Vallance) M. of Art, 22: 273.

— Beaten. (F. Miller) Art J. 50: 79.

— in Domestic Decoration. (H. B. Philpott) Artist (N. Y.) 32: 7.

— Light, for Amateurs. (C. H. L. Emanuel) Studio (Lond.) 7: 223.

Metal Workers' Exhibition. (J. S. Gardner) M. of Art, 22: 569.

Metallic Structures, Painting of. Am. Arch. 56: 93.

Metalliferous Deposits. (B. H. Brough) J. Soc. Arts, 48: 673, 689, 721. — Nature, 63: 18.

Metallography, Progress in. (T. K. Rose) Nature, 63: 232.

— Uses of. (A. Sauveur) Engin. M. 17: 977.

Metallurgy and Metal Mining in America, Progress of, since 1850. (J. Douglas) J. Soc. Arts, 46: 21, 134.

— Early, of Copper, Tin, and Iron in Europe and Primitive Processes surviving in Japan. (W. Gowland) Archæol. 56: 267.

— — of Silver and Lead. (W. Gowland) Archæol. 57: 359.

— Progress in, 1825-99. (C. Kirchhoff) J. Frankl. Inst. 148: 424.

Metals as Fuel. Nature, 64: 360.

— Bearing, Microstructure of. (G. H. Clamer) J. Frankl. Inst. 146: 138.

— Eighth Group of the Periodic System and Some of its Problems. (J. L. Howe) Science, n. s. 11: 1012. 12: 20.

— Electrified, Effect of Density of Surrounding Gas on Discharge of, by X-rays. (C. D. Child) Science, 5: 791.

— Melting Points and Latent Heats of Fusion, Relations between. (J. W. Richards) J. Frankl. Inst. 143: 379.

— Thermo-electricity in Certain. (L. Holborn and A. L. Day) Am. J. Sci. 158: 303.

— used by the Great Nations of Antiquity. (J. H. Gladstone) Nature, 57: 594.

Metamorphism, Contact, Contribution to the Study of. (J. M. Clements) Am. J. Sci. 157: 81.

Metamorphosis in Plants. (S. H. Vines) Sci. Prog. 7: 79.

Metamorphosis of Corpus Delicti; a story. (J. H. Cranson) McClure, 13: 259.

Metamorphosis of Mary Ann; a tale. (V. Sheard) Canad. M. 9: 190.

Metaphysics, Ethics, and Religion. (W. A. Heidel) Philos. R. 9: 30.

— Problem of, and its bearing upon Ethics. (A. E. Taylor) Internat. J. Ethics, 10: 352.

Metargon. Recently discovered Gases. (W. Ramsay) Science, n. s. 9: 273.

Metaurus, Campaign of the. (B. W. Henderson) Eng. Hist. R. 13: 417, 625.

Meteor, Parallax of a, determined by Photography. (J. M. Schaeberle and A. L. Colton) Pop. Astron. 5: 232.

Meteor-showers, Contemporary, of the Leonid and Bielid Meteor-periods. (A. S. Herschel) Nature, **61**: 222, 271.

Meteora, Convent of, in Thessaly. (R. P. Keep) Nation, **64**: 317. — (C. Angus) Eng. Illust. **20**: 173.

Meteoric Iron, New. (W. M. Foote) Am. J. Sci. **158**: 153.
— — near Iredell, Tex. (W. M. Foote) Am. J. Sci. **158**: 415.
— Platinum and Iridium in. (J. M. Davison) Am. J. Sci. **157**: 4.

Meteoric Shower of November. (H. C. Wilson) Pop. Astron. **6**: 502.
— Nov. 13, 1897. (W. H. Pickering) Pop. Astron. **6**: 294.

Meteorite, Farmington, Metallic Veins of. (O. C. Farrington) Am. J. Sci. **161**: 60.
— from Oakley, Kans. (H. L. Preston) Am. J. Sci. **159**: 410.
— New Kansas. (H. L. Ward) Am. J. Sci. **157**: 233. **158**: 225.

Meteorites. Chamb. J. **75**: 327. Same art. Liv. Age, **217**: 617.
— and Comets. (P. Kropotkin) 19th Cent. **46**: 934. Same art. Ecl. M. **134**: 376. Same art. Liv. Age, **224**: 20.
— A Century of the Study of. (O. C. Farrington) Pop. Sci. Mo. **58**: 429.
— Four New Australian. (H. A. Ward) Am. J. Sci. **155**: 135.
— in Ancient and Modern Times. (H. A. Miers) Sci. Prog. **7**: 349.
— in the Peabody Museum of Yale University, Catalogue of. Am. J. Sci. **153**: 83.
— Iron, as Nodular Structures in Stony Meteorites. (H. L. Preston) Am. J. Sci. **155**: 62.
— Jerome, Kansas. (H. S. Washington) Am. J. Sci. **155**: 447.
— New, from Allegan, Michigan, and Mart, Texas. (G. P. Merrill) Science, n. s. **10**: 770.
— Note on a New Meteorite from the Sacramento Mountains, Eddy Co., New Mexico. (W. M. Foote) Am. J. Sci. **153**: 65.
— Real Paths of Fireballs and Shooting Stars. (W. F. Denning) Knowl. **24**: 271.
— San Angelo. (H. L. Preston) Am. J. Sci. **155**: 269.
— Stability of a Swarm of, and of a Planet and Satellite. (A. Gray) Nature, **62**: 582.
— Two New American. (H. L. Preston) Am. J. Sci. **159**: 283.
— Worship and Folk-lore of. (O. C. Farrington) J. Am. Folk-Lore, **13**: 199. — (H. A. Newton) Am. J. Sci. **153**: 1. — (H. A. Newton) Nature, **56**: 355.

Meteorology, Applied. C. Abbe on. Nature, **61**: 448.
— Indian. Nature, **56**: 226.
— Progress of, during the Century. (H. S. Williams) Harper, **95**: 41.

Meteors, Bielid, Observations of, 1899. (G. W. Meyers) Pop. Astron. **8**: 13.
— Great Showers of. (Sir R. Ball) Strand, **18**: 562.
— Heights of. (W. F. Denning) Nature, **57**: 540.
— Leonid. (H. C. Wilson) Pop. Astron. **6**: 568.
— — of 1898. (C. D. Perrine) Pop. Astron. **6**: 553. — (W. F. Denning) Knowl. **20**: 249. — (W. F. Denning) Nature, **59**: 78.
— — November, 1899. (W. A. Cogshall) Pop. Astron. **7**: 71. — (E. C. Pickering) Pop. Astron. **7**: 412. — (L. Swift) Pop. Astron. **7**: 415. — (W. W. Payne) Pop. Astron. **7**: 475, 574. — Ed. R. **190**: 309. — (W. F. Denning and others) Nature, **61**: 81. — (E. C. Pickering) Knowl. **22**: 250. — (C. A. Young) Lippinc. **64**: 727. — (W. F. Denning) Nature, **60**: 592.

Meteors, Leonid, November, 1899, Chart of Radiant Points of. (W. F. Denning) Pop. Astron. **7**: 337.
— — — The Coming Star Shower. (J. E. Gore) Gent. M. n. s. **63**: 329.
— — — Failure of. (W. W. Payne) Pop. Astron. **8**: 15.
— — — The Great Bombardment. (C. F. Holder) Pop. Sci. Mo. **54**: 506.
— — — Non-appearance of. (W. H. Pickering) Pop. Astron. **7**: 523.
— — — Observations of. (L. G. Weld) Pop. Astron. **7**: 17. — (W. H. Pickering) Pop. Astron. **7**: 396. — (W. J. S. Lockyer) Nature, **61**: 132.
— — — — at Claremont, Cal. (F. P. Brackett) Pop. Astron. **7**: 30.
— — — Perturbations of. (G. J. Stoney; A. M. W. Downing) Pop. Astron. **7**: 227.
— — for 1901. (W. W. Payne) Pop. Astron. **9**: 559.
— — Observation of. (W. F. Denning) Nature, **56**: 613.
— — — from a Balloon. (D. Klumpcke) Cent. **38**: 276.
— — Orbit of. (W. W. Payne) Pop. Astron. **8**: 523.
— November. (A. L. Cortie) Month, **94**: 505.
— — 1898, '99, 1900. (J. K. Rees) Pop. Astron. **9**: 79.
— Shooting. (O. F. Bianco) Chaut. **28**: 351.

Meter, Venturi. J. Frankl. Inst. **147**: 108.

Methodism, American, Catholicity of. (E. R. Hendrix) Meth. R. **59**: 513.
— and the Age. (W. L. Watkinson) Lond. Q. **91**: 130.
— and Religious Thought. (W. C. Madison) Meth. R. **59**: 865.
— History of, Buckley's. (J. M. Whiton) Outl. **55**: 1036. Same art. Chr. Lit. **17**: 51. — (J. W. Chadwick) Nation, **65**: 134.
— Influence of, on Scotland. (R. Green) Lond. Q. **92**: 50.
— Is it Catholic? (H. K. Carroll) Meth. R. **58**: 177.
— Making of, Tigert's. (C. J. Little) Am. Hist. R. **4**: 555.
— Mission of. (W. L. Watkinson) Lond. Q. **91**: 343.
— New. (T. F. Wright) N. Church R. **5**: 447.
— Side-lights on. Lond. Q. **90**: 278.
— Spirit of Modern. (W. T. Davison) Contemp. **72**: 808.
— Unifying Factors in. (C. F. M'Kown) Meth. R. **59**: 732.

Methodist Book Concern, Reviews and Views of. (G. P. Main) Meth. R. **60**: 34.

Methodist Church, The. Outl. **65**: 110.
— in Italy. (S. M. Vernon) Meth. R. **57**: 604.
— Up-to-date Constitution for. (C. Sheard) Meth. R. **60**: 418.

Methodist Colleges, Self-help and Cost at. (J. M. Lee) Meth. R. **61**: 773.

Methodist Ecumenical Conference. (J. W. Johnston) R. of Rs. (N. Y.) **24**: 446.

Methodist Saints and Martyrs. (R. C. Nightingale) Contemp. **72**: 378.

Methodology and Truth. (J. E. Creighton) Philos. R. **10**: 45.

Methuen, Massachusetts. (C. H. Oliphant) New Eng. M. n. s. **23**: 97.

Metric System. (T. C. Mendenhall) Science, n. s. **10**: 196.
— and British and American Machine Shops. (C. Sellers) Cassier, **17**: 365.
— and International Commerce. (J. H. Gore) Forum, **31**: 739.
— from a Mechanical Point of View. (S. Webber) Cassier, **11**: 447.

Metropolitan Journalism, 1800-40, Rise of. (C. H. Levermore) Am. Hist. R. **6**: 446.

Metropolitan Love Incident. (J. Barker) Cosmopol. **28**: 679.

Metropolitan Museum, Rogers Bequest to. (F. J. Mather, jr.) Nation, 73: 25.

Metternich, Prince, and Napoleon. (G. Hill) Gent. M. n. s. 67: 164.

Metz, Restoration of, to France. Arena, 17: 293.

Meudon Astrophysical Observatory. (W. J. S. Lockyer) Nature, 56: 494.

Meunier, Constantin, Artist. (W. S. Sparrow) Studio (Internat.) 2: 73. — (Emile Verhaeren) M. of Art, 23: 496.

Meuse, Department of, Visit to. (E. V. Beaufort) Belgra. 96: 245.

Mexican Army, The. (F. H. Hardie) J. Mil. Serv. Inst. 15: 1203.

Mexican Codices, Recent Reproductions of. (M. H. Saville) Am. Anthrop. 3: 532.

Mexican Federal Palace Competition. Am. Arch. 57: 25.

Mexican Head-piece, Ancient, coated with Mosaic. (C. H. Read) Archæol. 54: 383.

Mexican War and Admission of Texas. (C. W. Hall) Nat'l M. (Bost.) 12: 72.

— Artillery in the. (G. W. Van Deusen) J. Mil. Serv. Inst. 17: 87.

Mexico. (C. Harcourt) Midland, 10: 3.

— and China, Religion of, compared. (J. Wickersham) Am. Antiq. 19: 319.

— and the Hispano-American Conflict. (L. D. Kocen) Westm. 150: 11.

— and the United States, Romero on. (F. Starr) Dial (Ch.) 26: 243. — (F. R. G. S.) Bk. Buyer, 18: 136.

— Archæological Studies in, Holmes's. (F. Starr) Dial (Ch.) 23: 44.

— Archivo General de. (G. P. Garrison) Nation, 72: 430.

— Awakening of a Nation. (C. F. Lummis) Harper, 94: 365, 498, 741.

— Buchanan's proposed Intervention in. (H. L. Wilson) Am. Hist. R. 5: 687.

— Conquests of, Coincidences of, 1520–1847. (H. Coppée) J. Mil. Serv. Inst. 5: 29.

— French Intervention in. (M. Romero) Cent. 32: 138. — (S. Y. Stevenson) Cent. 33: 113.

— Geology of, with Map. (P. Lake) Sci. Prog. n. s. 1: 609.

— Great Drainage Canal of. (B. G. Hunt) Cosmopol. 24: 595.

— Highlands of, Impressions in the. (C. De Kalb) Nation, 69: 277, 360, 464. 70: 68, 124.

— Holy Week in. (F. Starr) J. Am. Folk-Lore, 12: 161.

— its People and Ways. Nat'l M. (Bost.) 14: 151.

— Judicial Proceedings in, Mistakes about. (M. Romero) No. Am. 164: 639.

— Linguistic Families of. (O. T. Mason) Am. Anthrop. 2: 63.

— Lummis on. (F. Starr) Dial (Ch.) 24: 322.

— Maximilian's Empire in. (S. Y. Stevenson) Cent. 33: 420, 602.

— — Withdrawal of the French from Mexico. (J. M. Schofield) Cent. 32: 128.

— A Modern Arcadia. (E. F. Ames) Blackw. 162: 685. Same art. Ecl. M. 130: 66.

— Music in. (A. H. Noll) Lippinc. 60: 424.

— National Festival of, Sept. 16. (Clara S. Brown) Overland, n. s. 37: 1027.

— Native Races of. (H. S. Brooks) Lippinc. 67: 368.

— Notes of Travel. (C. G. Pringle) Garden & F. 10: 32, 42.

-- of To-day. Am. Arch. 59: 60. — (I. Mariscal) Indep. 51: 3059. — (J. N. Navarro) Nat. Geog. M. 12: 52, 176, 235.

Mexico, Oriental Influences in. (W. Hough) Am. Anthrop. 2: 66.

— Paganism in, Survivals of. Illus. (F. Starr and P Carus) Open Court, 13: 385.

— Peon System. (A. De Iturbide) No. Am. 168: 424.

— Pictorial Documents by Native Artists. Open Court, 12: 746.

— Prospecting in Western. (T. S. DeLay) Engin. M. 22: 247.

— Religion and the Church in. (C. E. Jeffery) Month, 92: 251.

— Romero on. (F. Starr) Dial (Ch.) 25: 131.

— Scenery and Architecture in. Am. Antiq. 22: 197.

— Society in, in Maximilian's Time. (S. Y. Stevenson) Cent. 33: 707.

— Spain's Legacy to. (J. J. O'Shea) Am. Cath. Q. 24: 91.

— Trip through. (L. M. Boulton) Canad. M. 15: 128.

— Women of. (M. Adams) Chaut. 27: 622.

Mexico, City of, to Acapulco. (T. P. Terry) Outing, 29: 593.

Mexico, Gulf of, and the Caribbean Sea, Strategic Features of. (A. T. Mahan) Harper, 95: 680.

Meyer, Adolphe von, as Photographer. (Isabel Brooke-Alder) Art J. 51: 270.

Meyer, Claus. Game at Cards; etched by Struck. Art J. 53: 142.

Meyer, Conrad Ferdinand. Acad. 55: 555.

Meyer, F. B., Work of, in South London. (M. Quiller-Couch) Sund. M. 27: 461.

Meyer, Herr; his Genius; a story. (A. M. Rose) Sund. M. 26: 687.

Meyer, Victor. Ath. '97, 2: 229. — Nature, 56: 449. — (H. C. Cooper) Science, 6: 449.

Meyerbeer, Giacomo, Composer. (M. Moszkowski) Cent. 37: 747.

Meynell, Alice. (K. T. Hinkson) Bk. Buyer, 18: 204.

— as a Judge of Poetry. Acad. 52: 391.

— Poems of. (T. B. Reilly) Cath. World, 73: 521.

— The Spirit of Place and Other Essays. (H. van Dyke) Bk. Buyer, 18: 206. — Sat. R. 87: 246.

Mezzotints, The Present Rage for. (W. Roberts) 19th Cent. 50: 257.

M. I.; a poem. (R. Kipling) McClure, 17: 525.

Miamu, Prehistoric Grotto at. (A. Taramelli) Am. J. Archæol. 2d s. 1: 287.

Mica Group, Minerals of, Crystal Symmetry of. (T. L. Walker) Am. J. Sci. 157: 199.

Mica Mining in District of Nellore, India. (R. W. Thompson) J. Soc. Arts, 46: 671.

Mi-careme in Paris. (J. Marlin) Canad. M. 13: 50.

Michailovsky, N. K. (V. S. Yarros) Bookman, 6: 292.

Michel and Angète; a story of Huguenot Exiles. (G. Parker) Harper, 101: 685, 895.

Michel Angelo Buonarroti. (J. La Farge) McClure, 18: 99.

— as a Poet. (T. B. Reilly) Cath. World, 65: 802.

— Painting of, with portrait and bibliography. Mast. in Art, 2: 417.

— Sculpture of, with portrait. Mast. in Art, 2: 416.

— Statue of, in the Congressional Library. (Russell Sturgis) Scrib. M. 25: 381. — Artist (N. Y.) 24: x.

Michelet, Jules. Acad. 54: 66. — (H. C. Macdowall) Macmil. 78: 254. — (W. M. Sloane) Critic, 33: 147.

— and the College of France. (T. Stanton) Nation, 67: 108.

— as an Historian. Quar. 193: 130.

— Intellectual Attachments. (R. Doumic) Ecl. M. 134: 20.

Michelstadt in Odenwald, Church Library at. Library, n. s. 2: 405.

Michigan, Farm in, Story of a. (A. B. Chalmers) Chaut. 32: 594.

Michigan, Lumber Region of. (L. Hubbard, jr.) Outing, 37: 676.
— Some Features of Pre-glacial Drainage in. (E. H. Mudge) Am. J. Sci. 154: 383.
— University of, Music in. (P. C. Lutkin) Music, 18: 392.
Michigan Schoolmasters' Club, Proceedings of the 27th Semi-annual Meeting. (E. C. Warriner) School R. 5: 95.
— — 28th Meeting. (E. C. Goddard) School R. 6: 116.
— — 29th Meeting. (E. C. Goddard) School R. 6: 419.
— — 30th Meeting. (W. H. Sherzer) School R. 6: 422.
Michigan State Normal College. (B. L. D'Ooge) Educa. R. 18: 387.
Michigan State Normal School, Putnam's History of. (G. H. Locke) School R. 8: 300.
Michilimackinac. (C. O. Ermatinger) Canad. M. 12: 437, 503. See Mackinac.
Micmac Legend, Taleak of the Soosoon. (P. W. Hart) Canad. M. 9: 277.
Micmac Mythology, Weather and the Seasons in. (S. Hagar) J. Am. Folk-Lore, 10: 101.
Micmac Raid in Acadie, A. (C. G. D. Roberts) Liv. Age, 224: 589.
Micro-organisms of Combustible Fossils. (B. Renault) Science, n. s. 13: 577.
Micro-biology as applied to Hygiene. Nature, 58: 15.
Microbe in Agriculture. (C. M. Aikman) 19th Cent. 43: 994.
Microbes and the Human Body, Dr. Metchnikoff on. Nature, 63: 621.
— and Medicine. (J. J. Walsh) Am. Cath. Q. 26: 287.
— and Mineral Waters. (Mrs. P. Frankland) Good Words, 38: 243.
— are they inherently Pathogenic? (M. L. Johnson) Westm. 145: 325.
— in Co-operation. (G. C. Nuttall) Knowl. 22: 151.
— in the Household. (G. M'Carthy) Chaut. 29: 230.
— Our Invisible Foes. (G. M. Sternberg) J. Mil. Serv. Inst. 6: 27.
— The War with. (E. A. de Schweinitz) Science, 5: 561.
Microcosm of Empire, A; a story. (H. C. MacIlwaine) Pall Mall M. 20: 193.
Micronesian Weapons, Dress, and Implements. (F. W. Christian) Anthrop. J. 28: 288.
Microphilus, Who was? (J. H. Slater) Ath. '00, 2: 250.
Microsclerometer, A. (T. A. Jaggar, jr.) Am. J. Sci. 154: 399.
Microscope, Home-life and the. Chamb. J. 75: 443.
— Simple Instrument for inclining a Preparation in. (T. A. Jaggar, jr.) Am. J. Sci. 153: 129.
Microtome, A New Rocking. Nature, 61: 115.
Microtomes, Automatic. (C. S. Minot) Nature, 5: 857.
Midas. (L. Parr) Longm. 33: 142.
Midday Moon, The; or, the Midnight Sun. (H. S. Wilson) Gent. M. n. s. 65: 88.
Middle Age, Some Difficulties Incidental to. (F. Bell) 19th Cent. 47: 459. Same art. Liv. Age, 225: 98. Same art. Ecl. M. 134: 819.
Middle-age Enthusiasms; a poem. (T. Hardy) Ecl. M. 132: 701.
Middle-aged Romance, A. (H. J. Arden) Sund. M. 29: 599.
Middle-aged Romance, A. (A. F. Robertsen) Cornh. 80: 366, 486. Same art. Liv. Age, 224: 116–165.
Middle Ages; Bibliotheca Historica Medii Ævi, Potthast's. (D. C. Munro) Am. Hist. R. 2: 710.
— Fisher's Mediæval Empire. (C. W. Colby) Nation, 69: 114. — Am. Hist. R. 4: 704.
— Jenks on Land and Politics in. (M. Smith) Pol. Sci. Q. 14: 141. — Sat. R. 85: 690. — (W. Rice) Dial (Ch.) 25: 71.

Middle Ages, Political Theories of, Gierke on. Ath. '01, 1: 133.
— Taylor's Classical Heritage of. (J. H. Robinson) Nation, 73: 171.
— Transition to. (J. S. Banks) Lond. Q. 96: 262.
Middlebury College, Sketch of. (C. B. Wright) Educa. 19: 594.
Middleman, The Triumph of. Dial (Ch.) 22: 349.
Middlesex Fells. (W. B. de Las Casas) New Eng. M. n. s. 19: 701.
Middleton, Alexander. (E. F. Ware) N. E. Reg. 52: 13.
Middletown, Ct. Story of a New England Town. (J. Fiske) Atlan. 86: 722.
Midland Railway, England, Railway Car Building on. (C. H. Jones) Cassier, 13: 227.
Midland University, The Proposed. Nature, 57: 277.
Midmar Castle. Antiq. n. s. 35: 139.
Midnight Express, The; a story. (L. McQuaid) Belgra. 95: 160.
Midnight Warning, A; a story. (T. F. O'Brien) Midland, 9: 434.
Midshipman, Mercantile, Training of. (S. D. Gordon) Un. Serv. M. 24: 114.
Midsummer Night's Trip, A; a railroad story. (J. A. Hill) McClure, 11: 365.
Mid-winter's Madcaps; a poem. (C. Turner) Outing, 33: 327.
Midwives, Registration of. (C. J. Cullingworth) Contemp. 73: 394.
Mierevelt's Portrait of Sir Thomas Roe. (W. Foster) Ath. '00, 2: 689.
Miersite. (L. J. Spencer) Nature, 57: 574.
Mifflin, Lloyd. At the Gates of Song. Poet-Lore, 11: 133.
Migration. (W. K. Brooks) Pop. Sci. Mo. 52: 784.
— Internal, in England and Wales. (A. W. Flux) Econ. J. 10: 141.
Migration in University Education. (R. M. Alden) Harv. Grad. M. 8: 309.
Migration Movements, Great. (W. Wheelock) Nation, 72: 484.
Migratory Impulse vs. Love and Home. (L. W. Kline) Am. J. Psychol. 10: 1.
Mikado, Personality of the. (W. E. Griffis) Outl. 68: 559.
Mike. (Mrs. B. Tanqueray) Good Words, 42: 679.
Mila Whendle; an "unpleasant play." (N. H. Musselman) Poet-Lore, 13: 22.
Milady's Maid; a story. (G. Fosbery) Argosy, 65: 508.
Milan, Castello of. (Julia Cartwright Ady) Monthly, R. 4, no. 2: 117.
— Cathedral. Am. Arch. 61: 46.
Milanese Art Foundation, A. (B. Berenson) Nation, 69: 49.
Milaraspa; a poet and mystic of Thibet. (G. Sandberg) 19th Cent. 46: 613.
Milburn, W. H., "the Blind Man Eloquent." (L. W. Lillingston) Sund. M. 26: 829.
Mildenhall, Suffolk, Church of St. Andrew, Roof of. (J. G. Waller) Archæol. 54: 255.
Miles, George H., with portrait. (T. E. Cox) Cath. World, 74: 48.
Miles, Manly, Sketch of, with portrait. Pop. Sci. Mo. 54: 834.
Militarism, Danger of. (U. Gohier) Indep. 52: 233.
— Fruits of. (A. G. Sedgwick) Nation, 67: 126.
Military Academy and the Education of Officers. (W. P. Richardson) J. Mil. Serv. Inst. 17: 170.
— as an Element in the System of National Defense. (J. Parker) Harper, 95: 295.
See West Point.
Military Administration in Gibraltar 100 Years ago. Chamb. J. 74: 238.

Militia Medical Service. (W. Tobin) Canad. M. 8: 527.

Militia Reform without Legislation. (T. F. Roden-bough) J. Mil. Serv. Inst. 2: 388.

Milk, Bacteria in. (E. Verney) Contemp. 72: 709. Same art. Liv. Age, 216: 198. Same art. Ecl. M. 130: 17.

— Dangers from, and their Remedies. (G. C. Frank-land) Longm. 29: 464.

— Microbes in. (E. C. Fincham) Chamb. J. 75: 548.

Milk Maids and their Melodies. (L. A. Smith) Belgra. 95: 393.

Milk Supply of Cities. (H. W. Conn) Pop. Sci. Mo. 55: 627.

— Improvement of. (R. A. Pearson) Am. J. Soc. Sci. 38: 19.

Milky Way, Best Way of Observing. (A. Pannekoek) Pop. Astron. 5: 524.

— Charts for Inserting. (A. Pannekoek) Pop. Astron. 5: 485.

— in Cygnus. (W. Maunder) Knowl. 23: 273.

Mill, John Stuart, with portrait. Gunton's M. 15: 341.

— and Romanes. The Heart and the Will in Belief. (J. G. Hibben) No. Am. 166: 121.

— Education of. (Mrs. M. West) Educa. 19: 434.

— Humanity of. (G. O. S. Pringle) Westm. 150: 159.

— Letter to. (W. M. Daniels) Atlan. 86: 664.

— Letters to A. Comte. (W. Lloyd) Westm. 153: 421.

— Letters to Professor Nichol. Fortn. 67: 660.

Mill Operatives in the South. (D. A. Willey) Chaut. 28: 458. — (L. B. Ellis) Forum, 31: 306.

Mill Town, Southern, Life in a. (H. Thompson) Pol. Sci. Q. 15: 1.

Millais, John Everett. Ed. R. 191: 182. — M. of Art, 24: 313. — Sat. R. 85: 73. — (R. A. M. Stevenson) Art J. 50: 1. — Spec. 80: 47.

— and his Works, Spielman on. Studio (Internat.) 5: 214.

— and Rossetti Exhibitions. (F. M. Hueffer) Fortn. 69: 189.

— Drawings. Sat. R. 91: 468.

— Exhibition of Paintings by. Acad. 53: 36. — Am. Arch. 59: 83. — Ath. '98, 1: 57.

— Millais's Life of. Acad. 57: 533. — (J. L. Gilder) Critic, 35: 1101.

— Memories of. (W. W. Fenn) Chamb. J. 78: 833.

— Painter of Men and Women. (W. Bayliss) Good Words, 40: 94.

— Portrait of Gladstone. (Benjamin-Constant) M. of Art, 24: 152.

— Religious Art of. (S. Beale) Am. Arch. 59: 75.

— Some Recollections of. Liv. Age, 224: 197.

— Some Reminiscences of. (Rudolf Lehmann) Art J. 51: 251.

— Works of, at Burlington House. (C. Phillips) 19th Cent. 43: 376.

Millais, Lady, Death of. Ath. '98, 1: 30.

Millard, Evelyn. What it must be like to be Beauti-ful. (M. C. Salaman) Eng. Illust. 18: 135.

Millennium, The. Spec. 84: 625.

— Is it Evolution? (B. F. Rawlins) Meth. R. 79: 925. — (E. L. Eaton) Meth. R. 80: 587.

Miller, James Russell. Lit. W. (Bost.) 31: 227.

Miller, Joaquin. Acad. 53: 181. — With portrait. Bk. Buyer, 17: 103.

Miller, John, Marriages of Daughters of. (W. R. Cut-ter) N. E. Reg. 51: 33.

Miller, Joseph, the Jester. (R. Bell) Eng. Illust. 18: 27.

Miller, Lewis. (J. H. Vincent) Chaut. 29: 139.

Miller, Valentine : a Rival of Blind Tom in California. (C. Kittredge) Overland, n. s. 35: 239.

Miller, Warner. Bank. M. (N. Y.) 58: 712.

Miller of Bolarque, The. Chamb. J. 74: 286.

Millers' Seal, The ; a story. (Alice W. French) Nat'l M. (Bost.) 8: 474.

Millet, Jean François, with portrait. (C. Yriarte) Pall Mall M. 23: 433. — With portrait and bibliography. Mast. in Art, 1: Pt. 8. — Idler, 12: 365.

— Mrs. Ady's. (H. Grenfel) Citizen, 3: 209.

— and Walt Whitman. (H. C. Merwin) Atlan. 79: 719.

— Less-known Pictures. (Arthur Tomson) Art J. 53: 308.

— Loan Exhibition at Hanover Gallery. Sat. R. 90: 45.

— Model of, — Adèle Moschener. Artist (N. Y.) 25: 129.

— Notable Masterpiece by ; the Wood-sawyers. (F. Keppel) Cent. 40: 457.

— Village of. (C. Johnson) Outl. 64: 275.

Milling Machines, British. (A. Herbert) Cassier, 18: 323.

Million-dollar Freight Train, The ; a story. (F. H. Spearman) McClure, 14: 380.

Millionaire, The Cult of the. Blackw. 170: 141. Same art. Ecl. M. 137: 518. Same art. Liv. Age, 230: 583.

— Education of the. (T. Beale) Forum, 30: 457.

— Extravagances of a. Eng. Illust. 16: 533.

Millionaire of Horinbrook Island. (Guy Boothby) Chamb. J. 74: Xmas supp. 1.

Millionaires Defended. (A. Shortt) Canad. M. 13: 493.

— Meanness of. Eng. Illust. 18: 103.

— Mischief of. Spec. 86: 525.

— Motives of. Spec. 86: 726.

— Studies in. (J. Burnley) Chamb. J. 78: 212-263.

— Ten Years of, in England. (H. S. Maclauchlan) Contemp. 71: 432.

Millionaires' Sons. Spec. 87: 118.

Mills, Benjamin Fay, in the Forum. (D. M. Morrell) Arena, 21: 201.

Mills, Charles Henry, Lord Hillingdon. Bank. M. (Lond.) 65: 751.

Mills College, College Life at. (Frances Smith) Over-land, n. s. 33: 456.

Mills of the Little Tin Gods ; a story. (Vaughan Kester) Cosmopol. 25: 101.

Mills' Hotel, The ; a paying philanthropy. (T. A. Hyde) Arena, 20: 76.

Millstones, Living. (R. Lydekker) Knowl. 24: 28.

Milltown. Sketches in a Northern Town. (Mrs. H. Birchenough) 19th Cent. 50: 479, 1001. Same art. Liv. Age, 231: 613.

Milman, Lieut. Gen. George Bryan, with portraits. Strand, 15: 54.

Milman, Henry Hart. Ed. R. 191: 510 Same art. Liv. Age, 225: 729. Same art. Ecl. M. 135: 193.

Milne, John ; observer of Earthquakes. (C. Moffett) McClure, 11: 17.

Milner, Sir Alfred. Eng. Illust. 22: 149. — Sat. R. 83: 213. — (E. B. Iwan-Mullen) National, 37: 178. — Sat. R. 91: 696.

— and Ruskin. Indep. 53: 2585.

Milton, John, Sr. (E. G. Atkinson) Ath. '97, 2: 160.

Milton, John, with portrait. (F. Thompson) Acad. 51: 357. — (W. P. Trent) Sewanee, 5: 1. — Acad. 59: 385.

— L'Allegro with Pictures by Maxfield Parrish. Cent. 41: 163.

— and London. Acad. 54: 201. Same art. Liv. Age, 219: 194.

— as seen in his Latin Poems. (G. Gerrell) Temp. Bar, 115: 547.

— England's Debt to. Spec. 83: 746. Same art. Liv. Age, 223: 845.

— Facsimile of MS. (W. E. Henley) Pall Mall M. 21: 135.

Mining, Gold and Silver. (C. C. Goodwin) Chaut. 24: 670.
— Iron, Edison's Method. (T. Waters) Idler, 19: 390.
— Placer Gold and how it is secured. (J. E. Bennett) Cosmopol. 26: 23.
— Practical Management of. (J. E. Hardman) Engin. M. 20: 665.
— Progress in, 1825-99. (C. Kirchhoff) J. Frankl. Inst. 148: 424.
Mining Activity, Prospective Resumption of. (D. T. Day) Engin. M. 12: 621.
Mining Camp, In a. (D. Vane) Good Words, 42: 551.
Mining-camps of the West. (S. Davis) Chaut. 25: 65.
Mining Industry, Italian. J. Soc. Arts, 45: 1173.
— Mechanical and Engineering Progress as influenced by. (J. Birkenbine) J. Frankl. Inst. 144: 61.
Mining Law in British Columbia, Mexico, and the United States. (R. W. Raymond) Engin. M. 14: 925.
Mining Machinery, Electricity in, Savings effected by the Utilization of. (C. Robinson) Engin. M. 13: 89.
Mining Statistics of the World. (B. H. Brough) Nature, 63: 551.
Minister, The Christian. (F. D. Altman) Luth. Q. 28: 301.
— Relation of, to Outside Movements and Organizations. (E. H. Delk) Luth. Q. 29: 374.
Ministerial Priesthood, Moberly on. (W. G. Craig) Presb. & Ref. R. 9: 771.
Ministerial Scholarship, Standard of. (C. F. Sanders) Luth. Q. 28: 419.
Ministerial Virility. Bib. World, 17: 3.
Minister's Man, The; a story. (A. W. Stewart) Gent. M. n. s. 60: 269.
Minister's Second. (H. A. Nash) New Eng. M. n. s. 18: 85.
Minister's Socks, The; a story. (M. C. Huntington) Outl. 66: 409.
Minister's Wife, Confessions of a. Atlan. 87: 202.
Ministers and Politics. (S. L. Krebs) Ref. Ch. R. 47: 343.
— Congregational, The Surplus of. (M. Pratt) Outl. 63: 162, 222.
— Salaries of. (W. S. Harwood) Outl. 61: 170.
— Young, Demand for. (N. J. M. Bogert) Presb. & Ref. R. 10: 636.
Ministry and the Newer Education. (W. J. Tucker) Bib. World, 12: 183.
— Call to the. (J. A. Clutz) Luth. Q. 31: 453.
— Christian, of the 20th Century. (F. H. Foster) Presb. & Ref. R. 12: 1.
— Doctrine of the. (G. U. Wenner) Luth. Q. 37: 200.
— Education for. (S. D. McConnell) World's Work, 2: 837.
— — Higher. (G. G. Findlay) Lond. Q. 95: 108.
— — Psychology in. (J. F. Flint) Bib. World, 13: 326.
— — Wanted, a Chair of Tent-making. (A. Brown) Atlan. 84: 794.
— Essential Qualifications for. (L. P. Mercer) N. Church R. 8: 1.
— for the Times. (C. Clever) Ref. Ch. R. 46: 321.
— Overcrowding of the. Pub. Opin. 22: 593.
— The Paradoxical Profession. (H. J. Barrymore) Forum, 29: 189.
— — The Preëminent Profession; a rejoinder. (H. A. Stimson) Forum, 29: 465.
— Practical Suggestions for. (L. P. Mercer) N. Church R. 8: 181.
— Priests and Prophets in the Modern Church. (L. Abbott) Ref. Ch. R. 47: 289.
— Sacrificial Office of. (C. A. Scott) Expos. 7: 130.
— Self-culture in. (H. Mosser) Ref. Ch. R. 47: 219.
— The Teaching. Bib. World, 15: 164.

Mink Story, The. (G. C. Teall) Midland, 7: 235.
Minneapolis and the Saloons. (W. S. Harwood) Outl. 63: 206.
— Arts and Crafts in. (C. Whitcomb) Brush & P. 7: 344.
— Author's Club of. (L. S. Mitchell) Writer, 12: 177.
— Music in. (E. Biorkman) Music, 12: 692.
— Public Library. Pub. Lib. 4: 35.
— Walker Art Collection. (C. M. White) Brush & P. 4: 181, 229.
Minneapolis Society of Fine Arts, 1st Exhibition. (C. M. White) Brush & P. 6: 83.
Minnesota and the Northern Securities Co. (W. D. Washburn, jr.) Outl. 69: 975.
— Board of Control in. (S. G. Smith) Am. J. Sociol. 6: 778.
— Moraines of, Revision of. (J. E. Todd) Am. J. Sci. 156: 469.
— Outing in the North Woods of. (C. W. Stiles) Midland, 10: 454.
— Primary Election Law. (A. L. Mearkle) R. of Rs. (N. Y.) 24: 464.
Minnesota State Library Association. Pub. Lib. 4: 27.
Minnie Baba and the Tiger Prince; a story. Midland, 8: 338.
Minogue, Anna C. Writer, 12: 155.
Minor, John Barbee, with portrait. (Sallie E. M. Hardy) Green Bag, 10: 119.
Minor Scales. (Carl Faelten) Music, 15: 347.
Minority Committee. (P. L. Dunbar) Lippinc. 68: 617.
Minos, Palace of. (A. J. Evans) Monthly R. 2, no. 3: 115.
Minsi-Delaware, Notes on the Modern Dialect of. (J. D. Prince) Am. J. Philol. 21: 295.
Minster Lovell, Small Holdings at. (A. G. Butler) Econ. J. 7: 423.
"Mint and Cummin;" a story. (A. Sherwill) Sund. M. 27: 410.
Mint, Canadian. (N. Patterson) Canad. M. 16: 209. 17: 197.
— The Largest, in the World. (C. G. Yale) Overland, n. s. 36: 558.
— Royal, Report for 1896. Bank. M. (Lond.) 64: 44.
— — for 1897. Bank. M. (Lond.) 66: 113.
— — for 1898. Bank. M. (Lond.) 68: 329.
— — for 1900. Bank. M. (Lond.) 72: 329.
Minting Machinery. (E. S. Church) J. Frankl. Inst. 152: 401.
Minussinsk and its Museum. (A. M. B. Meakin) Chamb. J. 78: 620.
Miquette's First Dinner-party. (Gyp) Liv. Age, 218: 557.
Mirabeau before the Revolution. (A. M. Wheeler) Chaut. 25: 23.
— in London. (W. B. Duffield) Macmil. 77: 459.
— in the Revolution. (A. M. Wheeler) Chaut. 25: 234.
— Secret Mission to Berlin. (R. M. Johnston) Am. Hist. R. 6: 235.
— a Victim of the Lettres de Cachet. (F. M. Fling) Am. Hist. R. 3: 19.
— P. F. Willert on. Bk. Buyer, 17: 141.
Miracle Joyeux; a legend. (F. Norris) McClure, 12: 154.
Miracles, Delusions concerning. (J. H. Denison) New World, 7: 543.
— Evidential Value of. (J. H. Bernard) Expos. 6: 331.
— in Religion have a Scientific Counterpart. (J. Cooper) Ref. Ch. R. 47: 302.
— Modern, A Town of. (C. Johnson) Outl. 65: 561.
— of the Bible. (John Stevens) Meth. R. 57: 65.
— Philosophy of. (A. B. Taylor) Luth. Q. 28: 510.
— Place of. (S. L. Blake) Bib. Sac. 56: 12.
— Real Meaning of the. (J. Reed) N. Church R. 4: 585.

Miraculous, The, in Church History. (J. Hogan) Am. Cath. Q. **23**: 382.

Mirage. (P. A. MacMahon) Nature, **59**: 259. — (J. Wells) Sund. M. **29**: 389. — (C. M. Charroppin) Pop. Astron. **5**: 23.

Miraglia Gullotti, Don Paolo. (A. P. Irby) National, **34**: 110.

Miranda, Francisco, and the British Admiralty. Am. Hist. R. **6**: 508.

Miranda Harlow's Mortgage. (H. B. Fuller) Atlan. **86**: 671.

Miriam Silberstein; a story. (Leslie Gurnell) Gent. M. n. s. **62**: 105.

Mirror of Justices, Authorship of. (I. S. Leadam) Law Q. **13**: 85.

Mirrors and Frames. (E. G. Dawber) Art J. **50**: 151. — Distorting. (L. S. Lewis) Strand, **14**: 313. — Magic, of Japan. (J. M. Wade) Open Court, **15**: 233. — Modern Patent. Am. Arch. **64**: 102.

"Miscegenation." Spec. **83**: 245.

Misdemeanors of the Lady Gertrude. (F. Forbes-Robertson) Liv. Age, **212**: 243.

"Miserre" Carvings. Gent. M. n. s. **58**: 204.

"Miseries of Human Life." (E. V. Lucas) Cornh. **78**: 390.

Misers, Motives of. Spec. **87**: 1021.

"Misery." (E. F. Tittle) Lippinc. **62**: 289.

Misery in Mis' Randolph's Knee. (R. Shackleton) Lippinc. **65**: 602.

Misogamy and its Causes. (R. Mulckow) Chaut. **28**: 563.

Misprision of Felony; a story. (A. Werner) Gent. M. n. s. **64**: 521. Same art. Liv. Age, **226**: 108.

Miss Almira Muggins. (B. S. Woolf) Chamb. J. **74**: 202.

Miss Atkinson's Charm. (E. K. Mackenzie) Good Words, **42**: 757.

Miss Belinda's Love-letters. (E. T. Fowler) Longm. **29**: 243. Same art. Ecl. M. **128**: 259.

Miss Bolt; a story. (C. M. Mew) Temp. Bar, **122**: 484.

Miss Carrington's Professional. (M. G. Cundill) Outing, **33**: 17.

Miss Cayley's Adventures; a story. (Grant Allen) Strand, **15**: 320 — **17**: 191.

Miss Champion de Pollinaxe; a tale. Argosy, **69**: 485.

Miss Constable's Nephew; a story. (A. Kenealy) Temp. Bar, **124**: 42.

Miss Crissie's Roup. Chamb. J. **75**: 264.

Miss Cullender's Lamb; a prison story. (T. Hopkins) McClure, **15**: 53.

Miss Davenant's Experiences; a story. (C. E. C. Weigall) Argosy, **63**: 161.

Miss Deborah's Easter House-party; a story. (M. Harland) Canad. M. **16**: 508.

Miss Eurita Fleason's Relaxation; a story. (E. A. Alexander) Harper, **95**: 266.

Miss Fanny; a story. (A. O'Hagan) Munsey, **26**: 431.

Miss Flook's Feelings; a story. Temp. Bar, **111**: 251.

Miss Gunton of Poughkeepsie. (H. James) Cornh. **81**: 603.

Miss Hetty's Carpet. (Flora H. Loughead) Overland, n. s. **33**: 128.

Miss Irene. (J. C. Harris) Scrib. M. **27**: 216.

Miss Jones and the Masterpiece. (Anne D. Sedgwick) Scrib. M. **23**: 661.

Miss Lady; a story. (N. V. McClelland) Harper, **100**: 20.

Miss Latimer's Lover. (E. T. Fowler) Argosy, **65**: 749.

Miss Lutimer's Resentment. (A. Moore) Temp. Bar, **121**: 595.

Miss Melissa's Miracle. (E. Meredith) Lippinc. **64**: 743.

Miss Mitty's Work; a story. Sund. M. **28**: 469.

Miss Moffett; a story. (M. Merington) Harper, **96**: 713.

Miss Morgan's Victory; a story. (W. A. White) Idler, **20**: 45.

Miss Multon; Staging of the Play. (C. Morris) McClure, **17**: 529.

Miss Mylrea's Last Journey. (B. Atkinson) Sund. M. **30**: 173. Same art. Liv. Age, **229**: 159.

Miss Noel's Reason; a story. (A. F. Redbranche) Harper, **103**: 556.

Miss Ophelia's Beau. (A. S. Winston) Outl. **63**: 362.

Miss Peckitt's Pincushion. (E. Nesbit) Longm. **32**: 364. Same art. Liv. Age, **218**: 889.

Miss Penelope's Pension; a story. (Anna B. Patten) Nat'l M. (Bost.) **6**: 82.

Miss Peniford's Prayer. (A. Wayte) Sund. M. **29**: 511.

Miss Peters's Indian Summer. (M. E. Pratt) New Eng. M. n. s. **19**: 357.

Miss Rosamond's Engagements. (P. W. Roose) Argosy, **67**: 402.

Miss Selina's Settlement. (Mrs. B. Harrison) Cent. **31**: 586.

Miss Smith's Book. Temp. Bar, **124**: 526.

Miss Sophia's Prescription. (Eliz. Stuart-Langford) Cornh. **81**: 205.

Miss 'Stacy's "Buryin'-money." (A. M. Ewell) Cent. **33**: 454.

Miss Temple's Game; a story. (F. W. Wharton) Cosmopol. **30**: 297.

Miss Twinch and her Pigs; a story. (Penley Reyd) Gent. M. n. s. **58**: 563.

Miss Van Cortlandt's Burglar; a story. Indep. **53**: 1481.

Miss Wynifred Fraser; a story. (H. J. T. Hill) Canad. M. **16**: 463.

"Missing;" a story of the South Pacific. (J. A. Barry) Cornh. **75**: 794. Same art. Ecl. M. **129**: 371.

Missing of the Stone, The; a sketch. (E. A. Maitland) Belgra. **98**: 273.

Missing Passenger, The; a story of early Mormonism. (J. J. Gray) Midland, **8**: 342.

Mission of Kitty Malone, The; a story. (K. M. Cleary) McClure, **18**: 88.

Mission Field, Trophies of the. (F. B. Broad) Sund. M. **29**: 16, 190, (J. D. Mullins) 292.

Mission Ruins of California. (J. M. Scanland) Open Court, **11**: 602.

Mission Work, 200 Years of. (S. E. A. Johnson) Sund. M. **30**: 410.

Missionaries and Governments. (L. C. Brown) Contemp. **78**: 870. — Catholic, in Central America. (B. J. Clinch) Am. Cath. Q. **23**: 260. — Christian, in China, Corea, Burma. (E. H. Parker) Dub. R. **120**: 351. — in Asia. (P. S. Grant) Outl. **66**: 161. — in China. See China. — in China and Elsewhere. (H. C. Macdowall) Macmil. **83**: 280. — Protestant, in the Far East. (F. Penman) Cath. World, **72**: 387. — Should be Native not Foreign Born. (E. F. Goerwitz) N. Church R. **8**: 102. — Some Truths about the. (J. Barrett) Outl. **66**: 462. — to Non-Catholics, Winchester Conference of. (W. L. Sullivan) Cath. World, **74**: 90.

Missionary, Foreign, Home Preparation of. (A. Oltmans) Bib. World, **13**: 185. — Modern Foreign, Equipment of. (G. W. Gilmore) Am. J. Theol. **2**: 561. — Roman Catholic, and his Topics. (W. Elliott) Cath. World, **74**: 97.

Missionary of the Cross; a story. (W. A. R. Kerr) Canad. M. **15**: 258.

Mitchell, Donald G., the Master of Edgewood. (L. R. Kimball) Scrib. M. 27: 184.

Mitchell, Maria, with portrait. Pop. Sci. Mo. 50: 544.

Mitchell, S. Weir. (T. Williams) Cent. 35: 136. — (H. S. Morris) Critic, 32: 119.

— The Adventures of François. Bk. Buyer, 17: 324.

— and his Work, with portrait. (S. G. Fisher) Bk. Buyer, 15: 193.

— Hugh Wynne. (W. Churchill) Bk. Buyer, 19: 369.

Mitford, Mary Russell. (Annie Fields) Critic, 37: 512.

— A Memory of. (C. E. Meetkerke) Argosy, 66: 462.

Mithræum at Spoleto, On the. (H. C. Coote) Archæol. 47: 205.

Mithridatic Drop, The; a story. (W. B. Wallace) Belgra. 97: 184.

Mitla, Mexico. (L. Viajero) Am. Arch. 61: 85.

— Pueblo of, Ruins in. (W. Corner) Anthrop. J. 29: 29.

Mivart, St. George. (R. Lydekker) Nature, 61: 569.

— Ath. '00, 1: 437.

— and the Church. (R. Ogden) Nation, 70: 142. — (G. M. Searle) Cath. World, 71: 353. — Outl. 64: 381, 392. — (H. H. Henson) National, 35: 646.

— — A Liberal Catholic View of. (R. E. Dell) 19th Cent. 47: 669.

— Recent Articles of, 1900. Month, 95: 113.

— Unchanging Dogma and Changeful Man. (W. Ward) Fortn. 73: 628.

Mixed; a California story. (W. L. Alden) Pall Mall M. 16: 83.

Mixed Proposal, A; a story. (W. W. Jacobs) Harper, 102: 255.

Mnium, Study of. (A. V. Jennings) Knowl. 21: 163.

Moabitish Woman; a story. (F. W. Wharton) Cosmopol. 29: 90.

Moat, The; a poem. (M. Blind) Ecl. M. 133: 146.

Mob and Military. (R. W. Young) J. Mil. Serv. Inst. 9: 67, 249.

Mobile and Fairhope, Alabama. (E. S. Gardner) Midland, 9: 291.

— West Florida's Attempts on, 1810–11. Am. Hist. R. 2: 699.

Mobs. The Mob Mind. (E. A. Ross) Pop. Sci. Mo. 51: 390.

Mockingbird, English. Spec. 86: 762.

— the King of the Woods. (N. Robinson) Pop. Sci. Mo. 52: 322.

Models, Artists and. (J. D. Hilton) Good Words, 40: 706.

— of the N. Y. Art Schools. (K. Jarboe) Munsey, 18: 202.

Modern Ananias, A; a story. (R. Neish) Pall Mall M. 18: 404.

Modern Cleopatra; a story. (C. B. Davis) Cosmopol. 27: 423.

Modern Fairy Tale; a story. (T. C. Crawford) Cosmopol. 22: 297, 421, 525.

Modern Fairy Tale, A; adapted from the French by C. H. Page. Bookman, 10: 360.

Modern Language Association; Meeting at New York. Nation, 70: 28.

Modern Language Text-books, Objections to the Use of Some. (A. Schinz) Educa. R. 19: 75.

Modern Languages, Neglect of. Blackw. 169: 262. Same art. Liv. Age, 228: 698.

— New Departure in the Study of. (E. H. Magill) School R. 6: 257.

— Teaching. (E. Lecky) Longm. 32: 158. Same art. Ecl. M. 131: 244.

— — Reform Movement in. (O. Thiergen) School R. 8: 230.

Modern Lorelei, A; a story. (C. S. Long) Nat'l M. (Bost.) 12: 776.

Modern Martyr, A; a story. (W. Graham) Eng. Illust. 16: 467.

Modern Music Series, Scott, Foresman & Co.'s. Music, 16: 515.

Modern Olympiad, A; a story. (I. J. Armstrong) Eng. Illust. 17: 53.

Modern Perseus; a sketch. (H. Duvar) Canad. M. 10: 445.

Modern Pirate; a story. (W. Bathon) Cosmopol. 29: 544.

Modern Political Institutions, Baldwin's. Bk. Buyer, 18: 401.

Modern Rifle-shooting. Un. Serv. (Phila.) 17: 98.

Modern Thought, Changing Temper of. (R. M. Wenley) Educa. R. 19: 10.

Modernity, The Craze for. (René Doumic) Liv. Age, 219: 341.

Modesty, and Clothing, Psychology of. (W. I. Thomas) Am. J. Sociol. 5: 246.

— Evolution of. (Havelock Ellis) Psychol. R. 6: 134.

— — Ellis on. (H. M. Stanley) Science, n. s. 9: 553.

Modjeska, Helena. (C. J. Phillips) Cath. World, 73: 609.

Moels, Origin of, and their Subsequent Dissection. (J. E. Marr) Geog. J. 17: 63.

Mogul, Mahratta, and Sikh Empires. (W. H. Rattigan) Asia. R. 29: 1.

Mohammed. (W. H. Rattigan) Lond. Q. 92: 291.

— and the Rabbis, Historical and Legendary Controversies of. (H. Hirschfeld) Jew. Q. 10: 100.

— a Great Asiatic Reformer. (W. H. Rattigan) Lond. Q. 92: 291.

Mohammedan Calendar, The. (L. L. Kropf and S. Lane-Poole) Eng. Hist. R. 13: 700.

Mohammedan Criticism of the Bible. (H. Hirschfeld) Jew. Q. 13: 222.

Mohammedan Era, The. (J. D. Bate) Asia. R. 29: 381.

Mohammedan Festival in Tunis. (H. Vivian) Idler, 14: 331.

Mohammedan Law, Scientific Study of. (W. H. Rattigan) Law Q. 17: 402.

Mohammedan University, A. (T. Morison) National, 32: 243.

Mohammedanism and Christian Missions. (W. P. Reeve) Open Court, 13: 279.

— Death and the Intermediate State in. (W. M. Patton) Meth. R. 61: 53.

— How an Empire was Built. (J. B. Walker) Cosmopol. 26: 464, 475.

— in the 19th Century. (O. Mann) No. Am. 171: 754.

— a Moslem's View of the Pan-Islamic Revival. (R. Ahmad) 19th Cent. 42: 517.

— Sources of, by W. St. Clair-Tisdale. (W. Muir) 19th Cent. 48: 1001.

Mohammedans; the Senussi Sect. Acad. 55: 282.

— Women among. (R. V. Rogers) Green Bag, 13: 466.

Mohawk Valley; the eastern gateway of the United States. (A. P. Brigham) Geog. J. 13: 513.

Mohawkite. (J. W. Richards) Am. J. Sci. 161: 457.

— Stibio-domeykite, Domeykite, Algodonite, and some Artificial Copper Arsenides. (G. A. Koenig) Am. J. Sci. 160: 439.

Mohonk, Lake, and its Conferences. (B. F. Trueblood) New Eng. M. n. s. 16: 447.

— Indian Conference at. Outl. 60: 476.

Mohonk Lodge, The; an experiment in Indian work. (W. C. Roe) Outl. 68: 176.

Mohun, Charles, Lord, Adventures of. Green Bag, 13: 562.

Moira, Gerald, Designer of Stained Glass. Studio (Internat.) 9: 18.

— Relief Painter. (G. White) Studio (Internat.) 3: 223.

Mojsisovics, E. von. Geog. J. 10: 545.

Molasses and Peat Fodder in Germany. J. Soc. Arts, 45: 1149.

Mole Antonelliana. (G. W. Percy) Am. Arch. 57: 3.

Moles. (A. Jessopp) 19th Cent. 42: 275.

Molesworth, Sir William. Acad. 61: 587.

Molière, J. B. P. de. Acad. 58: 249.

— as a Poet. (W. Platt) Westm. 152: 301.

— The House of. (W. E. G. Fisher) Fortn. 73: 557.

— Shakespeare and. (J. Clarétie) Fortn. 72: 317. Same art. Ecl. M. 133: 665.

— Tartuffe. (J. A. Harrison) Chaut. 32: 297.

Molkenboer, Antoon, Artist. (H. Hendrix) Studio, (Internat.) 13: 181.

Mollie's Birthday Text. (F. Nöel) Sund. M. 29: 740.

Molluscan Fauna of the Genesee River. (F. C. Baker) Am. Natural. 35: 659.

Molluscs, Cuenot's Excretion in. Am. Natural. 35: 151.

— Littoral, from Cape Fairweather, Patagonia. (H. A. Pilsbry) Am. J. Sci. 157: 126.

Molly Maguires. Macmil. 15: 110. Same art. Ecl. M. 128: 374.

Molteno, Sir John Charles. Life and Times. Sat. R. 89: 587.

Moltke, H. von, Strategy of, in the War with the French Republic. (A. E. Turner) Un. Serv. M. 20: 616.

Molybdenum, Estimation of, Iodometrically. (F. A. Gooch) Am. J. Sci. 153: 237.

— in the Rocks of the United States, Distribution and Quantitative Occurrence of. (W. F. Hillebrand) Am. J. Sci. 156: 209.

— Iodometric Determination of. (F. A. Gooch and J. T. Norton, jr.) Am. J. Sci. 156: 168.

Molybdic Acid reduced by Hydriodic Acid, Estimation of. (F. A. Gooch and O. S. Pulman, jr.) Am. J. Sci. 162: 449.

Moment of Clear Vision, The ; a story. (Octave Thanet) Scrib. M. 23: 311.

Moment's Madness, A ; a story. (Maud Diver) Pall Mall M. 13: 389.

Moment's Madness, A ; a story. (K. Guthrie) Idler, 14: 654.

Momerie, Alfred Williams. Outl. 67: 7.

Mon rêve ; a poem. (C. Hannan) Belgra. 95: 135.

Monaco, Madame de. (A. Laugel) Nation, 68: 256.

— The Story of. (W. Miller) Gent. M. n. s. 64: 22.

Monadnock, W. P. Phelps's Paintings of. (C. E. Hurd) New Eng. M. n. s. 17: 363.

Monarch or Monk ? — a legend of Tomsk. (J. Y. Simpson) Blackw. 161: 257. Same art. Liv. Age, 213: 325.

Monarchical Idea, Revival of. Church Q. 44: 1.

Monarchies and Republics. (F. M. Bird) Lippinc. 62: 370.

Monarchs at Home. (M. S. Warren) Eng. Illust. 18: 561, 579.

Monarchy in the 19th Century. (S. Low) 19th Cent. 49: 487. Same art. Ecl. M. 136: 701. Same art. Liv. Age, 229: 73.

Monasteries, English, The Internal Order of. Church Q. 45: 427.

— Greek Monachism. (Z. T. Sweeney) Cosmopol. 23: 297.

— Injunctions of Bishop of Lincoln to Certain. (E. Peacock) Archæol. 47: 49.

Monastery, An Anglican, near Alton, England. (A. Kelly) Idler, 12: 797.

— Changes and Chances of a. (S. M. C. Boevey) Reliquary, 39: 34.

— McCabe's Life in a Modern. Acad. 54: 238.

— Russian, Life in a. (A. M. Brice) Temp. Bar, 118: 230. Same art. Liv. Age, 224: 177.

Monastic Architecture in Russia. (C. A. Rich) Archit. R. 9: 21.

Monastic Orders up to Date. (E. Saint Genix) Contemp. 77: 437, 579.

Monastic Towns, English, Risings in, in 1327. (N. M. Trenholme) Am. Hist. R. 6: 650.

Monasticism, French, Problem of. (J. Manson) Fortn. 75: 682.

Monazite. (H. B. C. Nitze) J. Frankl. Inst. 144: 127.

— from Idaho. (W. Lindgren) Am. J. Sci. 154: 63.

— Notes on. (O. A. Derby) Am. J. Sci. 160: 217.

Monboddo and the Old Scottish Judges. (A. F. Shand) Cornh. 83: 482.

Monet, Claude, Impressionist Artist, with portrait. (W. Dewhurst) Pall Mall M. 21: 209. — Artist (N. Y.) 29: 57.

Monetary Chaos. (R. Giffen) 19th Cent. 42: 678. Same art. Ecl. M. 130: 52.

Monetary Commission, Indianapolis. Bank. M. (N. Y.) 55: 841. — (J. L. Laughlin) Forum, 24: 303. — (H. P. Willis) J. Pol. Econ. 6: 93.

— and its Work. (C. S. Fairchild) No. Am. 166: 172.

— Final Report of. (F. M. Taylor) J. Pol. Econ. 6: 293. — (F. A. Cleveland) Ann. Am. Acad. Pol. Sci. 13: 31.

— Open Letter to. (G. A. Groot) Arena, 19: 602.

— Plan of. Bank. M. (N. Y.) 56: 193.

— Questions for. Gunton's M. 13: 408.

Monetary Convention, Indianapolis, 1897. Gunton's M. 12: 110.

Monetary Outlook, 1898. Bank. M. (Lond.) 66: 1.

Monetary Reform in the United States. (F. M. Taylor) Econ. J. 8: 579.

— Progress of. (C. S. Hamlin) R. of Rs. (N. Y.) 20: 711.

Monetary Review for 1896. Bank. M. (Lond.) 63: 65.

— for 1900. Bank. M. (Lond.) 71: 259.

Monetary Securities, Transfer of. Bank. M. (N. Y.) 56: 406.

Monetary Standard, Historical Changes in. (W. W. Carlile) J. Pol. Econ. 7: 352.

Monetary System, Cure for a Vicious. (W. A. Peffer) Forum, 22: 722.

— Proposed Reforms of. (J. F. Johnson) Ann. Am. Acad. Pol. Sci. 11: 191.

Monetary Union, Latin, History of, Willis's. (W. W. Carlile) Econ. R. 11: 391. — (A. de Foville) J. Pol. Econ. 10: 113.

Money. (Leo Tolstoi ; J. L. Laughlin) Open Court, 14: 193.

— and its Vicissitudes, Bailey on. (C. W. Mixter) Q. J. Econ. 12: 343.

— and Prices. (R. Mayo-Smith) Pol. Sci. Q. 15: 196.

— and Social Problems, Harper on. Spec. 78: 516.

— Cheap, and Good. (R. Ewen) Westm. 149: 214.

— — Meaning of. Spec. 78: 233. Same art. Ecl. M. 129: 280.

— Coin of the Republic. (H. Wood and J. A. Collins) Arena, 23: 167.

— Common Sense on. Gunton's M. 16: 224.

— Congress and Monetary Relief. (W. C. Cornwell) Gunton's M. 17: 447.

— Distribution of. (C. A. Conant) J. Pol. Econ. 9: 47.

— Fiat, in N. E. (E. F. McLeod) Ann. Am. Acad. Pol. Sci. 12: 229.

— Figures made of Pressed Paper-. (G. Dollar) Strand, 17: 796.

— Functions and Qualities of. Bank. M. (N. Y.) 58: 27, 189.

— Functions of. (O. Lodge) Econ. R. 8: 433.

— Honest. (W. J. Bryan ; M. W. Howard, and others) Arena, 18: 57.

— in the Field. Spec. 84: 410.

Money in U. S. Treasury, 1894–96. (F. W. Taussig) Q. J. Econ. 13: 204.
— Limits of its Power. Sat. R. 88: 544.
— Meaning of the Term. (A. P. Andrew) Q. J. Econ. 13: 219.
— Measure of the Value of, according to European Economists. (G. M. Fiamingo) J. Pol. Econ. 7: 42.
— Modern Worship of. Spec. 79: 893. Same art. Ecl. M. 130: 277.
— The Monetary Chaos. (R. Giffen) 19th Cent. 42: 678.
— Multiple-Standard. (H. Winn) Arena, 19: 639. — (E. Pomeroy) Arena, 18: 318.
— Origins of. Bank. M. (N. Y.) 58: 346.
— Place of, in Economics. (W. W. Carlile) Econ. R. 10: 23.
— a poem. (H. T. Peck) Bookman, 5: 28.
— Prevailing Theories in Europe as to the Influence of, on International Exchange. (G. M. Fiamingo) Yale R. 6: 361.
— Problem of, Arbitration the only Solution of the. (A. R. Foote) Forum, 23: 208.
— Quantitative Theory of. (W.-W. Carlile) Econ. R. 8: 1.
— — from the Marxist Standpoint. (A. P. Hazell) J. Pol. Econ. 7: 78.
— Rise in Value of. Bank. M. (Lond.) 68: 569.
— Safety of the Legal Tender Paper. (C. F. Dunbar) Q. J. Econ. 11: 223.
— Science of. (L. Vann) Conserv. R. 4: 184.
— Shall we teach our Daughters the Value of? (A. L. B. Ide) Pop. Sci. Mo. 54: 686.
— Stable. (T. E. Will) J. Pol. Econ. 7: 85.
— Standard of, steadily appreciating. (C. M. Walsh) Q. J. Econ. 11: 280.
— Stock of. Bank. M. (Lond.) 64: 305.
— Value of. (W. Cunningham) Q. J. Econ. 13: 379.
— — and Prices. (G. J. F. Grant) Westm. 154: 95.
— — Law of. (C. A. Conant) Ann. Am. Acad. Pol. Sci. 16: 189.
— without Law. Bank. M. (N. Y.) 54: 382.
Money Articles, Mysteries of. (H. Withers) Cornh. 75: 684.
Money Controversy, Our Next. (F. L. McVey) J. Pol. Econ. 10: 119.
Money-lenders. Spec. 79: 39.
— and their Customers. Spec. 78: 621.
Money-lending Inquiry, The. (T. W. Russell) 19th Cent. 44: 234. — Chamb. J. 75: 502. — Spec. 81: 40.
Money Making, The Morality of. Spec. 83: 601.
Money Market, The. Bank. M. (Lond.) 63: 58.
— and the Stock Exchange. Bank. M. (Lond.) 65: 54.
— International. (C. Rosenraad) J. Statis. Soc. 63: 1.
— Modern Conditions in. Bank. M. (Lond.) 64: 1.
Money Power; the Invisible Empire. (J. C. Ridpath) Arena, 19: 828.
Money Reform of Austria-Hungary. Bank. M. (N. Y.) 55: 705.
Money Unit, Value of. (T. N. Carver) Q. J. Econ. 11: 429.
Monge, Gaspard, with portrait. (T. J. McCormack) Open Court, 12: 112.
Mongol-Mayan Constitution. (J. Wickersham) Am. Antiq. 20: 169.
Mongolia. (W. E. Gowan) Asia. R. 25: 387.
Mongols, Modern. (F. L. Oswald) Pop. Sci. Mo. 57: 618.
Mongoose in Jamaica. (C. W. Willis) Pop. Sci. Mo. 54: 86.
Monhegan, Historical and Picturesque. (A. G. Pettengill) New Eng. M. n. s. 19: 65.
Monier Construction. (J. B. Johnson) Am. Arch. 69: 37.

"Monica's" Chief Engineer; a story. (H. Bindloss) Gent. M. n. s. 61: 84. Same art. Liv. Age, 219: 371.
Monism and Pluralism. (D. G. Ritchie) Mind, 23: 449.
— (C. M. Bakewell) Philos. R. 7: 355.
— for the Multitude, Haeckel on. Nature, 63: 320.
— Lotze's. (W. J. Wright) Philos. R. 6: 57.
Monistic Psychology. (C. W. Rishell) Meth. R. 58: 863.
"Monitor," the U. S. Ironclad. (F. M. Bennett) Cassier, 13: 459.
— and the Navy under Steam, Bennett on. (H. C. Taylor) Am. Hist. R. 6: 820.
— and the Later Turret Ships. (G. L. Fowler) Engin. M. 14: 110.
Monk from the Ghetto. (M. Wolfenstein) Lippinc. 66: 131.
Monk of Baldwyn Priors; a ghost story. (A. S. Appelbee) Eng. Illust. 19: 452.
Monkey, An Invisible. (R. Lydekker) Knowl. 20: 129.
Monkey, The; a story. (M. E. Wilkins) Harper, 102: 109.
Monkey that Never Was, The. (C. B. Fernald) Cent. 36: 461.
Monkey-flowers; a story. (A. T. Quiller-Couch) Cosmopol. 31: 405.
Monkeys. Quar. 186: 394.
— at the Zoo. (F. G. Aflalo) Good Words, 42: 559.
— Brazilian Names of. (J. Platt) Ath. '01, 1: 695.
— Hand-prints of. (R. Lydekker) Knowl. 24: 3.
— Intelligence of. (E. L. Thorndike) Pop. Sci. Mo. 59: 273.
Monkhouse, Allan. Acad. 55: 485.
Monkhouse, William Cosmo. Acad. 61: 77. — (S. Lee) Ath. '01, 2: 125.
Monks and Monasteries, A. W. Wishart on. Outl. 65: 743.
— of Islam. (L. J. Garnett) Sund. M. 29: 655.
Monmouth, James, Duke of, Fea's Life of. (P. Bicknell) Dial (Ch.) 31: 511.
Monmouthshire, Bibliography of. (W. Haines) Library, 8: 239.
— Border Castles of. (C. Parkinson) Temp. Bar, 118: 421.
Monmouthshire Sketches, Some. (J. R. Larkby) Reliquary, 40: 145.
Monogamy, Historical and Ethical Basis of. (T. Williams) Internat. J. Ethics, 10: 156.
Monograms, Making of. (G. White) Studio (Lond.) 5: 185.
Monologue. An Enchantress, with illustrations. (Phœbe Hart) Pall Mall M. 19: 553.
Monopolies; the Amsterdam Avenue Fight, N. Y. City. Outl. 61: 623.
— and Combinations, Classification of. (N. H. Robinson) Yale R. 9: 324.
— and Fair Dealing. (C. S. Devas) Internat. J. Ethics, 12: 59.
— and the Law. (J. B. Clark) Pol. Sci. Q. 16: 463.
— and Trusts, Ely's. (F. C. Montague) Econ. J. 10: 519.
— — Nature and Significance of. (R. T. Ely) Internat. J. Ethics, 10: 273.
— Limitations of. (E. S. Meade) Forum, 31: 213.
— or Franchises — their Public Ownership and Operation. (H. E. Tremain) Ann. Am. Acad. Pol. Sci. 14: 310.
— Regulated. (D. MacG. Means) Nation, 72: 229.
— The War on. (D. MacG. Means) Nation, 70: 410.
Monopolists, Coming Contest with. (R. Ewen) Westm. 152: 516.
Monopoly and Economic Consolidation. (P. A. Robinson) Conserv. R. 4: 33.

Monopoly, Graziani on Mathematical Theory of. (F. Y. Edgeworth) Econ. J. **8**: 234.
— in British Industry. (H. W. Macrosty) Contemp. **75**: 364.
— *vs.* Competition. (M. Mannering) Nat'l M. (Bost.) **10**: 188.
Monotype, The. (G. W. Steevens) New R. **17**: 564.
Monotype Party, A, at the Salmagundi. (J. B. Carrington) Bk. Buyer, **15**: 1.
Monotypes. (W. A. Coffin) Cent. **31**: 517.
Monro, Dr. Thomas, 1759–1833. (Clara E. Coode) Art J. **53**: 133.
Monroe Doctrine. Westm. **150**: 171.
— American Policy and the. Liv. Age, **225**: 586.
— Americanism and. (J. C. Green) Westm. **149**: 237.
— and the Doctrine of Permanent Interest. (A. B. Hart) Am. Hist. R. **7**: 77.
— and Hay-Pauncefote Treaty. (J. G. Whiteley) Forum, **30**: 722.
— Beaumarchais on. (F. Bancroft) Pol. Sci. Q. **14**: 355.
— Birth of. (O. S. Borne) Nat'l M. (Bost.) **11**: 599.
— Notes on. (John Harold) Sat. R. **92**: 300.
— Olney Doctrine and America's New Foreign Policy. (S. Low) 19th Cent. **40**: 849. Same art. Ecl. M. **128**: 161.
— Original Intention of. (T. A. Cook) Fortn. **70**: 357.
— Reddaway on. (A. G. Sedgwick) Nation, **66**: 368. — Sat. R. **85**: 721. — (F. H. Hodder) Dial (Ch.) **25**: 41.
— Repeal of, and "Our Next War." (J. Chetwood) Arena, **23**: 247.
— Shall it be Modified? (W. Wellman) No. Am. **173**: 832.
— Some Aspects of. (S. Brooks) Fortn. **76**: 1013.
Monserrat. *See* Montserrat.
Monsieur Beaucaire; a novel. (B. Tarkington) McClure, **14**: 158, 247. Same art. Idler, **17**: 397, 499. **18**: 8.
Monsieur Bibi's Boom-boom; a story. (H. J. W. Dam) McClure, **14**: 81.
Monsieur Duval; a sketch from life. (F. Barry) Temp. Bar, **110**: 571. Same art. Liv. Age, **213**: 471.
M. Galleria. (J. Van Z. Belden) Lippinc. **65**: 476.
Monsieur le Colonel. Macmil. **76**: 444.
Monsieur le President. (E. Greck) Temp. Bar, **113**: 53.
Monson, New Hampshire. (A. E. Brown) New Eng. M. n. s. **24**: 652.
Monsoon, English. Spec. **87**: 383.
Monster, The; a story. (S. Crane) Harper, **97**: 343.
Monsters, Mythical. (D. S. Lamb) Am. Anthrop. **2**: 277.
Mont St. Michel, Graves and Ghosts of. (B. Gilman) Overland, n. s. **36**: 305.
Montagu, Lady Mary Wortley. Quar. **186**: 436. — (F. C. Hodgson) Gent. M. n. s. **59**: 426. — (S. G. Tallentyre) Longm. **33**: 336. Same art. Ecl. M. **132**: 709. Same art. Liv. Age, **221**: 11.
— and Mary Astell. (H. McIlquham) Westm. **151**: 289.
Montaigne, M. de. Acad. **54**: 3.
— and Essay Writing in France. (F. M. Warren) Chaut. **32**: 192.
— and Shakespeare. (J. C. Collins) Sat. R. **85**: 850.
— Romantic Side of. Temp. Bar, **110**: 26. Same art. Liv. Age, **212**: 620.
Montalembert, Charles F. de, with portrait. (J. G. Daley) Cath. World, **71**: 331. — Ed. R. **190**: 209.
— and French Education. (R. B. S. Blakelock) Dub. R. **126**: 102.
Montana and Idaho, Boundary Line. (R. U. Goode) Nat. Geog. M. **11**: 23.
— Northwestern; the Crown of the Continent. (G. B. Grinnell) Cent. **40**: 660.

Montana, the Treasure State. (J. H. Crooker) New Eng. M. n. s. **21**: 741.
Montanians, The. (R. L. Hartt) Atlan. **81**: 737.
Montauk, A Week at. (E. T. Devine) Char. R. **8**: 368.
Monte Carlo. (Jane Marlin) Overland, n. s. **35**: 353. — (P. C. Mitchell) Sat. R. **86**: 138.
Monte Oliveto. Temp. Bar, **116**: 254.
Montefiore Library, Hebrew MSS. of, Catalogue of. (H. Hirschfeld) Jew. Q. **14**: 159.
Montenegro. (F. A. Kirkpatrick) Longm. **31**: 163.
— and her Prince. (J. D. Bourchier) Fortn. **70**: 911.
— Code of Property of. (H. A. D. Phillips) Law Q. **13**: 70.
— In. (A. A. Coolidge) Nation, **69**: 239.
— Jubilee of, 1901. (W. Miller) Macmil. **84**: 342. Same art. Liv. Age, **231**: 385.
— Law and Order in. (S. F. Batchelder) Nation, **72**: 130.
— Visit to. (H. K. Scott) Belgra. **96**: 98.
— A Visit with the Prince of. (E. A. Steiner) Outl. **75**: 545.
Monterey, Cal. A California Plymouth Rock. (M. H. Field) Chaut. **31**: 388.
— The Artist in. (H. A. Culmer) Overland, n. s. **34**: 514.
— Siege of. J. Mil. Serv. Inst. **8**: 325.
Monterey Coast, Two Pictures of an Unknown Bit of the. (H. W. Fairbanks and L. M. Dixon) Overland, n. s. **30**: 291.
Montesquieu, Charles de Secondat, with portrait. (L. Levy-Bruhl) Open Court, **13**: 28.
— in Italy. Quar. **190**: 43.
Montfort, Thomas P. Writer, **14**: 74.
Montgomery Invincibles; a story. (H. G. Carleton) Cosmopol. **30**: 599.
Montgomery Race Conference. (B. T. Washington) Cent. **38**: 630. — (I. C. Barrows) Outl. **65**: 153, 160.
Montmorency, Duchess of. (A. Laugel) Nation, **66**: 421.
Montpelier, Vermont. (H. A. Huse) New Eng. M. n. s. **19**: 301.
— the Home of Dewey. (M. B. Thrasher) Nat'l M. (Bost.) **10**: 442.
Montreal. (W. D. Lighthall) New Eng. M. n. s. **19**: 233. — (S. Byrne) Cath. World, **73**: 494. — (F. Dolman) Idler, **15**: 467.
— and Quebec, Notes on. (E. P. Gould) Educa. **19**: 185.
— and Some of its Homes. (H. C. Walsh) Canad. M. **12**: 51.
— Bank of. (J. M. Oxley) Canad. M. **16**: 99.
— Chateau de Ramezay. (A. C. Yate) Asia. R. **29**: 163.
— The Maids of. (M. S. Pepper) Chaut. **32**: 249.
— Memorial Tablets of. (J. Maclean) Am. Antiq. **21**: 80.
— Municipal Government of. (F. H. McLean) Ann. Am. Acad. Pol. Sci. **18**: 359.
— Municipal Reform in. Canad. M. **12**: 457.
— a poem. (W. D. Lighthall) Canad. M. **15**: 73.
— to Ste. Anne, Bicycling from. (F. Farrington) Outing, **38**: 423.
— The Two Montreals. (L. W. Betts) Outl. **66**: 1047.
Montrose, James, Marquis of, The Heart of. Chamb. J. **78**: 499.
— and Argyll in Fiction. Blackw. **165**: 93. Same art. Liv. Age, **220**: 495.
Montrose, Scotland, St. Mary's Church. Woodward Memorial Reredos. (E. Pinnington) Art J. **53**: 282.
Montserrat. Maravilla de Cataluña. (Eleanor Lewis) Outl. **59**: 80.
— Monastery of. (Arthur Symons) Sat. R. **86**: 599.
Monumental Timekeepers. (J. M. Bacon) Good Words, **41**: 822.

Monuments, Brass, their Lettering and Ornament. (E. F. Strange) Art J. 50: 119.
— Christianized Megalithic. (A. de Mortillet) Pop. Sci. Mo. 53: 668.
— National, Two Centuries of. Liv. Age, 213: 91.
— Old and Modern. Idler, 14: 475.
— Unfinished. Am. Arch. 73: 54.
Monuments, History, Prophecy, and, McCurdy's. (C. H. Toy) Am. Hist. R. 2: 327.
Monvel, Boutet de, the Painter. (M. L. Van Vorst) Cent. 35: 572. — McClure, 10: 197. — (Th. Bentzon) Critic, 34: 129. — With portrait. Brush & P. 3: 257.
— Art of. (C. Hiatt) Studio (Lond.) 5: 157.
Moods, Ephemeral and Eternal. (T. Cleveland, jr.) Poet-Lore, 10: 235.
Moody, Dwight L. (A. M. Mitchell) New Eng. M. n. s. 16: 671. — Outl. 63: 1003. — With portrait. (G. P. Morris) R. of Rs. (N. Y.) 21: 163. — (G. F. Pentecost) Indep. 52: 10. — (J. Stalker) Sund. M. 29: 111. Same art. Liv. Age, 224: 690.
— His Northfield Home. (M. L. Osborne) Nat'l M. (Bost.) 11: 478.
— Inner Life of. (C. M. Stuart) Chaut. 30: 527.
— a Personal Tribute. (G. A. Smith) Outl. 64: 163.
— Power of his Ministry. (L. Abbott) No. Am. 170: 263.
Moody, Fannie. Animal Sketches. Artist (N. Y.) 26: 121.
Moody, William Vaughn. (G. B. Rose) Sewanee, 9: 332.
— Poems. Atlan. 88: 132. — (J. B. Gilder) Critic, 39: 224. — (W. M. Payne) Dial (Ch.) 30: 365.
— A Poet of Promise. Outl. 68: 664.
Moon; Adams's Lectures on the Lunar Theory. (P. H. Cowell) Knowl. 24: 155.
— Enlargement of, near Horizon, Ptolemy's Theorem on. (T. J. J. See) Pop. Astron. 8: 362.
— In the Northern Regions of. (A. Mee) Knowl. 21: 84.
— The Lunar Atmosphere. (W. H. Pickering) Pop. Astron. 8: 205.
— Origin of the Lunar Formations. (W. H. Pickering) Pop. Astron. 8: 147, 181.
— Photographic Atlas of. (L. Weinek) Pop. Astron. 5: 240. — Nature, 60: 491.
— Photographs of, taken at Paris Observatory. Nature, 56: 280.
— Ringed Plains of the Mare Nubium. (E. W. Maunder) Knowl. 24: 200.
— Schmidt-Dickert Model of. (O. C. Farrington) Science, n. s. 9: 35.
— "Seas" of; what are they? (J. G. O. Tepper) Knowl. 22: 251.
— Stereoscopic Study of. (G. K. Gilbert) Science, n. s. 13: 407.
— Sunrise on the Sea of Plenty. (E. W. Maunder) Knowl. 24: 61.
— Theory of Motion of, Brown's. Nature, 57: 88.
Moonlight in London; a poem. (W. Hogg) Spec. 80: 479.
Moon's Miracle, The; a story. (W. Ramal) Cornh. 75: 524.
Moonshiners, Glimpse of. (E. O. Peterson) Chaut. 26: 178.
— Raiding. (S. G. Blythe) Munsey, 25: 416.
" Moonshining " in Georgia. (W. M. Brewer) Cosmopol. 23: 127.
Moon-stricken; a story. (B. E. J. Capes) Cornh. 74: 795. Same art. Ecl. M. 128: 171.
Moor-hens, Our. (Clara Bensted) Chamb. J. 78: 795.
Moore, Albert. (A. L. Baldry) Studio (Lond.) 3: 3, 46. — (E. Radford) Idler, 14: 3.

Moore, Albert, An Embroidery by. Art J. 50: 109.
Moore, Alfred, with portrait. (J. Davis) Green Bag, 12: 325.
Moore, Charles Leonard. Ghost of Rosalys; a play. (W. N. Guthrie) Sewanee, 9: 215.
Moore, Clement C.; the Author of "A Visit from St. Nicholas." (Clarence Cook) Cent. 33: 198.
Moore, F. Frankfort. Writer, 48: 109. — With portrait. Bk. News, 16: 353.
Moore, George. (D. C. Murray) Canad. M. 9: 41.
— as a Critic of Stevenson. (V. Blackburn) Acad. 51: 476.
— Conversations with. (W. Archer) Critic, 39: 47. Same art. Pall Mall M. 24: 353.
— Evelyn Innes. Bk. Buyer, 17: 55. — (H. T. Peck) Bookman, 7: 498.
Moore, Henry, Animal Studies by. (A. L. Baldry) Studio (Internat.) 4: 223.
Moore, Sir John, at Corunna. (W. H. Fitchett) Cornh. 77: 1.
— in '98. (R. Staveley) Cornh. 78: 156.
Moore, Thomas, American Trip of, with portrait. (J. G. Daley) Cath. World, 73: 768.
— An Unpublished Poem by. (J. C. Johnson) Bookman, 7: 386.
Moore, T. Sturge. Vinedresser and other Poems. Sat. R. 88: 77.
Moore Families, of Litchfield and Merrimac, N. H. (E. S. Stearns) N. E. Reg. 55: 78.
— of Londonderry, N. H. (E. S. Stearns) N. E. Reg. 204: 488.
Moore Genealogy. (J. S. Sargent) N. E. Reg. 52: 72.
Moorefield, A Mass House in. (Scott Damant) Eng. Illust. 21: 579.
Moorish Art, Two Centres of. (E. L. Weeks) Scrib. M. 29: 433.
Moorish Service, Europeans in the. (B. Meakin) Un. Serv. M. 18: 552.
Moorish Treasure, The. (Capt. Cecil North) Chamb. J. 77: 625-702.
Moors, Influences left in Spain. Sat. R. 88: 194.
— Meakin's Land of the. (D. B. Macdonald) Nation, 73: 15.
Moose in Canada. (C. A. Bramble) Canad. M. 14: 55.
— My First Bull. (F. C. Selous) Outing, 39: 138.
— where it Lives and how. (A. J. Stone) Outing, 39: 258.
Moose-call, A Tragic. (A. A. Shute) Outing, 33: 184.
Moose-hunt. (C. G. D. Roberts) Outing, 37: 3.
Moose-hunting. Blackw. 168: 58. — (H. R. Wadsworth) Canad. M. 16: 56. — (P. Syms) Outing, 31: 156. — (F. H. Risteen) Outing, 33: 221.
— in the Maine Woods. (C. Bailey) Outing, 35: 127.
— in New Brunswick. (W. C. Gaynor) Canad. M. 8: 399.
— on Snow-shoes. (F. H. Risteen) Outing, 31: 249.
— William's Moose. (H. Sears) Harper, 97: 87.
— with the Tro-chu-tin [Klondike Indians]. (T. Adney) Harper, 100: 495.
Moose-land, Christmas in. (E. W. Sandys) Outing, 33: 400.
Moosilauke. (B. Torrey) Atlan. 87: 667.
Mooswa of the Boundaries; a tale. (W. A. Fraser) Canad. M. 15: 497. 16: 49, 157.
Moot System, The. (C. Walsh) Law Q. 15: 416.
Moplas, The, of Malabar. (F. Fawcett) Asia. R. 24: 288.
Moqui Indians, Sun Worship among. (J. W. Fewkes) Nature, 58: 295.
Moral, Essence and Extent of the. (W. Rupp) Ref. Ch. R. 48: 371.
Moral Adventuress. (J. L. Ford) Munsey, 22: 756.
Moral Character of Children, Influence of Puberal Development upon. (A. Marro) Am. J. Sociol. 5: 193.

Moral Education in a Democracy, Fouillée on. Educa. 19: 443.
— of Children. (P. Carus) Open Court, 13: 176.
— Some Aims of. (Frank C. Sharp) Int. J. Ethics, 9: 214.
— Study in. (J. R. Street) Pedagog. Sem. 5: 5.
Moral Evolution, Harris's. (G. S. Patton) Presb. & Ref. R. 8: 531.
Moral Impulses, Nurture of. (H. Sabin) Educa. 20: 259.
Moral Instinct, Sutherland on. (T. H. Giddings) Pol. Sci. Q. 14: 177. — (Hiram M. Stanley) Dial (Ch.) 25: 167. — Spec. 81: 17.
Moral Judgments, Objective Study of Some. (F. C. Sharp) Am. J. Psychol. 9: 198.
— Predicates of. (E. Westermarck) Mind, 25: 184.
Moral Law, The. (F. Thilly) Internat. J. Ethics, 10: 223.
— Possibilities of the. (H. W. Dresser) Arena, 21: 477.
Moral Life of the Early Romans. (F. Granger) Int. J. Ethics, 7: 281.
Moral Obligation, Some Defective Theories of. (C. C. Dove) Westm. 154: 432.
— Source of. (J. S. Mackenzie) Internat. J. Ethics, 10: 463. — (G. H. Joyce) Am. Cath. Q. 26: 41.
Moral Order, The. Outl. 61: 862.
— Bruce on. (A. Macalister) Crit. R. 10: 1.
Moral Progress, 1–300 A. D., Some Presuppositions for a History of. (W. R. Inge) Int. J. Ethics, 8: 203.
Moral Standard, Variability of the. (J. Rickaby) Month, 90: 183.
Moral Teaching in Ancient Egypt. (H. Osgood) Presb. & Ref. R. 8: 267.
Moral Training of Children, New Psychology and. (H. Davies) Internat. J. Ethics, 10: 493.
Moralities, Minor. (Lady Magnus) Good Words, 39: 91–308.
Morality and Belief in the Supernatural. (E. Ritchie) Int. J. Ethics, 7: 180.
— and Religion. (N. Wilde) Philos. R. 6: 64.
— — Vanishing Landmarks of. Contemp. 80: 136.
— Intuitive and Imperative. (T. Nichols) Presb. & Ref. R. 10: 511.
— Psychic Rudiments and. (G. E. Dawson) Am. J. Psychol. 11: 181.
— Relation between Early Religion and. (E. Buckley) Internat. Mo. 1: 577.
— Social, W. A. Watt on. (C. S. Devas) Dub. R. 129: 123.
— without Religion. (O. Pfleiderer) Am. J. Theol. 3: 225.
"Morality" Play, A Modern. (J. Lemaitre) Liv. Age, 212: 55.
Moralizing in Art, Against. (J. Burroughs) Atlan. 84: 229.
Morals. (F. Barnard) School R. 7: 222.
— American, History of. (S. E. Baldwin) Am. J. Soc. Sci. 36: 1.
— and Civilization. (H. G. Wells) Fortn. 67: 263.
— and Science. (P. M. Berthelot) Pop. Sci. Mo. 52: 326.
— at Home and Abroad. (E. P. Clark) Nation, 73: 163.
— Basis of. (G. G. Findlay) Chr. Lit. 16: 374, 395. — (D. D. Lum) Monist, 7: 554.
— Metaphysical, Basis of. (J. Fearnley) Sewanee, 3: 339.
— Personal Equation in. Overland, n. s. 34: 371.
Moran, Edward, Artist. Brush & P. 8: 188.
Moran, Mrs. Mary Nunmo, Etcher, with portrait. (M. T. Everett) Brush & P. 8: 3.
Moran, Thomas, Painter-etcher, with portrait. (F. W. Morton) Brush & P. 7: 1.

Morata, Olympia. (B. G. Johns) Good Words, 42: 267.
Moray, James Stuart, Earl of; A New View of the Good Regent. (O. Smeaton) Westm. 151: 310.
Moray, the Traitor; a story. (F. M. White) Pall Mall M. 18: 384.
More, Alex. Goodman. Knowl. 21: 187.
More, Hannah, Horace Walpole and. (H. Toynbee) Temp. Bar, 110: 371.
More, Henry, Ethical System of. (G. N. Dolson) Philos. R. 6: 593.
More, Mrs. Patty; a Mendip Annal. (M. J. H. Skrine) Temp. Bar, 114: 269.
More, Sir Thomas, The Gentle. (E. S. Saville) Westm. 156: 454.
— and the Persecution of Heretics. (H. G. Ganss) Am. Cath. Q. 25: 531.
More Dolly Dialogues. (A. H. Hawkins) McClure, 16: 110.
More Gracious Estate, The; a story. (Mrs. E. Nepean) Belgra. 95: 241.
More than enough Moa. (V. Waite) Cornh. 80: 604.
More Warm than Pleasant; a story. (O. Hall) Eng. Illust. 16: 449.
Moreau, Gen. J. V. (A. Laugel) Nation, 70: 107.
Moreau, Gustave. (H. Frantz) M. of Art, 24: 97. — (C. I. Holmes) Contemp. 74: 403.
— Hermelin's. Nation, 67: 463.
Morelia, Mexico, Cathedral of. (J. W. Perkins) Am. Arch. 64: 35.
Morelli, Domenico, Artist. (I. M. Anderson) Studio (Internat.) 15: 83.
Morelos, J. M., Hidalgo and. (H. C. Lea) Am. Hist. R. 4: 636.
Morgan, Alice. Writer, 14: 140.
Morgan, Charles Hill, with portrait. Cassier, 19: 158.
Morgan, Gen. Daniel, Some Letters of. Pennsyl. M. 21: 488.
Morgan, Sir Henry, and his Buccaneers. (C. T. Brady) Idler, 19: 69. Same art. McClure, 15: 502.
Morgan, J. Pierpont. (L. Denison) World's Work, 1: 610. — (R. S. Baker) McClure, 17: 507.
— and his Work. (E. E. Machen) Cosmopol. 31: 177.
— "Morganeering." (W. R. Lawson) National, 37: 538.
Morgan, Julius P. (J. P. Bock) Munsey, 24: 406.
Morgana mia; a poem. (F. Blake Crofton) Canad. M. 12: 244.
Morin, Louis, French Caricaturist, with portrait. (H. Boucher) Studio (Internat.) 10: 242. — (M. H. Spielmann) M. of Art, 25: 151.
Moriscos of Spain, Lea's. Nation, 72: 376.
Morison, Rev. John H. A Memoir. N. Church R. 4: 475.
Morisons of Perth, A Notable Publishing House. (J. Minto) Library, n. s. 1: 254.
Morituri: Teias. (H. Sudermann) Poet-Lore, 9: 330.
Morland, George. (J. C. Van Dyke) Cent. 37: 504.
Morlattan, Pa., Missions at, 1760. (B. F. Owen) Pennsyl. M. 25: 372.
Morley, Henry. Acad. 55: 326.
— Life of. Ath. '98, 2: 633.
Morley, John. (T. Bouran) Westm. 154: 117. — Fortn. 70: 249. — (N. Hapgood) Contemp. 72: 368.
— as Politician. Sat. R. 92: 581, 622.
— Opposed to British Imperialism. Sat. R. 87: 69.
— A Study by a Member of Parliament. Cent. 36: 874.
— Verdict of History on. Fortn. 76: 322.
— Warnings by. (R. Ogden) Nation, 68: 103.
Mormon, Book of, Origin of. (P. B. Pierce) Am. Anthrop. 1: 675.
— Law of the Book of. (J. Williams) Am. Law Q. 34: 219.

Mormon Power in America, The. (J. M. Scanland) Gunton's M. 18: 131.

Mormon Question, The. (J. E. Wing) Outl. 64: 884.
— Revival of the. (E. Young) No. Am. 168: 476.

Mormon Theogony. (J. D. Gillilau) Meth. R. 58: 777.

Mormonism, and the Mormon War in Missouri. (W. F. Switzler) Midland, 11: 296.
— Anti-polygamy. (H. Lesan) Midland, 8: 300.
— Congressman-elect Roberts's Position in Regard to. (J. M. Chapple) Nat'l M. (Bost.) 11: 377.
— Danger from. (R. W. Beers) Bib. Sac. 58: 469.
— Indictment against. (G. E. Ackerman) Meth. R. 61: 388.
— Its History, Doctrines, Strength, Methods, and Aims. (P. Anstadt) Luth. Q. 30: 228.

Mormons. (W. J. Larned) Lippinc. 60: 382. — (R. L. Hartt) Atlan. 85: 261. — (C. B. Spahr) Outl. 64: 305.
— in Mexico. (C. W. Kindrick) R. of Rs. (N. Y.) 19: 702.
— James J. Strang's Beaver Island Colony. (A. N. Somers) Nat'l M. (Bost.) 14: 115.
— Passing of. (A. L. Mearkle) Arena, 23: 378.
— Truth about. (C. C. Goodwin) Munsey, 23: 310.
— A Word for the. (T. W. Curtis) Arena, 21: 715.

Morning Calls; Mrs. Patrick Campbell. Eng. Illust. 17: 28.

Morning-glories, Wonderful, of Japan. (E. R. Scidmore) Cent. 33: 281.

Morning Musicale, The Year's Work of the. Music, 16: 509.

Morning's Imbroglio, A. Eng. Illust. 22: 69.

Morocco. (H. E. M. Stutfield) National, 37: 126.
— as an Independent Power, Possible Collapse of. Asia. R. 30: 63.
— Berbers of. (W. B. Harris) Anthrop. J. 27: 61.
— Cafés of. (S. L. Bensusan) Idler, 15: 583.
— Central, Nomadic Berbers of. (W. B. Harris) Geog. J. 9: 638.
— A Coming Problem of North Africa. (H. M. Grey) Monthly R. 1, no. 3: 75.
— The First Woman's Hospital in. (M. J. Meath) 19th Cent. 43: 1002.
— French Activity in. (A. Krausse) Indep. 52: 1544.
— French Interest in. Sat. R. 89: 450.
— Future of. (H. M. Grey) National, 33: 670. — Sat. R. 87: 518.
— in 1899, Present Aspect of Affairs in. Asia. R. 27: 338.
— Land of Woe. (M. J. Meath) 19th Cent. 49: 1050.
— Memories of. Cornh. 82: 75. Same art. Ecl. M. 135: 538. Same art. Liv. Age, 226: 495.
— Menelek and. Ecl. M. 135: 268.
— The Mogador Conflict. (I. Perdicaris) Asia. R. 29: 84.
— Notes on. (Isabella B. Bishop) Monthly R. 5, no. 1: 89.
— Past and Present. Quar. 192: 336.
— Piracy in. (I. Perdicaris) Asia. R. 24: 325.
— Pirates of. (B. Meakin) Scot. R. 33: 73.
— Question of. (W. B. Harris) Blackw. 168: 1.
— — and the War. (W. B. Harris) National, 32: 29.
— Riding and Camping in. Chamb. J. 78: 504.
— Russia and. Fortn. 73: 258.
— South, A Ride in. (F. W. Wynn) Macmil. 79: 348. Same art. Liv. Age, 221: 295.
— Spain and. (A. G. Spilsbury) Fortn. 76: 222.
— A Special Mission to. (E. Montet) Asia. R. 32: 306.
— A Swan's Song from. (A. J. Dawson) Fortn. 76: 117.
— Up-to-date. (H. R. Haweis) Fortn. 72: 270.
— Yesterday and To-day in. (B. Meakin) Forum, 30: 364.

Morocco City, The Imperial. (A. G. Aflalo) Pall Mall M. 20: 53.

Morphological Museum as an Educational Factor in the University System. (G. S. Huntington) Science, n. s. 13: 601.

Morphology, Experimental. (G. F. Atkinson) Nature, 57: 41. — (G. F. Atkinson) Science, 6: 538.
— — Davenport's. Am. Natural. 33: 514.
— of Higher Plants, Goebel on. (D. H. Campbell) Am. Natural. 32: 606.
— of Pennaria Tiarella, McCrady on. (Martin Smallwood) Am. Natural. 33: 861.

Morrant's Half-sovereign; a story. (E. Phillpotts) Cornh. 75: 487.

Morrell, Wm., Bigamist. (F. S. Potter) Cornh. 80: 95.

Morrill, Justin S. (H. White) Nation, 68: 5.
— and Popular Education. (H. Babson) Outl. 68: 81.
— Notable Letters from Political Friends. Forum, 24: 137, 267, 402.
— Oldest U. S. Senator. (E. J. Edwards) Chaut. 26: 515.

Morris, Clara. Her First Appearance on the New York Stage. (C. Morris) McClure, 16: 201.
— Life on the Stage. (I. A. Pyle) Dial (Ch.) 31: 322.
— Stage Notes. Critic, 38: 25, 445. 39: 59.

Morris, Harrison S., with portrait. Bk. News, 17: 386.

Morris, Wm. (S. Gwynn) Macmil. 78: 153. — Acad. 52: 394. — Ed. R. 185: 63. — (Walter Crane) Scrib. M. 22: 88. — (W. H. Winslow) New Eng. M. n. s. 16: 161. — (J. B. Renyon) Meth. R. 59: 386. — Blackw. 166: 16. — Quar. 190: 487. — (J. L. Gilder) Critic, 35: 620. — Library, n. s. 2: 113. — (F. Tiffany) New World, 9: 103.
— and the Arts and Crafts in London. (E. R. Pennell) Nation, 69: 313.
— and Dante Gabriel Rossetti. Ed. R. 191: 356.
— and Pre-Raphaelism. (A. Streeter) Month, 94: 595.
— and Reviewers. Citizen, 2: 362.
— and Some of his Books. (E. L. Cary) Bk. Buyer, 22: 309.
— Art of. (R. Sturgis) Archit. R. 7: 440.
— — Vallance's. (R. Sturgis) Nation, 66: 111. — (G. M. R. Twose) Dial (Ch.) 25: 343. — Spec. 81: 624.
— as a Poet, with portrait. Bk. Buyer, 13: 917.
— Bibliography of, Scott's. Ath. '97, 2: 591.
— The Books of, Forman on. Ath. '98, 1: 80.
— Commonweal. (L. D. Abbott) New Eng. M. n. s. 20: 428.
— Kelmscott Press. Critic, 35: 910.
— Labor Church at Leek; a sketch. (L. D. Abbott) Bk. Buyer, 16: 31.
— Last Romances of. (L. J. Block) Dial (Ch.) 24: 320.
— Life of, Mackail's. Bookman, 9: 533. — Acad. 56: 525. — Ath. '99, 1: 587.
— — A Study in Biography. (G. White) Conserv. R. 2: 347.
— Life-work of. (F. S. Ellis) J. Soc. Arts, 46: 618.
— Mackail on. Church Q. 51: 47.
— Poem to. (G. B. Stuart) Argosy, 63: 136.
— Poetry of. (N. Smith) Fortn. 68: 937.
— Printing of. (T. L. De Vinne) Bk. Buyer, 13: 920.
— Revolutionist and Poet. (D. F. Hannigan) Westm. 147: 117.
— Some Memories of. (K. Tynan) Bk. Buyer, 13: 925.
— The Sundering Flood. Acad. 53: 304.
— Water of the Wondrous Isles. Acad. 52: 343.
— Work and Life of. (W. Crane) M. of Art, 20: 89.

Morrison, Arthur. Acad. 52: 493.

Morrison, George Ernest. (H. A. Strong) Spec. 85: 75.

"Mors, Morituri te Salutamus;" a poem. (F. B. Money-Coutts) Ecl. M. 132: 728.

Mort à La Mode, La; a story. (A. Hope Hawkins) Idler, 14: 571.

Mort d'eté ; a poem. (A. E. Glase) Argosy, **64**: 544.

Mortality, The Great, in the 14th Century. (E. P. Cheney) Pop. Sci. Mo. **59**: 402.

— in Extreme Old Age. (H. Westergaard) Econ. J. **9**: 315.

Mortar, Roman. Am. Arch. **70**: 69.

Mortars, Domestic. (F. Peacock) Antiq. n. s. **33**: 243, 362.

Mortgage Guarantees. Bank. M. (Lond.) **68**: 789.

Mortgaged Nations. (G. E. Walsh) Gunton's M. **21**:61.

Mortgages and Trade Fixtures. Law Q. **15**: 165.

— Foreign. Bank M. (Lond.) **63**: 129.

— Taxation of. Outl. **64**: 243.

— — in New York, Proposed. (C. E. Sprague) Gunton's M. **18**: 218.

— — A Just Tax Law. Outl. **66**: 728.

Mortification of the Flesh. (P. L. Dunbar) Lippinc. **68**: 250.

Mortillet, Louis Laurent Gabriel de, Sketch of. Pop. Sci. Mo. **54**: 546.

Mortmain in Thought and Life. Spec. **85**: 365.

Morton, Alexander, and Co., Weavers. (J. L. Caw) Art J. **52**: 7, 78.

Morton, Martha. Critic, **30**: 80.

— Bachelor's Romance. (G. B. Shaw) Sat. R. **85**: 75.

Morton, Oliver P., Foulke's Life of. Am. Hist. R. **4**: 570.

Mortuary Chapel, Design for a. (Mrs. G. F. Watts) Studio (Internat.) **5**: 235.

Mosaic. (C. R. Lamb) Chaut. **30**: 246.

— Historic Development of. (G. W. Hayler) Am. Arch. **71**: 68, (G. Birdwood) **71**: 94. — (G. Birdwood) J. Soc. Arts, **49**: 265.

— recently discovered at Jerusalem. (F. J. Bliss) Bib. World, **18**: 46.

Mosaics, Improved Process of Manufacturing. (J. Frankl. Inst. **145**: 198.

— in Venice. Am. Arch. **70**: 87.

Mosasaur Skeleton, A Complete Osseous and Cartilaginous. (H. F. Osborn) Science, n. s. **10**: 919.

Mosasaurs, Lizards, and Sphenodon. (H. F. Osborn) Am. Natural, **34**: 1.

Moscheles, Ignaz, in Scotland. (J. C. Hadden) Scot. R. **33**: 94.

Moscow. (A. Symons) Liv. Age, **216**: 19.

— The Retreat from, and Passage of the Beresina. (Colonel Turner) Un. Serv. M. **14**: 335, 463, 585. **15**: 8, 113.

— — by One of the Old Guard. (A. J. Butler) Cornh. **78**: 218. Same art. Ecl. M. **131**: 388.

— A Review in. (C. W. G. Richardson) Un. Serv. M. **20**: 345.

Mose Martin's Temptation ; a story. (C. Lanier) Indep. **53**: 1067.

Moseley, Edward Strong. (W. C. Todd) N. E. Reg. **54**: 377.

Moser, Mary. (F. Miller) Eng. Illust. **19**: 434.

Moses and the Exodus. (G. F. Price) J. Mil. Serv. Inst. **7**: 327.

— as a Scholar. (H. H. Hall) Luth. Q. **27**: 531.

— Education of. Meth. R. **57**: 809.

— in Egypt, Story of, told for Children. (W. F. Adeney) Bib. World, **13**: 330.

— Religion of. (J. P. Peters) J. Bib. Lit. **20**: 101.

— Story of. (C. A. Powell) Nat'l M. (Bost.) **9**: 170.

Moses, Belle. Writer, **14**: 27.

Moses, the Tale of a Dog. (F. J. Hagan) Outing, **32**: 569.

Moslem Confraternities of North Africa. (W. B. Harris) Blackw. **170**: 545.

Mosquito, The, and Yellow Fever. (G. M. Sternberg) Am. J. Soc. Sci. **39**: 84.

Mosquito Coast, Sport on. (S. Vail) Outing, **30**: 246.

Mosquitoes. (W. S. Harwood) Outing, **38**: 572. — (Grant Allen) Strand, **15**: 395.

— and Malaria. Quar. **192**: 291. — (R. Ross) Nature, **61**: 522. — (R. Ross) J. Soc. Arts, **49**: 18. — (L. O. Howard) Cent. **39**: 941. — (P. H. Grimshaw) Knowl. **22**: 49. — Chamb. J. **76**: 678. — (R. Ross) Pop. Sci. Mo. **56**: 42.

— — Investigations on. (Dr. Daniels) Nature, **60**: 333.

— as Transmitters of Disease. (L. O. Howard) R. of Rs. (N. Y.) **24**: 192.

— Goldfish as Destroyers of Mosquito Larvæ. (W. L. Underwood) Science, **14**: 1017.

— How a Southern City Abolished. (N. T. Barton) Indep. **53**: 1660.

— Transmission of Yellow Fever by. (G. M. Sternberg) Pop. Sci. Mo. **59**: 225. — Nation, **72**: 351.

Mosquitos ; a story. (M. H. Robins) Temp. Bar, **120**: 352.

Mossback's Peril, A ; a story. (F. W. Calkins) Midland, **9**: 337.

Most Peculiar Man, The ; a story. (E. W. Cooley) Midland, **7**: 53.

Most Remarkable Case, A. (Mrs. H. A. Wales) Midland, **7**: 443.

Moth, The Codling. (F. W. Card) Garden & F. **10**: 302.

— Gypsy, in Massachusetts. New Eng. M. n. s. **21**: 677.

Mother. (M. L. Knapp) Atlan. **85**: 110.

Mother, The, in the Church. (L. R. Meyer) Meth. R. **61**: 716.

Mother, The ; a song-drama. (F. M. Hueffer) Fortn. **75**: 741.

Mother, The ; a story. (Maarten Maartens) Good Words, **39**: 51, 126, 195.

Mother and Child. (H. C. Potter) Harper, **104**: 102.

Mother-of-pearl and its Sources. (R. Lydekker) Knowl. **22**: 97.

"Mother Goose" and Baby-life. (J. Monteith) Educa. **19**: 206.

Mother's Touch ; a poem. (B. A. Macnab) Canad. M. **14**: 100.

Motherhood and Marriage spiritually considered. (Lydia F. Dickinson) N. Church R. **4**: 346.

— as a Profession. (J. B. Walker) Cosmopol. **25**: 89.

— Should the College train for ? (H. H. Backus) Outl. **61**: 461.

— Wild. (C. G. D. Roberts) Outing, **37**: 501.

Motherless Heroines in English Classics. (G. Withington) Poet-Lore, **11**: 259.

Mothers and Daughters. (Florence Bell) Monthly R. **4**, no. 1: 98. Same art. Ecl. M. **137**: 492. Same art. Liv. Age, **230**: 593. — Spec. **87**: 84.

— in Council. (Elaine G. Eastman) Outl. **58**: 281.

— in Israel. (T. L. Cuyler) Sund. M. **28**: 44.

— Modern. (D. Dale) Argosy, **68**: 145.

— National Congress of. (E. A. Richardson, J. W. Hoyt, and F. Reed) Arena, **17**: 857.

— Worldly, In Defence of. (E. Desart) National, **29**: 382.

Mothers of Honoré, The ; a story. (M. H. Catherwood) Harper, **99**: 136.

Mothers' Clubs of St. Paul. (Elaine G. Eastman) Outl. **58**: 725.

Moths and Tulips. (S. Olivier) Contemp. **75**: 343. Same art. Liv. Age, **221**: 241. Same art. Ecl. M. **132**: 866.

— Case. (M. T. D. Badenoch) Pop. Sci. Mo. **53**: 656.

Motion and its Reversal. (W. S. Franklin) Science, n. s. **9**: 70.

— in Animals and Plants, as related to Electricity. (J. Burdon-Sanderson) Nature, **60**: 343.

— Objective Presentation of Harmonic. (Carl Barus) Science, n. s. **9**: 385.

Motion of a Heavenly Body in a Resisting Medium. (G. A. Bliss) Pop. Astron. **6**: 20.

Motive Power. Steam Turbines and High Speed Navigation. (C. A. Parsons) Nature, **61**: 424.

Motley, John Lothrop, Bismarck and. (J. P. Grund) No. Am. **167**: 360, 569.

Motor, Diesel. J. Frankl. Inst. **152**: 371. — (E. D. Meier) J. Frankl. Inst. **146**: 241.

— Pelton, Efficiency Surface for. (W. K. Hatt) J. Frankl. Inst. **143**: 455.

Motor-cars, Flying. Spec. **87**: 277.

— Some Experiences with Modern. (Dawson Turner) Chamb. J. **77**: 341. Same art. Liv. Age, **225**: 636.

Motor Cycling vs. Motoring. (M. C. Krarup) Outing, **37**: 207.

Motor Impulse, Diffusion. (C. Wissler and W. W. Richardson) Psychol. R. **7**: 29.

Motor-poacher, The; a story. (A. S. Appelbee) Eng. Illust. **21**: 563.

Motor Traffic. (Sir D. Salomons) J. Soc. Arts, **45**: 581.

Motor Trucks, Steam. (J. G. Dudley) Engin. M. **21**: 260.

Motorman Cupid; a story. (Melville Chater) Cosmopol. **28**: 290.

Motors, Benzine and Petroleum. (G. Lieckfeld) Engin. M. **17**: 818.

Mott, Samuel, of Preston, Conn., Marriages by. (F. Palmer) N. E. Reg. **55**: 176.

Mottoes for a House. Acad. **58**: 171.

Mouat, F. J. Geog. J. **9**: 331. — J. Soc. Arts, **45**: 159.

Mouchrabiehs of Cairo. (I. B. Starr) Art J. **49**: 110.

Moujik, The, and his Home. (F. Whishaw) Chamb. J. **75**: 321.

Mould and Vase; poem. (E. Wharton) Atlan. **88**: 343.

Mould, The Maple. (A. S. Wilson) Knowl. **20**: 89.

Moulding Machine. (J. Horner) Cassier, **20**: 311.

Mouldings, The Theory of. (C. H. Walker) Archit. R. **6**: 83, 95, 108, 139. **7**: 5.

Moulton, Louise Chandler, Poetry of. (H. A. Clark) Poet-Lore, **12**: 114.

Moulton, William Fiddian. (P. W. Bunting) Sund. M. **27**: 245. — (E. D. Burton) Bib. World, **11**: 325. — (G. G. Findlay) Lond. Q. **93**: 52.

Mound, Ancient, at How Tallon. (R. A. Getty) Reliquary, **38**: 105.

Mound at Marathon, The; a poem. (A. E. Hanscom) Chaut. **31**: 625.

Mound-builder Remains in New York. (A. L. Benedict) Am. Antiq. **23**: 99.

Mound-dwelling, An Aberdeenshire. (D. MacRitchie) Antiq. n. s. **33**: 135.

Mounds, Aboriginal, of Georgia Coast, Moore on. Nature, **57**: 400.

— Aztec, Romance of Opening. (Dr. Gann) Chamb. J. **78**: 373.

— Fairy. (D. MacRitchie) Antiq. n. s. **36**: 52, 70.

Moung Tu's Revenge; a story. Eng. Illust. **19**: 483.

Mt. Caburn Camp, near Lewes, Excavations at. (A. L. Fox) Archæol. **46**: 423.

Mount Desert, Romance of. (S. A. Eliot) New Eng. M. n. s. **20**: 682.

Mount Edgcumbe House, England. (Lady Ernestine Edgcumbe) Pall Mall M. **12**: 5.

Mount Holyoke College. (H. E. Hooker) New Eng. M. n. s. **15**: 545.

Mt. Lowe Railway Observatory. (E. L. Larkin) Pop. Astron. **9**: 359.

Mt. Melleray Monastery, Ireland. (C. Johnson) Outl. **67**: 265.

Mt. St. Elias, Expedition of Prince Luigi of Savoy to, in 1897. Nat. Geog. M. **9**: 93.

Mountain Climbing, Practical. (A. S. Peck) Outing, **38**: 695.

Mountain Climbing; to the Summit of Mount Hood. (M. K. Locke) Cosmopol. **25**: 369.

Mountain Lion, Trapping a. (J. E. Badger, jr.) Outing, **35**: 268.

Mountain Moloch. (D. Osborne) Lippinc. **60**: 3.

Mountain-pine, The. (René Bazin) Liv. Age, **230**: 842.

Mountain Ranges of the Great Basin. (W. M. Davis) Science, n. s. **14**: 457.

Mountain Structure and its Origin. (J. Geikie) Internat. Mo. **3**: 17, 202.

Mountain Tourists, Women. (T. Girm-Hochberg) Chaut. **25**: 553.

Mountain Whites of the South. (C. J. Ryder) Educa. **18**: 67.

Mountaineering. Ascent of the Grand Teton. (W. O. Owen) Outing, **38**: 302.

— The Cup and the Lip in. (F. Connell) Cornh. **85**: 229. Same art. Ecl. M. **137**: 620. Same art. Liv. Age, **230**: 802.

— Modern. Ed. R. **186**: 33.

— Pioneer Climbers. (T. G. Bonney) Nature, **60**: 274.

— Recent. Quar. **194**: 126.

— Recent Achievements in. (W. M. Conway) No. Am. **164**: 537.

Mountaineers, Early. Spec. **83**: 222.

— Southern. (J. Fox, jr.) Scrib. M. **29**: 387-556.

Mountains, Age of. (L. J. Lobley) Knowl. **20**: 136.

— — of British. (J. L. Lobley) Knowl. **20**: 92.

— Concerning. (G. L. Bell) National, **38**: 616.

— Effect of, on the Quality of the Atmosphere. (A. E. Douglass) Pop. Astron. **7**: 354.

— Experiments among. Chamb. J. **74**: 95.

Mountains of the Moon, The; a story. (L. Housman) Pall Mall M. **18**: 78.

Mountebank, The; a story. (E. E. Peake) Nat'l M. (Bost.) **13**: 598.

Mountebanks, Strolling. (A. Castaigne) Harper, **103**: 841.

Mounted Infantry, Importance of. (A. M. Low) Forum, **30**: 310.

Mounted Troops in War. (E. T. H. Hutton) J. Mil. Serv. Inst. **16**: 344.

Mouravieff, Count, and his Successor. (W. T. Stead) Contemp. **78**: 326.

Mourne Mountains, The. (C. Edwardes) Gent. M. n. s. **65**: 128. — (G. A. J. Cole) Knowl. **21**: 121.

Mouse, Pocket, in Confinement. (J. A. Allen) Am. Natural. **32**: 583.

Mouse, The; a story. (E. Clifford) Temp. Bar, **113**: 604.

"Mouse, The;" a story of the Diplomatic Corps. (L. N. Clark) Cent. **38**: 297.

Mouse Club, The. (L. Wain) Eng. Illust. **20**: 398.

Mouse Cure, The; a story. (W. L. Alden) Idler, **12**: 457.

Moussorgsky, M. P., Russian Musician. (A. Pougin) Music, **13**: 438.

Mouthful of Husks, A; a story. (O. Barron) Pall Mall M. **15**: 529.

Movement, Irritability and. (W. Haacke) Chaut. **28**: 276.

— Sensation of, Does it originate in the Joint? (W. B. Pillsbury) Am. J. Psychol. **12**: 346.

Movements, American Fondness for. (E. L. Fell) Lippinc. **63**: 677.

— Development of, Comparative Observations on. (Kathleen C. Moore) Pedagog. Sem. **8**: 231.

Moving Finger, The; a story. (E. Wharton) Harper, **102**: 627.

Mowat, Sir Oliver, with portrait. (W. Clayton) Green Bag, **10**: 1.

Mowbray, Sir John. Parliamentary Reminiscences: Seventy Years at Westminster. Blackw. **167**: 26.

— Seventy Years at Westminster. Sat. R. **91**: 210.

Mowry Family Monument, Woonsocket, R. I. (W. A. Mowry) N. E. Reg. **52**: 207.

Moynton Prizes, Stories of the. (A. D. Savage) Outl. **67**: 211.

Mozart. (Edvard Grieg) Cent. **33**: 140.
— and his Manuscripts. (C. Malherbe) Music, **21**: 1.
— in France, with portraits. (H. Buffenoir) Music, **16**: 160.
— New Versions of. (Esther Singleton) Bookman, **11**: 31.

M. P. Errant, An; a story. Belgra. **94**: 257, 385.

Mr. Appleby's Vote. (C. V. Glen) Cent. **41**: 17.

Mr. Bawler. (H. B. Leatham) Sund. M. **27**: 766.

Mr. Bellou's Watch; a story. (H. Spender) Eng. Illust. **17**: 513.

Mr. Blakeley's Boomerang. Un. Serv. (Phila.) **17**: 263.

Mr. Braithwaite's Perplexity. (Mrs. H. Synge) Chamb. J. **76**: 81-120.

Mr. Brisher's Treasure. (H. G. Wells) Strand, **17**: 469.

Mr. Carter's Candidacy. (E. C. Shipman) New Eng. M. n. s. **15**: 721.

Mr. Cholmondeley's Indecision; a story. (E. G. Wheelwright) Argosy, **68**: 468.

Mr. Cornelius Johnson, Office Seeker; a story. (P. L. Dunbar) Cosmopol. **26**: 420.

Mr. Dawson; a sketch. (C. M. Priest) Belgra. **92**: 71.

Mr. Gedge's Cat's-paw. (C. Hyne) Canad. M. **11**: 493.

Mr. Grigsby's Way. (A. S. Winston) Cent. **38**: 897.

Mr. Hapgood's Gospel. (W. Payne) Atlan. **87**: 706.

Mr. No-Name. (R. Jackburns) Sund. M. **30**: 547.

Mr. Perkins's Wife; a story. (H. Fuller) Harper, **99**: 147.

Mr. Perry's Wooing; a story. (H. Godfrey) Pall Mall M. **15**: 305.

Mr. Potter's Speech. (J. Workman) Chamb. J. **74**: 497-517.

Mr. Skipper's Lodgers; a story. (J. E. Cussans) Gent. M. n. s. **61**: 353.

Mr. Smedley's Guest. (E. S. Chamberlayne) Atlan. **87**: 213.

Mr. Smith, Perthshire. (A. E. Brand) New Eng. M. n. s. **24**: 396.

Mr. Tumbledowndick; a story. (R. Jackbern) Sund. M. **29**: 813.

Mr. Willie's Wedding-veil; a story. (M. T. Earle) Harper, **96**: 131.

Mr. Wyatt; a story. (C. M. Nicklin) Gent. M. n. s. **67**: 74.

Mrs. Bingham's Foot; a story. (W. Pett Ridge) Idler, **11**: 716.

Mrs. Brown of Brownsville; a story. (F. W. Calkins) Midland, **10**: 145.

Mrs. Brown's Christmas. (J. T. Connor) Midland, **7**: 75.

Mrs. Clyde; a story. (Mrs. Van R. Cruger) Cosmopol. **23**: 495 — **24**: 413.

Mrs. Conyers to the Rescue; a story. (I. Coventry) Argosy, **71**: 416.

Mrs. Dimson's Diamond Jubilee; a story. (H. Stanford) Argosy, **71**: 150.

Mrs. Evans's Last Sensation; a story. (F. W. Wharton) Cosmopol. **32**: 199.

Mrs. Fenimore; a story. (J. W. Sherer) Gent. M. n. s. **60**: 586. Same art. Ecl. M. **131**: 224.

Mrs. Gaylord's Cellar Party. Lippinc. **67**: 242.

Mrs. H. Harrison Welles's Shoes. (J. L. Williams) Scrib. M. **24**: 688.

Mrs. Hiram Pointdexter's Front Door. (R. Smylie) New Eng. M. n. s. **18**: 600.

Mrs. Lawton's Little Dinner; a story. (Carolyn Wells) Cosmopol. **32**: 61.

Mrs. Luttrel's Husband. (E. Burrowes) Argosy, **70**: 207.

Mrs. McCafferty's Mistake. (S. MacManus) Cent. **40**: 430.

Mrs. Mary Chiddimore; a story. (E. M. O. Marshall) Temp. Bar, **113**: 436.

Mrs. Merington's Philosophy; a story. (C. O'C. Eccles) Pall Mall M. **17**: 335.

Mrs. Meriwether's Wedding. (C. P. Lamar) Lippinc. **60**: 522.

Mrs. Mills's Economy. Chamb. J. **76**: 573.

Mrs. Norton's Visitor. (L. Hardy) Sund. M. **28**: 189.

Mrs. Omadu's Totem; a story. (G. Leatherdale) Pall Mall M. **15**: 571.

Mrs. Oriel; a story. Temp. Bar, **123**: 206. Same art. Liv. Age, **230**: 103.

Mrs. Pettingrew's Question; a story. (E. D. Deland) Harper, **97**: 96.

Mrs. Portingale's Lunatic. (W. E. Cule) Chamb. J. **77**: 93.

Mrs. Rashleigh's Mistake; a story. (Lady V. Sanders) Argosy, **65**: 302.

Mrs. Russell's Sister. (A. E. Brand) Lippinc. **62**: 731.

Mrs. Simpson's Poodle; a story. (Laura B. Thornely) Midland, **9**: 77.

Mrs. Skimp joins the Army. (A. K. Spero) Overland, n. s. **36**: 257.

Mrs. Tea-meeting Smith. (E. S. Atkinson) Canad. M. **10**: 106.

Mrs. Tetlow's Thanksgiving Guests. (K. W. Patch) Nat'l M. (Bost.) **11**: 213.

Mrs. Thankful's Charge. (N. Brooks) Cent. **40**: 563.

Mrs. Upton's Device; a story. (J. K. Bangs) Harper, **95**: 726.

Mrs. Walton's Holiday; a story. Argosy, **64**: 423.

Mrs. Whin's Caddie. (R. Ramsay) Chamb. J. **74**: 347. Same art. Liv. Age, **214**: 105.

"Mrs. William;" a story. (H. R. Kent) Nat'l M. (Bost.) **11**: 420.

Mucha, Alphonse Marie; a great decorative artist. (Frederic Lees) M. of Art, **23**: 205. — Artist (N. Y.) **30**: 113.

Muckley, Louis Fairfax, Work of. Studio (Lond.) **4**: 146.

Muddy Corner, A. (R. C. Nightingale) Good Words, **40**: 307. Same art. Liv. Age, **222**: 36. Same art. Ecl. M. **133**: 255.

Mud-marks, Mystery of the. (L. James) Macmil. **81**: 59.

Mudie's Select Library, London. (T. W. Idle) Pub. Lib. **3**: 339.

Mueller, F. von; His Services to California. (C. H. Shinn) Garden & F. **10**: 381.

Mueller, Fritz. Nature, **56**: 546.

Mueller, George, with portrait. (S. M. Jackson) Char. R. **10**: 255. — With portrait. (W. T. Stead) R. of Rs. (N. Y.) **17**: 572.

Mueller, Max. (C. Bendall) Ath. '00, **2**: 580. — (W. Hopkins) Nation, **71**: 343. — (A. Lang) Contemp. **78**: 784. — With portrait. (T. J. McCormack) Open Court, **14**: 734. — (B. E. Smith) Critic, **37**: 510. — Dial (Ch.) **29**: 345. — Liv. Age, **227**: 520. — (K. Blind) Westm. **155**: 529.
— and his Work. (A. V. W. Jackson) Forum, **30**: 620.
— and the Religious Parliament. (Lady Blennerhassett) Open Court, **15**: 115.
— and Royalty. (H. Vivian) Sat. R. **84**: 283.
— at Oxford. Atlan. **87**: 867.
— Auld Lang Syne. (A. MacMechan) Citizen, **4**: 61.— Music, **14**: 111. — With portrait. (M. Kingsley) Bk. Buyer, **16**: 215.
— Autobiography. (E. G. Johnson) Dial (Ch.) **30**: 260.
— Estimate of. With portrait. (C. Johnston) R. of Rs. (N. Y.) **22**: 703.
— Memories of. (M. D. Conway) No. Am. **171**: 884.

Mueller, Max. Personal Reminiscences. (E. D. War-field) Outl. **66**: 655.

Muenster, Sebastian. (C. R. Beazley) Geog. J. **17**: 423.

Muensterberg, Hugo, on the New Education. (J. Lee) Educa. R. **20**: 123.

— on School Reform. (W. S. Jackman) Educa. R. **20**: 85.

— Psychology and Life. (R. S. Holdane) Mind, **25**: 205.

Muff, The. (M. S. Patterson) Cosmopol. **26**: 21.

Muffet, Thomas. Health's Improvement, Extracts from. Westm. **153**: 209.

Muggletonians, and their Religious Movement. (J. Hyde) N. Church R. **7**: 215.

Mugwump, Opportunity of the. Sewanee, **3**: 1.

Muhlenberg, Peter, Some Letters of. Pennsyl. M. **21**: 488.

Muir Glacier, The, Silent City of. (D. S. Jordan) Pop. Sci. Mo. **51**: 161.

Mule, The Common. (R. B. Townshend) 19th Cent. **47**: 130.

Mule, The; a story. (H. S. Scott) Cosmopol. **26**: 222.

Mules as Pack-animals. Spec. **80**: 619.

Müller. *See* Mueller.

Mullet Fishing. (L. R. Meekins) Outing, **36**: 551.

Mullion Church, Cornwall, Door in. (M. E. Hartland) Reliquary, **41**: 128.

Mulready, William. Art J. **51**: 65.

Mummers, Christmas, at Rugby. (W. H. D. Rouse) Folk-Lore, **10**: 186.

Mummies and Scarabs. (J. C. Haig) Chamb. J. **74**: 315.

Mummification, especially of the Brain. (D. S. Lamb) Am. Anthrop. **3**: 294.

Mummy, The, and the Moth. (A. W. McClelland) Overland, n. s. **35**: 304.

Munger, Nicholas, of Guilford, Conn. (R. D. Smyth) N. E. Reg. **54**: 46.

Munich, Exhibition at, 1900. Artist (N. Y.) **29**: 135.

— Festsaalbau; Gallery of Beauty. (Augustus Van Cleef) Cosmopol. **30**: 451.

— in Summer. (A. Lodeman) Nation, **65**: 127.

— Prince Regent Theatre, Opening of. (E. Hoffmann) Music, **20**: 289.

— St. George's Day in. (M. Maskell) Month, **91**: 386.

— "Secession" Exhibition, 1899. (G. Keyssner) Studio (Internat.) **8**: 178.

— — and Glas-Palast Exhibition. (A. Werschler) Artist (N. Y.) **24**: 24.

Municipal Administration, Bibliography of, 1897, 1898. (R. C. Brooks) Munic. Aff. **1**: 224-783. **2**: 157-802.

— of Public Utilities. (J. R. Commons) Indep. **53**: 2633.

Municipal Activities in Germany (F. S. Hoffman) Outl. **58**: 1063.

Municipal Æsthetics from a Legal Standpoint. Munic. Aff. **3**: 715.

Municipal and Private Distribution of Water, Gas, and Electricity, Investigation of, by Labor Bureaus. (C. D. Wright and others) Econ. Stud. **3**, supp. no. **1**: 57.

Municipal Art. (Elma Graves) Am. J. Sociol. **6**: 673.
— (Isabel McDougall) Brush & P. **3**: 302, 342. — (F. S. Lamb) Munic. Aff. **1**: 674. — (C. H. Caffin) Harper, **100**: 655. — (L. A. Mead) Brush & P. **6**: 220.

— Civic Architecture. (C. R. Lamb) Munic. Aff. **2**: 46.

— Color in. (F. S. Lamb) Munic. Aff. **2**: 110.

— Conference on, Baltimore. Munic. Aff. **3**: 706.

— in American Cities. Munic. Aff. **2**: 1.

— in the Netherlands. (A. French) New Eng. M. n. s. **18**: 267.

— in New York, Future of. (J. DeW. Warner) Munic. Aff. **2**: 123.

— Mural Painting. (E. H. Blashfield) Munic. Aff. **2**: 98.

Municipal Art; Sculpture. (K. Bitter) Munic. Aff. **73**.

— A Word for. (E. H. Blashfield) Munic. Aff. **3**: 582.

Municipal Board, State. (J. W. Jenks) Munic. Aff. **2**: 411.

Municipal Co-operation, Limitations of Legislative Control of. (E. McQuillan) Am. Law R. **34**: 505.

Municipal Control of Electric Lighting. (Con. R. R. Bowker) Munic. Aff. **1**: 605. — (Pro. J. R. Commons) Munic. Aff. **1**: 631.

Municipal Corporations, Public Control of. (E. B. Smith) Atlan. **87**: 583.

Municipal Corruption, Ethical Survivals in. (Jane Addams) Int. J. Ethics, **8**: 273.

Municipal Development, A Year's. (C. R. Woodruff) Am. J. Sociol. **6**: 532.

Municipal Elections, Non-partisan. (G. C. Wright) Munic. Aff. **4**: 363.

Municipal Employment and Progress. (J. R. Commons) Munic. Aff. **4**: 294.

Municipal Enterprise, Cost of. (D. H. Davies) J. Soc. Arts, **47**: 224, 265.

Municipal Enterprises: ought they to be allowed to yield a Profit? (E. Canaan) Econ. J. **9**: 1.

Municipal Expenditure and National, Growth of. (Lord Avebury) J. Statis. Soc. **64**: 73.

Municipal Finance and Municipal Enterprise. (Sir H. H. Fowler) J. Statis. Soc. **63**: 383.

— Uniformity in. (C. W. Tooke) Munic. Aff. **2**: 195.

Municipal Franchises, The Future of. (H. P. Willis) Nation, **73**: 371.

Municipal Frontiers, Rectification of. (W. M. Acworth) Econ. J. **8**: 454.

Municipal Government. Classification of Municipal Receipts and Expenditures. Ann. Am. Acad. Pol. Sci. **12**: 112.

— Eaton on. (J. Bryce) Nation, **70**: 74.

— in the United States. (J. Ford) No. Am. **172**: 751.

— Now and a Hundred Years Ago. (C. R. Woodruff) Pop. Sci. Mo. **58**: 60.

Municipal Industries and the Ratepayer. (W. Smart) Econ. J. **11**: 169.

Municipal League, National, 15th Annual Meeting, Columbus. Ann. Am. Acad. Pol. Sci. **15**: 122.

Municipal Life, Chamberlain on. Spec. **79**: 677.

Municipal Lighting. (E. W. Bemis) Outl. **62**: 884.

Municipal Misgovernment and Corruption. (Frank Moss) Cosmopol. **32**: 102.

Municipal Monopolies, Bemis on. (J. H. Gray) J. Pol. Econ. **7**: 563.

Municipal Neutrality Laws of the United States. (H. C. Carbaugh) J. Mil. Serv. Inst. **15**: 69.

Municipal Ownership. (D. MacG. Means) Nation, **65**: 26.

— All Sorts of. (C. R. Woodruff) Outl. **68**: 111.

— and Corruption in American Cities. (J. W. Martin) Contemp. **76**: 856. Same art. Ecl. M. **134**: 287.

— Failure of. (H. H. Vreeland) Indep. **52**: 1165.

— of Docks in N. Y. City. (B. S. Coler) Munic. Aff. **4**: 207.

— of Gas. (E. M. Grout) Munic. Aff. **1**: 225, 290.

— — Reply. (A. R. Foote) Munic. Aff. **1**: 245.

— of Natural Monopolies. (R. T. Ely) No. Am. **172**: 445.

— of Street Railways. (J. DeW. Warner) Munic. Aff. **1**: 421. — (E. E. Higgins) Munic. Aff. **1**: 458.

— — in Detroit. (C. Moore) Q. J. Econ. **13**: 453. **14**: 121.

— of Telephones. (F. Brocklehurst) Econ. J. **10**: 552.

— — in Amsterdam. (P. Falkenburg and J. H. Van Zanten) Munic. Aff. **4**: 24.

— A Successful Substitute for. (A. F. Potts) R. of Rs. (N. Y.) **20**: 576.

"Muscovy" Company, Story of the. (L. Hart) New R. **17**: 92. Same art. Ecl. M. **129**: 422.

Muscular Exercise, Psychical Aspects of. (L. Gulick) Pop. Sci. Mo. **53**: 793.

Muse's Tragedy, The. (Edith Wharton) Scrib. M. **25**: 77.

Museum Sermon, The. (V. L. Whitechurch) Good Words, **40**: 810.

Museums. (R. Meldola) Nature, **58**: 217.

— as Educational Institutions. (O. C. Farrington) Educa. **17**: 481.

— as retarding the Advance of Science. (F. A. Bather) Science, **5**: 677.

— Conducive to Extinction of Animals. (R. Nyana) Sat. R. **90**: 268.

— Essays on, Flower's. Sci. Prog. **7**: xxxix.

— Formative Period in. (L. P. Gratacap) Science, n. s. **14**: 168.

— in Connection with Public Libraries. (C. Adler; M. Medlicott) Lib. J. **23**: supp. 94.

— The Making of. (L. B. Gratacap) Archit. R. **9**: 376.

— Notes on European. (E. O. Hovey) Am. Natural. **32**: 697. — (O. C. Farrington) Am. Natural. **33**: 763.

— Open Air, in Sweden. (G. Bröchner) Studio (Internat.) **12**: 158.

Mushroom Caves of Paris. (D. Griffith) Strand, **16**: 507.

Mushrooms, Cultivation of. (E. O. Orpet) Garden & F. **10**: 435.

— Edible and Poisonous. (G. M'Carthy) Chaut. **27**: 394.

— French, and Mushroom-growing. (R. H. Wallace) Chamb. J. **74**: 676.

— Poisonous. (C. S. Sargent) Garden & F. **10**: 469.

Music, African, Survival of, in America. (J. R. Murphy) Pop. Sci. Mo. **55**: 660.

— American, and European Fallacies. (O. G. Sonneck) Music, **19**: 220.

— Americanism in. (J. S. Van Cleve) Music, **15**: 123.

— and Æsthetic Theory. (H. M. Davis) Music, **12**: 329, 462.

— and Common Life. (Helen Place) Music, **19**: 543.

— and Literature. Macmil. **75**: 267.

— and Matrimony. (J. C. Hadden) Cornh. **79**: 497. Same art. Liv. Age, **221**: 575. Same art. Ecl. M. **133**: 33.

— and Men of Genius. (Cunningham Moffett) Music, **17**: 273.

— and Words. (F. Ritchie) Longm. **34**: 219. Same art. Ecl. M. **133**: 552. Same art. Liv. Age, **222**: 558.

— Anglo-Saxon. (W. H. Sheran) Westm. **147**: 567. Same art. Liv. Age, **214**: 60.

— Artistic Development in, Maitland's. (J. F. Runciman) Sat. R. **87**: 269.

— as an Art rather than a Teacher. (J. F. Runciman) Sat. R. **88**: 355.

— as a Civilizing Agency. (C. C. Eaglesfield) Cath. World, **72**: 711.

— as an Educational Factor. (M. Reilly) Cath. World, **68**: 603.

— as Medicine. (P. Pastnor) Music, **15**: 651.

— as Revealer of National Character. (M. Beerbohm) Sat. R. **90**: 80.

— at the French Exposition, 1900. (C. Eddy) Music, **16**: 589.

— Bas-relief Symbolizing, in Cathedral of Rimini. (J. G. Waller) Archæol. **52**: 175.

— Beginnings in. (R. Foresman) Music, **20**: 259.

— Best Books about. (J. Huneker) Bk. Buyer, **21**: 99.

— Children's, Program of. Music, **12**: 246.

— Church. (W. S. B. Mathews) Music, **19**: 145. — (James Taft Hatfield) Meth. R. **58**: 404.

Music, Church, Catholic. (E. Dickinson) Am. Cath. Q. **24**, no. 2: 141.

— — English. (J. F. Runciman) Sat. R. **89**: 232.

— — Ideal of. (E. Dickinson) Bib. Sac. **54**: 320.

— — Novel Class in. Music, **12**: 122.

— — Reforms in. (W. F. P. Stockley) Cath. World, **74**: 283.

— Classical; great Composers compared. (W. S. B. Mathews) Music, **11**: 327 — **12**: 365.

— Debt of Poetry to. (J. B. Chapman) Music, **14**: 589.

— Deterioration of. (Cesar Cui) Music, **17**: 150.

— Earth, Sky, and Air in Song. (W. H. Neidlinger) Music, **19**: 553.

— Effect of, on Caged Animals. (F. C. Baker) Am. Natural. **31**: 460.

— Effect on Imagination. (E. Swayne) Music, **16**: 258. — (W. S. B. Mathews) Music, **16**: 292.

— English, contrasted with French. (J. F. Runciman) Sat. R. **90**: 791.

— English, Foreign Influence. (J. F. Runciman) Sat. R. **91**: 173.

— — and English Musical Criticism. (E. Newman) Contemp. **80**: 734.

— — in 19th Century. (J. F. Runciman) Sat. R. **89**: 45.

— — MS. of 16th Century, in Library of Eton College. Archæol. **56**: 89.

— Evolution of. (W. S. B. Mathews) Music, **15**: 1.

— Examinations in, Curse of. (J. F. Runciman) Sat. R. **92**: 458.

— Field. (A. H. Merrill) J. Mil. Serv. Inst. **16**: 84.

— for Grade and Rural Teachers. (J. L. Mathews) Music, **12**: 254.

— Formality or Freedom in. (F. B. Arndt) Music, **14**: 174.

— Benj. Franklin's Relation to. (O. G. Sonneck) Music, **19**: 1.

— French. (J. F. Runciman) Sat. R. **86**: 846.

— Grace Notes, Proper Performance of. (W. S. B. Mathews) Music, **20**: 250.

— History of, Study of. (E. Dickinson) Music, **18**: 18, 128, 323.

— Home Study of. (W. S. B. Mathews) Music, **13**: 541.

— How to Hear. (R. Welton) Music, **11**: 504.

— How to Memorize. (J. S. Van Cleve) Music, **18**: 290.

— How to Study, alone. Music, **14**: 660.

— in Beloit College. Music, **18**: 183.

— in Beloit Schools. (Amy Z. Peavey) Music, **20**: 270.

— in Bohemia, Hungary, and Poland. (Octavia Hensel) Music, **12**: 567.

— in Boulder, Colo. (C. H. Farnsworth) Music, **16**: 415.

— in Chicago High Schools. (W. H. Fairbanks) Music, **18**: 604.

— in the Church. (L. C. Elson) Internat. Mo. **4**: 166.

— in the Congressional Library. Music, **14**: 609. **17**: 270.

— in Country Schools. (C. Lagerquist) Music, **14**: 328.

— in Des Moines, Iowa. (S. Urban) Midland, **10**: 257.

— in England, Century of. (J. F. Runciman) Sat. R. **91**: 11.

— in Fiction. (C. W. James) Cornh. **84**: 631.

— in Finland. (Anna C. Stephens) Music, **12**: 521.

— in German Universities. (M. Emmanuel) Chaut. **27**: 520. — (M. Emmanuel) Music, **15**: 272.

— in High-schools. (Wm. L. Prince) Music, **19**: 547.

— in the Insect World. (Albert of Godesberg) Music, **20**: 179.

— in a Liberal Education. (R. H. Howland) Music, **19**: 138.

— in London at Queen's Accession. (J. S. Curwen) J. Soc. Arts, **45**: 375.

Music Teachers, National Association of. (W. S. B. Mathews) Music, 12: 223.

— — New York Meeting, 1897. (W. S. B.-Mathews) Music, 12: 482.

— — Cincinnati Meeting, 1899. Music, 16: 301.

Music Teachers' Associations, their Trials and Needs. (W. S. B. Mathews) Music, 18: 375.

Music Teachers' Convention, Illinois State. Music, 20: 202.

Music Teaching. (J. F. Runciman) Sat. R. 88: 516.

— Defects in. (W. S. B. Mathews) Music, 20: 254.

— Difficulty of using New Compositions. (W. S. B. Mathews) Music, 20: 431.

— Use of Imitation in. (Helen Place) Music, 20: 39.

Musical Books, The Best. (F. H. Marling) Bk. Buyer, 16: 329, 417, 510.

Musical Clubs, Illinois Federation of. Music, 19: 609.

— National Federation of. Music, 17: 438.

— Women's Amateur. (Rose F. Thomas) Music, 20: 90.

Musical Comedy, The Doom of. (E. Kuhe) Theatre, 39: 182.

Musical Composers and "Artistes." (H. R. Haweis) Harper, 94: 471.

— Modern, in the Light of Contemporary Criticism. (A. Moszkowski) Forum, 22: 547.

Musical Composition, Greek, of Third Century, B. C. (Ludvik Kuba) Music, 11: 398.

Musical Conception, Development of. (Bertram C. Henry) Music, 11: 403.

Musical Consciousness, The. (H. M. Davies) Music, 12: 25, 171.

Musical Criticism. (Charles Dennee) Music, 13: 167.

Musical Culture, by hearing Music. (R. Welton) Music, 11: 388.

Musical Degrees, Bogus. Music, 19: 648.

Musical Drama. (Saint-Saens) Music, 18: 516.

— Interpretation of. (V. Maurel) Music, 14: 573.

Musical Duel; a story. (W. L. Alden) Idler, 12: 231.

Musical Education in Conservatories. (W. S. B. Mathews) Music, 20: 189.

— New Ideals in. (W. S. Pratt) Atlan. 86: 826.

Musical Endowments, Fields for. (W. S. B. Mathews) Music, 19: 449.

Musical Æsthetics. (Prof. Meyer) Music, 20: 149.

Musical Expression, Limits of. (J. S. Van Cleve) Music, 12: 418.

Musical Festival, Cincinnati. (W. S. B. Mathews) Music, 18: 261.

Musical Instinct. (J. Moos) Music, 14: 460.

Musical Instruments, Brass and Percussion. (A. C. G. Weld) Music, 11: 406.

— Chinese. (L. B. Starr) Music, 14: 499.

— Native American Stringed. (D. G. Brinton) Am. Antiq. 19: 19.

— of Japan. (L. E. Dew) Music, 17: 445.

— Self-playing. (W. S. B. Mathews) Music, 20: 186.

Musical Interpretation; memorizing. (W. S. B. Mathews) Music, 19: 35.

Musical Journalism. (W. S. B. Mathews) Music, 12: 342.

Musical Life, Humors of. (M. V. White) Cornh. 78: 109.

Musical Memory. (J. S. Van Cleve) Music, 12: 636. 13: 158.

Musical Mind-training. (T. C. Whitmer) Music, 16: 572.

Musical Notation, A New. Music, 12: 381. — (C. C. Guilford) Music, 13: 403.

— Guilford's System. (W. S. B. Mathews) Music, 13: 641.

Musical Notation; Wagner's New System. (W. Erhardt) J. Soc. Art, 49: 501.

— upon Lines and Spaces, Earliest System of. Archæol. 46: 389.

Musical Notes on Great Composers. (H. Clark, jr.) Music, 12: 311.

Musical Overtones, or Upper Partials. (C. S. Wake) Music, 12: 409.

Musical Periodicals in America. Music, 14: 647.

Musical Pitch, New Philharmonic. (A. J. Hipkins) Nature, 60: 421.

Musical Programs. (W. S. B. Mathews) Music, 15: 75.

Musical Renaissance of Northern New England. (L. T. Bryant) Nat'l M. (Bost.) 13: 583.

Musical Science, Task of. (R. Wallaschek) Music, 11: 362.

Musical Study, Aims of. (Pauline Jennings) Music, 15: 40.

Musical Terminology. (Dr. H. C. Hanchett) Music, 16: 237. — (W. S. B. Mathews) Music, 16: 285.

Musical Therapeutics, The Key-note in. (H. W. Stratton) Arena, 25: 287.

Musical Traditions, Are there any? (H. T. Finck) Indep. 52: 2041.

Musical University wanted in America. (W. S. B. Mathews) Music, 16: 11.

Musical Wit and Humor. (J. C. Hadden) Chamb. J. 74: 262.

Musical without Practice, How to be. (J. S. Smith) Music, 16: 535.

Musicians, American, Group of Native. R. of Rs. (N. Y.) 19: 435.

— Great Feeble. (J. F. Runciman) Sat. R. 88: .323.

— Multiplication of. (J. C. Hadden) National, 29: 735.

— Narrowness of. (J. F. Runciman) Sat. R. 87: 78.

— Norwegian. (E. E. Simpson) Music, 19: 364.

— Noteworthy Modern. Music, 12: 208-705. 13: 82, 223.

— of the Restoration. (S. M. C. Boevey) Longm. 34: 403. Same art. Liv. Age, 223: 305.

— Some New York, Singers, Organists, Teachers. (S. H. Thinker) Music, 11: 664.

Musk, Wild. (W. H. Hudson) Argosy, 74: 279.

Musk-ox Hunting among the Iwilics. (A. H. Verrill) Outing, 38: 158.

— of Canada. (C. A. Bramble) Canad. M. 14: 122.

Musket, The, as a Social Force. (J. McElroy) J. Mil. Serv. Inst. 7: 199.

Musketeers, The; Criticism of the Play as produced by Beerbohm Tree, 1898. (A. Lawrence) Idler, 14: 805.

Musketry. (J. Chester) J. Mil. Serv. Inst. 12: 232.

— and Discipline. Un. Serv. M. 22: 611. 23: 365. 24: 186.

— and Tactics. (S. Murray) Un. Serv. M. 17: 653.

— The School of. Chamb. J. 74: 431.

Musketry Reform. Un. Serv. M. 23: 81.

Musketry Training and its Value in War. (J. Parker) J. Mil. Serv. Inst. 14: 61.

— of the Volunteers. (De La Bère) Un. Serv. M. 19: 58. — (D. Howie) Un. Serv. M. 19: 290.

Muskoka Lakes. (A. Blackwood) Longm. 37: 215.

— A Highland Holiday. (E. W. Sandys) Outing, 30: 323.

— A People's Playground. (E. W. Sandys) Outing, 32: 267.

Musolino, Giuseppe; an Italian Brigand of To-day. (I. P. Stevenson) Indep. 53: 1844.

Musri, North Arabian Land of, in Early Hebrew Tradition. (T. K. Cheyne) Jew. Q. 11: 551.

Mussels, Simpson's Synopsis of Pearly Fresh-water. (T. D. A. Cockerell) Science, n. s. 13: 983.

Musset, Alfred de. Lorenzaccio. (G. B. Shaw) Sat. R. 83: 713.

Mut in Asher, Temple of; Excavations by Benson and Gourlay. Sat. R. 87: 342.

Mutare Pulices. (K. F. Smith) Am. J. Philol. 22: 44.

Mutinies on American Ships. (J. R. Spears) Munsey, 25: 646.

Mutiny on the Flag-ship. (Anna A. Rogers) Scrib. M. 24: 297.

Muttra, India, the Sacred City. (J. MacCartie) Pall Mall M. 20: 334.

Mutual Aid Societies in France. (W. F. Willoughby) Yale R. 6: 169.

Muzafer-Ed-Din, Shah of Persia; the Shah at Home. (J. F. Fraser) Eng. Illust. 17: 3.

Mweru, Lake. (A. B. Watson) Geog. J. 9: 58.

Mweru District, Choma Division of the. (H. Croad) Geog. J. 11: 617.

My Affinity; a story. Temp. Bar, 114: 46.

My Book; the story of an Author's Vanity. Acad. 59: 387. Same art. Ecl. M. 136: 70. — Same art. Liv. Age, 227: 586.

My Boyhood Dreams; a sketch. (S. L. Clemens) Mc-Clure, 14: 286.

My Captive; a Tale of Tarleton's Raiders. (J. A. Altsheler) Lippinc. 66: 483.

My Castle. (W. H. Winslow) New Eng. M. n. s. 23: 86.

My Corn-cob Pipe; a poem. (T. D. Ashbaugh) Outing, 33: 366.

My Crank Client; a story. (W. B. Hutchinson) Cosmopol. 29: 217.

My Divinity; a story. (D. Monroe) Belgra. 98: 334.

My Dog; a poem. (C. Hawkes) Outing, 29: 487.

My Doris; a story. (Alice H. Rich) Midland, 7: 347.

My Experiences as a Collaborator. Chamb. J. 75: 335.

My Fifth in Mammy; a story. (W. L. Sheppard) Harper, 96: 121.

My First Play; a story. (J. Hickory Wood) Idler, 16: 633.

My Foreign Friend; a story. (A. M. Purser) Cornh. 75: 250.

My Friend Ah-Chy. (C. Ritchie) Atlan. 82: 197.

My Friend Donald. (M. Byrde) Longm. 37: 47.

My Friend Jack. (G. M. Fenn) Chamb. J. 76: 205.

My Heart's Haven; a poem. (A. Mackay) Argosy, 65: 300.

My H'intimate Friend. (H. A. Lincoln) Sund. M. 28: 592.

My Host of the Moor; a story. (A. K. Gill) Pall Mall M. 22: 191.

My Japanese Friends. (E. Hallam) Temp. Bar, 119:129.

My Lady Moon; a story. (Lady M. Majendie) Argosy, 63: 81, 736. 64: 86.

My Lady of Orange. (H. C. Bailey) Longm. v. 37, 38.

My Ladye's Bower; a tale. (E. Curtis-Plim) Argosy, 72: 433.

My Lady's Bower; a ghost story. (A. Hooper) Canad. M. 10: 530.

My Lady's Chamber; a story. (O. Thanet) Nat'l M. (Bost.) 13: 137, 275, 354.

My Lady's Honor; a story. (H. A. Hinkson) Idler, 15: 637.

My Late Widow; a story. (C. W. Stoddard) Cosmopol. 22: 393.

My Little Maid. (J. T. K. Tarpey) Temp. Bar, 121: 256.

My Little Schoolmaster. (E. Griffith-Jones) Sund. M. 27: 146. Same art. Liv. Age, 217: 265.

My Lord Duke. (E. W. Hornung) Chamb. J. 74: 1-331.

My Love-story. (J. R. Perry) Scrib. M. 28: 209.

My Mother's Diary. (M. Westenholz) Cornh. 83: 364. Same art. Liv. Age, 229: 510.

My Normandy; a poem. (M. Macleod) Argosy, 74: 170.

My Old Guitar; a sketch. Canad. M. 11: 58.

My Own Funeral. (G. Moore) Lippinc. 68: 601.

My Pennsylvanian. (J. A. Altsheler) Lippinc. 69: 707.

My Revenge; a story. Argosy, 63: 468.

My Saint Katharine; a tale. (C. Blackwell) Argosy, 69: 415.

My Share in the War. (F. N. Connell) Chamb. J. 74: 92.

My Son's Friends; a tale. (M. H. Spielmann) Argosy, 74: 37.

My Strange Mirror; a story. (M. C. Faville) Midland, 9: 424.

Mycenæ, The Arts at. (W. J. Stillman) Nation, 66: 182.

— Question of. (H. R. Hall) Nature, 64: 280.

Mycenæan Age, Tsountas and Manatt's. (F. B. Tarbell) Am. Hist. R. 2: 706. — (J. R. Smith) Dial (Ch.) 22: 304.

Mycenæan House of the Double-axe, The. (L. Dyer) Nation, 71: 86.

Mycenæan Vase, Notes on a. (P. Orsi) Am. J. Archæol. 2d s. 1: 251.

Mycetozoa, The. (Edward and Agnes Fry) Knowl. 22: 1-271.

Myers, Frederic W. H. Acad. 60: 88. — Ath. '01, 1: 113. — Dial (Ch.) 30: 95.

— Life-work of. (A. Boutwood) Lond. Q. 96: 98.

— Service to Psychology. (W. James) Pop. Sci. Mo. 59: 380.

Myles, John. (W. A. Slade) New Eng. M. n. s. 17: 342.

"Myrey's Fambly;" a Nova Scotian story. (A. Ashmore) Canad. M. 14: 377.

Myrick, Herbert, An Agricultural Editor. R. of Rs. (N. Y.) 15: 678.

Myrmecophaga and Didelphis. (O. Thomas) Am. Natural. 35: 143.

Mysia, Explorations in. (J. A. R. Munro and H. M. Anthony) Geog. J. 9: 151, 256.

— Gleanings from. (J. A. R. Munro) J. Hel. Stud. 21: 229.

Mysie; a story. (L. Towle) Pall Mall M. 17: 372.

Mysterious Fever, A; a story. (W. L. Alden) Pall Mall M. 14: 274.

Mysterious Miss Dacres. (Mrs. S. Crowninshield) Lippinc. 67: 385.

Mystery, The Evolution of. (M. Maeterlinck) Fortn. 73: 899.

Mystery of Mr. Cain. (L. McLaws) Lippinc. 63: 3.

Mystery of Fifty-fivers, The. (H. Seymour) Belgra. 98: 377.

Mystery of Hayward Castle; a story. (W. E. Boynton) Midland, 8: 77.

Mystery of the Mist; a poem. (K. Coolidge) Atlan. 86: 421.

Mystery of Red Light Island; a story of early Iowa. (W. S. Kerr) Midland, 10: 443.

Mystery of the Sword, A. (E. and H. Heron) Chamb. J. 75: 353-376.

Mystery Play, The; a story. (E. C. Waltz) Cent. 41: 182.

Mystery Plays. (E. F. L. Gauss) Open Court, 14: 415.

— Effect of, upon Subsequent Religious Thought. (C. J. Wood) Open Court, 15: 23.

— Greek, a Preparation for Christianity. (P. Carus) Monist, 11: 87.

— Pagan and Christian, Cheetham on. (J. B. Heard) Crit. R. 8: 141.

Mystic, Connecticut. (O. D. Tompkins) New Eng. M. n. s. 24: 152.

Mystic Music. (W. Richards) Temp. Bar, 124: 233.

Mysticism, Christian. Church Q. 49: 333.

— Essay on the Bases of the Mystic Knowledge, Récéjac's. (E. G. Martin) Bk. Buyer, 18: 319. — (H. C. Minton) Presb. & Ref. R. 10: 543.

Mysticism, Japanese, Hearn on. Spec. **79**: 736.
— Modern. Quar. **190**: 79.
— Münsterberg on. (J. H. Hyslop) Psychol. R. **6**: 292.
— (H. Münsterberg) Psychol. R. **6**: 408.
— The New. (E. Rhys) Fortn. **73**: 1045.
— Psychology and. (H. Münsterberg) Atlan. **83**: 67.
— True and False. (J. Lindsay) Presb. & Ref. R. **10**: 617.
— What is? (G. Tyrrell) Month, **90**: 601.
Mystics of the Middle Ages, Catholic. Ed. Rev. **184**: 298. Same art. Liv. Age, **212**: 19.
Myth, Philosophy of. (I. F. Russell) Meth. R. **58**: 726.
Mythology. (A. C. Thomas) Am. Antiq. **23**: 316.
— in teaching English. (Alice S. Randall) Educa. **22**: 166.
— Max Müller on Science of. (B. L. Hobson) Presb. & Ref. R. **9**: 139. — Acad. **51**: 297.
— Modern, Lang on. (B. L. Hobson) Presb. & Ref. R. **9**: 508. — Sat. R. **84**: 91.
— Norse. (H. Wunsh) N. Church R. **8**: 404.
— — Drawings illustrating. (N. Molkenboer) Studio (Internat.) **13**: 181.
Myths, Ethnic Variation of. (J. Fraser) Am. Antiq. **22**: 213.
— Pedagogy of, in the Grades. (Ezra Allen) Pedagog. Sem. **8**: 258.

Nachez, Tivadar, with portraits. Strand, **15**: 200.
Nadir of Temperature, and Allied Problems. (J. Dewar) Am. J. Sci. **162**: 168.
Nādir Shah, Legend of. Folk-Lore, **8**: 77.
Nagging. Spec. **79**: 334.
Nagid, Egyptian, Installation of the. (E. N. Adler) Jew. Q. **9**: 717.
Nai Yim, the Fish-fighter. (B. Thomson) New R. **17**: 710.
Nail Combine, Failure of. Gunton's M. **12**: 32.
Naivasha Lake to the Victoria Nyanza, Journey from. (G. H. Gorges) Geog. J. **16**: 78.
Naketah; a story. (S. Sheldrake) Canad. M. **17**: 375.
Name, Question of a. (J. London) Writer, **48**: 177.
Nameless; a poem. (A. Soumet) Argosy, **63**: 777.
Nameless One, A. (J. Reimers) Overland, n. s. **35**: 219.
Nameless Pickaninny. (F. H. Sweet) New Eng. M. **23**: 220.
Names. (H. T. Peck) Bookman, **8**: 334.
— and Numbers. (E. Mach) Open Court, **14**: 37.
— Bardsley's Dictionary of English and Welsh Surnames. (W. Canton) Good Words, **42**: 717. — (E. Whitaker) Macmil. **84**: 139. Same art. Ecl. M. **137**: 354.
— Cognominal Puzzles. (E. Whitaker) Good Words, **41**: 442.
— Household. (J. F. Cowan) Educa. **19**: 640.
— Inaccurate Use of. (F. W. Chapman) Educa. **19**: 304.
— Indian; Old Friends with a New Face. (St. J. E. C. Hankin) Fortn. **68**: 297.
— of Persons and Places, Significance of Some. (Ezra Brainerd) Educa. **19**: 140.
— of Places. (H. Maxwell) Blackw. **167**: 527.
— Surnames and Christian. (E. F. Watrous) Chaut. **31**: 631.
Nanak and the Faith of the Sikhs. (J. T. Bixby) New World, **7**: 704.
Nance, R. Morton, Sketches by. Studio (Internat.) **5**: 257.
Nancy; a story. (J. S. Wood) Cent. **31**: 930.
Nancy and I and the Girl; a story. (N. V. McClelland) McClure, **18**: 59.
Nancy of Chigwell Row. Ath. '00, **2**: 282.
Nancy, France, Art at. (H. Frantz) M. of Art, **21**: 92.

Nansen, F. (F. Hope) Canad. M. **8**: 479. — (L. Stephen) Int. J. Ethics, **8**: 1.
— and the Approach to the Pole. Ed. R. **186**: 307.
— and the "Fram." (W. H. Dall) Nation, **64**: 306.
— Arctic Expedition of '93-'96. (F. Nansen) Geog. J. **9**: 473.
— Farthest North. (A. W. Greely) Critic, **30**: 331. — (G. McDermot) Cath. World, **65**: 641. — (H. F. Witherby) Knowl. **20**: 57.
— — Diary of a Pagan. (H. Stuck) Sewanee, **6**: 193.
— Heroic Journey. (N. S. Shaler) Atlan. **79**: 610.
— in America. Critic, **31**: 290.
— Meeting for, in Albert Hall. Geog. J. **9**: 249.
— Originality of. Sat. R. **83**: 162.
— Story of Nansen's Achievement. Liv. Age, **212**: 870. See Arctic Regions.
Nantucket, Marriages in. (O. G. Hammond) N. E. Reg. **51**: 54, 161.
— Naval Manœuvres at, 1901. (H. H. Lewis) New Eng. M. n. s. **25**: 180.
— Secession and Annexation of. (C. Cornish) Green Bag, **11**: 124.
Naomi; a story. (J. Stafford) Gent. M. n. s. **66**: 1.
Naphtha Industry, Russian. J. Soc. Arts, **45**: 1136.
Napier, Sir Charles, Admiral. (J. K. Laughton) Ath. '01, **1**: 532. — (S. Gwynn) Cornh. **81**: 65.
Napier, Sir John. (G. Law) Jurid. R. **9**: 59, 173.
Napier, Robert C., Lord, of Magdala. (G. H. Trevor) Sund. M. **27**: 541.
Napiers, The Youth of the. (S. Gwynn) Cornh. **75**: 231. Same art. Liv. Age, **212**: 674.
Naples. (A. Symons) Liv. Age, **217**: 267.
— and the Gospel. (A. E. Keeling) Lond. Q. **94**: 119.
— Aquarium at. (F. G. Aflalo) Good Words, **39**: 756.
— Breakfast in. (M. Scott-Uda) Cent. **40**: 15.
— City Election, 1901. Ousting an Italian Tammany. (F. J. Mather, jr.) Nation, **73**: 393.
— Low Life in, as pictured by Neapolitans. (L. Wolffsohn) Gent. M. n. s. **64**: 84.
— Republicans of, Nelson and the. (F. P. Badham) Eng. Hist. R. **13**: 261.
— Sketches in. (C. Edwardes) Temp. Bar, **119**: 416.
— Witchcraft in. (J. B. Andrews) Folk-Lore, **8**: 1.
— Zoölogical Station. (E. H. Patterson) Pop. Sci. Mo. **54**: 668. — (W. A. Herdman) Nature, **63**: 68.
— — The Greatest Biological Station in the World. (W. A. Herdman) Pop. Sci. Mo. **59**: 419.
— — Some Unwritten History of. Am. Natural. **31**: 960.
Napoleon I. and Alexander I., Vandal's. (H. E. Bourne) Am. Hist. R. **2**: 352.
— and the Eagle. (Katharine H. Brown) Overland, n. s. **36**: 538.
— and England, Lumbroso's. Am. Hist. R. **3**: 144.
— and Josephine. (A. Laugel) Nation, **71**: 462.
— — at Bayonne. (W. H. James) Macmil. **78**: 185. Same art. Ecl. M. **131**: 607. Same art. Liv. Age, **218**: 671.
— and Prince Metternich. (G. Hill) Gent. M. n. s. **67**: 164.
— Aphorisms of. (R. G. Burton) Un. Serv. M. **20**: 567.
— Armies of, Economy of. (E. S. May) J. Mil. Serv. Inst. **20**: 126.
— as Novelist. Sat. R. **87**: 584. Same art. Liv. Age, **221**: 796.
— as Social Reformer, Sloane's. Spec. **78**: 407.
— at Elba. (A. Laugel) Nation, **64**: 355.
— at La Malmaison. (G. De Dubor) Pall Mall M. **24**: 468.
— at St. Helena. (R. H. Titherington) Munsey, **26**: 215. — (R. Doumic) Ecl. M. **133**: 264. Same art. Liv. Age, **222**: 45.

National Academy of Design; A Retrospect. Artist (N. Y.) 25: x.

National Archives, The. (W. MacDonald) Nation, 70: 393.

National Association of Manufacturers of the U. S. Banquet at Waldorf-Astoria Hotel, New York, Jan. 27, 1898. (J. C. Ridpath) Arena, 19: 686.

National Bank Law, Changes in the. Bank. M. (N. Y.) 56: 702.

— Deposit-reserve System of the. (E. S. Meade) J. Pol. Econ. 6: 209, 292.

National Banks, Insolvent, in City and Country. (W. A. Cutler) J. Pol. Econ. 7: 367.

National Capital, Expenditure of, Giffen on. Bank. M. (Lond.) 71: 891.

National Cash Register Factory, Dayton, O., Industrial System of. (P. Monroe) Am. J. Sociol. 3: 729.

National Character. Monthly R. 1, no. 2: 11.

— and National Growth. (W. J. McGee) Nat. Geog. M. 10: 185.

National Competition in Art, in English Schools, 1899. Artist (N. Y.) 26: 37.

National Debt, U. S., its Origin, History, and Peculiarities. (H. S. Boutell) Forum, 32: 138.

National Debts; Modern Loan-mongering. (A. J. Wilson) Contemp. 73: 326.

National Democratic Convention of Kentucky, 1897. Pub. Opin. 23: 101.

National Development, Theory of. Gunton's M. 15: 302.

National Educational Association, Milwaukee Meeting, 1897. Educa. R. 14: 191. — Pub. Opin. 23: 117.

— Washington Meeting, 1898. (N. M. Butler) Educa. R. 16: 200.

— Los Angeles Meeting, 1899. (W. S. Abbott) Overland, n. s. 34: 74. — (E. B. Payne) Arena, 22: 362. — School R. 7: 409.

National Expenditures and Municipal, Growth of. (Lord Avebury) J. Statis. Soc. 64: 73.

National Gallery, London, and Common Sense. (H. M. Paull) Fortn. 69: 592.

— Condition of. Sat. R. 85: 275. — (H. Bishop) Sat. R. 86: 240. — (L. Housman) Sat. R. 86: 272.

— Eastlake on. Sat. R. 83: 691.

— Five New Pictures in. (M. H. Witt) 19th Cent. 48: 648.

— Hall of Masterpieces at; Why not? Spec. 85: 557.

— in 1900, and its Present Arrangements. (M. H. Spielmann) 19th Cent. 48: 54.

— Poynter on. Art J. 52: 117.

— Some Pictures in, 1901. (J. Todhunter) Temp. Bar, 124: 447.

— Two Pictures recently acquired. (Herbert P. Horne) M. of Art, 23: 241.

National Geographic Society. (J. Hyde) Nat. Geog. M. 10: 220.

— President's Address. (A. G. Bell) Nat. Geog. M. 11: 401.

National Guard. (E. E. Britton) J. Mil. Serv. Inst. 26: 155.

— and its Value. (Col. Thos. Wilhelm) Overland, n. s. 38: 496.

— Congress and. (J. M. Rice) J. Mil. Serv. Inst. 19: 452.

— Did it Fail, in 1898 ? (H. F. Davis) J. Mil. Serv. Inst. 24: 417.

— Future of. (C. S. Clark) No. Am. 170: 730.

— How can it be made Effective to the Regular Army in both War and Peace. (H. Barry) J. Mil. Serv. Inst. 26: 189. — (D. M. Taylor) J. Mil. Serv. Inst. 26: 232. — (L. D. Greene) J. Mil. Serv. Inst. 27: 340. — (W. B. Beal) J. Mil. Serv. Inst. 27: 371.

National Guard, How to improve the Efficiency of. (H. A. Giddings) J. Mil. Serv. Inst. 21: 61.

— Limitations of. (L. C. Scherer) J. Mil. Serv. Inst. 18: 267.

— Proposed Reorganization of. (F. R. Coudert) J. Mil. Serv. Inst. 24: 239. — (J. Ruppert, jr.) Arena, 23: 225. — (E. MacPherson) J. Mil. Serv. Inst. 25: 329.

— What it is and its Use. (J. M. Rice) J. Mil. Serv. Inst. 15: 909.

National Hero, The True. (E. L. Godkin) Nation, 67: 270.

National Highway, The Old. (W. G. Irwin) Chaut. 29: 447.

National Honor, and the Morality of Statesmen. Spec. 80: 435.

National Hymns. Songs of Freedom. (L. Mead) Chaut. 31: 574.

National Ideals, Conscious and Unconscious. (G. Murray) Internat. J. Ethics, 11: 1.

National Liberal Club, London, Decorations. (A. L. Baldry) Art J. 51: 305.

National Life and Character. (T. Roosevelt) Sewanee, 2: 353.

— Religion in. (H. M. Scott) Presb. & Ref. R. 11: 555.

National Magazine, Boston; its Aims, and its Staff and Contributors. Nat'l M. (Bost.) 9: 503.

National Municipal League. (C. R. Woodruff) Yale R. 7: 213.

National Music Teachers' Association, Des Moines, 1900. Music, 18: 264.

— — Concerts. Music, 18: 272.

National Park in the Minnesota Pine Forests. (H. B. Hudson) R. of Rs. (N. Y.) 20: 698.

National Personality. Ed. R. 194: 132.

National Physical Laboratory, The. Nature, 60: 25.

— Aims of. (R. T. Glazebrook) Nature, 64: 290.

National Prison Association Congress, 1899. (C. P. Kellogg) Char. R. 9: 382.

National Prosperity, Conditions of. (J. S. Stahr) Ref. Q. 44: 52.

National Provident Institution. Bank. M. (Lond.) 63: 674.

National Repository for Science and Art, A. (F. Petrie) J. Soc. Arts, 48: 525.

National Resources, On the Calculation of. (V. V. Branford) J. Statis. Soc. 64: 380.

National Sculpture Society, Exhibition of. (Barr Ferree) Am. Arch. 60: 99.

National Social and Political Conference, '1901. (E. Pomeroy) Arena, 25: 588.

National-Social Movement in Germany, Social Objects of. (P. Göhre) Am. J. Sociol. 4: 765.

National Songs: "God Save the Queen." (J. C. Hadden) Argosy, 72: 93.

— U. S., and their Writers. (F. Wayne) Nat'l M. (Bost.) 11: 284.

National Stability founded on Morality. (C. W. Super) Bib. Sac. 54: 293.

National Types, Change of. Chamb. J. 78: 673.

National Unity, One View of. (E. E. Brown) Arena, 22: 186.

National University, A. Science, n. s. 14: 45. — (C. W. Dabney, jr.) Science, n. s. 5: 378. — (W. H. Smith) Educa. R. 17: 88.

— Constitutionality of a. (E. J. James) Educa. R. 18: 451.

— Need of a. (L. R. Harley) Educa. 19: 273.

— Our. (W. J. McGee) Harper, 96: 633. — (C. W. Eliot) Critic, 32: 414.

— Proposed Washington Memorial. (Susanna P. Gage) Outl. 58: 521.

Nelson, Horatio. (W. O'C. Morris) Scot. R. **30**: 55. — Lond. Q. **89**: 1.

— and his Biographers. (D. Hannay) Macmil. **76**: 92.

— and his St. Vincent Campaign. (W. O'C. Morris) Pall Mall M. **13**: 320.

— and his Times. (Lord Charles Beresford) Ath. '98, **1**: 820.

— at Copenhagen. (H. G. Hutchinson) Blackw. **166**: 323.

— at Naples in 1799. (J. K. Laughton ; F. P. Badham) Ath. '00, **1**: 498.

— at Trafalgar. (A. T. Mahan) Cent. **31**: 741.

— Birthplace of. Argosy, **69**: 32.

— Fatal Shot at Trafalgar. (A. M. Horwood) Chamb. J. **75**: 75.

— Genealogy of. (W. L. Clowes) 19th Cent. **42**: 755.

— How he looked in the Year of the Nile, with portraits. (D. Sladen) M. of Art, **22**: 529.

— in the Battle of the Nile. (A. T. Mahan) Cent. **31**: 435.

— Mahan's Life of. Quar. **187**: 126. — Am. Hist. R. **4**: 719. — Ed. R. **186**: 84. — Atlan. **80**: 264. — (W. O'C. Morris) Fortn. **67**: 895. Same art. Ecl. M. **129**: 152. — (G. S. Clarke) 19th Cent. **41**: 893. Same art. Liv. Age, **214**: 379. — (S. Wilkinson) National, **29**: 703. — (H. E. Bourne) Citizen, **3**: 160. — (E. G. Johnson) Dial (Ch.) **22**: 242. — (C. W. Colby) Nation, **64**: 285. — (P. H. Colomb) Sat. R. **83**: 363. — Spec. **78**: 545.

— Moral Riddle in the Life of. (P. Young) Un. Serv. M. **17**: 244.

— The Neapolitan Republicans and Nelson's Accusers. (A. T. Mahan) Eng. Hist. R. **14**: 471.

— Our Great Naval Hero. (W. C. Russell) Eng. Illust. **16**: 545 — **17**: 607.

Nelson, Mrs. Ann, a Queen of the Road. (Thormanby) Chamb. J. **78**: 360.

Nelson, British Columbia, a Typical Mining Town. (W. F. Brougham) Canad. M. **14**: 19.

Nelumbiums. (W. Tricker) Garden & F. **10**: 127.

Nemerteans, Times of Breeding of some Common. (W. R. Coe) Science, n. s. **9**: 167.

Nemesis, or The Divine Envy. (P. E. More) New World, **8**: 625.

"Neminism," President Jordan's. (A. Pangloss) Pop. Sci. Mo. **56**: 494.

Neminist, Education of the. (D. S. Jordan) Pop. Sci. Mo. **51**: 176.

Nencki, Marcel. Science, **14**: 889.

Neo-Hegelian "Self" and Subjective Idealism. (A. K. Rogers) Philos. R. **10**: 139.

Neolithic Cemetery in Cornwall, Discovery of. (J. Baker) Ath. '00, **2**: 383.

Neolithic Period in Northern Africa, Zaborewski's. Am. Natural. **33**: 423.

Neolithic Settlement, A Supposed. (J. Kenworthy) Reliquary, **41**: 121.

Neolithic Troglodytes, Reading and Writing of. (A. C. H.) Nature, **55**: 229.

Neon ; recently discovered Gas. (William Ramsay) Science, n. s. **9**: 273.

— and Metagon, New Elements. Pop. Astron. **6**: 345.

Neo-Pantheism and the Catholic Faith. (J. J. Elmendorf) Sewanee, **1**: 207.

Nepaul, Visit to. (L. de Forest) Cent. **40**: 74.

Nepenthes. (W. Watson) Garden & F. **10**: 382.

Nepheline Syenite in New Jersey, New Occurrence of. (F. L. Ransome) Am. J. Sci. **158**: 417.

נפש, Use of, in the Old Testament. (C. A. Briggs) J. Bib. Lit. **16**: 17.

Nepigon River, Fishing Trip to. (J. S. Stokes) Outl. **59**: 277.

Neoplatonism, Permanent Influence of, upon Christianity. (W. R. Inge) Am. J. Theol. **4**: 328.

Neotropical Region, History of the. (H. von Ihering) Science, n. s. **12**: 857.

Nepos, Cornelius, Lives of, Lindsay's. (J. R. Bishop) School R. **6**: 47.

Neptunian ; poem. (P. H. Savage) Atlan. **82**: 285.

Nerelle ; a tale of an Austral Maid. (G. F. Scott) Belgra. **93**: 159, 257. **94**: 26–423.

Nernst Lamp in America. Nature, **64**: 632.

Nero, True History of the Reign of. (C. P. Parker) New World, **7**: 313.

Nerval, Gérard de, Problem of. (A. Symons) Fortn. **69**: 81.

Nerve and Muscle, Prime Movers of. Knowl. **20**: 230.

— Some Recent Work upon. (Fs. Gotch) Sci. Prog. **7**: 430.

Nerves in the Nursery. Liv. Age, **224**: 659.

Nerve-activity, Theory of. (E. Hering) Monist, **10**: 167.

Nerve-wave, The. (Chas. Richet) Nature, **60**: 625.

Nervous Disease, Few Ethnic Features of. (I. C. Rosse) Am. J. Soc. Sci. **37**: 239.

Nervous System, Barker on. Am. Natural. **35**: 61.

— Artificial Formation of a Rudimentary. Illust. (A. L. Herrera) Nat. Sci. **13**: 333, 384.

— Education of the, Halleck's. (J. H. Hyslop) Bookman, **4**: 451.

— From Fundamental to Accessory in Development of. (F. Burk) Pedagog. Sem. **6**: 5.

— Maintenance of the Equilibrium as a Function of the Central. (H. Obersteiner) Am. Natural. **33**: 313.

Nescience ; a poem. (C. A. Lane) Open Court, **12**: 696.

— First Principles of. Spec. **85**: 233. — Liv. Age, **227**: 130.

Net Result, The. (H. Martley) Longm. **32**: 434.

Netherlands, Blok's History of the People of. (C. W. Colby) Nation, **72**: 515.

— Conquest of the. (F. Dixon) Temp. Bar, **111**: 475.

Nethersole, Olga. (Lavinia Hart) Cosmopol. **31**: 15.

— in The Termagant. (A. Lawrence) Idler, **14**: 324.

— My Struggles to succeed. Cosmopol. **28**: 193.

Netley Hospital ; when Tommy is Sick, and how he is Cured. Eng. Illust. **20**: 170.

Netsukes, Japanese. (E. Gilbertson) Studio (Lond.) **2**: 123.

Nettleship, R. L., Lectures of, Bradley's. Ath. '97, **2**: 780.

Neuchâtel. Musée des Beaux-arts, Decoration of the. Studio (Internat.) **6**: 254.

Neufeld, Charles, Captivity of, at Omdurman. Acad. **57**: 367.

Neuschwanstein Castle, Bavaria. (Anna Douglas) Art J. **53**: 364.

Neutrality Laws. (S. E. M. Hardy) Green Bag, **10**: 333.

Nevada, The Future of. (F. G. Newlands) Indep. **53**: 885.

— Shall it be deprived of its Statehood ? (C. W. E. Smythe) Forum, **23**: 228.

Nevada Silver Boom. Blackw. **165**: 735.

Never Again ; a story. (N. W. Williams) Gent. M. n. s. **63**: 105.

"Never the Lotos closes ;" a story. (E. and H. Heron) Cornh. **75**: 95. Same art. Liv. Age, **212**: 455.

Nevill, Sir Hugh de, Will of, written at Acre, 1267. (M. S. Giuseppi) Archæol. **56**: 351.

Nevill Holt. (Maud Cunard) Archit. R. **7**, no. **2**: 143.

Neville Princesses, The. (A. Buckler) Gent. M. n. s. **60**: 157.

Nevin, Ethelbert. (L. Campbell-Tipton) Music, **19**: 572.

New Academy of Complements (sic). (F. M. Parsons) Longm. **32**: 331.

New Amsterdam. Knickerbocker Days. (E. S. Martin) Cosmopol. **30**: 219.

— Mother City of Greater New York. (Mrs. Schuyler Van Rensselaer) Cent. **34**: 138.

New Anthem, A. (J. Crabtree) Belgra. **93**: 113.

New Britain, Connecticut. (M. C. Talcott) New Eng. M. n. s. **19**: 721.

— Institute Library Building. Lib. J. **26**: 276.

New Brunswick and its Scenery. (A. M. Belding) Canad. M. **15**: 49.

— In "the Pine-tree Province." (Rev. R. Wilson) Chamb. J. **78**: 381.

— Premiers since Confederation. (J. Hannay) Canad. M. **9**: 213.

— Representative Institutions in, Early. (J. G. Bourinot) Canad. M. **11**: 21.

New Century, A, and an Old Riddle. (Mrs. T. Chapman) 19th Cent. **49**: 7.

New Christmas Carol; a story. (W. Pett Ridge) Cosmopol. **32**: 165.

New Church, The, and the Holy Spirit. (E. J. E. Schreck) N. Church R. **6**: 497.

— Three Essentials of. (J. Reed) N. Church R. **8**: 321.

New Church Belief Simple not Abstruse. (T. F. Wright) N. Church R. **6**: 120.

New Church Conference of 1899, Manchester, England. (T. F. Wright) N. Church R. **6**: 593.

New Church Convention of 1899 in Boston. (J. Reed) N. Church R. **6**: 590.

New College and Oxford. (H. W. Mabie) Outl. **60**: 837.

New Curiosity Shop, A; a story. (J. Ayscough) Argosy, **68**: 34.

New "De Profundis," The; a poem. (S. Phillips) Bk. Buyer, **16**: 204.

New Earth, A; a story. (A. J. Raine) Sund. M. **28**: 531.

New England, Animals of. (F. E. Keay) New Eng. N. n. s. **24**: 535.

— Colonial Houses in. (V. H. Robie) Brush & P. **6**: 61.

— Council for, and the Merchant Venturers of Bristol. (M. Cristy) Am. Hist. R. **4**: 678.

— Country Towns in. (C. N. Hall) New Eng. M. n. s. **23**: 50.

— Decadence of Agriculture in. (C. S. Phelps) New Eng. M. n. s. **25**: 374.

— Early, Travel in. (A. L. Hill) New Eng. M. n. s. **17**; 82.

— England and. (E. P. Powell) New Eng. M. n. s. **16**: 466.

— in War-time. (A. G. Hyde) Macmil. **81**: 348. Same art. Liv. Age, **225**: 8. Same art. Ecl. M. **134**: 665.

— Influence of Hebrew Thought in the Development of the Social Democratic Idea in. (C. S. Allen) Arena, **18**: 748.

— Lakes of. (C. L. Whittle) New Eng. M. n. s. **16**: 605.

— Loyalists of. (C. Phillipps-Wolley) Longm. **30**: 116.

— Musical Life in, 1850–90. (M. D. Shepard) New Eng. M. n. s. **22**: 131.

— Popular Education in. (W. C. Lawton) New Eng. M. n. s. **17**: 115.

— Positive Pedigrees and Authorized Arms of. (W. S. Appleton) N. E. Reg. **52**: 185.

— Religious Life of, Walker's. (W. B. Weeden) Am. Hist. R. **3**: 374.

— Renaissance of. (F. W. Rollins) Indep. **53**: 69.

— Removals and Attempted Removals from, 1635–60. (F. Strong) New Eng. M. n. s. **20**: 184.

— Rural, Future of. (A. F. Sanborn) Atlan. **80**: 74.

— — Problems of. (P. Morgan and A. F. Sanborn) Atlan. **79**: 577.

— — Regeneration of. I. Economic. (R. L. Hartt) Outl. **64**: 504.

New England, Rural, Regeneration of. II. Social. (R. L. Hartt) Outl. **64**: 577.

— — — III. Religious. (R. L. Hartt) Outl. **64**: 628.

— — — Discussions. Outl. **64**: 745.

— Weather in. (E. T. Brewster) New Eng. M. n. s. **24**: 415.

New England Association of Colleges and Preparatory Schools, Report of, 1896. (R. G. Huling) School R. **5**: 641.

— — 1897. (R. G. Huling) School R. **6**: 691.

— — 1898. (R. G. Huling) School R. **7**: 577.

— — 1899. (R. G. Huling) School R. **8**: 569.

— — 1900. (R. G. Huling) School R. **9**: 613.

New England Character. (Sara C. Burnett) Nat'l M. (Bost.) **8**: 407.

New England Festival, A; a story. (A. Y. Keith) Indep. **53**: 1913.

New England Hill Town. (R. L. Hartt) Atlan. **83**: 561, 712.

New England Historic-Genealogical Society, Proceedings of. N. E. Reg. **54**: 220, 446.

New England Homestead, Recollections of. (C. Guild) New Eng. M. n. s. **21**: 117.

New England Magazine, First, and its Editor. (G. W. Cooke) New Eng. M. n. s. **16**: 103.

New England Poets, W. C. Lawton on. (C. Richter) Book R. **6**: 190.

New England Primer, Ford's History of. (W. Eames) Am. Hist. R. **3**: 372. — (W. de Groot Rice) Dial (Ch.) **24**: 139.

New England Statesmen. (H. B. Stimpson) Conserv. R. **1**: 184.

New England Type, The. Outl. **64**: 617.

New England Village. R. of Rs. (N. Y.) **24**: 462.

New English Art Club. (F. Wedmore) Studio (Lond.) **4**: 71. **6**: 213. **9**: 285.

— and British Artists' Exhibition, 1901. Art J. **53**: 190.

— Exhibition, 1893. Studio (Lond.) **2**: 79.

— — 1898. M. of Art, **22**: 227. — Sat. R. **85**: 552.

— — 1900. Sat. R. **89**: 525.

New-fire Ceremony, Lesser, at Walpi. (J. W. Fewkes) Am. Anthrop. **3**: 438.

New Forest, Birds in. (H. F. Witherby) Knowl. **20**: 130.

— Making of. (F. Baring) Eng. Hist. R. **16**: 427.

— Summer in. (W. H. Hudson) Longm. **35**: 263. Same art. Ecl. M. **135**: 110.

— A Village in. (C. Gleig) Blackw. **170**: 658.

New Gallery. (F. Bate) Studio (Lond.) **1**: 78. — (F. Khnopff) M. of Art, **22**: 428. — Ath. '97, **1**: 585, 686.

— and Old Masters. M. of Art, **22**: 222.

— Arts and Crafts Exhibition, 1893. (A. Vallance) Studio (Lond.) **2**: 3, 56.

— — 1899. Am. Arch. **66**: 52.

— Exhibition, 1897. Sat. R. **83**: 537.

— — Summer, 1897. Acad. **51**: 479.

— — 1898. Acad. **53**: 479. — Spec. **80**: 624. — Am. Arch. **63**: 69, 77.

← — Summer, 1899. Art J. **51**: 185.

— — Winter, 1899. Ath. '00, **1**: 54, 120.

— — 1900. Art J. **52**: 184. — M. of Art, **24**: 265.

— — 1901. M. of Art, **25**: 341, 403. — Art J. **53**: 183. — Sat. R. **91**: 535.

— Some Pictures criticised. (E. Aman-Jean) Studio (Lond.) **8**: 165.

— Watts's Pictures at. Spec. **78**: 17. — Ath. '97, **1**: 23, 89.

New Guinea, Birds of. (G. S. Mead) Am. Natural. **31**: 204.

— British, Studies in the Anthropogeography of. (A. C. Haddon) Geog. J. **16**: 265, 414.

New Guinea, Tribes inhabiting the Mouth of the Wanigela River in. (R. E. Guise) Anthrop. J. 28: 205.

New Hampshire and Massachusetts, Boundary Line of. (G. J. Varney) New Eng. M. n. s. 16: 347.

— Old Home Week in. (W. H. Burnham) New Eng. M. n. s. 23: 647. — (H. H. Williams) Nat'l M. (Bost.) 11: 145.

— Old Roads in. (W. H. Stone) New Eng. M. n. s. 18: 674.

— Opportunity of. (F. W. Rollins) New Eng. M. n. s. 16: 534.

— Part of, in Sullivan's Expedition of 1779. (W. E. Griffis) New Eng. M. n. s. 23: 355.

— Rebellion in, 1786. (F. B. Sanborn) New Eng. M. n. s. 23: 323.

— Whittier's. (D. L. Maulsby) New Eng. M. n. s. 22: 631.

New Haven. (W. Allen) New Eng. M. n. s. 20: 481.

New Hebrides, An Adventure in the. (L. Becke) Pall Mall M. 16: 547.

New Invasion; a poem. (H. H. Godfrey) Canad. M. 13: 147.

New Ipswich, New Hampshire. (P. C. Bouvé) New Eng. M. n. s. 22: 97.

New Jersey, Education in; system of public instruction. (J. M. Green) Educa. R. 16: 254.

New Jersey Highlands, Awheel over. (A. H. Godfrey) Outing, 33: 8.

New Jersey Precedent; Holmes vs. Walton. (A. Scott) Am. Hist. R. 4: 456.

New Learning, The. (H. Paul) 19th Cent. 42: 928.

New Mexico. (Edith M. Nicholl) Cornh. 82: 251.

New Minister, The; a story. (A. F. Robertson) Belgra. 97: 305.

New Netherland, English and Dutch Towns of. (A. E. McKinley) Am. Hist. R. 6: 1.

New Noah, A. (Fred Whishaw) Chamb. J. 76: 710.

New Organ; a story. (E. C. Hall) Cosmopol. 26: 411.

New Orleans. (E. S. Gardner) Midland, 9: 195.

— and Reconstruction. (A. Phelps) Atlan. 88: 121.

— Battle of. (S. Crane) Lippinc. 65: 405. — (C. Slack) Un. Serv. M. 21: 190. 27: 221.

— — Napoleon's Interest in. (W. H. Roberts) Cent. 31: 359.

— Conference of Charities. (F. H. Wines) Char. R. 6: 145.

— Fisk Free and Public Library. (W. Beer) Lib. J. 22: supp. 32. — Pub. Lib. 4: 54.

— Free Public Library. Lib. J. 22: 89.

— of G. W. Cable. (W. Hale) Bookman, 13: 136.

— The Old Cabildo of. (G. King) Harper, 102: 283.

— Under Side of. (F. A. Doughty) Lippinc. 60: 513.

"New Race," The; a prehistoric people of Egypt. (Wilfred M. Webb) Eng. Illust. 22: 135.

New Reporter, The. (J. L. Williams) Scrib. M. 23: 572.

New South Wales, Australia, Life on a Station in. (Hugh Henry) Gent. M. n. s. 58: 493. Same art. Ecl. M. 128: 813.

— Making of. Lond. Q. 89: 231.

New Steward, The. Liv. Age, 216: 255.

New Thought, The; What is it? (H. W. Dresser) Arena, 21: 29.

New Valet, The; a story. (H. Macfarlane) Eng. Illust. 20: 163.

New Waiter at the Boathouse Inn, The. (E. Kerns) Chamb. J. 77: 44.

New Wines and Old Bottles. Temp. Bar, 117: 389. Same art. Liv. Age, 223: 118. Same art. Ecl. M. 133: 888.

New World, Influence of, upon the Old. (W. T. Stead) Indep. 51: 1727.

— Payne's. (A. S. Gatschet) Nation, 70: 499.

New Year Wish; a poem. (E. Gibson) Argosy, 65: 64.

New Year's, With the Japanese Court at. (F. B. Hayes) Cosmopol. 24: 587.

New Year's Day; customs of various nations. (J. Wells) Sund. M. 28: 16.

New Year's Day, 1900; a poem. (E. M. Rutherford) Gent. M. n. s. 64: 308.

New Year's Greeting, A; a poem. (E. M. Alford) Argosy, 65: 128.

New York City and its Historians. (Mrs. S. Van Rensselaer) No. Am. 171: 724, 872.

— American Art in. (V. H. Robie) Brush & P. 7: 48.

— Appellate Court Building. (C. De Kay) Indep. 53: 1795. — (R. Ladegast) Outl. 67: 286. — (E. Knaufft) R. of Rs. (N. Y.) 22: 191.

— Aquarium, Treasures of the. (C. L. Bristol) Cent. 38: 553.

— Art World of. (D. C. Preyer) Brush & P. 8: 26, 91.

— at Night. (J. B. Carrington) Scrib. M. 27: 326.

— Ball-giving in. (C. Van Horne) Munsey, 21: 124.

— Battery and Castle Garden, Iconography of. (W. L. Andrews) Bk. Buyer, 22: 190, 304.

— Botanical Garden. (D. T. Macdougal) Pop. Sci. Mo. 57: 171.

— Broadway's Grenadiers. (J. W. Harrington) Munsey, 22: 43.

— Central Park in Winter. (R. S. Spears) Munsey, 22: 633.

— Chamber of Commerce; New York's Oldest Corporation. (W. L. Hawley) Munsey, 26: 38.

— Changes and Improvements in. Am. Arch. 73: 5.

— Charity Appropriations. (H. Folks) Char. R. 7: 869.

— Charter of. Ann. Am. Acad. Pol. Sci. 14: 136.

— Charter Revision, 1900. (E. P. Clark) Nation, 71: 439. — Outl. 65: 198. — (H. D. Baldwin) Munic. Aff. 4: 768.

— Children's Playgrounds in. (S. V. Tsanoff) Munic. Aff. 2: 293.

— City Magistrates' Courts. (R. C. Cornell) Scrib. M. 21: 221.

— City of Bridges. (J. D. Warner) Munic. Aff. 3: 651.

— Civic Assets of. (W. H. Tolman) R. of Rs. (N. Y.) 17: 55.

— Columbus Circle, Beautifying. (A. P. Doyle) Munic. Aff. 5: 722.

— Criminal Legislation by Proxy. (F. Moss) Forum, 28: 46.

— Cross Streets of. (Jesse L. Williams) Scrib. M. 28: 571.

— Daily Papers and their Editors. (J. Swinton) Indep. 52: 168.

— Debt Limit of, should be Amended. (B. S. Coler) Munic. Aff. 5: 664.

— Desperate Plight of. Cent. 40: 951.

— East Side Considerations. (E. S. Martin) Harper, 96: 853.

— East Side Living Conditions. Gunton's M. 15: 194.

— Education in the Charter of Greater. (F. A. Fitzpatrick) Educa. R. 13: 486.

— — Administration of. (N. M. Butler) Educa. R. 13: 195.

— — Public Education Association. (M. G. Van Rensselaer) Educa. R. 16: 209.

— Election, 1897. (J. Bryce) Contemp. 72: 751.

— — Lessons of. (N. M. Butler) Educa. R. 14: 514. — (D. F. Wilcox) Munic. Aff. 2: 207.

— — What is Involved in. Spec. 79: 587.

— Election of 1901. (M. R. Maltbie) R. of Rs. (N. Y.) 24: 551. — Outl. 69: 674. — Gunton's M. 21: 400. — (E. P. Clark) Nation, 73: 258.

— — Campaign for Decency. (H. Davis) Munsey, 26: 248.

Newspaper Notices; their use and abuse. (M. Watson) Theatre, **39**: 17.

Newspaper Press, The Government and the, in England. (E. Porritt) Pol. Sci. Q. **12**: 666.

— Half a Century's Survey. (F. Greenwood) Blackw. **161**: 704. Same art. Ecl. M. **129**: 62.

Newspaper Reporters and Oversupply. (J. L. Wright) Arena, **20**: 614.

Newspaper Reporting of Speeches and Sermons. (W. J. Fowler) Writer, **13**: 98.

Newspaper Science. Dial (Ch.) **26**: 233.

Newspaper Stopgap, A. (E. G. Henham) Cornh. **81**: 96.

Newspaper Work as a Career. (A. R. Kimball) Writer, **10**: 45.

— Limitations of Truth-telling. (E. F. Adams) Arena, **20**: 604.

— Practical. (H. S. Underwood) Writer, **10**: 29.

— Queerest Phase of. (J. Pendleton) Good Words, **42**: 277.

Newspaper Writers, Rules for. (E. H. Wood) Writer, **12**: 36.

Newton, Ernest, Architect. Studio (Internat.) **4**: 170.

Newton, Hubert Anson. (J. W. Gibbs) Am. J. Sci. **153**: 359.

Niagara Falls. (I. Trudell) Nat'l M. (Bost.) **6**: 461. — (Mrs. S. Van Rensselaer) Cent. **36**: 184.

— Age of, New Method of Determining. (G. F. Wright) Pop. Sci. Mo. **55**: 145.

— Another Episode in the History of. (J. W. Spencer) Am. J. Sci. **156**: 439.

— in Winter. (O. E. Dunlap) Cosmopol. **28**: 593.

— The New. (R. L. Hartt) McClure, **17**: 78.

— The Passing of. (M. B. Hartt) Outl. **68**: 21.

— Power from. (O. E. Dunlap) World's Work, **2**: 1052.

— Queen Victoria Park. (E. A. Meredeth) Canad. M. **9**: 228.

— Story of. (C. H. Hitchcock) Am. Antiq. **23**: 1.

— Use of. (R. L. Hartt) McClure, **17**: 78. — (W. C. Andrews) R. of Rs. (N. Y.) **23**: 694. — (H. W. Buck) Cassier, **20**: 3.

Niagara Fools, The, and their Feats. (G. Dollar) Strand, **14**: 332.

Niagara's Banks; a story. (J. W. Dafoe) Canad. M. **8**: 493.

Nibelungen Lied, The. (F. Thompson) Acad. **52**: 302. — (Margaret Watson) Dub. R. **126**: 297.

Nicæa, Greek Emperors of, at Nymphio. (E. Freshfield) Archæol. **49**: 382.

Nicanor Gate and the Brass Gate. (A. Büchler) Jew. Q. **11**: 46.

Nicaragua and Costa Rica, Location of Boundary between. (A. P. Davis) Nat. Geog. M. **12**: 22.

— and the Isthmian Routes. (A. P. Davis) Nat. Geog. M. **10**: 247.

— Naturalist in. (J, Crawford) Outing, **31**: 564.

— Northeast. (J. M. Nicol) Geog. J. **11**: 658.

Nicaragua Canal, The. (J. R. Chandler) Indep. **52**: 1106. — (W. Miller) Forum, **26**: 331. — (H. D. Money) Munsey, **18**: 747. — (H. White) Nation, **66**: 396. — Quar. **193**: 279. — Nat. Geog. M. **12**: 28. — (R. Bromley) 19th Cent. **49**: 100. — (E. R. Johnson) Indep. **51**: 179. — (T. B. Reed) No. Am. **168**: 552. — Liv. Age, **220**: 134. — (A. P. Davis) Munsey, **21**: 542. — (A. Shortt) Canad. M. **12**: 385.

— Advantages of. (A. S. Crowninshield) Cent. **35**: 458.

— and Clayton-Bulwer Treaty. (T. B. Strange) Canad. M. **12**: 480.

— and the Monroe Doctrine, Keasbey's. (A. G. Sedgwick) Nation, **64**: 90. — Spec. **78**: 837.

— and our Commercial Interests. (E. R. Johnson) R. of Rs. (N. Y.) **18**: 571.

Nicaragua Canal and Panama Canal compared. (A. P. Davis) Forum, **30**: 527.

— and the Treaty. (J. D. Whelpley) World's Work, **1**: 438. — (H. White) Nation, **73**: 294.

— and the West Indies. (O. Wachs) J. Mil. Serv. Inst. **15**: 1229.

— Bill for. Outl. **65**: 107.

— Commission on, a Trio of American Engineers. R. of Rs. (N. Y.) **16**: 292.

— Control of. (E. Van Dyke Robinson) Indep. **53**: 2962.

— Debate in Congress, Jan., 1897. (H. White) Nation, **64**: 81.

— Difficulties of Projected Route. (W. H. Hunter) Engin. M. **16**: 972.

— England and the Clayton-Bulwer Treaty. Spec. **81**: 264.

— How and by whom it should be Built. (L. M. Haupt) Engin. M. **15**: 550.

— in its Commercial and Military Aspects. (J. Nimmo, jr.) Engin. M. **15**: 720.

— in its Military Aspects. (G. P. Scriven) J. Mil. Serv. Inst. **15**: 1. — (W. R. Hamilton) J. Mil. Serv. Inst. **15**: 687. — (L. D. Green) J. Mil. Serv. Inst. **26**: 1.

— in the Light of Present Politics. (L. M. Keasbey) R. of Rs. (N. Y.) **18**: 566.

— Latest Aspects of the Project. (C. M. Stadden) No. Am. **167**: 698.

— Neutralization of. (J. R. Procter) Internat. Mo. **1**: 447.

— Our Diplomatic Relations with. (C. M. Stadden) R. of Rs. (N. Y.) **20**: 444.

— Question of Permanency of. (C. W. Hayes) Nat. Geog. M. **11**: 156.

— The Report on. (F. E. Leupp) Nation, **68**: 431.

— a Review. (C. B. Spahr) Outl. **60**: 431.

— Route of. (C. Willard Hayes) Science, n. s. **10**: 97.

— — Physiography of. (C. Willard Hayes) Nat. Geog. M. **10**: 233.

— — — Hayes on. (I. C. Russell) Am. Natural. **33**: 679.

— A Spanish View of. (J. G. Sobral) No. Am. **164**: 462.

— The Trans-isthmian Canal Problem. (W. Ludlow) Harper, **96**: 837.

— Water Supply for. (A. P. Davis) Nat. Geog. M. **11**: 363.

— West Indies in their relation to England and the U. S. (J. P. De Putron) Westm. **154**: 182.

See Interoceanic; Panama.

Nicene Creed in a Novelette. (W. Lloyd) Westm. **147**: 11.

— Scott on. (F. H. Foster) Presb. & Ref. R. **8**: 123.

Nicholas I. of Russia; his visit to England in 1844. (C. Murray) Cornh. **75**: 341.

Nicholas II. of Russia. (W. T. Stead) Cosmopol. **28**: 377. — (F. J. Dillon) Good Words, **41**: 446.

— and the French People. (P. Bigelow) Indep. **53**: 2464.

— Coronation of. (R. H. Davis) Harper, **94**: 335.

— Emperor of Peace. (W. T. Stead) R. of Rs. (N. Y.) **19**: 35.

— Monarchs at Home. (M. S. Warren) Eng. Illust. **19**: 304.

— Peace Proposal of. (E. E. Hale) New Eng. M. n. s. **19**: 580. — Spec. **81**: 823. — Contemp. **74**: 498. Same art. Liv. Age, **219**: 417. — (A. White) National, **32**: 201. — (J. G. Rogers) 19th Cent. **44**: 697.

— Rumored Abdication of. Spec. **83**: 209.

— Salutation to; a poem. (E. S. Phelps) Atlan. **83**: 97.

Nicholls, George, and the English Poor Law. (W. J. Ashley) Nation, **66**: 428.

Nicholls, Harry, Portrait of. Theatre, **39**: 118.

Nicholls Manslaughter Case. Spec. **80**: 650.

Nicholson, John ; hero of the Indian Mutiny. (Douglas Sladen) Idler, 11: 243, 314. — Blackw. 163: 207. Same art. Liv. Age, 217: 82.
— Trotter's Life of. Acad. 53: 5. — Sat. R. 85: 468. — Ath. '98, 1: 44.
Nicholson, William. (O. Uzanne) Bk. Buyer, 17: 293. — (Edna Harris) Brush & P. 3: 354.
— and his Work. (J. A. Reid) Art J. 52: 72.
Nicholson, W. P., Colored Prints of. (G. White) Studio (Internat.) 3: 177.
Nickel and Cobalt. (T. L. Phipson) Chamb. J. 74: 661.
— — Atomic Weights of. Nature, 57: 374.
— — Separation of, by Hydrochloric Acid. (F. S. Havens) Am. J. Sci. 156: 396.
— Mining, Smelting, and Refining. (T. Ulke) Engin. M. 16: 215, 451.
— On the Qualitative Separation from Cobalt. (P. E. Browning and J. B. Hartwell) Am. J. Sci. 160: 316.
Nickel Steel in Metallurgy, Mechanics, and Armor. (H. W. Raymond) Engin. M. 12: 838.
Nicknames of French Monarchs. (J. F. Cowan) Educa. 19: 500.
Nicobar Islands. (R. C. Temple) J. Soc. Arts, 48: 105.
Nicod, Paul. Spec. 80: 82.
Nicolas of Flüe. (M. E. Blake) Cath. World, 65: 658.
Nicolet, G., Painter. (T. Nicolet) M. of Art, 25: 97.
Nicolette ; a story. (C. K. Burrow) Idler, 13: 234.
Niecks, Frederick, Prof., Musician and Writer, with portrait. Music, 17: 249.
Niello Work. (C. Davenport) J. Soc. Arts, 48: 245.
Niese on the Two Books of the Maccabees. (I. Abrahams) Jew. Q. 13: 508.
Nieto de Silva, Don Felix, A Gentleman of Spain. (D. Hannay) Macmil. 78: 136. Same art. Liv. Age, 218: 461.
Nietzsche, Friedrich. Acad. 59: 175. — (T. B. Saunders) Ath. '00, 2: 281. — (O. Crawfurd) 19th Cent. 48: 592. — Acad. 60: 35, 479. — Acad. 57: 31. — (B. Hume) Lond. Q. 94: 338. — Acad. 54: 195.
— and Darwinism. (A. Fouillée) Internat. Mo. 3: 134.
— and his Philosophy. (S. Zeisler) Dial (Ch.) 19: 219.
— and Richard Wagner. (B. Marshall) Fortn. 69: 885.
— as Critic, Philosopher, Poet, and Prophet, with Selections, compiled by T. Common. Ath. '01, 1: 751.
— Beyond Good and Evil. (C. C. Everett) New World, 7: 684.
— Ethics of. (M. Adams) Internat. J. Ethics, 11: 82.
— Genealogy of Morals. Book R. 5: 265.
— Influence of Schopenhauer upon. (G. N. Dolson) Philos. R. 10: 241.
— Life and Works. (A. Seth) Blackw. 162: 476.
— a Mad Philosopher. (H. T. Peck) Bookman, 8: 25.
— A Nietzsche Breviary. Bookman, 8: 153.
— The Opinions of. (A. S. P. Pattison) Contemp. 73: 727.
— Philosophy of. Poet-Lore, 11: 622. — (H. Brooks) Book R. 6: 11.
— Teachings of. (Charles M. Bakewell) Int. J. Ethics, 9: 324.
— Tragedy of a Thinker. Macmil. 81: 106.
Niger, The French on the. (F. A. Edwards) Fortn. 69: 576. — (F. A. Edwards) Gent. M. n. s. 61: 275.
Niger, Hourst Expedition to. (E. de Sasseville) Nat. Geog. M. 8: 24.
— Question of. Spec. 79: 480.
— Source of. (J. K. Trotter) Geog. J. 10: 237, 386.
Niger Coast Protectorate, Jekris, Sobos, and Ijos of. (H. L. Roth) Anthrop. J. 28: 104.
Niger Country, Bindloss on. Ath. '99, 2: 280.
— Future of the. (F. A. Edwards) Westm. 151: 388.

Niger Delta, Ju-Ju Laws and Customs in. (C. N. De Cardi) Anthrop. J. 29: 29.
— Life and Death in. Blackw. 163: 451. Same art. Liv. Age, 217: 525.
Niger Lapis in the Comitium at Rome. (G. Boni) Archæol. 57: 175.
Niger-Soudan, With a Maxim in the. (W. D. Bird) Un. Serv. M. 15: 322.
Niger Trade, An Incident of the. (H. Bindloss) Chamb. J. 76: 154.
Nigeria. (A. S. Geden) Lond. Q. 92: 262.
— and its Trade. (H. Bindloss) Monthly R. 3, no. 3: 67.
— French Mutiny in. Spec. 83: 274.
— A Glance at. (H. Bindloss) Asia. R. 28: 327. Same art. Liv. Age, 223: 559. Same art. Ecl. M. 134: 40.
Nigger of the Narcissus ; a story. (J. Conrad) New R. 17: 125, 485, 605.
Night. (T. Fortebus) Argosy, 75: 300.
Night ; a poem. (R. Coolidge) Atlan. 82: 288.
Night and Sleep and Rest. (Myron Reed) Cosmopol. 22: 437.
Night in Austin Friars, A. (T. S. E. Hake) Chamb. J. 74: 705-756.
Night in a Cathedral, A. (W. O'C. Morris) Poet-Lore, 10: 473.
Night in the Clouds, A. (M. A. Morrison) Good Words, 42: 172.
Night in Devil's Gully. (O. Hall) Lippinc. 63: 272.
Night in the Desert ; a poem. (J. S. Phillimore) Argosy, 71: 361.
Night in a Hospital, A. Macmil. 79: 473.
Night in the Mountains, A ; a story. (R. E. Dean) Midland, 9: 28.
Night in Time of War ; a poem. (E. Gosse) Ecl. M. 131: 387.
Night in Venice ; a story. (M. P. Shiel) Cornh. 76: 500.
Night on the Moor, A ; a story. (R. M. Gilchrist) Pall Mall M. 22: 367.
Night on Urondi Kopje, A. Chamb. J. 74: 603.
Night Escape, A ; an episode of the war. (S. Vail) Scrib. M. 24: 630.
Night Piece ; a poem. (A. Colton) Atlan. 88: 428.
Night Run of the "Overland," The ; a story. (E. E. Peake) McClure, 15: 143.
Night Song in the Streets. (C. G. D. Roberts) Cosmopol. 26: 336.
Night Walk, The. (G. Meredith) Cornh. 80: 145.
Night's Adventure on the Pearl River. Blackw. 169: 806. Same art. Liv. Age, 230: 186. Same art. Ecl. M. 137: 346.
Nightingale, Florence. (W. H. Fitchett) Cornh. 78: 721. — (C. Middleton) Sund. M. 30: 702.
Nightjars, A Study of. (A. H. Japp) Gent. M. n. s. 67: 141.
Nightmare, Origin of. Science, n. s. 9: 455.
— The Riddle of. (L. Hearn) Liv. Age, 220: 332.
Nihilism and Anarchy. (C. Johnston) No. Am. 171: 302.
— Regicide, in the 19th Century. (S. B. Chester) Gent. M. n. s. 67: 382.
— Russian, of To-day. (A. Cahan) Forum, 31: 413.
Nijni Novgorod, Fair of. (F. J. Ziegler) Lippinc. 67: 727.
Nile, Battle of, Nelson in the. (A. T. Mahan) Cent. 31: 435.
— — Sir Thomas Foley's Action at the. (J. B. Herbert) Un. Serv. M. 15: 420.
— Campaign of the, 1798. (W. O'C. Morris) Pall Mall M. 14: 108.
— Dam at Assouan. (A. J. Liversedge) Cassier, 21: 140. — (F. C. Penfield) Cent. 35: 483. — Am. Arch. 60: 14.

Noke, Charles J., Pottery Enamel Work by. (K. Parkes) Artist (N. Y.) **31**: 210.

"Noli me Tangere;" a story. (B. Atkinson) Sund. M. **30**: 219.

Nome, Cape, Gold District. (F. C. Schrader) Nat. Geog. M. **11**: 15. — (W. J. Lampton) McClure, **15**: 134. — (C. Edgar Lewis) Outl. **64**: 784. — (A. Heilprin) Pop. Sci. Mo. **56**: 633.

— Gold Mining at. (Elizabeth Robins) Pall Mall M. **23**: 55. — (A. G. Kingsbury) Nat'l M. (Bost.) **14**: 505.

— Woman's Experience at. (E. B. Caldwell) Cosmopol. **30**: 81.

Nomenclature, Scientific. (T. Roosevelt) Science, **5**: 685.

— — The Merton Rules. (E. Coues and J. A. Allen) Science, **6**: 9.

— — Reform in. (A. L. Herrera) Science, n. s. **10**: 120.

— — Strange Practices in Plant Naming. (C. L. Pollard) Science, n. s. **14**: 280.

Nominating Caucus, Rise and Fall of. (M. Ostrogorski) Am. Hist. R. **5**: 253.

Nominating Conventions in Pennsylvania. (J. S. Walton) Am. Hist. R. **2**: 262.

— National. (J. M. Thurston) Cosmopol. **29**: 194.

Nominating System. (E. L. Godkin) Atlan. **79**: 450.

— in Philadelphia. (W. J. Branson) Ann. Am. Acad. Pol. Sci. **14**: 18.

Nomination of Candidates by the People. (J. S. Hopkins) Arena, **19**: 729.

Nominations, The Presidential, 1900. Nation, **70**: 491.

Non-combatant, The. (A. French) Scrib. M. **21**: 741.

Nonconformists and the Stage. (A. Halstead) Theatre, **39**: 78.

— Early, Education of. (F. Watson) Gent. M. n. s. **67**: 229.

Nonconformity, The Position of. Liv. Age, **213**: 675.

Nonius Marcellus, Leyden MS. of. (W. M. Lindsay) Am. J. Philol. **22**: 29.

Non-literary, The. Spec. **78**: 84.

Non-partisan Municipal Elections. (G. G. Wright) Munic. Aff. **4**: 363.

Nono, Luigi. (Lilian Priuli-Bon) Art J. **53**: 193.

Nonsense, The Sense of. (Carolyn Wells) Scrib. M. **29**: 239.

Nonsense Verses, Old and New. (St.J. E. C. Hankin) Idler, **14**: 90.

Noontide; a poem. (F. W. Bourdillon) Spec. **83**: 317. Same art. Ecl. M. **133**: 910.

Noose, The. (H. Hutchinson) Blackw. **163**: 665.

Norbury Church, Derbyshire. (G. Le Blanc Smith) Reliquary, **41**: 200.

Nordau, Max. Degeneration. Sewanee, **3**: 503. — (E. Garnett) Acad. **56**: 96.

Nordenskjöld, A. E. Von. (W. S. Bruce) Nature, **64**: 450. — With portrait. Geog. J. **18**: 449.

— "Periplus." (C. R. Beazley) Geog. J. **12**: 373.

Nordhoff, Evelyn H., in Memoriam. (Ellen D. Hale) Artist (N. Y.) **23**: xxxv.

Nordica, Madame; a study. (W. Armstrong) Music, **19**: 15.

Norfolk, England, History and Description of. Quar. **185**: 117.

— Broads of. (E. V. Beaufort) Belgra. **93**: 466. — (H. C. Shelley) New Eng. M. n. s. **16**: 195.

— Farming in. (H. R. Haggard) Longm. **32**: 401, 497. **33**: 220-500. **34**: 32-500.

— Meal-marshes of, Fish and Fowl in the. Liv. Age, **214**: 893.

— North, Fish and Fowl of. (C. J. Cornish) Cornh. **79**: 312.

Norfolk, Summering in. (J. W. White) Outing, **38**: 374.

— West, A Corner of. Blackw. **162**: 382.

— Wild Fowl Decoy in. (E. R. Suffling) Chamb. J. **75**: 77.

Norfolk, Va., Quaint Old. (Malinda C. Faville) Midland, **9**: 35.

Norfolk Island. Gent. M. n. s. **62**: 438.

Norland Lyrics; a foreword. (C. G. D. Roberts) Canad. M. **12**: 156.

Normal School and its Mission. (G. R. Pinkham) Educa. **18**: 538.

— Central Defect of the. (W. H. Mace) Educa. R. **21**: 132.

— in France. Educa. R. **13**: 291.

— Michigan State. (D. E. Smith) Educa. **17**: 563.

— Problems of, at Opening of 20th Century. (H. H. Seerley) Educa. **21**: 287.

Normal Schools and the Training of Teachers. (F. Burk) Atlan. **81**: 769.

— Continuous Sessions of. (I. Shepard) Educa. R. **15**: 363.

— Courses of Study for. (O. Chrisman) Arena, **22**: 56.

— Do we need Higher? (C. C. Ramsay) Educa. **19**: 183.

— Future of. (W. T. Harris) Educa. R. **17**: 1.

— of Massachusetts. (G. E. Gay) Educa. **17**: 513, (A. G. Boyden) 611. **18**: 55.

— of the South, Some Wornout Methods of. (F. H. Kasson) Educa. **18**: 633.

— Origin and Growth of. (F. H. Kasson) Educa. **19**: 343.

— Original Investigation in. (F. E. Bolton) Educa. **20**: 548, 603.

— The Relative Importance of Practice Teaching in. (J. W. Hall) Educa. R. **18**: 292.

— Report on, by a Committee of the National Educational Association. Educa. R. **20**: 72.

Normal School Problems of 20th Century. (A. G. Boyden; J. W. Cook; E. Conant; E. T. Pierce; J. G. Thompson) Educa. **21**: 1.

Normal School Teacher, A, "Confessions" of. (M. H. Leonard) Pop. Sci. Mo. **50**: 620.

Norman, Henry, Portrait of. Bk. Buyer, **16**: 466.

Norman, Mrs. Henry. (Ethel F. Heddle) Good Words, **42**: 15.

Norman Features in Wold Churches, Yorkshire. (E. M. Cole) Antiq. n. s. **37**: 294.

Normand, Ernest, Art Work of. (Fk. Rinder) Art J. **53**: 137.

Normand, Mrs. Ernest. See Rae, Henrietta.

Normandy, In. (I. P. Stevenson) Chaut. **31**: 169.

Normans, Characteristics of the. (C. Gibson) Cath. World, **65**: 506.

Normanton, Earl of. Collection of Pictures. (A. L. Baldry) Art J. **50**: 310, 325.

Norris, Frank, Realist, with portrait. (F. T. Cooper) Bookman, **10**: 234.

— The Octopus. (A. S. van Westrum) Bk. Buyer, **22**: 326.

Norris, John Pilkington. (F. D. How) Sund. M. **29**: 821.

Norse Remains and Indian Works, Points of Difference between. (G. Fowke) Am. Anthrop. **2**: 550.

North Adams, Massachusetts. See Adams.

— Public Library Building. (A. B. Jackson) Lib. J. **25**: 105.

North America, Second Book, Tarr and McMurry's. (R. D. Salisbury) School R. **8**: 627.

North and South. (S. Trotter) Pop. Sci. Mo. **51**: 367.

North Cape, A Jaunt to the. (Isabel McCrackan) Overland, n. s. **32**: 195.

North Carolina, Constitutional Amendment. Outl. 65: 841.

— Mineralogical Notes from. (J. H. Pratt) Am. J. Sci. 155: 126.

— Race War in. (H. L. West) Forum, 26: 578.

— Suffrage Amendment of. (A. J. McKelway) Indep. 52: 1955.

— Taxation in. (G. E. Barnett) J. H. Univ. Stud. 18: 77.

— Transition from Colony to Commonwealth. (E. W. Sikes) J. H. Univ. Stud. 16: no. 10–11.

North Central Association of Colleges and Preparatory Schools. School R. 5: 38.

North Clare; Leaves from a Diary. (E. Lawless) 19th Cent. 46: 603.

North Country of England, Notes from. Temp. Bar, 118: 336.

North Laos Mission, A Visit to the. (H. King) Indep. 53: 1721.

North Polar Stars, Catalogue of. (Caroline E. Furness) Pop. Astron. 9: 1.

North Pole, Attempt to reach the. (R. E. Peary) Mc-Clure, 12: 417.

— Nearer the. (S. Bompiani) Outl. 66: 573.

— Quest of. (H. C. Walsh) Munsey, 25: 613. — Blackw. 170: 476. Same art. Liv. Age, 231: 574.

— Waymarks to, Nansen's. (W. F. Hume) Knowl. 20: 33.

— Wellman Expedition, 1898–99. (W. Wellman) Idler, 19: 130, 206.

North Road, The Great, C. G. Harper on. Ath. '01, 1: 457.

North Sea Canal : a Great Dutch Waterwork. Chamb. J. 74: 673.

North-sea Fisheries. (W. Wood) Gent. M. n. s. 61: 256.

Northampton, Massachusetts. (S. E. Bridgman) New Eng. M. n. s. 21: 581.

Northamptonshire, England. (Alice Dryden) Pall Mall M. 13: 239.

— The Hidation of. (J. H. Round) Eng. Hist. R. 15: 78.

Northcote, James. Acad. 54: 31. 61: 377.

Northern Pacific R. R., Cataclysm in. (H. White) Nation, 73: 65.

Northern Pastoral, A. (B. Russell) Sund. M. 26: 118. Same art. Liv. Age, 212: 822.

Northfield, Massachusetts, Old Days and New in. (A. M. Mitchell) New Eng. M. n. s. 16: 671.

Northrop, Birdsey G. (E. B. Peck) New Eng. M. n. s. 22: 269.

Northumberland, Hinds's History of. Ed. R. 192: 140. — Ath. '98, 2: 123.

— Rustics of. (P. A. Graham) Longm. 29: 321.

Northumbrian Palatinates and Regalities. (W. Page) Archæol. 51: 143.

Northumbrian Worthies, Old. (B. W. Wells) Sewanee, 1: 419.

Northwest ; Conquest of the Country N. W. of the River Ohio, 1778–83, English's. (F. J. Turner) Am. Hist. R. 2: 363.

— Evolution of the. (W. A. Tenney) Overland, n. s. 35: 321.

— Henry and Thompson on the Greater. (B. A. Hinsdale) Dial (Ch.) 23: 40.

— Literary Development of the Far. (H. Bashford) Overland, n. s. 33: 316.

— The New. (J. A. Wheelock) Harper, 96: 299.

— under Three Flags, C. Moore's. (B. A. Hinsdale) Am. Hist. R. 6: 139.

— "Where Rolls the Oregon." (A. H. Bradford) Outl. 59: 1028.

— The Wonderful. (H. A. Stanley) World's Work, 2: 812.

Northwest, Canadian, In the. (Harold Bindloss) Good Words, 41: 117. Same art. Liv. Age, 224: 772.

Northwestern Railway. (John Pendleton) Good Words, 39: 381, 470.

Norton, Caroline E. S., and her Writings. (I. A. Taylor) Longm. 29: 231. Same art. Liv. Age, 212: 448.

Norton, Rev. John, of Middletown. (Z. S. Eldredge) N. E. Reg. 53: 87.

Norton, Thomas, of Guilford, Conn., Descendants of. (R. D. Smyth) N. E. Reg. 54: 269.

Norvins's Memorial. (H. M. Stephens) Am. Hist. R. 3: 360.

Norway, Arthur H. Highways and Byways in Devon and Cornwall. Studio (Internat.) 4: 127.

Norway, Agricultural. (R. H. Wallace) Econ. R. 7: 145.

— and Sweden, Quarrel between. (J. Moritzen) R. of Rs. (N. Y.) 19: 558. — (H. L. Bræfkstad) Fortn. 69: 96.

— — Relations of. (L. Stejneger) Conserv. R. 2: 317. 3: 114.

— Chápter on. New Eng. M. n. s. 22: 233.

— Cruise in the Fjords of. (C. M. O'Brien) Cath. World, 69: 533.

— Day in. (H. E. Scudder) Cent. 32: 546.

— — Another. (H. H. Boyesen) Cent. 32: 551.

— Glacier Excursion in. (H. H. Boyesen) Cosmopol. 23: 625.

— Glimpses of its Scenery. (W. Wilton) Canad. M. 9: 208–483.

— Letters from. (C. W. Wood) Argosy, 70: 57–403. 71: 41–444. 72: 23–386.

— Revisited. (E. Gosse) No. Am. 167: 534.

— The Romsdal. (H. Maxwell) Blackw. 168: 336.

— Wild. Lond. Q. 89: 289.

— A Woman's Trip through the Upper Saeterdal. (E. Taylor) Outing, 34: 367.

Norway Vidda, Crossing the. (E. Taylor) Outing, 36: 664.

Norwegian Literature, 1896–97. (C. Brinckmann) Ath. '97, 2: 24.

— 1897–98. (C. Brinckmann) Ath. '98, 2: 23.

— 1898–99. (C. Brinckmann) Ath. '99, 2: 24.

— 1899–1900. (C. Brinckmann) Ath. '00, 2: 24.

— 1900–01. (C. Brinckmann) Ath. '01, 2: 24.

Norwich, England, Government of. (Elsie Watson) Pol. Sci. Q. 16: 262.

Norwich Cathedral. (W. Lefroy) Sund. M. 26: 183.

Norwich Union Life Insurance Society. Bank. M. (Lond.) 63: 141.

Norwich University, Norwich, Vt. (N. L. Sheldon) New Eng. M. n. s. 20: 65.

Nosairîs, Dussaud's History and Religion of. Ath. '01, 1: 10.

Nose, Scientific Opinions of the. (E. Schutz) Chaut. 24: 594.

Noses of Apes, Contrasts in. (R. Lyddeker) Knowl. 22: 174.

Noses and Minds. (L. Robinson) Blackw. 169: 796. Same art. Ecl. M. 137: 484. Same art. Liv. Age, 230: 347.

Not in the Signal Code. (Edith L. Wood) Scrib. M. 27: 372.

Not made in Germany ; a story. Macmil. 75: 201. Same art. Liv. Age, 212: 557.

Not on the Passenger-list ; a story. (J. V. Z. Belden) Harper, 99: 291.

Not Peace, but a Sword ; a story. (J. D. Hilton) Sund. M. 28: 234. Same art. Liv. Age, 221: 556.

Not Poppy nor Mandragora ; a story. (M. L. Luther) Nat'l. M. (Bost.) 10: 413.

Not Servants but Friends. (L. Abbott) Outl. 60: 128.

Octopus or Devil Fish. (C. F. Holder) Outing, **38:** 396.

Odd Notions. (A. K. H. Boyd) Longm. **31:** 49.

Odd People I have met. (S. Baring-Gould) Sund. M. **28:** 52, 202, 547, 693.

Oddingley Murders, The. (E. P. Thompson) Gent. M. n. s. **66:** 56.

Oddment, An; a story. (Mrs. J. H. Perks) Temp. Bar, **115:** 564. Same art. Liv. Age, **220:** 254.

Odds beyond Arithmetic. Temp. Bar, **122:** 381. Same art. Liv. Age, **229:** 238.

Ode to a Nightingale, Keats's. (W. C. Wilkinson) Bookman, **5:** 377.

Odell, Benjamin B., jr. Governor-elect of New York. (L. Abbott) R. of Rs. (N. Y.) **22:** 687. — (R. Ogden) McClure, **17:** 283.

— Executive Work of; with portrait. World's Work, **1:** 922.

— a Practical Politician. Outl. **69:** 97.

Oder, The River. Geog. J. **9:** 422.

Odile; a story. (R. Mackay) Temp. Bar, **115:** 298.

Odin and the Royal Family of England. (K. Blind) Scot. R. **33:** 371.

O'Donnells in Spain. Temp. Bar, **114:** 488.

Odors. (E. Duvall) Lippinc. **61:** 269.

Odysseus, Inner Life of. (H. N. Fowler) Chaut. **32:** 640.

Odyssey of the North, An; a story. (J. London) Atlan. **85:** 85.

Odyssey of Sandy M'Pherson; a story. (H. E. Warner) Midland, **8:** 237.

Oehlenschlager, Adam Gottlob. (W. M. Payne) Sewanee, **8:** 129.

O'er Sea and Land. (Mrs. W. C. Hawksley) Chamb. J. **74:** 625–691.

Of Autumn Downs; a poem. (E. W. Barnard) Outing, **31:** 19.

Of the Golden Age; a poem. (L. I. Guiney) Cosmopol. **26:** 513.

Of Janet; a poem. (J. Rhoades) Ecl. M. **132:** 306.

Of Men and Matters in Our Village; a story. Blackw. **169:** 637.

Of the Old Guard; a story. (F. H. Spearman) McClure, **17:** 450.

Of Royal Blood. (W. Le Queux) Chamb. J. **77:** 1–404.

"Of the Stock Exchange, London, Gentleman." (E. Davies) Argosy, **64:** 377.

Offa's Dyke, On. Archæol. **53:** 465.

Offertories. Spec. **80:** 536.

Office, Corruption in. (A. G. Sedgwick) Nation, **67:** 107.

— Federal, Power of Removal from. (J. W. Stillman) Green Bag, **10:** 164.

— Public Service without. (E. P. Clark) Nation, **72:** 310.

Office-seeking during the Administration of John Adams. (G. Hunt) Am. Hist. R. **2:** 241.

— during Jefferson's Administration. (G. Hunt) Am. Hist. R. **3:** 270.

Officers at Posts, Practical Instruction of. (J. P. Wisser) J. Mil. Serv. Inst. **9:** 198.

— in the Field, Personal Equipment of. (W. C. Brown) J. Mil. Serv. Inst. **14:** 1219.

— on the Retired List. (G. N. Lieber) J. Mil. Serv. Inst. **22:** 62.

Officers' Quarters, Furniture for, Earl's Court Exhibition, 1901. Artist (N. Y.) **31:** 84.

Ogden, Ruth, with portrait. Bk. News, **16:** 113.

Ogilvie, G. Stuart. Master. (G. B. Shaw) Sat. R. **85:** 592.

— White Knight. (G. B. Shaw) Sat. R. **85:** 324.

Oglethorpe, Anne and Eleanor. Blackw. **163:** 196.

Oglethorpe, James Edward. (A. Dobson) Longm. **33:** 253. Same art. Ecl. M. **132:** 570. Same art. Liv. Age, **220:** 537.

O'Gorman, Camila. (F. A. Kirkpatrick) Cornh. **77:** 535.

O'Higgins, Bernard, Dictator of Chili. Temp. Bar, **15:** 263.

Ohio, Early Pioneer Life in. (B. F. Stone) New Eng. M. n. s. **16:** 210.

— Emigration to, 1798–1800. (G. T. Ridlon) New Eng. M. n. s. **21:** 695.

— in National Affairs. (C. M. Harvey) Chaut. **26:** 392.

— in 1790. (E. W. Latimer) Lippinc. **62:** 242.

— The Legislature that elected Mr. Hanna. (J. T. Kenny) Arena, **21:** 311.

— Municipal Code Commission. (E. Kibler) Munic. Aff. **3:** 528.

— The Ohioans. (R. L. Hartt) Atlan. **84:** 679.

— School System of. (E. E. White) Educa. R. **17:** 465.

— Tax Inquisitor Law. (T. N. Carver) Econ. Stud. **3:** 167.

Ohio Coal Measures, Names for the Formations of. (C. S. Prosser) Am. J. Sci. **161:** 191.

Ohio Library Association, Sixth Annual Meeting of. Pub. Lib. **5:** 355.

Oil. (C. W. Mason) Argosy, **69:** 98. — (J. Croskey) Chamb. J. **76:** 657.

— Lubricating, Purification of. (G. W. Bissell) Cassier, **12:** 126.

Oil and Water; a story. (C. B. Loomis) Munsey, **25:** 287.

Oil-fields, New, of the U. S. (D. T. Day) R. of Rs. (N. Y.) **23:** 711.

— of Texas and California. Nat. Geog. M. **12:** 276. — (E. R. Treherne) Cosmopol. **31:** 251.

— of the U. S., Story of. (G. E. Walsh) Cassier, **12:** 663.

Oil Kings, Defeat of, in England. (R. Donald) Contemp. **74:** 232.

Oil-wells at Oil City, Pa. (W. Fawcett) Nat'l M. (Bost.) **12:** 483.

— Boring, in the Sea. Chamb. J. **75:** 224.

Okapi, The, African Quadruped. (F. E. Beddard) Pall Mall M. **24:** 569. — (H. H. Johnston) McClure, **17:** 497.

Oklahoma. (H. C. Candee) Atlan. **86:** 328.

— The Government's Gift of Homes. (C. M. Harger) Outl. **68:** 907.

— Land Lottery in. (J. G. Speed) Outl. **68:** 667.

— The Next Commonwealth. (C. M. Harger) Outl. **67:** 273.

Oklahoma Boomers. (G. Dollar) Strand, **14:** 137.

Oklahoma Claims. (H. C. Candee) Lippinc. **62:** 557.

Oklahoma Territory. (J. M. Miller) New Eng. M. n. s. **18:** 393.

— Social Conditions. (H. C. Candee) Forum, **25:** 426.

Okuma, Count; a famous Japanese statesman. (F. E. Clark) Indep. **53:** 91.

Olbreuse, Elénore d', and Queen Victoria. (A. van Amstel) 19th Cent. **43:** 625.

Olbrich, J., Vienna Architect. (O. Stoessl) Artist (N. Y.) **32:** 34.

Olbrich, J. M., Work of, at Darmstadt Artists' Colony. (W. Fred) Studio (Internat.) **15:** 91.

Olcott, Eben Erskine. Cassier, **20:** 175.

Old Age. (J. Payn) 19th Cent. **42:** 402. Same art. Ecl. M. **129:** 768.

— Browning's Vision of. (C. W. Hodell) Meth. R. **61:** 99.

— Deferment of. (W. A. Hollis) Indep. **51:** 935.

— Elders of Arcady. (A. Jessopp) 19th Cent. **47:** 776. Same art. Ecl. M. **135:** 347.

— an Investment for. Chamb. J. **75:** 815.

Old Age, Pensions for. (B. Holland) Econ. J. 8: 333. — Spec. 81: 75, 516. — (J. H. Schooling) Eng. Illust. 20: 97. — Chamb. J. 75: 593. — (L. Holland) National, 31: 868. — (W. D. MacGregor) Westm. 154: 276. —(H. H. Lusk) Arena, 23: 635. — (A. M. Brice) Temp. Bar, 124: 26. — (C. S. Loch) Econ. J. 9: 520. — (H. W. Wolff) Econ. R. 9: 321. — Ed. R. 190: 332. — (E. Tregear) Indep. 51: 799. — (D. MacG. Means) Nation, 69: 146. — (S. Walpole) 19th Cent. 45: 681. — (J. Trist) Westm. 152: 533. —(V. Nash) Contemp. 75: 495. — Spec. 82: 672. —(A. Murray) Bank M. (Lond.) 168: 740.

— — Denmark and its Aged Poor. (A. W. Flux) Yale R. 7: 434.

— — Fallacies about. (C. S. Loch) 19th Cent. 44: 807.

— — from a Socialist's Standpoint. (J. C. Chase) Lippinc. 64: 748.

— — in Denmark. (E. Sellers) Contemp. 78: 430.

— — in France. (A. F. Wood) 19th Cent. 46: 131.

— — in Italy. (H. W. Wolff) Econ. R. 10: 86.

— — in New Zealand. (W. H. Montgomery) Canad. M. 12: 296. — Bank M. (Lond.) 66: 804.

— — Is Unionist Party committed to? (C. A. Whitmore) National, 33: 709.

— — The Landlords to pay. (W. C. Wright) Westm. 151: 501.

— — made Easy. Fortn. 71: 445.

— — Outline of a Practical Scheme of. (J. C. Haig) National, 38: 432.

— — Plea for. (M. Davitt) Forum, 28: 677.

— — Poor Law Statistics as used in Connection with. (C. Booth) Econ. J. 9: 212.

— — Report on. Bank. M. (Lond.) 66: 285.

— — Report of the Committee on. (T. Scanlon) Fortn. 70: 575.

— — Shall we give? (W. E. H. Lecky) Indep. 51: 2662.

— — A State Crutch. (A. E. Spender) Westm. 152: 44.

— — Why I oppose. (W. E. H. Lecky) Forum, 28: 687.

— a poem. (R. G. A. S. Prudhomme) Argosy, 67: 290.

Old and the New; a poem. (A. B. Willits) Cosmopol. 25: 64.

Old and New Music; a story. (Julian Hawthorne) Cosmopol. 25: 303.

Old Bachelor's Story, The. (Mattie A. Curl) Midland, 11: 150.

Old Bailey, The. (J. C. Thornley) Chaut. 28: 323.

Old Betty and her Ladyship. (L. G. Moberly) Temp. Bar, 120: 406. Same art. Ecl. M. 135: 497. Same art. Liv. Age, 226: 453.

Old Brigadier. (Ivan Turgénief) Scot. R. 32: 272.

Old Broideries; poem. (J. P. Peabody) Atlan. 82: 286.

Old Cab-driver, The. (Jacques Normauth) Liv. Age, 226: 298.

Old Captain; a story. (M. Hemenway) Harper, 98: 3.

Old Captive, The; a poem. (J. D. Daskam) Atlan. 84: 429.

"Old Carnations." (A. B. Paine) Scrib. M. 28: 146.

Old Catholic Movement, Incidents in the Inception of. (A. T. Brook) Am. J. Theol. 2: 632.

— Origin and Development of. Am. J. Theol. 2: 481.

Old Catholics and the Lambeth Conference. Spec. 79: 206.

Old Cavalier, The; a poem. (T. Roberts) Canad. M. 12: 485.

Old Chester Tales. (M. Deland) Harper, 96: 664 — 98: 142.

Old Cinder Cat; a story. (V. F. Boyle) Harper, 101: 416.

Old Commoner, An. Argosy, 70: 92.

Old Don's Honor, The. (F. L. Wheeler) Overland, n. s. 33: 202.

Old Earth; a poem. (J. E. Downey) Poet-Lore, 11: 354.

Old Elm's Story, The. (M. E. Hall) Midland, 7: 529.

Old English Words, Revival of. (M. H. Leonard) Writer, 13: 22.

Old Esther's Easter Bonnet; a story. (E. Atkinson) Canad. M. 14: 519.

Old-fashioned Wooing, An; a story. (E. E. Kelley) McClure, 17: 139.

Old Flame, An; more adventures of the amateur cracksman. (E. W. Hornung) Scrib. M. 29: 707.

Old Friends. (E. Brower) Lippinc. 59: 274.

Old Glory, 1898; a poem. (J. W. Riley) Atlan. 82: 727.

Old Grand Army Man, An; a story. (A. French) McClure, 11: 162.

Old Homes; a poem. (M. Cawein) Atlan. 82: 855.

Old House, The; a romance. Liv. Age, 222: 1-225.

Old Jim Horse, The; a sketch. (J. L. Steffens) McClure, 15: 32.

Old Ladies, In Praise of. (L. M. Donnelly) Atlan. 84: 852.

Old Lady, The; a story. Temp. Bar, 111: 408.

Old Lamps for New Ones, Dickens's. (Ellen Duvall) Citizen, 4: 11.

Old Land and the Young Land, The; a poem. (A. Austin) Ecl. M. 134: 268. Same art. Liv. Age, 223: 787.

Old Love and Young; a story. (E. A. Gillie) Gent. M. n. s. 65: 105.

Old Lovers; a poem. (E. Nesbit) Argosy, 64: 564.

Old Maid's Canvassing Experience; a story. (Mrs. C. A. Scarff) Midland, 7: 58.

Old Man Dawson's Ploughing Bee. Chamb. J. 77: 550.

Old Man's Love Song; Indian story, with music. (A. C. Fletcher) Music, 18: 137.

Old Man's Son, The. (H. A. Vachell) Cornh. 80: 31.

Old Masters, Renaissance of the. (A. Hoeber) Bookman, 11: 229.

Old Mr. Jellicoe's Plan. (W. E. Cule) Chamb. J. 78: 641-691.

Old Mrs. Jenkins. (E. K. Mackenzie) Good Words, 42: 111.

Old No. 7; a railway tale. (W. E. Hunt) Canad. M. 11: 101.

Old Novels, Some. Spec. 78: 57.

"Old Oaken Bucket," and its Author. (J. S. Gibson) Outl. 63: 367.

Old Pine Tree. (A. M. Douglas) New Eng. M. n. s. 24: 643.

Old Quilt, An; a story. (J. H. Vincent) Outl. 64: 873.

Old Schoolhouse; a poem. (M. E. Sangster) Cosmopol. 22: 335.

Old Sile's Clem; a story. (P. H. Coggins) Harper, 96: 922.

Old Story, An; a New England story. (H. A. Nash) McClure, 14: 255.

Old Testament Religion, Dillmann on. (F. B. Denio) Bib. World, 9: 349.

Old Things that Pass away. (H. Le Roux) Liv. Age, 223: 130.

Old Tom of Nantucket. (J. Altsheler) Lippinc. 59: 240.

Old Tories, Revolt of. Spec. 79: 545.

"Old Venny;" a story. (G. Gamble) Eng. Illust. 20: 589.

Old Violin, An. (Hélen Nyblom) Liv. Age, 221: 695-770.

Old World in the New. (B. I. Wheeler) Atlan. 82: 145.

Old-world Wooing, An. (A. M. Jenney) Cent. 39: 605.

Oldbuck, Mr., My Boyhood's Friend. (N. Brooks) Bk. Buyer, 17: 221.

Oldys, William, A Relic of. (C. I. Elton) Cornh. 77: 786.

Ole Mis' Anne; a story. (E. T. Hewitt) Eng. Illust. 20: 194.

Oleomargarine. Pure-food Legislation. (A. I. Chamberlain) Outl. 66: 954.

O'Leary, Rev. Arthur. (J. J. O'Shea) Cath. World, 68: 195.

Oligocene, White River, So. Dakota, Aqueous vs. Æolian Deposition of. Science, n. s. 14: 210.

Oligochæta, Parasitic or Commensal, in New England. (M. A. Willcox) Am. Natural. 35: 905.

Oliphant, Mrs. Margaret Wilson. Acad. 52: 15. — Ath. '97, 2: 35. — Lit. W. (Bost.) 28: 239. — Blackw. 162: 161. — (A. L. Coghill) Fortn. 68: 277. Same art. Ecl. M. 129: 492. — (H. W. Preston) Atlan. 80: 424. — Spec. 79: 12. Same art. Liv. Age, 214: 403. — (W. R. Nicoll) Bookman, 5: 484. — (W. A. Guerry) Sewanee, 8: 64. — (M. Townsend) Cornh. 79: 773. Same art. Critic, 35: 812.

— and her Rivals. Scot. R. 30: 282. Same art. Liv. Age, 216: 44.

— An Appreciation. Lond. Q. 89: 85.

— Autobiography. Acad. 56: 553. — (H. W. Preston) Atlan. 84: 567. — Blackw. 165: 895. Same art. Ecl. M. 133: 224. Same art. Liv. Age, 222: 27. — Quar. 190: 255. Same art. Ecl. M. 133: 752. Same art. Liv. Age, 223: 1. — Scot. R. 34: 124. — Church Q. 49: 140. — (W. Canton) Good Words, 40: 429. — (E. Fuller) Bookman, 9: 528. — With portrait. Bk. Buyer, 19: 110.

— as a Biographer. Blackw. 163: 501.

— as a Novelist. Blackw. 162: 305. Same art. Liv. Age, 215: 74.

— as a Realist. (G. Slater) Westm. 148: 682.

— Coghill's. (F. W. Halsey) Bk. Buyer, 19: 111.

— Life and Writings of. Ed. R. 190: 26.

— A Sketch from Memory. (H. O. Sturgis) Temp. Bar, 118: 233.

Oliphant, Laurence. Sympneumata. (S. A. Underwood) Arena, 20: 526.

Olive Branch of the Civil War ; a story. (L. C. Pickett) Arena, 17: 694.

Olive Cultivation in Persia. J Soc. Arts, 45: 52.

Olives and Oil-making at Sorrento. Chamb. J. 75: 573.

Oller, Galofre. Boria Avall. (D. A. Hart) Art J. 50: 5.

Olympian Games, at Paris, 1900. (P. de Coubertin) No. Am. 170: 802.

Olympus, The Shepherds of. Macmil. 78: 284.

Omaha Exposition, 1898. (C. H. Walker) Cent. 33: 518. — (A. Shaw) Cent. 34: 836. — (H. W. Lanier) R. of Rs. (N. Y.) 18: 52. — (W. S. Harwood) Outl. 59: 428. — (J. J. Ingalls) New Eng. M. n. s. 18: 517. — (Elsie Reasoner) Overland, n. s. 3: 446. — (Elsie Reasoner) Midland, 9: 258. — (Alice French) Cosmopol. 25: 599. — (C. H. Walker) Archit. R. 5: 11.

— and the West. (W. A. White) McClure, 11: 575.

— Architecture. Midland, 8: 555.

— Indian Life at, Glimpses of. R. of Rs. (N. Y.) 18: 436.

Omar Khayyam. (J. A. Murray) Fortn. 66: 848. Same art. Ecl. M. 128: 65. — (J. Hay) Critic, 31: 401. — (J. Hay) Critic, 33: 484.

— as a Bore. (A. Lang) Critic, 37: 216.

— Cult of. Acad. 59: 55, 77.

— Rubáiyát of. Acad. 52: 475.

— — and Kipling's Seven Seas. (P. E. More) Atlan. 84: 800.

— — Fitzgerald's Translation. Critic, 33: 487. — Gent. M. n. s. 60: 413. Same art. Ecl. M. 131: 287.

— — Influence of. Spec. 82: 816.

— — New Rendering of ; a poem. (Richard Le Gallienne) Cosmopol. 23: 247, 385.

— — Paraphrase of. (C. P. Murphy) Nat'l M. (Bost.) 11: 253.

Omar Khayyam, Rubáiyát of, Present Popularity of. (B. Holland) National, 33: 643. Same art. Liv. Age, 222: 363.

— — Recent Notes upon. (E. Radford) Idler, 14: 198.

— — Sibleigh's French Translation of Fitzgerald's Version. (F. A. H. Morgan) Critic, 38: 335.

Omayyads, The, and the Eastern Empire. (S. K. Bukhsh) Asia. R. 32: 134.

Omdurman and Havana. (R. Ogden) Nation, 68: 40.

— and the Moslem World. (R. Ahmad) 19th Cent. 44: 688. Same art. Liv. Age, 219: 565.

— Battle of. (F. Maurice) 19th Cent. 44: 1048. — (W. Huyshe) Sat. R. 86: 332. Same art. Liv. Age, 219: 121.

— — Slaughter of Wounded after. (E. N. Bennett) Contemp. 75: 18. — (Sir W. Gatacre) Contemp. 75: 299.

Omen Animals of Sarawak. (A. C. Haddon) Pop. Sci. Mo. 60: 80.

Omitlan, a Prehistoric City in Mexico. (W. Niven) Am. Antiq. 19: 187.

Omnibus Driving in London. (G. E. Mitton) Eng. Illust. 18: 314.

On Board the Rose Marie ; a story. (S. R. Tarr) Nat'l M. (Bost.) 5: 385.

On a Boy's First Reading of "King Henry V. ;" a poem. (S. W. Mitchell) Cent. 35: 333.

On the Coast of Acadie ; a poem. (A. J. Chipman) Canad. M. 14: 7.

On Credulity ; a story. (A. Hood) Temp. Bar, 122: 219.

On de Rapide. (M. K. Bartlett) Cent. 38: 609.

On Deck. (H. B. Fuller) Liv. Age, 217: 488.

On a Diamond Jubilee ; a poem. (Lewis Morris) Acad. 51: 631.

On the Divide ; a story. (L. Wasson) Chaut. 29: 472.

On the Echo o' the Morn. (J. B. Connolly) Scrib. M. 29: 659.

On Egoism ; a story. (A. Hood) Temp. Bar, 124: 358.

On Enchanted Ground. (E. Cox) Temp. Bar, 118: 108.

On the Fever Ship. (R. H. Davis) Scrib. M. 25: 21.

On Georgian Bay ; a story. (J. N. McIlwraith) Cornh. 82: 179.

On the Gonzales Ranch. (Viola Bruce) Overland, n. s. 34: 326.

On a Grecian Urn, Keats's Ode. (W. C. Wilkinson) Bookman, 5: 217.

"On Her Majesty's Service ;" a story of West Africa. (H. Bell) Idler, 12: 644.

On Her Majesty's Service ; a story. (A. B. Fletcher) Blackw. 167: 551. Same art. Liv. Age, 225: 481.

On the Highlands ; a poem. (H. Ibsen) Poet-Lore, 13: 335.

"On the Hip." (W. H. Browne) Nation, 79: 397.

On the Hire System ; a Drawing-room Comedy. (L. L. Lang) Blackw. 170: 591.

On the Housetop ; a story. (R. Barr) Canad. M. 15: 363.

On the Inside Track ; a story. (Marion Hill) Nat'l M. (Bost.) 7: 44.

On a Little Music ; a story. (A. Hood) Temp. Bar, 123: 85. Same art. Liv. Age, 231: 316.

On Memory's River ; a poem. (W. H. Woods) Outing, 33: 490.

On the Monks' Island ; a tale. (Z. de Ladeveze) Gent. M. n. s. 67: 125.

On the Night Desk ; a story. (A. B. Paine) Munsey, 22: 225.

On the Night Train. (M. T. Earle) Atlan. 85: 748.

On the Pages of an Old Reading-book. (N. J. Welles) New Eng. M. n. s. 16: 118.

On a Picture of Dante and Beatrice ; a poem. (A. Mackay) Argosy, 64: 503.

On Primrose Hill. (A. E. P. Searing) New Eng. M. n. s. 23: 653.

Oratory, Irish. (J. F. Taylor) Cornh. **75**: 321.
— Parliamentary, Interest in. Nation, **72**: 369.
Orbit of Bodies under the Action of a Central Attraction. (R. W. Wood) Pop. Astron. **8**: 32.
— Parabolic, Graphical Method of Finding Elements. Pop. Astron. **7**: 193.
Orbits, Periodic. Nature, **57**: 394.
Orcady, Road in. (D. J. Robertson) Ecl. M. **131**: 496.
Orchar Collection of Pictures. Illus. Good Words, **38**: 811.
Orchards, English. (G. Gordon) J. Soc. Arts, **45**: 305.
Orchardson, William Quiller. (C. Monkhouse) Scrib. M. **21**: 399. — (R. W. Maude) Strand, **15**: 483.
— Parting of the Ways. Art J. **53**: 72.
Orchestra, Drawing-room. Belgra. **97**: 253.
— Growth of. (J. F. Runciman) Sat. R. **91**: 369.
— Local, at Bangor, Me. (Abbie N. Garland) Music, **12**: 113.
— Prout's. (J. F. Runciman) Sat. R. **86**: 635. **89**: 76, 104.
Orchestral Conductors. (W. S. B. Mathews) Music, **13**: 384. — (C. Eddy) Music, **13**: 411.
Orchestras in Chicago. Music, **18**: 95.
Orchestration. (J. P. Sousa) Music, **11**: 501.
Orchid, The; a poem. (M. A. Mason) Outing, **32**: 284.
Orchid Breeding, Curiosities of. (C. C. Hurst) Nature, **59**: 178.
Orchids, A Few Native, and their Insect Sponsors. (W. H. Gibson) Harper, **94**: 861.
— Meditation on. Sat. R. **87**: 746.
— Story of the. (A. S. Wilson) Knowl. **22**: 149, 210, 259.
Orcutt, Emma Louise. Lit. W. (Bost.) **32**: 182.
Ordeal, Modern Survival of. (G. H. Westley) Green Bag, **12**: 624.
Order, The Notion of. (B. Russell) Mind, **26**: 30.
— The Price of. (T. Williams) Atlan. **86**: 219.
Order of the Yellow Robe; a story. (Helen F. Huntington) Nat'l M. (Bost.) **6**: 526.
Orders and Decorations, Royal. (F. Cunliffe-Owen) Munsey, **26**: 32.
— Knightly, of France. (J. F. M. Fawcett) Gent. M. n. s. **60**: 276.
— Sacrament of, in the 17th Century. (F. A. Gasquet) Am. Cath. Q. **25**: 625.
Ordination, The. (M. S. Harpel) New Eng. M. n. s. **24**: 672.
Ordnance Department. (C. E. Dutton) J. Mil. Serv. Inst. **15**: 1083.
Ordnance Factories, The Royal. (C. H. Owen) Un. Serv. M. **19**: 243.
Ordnance Manufacture in France. (Col. Gun) J. Mil. Serv. Inst. **14**: 1291.
Ordnance Survey, British, Twelve Years' Work of, 1887-99. (J. Farquharson) Geog. J. **15**: 565.
Ordsall Hall, Manchester, Eng. Am. Arch. **69**: 16.
Ordway, Alfred. (L. W. Usher) New Eng. M. n. s. **18**: 3.
Ore Deposits, Geology of. (C. R. Van Hise) Science, n. s. **14**: 745, 785.
Ore Dock Machinery, American. (A. C. Johnston) Cassier, **18**: 355.
Ores, Analysis of. (J. Parry) Nature, **58**: 149.
— Magnetic Concentration of. (W. A. Anthony) Cassier, **13**: 433.
— Science of. (H. Louis) Nature, **63**: 510.
— — Beck on. (H. Louis) Nature, **63**: 245.
— Zone of Maximum Richness in Ore Bodies. (C. R. Keyes) Science, n. s. **14**: 577.
Oregon, Illinois, Artist Life in. Brush & P. **2**: 271.
Oregon, Southern, Glimpses of. (W. H. Dall) Nation, **65**: 201, 221.
— — Hunting in. (J. E. Bennett) Overland, n. s. **30**: 146.

Oregon Election, 1898, Significance of. (W. McCamant) Forum, **26**: 41.
"Oregon," Great Voyage of the. (E. W. Eberle) Cent. **36**: 912.
O'Reilly, John Boyle, Writings of. (R. E. Connell) Cath. World, **65**: 751.
Organ, The, as an Instrument of Musical Expression. (W. S. B. Mathews) Music, **19**: 150.
— The Boston. (W. F. Gates) Music, **16**: 560.
— Enharmonic, Joseph Alley's, Sketch of the Inventor. (S. H. Hooker) Music, **11**: 677.
— Mediæval, at Lübeck and others. (A. G. Hill) Archæol. **51**: 419.
— of Jewish Temple, Washington, D. C. (W. S. B. Mathews) Music, **18**: 575.
Organ-blowers, Humors of. (J. C. Hadden) Longm. **35**: 366. Same art. Liv. Age, **224**: 824.
Organ Builders, Early, of Pennsylvania. (J. W. Johnson) Pennsyl. M. **22**: 231.
Organ Concert in Chicago, Description of. Music, **15**: 584.
Organ Music Abroad. (P. C. Lutkin) Music, **20**: 296.
— and Organ Playing. (A. Guilmant) Forum, **25**: 83.
Organ Pipes, Behavior of Small Closed Cylinders in. (B. Davis) Am. J. Sci. **162**: 185.
— Mediæval, and the Musical Scale. (C. K. Wead) Music, **15**: 387.
Organ Recitals, Free Public, in Boston. (W. I. Cole) R. of Rs. (N. Y.) **16**: 579.
Organist, The American. (E. Swayne) Music, **17**: 185.
Organist of Ponikila, The. (H. Sienkiewicz) Munsey, **18**: 557.
Organists and Organ Playing in the United States. (W. S. B. Mathews) Music, **13**: 615.
— French, Celebrated. (C. Eddy) Music, **13**: 589.
Organist's Trials in India. Music, **19**: 478.
Organization, Economic. (C. R. Flint) Cosmopol. **26**: 345.
— of Mankind. (E. W. Cook) Contemp. **80**: 395.
— Waste of Energy in. (Ellen H. Richards) Outl. **63**: 928.
Organized Bodies, Molecular Structure of. (F. W. Jones) Nature, **61**: 273.
Organized Matter, Central Element of. (L. H. Batchelder) Chaut. **28**: 341.
Organs, American. (C. Eddy) Music, **15**: 615.
— and Hurdy-gurdies in Streets; Boston's New "in Tune" Law. (H. C. Lahee) Nat'l M. (Bost.) **9**: 347.
— and Organ-building in New England. (H. C. Lahee) New Eng. M. n. s. **17**: 485.
— and Organists of Europe. (T. C. Whitmer) Music, **21**: 12.
— Elliston on. (J. F. Runciman) Sat. R. **91**: 301.
Orient, A Reading Journey in the. (M. Jadwin and others) Chaut. **32**: 59-623. **33**: 54, 164.
Oriental Studies in England, Endowment of. Acad. **52**: 222.
Orientals, Two Westernized. (G. Lynch) Outl. **67**: 671.
Orientalists, International Congress of, 1897. (A. V. W. Jackson) Nation, **65**: 258.
— — 1900. (E. Montet) Asia. R. **29**: 113, 323.
— International Congresses of. (R. N. Cust) Asia. R. **24**: 79.
Orientation, Sensations of. (E. Mach) Monist, **8**: 79.
Origen. Theory of Knowledge. (H. H. Davies) Am. J. Theol. **2**: 737.
Original, An; a story. Cornh. **79**: 80.
Original Package Doctrine, Latest Phase of. (S. Miller) Am. Law R. **35**: 364.
— What is the? (M. M. Townley) Am. Law R. **35**: 669.

Orinoco, In the Valley of the. (S. Paterson) Geog. J. 13: 39.
— With a Steam-launch on the. (S. Paterson) Chamb. J. 74: 385-404.
Oriole, Orchard. (E. Ingersoll) Harper, 95: 75.
Orion, A Night with. (W. Noble) Pop. Astron. 4: 428.
Oriskany Fauna. Camden Chert of Tennessee and its Lower Oriskany Fauna. (J. M. Safford and C. Schuchert) Am. J. Sci. 157: 429.
Orkney Foray, An. Blackw. 164: 375.
Orkney Islands, A Road in. (D. J. Robertson) Longm. 32: 265.
Orleans, Henry, Prince of. Geog. J. 18: 318. — (F. Lees) Idler, 15: 183.
Orleans, Princes of. (C. Sutcliffe) Fortn. 68: 119.
Orleans, Sophie Charlotte d', Duchesse d'Alençon, a Heroine of Charity. ·(M. M'Shane) Month, 89: 620.
Orleans Pretenders, The. (A. D. Vandam) Contemp. 72: 253. Same art. Liv. Age, 214: 728.
Orlik, Emil, Artist. (R. Mather) Studio (Internat.) 11: 159.
Ormerod, Eleanor A. Ath. '01, 2: 161. — (W. F. Kirby) Nature, 64: 330.
Ormon, the Gulfer. (J. A. Barry) Chamb. J. 75: supp. 1.
Ormuzd, or the Ancient Persian Idea of God. (A. V. W. Jackson) Monist, 9: 161.
Ornament. (L. F. Day) Art J. 53: 18, 49.
— and Decorative Arts, Reference Books on. Library, 9: 251.
— Natural, The Place of. Spec. 82: 305. Same art. Liv. Age, 221: 322.
Ornament Motives; Trefoil and Palmette. (A. D. F. Hamlin) Archit. R. 8: 27.
Ornithology, Economic, Methods in, with special reference to the Cat Bird. (S. D. Judd) Am. Natural. 31: 392.
Oroya Railway, Climatic Contrasts along. (R. DeC. Ward) Science, n. s. 7: 133.
Orpen, Wm. (W. Meynell) Artist (N. Y.) 31: 177.
Orphan, The; a whale story. (F. T. Bullen) Cornh. 79: 615.
Orpheus and Eurydice; a famous old pantomime. (W. J. Lawrence) Theatre, 38: 31.
Orpheus Relief, The. (J. Pickard) Am. J. Archæol. 2d s. 2: 169.
Orr, Monro S. Drawings. (W. Sharp) Art J. 52: 310.
Orsay, Alfred d'; Beau Brummel's Successor. (Albert L. Cotton) Gent. M. n. s. 62: 503.
"'Orse," The; a story. (M. L. Pendered) Longm. 30: 136. Same art. Liv. Age, 214: 199.
Orthoclase as Gangue Mineral in a Fissure Vein. (W. Lindgren) Am. J. Sci. 155: 418.
Orthodoxy, After, — What? (M. J. Savage) No. Am. 170: 585.
— What is? (F. Brown) No. Am. 168: 409.
Orton, Edward. (T. C. Mendenhall) Science, n. s. 11: 1. — (G. K. Gilbert) Science, n. s. 11: 6. — Pop. Sci. Mo. 56: 607.
Orvieto, Corpus Christi Day at. (H. D. Rawnsley) Contemp. 74: 737. Same art. Ecl. M. 132: 176.
Orwell Hall; a poem. (E. A. Newton) Pall Mall M. 12: 193.
Osborne, Francis, Author. (C. C. Osborne) Gent. M. n. s. 66: 351.
— a 17th Century Chesterfield. (S. Peel) 19th Cent. 40: 944. Same art. Liv. Age, 212: 206.
Osborne Family, Military Services of. (W. H. Osborne) N. E. Reg. 54: 283.
Osborne House. Eng. Illust. 17: 461.
Osbourne, Lloyd, with portrait. Bk. Buyer, 21: 179.

Oscar II., King of Norway and Sweden, with portraits. Strand, 15: 198. — (W. H. Harvey) Good Words, 41: 750.
Oscar and Louise. (Margaret S. Briscoe) Scrib. M. 30: 436.
Oscillographs. Nature, 63: 142.
Osiris and the Resurrection. (E. R. Emerson) Am. Antiq. 20: 129, 261.
— The Tomb of. Liv. Age, 217: 407.
Osmotic Pressure. (Lord Kelvin) Nature, 55: 272.
— Theory of. (J. Larmor) Nature, 55: 545.
Osprey, The. Sat. R. 88: 701.
Ossian, Poems of. Sharp's Edition. Spec. 78: 273.
Ossianic Ballads. (W. A. Craigie) Scot. R. 34: 260.
Osterley Park and Manor, England. (M. E. Jersey) Pall Mall M. 14: 4.
Ostertag, Blanche, Artist. (Helen Underwood) Brush & P. 1: 55. — (Isabel McDougal) Brush & P. 3: 129.
Ostracoda, Giant, Old and New. (T. R. R. Stebbing) Knowl. 24: 100.
Ostrich, The American. (W. M. Gray) Cosmopol. 22: 377.
Ostrich Inn, Colnbrook, England. (R. Waybrook) Idler, 15: 413.
Ostrich Ranching in California. (S. M. Kennedy) Overland, n. s. 32: 531. — (A. Inkersley) Good Words, 41: 232.
Ostwald, Wilhelm, Laboratory of. (F. H. Neville) Nature, 64: 428.
Oswego County, N. Y., Swamps of, and their Flora. (W. W. Rowlee) Am. Natural. 31: 690, 792, 864.
Oswell, William Cotton, as Hunter and Explorer. Sat. R. 91: 776.
Other Grace, The. (J. H. Findlater) National, 29: 130. Same art. Liv. Age, 213: 125.
Other Man, The; a story. (S. C. Bryant) McClure, 17: 519.
Other Man, The; a story. (E. O. Petersen) Nat'l M. (Bost.) 6: 276.
Other Maumer, The; a story. (V. F. Boyle) Harper, 101: 749.
Other Mr. Smith. (E. D. Deland) Lippinc. 63: 97.
Other Side, The; a tale. (I. E. Mackay) Canad. M. 16: 375.
Other Vagrant. (A. E. Herrick) New Eng. M. n. s. 18: 182.
Othin, The Cult of, Chadwick on. (F. Y. Powell) Folk-Lore, 11: 81.
Otis, Albert Boyd. (J. Williamson) N. E. Reg. 52: 9.
Otis, Amos, of Yarmouth Port, Mass., Ancestry of. (F. W. Sprague) N. E. Reg. 51: 328.
Otis, Maj.-Gen. Elwell Stephen. (W. C. Church) R. of Rs. (N. Y.) 19: 299. — (C. A. Woodruff) Indep. 51: 595.
Ottawa, Canada. (McLeod Stewart) Pall Mall M. 15: 185. — (J. M. Oxley) New Eng. M. n. s. 24: 181.
— and Hull, Fire at, April 26, 1900. (F. Gadsby) Canad. M. 15: 195.
— and Rideau Hall. (F. H. Randal) Canad. M. 12: 149.
Ottawa County, Kansas, Remarkable Concretions of. (W. T. Bell) Am. J. Sci. 161: 315.
Ottawa River, The Upper. Where the Water runs Both Ways. (F. Irland) Scrib. M. 26: 259.
Ottawa Valley, Canada. (N. H. Smith) Canad. M. 15: 57.
Ottenhausen's Coup; a story. (J. W. Harrington) Idler, 20: 20. Same art. McClure, 10: 475.
Otter, Sea-. Chamb. J. 75: 589.
Otter-hunting. Sat. R. 86: 9. — (W. P. Collier) Temp. Bar, 117: 560. —Sat. R. 84: 161.
— in England. (F. A. Roller) Pall Mall M. 12: 45.
Otterbein, P. W., and the Reformed Church. (W. J. Hinke) Presb. & Ref. R. 12: 437.

Otterburne's Heir ; a story. (A. de L. Kirkpatrick) Argosy, 69: 85.

Ottoboni, Cardinal, Letters of. (R. Graham) Eng. Hist. R. 15: 87.

Ottoman Empire, Integrity of the. (J. G. Rogers) 19th Cent. 41: 671. Same art. Liv. Age, 213: 563.

Ottoman Poetry, Gibbs's History of. (D. B. Macdonald) Nation, 72: 15.

Ottoman Provincial Government. (H. H. Johnson) Westm. 153: 13.

Ottway, Thomas. (H. M. Sanders) Temp. Bar, 118: 372.

Ouananiche Fishing in Canada. (E. W. Sandys) Outing, 34: 237.

Oudeypore ; an Indian jewel. (J. Ralph) Harper, 100: 272.

Oudinot, N. C., Memoirs of, comp. by G. Stiegler. (E. G. Johnson) Dial (Ch.) 22: 302.

Ouida [Louisa de La Ramée]. Acad. 51: 549.
— Massarenes. (M. Beerbohm) Sat. R. 84: 8.

Oulton, John, Merchant. (A. Titus) N. E. Reg. 53: 391.

Our Automotor Omnibus ; a story. Macmil. 81: 62.

Our Brother, the Mountain. (F. Converse) Atlan. 88: 278.

Our Cattleman at Zootvaal Homestead ; a story. (F. Selous) Belgra. 99: 641.

Our Comrades of Greater Britain. (G. T. H. Hutton) Un. Serv. M. 14: 527.

Our Family Tree ; a story. (E. D. Roberts) Munsey, 16: 468.

Our Inaugural Guest ; a story. (I. C. Emery) Nat'l M. (Bost.) 12: 66.

Our L.-T. ; a story. Blackw. 170: 419.

Our Lady of Antibes. (E. D'Arcy) Cent. 37: 51.

Our Lady of Deliverance. (J. Oxenham) Chamb. J. 77: 417–804.

Our Lady of the Foam ; a poem. (F. Savile) Argosy, 72: 272.

Our Lady of Little Cañon. (J. Ayscough) Macmil. 84: 304.

Our Little All. (F. J. Davey) Good Words, 41: 846.

Our Lord and St. Peter. (S. Lagerlof) Ecl. M. 134: 296. Same art. Liv. Age, 224: 82.

Our M. P. ; a story. (E. S. Atkinson) Canad. M. 10: 70.

Our Mantua-maker. (V. Roseboro) Cent. 36: 143.

Our Marching ; a poem. (T. Roberts) Canad. M. 14: 272.

Our Mary. (M. E. Mann) Longm. 33: 163.

Our Match at the Park. Macmil. 82: 283. Same art. Liv. Age, 227: 111.

Our Music-master. Temp. Bar, 118: 569.

Our Novel ; a story. (A. E. W. Mason) Eng. Illust. 16: 531.

Our Queer Old World ; a poem. (J. W. Riley) McClure, 9: 883.

Our Soldier. (H. L. Bradley) Atlan. 80: 363.

Our Square. (Mrs. B. Bosanquet) Cornh. 80: 790.

Our Two Uncles. (S. H. Preston) Scrib. M. 29: 336.

Our Typewriter ; a story. (E. P. Butler) Nat'l M. (Bost.) 9: 122.

Our Venetian Baby ; a story. (H. L. Montgomery) Temp. Bar, 111: 120.

Our Village ; a story. (E. B. Harrison) Temp. Bar, 114: 417.

Our War Veteran. (R. A. Norris) Arena, 19: 850.

Our Witch. (R. M. Johnston) Cent. 31: 760.

Our Youngest "Pup." (J. H. Bridge) Overland, n. s. 30: 354.

Ouse River, Cowper and. (J. C. Tarver) Macmil. 82: 135. Same art. Ecl. M. 135: 364.

Ouseley, Sir Fred Gore. (A. F. Ferguson) Sund. M. 28: 197.

Out of Bondage. (R. E. Robinson) Atlan. 80: 200.

"Out of the Deep." (F. W. Wharton) Lippinc. 64: 777.

Out-of-door Books, Old. (G. A. B. Dewar) Longm. 35: 342.

Out-of-door Literature, American. (H. L. West) Forum, 29: 632.

Out-of-doors, Americans. Outl. 65: 243.

Out of the Fog. (E. Marshall) Cent. 37: 213.

Out of Meeting. (T. Wharton) Lippinc. 60: 683.

Out of Muhlqueen's Alley ; a story. (A. L. Provost) Chaut. 31: 508.

Out of Season ; a story. Argosy, 67: 377.

Out of the Shadow ; a story. (E. E. Peake) Cosmopol. 27: 642.

Out of the Silence, Speak ! a poem. (J. C. R. Dorr) Atlan. 86: 707.

Out of Tune ; a story. (A. L. Kielland) Liv. Age, 212: 123.

Out Past the City Gates ; a story. (A. J. Dawson) Temp. Bar, 116: 48.

Out-patients ; a sketch. Macmil. 84: 114. Same art. Liv. Age, 230: 577. Same art. Ecl. M. 137: 512.

Outcast, The ; a poem. (H. Seymour) Belgra. 98: 126.

Outdoor Life. (H. Hendry) Sat. R. 86: 265.

Outdoor Recreation League. (A. Henry) Outl. 64: 47.

Out-door Relief, Effect of, in England. Sat. R. 85: 454.
— in Canada. (A. M. Machar) Char. R. 6: 457.
— in Ohio. (L. B. Gunckel) Char. R. 7: 755.
— in the West. (R. Hunter) Char. R. 7: 687.
— — The Grievance of. (J. H. Hyslop) Forum, 23: 476.
— Official. (E. Bicknell) Char. R. 6: 449.
— Public. (C. A. Elwood) Am. J. Sociol. 6: 90. — (E. T. Devine) Char. R. 8: 186.
— — in New York. (E. T. Devine) Char. R. 8: 129.
— Relation between Public and Private. (F. Almy) Char. R. 9: 22, 65.

Outing, Seven Years'. (Frances B. Perkins) New Eng. M. n. s. 22: 592.

Outlaw, The ; a story. (H. B. M. Watson) Pall Mall M. 21: 42, 167, 322, 492. 22: 34.

Outrageous Fortune ; a novel. (S. M. Düring) Argosy, 73: 1, 124, 283. 74: 49, 119, 230.

Outsider, The ; a story of the Boer war. (R. Kipling) McClure, 15: 210.

Outsiders. (J. Ayscough) Temp. Bar, 117: 585. 118: 135, 153.

Outwitting a Grizzly. (W. Thomson) Lippinc. 61: 279.

Outwitting of the King. (Winona Godfrey) Overland, n. s. 34: 177.

Over the Border. (X. Wraigh) Westm. 149: 329.

Over Hermon ; a poem. (C. Scollard) Atlan. 88: 519.

Over-nutrition and its Social Consequences. (S. N. Patten) Ann. Am. Acad. Pol. Sci. 10: 33.

Over-production, Measurement of. (G. C. Selden) Q. J. Econ. 15: 138.

Over the Roses and under the Vines ; a comedietta. (E. Durand) Canad. M. 11: 399.

Over Sunday. (Carolyn Wells) Scrib. M. 30: 476.

Overbeck, Johannes. (Walter Miller) Am. J. Archæol. 11: 361.

Overland Monthly, Beginnings of. (A. Roman) Overland, n. s. 32: 72.
— Conditions in the '80's. (Milicent W. Shinn) Overland, n. s. 32: 66.
— Early Days of. (Noah Brooks) Overland, n. s. 32: 3.
— Reminiscences of. (W. C. Bartlett) Overland, n. s. 32: 41.

Overton, J. H. The Church in England. Church Q. 45: 471.

Overtures, Notes on. Sat. R. 83: 347.

Ovid, Fasti, Principal MSS. of. (G. J. Laing) Am. J. Archæol. n. s. 3: 212.

Owakülti Altar at Sichomovi Pueblo. (J. W. Fewkes) Am. Anthrop. 3: 211.

Pacific Coast, Northern, Archæological Investigations on, 1899. (H. I. Smith) Am. Anthrop. **2**: 563.

— A Psychological Study of Influence. (J. Royce) Internat. Mo. **2**: 555.

Pacific Isles, Sketches of, Becker's. Ath. '98, **1**: 116.

Pacific Ocean, America in the. (J. Barrett) Forum, **30**: 478.

— and Far East, America in. (J. Barrett) Harper, **99**: 917.

— and Our Future there. (W. E. Griffis) Outl. **61**: 110.

— Coming Struggle in. (B. Taylor)·19th Cent. **44**: 656. Same art. Ecl. M. **131**: 662.

— Date Line in. Geog. J. **15**: 415. — (B. E. Smith) Cent. **36**: 742.

— A First Day in ; Passages from a Diary. (John La Farge) Scrib. M. **29**: 670.

— Gains and Losses in. (J. G. Leigh) Fortn. **73**: 45.

— The New. Sat. R. **88**: 253. Same art. Liv. Age, **223**: 264.

— Our Future on ; what we have to hold and win. (G. W. Melville) No. Am. **166**: 281.

— Partition of the Western. Ed. R. **191**: 478.

— South, In the. (F. M. Price) Indep. **51**: 1473.

— United States, the Paramount Power of. (J. Barrett) No. Am. **169**: 165.

Pacific Railroads, Settlements with. (H. R. Meyer) Q. J. Econ. **13**: 427.

Pacific States, Industries of, The Urgent Need of. (E. Berwick) Arena, **17**: 831.

Pack Service in the U. S. Army. (A. C. Cantley) Chaut. **27**: 591.

Packing Industry, Chicago. (Theodore Dreiser) Cosmopol. **25**: 615.

Paderewski, Ignace Jan. (J. F. Runciman) Sat. R. **87**: 651.

— an Appreciation. Critic, **36**: 87.

— in London. (J. F. Runciman) Sat. R. **91**: 800.

— Piano Playing of. (W. S. B. Mathews) Music, **17**: 509. — (J. F. Runciman) Sat. R. **88**: 735.

Padlock, Ancient. (F. Peacock) Reliquary, **40**: 191.

Padmaja, the Lotus-born ; a story. (M. S. Naidus) Canad. M. **16**: 70.

Padre Ignazio ; a story. (O. Wister) Harper, **100**: 692.

Padrone System, The. Gunton's M. **12**: 342.

Padstow Church. (S. Barber) Reliquary, **40**: 182.

Padua, Art of. (H. Mereu) Am. Arch. **55**: 68, 83.

— Municipal Government of. (L. Einaudi) Munic Aff. **3**: 215.

Pæstum ; remnant of Paganism. (F. C. Dunlop-Wallace-Goodbody) Gent. M. n. s. **65**: 491.

Pagan Literature, Popular, of the 2d Century. (J. Reinhard) Sewanee, **6**: 325.

Pagan Myths and Christian Figures. (W. H. Jewitt) Antiq. n. s. **37**: 74–337.

Paganini and Chopin. (H. Marteau) Music, **15**: 57.

Paganism, Judaism, and Christianity. Outl. **61**: 107.

— Modern. Outl. **66**: 544.

— Two Remnants of. (F. C. Dunlop-Wallace-Goodbody) Gent. M. n. s. **65**: 491.

Page, Mary Bowdoin. Writer, **14**: 9.

Page, Thos. Nelson, English of. (V. T. Artz) Writer, **11**: 69.

— The Old Gentleman of the Black Stock. (G. W. Cable) Bk. Buyer, **21**: 378.

— Red Rock. (M. T. Earle) Bk. Buyer, **17**: 297. — (R. T. W. Duke) Conserv. R. **1**: 339.

Pages from the Diary of Parson Parlett. Liv. Age, **212**: 626. Same art. Ecl. M. **128**: 419.

Pages from a Private Diary. Cornh. **75**: 114 — **77**: 541.

Paget, Sir James. (F. W. Tunnicliffe) Nature, **61**: 256.

Pahlavi, Items from the Gathic. (L. H. Mills) Am. J. Philol. **21**: 287.

Paige, Rev. Lucius Robinson. (A. E. White) N. E. Reg. **52**: 297.

Pain, Barry. Acad. **52**: 494.

Pain and Death, Some Thoughts on. (H. B. Marriott-Watson) No. Am. **173**: 540.

— and Strength Measurements of School Children. (Ada Carman) Am. J. Psychol. **10**: 392.

— The Ethics of. (W. Barry) Liv. Age, **219**: 861. Same art. Ecl. M. **132**: 252.

— of the World, The. (W. O. McGeehan) Overland, n. s. **36**: 150.

— Philosophy of. (W. H. Johnson) Cath. World, **73**: 104.

— Physical Basis of. (H. C. Warren) Am. Natural. **31**: 1057.

— Sensibility to. (E. J. Swift) Am. J. Psychol. **11**: 312.

— Value of. (W. Hutchinson) Monist, **7**: 494.

Paine, Albert Bigelow, with portrait. Bk. News, **16**: 183.

Paine, Thomas, Americanism of. (M. D. Conway) Arena, **21**: 205.

— Monument to, at New Rochelle. (E. H. Shaw) Bk. Buyer, **18**: 371.

— Political Theories of. (C. E. Merriam, jr.) Pol. Sci. Q. **14**: 389.

— Residences in Paris. (M. D. Conway) Ath. '99, **1**: 398.

Paine, Timothy O., Selections from the Poems of. N. Church R. **4**: 636.

Paint and Painting. (E. H. Brown) Am. Arch. **65**: 35, 59. **68**: 27.

— and Powder. (I. A. Taylor) 19th Cent. **46**: 633. Same art. Ecl. M. **134**: 236.

Painted Skeleton from Northern Mexico. (A. Hrdlička) Am. Anthrop. **3**: 701.

Painter vs. Poet in portraying Nature. (Claude Phillips) Art J. **52**: 1.

Painter-etchers, Royal. (F. Wedmore) M. of Art, **21**: 78.

Painters behind the Scenes. Ed. R. **185**: 487. Same art. Liv. Age, **213**: 705.

— Dutch, of To-day. M. of Art, **24**: 280. — (E. W. Champney) Cent. **34**: 395.

— Florentine, of the Renaissance, Berenson's. (H. P. Horne) Sat. R. **90**: 237.

— of Seville. (A. Symons) Fortn. **75**: 48. Same art. Ecl. M. **136**: 656. Same art. Liv. Age, **228**: 798.

— Scandinavian, Modern Group of. (Cecilia Waern) Scrib. M. **25**: 643.

— who would Express themselves in Words, Concerning. (J. La Farge) Scrib. M. **26**: 254.

Painters' Club, A. (L. Grier) Studio (Lond.) **5**: 110.

Painting. The Academy, the New Gallery, and the Guildhall. (H. H. Statham) Fortn. **72**: 101.

— Art vs. Realism in. Sat. R. **87**: 77.

— Barbizon School. Mast. in Art, **1**: Pt. 8.

— British Contemporary. (G. B. Rose) Sewanee, **8**: 193.

— The Building-up of a Picture. (F. Leighton) M. of Art, **22**: 1.

— A Century of. Idler, **11**: 153, 571. **12**: 41–772. **13**: 39.

— Decorative, by J. D. Linton. Studio (Internat.) **11**: 243.

— Decorative Tendency in. Sat. R. **89**: 425.

— Dutch Masters at Burlington Fine Arts Club. Sat. R. **89**: 777.

— Dutch School. Mast. in Art, **1**: Pt. 6.

— English School. Mast. in Art, **1**: Pt. 7.

— Flemish School. Mast. in Art, **1**: Pt. 1.

— Florentine, of the 14th Century. (R. E. Fry) Monthly R. **3**, no. 3: 112.

Palu, The, of the Equatorial Pacific. (L. Becke) Chamb. J. **77**: 37.

Pamir Boundary Commission, Proceedings of. Geog. J. **13**: 50.

Pampanga Province, In. (P. Whitmarsh) Outl. **64**: 395.

Pamphlet, The English Political. Acad. **51**: 623.

Pamphlet-case. (F. A. Bather) Science, n. s. **9**: 720.

Pamphlets and the Pamphlet Duty of 1712. (J. Macfarlane) Library, n. s. **1**: 298.

— Care of. (C. H. Foye) Lib. J. **24**: 13.

— Literary. Spec. **80**: 169.

— The Uses of. (F. Weitenkampf) Bk. Buyer, **23**: 277.

Pan and a Memory ; a story. (K. Leeds) Pall Mall M. **14**: 444.

Pan-American Congress, The. (R. Ogden) Nation, **73**: 332.

— and Mexican Hospitality. (T. R. Dawley, jr.) Outl. **69**: 971.

— The Next. (W. C. Fox) Forum, **30**: 294.

— A South American on. (R. Ogden) Nation, **72**: 505.

— What can it Accomplish ? (W. E. Curtis) Gunton's M. **18**: 497.

Pan-Celtic Congress. Ath. '01, **2**: 285, 318.

Panama, City of, Old and New. (M. MacMahon) Cath. World, **73**: 653.

Panama, Isthmus of, Hill's Geological History of. Am. Natural. **33**: 350.

Panama Canal, The. (H. H. Lewis) Munsey, **23**: 360.

— Actual Condition of. (C. Paine) Engin. M. **18**: 681.

— and Nicaragua Canal compared. (A. P. Davis) Forum, **30**: 527.

— Best Isthmian Canal. (H. L. Abbot) Atlan. **86**: 844.

— Commercial Aspects of the. (W. C. Ford) Harper, **96**: 761.

— Compared with Nicaraguan. (G. A. Burt) Engin. M. **19**: 19.

— The New. (H. L. Abbot) Forum, **26**: 343.

— Plans for Completion of. (W. H. Hunter) Engin. M. **16**: 711.

— Scheme for. (E. V. Smalley) Outl. **60**: 911.

Panama Canal Co., Surrender of. (R. Ogden) Nation, **73**: 486.

Panama Scandals, Revival of. Spec. **78**: 467.

Pancho's Happy Family ; a story. (H. D. Skinner) Harper, **97**: 840.

Pandects, Discovery of the. Green Bag, **12**: 183.

Pandora. (C. Foley) Outl. **66**: 215.

— and Prometheus. (Arthur, Duke of Wellington) Un. Serv. M. **16**: 317.

Pandora Vase, A New. (P. Gardner) J. Hel. Stud. **21**: 1.

Pandora's Box. (Jane E. Harrison) J. Hel. Stud. **20**: 99.

Panel, Painting of the Doom, discovered in 1892. (C. E. Keyser) Archæol. **54**: 119.

Panel Paintings of Saints on the Devonshire Screens. (C. E. Keyser) Archæol. **56**: 183.

Panics and Prices. (G. Yard) Cornh. **77**: 757. Same art. Ecl. M. **131**: 80.

— How can their Severity be Ameliorated ? Bank. M. (N. Y.) **55**: 892.

Panizzi, Antony. Library, n. s. **2**: 225.

Panjab. See Punjab.

Panoramas, Painting of. (W. Telbin) M. of Art, **24**: 555.

Pantheon, The Paris. Am. Arch. **58**: 18.

— Roman. (Alfredo Melani) Am. Arch. **65**: 27.

— — Gilt-bronze Tiles of. (F. G. Moore) Am. J. Archæol. 2d s. **3**: 40.

Pantomime. (J. Knight) Theatre, **38**: 70.

— of 1898–99 at Drury Lane Theatre, London. (A. Lawrence) Idler, **15**: 83.

Pantomime Music and Songs, Old-time. (W. J. Lawrence) Gent. M. n. s. **63**: 553.

Pantomimes, Poor. (G. B. Shaw) Sat. R. **85**: 11.

Paolo ; a story. (C. Smith) Temp. Bar, **114**: 292. Same art. Liv. Age, **218**: 311.

Paolo, Fra [Pietro Sarpi]. (H. F. Brown) Scot. R. **30**: 251.

Pap's Mules. (S. M. Peck) Bk. News, **15**: 549.

Papacy, The. Spec. **82**: 334.

— and the Italian Government. (W. Ward) Fortn. **71**: 475.

— and Mediæval Empire, Final Conflict of. (D. S. Schaff) Bib. Sac. **58**: 491.

— and Pelagianism. Dub. R. **120**: 88. — (J. Chapman) Dub. R. **121**: 99.

— and the Temporal Power. (F. M. Crawford) Indep. **53**: 361.

— Claims of, Puller on. Church Q. **51**: 350.

— The College of Cardinals. (D. S. Muzzey) Outl. **62**: 566.

— in the 19th Century. (G. McDermot) Cath. World, **68**: 435.

— in 1897. (W. J. D. Croke) Am. Cath. Q. **22**: 330.

— in Rome in the 20th Century. (S. Cortesi) Internat. Mo. **4**: 68.

— Intolerable Situation in Rome. (H. M. Vaughan) Westm. **156**: 178. — Reply. (G. della Vecchia) Westm. **156**: 446.

— Italy's Quarrel with. (G. della Vecchia) Westm. **155**: 402.

— Last Ten Years of Temporal Power. (Donat Sampson) Am. Cath. Q. **24**, no. 3: 131, no. 4: 142.

— The Policy of the Holy See. (G. M. Fiamingo) Contemp. **75**: 290.

— Practical Aspect of. Church Q. **52**: 188.

— Primacy of, St. Peter and. (F. Bacchus) Dub. R. **121**: 314.

— Rivington on the Roman Primacy. Church Q. **49**: 1.

Papagueria. Illus. (W. J. McGee) Nat. Geog. M. **9**: 345.

Papal Authority, Puller and Rivington on. (J. P. Sheraton) Presb. & Ref. R. **8**: 126.

Papal Conclave, The Next. (G. Fiamingo) Open Court, **11**: 135.

— of 1740. (W. K. Stride) Argosy, **71**: 21.

Papal Independence and Italy's Prosperity. (A. Diarista) Cath. World, **73**: 97.

Pape, Eric, Painter and Illustrator. (Dora M. Morrell) Brush & P. **3**: 321.

Paper, Adaptability of. (T. L. de Vinne) Bookman, **5**: 222.

— and Paper-marks, On. (W. Blades) Library, **1**: 217.

— and Paper Standards. (C. F. Cross) Sci. Prog. **7**: 395.

— Cellulose in. Nature, **55**: 241.

— Deterioration of, Report of Committee on. J. Soc. Arts, **46**: 597.

— Embossed, Work in. (H. Frantz) M. of Art, **21**: 332.

— Fine, in England in the 18th Century. (R. Garnett) Library, **9**: 133.

— From Logs to. (A. D. Adams) Cassier, **20**: 420.

— Mexican. (F. Starr) Am. Antiq. **22**: 301.

— Modern Book, Durability of. (J. Y. W. MacAlister) Library, **10**: 295.

Paper Currency in Colonial South Carolina. (B. W. Wait) Sewanee, **5**: 277.

Paper-hangings and Textile Fabrics. (Walter S. Sparrow) M. of Art, **23**: 416.

Paper-making, Recent History of. (C. Beadle) J. Soc. Arts, **46**: 405.

Paper Money as a Standard of Value. (A. R. Wallace) Acad. **55**: 549.

— in the Light of Political Economy and Experience. Bank. M. (N. Y.) **57**: 922.

Parks, Country, Future of. Spec. **79**: 78.
— Maintenance of, Cost of. (C. S. Sargent) Garden & F. **10**: 271.
— Making of. (C. S. Sargent) Garden & F. **10**: 489.
— National, of California, Uncle Sam's Troopers in. (Capt. J. A. Lockwood) Overland, n. s. **33**: 356.
— of Minneapolis and St. Paul. (M. C. Robbins) Garden & F. **10**: 162.
— One Way to make Attractive. (C. S. Sargent) Garden & F. **10**: 201.
— Open Spaces of the Future. (O. Hill) 19th Cent. **46**: 26.
— Public, New Dangers to. (C. S. Sargent) Garden & F. **10**: 439.
— — True Purpose of Large. (J. C. Olmsted) Garden & F. **10**: 212.
— Three Natural, at Halifax, Truro, and St. John. (G. N. Hay) Garden & F. **10**: 3.
— Urban, Natural Beauty in. (C. S. Sargent) Garden & F. **10**: 251.
Park-making as a National Art. (M. C. Robbins) Atlan. **79**: 86. — (C. S. Sargent) Garden & F. **10**: 11. — (H. B. Merwin) World's Work, **1**: 293.
Parkways and Boulevards in American Cities. (Sylvester Baxter) Am. Arch. **62**: 11, 27, 35.
Parlaghy, Vilma. (C. Ruge) Munsey, **23**: 529.
Parliament of Paris, The. (G. W. Prothero) Eng. Hist. R. **13**: 229.
Parliament and Convocation. Spec. **78**: 689.
— and Government. Spec. **83**: 744.
— Congress and ; a Contrast. (S. Brooks) No. Am. **170**: 78.
— Dissolution of, Prerogative of. (E. Robertson) 19th Cent. **48**: 137.
— English and French, Two Days in. (J. S. Crawford) Gunton's M. **21**: 320, 422.
— English, and the Party System. Macmil. **84**: 471.
— From behind the Speaker's Chair. Strand, v. **14-18**.
— Front Bench Invertebrates. (H. W. Wilson) National, **31**: 292.
— Great Britain's Law-makers. (P. Alden) Outl. **61**: 519.
— Is it so Shocking ? (G. A. B. Dewar) Westm. **149**: 324.
— Lawyers in. (E. Porritt) Green Bag, **11**: 131.
— Leaders in. (F. J. Higginbottom) Pall Mall M. **18**: 96, 266, 396, 566.
— Long, Diary of Early Days of. (W. A. J. Archbold) Eng. Hist. R. **16**: 730.
— Loquacity in. Spec. **78**: 687.
— A New Member's First Impression of. (H. Norman) Outl. **67**: 105.
— of 1264. (J. P. Gilson) Eng. Hist. R. **16**: 499.
— Payment of Members at Home and Abroad. (W. Miller) Westm. **149**: 25.
— Quaint Side of. (M. MacDonagh) 19th Cent. **43**: 197. Same art. Liv. Age, **217**: 230. Same art. Ecl. M. **130**: 462. Same art. Green Bag, **12**: 555.
— The Queen's Parliaments. (H. W. Lucy) No. Am. **164**: 741. **165**: 99.
— Recollections in and out of. (Sir C. Dalrymple) Good Words, **42**: 27.
— Redistribution. (C. A. Whitmore) National, **34**: 439.
— Shortening of. (T. C. Snow) Contemp. **73**: 115.
— Significant Acts of. (H. T. S. Forbes) Cornh. **78**: 811.
— Violence and Disorder in. (J. Sykes) Good Words, **42**: 675.
— Visit to House of Commons. (A. R. Carman) Canad. M. **18**: 122.
Parliamentary Election in England, The. (A. V. Dicey ; A. Webb) Nation, **71**: 362.
Parliamentary Oath, Evolution of the. (M. MacDonagh) 19th Cent. **46**: 316.

Parliamentary Privilege. Spec. **81**: 139.
Parliamentary Sketches in Ottawa. (C. L. Shaw) Canad. M. **13**: 438.
Parliaments of the World. (T. B. Reed) Munsey, **18**: 211.
Parmelee, John, Descendants of. (R. D. Smyth) N. E. Reg. **53**: 405.
Parnassian Scramble, A. (F. Lynde) Atlan. **84**: 88.
Parnassus, Grass of. (Hugh Macmillan) Good Words, **39**: 673.
Parnell, Charles Stewart. (L. Johnson) Acad. **55**: 293. — Blackw. **165**: 138. — (A. Webb) Conserv. R. **2**: 65. — (A. Webb) Nation, **68**: 106, 123. — Westm. **151**: 1.
— and Cromwell ; a dialogue between their ghosts. (D. F. Hannigan) Westm. **152**: 244.
— and his Power. (L. Garvin) Fortn. **70**: 872.
— and his Work. Ed. R. **189**: 543.
— O'Brien's Life of. Spec. **81**: 740, 776. — Ath. '98, **2**: 667. — (J. J. O'Shea) Am. Cath. Q. **24**: 40. — (C. De Kay) Critic, **35**: 729. — (E. G. Johnson) Dial (Ch.) **26**: 74.
Parnellism and Practical Politics. Westm. **149**: 40.
Parodies. (H. M. Sanders) Temp. Bar, **119**: 237. Same art. Liv. Age, **225**: 250.
Parodists, Some American. (W. T. Larned) Bookman, **14**: 21.
Parody, A Plea for. (P. Pollard) Bookman, **14**: 47.
Parol Evidence in respect to Writings under the Statute of Frauds. (I. Browne) Am. Law R. **30**: 863.
Parr, Samuel. (J. M. Attenborough) Westm. **155**: 54.
Parried ; a dialogue. (T. Jenks) Cent. **36**: 318.
Parrish, Maxfield, Artist and Illustrator. Studio (Internat.) **9**: xxii.
— The Work of. (J. B. Carrington) Bk. Buyer, **16**: 220.
Parrot, The ; a story. (M. E. Wilkins) Harper, **101**: 603.
Parrot and the Melodrama, The ; a story. (E. Nesbit) McClure, **12**: 249.
Parrot Story, An African. (M. H. Kingsley) Cornh. **76**: 389.
Parrots. (W. H. Hudson) Sat. R. **91**: 765.
— Wild, In Haunts of. (F. A. Ober) Indep. **53**: 1373.
Parry, Caleb Hillier. Quar. **185**: 94.
Parry, Charles Hubert, Composer ; with portrait. Music, **14**: 195.
Parry, Joshua. Quar. **185**: 94.
Parsi Tower of Silence, A Special Visit to a. (A. V. W. Jackson) Nation, **72**: 449.
Parsism and Judaism, Stave on. (J. H. Moulton) Crit. R. **10**: 323.
Parsimony, Law of. Meth. R. **57**: 455.
Parson, John. (L. G. Moberly) Sund. M. **29**: 413.
Pars'n Dan'l ; a story. (A. Baird) Temp. Bar, **112**: 94.
Parson Kelly. (A. E. W. Mason and Andrew Lang) Longm. **33**: 193-481. **34**: 1-481. **35**: 59.
Parson of Cactus Flats, The. (E. Day) Munsey, **16**: 474.
Parson Punchard's Pigs ; a Suffolk sketch. (Mrs. Isabel Smith) Chamb. J. **77**: 446.
Parsonages, Country, in England. (M. G. Watkins) Gent. M. n. s. **66**: 48.
Parson's Barrel, The. (T. L. Cuyler) Sund. M. **30**: 577.
Parson's Duty ; a story. (C. Dutton) Belgra. **92**: 58. Same art. Liv. Age, **212**: 746.
Parson's Indication, The ; a story. (B. Marnan) Pall Mall M. **19**: 317.
Parson's Letter-bag, The. Chamb. J. **76**: 825.
Parson's Revels, The ; a story. (H. M. Batson) Cornh. **75**: 757.
Parson's Sermon, The ; a story. (H. F. Hetherington) Sund. M. **27**: 511.
Parsons, Alfred, Artist. (A. L. Baldry) Studio (Internat.) **7**: 149.

Parsons, Beatrice. Artist (N. Y.) **24**: 140.

Parsons, Charles Algernon. Cassier, **17**: 246.

Parsons, Frank; an Economist with 20th Century Ideals. (B. O. Flower) Arena, **26**: 154.

Parsons, Father Robert, The Portrait of. (J. H. Pollen) Month, **98**: 113.

Parsons, Thomas William. (M. S. Porter) Cent. **40**: 934.

Parsons, Prevalence of. (G. S. Lee) Bk. Buyer, **14**: 373.

Part Payment by one of several Joint Debtors; does it affect the right of the others to take advantage of the Statute of Limitations? (M. S. Gunn) Am. Law R. **32**: 846.

Parthenon, The. Am. Arch. **55**: 36.

— Decay of. (J. R. S. Sterrett) Nation, **64**: 220, (E. Robinson) 243.

— Horizontal Lines of. (W. F. Decker) Am. Arch. **69**: 51.

— How an Inscription was Unraveled. (E. P. Andrews) Cent. **32**: 301.

— Metopes of the West End of. (W. S. Ebersole) Am. J. Archæol. 2d s. **3**: 409.

Parthenon Sculptures, New Light on. (C. Waldstein) Harper, **104**: 12.

Parties, American, Defence of. (W. G. Brown) Atlan. **86**: 577.

— and Principles. Monthly R. **1**, no. **1**: 25.

— Changes in. (E. P. Clark) Nation, **69**: 461.

— Disintegration of. (G. Smith) No. Am. **164**: 753.

— Failure of Two-party System. (A. Watkins) Forum, **31**: 643.

— Future of. (C. A. Conant) Atlan. **88**: 365.

— Influence of Issues on. Gunton's M. **12**: 46.

— Non-partisanship, Theory and Practice of. Gunton's M. **13**: 259.

— Oscillations in Power of. (A. L. Lowell) Ann. Am. Acad. Pol. Sci. **12**: 69.

Parties and Dinner-parties in England. (J. McCarthy) Indep. **53**: 1848.

Parting, The; a poem. (J. V. Cheney) Cosmopol. **27**: 598.

Parting of the Ways; a poem. (C. Burke) Argosy, **68**: 360.

Partisan or Non-partisan, Which? Outl. **69**: 399.

Partisanship and Cosmopolitanism. (W. P. Trent) Sewanee, **7**: 342.

Partnership, Some Recent Massachusetts Decisions in. (L. M. Freedman) Am. Law R. **32**: 244.

Parton, Sarah Willis [Fanny Fern]. (E. Parton) New Eng. M. n. s. **24**: 94.

Partridge, Bernard, Artist. (H. G. Daniels) Idler, **11**: 359.

Partridge, William Ordway. (W. C. Langdon) New Eng. M. n. s. **22**: 383. — (C. C. Sargent, jr.) Munsey, **19**: 436.

Partridge, Norfolk. Spec. **86**: 47.

Partridge Cooking. Sat. R. **90**: 266.

Partridge Shooting. (Ernest Hamilton) Pall Mall M. **13**: 177. — Sat. R. **88**: 289.

Parts of Speech, Psychological Significance of. (Gertrude Buck) Educa. **18**: 269.

Party, Burke on. (C. W. Colby) Nation, **65**: 512.

— Nemesis of. (A. B. C.) Fortn. **69**: 1.

— Political Degeneracy in. (G. Gunton) Gunton's M. **20**: 414.

— Possible New, in England, 1900. Monthly R. **1**, no. **3**: 1.

Party at Madeira's, A; a story. (E. S. Martin) Harper, **103**: 590.

Party Government. (W. Trant) Canad. M. **8**: 442.

— in the Cities of New York State. (D. F. Wilcox) Pol. Sci. Q. **14**: 681.

Party Government, The Price of. (W. S. Lilly) Fortn. **73**: 922.

Party System, The. (B. N. Langdon-Davies) Macmil. **84**: 373.

— Break-up of. (H. C. Garrod) Westm. **155**: 209.

— is it Breaking up? (T. E. Kebbel) 19th Cent. **45**: 502.

Pascal, Blaise. (L. Stephen) Fortn. **68**: 1. Same art. Liv. Age, **214**: 517. — Acad. **51**: 139.

— Boutroux's. (A. Laugel) Nation, **71**: 129, 148.

— Inner Life of. (N. Luccock).Chaut. **32**: 197.

— Scientific Achievements of. (T. J. McCormack) Open Court, **12**: 595.

— A Visit to. (A. Suarés) Liv. Age, **227**: 73-150.

— with Three Portraits. (L. Lévy-Bruhl) Open Court, **12**: 582.

Pasha's Prisoner, The; a story of modern Turkey. (R. Barr) McClure, **15**: 35.

Pasigraphy, and the Pasigraphic Movement in Italy. (E. Schroeder) Monist, **9**: 44.

Pasquale's Stratagem. (W. McVeigh) Munsey, **17**: 696.

Passage-at-arms, A. (W. E. Cule) Chamb. J. **75**: 156.

Passage-at-arms, A; a story. (J. J. á Becket) Harper, **94**: 360.

Passages from the Diary of Parson Parlett. (B. Pardepp) Longm. **29**: 336.

Passamaquoddy Bay, Dialect of. (A. S. Gatschet) Nat. Geog. M. **8**: 16.

Passenger to Cudgellico; a story. (M. Roberts) Eng. Illust. **16**: 575.

Passeur; a story. (R. W. Chambers) Eng. Illust. **18**: 62.

Passing of Cat Alley. (J. A. Riis) Cent. **35**: 166.

Passing of Empires, Maspero's. (J. P. Peters) Nation, **70**: 380.

Passing of Enriquez. (Bret Harte) Cent. **34**: 230.

Passing of MacIvor, The; a story. (C. Warman) McClure, **11**: 484.

Passing of Mother's Portrait. (R. Field) Atlan. **87**: 523.

Passing of a Poet. (C. Scollard) Lippinc. **66**: 795.

Passing of Ronald Carew. (F. G. Aflalo) Chamb. J. **78**: supp. 38.

Passing of Thorndale. (C. Ticknor) New Eng. M. n. s. **22**: 209.

Passing of Thomas, The. (Grace Luce) Overland, n. s. **34**: 444.

Passing of Two Angora Rugs, The. (Matie E. Dudley) Overland, n. s. **35**: 505.

Passing of Zaxtia, The; a story. (E. H. Wilcox) Outing, **29**: 345.

Passing Strange if True; a tale. (G. F. F.) Argosy, **64**: 249.

Passion-flowers. (A. E. P. R. Dowling) Am. Cath. Q. **22**: 724.

Passion Play at Selzach. (A. G. Hopkins) Belgra. **92**: 263. — (C. T. Herrick) Lippinc. **65**: 956.

— An English. (R. H. Davis) Cent. **39**: 622.

— The Gospel on the Parisian Stage. (M. D. Conway) Open Court, **13**: 449.

— in Switzerland. (R. H. E. Starr) Cosmopol. **24**: 131.

— Mexican Indian. (L. M. Terry) Overland, n. s. **37**: 817.

— Ober-Ammergau. *See* Ober-Ammergau.

Passion Study. (Irving Bacheller) Cosmopol. **22**: 320.

Passmore Edwards Settlement in Bloomsbury. Spec. **80**: 267.

— Architecture of. (G. L. Morris) Studio (Internat.) **7**: 11.

Passon's Dilemma. (E. C. M. Dart) Longm. **38**: 435. Same art. Liv. Age, **231**: 309.

Passover, Chronology of, Mr. Lewin and Prof. Bacon on. (W. M. Ramsay) Expos. **6**: 431.

— Time of, Ramsay on. (B. W. Bacon) Expos. **8**: 1.

"Past Carin';" a story. (H. Lawson) Blackw. **169**: 684. Same art. Liv. Age, **230**: 504.

Pastel Drawing. (F. Wedmore) Studio (Lond.) **5**: 100.

— its Value and Present Position. (A. L. Baldry) M. of Art, **24**: 277.

Pastel Society Exhibition. (R. A. M. Stevenson) Art J. **51**: 119. — Sat. R. **87**: 170.

Pastellist, Art of the. (F. Wedmore) Studio (Lond.) **5**: 100.

Pasteur, Louis. (E. Priestley) 19th Cent. **42**: 113. — Acad. **61**: 455.

— and his Discoveries. Quar. **193**: 384.

— Radot's Life of. (G. C. Frankland) Nature, **65**: 97.

— a sketch. (G. C. Frankland) Good Words, **38**: 490.

— Tomb of. Nature, **55**: 275.

— Work of, and Modern Conception of Medicine. (C. Richet) Nature, **56**: 508.

Pastimes in Moderation. (F. G. Aflalo) Chamb. J. **77**: 582.

Paston, George, *pseud.* Acad. **55**: 520.

Paston Letters. (C. W. Turner) Sewanee, **5**: 425. — (E. B. Stone) Lippinc. **59**: 107. — (J. W. Thompson) Dial (Ch.) **31**: 132.

Pastor, Ludwig, German Historian, with portrait. Cath. World, **67**: 55.

Pastor, Charge to a. (T. F. Dornblaser) Luth. Q. **28**: 61.

— What he owes to his Pulpit. (T. B. Birch) Luth. Q. **28**: 325.

Pastoral Drama on the Elizabethan Stage. (W. W. Greg) Cornh. **80**: 202.

Pastoral Work, Joy of. (R. F. Horton) Sund. M. **28**: 793.

Pastorate, City, Discouragements and Encouragements of. (F. M. Porch) Luth. Q. **30**: 533.

Pat Mullarkey's Reformation. (H. van Dyke) Cent. **33**: 233.

Patagonia, Explorations in. (F. P. Moreno) Geog. J. **14**: 241, 353.

— Journey in Northwestern. (O. Nordenskjold) Geog. J. **10**: 401.

— New Fossils from. (F. P. Moreno) Nature, **60**: 396.

— Southern, and Adjoining Islands, Indian Tribes of. (J. B. Hatcher) Nat. Geog. M. **12**: 12.

— — Geographic Features of. (J. B. Hatcher) Nat. Geog. M. **11**: 41.

— — Geology of. (J. B. Hatcher) Am. J. Sci. **154**: 327.

Patagonian Personalities. Science, n. s. **14**: 693.

Patchwork; a story. (A. Pain) Idler, **18**: 191.

Pâte-sur-pâte. (L. Solon) Art J. **53**: 73.

Patent Law, English, its History, Literature, and Library. Library, **10**: 42.

— International. (J. S. Fairfax) Engin. M. **15**: 952.

— Reform of. (A. Siemens) J. Soc. Arts, **49**: 431.

Patent Office, United States. (E. V. Smalley) Cent. **39**: 346.

Patent Office Library, The British. (J. B. C. Kershaw) Chamb. J. **75**: 102.

Patent System as a Factor in National Progress. (W. C. Dodge) Engin. M. **13**: 542.

— British and American. (G. C. Marks) Cassier, **19**: 207.

— History of the. (E. W. Hulme) Law Q. **16**: 44.

— U. S., Benefits of. (W. C. Dodge) Cassier, **18**: 198.

Patents, Grant of, Past and Present, in Great Britain. (E. W. Hulme) Law Q. **13**: 313.

— Infringement of, by Intention. (J. M. Lainé) Law Q. **17**: 201.

— Is it Worth while to take out a Patent? (H. Huntington) Forum, **24**: 606. — (E. J. Prindle) Forum, **25**: 95.

— A Talk on. (E. H. Mullin) Cassier, **14**: 81.

— Working of Patent Acts. (R. H. Thurston) Science, n. s. **13**: 669.

Pater, Walter. Acad. **53**: 13. — (Stanley Addleshaw) Gent. M. n. s. **58**: 227. — (L. Johnson) Acad. **51**: 78. — (W. Mountain) Poet-Lore, **13**: 275.

— An Appreciation of. (H. L. Eno) Citizen, **3**: 248.

— as a Writer. Acad. **59**: 314.

— a Study. (A. D. Malley) Cath. World, **70**: 602.

— Theology of. Chr. Lit. **16**: 406.

Paternalism *vs.* Fraternalism in Government. (R. T. Ely) Cent. **33**: 780.

Paternoster Row. (W. Besant) Liv. Age, **222**: 291.

Paterson, A. B., Poetry of. Acad. **53**: 555.

Paterson, Oscar, Artist in Stained-glass. (G. White) Studio (Internat.) **4**: 12.

Paterson, William Romaine. Acad. **52**: 490.

Path of the Storm. (M. Van Vorst) Harper, **99**: 877.

Pathology. Adaptation in Pathological Processes. (W. H. Welch) Science, **5**: 813.

Pathos, The New. (R. Ogden) Atlan. **79**: 856.

— Pathetic Lines from English Literature. Acad. **53**: 175, 214.

Pathrick's Proxy; a story. (S. MacManus) Cosmopol. **28**: 343.

Paths of Glory. (J. Jacobs) Fortn. **73**: 59. Same art. Liv. Age, **224**: 515.

Pathway Round. (F. K. Johnson) Atlan. **86**: 229.

Patience; a story. (H. Akroyd) Gent. M. n. s. **66**: 398.

Patience of Prudence Morrison. (M. M. Hickson) Longm. **33**: 446.

Patient Love; a story. (F. H. Spearman) Cosmopol. **28**: 454.

Patmore, Coventry. Acad. **59**: 399, 493. — With portrait. (H. E. O'Keeffe) Cath. World, **69**: 646. — (E. Gosse) Contemp. **71**: 184. Same art. Liv. Age, **212**: 795. Same art. Ecl. M. **128**: 581. — (A. Symons) New R. **16**: 71. Same art. Ecl. M. **128**: 244. — With portrait. Bk. Buyer, **13**: 970. — (V. M. Crawford) Fortn. **75**: 304. — (A. T. Quiller-Couch) Monthly R. **2**, no. 1: 149. — (G. Tyrrell) Month, **96**: 561. — Lond. Q. **88**: 56.

— Champney's Memoirs and Correspondence of. (E. G. Johnson) Dial (Ch.) **30**: 37. — (F. M. Bird) Nation, **72**: 71.

— The Praise of the Odes. (L. Garvin) Fortn. **67**: 207.

Paton, Dr. J. B., at Home. (J. A. Hammerton) Sund. M. **26**: 599.

Patricia. (C. K. Burrow) Chamb. J. **75**: 493.

Patriot, The; a story of the war. (H. Fuller) Arena, **20**: 658.

Patriot's Progress, The; a story. (S. Gwynn) Cornh. **75**: 516.

Patriotic Association of Phila., 1778. Roll of Members. Pennsyl. M. **23**: 356.

Patriotic Impulse, The New. Dial (Ch.) **27**: 265.

Patriotic Societies of America. (Marion Howard) Nat'l M. (Bost.) **7**: 249.

Patriotism. (W. Everett) Harv. Grad. M. **9**: 1.

— and Ethics. Ecl. M. **137**: 366. Same art. Liv. Age, **230**: 258.

— by Manual. (F. J. Mather, jr.) Nation, **71**: 439.

— Chamberlain on. Spec. **79**: 640.

— Decadence of, and what it means. (H. E. Foster) Arena, **19**: 740.

— The History of a Poem. (E. Gosse) No. Am. **164**: 283.

— in the Public Schools. (H. E. Perrin) Educa. **20**: 404.

— Its Defects, its Dangers, and its Duties. (W. C. Doane) No. Am. **166**: 310.

— Love of Country. (D. MacG. Means) Nation, **66**: 83.

— The New. (S. Jones) Munic. Aff. **3**: 455.

— Pseudo-, The Menace of. (E. M. Chapman) No. Am. **164**: 250.

Patriotism, Recollections of. Liv. Age, 212: 61.
— Renaissance of. (G. J. Manson) Indep. 52: 1612.
— Spurious *vs.* Real, in Education. (W. Wilson) School R. 7: 599.
Patrocles and the Oxo-Caspian Trade Route. (W. W. Tarn) J. Hel. Stud. 21: 10.
Patrols, Independent. (C. Miller) J. Mil. Serv. Inst. 23: 185.
Patron, Literary. Spec. 86: 45.
Patrons, Last of the. Quar. 188: 504.
Patron Saints of England. Acad. 57: 596.
Patronage, Corrupting Power of Public. (O. W. Underwood) Forum, 31: 557.
Patronage of High Bear; a story. (Owen Wister) Cosmopol. 30: 250.
Patten, Simon N., Psychological Doctrines of. (W. Fite) J. Pol. Econ. 7: 384.
Patten, Willard, and his Oratorio, Isaiah. (W. S. B. Mathews) Music, 11: 573.
Pattern Design, Animals in. (Walter Crane and L. F. Day) Art J. 53: 212.
Patterson, Wm., and Macpherson, John. Letters, 1766–73. (W. M. Hornor) Pennsyl. M. 23: 51.
Patti, Adelina, An Afternoon with. (W. Armstrong) Music, 12: 632.
Pattison, Dorothy Wyndlow, "Sister Dora." (S. M. Jackson) Char. R. 8: 413.
Paul, St., Abbott's Life and Letters of. (G. F. Greene) Presb. & Ref. R. 11: 527.
— Address on Mars' Hill, Elements of Persuasion in. (J. M. English) Am. J. Theol. 2: 97.
— and the Jerusalem Church. (J. Warschauer) New World, 7: 722.
— and our Modern Life. (J. McSorley) Cath. World, 72: 428.
— and Silas at Philippi. (E. C. Selwyn) Expos. 9: 415. 10: 29.
— and Social Relations. (W. E. McLennan) Meth. R. 58: 738.
— and the Twelve. (E. P. Gould) J. Bib. Lit. 18: 184.
— Attitude towards Greek Philosophy. (A. Carr) Expos. 5: 372.
— Back to Christ through. (W. Rupp) Ref. Ch. R. 46: 553.
— Chronology of Life of, Review of. (A. G. Maas) Am. Cath. Q. 24, no. 3: 57, no. 4: 61.
— — Second Fixed Point in. (W. M. Ramsay) Expos. 8: 81.
— Conversion of. (G. Elliott) Meth. R. 60: 345.
— Data on, Some. (J. B. Young) Meth. R. 60: 232.
— Doctrine of, Structure of. Lond. Q. 88: 272.
— Doctrine of Salvation, in Romans. (W. Rupp) Ref. Church R. 45: 52.
— Emancipation of Saul, According to. (G. A. Derby) Expos. 3: 69.
— Family and Rank of. (W. M. Ramsay) Expos. 10: 328.
— First Galatian Ministry of. (F. Rendall) Expos. 9: 241.
— Fouard's Last Years of. (W. H. Johnson) Cath. World, 72: 638.
— From Paul to John. (J. Warschauer) New World, 9: 49.
— Gospel according to. (C. A. Scott) Expos. 8: 202.
— — Feine on. (J. Macpherson) Crit. R. 11: 49.
— History of, Acts and Galatians. (S. S. Stewart) Meth. R. 58: 86.
— identified with Antichrist by the Jews. (E. C. Selwyn) Expos. 10: 115.
— Imprisonment in Rome, Was there a Second? (J. Macpherson) Am. J. Theol. 4: 23.
— Influence of the Damascus Vision upon his Theology. (E. I. Bosworth) Bib. Sac. 56: 278.

Paul, St.; is he a Competent Witness? (E. F. Williams) Bib. Sac. 56: 657.
— Life and Letters of. (L. Abbott) Outl. 58: 61–971.
— The Many-sided Apostle. (H. van Dyke) Outl. 61: 640.
— New Chronology of. (G. H. Gilbert) Bib. Sac. 55: 244.
— Portraits of, Have we Authentic? (W. H. Bradley) Bib. World, 9: 179.
— Sermons of. Spec. 86: 965.
— Spiritual Development of. (G. A. Barton) New World, 8: 111.
— Statesmanship of. (W. M. Ramsay) Contemp. 79: 377, 544.
— Supernaturalism of. (O. Cone) New World, 7: 483.
— Teaching of, Schäder on. (G. Vos) Presb. & Ref. R. 11: 355.
— Touch of Nature in. Spec. 87: 981.
— An Unrecorded Sermon of. Spec. 87: 417.
Paul of Burgos in London. (I. Abrahams) Jew. Q. 12: 255.
Paul Petrovetsky; a story. (W. Hayward) Midland, 8: 539.
Paul Poirier's Bear-trap; a sketch. (F. Baird) Canad. M. 13: 165.
Paula's Quest. (J. H. Durham) Overland, n. s. 35: 211.
Paulicians, Conybeare on the. Church Q. 47: 365.
— Manual of their Church; tr. by F. C. Conybeare. Ath. '98, 1: 814.
Paulist Fathers and their Work. (R. Everett) Arena, 21: 407.
Paulitschke, Dr. Philipp. Geog. J. 15: 186.
Paulsen, F., "Philosophia Militans" of. (K. Francke) Nation, 72: 352.
Paulus Diaconus, Historical Congress in Honor of. (T. Hodgkin) Contemp. 76: 673.
Pauncefote, Lord, of Preston. (C. Roberts) Harper, 100: 687.
Pauper Child, Psychology of the. (P. Lombroso) Ecl. M. 135: 214.
Pauper Children in Reign of George I. (E. Sellers) Sund. M. 30: 229.
Pauperism; Bibliography. Chaut. 33: 95.
— the Grievance of the West. (J. H. Hyslop) Forum, 23: 476.
— How far is it a Necessary Element in a Civilized Community? (T. Mackay) Econ. R. 10: 417.
— in England, Changes in. (G. U. Yule) J. Statis. Soc. 62: 249.
— Making Paupers and making Men. Outl. 63: 147.
— Problem of. (F. H. Wines) Char. R. 7: 545. — (J. T. Baylee) Westm. 147: 274.
— — in America. (F. de L. Booth-Tucker) Char. R. 6: 127.
— Progress of. Spec. 85: 958.
Pausanias. (W. B. Wallace) Un. Serv. M. 21: 302.
— Description of Greece. (H. N. Fowler) Am. J. Archæol. 2d s. 2: 357.
— Frazer's. Ed. R. 188: 358. — (H. F. Tozer) Geog. J. 12: 158. — Spec. 80: 580. — (P. Shorey) Dial (Ch.) 24: 318. — (C. Whibley) Macmil. 77: 415. Same art. Liv. Age, 217: 549. — (W. Cantor) Good Words, 39: 818. — Nation, 67: 468, 487. — Ath. '98, 1: 411, 442. — (J. I. Manatt) Am. Hist. R. 4: 137.
Pavement, Wood, and where it comes from. Chamb. J. 75: 605.
Pavement Artists and their Work. (C. L. M. Stevens) Eng. Illust. 20: 201.
Pavements, Glass for. Am. Arch. 63: 76.
Pavia, Certosa of, Minor Sculptures of the. (Alfredo Melani) Art J. 53: 312.
Paving, Good, and Street Cleaning. (G. E. Waring) Engin. M. 12: 781.

Paving, Wood. (B. S. Wheeler) Am. Arch. **74**: 93.

Paving Brick in the Middle West. (H. F. Bain) R. of Rs. (N. Y.) **20**: 60.

Pawned Kingdom, A; a story. (M. Roberts) Eng. Illust. **18**: 15.

Pawnee Ceremony of Giving Thanks. (Alice C. Fletcher) J. Am. Folk-Lore, **13**: 261.

Pawnee Ritual used when changing a Man's Name. (Alice C. Fletcher) Am. Anthrop. **1**: 82.

Pawnee Rough Rider. (H. W. Ball) Midland, **10**: 452.

Pawnees, Last Hunt of the. (J. F. Bixby) Overland, n. s. **29**: 52.

Pawns; a sketch. (E. S. Chamberlayne) Harper, **103**: 240.

Pawnshop, Philanthropic, in Vienna. (E. Sellers) National, **29**: 243. Same art. Ecl. M. **128**: 706. Same art. Liv. Age, **213**: 397.

Pawtucket, R. I., Public Library Building. Lib. J. **24**: 258.

Pax, Ebony, bearing the Legend of St. Veronica. (G. Stephens) Archæol. **46**: 266.

— Instrument of. (H. J. Feasey) Antiq. n. s. **33**: 209.

Paying Concern, A; a story. (G. Roscoe) McClure, **14**: 189.

Paymaster's Boy, The. (N. Munro) Good Words, **40**: 1-793.

Paymaster's Escort, The. (J. A. Lockwood) Overland, n. s. **33**: 109.

Payment Time; a story. (P. Bourget) Poet-Lore, **11**: 479.

Payn, James. Spec. **80**: 474. — Acad. **53**: 373. — Bookman, **7**: 313. — With portrait. Bk. Buyer, **16**: 389. — (L. Stephen) Cornh. **77**: 590. Same art. Liv. Age, **217**: 656. — Critic, **32**: 236.

Payne, Charles H. (W. F. Anderson) Meth. R. **61**: 177.

Payne, Roger, Characteristics and Peculiarities of. (S. T. Prideaux) M. of Art, **22**: 607.

— and Thomas; the Two Paynes. (A. Dobson) Studio (Lond.) **2**: 155.

Payne, William H., with portrait. (Sallie E. M. Hardy) Green Bag, **10**: 158.

Peabody, Josephine Preston. The Wayfarers. Poet-Lore, **11**: 132.

Peabody Education Fund. (J. L. M. Curry) Educa. R. **13**: 226.

— Thirty Years of. (D. C. Gilman) Atlan. **79**: 161.

Peabody Institute, Baltimore, Catalogue of Library. Library, **6**: 69.

Peace as a Factor in Social and Political Reform. (F. Smith) Pop. Sci. Mo. **53**: 225.

— Democracy and. (S. M. Macrane) Yale R. **9**: 9.

— of the World. (Charles Macksey) Am. Cath. Q. **24**, no. 4: 28.

— Prepare the World for. (E. S. Wicklin) Arena, **25**: 163.

— a Problem of Practical Diplomacy. (P. Carus) Open Court, **13**: 360.

— that cometh of Understanding; a discourse for Necessitarians. (J. MacCunn) Int. J. Ethics, **10**: 89.

— Twentieth Century Peacemakers. (A. W. Tourgée) Contemp. **75**: 886.

— Universal. (F. A. White) Westm. **156**: 357. — Westm. **151**: 357.

— — Cause against. Sat. R. **87**: 70.

— — The Czar's Project. (B. O. Flower) Nat'l M. (Bost.) **9**: 180. — Contemp. **74**: 498. — Sat. R. **86**: 300.

— — From a Woman's Standpoint. (B. von Süttner) No. Am. **169**: 50.

— — Impossibility of. Sat. R. **87**: 645.

— — Prospects of. (W. Cunningham) Atlan. **84**: 236.

— — The Vanishing of. Fortn. **71**: 871.
See also Disarmament.

Peace of God; a poem. (S. Sterne) Atlan. **81**: 839.

Peace Commission in Paris. Outl. **60**: 572.

Peace Conference, International, 1899. New Eng. M. n. s. **22**: 121. — (E. E. Hale) Forum, **31**: 197. — (E. E. Hale) Outl. **61**: 472. — (Percy Alden) Outl. **62**: 22, 837. — (W. Broadfoot) Blackw. **166**: 417. — (L. Courtney) Contemp. **75**: 609. — (W. T. Stead) Forum, **28**: 1. — Gunton's M. **17**: 1. — (L. Tolstoi) Indep. **51**: 997. — (R. Ogden) Nation, **68**: 270. — (T. F. Wright) N. Church R. **6**: 601. — (B. F. Trueblood) New Eng. M. n. s. **20**: 651. — (S. Low) No. Am. **169**: 625. — (E. M. Bliss) R. of Rs. (N. Y.) **19**: 432.

— and Arbitration. Ed. R. **190**: 190. Same art. Ecl. M. **133**: 481. Same art. Liv. Age, **222**: 465.

— and its Effect on "Custom of War." (W. D. Thompson) J. Mil. Serv. Inst. **28**: 404.

— and its Results. (J. H. Vickery) Indep. **51**: 2533.

— and the Monroe Doctrine. (F. W. Holls) R. of Rs. (N. Y.) **20**: 560.

— and the Moral Aspect of War. (A. T. Mahan) No. Am. **169**: 433.

— and what it might have been. Cath. World, **69**: 577.

— The Czar and. (P. Fiore) Chaut. **29**: 242.

— The Czar's Details. (R. Ogden) Nation, **68**: 41.

— The Czar's Rescript. (T. J. Lawrence) Int. J. Ethics, **9**: 137.

— Dangers of Mediation. Sat. R. **87**: 742.

— Holls on. (T. S. Woolsey) Yale R. **9**: 457. — (E. E. Hale) Outl. **67**: 919, 965. — (W. H. Buckler) Nation, **72**: 318.

— The House in the Wood. (G. Lecky) 19th Cent. **45**: 795. Same art. Liv. Age, **221**: 701. Same art. Ecl. M. **133**: 113.

— Hypocrisies of. (S. Low) 19th Cent. **45**: 689.

— International Law and the. (J. H. Vickery) Pop. Sci. Mo. **57**: 76.

— Its Possible Practical Results. No. Am. **168**: 771.

— Lack of Results. Sat. R. **88**: 156.

— Note on. Quar. **190**: 537.

— Outcome of. (W. T. Stead) R. of Rs. (N. Y.) **20**: 312.

— Some Lessons of. (T. E. Holland) Fortn. **72**: 944.

— Some Plain Words about the Tsar's New Gospel of Peace. (H. H. Howorth) 19th Cent. **45**: 202. Same art. Liv. Age, **221**: 75.

— U. S. Delegation to. R. of Rs. (N. Y.) **19**: 545.

Peace Demonstrations, The Present. (V. Tchertkoff) Fortn. **71**: 593.

Peace Movement. Westm. **151**: 124.

— Advance of, throughout the World. (F. Passy) R. of Rs. (N. Y.) **17**: 183.

— Evolution of. (W. F. Gill) Arena, **22**: 228.

— Present Status and Prospects of. (B. von Süttner) No. Am. **171**: 653.

Peace Offering, The; a story. (A. French) McClure, **11**: 458.

Peace Society of England. (W. E. Darby) Pall Mall M. **19**: 264.

Peace with Honor; a story. (S. C. Grier) Argosy, **63**: 22-657. **64**: 1-641.

Peacemaker; a story. (V. Sheard) Canad. M. **16**: 126.

Peacemaker, The. (Bliss Perry) Scrib. M. **26**: 643.

Peacemaker of Lamont. (G. Zollinger) New Eng. M. n. s. **19**: 383.

Peacemakers, The. (H. Bindloss) Good Words, **42**: 814.

Peach Families, of Marblehead. (R. W. Peach) N. E. Reg. **54**: 276.

Peach, The. (A. C. Smith) Scrib. M. **25**: 85.

Peach Farm, Maryland, Balance-sheet of a Small. (W. B. Stottlemyer) R. of Rs. (N. Y.) **21**: 317.

Peacham, Henry, the younger, as an Educationist, 1622. (F. Watson) Gent. M. n. s. **60**: 507.

Peaches, Varieties of. (R. H. Price) Garden & F. 10: 12.

Peacock, Ralph, Artist. Studio (Internat.) 12: 3.

Peacocks. Spec. 82: 232.

Peak Forest, Eng., a Mid-country Gretna Green. (J. Hyde) Gent. M. n. s. 58: 81.

Peakland, Township in; Fairfield. (J. Hyde) Gent. M. n. s. 66: 238.

— — Some Bygone Happenings in. (J. Hyde) Gent. M. n. s. 67: 389.

Peal, Samuel E. Nature, 56: 421.

Pean, Angelique des Meloises, Mme. de. The Two Pompadours. (M. S. Pepper) Chaut. 32: 381.

Pear Trees, Body Blight in. (W. Paddock) Science, n. s. 10: 85.

Pearl; a story. (R. Neish) Pall Mall M. 19: 535.

Pearl of Pevynsy, The; a story. (W. Kendrick) Belgra. 92: 80.

Pearl Diving. Working under Water. (H. P. Whitmarsh) Outl. 61: 124.

Pearl-seeking. (F. H. Sweet) Lippinc. 61: 375.

Pearls, Fresh-water, of America. Nature, 60: 150.

— Production of Fine. (A. Dastre) Chaut. 29: 173.

Pearls; a story. (Francis Prevost) Pall Mall M. 12: 252.

Pears, Charles. (H. W. Bromhead) Art J. 50: 306.

Pearson, Charles Henry. Church Q. 52: 211. — Acad. 58: 550.

— Stebbing's Memorials of. (W. J. Ashley) Nation, 71: 331.

Pearson, Fred Stark, with portrait. Cassier, 18: 446.

Pearson, John Loughborough, Architect, with portrait. (C. Monkhouse) Pall Mall M. 15: 93. — Ath. '97, 2: 861.

Pearsons, D. K., Friend of the American Small College. (G. P. Morris) R. of Rs. (N. Y.) 24: 580.

Peary, Robert E., Explorations of. Acad. 54: 288.

— His Latest Work in the Arctic. (H. L. Bridgman; R. E. Peary) McClure, 14: 235.

— Northward over the Great Ice. Bookman, 7: 413.

— Portrait of. Bk. Buyer, 16: 111.

— Work of, in 1900 and 1901, with portraits. Nat. Geog. M. 12: 357.

Peasant Mother, A; a recollection of the Siege of Paris. (N. Iasigi) Outl. 67: 65.

Peat, Commercial Uses of. (W. H. Wheeler) Nature, 63: 590.

Peck, Harry Thurston, with portrait. Bk. News, 19: 452.

Peck, Maude, Singer, with portrait. Music, 14: 625.

Peck, Samuel Minturn, with portrait. Bk. News, 15: 556. — Lit. W. (Bost.) 28: 374.

Pectolite, Prophyllite, etc., Experiments relative to Constitution of. (F. W. Clarke and G. Steiger) Am. J. Sci. 158: 245.

Peculiar Attack, A; a monologue. (P. Hart) Pall Mall M. 16: 555.

Pedagogical Type, The. (G. M. Hyde) Bookman, 6: 514.

Pedagogue, A. (Mary J. H. Skrine) Temp. Bar, 124: 89. Same art. Liv. Age, 231: 34.

Pedagogue's Romance, A; a story. (H. C. Bradby) Ecl. M. 136: 518. Same art. Liv. Age, 228: 356.

Pedal, Loud, or Damper. (H. A. Kelso) Music, 12: 231.

Pedigrees, The Amateur Monger of. (P. E. Lewin) Gent. M. n. s. 67: 339.

— Positive, in New England. (W. S. Appleton) N. E. Reg. 52: 185.

Pedrell, Filippo, and the Spanish Lyric Drama. (G. Tebaldini) Music, 13: 679.

Pedro, Case of, "Public Property." (C. S. Clark) Un. Serv. M. 18: 650.

Peek, Sir Cuthbert. Geog. J. 18: 222.

Peel, Sir Robert. (H. M. Stephens) Chaut. 28: 231. — (A. Birrell) Contemp. 75: 747. Same art. Ecl. M. 133: 241. Same art. Liv. Age, 221: 735. — Ed. R. 189: 285. — (F. A. Channing) Fortn. 71: 551. — (W. O'C. Morris) Scot. R. 33: 203.

— and William Pitt. Quar. 189: 359.

— Library of. (W. Roberts) Ath. '00, 1: 627.

— C. S. Parker's. (E. Porritt) Am. Hist. R. 4: 721. — Spec. 82: 238. — Sat. R. 87: 179.

Peel Act: Should it be modified ? Bank. M. (Lond.) 69: 192.

Peel Heirlooms, Sale of the. Ath. '00, 1: 631.

Peerage, The Story of a Claim to a. (B. Borret) Green Bag, 11: 449.

Peg-legged Romance, A. (J. A. Hill) McClure, 11: 469.

"Peggy Stewart," the, Destruction of, at Annapolis, 1774. Pennsyl. M. 25: 248.

Peggy Travels. (F. Lewis) New Eng. M. n. s. 21: 60.

Pegram, Fred., Artist. (Roy Compton) Idler, 11: 673.

Peignot, Gabriel, Letters of. (R. Harrison) Library, 6: 159.

Pekenino, Michel-Louis. (Alfredo Melani) Am. Arch. 69: 100.

Peking and London. (A. Little) Fortn. 71: 943. Same art. Liv. Age, 222: 340.

— Besieged in. (C. E. Payen) Cent. 39: 453.

— British Capture of. J. Mil. Serv. Inst. 27: 245.

— Disestablishment of. Spec. 80: 816.

— Diplomatic Life in. (E. von Heyking) Internat. Mo 4: 359.

— Fall of. (G. Reid) Forum, 30: 578.

— Foreign Legations in. Liv. Age, 228: 26.

— The Last Palace Intrigue at. (R. S. Gundry) Fortn. 73: 958. Same art. Liv. Age, 226: 1.

— Legation Street in. (Eliza R. Scidmore) Liv. Age, 226: 325.

— A Prisoner in. (L. Miner) Outl. 66: 641-734.

— The Punishment of. (A. H. Smith) Outl. 66: 493.

— Revisited. (Mrs. Archibald Little) Cornh. 84: 169. Same art. Ecl. M. 137: 501. Same art. Liv. Age, 230: 602.

— Siege of the Foreign Legations in. (R. Allen) Cornh. 83: 202. — Liv. Age, 227: 401-642. 228: 265. — (Sir R. Hart) Cosmopol. 30: 121.

— — American Marines in. (C. H. Fenn) Indep. 52: 2845.

— — Causes of. (R. Allen) Cornh. 82: 669, 754. — (W. A. P. Martin) Nat. Geog. M. 12: 53.

— — Causes which led to the Preservation of the Legations. (R. Allen) Ecl. M. 136: 232.

— — Chinese Account of. (Chuan Sen) Indep. 52: 2776.

— — Defense of the Legations. (J. H. Ingram) Indep. 52: 2979.

— — a National Uprising and International Episode. (Sir R. Hart) Fortn. 74: 713.

— — Personal Side of. (M. S. Woodward) Indep. 52: 2782.

— — Struggle on the Wall. (W. N. Pethick) Cent. 39: 308.

— — With the Relief Column. (F. Palmer) Cent. 39: 302.

— — With the Relief Force, 1900. (H. C. Thomson) National, 37: 270.

— — A Woman's Diary of. (K. M. Lowry) McClure, 16: 65.

— Streets of. (E. R. Scidmore) Cent. 36: 859.

— Transformation of. (A. H. Smith) Outl. 68: 157.

— Visit to, in 1899. Good Words, 41: 615. Same art. Ecl. M. 135: 752. Same art. Liv. Age, 227: 105.

Peking Gazettes, A Précis of the. Liv. Age, 227: 677.

Pelagian Controversy, Augustine and. (B. B. Warfield) Chr. Lit. 16: 248.

Pelagianism and the Holy See. Dub. R. **120**: 88. — (J. Chapman) Dub. R. **121**: 99.

Pelargoniums at Cornell University. Garden & F. **10**: 184.

Pelatan-clerici Process for the Extraction of Gold and Silver. (E. G. Spilsbury) Cassier, **15**: 282.

Pele Towers and Border Castles, Ansted's. Artist (N. Y.) **25**: 186.

Pelican, The; a story. (Edith Wharton) Scrib. M. **24**: 620.

Pelopidæ Papers, The. (G. H. Powell) Gent. M. n. s. **63**: 457.

Peloponnesian War, A Southerner in the. (B. L. Gildersleeve) Atlan. **80**: 330.

Pelota, Game of, in Madrid. (Poultney Bigelow) Cosmopol. **26**: 578. — (C. Edwardes) Cornh. **76**: 515.

Pelzer, S. C.; a Model Factory Town. (L. B. Ellis) Forum, **32**: 60.

Pemberton, Max. (M. Beerbohm) Sat. R. **84**: 509.

Pemberton, J. C., Gen., Regime of. Nat'l M. (Bost.) **9**: 583.

Pembroke, George, 13th Earl of. (A. V. Dicey) National, **28**: 616.

Pemosis, Physiological. (George Macloskie) Science, n. s. **9**: 206.

Pen, Mightiness of the. (H. Macfarlane) Good Words, **40**: 487.

Pen and Brush Club, New York. (M. Tracy) Writer, **11**: 97.

Pen-drawing for Reproduction. (C. G. Harper) Studio (Lond.) **1**: 152, 197.

— Pennell on. Studio (Internat.) **4**: 59.

Penal Code for the Army. (R. M. Power) J. Mil. Serv. Inst. **8**: 319.

— The Modern. (C. T. Lewis) Charities, **7**: 119.

Penal Institutions; a study in nativities. (B. C. Mathews) Forum, **26**: 621.

Penal Sentences. (E. F. DuCane) Chamb. J. **75**: 704.

Penal Servitude, Past and Future of. (H. B. Simpson) Law Q. **15**: 33.

Penal System, California. (C. H. Shinn) Pop. Sci. Mo. **54**: 644.

— Evils of. (P. C. Garrett) Citizen, **3**: 176.

Penalized; a story. (Bernard Pares) Gent. M. n. s. **58**: 417.

Penalties and Substituted Contracts. (A. I. Clark) Law Q. **16**: 117.

Penang, India. (P. C. Standing) Idler, **12**: 314.

Pendleton, Edmund. (Sallie E. M. Hardy) Green Bag, **10**: 14.

Pendulum, Physical, New Form of. (J. S. Stevens) Am. J. Sci. **155**: 14.

Penelope's Irish Experiences. (K. D. Wiggin) Atlan. **86**: 629, 779. **87**: 30–485.

Penelope's Progress. (K. D. Wiggin) Atlan. **80**: 561, 702, 833. **81**: 90, 232, 366.

Peneplain, The. (R. A. Daly) Am. Natural. **33**: 127.

Penfield, Edward, and his Art. (C. B. Davis) Critic, **34**: 232.

Pengelly, Wm., Memoir of, ed. by H. Pengelly. Nature, **57**: 4.

— Sketch of, with portrait. Pop. Sci. Mo. **55**: 113.

Penguins on Macquaire Islands, S. Pacific Ocean. (W. H. Bickerton) Pall Mall M. **13**: 363.

Peninsular and Oriental Steamship Line. Tenting on Two Seas. (J. Ralph) Harper, **99**: 747.

Peninsular War, Diary of a Soldier in. (W. Verner) Macmil. **77**: 1.

Penitent, A. (L. E. Smith) Longm. **36**: 133. Same art. Liv. Age, **226**: 314.

Penitent Thief, The; from the Pali. (A. J. Edmunds) Open Court, **14**: 628.

Penitential Discipline in the Early Church. (J. Hogan) Am. Cath. Q. **25**: 417.

Penitential Hymn. (J. E. Spingarn) Cosmopol. **27**: 195.

Penn, William, and Gulielma, Early Homes of. Temp. Bar, **115**: 104. Same art. Ecl. M. **131**: 553.

— Burial-place of. (H. C. Shelley) New Eng. M. n. s. **20**: 548. Same art. Canad. M. **13**: 418.

— Family of. (H. M. Jenkins) Pennsyl. M. **21**: 1–402. **22**: 71, 171, 326.

— Letter to Robert Harley, 1701. Pennsyl. M. **25**: 282.

— Return of, December, 1699. (W. Perrine) Lippinc. **64**: 929.

— Sermon by, Abstract of. Pennsyl. M. **22**: 128.

Penn Family, and the Taxation of their Estates. Pennsyl. M. **23**: 290, 420. **24**: 165, 308.

— General Title to Pennsylvania. (W. B. Rawle) Pennsyl. M. **23**: 60–479. **25**: 80.

Pennell, Joseph, and his Drawings. (Arthur Tomson) Art J. **52**: 225.

— Work of. Brush & P. **8**: 72.

Pennsylvania and the English Government, 1699–1704. (H. V. Ames) Pennsyl. M. **24**: 61.

— and South Africa; a contrast. (H. Hodgkin) Westm. **155**: 614.

— Colonial, German and Swiss Settlements of, Kuhns on. (M. D. Learned) Am. Hist. R. **6**: 813.

— Colony and Commonwealth of, Fisher's. (J. G. Rosengarten) Citizen, **3**: 137.

— Constitution of 1776. Last General Assembly. (W. B. Rawle) Pennsyl. M. **25**: 220.

— Description; Notes of Travel in 1772. (J. W. Jordan) Pennsyl. M. **25**: 208.

— The Fight for Honesty in. (J. T. Newcomb) Nation, **73**: 145.

— First Charter of Liberties given to. (R. Almack) Archæol. **47**: 83.

— History of Quaker Government in, I. Sharpless's. (H. M. Jenkins) Am. Hist. R. **5**: 767.

— Ills of. Atlan. **88**: 558.

— Legislation in, Local and Special. Ann. Am. Acad. Pol. Sci. **14**: 269.

— Legislative History of. (C. R. Hildeburn) Pennsyl. M. **22**: 393.

— Origin of Surnames in. (L. O. Kuhns) Lippinc. **59**: 395.

— Political Situation in. (R. Evans) Nation, **67**: 185.

— Proprietary Government in, Shepherd's. (H. M. Jenkins) Am. Hist. R. **2**: 735.

— The Quaker and Palatine as Commonwealth Builders. (F. R. Diffenderffer) Ref. Ch. R. **46**: 145.

— Representation in, Prior to the Revolution. (C. H. Lincoln) Pennsyl. M. **23**: 23.

— Religious Condition of, J. Falckner's Missive on, tr. by J. F. Sachse. Pennsyl. M. **21**: 216.

— The Riots in. Spec. **79**: 361.

— Sachse's German Sectarians of. (M. Merriman) Nation, **72**: 301.

— School System of. (L. R. Harley) Educa. **20**: 389.

— Schools of. (W. A. Mowry) Educa. **17**: 463.

— State Regiment of Foot, May 10 to August 16, 1777, Orderly Book of. (J. W. Jordan) Pennsyl. M. **22**: 57–457.

— University of, Observatory. *See* Flower Observatory.

— "Translations and Reprints of Original Sources of European History" criticised. (H. T. Henry) Am. Cath. Q. **23**: 449.

Pennsylvania Academy of Fine Arts, 67th Exhibition, 1898. Citizen, **3**: 273.

— 68th Exhibition, 1899. Artist (N. Y.) **24**: xxiii. — Brush & P. **3**: 288.

Pennsylvania Academy of Fine Art 70th Exhibition, 1901. Brush & P. 5: 262. — Artist (N. Y.) 30: iii.

Pennsylvania Dutchman and wherein he has excelled. (S. W. Pennypacker) Pennsyl. M. 22: 452.

Penny, Value of a, in 1695. (H. N. Williams) Argosy, 74: 301.

Penny Wise. (V. F. Boyle) Atlan. 85: 518.

Penobscot Indians, The. (G. J. Varney) Green Bag, 12: 662.

Penology, Progress in. (S. J. Barrows) Forum, 30: 442.

Penshurst, Kent. (H. C. Shelley) New Eng. M. n. s. 23: 275.

Penshurst Place. (C. S. Sargent) Garden & F. 10: 389.

Pension Bureau, South and the. (T. A. Broadus) R. of Rs. (N. Y.) 23: 203.

Pension Frauds, Alleged. (G. R. Scott) Arena, 20: 409.

Pension Funds and Banking Superannuation. Bank. M. (Lond.) 72: 702.

Pension Love-story, A. (R. Herrick) Scrib. M. 22: 740.

Pension System, Defects in our. (F. E. Leupp) Forum, 31: 670.

— of the Chicago and Northwestern Railway Co. (G. G. Tunell) J. Pol. Econ. 9: 271.

Pensions; Cash vs. Glory. (E. P. Jackson) No. Am. 167: 382.

— Military and Naval, of the United States. (O. O. Howard) J. Mil. Serv. Inst. 11: 1. — (H. C. King) J. Mil. Serv. Inst. 11: 158.

— The New Raid. (J. E. Leupp) Nation, 69: 86.

— Old Age. See Old Age.

— Problem of. (H. C. Evans) Munsey, 19: 697.

— Some Weak Places in our System. (S. N. Clark) Forum, 26: 306.

— Teachers'. The Story of a Women's Campaign. (E. A. Allen) R. of Rs. (N. Y.) 15: 700.
  See also Teachers.

— To purge the Pension List. (J. H. Girdner) No. Am. 166: 374.

— Voluntary vs. State. (J. T. Baylee) Westm. 151: 620.

— Workingmen's. (P. Monroe) Am. J. Sociol. 2: 501.

Pentathlum, The Modern. Liv. Age, 214: 307.

Pentecost, Day of. (E. Huber) Luth. Q. 27: 406.

— the Birthday of the New Testament Church. (C. Cort) Ref. Ch. R. 46: 227.

Penury, Cure of. (W. Gladden) Bib. Sac. 57: 135.

Penycuik Breeding Experiments. Nature, 60: 272. — Pop. Sci. Mo. 57: 126.

Penzance and Vicinity. (J. Shaylor) Idler, 16: 175.

People, Sovereignty of the. (H. Seal) Westm. 147: 524.

People I have known. Ecl. M. 134: 84.

People in my Watch, The. (T. K. Beecher) Outl. 69: 509.

People of the Buffalo, The; a story. (H. Garland) McClure, 16: 153. Same art. Idler, 19: 29.

People who Disappointed one. (A. K. H. Boyd) Ecl. M. 131: 700.

People's Palace Art School. (A. Fish) M. of Art, 21: 252.

People's Party, The. (M. Butler) Forum, 28: 658.

— Passing of the. (W. A. Peffer) No. Am. 166: 12.

Peoria, Ill., Fort Créve-Cœur. (F. J. O'Reilly) Cath. World, 71: 88.

— Public Library. Lib. J. 22: 145.

Pepper, Herbert S. New Designer for Metal-work. (E. F. Strange) Studio (Lond.) 3: 142.

Pepper, Dr. William; a remarkable American. (F. N. Thorpe) Cent. 39: 579.

— Sketch of. (L. R. Harley) Pop. Sci. Mo. 55: 836.

Peppercorn, A. D., Artist. (A. M. Stevenson) Studio (Internat.) 12: 77.

Pepys, Samuel, with portrait. Acad. 51: 284.

— and his Wife. (M. Dale) Westm. 153: 547.

— Marriage of, Date of. (S. R. Gardiner) Ath. '00, 1: 786.

— Our Inimitable Diarist. (R. M. Sillard) Westm. 155: 323.

— Will of. (G. A. Aitken) Ath. '97, 1: 214.

Pepys, Mrs. Samuel. Temp. Bar, 118: 91. Same art. Ecl. M. 133: 936. Same art. Liv. Age, 223: 193.

Pepys visits Bayreuth; a story. (W. Bendall) Idler, 16: 20.

Perception, Fallacies of. (J. W. Powell) Open Court, 12: 720.

— of Horizontal and of Vertical Lines. (B. O. Peirce) Science, n. s. 10: 425.

Perch, Educability of the. (N. Triplett) Am. J. Psychol. 12: 354.

Percival, John, with portraits. Strand, 16: 432.

Percy, Lady Elizabeth. (J. M. Bulloch) Eng. Illust. 18: 523.

Percy, George W. (G. A. Wright) Am. Arch. 72: 31.

Percy, Josceline, Vice-Admiral. (Mrs. C. Bagot) Blackw. 165: 461. Same art. Ecl. M. 132: 806.

Perdita; a story. (H. Hawthorne) Harper, 94: 557.

Père Lachaise Cemetery, In. (J. Stafford) Chamb. J. 75: 582.

Père Michel; a story. (L. G. Moberly) Belgra. 93: 128.

Pereira, Nuño Alvares. (C. J. Willdey) Scot. R. 32: 37.

Père Raphaël. (G. W. Cable) Cent. 40: 545.

Perez, Francesco. (G. A. Cesareo) Liv. Age, 220: 744.

Perfect Cure, A. (R. Stephens) Chamb. J. 75: supp. 39.

Perfect Things, Hiddenness of. (F. A. Fulcher) Argosy, 68: 238.

Perfection, Christian. (R. H. Story) Expos. 9: 73.

Perfidy of Mrs. Tucker. (M. Brodie) Idler, 13: 620.

Perfume of the Rose; a story. (F. A. Steel) Lippinc. 64: 935.

Perfume-manufacture. Grasse, the "Sweetest" Town in the World. (E. Hodgens) Chaut. 29: 419.

Perfumery. From Petal to Perfume. (E. Brewer) Strand, 16: 232.

— Morality of. (H. T. Peck) Cosmopol. 25: 585.

Perfumes, Natural and Artificial. (J. Passy) Pop. Sci. Mo. 52: 86.

Perichola, La, True Story of. (May Crommelin) Theatre, 39: 298.

Peridotites in North Carolina, Origin of the Corundum associated with. (J. H. Pratt) Am. J. Sci. 156: 49.

Périgueux, St. Front. (J. C. Paget) Temp. Bar, 115: 127.

Peril of Fan-way-chin. (G. S. Hays) Cent. 39: 60.

Perilous Adventure, A. Argosy, 65: 637.

Perilous Journey. (C. M. Vaile) New Eng. M. n. s. 17: 408.

Perils of the Red-box; a novel. (H. Hill) Canad. M. 17: 18.

Periodic Law. (J. L. Howe) Pop. Sci. Mo. 59: 152.

Periodical Literature, Bibliography of. (F. Campbell) Library, 8: 49.

— Early, in the Ohio Valley. (L. Mendenhall) Midland, 8: 144.

Periodical Press of France. (T. B. Preston) Chaut. 24: 415.

Periodicals, American, 1880–1900. (H. L. Nelson) Dial (Ch.) 28: 349.

— and Transactions of Societies, Lists of. (C. W. Andrews) Lib. J. 24: supp. 29.

— Availability of Contributions. (R. Hall) Writer, 10: 13.

— Union List of, in Chicago Libraries. Pub. Lib. 5: 60.

— Use of, in Reference Work. (F. W. Faxon) Pub. Lib. 3: 207.

Perishing Land, The. (Réné Bazin) Liv. Age, **223**: 267–814. **224**: 26–483.

Perjury in Judicial Proceedings. (J. J. McCarthy) Am. Law R. **35**: 684.

— Is it excusable under any Circumstances ? (B. Borret) Green Bag, **13**: 141.

Perkin, Wm. Henry. (S. Young) Good Words, **41**: 256.

Perkins, George W., with portrait. (W. J. Boies) World's Work, **3**: 1538.

Perley, Samuel, Marriages by, 1767–82. (H. O. Thayer) N. E. Reg. **204**: 460.

Perosi, Lorenzo, Music. (J. F. Runciman) Sat. R. **87**: 557.

Perpetua ; a Tale of Nîmes in A. D. 213. (S. Baring-Gould) Sund. M. **26**: 26–846.

Perpetuities. (C. Sweet) Law Q. **15**: 71.

Perpetuity and Entry, Powers of. (A. J. Mackey) Law Q. **17**: 32.

Perraud, Cardinal, and the Lacordaire Group. (J. O'Reilly) Cath. World, **65**: 381.

Perry, Amos. (C. S. Brigham) N. E. Reg. **54**: 245.

Perry, Bliss. Lit. W. (Bost.) **30**: 264.

Perry, Stephen Joseph, with portrait. Pop. Sci. Mo. **50**: 835.

Perry, Thomas Sergeant. (M. C. S.) Bookman, **7**: 288.

Persecution, Relic of the Times of. (J. H. Pollen) Month, **96**: 46.

— Religious. Spec. **83**: 745.

Perseids of 1899. (J. A. Miller) Pop. Astron. **7**: 406.

— August, of 1900. (W. F. Denning) Nature, **62**: 398.

— Outlying Clusters of. (A. S. Herschel) Nature, **56**: 540.

Perseus, New Star in. *See* Stars.

Persia. Liv. Age, **225**: 442. — (L. Griffin) Asia. R. **29**: 225.

— and Afghanistan, Problem of. (T. E. Gordon) 19th Cent. **47**: 413.

— Attack on a Telegraph Station in. (B. Williams) Longm. **30**: 158. Same art. Ecl. M. **129**: 236.

— Coming Struggle for. (R. P. Lobb) Asia. R. **28**: 284.

— An Economist's Notes on. (J. Rabino) J. Statis. Soc. **64**: 261.

— England's Trade with. (J. F. Fraser) Contemp. **72**: 86.

— English Enterprise in. (F. E. Crow) 19th Cent. **41**: 124.

— Journeys in. (P. M. Sykes) Geog. J. **10**: 568.

— My First Morning at a Persian Court. (W. Sparroy) Fortn. **76**: 281.

— Russia's Lien on. (T. Beale) Forum, **29**: 147.

— Russian Policy toward. Sat. R. **91**: 69.

— Shah of, Elder Brother of. (W. Sparroy) Blackw. **168**: 264.

— Some English Interests in. Sat. R. **86**: 198.

— Spinning in. Reliquary, **39**: 46.

— Sufism, or Persian Mysticism. (J. H. Parsons) Gent. M. n. s. **59**: 279.

— Sykes's Through Persia in a Side-saddle. Spec. **81**: 151. — Ath. '98, **1** : 592. — Bk. Buyer, **18**: 411.

— Trade Routes in. (A. Hotz) J. Soc. Arts, **47**: 341.

— Tutor's Experience in. Blackw. **167**: 749.

— under Darius and Artaxerxes. (G. S. Goodspeed) Bib. World, **14**: 250.

Persian Apparatus, Study in the. (W. Sparroy) Macmil. **82**: 337.

Persian Embassy to Europe in 1287–88. (N. McLean) Eng. Hist. R. **14**: 299.

Persian Emperors, Edicts of, in the Old Testament. (L. H. Mills) Crit. R. **11**: 344.

Persian Epigram, A. (E. H. Keen) Outl. **69**: 1036.

Persian Folk-lore. (L. C. Sykes) Folk-Lore, **12**: 261.

Persian Gulf, Ancient Trading Centres of. Geog. J. **9**: 309, (A. W. Stiffe) 608. — (A. W. Stiffe) Geog. J. **16**: 211. **18**: 291.

— Notes on. (A. W. Stiffe) Geog. J. **12**: 179.

Persian Literature, Modern. (E. D. Ross) No. Am. **170**: 827.

Persian Poets. (W. Canton) Good Words, **40**: 357.

Persius Flaccus ; a Roman Puritan. (F. F. Abbott) New Eng. M. n. s. **18**: 577.

Perso-Baluch Boundary, The. (T. H. Holdich) Geog. J. **9**: 416.

Person, A, and a Picture. (G. Morris) Cent. **32**: 630.

Personal Effects. Spec. **86**: 966.

Personal Equation, Psychology of. (T. H. Safford) Science, **6**: 784.

Personal Equation ; a story of Cornell College. (J. G. Sanderson) Lippinc. **67**: 86.

Personal Experience, A. (T. W. Wilkinson) Chamb. J. **75**: 555. Same art. Liv. Age, **219**: 463.

Personality, Alterations of, Binet's. Spec. **78**: 172.

— Aspects of. (F. Gill) New World, **7**: 229.

— Double. (A. Wilson) Longm. **31**: 151. Same art. Ecl. M. **130**: 78.

— from the Monistic Point of View. (G. F. Genung) Am. J. Theol. **3**: 473.

— The Loss of. (E. D. Puffer) Atlan. **85**: 195.

— Multiple ; Plural States of Being. (A. Binet) Pop. Sci. Mo. **50**: 539.

— of Places. Sat. R. **88**: 513.

— People with Two Personalities. Ecl. M. **129**: 716.

— Problem of. (W. Seton) Cath. World, **68**: 652.

Personifications, Strange. (T. Flournoy) Pop. Sci. Mo. **51**: 112.

Personifying Passion in Youth, and the Sex and Gender Problem. (J. H. Leuba) Monist, **10**: 536.

Perspective, Problems in. (W. R. Ware) Am. Arch. **73**: 11, 30, 88.

Persulphates, Determination of. (C. A. Peters and S. E. Moody) Am. J. Sci. **162**: 367.

Perturbations, and the Perturbative Function. (J. Morrison) Pop. Astron. **8**: 309. **10**: 130, 249, 436.

— of Heavenly Bodies. (F. R. Moulton) Pop. Astron. **6**: 88.

Peru, Antiquities, Terra-cotta, from. (A. F. Berlin) Am. Antiq. **21**: 271.

— Social Condition of. (C. E. George) Gunton's M. **21**: 354.

Perugia. (R. E. D. Sketchley) Argosy, **75**: 24.

— The Heavenly Choir of. (K. S. Macquoid) Sund. M. **26**: 510.

— Story of. (Margaret Symonds) Ath. '98, **1**: 820.

Perugini, C. E. (M. H. Spielmann) M. of Art, **22**: 457.

Perugino, Williamson's. (K. Cox) Nation, **71**: 496.

Peshittâ Version of the New Testament, Growth of. (F. C. Conybeare) Am. J. Theol. **1**: 883.

Pessimism and Thomas Hardy's Poems. (M. Kendall) Lond. Q. **91**: 223.

— and Tragedy. (W. Archer) Fortn. **71**: 390. Same art. Ecl. M. **132**: 899. Same art. Liv. Age, **221**: 331.

— Aspects of. (J. Kendal) Am. Cath. Q. **22**: 74.

— British. (A. Carnegie) 19th Cent. **49**: 901. Same art. Liv. Age, **230**: 137. Same art. Ecl. M. **137**: 328.

— Evolutional, Leopardi and. (W. N. Guthrie) Sewanee, **4**: 129.

— A German Movement against. (Count S. C. de Soissons) Contemp. **79**: 397. Same art. Liv. Age, **229**: 322.

— Health, and Courage. Outl. **61**: 444.

— its relation to Ultimate Philosophy. (F. C. S. Schiller) Int. J. Ethics, **8**: 48.

— Modern. (G. White) Sewanee, **4**: 102, 334.

Pessimism, Personal Element in. (G. A. Gordon) Liv. Age, 209: 64.
— Some Sources of. Outl. 61: 393.
Pestalozzi, Johann Heinrich. A Pestalozzian Pilgrimage. (S. L. Patteson) Chaut. 33: 610.
— Doctrine and Method of. (N. C. Schaeffer) Ref. Q. 45: 334.
— Swiss Educational Reformer. (N. C. Schaeffer) Ref. Q. 44: 190.
Pests. (W. Cooper) Strand, 14: 542.
Pet Animals. (F. G. Aflalo) Chamb. J. 78: 484.
Pet of the Gods. (C. K. Eichler) New Eng. M. n. s. 17: 245.
Pets in the Sea. (C. F. Holder) Outl. 58: 181.
— Care of. (F. L. Oswald) Chaut. 31: 36.
— Nuisance of. (J. S. Wise) Outing, 38: 558.
Peten, Yucatan; an island city. (T. R. Dawley, jr.) Harper, 96: 774.
Peter, St., the Man and the Epistle. (G. M. Harmon) J. Bib. Lit. 17: 31.
— Sojourn in Rome. (A. C. McGiffert) Am. J. Theol. 1: 145.
— Twenty-five Year Episcopate of, in Rome. Dub. R. 120: 386.
— — Barnes on. (H. Thurston) Month, 95: 402,
— A Type of Theological Transition. (S. Mathews) Bib. World, 17: 348.
Peter the Great. Ed. R. 187: 460. — Lond. Q. 89: 26. — (J. Fitzmaurice-Kelly) New R. 17: 163. Same art. Ecl. M. 129: 546. — (A. Laugel) Nation, 65: 296, 317.
— After. (A. Laugel) Nation, 71: 48, 68.
— Bain's Daughter of. (I. F. Hapgood) Nation, 71: 292.
— on the Stage. (F. Ormathwaite) Theatre, 39: 119.
— Waliszewski on. Ath. '97, 2: 58. — (H. E. Bourne) Citizen, 3: 255.
Peter, Thomas, of Saybrook and Mylor. (E. B. Peters) N. E. Reg. 54: 339.
Peter and the Interviewer; a story. (P. Reyd) Gent. M. n. s. 60: 167.
Peter and Number Six. (F. C. Williams) Lippinc. 68: 509.
Peter on Cookery Lessons; a story. (P. Reyd) Gent. M. n. s. 62: 254.
Peter on Matrimony; a story. (P. Reyd) Gent. M. n. s. 63: 417.
Peterborough Cathedral. (W. C. Ingram) Sund. M. 27: 269, 295. — (Cecilia Waerm) Am. Arch. 55: 27.
— Restoration of. Acad. 51: 28, 49.
Peters, Carl. (E. Sellers) Fortn. 67: 125.
Peters, Charles Rollo, Artist, with portrait. (F. W. Ramsdell) Brush & P. 4: 205.
Peters, Judge Richard, Puns and Witticisms of. Pennsyl. M. 25: 366.
Petersham; a poem. (R. B. Fiske) Atlan. 84: 428.
Petite Blanchisseuse, La; a story. (A. Beaumont) Belgra. 93: 445.
"Petite Chanteuse." (Ella S. Partridge) Nat'l M. (Bost.) 6: 86.
Petition, A; a poem. (R. G. A. S. Prudhomme) Argosy, 65: 190.
Petitioner, A. (M. S. Briscoe) Harper, 97: 232.
Petöfi, Alexander. (A. Hegedus, jr.) Critic, 36: 431. — Temp. Bar, 109: 405. Same art. Liv. Age, 212: 256.
— Memoirs of, Ferenczi's. Ath. '97, 1: 832.
Petra, Arabia, "High Place" at. (G. L. Robinson) Am. Antiq. 23: 229.
— Ruined Capital of Edom. (A. Forder) Bib. World, 18: 328.
Petrarch, Carducci's. (J. W. Mario) Nation, 68: 254.
— Letters to Cicero. (F. Abbott) Sewanee, 5: 319.
— Trials of a Man of Letters. Liv. Age, 221: 64.

Petrified Indian. (G. K. Turner) New Eng. M. n. s. 22: 525.
Petroglyphs on the Amoor River. (B. Laufer) Am. Anthrop. 1: 746.
Petrography. Rock Composition and Rock Classification. Am. Natural. 35: 235.
Petrolene. (S. F. Peckham) J. Frankl. Inst. 151: 50.
Petroleum, Asphalt, and Bitumen. (A. Jaccard) Pop. Sci. Mo. 50: 380.
— in California. (W. L. Watts) Cassier, 21: 123.
— Thomson and Redwood's Handbook on. (W. T. Lawrence) Nature 64: 441.
Petroleum District of Baku. (D. A. Louis) Engin. M. 15: 986.
Petroleum Fuel, Safety of. (J. Holden) Cassier, 17: 21.
Petroleum Industry. (G. T. Holloway) Knowl. 21: 124, 151, 169.
Petroleum Pipe Line, Russian. (E. H. Foster) Cassier, 19: 3.
Petroleums, Crude, Classification of. (S. F. Peckham) J. Frankl. Inst. 15: 114.
Petronius. Cena Trimalchionis, Peck's Translation of. (A. G. Durno) Bk. Buyer, 18: 54.
— A Study in Ancient Realism. (F. F. Abbott) Sewanee, 7: 435.
Pettenkofer, Max Josef von. (W. H. Corfield) Nature, 63: 399.
Petticoat Trail, The; a story. (E. E. Peake) Nat'l M. (Bost.) 13: 234.
Pettie, John. The Threat; etched by Heydemann. Art J. 50: 358.
Petty, Sir Wm., Economic Writings of. Ath. '99, 2: 793.
— Father of English Economics. (W. H. Mallock) National, 37: 548.
— Place of, in the History of Economics. (C. H. Hull) Q. J. Econ. 14: 307.
Petty Sessions, At. (E. Porritt) Green Bag, 11: 472.
Petunia-baby, The. (C. W. Bullwinkle) New Eng. M. n. s. 24: 369.
Pevensey Marsh, Round. (T. H. B. Graham) Gent. M. n. s. 58: 359.
Pew-ends, Poppy-heads and. (D. M. Image) Artist (N. Y.) 26: 11. See Bench-ends.
Pews, Church, History of. Sat. R. 88: 386.
Pewter-ware, Some Rare. (R. D. Benn) Art J. 51: 313, 347.
Pewter Work. (H. Frantz) M. of Art, 20: 98.
Ph. D. Degree, Examination for. (W. F. Magie) Educa. R. 22: 18.
Phæstos, A Visit to. (A. Taramelli) Am. J. Archæol. n. s. 5: 418.
Phagocytes; the Scavengers of the Body. (M. A. Dastre) Pop. Sci. Mo. 56: 379.
Phantasies. (C. F. Keary) New R. 16: 50, 337, 383.
Phantasmatograph, The. (W. H. Pollock) Longm. 34: 58.
Phantom Army; poem. (W. P. Foster) Atlan. 87: 631.
Phantom Kangaroo. (O. Hall) Lippinc. 59: 420.
Phantom Painting, The; a story. (J. M. Chapple) Nat'l M. (Bost.) 8: 464.
Phantomnation. (F. Hall) Nation, 70: 127.
Pharaoh and the Sergeant; a poem. (R. Kipling) McClure, 9: 925.
Pharaoh's Curse; a story. (L. Sorrel) Argosy, 63: 598.
Pharaoh's Daughter, Story of, as translated from a 12th Cent. MS. at Patmos. (W. W. Astor) Pall Mall M. 22: 521.
Pheasant, Mongolian, in Oregon. (T. C. Farrell) Outing, 32: 596.
Pheasant Farming. Chamb. J. 75: 86.
Pheasant Shooting. (Ernest Hamilton) Pall Mall M. 13: 399.

Pheasants on the Table. (A. I. Shand) Sat. R. **92**: 457.

Phelps, Edward J., with portrait. (S. E. Baldwin) Green Bag, **12**: 213.

— as seen in his Letters. (E. B. Sherman) Critic, **36**: 405.

— Orations and Essays. (D. Mowry) Dial (Ch.) **31**: 132.

Phelps, William Preston. (C. E, Hurd) New Eng. M. n. s. **17**: 363.

Phenomenalism in Psychology, Defence of. (F. H. Bradley) Mind, **25**: 26.

Phil. Burton's Ducks ; a tale. (G. N. Weekes) Canad. M. **12**: 367.

Phil's Pard. (W. C. Platts) Chamb. J. **74**: 81-136.

Philadelphia ; Art Exhibitions. (M. E. Wright) Brush & P. **7**: 257.

— Assessment of Damages done by the British, 1777-78. Pennsyl. M. **25**: 323.

— Campaign against Machine Rule in. (C. R. Woodruff) R. of Rs. (N. Y.) **24**: 558.

— Centennial of, 1876, Reminiscences of. (T. G. Alvord) Nat'l M. (Bost.) **11**: 277.

— a Century ago. (K. M. Rowland) Lippinc. **62**: 804.

— Commercial Museum. (R. A. Foley) World's Work, **2**: 1258. — (W. C. Betts) J. Pol. Econ. **8**: 222. — (W. P. Wilson) Forum, **28**: 113.

— Congress (of Societies) at, 1900. (W. Hopkins) Nation, **72**: 7.

— Country Life about. Outing, **37**: 398.

— Defences of, 1777. (W. C. Ford) Pennsyl. M. **21**: 51.

— Election Frauds in. (C. R. Woodruff) Arena, **24**: 397.

— Election Methods and Reforms in. (C. R. Woodruff) Ann. Am. Acad. Pol. Sci. **17**: 181.

— Financial Institutions. Bank. M. (N. Y.) **60**: 480.

— Gas Franchise in. (F. W. Spiers) Citizen, **3**: 201.

— Gas Lease. (F. W. Spiers) Munic. Aff. **1**: 718.

— Gas Works. (C. R. Woodruff) Am. J. Sociol. **3**: 601. — (J. I. Rogers) Munic. Aff. **1**: 730.

— — Lesson of. (J. H. Stallard) Overland, n. s. **33**: 175.

— Girlhood in, 1820-40. (E. D. Gillespie) Lippinc. **67**: 327.

— International Commercial Congress, 1899. (W. H. Schoff) Ann. Am. Acad. Pol. Sci. **15**: 81.

— List of Foreigners who arrived at, 1791-92. (L. R. Kelker) Pennsyl. M. **14**: 187, 334.

— National Export Exposition, 1899. (W. P. Wilson) Lippinc. **64**: 464. — R. of Rs. (N. Y.) **120**: 447.

— Negro in, W. E. B. DuBois on. Am. Hist. R. **6**: 162. *See* Negro in Philadelphia.

— Old, Glimpse of. (E. P. Weaver) Lippinc. **59**: 557.

— — Salon in. (A. H. Wharton) Lippinc. **64**: 92, 311.

— Photographic Salon. (W. B. Dyer) Brush & P. **7**: 115. — (J. F. Ziegler) Brush & P. **5**: 108.

— Reform in. (E. P. Clark) Nation, **70**: 159.

— Republican Tammany of. (C. R. Woodruff) Outl. **69**: 169.

— Ship Registers, 1726-75. Pennsyl. M. **23**: 498. **24**: 108, 212, 348. **25**: 118-400.

— State House of, in 1774. (J. W. Jordan) Pennsyl. M. **23**: 417.

— Street Railway System of, Spiers's. Citizen, **3**: 183.

— Water-color Exhibition. (W. P. Lockington) Brush & P. **8**: 65.

— Water Supply of, and of London. (M. R. Maltbie) Munic. Aff. **3**: 193.

— — A Story of Procrastination. (C. R. Woodruff) Forum, **28**: 305.

Philadelphia Farmer's Club. Outing, **37**: 398.

Philæ, Capt. Lyons's Report on. Nature, **56**: 122.

Philanthropic Work, Summer School in. (P. W. Ayres) Ann. Am. Acad. Pol. Sci. **15**: 297.

Philanthropists, Legislative Function of. (J. Lee) New Eng. M. n. s. **20**: 51.

Philanthropy and Wage-paying. (V. M. Crawford) Econ. J. **11**: 96.

— by Circular. Bank. M. (Lond.) **70**: 725.

— Mechanism of. Spec. **78**: 235.

— Practical. (H. A. Townsend) Pop. Sci. Mo. **55**: 534.

— A School of. (P. W. Ayres) Char. R. **9**: 250.

— Science in. (C. R. Henderson) Atlan. **85**: 249.

— A Training Class in. (P. W. Ayres) Char. R. **8**: 315.

— Training for Practical. (P. W. Ayres) R. of Rs. (N. Y.) **19**: 205.

— *vs.* Legislation. (A. Ogilvie) Westm. **154**: 510.

— Wise Methods in. (J. P. Poole) Westm. **152**: 691.

Philbin, Eugene A. Outl. **67**: 795.

Philip and Alexander of Macedon, Hogarth's. (B. Perrin) Am. Hist. R. **3**: 128.

Philip and Constance ; a story. (W. S. Harwood) Music, **12**: 12.

"Philip Herbert," Loss of the. (A. H. Norway) Cornh. **76**: 810.

Philip of Pokanoket, King, Country of. (W. A. Slade) New Eng. M. n. s. **18**: 605.

Philippine Islands. Am. Antiq. **20**: 558. — (J. A. Osborne) Chaut. **27**: 375. — (F. F. Hilder) Forum, **25**: 534. — (R. R. Lala) Outl. **59**: 265. — Maps and Illus. (F. F. Hilder) Nat. Geog. M. **9**: 257. — Bank. M. (N. Y.) **56**: 852. — Month, **98**: 96. — (J. Parker) J. Mil. Serv. Inst. **27**: 317.

— Aborigines of. (P. Whitmarsh) Outl. **65**: 435.

— After the Capture of Manila. (F. R. Roberson) Cosmopol. **26**: 379.

— American Occupation of, Claims arising from. (W. F. Norris) Green Bag. **13**: 336.

— Among the Wild Igorrotes. (P. Whitmarsh) Outl. **65**: 213.

— and American Capital. (J. R. Smith) Pop. Sci. Mo. **55**: 186.

— and China. (P. Carus) Open Court, **14**: 108.

— and Cuba ; the Territory with which we are Threatened. (W. Reid) Cent. **34**: 788.

— and their Future. Quar. **190**: 198. Same art. Ecl. M. **133**: 801. Same art. Liv. Age, **223**: 139.

— and their People, Worcester's. (J. E. Stevens) Nation, **67**: 415.

— Annexation of, justified by our History, Constitution, and Laws. (I. M. Scott) Overland, n. s. **34**: 310.

— — Objections to. (G. G. Vest) No. Am. **168**: 112.

— — Shall they be annexed ? (A. H. Whitfield) Cosmopol. **26**: 351.

— Apropos of the. (E. L. Godkin) Nation, **67**: 216.

— Architecture in. Our Acquired Architecture. (M. Schuyler) Archit. R. **9**: 277.

— Are they Worth having ? (G. F. Becker) Scrib. M. **27**: 739.

— Army in. (R. Ogden) Nation, **72**: 22.

— An Army of Wealth Creators *vs.* an Army of Destruction. (B. O. Flower and others) Arena, **25**: 521.

— as a Fulcrum. (D. MacG. Means) Nation, **67**: 161.

— Balance-sheet in, Our. (R. Ogden) Nation, **72**: 124.

— Banking and Finance in. Bank. M. (N. Y.) **60**: 834.

— Blumentritt's Studies of. (D. G. Brinton) Am. Anthrop. **1**: 122.

— Burden of. (R. Ogden) Nation, **73**: 486.

— Campaign in. (W. G. Irwin) Chaut. **28**: 158.

— Campaigning in. (P. Ralli) Overland, n. s. **33**: 154-220. **34**: 230.

— The Case of. Blackw. **165**: 1016.

— Catechism on. (A. G. Sedgwick) Nation, **67**: 178.

— Catholic Church in. A Leaf out of the Latin Book. (L. W. Bacon) Outl. **64**: 971.

Philippine Islands, Catholicism in. (W. Weber) Nation, 67: 148.

— Chinese Exclusion from. (S. W. Belford) Arena, 23: 449.

— Church Problems in. (P. Whitmarsh) Outl. 64: 443.

— Church Property in. (A. G. Robinson) Indep. 52: 2377.

— Church Question in. Outl. 64: 388.

— Civil Government in, Preparing. (J. A. Le Roy) Indep. 53: 1525.

— — Inauguration of. (J. W. Hillman) Indep. 53: 2017.

— Civil Service in. (O. G. Villard) Nation, 72: 289.

— Civilization and Barbarism in Luzon. (M. L. Todd) Nation, 73: 221.

— Commerce of. (J. Hyde) Nat. Geog. M. 9: 301.

— Commission, Taft, Report of. Ann. Am. Acad. Pol. Sci. 17: 381. — (J. T. Creagh) Cath. World, 73: 6. — (R. Ogden) Nation, 69: 346. — Outl. 63: 621, 630.

— — Work of. (B. J. Clinch) Am. Cath. Q. 26: 625. — World's Work, 2: 1144.

— Commission's Proclamation. Outl. 61: 860, 890.

— Common Schools in. (C. G. Calkins) Indep. 52: 1489.

— Congress, the President and. (P. Belmont) No. Am. 169: 894.

— "Consent of the Governed." Cath. World, 70: 253.

— — and the Filipinos. (E. B. Briggs) Cath. World, 70: 794.

— Cuba and. Outl. 67: 567.

— The Cuba of the Far East. (J. Barrett) No. Am. 164: 173.

— The Currency Situation in. (P. Willis) Nation, 72: 269.

— Customs and Oddities in. (M. A. Hamm) Indep. 51: 961.

— Disposition of. (C. E. Howe) Nat. Geog. M. 9: 304.

— Do we owe Independence to the Filipinos? (C. Denby) Forum, 29: 401.

— Duty of U. S. in. (E. D. Weed) Arena, 20: 453.

— Economic Condition of. (Max L. Tornow) Nat. Geog. M. 10: 33.

— Education in. (P. Whitmarsh) Outl. 66: 986. — (F. W. Nash) Educa. R. 22: 217.

— Efforts to determine Area and Population of. (W. F. Willcox) Am. Statis. Assoc. 6: 346.

— Empire of. (J. Foreman) National, 32: 392.

— Environment of. (J. Barrett) Nat. Geog. M. 11: 1.

— Excursion in. (M. L. Todd) Nation, 73: 241.

— An Execution in. Green Bag, 10: 470.

— The Facts. Outl. 61: 620.

— Facts about, with a Discussion of Pending Problems. (F. A. Vanderlip) Cent. 34: 555.

— Fate of. Spec. 80: 646. Same art. Liv. Age, 217: 837. Same art. Ecl. M. 131: 138.

— Filipino Petition, The. (R. Ogden) Nation, 72: 42. — (W. F. Norris) Green Bag, 13: 450.

— Filipino Responsibility. (P. Whitmarsh) Outl. 64: 674.

— Filipinos, The. (E. Wildman) Munsey, 21: 32. — (R. R. Lala) Forum, 28: 29. — Month, 97: 93.

— — The Backwoods. (L. R. Sargent) Outl. 63: 17.

— — Formation of. (B. J. Clinch) Yale R. 10: 53.

— — The Military. (L. R. Sargent) Outl. 63: 202.

— — View Point of the. (H. L. Hawthorne) R. of Rs. (N. Y.) 24: 567.

— Firmament in. (R. O'Halloran) Pop. Astron. 7: 201.

— The First Book on. (L. S. Livingston) Bookman, 9: 263.

— Friars in, as Missioners. (Bryan J. Clinch) Am. Cath. Q. 24, no. 4: 73.

— — Case against. (A. Regidor) Indep. 53: 317.

Philippine Islands, Friars in, Filipinos, and Land. (J. B. Rodgers) R. of Rs. (N. Y.) 23: 71.

— — The Way out. Outl. 63: 668.

— From Manila to Bacalor. (P. Whitmarsh) Outl. 64: 347.

— Games of. (S. Culin) Am. Anthrop. 2: 643.

— Geographic Facts from Report of Taft Philippine Commission. Nat. Geog. M. 12: 114.

— Germany in. Liv. Age, 218: 277.

— Give the Country the Facts. Atlan. 87: 424.

— Gold in. (R. R. Lala) R. of Rs. (N. Y.) 20: 74. — (F. F. Hilder) Nat. Geog. M. 11: 465.

— Higher Administration in. (J. A. Le Roy) Indep. 53: 2390.

— The Hill-men of. (L. M. J. Garnett) Nation, 67: 127.

— History of the Affair. Outl. 61: 904.

— History of, 1899–1903. Outl. 61: 688.

— Holding. (H. White) Nation, 66: 438.

— Home Rule in. (J. A. Le Roy) Indep. 53: 1955.

— How may the U. S. govern? (W. W. Cook) Pol. Sci. Q. 16: 68.

— Improving Opinion on. Gunton's M. 16: 91.

— In the. (L. R. Sargent) Indep. 51: 2477.

— in History. (C. Johnston) R. of Rs. (N. Y.) 17: 698.

— in November, 1897. (A. Bellessort) Ecl. M. 133: 1.

— An Incident in. (M. O. Wilcox) Idler, 19: 181.

— Independence of. The Filipinos' Vain Hope. (M. Wilcox) No. Am. 171: 333.

— Insurrection in, and the Voice of the Courts. (E. B. Briggs) Cath. World, 69: 544.

— — written from a Study of the Spanish Archives left in Manila. (C. G. Calkins) Harper, 99: 469.

— International Brotherhood. (L. Abbott) Outl. 61: 865.

— Japan and. (A. M. Knapp) Atlan. 83: 737.

— Johns Hopkins' Expedition to, to investigate Diseases. (S. Flexner; L. F. Barker) J. Mil. Serv. Inst. 26: 421.

— Justice in. (P. Ralli) Outl. 68: 19.

— Katipunan Society of. (L. W. V. Kennon) No. Am. 173: 208. — (R. R. Lala) Indep. 51: 2207.

— Knotty Problems of. (D. C. Worcester) Cent. 34: 873.

— Lala on. (I. M. Price) Dial (Ch.) 26: 394.

— Land of the Igorrotes. (P. Whitmarsh) Outl. 64: 960.

— Legend of. Poet-Lore, 11: 151.

— Letters from. (M. L. Todd) Nation, 73: 221, 242.

— Lifting the Veil. (R. Ogden) Nation, 72: 189.

— Malay Pirates of. (D. G. Worcester) Cent. 34: 690.

— Manila and. (A. Falkner von Sonnenburg) Nat. Geog. M. 10: 65.

— Markets in, for U. S. Products. Nat'l M. (Bost.) 15: 319.

— Material Problems in. (S. W. Belford) R. of Rs. (N. Y.) 19: 454.

— Martial Law in. Chamb. J. 74: 245.

— The Men behind the Plow. (P. Whitmarsh) Outl. 66: 932.

— The Military Commission in. (M. A. Hildreth) Green Bag, 12: 179.

— The Military Position in. Liv. Age, 223: 397.

— Millett's Expedition to. (J. D. Cox) Nation, 70: 14.

— Mineral Deposits of. (F. L. Strong) Engin. M. 21: 256.

— Missionary Union in. Outl. 68: 433.

— More Truth about. (R. Ogden) Nation, 72: 82.

— Must we obtain the Consent of the Governed? Educa. 20: 311.

— The "National Duty" Delusion. (W. H. Davis) Arena, 21: 736.

Philippine Islands, To-day in. (O. K. Davis) Munsey, 21: 193.
— Transportation in. (W. G. Irwin) Cassier, 17: 423.
— Trooper's Diary in. (E. H. Blatchford) Outl. 59: 775—60: 908.
— Two Philippine Sketches. (H. P. Whitmarsh) Atlan. 86: 364.
— 200 Years ago. (E. E. Slosson) Pop. Sci. Mo. 58: 393.
— Types and Characteristics in. R. of. Rs. (N. Y.) 19: 302.
— Uncle Sam's Legacy of Slaves. (H. O. Dwight) Forum, 29: 283.
— An Unknown Empire. Gunton's M. 14: 384.
— The United States and. (J. Foreman) National, 36: 52. — (J. H. Marble ; F. S. Baldwin ; R. R. Lala) Arena, 22: 554. — (M. von Brandt) Liv. Age, 221: 261. — (W. H. Fleming) Conserv. R. 1: 499.
— U. S. Army in. (J. C. Gillmore) Idler, 19: 359, 429. — (S. S. Long) J. Mil. Serv. Inst. 25: 125.
— U. S. Senators' Views on Disposition of. Nat'l M. (Bost.) 9: 118.
— U. S. Title to. (J. S. Mosby) Nation, 70: 50.
— The U. S. vindicated. (W. E. Chandler) Indep. 51: 1807.
— Value of. (J. Barrett) Munsey, 21: 689.
— Visit to, in 1894. (C. Ericsson) Contemp. 73: 829. Same art. Ecl. M. 131: 95. Same art. Liv. Age, 218: 269.
— Volcanic Eruptions in, Remarkable. (R. L. Packard) Pop. Sci. Mo. 56: 374.
— War Claims arising from Occupation of. (W. F. Morris) Green Bag, 12: 215.
— War in. (P. MacQueen) Nat'l M. (Bost.) 10: 3-590.
— — Filipino Appeal to the People of the United States. (A. Mabini) No. Am. 170: 54.
— — Half Year of. (J. Barrett) R. of Rs. (N. Y.) 20: 290.
— — Mistakes of the Campaign. (J. M. Miller) Indep. 51: 1857.
— — Visits to Various Islands during. (P. MacQueen) Nat'l M. (Bost.) 11: 19.
— — When will it cease ? (P. MacQueen) Arena, 22: 697.
— Warfare in. (P. B. Malone) Cath. World, 73: 348.
— Wealth of. (J. A. Adams) Munsey, 19: 665.
— Week in, in November, 1897. (André Bellessort) Liv. Age, 221: 469-562.
— What an American saw in. (J. T. Mannix) R. of Rs. (N. Y.) 17: 689.
— What shall we do with ? (J. T. Morgan) No. Am. 166: 641. — (E. L. Godkin) Nation, 67: 253. — (C. Denby) Forum, 27: 47. — (W. F. More) Ref. Ch. R. 46: 237.
— White Man and Brown Man in. (F. Palmer) Scrib. M. 27: 76.
— Why the Treaty should be Ratified. (C. Denby) Forum, 26: 641.
— Why we do not Want. (Mrs. J. Davis) Arena, 23: 1.
— Will they Pay ? (F. Doster) Arena, 25: 465.
— Worcester on. Outl. 61: 114.
— Worcester's Report on. Outl. 62: 376.
— Work of our Army-supply Departments in. (J. W. Pope) R. of Rs. (N. Y.) 20: 442.
— Yesterdays in the, Stevens's. Bk. Buyer, 17: 104.
— Younghusband on. (I. M. Rice) Dial (Ch.) 26: 394.
Phillip, Admiral Arthur, Memoir of, Becke and Jeffery's. Ath. '99, 2: 411.—Sat. R. 88: 427.
Phillips, George Faudel, Portraits of. Strand, 13: 65.
Phillips, Henry Wallace. Writer, 14: 9.
Phillips, J., Wood-carving of. (F. H. Jackson) M. of Art, 25: 515.

Phillips, Stephen. (E. Gosse) Cent. 39: 430. — (R. A. Streatfield) Monthly R. 2, no. 3: 93. — With portrait. (W. Archer) Pall Mall M. 24: 246. — (C. F. Smith) Sewanee, 9: 385. — (E. A. Savage) Westm. 156: 187. — Blackw. 163: 569. Same art. Liv. Age, 217: 371. — Acad. 52: 492.
— and his Fears for the Drama. (M. Beerbohm) Sat. R. 91: 669.
— and Tragedy. (W. Watson) Outl. 58: 765. — (W. Watson) Fortn. 69: 432.
— Herod, a Tragedy. Acad. 59: 640. — (M. Beerbohm) Sat. R. 90: 584, 614. — Spec. 85: 616. Same art. Ecl. M. 136: 394. — (W. C. Brownell) Bk. Buyer, 22: 33. — (S. Gwynn) Contemp. 79: 32. — (J. B. Gilder) Critic, 38: 251.
— — at Her Majesty's Theatre. Fortn. 75: 178.
— Metrical Defects in the Poetry of. Acad. 54: 301.
— Paola and Francesca. (H. Seal) Westm. 156: 393. — (S. Colvin) 19th Cent. 46: 915. — Atlan. 85: 278. — (E. R. Peacock) Canad. M. 15: 146. — (W. Archer) Critic, 36: 156. — (W. P. Trent) Forum, 29: 116. — (W. E. Henley) Pall Mall M. 20: 423. — (C. Porter) Poet-Lore, 12: 126.
— Poetry of. (R. Le Gallienne) Bookman, 13: 24. — Acad. 53: 3, 47. — Sat. R. 85: 21. — Spec. 80: 48. — Ed. R. 191: 51. Same art. Ecl. M. 134: 571. Same art. Liv. Age, 224: 665.
— Real Conversations. (W. Archer) Critic, 38: 505.
Phillips, Theodore Leonard, Artist. Brush & P. 2: 284.
Phillpots, Eden, with portrait. Bk. News, 18: 89. — Acad. 55: 431. — (Joseph B. Gilder) Critic, 38: 22.
— The Human Boy ; a review. Spec. 83: 319. Same art. Ecl. M. 134: 128.
— Sons of the Morning. (C. Hovey) Bookman, 12: 233.
Philo Judæus, and St. John. (W. E. Ball) Contemp. 73: 219.
Philo of Alexandria, Apocryphal Work ascribed to. (L. Cohn) Jew. Q. 10: 277.
Philologia Flats. (E. Hope) Temp. Bar, 120: 386.
Philology, Amenities of. (E. W. Bowen) No. Am. 164: 379.
— Modern, and Secondary Education. (O. L. and H. H. Manchester) Educa. R. 16: 262.
— or, the Science of Expression. (J. W. Powell) Am. Anthrop. 2: 603.
Philomèle. Liv. Age, 214: 41.
Philoméne ; a tale. (J. F. Taylor) Canad. M. 12: 454.
Philosopher's Romance, A ; a story. (J. Berwick) Macmil. 77: 27—78: 1.
Philosophic Faith. (M. G. Husband) Int. J. Ethics, 7: 464.
Philosophical Disciplines, Suggestions toward a Theory of the. (G. H. Mead) Philos. R. 9: 1.
Philosophical Literature of Germany in the Years 1899 and 1900. (E. Adickes) Philos. R. 10: 386.
Philosophical Method, Prof. James on. (D. S. Miller) Philos. R. 8: 166.
Philosophical Parties. (P. Carus) Open Court, 11: 564.
Philosophical Talks in Secondary Schools. (T. F. Willis) Month, 93: 371.
Philosophical Terminology. (F. Tönnies) Mind, 24: 289, 467. 25: 46.
— Notes on the Welby Prize Essay by Dr. Tönnies. (V. Welby) Mind, 26: 188.
Philosophy and the Activity-experience. (W. Caldwell) Int. J. Ethics, 8: 460.
— and Modern Culture. (J. Sully) Fortn. 73: 121.
— and the Study of Philosophers. (D. G. Ritchie) Mind, 24: 1.
— and Theology. (E. H. Griffin) Presb. & Ref. R. 12: 377.

Photographic Snapshot at a Bear. (S. Stokes) Outing, 38: 216.

Photographic Story of a Boy's Trip to Europe. Cosmopol. 22: 541.

Photographic Surveying. Nature, 57: 563.

Photographing by the Light of Venus. (W. R. Brooks) Cent. 40: 529.

— Cedar Birds. (R. W. Shufeldt) Am. Natural. 31: 120.

— Fishes. (R. W. Shufeldt) Cosmopol. 30: 43.

— Living Fish under Water. (R. W. Shufeldt) Outing, 38: 543.

— Through a Fly's Eye. (F. W. Saxby) Knowl. 21: 187.

— a Wounded African Buffalo. (A. C. Humbert) Harper, 96: 655.

Photographs, Annual Exhibitions of. (H. S. Ward) Art J. 50: 348.

— Geological. (W. W. Watts) Nature, 57: 437.

— More Amateur; result of the sixth contest. Overland, n. s. 33: 55.

— Notes on. (H. S. Ward) Art J. 49: 285.

— of the Civil War, The Government Collection of. (A. W. Greely) McClure, 10: 18.

— of Moving Objects. (T. C. Hepworth) Chamb. J. 75: 228.

Photography, Amateur. (E. W. Newcomb) Chaut. 25: 305.

— and Color-printing in Japan. (M. R. Hill-Burton) Studio (Internat.) 5: 245.

— Animal. (R. Lydekker) Nature, 65: 33.

— Animated Pictures. (J. M. Barr) Pop. Sci. Mo. 52: 177.

— Another View of. (R. de La Sizeranne) Liv. Age, 217: 22–109.

— Artistic. (H. S. Ward) Art J. 49: 295. 52: 341.

— — Awheel. (J. Nicol) Outing, 30: 339.

— — in Portraiture. (M. Burnside) Brush & P. 6: 122.

— as a Fine Art. (C. W. Hearn) Nat'l M. (Bost.) 15: 195. — (F. H. Day) Lippinc. 65: 83.

— Astronomical. (H. Jacoby) Internat. Mo. 1: 544. — (F. L. O. Wadsworth) Knowl. 20: 193, 218.

— — as applied to Surface Markings of Celestial Objects. (F. L. O. Wadsworth) Pop. Astron. 5: 200.

— — of Meteors. (E. E. Barnard) Pop. Astron. 5: 282.

— — Reflector and Portrait Lens in. (M. Wolf) Nature, 55: 582.

— — Wide-angle. (E. W. Maunder) Knowl. 22: 86.

— at the Crystal Palace. Nature, 58: 14.

— Best Pictures in our Amateur Competition. Eng. Illust. 21: 601.

— Child. (M. C. Blossom) Cosmopol. 30: 513.

— Color. (E. S. Shepherd) J. Soc. Arts, 48: 758–793.

— — Diffraction Process of. (R. W. Wood) J. Soc. Arts, 48: 285. — (R. W. Wood) Science, n. s. 9: 859. — (R. W. Wood) Nature, 60: 199.

— — McDonough-Joly Process. (H. S. Ward) Knowl. 24: 6.

— — The Sun as Painter in Water Colors. Chamb. J. 78: 364. Same art. Ecl. M. 137: 403. Same art. Liv. Age, 230: 97.

— — Wood's Method. Science, n. s. 9: 422.

— Curiosities of. Sund. M. 29: 54–832.

— Curiosities of the Camera. Sund. M. 30: 15–808.

— Disappearance of Images on Plates. (W. J. S. Lockyer) Nature, 63: 278.

— Film. (T. C. Hepworth) Chamb. J. 75: 437. Same art. Liv. Age, 218: 528.

— for Amateurs. (J. Le Couteur) Artist (N. Y.) 23: 50, 113, 241.

— for Preserving Legal Records. (H. Leffmann) J. Frankl. Inst. 152: 351.

— for Sportsmen. (J. Nicol) Outing, 36: 451.

Photography; Gum-bichromate Process. (H. S. Ward) Art J. 49: 377.

— Holiday Work in. (J. Nicol) Outing, 34: 512.

— — with a "Frena." Artist (N. Y.) 26: 18.

— How to secure Expression in. Illus. (C. F. Jenkins) Cosmopol. 27: 131.

— in Architecture. (Hugo Erichsen) Am. Arch. 58: 73.

— in Astronomy, Development of. (E. E. Barnard) Pop. Astron. 6: 425.

— in the Dark. (M. I. Wilbert) J. Frankl. Inst. 150: 388. — (W. J. Russell) Nature, 60: 208.

— — Russell's Experiments. Sat. R. 84: 258.

— in Illustration. (H. S. Ward) Knowl. 20: 253.

— in Natural Colors. Am. Arch. 69: 62. — (H. S. Ward) Knowl. 20: 177. Same art. Liv. Age, 214: 746. — (W. W. Abney) Nature, 55: 318. — (H. T. Wood) J. Soc. Arts, 45: 158. Same art. Ecl. M. 129: 692. — (S. Thompson) Sat. R. 83: 239. — Liv. Age, 213: 273.

— — Bibliography of. (T. Bolas) J. Soc. Arts, 45: 531.

— — Notable Advance in. World's Work, 1: 200.

— Insect Studies. (C. M. Weed) Outing, 37: 163.

— Is the Camera the Friend or Foe of Art? Studio (Lond.) 1: 96.

— Is it among the Fine Arts? (R. de La Sizeranne) M. of Art, 23: 102, (Fernand Khnopff) 156, (A. L. Baldry) 206, (H. P. Robinson) 253, (G. A. Storey) 369. — (J. Pennell) Contemp. 72: 824. Same art. Liv. Age, 216: 99. Same art. Ecl. M. 130: 329.

— Making of. (C. F. Himes) Pop. Astron. 8: 26. — (C. F. Himes) J. Frankl. Inst. 148: 401.

— Monotypes. (W. A. Coffin) Cent. 31: 517.

— Naissance of Art in. (A. Pringle) Studio (Lond.) 1: 87.

— Nature Camera Studies. (E. H. Baynes) Outing, 38: 8.

— The New. (A. Maskell) Studio (Lond.) 4: 28.

— Newark (Ohio) Camera Club. (Ema Spencer) Brush & P. 3: 93.

— Nude in. Studio (Lond.) 1: 104.

— of Flowers, Artistic, by Henry Troth. (L. A. F. Lamb) Brush & P. 8: 281.

— of Nebulæ. (R. A. Gregory) Nature, 57: 443.

— Our Photographic Corner. Sund. M. 28: 240–815.

— Painter's Views on. (A. Hartley) Studio (Lond.) 4: 59.

— Phosphorescence as a Source of Illumination in. (Jervis-Smith) Nature, 63: 421.

— Pictorial. (A. Stieglitz) Scrib. M. 26: 528.

— — Suppression and Modification in. Studio (Lond.) 3: 13.

— Picture Possibilities of. (Laura M. Adams) Overland, n. s. 36: 241.

— Pinhole. Chamb. J. 76: 263.

— Portrait, Art in. (Rupert Hughes) Cosmopol. 26: 123.

— Portraiture by. (W. B. Dyer) Brush & P. 5: 20.

— Positive, in Eclipse Work. (F. E. Nipher) Pop. Astron. 9: 24.

— Preservation of Photographic Records. (C. Jones) Nature, 63: 378.

— Quick. (J. Nicol) Outing, 29: 523.

— Rebellion in. (A. Genthe) Overland, n. s. 38: 93.

— Recent Progress in. (C. Jewett) Nature, 61: 416.

— Reproduction by Photographic Processes. (T. Bolas) Nature, 58: 149.

— Scientific Value of, for Astronomical Investigations. (G. Clark) Pop. Astron. 9: 294.

— Snow as a Subject for the Camera. (R. Briant) Studio (Lond.) 5: 32.

— Some Uses of the Camera in Zoölogy. (R. W. Shufeldt) Pop. Sci. Mo. 53: 443.

Pidgin-English. (W. T. Dobson) Argosy, 73: 105.

Piece of Crumpled Paper, A. (Mrs. S. Garrett) Good Words, 40: 764.

Piece Work. Taylor Differential-rate System. (S. E. Thompson) Engin. M. 20: 617.

— and the Premium Plan. (Sir B. C. Browne) Engin. M. 20: 913.

Piece-work Pricing. (D. Carnegie) Cassier, 18: 74.

Piedmont Springs. (Carlotta L. Sessions) Overland, n. s. 38: 511.

Piedmontese Sanctuaries, Some. (J. S. Fiske) Nation, 71: 10.

Pierce, Henry L. Critic, 30: 22.

— An American Citizen. (T. T. Munger) Cent. 32: 463.

Pierce, Phebe, of Woburn, Ancestry of. (W. R. Cutter and A. G. Loring) N. E. Reg. 52: 52.

Piero della Francesca vs. Desiderio da Settignano. Three Mysterious Profiles. (M. Cruttwell) Art J. 49: 312.

Pierre Cournet's Last Run. (V. L. Whitechurch) Strand, 18: 741.

Pierrot, Character of. (Sylvanus Urban) Gent. M. n. s. 59: 205.

Piers Ploughman and English Life of the 14th Century. (J. W. Mackail) Cornh. 76: 42.

Pietism, Halle School, Influence of, in Pennsylvania. (J. F. Sachse) Luth. Q. 31: 170.

Pietro; a story. (F. Lynde) Nat'l M. (Bost.) 6: 515.

Piezometry. (C. Barus) Science, 6: 350.

Pig, The New. Spec. 79: 307.

Pig Iron, Relation of Price of, to Commercial Prosperity. (G. H. Hull) No. Am. 169: 101.

Pig-sticking at Tangier. ("Frias") Pall Mall M. 20: 485.

— in India. (Major Dalbac) Eng. Illust. 22: 87.

— in Northern India. ("Griff") Outing, 31: 549.

Pigs drawn by Celebrities. (Gertrude Bacon) Strand, 17: 338.

Pigeon, Carrier, Evolution of the. (G. Renaud) Pop. Sci. Mo. 50: 369.

Pigeon Post in the Service of the Army and Navy. (B. Denninghoff) Chaut. 29: 182. — (E. J. Larner) 19th Cent. 45: 815.

Pigeon Post; a poem. (J. Lincoln) Chaut. 31: 137.

Pigeons, Carrier. (L. W. Lillingston) Good Words, 39: 311.

— — Flight of. (W. J. Lautz) Cosmopol. 24: 645.

— — in Local Lofts. (T. Gontz) Overland, n. s. 37: 1093.

— — in Warfare. (G. J. Larner) Un. Serv. M. 22: 528.

— — Practical Hints on. (C. H. Elgee) Un. Serv. M. 22: 630.

Pigeonneau's Inadvertent Romance. (A. France) Poet-Lore, 11: 28.

Pigou, Francis. Phases of my Life. Spec. 81: 803.

Pike, Albert, High Play of, at Washington. (G. Selwyn) Overland, n. s. 37: 623.

Pike, Robert. (N. N. Withington) New Eng. M. n. s. 17: 26.

Pike's Peak or Bust; a story. (E. Lefèvre) McClure, 17: 153.

Pilaf-Tepe, Tumulus of. (C. D. Edmonds) J. Hel. Stud. 20: 20.

Pilchard Fishing. (S. Gwynn) Blackw. 170: 331. Same art. Liv. Age, 231: 289. — (F. G. Aflalo) Sat. R. 86: 338.

Pilcher, Percy S. Nature, 60: 546.

Pile Driving. Am. Arch. 62: 31.

— Cost of. (E. N. Pagelsen) Am. Arch. 60: 78.

Piles and Pile Driving. (H. J. Howe) Am. Arch. 60: 83 — 61: 36.

Pilgrim and the Puritan, Difference between. (E. S. Cranden) N. Church R. 6: 62.

Pilgrim Fathers, Medical History of. (E. E. Cornwall) New Eng. M. n. s. 15: 662.

Pilgrimage, A Fin-de-siècle. (F. W. Lockwood) Gent. M. n. s. 64: 494.

Pilgrimage of Truth, The. (E. Bögh) Harper, 102: 3.

Pilgrims; a poem. (Sir Lewis Morris) Cosmopol. 22: 445.

— and Emigrants. (Emile Bertaux) Liv. Age, 216: 499.

— Old, and Pilgrimages. (W. C. Sydney) Gent. M. n. s. 58: 479.

— Pilgrim Press in Leyden. (W. E. Griffis) New Eng. M. n. s. 19: 559.

— Story of, Arber's. (E. D. Warfield) Citizen, 3: 259.

Pilgrims to Mecca. (M. H. Foote) Cent. 35: 742.

Pillager Indians, Protest of. (F. E. Leupp) Forum, 26: 471.

Pillar of the Truth. (W. Loehe) Luth. Q. 37: 84.

Pillars of the Old Meeting-house; a sketch. (E. S. Atkinson) Canad. M. 9: 248, 426.

Pilot, The. (L. W. Lillingston) Good Words, 39: 752.

Pilot, The; a story. (Morley Roberts) Pall Mall M. 13: 354.

Pilot of the "Sadie Simmons;" a story. (J. M. Hanson) Cosmopol. 28: 577.

Pilot Charts. Nature, 63: 494.

Pilot Service, A National. (C. E. Naylor) Overland, n. s. 31: 25.

Pilot's Daughter, The; a story. (E. Elliott) Outing, 30: 160.

Pilots and their Life on the Ocean. (E. Gannet) Nat'l M. (Bost.) 12: 491.

Pin and Clock Making. Chamb. J. 76: 495.

Pin Luck. (Clara Vostrovsky) Educa. 18: 431.

Pinckney, Eliza. Quar. 186: 53.

Pindar, From; translation. Chaut. 32: 585.

Pine, Corsican, at Home. (M. L. de Vilmorin) Garden & F. 10: 411.

— Second-growth White, in Pennsylvania. (C. A. Keffer) Garden & F. 10: 92. — (A. K. Mlodziansky) Garden & F. 10: 172, 272.

— White, Œcology of. (E. J. Hill) Garden & F. 10: 331.

Pine Forests of Arizona. (J. W. Tuomey) Garden & F. 10: 152.

Pine Trees of Michigan. (L. Hubbard, jr.) Outing, 37: 676.

Pineapple, The; the King of Tropical Fruits. (R. W. Cater) Chamb. J. 78: 781.

Pineapple-growing in Florida. Chamb. J. 76: 63.

Pinebluff (N. C.) Sanitary School. Educa. 18: 379, 442, 501.

Pinehurst, North Carolina. (H. Redan) New Eng. M. n. s. 25: 256.

Pinero, Arthur W., with portrait. (W. Archer) Pall Mall M. 23: 388. — (W. Kingsley Tarpey) Critic, 37: 117. — With Bibliography of his Plays. (G. M. Hyde) Bk. Buyer, 17: 301.

— and Carr, J. C. Beauty Stone. (M. Beerbohm) Sat. R. 85: 744.

— Dandy Dick. (M. Beerbohm) Sat. R. 89: 200.

— Mrs. Ebbsmith. (M. Beerbohm) Sat. R. 91: 300.

— The Gay Lord Quex. Acad. 56: 436. — (M. Beerbohm) Sat. R. 87: 459. — (J. Rankin Towse) Critic, 38: 38.

— — and the Idea of Comedy. (W. L. Courtney) Fortn. 67: 746.

— Iris. (W. L. Courtney) Fortn. 76: 902.

— Plays of. (G. Kobbé) Forum, 26: 119.

— Princess and the Butterfly. (G. B. Shaw) Sat. R. 83: 348.

— Trelawny of the "Wells." (G. B. Shaw) Sat. R. 85: 170.

Pines, The; a poem. (B. K. Daniels) Canad. M. 9: 276.

Plagiarism. (E. F. Benson) 19th Cent. 46: 974.
— Fortunes of a. (F. Hall) Nation, 71: 170.
— Real and Apparent. (B. Samuel) Bookman, 12: 24, 122.
Plagioclase Feldspars in Rock Sections, Determination of. (G. F. Becker) Am. J. Sci. 155: 349.
Plague, The. (M. Lubbock) 19th Cent. 41: 184. Same art. Liv. Age, 212: 817.
— and Cholera, Common Salt as a Preventive of. (C. G. Gümpel) Asia. R. 31: 344.
— and the European. (W. Hopkins) Nation, 69: 185.
— Approach of. Sat. R. 88: 193. Same art. Liv. Age, 222: 849.
— at Oporto. (A. Calmette) No. Am. 171: 104.
— Bubonic. Quar. 194: 539. — (V. C. Vaughan) Pop. Sci. Mo. 51: 62. — (C. Edson) Internat. Mo. 2: 94.
— — History and Geographic Distribution of. (G. M. Sternberg) Nat. Geog. M. 11: 97.
— — in Honolulu. (R. D. Silliman) R. of Rs. (N. Y.) 21: 566.
— Danger from, in America. (V. C. Vaughan) Pop. Sci. Mo. 55: 577.
— Dangers of, Minimized. Sat. R. 88: 193.
— Fighting the World's Epidemic of. R. of Rs. (N. Y.) 21: 571.
— The Great Pestilence, 1348-49. (Arthur Dimock) Gent. M. n. s. 59: 168.
— in Bombay. (H. M. Birdwood) J. Soc. Arts, 46: 305.
— — 1897. (F. E. Clark) Lippinc. 60: 133.
— — Political Aspects of. (E. W. Hopkins) Forum, 23: 737.
— in Great Britain. Spec. 85: 297.
— in India. (J. Ferguson) Canad. M. 8: 525. — (A. Lustig) Chaut. 26: 613. — (K. M. Hunter) 19th Cent. 43: 1008.
— — Quarantine Camp. Blackw. 166: 188.
— — Under the Vultures' Wings. (J. Ralph) Harper, 100: 125.
— Literature of. (H. R. Plomer) Library, 3: 209.
— Present Danger from. (J. J. Walsh) Indep. 51: 2547.
Plague Bacillus. (G. A. Buckmaster) Sci. Prog. 7: 105.
Plague Ship, The. (S. Bonsal) Scrib. M. 29: 106.
Plague-stricken City [Bangalore]. (H. C. Gordon) Eng. Illust. 22: 17.
Plain Girl, The ; a sketch. (M. MacMurchy) Canad. M. 12: 69.
Plain Girl's Romance, A. (V. Wood) Belgra. 96: 213.
Plain Living and High Thinking ; a story. Temp. Bar, 110: 488.
Plains and Escarpments, English. (R. Lydekker) Knowl. 20: 263.
Plains, A Tragedy of the. (E. Hough) Liv. Age, 215: 146.
Plains, Providence, A ; a story. (G. M. Cooke) Munsey, 18: 403.
Plainville Sensation, A. (H. A. Nash) New Eng. M. n. s. 18: 752.
Plancon, Pol, Opera-singer, with portrait. Music, 15: 316.
Planet [D Q], The New. Acad. 56: 129. Same art. Ecl. M. 132: 597. — Liv. Age, 220: 530. — (Gustave Ravene) Pop. Astron. 6: 558.
— — Notes on. (Asaph Hall) Pop. Astron. 6: 567.
Planetary Work at Lowell Observatory. (A. E. Douglass) Pop. Astron. 7: 74.
Planets and the Weather. (T. Lindsay) Pop. Astron. 7: 181.
— Are there Planets among the Stars ? (G. P. Serviss) Pop. Sci. Mo. 52: 171.
— How they are Weighed. (S. Newcomb) McClure, 14: 290.

Planets, Inhabited ; a New Church Point of View. (T. F. Wright) N. Church R. 4: 117.
— Intra-mercurial, Four. (S. J. Corrigan) Pop. Astron. 4: 414.
— Life on. (J. Janssen) Pop. Sci. Mo. 50: 812. — (D. T. MacDougal) Forum, 27: 71. — (D. T. MacDougal) Pop. Astron. 7: 420.
— Micrometrical Determination of Dimensions of. (E. E. Barnard) Pop. Astron. 5: 285.
— Minor, Some Facts about the. (J. K. Rees) Pop. Astron. 6: 339.
— Scenes on. (G. P. Serviss) Pop. Sci. Mo. 56: 337.
— Spheres of Activity of. (F. R. Moulton) Pop. Astron. 7: 281.
— Study of Details of. (T. J. J. See) Pop. Astron. 4: 550.
— Supposed Early Conjunction of. (W. H. S. Monck) Pop. Astron. 8: 238.
Planisphere, Astrolabe, of English Make. (Ferguson) Archæol. 52: 75.
Planktology, Methods in. (G. W. Field) Am. Natural. 32: 735.
Plankton of Fresh Water Lakes. (C. D. Marsh) Science, 82: 374.
— of Lake Mendota. Nature, 58: 259.
Plankton Method, The. (C. A. Kofoid) Science, 6: 829.
Planning, Common-sense. (R. Sturgis) Archit. R. 5: 44.
Plant Doctors Wanted. (J. B. Carruthers) Contemp. 76: 573.
Plant Geography, Ecological. (A. S. Hitchcock) Am. Natural. 31: 435.
Plant Life, Alternations of Generations in. (E. Fry) Nature, 55: 422.
Plant Morphology. (G. F. Atkinson) Science, n. s. 13: 530.
— and Physiology, Society for, 1st Annual Meeting. (E. F. Smith) Am. Natural. 32: 96.
Plant Pests, Legislation against. (C. S. Sargent) Garden & F. 10: 281.
Plant Physiology, Progress and Problems of. (C. R. Barnes) Science, n. s. 10: 316.
Plant Relations, Coulter's. (E. A. Schultze) School R. 7: 491.
Plant Structures, Coulter's. (H. C. Cowles) School R. 8: 364.
Plantagenets, Self-styled. (A. M. Hyamson) Gent. M. n. s. 67: 503.
Plantain, The. (H. Macmillan) Sund. M. 30: 699.
Plantation Hymns. (W. E. Barton) New Eng. M. n. s. 19: 443.
Plantation Memories. (A. G. Bradley) Blackw. 161: 331. Same art. Ecl. M. 128: 655.
Plantations and Trade, Lords of, Papers of. Citizen, 3: 34.
— Sent to the. (W. H. S. Aubrey) Chamb. J. 78: 812.
Planters, The ; a story. (S. F. Bullock) McClure, 14: 19.
Plantin, Christopher. (R. S. Faber) Library, 2: 12, 38, 87, 133.
Planting for the Future. (H. A. Caparn) Garden & F. 10: 312.
Plants and Animals, How they spend the Winter. (W. S. Blatchley) Pop. Sci. Mo. 50: 496.
— — on the Spread of Introduced. Chamb. J. 78: 389.
— and their Food. (H. H. W. Pearson) Knowl. 23: 2-244.
— as Water-carriers. (B. D. Halsted) Pop. Sci. Mo. 59: 492.
— Bacterial Diseases of. (E. F. Smith) Am. Natural. 31: 34, 123.
— Brain-power of. (A. Smith) Gent. M. n. s. 61: 185. Same art. Ecl. M. 131: 449. Same art. Liv. Age, 219: 55.

Plants, Common. (C. S. Sargent) Garden & F. 10: 211.

— Common Carnivorous. Chamb. J. 74: 293.

— Evolution of, Campbell's Lectures on. (C. E. Bessey) Science, n. s. 9: 618.

— Flowering and Flowerless, Link between. (J. B. F.) Nature, 55: 396.

— — with Illustrations from British Wildflowers. (R. L. Praeger) Knowl. 24: 25-217.

— Freezing of. (J. B. Dandeno) Science, n. s. 13: 916.

— Garden, New; a Study in Evolution. Nature, 64: 446.

— Geography of, in North America. Science, n. s. 12: 708-870.

— Green Color of. (D. T. MacDougal) Harper, 94: 803.

— Metamorphosis in. (S. H. Vines) Sci. Prog. 7: 79.

— Movements of. (F. Darwin) Nature, 65: 40.

— Names of, Popular American. (Fanny D. Bergen) J. Am. Folk-Lore, 11: 221.

— Native, The Improving of. (C. S. Sargent) Garden & F. 10: 359.

— Sensory Mechanism of. (D. T. MacDougal) Pop. Sci. Mo. 60: 173.

— Study of. (T. Cooke-Trench) Longm. 36: 47. Same art. Ecl. M. 135: 324. Same art. Liv. Age, 226: 189.

— Unusual Forms in. (B. D. Halsted) Pop. Sci. Mo. 55: 371.

— Vernal Phenomena in the Arid Region. (T. D. A. Cockerell) Am. Natural. 33: 39.

Plassey, Battle of. Eng. Illust. 19: 79.

Plasterwork, Decorative. (E. P. Warren) Archit. R. 8: 13.

Plastic Art in Education. (M. L. H. Unwin) Westm. 147: 446.

Plastic Word, The. (A. C. Stephens) Poet-Lore, 12: 384.

Plastilene. (C. R. Eastman) Science, n. s. 9: 211.

Plate, Gold and Silver, at Windsor Castle. Pall Mall M. 15: 439.

Plateau Implements, Authenticity of. I. (R. A. Bullen) II. (W. J. S. Abbott) Nat. Sci. 12: 106.

Plateau Man, Authenticity of. (A. S. Kennard) Nat. Sci. 12: 27.

Plato and his Republic. (P. Shorey) Chaut. 25: 592.

— as an Educationist. Acad. 59: 238.

— Growth of a Thinker's Mind. (L. Campbell) Fortn. 69: 36.

— Logic of, Lutoslawski on. Ath. '98, 1: 145.

— Parmenides. [3d article.] (A. E. Taylor) Mind, 22: 9.

— Republic, Stoical Vein in. (A. Fairbanks) Philos. R. 10: 12.

Platonic Friendship. (N. Hapgood) Atlan. 84: 835.

Platonic Idea elucidated by Composite Photograph. (J. Cooper) Meth. R. 60: 560.

Platonists, Neo-, Whittaker on. (W. L. Davidson) Crit. R. 11: 316.

— of Cambridge. (F. J. Powicke) Bib. Sac. 54: 646.

Platt, Thomas Collier. (W. A. White) McClure, 18: 145. — (G. Myers) National, 38: 219.

— City Saver. (R. Ogden) Nation, 71: 400.

Plattsburg, Battle of. (A. Macomb) J. Mil. Serv. Inst. 12: 76.

Plautus, Notes and Queries on. (E. W. Fay) Am. J. Philol. 18: 168.

— Subjunctive in. (E. R. Morris) Am. J. Philol. 18: 383.

— Truculentus. (W. M. Lindsay) Am. J. Philol. 17: 438.

— Two Recensions of, A and P^A. (W. M. Lindsay) Am. J. Philol. 21: 23.

Play. Amusements of Worcester School Children. (T. R. Crosswell) Pedagog. Sem. 6: 314.

Play as a Factor in Social and Educational Reforms. (E. A. Kirkpatrick) R. of Rs. (N. Y.) 20: 192.

— Educational Value of. (G. E. Johnson) Pedagog. Sem. 6: 513.

— Professor Groos and Theories of. (Hiram M. Stanley) Psychol. R. 6: 86.

— in Institutions for Children, Value and Direction of. (Frances A. Kellor and F. H. Nibecker) Charities, 6: 297-302.

— in Relation to Character. (J. E. Bradley) Educa. 19: 406.

— Instruction by, and Genius. (P. Carus) Open Court, 13: 567.

— of Man, Groos on. (F. Starr) Dial (Ch.) 31: 237.

Play, The, 's the Thing. (A. W. Vorse) Scrib. M. 26: 167.

Play-bill, The; its Growth and Evolution. (P. Fitzgerald) Gent. M. n. s. 64: 529.

Play Devil, The. (E. A. Walcott) Cent. 39: 588.

Play Life of South Carolina Children. (Z. McGhee) Pedagog. Sem. 7: 459.

Play-writing to Order. (M. Beerbohm) Sat. R. 86: 405.

Players and Old Plays, Notes on. (F. Wedmore) 19th Cent. 48: 249.

— French, Intrusion of. Theatre, 39: 75.

— The Onslaught on. Theatre, 38: 63.

Playfair, Lyon. Ecl. M. 135: 455. Same art. Liv. Age, 226: 363. — (M. W. Hazeltine) No. Am. 171: 65. — Acad. 57: 567. — Nature, 58: 128.

— Reid's Memoirs of. (C. S. Peirce) Nation, 70: 114.

Playfair, Sir R. Lambert. Geog. J. 13: 439.

Playgrounds, Baths, and Gymnasia. (J. Quincy) Am. J. Soc. Sci. 36: 139.

Playgrounds, City. (C. S. Sargent) Garden & F. 10: 479.

— Education in. (J. Lee) Educa. R. 22: 449.

— in New York. (S. V. Tsanoff) Munic. Aff. 2: 293.

— Municipal, in Chicago. (C. Zueblin) Am. J. Sociol. 4: 145.

— of Rural and Suburban Schools. (I. G. Oakley) Pop. Sci. Mo. 54: 176.

— Progress in Seward Park. (C. B. Stover) Charities, 6: 386-393.

— Small, The Movement for. (Sadie American) Am. J. Sociol. 4: 159.

— — Stoyan Tsanoff and. (A. Truslow) Outl. 58: 772.

Playing Cards and Card-playing, History of. (Louisa Parr) Pall Mall M. 13: 207.

— Early, their Design and Decoration. (R. Steele) J. Soc. Arts, 49: 317.

Playing of the Game; a story. (M. MacMurchy) Canad. M. 14: 157.

Plays and Novels. (E. E. Hale, jr.) Atlan. 79: 858.

— and Players, Some Recent. (G. Kobbé) Forum, 29: 377.

— English, Woodcuts in, printed before 1660. (A. W. Pollard) Library, n. s. 1: 71.

— Founded on Old Novels. (M. Mannering) Nat'l M. (Bost.) 11: 608.

— Immoral. (S. P. Kerr) Westm. 155: 444.

— Modern. (E. E. Hale, jr.) Dial (Ch.) 26: 334.

Playthings of Kings. (K. DeForest) Harper, 100: 760.

Playwrights, Problems and. Fortn. 74: 858.

Plea to Peace; a poem. (E. W. Wilcox) Cosmopol. 26: 355.

Pleading, Legal. (C. S. Dickson) Jurid. R. 9: 14.

Pleasant Blunder, A. (A. D. Romney) Temp. Bar, 118: 540.

Pleasure as Ethical Standard. (E. C. Moore) Am. J. Sociol. 6: 255.

— Disenchantment of. Sat. R. 89: 453.

— Place of, in a System of Ethics. (F. J. E. Woodbridge) Int. J. Ethics. 7. 475.

Pleasure, The Pursuit of ; a poem. (E. H. Keen) Outl. 65: 725.

Pleasure-grounds, Public, Need of More. (C. S. Sargent) Garden & F. 10: 31.

— Seaside, for Cities. (S. Baxter) Scrib. M. 23: 676.

Pleasure-seeking. (W. Hutchinson) Monist, 8: 342.

Pleasures, Can there be a Sum of ? (H. Rashdall) Mind, 24: 357.

Pleasures of Poverty. (P. Blouet) No. Am. 169: 285.

Pleiades, Exterior Nebulosities of the. (H. C. Wilson) Pop. Astron. 7: 57.

— Onondaga Tale of. (W. M. Beauchamp) J. Am. Folk-Lore, 13: 281.

Plesse, Princess Henry of. Critic, 37: 99.

Plevna, Siege of. (S. Crane) Lippinc. 65: 759. — (T. H. Bliss) J. Mil. Serv. Inst. 2: 11.

Plots and Counterplots. (S. J. Weyman) Liv. Age, 216: 768.

— for Literary Use. (B. Capes) Cornh. 82: 101.

Ploughing ; a study of farm life. (M. M. Williams) McClure, 16: 577.

Ploughing of th' Owd Lad's Bit ; a tale. (C. L. Antrobus) Argosy, 72: 102. Same art. Liv. Age, 227: 312.

Plouharnac ; a tale. (W. B. Wallace) Belgra. 95: 148.

Plover and Plover-shooting. (E. W. Sandys) Outing, 34: 181.

— Killdeer, and her Young. (H. W. Gleason) Outing, 36: 134.

Plumbing. (W. P. Gerhard) Am. Arch. 73: 35, 44.

— Back-airing. (W. P. Gerhard) Am. Arch. 73: 14.

Plummer, Alfred. Commentary on St. Luke. Church Q. 45: 409.

Plums and Plum-culture. Chamb. J. 76: 389.

Plumularidæ, Sarcostyles of the. (C. C. Nutting) Am. Natural. 32: 220.

Plural States of Being. (A. Binet) Pop. Sci. Mo. 50: 539.

Pluralism and the Credentials of Monism. (C. M. Bakewell) Philos. R. 7: 355.

Plutarch and his Age. (R. M. Wenley) New World, 9: 263.

Plutocracy, Menace of. Sat. R. 87: 486.

Plymouth, England. (E. D. Mead) New Eng. M. n. s. 25: 395. — (E. Radford) Art J. 49: 147.

— An Enemy's Fleet off. (S. Gwynn) Macmil. 80: 114.

— Marine Biological Laboratory. (E. G. Gardiner) Science, n. s. 9: 488.

Plymouth, Mass., Antislavery Times in. (A. M. Diaz) New Eng. M. n. s. 20: 216.

Pneumatic Despatch. (C. A. Carus-Wilson) J. Soc. Arts, 48: 309.

Pneumatic Shop Appliances. (W. P. Pressinger) Cassier, 15: 259.

Pneumatic Tubes, Recent Progress in Development of. (B. C. Batcheller) J. Frankl. Inst. 146: 81.

Pneumatics. (J. H. Kinealy) Cassier, 20: 317.

Pneumatology ; Science of Spirit. (L. S. Crandall) Arena, 17: 439.

Po, River, Stanzas to. (R. Edgcumbe) Ath. '01, 2: 252.

Poacher, Amateur. (H. G. Hutchinson) Longm. 38: 231. Same art. Liv. Age, 230: 497.

Poachers and their Ways. Chamb. J. 76: 529.

Pobedonostzeff, Constantine ; a Statesman of Russia. (A. D. White) Cent. 34: 111.

Pocock, Nicholas. Ath. '97, 1: 349.

Poe, Edgar Allan. (M. A. D. Howe) Bookman; 5: 205. — Acad. 57: 137. 61: 263. — (H. Austin) Dial (Ch.) 27: 307. — (C. L. Moore) Dial (Ch.) 26: 236. — (H. W. Mabie) Outl. 62: 51.

— after Fifty Years. (W. F. Gill) Arena, 22: 526.

Poe, Edgar Allan, American Rejection of. (C. H. Moore) Dial (Ch.) 26: 40. — (A. C. Barrows ; C. Sheldon) Dial (Ch.) 26: 110.

— and the Raven. (Della Courson) Educa. 20: 566.

— and Recent Poetics. (G. L. Swiggett) Sewanee, 6: 150.

— Did he plagiarize from Chivers ? (J. Benton) Forum, 23: 363.

— Fifty Years after. (E. W. Bowen) Forum, 31: 501.

— First Books of. (L. S. Livingston) Bookman, 8: 232.

— Grave of. (J. B. Dugdale) Poet-Lore, 11: 583. — (L. R. Meekyns) Critic, 33: 39.

— Memorials of. (J. G. Wilson) Indep. 53: 940.

— New Glimpses of. (J. A. Harrison) Indep. 52: 2158, 2259.

— Obsession of. (J. P. Fruit) Poet-Lore, 12: 42.

— Personality of. (A. Morgan) Munsey, 17: 522.

— Place of, in American Literature. (H. W. Mabie) Atlan. 84: 733.

— Plea for. (G. L. Swiggett) Poet-Lore, 13: 379.

— The Raven, Poe's Opinion of. (J. Benton) Forum, 22: 731.

— Student Days at the University of Virginia. (C. W. Kent) Bookman, 13: 430.

— Ulalume. (F. L. Pattee) Chaut. 31: 182.

— Zolnay's Bust of. Bk. Buyer, 19: 247.

Poem, The. (H. B. Merwin) Atlan. 84: 428.

Poems for Music. (F. Attenborough) Music, 18: 16

— Unwritten and Unended. (E. G. Gardner) Month, 95: 588.

Poet, The, as a Prophet. (W. N. Guthrie) Sewanee, 6: 402.

— Minor, Tragedy of the. Liv. Age, 225: 261.

— What is a ? (Lane Cooper) Ref. Ch. R. 47: 213.

Poet and Diplomatist ; a story. (K. L. Johnston) Canad. M. 10: 128.

Poet-Lore, the Periodical. Acad. 59: 95.

Poeta Nascitur ; a story. (D. May) Idler, 16: 763.

Poetic, The, in Paint. Studio (Lond.) 3: 101.

Poetic Justice ; a story. (H. T. George) Nat'l M. (Bost.) 11: 97.

Poetry, American, of 1900. (H. A. Clarke) Poet-Lore, 13: 123. See American Poetry.

— and Landscape. Spec. 78: 331.

— and Philosophy, Old Quarrel between. (R. M. Wenley) Poet-Lore, 10: 365.

— and Pipes. (G. Greenwood) Temp. Bar, 113: 128. 118: 124.

— and Prose. Spec. 86: 233.

— Beginnings of, F. B. Gummere on. Outl. 69: 1082.

— Conditions of Great. Quar. 192: 156.

— Debt of, to Music. (J. B. Chapman) Music, 14: 589.

— A Decade of, 1869–79. (S. H. Ward) Indep. 51: 1366.

— English Patriotic. Quar. 192: 520.

— Enjoyment of. (S. M. Crothers) Atlan. 83: 268.

— Essentials of. Acad. 58: 199.

— Ethics of Verse-writing. (C. Urmy) Writer, 14: 97.

— Expression in. (H. C. Beeching) National, 36: 110.

— for Children. (F. MacCunn) Good Words, 42: 490. Same art. Liv. Age, 230: 446.

— Freemasonry of. Spec. 86: 307.

— Have we still Need of ? (C. Thomas) Forum, 25: 503.

— In Regard to. (C. L. Moore) Dial (Ch.) 24: 217.

— Life in, and Law in Taste, Courthope's. Ed. R. 194: 320.

— — Poetical Expression. (W. J. Courthope) 19th Cent. 41: 270. 42: 113.

— Lyric, Claims of. (F. L. Thompson) Dial (Ch.) 24: 286.

— John Stuart Mill on. Acad. 51: 298.

Police Power, Abuse of the. (H. C. Kudlich) Forum, 23: 487.

Policeman, Itinerant, Notes of. (J. Flynt) Indep. 51: 2730-3212.

Policeman Flynn's Adventures. (E. Flower) Cent. 41: 306.

Policemen of the World. (C. S. Pelham-Clinton) Strand, 13: 214.

Policy Holders, Constitutional Rights of. Green Bag, 11: 571.

Policy or Grab; Jingo or pro-Boer. (F. W. Tugman) Westm. 155: 624.

Polis, Game of, and Plato's Rep. 422 E. (W. Ridgeway) J. Hel. Stud. 16: 288.

Polish. (Lord Rayleigh) Nature, 64: 385.

Polish Danger in Prussia. (H. W. Wolff) Westm. 155: 375.

Polish Drama, Early. (H. Modjeska) Critic, 35: 1118.

Polish Literature, 1896-97. (A. Belcikowski) Ath. '97, 2: 25.

— 1897-98. (A. Belcikowski) Ath. '98, 2: 24.

— 1898-99. (A. Belcikowski) Ath. '99, 2: 24.

— 1899-1900. (A. Belcikowski) Ath. '00, 2: 24.

— 1900-01. (A. Belcikowski) Ath. '01, 2: 25.

Polish Musicians. (M. Aronson) Music, 13: 754.

Politarchs, The. (E. DeW. Burton) Am. J. Theol. 2: 598.

Political Campaigns in Western Country Districts. (G. M. Burnham) Nat'l M. (Bost.) 9: 344.

— Time Element in. (L. G. McConachie) Am. J. Sociol. 5: 51.

Political Clubs in Prussian Cities. (R. C. Brooks) Munic. Aff. 4: 375.

Political Conspiracy, A. (E. W. Sargent) New Eng. M. n. s. 25: 306.

Political Crime, L. Proal on. Bk. Buyer, 17: 227.

Political Deal, A; a story. (E. F. Andrews) Arena, 18: 840.

Political Economy, George's. (O. T. Morton) Dial (Ch.) 24: 226.

— Handbook of, 1723, by an Unknown Writer. (L. Katscher) J. Pol. Econ. 9: 423.

-- Manchester School and To-day. (A. Carnegie) 19th Cent. 43: 277. Same art. Ecl. M. 130: 476.

— New. (F. Parsons) Bib. Sac. 56: 120.

— Nicholson on. (M. B. Hammond) Dial (Ch.) 24: 377.

— Origins of. Scot. R. 33: 353.

— Palgrave's Dictionary of. (W. J. Ashley) Nation, 71: 53.

— Problems in, Pressing. (A. H. McKnight) Gunton's M. 14: 104.

— Some Unpublished Notes on. (J. Rae) Q. J. Econ. 16: 123.

— Value of, to Christian Minister. (J. R. Commons) Meth. R. 58: 696.
  See Economics.

Political Education. (A. T. Hadley) Atlan. 86: 145.

— President Hadley on. Gunton's M. 19: 365.

Political Events, Record of. November 12, 1896, to May 8, 1897. (W. A. Dunning) Pol. Sci. Q. 12: 352.

— Nov., 1897, to May, 1898. (W. A. Dunning; M. Smith) Pol. Sci. Q. 13: 364, 745.

— Nov. 11, 1898, to May 10, 1899. (M. Smith) Pol. Sci. Q. 14: 357.

— Nov., 1899, to May, 1900. (W. R. Shepherd) Pol. Sci. Q. 15: 356, 646.

— Nov. 10, 1900, to May 10, 1901. (W. R. Shepherd) Pol. Sci. Q. 16: 370, 741.

Political Evolution. Gunton's M. 15: 388.

Political Impracticables. (T. Roosevelt) Liv. Age, 227: 589.

Political Morality, Our Standards of. (A. T. Hadley) Indep. 52: 97.

Political Movement of Our Time, Causes of. (F. Parsons) Arena, 26: 466.

Political Oratory. Liv. Age, 212: 350.

Political Parties, State Control of. (F. D. Pavey) Forum, 25: 99.

Political Pessimist, The. (T. W. Roper) Westm. 147: 686.

Political Philosophy, Value of. (W. W. Willoughby) Pol. Sci. Q. 15: 75.

Political Phrases, Some Famous. (J. Sykes) Gent. M. n. s. 60: 85. Same art. Liv. Age, 216: 745.

Political Principles. (F. Thomasson) Westm. 155: 366.

Political Prophecy. Spec. 83: 652.

Political Reminiscences, Some. (G. F. Hoar) Scrib. M. 25: 285-555.

Political Science and History. (J. W. Burgess) Am. Hist. R. 2: 401.

— Problems of. (L. S. Rowe) Ann. Am. Acad. Pol. Sci. 10: 165.

Political Sense, Growing. Gunton's M. 15: 241.

Political Society and Utilitarianism. (J. M. A. Brown) Westm. 156: 273.

Political Tenacity. (E. L. Godkin) Nation, 71: 284.

Political Tendencies, Present. (W. L. Cook) Ann. Am. Acad. Pol. Sci. 18: 189.

Political Terms, Lewis on the Use and Abuse of Some. Spec. 80: 862.

Political Theory and Practice, Recent. Quar. 192: 359.

Political Union, Forms of. (W. H. Moore) Law Q. 16: 369.

Political Venture, A; a story. (E. D. Troup) Midland, 10: 37.

Politician, The, as Literary Material. (A. B. Maurice) Bookman, 11: 120.

— Current Coin of. (M. MacDonagh) Macmil. 82: 113. Same art. Liv. Age, 226: 98.

— Decline of the. (J. Annand) New R. 17: 699. Same art. Ecl. M. 130: 206.

— Peculiarities of Leading. (E. J. Mozle) Chamb. J. 78: 806.

Politics and Administration. (H. J. Ford) Ann. Am. Acad. Pol. Sci. 16: 177.

— — Goodnow on. (W. J. Braithwaite) Econ. R. 10: 541.

— and Education. Gunton's M. 17: 98.

— as a Form of Civil War. (F. Smith) Pop. Sci. Mo. 54: 588.

— John Jay Chapman on Causes and Consequences in. (G. E. Waring, jr.) Bk. Buyer, 17: 289.

— Commercialism in. (B. S. Coler) Indep. 53: 2561.

— Eighth and Ninth Commandments in. (T. Roosevelt) Outl. 65: 115.

— Ethics of. The Law of the Beasts. (F. Greenwood) 19th Cent. 42: 532.

— — The Modern Machiavelli. (F. Harrison) 19th Cent. 42: 462.

— First Principles of, Lilly on. Ath. '99, 2: 611.

— in the Last Half Century. (P. S. Reinsch) Conserv. R. 4: 340.

— in State Institutions. (H. White) Nation, 73: 411.

— in the United States. McClure, 15: 483.

— Moral Ideas in, Use of. (J. S. Mackenzie) Internat. J. Ethics, 12: 1.

— Prosperity and. (H. White) Nation, 69: 274.

— Right and Wrong in. (L. Stephen) Monthly R. 2, no. 1: 33.

— Science in. Monthly R. 1, no. 3: 10.

— Secrecy in. Spec. 79: 890.

— Slow Growth of Moral Influence in. (J. Hereford) 19th Cent. 48: 226. Same art. Liv. Age, 226: 665.

— Studies in Political Areas. (F. Ratzel) Am. J. Sociol. 4: 366.

Politics, Tricks and Tribulations of. (A. Hendricks) Lippinc. 60: 505.
— Value of a Significant Name in. Sat. R. 91: 229.
— A Wholesome Stimulus to Higher. Atlan. 83: 289.
— Young Man in. (J. B. Foraker) Munsey, 18: 398.
Politics in Magnolia; a story. (E. E. Peake) Nat'l M. (Bost.) 13: 455.
Polity of Nature. (R. Herrick) Lippinc. 68: 458.
Polk, Leonidas, Polk's Life of. (W. P. Trent) Sewanee, 2: 377.
Polks, The. (C. Burrows) Munsey, 16: 397.
Pollen, Potency and Prepotency of. (H. M. Ward) Nature, 61: 470.
Pollen-bearing vs. Plant Vigor. (M. G. Kains) Garden & F. 10: 380.
Pollock, Charles Edward, Baron. (M. Moscow) Good Words, 39: 342.
Pollock, Frank Lillie. Writer, 14: 42.
Polly; a story. Temp. Bar, 123: 531.
Polly's Past; a story. (G. E. Moysey) Gent. M. n. s. 64: 313.
Polly Vernon's Birthday. (F. T. Dickson) Belgra. 98: 69.
Polo, Marco, Adventures of. (E. S. Holden) Outing, 37: 55.
Polo and Politics. Blackw. 165: 1030. Same art. Liv. Age, 222: 174.
— English, of To-day. (T. F. Dale) Outing, 38: 501.
— Glorious Sport of. (R. Newton, jr.) Munsey, 24: 44.
— in Play. (A. H. Godfrey) Outing, 30: 478.
— of the Ancients. (J. Tyler) Outing, 37: 312.
— Water-. (A. H. Broadwell) Strand, 18: 315.
Polo Pony, Educating the. (O. Wister) Outing, 36: 296.
Polotsk, Battles of, Swiss Contingent in. (W. Westall) Cornh. 82: 529.
Polybius. (W. B. Wallace) Un. Serv. M. 19: 485.
Polycarp, Prayer of, Liturgical Echoes in. (J. A. Robinson) Expos. 5: 63.
Polycarp; a poem. (R. C. Seaton) Month, 90: 147.
Polydactylism, A Case of. (H. L. Osborn) Am. Natural. 35: 681.
Polygamy. Shall a Mormon sit in U. S. Congress? (T. F. Wright) N. Church R. 6: 279.
Polynesia, a Drowned Continent. (R. Lydekker) Knowl. 21: 3.
Polynesian Languages, Dialect Changes in. (S. Ella) Anthrop. J. 29: 154.
Polyphase Electric Working. (A. C. Eborall) J. Soc. Arts, 49: 749–833.
Polyphemus; a poem. (Alfred Austin) No. Am. 173: 1.
Polytechnic, Northern, Halloway, London. (A. T. Simmons) Nature, 59: 449.
Polytechnics. (Q. Hogg) J. Soc. Arts, 45: 857.
— Work of. (W. Garnett) J. Soc. Arts, 45: 863.
Polypterus, Life Habits of. (N. R. Harrington) Am. Natural. 33: 721.
Pomegranates and Oleanders in California. (C. H. Shinn) Garden & F. 10: 263.
Pomeroy, F. W., Artist, with portrait. (A. L. Baldry) Studio (Internat.) 6: 77.
Pomerium, The, and Roma Quadrata. (S. H. Platner) Am. J. Philol. 22: 420.
Pomona and Jonas tell a Story. (F. R. Stockton) Cent. 39: 120.
Pomp, Ecclesiastical. Spec. 78: 83.
Pompeian Gentleman's Home-life. (E. Neville-Rolfe) Scrib. M. 23: 277.
Pompeian House, Interior of a. (H. G. Huntington) Cosmopol. 24: 521.
Pompeii, Excavations at. Am. Arch. 64: 54.

Pompeii, Five-storied Cliff Houses of. (H. P. F. Marriott) Antiq. n. s. 33: 20.
— Gusman's. (J. C. Egbert, jr.) Bookman, 13: 243.
— House of Aulus Vettius recently discovered at. (T. Ely) Archæol. 55: 301.
— Mau's. (J. C. Egbert, jr.) Bookman, 12: 48.
— Odds and Ends in. (L. Wolffsohn) Gent. M. n. s. 67: 298.
— Reborn and Regenerate. (J. J. O'Shea) Cath. World, 64: 484.
— Study of. (H. P. F. Marriott) Antiq. n. s. 36: 206.
Pompeii; a poem. (M. A. M. Marks) Argosy, 65: 639.
Pompeii; a poem. (Edgar Fawcett) Cosmopol. 24: 182.
Pompilia, Francesca, The Murder of. (W. H. Griffin) Monthly R. 1, no. 2: 114.
"Pom-pom," The. (E. L. Zalinski) Cassier, 19: 133.
Pond, James B., a Pioneer Boyhood. Cent. 36: 929.
— Eccentricities of Genius. (I. A. Pyle) Dial (Ch.) 30: 40.
Ponds, The Beauty of. Spec. 83: 407.
Ponsonby, Sara. (H. M. North) Cent. 31: 424.
Pontiac, Siege of, Henry Gladwin and. (C. Moore) Harper, 95: 77.
Pontifical Manuscript of a Bishop of Metz of the 14th Century. (E. S. Dewick) Archæol. 54: 411.
Pontine Marshes. Am. Arch. 72: 53.
Pontus, Greece, Archæology in, 1899-1900. (R. C. Bosernquet) J. Hel. Stud. 20: 167.
— Milestones, Pontic. (J. A. R. Munro) J. Hel. Stud. 20: 159.
— Pontica. (J. G. C. Anderson) J. Hel. Stud. 20: 151.
— Roads in, Royal and Roman. (C. Waldstein) J. Hel. Stud. 21: 52.
Pony, How to choose a Child's. (Francis Trevelyan) Cosmopol. 31: 129.
Pony Express. (W. F. Bailey) Cent. 34: 882.
Ponies. Outing, 32: 125.
— Connemara. Chamb. J. 78: 609.
Pool, Maria Louise. Critic, 32: 364.
Poole, W. F., and the New England Clergy. (Z. S. Holbrook) Bib. Sac. 57: 282.
— Memorial to. Pub. Lib. 1: 192.
Poole's Index, Origin of. (Z. S. Holbrook) Nation, 67: 12, (J. Edmands) 71.
Pooling Contracts and Public Policy. (C. W. Willard) Am. Law R. 31: 236.
Poor, Aged. (J. Hutton) National, 33: 99.
— — Cottage Homes for. (J. Hutton) 19th Cent. 43: 633.
— Caring for, by Contract. Char. R. 8: 552.
— The Cry of the. (J. C. Ridpath) Arena, 18: 407.
— Dwellings of, and their Morality. (G. McDermot) Cath. World, 64: 573.
— Imperial Influence of. (W. Williams) Lond. Q. 94: 83.
— Improved Housing of. (G. McDermot) Cath. World, 64: 719.
— in Summer. (R. A. Stevenson) Scrib. M. 30: 259.
— The Insolvent. (E. A. Parry) Fortn. 69: 797.
— Lawyers' Work among the. (R. Loew) Am. J. Soc. Sci. 39: 17.
— Relief and Care of, in their Homes. (E. T. Devine) Char. R. 10: 118–334.
— Relief of. (Mrs. A. K. Terrel) Midland, 7: 330.
Poor Buckra; a Singular Literary Survival. (C. E. Means) Outl. 63: 119.
Poor Chola. (J. P. Dabney) Lippinc. 60: 723.
Poor "Fairly Rich" People. (H. E. Foster) Arena, 18: 820.
Poor Gentleman, A; a story. (G. Gissing) Pall Mall M. 19: 177.
Poor Janey; a story. (M. Collier) Belgra. 94: 235.

Portaleone, Leone de Sommi. (D. Kaufmann) Jew. Q. 10: 445.

Portate Ultimatum, The. (A. Colton) Scrib. M. 26: 713.

Porter, Edgar G., Passing into History. (H. C. Graves) N. E. Reg. 54: 202.

Porter, Rev. Edward Griffin, Memoir of. (M. S. Dudley) N. E. Reg. 55: 11.

Porter, Endymion. (G. Serrell) Temp. Bar, 114: 538.

Porter, Gen. Horace. (R. H. Titherington) Munsey, 17: 120. — Critic, 30: 215.

— Reply to Articles of. (H. H. Humphries) J. Mil. Serv. Inst. 23: 1.

Porter, Jane, Diary of. (I. M. White) Scot. R. 29: 321.

Porter, Sarah ; her unique educational work. (W. M. Sloane) Cent. 38: 345.

Portion of Labor ; a novel. (M. E. Wilkins) Harper, 102: 510–881. 103: 69–957.

Portland, Duke of, most Mysterious of Millionaires. Eng. Illust. 20: 291.

Portland, England. (M. Byron) Blackw. 170: 243.

Portland, The Isle of. Liv. Age, 227: 395.

Porto Rico. (F. W. Mansfield) J. Mil. Serv. Inst. 27: 30. — (W. A. Glassford) J. Mil. Serv. Inst. 28: 15. — (W. V. Pettit) Atlan. 83: 634. — (R. J. Hill) Nat. Geog. M. 10: 93. — (F. A. Ober) Cent. 34: 546.

— Alone in ; a War Correspondent's Adventure. (E. Emerson, jr.) Cent. 34: 666.

— and the Capture of San Juan. (W. Winthrop) Outl. 59: 675.

— and the Constitution. (G. H. Smith) Arena, 23: 626.

— — Are you not too Dogmatic ? (F. L. Norton) Outl. 64: 645.

— and Cuba, Spanish Population of, (C. M. Pepper) Ann. Am. Acad. Pol. Sci. 18: 163.

— and Hawaii as Colonies. (G. L. Bolen) Gunton's M. 18: 26.

— and its Future. (R. Stone) Munsey, 23: 620.

— and the Porto-Ricans. (M. W. Harrington) Cath. World, 70: 161.

— as seen Last Month, June, '98. (E. Emerson, jr.) R. of Rs. (N. Y.) 18: 42.

— Be Honest with. (R: Stone) Outl. 64: 470.

— Bill for Governing. Outl. 64: 569, 899.

— Byways in. (A. Rhodes) Outl. 61: 502.

— Campaign in. (R. H. Davis) Scrib. M. 24: 515.

— Census of. (W. C. Mitchell) J. Pol. Econ. 9: 282.

— Characteristics of the People. (G. G. Groff) Indep. 53: 1552.

— Civil Government in, Results of. (W. H. Hunt) World's Work, 2: 1170.

— The Closed Door in. (R. Ogden) Nation, 67: 383.

— Condition of. (W. H. Ward) R. of Rs. (N. Y.) 19: 313.

— Currency of. (J. D. Whelpley) Forum, 27: 564.

— Cycling in. (L. H. Ives) Outing, 36: 45.

— Decision of the Supreme Court. Outl. 68: 337.

— Education in. (V. S. Clark) Forum, 30: 229.

— Election in, 1900. Outl. 66: 906.

— Fauna and Flora of. (M. H. Harrington) Science, n. s. 10: 286.

— Finances of. (J. H. Hollander) Pol. Sci. Q. 16: 553. — (J. H. Hollander) Indep. 53: 2402.

— Financial Problems of. (T. S. Adams) Ann. Am. Acad. Pol. Sci. 17: 444.

— Financial Wrong in. (C. Wiener) No. Am. 167: 754.

— Fine Water-power of. (H. M. Wilson) Engin. M. 17: 602.

— from a Woman's Point of View. (Mrs. G. V. Henry) R. of Rs. (N. Y.) 20: 177.

— Ex-President Harrison on. (H. White) Nation, 71: 302.

Porto Rico, Home Life in. (H. L. Watson) Nat'l M. (Bost.) 11: 585.

— How shall it be Governed ? (H. K. Carroll) Forum, 28: 258.

— In Streets of. (A. Halliday-Antona) Indep. 52: 1443.

— In, with General Miles. (W. P. Sutton) Cosmopol. 26: 13.

— Independence Day in. (T. S. Adams) Nation, 73: 47.

— Industrial Development of. (A. W. Buel) Engin. M. 19: 683.

— Inhumanity in. (R. Ogden) Nation, 70: 122.

— Is it a Part of the United States ? (J. D. Richardson) Indep. 52: 467.

— The Land and the People. (W. H. Ward) Indep. 51: 543.

— Last Spanish Budget in. (J. D. Whelpley) Indep. 52: 2206.

— Legislature of, The First. (T. S. Adams) Nation, 72: 191.

— Military Training as a Factor in the Civic Reorganization of. (L. S. Rowe) R. of Rs. (N. Y.) 23: 334.

— The Moral of. (R. Ogden) Nation, 73: 84.

— Need of Electric Tramways in. (A. M. Lluveras) Engin. M. 16: 799.

— Needs and Possibilities of. (A. Hopkins) Outl. 68: 629. — (Roy Stone) Outl. 63: 1023.

— New United States Colony. (P. MacQueen) Nat'l M. (Bost.) 9: 3.

— Occupation of. (J. A. Church) R. of Rs. (N. Y.) 18: 282.

— or Puerto Rico ? (Robert T. Hill) Nat. Geog. M. 10: 516.

— Our Duty in. (G. V. Henry) Munsey, 22: 223.

— Our New Island. (E. Deland) Chaut. 27: 669.

— Political Beginnings in. (J. Finley) R. of Rs. (N. Y.) 22: 571.

— Political Problems in. (T. S. Adams) Nation, 72: 334.

— Problem of, Significance of. (L. S. Rowe) No. Am. 173: 35.

— Progress of Government in. Ann. Am. Acad. Pol. Sci. 18: 383.

— Public Instruction in. (C. E. Waters) Educa. 19: 238.

— Question of. Yale R. 8: 355.

— Relief Bill. (A. J. Hopkins) Forum, 29: 139.

— Sanitary Work in. (L. P. Davison) Indep. 51: 2128.

— School System. (A. P. Gardner) Forum, 26: 711.

— Spain's Last Outpost. Gunton's M. 15: 95.

— Status of. (H. G. Curtis) Forum, 28: 403.

— Status of People of, in our Polity. (S. Pfeil) Forum, 30: 717.

— Successful Colonial Government of. (G. G. Groff) Indep. 52: 102.

— Tariff for. Outl. 64: 436.

— — Effect of Proposed. (A. Ames) Indep. 52: 637.

— The United States and. (J. B. Foraker) No. Am. 170: 464.

— Value of. (R. T. Hill) Forum, 27: 414.

— What has been done under Military Rule. (H. K. Carroll) R. of Rs. (N. Y.) 20: 705.

— With Gen. Miles in. (B. T. Clayton) Indep. 51: 679.

Portrait by Cabanel, A ; a story. (R. C. V. Meyers) Harper, 95: 287.

Portrait, What is a ? (B. M. Hacker) Artist (N. Y.) 24: xlviii.

Portrait of a Lady ; a story. (J. K. Jerome) Idler, 11: 282.

Portrait Art by a Portrait Painter. (Geo. Butler) Scrib. M. 27: 125.

Portrait Fiction. Spec. 86: 82. Same art. Liv. Age, 228: 844.

Portrait Painters, Famous. Munsey, **16**: 448. **18**: 432.

— Four Living. (E. F. Baldwin) Outl. **61**: 543.

— Society of. New Gallery Exhibition. Ath. '00, **2**: 689.

— Some British. (C. Monkhouse) Art J. **49**: 34.

Portrait-painting and Some Early English Painters. (Frank Fowler) Cosmopol. **29**: 495.

— and the State. (Frank Fowler) Scrib. M. **28**: 765.

— in Words. (G. Paston) Cornh. **76**: 207.

— Recent. (F. Wedmore) Studio (Lond.) **5**: 119.

Portraits, American, Index to. (B. Samuel) Pennsyl. M. **25**: 47, 228, 384.

— and Phantoms. (S. Olivier) Contemp. **75**: 687. Same art. Ecl. M. **133**: 451. Same art. Liv. Age, **222**: 214.

— at Eton. (B. W. Cornish) Pall Mall M. **21**: 501.

— Collection of, in New York City Hall and Municipal Offices. Scrib. M. **22**: 783.

— Early Italian. (Walter Armstrong) Art J. **53**: 46.

— Electric Auto-. (A. Thurburn) Knowl. **23**: 51.

— English, of 18th Century at Birmingham. Art J. **53**: 89.

— of the Flavian Age. (J. W. Crawfoot) J. Hel. Stud. **20**: 31.

— seen this Season. (F. Wedmore) Studio (Lond.) **5**: 119.

Portraiture, Analytical. (F. Galton) Nature, **62**: 320.

— Artistic Photography in. (M. Burnside) Brush & P. **6**: 122.

— in Recumbent Effigies, Hartshorne on. Ath. '00, **2**: 286, 352, 418.

— Mortimer Menpes on. (R. Blathwayt) Pall Mall M. **20**: 217.

Portsmouth, N. H., Inhabitants of, 1711. (G. A. Gordon) N. E. Reg. **51**: 43.

Portugal, Hotels in, Cheapness of. (C. Edwardes) Chamb. J. **78**: 725.

Portuguese Population in U. S. (F. L. Hoffman) Am. Statis. Assoc. **6**: 327.

Pose. Spec. **82**: 636.

— of Body. (G. T. Stevens) Pop. Sci. Mo. **59**: 390.

Poseidippus, Notes on the Newly-discovered Elegy of. (R. Ellis) Am. J. Philol. **21**: 76.

Posing. Citizen, **3**: 57.

— the Artist and his Model. (Gustave Kobbé) Cosmopol. **31**: 115.

— Women who Pose. (Vance Thompson) Cosmopol. **32**: 179.

Position, Payment in. Spec. **78**: 692.

Position-finding Service in Sea-coast Defenses. (J. Chester) J. Mil. Serv. Inst. **13**: 227.

Positivism, Fouillée on. Ath. '97, **2**: 345.

— its Position, Aims, and Ideals. (F. Harrison) No. Am. **172**: 456.

Post-Apostolic Age, Waterman's. (T. J. Shahan) Am. Hist. R. **5**: 107.

Post-cards, Pictorial. (N. Alliston) Chamb. J. **76**: 745.

Post Mess, The. (C. J. T. Clarke) J. Mil. Serv. Inst. **15**: 545.

Post Office, and the Public in 1837. (W. B. Paley) Gent. M. n. s. **61**: 590.

— Case for Inquiry in. (C. H. Garland) Westm. **156**: 332.

— English, Banking Business of. Bank. M. (Lond.) **66**: 556.

— — Reforms Needed. (J. H. Heaton) 19th Cent. **43**: 764.

— English Report of 1899, and the Hints it contains for Bankers. Bank. M. (Lond.) **70**: 565.

— — Report for 1900. Bank. M. (Lond.) **72**: 449.

Post-office Curiosities. (H. T. Churchill) Canad. M. **16**: 220.

Post-office Department of U. S., Maladministration of. (W. Clark) Arena, **17**: 947.

— Publishers and the. (C. H. Howard) Arena, **26**: 570.

Postage for Library Books, Demand for Reduced. Educa. **20**: 177.

— Imperial Penny, at Last. (J. H. Heaton) Fortn. **70**: 385. — Spec. **81**: 76.

Postage Stamps and their Collection. Chamb. J. **74**: 504.

— of Canada. (A. C. Casselman) Canad. M. **11**: 242.

— pictorially considered. (E. C. Fincham) Pall Mall M. **19**: 126.

Postal and Telegraphic Progress under Queen Victoria. (J. H. Heaton) Fortn. **67**: 839.

Postal Commission, Work of the. (W. H. Moody) Indep. **53**: 195.

Postal Currency for Small Remittances. (C. W. Post) No. Am. **167**: 628.

Postal Delivery, Rural Free. (C. B. Todd) Gunton's M. **19**: 232.

Postal Reform, American, Side Lights on. (O. J. Victor) Forum, **24**: 723.

— — Need of. (E. F. Loud) No. Am. **166**: 342.

Postal Savings Banks. (J. A. Gary) Munsey, **19**: 387.

— Bank. M. (N. Y.) **56**: 37.

Postal Service, U. S., and the Railroads. (J. L. Cowles) Outl. **58**: 469, 715.

— — Charge for Railway Mail Carriage. (G. G. Tunell) J. Pol. Econ. **7**: 144.

— — Cowles's General Freight and Passenger Post. (G. G. Tunell) J. Pol. Econ. **7**: 396.

— — Reasonable Railway Mail Pay. (G. G. Tunell) J. Pol. Econ. **8**: 203.

— — A Step toward Economy in. (E. F. Loud) Forum, **24**: 471.

— — Transportation of Mail. (G. G. Tunell) J. Pol. Econ. **7**: 468.

Poster, Age of the. (M. Talmeyer) Chaut. **24**: 457.

— The Modern. (N. A. Flood) Chaut. **29**: 561.

— Passing of the. (Mabel Key) Brush & P. **4**: 12.

Poster Designing, Suggestions on. (A. G. Byrns) Brush & P. **9**: 154.

Posters. (G. R. Sparks) Brush & P. **1**: 10. — (P. L. Barnard) Brush & P. **9**: 107.

— Another Word on. (A. Fish) Studio (Lond.) **5**: 215.

— Collecting of. (C. T. J. Hiatt) Studio (Lond.) **1**: 61.

— of Louis Rhead. (G. White) Studio (Lond.) **8**: 156.

— Some American. Artist (N. Y.) **23**: 16.

Posterity, A Plea for. (H. Giffard-Ruffe) Westm. **156**: 26.

Posthumous Fortune, A. (Mary T. Van Denburgh) Overland, n. s. **34**. 123.

Postmaster-General's Report, English, 1898. Bank. M. (Lond.) **68**: 465.

Postmen of the World. (T. Lake) Strand, **15**: 745.

Pot of Gold ; a story. (M. Austin) Munsey, **25**: 491.

Pot Cranes and their Adjustments. (J. R. Allen) Reliquary, **38**: 145.

Potato, Bacterial Diseases of. (E. F. Smith) Am. Natural. **31**: 123.

Potato Bug, Colorado, Collops Bipunctatus as an Enemy of. (C. E. Mead) Am. Natural, **33**: 927.

Poteen-hunting in the Wild West of Ireland. Chamb. J. **76**: 761.

Potentates in Pinafores. Eng. Illust. **19**: 493.

Potential Things. (D. Bright ; P. Carus) Monist, **10**: 282.

Potocka, Countess Claudina. Memoirs. Sat. R. **92**: 528.

Potomac Formation, Age of, Fontaine and Newberry on. (L. F. Ward) Science, **5**: 411.

Potomac River Bridge at Washington. (George Keeler) Am. Arch. **70**: 77.

Potsdam, New Photographic Telescope at. Pop. Astron. **8**: 1.

Pottawatomies, The, in the War of 1812. (S. Po-Ka-Gon) Arena, **26**: 48.

Potter, Bessie, Sculptor, with portrait. (Lucy Monroe) Brush & P. **2**: 29.

— Statuettes by. (A. Hoeber) Cent. **32**: 732.

— Work of. M. of Art, **24**: 522.

Potter, Mrs. Brown, Portrait of. Theatre, **39**: 280.

Potter, Henry C., Letter of, to Mayor Van Wyck. Outl. **66**: 733.

— The Scholar and the State. (J. Bryce) Bk. Buyer, **15**: 637.

Potter, Margaret Potter, with portrait. Bk. News, **20**: 145.

Potter, Reuben Marmaduke. J. Mil. Serv. Inst. **11**: 504.

Potter Family, of New Haven, Conn. (J. Shepard) N. E. Reg. **54**: 20.

Potteries at Lambeth, Samples from. (W. T. Whitley) Art J. **50**: 58.

— Two Devonshire. (H. S. Ward) Art J. **52**: 119.

Potter's Art, The. (G. Mourey) Studio (Internat.) **3**: 112.

Pottery, American Historical. Nat'l M. (Bost.) **14**: 265.

— Ancient Peruvian. (W. M. Webb) Artist (N. Y.) **32**: 93.

— and Plumbism. (T. E. Thorpe) Nature, **62**: 42.

— and Porcelain at Bethnal Green Museum. Art J. **51**: 254.

— Art from the Kilns. (C. DeKay) Munsey, **26**: 46.

— as a Historical Document. (Sir G. Birdwood) J. Soc. Arts, **47**: 689.

— Birkenhead. (W. T. Whitley) Art J. **50**: 27.

— Decoration of, Recent Advances in. (W. Burton) J. Soc. Arts, **49**: 213.

— Eastern. (C. Holme) Studio (Internat.) **15**: 48.

— Fabric-marked. (F. S. Dellenbaugh) Pop. Sci. Mo. **52**: 674.

— Fremington. (Francesca M. Steele) Art J. **52**: 28.

— from Mississippi Valley, Decorations upon. (C. C. Willoughby) J. Am. Folk-Lore, **10**: 9.

— Mr. Hadley's. M. of Art, **22**: 672.

— Indian. (G. W. James) Outing, **39**: 154.

— Kaipien. Brush & P. **5**: 177.

— Material and Design in. (W. Burton) J. Soc. Arts, **45**: 1127, 1139, 1157.

— Newcomb. Brush & P. **6**: 15.

— Persian, 13th Century. (H. Wallis) 19th Cent. **46**: 560.

— Primitive Painted, in Crete. (D. G. Hogarth) J. Hel. Stud. **21**: 78.

— Pseudo-Samian, Imitations of. Reliquary, **38**: 183.

— Some Dutch. (F. Rhead) Artist (N. Y.) **24**: 34, 64, 198.

— Staffordshire, for America. (J. M. O'Fallon) Art J. **49**: 340. — (C. Monkhouse) Scrib. M. **22**: 701.

— Textiles used in Making and Embellishing. (W. H. Holmes) Am. Anthrop. **3**: 397.

— Van Briggle. (G. D. Galloway) Brush & P. **9**: 1.

— Wileman & Co.'s. Artist (N. Y.) **26**: 76.

Pottery Industry, Chemistry of. (K. Langenbeck) J. Frankl. Inst. **143**: 321.

Pouget, Baron. (A. J. Butler) Cornh. **75**: 660. Same art. Ecl. M. **128**: 817.

Poulett vs. Poulett; a coming Cause Celèbre. (J. De Morgan) Green Bag, **11**: 255.

Poultry, Prize, as a Hobby. (A. H. Blair) Chamb. J. **77**: 405.

Poultry Breeding. (H. S. Babcock) Outing, **38**: 404.

— in the U. S. (H. S. Babcock) Outing, **37**: 38.

Poultry Farming. (J. B. Walker, jr.) Cosmopol. **23**: 177.

— for Profit. Chamb. J. **76**: 183.

Poultry Farming in England. Sat. R. **88**: 70.

Poussin, Nicholas, Denio's Life of. (E. E. Hale, jr.) Dial (Ch.) **27**: 421.

Poverty and Social Decay. (A. M. Colwick) Arena, **26**: 34.

— Cause and Cure of. (E. B. Randle) Meth. R. **61**: 911.

— Causes of. (F. A. Walker) Cent. **33**: 210. — Ann. Am. Acad. Pol. Sci. **11**: 130.

— — Statistical Study in. (A. M. Simons) Am. J. Sociol. **3**: 614.

— The Power of. (H. M. Buller) Sund. M. **28**: 505.

Poverty of Fortune, The. (Douglas Tilden) Overland, n. s. **31**: 195.

Poverty Corner. (Jas. Bayfield) Good Words, **39**: 320.

Powder and Paint. (Ida Taylor) 19th Cent. **46**: 633. Same art. Ecl. M. **134**: 236.

Powder, Essentials of, as distinguished from Explosives. (W. J. Williams) J. Frankl. Inst, **151**: 194.

— Smokeless. (J. Castner) J. Mil. Serv. Inst. **11**: 786.

— — in the Light of the most Recent Discoveries. (Hudson Maxim) Forum, **30**: 595.

— — in Warfare. (Hudson Maxim) J. Frankl. Inst. **146**: 375, 457.

— — Story of. (Hudson Maxim) Cassier, **16**: 239.

Powell, John W., Extension of Bacon's Work. (W. J. McGee) Forum, **27**: 168.

Powell, Maud, Violinist, with portrait. Music, **20**: 127.

Powellite Crystals, from Michigan. (C. Palache) Am. J. Sci. **157**: 367.

Power and Industry. (A. D. Adams) Cassier, **19**: 129.

— Cost of. (C. D. Gray) J. Frankl. Inst. **152**: 275, 331, 421.

— Hydraulic, Applications of. (G. W. Dickie) Cassier, **13**: 138.

— in a Pound of Coal. (E. D. Meier) Cassier, **18**: 65.

— Motive, from High-furnace Gases. (B. Donkin) Engin. M. **20**: 422.

— Problem of, The Future. (T. C. Mendenhall) Cassier, **21**: 41.

— Rope Transmission of, American System. (R. D. O. Smith) Cassier, **13**: 153.

— — from Niagara. (O. E. Dunlap) Cassier, **11**: 197.

— Small Motive. (A. D. Adams) Am. Arch. **66**: 11.

— Transmission of, by Belts and Pulleys. (C. L. Redfield) Engin. M. **14**: 641.

— — in American Warships. (G. W. Dickie) Cassier, **14**: 241.

See Electric Transmission.

Power behind the Throne, The; a story. (C. Dawe) Pall Mall M. **20**: 225.

Power of a Will, The; a story. (M. C. Sidgwick) Belgra. **98**: 132.

Power Development, Future of. (W. D. Ennis) Engin. M. **19**: 728.

Power Losses in the Machine-shop. (C. H. Benjamin) Cassier, **17**: 215.

Power Plant, Care and Oversight of the. (T. C. Smith) Engin. M. **13**: 742.

Power Tool, Industrial Revolution of the. (C. Barnard) Cent. **37**: 941.

Powers, Hiram. (H. Boynton) New Eng. M. n. s. **20**: 519.

Powers, Three Great. (A. Bierbower) Lippinc. **63**: 251.

— The Minor. Spec. **78**: 329.

Pownalboro', Maine. (C. E. Allen) New Eng. M. n. s. **24**: 516.

Poynter, Edward J., with portrait. (M. H. Spielmann) M. of Art, **20**: 111. — With portrait. (H. Sharp) Studio (Lond.) **7**: 3.

— Roman Boat-race. Art J. **50**: 12.

— Studies by. (M. H. Spielmann) M. of Art, **21**: 1, 289.

Poznanski, S. Ibn Chiquitilla, nebst dem Fragmenten seiner Schriften. (G. G. Cameron) Crit. R. **8**: 86.

Practical Marches of Light Artillery. (E. M. Blake) J. Mil. Serv. Inst. 19: 102.

Practice and Habit, Researches in. (W. S. Johnson) Science, n. s. 10: 527.

Pradella, Francisco, Spanish Painter. (D. A. Hart) Studio (Internat.) 13: 174.

Præsos, Crete, Researches at. (F. Halbherr) Am. J. Archæol. n. s. 5: 371.

Pragmatism. (W. Caldwell) Mind, 25: 433.

Prague. (A. Symons) Harper, 103: 509.

Prairie Cabin. (G. E. Tufts) New Eng. M. n. s. 24: 174.

"Prairie-chicken." (H. S. Canfield) Outing, 36: 638.

Prairie Chicken Hunt, Old-time. (E. Hough) Outing, 37: 319.

Prairie Chicken Hunting. (C. H. Morton) Outing, 39: 62.

Prairie Chums of Mine. (W. Hutchinson) Contemp. 76: 347. Same art. Liv. Age, 223: 164.

Prairie Dog Tales; a story of U. S. S. "Prairie." (W. Packard) Nat'l M. (Bost.) 10: 135.

Prairie Fire; a story. Temp. Bar, 114: 33ʂ.

Prairie Twilight; a poem. (M. Baldwin) Atlan. 86: 424.

Praise-God Barebones. (E. G. Atkinson) Ath. '97, 2: 257.

Prato, Day at. (H. Monroe) Lippinc. 65: 443.

Pratt, Dr. John F. (C. E. Bangs) N. E. Reg. 53: 354.

Pratt Institute Free Library, Brooklyn, N. Y. Photograph Collection. (M. W. Plummer) Lib. J. 25: 7.

Prawns, Changes of Color of. Nature, 61: 552.

Pray, Joseph. Capt. Pray's Company. N. E. Reg. 54: 98.

Prayer, Answers to. Sund. M. 26: 73-685.

— Books of Common, First and Second. (W. Fleming) Am. Cath. Q. 26: 338.

— An Early Christian. (E. J. Goodspeed) Bib. World, 17: 309.

— The Efficacy of. (V. Y. Remnitz and A. G. Brown) Arena, 20: 370.

— — in the Light of Evolution. (W. W. Battershall) No. Am. 167: 251.

— Fallacies concerning. (J. M. Whiton) Forum, 23: 351.

— History of; a sermon. (L. Abbott) Outl. 61: 456.

— in War-time. (E. M. Chapman) Bib. Sac. 56: 532.

— Meaning of. (J. Bigham) Meth. R. 57: 356.

— Worship by, of Great Use. (J. Worcester) N. Church R. 7: 1.

Prayer; a poem. (M. A. M. Marks) Argosy, 65: 499.

Prayer-book as a Rule of Life. Church Q. 49: 292.

— English, Pullan on. Church Q. 50: 395.

Prayer-books, National Collection of. (L. W. Lillingston) Sund. M. 28: 695.

Prayers for the Dead. Sat. R. 87: 362.

Praying-match, The. (E. C. Waltz) Cent. 38: 450.

Preacher, The, and his Message. (E. V. Du Bois) Meth. R. 61: 875.

— and the Out-of-doors. (D. L. Sharp) Meth. R. 61: 524.

— Great, The Making of a. Lond. Q. 90: 37.

— Inner Life of. Meth. R. 59: 444.

— 20th Century. (A. H. Tuttle) Meth. R. 61: 374.

Preachers who have impressed me. (W. R. Nicoll) Sund. M. 26: 145.

Preaching. (W. Kirkus) New World, 9: 226.

— Aim of. (D. B. Lady) Ref. Q. 45: 348.

— Apprenticeship of. (W. L. Watkinson) Meth. R. 57: 37.

— Art of, in Mediæval Times. (L. Johnston) Cath. World, 74: 210.

— Christ. Ref. Q. 44: 380.

— Christlieb's Lectures on. (G. B. Carr) Presb. & Ref. R. 10: 167.

Preaching during the Renaissance. (L. Johnston) Cath. World, 74: 334.

— Efficiency in. (R. F. Sample) Presb. & Ref. R. 8: 279.

— Expository. (W. H. P. Faunce) Bib. World, 11: 81, 317. 12: 320.

— — a New-Church View. (T. A. King) N. Church R. 4: 513.

— for a Theological Crisis. (D. H. Bauslin) Luth. Q. 27: 341.

— The Imagination in. (W. L. Ledwith) Presb. & Ref. R. 12: 284.

— Impressionist. (W. L. Watkinson) Meth. R. 57: 743.

— Inspiration of. (J. T. Gladhill) Luth. Q. 29: 361.

— The Modern Prophet and his Bible. (G. A. Schwedes) Ref. Ch. R. 46: 447.

— Must be Biblical. Bib. World, 12: 289.

— Office of the Preacher. (S. K. Davis) Arena, 26: 503.

— Personal Element in. (G. W. Richards) Ref. Q. 44: 324.

— Positive Note in. (J. Watson) Chr. Lit. 17: 44.

— Primary Impression of. (T. W. Hunt) Meth. R. 57: 545.

— Proper Use of Science in. (J. M. Coulter) Am. J. Theol. 3: 641.

— Qualifications Necessary for. (P. B. Cabell) N. Church R. 6: 365.

— Sophistical Element in. (C. S. Nash) Bib. Sac. 58: 242.

— Teaching Element in. (A. H. Tuttle) Meth. R. 58: 205.

— Yale Lectures on, 1899. Meth. R. 59: 106.

Prebendary's Daughter, The; a story. (Mrs. H. Wood) Argosy, 63: 429.

Precedents, Judicial, Theory of. (J. W. Salmond) Law Q. 16: 376.

Precious Metals, Del Mar's History of. (H. C. Bolton) Science, 14: 893.

— Production of. (F. B. Forbes) Gunton's M. 13: 182.

Precious Stones. Ed. R. 186: 331.

— Geography of. (G. F. Kunz) J. Frankl. Inst. 145: 24, 133.

Prede Claudo; a story. (J. Hazard) Temp. Bar, 124: 72.

Predestination, A. (Frances Campbell) Good Words, 41: 702.

— and Determinism in Light of New Church. (T. M. Martin) N. Church R. 5: 459.

— in the Reformed Confessions. (B. B. Warfield) Presb. & Ref. R. 12: 49.

Preece, William Henry. (J. W. Curra) Cassier, 14: 356.

Prefaces and the Colophon. (J. Benton) Writer, 13: 70.

Preglacial Drainage in Michigan. (E. H. Mudge) Am. J. Sci. 154: 383. 160: 158.

Prehistoric Age, Common Things of the. (S. D. Peet) Am. Antiq. 23: 395.

Prehistoric Archæology, Canon in. (T. Wilson) Am. Antiq. 19: 125.

Prehistoric Arrowheads and Banner-stones. (S. D. Peet) Am. Antiq. 19: 26.

Prehistoric Art and Crafts. Quar. 187: 400.

Prehistoric Copper Implements of Ontario. (G. E. Laidlaw) Am. Antiq. 21: 83.

Prehistoric Man in the Neighborhood of the Kent and Surrey Border. (G. Clinch) Anthrop. J. 29: 124.

Prehistoric Monuments. (A. L. Lewis) Anthrop. J. 27: 194.

Prehistoric Remains, Sequences in. (W. M. F. Petrie) Anthrop. 29: 295.

— at Cambusnethan. Reliquary, 39: 49.

Prehistoric Workshops at Mt. Kineo, Me. (C. C. Willoughby) Am. Natural. 35: 213.

Prester John; a story. (J. Buchan) Chamb. J. 74: 362.

Preston, Margaret J. (J. A. Harrison) Critic, 30: 291. — (Sophia B. Gilman) Lit. W. (Bost.) 28: 125.

Preston, Samuel, Extracts from Journal of, 1787. Pennsyl. M. 22: 350.

Preston, Dr. Thomas. Nature, 61: 474.

Preston, William Campbell, with portrait. (W. L. Miller) Green Bag, 11: 393-586. 12: 37.

Prestwich, Sir Joseph, with portrait. Pop. Sci. Mo. 52: 254. — Sat. R. 88: 270.

— and Practical Geology. Nature, 60: 265.

Presumption of Jonathan Dawes; a story. (M. Scott) Idler, 14: 365.

Pretenders. Men who would be Kings. (A. de St. André and G. G. Thomas) Eng. Illust. 19: 129.

Pretending. (M. Beerbohm) Sat. R. 85: 103.

Preternatural Suspicion. Spec. 79: 765.

Pretoria before the War. (H. C. Hillegas) Harper, 100: 548.

— The British at. (J. Barnes) Outl. 66: 41.

— How we escaped from. (Capt. A. Haldane) Blackw. 168: 155, 305.

— in War-time. (R. H. Davis) Scrib. M. 28: 173.

— Last Days of. (R. H. Davis) Scrib. M. 28: 407.

— The March to. Fortn. 74: 152.

— Outside Pretoria; a Typical Fight. (J. Barnes) Outl. 66: 112.

"Pretty Rose;" a story. (Minnie Moffat) Nat'l M. (Bost.) 6: 235.

Preventive Work in Charity. (J. Lee) Char. R. 10: 376-586. — Charities, 6: 176-485. 7: 37.

Prévost, Abbé, Author of Manon Lescaut. (W. B. Wallace) Idler, 18: 118.

— in England. (F. B. de Bury) Scot. R. 33: 27.

— Le Jardin secret. (H. T. Peck) Bookman, 5: 291.

Prevost, Augustus. Bank. M. (Lond.) 71: 728.

Preyer, T. W. Nature, 56: 296.

Price of the Grindstone and the Drum; a story. (G. Parker) Pall Mall M. 19: 149.

Price of the Harness. (S. Crane) Blackw. 164: 829.

Price of an Inspiration, The; a story. (E. A. Smith) Argosy, 71: 67. Same art. Liv. Age, 225: 708.

Price of a Necklace; a story. (E. Gerard) Eng. Illust. 12: 723.

Price of a Wife. (J. S. Winter) Lippinc. 60: 579.

Prices and Charges, Power of State to regulate. (G. A. Finkelnburg) Am. Law R. 32: 501.

— and Index Numbers. (R. S. Padan) J. Pol. Econ. 8: 171.

— at Woodstock in 1604. (E. A. M'Arthur) Eng. Hist. R. 13: 711.

— Determination of. Gunton's M. 14: 90.

— Fall in, since 1872, Causes of. (J. W. Jenks) Am. J. Soc. Sci. 35: 31. — Bank. M. (N. Y.) 55: 547.

— Falling. (Gordon Dean) Arena, 17: 633.

— — and Impoverishment. (H. Fuller) Arena, 17: 940.

— Gold and Silver, Stability of. (L. Darwin) J. Statis. Soc. 62: 348.

— in the Confederate States, 1861-65. (J. C. Schwab) Pol. Sci. Q. 14: 281.

— Level of, Who shall control the? (G. H. Shibley) Arena, 23: 68.

— Money and. (R. Mayo-Smith) Pol. Sci. Q. 15: 196.

— Movements of. (R. Mayo-Smith) Pol. Sci. Q. 13: 477.

— — and Individual Welfare. (R. Mayo-Smith) Pol. Sci. Q. 15: 14.

— of Commodities in 1898. (A. Sauerbeck) J. Statis. Soc. 62: 170.

Prices of Commodities in 1899. (A. Sauerbeck) J. Statis. Soc. 63: 92.

— — in 1900. (A. Sauerbeck) J. Statis. Soc. 64: 87.

— Round Numbers in. (E. D. Jones) Am. Statis. Assoc. 5: 111.

Prichard, J. C., Anticipation of Modern Views of Evolution by. (E. B. Poulton) Sci. Prog. n. s. 1: 278.

Pride of Jennico, The. (A. and E. Castle) Temp. Bar, 111: 305, 449. 112: 1, 145.

Priene, a Recovered City of Alexander the Great. (A. L. Frothingham, jr.) Cent. 40: 103.

Priest and People. (E. T. Hargrove) Arena, 18: 772.

Priest of Mahadev, A; a story. (F. A. Spencer) Argosy, 74: 224.

Priesthood, Ancient Teutonic. (H. M. Chadwick) Folk-Lore, 11: 268.

— and Sacrifice, Oxford Conference on. (J. S. Banks) Lond. Q. 95: 359.

— — Sanday on. Church Q. 52: 100.

— The Levitical. (D. A. Walker) J. Bib. Lit. 19: 124.

— Ministerial, by R. C. Moberly. Church Q. 46: 1.

— of David's Sons. (T. K. Cheyne) Expos. 5: 453.

Priestly Prerogative; Sixth of the "Malemute Kid" Stories. (Jack London) Overland, n. s. 34: 59.

Priestman, Bertram, Artist. (A. L. Baldry) Studio (Internat.) 5: 77.

Priests and Prophets in the Modern Church. (L. Abbott) Ref. Ch. R. 47: 289.

Priests' Bargain, The; a story. (E. P. Larkin) Pall Mall M. 12: 72.

Prima Donna, Decline of the. Spec. 84: 89.

Prima Donnas. (J. F. Runciman) Sat. R. 89: 807.

— Advertising Famous. (H. C. Lahee) Nat'l M. (Bost.) 9: 104.

— of the Past, with portraits. (G. L. Norgate) Pall Mall M. 22: 357.

Primal Instinct; a story of the East. (C. Holland) Idler, 16: 491.

Primaries, Direct and Indirect. Outl. 66: 91.

— Minnesota Law governing. (A. L. Mearkle) R. of Rs. (N. Y.) 24: 464. — (F. L. McVey) Yale R. 9: 450.

— Movement for Better. (W. H. Hotchkiss) R. of Rs. (N. Y.) 17: 583.

— Municipal, in the South. (S. S. P. Patterson) Sewanee, 2: 449.

— Reform of. Gunton's M. 14: 152. — (G. Gunton) Gunton's M. 20: 323.

Primary Education Fetich. (J. Dewey) Forum, 25: 315.

Primary Schools, French. (W. Burnet) Gent. M. n. s. 62: 594.

Primates, Successors of North American. (J. L. Wortman) Science, n. s. 13: 209.

Prime Minister's Coup; a story. (W. Le Queux) Cosmopol. 28: 461.

Prime Ministers I have known. (T. H. S. Escott) Chamb. J. 75: 577.

Primers, Sarum, York, and Roman. Ath. '01, 2: 245.

Primordial; a story. (M. Robertson) Harper, 96: 693.

Primroses and Wordsworth. Acad. 53: 449.

Prince, Thomas. Brief Memoirs of Prince's Subscribers. (J. R. Kemble) N. E. Reg. 52: 360.

Prince. (R. L. Brock) New Eng. M. n. s. 23: 616.

Prince Edward Island. (A. E. Mellish) Canad. M. 17: 220.

— In the Garden of the Gulf. Chamb. J. 76: 721.

— Premiers of. (W. L. Cotton) Canad. M. 9: 468.

— Scenery of. (B. Rosamund) Canad. M. 15: 62.

Prince George's Creek, Cape Fear, North Carolina, Plantation on. (S. B. Doggett) N. E. Reg. 52: 469.

Psychology of Fishes, Note on. (E. Thorndike) Am. Natural. **33**: 923.

— of Religion, Starbuck on. (J. H. Leuba) Psychol. R. **7**: 509.

— of Society. (F. H. Giddings) Science, n. s. **9**: 16.

— Physical. (A. H. Lloyd) Psychol. R. **7**: 172.

— Physiological. (J. J. Walsh) Am. Cath. Q. **25**: 497.

— Physiological Basis of Mental Life. (H. Münsterberg) Science, n. s. **9**: 442.

— Popular, More Books on. (E. W. Scripture) Bk. Buyer, **13**: 992.

— Postulates of a Structural. (E. B. Titchener) Philos. R. **7**: 449.

— Practical Aspects of. (J. Jastrow) Educa. R. **17**: 135.

— Progress of, in America, Hindrances to. (G. T. Ladd) Psychol. R. **6**: 121.

— Recent Advance in. (E. B. Titchener) Internat. Mo. **2**: 154.

— Recent Books on, 1898. (J. Jastrow) Dial (Ch.) **24**: 145.

— Relation of Logic to. (D. G. Ritchie) Philos. R. **6**: 1.

— Significance of the Parts of Speech. (G. Buck) Educa. **18**: 269.

— Stout's Analytic. (J. R. Angell) Philos. R. **6**: 532.

— Stout's Manual of. (J. Jastrow) Psychol. R. **7**: 64.

— Structural and Functional. (E. B. Titchener) Philos. R. **8**: 290.

— — Postulates of a. (W. Caldwell) Psychol. R. **6**: 187.

— Talks to Teachers on. (W. James) Atlan. **83**: 155–617.

— — James's. (C. H. Thurber) School R. **7**: 434.

— The Teacher and the Laboratory; a reply. (H. Münsterberg) Atlan. **81**: 824.

— Teacher's Attitude towards. (H. Davies) Educa. **19**: 476.

— Teaching of. (Hiram M. Stanley) Educa. R. **16**: 177.

— — Advances in. (H. Münsterberg) Science, n. s. **9**: 91.

— Weir's Dawn of Reason. (R. MacDougall) Am. Natural. **33**: 611.

Psychophysical Measurement Methods, English of. (E. B. Titchener) Am. J. Psychol. **9**: 327.

Psychrometer Applicable to the Study of Transpiration. (R. G. Leavitt) Am. J. Sci. **155**: 440.

Ptyctodontidæ, Dentition of Devonian. (C. R. Eastman) Am. Natural. **32**: 473, 545.

Puberal Development, Moral Influence of. (A. Marro) Am. J. Sociol. **5**: 193.

Puberal Hygiene, in relation to Pedagogy and Sociology. (A. Marro) Am. J. Sociol. **6**: 224.

Pubescent Period. (Oscar Chrisman) Educa. **19**: 342.

Public Art in St. Louis. (J. L. Mauran) Munic. Aff. **3**: 702.

Public Buildings, Grouping of. (C. H. Walker) Am. Arch. **71**: 11.

Public Defenders. (Mrs. C. Foltz) Am. Law R. **31**: 393.

Public Documents. (M. Mann) Pub. Lib. **4**: 405.

— How made more Useful. (A. R. Hasse) Lib. J. **26**: 8. Same art. Pub. Lib. **6**: 28.

Public Franchises in N. Y. City. (G. Meyers) Munic. Aff. **4**: 71.

Public House, An English Village. (O. Mordaunt) Outl. **63**: 553.

Public Houses. (N. Buxton) Contemp. **77**: 556.

— Reformed. (O. Mordaunt) Econ. R. **9**: 93.

Public-house Management, Experiment in. (Wm. Booth) Contemp. **76**: 379.

Public Institutions of Charity and Correction, Politics in. (C. R. Henderson) Am. J. Sociol. **4**: 202.

Public Life, On the Outskirts of. (T. W. Higginson) Atlan. **81**: 188.

Public Opinion, Growth and Expression of. (E. L. Godkin) Atlan. **81**: 1.

— in England and America. (E. Porritt) New Eng. M. n. s. **19**: 742.

— in Public Affairs. (F. Greenwood) Macmil. **79**: 161.

— International. Nation, **72**: 410.

Public Ownership and the Social Conscience. (R. F. Cutting) Munic. Aff. **4**: 3.

— of Natural Monopolies, Advantages and Management of. (R. T. Ely) Cosmopol. **30**: 556.

— Outlook for. (A. Watkins) Forum, **32**: 201.

Public Reservations, Trustees of, in Mass. A Trust to protect Nature's Beauty. (S. Baxter) R. of Rs. (N. Y.) **23**: 42.

Public Schools. (W. H. Maxwell) Munic. Aff. **4**: 742.

— and Community Life. (J. K. Paulding) Educa. R. **15**: 147.

— and Parents' Duties. (J. Hawthorne) No. Am. **168**: 399. — Reply. (M. G. Van Rensselaer) No. Am. **169**: 77.

— and the Public Services. (J. C. Tarver) Fortn. **74**: 589.

— English. The Education of Englishmen. (M. A. De Morgan) Chaut. **28**: 427.

— False and True in Criticism of Public School Work. (E. B. Andrews) Educa. R. **21**: 258.

— First American. (W. A. Mowry) Educa. **21**: 535.

— Influence of Public Press on. (E. L. Cowdrick) Educa. **21**: 100.

— Lock-step of the. (W. J. Shearer) Atlan. **79**: 749.

— Parents and. (C. N. Chadwick) Outl. **60**: 386.

— Perils of. (W. Gladden) Indep. **51**: 2125.

— Politics and. (G. W. Anderson) Atlan. **87**: 433.

— Product of. (H. H. Almond) New R. **16**: 84.

— Relations of State to. (J. W. Dickinson) Educa. **20**: 5.

— Roman Catholic Church and. (P. R. McDevitt) Cath. World, **73**: 695.

— Shall they train Home-makers? (Julia Richman) Outl. **59**: 1022.

— Some Opponents and Friends. Educa. **20**: 50.

— Uniform Financial Reports for; Report of a committee of the Nat. Educa. Assoc. Educa. R. **17**: 380.

Public School Politician, The. (A. H. Nelson) Educa. R. **19**: 187.

Public School Problems at Opening of 20th Century. (A. Gove; J. M. Greenwood; C. B. Gilbert; A. D. Mayo) Educa. **21**: 193.

Public School System, Evils in our. (W. F. Edwards) Gunton's M. **16**: 269.

— How High should it go? Educa. **20**: 634, 635.

— Reforms in our. (W. F. Edwards) Gunton's M. **17**: 43.

Public Service, Administrative Reform in. (P. L. Gell; A. West) 19th Cent. **48**: 42, 625.

— Amateurism and Mental Inertia in. (R. H. Thurston) Science, n. s. **13**: 594.

Public Service Companies and City Governments. (W. Gladden) Outl. **66**: 502.

Public Services; Rights of the Public over Quasi-public Services. (W. Clark) Arena, **18**: 470.

Public Speaking, Hints on. Green Bag, **9**: 379.

Public Work directly performed. (S. Baxter) R. of Rs. (N. Y.) **15**: 435.

Public Works, Plan for the Control of Quasi-. (J. D. Forrest) Am. J. Sociol. **3**: 837.

Publisher's Methods, Changes in. R. of Rs. (N. Y.) **24**: 599.

Puritan in History. (A. M. Fairbairn) Liv. Age, 212: 58.

Puritan Colony, A Forgotten. Blackw. 165: 868.

Puritan Preaching, Dr. John Brown on. (C. S. Macfarland) Outl. 63: 640.

Puritan Principles and the Modern World. (A. H. Bradford) Chaut. 27: 608.

Puritan Settlements in New England. Lond. Q. 87: 328.

Puritan Theology of New England, 1620-1720. (F. H. Foster) Am. J. Theol. 1: 700.

Puritanism and English Literature. (E. Dowden) Contemp. 76: 22. Same art. Ecl. M. 133: 605. Same art. Liv. Age, 222: 593.

— Message of. (N. D. Hillis) Bib. Sac. 55: 342.

Puritans and Richard Hooker, Paget on. Church Q. 49: 116.

Purple-eyes. (J. L. Long) Cent. 34: 354.

Purple Fly, The. (J. S. Thomson) Good Words, 41: 544.

Purple Terror, The. (F. M. White) Strand, 18: 243.

Pursuit of the Piano, The; a story. (W. D. Howells) Harper, 100: 725.

Pusey, Edward B., and the Oxford Movement. Blackw. 162: 795. Same art. Ecl. M. 130: 237.

— and Wiseman. Quar. 187: 299.

— as a Correspondent. Church Q. 50: 282.

— as a Devotional Writer. (F. Platt) Lond. Q. 94: 263.

— Eirenicon. Why is it a Failure? Dub. R. 122: 391.

— Last Years of. Month, 90: 561.

— Letters of. (J. Rickaby) Month, 93: 166.

— Liddon's Life of. Acad. 52: 417. — Church Q. 45: 279. — (J. W. Chadwick) New World, 7: 183.

— Private Life of. Acad. 59: 355.

— Spiritual Letters of; a Review. Church Q. 48: 344.

Puseyism, Latest Light on the Practical Influence of. Lond. Q. 90: 205.

Pushkin, Alex. S. Temp. Bar, 116: 519. — (I. F. Mayo) Argosy, 68: 26. — Acad. 56: 676.

— and his Work. (Z. A. Ragozin) Cosmopol. 28: 307.

Pusterthal Festival, A. (C. L'Estrange) Belgra. 92: 398.

Put up the Sword; a poem. (J. J. Roche) Cent. 37: 315.

Putnam, Frank, and his Poems; with portrait. Nat'l M. (Bost.) 12: 472.

Putnam, Frederick W., with portrait. Nat. Geog. M. 9: 429.

Putnam, Herbert, with portrait. (M. B. Thrasher) Nat'l M. (Bost.) 10: 200.

— Appointment to Library of Congress. (S. C. Fairchild) Library, n. s. 1: 100.

— Librarian of Congress. Library, n. s. 1: 241.

Putnam, Israel, Homes and Haunts of. (W. F. Livingston) New Eng. M. n. s. 17: 193.

Putting away of the McPhersons. (C. H. Pemberton) Arena, 20: 417.

Puvis de Chavannes, P. C. (D. L. Murdoch) Conserv. R. 1: 407. — With portrait. (G. Mourey) Studio (Internat.) 6: 206. — With portrait. (M. van Vorse) Pall Mall M. 17: 313. — (G. Mourey) Studio (Lond.) 4: 171. — (J. La Farge) Scrib. M. 28: 672. — (C. J. Holmes) Contemp. 74: 864. — (S. Beale) Am. Arch. 62: 80. — (R. Riordan) Critic, 33: 455.

— and Detaille. (B. Karageorgevitch) M. of Art, 22: 659.

— Appreciation of. (W. Sharp) Art J. 50: 377.

— at the Panthéon. Am. Arch. 63: 11.

— in Boston. (C. Waern) Atlan. 79: 251.

— Personal Recollections of. Liv. Age, 220: 203. Same art. Ecl. M. 132: 429.

Puvis de Chavannes, P. C., Sketches by. (G. Mourey) Studio (Internat.) 9: 12.

Puzzle-cards, Old. Strand, 18: 580.

Puzzles, A Study of. (E. H. Lindley) Am. J. Psychol. 8: 431.

Puzzolana and its Practical Use. (Josef Zervas) Am. Arch. 56: 99.

Pygmies, African. Pub. Opin. 23: 591. — (S. P. Verner) Conserv. R. 2: 306.

— and Prehistoric Libya. (N. Patterson) Canad. M. 11: 381.

— Lloyd's Journey across the Great Pygmy Forest. Nat. Geog. M. 10: 26.

— of Asia. (R. Lydekker) Knowl. 23: 196.

— of the Great Forest. (R. Lydekker) Knowl. 23: 259.

Pylos and Sphateria. (H. Awdry) J. Hel. Stud. 20: 14.

Pyramid of Ghizeh, The Top of the Great. Illus. (Hugh Macmillan) Good Words, 38: 672.

Pyramid Lake, Nevada. (H. W. Fairbanks) Pop. Sci. Mo. 58: 505.

Pyramids, How they were Erected. (W. F. Durfee) Cassier, 15: 213.

— of Egypt, Great. (B. I. Wheeler) Cent. 34: 107.

— The Pharaohs have Vanished, the Pyramids Remain. Eng. Illust. 20: 11.

Pyrenees, Customs of the Western. (A. R. Whiteway) Eng. Hist. R. 15: 625.

— West; Doctors in the Middle Ages. (A. R. Whiteway) Gent. M. n. s. 65: 450.

— — Curé of the Past. (A. R. Whiteway) Gent. M. n. s. 66: 191.

— — Lawyers in the Past. (A. R. Whiteway) Gent. M. n. s. 66: 90.

— — Marriages in. (A. R. Whiteway) Gent. M. n. s. 65: 404.

— — Mediæval Penology. (A. R. Whiteway) Gent. M. n. s. 66: 380.

— — Peasant Proprietor. (A. R. Whiteway) Gent. M. n. s. 66: 226.

— — Sources of Law. (A. R. Whiteway) Gent. M. n. s. 67: 83.

— — Women of, Mediæval. (A. R. Whiteway) Gent. M. n. s. 65: 272.

— Spender's Through the High. Ath. '98, 2: 634.

Pyrite and Marcasite. (H. N. Stokes) Am. J. Sci. 162: 414.

Pyrography, Art of. (E. H. Reed) Brush & P. 4: 79.

Pyrogravure, Possibilities of. (A. M. Harcolm) Brush & P. 7: 249.

Pyrometry, Methods of. (C. Barus) Science, 6: 338, 528.

Pythagoras, Life of. (M. Cantor) Open Court, 11: 321.

Quack's Triumph, A; a story. Cornh. 78: 94. Same art. Ecl. M. 131: 414. Same art. Liv. Age, 218: 596.

Quail of the Pacific Coast. (T. S. Van Dyke) Outing, 39: 327.

— Intelligence of. (T. S. Van Dyke) Outing, 37: 432.

Quail Hunting in the South. (W. Howe) Outing, 33: 245.

Quail Shooting. (M. Southey) Outing, 33: 54.

— in December. (E. W. Sandys) Outing, 31: 284.

— in Southern California. (H. A. Vachell) Pall Mall M. 17: 115.

— on the Snow. (D. W. Huntington) Outing, 29: 366.

Quails. Sat. R. 87: 617.

— an International Question. Liv. Age, 220: 465.

Quain, Sir Richard. Nature, 57: 467.

— Sketch of. Pop. Sci. Mo. 53: 835.

Quaker Boy, Recollections of a. (R. E. Robinson) Atlan. 88: 100.

Quakerism, The Attraction of. Spec. **84**: 801.
— Present Position of. (E. Grubb) Lond. Q. **95**: 61.
— Power and Function of. Spec. **86**: 416.
Quakers and Palatines as Commonwealth Builders. (F. R. Diffenderffer) Ref. Ch. R. **46**: 145.
— Anecdotes of the. (R. Tangye) Chamb. J. **78**: 90.
— Customs of. (A. M. Earle) New Eng. M. n. s. **19**: 18.
— Hazard on. (B. A. Hinsdale) Dial (Ch.) **28**: 11.
— London, Haunts of. (B. Holmes) Antiq. n. s. **35**: 11-334.
— Oxford and. (A. M. Gummere) Pennsyl. M. **23**: 273.
— Persecution of, 1662. (E. B. Smith) New Eng. M. n. s. **22**: 157.
— Philadelphia. (T. Wharton) Lippinc. **60**: 683.
— Rhode Island, Social Life of, 1810-25. (E. B. Chace) New Eng. M. n. s. **16**: 655.
— Two Generations of. (L. P. Smith and R. E. Robinson) Atlan. **88**: 92.
— A Vanished Race. (J. D. Hilton) Sund. M. **27**: 586.
Qualichin and the Cultus Trader; a British Columbia story. (H. Sands) Canad. M. **18**: 151.
Quantity Theory, The. (W. A. Scott) Ann. Am. Acad. Pol. Sci. **9**: 212.
Quantrell, William C., the Guerrilla Chief. (J. J. Lutz) Midland, **7**: 509.
Quarantine against Insects and Plant Diseases. (C. S. Sargent) Garden & F. **10**: 91.
— and Sanitation. (W. Wyman) Forum, **26**: 684.
— for Cattle. (H. H. Bowen) Lippinc. **60**: 120.
— in England, The Last of. Liv. Age, **212**: 767.
— Methods of. (A. H. Doty) No. Am. **165**: 201.
Quaritch, Bernard. Acad. **57**: 748. — (E. D. North) Bk. Buyer, **20**: 50. — (D. Sage) Atlan. **85**: 843. — Bookman, **10**: 568.
Quartermaster's Department. (J. G. C. Lee) J. Mil. Serv. Inst. **15**: 257.
— Reform in the. (A. M. Palmer) J. Mil. Serv. Inst. **16**: 25.
— Special Service Corps for. (E. F. Ladd) J. Mil. Serv. Inst. **14**: 1008.
Quartet Party, The. (Maud A. Bulmer) Temp. Bar, **124**: 113.
Quartz-muscovite from Belmont, Nev. (J. E. Spurr) Am. J. Sci. **160**: 351.
Quaternary Era, Inferior Boundary of the. (O. H. Hershey) Am. Natural. **31**: 104.
Quatrain. (A. Phelps) Atlan. **84**: 458.
Quay, Matthew, and the Constitution. (E. P. Clark) Nation, **68**: 327.
— Latest Exposure of. (E. P. Clark) Nation, **67**: 271.
Quebec. (G. Stewart) New Eng. M. n. s. **21**: 33.
— and the American Revolution; a reply. (V. Coffin) Canad. M. **9**: 56.
— as a Sketching Ground. (B. G. Goodhue) Studio (Lond.) **5**: 200.
— Attractions of. (B. Nicholson) Canad. M. **16**: 554.
— Capture of, 1759. (C. T. Brady) McClure, **15**: 267.
— the Crowned City. (L. W. Betts) Outl. **67**: 521.
— Did Wolfe or Townsend capture? (A. H. V. Colquhoun) Canad. M. **17**: 471.
— Fall of. (C. T. Brady) Idler, **20**: 28.
— Foreign Partnerships and Corporations in the Province of. (E. F. Surveyer) Am. Law R. **35**: 413.
— "Journal of the most Remarkable Occurrences in Quebec, 1775." (J. Bain, jr.) Am. Hist. R. **4**: 129.
— Pioneer Women of. (M. S. Pepper) Chaut. **32**: 130.
— Premiers of, since 1867. (G. Stewart) Canad. M. **8**: 289.
— Provincial Elections. Pub. Opin. **22**: 616.
Queen, The; a poem. (O. Seaman) Ecl. M. **136**: 486.
Queen Elma. (A. Eyre) Chamb. J. **75**: 481-550.
Queen, The, in her Counting-house. (Henry W. Lucy) Chamb. J. **77**: 817.

Queen of the Heap. (V. L. Whitechurch) Good Words, **42**: 455.
Queen of Heaven, A Symbolic Figure of. (T. F. Wright) Bib. World, **17**: 447.
Queen of Penwinnoc, The. (C. K. Burrow) Temp. Bar, **123**: 136. Same art. Liv. Age, **230**: 366.
Queen of Quelparte, The. (A. B. Hulbert) Chaut. **33**: 370, 461, 563.
Queen of Spades; a tale. (H. Seymour) Belgra. **97**: 387.
Queen, The, vs. Billy; a story. (Lloyd Osbourne) Scrib. M. **23**: 69.
Queen's English, The. (W. E. Hodgson) Acad. **52**: 499.
Queen's Favor, A; a story. (Hamilton Drummond) Eng. Illust. **21**: 529.
Queen's Ferry, The. (G. Law) Jurid. R. **12**: 268.
Queen's Flight. (E. Gore-Booth) Longm. **35**: 350.
Queen's Harper, The; a story. (Nora Hopper) Gent. M. n. s. **59**: 387.
Queen's Jewels, The; a story. (C. E. C. Weigall) Temp. Bar, **15**: 242.
Queen's Own Guides. Blackw. **161**: 625. Same art. Ecl. M. **129**: 457.
Queen's Twin. (S. O. Jewett) Atlan. **83**: 235. Same art. Cornh. **79**: 145. Same art. Outl. **67**: 455.
Queens as Sovereigns. Spec. **81**: 331.
— Asiatic. Spec. **81**: 645.
— Charities of. (M. A. Belloc) Sund. M. **30**: 649.
— of Europe, Personal Aspects of. With portraits. (G. E. Kenton) Nat'l M. (Bost.) **6**: 164.
Queensland, A Flower-hunter in. Lond. Q. **90**: 247.
— Industrial Expansion in. (T. M. Donovan) Westm. **147**: 254.
Queenslander; how he rides and shoots. (F. Campbell) Temp. Bar, **119**: 433.
Quentin Harcourt, Q. C.: his love story. (Mrs. J. H. Needell) Chamb. J. **77**: 145-202.
Quero, Cruise of the. (R. S. Rantoul) Cent. **36**: 714.
Quest after Music; a poem. (M. B. Hinton) Atlan. **86**: 450.
Quest of "Burotu," The. Chamb. J. **78**: 600.
Quest of Summer, The; a poem. (R. Burton) Poet-Lore, **9**: 1.
Quests; poem. (M. Vandegrift) Atlan. **88**: 281.
Question of Courage, A; a story. (W. McLennan) Harper, **97**: 190.
Question of Habit, A. (W. W. Jacobs) Strand, **17**: 381.
Question of Happiness. (G. M. Gallaher) Cent. **35**: 105.
Question of Precedence; a story. (H. H. Bennett) Temp. Bar, **116**: 76. Same art. Lippinc. **63**: 520.
Question of Religion, A; a story. (G. K. Turner) McClure, **13**: 150.
Quick, Robert Herbert, an Educational Reformer. (W. L. Bevan) Sewanee, **8**: 147.
— An Interpretation. (C. F. Thwing) Educa. R. **19**: 1.
— Storr's Life and Remains of. Educa. **20**: 118. — (A. E. Bernays) School R. **7**: 424.
Quick and the Dead, The; a poem. (A. Lamont) Argosy, **65**: 115.
Quicke, Major F. C. Geog. J. **18**: 628.
Quicken Tree of Dubhros; a folk-tale. (L. L. Duncan) Folk-Lore, **7**: 321.
Quiet, The; a poem. (J. P. Peabody) Atlan. **86**: 422.
Quiet, Value of. Spec. **80**: 723.
Quilt, A Remarkable. Illus. Strand, **18**: 233.
Quilter, W. Cuthbert, Collection of. (F. G. Stephens) M. of Art, **20**: 121-316. **21**: 64, 128.
Quimper, France. Cath. World, **72**: 751.
Quin Abbey. (D. C. Parkinson) Reliquary, **37**: 129.
Quinahtsk's Quits, The; a tale. (F. Leather) Outing, **36**: 589.

Rani, Concerning an Imprisoned. (C. Sorabji) 19th Cent. 50: 623.

Rank, Magic of. Spec. 87: 554.

Ranke, Leopold von. (E. G. Bourne) Sewanee, 4: 385.

Ransome, Stafford. Japan in Transition. (A. Kinnosuké) Critic, 36: 454.

Ranunculus Repens, Variations of Parts in. 2d Paper. (J. H. Pledge) Nat. Sci. 12: 179.

Raoult, François Marie. (W. Ramsay) Nature, 64: 17.
— (H. C. Jones) Science, n. s. 13: 881.

Raousset-Boulbon, Gaston de. (D. Sampson) Gent. M. n. s. 64: 292.

Rapagnetta. See Annunzio, Gabriele d', pseud.

Rape of the Baron's Wine; a poem. (Dora S. Shorter) Pall Mall M. 13: 221.

Raphael, with portrait and bibliography. Mast. in Art, 1: Pt. 12.
— Madonna di Sant' Antonio. (Julia Cartwright) Art J. 53: 284.
— Palace at Rome. Am. Arch. 62: 19.

Raphael, Mother Francis, with portrait. (L. W. Reilly) Cath. World, 65: 366.

Raphael, Mrs. Mary F. (F. Rinder) Art J. 51: 257.

Rapid Transit in Boston. Ann. Am. Acad. Pol. Sci. 11: 278.
— in New York City. Ann. Am. Acad. Pol. Sci. 11: 274.

Rapid Transit Subways in Metropolitan Cities. Munic. Aff. 4: 458.

Rappahannock, Song of ; a battle experience. (I. Seymour) McClure, 8: 314.

Rapping and Talking Table. Ecl. M. 129: 864.

Rare Books, Notes of. (E. D. North) Bk. Buyer, 21: 212.

Rascal as Hero. (E. K. Dunton) Atlan. 86: 135.

Rash Experiment, A ; a story. (W. W. Jacobs) Idler, 11: 102.

Rat, Mental Processes of the. (W. S. Small) Am. J. Psychol. 11: 133. 12: 206.
— Psychic Development of the Young White. (W. S. Small) Am. J. Psychol. 11: 80.

Rat of Funafuti, The. Chamb. J. 76: 395.

Rats, A War on. Spec. 86: 563.

Rats of Sacramento, The. (W. K. McGraw) Overland, n. s. 36: 235.

Ratification and the Rights of Third Parties. (C. H. Tuttle) Am. Law R. 35: 864.

Ration, Ideal, for an Army in the Tropics. (C. A. Woodruff) J. Mil. Serv. Inst. 27: 1.
— Meat, in the Tropics. (P. R. Egan) J. Mil. Serv. Inst. 29: 24.
— United States Army and its Adaptability to Tropical Climates. (L. L. Seaman) J. Mil. Serv. Inst. 24: 375.

Rations in the Tropics. (L. L. Seaman) J. Mil. Serv. Inst. 28: 83.

Rationalism in Religion. (G. Tyrrell) Month, 93: 1.

Ratisbonne, Louis. (W. Roberts) Ath '00, 2: 443.

Rattlesnakes. Daring the Rattler in his Den. Illus. (S. W. Matteson) Cosmopol. 26: 665.
— Pre-Cambrian. (J. F. Kemp) Science, n. s. 12: 81.

Rattlesnake Oil. Chamb. J. 75: 159.

Raven of Flamboro', The. (Alick Munro) Chamb. J. 76: 603.

Raven, Strange Habit of the. (G. Gordon) Chamb. J. 78: 128.

Raven-Hill, L., Artist. (A. Lawrence) Idler, 15: 525.
— Bk. Buyer, 14: 353.

Ravenna. (H. Spender) Fortn. 76: 615. Same art. Liv. Age, 231: 580. — (H. Mereu) Am. Arch. 74: 35.
— Theodoric's Palace at. (Alfred Melani) Am. Arch. 66: 3.

Ravens, The ; a poem. (J. R. Taylor) Atlan. 88: 138.

Rawlinson, Sir Henry C., and Cuneiform Inscriptions. Acad. 53: 411.

Rawlinson, Sir Henry C., Rawlinson's Life of. Ath. 98, 1: 333. —(L. Griffin) Sat. R. 85: 433. — (J. P. Peters) Nation, 67: 15. — (P. F. Bicknell) Dial (Ch.) 25: 259.

Rawlinson MSS. in the Bodleian Library. (N. D. Davis) Nation, 65: 372, 394.

Rawson, William Rawson. Geog. J. 15: 74.

Ray, Anne. (F. D. How) Sund. M. 30: 186.

Ray's Daughter. (C. Vring) Lippinc. 65: 803.

Ray's Recruit. (C. King) Lippinc. 59: 435.

Rayleigh, J. W. S., Scientific Work of. (O. Lodge) National, 32: 89.

Raymond, Daniel ; An Early Chapter in the History of Economic Theory in the United States. (C. P. Neill) J. H. Univ. Stud. 15: 217.

Raynham, Mass. First Book of Records. N. E. Reg. 53: 59. 54: 15. 55: 41.
— Marriages and Baptisms in. (F. E. Blake) N. E. Reg. 51: 290, 315, 437.

Raynham, Norfolk, Eng., Records, Material from. (C. H. Townshend) N. E. Reg. 52: 318.

Reading and Composition, How to teach, Burns on. (B. F. Armitage) School R. 9: 550.
— and Talking. How naturally learned. (Harriet Iredell) Educa. 19: 233.
— and Thinking. (F. W. Osborn) Educa. 17: 523.
— and Writing, Should Children under Ten learn? (G. T. W. Patrick) Pop. Sci. Mo. 54: 382.
— by Sample. (H. S. Pancoast) Educa. R. 18: 30.
— Children's. (C. Welsh) Dial (Ch.) 31: 427.
— — Supplementary. (May Lowe) Educa. 22: 45.
— Children's Tastes in. (C. Vostrovsky) Pedagog. Sem. 6: 523.
— Do Readers read ? (A. E. Bostwick) Critic, 39: 67.
— for Boys and Girls. (E. T. Tomlinson) Atlan. 86: 693.
— for Children. (J. C. Dana) Lib. J. 22: 187.
— — Good, Importance of. (W. C. Lane) N. Church R. 4: 424.
— for the Young. (H. V. Weisse) Contemp. 79: 829. Same art. Liv. Age, 230: 178.
— — Best. (G. E. Upton) Pub. Lib. 6: 88.
— Good, To interest Children in. (A. B. Hervey) Chaut. 30: 367.
— How to not read. (G. Burgess) Critic, 36: 33.
— How to read Aloud, Clark on. (A. F. Nightingale) School R. 5: 404.
— in Elementary Schools, Interest of Children in. (C. Wissler) Pedagog. Sem. 5: 523.
— in the Racine High School. (C. H. Thurber) School R. 5: 36.
— A Lady's, Eighty Years ago. (R. H. Sessions) New Eng. M. n. s. 21: 145.
— Manual for Teachers, Laing's. (B. F. Armitage) School R. 9: 550.
— of a Community, Librarian's Influence on. (A. L. Peck) Lib. J. 22: 77.
— Over-praise of. Acad. 61: 635.
— Physiology and Psychology of. (E. B. Huey) Am. J. Psychol. 9: 575. 11: 283. 12: 292.
— Psychology of. (R. Dodge) Psychol. R. 8: 596.
— Public, Art of. (S. C. LeMoyne ; C. Shipman) Critic, 39: 266.
— The Question of. (B. Winchester) Sewanee, 8: 457.
— Visual. (W. B. Secor) Am. J. Psychol. 11: 225.
— What the People read. Acad. 52: 283-577. 53: 59-689. 54: 91-156.
— with a Purpose. (A. Bierbower) Chaut. 31: 146.
— "without Tears." (E. K. Robinson) Good Words, 40: 235.

Reading of Life, A ; a poem. (G. Meredith) Monthly R. 2, no. 3: 155. Same art. Critic, 38: 213.

Reform Bill, An Ideal; by John Bull, jr. Macmil. 83: 222.

Reform Club's Feast of Unreason. (C. A. Towne) Arena, 18: 24.

Reform Party in U. S. Politics; unite or perish. (W. D. P. Bliss) Arena, 22: 78.

Reformation, Counter-. (J. H. Dubbs) Ref. Q. 44: 298.

— French, and the French People in the 16th Century. (H. Hauser) Am. Hist. R. 4: 217.

— in England, The Beginnings of. Church Q. 48: 406.

— — Gasquet on. Church Q. 50: 405. — (W. H. Kent) Dub. R. 126: 121 — (E. E. Emerton) Nation, 70: 382.

— — Sidelights of. (D. Baxter) Month, 90: 635.

— in a London Parish. (J. V. Kitto) Ath. '00, 2: 120.

— Modern Lights on the. (J. Lindsay) Bib. Sac. 55: 281.

— Scottish, Papers of. (A. Lang) Fortn. 74: 217.

— — Story of. (M. Barrett) Am. Cath. Q. 25: 584.

— Some Fruits of the. (A. W. Kennedy) Chaut. 29: 369, 429, 533.

— Walker's History of. (C. A. Scott) Crit. R. 11: 202.

Reformation of Lord Cecil; a story. (J. G. Menard) Nat'l M. (Bost.) 10: 370.

Reformation of Maurice Galvin; a story. (L. Macnamara) Pall Mall M. 16: 222.

Reformation of Uncle Billy. (E. P. Butler) Cent. 35: 538.

Reformation Period, Pictures of the. (J. M. Stone) Dub. R. 128: 46.

Reformatories, Catholic. (J. J. Delaney) Char. R. 6: 441.

— Juvenile, Discipline and Management of. Char. R. 9: 436.

— — Essential Work of. (F. H. Niebecker) Char. R. 9: 450.

— — Methods of Discipline in. (S. Smith) Indep. 51: 2561, 2612.

Reformatory and Industrial Schools. (Lord Monkswell) Fortn. 67: 229.

— An Open-air. (E. Sellers) National, 33: 980.

Reformed Church in America, Synod of. (J. B. Drury; J. I. Good) Presb. & Ref. R. 8: 745. 9: 711. 10: 658. 12: 688.

— 1747–92. (J. I. Good) Presb. & Ref. R. 8: 609.

— — Sesqui-centennial Celebration of. Ref. Q. 44: 531.

— Philosophy in the Educational System of. (J. S. Stahr) Ref. Church R. 45: 88.

— Relation of, to the New Theology. (J. C. Bowman) Ref. Q. 44: 141.

Reformed Church in South Africa. (J. I. Marais) Presb. & Ref. R. 11: 608.

Reformed Churches, Alliance of. (W. H. Roberts) Presb. & Ref. R. 11: 137.

Reformed Church Review. (W. Rupp) Ref. Q. 44: 1.

Reformed Presbyterians, Political Dissent of. (J. M. Foster) Outl. 66: 1008.

Reformer, Confessions of a. Indep. 53: 1963.

Reformers, Asiatic, Three Great. (W. H. Rattigan) Lond. Q. 92: 291.

— Eccentricities of. (T. W. Higginson) Outl. 62: 510.

— Futilities of. (J. D. Miller) Arena, 26: 481.

— Latitude and Longitude among. (T. Roosevelt) Cent. 38: 211.

Reforms, Doorway of. (E. Pomeroy) Arena, 17: 711.

Refraction, Effect of, on Measures of Double Stars. (E. Doolittle) Pop. Astron. 5: 143.

— within Telescope Tube. (J. Renton) Nature, 63: 334.

Refrain, A; a poem. (M. A. Curtois) Gent. M. n. s. 66: 603.

Refreshments at Entertainments. Sat. R. 90: 43.

Refrigerating; Linde's Method. (J. A. Ewing) J. Soc. Arts, 46: 375.

Refrigerating Methods, Modern. (E. H. G. Brewster) Cassier, 13: 168.

Refrigerating Plants, Small. (W. C. Kerr) Cassier, 11: 171.

Refrigeration. (Albert Siebert) Am. Arch. 56: 28.

— Principles of. (G. Richmond) Cassier, 17: 411.

Refunding Law in Operation. (C. A. Conant) R. of Rs. (N. Y.) 21: 711.

Refuse, Electric Light from, in Shoreditch. (N. W. Perry) Cassier, 13: 99.

— of New York City. (E. B. Baker) Munsey, 23: 81.

Refuse Disposal in Great Britain, Town. (W. F. Goodrich) Cassier, 21: 99.

Regalia of England. (C. Davenport) J. Soc. Arts, 46: 349.

Regeneration and Justification in Lutheran Theology. (F. H. Knubel) Luth. Q. 37: 175.

Regeneration and Liability to Injury. (T. H. Morgan) Science, n. s. 14: 235.

— in the Egg. (T. H. Morgan) Am. Natural. 35: 949.

— Weismann on. (J. A. Thompson) Nature, 60: 242.

Regent's Park Zoo, London. (F. E. Beddard) Pall Mall M. 24: 159.

Regia, The, the Atrium Vestræ. Archæol. 50: 227.

Regicide in the 19th Century. (S. B. Chester) Gent. M. n. s. 67: 382.

Regiment, The Making of a. (I. Seymour) McClure, 9: 1031.

Regimental Colors in Canada. (T. E. Champion) Canad. M. 9: 223.

Regimental Pets. (E. W. Low) Eng. Illust. 18: 399.

Regiments, Three Famous Fighting. (George Douglas) Eng. Illust. 22: 165.

Registration Reform and Women's Suffrage. Westm. 156: 68.

Regnault's Caloric, Concerning. (G. P. Starkweather) Am. J. Sci. 157: 13.

Regnier, Henri de. Critic, 36: 102. — With portrait. Harv. Grad. M. 8: 372. — (Jane G. Cooke) Bookman, 11: 136.

Reichstag, A Session of the. (R. Nordhausen) Liv. Age, 216: 563.

Reid, Eadie, an English Church Artist. (F. J. Crowest) Sund. M. 29: 693.

Reid, Captain Mayne. Acad. 59: 643.

Reid, Captain Samuel Chester. (C. T. Brady) McClure, 15: 186.

Reigate, England. (F. G. Kitton) Art J. 50: 238.

Reign of Terror, A Royalist Spy during. (J. H. Clapham) Eng. Hist. R. 12: 67.

Reigning, Art of. Spec. 79: 76.

Reigns, Longest, in the World. Eng. Illust. 17: 401.

Reimann, Albert, Artist in Metal. M. of Art, 26: 65.

Reinagle, Philip. (G. D. Leslie and F. A. Eaton) Art J. 50: 140.

Reincarnation not taught by Swedenborg. N. Church R. 4: 294.

Reincarnation of Smith. (B. Harte) New Eng. M. n. s. 25: 17.

Reincarnations of a Prize Novel, The; a story. (F. M. Bicknell) Nat'l M. (Bost.) 8: 424.

Reindeer for Klondike. Spec. 80: 113.

— of the Jotanheim. (H. Sears) Harper, 96: 99.

Reinhard, Mme. Reminiscences. (A. Laugel) Nation, 72: 311, 354.

Reinicke, René, with portrait. (J. B. Carrington) Bk. Buyer, 15: 673.

Réjane, Madame, Portrait of, as Mme. Sans-Gêne. Theatre, **39**: 5.

Rejected Titian, A. (R. Herrick) Scrib. M. **22**: 29.

Rejuvenation of the Tenth Man; a story. (F. Furbush) Nat'l M. (Bost.) **10**: 55.

Relatives, Logic of. (C. S. Peirce) Monist, **7**: 161.

Relaxation, The Gospel of. (Wm. James) Scrib. M. **25**: 499.

Release of Benjamin Cudd, The; a prison story. (T. Hopkins) McClure, **15**: 116.

Relics; a poem. (G. B. Stuart) Argosy, **63**: 177.

Relics of Celebrities, Value of. (H. Macfarlane) Cornh. **81**: 367.

Relief, Material, Uses and Limitations of. (F. Tucker) Char. R. **10**: 249.

Relief Funds, War. (C. G. Lang) 19th Cent. **47**: 121.

Relief Sculpture, Early Christian, Symmetry in. (C. L. Meader) Am. J. Archæol. 2d s. **4**: 126.

Religio Laici. (H. C. Beeching) Monthly R. **1**, no. 2: 83.

Religio Peccatoris. Month, **89**: 245.

Religion, Abiding Realities of. (J. H. Barrows) Bib. Sac. **56**: 543.

— Advances of, in the Present Age. (W. Goddard) N. Church R. **8**: 547.

— Ancestor-worship the Origin of. (G. McDermot) Cath. World. **66**: 20.

— and Art. (W. Holman Hunt) Contemp. **71**: 41. Same art. Liv. Age, **212**: 440.

— and Honesty. Nation, **72**: 209.

— and the Larger Universe. (J. T. Bixby) New World, **9**: 285.

— and Magic, Primitive. (F. Legge) Scot. R. **29**: 226.

— and Modern Culture. (A. Sabatier) New World, **8**: 91.

— and Morality, Relation between Early. (E. Buckley) Internat. Mo. **1**: 577.

— and Mythology, Egyptian and Babylonian. (F. R. Fowke) Nature, **61**: 437.

— and National Success, Relation between. Spec. **81**: 590.

— and Philosophy, Modern diluted. Sat. R. **88**: 95.

— and Politics. (J. W. Appel) Ref. Ch. R. **48**: 48.

— and Science at the Dawn of the 20th Century. (W. H. Mallock) Fortn. **76**: 395–812.

— — Prof. Fiske and the New Thought. (R. O. Mason) Arena, **25**: 365.

— and Theology. (A. Burnell) Westm. **155**: 329.

— Anthropology and the Evolution of. (W. W. Peyton) Contemp. **80**: 213, 435.

— as a Personal Relation. (H. C. King) Bib. Sac. **57**: 553.

— As to the Reality of. (John Fiske) Liv. Age, **221**: 662.

— Authority in. (H. C. Minton) Presb. & Ref. R. **11**: 201. — (R. E. Day) Cath. World, **72**: 75.

— — and Protestants. (F. W. Grey) Am. Cath. Q. **22**: 141.

— becoming Broader with Time. N. Church R. **4**: 271.

— Brinton on the Origin of. (I. W. Howerth) Monist, **10**: 293.

— Christian Philosophy of. Lond. Q. **88**: 108.

— Comparative, Practical Value of the Science of. (M. M. Snell) Bib. World, **13**: 88.

— Conservatism in. (S. M. Woodbridge) Presb. & Ref. R. **8**: 702.

— The Development of. Church Q. **45**: 110.

— Doctrine of Final Causes. (F. Sewall) N. Church R. **8**: 560.

— The Essential in. (E. Ritchie) Philos. R. **10**: 1.

— Essential Nature of. (L. F. Ward) Int. J. Ethics, **8**: 169.

— Ethics and Relation of. (W. G. Everett) Internat. J. Ethics, **10**: 479.

Religion, Evolution of. (J. W. Powell) Monist, **8**: 183.

— The Family and the Propagation of. (G. B. Stevens) Ref. Ch. R. **48**: 363.

— History of, F. B. Jevons on. Church Q. **44**: 73.

— How we Abuse. (J. McSorley) Cath. World, **70**: 81.

— Impulses and Ends of. (J. H. Leuba) Bib. Sac. **58**: 751.

— in Fiction. Spec. **86**: 453.

— in Germany, The Status of. (R. Eucken) Forum, **32**: 387.

— in Greek Literature. (J. Iverach) Lond. Q. **93**: 85.

— — Campbell on. (B. F. Wheeler) Philos. R. **8**: 622.

— in the Schools in the Philippines. Educa. **21**: 374.

— Is it Declining? (J. Whitehead) N. Church R. **8**: 419.

— Is it a Feeling of Dependence? (P. Carus) Open Court, **13**: 564.

— Jevons's Introduction to History of. (W. B. Greene, jr.) Presb. & Ref. R. **9**: 136.

— Lang on the Making of. (B. B. Warfield) Presb. & Ref. R. **9**: 744. — Ed. R. **188**: 311. — (E. Clodd) Acad. **53**: 651. — (J. Iverach) Crit. R. **8**: 389. — Nation, **67**: 74. — Spec. **81**: 86. — Ath. '98, **1**: 782. — (G. Tyrrell) Month, **92**: 225, 347.

— Liberal Congress of. R. of Rs. (N. Y.) **18**: 434.

— Magic and, Lang on. Ed. R. **194**: 343.

— Methods of Studying. (G. A. Coe) Meth. R. **61**: 532.

— of Childhood. (J. A. Story) Meth. R. **60**: 524.

— of Low Savages. (A. Lang) Ath. '01, **2**: 221.

— of our Ancestors. (P. Carus) Open Court, **11**: 177.

— of Primitive Peoples, Brinton's. (C. M. Tyler) Am. Hist. R. **3**: 335.

— of Science. (J. Odgers) Open Court, **11**: 671.

— of the Spirit, Society of the [led by Prof. E. H. Smith]. (E. H. Crosby) Arena, **20**: 511.

— Personal, A Study in the Dynamics of. (G. A. Coe) Psychol. R. **6**: 484.

— Philosophy of. (F. Aveling) Dub. R. **129**: 281.

— — and Judaism. (R. M. Wenley) Jew. Q. **10**: 18.

— — and the Endowment of Natural Theology. (R. M. Wenley) Monist, **12**: 21.

— — in England and America, Caldecott on. (W. Johnston) Crit. R. **11**: 306.

— — Otto Pfleiderer on. (A. M. Fairbairn) Crit. R. **7**: 131.

— — Recent Work in. (C. H. Toy) Internat. Mo. **1**: 217.

— — Sabatier's. (W. B. Greene, jr.) Presb. & Ref. R. **10**: 144. — Outl. **60**: 533.

— — Herbert Spencer's. (E. S. Carr) Bib. Sac. **54**: 232.

— — Theistic, Lindsay on. Ath. '97, **2**: 666. — (H. C. Minton) Presb. & Ref. R. **9**: 129.

— Practical; reply to L. Irwell. (C. G. Henderson) Westm. **151**: 93.

— Pre-animistic. (R. R. Marett; A. Lang) Folk-Lore, **11**: 162.

— Present-day, and Philosophy. (J. S. Banks) Lond. Q. **91**: 235.

— Psychological Study of. (J. H. Leuba) Monist, **11**: 195.

— Questionings from the Pews concerning. (B. F. Burnham) Arena, **19**: 68.

— Recent Books on, 1898. (J. Bascom) Dial (Ch.) **24**: 261. **25**: 46.

— the Reconciler of Thought and Action. Sat. R. **88**: 352.

— Reconstruction in. (E. G. Murphy) Outl. **67**: 682.

— Science of. (F. B. Jevons) Internat. Mo. **3**: 464, 550. — (F. Max Müller) Acad. **55**: 335. Same art. Liv. Age, **219**: 909.

Rembrandt, Genius of, with portrait. Cath. World, 74: 304.
— The Painter at the Clinic. (W. C. Larned) Liv. Age, 220: 329.
— Prints and Drawings. Sat. R. 87: 299, 363.
— Work of. Sat. R. 87: 43.
Rembrandt, The; a story. (E. Wharton) Cosmopol. 29: 429.
Re-meeting, The. (R. V. Risley) Lippinc. 66: 476.
Remenyi, Edouard, Last Appearance in Boston. (J. L. Mathews) Music, 14: 284.
Remey, Rear-Admiral George Collier. Outl. 65: 835.
Reminiscences, Legal. (L. E. Chittenden) Green Bag, 9: 7.
— The Popularity of. Acad. 58: 451. Same art. Liv. Age, 225: 846.
Reminiscences of "Big Ravine." (W. K. McGrew) Overland, n. s. 36: 28.
Reminiscences of Early Days, Some. (G. Selwyn) Overland, n. s. 37: 842.
Reminiscences of a Young French Officer. (M. O'Rell) No. Am. 166: 535.
Reminiscent Honeymoon, A. (K. G. Wells) New Eng. M. n. s. 18: 413.
Remittance Man, The. (D. W. Duthie) 19th Cent. 46: 827.
Remsen, Ira. Outl. 68: 817.
Renaissance, The. (G. H. Dryer) Meth. R. 58: 614.
— Aspects of. (J. M. Stone) Month, 89: 65.
— French. (B. W. Wells) Sewanee, 4: 153.
— An Idyll of the. (M. D. Walsh) Archit. R. 10: 113.
— Italian. (H. Mereu) Am. Arch. 69: 59, 67.
— — Art of. (G. B. Rose) Sewanee, 6: 129.
— The Later, Hannay's. (F. E. Shelling) Citizen, 4: 85.
— Philosophy of. (W. H. Kent) Dub. R. 122: 372
Renan, Ary. (E. F. S. Dilke) Ath. '00, 2: 194.
Renan, Ernest. (J. F. Kelly) New R. 17: 525.
— and Duc d'Aumale; a dialogue. (C. Bastide) New R. 17: 53.
— and Berthelot, Correspondence of. Sat. R. 85: 496. — (A. Laugel) Nation, 66: 319, 340.
— and Newman. (W. Barry) National, 29: 557.
— and the Soul of the Celt. (L. Marillier) Internat. Mo. 4: 577.
— Life of, Darmesteter's. Ath. '97, 2: 663. — (A. Laugel) Nation, 67: 109, 117, 183. — (C. M. Bakewell) New World, 7: 190.
— Tragedy of Life of. (C. M. Bakewell) New World, 6: 664.
Renduel, Eugene; an honest publisher. (C. E. Meetkerke) Gent. M. n. s. 62: 368.
Renegade, The; a story. (C. J. Cutcliffe Hyne) Pall Mall M. 16: 301.
Renegade, A; a story. (M. Wolfenstein) Outl. 66: 34.
Renegade, A. (Mrs. Isabel Smith) Chamb. J. 78: 46.
Renegade Rebel, A. (W. McL. Raine) New Eng. M. n. s. 25: 193.
Renegado, The. (G. G. Farquhar) Chamb. J. 74: 478.
Rennes. Sat. R. 88: 224.
Renouard, Paul, Draughtsman. (G. Mourey) Studio (Internat.) 10: 165.
Renouf, Sir P. Le P. Ath. '97, 2: 562.
Rensselaerwyck, Relics of. (Cuyler Reynolds) Cosmopol. 24: 136.
Rent, Concept of Price-determining. (A. M. Hyde) J. Pol. Econ. 6: 368.
— Curiosities of. Green Bag, 12: 404.
— Ground-, in relation to Income Tax. (E. C. Fitzwilliam) Westm. 152: 152.
— Interests, and Profit. (A. South) Westm. 147: 192. Same art. Ecl. M. 128: 532.

Rent, Passing of the Old Doctrine of. (F. A. Fetter) Q. J. Econ. 15: 418.
— Some Aspects of the Theory of. (R. P. Falkner) Ann. Am. Acad. Pol. Sci. 12: 98.
Rent Charges in Fee, Landowners' Liability to pay. (T. C. Williams) Law Q. 13: 288.
Rent Question in London. (G. B. Shaw) Sat. R. 88: 328.
— Liable to become a Political Question. Sat. R. 88: 126, 159.
Rented House, The; a story. (Alice French) Harper, 98: 630.
Repair Ships, Naval. (A. B. Willits) Cassier, 14: 427.
Repartees. Month, 93: 82.
Repeal, Reasons against. (J. Madge) Meth. R. 58: 387.
Repentance. (C. E. Hay) Luth. Q. 29: 334.
Repentance, A; a drama. (P. M. Craigie) Acad. 56: 329. — Critic, 35: 691.
Reporter, The, and Literature. (N. Hapgood) Bookman, 5: 119.
— Police. (V. Thompson) Lippinc. 62: 283.
Reporters, Anecdotes of. (M. Macdonagh) Cornh. 80: 505.
— Recollections of. (J. L. Sprogle) Lippinc. 63: 136.
Reporting, Society. (J. M. Coard) Writer, 10: 97.
Reports, Old, Romance of. (F. J. Hagan) Green Bag, 10: 98.
Repoussé Metal Work. (N. Dawson) Studio (Lond.) 2: 195.
— Methods of Treating. (F. Miller) Art J. 50: 79.
Representation, Delusion of. Sat. R. 87: 230.
— in State Legislatures. (G. H. Haynes) Ann. Am. Acad. Pol. Sci. 15: 204, 405. 16: 93, 243.
— Origin of Political. (E. Jenks) Contemp. 74: 882.
— Proportional, in Belgium. (J. R. Commons) R. of Rs. (N. Y.) 21: 583. — (E. Mahaim) Ann. Am. Acad. Pol. Sci. 15: 381.
Representative of Bernadotte; a story. (C. J. C. Hyne) Pall Mall M. 11: 269.
Representative Government, Weakest Point of. Spec. 80: 567. — Ecl. M. 131: 142, 325.
Representative Principle in Danger. Spec. 79: 887.
Representative Systems; rotten boroughs of Old and New England. (E. Porritt) Yale R. 7: 449.
Representatives, Federal, First Apportionment of, in U.S. (E. J. James) Ann. Am. Acad. Pol. Sci. 9: 1.
Reprisal, The; a story. (H. W. McVickar) Harper, 97: 925.
Reprisals; a story. (G. Montbard) Eng. Illust. 20: 383.
Reproduction, Asexual, in Hymenopterous Insects. (P. Marchal) Nat. Sci. 12: 316.
— in Plants, Physiology of. (H. M. Ward) Sci. Prog. n. s. 1: 241.
— Is there any Distinction between Sexual and Asexual? (W. C. Curtis) Science, n. s. 12: 940.
Reproductive or Genetic Selection. (Karl Pearson) Science, n. s. 9: 283.
Reptiles, New Classification of, Fürbringer on. (G. A. Boulenger) Nature, 63: 462.
— Significance of Certain Changes in the Temporal Region of the Primitive. (E. C. Case) Am. Natural. 32: 69.
Republic, Future of the. Spec. 83: 741.
— in Name only. Sat. R. 88: 94.
— in War Time. (J. B. Walker) Cosmopol. 25: 463.
Republican National Committee, How it works for Votes. R. of Rs. (N. Y.) 22: 549.
Republican National Convention, First. (G. W. Julian) Am. Hist. R. 4: 313.
— 1900. Outl. 65: 472. — (F. A. Munsey) Munsey, 23: 671.
— — from Opposite Points of View. Outl. 65: 480.
Republican Party and Party Government in the U. S. (G. F. Hoar) Internat. Mo. 2: 418.

Republican Party, Early Years of. (H. A. Cushing) Bookman, 12: 59.

— Origin of. (C. M. Harvey) Chaut. 25: 643.

Republican Platform, 1900; full text. Outl. 65: 491.

Republican Shorter Catechism, A. (R. Ogden) Nation, 73: 84.

Republicanism; does Mistrust give Strength to Authority? (Count de Fronsac) Canad. M. 8: 337.

Republics, Mistaken Sympathy with. (T. G. Shearman) No. Am. 170: 480.

— Monarchies and. (F. M. Bird) Lippinc. 62: 370.

— Saintsbury's Thoughts on. (Elizabeth C. Birney) Citizen, 3: 7.

Reputation, A; a story. (J. B.) Macmil. 77: 294. Same art. Liv. Age, 217: 58.

Reputations, Dead. Chamb. J. 77: 161.

Requiem of the Drums; a story. Cosmopol. 30: 401.

Requital. (M. Diver) Temp. Bar, 124: 485.

Re-reading of Books. (John Burroughs) Cent. 33: 146.

Resch, D. A. Die Sprüche Jesu. Eine kritische Bearbeitung von J. H. Ropes. (J. T. Marshall) Crit. R. 8: 56.

Rescue, The. (A. D. Sedgwick) Cent. 41: 296.

Rescue, The; a story. (E. Wood) Harper, 103: 94.

Rescue, Story of a. (L. H. Carpenter) J. Mil. Serv. Inst. 17: 267.

Research, French and English Treatment of. (E. Priestley) 19th Cent. 42: 113. Same art. Ecl. M. 129: 625.

Research Fellowships. (A. Gray) Nature, 58: 600.

Resemblance; a poem. (R. G. A. S. Prudhomme) Argosy, 65: 693.

Reservations, Public, Mass. Trustees of. (C. S. Sargent) Garden & F. 10: 369.

Reserves, Efficiency of. Bank. M. (Lond.) 71: 404.

Reservoirs, Storage, Schuyler on. Nature, 64: 154.

Resignation; a sonnet. (P. McArthur) Atlan. 87: 865.

Resins, Recent Advances in Study of. (H. Trimble) J. Frankl. Inst. 143: 178.

Resorcinol, Heat of Solution of, in Ethyl Alcohol. (C. L. Speyers and C. R. Rosell) Am. J. Sci. 160: 449.

Respectable Sins. (J. Watson) Sund. M. 30: 235-516.

"Respectfully Jones;" a story. (C. Cotterell) Argosy, 65: 116.

Respice Finem; a poem. (L. Morris) Cosmopol. 24: 204.

Respiration, Forced, Influence of, on Psychical and Physical Activity. (G. M. Whipple) Am. J. Psychol. 9: 560.

— Normal and Intramolecular. (G. J. Peirce) Am. Natural. 35: 463.

Respiration Apparatus; How food is used in the body. (W. O. Atwater) Cent. 32: 246.

Responsibility, Law and. (T. W. Taylor, jr.) Philos. R. 7: 276.

— Necessity and. (A. Sutherland) No. Am. 168: 269.

Responsibility of Mr. Weatherstone, a story. (V. Sheard) Canad. M. 15: 44.

Restaurants, American, Characters seen in. (J. M. Chapple) Nat'l M. (Bost.) 7: 346.

Restigouche River, Reminiscences of. (E. J. Myers) Outing, 37: 24.

Restoration of Aunt Eliza, The; a story. (K. Silvester) Gent. M. n. s. 60: 521.

Restored to Life; a tale. (T. Shairp) Belgra. 92: 169.

Result of an Interview; a story. (M. Penrose) Argosy, 63: 492.

Result of Miss Knight's Temper; a story. (W. P. Ridge) Eng. Illust. 18: 361.

Resurgam; a poem. (A. B. Paine) Outing, 31: 22.

Resurrection, The. (W. W. Peyton) Contemp. 75: 123. Same art. Liv. Age, 220: 671.

— and the Ancient World. (J. V. Tracy) Cath. World, 69: 46.

Resurrection, Death and. (P. Carus) Open Court, 13: 495.

— of the Body. Spec. 81: 594. — (J. Watson) Expos. 9: 62.

— of the Body of Christ. (J. B. Keene) N. Church R. 6: 511.

Resurrection of Jonathan Slater; a tale. (E. S. Atkinson) Canad. M. 10: 490.

Resurrection of Lazarus; a poem. (A. Graf) Ecl. M. 137: 678.

Reszke, Edouard de, Operatic Singer, with portrait. Music, 15: 315.

Retainer, An Old. (H. A. Bryden) Sat. R. 83: 654.

Retene. (S. F. Peckham) J. Frankl. Inst. 151: 50.

Retinal Circulation, Mapping, by Projection. (R. M. Ogden) Am. J. Psychol. 12: 281.

Retinal Image, Experiment on Reinversion of. (H. C. Warren) Am. Natural. 31: 86.

— Projection of. (W. B. Pillsbury) Am. J. Psychol. 9: 56.

Retirement from Business, Early. (T. Cushman) Arena, 24: 145.

Retirement of Signor Lambert; a story. (A. C. Doyle) Cosmopol. 26: 173.

Retiring of Domsie, The; a story. (J. Watson) McClure, 8: 550.

Retouches; a reply. (H. T. Peck) Bookman, 9: 157.

Retribution, Divine, Doctrine of. (C. V. Anthony) Meth. R. 61: 105.

Retrievers. (Sir H. Smith) Blackw. 168: 204.

— and How to break Them. (H. Smith) Blackw. 161: 743.

Retrogression, Theory of. (G. A. Reid) Nat. Sci. 13: 396.

Retrospection; a poem. (A. Mackay) Argosy, 65: 685.

Return, The; a Christmas story. (Rene Bazin) Liv. Age, 219: 803.

Return of Dick Weemins; a story. (Frank Baum) Nat'l M. (Bost.) 6: 366.

Return of his Youth. (V. Wilmot) New Eng. M. n. s. 24: 546.

Return of Shakespeare to Stratford; a poem. (L. Vintras) Belgra. 98: 217.

Return to John Abney, The; a story. (M. B. Hardie) Eng. Illust. 20: 469.

Reuchlin, Johann. Quar. 188: 1.

Rev. Harry, The; a story. (C. Young) Belgra. 97: 364.

Reveille; a poem. (F. E. Coates) Bk. Buyer, 16: 300.

Reveille to the Breaking Morn. (W. A. Somerville) Chamb. J. 78: 369.

Reveillon d'Artistes. (H. Lafontaine) Music, 16: 568.

Revelation; an exposition. (W. Rauschenbusch) Bib. World, 10: 94.

— and Discovery. (C. E. St. John) New World, 7: 264.

— Divine. (H. King) Luth. Q. 31: 66.

— Divine Element in Scripture. (C. J. Grannan) Am. Cath. Q. 26: 353.

— or Discovery. (W. Rupp) Ref. Ch. R. 47: 384.

— Primitive. (J. H. Wilson) N. Church R. 6: 24.

— Principle of Adaptation in. (G. S. Rollins) Bib. World, 16: 259.

Revelations of Divine Love made to Mother Juliana, Anchoress of Norwich. (G. Tyrrell) Month, 95: 12, 250.

Revelstoke, Lord. Bank. M. (Lond.) 69: 719.

Revenge, Essence of. (E. Westermarck) Mind, 23: 289.

Revenge of the "Adolphus." (S. Crane) Strand, 18: 724.

Revenge of the Bear, The; a story. (H. A. Kennedy) Pall Mall M. 22: 383.

Revenge of the Four, The; a story. (J. Flynt and F. Walton) McClure, 16: 229. Same art. Idler, 19: 46.

Revenge of "Freckles"; a story. (Eden Phillpotts) Idler, 11: 560.

Revenue, National, Sources of. (N. Dingley) No. Am. 168: 297.

Revenue of the Crown, The; a story. (W. M. Browne) Scrib. M. 27: 344.

Revenue without Taxation. (R. Ewen) Westm. 153: 577.

Revenue-cutter Service. (H. D. Smith) Cent. 33: 573.

Revere, Paul, and his Engraving. (W. L. Andrews) Scrib. M. 30: 333.

Reverence, The Value of. (G. Hibbard) Conserv. R. 5: 264.

Reverie. (G. E. Partridge) Pedagog. Sem. 5: 445.

Reverie; a poem. (C. E. Meetkerke) Gent. M. n. s. 66: 621.

Reversions; a story. (J. Ayscough) Argosy, 70: 19, 154, 266.

Review, Wanted — A Retrospective. Atlan. 86: 428.

Reviewing, Twenty Years of. (G. Saintsbury) Blackw. 161: 21. Same art. Ecl. M. 128: 303.

Revision, The Malady of. Atlan. 85: 140.

Revivalist, Passing of the. (D. Utter) Arena, 21: 107.

Revolt of the Blackfoot, The; a story. (W. A. Fraser) McClure, 14: 88.

Revolt of a Hard-shell; a story. (M. Penrose) Temp. Bar, 113: 193.

Révolte, La; drama. (V. de l'I. Adam) Fortn. 68: 862.

Revolver Shooting, Practical. (W. Winans) Outing, 38: 37.

Revue des Deux Mondes. (M. T. Blanc) McClure, 9: 710.

Rey, Guido, Photographs by. Studio (Internat.) 15: 39.

Reykjavik to Gloucester. (J. M. Connolly) Scrib. M. 30: 216.

Reynolds, Arthur. Bank. M. (N. Y.) 56: 536.

Reynolds, Mrs. Belle, Major U. S. A. (C. S. Brown) Midland, 10: 106.

Reynolds. George M. Bank. M. (N. Y.) 54: 65.

Reynolds, Sir Joshua. (J. C. Van Dyke) Cent. 32: 815. — Munsey, 16: 448, 560. — With portrait and bibliography. Mast. in Art, 1: Pt. 7.

— and Kauffmann, Angelica; painting by Margaret Dicksee. (F. Gerard) Art J. 49: 82.

— Armstrong's Life of. (D. S. M.) Sat. R. 90: 788.

— "Contemplation." M. of Art, 22: 88.

— Defense of. (T. S. Moore) Monthly R. 3, no. 1: 120.

— London House. Am. Arch. 61: 86.

— Paintings at Longford Castle. (C. Phillips) Art J. 49: 363.

Reynolds-Stephens, W., with portrait. (M. H. Spielmann) M. of Art, 21: 71. — (A. L. Baldry) Studio (Internat.) 8: 75.

— "Launcelot and the Nestling." (A. L. Baldry) Art J. 53: 9.

Rhead, Louis, Posters of. (G. White) Studio (Lond.) 8: 156.

Rheinfelden, Germany, Electric Power at. (E. Rathenau) Cassier, 12: 98.

Rhetoric, Art of. (E. Manson) Westm. 148: 630.

— Constructive, Hale's. (R. W. Thomas) School R. 5: 402.

— in Secondary Schools. (L. May McLean) Educa. 18: 158.

— Science of Discourse, Tompkins's. (C. S. Doolittle) School R. 6: 548.

Rhine, Down the. (A. Birrell) Cent. 39: 206, 682, 819. — Old-time Travel on. Sat. R. 92: 234.

Rhine Country, The. (H. A. Guerber) Chaut. 26: 467.

Rhine-Elbe Canal; a feature in German politics. (J. H. Gore) R. of Rs. (N. Y.) 21: 457.

Rhine Valley, Notes on. (G. A. T. Middleton) Archit. R. 9: 325.

Rhinoceros Hunting in Africa. (H. A. Bryden) Eng. Illust. 20: 361.

Rhoades, John Harsen. Bank. M. (N. Y.) 58: 864.

Rhode Island and the Formation of the Union, Bates's. (J. H. Stiness) Am. Hist. R. 5: 146.

— Constitutional Imbroglio in. (D. MacG. Means) Nation, 69: 255.

— Libraries of. (H. R. Palmer) New Eng. M. n. s. 22: 478.

— Old Plantation Life in. (G. C. Mason) New Eng. M. n. s. 21: 735.

— Old Quaker Days in. (E. B. Chace) New Eng. M. n. s. 16: 655.

— Sunset Lands of the Narragansetts. New Eng. M. n. s. 20: 777.

Rhode Island Historical Society. (E. Fuller) New Eng. M. n. s. 23: 483.

Rhodes, Cecil. (E. S. Grogan) World's Work, 1: 367. — (C. D. Baynes) Fortn. 67: 632. — Monthly R. 1, no. 2: 21.

— a Character Sketch. (W. T. Stead) R. of Rs. (N. Y.) 20: 547.

— and the Privy Council. Spec. 79: 69.

— as a Personage. Spec. 78: 160.

— as a Pirate. (R. Ogden) Nation, 64: 198.

— Evidence of. Spec. 78: 366.

— Future of. (C. Radziwill) No. Am. 170: 857.

— Home of. (G. Ralling) Good Words, 40: 324.

— Political Future of. Sat. R. 84: 9.

— Political Life and Speeches of. Sat. R. 89: 749.

— Position and Policy of. (Imperialist) Fortn. 69: 805.

— Position of. Fortn. 67: 33.

— Responsibility of. (A British Officer) No. Am. 170: 348.

— Rhodes Redivivus. (E. Dicey) Fortn. 70: 605.

— Some Reputations in the Crucible of 1896. (W. T. Stead) R. of Rs. (N. Y.) 15: 56.

— Speeches. (E. Dicey) Fortn. 67: 467.

Rhodes, James Ford. Lit. W. (Bost.) 31: 109.

Rhodesia and Bechuanaland, Travels in. (C. E. Fripp) J. Soc. Arts, 45: 515.

— and its Government, Thomson's. Sat. R. 87: 116.

— and its Mines in 1898. (W. F. Wilkinson) J. Soc. Arts, 47: 209.

— and Northwards. (S. C. Norris) Macmil. 83: 272.

— Golden. (J. Y. F. Blake) National, 29: 839.

— Native. (J. Y. F. Blake) National, 30: 217.

— Second Thoughts on. (J. Y. F. Blake) National, 31: 118.

— Some Home Truths about. (W. E. Fairbridge) National, 29: 3.

— Travels and Researches in. (H. Schlichter) Geog. J. 13: 376.

— What to do with. (D. F. DuToit) New R. 16: 218.

Rhododendrons, Hardy. (T. D. Hatfield) Garden & F. 10: 237.

Rhodolite. (W. E. Hidden and J. H. Pratt) Am. J. Sci. 155: 294.

— Associated Minerals of. (W. E. Hidden and J. H. Pratt) Am. J. Sci. 156: 463.

Rhone, Valley of the. (C. W. Wood) Argosy, 63: 51-707. 64: 53-706. 66: 546, 655.

Rhopalocera, Neuration of. Illus. (A. Quail) Nat. Sci. 13: 396.

Rhubarb, the Rheum-foe. Chamb. J. 75: 316.

Rhyme. (F. Ritchie) Longm. 37: 114.

— Does it connect Ideas? Acad. 61: 389.

— Enquiry as to. (B. Matthews) Longm. 32: 449. Same art. Bookman, 8: 32.

— Genetic Study of. (C. R. Squire) Am. Psychol. 12: 493.

Rifles, Military, and Rifle Firing. J. Mil. Serv. Inst. 1: 287.

— Modern Small-calibre, Effect of ; Surgery in Future Wars. (A. C. Girard) J. Mil. Serv. Inst. 20: 55.

— Some Stray Shots and a Moral. (R. B. Townshend) 19th Cent. 47: 321.

Rifling Ships on the Australian Coast. Chamb. J. 75: 175.

Rig-Veda, x. 40, 10 ; the Wedding Stanza. (M. Bloomfield) Am. J. Philol. 21: 411.

Right, Hegel's Philosophy of. (W. T. Harris) Philos. R. 6: 288.

" Right-and-left," A. (F. Whishaw) Longm. 37: 416.

Right Guard's Rush, The ; a story. (H. C. Pierson) Outing, 31: 185.

Right of Way, The ; a novel. (G. Parker) Harper, 102: 204-843. 103: 20-208.

Right Promethean Fire, The ; a story. (G. M. Martin) McClure, 17: 85.

Right Wing, The Unlucky. (G. Tompkins) No. Am. 167: 639.

Righteousness, Personal. (P. S. Moxom) Bib. Sac. 57: 54.

Rights, Natural. (A. I. Clark) Ann. Am. Acad. Pol. Sci. 16: 213.

— of Man. (L. Abbott) Outl. v. 67, 68. — (W. A. Northcott) Arena, 26: 561.

— — French Declaration of, 1789. (J. H. Robinson) Pol. Sci. Q. 14: 653.

Rigidity, Magnetic Increment of, in Strong Fields. (H. D. Day) Am. J. Sci. 153: 449.

Rigo, Stage-manager for Grand Opera. (J. L. Mathews) Music, 15: 296.

Riis, Jacob A. Making of an American. Outl. 67: 497-901. 68: 31-922. 69: 35-301.

Riley, James Whitcomb. Acad. 55: 472. — (M. Thompson) Critic, 33: 460.

— as a Poet of Childhood, with portrait. (C. E. Laughlin) Bk. Buyer, 17: 181.

— at Home, with portrait. (J. M. Chapple) Nat'l M. (Bost.) 9: 322.

— Poetry of. (B. Carman) Atlan. 82: 424.

Rimbaud, Jean Arthur. (C. Whibley) Blackw. 165: 402. — (Arth. Symons) Sat. R. 85: 706.

Rimington, A. Wallace. Drawings of Spain. Studio (Lond.) 2: 134.

Rimini, Church of St. Francis. (A. Higgins) Archæol. 53: 171.

Rimmer, Caroline Flint. (D. M. Morrell) Arena, 21: 72.

Rimsky-Korsakow, Russian Musician, with portrait. (A Pougin) Music, 14: 17.

Rinderpest, Koch on. Nature, 55: 450.

Ring and the Deer, The. (W. H. Boardman) Harper, 102: 963.

Ringmer, Sussex, Church of. (W. H. Legge) Reliquary, 38: 225.

Rings, Magic. (D. Sampson) Argosy, 69: 147.

Ringwood as a Sketching Ground. (E. W. Charlton) Studio (Lond.) 5: 140.

" Rio de Janeiro," Loss of the. (Alex. Woolf) Overland, n. s. 37: 847.

Rio Grande, Running the Cañons of the. (R. T. Hill) Cent. 39: 371.

Riordan's Last Campaign. (Anne O'Hagan) Scrib. M. 25: 228.

Riot Duty, Ten Years of. (W. Alexander) J. Mil. Serv. Inst. 19: 1.

Riots in Cities and their Suppression. (E. L. Molineux) J. Mil. Serv. Inst. 4: 335.

— Law of. (J. Taylor) Green Bag, 13: 379.

— of 1877, Army in connection with Labor. (E. S. Otis) J. Mil. Serv. Inst. 5: 292. 6: 117.

Riots, Some Famous Theatrical. (N. Williams) Argosy, 72: 224.

— Use of Troops in. (W. N. Blow) J. Mil. Serv. Inst. 23: 45.

— Uses of Cavalry in Time of. (A. Gray) J. Mil. Serv. Inst. 19: 108.

Rip and my Recantation ; a story. (A. Slade) Eng. Illust. 17: 251.

Ripening, The ; a poem. (W. M. Gamble) Atlan. 84: 855.

Ripon Cathedral. (W. Danks) Sund. M. 454, 535.

Riquer, Alijandro de, Spanish Painter. (F. de Arteaga y Pereira) Studio (Internat.) 10: 180.

Rise of the Morning Star, The. (P. Shoup) Overland, n. s. 35: 127.

Rising Early and Marrying Early. (E. J. Hardy) Argosy, 69: 52.

Rising of Caleb Ballard. (F. T Cox) New Eng. M. n. s. 19: 54.

Rising Wolf, — Ghost Dancer ; a story. (H. Garland) Idler, 20: 471.

Risks, Assumption of, Relation between, and Contributory Negligence. (C. B. Labatt) Am. Law R. 31: 667.

Ristori, Adelaide. My Art. (A. Ristori) Macmil. 83: 182.

Rita da Cascia, St., Life of. (M. E. Herbert) Dub. R. 128: 36.

Rites, Meaning of. Ed. R. 190: 97.

Ritschl, Albert. (F. H. Foster) Presb. & Ref. R. 8: 369.

— A Plea for. (L. H. Schwab) Am. J. Theol. 5: 18.

— Theology of. (J. H. W. Stuckenberg) Am. J. Theol. 2: 268.

Ritschlian Doctrine of Justification and Reconciliation. (J. Orr) Crit. R. 11: 3.

— of Theoretical and Religious Knowledge. (H. R. Mackintosh) Am. J. Theol. 3: 22.

Ritschlian Reform Movement in Germany and Sweden. (R. von Koch) Chr. Lit. 16: 361.

Ritschlian Theology. (A. S. Weber) Ref. Church R. 45: 145.

— in Kaftan's Dogmatik. (W. P. Paterson) Crit. R. 8: 407.

— Orr's. (B. B. Warfield) Presb. & Ref. R. 9: 181.

Ritschlianism and Church Doctrine. Church Q. 51: 22.

— Garvie's Lectures on. (H. C. Minton) Presb. & Ref. R. 11: 547. — (H. R. Mackintosh) Crit. R. 10: 37.

Ritual in the Reign of Maximin. (J. Rickaby) Am. Cath. Q. 25: 437.

— Value and Danger of. Spec. 78: 167.

Ritual Ordinance of Neophytus. (F. E. Warren) Archæol. 47: 1.

Ritualism and the General Election, 1900. (C. Wimborne) 19th Cent. 48: 536.

— and Prosecution. Spec. 85: 703.

— Dangers of. (G. della Vecchia) Westm. 150: 333.

— Development of. (H. C. Corrance) Contemp. 74: 91.

— in the Church of England. (E. L. Godkin) Nation, 68: 141. — (D. H. Bauslin) Luth. Q. 29: 421.

— — and Disestablishment. (G. W. E. Russell) 19th Cent. 45: 188.

— — Chelsea Manuscript, A. (R. McNeill) Macmil. 80: 196.

— — Controversy on. (K. C. Anderson) New World, 9: 201.

— — Fallacies in the Controversy. (H. C. Beeching) National, 33: 449.

— — Kensit Case. (H. Henson) National, 31: 694.

— — The Lambeth Decision. (M. MacColl) Fortn. 72: 644. — (L. T. Dibdin) Fortn. 73: 524.

— — — and the Law. (M. MacColl) Fortn. 73: 224.

— — The Nation and the Ritualists. (J. G. Rogers) 19th Cent. 45: 341.

Ritualism in the Church of England, Troubles about. Sat. R. 87: 102.

    See Church of England.

— — The Ritualist Conspiracy. (C. Wimborne) 19th Cent. 44: 531.

— What is ? (A. Barry) Contemp. 74: 643.

Ritualists and the Electorate. (Austin Taylor) Contemp. 76: 482.

— The Archbishops and the. (J. G. Rogers) Contemp. 76: 305.

Rival Physicians, The ; a story. (N. P. Murphy) Gent. M. n. s. 67: 406.

Rivalry, School. (J. B. Mowry) Educa. 22: 95.

Rivals. (W. Barry) Liv. Age, 220: 593. — (P. B. Mackie) Liv. Age, 231: 653.

Rive-King, Julia, Pianist. Music, 17: 301.

River, Description of a. (E. W. Sandys) Outing, 32: 176.

— Gift of the. (S. H. Dunn) Month, 97: 29.

River-basins, African and Asiatic, Areas of. (A. Bludau) Geog. J. 11: 61. 12: 182.

River Monnow, The ; a poem. (M. G. Watkins) Gent. M. n. s. 61: 301.

River People, The. (D. Marshall) Scrib. M. 28: 101.

River Water, Clarification of. (A. Hazen) J. Frankl. Inst. 147: 177.

Rivers, Augustus Pitt. (L. Gomme) Folk-Lore, 11: 185.

Rivers of England, Forgotten. Spec. 80: 904.

— of North America, Russell's. (R. E. Dodge) Science, n. s. 9: 214.

Riverside, Cal., to Santa Ana, Cal. (L. W. Garland) Outing, 29: 580.

Riveting Machinery, Electric. (F. von Kodolitsch) Cassier, 18: 71.

Riviera, Along the, awheel. (P. E. Jenks) Outing, 30: 365.

— The English. (W. J. Stillman) Nation, 68: 473.

— French. (W. G. Blaikie) No. Am. 168: 445.

— On the. Chamb. J. 78: 39.

— Peasant Life on the. (E. F. Baldwin) Outl. 63: 60.

Riviere, Briton, Artist. (H. Sharp) Studio (Lond.) 5: 124.

— King's Libation. Art J. 49: 246.

— Sketches by. (H. Sharp) Studio (Lond.) 5: 124.

Rivière, Henri, Artist, Chromo-xylographs of. (G. Mourey) Studio (Lond.) 7: 83.

Rivière, Théodore, Statuettes of. (Henri Frantz) M. of Art, 23: 136.

Rivington, Luke, as a Roman Catholic Controversialist. Church Q. 44: 21.

Road, The Open. Spec. 83: 214.

— Resurrection of the. Spec. 83: 372.

Road 'twixt Heaven and Hell ; poem. (Anna H. Branch) Cent. 35: 305.

Road-hymn for the Start ; poem. (W. V. Moody) Atlan. 83: 840.

Roadmaster's Story, The. (F. H. Spearman) McClure, 17: 594.

Roadside Rest ; a poem. (A. Ketchum) Atlan. 86: 712.

Roadway, A Transcontinental. (J. Hawthorne) Cosmopol. 28: 125.

Roadways, Modern City. (N. P. Lewis) Pop. Sci. Mo. 56: 524.

Roads, American. (C. A. Bell) Chaut. 25: 356.

— Artistic Country. (A. W. Campbell) Canad. M. 8: 214.

— Building of American Highways. (G. E. Walsh) Gunton's M. 21: 129.

— Canals and Bridges, Ancient. (S. D. Peet) Am. Antiq. 21: 151.

— Genesis of. Spec. 87: 151.

Roads, Good, and State Aid. (O. Dorner) Forum, 26: 668.

— — Economy of. (A. A. Pope) Outl. 58: 168.

— — a Good Investment. (E. Mayo) World's Work, 2: 1285.

— — The Government and. (M. Dodge) Forum, 32: 292.

— — Movement for, in Middle West. (H. W. Perry) Midland, 7: 524.

— Highway Construction in Massachusetts. (C. L. Whittle) Pop. Sci. Mo. 51: 73.

— Improvement of, in England. (A. M. White) J. Soc. Arts, 48: 506.

— National Good Roads Association. (E. Mayo) World's Work, 1: 956.

— Roman Highways. (D. R. McAnally) Pop. Sci. Mo. 53: 255.

— — of Britain. (W. B. Paley) 19th Cent. 44: 480.

Roan Barbary ; a novelette. (G. Hibbard) Harper, 96: 395.

Roanoke College, Salem, Va. Lit. W. (Bost.) 28: 341.

Robari. [Yonnie War of 1887.] Macmil. 81: 99.

Robber and the Burglar ; a story. (E. Nesbit) Pall Mall M. 19: 107.

Robber-thief ; a monologue. (P. Hart) Pall Mall M. 22: 452.

Robbers, The Two, in the Gospel, Note on the Names of. (J. R. Harris) Expos. 7: 304.

Robbia, Andrea and Luca della. Good Words, 42: 823. — With portraits. Mast. in Art, 2: Pt. 21.

— Madonnas ; poem and illus. Critic, 39: 545.

Robbia, Luca della. (E. Hutton) Idler, 13: 379.

— Work of. (Florence Eversham) Music, 11: 348. 12: 81.

Robert Houdin, Conjuror, Author, and Ambassador. (H. R. Evans) Cosmopol. 28: 645.

Robert, Hubert-, Paintings of, in Chicago. (A. V. Clarke) Brush & P. 9: 79.

Robert the Devil. (C. M. Girardeau) Lippinc. 59: 113.

Robert Aikman's Chastisement. (Mrs. A. K. H. Forbes) Sund. M. 28: 301.

Roberts, Arthur, as a Comedian. (Max Beerbohm) Sat. R. 86: 845.

Roberts, Brigham H., Case of. Outl. 63: 669. 64: 201.

— — a Word of Dissent. Outl. 64: 134.

— — Polygamy in Congress. (A. T. Schroeder and T. W. Curtis) Arena, 23: 113.

— The Cleveland Petition. Outl. 61: 472.

— Shall a Mormon sit in the U. S. Congress ? (T. F. Wright) N. Church R. 6: 279.

Roberts, Charles G. D., and Carman, Bliss. (G. White) Sewanee, 7: 48.

— Book of the Native. (T. G. Marquis) Canad. M. 8: 452.

Roberts, Elizabeth Wentworth, Religious Paintings of. (W. H. Downes) New Eng. M. n. s. 24: 487.

Roberts, Ellis, as Portrait Painter. (F. Miller) Art J. 51: 321.

Roberts, Lord Frederick S. (W. S. Churchill) World's Work, 1: 309. — (G. Grey) Sund. M. 29: 246. — Outl. 64: 54. — Canad. M. 14: 328. — (W. J. Mathams) Good Words, 41: 326. — With portrait. R. of Rs. (N. Y.) 21: 187.

— and the Indian Frontier Policy. (J. M'L. Innes) Fortn. 68: 750. — Spec. 78: 58. — Ath. '97, 1: 39, 75. — (F. A. Steele) Acad. 51: 169.

— and his March through the Orange Free State. (J. Barnes) Outl. 65: 205.

— as Commander-in-chief. Sat. R. 91: 4.

— Forty-one Years in India. Asia. R. 23: 381.

Roberts, George E. Bank. M. (N. Y.) 58: 869.

Roberts, Ina Brevoort. Writer, 14: 121.

Roberts, Mt., British Columbia, Summit of. (J. M. Baltimore) Canad. M. 17: 429.

Roberts Family; five poets. (A. B. De Mille) Canad. M. 15: 426.

Robertson, Alexander. The Bible of St. Mark. Studio (Internat.) 6: 142.

Robertson, Frederick W. (T. H. S. Escott) Fortn. 72: 991.

Robertson, Forbes, as Hamlet. (G. B. Shaw) Sat. R. 84: 364.

— — Portrait of. Theatre, 39: 222.

Robertson, Percy. (Godalming) Art J. 50: 338.

— Shere; an etching. Art J. 51: 304.

Robertson, T. W. Caste, performed in 1897. (G. B. Shaw) Sat. R. 83: 685.

Robertson, W. Graham. (M. H. Spielman) M. of Art, 24: 74.

Robertson, William J. (Sallie E. M. Hardy) Green Bag, 10: 154.

Robespierre. Acad. 56: 433.

— and the Red Terror, Hedeman's. Ath. '99, 2: 245.

— Brink's. Sat. R. 88: 7.

— Fall of. (J. G. Alger) Scot. R. 31: 298.

Robespierre, M'lle. (A. Laugel) Nation, 72: 67.

Robethon, John de. (J. F. Chance) Eng. Hist. R. 13: 55.

Robida, Albert, Artist, Illustrator of Rabelais. (C. H. Heydemann) Idler, 11: 497.

Robin, My Friend the. (G. Coleridge) Fortn. 69: 92. Same art. Liv. Age, 216: 455. Same art. Ecl. M. 130: 274. — (R. S. Wishart) Sund. M. 30: 152.

Robin Adair; the story of a famous song. (S. J. A. FitzGerald) McClure, 8: 361.

Robin Hood. (Maud E. Kingsley) Educa. 22: 39.

— and his Merry Men; stories. (B. Pain) Eng. Illust. 18: 33 — 19: 551.

Robina's Idea; a story. (L. Street) Argosy, 63: 345.

Robins, Elizabeth. Acad. 55: 428, 462.

— in Hedda Gabler. Critic, 32: 254.

— Open Question. (J. B. Perry) Critic, 34: 157.

Robin's Nest. (S. J. Eddy) New Eng. M. n. s. 22: 161.

Robinson, Charles, Book Illustrator. Studio (Lond.) 5: 146.

— Drawings of, with portrait. (L. Wood) Bk. Buyer, 13: 972.

— Recent Work. Brush & P. 8: 192.

Robinson, Conway, with portrait. (Sallie E. M. Hardy) Green Bag, 10: 67.

Robinson, Frederick William. Acad. 61: 618. — (T. Watts-Dunton) Ath. '01, 2: 812.

Robinson, Henry Crabb. (J. Fyvie) Temp. Bar, 120: 26.

— A Successful Bachelor. (L. H. Vincent) Atlan. 81: 805.

Robinson, Rev. John, of Duxbury, Parentage and Birth of. (J. S. Hotchkiss) N. E. Reg. 53: 198.

Robinson, Joseph. (C. V. Stanford) Cornh. 78: 795.

Robinson, Phil. In Garden, Orchard, and Spinney. (F. Danby) Sat. R. 84: 17.

Robinson, Rowland Evans. (J. C. R. Dorr) Atlan. 87: 117. — (H. L. Bailey) New Eng. M. n. s. 23: 430.

Robinson, Theodore, Painter. (H. Garland; P. H. Campbell) Brush & P. 4: 285, 287.

Robinson Crusoe, The Making of. (J. C. Hadden) Cent. 36: 387.

Robinson, the Village in the Tree-tops, near Paris. (E. Douglass) Strand, 17: 202.

Robsart, Amy, Death of. (J. Gairdner) Eng. Hist. R. 13: 83.

Roccamonfina, In the Woods of. (L. Wolffsohn) Gent. M. n. s. 65: 336.

Rochdale Pioneers, The. (W. S. Harwood) Outl. 64: 533.

Roche, Sir Boyle. (C. L. Falkiner) Cornh. 76: 624.

Roche, Deserter and Prime Minister; a story. Idler, 16: 697.

Rochefort, Charles César de. (G. Brenan) Macmil. 83: 306.

Rochefort, Henri, Adventures of. Lond. Q. 88: 69. Same art. Liv. Age, 213: 668.

— Life. (E. G. Johnson) Dial (Ch.) 22: 10.

Rochester, Eng., Norman Cathedral Church at. Archæol. 49: 323.

Rochester Cathedral. (W. Benham) Good Words, 41: 757, 835.

Rochester, Diocese of, Reconstruction of the. (H. Southwark) 19th Cent. 43: 457.

Rochester, Mass., and her Daughter Towns. (M. H. Leonard) New Eng. M. n. s. 20: 613.

— Revolutionary Records of. (M. H. Leonard) New Eng. M. n. s. 19: 289.

Rochester, N. Y. (R. H. Arnot) New Eng. M. n. s. 24: 31.

Rock, Miles. (W. Eimbeck) Science, n. s. 13: 978.

Rock Analysis, Statement of. (H. S. Washington) Am. J. Sci. 160: 59.

Rock Differentiation, Some Queries on. (G. F. Becker) Am. J. Sci. 153: 21.

Rock Excavation, Subaqueous, by means of Rock Cutters. (F. Lobnitz) Cassier, 15: 204.

Rock Mountain Stream; a poem. (F. J. Wilson) Canad. M. 8: 474.

Rock-weathering, Merrill on. Nature, 56: 97.

Rockall. Geog. J. 11: 48.

Rocked in the Wind's Cradle. (M. Thompson) Indep. 53: 1285.

Rockhill, William Woodville, with portrait. (J. Barrett) Indep. 53: 2564. — Outl. 67: 783.

Rockingham, Vt., Records of the First Church of. N. E. Reg. 54: 197, 289, 435. 55: 58, 425.

Rockets, About. Chamb. J. 74: 607.

Rocks, Ancient Crystalline. (G. M. Dawson) Nature, 56: 396.

— and Rock Flowage, Metamorphism of. (C. R. Van Hise) Am. J. Sci. 156: 75.

— Architectural Forms in Nature. (F. S. Dellenbaugh) Pop. Sci. Mo. 54: 63.

— Bacteria and the Decomposition of. (J. C. Branner) Am. J. Sci. 153: 438.

— Fractional Crystallization of. (G. F. Becker) Am. J. Sci. 154: 257.

— Igneous, Natural History of. Part 2. (A. Harker) Sci. Prog. 7: 203.

— Pre-glacial Decay of, in Eastern Canada. (R. Chalmers) Am. J. Sci. 155: 273.

— with Funny Faces. Eng. Illust. 20: 49.

Rocks of Moraga, The; a story of the Philippines. (M. O. Wilcox) McClure, 16: 214.

Rocky Mts., At the Foot of the. (Abbie C. Goodloe) Scrib. M. 22: 359.

— Canadian, Exploration in the. (Norman Collie) Geog. J. 13: 337. 17: 252. — (H. E. M. Stutfield) Blackw. 165: 540. — (G. M. Dawson) Science, n. s. 13: 401.

— Unclimbed Peaks of. (A. C. Laut) Outing, 37: 530.

— Winter Hunting in. (J. W. Schultz) Outing, 37: 437.

Rod, Edouard. (T. Bentzon) Critic, 34: 335. — Lit. W. (Bost.) 30: 40. — With portrait. (F. T. Cooper) Bookman, 9: 152, 255.

— La-Haut. Acad. 51: 260.

— Au Milieu du Chemin. Acad. 58: 188.

Rodbertus, Gonner's Social Philosophy of. (J. Bonar) Econ. J. 10: 67.

Roden's Corner; a novel. (H. S. Merriman) Harper, 96: 169. 97: 437.

Rodents, Generic and Family Names of. Am. Natural. 33: 70.

Rodger, J. W. Nature, 56: 129.

Rodin, Auguste, Sculptor. (G. Mourey) Studio (Internat.) 4: 215. — (C. Quentin) Art J. 50: 193. — (G. Borghum) Artist (N. Y.) 32: 190. — (W. C. Brownell) Scrib. M. 29: 88. — (Count de Soissons) 19th Cent. 49: 693. — (Penguin) Am. Arch. 72: 39. — With portrait. (Marie Van Vorst) Pall Mall M. 23: 17. — Studio (Internat.) 11: 88.

— Exhibition of his Works. (C. Quentin) Art J. 52: 213.

— Great New Doorway by. (H. Frantz) M. of Art, 22: 274.

— his Decorative Sculpture. (C. Mauclair) Internat. Mo. 3: 166.

— His Statue of Balzac. M. of Art, 22: 617. — Studio (Internat.) 5: 107.

— St. John the Baptist Preaching. (D. S. MacColl) Art J. 53: 59.

— Some Recent Work of. ' (C. Quentin) Art J. 50: 321. — Scrib. M. 23: 125.

— Visit to. (Ernest Beckett) Sat. R. 91: 328.

Rodney, George Brydges, Lord. (W. Grey) Un. Serv. M. 22: 72.

— and De Grasse at the Battle of the Saints. (W. H. Fitchett) Cornh. 77: 433.

Roe, Sir Thos., an Ambassador to the Sultan, 1621. (S. L. Poole) Cornh. 80: 468.

Roeblingite, a New Silicate from Franklin Furnace, N. J., containing Sulphur Dioxide and Lead. (S. L. Penfield and H. W. Foote) Am. J. Sci. 153: 413.

Roebuck, John A., Life of. Spec. 79: 737.

— Life and Letters of, Leader's. Ath. '97, 2: 847.

— Radical of the Old School. (C. B. Roylance-Kent) Macmil. 78: 32. Same art. Liv. Age, 217: 665.

Roentgen Ray Photographs, Polarization Effects in. (W. L. Robb) Am. J. Sci. 154: 243.

Roentgen Ray Tubes, Recent Improvements in. (H. L. Sayen) J. Frankl. Inst. 145: 441.

Roentgen Rays. (John Trowbridge) Cent. 34: 128. — (J. Trowbridge) Harv. Grad. M. 5: 511. — (A. W. Goodspeed) J. Frankl. Inst. 150: 472. — (J. J. Thomson) Harper, 103: 564.

— and Mineral Phosphorescence. (J. E. Burbank) Am. J. Sci. 155: 53.

— and some Related Phenomena. (Ernest Merritt) Science, n. s. 12: 41, 98.

— and Ultra-violet Light, Conductive Effect of. (Kelvin and others) Nature, 55: 343.

— Apparatus and Methods. (E. G. Willyoung and H. L. Sayen) J. Frankl. Inst. 143: 211.

— Energy of. (J. G. McPherson) Knowl. 22: 148.

— in the Edison Laboratory. (Jas. Nairn) Good Words, 38: 50.

— in Medicine. (F. H. Williams) Internat. Mo. 3: 42.

— in Military Surgery. J. Mil. Serv. Inst. 24: 313.

— in Warfare. (H. C. Fyfe) Strand, 17: 777.

— Induction-coil Method for. (C. L. Norton and R. R. Lawrence) Science, 5: 796.

— Latest Developments with. (J. Trowbridge) Pop. Sci. Mo. 56: 659.

— Psychical Research and. (N. W. Sibley) Westm. 149: 211.

— Sources of. (J. Trowbridge and J. E. Burbank) Am. J. Sci. 155: 129.

— Tubes for Production of. Nature, 55: 296.

— Work with, Use of Sensitive Paper in. (M. I. Wilbert) J. Frankl. Inst. 152: 463.

— A Year of. (D. W. Hering) Pop. Sci. Mo. 50: 654.

Roger of Salisbury, First Bishop of Bath and Wells, 1244–47. (C. M. Church) Archæol. 52: 89.

Rogerenes, The. (A. M. Earle) Indep. 51: 3078.

Roger's Romance. (W. L. Alden) Belgra. 93: 153.

Rogers, Ezekiel. (J. L. Ewell) New Eng. M. n. s. 21: 3.

Rogers, Hope. (J. S. Rogers) N. E. Reg. 55: 47.

Rogers, Joseph M., Autobiography of. New Eng. M. n. s. 16: 720.

Rogers, W. M. B. (T. C. Mendenhall) Science, 6: 1.

Rogue's Errand, A. (T. W. Speight) Chamb. J. 74: 183–199.

Rohan, The Chevalier de. (A. Laugel) Nation, 69: 7.

— Plot of. (H. Hall) Ath. '99, 1: 146. Same art. Liv. Age, 220: 724.

Rojas, Fernando de. Celestina ; tr. by Mabbe. (R. B. C. Graham) Sat. R. 84: 116, 144.

Roland, Madame. Argosy, 67: 387.

Roland, The Song of. (F. M. Warren) Chaut. 32: 71.

Rolandstein Duel, The. (H. Vallings) Temp. Bar, 123: 29.

Rolfe, William James. Critic, 33: 357.

Rolle, Richard, the Hermit. (T. E. Bridgett) Dub. R. 121: 284.

Roller Bearing, Hyatt. J. Frankl. Inst. 147: 145.

Roller Boat of Mons. Bazin. (E. Gautier) J. Soc. Arts, 45: 137. — (J. H. Cuntz) Cassier, 11: 279.

Rolling-mill Practice, British and American. (W. Garrett) Cassier, 20: 157.

Rollins, Alice Wellington. Critic, 31: 368. — (J. D. Barry) Lit. W. (Bost.) 28: 458.

Rolls House and Chapel, London. (S. Beale) Am. Arch. 69: 30.

Romagna, Peasants of. (E. M. Phillipps) Fortn. 68: 407. Same art. Liv. Age, 215: 267.

Roman Aqueducts as Monuments of Architecture. (H. C. Butler) Am. J. Archæol. 2d s. 5: 175.

Roman Art, Native Vigor of. (F. M. Day) Internat. Mo. 3: 602.

— Wickhoff's. (G. N. Olcott) Bookman, 13: 74.

Roman Britain in 1899. Ath. '00, 1: 56.

— in 1900. (F. Haverfield) Ath. '01, 1: 24.

— New Points in the History of. (A. Tylor) Archæol. 48: 221.

Roman Busts in the Museum of the Syllogos of Candia. (L. Mariani) Am. J. Archæol. 2d s. 1: 266.

Roman Catholic Apologists, Some Recent. (St.G. Mivart) Fortn. 73: 24.

Roman Catholic Books for Public Libraries, List of. (J. H. McMahon) Lib. J. 24: 255.

Roman Catholic Catechism and its Requirements. (A. L. A. Klauder) Cath. World, 73: 803.

Roman Catholic Church, Activity in. (W. Gibson) 19th Cent. 45: 785.

— and English Politics. (J. McCarthy) Outl. 64: 669.

— and Expansion. (H. A. Stimson) Indep. 51: 396.

— and Fraternal Societies. (H. A. Brann) Cath. World, 68: 471.

— and the Future. (Judge Cortright) Cath. World, 72: 562.

— and Heresy, Ward on. Spec. 80: 115–166.

— and the Novelists. Ed. R. 194: 276.

— as an Organism. (W. H. Mallock) Sat. R. 89: 740.

— as a Political Bogey. (W. S. Davis) World's Work, 1: 30.

— as She is, and as We present Her. (W. F. P. Stockley) Cath. World, 72: 606.

— The Belligerent Papacy. (W. J. Stillman) National, 33: 389.

— Brothers of the Christian Schools. (M. Mendel) Cath. World, 70: 737.

— — in the United States. Cath. World, 73: 721.

— Catholic Christianity. (J. Card. Gibbons) No. Am. 173: 78.

— Catholic Women's Association. (L. Girod) Cath. World, 72: 497.

— Danger from. (R. F. Horton) National, 34: 932.

— Democracy in. (W. Barry) Contemp. 76: 70. Same art. Liv. Age, 222: 671. Same art. Ecl. M. 133: 706.

Roman Catholic Church, Education of the Priests of. Cath. World, 70: 51.

— Encyclicals : Consecration to the Sacred Heart ; Year of Jubilee. (Leo XIII.) Am. Cath. Q. 24, no. 3: 69.

— England's Conversion and the Hierarchical Jubilee. (Father Cuthbert) Cath. World, 72: 1.

— Experiences of a Convert. Contemp. 77: 817.

— Five Letters on. (J. H. Newman) Contemp. 76: 357.

— Foster on. Presb. & Ref. R. 11: 195.

— Hinton's The Scale of Perfection. (J. McSorley) Cath. World, 74: 33.

— Holy See and the Council of Ephesus. (W. H. Johnson) Cath. World, 73: 777.

— Holy Year in Rome. Cath. World, 70: 773.

— in America. (R. Norton) Nation, 68: 236.

— — as depicted in the Pope's Letter on Americanism. (W. Rupp) Ref. Ch. R. 46: 389.

— in China. Cath. World, 71: 737. — (B. Cothonay) Cath. World, 73: 415.

— in Early Britain. (J. A. Floyd) Cath. World, 66: 173.

— in the Early Years of Henry VIII. (G. McDermot) Cath. World, 70: 821.

— in England, and Anglicans. Spec. 80: 439.

— — A New Oxford Movement. (J. Kendal) Am. Cath. Q. 22: 578.

— — Pastoral of 1901. (Viscount Halifax) 19th Cent. 49: 736.

— — Progress of. (J. Britten) Month, 94: 143.

— in France, End of "Americanism" in. (P. L. Péchenard) No. Am. 170: 420.

— — Persecution of, under Third Republic. (Reuben Parsons) Am. Cath. Q. 24, no. 4: 1.

— in French Fiction. Macmil. 75: 140. Same art. Liv. Age, 212: 116.

— in French Politics ; Catholic View. (Herbert Thurston) Sat. R. 91: 829.

— in Kerkyra. (D. Quinn) Cath. World, 71: 17.

— in relation to Material Progress. (R. F. Clarke) Am. Cath. Q. 25: 791.

— in South Africa. (E. M. Clerke) Dub. R. 126: 46.

— in the United States. (H. D. Sedgwick, jr.) Atlan. 84: 445.

— Italy and the. Spec. 80: 783.

— King's Facing the 20th Century. Cath. World, 70: 118.

— Latin and American in. (J. Murphy) Open Court, 12: 664.

— Ministry of, Gibbons on. (S. McLanahan) Presb. & Ref. R. 8: 828.

— Mivart on the Continuity of. (J. J. Fox) Cath. World, 70: 725.

— Neglect of, by Historians. (J. H. Robinson) Pol. Sci. Q. 15: 667.

— Paganism in. (T. Trede) Open Court, 13: 321.

— Peril of. Spec. 83: 557.

— Pioneer Catholic Mission in the Northwest. (E. A. Bridger) Cath. World, 71: 842.

— Political and Social Evolution of. (H. A. Stimson) Indep. 53: 1107.

— Progress in the Reign of Victoria. (E. M. Clerke) Dub. R. 128: 227.

— Puller's Primitive Saints of the See of Rome. (W. T. Davison) Crit. R. 11: 394.

— Reform within. Contemp. 78: 693.

— Reforms in Church Music. Cath. World, 74: 283.

— Religious Communities and their Critics. Cath. World, 72: 701.

— Ritual Song in. (E. Dickinson) Music, 13: 183, 301, 445.

— Rôle of. (U. Gohier) National, 34: 358.

— A Russian Champion of. (W. H. Kent) Dub. R. 127: 95.

Roman Catholic Church, Weapon of Fiction against. (W. Lecky) Cath. World, 66: 755.

— Why I left. (A. Galton) National, 35: 580.

— — Some Final Impressions. (A. Galton) National, 35: 850.

Roman Catholic Citizens and Constitutional Rights. (T. H. Malone) No. Am. 171: 594.

Roman Catholic Collegiate Education in the United States. (A. O'Malley) Cath. World, 67: 289.

Roman Catholic Congregations and Modern Thought. (St.G. Mivart) No. Am. 170: 562.

Roman Catholic Controversialists. Church Q. 44: 21.

Roman Catholic Counter-reformation in Bohemia. (L. F. Miskovsky) Bib. Sac. 57: 532.

Roman Catholic Educated Women, Opportunities of. (J. T. Murphy) Am. Cath. Q. 23: 611.

Roman Catholic Education in India. Cath. World, 65: 289.

Roman Catholic Faith and Modern Science. (H. H. Wyman) Cath. World, 71: 1.

Roman Catholic Hierarchy in Australia. (An English Catholic) National, 36: 286.

Roman Catholic Life in Boston. (A. A. McGinley) Cath. World, 67: 20.

— in Chicago. (K. Prindiville) Cath. World, 67: 476.

— in New York City. (R. H. Clarke) Cath. World, 67: 192.

— in St. Louis. (L. H. Bugg) Cath. World, 68: 15.

— in St. Paul, Minn. (M. I. Cramsie) Cath. World, 68: 323.

— in Washington, D. C. (M. T. Waggaman) Cath. World, 66: 821.

— Two Estimates of. (G. Tyrrell) Month, 93: 446.

Roman Catholic Literature, A Century of. (W. H. Kent) Dub. R. 128: 1, 256. 129: 42, 345.

Roman Catholic Missionaries from France and Germany. (T. J. Shahan) Cath. World, 72: 34.

— in Texas. (T. O'Hagan) Cath. World, 71: 340.

Roman Catholic Missions in Arizona. (A. M. Clark) Cath. World, 65: 154.

— among the Indians. Cath. World, 65: 343.

— in the Pacific. (B. G. Clinch) Am. Cath. Q. 23: 562.

Roman Catholic Prelates as American Diplomats. (M. F. Sullivan) Cath. World, 68: 752.

Roman Catholic Secondary Schools. (J. A. Burns) Am. Cath. Q. 26: 485.

Roman Catholic Social-reform Movement, The. (M.-M. Snell) Am. J. Sociol. 5: 16.

Roman Catholic Society of the Queen's Daughters, Work and Aims of. (M. V. Toomey) Cath. World, 67: 610.

Roman Catholic Truth, Witness of Protestantism to. (H. C. Corrance) Cath. World, 68: 767.

Roman Catholic University. Contemp. 75: 629.

— English, The Refusal to grant a. Liv. Age, 225: 318.

— for Ireland, Proposed. (W. Nicholas) Lond. Q. 91: 250.

— Should it be established in Ireland ? (D. S. A. Cosby) Westm. 155: 293. — (T. E. Naughten) Westm. 155: 672. — (M. C. Stratton) Westm. 156: 324.

Roman Catholic Ways in the Tyrol. (M. S. Dalton) Month, 96: 489.

Roman Catholic Women, Charitable Work of. (S. L. Emery) Cath. World, 68: 451.

Roman Catholicism, An American Religious Crusade. (W. Barry) National, 33: 115.

— Americanism vs. (V. Charbonnel) Outl. 61: 584.

— and Anglicanism. (R. Richardson) Cath. World, 69: 359.

— and Scripture. (St.G. Mivart) 19th Cent. 47: 425.

— and Spiritualism. (H. C. Corrance) Dub. R. 124: 107.

Roman Catholicism, British Converts to, in Paris, 1702-1789. (J. G. Alger) Eng. Hist. R. 13: 323.

— Continuity of. (St.G. Mivart) 19th Cent. 47: 51, 244.

— Exit Liberal. (T. E. Naughten) Westm. 155: 311.

— Fairbairn on. (W. H. Hent) Dub. R. 124: 384.

— the Faith of the Millions, Tyrrell's. Cath. World, 74: 345.

— in England, Crisis of, Fifty Years ago. (C. L. Walworth) Cath. World, 69: 396, 549, 662, 812. 70: 59, 239, 412.

— — Will England become Catholic ? (R. Bagot) Liv. Age, 222: 265. Same art. Ecl. M. 133: 321.

— in Fiction. (W. Sichel) Fortn. 71: 604.

— in France, Renascence of, 1796-1861. (M. O'Connor) Dub. R. 125: 296.

— in Italy. (G. Fiamingo) Open Court, 11: 412.

— in New York City, Progress of. Cath. World, 67: 146.

— in the Philippines. (C. Shane) Cath. World, 67: 695.

— in the U.S., Brunetière on. (R. Ogden) Nation, 67: 385.

— in the West. (L. H. Bugg) Cath. World, 66: 302.

— Intellectual Future of. (W. H. Mallock) 19th Cent. 46: 753.

— Liberal. Contemp. 72: 854.

— The New Liberal. Spec. 83: 564.

— 19th Century. Month, 94: 406.

— of France. (T. J. Shahan) Conserv. R. 3: 278.

— Progress of, in Northern Europe. (C. W. Dowd) Cath. World, 71: 646.

— The Prospects of. (W. Barry) National, 38: 226.

— restored in Geneva. (T. L. L. Teeling) Am. Cath. Q. 23: 284, 487.

— Unchanging Dogma and Changeful Man. (W. Ward) Fortn. 73: 628.

— The Vatican at Work. (R. Bagot) National, 34: 515.

Roman Catholics and American Citizenship. (J. A. M'Faul) No. Am. 171: 320.

— and the American Revolution. (F. T. Furey) Cath. World, 65: 495.

— in England, Cry of, for Tolerance. (R. Bagot) National, 37: 270.

— in the United States. "As Others see us." (W. F. P. Stockley) Am. Cath. Q. 26: 278.

— What should they read ? Am. Cath. Q. 22: 673.

Roman Chorus, Middlebury College. (M. R. Sanford) Cent. 36: 842.

Roman Congregations. (W. Humphrey) Month, 90: 927. 91: 64-395.

Roman Constitutional History in our High Schools. (J. H. Drake) School R. 8: 146.

Roman Corn-mill. Reliquary, 39: 54.

Roman Country House, The. (A. D. F. Hamlin) Archit. R. 4: 19.

Roman Criminal Law, Mommsen's. (J. L. Strachan-Davidson) Eng. Hist. R. 16: 219.

Roman-Dutch Procedure, Some Points in. (Sir D. P. Chalmers) Green Bag, 10: 401.

Roman Emperors. Un. Serv. M. 24: 293.

Roman Haunting, A; a story. (J. Ayscough) Temp. Bar, 123: 68.

Roman Law, Dutch, in the Colonies. (Sir D. P. Chalmers) Jurid. R. 9: 409.

— Influence on English Law. (H. W. Rogers) Chaut. 26: 496.

— Reception of, in Scotland. (J. D. Wilson) Jurid. R. 9: 361.

— Wardour Street. (W. W. Buckland) Law Q. 17: 179.

Roman Letter-writers of To-day. (M. Oxenden) Temp. Bar, 115: 454.

Roman Orators. (C. J. Little) Chaut. 27: 11.

Roman Pavement at Leicester, Eng. Ath. '98, 2: 459.

Roman Potter's Kiln at Stockton Heath near Warrington. Reliquary, 40: 263.

Roman Private Law, Muirhead's Historical Introduction to. (W. H. Bucklar) Nation, 70: 75.

Roman Remains at Inchtuthill. (F. Haverfield) Ath. '01, 2: 325.

— in Bath, Eng. (S. Beale) Am. Arch. 32: 37.

— in Lincoln, Discoveries of. (G. E. Fox) Archæol. 53: 233, 539.

Roman Roads and Milestones in Asia Minor. (J. R. S. Sterrett) Nation, 69: 204.

— of Britain. (W. B. Paley) 19th Cent. 44: 840.

Roman Sarcophagi at Clieveden. (C. Robert) J. Hel. Stud. 20: 81.

Roman Sculptured and Inscribed Stones at Cirencester. Reliquary, 39: 196.

Roman Silver Refinery at Silchester, Remains of a. (W. Gowland) Archæol. 57: 113.

Roman Town of Doclea in Montenegro. Archæol. 55: 33.

Roman Villa in Spoonley Wood, Gloucestershire, and Romano-British Houses. Archæol. 52: 651.

Romance against Romanticism. (B. Matthews) Bookman, 12: 463.

— and Allegory, Saintsbury on. (W. M. Payne) Dial (Ch.) 23: 45.

— and Science. (L. Stephen) Pall Mall M. 24: 105.

— Apologetics of. (J. Buchan) Acad. 52: 203.

— Confession of a Lover of. Atlan. 80: 281.

— Ideals of. Ed. R. 186: 381. Same art. Liv. Age, 216: 83.

— New Phases of. (J. O. Pierce) Dial (Ch.) 26: 69.

Romance, A, Invaded. (G. Burgess) Cent. 36: 436.

Romance amongst the Rice-birds, A. (E. E. Peake) Outing, 30: 567.

Romance Duo ; a poem. (C. E. Meetkerke) Argosy, 66: 97.

Romance of Barker's Buildings ; a story. (A. L. Harris) Cornh. 76: 672.

Romance of Chinkapin Castle, The ; a story. (R. McE. Stuart) Harper, 98: 297.

Romance of the Frozen North, A. (J. A. Hill) Idler, 20: 3.

Romance of a Gift Ring ; a story. (A. G. Tait) Canad. M. 10: 249.

Romance of a Glove ; a story. Cornh. 77: 471.

Romance of the Gold-fields, A. (W. Thomson) Overland, n. s. 34: 408.

Romance of the House of Commons, A. (H. G. Hutchinson) Cornh. 79: 757.

Romance of the Institute. (A. Colton) Cent. 38: 415.

Romance of a Jock Scott. (M. G. Cundill) Outing, 32: 467.

Romance of a Mexican Dollar ; a story. (C. M. Rettock) Nat'l M. (Bost.) 10: 25.

Romance of a Mule-car. (F. R. Stockton) Cent. 33: 127.

Romance of Mutby Workhouse, The. (Isabel Smith) Chamb. J. 76: 254.

Romance of Old Paris. (Jennie B. Waterbury) Nat'l M. (Bost.) 6: 226.

Romance of a Promissory Note, The. (W. Scott King) Chamb. J. 76: 691.

Romance of Quill's Inn. (F. G. Aflalo) Chamb. J. 78: 289-314.

Romance of Porthaven Harbor, A. (V. L. Whitechurch) Good Woods, 40: 455.

Romance of a School Inspection ; a story. (N. Powys) Temp. Bar, 114: 231. Same art. Ecl. M. 131: 470.

Romance of Thatmaiyo Bridge, The. (H. Bindloss) Gent. M. n. s. 66: 593. Same art. Ecl. M. 137: 466.

— Liv. Age, 230: 624.

Romance on Wheels; a story. (E. B. Piercy) Eng. Illust. **17**: 535.

Romance that Failed; a story. (W. R. Stewart) Canad. M. **15**: 236.

Romance Writing among the Greeks. (C. J. Goodwin) Sewanee, **5**: 290, 409.

Romanes, George John, and Mill; The heart and the will in belief. (J. G. Hibben) No. Am. **166**: 121.

— Religious Poems of. [Spec.] Liv. Age, **212**: 273.

Romanesque Architecture in North Italy, Some Examples of. (H. Stannus) J. Soc. Arts, **49**: 369.

Romano-British Fibulæ showing Late-Celtic Influence. (J. R. Allen) Reliquary, **41**: 195.

Romantic School in France, Rise of. (C. Yriarte) Pall Mall M. **23**: 146.

Romanticism among German Women. (G. Valbert) Liv. Age, **212**: 809.

— English, in the 19th Century, Beers on. (E. E. Hale, jr.) Dial (Ch.) **31**: 433. — (H. B. Hinckley) Bookman, **9**: 347. — Ath. '99, **2**: 312.

Romaunt of ye Bicycle, A; a poem. (M. Park) Outing, **33**: 585.

Rome. (F. W. Fitzpatrick) Øpen Court, **15**: 399. — Liv. Age, **215**: 28.

— American Academy at. (J. La Farge) Scrib. M. **28**: 253.

— Ancient, Chief Methods of Construction used in. (J. H. Middleton) Archæol. **51**: 41.

— — Destruction of, Lanciani's. (A. L. Frothingham) Am. Hist. R. **5**: 731.

— — Notes on, made between 1550 and 1570. (J. H. Middleton) Archæol. **51**: 489.

— and Byzantium. Quar. **192**: 129.

— and her Dutch Rebels. (R. B. Townshend) Westm. **155**: 386.

— and the Popes, Grisar's History of. (T. B. Scannell) Dub. R. **129**: 297.

— Basilicas of. Temp. Bar, **109**: 471. Same art. Ecl. M. **128**: 526.

— Bishops of, Succession of the First. (F. Bacchus) Dub. R. **123**: 276. **124**: 373.

— British School at. Antiq. n. s. **36**: 26.

— Christian House at, The Early. Illus. (S. Baring-Gould) Good Words, **38**: 622, 699.

— Christmas in. (G. V. Christmas) Cath. World, **70**: 341.

— Constitutional and Political History of, Taylor's. Ath. '99, **2**: 795.

— Crawford's Ave Roma Immortalis. (A. L. Frothingham, jr.) Am. Hist. R. **4**: 508. — (W. Sharp) Good Words, **40**: 167.

— during Holy Week. (C. R. Boulton) Canad. M. **10**: 470.

— Election in. (F. W. Pelly) Cath. World, **64**: 584.

— — in 1900. Ed. R. **191**: 106.

— — The Muddles of. (J. B. Hodge) Un. Serv. M. **21**: 585. Same art. J. Mil. Serv. Inst. **27**: 402.

— English National Establishments in, during Middle Ages. (W. J. D. Croke) Dub. R. **123**: 94, 305.

— Excavations in, 1898. (R. Norton) Indep. **52**: 1550.

— Fall of the Empire, and its Lessons. (T. Hodgkin) Contemp. **73**: 51. Same art. Ecl. M. **130**: 289.

— A Festal Day in. (W. Irving) Outl. **61**: 322.

— Flood in. (S. Cortesi) Indep. **53**: 80.

— Forum, The. (R. Norton) Nation, **67**: 425. — (H. Mereu) Am. Arch. **70**: 5.

— — Excavations in. (R. Norton) Nation, **68**: 124. — (L. Borsari) Ath. '99, **1**: 24. — (G. Boni) 19th Cent. **47**: 637. — (M. D. Gray) Bib. World, **17**: 199. — Am. Arch. **73**: 93.

— — History of the Column of Phocas in. (F. M. Nichols) Archæol. **52**: 183.

Rome, Forum, Progress in. (R. Norton) Nation, **69**: 67. **70**: 277.

— — Strata in. (G. Boni) 19th Cent. **49**: 461.

— Genius of. Quar. **191**: 30.

— The Glory that was. Liv. Age, **224**: 661.

— Higher Life of. (R. Lanciani) Outl. **57**: 25.

— History of, to Death of Cæsar, How and Leigh's. (T. J. Shahan) Citizen, **3**: 91.

— — Topical Outlines of, Burdick's. (W. J. Chase) School R. **6**: 51.

— in the Middle Ages, Gregorovius on. Ath. '97, **1**: 500.

— its Rise and Fall, Myers's. (G. S. Goodspeed) School R. **9**: 551.

— Literary Landmarks of. (L. Hutton) Harper, **94**: 281.

— Noble Christian Families in, under Pagan Emperors. (J. A. Campbell) Dub. R. **126**: 356.

— Notes from. (R. Lanciani) Ath. '99, **1**: 313–696. **2**: 766, 841. '00, **1**: 56, 153, 280, 342, 471, 599, 759. **2**: 352, 764, 865.

— of Tacitus. (B. K. Hudson) New Eng. M. n. s. **22**: 21.

— Old, and the New, Stillman's. (K. Cox) Nation, **66**: 31, 128.

— Palace of Justice. Am. Arch. **71**: 15.

— Policlinico Umberto I. (James Gilmore) Am. Arch. **73**: 51.

— Religious Life in. (M. Joseph) Jew. Q. **14**: 64.

— Ruins and Excavations of. (G. McDermott) Cath. World, **66**: 465.

— St. Peter's. (A. J. C. Hare) Argosy, **73**: 25.

— — Crypt of. Cath. World, **65**: 739.

— See of, Puller and Rivington on. (J. P. Sheraton) Presb. & Ref. R. **8**: 126.

— Serrao's Conquest of. (A. Laugel) Nation, **70**: 87.

— Short History of, Wells's. (W. J. Chase) School R. **5**: 474.

— Society in, at the Fall of the Western Empire, Dill on. Church Q. **48**: 174. — (T. M. Lindsay) Crit. R. **9**: 153. — Sat. R. **87**: 86. — Acad. **56**: 10. — (W. C. Lawton) Dial (Ch.) **26**: 307. — Ed. R. **190**: 170.

— Tivoli Electric Plant. (A. O. Dubsky) Cassier, **15**: 331.

— The Squalor of. Chamb. J. **77**: 374.

— Tribunal Aurelium. (C. J. O'Connor) Am. J. Archæol. 2d s. **4**: 303.

— Under Pius IX., Reminiscences of. (D. Macleod) Good Words, **42**: 546.

— Villas of. (M. T. Reynolds) Archit. R. **6**: 256. **7**: 1.

— A Walk in. (L. O. Kuhns) Chaut. **34**: 45.

Romeo and Juliet, A Spanish. (A. M. Huntington) Bookman, **5**: 463.

Romney, George. Munsey, **17**: 728. — (J. C. Van Dyke) Cent. **34**: 350.

— Portrait of Cowper by. (W. Roberts) Ath. '00, **1**: 215.

— Portrait of Mrs. Mark Currie. Art J. **50**: 38.

— Portraits at the Grafton Gallery. (R. C. Witt) 19th Cent. **49**: 523. Same art. Ecl. M. **136**: 733. Same art. Liv. Age, **229**: 190. — Sat. R. **89**: 711. — (L. Cust) M. of Art, **24**: 449.

Romsey Abbey. (S. Beale) Am. Arch. **67**: 52.

— Recent Discoveries in. (C. R. Peers) Archæol. **57**: 317.

Roncoux, Campaign of. (F. Dixon) Temp. Bar, **111**: 475.

Rondeau for a Lawyer; a poem. (P. L. Dunbar) Green Bag, **9**: 294.

Rondeau Bay Park. (A. P. McKishine) Canad. M. **9**: 405.

Ronner, Alfred; a New Humorist. Illus. M. of Art, **23**: 40.

— Picture "The Street Singers." M. of Art, **26**: 90.

Roses, Feast of. (E. C. Vansittart) Antiq. n. s. **36**: 134.
— Yellow and Blue. (B. Milne) Eng. Illust. **20**: 103.
Roses in the Garden ; a poem. Ecl. M. **129**: 680.
Rosebery, Archibald P. P., Lord. (J. McCarthy) Outl. **64**: 777. — (N. Hapgood) Contemp. **71**: 227.
— Addresses. Ath. '99, **2**: 55. Same art. Ecl. M. **133**: 780. Same art. Liv. Age, **222**: 785.
— and English Politics. (R. Ogden) Nation, **73**: 468.
— and his Followers. (W. L. Stobart and Academicus) Fortn. **69**: 910.
— and Home Rule. Fortn. **71**: 175.
— and the Liberal Imperialists. Fortn. **75**: 35.
— and London. Spec. **83**: 743.
— and a National Cabinet. Fortn. **73**: 1069.
— and the Premiership. (H. W. Lucy) Forum, **27**: 513.
— Apostasy of. Fortn. **68**: 845.
— as ex-Premier. Sat. R. **92**: 68.
— as Literary Critic. (J. F. Hogan) Chamb. J. **76**: 433.
— as an Orator. Acad. **57**: 32.
— as a Political Leader, Recrudescence of. Spec. **80**: 683.
— Chance of, 1900. (J. A. R. Marriott) Fortn. **74**: 935.
— The Disraeli of Liberalism. Fortn. **71**: 129. Same art. Ecl. M. **132**: 524. Same art. Liv. Age, **220**: 405.
— Escape from Houndsditch. (S. Webb) 19th Cent. **50**: 366.
— Foreign Policy of. Contemp. **80**: 1, 153.
— The Future of. (H. W. Massingham) 19th Cent. **46**: 729.
— Napoleon ; the Last Phase. (Goldwin Smith) Atlan. **87**: 166.
— Open Letter to. Fortn. **76**: 375.
— a Palmerston — with Nerves. Fortn. **72**: 1.
— Reënters Politics. Sat. R. **87**: 549.
Rosecrans, William S., Defence of. (H. M. Beadle) Cath. World, **67**: 684.
Rosegger, Peter. (K. Francke) Bookman, **8**: 236.
— Autobiographical Sketch. Critic, **37**: 451.
Rosenberg Library, Galveston, Competition for. Am. Arch. **74**: 5.
Rosenfeld, Morris. (H. Hapgood) Critic, **36**: 257. — With portrait. Bk. Buyer, **16**: 305.
— Songs from the Ghetto. (R. Burton) Bk. Buyer, **18**: 58.
Rosicrucianism. (F. C. Penfield) Forum, **27**: 621.
Rosmini, Antonio. (W. D. McCrackan) Am. J. Soc. Sci. **35**: 112.
Rosny, J. H. Social Psychology in Contemporary French Fiction. (L. Marillier) Fortn. **76**: 520.
Ross, Clinton, with portrait. Bk. News, **16**: 8.
Ross, George C., Monarch of all he surveys. Eng. Illust. **20**: 629.
Ross, John, of Philadelphia, 1729–1800. Pennsyl. M. **23**: 77.
Rossellino, Antonio. Madonna and Child. (Claude Phillips) Art J. **51**: 33.
Rossetti, Christina Georgina. (Florence L. Snow) Midland, **7**: 120.
— at Home. Liv. Age, **217**: 141.
— Bell's Life of. Acad. **53**: 88.
— Devotional Prose of. Meth. R. **58**: 798.
Rossetti, Dante Gabriel. (W. M. Rossetti) Pall Mall M. **16**: 480. — Am. Arch. **60**: 35.
— and Christina. (E. L. Cary) Critic, **37**: 320.
— — First Books of. (L. S. Livingston) Bookman, **10**: 245.
— and Millais Exhibitions. (F. M. Hueffer) Fortn. **69**: 189. — (E. R. Pennell) Nation, **66**: 65, 86.
— and the Pre-Raphaelites. (J. C. Hume) Midland, **7**: 42.

Rossetti, Dante Gabriel, and William Morris. Ed. R. **191**: 356.
— Blessed Damozel ; ed. by W. M. Rossetti. Sat. R. **85**: 851.
— Dante's Vision. (F. B. Sawvel) Educa. **21**: 32.
— His Use of Chloral. (W. J. Stillman) Acad. **53**: 333.
— Letters. Spec. **80**: 238.
— — to Wm. Allingham. Ath. '98, **1**: 395.
— Marillier's Record of. (W. M. Rossetti) M. of Art, **24**: 217.
— Poetry of. (C. A. L. Morse) Cath. World, **65**: 633.
— Recollections of. (H. H. Gilchrist) Lippinc. **68**: 571.
— Salutations of Beatrice. (H. C. Marillier) Art J. **51**: 353.
Rossettis, The. (A. B. McGill) Bk. Buyer, **20**: 378.
— Hill, Caine, and Bell on. (F. J. Gregg) Bk. Buyer, **16**: 315.
Rossi, Moses di, Letter by, from Palestine, 1535. (D. Kaufmann) Jew. Q. **9**: 491.
Rossini, G. A. Barber of Seville. (J. F. Runciman) Sat. R. **90**: 113.
Rossiter, Dr. Bryan (or Bray), of Guilford, Conn., and his Descendants. (R. D. Smyth) N. E. Reg. **55**: 149.
Rossland : a Great Mountain Gold-camp. Chamb. J. **76**: 88.
Rostand, Edmond. (H. James) Cornh. **84**: 577. Same art. Critic, **39**: 437. — (C. Moffet) McClure, **14**: 437. — (A. Filon) Fortn. **70**: 98. — (E. Sedgwick) Atlan. **82**: 826. — (S. Young) 19th Cent. **44**: 102.
— and the Literary Prospects of the Drama. Ed. R. **192**: 307. Same art. Liv. Age, **228**: 1. Same art. Ecl. M. **136**: 221.
— Cyrano de Bergerac. (G. McDermot) Cath. World, **69**: 181. — (L. Strachey) Lippinc. **63**: 264. — With portrait. Bk. Buyer, **17**: 97. — (C. H. Genung) Bk. Buyer, **17**: 201. — (E. E. Hale, jr.) Dial (Ch.) **25**: 340. — (G. Kobbé) Forum, **26**: 502. — (H. S. Wilson) Gent. M. n. s. **61**: 62. — Acad. **54**: 51. — (W. F. S. Wallace) Idler, **13**: 417. — (C. de Kay) Critic, **33**: 152. — Outl. **60**: 440. — (M. Beerbohm) Sat. R. **86**: 42.
— — Coquelin's French Version of the Play. (P. S. Vimbert) Nat'l M. (Bost.) **9**: 471.
— — Richard Mansfield's Production of the Play. Midland, **11**: 159.
— — on the London Stage. (M. Beerbohm) Sat. R. **89**: 524.
— — Some Footnotes to. (P. Wilstach) Bookman, **10**: 363.
— — What it is and is not. Poet-Lore, **11**: 118.
— Fantasticks. (M. Beerbohm) Sat. R. **89**: 680.
— L'Aiglon. (M. Beerbohm) Sat. R. **91**: 767. — (E. E. Hale, jr.) Dial (Ch.) **29**: 354. — Liv. Age, **225**: 321. — Acad. **58**: 255.
— Plays of. (Eveline C. Godley) National, **37**: 564.
Rostock, the Lantern, Child-life of. (M. Boileau) Sund. M. **30**: 407.
Rostra and Græcostasis. (J. H. Middleton) Archæol. **49**: 424.
Rotary Engine, Principles and Development of the. (E. S. Farwell) Engin. M. **13**: 263.
Rothe, Richard, Centenary of. (J. Laidlaw) Expos. **6**: 439.
Rothenberg, Germany. (Anna Douglas) Art J. **53**: 244.
Rothenstein, W. Goya. Sat. R. **90**: 583.
Rothley, County of Leicester, Customary of. (G. T. Clark) Archæol. **47**: 89.
Rothrock Genealogy. Pennsyl. M. **21**: 499.
Rothschild, Alfred : Caricature Portrait. Idler, **17** 205.

Rothschild, Nathan Meyer, Lord, Portraits of. Strand, 14: 53.

Rothschild, The House of. Bank. M. (N. Y.) 63: 236. — Idler, 15: 97.

Rotifera, Research on the Reproduction of. (W. T. Calman) Nat. Sci. 13: 52.

Rotuma, Natives of. (J. S. Gardiner) Anthrop. J. 27: 396, 457.

Roty, Oscar, with portrait. (H. Frantz) M. of Art, 22: 356.

— and the Art of the Medallist. Studio (Lond.) 7: 158.

Rouen. (J. A. Cook) Idler, 13: 555, 661.

— Old Churches of. (E. Endres) Cath. World, 68: 628.

Rouge-et-noir. (W. LeC. Beard) Scrib. M. 22: 569.

Rougemont, Louis de, Veracity of. (Aylmer Pollard) Sat. R. 86: 403.

Rough Riders. (W. F. Cody) Nat'l M. (Bost.) 8: 338. — (T. Roosevelt) Scrib. M: 25: 1–677.

— Roosevelt's. (J. A. Dodge) Am. Hist. R. 5: 376.

— — Fight of. Outl. 59: 518. — (J. G. Winter, jr.) Outl. 60: 19.

Roumania as a Persecuting Power. (F. C. Conybeare) National, 36: 818.

— in 1900, Benger on. Ath. '01, 1: 203.

— Life in. (Hélène Vacaresco) Contemp. 80: 645.

Roumanians, History of. (J. B. Bury) Scot. R. 29: 30.

Round vs. Russell. Month, 89: 358.

'Round Craige's Pond ; a tale. (J. O. Whittemore) Outing, 39: 82.

Round the Far Rocks ; poem. (A. Fields) Atlan. 81: 70.

Round the Fire. (A. C. Doyle) Strand, 17: 3.

Round my Smoking-room. (H. F. Abell) Temp. Bar, 119: 220.

Round Table Conference. Month, 97: 7.

Rouss, Charles Broadway, the Blind Millionaire, with portrait. (G. Willets) Nat'l M. (Bost.) 11: 307.

Rousseau, Jean Jacques. (W. Emm) Westm. 151: 269. — With portrait. (L. Levy-Bruhl) Open Court, 13: 193. — (T. Delta) Acad. 53: 404.

— and the French Revolution. (C. H. Lincoln) Ann. Am. Acad. Pol. Sci. 10: 54.

— Country of. Spec. 85: 522.

— Emile, The Key to. (S. Wier) Educa. R. 16: 61.

— his Position in the History of Philosophy. (J. C. Murray) Philos. R. 8: 357.

— in England. Quar. 188: 381.

Rousseau, Jean-Jacques, Painter. (Jean Bernac) Art J. 53: 198.

Roussel, Theodore. (S. C. de Soissons) Artist (N. Y.) 30: 57.

— Paintings. Sat. R. 88: 99.

Routine Process. (G. Spiller) Mind, 24: 439.

Row of Dominoes, The ; a story. (F. Crane) McClure, 10: 525.

Rowing ; Brockville, Ont., rowing club. (W. S. Buell) Outing, 34: 69.

— Experiments in. (E. C. Atkinson) Nat. Sci. 13: 89.

— in American Universities. (C. Mellen) Outing, 36: 375.

— in Canada. (R. K. Barker) Canad. M. 11: 483.

— Inter-university, in 1897. (C. Mellen) Outing, 30: 237.

Rowing Season of 1901 in Canada. (R. K. Barker) Canad. M. 18: 33.

Rowland, Henry Augustus, with portrait. R. of Rs. (N. Y.) 23: 697. — (R. T. Glazebrook) Nature, 64: 16. — (T. C. Mendenhall) Science, 14: 865. — (H. F. Reid) Am. J. Sci. 161: 459.

Rowley, Massachusetts. (J. L. Ewell) New Eng. M. n. s. 21: 3.

Rowton House for Clerks wanted. (R. White) 19th Cent. 42: 594.

Rowton House ; the Poor Man's Hotel, London. Chamb. J. 76: 257. — (W. A. Sommerville) 19th Cent. 46: 445.

Roy, Charles Smart. Nature, 56: 591.

Royal Academy, The. (H. H. Statham) Fortn. 73: 1023. — (M. H. Spielmann) M. of Art, 23: 451. — (Marian E. Jones) Music, 16: 482. — Ath. '97, 1: 581–846. 2: 41, 72. — Acad. 51: 502, 526. — (D. S. MacColl) National, 29: 536. — Liv. Age, 218: 729.

— Collections. Sat. R. 91: 599, 632, 667, 766.

— Criticism of. Sat. R. 85: 615.

— Current Art. (M. H. Spielmann) M. of Art, 23: 337, 386.

— Exhibition, 1893. (A. Besnard) Studio (Lond.) 1: 75, 110.

— — — First Impression. (A. Tomson) Studio (Lond.) 1: 77.

— 1897. (A. C. R. Carter) Art J. 49: 161. — M. of Art, 21: 57, 151.

— 1898. (A. C. R. Carter) Art J. 50: 161. — M. of Art, 22: 421, 463, 547. — Acad. 53: 504, 530. — Spec. 80: 654–694.

— 1899. (A. C. R. Carter) Art J. 51: 161. — Ath. '99, 1: 55, 693, 760.

— Winter, 1900. Ath. '00, 1: 25, 88, 152.

— 1900. M. of Art, 24: 337, 385. — (F. Rinder) Art J. 52: 161. — Knowl. 23: 128. — Ath. '00, 1: 568, 597, 662, 726, 758, 791. 2: 31.

— Winter, 1901. Ath. '01, 1: 152, 182.

— 1901. (F. Rinder) Art J. 53: 161. — Acad. 60: 407. — M. of Art, 25: 341, 403, 439, 499.

— — Behind the Scenes at. (M. H. Spielmann) Pall Mall M. 24: 94.

— in 19th Century. (G. D. Leslie and F. A. Eaton) Art J. 49: 185. 50: 137. 51: 40–310.

— Leighton's Pictures at. Ath. '97, 1: 53, 189, 252.

— the New Gallery and the Guildhall. (H. H. Statham) Fortn. 72: 101.

— Painting at, 1897. Sat. R. 83: 571.

— The Salon and the. (H. H. Statham) Fortn. 75: 1079. Same art. Ecl. M. 137: 301.

— School of. M. of Art, 22: 229.

— Some Pictures criticised. (E. Aman-Jean) Studio (Lond.) 8: 109.

— Varnishing Day. (O. D. Grover) Brush & P. 2: 156.

Royal Ally, A. (W. M. Browne) Scrib. M. 26: 221.

Royal Archæological Institute, Meeting, 1900. Ath. '00, 2: 128, 161.

Royal Art in Scotland. M. of Art, 22: 334.

Royal Assent in England. Green Bag, 12: 602.

Royal Cambrian Academy, Conway. (E. W. Haslehurst) M. of Art, 25: 444.

Royal Canadian Academy. (J. Smith) Canad. M. 9: 300.

— Exhibition, 1898. (N. Patterson) Canad. M. 10: 509. — Canad. M. 11: 56.

Royal Collections at Buckingham Palace. (F. B. Robinson) M. of Art, 24: 16.

— English. (W. Y. Fletcher) Library, n. s. 1: 305.

Royal College of Surgeons, Centenary of. (V. Plarr) Nature, 62: 294.

— Library of. (J. B. Bailey) Library, 1: 249. — (J. R. Boosé) Library, 6: 191.

Royal Declaration, The, at Accession. Month, 97: 440.

Royal Geographical Society. (W. G. Fitzgerald) Strand, 13: 137.

— Anniv. Address. (C. R. Markham) Geog. J. 9: 589.

— Meetings of, '96–'97. Geog. J. 10: 107.

— President's Address, 1897. (C. R. Markham) Geog. J. 10: 565.

— 1900. (C. R. Markham) Geog. J. 16: 1.

Royal Glasgow Institute of the Fine Arts. Art J. 49: 91.

Royal Hibernian Academy Exhibition. M. of Art, 22: 558.

Royal Houses, The Extinction of. (J. C. Ridpath) Arena, 20: 378.

Royal Humane Society, A Chat about. (C. Middleton) Sund. M. 27: 99.

Royal Institute of British Architects, Admission of Women to Associateship in. Am. Arch. 63: 20.

Royal Institute Exhibition, 1900. (F. Rinder) Art J. 52: 379.

Royal Institution, Centenary of. Nature, 60: 129.
— Faraday Laboratory. (J. Mills) Knowl. 20: 41.
— History of. Science, n. s. 9: 838.

Royal Intent, The. (W. M. Browne) Scrib. M. 26: 496.

Royal Library, British. (J. M. Stone) Scot. R. 34: 213.

Royal Mésalliances. (A. de Burgh) Strand, 18: 56.

Royal Navy and Merchant Shipping, Oppenheim's. (A. T. Mahan) Am. Hist. R. 2: 719.

Royal Observatory, Greenwich. Ath. '00, 1: 819.
— Maunder on. (H. H. Turner) Nature, 63: 271.

Royal Palaces, London. (L. Viajero) Am. Arch. 73: 19.

Royal Romance, A. Liv. Age, 220: 435.

Royal Scottish Academy; art in Scotland. (W. M. G.) M. of Art, 22: 335. — M. of Art, 23: 328. — Art J. 51: 124.
— Exhibition, 1901. Art J. 53: 100.

Royal Slave. (Lady V. Welby) Fortn. 68: 432.

Royal Society, Anniversary Meeting of. Nature, 63: 135.

Royal Society of Canada. (J. G. Bourinot) Canad. M. 9: 488.
— 20th General Meeting. (H. M. Ami) Science, n. s. 13: 1015.

Royal Society of Painters in Water-colors. (F. Wedmore) Studio (Lond.) 4: 121.

Royal Society of Painter-Etchers, 1895. (F. Wedmore) Studio (Lond.) 5: 22.
— 1896. Studio (Lond.) 7: 165.

Royal Societies Club, London, Decorations. (A. L. Baldry) Art J. 51: 339.

Royal Statistical Society. J. Statis. Soc. 64: 363.

Royal Supremacy, The. (A. W. Renton) Green Bag, 11: 522.
— Rebellion against. (Earl of Portsmouth) No. Am. 169: 720.

Royal Wooing, A. (Evelyn Wills) Idler, 14: 106.

Royal Worcester, Recent. M. of Art, 22: 388.

Royalties. (F. Max Müller) Liv. Age, 214: 411 — 215: 155.
— I have seen. (T. H. S. Escott) Chamb. J. 75: 737. Same art. Liv. Age, 219: 554.

Royalty, Home Life of English. (A. H. Beavan) Cosmopol. 26: 185.
— Influence of. Sat. R. 88: 636.
— Reminiscences of. (M. J. Plarr) Argosy, 64: 50.

Royce, Josiah. Studies of Good and Evil. (J. W. Chadwick) Nation, 67: 263. — (C. K. Sherman) Dial (Ch.) 26: 121.
— The World and the Individual. (R. C. Cabot) Harv. Grad. M. 8: 317. — (J. E. McTaggart) Mind, 25: 258.

Roycroft Colony. (A. B. McGill) Cath. World, 73: 785.

Royer, Madame Clemence, with portrait. (T. J. McCormack) Open Court, 14: 562.
— Sketch of. (M. T. Boyer) Pop. Sci. Mo. 54: 690.

Rozwadowski, Count, Musician, and Italian Consul to Chicago, with portrait. Music, 14: 301.

Rubáiyát of Doc Sifers; a poem. (J. W. Riley) Cent. 33: 103, 217.

Rubber Industry of the Amazon Valley. J. Soc. Arts, 48: 748.

Rube. (H. Heimburg) Liv. Age, 224: 816. 225: 16.

Rubens, Peter Paul, with portrait, life, and bibliography. Mast. in Art, 2: Pt. 13.
— Michel's. (K. Cox) Nation, 69: 448.
— Paintings at Longford Castle. (C. Phillips) Art J. 49: 297.

Rubidium, Cæsium and, Certain Double Halogen Salts of. (H. L. Wells and H. W. Foote) Am. J. Sci. 153: 461.

Rubinstein, Anton Gregorovich. (A. E. Keeton) Gent. M. n. s. 66: 116. — Liv. Age, 222: 370.
— in Milan. Music, 18: 176.
— Incidents in the Life of. (I. Martinoff) Music, 13: 34.
— Personal Recollections, with portrait. (H. Ritter) Music, 19: 577.

Rubricas, Peculiar, attached to Various Early Spanish Signatures. (W. M. Wood) Overland, n. s. 30: 30.

Rubruquis, Rockhill's Edition of. (C. R. Beazley) Geog. J. 17: 298.

Ruby. New mode of occurrence in North Carolina. (J. W. Judd and W. E. Hidden) Am. J. Sci. 158: 370.

Ruby Heart, The; a story. (E. Nesbit) Argosy, 64: 702.

Ruby Jewels. (G. W. Thornley) Art J. 52: 365.

Ruby Mines of Upper Burma. (Mrs. H. C. Paget) Cornh. 84: 812.

Ruby Necklace, The; a story. (Helen W. Pierson) Nat'l M. (Bost.) 5: 571.

רוח, Use of, in the Old Testament. (C. A. Briggs) J. Bib. Lit. 19: 132.

Ruder, Pierre de, Case of. (C. Lattey) Month, 96: 500.

Rudolf, Lake, Mr. Cavendish on his Journey to. Nature, 57: 331.
— Expedition to. (Maj. H. H. Austin) Geog. J. 14: 148.

Ruetimeyer, L. (R. Burckhart) Science, 6: 985.

Rufford Abbey, England. (Lord Savile) Pall Mall M. 14: 435.

Ruffs and Reeves [birds]. Sat. R. 89: 553.

Rugby School, 1869–74. (H. Hayman) Bib. Sac. 56: 505. 57: 95, 218.
— Art Museum of. (T. M. Lindsay) M. of Art, 22: 590.
— Rouse's History of. Ath. '98, 2: 482.

Rugs, Fine. (Dinah Sturgis) Overland, n. s. 36: 71.
— Holt on. (F. W. Gookin) Dial (Ch.) 31: 232.
— Oriental. (W. G. Marquis) Brush & P. 8: 301.
— — Mumford on. (F. W. Gookin) Dial (Ch.) 30: 137. — (R. Sturgis) Internat. Mo. 3: 732. — (G. H. Ellwanger) Bk. Buyer, 21: 563.

Ruifrock, Henry, Pianist and Composer, with portrait. Music, 18: 465.

Ruined House, The; a story. (A. E. Barr) Sund. M. 28: 73.

"Rule Britannia," Authorship of. (J. C. Collins) Sat. R. 83: 189.

Rule Britannia; a story. (John Le Breton) Pall Mall M. 12: 129.

Rulers at Work. Illus. (F. Cunliffe-Owen) Munsey, 25: 801.

Rules for undermining a Flourishing Republic. (P. F. Bicknell) Nation, 68: 143.

Ruling-classes in a Democracy. (H. van Dyke) Outl. 69: 774.

Ruling Passion, The; a story. (Constance Smith) Good Words, 39: Xmas no.

Rumford, B. Thompson, Count. Temp. Bar, 117: 32.
— and his Work. (E. Gilman) Char. R. 6: 211.

Rummell, Franz, Pianist, with portrait. Music, 13: 750.

Run, The. (H. M. Steele) Cent. 39: 864.

Run of Luck, A. (J. C. Harris) Scrib. M. 22: 682.

Run of the Rosemere. (E. J. Devine) Month, 90: 190, 280.

Run of the Yellow Mail ; a railroad story. (F. H. Spearman) McClure, 17: 93.

Runaway Girls, The ; a story. (I. Allen) Idler, 16: 589.

Runciman, J. F., as Musical Critic. Acad. 56: 13.

— Old Scores and New Readings. (Alfr. Kalisch) Sat. R. 87: 73.

Runes of Nature. (H. Macmillan) Sund. M. 28: 624.

Runkelstein, Frescoes of. (W. D. McCrackan) Harper, 96: 222.

Runner, The ; a story. (B. Capes) Blackw. 166: 369.

Rupee, A Stable. Chamb. J. 77: 193.

Rupert, Prince. Journal, 1642–46. Eng. Hist. R. 13: 730.

— Marriage of. (E. Scott) Eng. Hist. R. 15: 760.

Rupert, A, from the South. (P. C. Standing) Un. Serv. M. 22: 41.

Rupert of Hentzau ; a story. (Anthony Hope) Pall Mall M. 13: 475. 14: 49–503. 15: 112–375. Same art. McClure, 10: 128 — 11: 270.

Rural Exodus. (E. A. S. Lowndes) Westm. 156: 168.

Rural Industries, Some Minor. Chamb. J. 76: 183–248.

Rural Life, The Study of. (K. L. Butterfield) Chaut. 32: 26.

Rural Prosperity. (E. Verney) Ecl. M. 128: 827.

Rural Visitor, A ; a story. (W. N. Harben) Bk. News, 16: 523.

Rus in Urbe. Month, 89: 178, 289, 413.

Rush, Mrs. James. (A. H. Wharton) Lippinc. 64: 92, 311.

Rush-Bagot Convention ; is it Immortal ? (H. S. Boutell) No. Am. 173: 331.

Ruskin, John. (T. F. Gailor) Sewanee, 1: 491. — (W. P. P. Longfellow) Archit. R. 7: 42. — (R. F. Horton) Lond. Q. 93: 289. — (M. H. Spielman) Library, n. s. 1: 225. — (C. T. Winchester) Meth. R. 60: 210. — (S. Beale) Am. Arch. 67: 45. — Blackw. 167: 340. — (J. Wedgwood) Contemp. 77: 334. Same art. Ecl. M. 134: 658. — (R. W. Bond) Contemp. 78: 118. Same art. Liv. Age, 225: 1. — (R. Riordan) Critic, 36: 230. — Econ. J. 10: 274. — (W. P. P. Longfellow) Forum, 29: 298. — (W. S. B. Mathews) Music, 18: 55. — (W. J. Stillmann) Nation, 70: 66. — (L. Stephen) National, 35: 240. Same art. Liv. Age, 225: 423. — (C. Waldstein) No. Am. 170: 553. — (H. D. Rawnsley) Outl. 64: 511. — Outl. 64: 202. — Quar. 191: 393. — With portrait. (L. Tavener) R. of Rs. (N. Y.) 21: 289. — (W. C. Brownell) Scrib. M. 27: 502. — Spec. 84: 133. — (W. H. Winslow) New Eng. M. n. s. 21: 274. — (B. O. Flower) Arena, 18: 70.

— Address on 80th Birthday of. (W. White) M. of Art, 25: 260.

— and the "Hinksey Diggers." Atlan. 85: 572.

— and his Critics. Sat. R. 90: 455, 487.

— and his Home in English Lake District. (J. M. Chappie) Nat'l M. (Bost.) 7: 241.

— and Millais. (W. J. Stillman) Nation, 69: 9.

— and Milner at Oxford. Indep. 53: 2585.

— and Modern Business. Spec. 84: 234.

— and the Royal Gold Medal. Am. Arch. 67: 94.

— and Venice. Am. Arch. 67: 55. — (Alex. Robertson) Good Words, 41: 472.

— Art and Truth. (J. La Farge) Internat. Mo. 2: 510.

— as an Art Critic. (C. H. Moore) Atlan. 86: 438.

— as an Artist. (M. H. Spielmann) M. of Art, 24: 241. — (F. Rinder) Argosy, 73: 305. — (M. H. Spielmann) Scrib. M. 24: 659.

Ruskin, John, as an Artist and Art Critic. (E. T. Cook) Studio (Internat.) 10: 77.

— as Economist. (P. Geddes) Internat. Mo. 1: 280.

— as a Lecturer. Atlan. 85: 571.

— as an Oxford Lecturer. (J. M. Bruce) Cent. 33: 590.

— as a Revolutionary. (L. D. Abbott) Indep. 52: 301.

— as a Writer, with portrait. (M. H. Spielmann) Bk. Buyer, 19: 161, 260.

— at Farnley. (E. M. Fawkes) 19th Cent. 47: 616.

— at Home. Acad. 56: 462. — (A. O'Hagan) Munsey, 25: 441.

— Chief Writings of. Lit. W. (Bost.) 31: 40.

— Education of. (A. H. Sotheran) Arena, 22: 630.

— Exhibition of Drawings. Sat. R. 91: 202.

— Hobson on. (M. West) Dial (Ch.) 26: 396.

— Influence of. (L. P. Jacks) New World, 9: 601.

— Is he out of Date ? (R. de La Sizeranne) M. of Art, 24: 258.

— Lessons from. (C. S. Devas) Econ. J. 8: 28.

— On Two Rare Works of. (E. Gosse) Indep. 52: 526.

— "Pathetic Fallacy" of and Keats's Treatment of Nature. (E. P. Morton) Poet-Lore, 12: 58.

— the Reformer ; a poem. (J. Brigham) Chaut. 30: 592.

— Religion of. Liv. Age, 224: 726.

— Reminiscences of. (C. Chapman) Sund. M. 29: 197.

— Rossetti and Pre-Raphaelitism. (M. S. Anderson) Dial (Ch.) 26: 336.

— Social Reforms of. (A. R. Marble) Arena, 23: 538.

— The Truth about. (H. H. Statham) Fortn. 73: 418.

Ruskin College ; a College for the People. (T. E. Will) Arena, 26: 15.

— The Poor Man's College. (M. Berkeley) Gent. M. n. s. 64: 273.

Ruskin Co-operative Colony. (H. N. Casson) Indep. 51: 192.

— Failure of. (W. G. Davis) Gunton's M. 21: 530.

"Ruskin Hall" Movement. Gunton's M. 20: 163. — (L. T. Dodd and J. A. Dale) Fortn. 73: 325. — Am. Arch. 69: 7.

Ruskin-land. (L. D. Abbott) Cosmopol. 28: 501.

Ruskin Mosaic, A. (J. Telford) Meth. R. 60: 601.

Ruskin's Social Experiment. Liv. Age, 213: 263.

Ruskiniana. Critic, 36: 233.

Russell, George H. Bank. M. (N. Y.) 57: 777.

Russell, Charles, of Killowen. (G. McDermott) Am. Cath. Q. 25: 636. — (E. Dicey) Fortn. 74:' 577. Same art. Liv. Age, 227: 433. Same art. Ecl. M. 136: 38. — With portrait. Green Bag, 12: 549. — (J. McCarthy) Indep. 52: 2164. — Liv. Age, 226: 842. — With portrait. (W. T. Stead) R. of Rs. (N. Y.) 22: 425. — Sat. R. 90: 199.

— R. B. O'Brien's Life of. Ath. '01, 2: 726.

Russell, Miss Ella, Interview with. Music, 12: 305.

Russell, Giles. (J. R. Kemble) N. E. Reg. 52: 360.

Russell, Capt. Peter, Journal of, 1780. Am. Hist. R. 4: 478.

Russell, W. Clark. (D. C. Murray) Canad. M. 9: 281.

Russia after the Completion of the Siberian Railway. (A. Vambéry) Pall Mall M. 19: 70.

— Aims of. Blackw. 169: 548.

— America's Agricultural Regeneration of. (A. H. Ford) Cent. 40: 501.

— American Treaty with. (W. M. Jones) R. of Rs. (N. Y.) 17: 549.

— Amusements in. (F. Whishaw) Chamb. J. 74: 166. Same art. Ecl. M. 129: 139.

— and China, Treaty between, 1900, Secret History of. Contemp. 71: 172.

— and Constantinople. (R. K. Wilson) Contemp. 71: 265.

— and Disarmament. (E. J. Dillon) Contemp. 74: 609.

— and England. Spec. 82: 496. — (R. Blennerhassett) National, 37: 21.

Russians and Antichrist, The. (G. L. Cotel) Temp. Bar, 112: 114.

— Impressions of. (Arthur Symons) Sat. R. 90: 76.

— in Oriental Warfare. (F. H. Tyrrell) Un. Serv. M. 16: 167.

Russo-Turkish Border, The. (G. F. Wright) Nation, 72: 211.

Rustic Argus, A. (M. E. Francis) Longm. 35: 521.

Rustic Comedy, A; a story. (Mrs. A. Baldwin) Idler, 13: 724.

Rustic's Goal, A; a story. (S. E. Cartwright) Temp. Bar, 110: 513.

Rusticus in Urbe. Blackw. 165: 974. Same art. Liv. Age, 222: 312.

Rustle of the Leaves, The; a poem. (J. Stafford) Argosy, 69: 31.

Ruth and Boaz, Case of. (D. W. Amram) Green Bag, 13: 313.

— Story of. (C. A. Dickinson) Nat'l M. (Bost.) 8: 162.

Rutherford, Mark, pseud. See White, William Hale.

Rutherford, Samuel; a Little Master of English. Acad. 56: 376. Same art. Ecl. M. 132: 941. Same art. Liv. Age, 221: 328.

Rutherford Astronomical Photographs. (F. E. Harpham) Pop. Astron. 8: 129.

Ruthwell Cross, The. Month, 89: 506.

Rutland, Vermont. (J. C. R. Dorr) New Eng. M. n. s. 18: 201.

Rutledge, John, with portrait. (F. R. Jones) Green Bag, 13: 325.

Rutter, F. W. P. Bank. M. (Lond.) 67: 503.

Ruyter, M. A. de, Life of, Grinnell-Milne's. Spec. 79: 343.

Rye, Eng. (G. F. Scott) Artist (N. Y.) 29: 29.

— Description of. (S. Rawson) Acad. 58: 364.

Ryland, Henry, Art Worker. Illus. Artist (N. Y.) 23: 9.

Ryland, William Wynne, an Artist who was hanged. (F. Miller) Eng. Illust. 17: 555.

Saadiah Gaon, Anti-Karaite Writings of. (S. Poznański) Jew. Q. 10: 238. — (A. Harkavy) Jew. Q. 13: 655.

— Sefer Ha-Galuy not written by? (D. S. Margoliouth and A. Harkavy) Jew. Q. 12: 502, 703.

Sabatier, Auguste, Newman and. (W. Ward) Fortn. 75: 808.

Sabatiers, The. (J. C. Bracq) Outl. 68: 212.

Sabbath, The American. (J. R. Howard) Outl. 68: 638.

— Earliest Form of. (C. H. Toy) J. Bib. Lit. 18: 190.

— Original Character of. (M. Jastrow) Am. J. Theol. 2: 312.

— Prehistoric Man's Day of Rest. (R. G. Haliburton) Canad. M. 9: 454.

Sabbionetta, Italy. (C. Buckingham) Am. Arch. 65: 107.

Sabina, Princess Palatine of Bavaria and Countess of Egemont. (E. Peyton) Gent. M. n. s. 64: 381.

Sabines, A Summer amidst the. (E. Mariotti) Temp. Bar, 115: 422.

Sabre and Bayonet Question. (J. Bigelow) J. Mil. Serv. Inst. 3: 65.

Sabrinæ Corolla. Macmil. 84: 292. Same art. Liv. Age, 230: 717.

Sacerdotalism. Church Q. 47: 424.

— in England. (S. Smith) Outl. 63: 497.

— True and False. (E. W. Donald) Outl. 62: 432.

Sachs, E. D. Art and Architecture in Modern Opera Houses and Theatres. (R. P. Spiers) M. of Art, 22: 476.

Sachs, Julius. (K. Goebel) Sci. Prog. 7: 150. — (F. Darwin) Nature, 56: 201.

Sacrament, Blessed, Benediction of the. (H. Thurston) Month, 97: 587.

Sacramental Rite, Has the Church a Share in determining the? (F. Rankin) Am. Cath. Q. 23: 720.

Sacramento Valley, The; its resources and industries. (N. P. Chipman) Overland, n. s. 37: 887.

Sacraments, Institution of. (H. J. C. Knight) Expos. 6: 54.

— Use of. (W. E. Parson) Luth. Q. 30: 326.

— — Parson on. (S. G. Hefelbower) Luth. Q. 31: 216.

Sacred Books, Natural History of. (A. Menzies) Am. J. Theol. 1: 71.

Sacred Heart, Devotion to, in Mediæval England. (G. Dolan) Dub. R. 120: 373.

Sacrifice, Idea of, as developed in the Old Testament. (F. A. Gast) Ref. Ch. R. 47: 1.

— Significance of, in the Old Testament. (H. Schultz) Am. J. Theol. 4: 257.

Sacrifice of Ventris Perugini. (W. Graham) Canad. M. 10: 401.

Sacrifice to Bhowani, A. (J. Reid) Cornh. 81: 393.

Sacrifices in the Bible, Origin of. (C. G. Hubbell) N. Church R. 5: 221.

Saddling, Principles and Practice of. (M. J. Treacy) J. Mil. Serv. Inst. 16: 77.

Safety-fund System, The. Bank. M. (N. Y.) 58: 343.

Saga of the Seas, A. (K. Grahame) Scrib. M. 24: 194.

Sagebeer, Joseph Evans. Lit. W. (Bost.) 31: 58.

Saginaw Valley, Mich., Archæology of. (H. I. Smith) Am. Anthrop. 3: 286, 501, 726.

Sagittarius, New Star in. (E. C. Pickering) Knowl. 22: 105.

Saguenay, Le; a poem, with translation. (L. Frechette) Canad. M. 10: 119.

Sahara, the, Aspects of Nature in. (A. Heilprin) Pop. Sci. Mo. 52: 577. 53: 174.

— from Algeria to the French Congo. (M. F. Foureau) Geog. J. 17: 135.

— Tunisian, A Journey through. (Sir H. H. Johnston) Geog. J. 11: 581.

— Western, A Visit to. (Harold Bindloss) Gent. M. n. s. 59: 400. Same art. Ecl. M. 129: 778.

Sailing alone around the World. (J. Slocum) Cent. 36: 680, 938. 37: 134, 243-755.

Sailing Rules, British, revised. (J. C. Macdonald) Jurid. R. 9: 332.

Sailor, The American, under the Law. (W. MacArthur) Forum, 26: 718.

Sailor Princes of To-day. (F. Morris) Munsey, 22: 669.

Sailors and the Law. (J. H. Williams) Indep. 52: 2733.

— Old-time. (A. R. McMahon) Un. Serv. M. 16: 417.

— Training of. (R. W. Bulkeley) Sat. R. 90: 555.

— Work Songs of. (J. E. Patterson) Good Words, 41: 391.

Sailors' Pets. Spec. 83: 182.

Sailors' Sports. (S. D. Gordon) Belgra. 97: 266.

Saint and Sinner. (B. Atkinson) Sund. M. 28: 578.

— English Abbreviation for. (F. C. Burkitt) Ath. '01, 2: 702.

St. Agnes, Eve of, Surette's. (J. H. Ingham) Citizen, 3: 274.

St. Andrew, Alien Priory of, and its Transfer to Winchester College in 1391. Archæol. 50: 251.

St. Andrews, Scotland, the Golfer's Paradise. (D. D. Fletcher) Nat'l M. (Bost.) 12: 341.

St. Andrew's University. (Mrs. R. Ritchie) Critic, 38: 241.

— The Oxford of Scotland. Chamb. J. 75: 678.

St. Augustine, Florida. (A. M. Brice) Temp. Bar, 119: 339.

St. Augustine's Monastery, Canterbury, Boggis's History of. Ath. '01, 2: 559.

Sarcophagi, Early Christian, at Zara, Dalmatia. Reliquary, 40: 194.

Sardine Industry, The French. (H. M. Smith) Pop. Sci. Mo. 59: 542.

Sardou, Victorien. Peril. (M. Beerbohm) Sat. R. 91: 234.

— Spiritisme. Sewanee, 2: 192.

— Visit to. (E. de Amicis) Chaut. 24: 701.

Sargasso Sea, Amid the Islets of. (C. Parkinson) Cornh. 80: 533. Same art. Liv. Age, 223: 720. Same art. Ecl. M. 134: 253.

Sargasso Weed; a poem. (E. C. Stedman) Atlan. 80: 493.

Sargent, Charles S., Suburban Country Place of. (Mrs. S. Van Rensselaer) Cent. 32: 3.

Sargent, John S., Artist. (A. L. Baldry) Studio (Internat.) 10: 3, 107.

— as a Portrait Painter. (Marion H. Dixon) M. of Art, 23: 112.

— at the Royal Academy. (H. H. Fyfe) 19th Cent. 49: 1022.

— Exhibition, 1899. Artist (N. Y.) 24: xliii.

— Portraits by. Sat. R. 89: 583.

Sarmiento, Domingo Faustino. (H. H. Barroll) Educa. 21: 257.

Sarmiento, Mt. (Sir W. M. Conway) Harper, 100: 223.

Sarsfield, Patrick. (R. B. O'Brien) Cornh. 82: 609.

Sartain, John, Reminiscences of. (R. H. Stoddard) Bk. Buyer, 19: 373. — (J. L. Gilder) Critic, 35: 1041. — (N. Angier) Dial (Ch.) 27: 359.

Sarto, Andrea del. Life, Works, and Bibliography, with portrait. Mast. in Art, 2: Pt. 22.

— Virgin and Child, with St. John. (Claude Phillips) Art J. 53: 102.

Sartoris, Nellie Grant, and her Children. (Juliette M. Babbitt) Midland, 7: 99.

Saskatchewan, Sources of the. (W. D. Wilcox) Nat. Geog. M. 10: 113. Same art. Geog. J. 13: 358.

Saskatchewan Country. (S. Bray) Canad. M. 13: 26.

Satan, Delivering to. (H. A. Redpath) Expos. 4: 322.

Satellites, Ephemerides of. (J. Morrison) Pop. Astron. 6: 165.

— Evolution of. (G. H. Darwin) Atlan. 81: 444.

— which have Measurable Discs, Investigations of. (T. J. J. See) Pop. Astron. 9: 471.

Satire, A Plea for. Atlan. 85: 855.

— Political, in New York. Critic, 32: 11.

— Social Pictorial. (G. Du Maurier) Harper, 96: 331, 505.

— Why have we No? Atlan. 84: 143.

Satirists, English. Acad. 57: 479.

Satolli, Cardinal; Results of his Mission. (E. McGlynn) Forum, 22: 695.

Sattler, Joseph, Designer. (C. Hiatt) Studio (Lond.) 4: 92.

Saturdarianism. (S. W. Gamble) Meth. R. 57: 867.

Saturn, The Planet. (C. A. Howes) Pop. Sci. Mo. 51: 357. — (E. M. Antoniadi) Knowl. 22: 9.

— New Satellite of. (E. C. Pickering) Knowl. 22: 131. — (E. C. Pickering) Pop. Astron. 7: 233. — (C. P. Butler) Nature, 59: 489.

Saturn's Rings, Ephemeris of. (J. Morrison) Pop. Astron. 6: 389.

Saturday Club, Boston. (G. W. Cooke) New Eng. M. n. s. 19: 24.

Saturnalia and Kindred Festivals. (J. G. Frazer) Fortn. 74: 653, 825.

Satyr-drama and Euripides' Cyclops. (John Patterson) Scot. R. 31: 349.

Sauber, Robert, Work of. (A. L. Baldry) Art J. 51: 1.

Saul and Macbeth. (H. W. Blanc) Sewanee, 1: 273.

Saul Stevens's Daughter. (Sara Dean) Overland, n. s. 30: 243.

Sault Ste. Marie, Industries at. Am. Arch. 68: 69.

— Locks at. (W. P. Kibbee) Engin. M. 13: 600.

Saunders, F. (G. J. Manson) Bookman, 4: 422.

— Recollections of. Critic, 30: 276.

Saunders, Marshall. Lit. W. (Bost.) 29: 325.

Saurians, Gigantic, of the Past. (W. H. Ballou) Cent. 33: 15.

— Serpentlike. (W. H. Ballou) Pop. Sci. Mo. 53: 209.

Saurocephalus, Species of. (O. P. Hay) Am. J. Sci. 157: 299.

Sauropodous Dinosauria, Families of. (O. C. Marsh) Am. J. Sci. 156: 487.

Sauter, George. (S. C. de Soissons) Artist (N. Y.) 30: 169.

Savage, Arthur, a Loyalist. (A. I. Appleton) N. E. Reg. 204: 472.

Savage, Minot J. (D. McDermid) Arena, 18: 23.

Savage Tribes, Government of. (J. W. Powell) Forum, 25: 712.

Savages. (J. Rickaby) Month, 98: 277.

— and Criminals. (W. Ferrero) Indep. 52: 2688.

— Capacity of. (F. Boyle) Macmil. 79: 36.

— Civilization brings Death to. (R. B. C. Graham) Sat. R. 86: 431.

— Love among the. (Tighe Hopkins) Chamb. J. 78: 238.

Savannah Yacht Club. (W. G. Sutlive) Outing, 33: 458.

Savaric, Bishop of Bath and Glastonbury, 1192-1205. (C. M. Church) Archæol. 51: 73.

Savart, Pierre. (W. L. Andrews) Bk. Buyer, 18: 309.

Saved by a Mosquito. (F. H. Major) Overland, n. s. 37: 637.

Saved by a Train Wrecker. (V. L. Whitechurch) Strand, 18: 170.

Savernake Forest, Early Spring in. (W. H. Hudson) Longm. 29: 512.

Savile, George. See Halifax, George S., Marquis of.

Saving and Spending. (A. W. Flux; J. A. Hobson) Econ. R. 9: 174, 342.

— Educational Aspect of. (J. H. Hamilton) Q. J. Econ. 13: 45.

— Function of. (L. G. Bostedo) Ann. Am. Acad. Pol. Sci. 17: 95. — (E. von Böhm-Bawerk) Ann. Am. Acad. Pol. Sci. 17: 454.

Saving Grace, The; a story. (S. E. White) McClure, 13: 398.

Saving Knowledge, Sum of. (D. H. Fleming) Presb. & Ref. R. 10: 318.

Saving of Judas, The; a poem. (H. P. Kimball) Poet-Lore, 9: 161.

Saving of Wyllard's Wheat; a story. (H. Bindloss) Argosy, 71: 264. Same art. Liv. Age, 226: 442.

Savings, Marginal Theory of. (C. W. Mixter) Q. J. Econ. 13: 245.

Savings Banks at Home and Abroad. (H. W. Wolff) J. Statis. Soc. 60: 278.

— Humor and Pathos of. (R. Broughton) Cent. 39: 483.

— Money in the Wrong Place. (H. W. Wolff) Econ. R. 8: 289.

— Postal. (J. P. Townsend) Gunton's M. 14: 73. — Bank. M. (N. Y.) 56: 388. 64: 615, 685. 68: 580.

— — for U. S. (I. Loughlin) Nat'l M. (Bost.) 10: 420.

— — Problem of. Bank. M. (Lond.) 71: 78.

— — relation to Commercial Banks. (J. H. Hamilton) Ann. Am. Acad. Pol. Sci. 11: 44.

— — Should the U. S. Government establish? Chaut. 26: 408.

Savings Bank Deposits in England. (H. W. Wolff) Contemp. 79: 278.

Savings Society of Newport, The. (Anna F. Hunter) Char. R. 9: 333.

Savonarola. Acad. 57: 127. Same art. Liv. Age, 222: 907. — (A. Reinhart) Am. Cath. Q. 23: 692.
— and Jesus. (J. W. Buckham) Bib. Sac. 57: 748.
— and Rome. (C. C. Starbuck) Meth. R. 58: 919.
— A 15th Century Revival. (D. J. H. Hobart) Harper, 104: 58.
— 400th Anniversary of his Martyrdom. Open Court, 12: 274.
— Monk, Patriot, Martyr. (F. M. Edselas) Cath. World, 66: 487.
Savoy, The House of. (T. L. I. Teeling) Month, 92: 513.
Savrola; a story. (W. S. Churchill) Macmil. 80: 67-401. 81: 1-81.
Saw-mill, The Modern. (W. H. Trout) Cassier, 11: 184.
Sawing of Logs, American Machinery for. (J. Richards) Engin. M. 16: 932.
— European Machinery for. (J. Richards) Engin. M. 17: 88.
Saws [i. e. Proverbs]. (P. Kent) Gent. M. n. s. 60: 145.
Saxe, Maurice, Marshal of France. (F. Dixon) Temp. Bar, 111: 475.
Saxe-Coburg and Gotha, Alfred E. A., Duke of. Geog. J. 16: 358.
Saxon Cross-shaft and Silver Ornament, Fragments of. Reliquary, 39: 129.
Saxton, Major-General G. H. Geog. J. 17: 539.
Sayce, A. H. Early History of the Hebrews. (A. A. Bevan) Crit. R. 8: 131.
Sayward's Raid; a tale of the Behring Sea. (H. B.) Macmil. 77: 220.
Scaffold, Forgotten Sights of the. (F. G. Walters) Gent. M. n. s. 59: 502.
Scale Insect; Aspidiotus Ostreœformis. (C. L. Marlatt) Science, n. s. 10: 18.
— A Dangerous. (C. L. Marlatt) Science, n. s. 10: 18.
— Date-palm. (T. D. A. Cockerell) Science, n. s. 9: 417.
— Sources of Error in Recent Works on Coccidæ. (C. L. Marlatt) Science, n. s. 9: 835. — Reply. (T. D. A. Cockerell) 10: 86.
    See San José Scale Insect.
Scalp-Lock, Significance of. (A. C. Fletcher) Anthrop. J. 27: 436.
Scalping, Ticket, Bill to prevent. (H. T. Mathers) Forum, 30: 684.
Scandinavia and her King. (C. Sutcliffe) Fortn. 68: 592.
— The New Mysticism in. (H. Ramsden) 19th Cent. 47: 279.
— Poets of. (E. Brausewetter) Cath. World, 73: 477.
Scandinavian Decorative Art. (S. Frykholm) Studio (Internat.) 12: 190.
Scandinavian Exhibition at Stockholm. (J. Douglas) Nation, 65: 352.
Scandinavian Literature. (David Anderson) Scot. R. 30: 322. Same art. Liv. Age, 216: 320.
Scandinavians, Nelson's. (A. Estrem) Am. Hist. R. 3: 161.
Scapegoat, The; a story. (Mrs. Henry Wood) Argosy, 67: 34.
Scapolite Rocks, from Alaska. (J. E. Spurr) Am. J. Sci. 160: 310.
Scapulæ of Northwest Coast Indians. (G. A. Dorsey) Am. Natural. 31: 736.
Scarab from Cyprus, A. (G. D. Pierides) J. Hel. Stud. 16: 272.
Scarlet Sin, A; a story. (E. Hamilton) Pall Mall M. 14: 292.
Scarlet Woman, The. (R. J. Walling) Idler, 18: 142, 220, 336. — (J. Britten) Month, 95: 61.
Scarning House; a story. Macmil. 83: 433.

Scarron, Paul. Temp. Bar, 110: 393.
Scartazzini, John Andrew. Ath. '01, 1: 242.
Scavenger Boy, Life of. (J. D. Symon) Eng. Illust. 20: 305.
Scavengers, Nature's, Plea for. (F. G. Aflalo) Sat. R. 80: 235. Same art. Liv. Age, 218: 837.
Scenery, Beautiful. (C. W. Dilke) Sat. R. 83: 707.
— Best. (H. A. Bryden and others) Sat. R. 84: 6-339.
— Desecration of. Spec. 85: 202.
— Romantic, Development of the Love of, in America. (M. E. Woolley) Am. Hist. R. 3: 56.
— Stage, True Principles of. (P. Fitzgerald) J. Soc. Arts, 49: 445.
Scenes in a Novelist's Landscape. (G. Morley) Argosy, 68: 272.
Scenes of Real Life, Country Pleasures; a short dialogue. (Gyp) Liv. Age, 215: 46.
Schaeffer, Rev. Solomon. (J. A. Brown) Luth. Q. 29: 277.
Schaff, Philip. (T. Appel) Ref. Ch. R. 46: 90.
— Letters to L. H. Steiner. (B. C. Steiner) Presb. & Ref. R. 11: 131.
— Schaff's Life of. (H. W. Reed) Dial (Ch.) 24: 44.
— (W. E. Griffis) New World, 7: 185.
Schandorph, Sophus. (E. Gosse) Ath. '01, 1: 51.
Scharwenka, Xaver. Mataswintha. Music, 12: 108.
Schaumburg, Emilie. (V. T. Peacock) Lippinc. 65: 102.
Schenck, Edwin S. Bank. M. (N. Y.) 58: 410.
Scherer, Gideon. (J. A. Brown) Luth. Q. 27: 544.
Schering, Ernst Christian Julius. (W. H. G. C. Young) Nature, 57: 416.
Scheurer-Kestner, Auguste. A Noble Life. Outl. 63: 243.
Schieffelin, Jacob and Hannah (Lawrence), of New York. (I. J. Greenwood) N. E. Reg. 204: 449.
Schiller as a Prophet. (P. Carus) Open Court, 11: 214.
— The Invincible Armada, Translated. (A. C. Orr) Canad. M. 9: 138.
— A Study of. (J. Forster) Chaut. 26: 251.
Schiller, Hans von, Pianist, with portrait. Music, 15: 320.
Schimper, Wilhelm A. F., Prof. (P. Groom) Nature, 64: 551.
Schirner, Eduard, Pianist, with portrait. (Charlotte Teller) Music, 16: 549.
Schists of the Gold and Diamond Regions of Eastern Minas Geraes, Brazil, Notes on. (O. A. Derby) Am. J. Sci. 160: 207.
Schleiermacher, Friedrich. (J. Lindsay) Presb. & Ref. R. 10: 58.
Schleswig-Holstein. The Home of our Forefathers. (M. Todhunter) Westm. 148: 396.
— Question of. (F. M. Müller) 19th Cent. 41: 707. — (A. D. Jörgensen) 19th Cent. 42: 918.
Schley, Winfield Scott, with portrait. (P. Benjamin) R. of Rs. (N. Y.) 24: 292.
— Court of Inquiry, with portrait. (P. Benjamin) Indep. 53: 2086.
— — The Verdict. (R. Ogden) Nation, 73: 466.
Schlichter, Henry. Geog. J. 17: 540.
Schmedtgen, William, Artist. (M. McDowell) Brush & P. 1: 141.
Schmidt, Arthur P., Music Publisher. Music, 19: 171.
Schmidt, Oscar, Sketch of. Pop. Sci. Mo. 55: 693.
Schnaderhuepfeln : the impromptu songs of Tyrol. (C. A. Gunnison) Overland, n. s. 34: 20.
Schneider, C. P. Eugéne. (G. K. Lemmy) Cassier, 19: 415.
Schneider, Otto J., Etcher, with portrait. (M. T. Everett) Brush & P. 7: 65.
Schneider, Sascha. (S. C. de Soissons) Artist (N. Y.) 32: 16.

Schuetzenberger, Paul. Ath. '97, 2: 37.

Schultze-Naumburg, Mme. M. of Art, 22: 336.

Schumann, Robert, and Clara Wieck. (R. Aldrich) Music, 18: 113.

— Memories of. (C. Reinecke) Music, 13: 581.

— Song-cycles. (M. Aronson) Music, 11: 552.

Schumann-Heink, Mrs., Singer, with portrait. Music, 15: 187. 18: 161.

— at Maine Festival. (B. H. Dingley) Music, 18: 586.

Schur, Wilhelm, Prof. (W. J. S. Lockyer) Nature, 64: 380.

Schurz, Carl. (E. L. Godkin) Nation, 68: 179.

— at Home. (O. G. Villard) Critic, 33: 247.

Schuster, Felix. Bank. M. (Lond.) 71: 423.

Schutt, Eduard, Artist and Man. (Lilian Apel) Music, 13: 16.

Schuyler, Catherine V. R., a Godchild of Washington, K. S. Baxter on. Bk. Buyer, 1: 138.

Schuyler, Eugene. (E. W. Blashfield) Bk. Buyer, 22: 117. — (J. S. Fiske) Nation, 72: 491.

— Essays. (E. G. Johnson) Dial (Ch.) 30: 184.

Schuylkill River. (O. C. S. Carter) J. Frankl. Inst. 144: 366.

Schwab, Charles M. Cassier, 17: 526.

Schwalbe, Dr. Ludwig, South Sea Savant. (L. Becke) Idler, 11: 204.

Schwann, Theodor, with portrait. (J. J. Walsh) Cath. World, 71: 198.

Science, An American Senate of. Science, n. s. 14: 277.

— and Education. Nature, 60: 324.

— and Faith. (J. C. Hedley) Dub. R. 123: 241. — (P. Topinard) Monist, 7: 218.

— and the Government. (J. R. Eastman) Science, 5: 525. — (S. Newcomb) No. Am. 170: 666.

— and History, Constructive Value of. (A. C. Armstrong) Meth. R. 59: 345.

— and Modern Civilization. (W. Roberts) Nature, 56: 621.

— and Morals. (P. M. Berthelot) Pop. Sci. Mo. 52: 326.

— and Philosophy. (R. M. Wenley) Pop. Sci. Mo. 59: 361.

— and Politics. Spec. 79: 817.

— and Providence. (F. M. Bristol) Open Court, 12: 509.

— and Realism. (Mary Fisher) Liv. Age, 215: 771.

— and Religion. (C. P. Gasquoine) Westm. 155: 92.

— — at End of 19th Century. (M. J. Griffin) Canad. M. 16: 313.

— — Reply to " The Final Seat of Authority." (A. Burnell) Westm. 154: 440.

— and Theology, Warfare of, White on. Church Q. 46: 121. — Ed. R. 186: 357. — (J. Hogan) Am. Cath. Q. 22: 382. — (W. Battershall) No. Am. 165: 87.

— and the U. S. Government. Dial (Ch.) 22: 73.

— and War. (R. Ogden) Nation, 69: 254.

— Applied, Teaching of. (C. Lauth) Pop. Sci. Mo. 52: 247.

— as an Instrument of Education. (P. E. Berthelot) Pop. Sci. Mo. 51: 253.

— as a Moral Guide. (H. E. Harvey) Westm. 149: 186.

— at the Beginning of the Century. (H. S. Williams) Harper, 94: 217.

— Century's Progress in. (W. Seton) Cath. World, 69: 146. — (M. Foster) Educa. R. 18: 313.

— Church and. (G. McDermot) Cath. World, 70: 527.

— Dawn of a Brilliant Era, 1837. (J. Mills) Knowl. 20: 2.

— Development of the Exact Natural Sciences in the 19th Century. (H. C. Jones) Science, n. s. 13: 338.

Science, England's Neglect of, Perry on. (G. M. Minchin) Nature, 64: 226.

— Ethics and. (J. Wedgwood) Contemp. 72: 218.

— Faith of. (G. S. Fullerton) Science, n. s. 12: 587. — (J. W. Diggle) Expos. 3: 521.

— Fifty Years of American. (W. J. McGee) Atlan. 82: 307.

— Foundation of. (W. J. McGee) Forum, 27: 168.

— Graduate Course in. (G. B. Germann) Science, n. s. 14: 413.

— How it serves the People. (E. Renan) No. Am. 172: 701.

— in Education. (A. Geikie) Pop. Sci. Mo. 54: 672. — (A. Geikie) Nature, 59: 108.

— — Mission of. (J. M. Coulter) Science, n. s. 12: 281.

— in 1896, Review of. Acad. 51: 27.

— in England at the Beginning of the 20th Century. Nature, 63: 221. Same art. Ecl. M. 136: 439.

— in Italy, Recent. (G. H. Bryan) Nature, 60: 9.

— in the 19th Century. Sat. R. 88: 350. — Spec. 85: 961. — (B. O. Flower) Arena, 26: 178.

— in the 20th Century. Nature, 63: 221.

— in Preparatory Schools, Specialization in. (C. S. Palmer) School R. 6: 659.

— — What is the Consensus of Opinion as to the Place of ? (C. C. Wilson) School R. 6: 203.

— in relation to Art and Industry. (N. Lockyer) Nature, 62: 32.

— in Religious Instruction. (F. W. Very) N. Church R. 7: 346.

— in the Schools. (W. M. Davis) Educa. R. 13: 429.

— Mivart's Groundwork of. (W. K. Brooks) Pop. Sci. Mo. 54: 450.

— The Old and the New. (E. W. Adams) Gent. M. n. s. 67: 493.

— on the Conduct of Life. (G. B. Halstead) Open Court, 12: 65.

— Paradoxes of. (G. F. Wright) Bib. Sac. 54: 205.

— Pearson's Grammar of. (C. S. Peirce) Pop. Sci. Mo. 58: 296.

— Physical, Recent Advance in. (J. Trowbridge) Internat. Mo. 1: 123.

— — vs. Matter and Form. (J. Bredin) Dub. R. 126: 343. — Reply. (C. Aherne) Dub. R. 127: 278.

— Progress of, Pres. Address at Denver Meeting of A. A. A. S., 1901. (R. S. Woodward) Nature, 64: 498. Same art. Science, n. s. 14: 305. Same art. Pop. Sci. Mo. 59: 513.

— Pure, Plea for. (H. A. Rowland) Pop. Sci. Mo. 59: 170.

— Recent, 1897. (P. Kropotkin) 19th Cent. 41: 250. 42: 22, 799. Same art. Ecl. M. 128: 394. Same art. Liv. Age, 214: 499. 215: 691.

— — 1898. (P. Kropotkin) 19th Cent. 44: 259.

— — 1899. 1. Biological Chemistry ; 2. Weather Prediction. (P. Kropotkin) 19th Cent. 45: 404. Same art. Ecl. M. 132: 910.

— — 1900. (P. Kropotkin) 19th Cent. 48: 919.

— — 1901. (P. Kropotkin) 19th Cent. 50: 417. Same art. Ecl. M. 136: 336. Same art. Liv. Age, 231: 401.

— Recent Advances in. (W. Crookes) Pop. Astron. 7: 3.

— Religious Significance of. (J. LeConte) Monist, 10: 161.

— Sadness of. (D. S. Jordan) Indep. 52: 2839.

— Social Service of. (W. H. Norton) Science, n. s. 13: 644.

— Some Forecasts of. Chamb. J. 77: 593.

— Some Unscientific Reflections upon. (A. H. Lloyd) Science, n. s. 14: 13.

— South Sea Bubbles in. (J. Trowbridge) Pop. Sci. Mo. 56: 404.

Science, Study of, and National Character. (A. B. Crowe) Pop. Sci. Mo. 57: 90.
— Superstitions of. (L. Tolstoi) Arena, 20: 52.
— Superstructure of. (W. McGee) Forum, 29: 171.
— Teachers' School of. (F. Zirngiebel) Pop. Sci. Mo. 55: 451.
— Teaching, in Higher Grade Schools. (A. T. Simmons) Westm. 154: 64.
— — Sentimentality in. (E. Thorndike) Educa. R. 17: 57.
— Testimony to Religion. (A. A. McGinley) Cath. World, 72: 235.
— Threshold of a New Era, 1897. Knowl. 20: 158.
— vs. Matter and Form. (C. Aherne) Dub. R. 125: 315.
— vs. Religion in 1900. Sat. R. 90: 321.
— Western, from an Eastern Standpoint. Westm. 156: 207.
Science Course for Secondary Schools, Introductory. (H. C. Cooper) School R. 9: 440.
Science Teachers, Conference of, Lond., Jan. 1900. Ath. '00, 1: 86.
Sciences, Classification of. (G. A. Cogswell) Philos. R. 8: 494.
— in the High School. (C. R. Barnes) School R. 6: 643.
— in the Higher Schools of Germany. (J. E. Russell) School R. 5: 18, 65.
— Influence of, on the Intellectual Life of the Age. (R. C. Shiedt) Ref. Ch. R. 48: 88, 145, 351.
— School and College Work in, Articulation of. (A. Smith) School R. 7: 411, 453, 527.
Scientific Apparatus, German. (J. K. Rees) Science, n. s. 12: 777.
Scientific Congresses at Cambridge. (J. M. Baldwin) Nation, 67: 199.
Scientific Education. (J. Sutherland) Nature, 63: 275.
— (Duke of Devonshire) Nature, 56: 580.
— Seminars and Conferences. (R. E. Dodge) Science, n. s. 9: 520.
Scientific Geography for Schools. (R. E. Dodge) Geog. J. 11: 159.
Scientific History in Great Britain during the Queen's Reign. (E. Clodd) Eng. Illust. 17: 567.
Scientific Ideas, Life History of. (G. Le Bon) Pop. Sci. Mo. 52: 251.
Scientific Institutions of Europe, Visits to. (E. W. Morley) Am. Arch. 59: 12.
Scientific Instruction in Girls' Schools. (C. W. Latimer) Pop. Sci. Mo. 53: 246.
— A Short History of. (J. N. Lockyer) Nature, 58: 597. Same art. Pop. Sci. Mo. 54: 372, 529.
Scientific Investigation, Attitude of the State toward. (H. F. Osborn and others) Science, n. s. 13: 81.
— National Aspects of. Nature, 63: 356.
Scientific Joy. (H. T. Peck) Cosmopol. 30: 389.
Scientific Law and Scientific Explanation, Nature of. (T. J. Cormack) Monist, 10: 549.
Scientific Literature, International Catalogue of. (C. Adler) Lib. J. 22: supp. 58. — Lib. J. 25: 583, 630.
— — Second Conference at London. (C. Adler) Science, n. s. 9: 761, 799.
— — Prospective Arrangement. (J. V. Carus and others) Science, n. s. 9: 825, 864, 907. 10: 46, 133.
— — Columbia University Report. Science, n. s. 10: 165.
— Study and Use of. (R. Lydekker) Knowl. 20: 273.
Scientific Method, Limitation of. (R. C. Schiedt) Ref. Ch. R. 47: 164. — (E. V. Gerhart) Ref. Ch. R. 46: 213, 512.
Scientific Nomenclature, Reform in. (A. L. Herrera) Science, n. s. 10: 120.
Scientific Opinion, Need of Organizing. (H. E. Armstrong) Nature, 55: 409, 433.

Scientific Positions under the Government. Science, n. s. 13: 994.
Scientific Problems, Some Unsolved. (H. S. Williams) Harper, 100: 774.
Scientific Progress in the 19th Century. (L. Büchner) Pop. Sci. Mo. 52: 486.
Scientific Proofs vs. à Priori Assumptions. (G. Henslow) Nat. Sci. 13: 103.
Scientific Reader, A. (R. Ogden) Lippinc. 63: 858.
Scientific Research and Church Authority. Month, 93: 577.
— Balfour on. Nature, 61: 395.
Scientific Societies in England, Origin and History of. (C. M. Kennedy) J. Soc. Arts, 49: 7.
— Origin and Progress of. (J. Evans) Nature, 63: 119.
Scientific Speculation and the Unity of Truth. (R. E. Froude) Dub. R. 127: 353.
Scientific Studies. Are they Dangerous to Religion? (J. T. Bixby) Arena, 25: 241.
Scientific Thought, Basis of. (C. Baskerville) Science, n. s. 14: 165.
— in 19th Century. (W. N. Rice) Science, n. s. 10: 945.
Scientific Work, Government, Education for. (H. S. Pritchett) Educa. R. 21: 109.
Scilly Isles The. (Sir G. Newnes) Strand, 13: 203.
Scinde Horse, The, at Meeanee and Hyderabad. (L. Fitzgerald) Un. Serv. M. 16: 207.
Scion of the Covenant. (A. E. Crockett) New Eng. M. n. s. 19: 155.
Sciosophy, Principles of. (D. S. Jordan) Science, n. s. 11: 763.
Scolds, Cure of, in the "Good Old Days." Illus. (L. Jewitt) Green Bag, 10: 473.
"Scores." (S. Gwynn) Cornh. 77: 367.
Scoring of the Raja; a story. (W. A. Fraser) Outing, 37: 151.
Scorpions; are they Matricides and Suicides? (J. Villaró) Pop. Sci. Mo. 51: 398.
Scorn of Woman, The. (Jack London) Overland, n. s. 37: 979.
Scorpion, My Pet. (N. Robinson) Pop. Sci. Mo. 54: 605.
Scot, Capt. Walter, of Satchells. Sat. R. 85: 72.
Scot, The, of Fiction. (J. H. Findlater) Atlan. 84: 298.
Scotch, The, Humorous Characteristics of. (A. W. Cross) Arena, 19: 680.
Scotch Express, The; a railroad sketch. (S. Crane) McClure, 12: 273.
Scotch Lady of the Olden Time. (Campbell Smith) Good Words, 38: 561.
Scotch Silver Spoon, An Old. Antiq. n. s. 33: 184.
Scotch Sport and Highland Prosperity. (A. Grimble) Chamb. J. 77: 97.
Scotch Teacher, A, in New York. Chamb. J. 75: 379.
Scotland, Art in. (J. L. Caw) Art J. 50: 45, 69.
— Bibliography of. (H. G. Aldis) Scot. R. 29: 101.
— Brown's History of, vol. 1. (G. T. Lapsley) Am. Hist. R. 5: 113.
— Church and Creed in, Future of. (W. Wallace) Fortn. 75: 1055.
— Church of, and the Scottish People. (A. M. Fairbairn) Contemp. 79: 129.
— — History of, Macpherson's. (C. G. M'Crie) Crit. R. 11: 205. — Ath. '01, 1: 523.
— — M'Crie on. (W. Beveridge) Crit. R. 11: 332.
— — Pre-reformation. (M. Barrett) Am. Cath. Q. 23: 779 — 24, no. 2: 58.
— Churches of, Father of the. (A. W. Stewart) Sund. M. 30: 85.
— — Union of the. (A. R. MacEwen) Sund. M. 30: 51. — (J. Denny) Lond Q. 94: 193. — Spec. 85: 555.
— Early History. Quar. 192: 455.

Scotland, Ecclesiastical Situation in, 1900. Blackw. **168:** 585.

— Educational Peace of. (J. Shaw) 19th Cent. **41:** 113.

— Graham's Social Life of. Acad. **57:** 477.

— Highlands of, in 1750. Spec. **80:** 448.

— Historians of, Patriotic. (V. V. Branford) Macmil. **76:** 268.

— History of, Craik's A Century of. (R. S. Rait) Crit. R. **11:** 228. — Macmil. **84:** 21. — Blackw. **169:** 293.

— — from the Roman Occupation, Lang's. (G. T. Lapsley) Am. Hist. R. **6:** 121. — (S. D. F. Salmond) Crit. R. **10:** 349. — Blackw. **167:** 599. — (J. Bryce) Nation, **71:** 15.

— — Studies of "The Forty-Five." Quar. **190:** 442.

— The Honors of. Chamb. J. **74:** 113.

— Hunting in. (J. W. Lyall) Pall Mall M. **24:** 541.

— Legal Provisions and Intestate Succession in. (J. D. Wilson) Jurid. R. **13:** 18.

— Local Finance in. (J. A. Row-Fogo) Econ. J. **9:** 184.

— Lochs of, Bathymetrical Survey of. (J. Murray) Geog. J. **15:** 309. **17:** 273.

— National Gallery of. (E. Pinnington) Good Words, **42:** 445, 532.

— National Sentiment of. Acad. **52:** 49.

— Origins of Modern. Quar. **194:** 581.

— Parliament of, before the Union of the Crowns. (R. S. Rait) Eng. Hist. R. **15:** 209, 417.

— Political Transformation of. Quar. **185:** 269. — (W. Wallace) National, **36:** 735.

— Politics in. Fortn. **69:** 927.

— Railways of. Sat. R. **90:** 747, 816.

— Religious Thought in, in the Victorian Era. (J. Lindsay) Bib. Sac. **56:** 455.

— Restoration Régime in. Ed. R. **195:** 478.

— The Sheriff in. (R. V. Campbell) Jurid. R. **12:** 15.

— Goldwin Smith and. (A. Lang) Blackw. **167:** 541.

— Social Life in 18th Century. Scot. R. **35:** 36.

— Soldier's Chronicle. (H. Maxwell) Blackw. **161:** 45. Same art. Ecl. M. **128:** 471.

— Song Schools of. (J. T. Fyfe) Gent. M. n. s. **65:** 283.

— Sport and Autumn House Parties in. Lippinc. **64:** 609.

— Statistical Accounts of. (J. T. Clark) Library, **6:** 130.

— Will it become Conservative? Spec. **78:** 6.

— Wyntoun's Chronicle of. (W. A. Craigie) Scot. R. **30:** 33.

Scotland Yard, New, Customs and Curiosities of. Eng. Illust. **18:** 355.

Scots Conveyancers, The Old. (H. P. Macmillan) Jurid. R. **11:** 41.

Scots Law in the Victorian Era. (W. C. Smith) Jurid. R. **13:** 152.

Scotsmen in London. (W. C. Mackenzie) Chamb. J. **76:** 321.

Scott, Clement. Sisters by the Sea. (M. Beerbohm) Sat. R. **84:** 254.

Scott, C. Anderson. Evangelical Doctrine Bible Truth. (D. Somerville) Crit. R. **11:** 339.

Scott, Forrester, artist. Studio (Internat.) **8:** 165.

Scott, Francis M., with portrait. (A. O. Hall) Green Bag, **10:** 45.

Scott, Frederick George. (T. Adams) Canad. M. **11:** 160.

Scott, Hugh S. Acad. **52:** 490.

Scott, Robert Taylor. (Sallie E. M. Hardy) Green Bag, **10:** 151.

Scott, Thomas, Walter Scott's Brother. (Frank Yeigh) Bk. Buyer, **17:** 308.

Scott, Walter. Spec. **78:** 762.

— and Blair Adam House. (W. Stephen) Scot. R. **36:** 35.

Scott, Walter, and his Country. Good Words, **38:** 235.

— and his French Pupils. Quar. **190:** 423. Same art. Ecl. M. **134:** 353. Same art. Liv. Age, **224:** 212.

— Bride of Lammermoor. (H. Craik and G. Saintsbury) Blackw. **162:** 853.

— Bust of, in Westminster Abbey. Critic, **30:** 374.

— Catholic Tribute to. (H. E. Walton) Month, **92:** 457, 568.

— Chronology of Waverley Novels. (J. Foster) Library, **4:** 117.

— His First Love, Williamina Stuart. (F. M. F. Skene) Cent. **36:** 368.

— Hudson's Life of. (P. A. Graham) Acad. **60:** 109. — (A. Lang) Critic, **38:** 338.

— Ivanhoe, Outline Study of. (Maud E. Kingsley) Educa. **21:** 308.

— Last Links with. (Eve B. Simpson) Chamb. J. **78:** 644.

— Letter-bag of. (G. C. G. Norgate) Temp. Bar, **112:** 77.

— Manuscripts of, Fate of. Chamb. J. **75:** 17–37.

— Methods and Originals of. Quar. **186:** 464.

— A Poem. Cent. **36:** 367.

— Poetical Works, Heraldic Aspect of. (J. G. Pedrick) Gent. M. n. s. **61:** 470.

— Redgauntlet, Proof-sheets of. (D. MacRitchie) Longm. **35:** 416.

— Story of his Ruin. (L. Stephen) Cornh. **75:** 448. Same art. Liv. Age, **213:** 577.

— Unpublished Portraits of. (J. Thomson) Cent. **36:** 364.

Scott, William, Artist. Studio (Internat.) **13:** 113.

Scotter, Manor of, Court Rolls of. (E. Peacock) Archæol. **46:** 371.

Scottish Anecdotes. (F. B. Harrison) Cornh. **80:** 234.

Scottish Art. Art J. **49:** 23.

Scottish Border Clan. Ed. R. **187:** 485.

Scottish Churches. Quar. **190:** 176.

Scottish Constitution, Notes on the History of the. (C. R. A. Howden) Jurid. R. **11:** 209.

Scottish Cruisies, Torches, and Rushlights. (J. Cameron) Good Words, **40:** 184.

Scottish Equitable Life Assurance Company. Bank. M. (Lond.) **63:** 143.

Scottish Forest, Summer-tide in. (H. Maxwell) Blackw. **166:** 309.

Scottish Historians, Recent. (A. H. Millar) Scot. R. **36:** 1.

Scottish King's Household. (M. Bateson) Jurid. R. **13:** 405.

Scottish Literature. Liv. Age, **214:** 837.

Scottish Monarch, Constitutional Position of, prior to the Union. Law. Q. **17:** 252.

Scottish National Gallery. Exhibition, 1901. Art J. **53:** 71.

Scottish People, Characteristics of. (W. W. Smith) Chaut. **27:** 647.

Scottish Provident Institution. Bank. M. (Lond.) **63:** 838.

Scottish Reformation, Story of the. (D. M. Barrett) Am. Cath. Q. **25:** 738.

Scottish Serjeanties, On. (G. Neilson) Law Q. **15:** 405.

Scottish Songs. (C. Moffet) Music, **13:** 691.

— and Irish Melodies. (Cunninghame Moffet) Music, **19:** 510.

— Anonymous. (J. A. Duncan) Scot. R. **30:** 361.

Scottish Spindles and Whorls, Decoration of. (F. R. Coles) Reliquary, **39:** 80.

Scottish Theology, Recent. (O. Smeaton) Westm. **148:** 654.

Scottish Universities. Quar. **188:** 139.

Scottish Universities, A Rectorial Election at the. Educa. R. **13**: 172.

Scotus Erigena, Joannes. (W. Larminie) Contemp. **71**: 557.

— Gardner on. Sat. R. **91**: 179.

Scouting. Un. Serv. M. **24**: 60.

— and Reconnaissance. (Von der Goltz) J. Mil. Serv. Inst. **7**: 72. — (W. Green) Un. Serv. M. **21**: 22.

— Col. Baden-Powell on. Acad. **58**: 127.

Scouts ; the Eyes of an Army. Spec. **83**: 747.

— in the Indian Cavalry. Un. Serv. M. **24**: 63.

— Western. (E. B. Osborn) Macmil. **82**: 201.

Scoville Institute Library, Children's Room at. Pub. Lib. **4**: 9.

Scrapbooks, Indexing. (C. S. Wady) Writer, **6**: 177.

Screamers, Osteology and Systematic Position of. (R. W. Shufeldt) Am. Natural. **35**: 455.

Screw-machine, Automatic Development of. (H. Roland) Engin. M. **18**: 177.

Screws ; Report of the Screw Gauge Committee of the British Association, 1900. J. Soc. Arts, **48**: 805.

— Theory of, Ball on. (J. D. Everett) Nature, **63**: 246.

— Triple, for Warships. (G. W. Melville) Cassier, **16**: 682.

Scribbler, The, and his Paymasters. Indep. **53**: 1840.

Scribblers, Sorrows of. National, **31**: 63. Same art. Ecl. M. **130**: 565.

Scriptores Historiæ Augustæ. (J. H. Drake) Am. J. Philol. **20**: 40.

Scriptorium, The Monastic. (J. Taylor) Library, **2**: 237, 282.

Scrivener's Tale, The. (M. Hewlett) Fortn. **76**: 332.

Scrooby, First American Visit to. (H. M. Dexter) New Eng. M. n. s. **21**: 182.

Scrupulous Father, The. (G. Gissing) Cornh. **83**: 175.

Scudéry, Georges de, and LaCalprenède, G. (B. W. Wells) Sewanee, **6**: 439.

Sculptors, American, Triumph of. (K. De Forest) World's Work, **1**: 181.

— French, of the 18th Century, Dilke's. Sat. R. **91**: 13.

Sculpture, American, A New Note in ; Statuettes by Bessie Potter. (A. Hoeber) Cent. **32**: 732.

— American School. (W. O. Partridge) Forum, **29**: 493.

— and Architecture, True Relation of. (W. O. Partridge) Forum, **29**: 44.

— at the Paris Salons, 1897. (M. H. Spielmann) M. of Art, **21**: 318.

— at the Royal Academy. Acad. **51**: 552.

— Celtic. (J. R. Allen) Studio (Internat.) **5**: 163.

— Christian Relief, Symmetry in Early. (C. L. Meader) Am. J. Archæol. 2d s. **4**: 126.

— Coloring. (G. Frampton and M. Webb) Studio (Lond.) **3**: 78.

— Decorative, by Alfred Drury. (A. L. Baldry) M. of Art, **22**: 442.

— Greek, Some Characteristics of. (H. C. Pearson) Educa. **18**: 596.

— in 1897. (A. L. Baldry) M. of Art, **22**: 65.

— in London and Paris. Artist (N. Y.) **26**: 8.

— New. M. of Art, **20**: 101.

— Norman, at Langridge. Reliquary, **39**: 56.

— Some Modern German. (A. Werschler) Artist (N. Y.) **24**: 73.

Sculptured Face ; a poem. (H. M. Richardson) Cosmopol. **25**: 439.

Sculptured Stone Ball found at Glas Hill, Aberdeenshire. Reliquary, **37**: 102.

Sculptures from under the Sea off Cythera. (W. Huyshe) Artist (N. Y.) **31**: 29. — (P. Kabbadias) J. Hel. Stud. **21**: 205. — Am. Arch. **72**: 15. — (G. P. Byzantinos) Indep. **53**: 704. — (R. B. Richardson) Indep. **53**: 701. — (C. Waldstein) Monthly R. **3**, no. **2**: 110.

Sea, Autumn by the. (F. Whishaw) Longm. **38**: 359.

— Bottom of the. (C. C. Nutting) Harper, **103**: 861.

— Deep- ; Expedition of the "Albatross," 1899. Nature, **60**: 378.

— — Exploration of East Indian Archipelago. Geog. J. **13**: 57.

— Disasters at, Inventions for preventing. (H. H. Lewis) World's Work, **1**: 771.

— Empire of. (D. Lever) Un. Serv. M. **17**: 482.

— Etiquette at. (F. T. Bullen) Spec. **82**: 747.

— Exploration of the. (C. M. Blackford) No. Am. **167**: 341.

— Floor of the. (F. T. Bullen) Spec. **83**: 527. Same art. Ecl. M. **134**: 112.

— Harvest of the. Spec. **82**: 376.

— How Sailors find their Way at. (C. C. Marriott) Chamb. J. **76**: 484.

— in the New Testament. (F. T. Bullen) Spec. **85**: 455.

— Life in the. (C. M. Blackford) No. Am. **173**: 246.

— Literature at. (F. T. Bullen) Spec. **87**: 12. Same art. Ecl. M. **137**: 546. Same art. Liv. Age, **230**: 397.

— Man and. (G. H. Scull) Atlan. **80**: 422.

— Messages from. (W. Allingham) Chamb. J. **74**: 715. Same art. Ecl. M. **130**: 104.

— Natural History. (G. Murray) Sci. Prog. n. s. **1**: 379.

— Poetry of. Liv. Age, **229**: 656.

— Privacy of. (F. T. Bullen) Spec. **84**: 627.

— Romance of, Undying. (F. T. Bullen) Spec. **84**: 547.

— Tales of. (E. G. Festing) Un. Serv. M. **15**: 384.

Sea-bat, Trailing the. (C. F. Holder) Outing, **36**: 22.

Sea-beaches and Sandbanks. (V. Cornish) Geog. J. **11**: 528, 628. Same art. Nature, **58**: 42.

Sea Change, A ; a story. (A. Brown) Atlan. **86**: 180.

Sea Coast Defence and the National Guard. (J. C. Ayres) Forum, **24**: 416.

Sea Coast Destruction and Littoral Drift. (W. H. Wheeler) Nature, **62**: 400.

Sea Fight with the Turks, First English. (F. T. Jane) Good Words, **39**: 334.

Sea Fights, Logs of the Great, 1794–1805. Un. Serv. M. **20**: 207.

— Old American. (H. H. Boyesen, 2d) Cosmopol. **32**: 189.

Sea-fish in the River, A ; a story. (E. Harling) Belgra. **95**: 439.

Sea Fisheries Congress, International, at Dieppe, 1898. Nature, **58**: 511.

Sea-fishing, Memories of. (F. G. Aflalo) Cornh. **82**: 624.

Sea Fog ; a poem. (T. H. Rand) Bk. Buyer, **16**: 128.

Sea-going Rafts on the Pacific. (E. K. Bishop) Engin. M. **16**: 90.

Sea-gull ; a poem. (S. W. Mitchell) Cent. **36**: 666.

Sea Life. Silent Warfare of the Submarine World. Spec. **80**: 233.

Sea Lingo. (W. K. Stride) Argosy, **75**: 58.

Sea Mills of Cephalonia. (F. W. and W. O. Crosby) Cassier, **11**: 388.

Sea-monster, Florida. (A. E. Verrill) Am. Natural. **31**: 304.

Sea Mystery, A. (T. A. Janvier) Liv. Age, **218**: 490.

Sea-otter, The, and its Extermination. (R. Lydekker) Knowl. **21**: 78.

Seaports in England, Growth of. (J. Ackland) 19th Cent. **42**: 411.

Sea Power. (E. L. Godkin) Nation, **67**: 198.

— and Sea-carriage. (B. Taylor) 19th Cent. **45**: 991.

— at the End of the 19th Century. (W. L. Clowes) Engin. M. **15**: 539.

— Essential Elements of Modern. (P. H. Colomb) Engin. M. **15**: 889.

— Mahan's Interest of America in. (J. D. Cox) Nation, **67**: 34. — R. of Rs. (N. Y.) **17**: 71.

Sea Power, Maritime Expeditions in relation to. (F. C. Ormsby-Johnson) Fortn. 72: 815.

Sea Prince, The; a fairy story. (E. P. Larken) Pall Mall M. 13: 437.

Sea Rhapsody; a poem. (R. Burton) Atlan. 88: 373.

Sea-sauce. (S. D. Gordon) Cornh. 79: 362.

Sea-shell; a poem. (G. E. Woodberry) Atlan. 79: 779.

Seashore House, Devonshire, Design for. (C. H. Townsend) Studio (Internat.) 4: 239.

Seaside Garden; a poem. (J. M. Falkner) Temp. Bar, 113: 136. Same art. Ecl. M. 130: 600.

Seaside Life in America. (F. H. Hardy) Cornh. 74: 605. Same art. Ecl. M. 128: 37.

Seaside Resorts, Past and Present. Eng. Illust. 21: 569.

Sea Song. (I. E. Mackay) Canad. M. 16: 369.

Sea-squirt, The. (E. Stenhouse) Knowl. 21: 220.

Sea Thoughts; a poem. (E. Gibson) Argosy, 63: 784.

Sea-trout, The Silver. Chamb. J. 76: 327.

Sea Turn, A; a story. (T. B. Aldrich) Harper, 103: 4.

Sea Urchins. Variations in the Apical Plates of Arbacia Punctulata. (H. L. Osborn) Science, n. s. 13: 938.

Seal, The. A Legal Relic. (M. M. Johnson) Green Bag, 9: 544.

— of England, The Great. Temp. Bar, 118: 513. Same art. Liv. Age, 225: 107. — Green Bag, 10: 245. — Illus. Green Bag, 10: 293. — (J. H. Schooling) Pall Mall M. 14: 37, 205. — (A. Wyon) J. Soc. Arts, 48: 42.

Seal of Confession, The. (P. Rosegger) Liv. Age, 225: 140.

Seals, Babylonian, Two. (W. H. Ward; W. St.C. Boscawen) Ath. '00, 1: 248, 312, 440, 535, 696.

Seal, Fur, as an Animal. (D. S. Jordan; G. A. Clark) Forum, 23: 192.

— — Herds of the North Pacific. Nature, 60: 354.

— — Hunting. (W. G. Emery) Outing, 31: 537.

— Gray, Breeding Habits of. (J. E. Harting) Nature, 57: 465.

Seal Fishery; the American Case. Fortn. 68: 679. Same art. Ecl. M. 130: 108. — Contemp. 72: 846.

— and Habits of the Fur Seal. (W. G. Emery) Nat'l M. (Bost.) 6: 99.

— Investigation of 1896. Science, 5: 453.

— — of 1897. (F. A. L.) Science, 6: 568.

— Passing of the Fur Seal. Sat. R. 83: 436. Same art. Liv. Age, 213: 557.

— Question of, Sherman and. Pub. Opin. 23: 99.

— United States and. R. of Rs. (N. Y.) 15: 561.

Seal Hunting in Newfoundland. (J. Harvey) Canad. M. 16: 195.

Seals, Bachelor. Spec. 79: 178. Same art. Liv. Age, 214: 749.

— Marathon of the. (F. T. Bullen) Spec. 82: 516.

Sealed Orders. (L. G. Giltner) New Eng. M. n. s. 24: 99.

Sealed Orders. (R. Ramsay) Chamb. J. 78: 273.

Sealed Packet, The. (T. St.E. Hake) Chamb. J. 77: extr. no. 22.

Sealed Packet, The; a story. (Clinton Ross) Bk. News, 16: 1.

Seaman, Owen. Acad. 52: 491.

— as a Parodist. Acad. 58: 11.

— Humorous Verse of. (H. Harland) Acad. 51: 453.

— In Cap and Bells. (W. E. Henley) Pall Mall M. 20: 566.

— A Modern Satirist. (H. M. Belden) Citizen, 4: 50.

Seamanship, Knight's Modern. (C. F. Goodrich) Nation, 73: 54.

Seamanship-training for the Naval Executive. (H. Noel) Un. Serv. M. 21: 40.

Seamen, British Supply of. (A. Cowie) Contemp. 73: 855.

Search, The. (H. S. Merriman) Liv. Age, 227: 325.

Search-light Letters. (Robert Grant) Scrib. M. 25: 96 — 26: 364.

Season of the Year. (Grant Allen) Longm. 31: 447. Same art. Liv. Age, 217: 204.

Season's Pageant, The; a poem. (J. Garraway) Argosy, 64: 631.

Seasons, The. (Grant Allen) Pop. Sci. Mo. 54: 230.

— Changes of the. (N. S. Shaler) Chaut. 27: 16.

— Return of the. (J. M. Bacon) Macmil. 82: 45. Same art. Ecl. M. 135: 180. Same art. Liv. Age, 225: 761.

Seattle, Part of, in the Cape Nome Rush for Gold. (A. G. Kingsbury) Nat'l M. (Bost.) 12: 162.

Seaward Hill, The; a poem. (W. Packard) Outing, 33: 584.

Seaweed; its Uses and Possibilities. (W. C. Mackenzie) Good Words, 41: 315.

Seb, Family of. (G. St. Clair) Westm. 147: 156.

Sebastopol during the Siege. (W. Simpson) Eng. Illust. 17: 297.

— The Fall of; the 8th of Sept., 1855. (I. S. A. Herford) Chamb. J. 76: 426.

— revisited. Un. Serv. M. 20: 85.

— To-day. (A. Kinnear) Chamb. J. 76: 103.

"Secessionists" of Germany. Studio (Lond.) 4: 24.

Sechuan, Southwest, Journey through. (E. Amundsen) Geog. J. 15: 620. 16: 531.

Seclusion, Ethics of. Sat. R. 88: 824.

Second Advent, Can we see Preparation for? (A. S. Lewis) Lond. Q. 94: 89.

Second Generation. (S. Crane) Cornh. 80: 734.

Second Marriage, A. (A. Brown) Atlan. 80: 406.

Second Mrs. Blaire; a story. (M. Merton) Canad. M. 9: 326.

Second Probation of Rev. Kid McHugh; story. (W. F. Gibbons) Chaut. 33: 522.

Second Shot, The; story of a Strange Retribution. (V. L. Whitechurch) Good Words, 41: 772.

Second Violin, The; a story. (W. A. Burrows) Music, 17: 593.

Second Wooing of Salina Sue; a story. (R. McE. Stuart) Harper, 98: 49.

Secondary Curriculum in France, Differentiation of. (J. D. E. Jonas) School R. 8: 244.

Secondary Education. (C. Brereton) Fortn. 70: 765. — Church Q. 47: 392. — (P. H. Hanus) Educa. R. 17: 346.

Secondary School and College. (C. W. Eliot) Educa. R. 13: 465.

— and Higher Education, Relative Values in. (M. V. O'Shea) School R. 6: 289.

— as regards General Culture. (D. W. Abercrombie) Educa. R. 17: 417.

— as regards Training for Citizenship. (F. W. Taussig) Educa. R. 17: 431.

— as regards Training for Vocation. (J. P. Munroe) Educa. R. 17: 440.

— at the Paris Exposition of 1900. (H. L. Taylor) School R. 9: 1, 269.

— Catholic, in the United States. (J. T. Murphy) Am. Cath. Q. 22: 449.

— Discipline vs. Dissipation in. (P. Shorey) School R. 5: 217.

— A French Critic on. (H. Milborne) Westm. 154: 645.

— A Freshman at Nineteen. (A. Flexner) Educa. R. 18: 353.

— Higher Ideals in. (F. Whitton) School R. 8: 261.

— in England. Chamb. J. 76: 502.

— in France, Commission on, Some Recommendations of. (G. H. Locke) School R. 8: 254.

— in the United States, with Bibliography. (E. E. Brown) School R. 5: 84-269. 6: 225, 357, 527. 7: 36, 103, 286. 8: 485, 540. 9: 34.

Seippel, Paul, Swiss Tourist. (G. Valbert) Liv. Age, 213: 235.

Seismological Observatory and its Objects. (J. Milne) Nature, 59: 487.

Seismology in Japan. (J. Milne) Nature, 63: 588. — Milne's. Ath. '98, 2: 640.

Selaginella, A Study of. (A. V. Jennings) Knowl. 21: 259.

"Selah," Inductive Study of. (C. A. Briggs) J. Bib. Lit. 18: 132.

Selborne, Roundell Palmer, Earl of. (W. O'C. Morris) Scot. R. 34: 39. — Church Q. 43: 317. — Lond. Q. 87: 355. — (J. H. Rigg) Lond. Q. 91: 261.

— as a Statesman. Ed. R. 190: 459.

— Memorials. (E. G. Johnson) Dial (Ch.) 26: 149.

Selborne. (H. C. Shelley) New Eng. M. n. s. 21: 548. — (Mrs. John Lane) Lippinc. 64: 589.

Selden, John, the Autocrat of the Dinner Table. (H. Paul) 19th Cent. 47: 624. Same art. Ecl. M. 135: 40.

Selection, Doctrine of, bearing upon the Social Problem. (W. M. Daniels) Int. J. Ethics, 8: 203.

— Election and. Ref. Ch. R. 47: 225.

— in Man. (J. Beddoe) Sci. Prog. 7: 403. n. s. 1: 167.

— Natural and Social, and Heredity. (J. R. Commons) Arena, 18: 90.

— — Divine Action in. (W. Seton) Cath. World, 70: 625.

— — Improvements in the Theory. (G. W. Bulman) Westm. 150: 688.

— — in Ethics. (D. Irons) Philos. R. 10: 271.

— — Plate on. (F. A. Dixey) Nature, 64: 49.

— — True Critical Test of. (S. Fitzsimmons) Am. Cath. Q. 26: 559.

— Organic. (J. M. Baldwin) Science, 5: 634. — (H. F. Osborn and E. B. Poulton) Science, 6: 583.

— — Limits of. (H. F. Osborn) Am. Natural. 31: 944.

Selenium Interference Rings. (A. C. Longden) Am. J. Sci. 160: 55.

Self, Early Sense of. (G. Stanley Hall) Am. J. Psychol. 9: 351.

— Concept of the. (J. D. Stoops) Philos. R. 10: 619.

— Genesis of the Ethical. (J. M. Baldwin) Philos. R. 6: 225.

— Identification of. (S. Baker) Psychol. R. 4: 272.

— Mueller's Theory of. (P. Carus) Monist, 8: 123.

— Neo-Hegelian; and Subjective Idealism. (A. K. Rogers) Philos. R. 10: 130.

— The Normal. (R. R. Marett) Mind, 9: 496.

Self-consciousness, Modern. Atlan. 86: 573.

— Uses of. Spec. 86: 761.

— Variety of Extent, Degree, and Unity in. (S. Bryant) Mind, 22: 71.

Self-glorification. Spec. 80: 299.

Self-government in the Colonies. Outl. 64: 244.

— What is it? Outl. 65: 672.

Selfhood and the 107th Psalm. (J. K. Smyth) N. Church R. 5: 18.

— Development of Moral. (W. I. Crane) School R. 9: 347.

Self-knowledge, Nature of. (S. H. Mellone) Mind, 26: 318.

Self-made Man, A. (S. Crane) Cornh. 79: 324.

Self-made Men, Two Types of. Spec. 79: 241.

Self-realization as a Working Moral Principle. (H. Sturt) Int. J. Ethics, 8: 328.

Selfishness; Apostles of Autolatry. (J. D. Miller) Arena, 24: 608.

— of Ill-health. (A. K. H. Forbes) Sund. M. 26: 163.

Seligman, Henry. Bank. M. (N. Y.) 58: 418.

Seligman, Isaac Newton. Bank. M. (N. Y.) 58: 415.

Seljuks before the Crusades. (S. Khuda Bukhsh) Westm. 156: 90.

Selkirk, Alexander, Will of. (Facsimile) N. E. Reg. 51: 150.

Selkirk, Earl of, in Canada. (G. Johnson) Canad. M. 13: 395.

Selkirk Mountains, Camp Sketches in. (D. O. Lewis) Canad. M. 8: 199.

Sellin, E. Studies in Jewish History. (D. Eaton) Crit. R. 11: 324.

Selous, F. C., Sketch of. Pop. Sci. Mo. 51: 258.

Selukwe Gold District, Woman's Tour in. (S. Chambers) Temp. Bar, 119: 73.

Selwyn, George. Acad. 58: 28. — Spec. 84: 56.

— Letters. (G. S. Street) Blackw. 167: 74.

Selwyn, Bishop John. (W. Seabrooke) Sund. M. 28: 659.

— How's Memoir of. Ath. '99, 2: 483.

Selzach, Passion Play at. (K. Francke) Nation, 73: 278. — (A. G. Hopkins) Belgra. 92: 263. — (C. T. Herrick) Lippinc. 65: 956.

Semantics, Bréal on. (P. Shorey) Dial (Ch.) 30: 298. — (A. J. Bell) School R. 9: 379.

Semasiological Possibilities. (F. A. Wood) Am. J. Philol. 19: 40. 20: 254.

Sembrich, Marcella, Opera Singer, with portrait. Music, 15: 190.

Semitic Bibliography. (W. Muss-Arnolt) Bib. World, 12: 1.

Semitic Deities, West-, with Compound Names. (G. A. Barton) J. Bib. Lit. 20: 22.

Semitic Studies and Orientalism. (E. Montet) Asia. R. 24: 68. 28: 124, 136, 383.

Semper, Carl, with portrait. Pop. Sci. Mo. 52: 837.

Semper Idem; a poem. (W. J. Lampton) Cosmopol. 22: 288.

Senancour, E. P. de, Author of Obermann. (J. P. Frothingham) Atlan. 88: 539.

— Obermann, and Matthew Arnold. (W. N. Guthrie) Sewanee, 2: 33.

Senate, U. S. (W. E. Mason) Munsey, 19: 504.

— The All-powerful. (R. Ogden) Nation, 72: 4.

— and House of Lords. Spec. 78: 431.

— and Mr. Cleveland. (J. Schouler) Forum, 23: 65.

— and the Tariff Bill. (H. L. West) No. Am. 164: 754.

— A Citizen to the. Nation, 68: 87.

— Has it degenerated? (G. F. Hoar) Forum, 23: 129.

— — A Reply to Senator Hoar. (C. R. Miller) Forum, 23: 271. — Pub. Opin. 22: 485.

— In the Seats of the Mighty. (C. Crane) Outl. 61: 27.

— its Origin, Personnel, and Organization. (W. A. Peffer) No. Am. 167: 48.

— its Place in our Government. (H. L. West) Forum, 31: 423.

— its Privileges, Powers, and Functions, its Rules and Methods of doing Business. (W. A. Peffer) No. Am. 167: 176.

— Power of the. (J. B. Fry) J. Mil. Serv. Inst. 12: 225.

— Veto-power of. (R. Ogden) Nation, 65: 42.

Senators, U. S., The House and the Election of. (B. Winchester) Arena, 24: 14.

Senatorships, Money and. (E. P. Clark) Nation, 70: 295.

Senior, Nassau W. Many Memories of Many People. Ed. R. 188: 273.

Senior, Mrs. Nassau W. (F. D. How) Sund. M. 30: 561.

Senior Reader, The. (A. C. Smith) Scrib. M. 26: 725.

Sensation and the Datum of Science. (E. A. Singer, jr.) Philos. R. 7: 485.

— Attributes of. (M. Meyer) Psychol. R. 6: 506.

— Criterion of. (G. S. Fullerton) Psychol. R. 7: 159.

— Relation of Stimulus to. (M. Meyer) Am. J. Psychol. 11: 530. — Reply. (F. E. Barrell) Am. J. Psychol. 12: 135.

— Studies in. (E. A. Singer) Psychol. R. 4: 250.

Sensations, Cutaneous. (L. M. Solomons) Psychol. R. 4: 246.

Sensational Serial, The. Liv. Age, 230: 129.

Sense, Kant's Theory of. (J. G. Schurman) Philos. R. 8: 1, 113.

"Sense of Humor, A;" a story. (J. H. Wood) Idler, 7: 215.

"Sense of Injury," Morbid. (W. F. Becker) Pop. Sci. Mo. 56: 596.

Sense of Spring, a poem. (J. S. Thomson) Canad. M. 10: 400.

Sense-perception, A B C of, Herbart on. (C. De Garmo) School R. 5: 53.

Sensibility, Decay of. (S. Gwynn) Cornh. 80: 18. Same art. Ecl. M. 133: 523. Same art. Liv. Age, 222: 419.

— a Forgotten Grace. (A. S. Winston) Lippinc. 60: 833.

Sensitiveness. Spec. 79: 551.

Sent Back by the Sea; a story. (E. L. Arnold) Temp. Bar, 111: 81.

Sentence, Apperception of the Spoken. (W. C. Bagley) Am. J. Psychol. 12: 80.

Sentences, Penal, Can they be standardized? (M. Crackanthorpe) 19th Cent. 47: 103.

— — Indeterminate; an evasion of law. Outl. 69: 1014.

Sentiment; is it declining? (A. G. Mason) Cent. 39: 626.

— Losses of. (R. Ogden) Nation, 73: 105.

— Tyranny of. (F. Greenwood) Blackw. 165: 1038.

Sentiment and "Feelin'"; a story. (M. E. Francis) Cornh. 79: 230.

Sentimental Journey, Notes from a. Macmil. 83: 112. Same art. Ecl. M. 136: 325.

Sentimentalists, The. (Garnett Smith) Macmil. 80: 449. Same art. Liv. Age, 223: 625. Same art. Ecl. M. 134: 192.

— Pier on the. (Flora M. Holly) Bookman, 13: 249.

Sentimentality, Popular English. Sat. R. 92: 41.

Sentries, Outpost. Un. Serv. M. 24: 180.

Senussi, and his threatened Holy War. (T. R. Threlfall) 19th Cent. 47: 400.

Separ's Vigilante; a story. (O. Wister) Harper, 94: 517.

Seppilli, Mr., Musical Conductor, with portrait. Music, 16: 64.

Septuagint, Lucian's Recension of the. Church Q. 51: 379.

Sequels. (K. Erskine) New Eng. M. n. s. 16: 599.

Serampore, A Portrait at. (A. L. Cotton) Nation, 69: 482.

Serao, Matilde. (H. James) No. Am. 172: 367.

Serena Ann's First Valentine. (M. E. Wilkins) Eng. Illust. 17: 235.

Serfdom, English, Disappearance of. (E. P. Cheyney) Eng. Hist. 15: 10.

Sergeant Harding's Grandfather; a tale. (G. S. Ellis) Belgra. 97: 112.

Sergeant Harding's Wedding-day. (G. S. Ellis) Pall Mall M. 20: 387.

Seri Indians, The. Nat. Geog. M. 12: 278.

— McGee's Memoir on. (F. Russell) Am. Natural. 35: 853.

Series, Manufacture of a. Ath. '00, 2: 155.

Seringapatam, Centenary of. (J. J. Cotton) Macmil. 81: 119.

— Night Attack in. Un. Serv. M. 18: 44.

— Taking of, May 4, 1799. (M. Barrett) Month, 93: 505.

Seriousness, Eclipse of, in Contemporary Literature. (W. B. Harte) Poet-Lore, 9: 36.

Serjeants-at-law. (J. E. R. Stephens) Gent. M. n. s. 59: 603. — (G. H. Westley) Green Bag, 12: 275.

Sermon, The, Layman's View of. (Mary A. Jordan) Outl. 58: 1066.

Sermon of the Rose; a poem. (J. W. Riley) Atlan. 82: 429.

Sermon on the Mount, Gore on. Sat. R. 84: 297.

— Heinrici on. (L. A. Muirhead) Crit. R. 11: 426.

— Is it Evangelical? (J. Luccock) Meth. R. 60: 108.

— Study of. (C. E. Creitz) Ref. Ch. R. 47: 90.

Sermon-text, Humor in the. Chamb. J. 74: 601.

Sermonizing. (A. E. Truxal) Ref. Q. 44: 201.

Sermons on Social Conditions Unwise. (W. L. Gladish) N. Church R. 4: 555.

Serpent and Tree. (S. D. Peet) Am. Antiq. 23: 179.

— in Literature. Acad. 61: 235.

— Story of. (W. H. Ward) Am. Antiq. 20: 211.

Serpent of Old Nile, The; a study of the Cleopatra of tragedy. (G. Bradford, jr.) Poet-Lore, 10: 514.

Serpents and how to recognize them. (L. Jervis) Knowl. 21: 7.

— Evolution of the Venom-fang. (L. Jervis) Knowl. 21: 91.

Serpent-worshippers of India. (W. H. Tribe) Harper, 102: 681.

Servant of Jehovah, The. (F. B. Denio) Am. J. Theol. 5: 322.

Servant Class, The, on the Farm and in the Slums. (B. Hale) Arena, 20: 373.

Servant Question. (F. M. Thompson) Cosmopol. 28: 521.

— The Ever-present Problem. Outl. 61: 481.

— A Suggested Solution. Outl. 61: 708.

— in Social Evolution. (A. L. Vrooman) Arena, 25: 643.

Servants and Served. (M. E. Haweis) Contemp. 75: 505. Same art. Liv. Age, 221: 481.

— and some 16th Century Educational Notes. (J. J. Walsh) Am. Cath. Q. 26: 714.

— in the Colonies. (Lady Broome) Cornh. 82: 796. Same art. Liv. Age, 228: 117.

— in Germany. (W. Cummings) Canad. M. 17: 572.

— Mistresses and. (C. W. Earle) Cornh. 77: 155.

— Training-school for. (M. H. Abel) Outl. 63: 501.

— Under what Circumstances do they accept the Risks of their Employment? (S. D. Thompson) Am. Law R. 31: 82.

Servetus, Schaff's Account of. (W. A. Stevens) Am. Theol. 1: 450.

Servia, Adventures in, during War with Turkey. (F. Villiers) Canad. M. 14: 217.

— Alexander's Successor. Possible Danger in Eastern Europe. Spec. 80: 783.

— A Plea for. (A. H. E. Taylor) Westm. 148: 1.

Service Books of Aquitaine, Mediæval. (R. Twigge) Dub. R. 121: 355.

Serving-man, The, in Literature. Macmil. 84: 193. Same art. Liv. Age, 230: 410.

Serving Two Masters; a story. (J. W. Sherer) Gent. M. n. s. 63: 521.

Servius, and the Scholia of Daniel. (R. B. Steele) Am. J. Philol. 20: 272.

— Notes on. (R. B. Steele) Am. Anthrop. 21: 170.

Sessions Paper Two Hundred Years ago. (C. H. Vellacott) Westm. 148: 449.

Seton, Ernest Thompson, with portrait. Bk. News, 18: 490. — (W. W. Whitelock) Critic, 39: 320.

Settlement of Solid Matter in Fresh and Salt Water, with Bibliography. (H. S. Allen) Nature, 64: 279.

Settlement [Social], Inner Life of the. (M. B. Loomis) Arena, 24: 193.

Settlement Houses and City Politics. (R. A. Woods) Munic. Aff. 4: 395.

Settlement Work in New York, Women in. (M. M. Kingsbury) Munic. Aff. 2: 458.

Shakespeare, Wm., The True. (F. Harris) Sat. R. 85: 384, 421, 455. 86: 38-776.
— Twelfth Night. (M. Beerbohm) Sat. R. 91: 171.
— Use of the Bible. (M. H. Liddell) Nation, 71: 189.
— Van Dam and Stoffel's. (M. H. Liddell) Nation, 71: 351.
— Verses written in a Copy of. (J. R. Lowell) Cent. 37: 49.
Shakespeare Reading, A, and the Reader's Shakespeare. (Sir Wyke Bayliss) Good Words, 39: 740.
Shakespeare's Copy of Montaigne. (Arthur Nicholson) Gent. M. n. s. 59: 349.
Shakespeare's Garden, A Rose from. (C. Hope) Month, 94: 573.
Shakespeare's Greenwood, The Superstitions of. (G. Morley) Knowl. 20: 172. Same art. Liv. Age, 215: 60.
Shakespeare's Land, Cycling thro'. (W. Hale) Outing, 36: 490.
Shakespeares of London, about the Poet's Time. (C. C. Stopes) Ath. '00, 1: 763.
Shakespearean Names, Some. (G. L. Apperson) Gent. M. n. s. 63: 278.
Shakespearean Pantomime, A. (W. J. Lawrence) Gent. M. n. s. 60: 97.
Shakespearean Questions. (W. J. Rolfe) Poet-Lore, 12: 551.
Shakespearean Theatre, A Permanent. (H. H. Fyfe) Fortn. 73: 807. Same art. Liv. Age, 225: 609. Same art. Ecl. M. 135: 222.
Shakespeariana, Certain Modern. (F. G. Fleay) Library, 2: 277.
Shakespere, Wm., Singing-teacher, Conductor, and Composer. (F. W. Wodell) Music, 13: 291. — Music, 17: 94, 525.
Shakings. Un. Serv. M. 22: 123.
Shallow Spirit of Judgment, The; a story. (E. Wyatt) McClure, 15: 423.
Shamanism. (J. Stadling) Contemp. 79: 86.
Shame of William Danby, The; a story. (F. Langbridge) Ecl. M. 135: 334. Same art. Liv. Age, 226: 168.
Shan States, The. Chamb. J. 75: 310.
— Chinese, Journeys in. (F. W. Carey) Geog. J. 14: 378. 15: 486.
— Southern; a new field for enterprise. Chamb. J. 78: 478.
Shanghai, A Glimpse at. (E. M. Allaire) Outing, 35: 134.
Shankara. (C. Johnston) Open Court, 11: 559.
Shannon, Charles Hazelwood, as an Artist. (W. Rothenstein) Sat. R. 83: 437.
Shannon, J. J., Artist, with portrait. (L. Hind) Studio (Lond.) 8: 67.
— as Portrait Painter. (F. Rinder) Art J. 53: 41.
Shantung, Martyrs of. (H. D. Porter) Outl. 64: 747.
Shapleigh, Waldron, Obituary of. J. Frankl. Inst. 152: 312.
Shareholders, What are the Interests of? (H. A. Dallas) Econ. R. 7: 182.
Shark, Johnny. (T. J. Hains) Harper, 103: 626.
Shark, Plea for the. Spec. 80: 688. Same art. Liv. Age, 218: 57.
Sharks. (M. Dunn) Contemp. 78: 213. Same art. Ecl. M. 135: 679. Same art. Liv. Age, 227: 20.
— as Game. (C. F. Holder) Outing, 37: 50.
— Concerning. (F. T. Bullen) National, 32: 401.
— in the English Channel. Sat. R. 86: 375.
— The Tănifa of Samoa. (Louis Becke) Chamb. J. 78: 343.
Shark-fishing with a Rod. (W. A. Michael) Outing, 31: 49.

Sharp, Joel, with portrait. Cassier, 14: 544.
Sharpe, Charles Kirkpatrick, A Virtuoso of the Old School. (L. H. Vincent) Atlan. 84: 36.
Sharpers. (D. E. W. Spratt) Lippinc. 61: 250.
Sharpshooting, Scientific. (H. Kephart) Cassier, 17: 418.
Shasta. (Benj. Shurtliff) Overland, n. s. 36: 153.
Shaughnessy, Thomas G., and the Canadian Pacific Railway. Canad. M. 12: 528.
Shaw, Byam, Artist. (G. White) Studio (Internat.) 1: 209. — Studio (Internat.) 7: 259. — With portrait. (A. L. Baldry) M. of Art, 22: 633.
— Sketches by. Studio (Internat.) 3: 173.
Shaw, George Bernard. Acad. 60: 127-192. — (G. S. Street) Blackw. 167: 832. — (W. K. Tarpey) Critic, 37: 124.
— and his Plays. (T. R. Sullivan) Bk. Buyer, 16: 502.
— as a Playwright. Acad. 53: 461, 490, 613.
— Cashel Byron's Profession. (M. Beerbohm) Sat. R. 92: 556.
— Correspondence with Harper & Brothers. Critic, 37: 114.
— Devil's Disciple. (M. Beerbohm) Sat. R. 88: 450.
— Plays. (E. E. Hale, jr.) Dial (Ch.) 25: 43. — Ath. '98, 1: 763.
— Three Plays for Puritans. (M. Beerbohm) Sat. R. 91: 107.
— Mrs. Warren's Profession. (M. Beerbohm) Sat. R. 85: 651, 679.
— Writings of. (J. B. Perry) Critic, 38: 453.
Shaw, Henry Wheeler [Josh Billings]. (E. P. Thomson) New Eng. M. n. s. 19: 696.
Shaw, James. (W. Jack) Good Words, 40: 692.
Shaw, R. Norman, Work of. Studio (Lond.) 7: 21, 98.
Shaw, Robert Gould. (H. L. Higginson; W. James; B. T. Washington) Harv. Grad. M. 6: 28.
— Memorial of. (E. Atkinson) Cent. 32: 176. — Am. Arch. 57: 88.
— A poem. (P. L. Dunbar) Atlan. 86: 488.
Shaw Family, Middleborough, Mass., Winthrop, Me. (A. L. Talbot) N. E. Reg. 51: 191.
Shaw's Folly; a story. (T. B. Aldrich) Harper, 102: 81.
Shawneetown, Flood at, 1898. (F. H. Wines) Char. R. 8: 175.
Shays's Rebellion, 1787, Documents relating to. Am. Hist. R. 2: 693.
— Reminiscences of. (P. Holland) New Eng. M. n. s. 23: 538.
She and I; a sketch. (E. Callaghan) Canad. M. 15: 33.
She Danced before him; a story. (M. C. Fraser) Pall Mall M. 15: 148.
Sheafe Family of Guilford, Conn. (W. K. Watkins) N. E. Reg. 55: 208.
Sheelia; a story. (R. M. Gilbert) Eng. Illust. 20: 619.
Sheep and the Forest Reserves. (C. S. Newhall) Forum, 30: 710. 31: 311.
— and Goats, Wild, of Canada. (C. A. Bramble) Canad. M. 14: 543.
— Development of Supernumerary Mammæ in. (A. G. Bell) Science, n. s. 9: 637.
— Four-horned. (R. Lydekker) Knowl. 24: 150.
— Hunting Alaskan White Sheep. (Dall de Weese) Outing, 34: 338.
— Rocky Mountain, Hunting. (E. E. Bowles) Outing, 36: 53.
— Winter Hunting in the Rockies. (J. W. Schultz) Outing, 37: 437.
Sheep and the Goats; a sermon on Matt. xxv. 31-33. (W. Lack) Expos. 6: 401.
Sheep Dog Competition. (J. W. Smith) Strand, 16: ··°

Sheep-stealers ; a children's story. (C. Clare) Eng. Illust. 20: 342.

Sheffield in the 18th Century, R. E. Leader on. Ath. '01: 752.

Sheffield Society of Artists. Artist (N. Y.) 23: 108.

Sheikh Said, Jurisdiction over. (E. de Sasseville) Nat. Geog. M. 8: 155.

Shelburne Farms, Vermont. (H. I. Hazleton) New Eng. M. n. s. 25: 267.

Sheldon, Charles M. (J. P. Fritts) Critic, 34: 540.

Sheldon, E. A. (L. H. Jones) Educa. R. 14: 428.
— and the Oswego Movement. (A. P. Hollis) Educa. 18: 545.

Shell-fish, Minor. Spec. 79: 242.

Shell Pagoda. (H. A. Nash) New Eng. M. n. s. 25: 147.

Shelley, Percy Bysshe, with portrait. Acad. 51: 548.
— and Carlyle. (W. Larminie) Contemp. 77: 728.
— and Catullus. (E. W. Bowen) Sewanee, 7: 337.
— and Elizabeth. (A. T. Quiller-Couch) Liv. Age, 219: 595.
— and Godwin. (W. G. Kingsland) Poet-Lore, 10: 389.
— Edinburgh Marriage of ; a discovery. Chamb. J. 77: 273.
— First Books of. (L. S. Livingston) Bookman, 12: 379.
— Italian Villa of (Casa Magni), and its Neighborhood. (E. A. Reynolds-Ball) Eng. Illust. 17: 121.
— Last Days of. Acad. 55: 512.
— Portraits of, in National Portrait Gallery. (R. Garnett) M. of Art, 25: 492.
— Some Unpublished Letters of. (E. D. North) Indep. 49: 737-1037.
— Victor and Cazire. (A. T. Quiller-Couch) Ecl. M. 132: 74.
— Youthful Poems. Acad. 55: 42, 113.

Shells as Ornaments, Implements, and Articles of Trade. (R. Lydekker) Knowl. 22: 242.
— Choice, from the Santa Barbara Channel. (L. G. Yates) Overland, n. s. 30: 128.
— in Art. (L. B. Thompson) Art J. 49: 266.
— Mid-ocean. (C. Parkinson) Chamb. J. 76: 534.
— of the River Thames. Spec. 84: 835.
— Sea, on the Colorado Desert. (J. E. Bennett) Overland, n. s. 29: 535.

Shelter, Poetry of. (C. C. Abbott) Lippinc. 61: 265.

Shelter Island, N. Y., A Tradition of. (C. Horsford) J. Am. Folk-Lore, 12: 43.

"Shenandoah," the Last of the Confederate Cruisers. (J. T. Mason R) Cent. 34: 600.

Shenandoah Valley, Cycling thro'. (D. F. Gay) Outing, 32: 232.

Shenstone, William. (L. Morison) Gent. M. n. s. 65: 196.

Shepard, Rev. Ambrose. (A. W. Stewart) Sund. M. 29: 351.

Shepard, Edward Morse. (G. F. Peabody) R. of Rs. (N. Y.) 24: 548.

Shepard, Thomas, Letter of, to Hugh Peters, 1645. (C. H. Firth) Am. Hist. R. 4: 105.

Shepherd of the Sierras. (M. Austin) Atlan. 86: 54.

Shepherds of Olympus, The. Macmil. 78: 284. Same art. Liv. Age, 218: 881.

Shepherd's Year, The. (T. S. Palmer) Gent. M. n. s. 63: 539. Same art. Liv. Age, 224: 356.

Sherborn, Mass., Women's Prison. (J. C. Barrows) New Eng. M. n. s. 21: 614. — (Ellen C. Johnson) Char. R. 9: 452.
— — Establishment of. (Susan D. Nickerson) Char. R. 9: 326.

Sheridan, Charles Francis. (W. F. Rae) Temp. Bar, 119: 396.

Sheridan, Gen. Philip H. His Bad Temper. (F. Williams) Indep. 53: 2397.

Sheridan's Ride. (G. A. Forsyth) Harper, 95: 165. — (C. W. Evans) Chaut. 31: 247.

Sheridan, Richard Brinsley. (T. B. Reed) Cosmopol. 26: 534. — (J. Grahame) Westm. 147: 515. Same art. Ecl. M. 129: 416. — Lond. Q. 87: 230. Same art. Liv. Age, 212: 726.
— and Shaw, George Bernard. (G. S. Street) Blackw. 167: 832.
— More about. (W. F. Rae) 19th Cent. 43: 256.
— Rivals, performed in 1900. (M. Beerbohm) Sat. R. 89: 424.
— Sisters of. (W. F. Rae) Temp. Bar, 118: 45.
— Sons of. (W. F. Rae) Temp. Bar, 116: 407.

Sheriff of Elbert ; a story. (C. Thomas) McClure, 12: 556.

Sheriffs and Coroners. (Hugh Cowan) Scot. R. 30: 235.
— Pricking the. Chamb. J. 74: 671.

Sherman, Frances. Matins. (J. Davidson) Canad. M. 8: 374.

Sherman, John. (G. F. Hoar) Indep. 52: 2610.
— as Secretary of State. Pub. Opin. 22: 101.
— Recollections of Forty Years. Sat. R. 84: 82.

Sherman, Rev. John, and Sherman, Capt. John, Ancestry of. N. E. Reg. 51: 309.

Sherman, Roger, Boutell's Life of. (C. H. Cooper) Dial (Ch.) 22: 246. — (S. E. Baldwin) Am. Hist. R. 2: 536. — (F. J. Stimson) Bk. Buyer, 14: 179.

Sherman, Thomas W., Major-General. J. Mil. Serv. Inst. 1: 103. — (E. S. Ellis) Chaut. 27: 474.

Sherman, Gen. Wm. Tecumseh. J. Mil. Serv. Inst. 25: 149.
— and Johnston, Gen., Convention between. (J. D. Cox) Scrib. M. 28: 489.
— Force's. Am. Hist. R. 5: 153.
— in Russia ; extracts from diary. Cent. 35: 866.
— March to the Sea. (J. F. Rhodes) Am. Hist. R. 6: 466.
— Opinion of General Grant. (W. T. Sherman) Cent. 31: 821.
— Recollections and Letters of. (M. Halstead) Indep. 51: 1610, 1682.
— Tour of Europe ; extracts from diary. Cent. 35: 729.
— Unpublished Letters of. (E. F. Weller) McClure, 8: 546.
— Why he declined the Nomination in 1884. No. Am. 171: 243.

Sherman Family, of Taxley, Eng., Wills of. N. E. Reg. 54: 62.

Sherwood, Mrs. Model Youths in her Writings. (F. Anstey) Pall Mall M. 13: 541.

Sherwood, William H., Pianist. (W. S. B. Mathews) Music, 11: 339.

Shetland Ponies. (G. Hendry) Eng. Illust. 17: 519.

Shetland Wool. Chamb. J. 74: 487.

Shiel, Loch. (M. G. Watkins) Gent. M. n. s. 60: 334.

Shield-wall and the Schieltrum. (G. Neilson) Antiq. n. s. 33: 341.

Shields in War. Spec. 84: 8, 16, 50, 51.

Shiftless Reader, A Plea for the. (M. B. Dunn) Atlan. 85: 131.

Shilling of Massachusetts Bay. (W. G. Sumner) Yale R. 7: 405.

Shiloh, The Sanctuary at. (L. W. Batton) J. Bib. Lit. 19: 29.

Shiloh, Battle of. (W. W. Wallace) J. Mil. Serv. Inst. 25: 14.
— a Spectacular Battle and its " Ifs." (Ben C. Truman) Overland, n. s. 34: 155.

Shimabara, Japan, Overthrow of Christians at. (R. B. Perry) Luth. Q. 28: 58.

Shine, J. L., Portrait of. Theatre, 38: 218.

Signal Service. (L. E. Van Norman) Outl. **59**: 336.
— Use and Organization of. Un. Serv. M. **19**: 522.
Signalling, Ætheric. J. Mil. Serv. Inst. **28**: 256.
— Ancient Methods of. (C. Bright) Cornh. **77**: 89. Same art. Ecl. M. **130**: 249.
— Electric, without Wires. (W. H. Preece) Science, **6**: 889.
— in the Army and Navy. (H. C. Fyfe) Strand, **18**: 714.
— in War-time. (G. J. Varney) Lippinc. **62**: 277.
Si-gnan, China. (R. S. Gundry) Sat. R. **90**: 263, 291. Same art. Ecl. M. **135**: 772. Same art. Liv. Age, **227**: 181.
Signatures, Law of. (Wm. Arch. McClean) Green Bag, **11**: 404.
Signet of Navarre. (N. P. Murphy) Good Words, **42**: 527.
Signets, Badges, and Medals. (P. Carus) Open Court, **14**: 284.
Signifying Nothing; a sketch. (M. Geoghegan) Belgra. **97**: 50.
Signor Patrichelli Leading; a story. (S. Jordan) Music, **18**: 334.
Signorelli. "School of Pan," Symbolism of. (R. E. Fry) Monthly R. **5**, no. 3: 110.
Signorini, Telemaco. (W. Mercer) Ath. '01, **1**: 602.
Signs, Dignity and Humor of. (A. C. Sage) Lippinc. **59**: 236.
— of Public Houses, Old English. (E. G. Dawber) Art J. **49**: 247.
— Professor of, A Modernized Myth in Court. (W. Barber) Green Bag, **9**: 252.
— Reading. (J. Gibbon) J. Mil. Serv. Inst. **5**: 396.
— Tradesmen's. (J. S. Gardner) Am. Arch. **65**: 21, 28. Same art. J. Soc. Arts, **47**: 613.
Sigsbee, Capt. Charles D., with portrait. (H. Garnett) Nat. Geog. M. **9**: 250.
Sikh Military Colonies. Un. Serv. M. **18**: 432.
Sikh Soldiers, Bravery of the. (H. Pearse) Macmil. **77**: 360.
— Record of. (F. P. Gibbon) Gent. M. n. s. **61**: 214.
Sikhism and the Sikhs. (L. Griffin) No. Am. **172**: 291.
Sikhs, Holy Writings of the. (M. Macauliffe) Asia R. **26**: 98, 357.
Silas Trustgore's Gift. Liv. Age, **223**: 593.
Silchester, Excavations at. (J. G. Joyce; G. E. Fox) Archæol. **46**: 329. **50**: 263. **52**: 733. **53**: 263. **54**: 173, 439. **55**: 215, 409. **56**: 103, 229. **57**: 87.
— Ath. '97, **1**: 721. '00, **1**: 792.
— Iron Tools found at. (J. Evans) Archæol. **54**: 129.
Silence, Moral Value of. (F. Adler) Int. J. Ethics, **8**: 345.
— of the Sea. (E. A. Smith) Good Words, **42**: 743.
— Pinchbeck. Spec. **87**: 474.
"Silent Sisters" Convent, near Bayonne. (L. Dennehy) Idler, **16**: 790.
Silhouette; a story. (A. E. Lawrence) Cosmopol. **23**: 401.
Silhouettes. (P. E. Morrell) Eng. Illust. **21**: 547.
— and Shadow Pictures. (M. L. Mayo and others) Munsey, **20**: 288.
Silhouettists, Last of the. (C. H. Hart) Outl. **66**: 329.
Silk, Artificial. (J. Cash) J. Soc. Arts, **48**: 61.
— Vegetable, Cultivation of, in Central America. (R. W. Cater) Chamb. J. **76**: 778.
— Weighted. (T. L. Phipson) Chamb. J. **75**: 44.
Silk Culture in the United States. (A. M. Earle) New Eng. M. n. s. **22**: 557.
Silk Industry, British, Revival of. M. of Art, **22**: 393.
— Japanese. J. Soc. Arts, **45**: 557.
— of Lyons. J. Soc. Arts, **48**: 750.
Silk-making in France. (G. d'Avenel) Chaut. **24**: 685.

Silk-worm Industry in America. (E. A. Samuels) Nat'l M. (Bost.) **10**: 183.
Silks and Brocades, English. Art J. **52**: 377.
Silliman, Benjamin, Sr., and James D. Dana, Reminiscences of, with portraits. (F. J. Kingsbury) Indep. **53**: 2385.
Silliman, Benj. Douglas, with portrait. (A. O. Hall) Green Bag, **9**: 1. — (W. G. Low) Am. Law R. **35**: 259.
Silurian-Devonian Boundary in North America. (H. S. Williams) Am. J. Sci. **159**: 203.
Silurian Fish Remains, Recently Discovered. (G. B. Howes) Nature, **61**: 307.
Silva of North America, Sargent's. (G. L. Goodale) Nation, **66**: 409.
Silver, Arthur, Studio of. Studio (Lond.) **3**: 117.
Silver and the Bank Reserve. Bank. M. (Lond.) **64**: 429.
— and Prices. (M. Frewen) J. Soc. Arts, **45**: 636.
— E. Atkinson on Cost of producing. Gunton's M. **15**: 247.
— Bank of England and. (H. White) Nation, **65**: 218.
— The "Crime of '73." (B. Carter) Nation, **70**: 162.
— English Cabinet on. Spec. **79**: 546.
— Fall in the Price of, since 1873. (E. S. Meade) J. Pol. Econ. **5**: 316.
— Free Coinage by the U. S. alone. (J. S. Morrill) Forum, **26**: 136.
— — and Legal Tender Decisions. (C. G. Tiedeman) Ann. Am. Acad. Pol. Sci. **9**: 198.
— — The Great Question in Retrospect. (W. M. Fishback) Arena, **20**: 289.
— Free Silver Campaign, Ethical Side of. (F. J. Stimson) Int. J. Ethics, **7**: 401.
— Free Silver Fiasco, Another. Bank. M. (Lond.) **64**: 553.
— in China. (T. Williams) Ann. Am. Acad. Pol. Sci. **9**: 359.
— in India. (J. C. Harrison) Pol. Sci. Q. **12**: 603.
— India's Case for. (A. S. Ghosh) No. Am. **165**: 477.
— John Bull and. (F. J. Faraday) National, **29**: 118.
— Mining and Minting of. (A. E. Outerbridge, jr.) J. Frankl. Inst. **146**: 401.
— Question of, Great Britain's Opportunity. (E. Sassoon and others) National, **30**: 233.
— — in Canada. (J. Davidson) Q. J. Econ. **12**: 139.
— — in the U. S. (W. Fisher) Econ. J. **7**: 111.
— — Is it Dead? Gunton's M. **13**: 267.
— — Present Status of. (R. P. Bland) No. Am. **165**: 469.
— Recent Production of, and its Probable Future. (E. S. Meade) Ann. Am. Acad. Pol. Sci. **14**: 327.
— Sinking. (W. R. Lawson) Contemp. **72**: 355.
— Standard, its History, Properties, and Uses. (E. A. Smith) Knowl. **24**: 102, 134, 163.
Silver Certificates and Standard Dollars. Bank. M. (N. Y.) **54**: 825.
Silver Currency, How it may be restored. (H. Boies) Arena, **21**: 757.
Silver Fans, The. Temp. Bar, **117**: 95. Same art. Liv. Age, **222**: 177.
Silver Joss, The. (Charles Edwardes) Chamb. J. **75**: supp. 14.
Silver Lining in the Cloud, The. Chamb. J. **76**: 755.
Silver Lotah, The. (Mayne Lindsay) Chamb. J. **77**: 705-763.
Silver Mines of Nertchinsk. (J. Y. Simpson) Blackw. **162**: 271.
Silver Ores, Reduction Works for, at Aduana. (M. T. Armas) J. Frankl. Inst. **146**: 293, 349.
Silver Plate, Evolution of Form in English. (P. Macquoid) J. Soc. Arts, **49**: 323.
Silver Prices in India. (F. J. Atkinson) J. Statis. Soc. **60**: 84.

Silver Skull, The; a story. (S. R. Crockett) Pall Mall M. **15**: 538. **16**: 73-571. **17**: 121-588. **18**: 124.

Silversmith, The; the beauty of his art. M. of Art, **23**: 377.

"Silverspot," the Story of a Crow. (E. S. Thompson) Scrib. M. **23**: 212.

Silverwork, Examples of Old. (A. Vallance) Artist (N. Y.) **31**: 72.

Silver Work; Virgil shield. (J. M. O'Fallon) Art J. **49**: 138.

Silver Work Exhibition of Burlington Fine Arts Club. Sat. R. **91**: 299. — Art J. **53**: 125.

Sime, S. H., Black and white artist. (A. H. Lawrence) Idler, **12**: 755.

Similitudes, Use of, by the Early Poets of the 19th Century. (L. Jervis) Westm. **154**: 334.

Simmonds, Peter L. J. Soc. Arts, **45**: 1150.

Simmons, Edward Emerson, Artist. (A. Hoeber) Brush & P. **5**: 241.

Simmons, Sir John L., Portraits of. Strand, **14**: 687.

Simon, O. J., A Letter from, to the Jesuit Fathers. Month, **93**: 319.

Simple Story, A. (Marguerite Poradowzka) Liv. Age, **216**: 293-372.

Simplicity of Susan, The; a story. (M. L. Pendered) Belgra. **98**: 108.

Simplon Tunnel. (A. L. Frankenthal) Am. Arch. **69**: 54. — (A. Larsen) Cassier, **17**: 179. — Nature, **55**: 617. **64**: 235.

Simpson, Edgar, Repoussé Work of. Illus. Artist (N. Y.) **23**: 157.

Simpson, Ellen H. Meth. R. **58**: 294.

Simpson, Emma, Mrs., Case of. (B. Borret) Green Bag, **13**: 539.

Simpson, Sir J. Y., and Chloroform, Gordon on. Nature, **57**: 361.

Sims, George R., Playwright. (A. H. Lawrence) Idler, **12**: 683.

Sin, Christian Science View of. (A. Farlow) Outl. **68**: 745.

— Pagan and Christian Conception of. (W. Rupp) Ref. Ch. R. **46**: 542.

— Pauline Doctrine of. (O. Cone) Am. J. Theol. **2**: 241.

— Vanishing Sense of. (J. H. Edwards) Presb. & Ref. R. **10**: 606.

— within the Church. (S. Z. Beam) Ref. Q. **45**: 357.

Sin of the Prince-bishop. (W. Canton) Sund. M. **27**: 224.

Sincerity. (Arthur Symons) Sat. R. **89**: 357.

Sind, India, Reminiscences of. Sat. R. **91**: 700.

Sindban and the Seven Wise Masters; translated from the Syriac. (H. Gollancz) Folk-Lore, **8**: 99.

Sinding, Christian, Musical Composer, with portrait. (Mary W. Chase) Music, **20**: 371.

Sinding, Stephan, Danish Sculptor. (W. R. Prior) M. of Art, **25**: 448.

Singan, Capital of Chinese Empire in 1900. (J. M. Hubbard) Nat. Geog. M. **12**: 63.

Singapore. (A. Bellesort) Liv. Age, **223**: 735. — (H. Clifford) Argosy, **73**: 277. — (M. L. Todd) Nation, **72**: 469.

— and Hong Kong. (A. Bellesort) Ecl. M. **134**: 165.

— Visit of the Duke of Cornwall and York. (H. Clifford) Blackw. **170**: 115. Same art. Ecl. M. **137**: 539.

— White Man's Rule in. (P. Bigelow) Harper, **100**: 443.

Sing Kee's China-Lily. (Mary Bell) Overland, n. s. **30**: 531.

Sing-Sing Prison. (J. M. Price) Eng. Illust. **18**: 57.

Singer and Song; a poem. (W. V. B. Thompson) Canad. M. **10**: 120.

Singers, Advertising Famous. (H. C. Lahee) Nat'l M. (Bost.) **9**: 104.

— Italian Tenor Opera. (H. C. Lahee) Nat'l M. (Bost.) **9**: 542.

— Popular, of this Century. (Egbert Swayne) Music, **11**: 288.

— Some Old. (J. Todhunter) Temp. Bar, **120**: 225.

Singing, Art of. (S. Reeves) Idler, **16**: 678, 729, 882.

— at Sight. (W. S. B. Mathews) Music, **20**: 443.

— — Song Method. (F. E. Howard) Educa. **21**: 531.

— by Note in Primary Schools. (J. E. Crane) Music, **14**: 332.

— Congregational. (J. F. Runciman) Sat. R. **89**: 265.

— Decline of the Art of. (R. Davey) 19th Cent. **45**: 944.

— Defects of Instruction in. Music, **17**: 62.

— Enunciation of Words in. (W. S. B. Mathews) Music, **19**: 69.

— A Few Ideas about. (A. S. Thompson) Music, **18**: 348.

— Forward Tone. (J. D. Mehan) Music, **13**: 568.

— Hints on. (M. Garcia) Music, **18**: 293.

— How to practice. (Karleton Hackett) Music, **15**: 145.

— in Public Schools. (Jennie L. Thomas) Music, **15**: 97.

— Instruction of Children in. (Carl Faelten) Music, **12**: '508.

— Laryngoscope in. (K. Hackett) Music, **12**: 39. — (A. D. Duvivier) Music, **13**: 102.

— Larynx in. (J. D. Mehan) Music, **15**: 134.

— Method of using Voice in. (W. L. Tomlins) Music, **14**: 651.

— Methods of. (W. J. Baltzell) Music, **14**: 271.

— Musical, in Schools. (Margaret P. Goodell) Music, **20**: 437.

— Paradoxes and Principles of. (J. D. Mehan) Music, **13**: 472.

— Rhythm in. (Bicknell Young) Music, **19**: 567.

— School and Chorus, J. D. Mehan's Opinions on. Music, **11**: 702.

— Should it be taught in Graded Schools? (Mrs. G. Boyd) Music, **15**: 601.

— Study of, Abroad. (Mr. Wilson) Music, **18**: 394.

— — in Italy. (F. Walker) Music, **13**: 363.

— taught to Children without Ear or Voice. (Theodosia Harrison) Music, **19**: 629.

— Tremolo in. (F. W. Root) Music, **18**: 140.

Singing of a Bird, The; a story. (J. Hawthorne) Harper, **101**: 125.

Singing of the Frogs, The. (J. G. Neilbardt) Overland, n. s. **38**: 226.

Singing Flames, Theory of. (H. V. Gill) Am. J. Sci. **154**: 177.

Singing Teachers, Prominent European. (P. D. Aldrich) Music, **16**: 169.

Single Tax, The. (L. Abbott) Outl. **68**: 171.

— Ethics of. (W. L. Garrison; S. S. Craig; C. B. Fillebrown) Arena, **21**: 51.

Singular Experience, A. (Lucy Hardy) Chamb. J. **75**: 318.

Sinner and the Problem, The; a story. (E. Parker) Macmil. **83**: 1-461.

Sins of the Fathers. (A. Provost) New Eng. M. n. s. **21**: 728.

Sion College, Library of. (W. H. Milman) Library, **2**: 55.

Sioux Campaign of 1890-91. (W. P. Richardson) J. Mil. Serv. Inst. **18**: 512.

Sioux Indians, Mythological Tales of. (L. L. Meeker) J. Am. Folk-Lore, **14**: 161.

— Quarter-century with the. (H. S. Houston) Outl. **60**: 323.

Sluis, Battle of. (W. L. Clowes) Cornh. **75**: 72. — (A. T. Storey) National, **28**: 681.

Slum, The Battle with the. (J. A. Riis) Atlan. **83**: 626.

Slum Movement in Fiction, The. (Jane H. Findlater) National, **35**: 447. Same art. Liv. Age, **225**: 755.

Slums, Incidents of the. (W. A. Wyckoff) Scrib. M. **30**: 486.

— Some, in Boston. (H. K. Estabrook) Char. R. **8**: 242.

Sly Biddy Machree; a story. (E. E. Garnett) Outl. **66**: 460.

Smallpox and Hydropathy. Westm. **152**: 101.

— and Sanitation. (W. Lloyd) Westm. **150**: 548.

— and Vaccination Statistics, with reference to Age-incidence, Sex-incidence, and Sanitation. (N. A. Humphreys; A. Milnes) J. Statis. Soc. **60**: 503, 552.

— Epidemic in Gloucester. Nature, **57**: 221.

— — in the U. S., 1901. (J. N. Hyde) Pop. Sci. Mo. **59**: 557.

Small Voices of the Town. (C. M. Skinner) Atlan. **88**: 550.

Smallwood, Wm. Ath. '97, **2**: 234.

Smart, Christopher. Temp. Bar, **112**: 268.

Smart Woman, A; a story. Belgra. **97**: 122.

Smell, Applicability of Weber's Law to. (E. A. M. Gamble) Am. J. Psychol. **10**: 82.

— Theories regarding Scent. (J. T. Bailey) Outing, **39**: 305.

Smile and Laugh, Nature of the. (G. V. N. Dearborn) Science, n. s. **11**: 851.

Smirke, Sir Robert. (G. D. Leslie and F. A. Eaton) Art J. **50**: 137.

Smith, Ada. Acad. **55**: 487.

Smith, Adam, with portrait. Gunton's M. **15**: 108.

— Consistency of. (A. Oncken) Econ. J. **7**: 443.

— Lectures on Justice, Police, Revenue, and Arms. (W. Hasbach) Pol. Sci. Q. **12**: 684.

— Two Letters of. (E. Cannan) Econ. J. **8**: 402.

Smith, Alexander, a Forgotten Poet. (J. C. Hadden) Argosy, **70**: 196. — Acad. **61**: 55.

— Life Drama. (J. Luccock) Meth. R. **61**: 418.

Smith, Sir Archibald Levin, with portraits. Strand, **15**: 570.

Smith, Arthur Donaldson, with portrait. Bk. News, **15**: 383.

Smith, Charles E., Obituary of. (E. A. Scott) J. Frankl. Inst. **152**: 300.

Smith, Edwards Porter, with portrait. (J. M. Pereles) Green Bag, **12**: 437.

Smith, Miss Eleanor. Song Primer for Children. Music, **18**: 104.

Smith, Elizabeth. (Mary D. Steele) Educa. **17**: 411.

— A Woman Learned and Wise. (A. H. Japp) Temp. Bar, **113**: 109. Same art. Liv. Age, **216**: 400. — (L. B. Lang) Longm. **31**: 404.

Smith, F. Hopkinson, in New York. (R. Riordan) Critic, **32**: 225.

— In Three Professions. (G. Willets) Arena, **22**: 68.

Smith, George Adam, and the Lyman Beecher Lectures. (C. S. Macfarland) Outl. **61**: 966.

Smith, George Murray. Ath. '01, **1**: 467, 567. — (L. Stephen) Critic, **38**: 501.

— and "National Biography." (W. E. G. Fisher) Fortn. **75**: 880.

— In Memoriam. (L. Stephen) Cornh. **83**: 577.

— Recollections of Authors. (G. M. Smith) Critic, **38**: 48, 155, 256.

Smith, Goldwin, and the Riddle of Existence. Liv. Age, **213**: 488.

— at Home. (F. Yeigh) Bk. Buyer, **18**: 195.

— on the United States. (W. P. Trent) Sewanee, **2**: 1.

Smith, Sir Harry. A Reminiscence of the Boer War in 1848. (G. F. H. Berkeley) Fortn. **72**: 1032.

Smith, Hugh Colin. Bank. M. (Lond.) **63**: 901.

Smith, J. Caswall, Artistic Photographic Work of. (J. T. Nettleship) Art J. **51**: 212.

Smith, James Foster, 1813–98, Obituary of. J. Frankl. Inst. **145**: 468.

Smith, James M., Judge, with portrait. (A. O. Hall) Green Bag, **9**: 1.

Smith, Captain John. (K. M. Rowland) Conserv. R. **1**: 113.

Smith, Col. Nicholas; stories of our Great National Songs. (F. Wayne) Nat'l M. (Bost.) **11**: 284.

Smith, Norton B. (A. H. Broadwell) Strand, **16**: 386.

Smith, Oliver, of Hatfield, Mass. (G. B. Stebbins) New Eng. M. n. s. **19**: 166. — (C. S. Walker) New Eng. M. n. s. **21**: 718.

Smith, Oliver H. P., and his Music to Poem "God is Love." Open Court, **12**: 702.

Smith, Pamela Colman, Artist. Brush & P. **6**: 135.

Smith, Richard Baird, Vibart on. Ath. '97, **2**: 816.

Smith, Robert, of Boxford. (E. S. Bolton) N. E. Reg. **55**: 267.

Smith, Sir Robert Murdoch, Dickson's. (F. J. Goldsmid) Geog. J. **16**: 237. — Blackw. **170**: 626.

Smith, Sophia, of Hatfield, Mass. (G. B. Stebbins) New Eng. M. n. s. **19**: 166.

Smith, Southwood. (Mrs. J. T. Fields) Char. R. **10**: 28.

Smith, Sydney. Primate of the Wits. Temp. Bar, **113**: 489. Same art. Ecl. M. **130**: 762.

Smith, Elder & Co., in the early '40's. (Geo. M. Smith) Cornh. **82**: 577. Same art. Liv. Age, **227**: 545.

Smith, Ancient Name of. (J. P. Mahaffy) Ath. '00, **1**: 465.

Smith of "Pennsylvania." (F. C. Williams) Lippinc. **67**: 210.

Smith College, Botanic Garden of. (W. F. Ganong) Garden & F. **10**: 512.

— Life at. (D. Z. Doty) Munsey, **17**: 865.

— Undergraduate Life at. (Alice K. Fallows) Scrib. M. **24**: 37.

Smith College Celebration, 1901. (H. W. Mabie) Outl. **66**: 394.

Smithfield; St. Bartholomew's. (W. J. Ferrar) Sund. M. **27**: 149.

Smithson, G. E. T. Geog. J. **13**: 545.

Smithsonian Institution, First Half Century of. Ath. '98, **1**: 505. — Nation, **67**: 16. — (S. H. Peabody) Dial (Ch.) **24**: 107. — Am. Natural. **32**: 201.

— History and Publications. (J. F. Hewitt) Westm. **150**: 174.

— Story of. (G. B. Goode) Nature, **58**: 271.

Smoke, Abatement of. (W. H. Bryan) Cassier, **19**: 17.

— from a Great City, The. (C. H. Benjamin) Cassier, **20**: 129.

— Suppression of. (R. H. Thurston) Science, n. s. **9**: 55–57. — (F. H. Mason) Am. Arch. **65**: 36.

Smoke Nuisance. J. Frankl. Inst. **144**: 401.

— and its Regulation. J. Frankl. Inst. **143**: 393. **144**: 17. **145**: 1, 107.

Smokeless Powder; Bernadou's Theory of the Cellulose Molecule. (C. E. Munroe) Science, n. s. **14**: 767.

Smoking Concert. (M. M. Hickson) Longm. **30**: 354.

"Smoky Pilgrims," The. (F. W. Blackmar) Am. J. Sociol. **2**: 485.

Smollett, Tobias. Acad. **51**: 276.

— and the Old Sea-dogs. Blackw. **164**: 231.

— Smelfungus goes South. (T. Seccombe) Cornh. **84**: 192.

Smooth Bore, The. (R. E. Robinson) Liv. Age, **226**: 331.

Social Conditions, How not to better. (T. Roosevelt) R. of Rs. (N. Y.) **15**: 36.

Social Conscience, Genesis of, Nash on. (E. Cummings) New World, **7**: 145.

Social Control. (E. A. Ross) Am. J. Sociol. **2**: 547, 823. **3**: 64, 236, 328, 649. **5**: 475, 604. **6**: 29-550.

— Ideals in. (E. A. Ross) Am. J. Sociol. **2**: 547.

— Primitive, Relation of Sex to. (W. I. Thomas) Am. J. Sociol. **3**: 754.

Social Convulsion, A ; a story. (W. Mills) Midland, **8**: 332.

Social Decadence. (S. E. Simons) Ann. Am. Acad. Pol. Sci. **18**: 251.

Social Democracy. (E. V. Debs) Nat'l M. (Bost.) **9**: 54.

— in Germany. (S. I. Tonjoroff) Arena, **22**: 89. — (J. W. Perrin) Chaut. **26**: 483.

— — and the Church. (R. Heath) Contemp. **74**: 547.

— — Evolution of. Spec. **79**: 510.

— — Present Condition of. (C. Schmidt) J. Pol. Econ. **6**: 488.

— — Russell on. (S. Ball) Econ. R. **7**: 230.

— The New. (J. H. Harley) Contemp. **80**: 723.

— What it stands for. Outl. **64**: 480.

Social Democrats, Some German. (E. A. Steiner) Outl. **64**: 546.

Social Development, Logical Process of, Crowell on. (A. W. Small) Am. J. Sociol. **4**: 257.

Social Discontent. (E. P. Wheeler) Char. R. **6**: 332.

Social Economy at the Paris Exposition. Ann. Am. Acad. Pol. Sci. **16**: 328.

— since 1874. (F. B. Sanborn) Am. J. Soc. Sci. **35**: 50.

Social Education Congress, Paris, 1900. Gunton's M. **18**: 43.

Social Ethics for Church Leaders. (C. R. Henderson) Bib. World, **16**: 424.

— in the Schools. (J. E. Bulkley) Forum, **26**: 615.

Social Evil, The ; a needed reform. Outl. **67**: 620.

Social Evils and their Cure. (F. H. Wines) Char. R. **6**: 193. — (S. Z. Beam) Ref. Q. **44**: 285.

Social Evolution. (H. Thomas) Westm. **152**: 577.

— and the Churches. (H. Davies) Bib. Sac. **54**: 714.

— Kidd's. (C. E. Corwin) Ref. Church R. **45**: 24.

— What is ? (H. Spencer) Pop. Sci. Mo. **54**: 35.

Social Forces, Theory of, Patten's. (W. Caldwell) Int. J. Ethics, **7**: 345.

Social Functions. Spec. **79**: 44.

— American. Liv. Age, **213**: 147.

Social Genesis. (L. F. Ward) Am. J. Sociol. **2**: 532.

Social Groups, Persistence of. (G. Simmel) Am. J. Sociol. **3**: 662, 829. **4**: 35.

Social Ideal, The Broadening. (B. O. Flower) Arena, **25**: 653.

Social Individual, The. (A. T. Ormond) Psychol. R. **8**: 27.

Social Institutions, Sociological Treatment of Some American. (S. W. Dike) Am. J. Sociol. **7**: 405.

Social Justice, Willoughby's. (D. MacG. Means) Nation, **72**: 456.

Social Law of Service, Ely's. (F. P. Manhart) Luth. Q. **28**: 430.

Social Life in England, Traill on. (O. B. Woodford) Dial (Ch.) **24**: 141.

— and Morality in India. (M. A. Ghani) Int. J. Ethics, **7**: 301.

— Some Changes in, during the Queen's Reign. 19th Cent. **41**: 639. Same art. Liv. Age, **213**: 499. — Spec. **78**: 503. Same art. Ecl. M. **129**: 430.

Social Mind, The Concept of the. (C. A. Ellwood) Am. J. Sociol. **5**: 220.

Social Movement, Meaning of. (A. W. Small) Am. J. Sociol. **3**: 340.

Social Museum, Paris, with portrait of Count Chambrun. (T. Stanton) Open Court, **12**: 505.

Social Ne'er-do-weel. (H. G. Wortley) Westm. **153**: 333.

Social Organization, Psychology of. (J. M. Baldwin) Psychol. R. **4**: 482.

Social Passion in Modern English Essayists. (V. D. Scudder) Chaut. **27**: 595.

Social Philosophy. (L. F. Ward) Am. J. Sociol. **2**: 532, 699, 801.

Social Problem, The. (P. Topinard) Monist, **8**: 556. **9**: 63.

— and the Gospel. (H. King) Luth. Q. **31**: 370.

— Hobson on the. (C. R. Henderson) Am. J. Sociol. **7**: 125.

Social Problems. (W. B. Columbine) Westm. **151**: 375.

— Methodology of. (A. W. Small) Am. J. Sociol. **4**: 113, 235, 380.

Social Progress. (R. T. Ely) Cosmopol. **31**: 61.

— and Race Degeneration. (F. A. Fetter) Forum, **28**: 228.

— Psychology of. (H. Bosanquet) Internat. J. Ethics, **7**: 265.

— Suggestion as a Factor in. (E. Noble) Internat. J. Ethics, **8**: 214.

Social Psychology, The Fundamental Fact in. (C. A. Ellwood) Am. J. Sociol. **4**: 807.

— Nature and Task of. (C. A. Ellwood) Am. J. Sociol. **5**: 98.

— Need of the Study of. (C. A. Ellwood) Am. J. Sociol. **4**: 656.

— Prolegomena to. (C. A. Ellwood) Am. J. Sociol. **5**: 98, 220.

Social Reform and the Education of the Clergy. (H. Rashdall) Econ. R. **8**: 44.

— and the [English] General Election. (T. Burke) Forum, **29**: 523.

— Animated Moderation in. (N. P. Gilman) New World, **6**: 684.

— Modern, and Old Christian Ideals. (L. G. Powers) Yale R. **6**: 421.

— An Object Lesson in. (F. Smith) Pop. Sci. Mo. **50**: 305.

— Practical Study in. (G. Wallas) Citizen, **3**: 36.

— Publicity as a Means of. (W. H. Baldwin, jr.) No. Am. **173**: 845.

— The Working Hypothesis in. (G. H. Mead) Am. J. Sociol. **5**: 367.

Social Reform Movement, Catholic. (M. M. Snell) Am. J. Sociol. **5**: 16.

Social Reform Union, The. (W. D. P. Bliss) Arena, **22**: 272.

Social Reformers and Presidential Campaign. (W. J. Ghent) Indep. **52**: 1439.

Social Reforms. Gunton's M. **14**: 257.

Social Relations in the United States. (F. B. Sanborn) Am. J. Soc. Sci. **37**: 69.

Social Restoration. (J. H. Williams) Month, **90**: 627.

Social Rights and Duties, Stephen's. (C. C. Closson) J. Pol. Econ. **6**: 115.

Social Science, Point of View in, Dangers of Wrong. Gunton's M. **13**: 17.

Social Sciences in Secondary Schools. (E. E. Hill) Educa. **21**: 497.

Social Self-knowledge. (I. W. Howerth) Open Court, **12**: 224.

Social Service, League for. (W. H. Tolman) Arena, **21**: 473.

Social Settlement, A Function of the. (J. Addams) Ann. Am. Acad. Pol. Sci. **13**: 323.

— The Primary. (K. K. Ide) Pop. Sci. Mo. **52**: 534.

Social Settlements, New Departure in, at Hazard, Ky. (E. C. Semple) Ann. Am. Acad. Pol. Sci. **15**: 301.

Society, Economic Foundations of, Loria's. (A. F. Gaskell) Econ. R. **10**: 263.

— The Institution of. (L. M. Keasbey) Internat. Mo. **1**: 355.

— London's Enlarged. Sat. R. **89**: 552.

— Modern, A Russian Statesman on. (G. Valbert) Liv. Age, **219**: 673. Same art. Ecl. M. **132**: 111.

— Organic Theory of. (A. H. Lloyd) Am. J. Sociol. **6**: 577.

— Psychology of. (F. H. Giddings) Science, n. s. **9**: 16.

— Ultimate, Studies in. (L. Gronlund and K. T. Takahashi) Arena, **18**: 351.

— What shall Society do to be saved? Overland, n. s. **35**: 530.

— Your True Relation to. (J. W. Bennett) Cosmopol. **27**: 369.

Society Croakers. Quar. **194**: 172. Same art. Ecl. M. **137**: 639. Same art. Liv. Age, **231**: 1.

Society for Plant Morphology, 2d Annual Meeting. (E. F. Smith) Am. Natural. **33**: 199.

Society for Promotion of Engineering Education, Presidential Address before. (T. C. Mendenhall) Science, n. s. **10**: 196.

Society for the Propagation of the Gospel in New England, Discovery of First Cash-book of the. (C. A. Briggs) Scrib. M. **23**: 363.

Society for the Study of Life, The. (A. Hensley; M. M. Irwin) Arena, **22**: 614.

Society of American Artists. (S. A. Walker) Indep. **53**: 1076.

— 21st Exhibition. Artist (N. Y.) **24**: lviii.

Society of Arts, London, 1754–1899. J. Soc. Arts, **47**: 815. — Am. Arch. **66**: 69.

Society of Landscape Painters, 1st Annual Exhibition. Artist (N. Y.) **24**: lxi.

Society of Oil Painters, Piccadilly, 18th Exhibition of. Ath. '01, **1**: 23. — Art J. **53**: 61.

Society Mystery; a story. (C. M. Keys) Canad. M. **15**: 164.

Society's Rules of Good Form. (N. Davis) Pall Mall M. **25**: 466.

Sociological, Medical, and Jurisprudential Purposes, Laboratory for. (A. McDonald) Am. Law R. **35**: 831.

Sociology and Economics. (L. F. Ward) Ann. Am. Acad. Pol. Sci. **13**: 230.

— and the Epic. (A. G. Keller) Am. J. Sociol. **6**: 267.

— and Philanthropy. (F. H. Wines) Ann. Am. Acad. Pol. Sci. **12**: 49.

— Bibliography of, 1896–97. (C. H. Hastings) Am. J. Sociol. **2**: 752. **3**: 129.

— Christian, Prerequisites of a. (W. H. Butler) Meth. R. **59**: 569.

— Current. (S. Hall) Mind, **26**: 145.

— Demands of, upon Pedagogy. Am. J. Sociol. **2**: 839.

— Exact Methods in. (F. H. Giddings) Pop. Sci. Mo. **51**: 145.

— Field Work in Teaching. (E. W. Clews) Educa. R. **20**: 159.

— Giddings's Inductive. (H. Sidgwick) Econ. J. **9**: 410. — Outl. **69**: 789.

— in Germany, Present Status of. (O. Thon) Am. J. Sociol. **2**: 567, 718, 792.

— Instruction in, at Paris. (C. W. A. Veditz) Am. J. Sociol. **3**: 206.

— An Italian Sociologist in Northern Countries. (B. W. Henderson) Econ. R. **8**: 15.

— Modern. (F. Giddings) Internat. Mo. **2**: 536.

— or the Science of Institutions. (J. W. Powell) Am. Anthrop. **1**: 475, 695.

— Partingtonian. Library, **3**: 103.

Sociology, Philosophy and the Newer. (W. Caldwell) Contemp. **74**: 411.

— a Psychological Study. (W. E. C. Wright) Bib. Sac. **58**: 370.

— Point of View in. (A. W. Small) Am. J. Sociol. **3**: 145.

— Present Position of. (F. S. Baldwin) Pop. Sci. Mo. **55**: 811.

— Relations to Philosophy. (B. Bosanquet) Mind, **22**: 1.

— Scope of. (A. W. Small) Am. J. Sociol. **5**: 506–778. **6**: 42–487.

— Sentimental. (G. L. Cady) Bib. Sac. **56**: 100.

— Study and Needs of. (W. H. Van Ornum) Arena, **24**: 328.

— Study and Teaching of. (S. M. Lindsay) Ann. Am. Acad. Pol. Sci. **12**: 1.

— Theory of Imitation in. (C. W. A. Veditz) Ann. Am. Acad. Pol. Sci. **18**: 367.

— Unit in. (A. W. Small; S. M. Lindsay) Ann. Am. Acad. Pol. Sci. **13**: 81.

— Unit of Investigation in. (S. M. Lindsay) Ann. Am. Acad. Pol. Sci. **12**: 214.

— What is? (C. Bouglé) Chaut. **26**: 291.

— Value of, to Working Pastors. (A. W. Small) Outl. **62**: 389.

Socotra, Island of. (J. T. Bent) 19th Cent. **41**: 975.

— (S. E. Saville) Temp. Bar, **113**: 562.

— English Expedition to. (H. O. Forbes) Geog. J. **13**: 633.

— — Results of. Nature, **60**: 116.

— Sea-girt. Chamb. J. **75**: 22.

— Southern Arabia and, Austrian Expedition to. (D. Müller; O. Simony; F. Kossmat) Geog. J. **13**: 638.

— Two Months in. (E. N. Bennett) Longm. **30**: 405.

Socrates. The Gadfly of the State. Spec. **84**: 834.

— Inner Life of. (H. N. Fowler) Chaut. **33**: 184.

— Philosopher, Seer, and Martyr. (B. O. Flower) Arena, **20**: 261.

Socratic Dialogue, A. (R. Ogden) Nation, **71**: 25.

"Sod o' Turf;" a story. (H. T. Gillaphin) Cosmopol. **27**: 375.

Sodic Sulphate, Transition Temperature of. (T. W. Richards) Am. J. Sci. **156**: 201.

Sodium Lines, Preliminary Note on the Broadening of, by Intense Magnetic Fields. (A. S. Dunstan, M. E. Rice, and C. A. Kraus) Am. J. Sci. **153**: 472.

Sodium Thiosulphate, Action of, on Solutions of Metallic Salts at High Temperatures and Pressures. (J. Dewar) Am. J. Sci. **162**: 115.

— Titration of, with Iodic Acid. (C. F. Walker) Am. J. Sci. **154**: 235.

— Titrations by. (J. T. Norton) Am. J. Sci. **157**: 287.

Sodoma, Influence of Quercia on. (Louise M. Richter) Artist (N. Y.) **32**: 89.

Soft-hearted Sioux, The; a story. (Zitkala-Ša) Harper, **102**: 505.

Softy; a story. (A. Griffiths) Eng. Illust. **16**: 643.

Soho, Past Days in. Chamb. J. **74**: 399.

Soil, Soluble Mineral Matter in. (T. H. Means) Am. J. Sci. **157**: 264.

Soil Ferments Important in Agriculture. (H. W. Wiley) J. Frankl. Inst. **143**: 293.

Soil-song; a poem. (J. B. Tabb) Atlan. **82**: 393.

Soils and Fertilizers. (C. M. Blackford) Pop. Sci. Mo. **54**: 392.

Sokotra. See Socotra.

Solange of the Wolves. (M. Prévost) Bookman, **12**: 354.

Solar Calorimeter depending on the Rate of Generation of Steam. (J. Y. Buchanan) Nature, **63**: 548.

Solar Motion, Problem of. (M. W. Whitney) Pop. Astron. **5**: 309.

Solar Radiometer, Registering, and Sunshine Recorder. (G. S. Isham) Am. J. Sci. 156: 160.

Solar System in the Light of Recent Discoveries. (T. J. J. See) Atlan. 83: 464.

— Origin of. (A. L. Cortie) Am. Cath. Q. 24, no. 4: 19.

Soldan, Myth of. (S. Lane-Poole) Longm. 32: 349.

Soldanella, The Alpine. (Grant Allen) Strand, 14: 129.

Soldier, The American. (H. S. Kilbourne) J. Mil. Serv. Inst. 22: 50.

— Daily Life at Aldershot. (P. Wales) Canad. M. 14: 305.

— Diet of the. (W. E. Waters) J. Mil. Serv. Inst. 11: 697.

— Education of the. (C. D. Parkhurst) J. Mil. Serv. Inst. 11: 946. 12: 64.

— The Enlisted. (R. I. Dodge) J. Mil. Serv. Inst. 8: 259.

— — Prize Essay. (A. A. Woodhull) J. Mil. Serv. Inst. 8: 18.

— Hygiene of, Personal. (W. Hill-Climo) Un. Serv. M. 15: 130.

— in Camp, Garrison, and Field, Care of. (H. S. F. Harris) J. Mil. Serv. Inst. 23: 63.

— of Fiction. (H. Wyndham) Un. Serv. M. 17: 317.

— on Service in the Tropics, Clothing and Equipment of. (M. F. Steele) J. Mil. Serv. Inst. 29: 14.

— Physical Training of. (G. F. E. Harrison) J. Mil. Serv. Inst. 13: 951.

— Private Life of a British. (P. Wales) Canad. M. 14: 439.

Soldier of Misfortune. (Philippa Bridges) Cornh. 84: 742.

Soldiers, American Volunteer, at Different Periods of Time. (R. C. Kempton) Nat'l M. (Bost.) 8: 243.

— Amusements of, during War. (G. H. Scull) Outing, 37: 330.

— Can they be Christians? (Martin Luther) Open Court, 13: 525.

— Discharged, Civil Employment of. (R. J. B. Mair) Un. Serv. M. 19: 644.

— — and Reserve, Civil Employment of. (W. T. Dooner) Un. Serv. M. 20: 196.

— — Meritorious. (J. E. Bloom) J. Mil. Serv. Inst. 11: 751, 1024.

— I have met. (E. J. Hardy) Chamb. J. 74: 84.

— in City Hospitals. (L. Veiller) Char. R. 8: 374.

— Leisure Hours in a Western Army Post. (W. W. Price) Un. Serv. (Phila.) 17: 226.

— Praying. (E. J. Hardy) Un. Serv. M. 15: 619.

— Tommy Atkins, the Yankee, and the Boer. (P. Bigelow) Indep. 52: 417.

— Training and Employment of, Military Specialists' Thought on. (J. W. Hess) J. Mil. Serv. Inst. 14: 41.

Soldiers of Fortune. (R. H. Davis) Scrib. M. 21: 29–693.

Soldiers' and Sailors' Monument, N. Y. Am. Arch. 70: 55.

Soldiers' Children. (G. Forrest) Un. Serv. M. 16: 147.

Soldiers' Home, National. (E. O. Stevens) New Eng. M. n. s. 22: 285.

Soldiers' Songs. Acad. 54: 65.

Soldiers' Wives. (E. J. Hardy) Un. Serv. M. 16: 249.

Solferino, Battle of. (S. Crane) Lippinc. 66: 613.

Solicitors of England, Tardy Punishment for Dishonest. Sat. R. 91: 103.

Solidarity and Personality, Human. (W. Rupp) Ref. Ch. R. 46: 119.

Solids, Physical and Chemical Properties of. (R. H. Bradbury) J. Frankl. Inst. 152: 321.

Soliloquies in Drama. (M. Beerbohm) Sat. R. 92: 709.

Soliloquy, Dramatic Convention with special reference to the. (H. M. Paull) Fortn. 71: 863.

Solita Lavegne ; a tale of Jokio Rancho. (J. A. Rhodes) Overland, n. s. 33: 552.

Solitary Thanksgiving, A. (M. A. Bacon) New Eng. M. n. s. 23: 337.

Solitude, Luxury of. Chamb. J. 74: 577.

Solo Orchestra, The ; a story. (B. Matthews) Harper, 94: 790.

Solomon in Tradition and in Fact. (B. W. Bacon) New World, 7: 212.

— The Judgment of. (M. D. Conway) Open Court, 12: 72.

— The Testament of. (F. C. Conybeare) Jew. Q. 11: 1.

— Wives of. (M. D. Conway) Open Court, 12: 200.

Solomon, Solomon J., with portraits. Strand, 15: 197.

— Work of. (A. L. Baldry) Studio (Lond.) 8: 3.

Solomon Islands, Ethnographical Notes in. (B. T. Somerville) Anthrop. J. 26: 357.

Solomonic Literature. (M. D. Conway) Open Court, 12: 1, 321, 385, 556.

Solomons, Sir David, Electrician, Motor Carriages. (Isabel Marks) Idler, 11: 477.

Solpuga, Nature and Habits of Pliny's. (R. I. Pocock) Nature, 57: 618.

Solution, New, for the Copper Voltameter. (W. K. Shepard) Am. J. Sci. 162: 49.

Solutions, Theory of. (Lord Rayleigh) Nature, 55: 253.

Solving the Difficulty. (A. Cambridge) Longm. 31: 41.

Solway Fishery. (T. A. G. Strickland) Knowl. 23: 123.

Somali-land, Affairs in. (Sir R. Lambert-Playfair) Chamb. J. 76: 161.

— Northern, Two Recent Journeys in. (F. B. Parkinson ; Lieut. Brander-Dunbar) Geog. J. 11: 15.

— — Volcanic Crater in. (A. E. Pease) Geog. J. 11: 138.

Somatology, Laboratory Outline of. (F. Russell) Am. Anthrop. 3: 28.

Some Americans Abroad. (C. B. Loomis) Cent. 39: 469–904. 40: 134.

Some Experiments with Jane ; a story. (M. A. Curtois) Gent. M. n. s. 67: 313. Same art. Liv. Age, 231: 642.

Some of my Shipmates. (R. Sendall) Un. Serv. M. 20: 13, 128.

Some one had Blundered ; a story. (P. Millington) Temp. Bar, 115: 362. Same art. Liv. Age, 220: 109. Same art. Ecl. M. 132: 284.

Some Recollections of a Sketcher. (H. F. Abell) Temp. Bar, 121: 371. Same art. Liv. Age, 227: 778.

Some Victims of a Plot ; a story. (T. Garrison) Nat'l M. (Bost.) 11: 316.

Some Ways of Love ; a story. (Charlotte M. Mew) Pall Mall M. 24: 301.

Somerset, Edward, Duke of, the Protector, and Scotland. (A. F. Pollard) Eng. Hist. R. 13: 464.

Somerset, Lady Henry, and her Homes. (Alice R. Willard) Midland, 8: 387.

Somerset, Leveson E. H. Geog. J. 15: 430.

Somersetshire, Old Buildings in. (W. Raymond) Idler, 13: 629.

Somerville, Guy. Writer, 14: 60.

Something in the Air ; a tale. Argosy, 69: 409.

Somewhere within that Sea of Fire ; a railroad story. (A. E. Lawrence) Nat'l M. (Bost.) 9: 379.

Son of a Convict, The. (F. H. Loughead) Overland, n. s. 29: 128.

Son of Ham, A. (O. A. Ward) Overland, n. s. 32: 152.

Son of Man, Title of. (M. G. Evans) Bib. Sac. 57: 680.

— in the Book of Daniel. (N. Schmidt) J. Bib. Lit. 19: 22.

Son of a Tory ; a story. (C. Scollard) Chaut. 24: 554–674. 25: 41–278.

Son of the Wolf, The ; Third of the "Malemute Kid" Stories. (Jack London) Overland, n. s. 33: 335.

Sonata, A; a story. (W. I. Andrus) Music, 11: 531.

Sonata in A Flat, Op. 13; a story. (F. Crane) Music, 13: 284.

Song; a poem. (W. Watson) Bk. Buyer, 16: 235.

Song; a poem. Argosy, 67: 227.

Song, The Burden of the. (May Byron) Temp. Bar, 123: 39.

Song in Winter, A; a poem. (A. St. J. Adcock) Chamb. J. 74: 416. Same art. Ecl. M. 129: 466.

Song of Autumn; a poem. (E. Root) Outing, 31: 173.

Song of the Camp, A; a poem. (B. Taylor) Nat'l M. (Bost.) 8: 223.

Song of the Canadian Pioneer; a poem. (A. Bridle) Canad. M. 14: 374.

Song of the Centaur. (B. M. Channing) Poet-Lore, 13: 248.

Song of Cheiron. (T. S. Moore) Sat. R. 90: 82.

Song of a Commonplace Soul. (A. E. Jameson) Argosy, 74: 270.

Song of the Four Winds; a poem. (C. Burke) Ecl. M. 130: 796.

Song of the Gatherer. (P. L. Dunbar) Green Bag, 10: 355.

Song of the Gray Nut-pine. (E. T. Hoffman) Outing, 38: 248.

Song of the Moor. (J. Buchan) Macmil. 76: 215. Same art. Liv. Age, 214: 441.

Song of the Muse of Labor; a poem. (E. Markham) McClure, 14: 123. Same art. Idler, 19: 191.

Song of the Past, A; a poem. (F. B. Doveton) Gent. M. n. s. 59: 25. Same art. Ecl. M. 129: 633.

"Song o' Steam." (A. Bates) Atlan. 79: 476.

Song of Subscriptions; a poem. (I. Zangwill) Cosmopol. 24: 354.

Song of Summer. (J. A. Coll) Outing, 36: 310.

Song of the Unsuccessful; a poem. (R. Burton) Outl. 64: 541.

Song of the Wandering Dust. (A. H. Branch) Atlan. 81: 697.

Song of the Wheel; a poem. (G. L. Richardson) Outing, 29: 455.

Song Settings, Poems for. (Wm. Armstrong) Music, 16: 473.

Songs and Song Writers, Finck on. (I. A. Pyle) Dial (Ch.) 30: 107. — (Egbert Swayne) Music, 19: 386.

— Celebrated, Victor Maurel on. Music, 15: 179.

— Composition of. (W. J. Baltzell) Music, 11: 259.

— How to appreciate. (W. J. Baltzell) Music, 14: 478.

— Lack of Modern English. (J. F. Runciman) Sat. R. 88: 11.

— of the Chase. (Laura A. Smith) Idler, 15: 847.

— of Freedom. (L. Mead) Chaut. 31: 574.

— of the Ships of Steel; poems. (J. Barnes) McClure, 11: 115.

— Old. (L. Vernon) Music, 18: 440. — (P. Erskine) Liv. Age, 230: 656.

— Popular Cradle-. (E. de Schoultz-Adiewsky) Music, 11: 561. 12: 19.

— Popular, Vogue of. (H. T. Finck) Lippinc. 65: 298.

— Romances connected with. (J. C. Hadden) Chamb. J. 78: 186.

— Sea. (A. Walters) Temp. Bar, 120: 485. Same art. Liv. Age, 226: 800.

— War. (F. M. Butler) Lippinc. 62: 411.

Sonnet and Sonnetteer; a study. (G. A. Pierce) Chaut. 33: 501.

Sonnet of Revolt. Fortn. 75: 1030.

Sonnets. (R. Hovey) Atlan. 86: 534.

— A Group of. (Phillips Brooks) Liv. Age, 228: 589.

— A Plea for the Study of. (E. G. Kemp) Temp. Bar, 111: 277. Same art. Liv. Age, 214: 366.

Sonora. (G. Holms) Chamb. J. 78: 657.

Sons beyond the Border; a poem. (A. J. Stringer) Canad. M. 14: 128.

Sons of the Revolution, Massachusetts Society of. (W. G. Page) New Eng. M. n. s. 20: 3.

Sons of R. Rand. (A. W. Colton) New Eng. M. n. s. 17: 52.

Sop for a Saurian, A. (F. R. H. Chapman) Chamb. J. 77: 173.

Sophia, Queen of Norway and Sweden, with portraits. Strand, 15: 199.

Sophia; a story. (S. J. Weyman) Munsey, 21: 339 — 23: 115.

Sophia Dorothea. Love of an Uncrowned Queen. Ed. R. 193: 56.

Sophie Charlotte, Queen of Prussia. (W. H. Wilkins) 19th Cent. 49: 666.

Sophiology. (J. W. Powell) Am. Anthrop. 3: 51.

Sophocles. Ajax; ed. and tr. by Jebb. Sat. R. 83: 72.

— Antigone as performed at Bradfield. Acad. 53: 691.

— — Archæological Study of. (J. H. Huddilston) Am. J. Archæol. 2d s. 3: 183.

— Œdipus Story, Fatherhood in. (C. Porter and H. A. Clarke) Poet-Lore, 11: 102.

— Two Notes on. (G. Young) J. Hel. Stud. 21: 45.

Sophocles, Evangelinus Apostolides, a Harvard Ascetic. (F. B. Sanborn) Harv. Grad. M. 10: 207.

Sorata, Mt., Climbing. (Sir M. Conway) Harper, 99: 863.

Sorbonne, New Psychical Laboratory at. Nature, 58: 12.

Sorel, Charles. Francion; Counterblast to Urfé's Astree. (B. W. Wells) Sewanee, 8: 279.

Sorrow of Don Tomas Pidal, Reconcentrado; a story. (F. Remington) Harper, 99: 393.

Sorrows of Little Tillottson; a story. (E. A. Opper) Munsey, 26: 259.

Sorry Affair, A; a story. (S. Haynes) Engl. Illust. 20: 125.

Sothern, E. H., in Hamlet. (J. R. Towse) Critic, 37: 427.

Soto, Hernando de. (C. T. Brady) McClure, 16: 375.

— and his Last Expedition. (C. T. Brady) Idler, 19: 244.

— Expedition through Florida. (T. H. Lewis) Am. Antiq. 22: 351. 23: 107, 242.

Soubirous, Bernadette. (S. E. Saville) Belgra. 98: 58.

Soubrette, The; a poem. (R. Burton) Poet-Lore, 11: 13.

Soudan, The, and Egypt. (U. A. Forbes) Lond. Q. 91: 98.

— — in 1897-98. (W. T. Mand) J. Soc. Arts, 47: 57.

— British Influence in. (R. P. Lobb) Asia. R. 26: 322.

— Christianity in. (L. M. Butcher) Contemp. 75: 854.

— England and. Quar. 188: 546. — Spec. 80: 105.

— — Our Policy on the Upper Nile. Spec. 81: 328.

— England in Egypt and. (C. C. Long) No. Am. 168: 570.

— English Expedition of 1898. Advance on Khartoum. Spec. 81: 265-328. — (C. Williams) National, 31: 351.

— French, Mahdi of. (P. C. Standing) Un. Serv. M. 21: 155.

— A Glimpse at Nubia, miscalled "The Soudan." (T. C. S. Speedy) Harper, 98: 242.

— Gordon's Autograph Map. Contemp. 74: 480.

— How conquered. (F. A. Edwards) Westm. 150: 609.

— Khartoum in Sight. (A. Griffiths) Fortn. 68: 481.

— Last of the Dervishes. (F. I. Maxse) National, 34: 683.

— Loss and Recovery of, Alford and Sword on. Westm. 151: 53.

— My Journey from the Nile to Suakim. (F. Villiers) J. Soc. Arts, 46: 233.

South, The, since the War. (I. S. A. Herford) Cornh. 81: 685.

— — Historical Studies in. (J. B. Henneman) Sewanee, 1: 320.

— Social and Economic Revolution in. (P. A. Bruce) Contemp. 78: 58.

— Social Changes in the Black Belt. (C. Meriwether) Sewanee, 5: 203.

— Solid, Dissolution of. (B. J. Ramage) Sewanee, 4: 493.

— — Will it be Solid again? (M. L. Dawson) No. Am. 164: 193.

— Some Types in Dixie-land. (D. B. Dyer) Cosmopol. 22: 235.

— Songs of, Clarke's. (S. Axson) Citizen, 3: 206.

— Tendencies of Higher Life in the. (W. P. Trent) Atlan. 79: 766.

— Women in; forgotten white woman. (P. V. Pennybacker) Outl. 64: 133.

— Yankee of. (E. Greene) Chaut. 25: 636.

— Yankee Teacher in. (E. G. Rice) Cent. 40: 151.

South Africa. See Africa, South.

South African Hospitals Commission. (F. Treves) 19th Cent. 49: 396.

South America. (G. E. Church) Nature, 64: 353.

— Collapse of. Chamb. J. 76: 147.

— Coming Revival of. (H. H. Bassett) Chamb. J. 74: 33.

— Future of. (Ignotus) National, 38: 289.

— German Colonies and Interests in. Sat. R. 91: 530.

— in 1901, The Position in. Liv. Age, 230: 846.

— Our Trade with. (R. Mitchell) Harper, 94: 796.

— Physical Geography of. (G. E. Church) Geog. J. 17: 333.

— Political Affairs. (R. B. C. Graham) Sat. R. 92: 398.

— Republics in. (J. L. McLaurin) Indep. 53: 2445.

— Steppes of. Spec. 82: 48.

— Supposed Discovery of, before 1448. (J. Batalha-Reis) Geog. J. 9: 185.

— Trade of. Outl. 68: 900.

— — with United States. (E. H. Walker) Nat'l M. (Bost.) 15: 281.

— Western; relation to American trade. (J. R. Smith) Ann. Am. Acad. Pol. Sci. 18: 446.

South American Indian Therapeutics. Chamb. J. 76: 94.

South American Revolution, A. (J. H. Sears) J. Mil. Serv. Inst. 15: 468.

South American Trade of Baltimore. (F. R. Rutter) J. H. Univ. Stud. 15: 371.

South Carolina, Applied Physiography in. (L. C. Glenn) Nat. Geog. M. 8: 152.

— Constitutional Convention and Constitution of 1895. (A. M. Eaton) Am. Law R. 31: 198. — (D. D. Wallace) Sewanee, 4: 348.

— History of, McCrady's. (D. D. Wallace) Sewanee, 7: 182. 9: 435. — (H. L. Osgood) Am. Hist. R. 5: 358.

— in the Presidential Election of 1800. Am. Hist. R. 4: 111.

South Dakota, Bad Lands of. (N. H. Darton) Nat. Geog. M. 10: 339.

South Downs as a Sketching Ground. (W. W. Fenn) Studio (Lond.) 5: 26.

South Hampton, N. H., Church Records. (G. A. Gordon) N. E. Reg. 52: 427. 53: 162, 275, 411.

South Ferriby, Lancashire, Sculptured Tympanum at. Archæol. 47: 161.

South Kensington Museum, Additions to. Art J. 51: 58.

— Architecture at. (G. A. T. Middleton) Archit. R. 8: 389.

South Kensington Museum; Ashbee Bequest. (F. Rinder) Art J. 53: 90.

— Circulation Department of. (Lord Balcarres) National, 33: 885.

— Collections of Natural History at. Science, n. s. 10: 605.

— Sir John Donnelly and. M. of Art, 23: 362.

— National Competition, 1895. Studio (Lond.) 6: 42.

— — 1896. (G. White) Studio (Lond.) 8: 224.

— Science and Art Department. Spec. 81: 173.

— — Exposure of. M. of Art, 22: 79. — (M. H. Spielmann) M. of Art, 22: 666.

— — Poor Management of. Art J. 50: 316.

— Students' Work, 1893. Studio (Lond.) 1: 208.

— Two Oriental Carpets in. (A. B. Skinner) M. of Art, 23: 269.

South Kensington Sketching Club. Artist (N. Y.) 32: 202.

South Pole, The. Quar. 194: 451.
    See Antarctic.

South Sea Arcady. (Mrs. A. S. Boyd) Blackw. 166: 668.

South Sea Island Story. (Lloyd Osborne) Cosmopol. 27: 249.

South Shields, Excavations at Durham. (J. C. Bruce) Archæol. 46: 163.

Southampton, Henry Wriothesley, Earl of. (J. Vaughan) Temp. Bar, 110: 109.

Southampton, England. (E. D. Mead) New Eng. M. n. s. 25: 395.

— to London. (W. Hale) Outing, 38: 275.

Southern Association of Colleges and Secondary Schools, Proceedings, 1898. (W. E. Boggs) School R. 7: 145.

— — 1899. School R. 8: 72.

— — 1900. School R. 9: 79.

Southern Confederacy, In the Last Days of the. (S. M. Handy) Atlan. 87: 104.

— Resources of. (W. G. Brown) Atlan. 88: 827.

— Surviving Leaders of, with portraits. (F. A. Newton) Nat'l M. (Bost.) 5: 553.

— Veterans of. (M. Laud; L. A. Mayo) Munsey, 18: 753.

— Why it failed. (S. D. Lee; J. Wheeler; E. P. Alexander; E. M. Law; Don C. Buell; O. O. Howard; J. D. Cox) Cent. 31: 626.

Southern Cross, Under the. (E. A. Richings) Belgra. 97: 320.

"Southern Cross" Expedition to the Antarctic, 1899-1900. (C. E. Borchgrevink) Geog. J. 16: 381.

Southern Mountaineer. (W. G. Frost) R. of Rs. (N. Y.) 21: 303.

Southern Poetry prior to 1860, Bradshaw on. (O. L. Triggs) School R. 9: 125.

Southern Seas, Islands of the; Hawaii, Samoa, New Zealand, Tasmania, Australia, and Java, Shoemaker on. (J. K. Goodrich) Bk. Buyer, 16: 149.

Southern Statesmen of Old Regime, Trent's. (E. D. Warfield) Citizen, 3: 138.

Southey, Robert, with portrait. Acad. 51: 152.

— A Letter of. (H. M. Poynter) Ath. '00, 2: 512.

— Letters. (L. Stephen) National, 33: 740. Same art. Ecl. M. 133: 509. Same art. Liv. Age, 222: 529.

— — Some Unpublished. (E. B. Williams) Blackw. 164: 167. Same art. Liv. Age, 218: 843.

Southey, Mrs., Letters from. (M. Howitt) Good Words, 40: 768.

Southwest, From the Far. (Mary W. Roe) Outl. 59: 924.

Sovereignty and the Consent of the Governed. (E. B. Briggs) Am. Law R. 35: 49.

— in America, France, and England. Spec. 80: 900.

— Sociological View of. (J. R. Commons) Am. J. Sociol. 5: 1-814. 6: 67.

Sowams, the Home of Massasoit; where was it? (V. Baker) N. E. Reg. 53: 317.

Sower, The; a poem. (G. M. Whicher) Educa. 21: 290.

Space and Science. (H. M. Stanley) Philos. R. 7: 615.

— and Time. (H. Seal) Westm. 152: 675.

— — Doctrine of. (G. S. Fullerton) Philos. R. 10: 375, 488, 583.

— Hyper-, Philosophy of. (Simon Newcomb) Pop. Astron. 6: 380.

— Kant's Conception of the Leibnitz Space and Time Doctrine. (M. W. Calkins) Philos. R. 6: 356.

— Kantian Doctrine of. (G. S. Fullerton) Philos. R. 10: 113.

— — Difficulties connected with. (G. S. Fullerton) Philos. R. 10: 229.

— Measuring. Blackw. 169: 629. Same art. Ecl. M. 137: 257. Same art. Liv. Age, 230: 25.

— Perception of. (E. A. Kirkpatrick) Psychol. R. 8: 565.

— — Visual. (J. M. Cattell) Science, n. s. 14: 263.

— Physiological and Geometrical. (E. Mach) Monist, 11: 321.

— Star strewn; is it infinite? (A. M. Clerke) Pop. Astron. 4: 431.

Spain after the War of 1898. (J. Douglas) Nation, 71: 424. — (F. G. Smith) Lond. Q. 91: 289.

— America, and France. (E. Ollivier) Cent. 34: 776.

— and Cuba. Spec. 79: 511.

— and France. Spec. 80: 262. 81: 728.

— and her American Colonies. (T. S. Woolsey) Cent. 34: 715.

— and Modern Civilization. (P. H. Swift) Meth. R. 58: 513.

— and Spanish Colonies, a List of Books relating to. (Miss T. L. Kelso and J. N. Wing) Bk. Buyer, 16: 414.

— and the United States. Spec. 79: 392, 585, 641. — (C. Benoist) Liv. Age, 217: 627.

— — in 1795. (G. L. Rives) Am. Hist. R. 4: 62.

— — in 1813–14. (E. B. Morris) Nation, 66: 281.

— Army of, in 1897. (L. Williams) Un. Serv. M. 15: 449. — (L. Williams) J. Mil. Serv. Inst. 21: 349.

— — Medical Statistics of, 1896. J. Mil. Ser. Inst. 25: 434.

— as a Naval Power. Liv. Age, 217: 436.

— as a Republic. (W. M. Handy) Chaut. 27: 598.

— Bank of. (W. C. Ford) Nation, 66: 317.

— Bates's Spanish Highways and Byways. (D. B. Macdonald) Nation, 72: 300.

— Bicycle Trip in. (J. Pennell) Contemp. 73: 714.

— Brief History of our Late War with [Fiction]. Cosmopol. 24: 53–441.

— Can Sagasta save? (L. Williams) Fortn. 68: 884.

— The Carlist Cause. (Marquis de Ruvigny and C. Metcalfe) Fortn. 68: 875.

— Carlist Policy in. (Marquis de Ruvigny and C. Metcalfe) Fortn. 70: 429. Same art. Ecl. M. 131: 648.

— Collapse of, and the Rise of the Anglo-Saxon. (J. H. Bridge) Overland, n. s. 32: 87.

— Colonial Methods of. (P. Bigelow) Chamb. J. 78: 454.

— Colonial Policy of. (J. Foreman) Westm. 148: 373. Same art. Ecl. M. 129: 745. — Liv. Age, 212: 283.

— Colonies of; how treated. (P. MacQueen) Nat'l M. (Bost.) 9: 204.

— Cosas d'Espana. (M. von Brandt) Liv. Age, 218: 449.

— Crisis in, 1898. Blackw. 163: 238. Same art. Liv. Age, 216: 779. Same art. Ecl. M. 130: 433.

— — 1901. (R. Ogden) Nation, 72: 150.

— A Dangerous Mission to. Cosmopol. 26: 3, 193.

— Debt of. (A. Houghton) No. Am. 173: 862.

Spain. Decadence of. (H. C. Lea) Atlan. 82: 36. — Spec. 80: 615.

— — Dry-rot in Spain. Spec. 80: 850.

— Decline and Fall of. (J. M. Scanland) Arena, 21: 142. — (P. Zendrini) Westm. 151: 172.

— Dilemma of. (R. Ogden) Nation, 65: 293.

— Downfall of, H. W. Wilson's. (H. C. Taylor) Am. Hist. R. 6: 159.

— Drawings by A. W. Rimington. Studio (Lond.) 2: 134.

— Dynastic Crisis in. Fortn. 70: 175.

— Europe's New Invalid. (J. Foreman) National, 29: 721. Same art. Ecl. M. 129: 616. Same art. Liv. Age, 214: 661.

— Finances of. (W. C. Ford) Nation, 66: 259.

— "For the Glory has departed." (K. J. Spalding) Gent. M. n. s. 60: 184.

— From France into. (R. C. Super) Nation, 73: 204.

— Girl Graduate of, in 1784. Macmil. 82: 362. Same art. Ecl. M. 135: 765.

— Government vs. the Nation. (H. B. Clarke) Forum, 27: 156.

— Historic Monuments of. (J. L. Powell) Antiq. n. s. 33: 326, 370. 34: 13, 40, 84.

— Historical Buildings of, Preservation of. Am. Arch. 60: 54.

— Impressions of. (J. R. Lowell) Cent. 35: 140.

— In Andalusia with a Bicycle. (J. Pennell) Contemp. 73: 714. Same art. Ecl. M. 131: 24.

— in the 19th Century, Latimer on. (C. H. Cooper) Dial (Ch.) 24: 144.

— in 1901, Outlook in. (L. Holland) National, 36: 899. Same art. Ecl. M. 136: 598. Same art. Liv. Age, 228: 627.

— In Southern, during the War. (Grant Lynd) Cosmopol. 26: 549.

— Indian Policy of. (H. C. Lea) Yale R. 8: 119.

— International Position at Close of 19th Century. (A. E. Houghton) Internat. Mo. 2: 397.

— its Politics and Liberalism. (T. Hughes) Am. Cath. Q. 22: 493.

— Living or Dying? (J. L. M. Curry) Forum, 28: 268.

— Modern. (H. Ellis) Argosy, 75: 180. Same art. Ecl. M. 137: 779. Same art. Liv. Age, 231: 236, 601.

— a National Derelict. (F. P. Powers) Lippinc. 62: 145.

— The Nobility of. (R. R. Lala) Indep. 51: 2738.

— Northern, Huntington's. Sat. R. 85: 687.

— Our Certificate from. (R. Ogden) Nation, 67: 162.

— The Outlook in. Spec. 79: 203.

— Pastels from. (Mrs. M. L. Woods) Cornh. 82: 289, 586.

— People of. (C. Edwardes) Macmil. 78: 205. Same art. Ecl. M. 131: 464. Same art. Liv. Age, 218: 522.

— Political Future of. (H. Taylor) No. Am. 166: 686.

— Political Ideals and Realities in. (E. Castelar) Liv. Age, 212: 475.

— Possible Salvation of. (R. Ogden) Nation, 67: 67.

— A Recent Glance at. (J. Foreman) National, 29: 238.

— Recuperation of. (R. Ogden) Nation, 68: 23.

— Resources and Industries of. (E. D. Jones) No. Am. 167: 39.

— Rise and Fall of. (R. H. Titherington) Munsey, 19: 713.

— Royalty in, Romance of. (S. Bonsal) Munsey, 18: 336.

— The Ruin of. (E. J. Dillon) Contemp. 73: 876. Same art. Ecl. M. 131: 58.

— A Secret Mission to. (P. H. Bagenal) National, 32: 552.

— The Situation in. (S. Bonsal) R. of Rs. (N. Y.) 16: 555.

Specie Payments, Resumption of, by U. S., 1879. (J. K. Upton) World's Work, **1**: 202.

— — in Russia. Q. J. Econ. **11**: 212.

Species and Sub-species, Discrimination of. (C. Merriam) Science, **5**: 753.

— Conception of, as affected by Recent Investigations on Fungi. (W. G. Farlow) Am. Natural. **32**: 675.

— Formation of. (T. Eimer) Monist, **8**: 97.

— Four Categories of. (O. F. Cook) Am. Natural. **33**: 287.

— or Sub-species. (R. Lydekker) Nature, **56**: 256.

— Sex, and the Individual. (J. T. Cunningham) Nat. Sci. **13**: 184, 233.

— Tendency of, to form Varieties. (C. Darwin and A. Wallace) Pop. Sci. Mo. **60**: 5.

Specific Gravity of Animals. (S. R. Williams) Am. Natural. **24**: 95.

Spectacles, Public, Ancient and Modern. Cosmopol. **28**: 13.

Spectra of Hydrogen, and Spectrum of Aqueous Vapor. (J. Trowbridge) Am. J. Sci. **160**: 222.

— Series in. (E. A. Partridge) J. Frankl. Inst. **149**: 193.

Spectre in the Cart, The. (T. N. Page) Scrib. M. **26**: 179.

Spectre of Lavington ; a story. (K. M. Fitz-Gerald) Temp. Bar, **115**: 42. Same art. Liv. Age, **219**: 493. Same art. Ecl. M. **132**: 29.

Spectres of the German and Austrian Courts, The. Chamb. J. **76**: 772.

Spectroscope, Adjustment of the. (C. A. Young) Pop. Astron. **5**: 318.

— and its Teachings. Illus. (N. Lockyer) Nature, **59**: 371-391.

— in Eclipse Work. (E. W. Maunder) Pop. Astron. **6**: 376.

— Michelson Echelon. (C. P. Butler) Nature, **59**: 607.

— The Objective Prism, the Flash, and the Reversing Layer. (E. W. Maunder) Knowl. **21**: 184.

— without Prisms or Gratings. (A. A. Michelson) Am. J. Sci. **155**: 215.

Spectrum ; Magnetic Perturbations of the Spectral Lines. (T. Preston) Nature, **60**: 175.

— Mechanical Illustration of Kirchhoff's Principle. (William Hallock) Science, n. s. **9**: 210.

— New. (S. P. Langley) Am. J. Sci. **161**: 403. — (S. P. Langley) Pop. Astron. **9**: 415.

Spectrum Analysis relating to Inorganic and Organic Evolution. (N. Lockyer) Nature, **60**: 103.

— Science of, Kayser on the. (A. Schuster) Nature, **63**: 317.

Spectrum Series. (N. Lockyer) Nature, **60**: 368, 392.

Spectrum Top, The. (T. L. Alger) Knowl. **20**: 8.

Speculating in Differences. Chamb. J. **77**: 363.

Speculating on a Double Event ; a story. Blackw. **170**: 252.

Speculation and Agitation. Bank. M. (N. Y.) **56**: 805.

— and Government Officials ; a question of ethics. Cosmopol. **25**: 345, 471, 591.

— an Incident in National Development. (J. Weare) Gunton's M. **20**: 142.

— Mania for Wild. (C. W. Hall) Nat'l M. (Bost.) **9**: 605.

— Temptation of Ten Per Cent. (W. L. Hawley) Munsey, **22**: 759.

— Uses of. (C. A. Conant) Forum, **31**: 698.

Speculum, Story of a. (A. W. Quimby) Pop. Astron. **5**: 26.

Speech ; Abstraction, Higher Forms of. (T. Ribot) Open Court, **13**: 433.

— — Intermediate Forms of. (T. Ribot) Open Court, **13**: 349.

Speech, Abstraction Prior to. (T. Ribot) Open Court, **13**: 14.

— Evolution of. (T. Ribot) Open Court, **13**: 267.

— Organs of, Care of. (Dr. Nitsche) J. Mil. Serv. Inst. **13**: 977.

— Origin of. (T. Ribot) Open Court, **13**: 202.

— Survivals in American Educated. (S. D. McCormick) Bookman, **11**: 446. **12**: 243.

Speeches, Best ever made. Bk. News, **20**: 53.

— Long, and Bores. (F. C. Rasch) Fortn. **68**: 961.

— Maiden. Liv. Age, **221**: 449. — (M. MacDonagh) Macmil. **84**: 206. Same art. Liv. Age, **230**: 470.

— — Some Famous. (Alfred F. Robbins) Gent. M. n. s. **59**: 8. Same art. Ecl. M. **129**: 484.

Speed, Harold, Artist, Work of. (A. L. Baldry) Studio (Internat.) **6**: 151.

"Speedy," H. M. S. (W. J. Fletcher) Pall Mall M. **25**: 264.

Spell of the Bird, The ; a strange tale. (F. Aubrey) Eng. Illust. **22**: 24.

Spellbinder, The ; a story. (A. French) McClure, **8**: 529.

Spellbinders, The. (W. D. Foulke) Forum, **30**: 658.

Spellbound ; a story. (G. Gissing) Eng. Illust. **18**: 49.

Spelling ; "Chestnut," for Example. (J. M. Parker) No. Am. **164**: 505.

— Futility of the Spelling Grind. (J. M. Rice) Forum, **23**: 163, 409.

— a Lost Art. (W. E. Mead) Educa. R. **19**: 49.

— of English. (B. Matthews) Internat. Mo. **4**: 134.

— — Simplification of. (B. Matthews) Cent. **40**: 617.

— Our Curse from Cadmus. (M. B. Wright) Temp. Bar, **114**: 93.

— Psychology of Misspellings. (T. LeM. Douse) Mind, **25**: 85.

Spelling Reform, H. T. Peck vs. (B. E. Smith) Critic, **31**: 311.

— Progress of. (H. T. Peck) Bookman, **6**: 196.

Spencer, Herbert. Liv. Age, **212**: 220. — (Grant Allen) Pop. Sci. Mo. **50**: 815. — Acad. **58**: 369, 424.

— and Darwin. (Grant Allen) Fortn. **67**: 251. Same art. Liv. Age, **212**: 834. Same art. Ecl. M. **128**: 463.

— and Kant, Some Views of. (S. T. Preston) Mind, **25**: 234.

— and Lord Salisbury on Evolution. 19th Cent. **41**: 387, 569. Same art. Liv. Age, **213**: 354-457.

— as a Novelist. Atlan. **85**: 719.

— at Seventy-nine. Pop. Sci. Mo. **55**: 542.

— Biology, Principles of. (C. L. Morgan) Nat. Sci. **13**: 377.

— Bookselling Plan of. Lit. W. (Bost.) **29**: 57.

— Buckle, and Comte. (L. Gambetta) No. Am. **171**: 55.

— a Causerie. (T. E. Brown) New R. **16**: 393.

— an Episode. (F. Coates) Chaut. **25**: 538.

— Ethics of. (T. B. Stork) Luth. Q. **30**: 1.

— German Appreciation of. (R. Didden) Westm. **148**: 604.

— in Self-defence. (W. H. Mallock) 19th Cent. **44**: 314. — (H. Spencer) 19th Cent. **44**: 339.

— H. McPherson on. (O. Smeaton) Westm. **154**: 58.

— The Man and his Work. (W. H. Hudson) Pop. Sci. Mo. **50**: 433.

— The Man and the Philosopher, with portrait. (W. Knight) Bookman, **14**: 156.

— Philosophy of. (G. McDermot) Am. Cath. Q. **26**: 643.

— — vs. the Known God. (D. S. Gregory) Presb. & Ref. R. **10**: 413.

— Philosophy of Religion. (E. S. Carr) Bib. Sac. **54**: 232.

— Principles of Sociology. **Gunton's M. 12**: 291.

Spencer, Herbert, Psychology of. (J. M. Baldwin) Am. Natural. **31**: 553.
— Reply to. (J. Ward) Fortn. **73**: 464.
Spenser, Edmund. Acad. **56**: 67.
— and the English Reformation. (T. H. Hunt) Bib. Sac. **57**: 39.
— as an English Official in Ireland. (L. Einstein) Ath. '00, **2**: 57.
— Faerie Queene. (W. S. Kennedy) Poet-Lore, **10**: 492.
— Tercentenary of. (A. E. Spender) Westm. **151**: 85.
— (H. C. Shelley) Outl. **61**: 35.
Spenser's Grave; a poem. (Adeline M. Banks) Gent. M. n. s. **62**: 443.
Spermatogenesis of Oniscus Asellus-linn. (M. L. Nichols) Am. Natural. **35**: 919.
Sperrylite, Occurrence of, in North Carolina. (W. E. Hidden) Am. J. Sci. **156**: 381.
Sphalerite Crystals, from Galena, Kans. (A. F. Rogers) Am. J. Sci. **159**: 134.
Sphenodon, Mosasaure Lizards and. (H. F. Osborn) Am. Natural. **35**: 1.
Sphinx of Ghizeh, The Great. (H. Macmillan) Sund. M. **27**: 369.
— An Old Friend with a New Face. (J. Ward) Good Words, **40**: 824.
Spider, British Trap-door. (F. Enock) Knowl. **20**: 250, 300.
Spider of Guiana. (Erckmann-Chatrian) Strand, **17**: 81.
Spider Bites and Kissing Bugs. (L. O. Howard) Pop. Sci. Mo. **56**: 31.
Spiders, African, Stridulation in Some. Nature, **57**: 356.
— and Pitcher-plants. (R. I. Pocock) Nature, **58**: 274.
— and their Ways. (M. W. Leighton) Pop. Sci. Mo. **50**: 373.
— Garden. (Grant Allen) Strand, **14**: 287.
— Insect Cave-dwellers. (C. F. Holder) Outl. **58**: 431.
— of Hungary. (R. I. Pocock) Nature, **58**: 365.
— Stridulating, Smallest of. (G. H. Carpenter) Nat. Sci. **12**: 319.
— Trap-door, in England. (T. Wood) Sund. M. **29**: 677.
— Weaving. (N. H. Moore) Chaut. **33**: 533.
Spiering, Theodore, Violinist and Conductor. (W. S. B. Mathews) Music, **20**: 105.
Spies. (A. Lang) Cornh. **76**: 526.
— a Dangerous Mission to Spain. Cosmopol. **26**: 3, 193.
Spifame, Raoul, an Unfortunate French Lawyer. (G. H. Westley) Green Bag, **11**: 77.
Spilimbergo, Irene da, a Pupil of Titian. (A. Werner) Gent. M. n. s. **62**: 492.
Spilsbury, Edmund Gybbon. Cassier, **14**: 95.
Spinal Cord, Cocaine Analgesia of the. (S. E. Jelliffe) Pop. Sci. Mo. **59**: 280.
Spines, Origin and Significance of. (C. E. Beecher) Am. J. Sci. **156**: 1–329.
Spinges, Battle of. (W. Westall) Cornh. **75**: 803.
Spinoza. Acad. **57**: 7. **61**: 500.
— and Leibnitz, Philosophy of. (R. Latta) Mind, **24**: 333.
— Coleridge on. (W. H. White) Ath. '97, **1**: 680.
Spinster, A, of the 18th Century. (G. Festing) Temp. Bar, **120**: 267.
Spinsters and Bachelors, Noted. (F. A. Doughty) Cath. World, **67**: 650.
Spion Kop, Battle of. Blackw. **169**: 441. Same art. Ecl. M. **137**: 25. Same art. Liv. Age, **229**: 477.
— Thorneycroft's Mounted Infantry on. (L. Oppenheim) 19th Cent. **49**: 39.
Spiral Stone, The. (A. Colton) Atlan. **88**: 268.

Spire of St. Ignatius; a sketch. (F. H. Randal) Canad. M. **13**: 169.
Spirit and its Struggle after a Definition. Month, **97**: 484.
— and Matter. (W. E. Krebs) Ref. Q. **45**: 311.
— Biography of. (G. M. Hammell) Meth. R. **57**: 617.
Spirit of Crow Butte, The. (J. G. Neihardt) Overland, n. s. **38**: 355.
Spirit of the Gift, The; a poem. (E. V. Cheney) Chaut. **32**: 244.
Spirit of Mahonqui, The; a story. (F. Remington) Harper, **97**: 53.
Spirit of Revolution, The; a story. (N. Duncan) McClure, **15**: 466.
Spirits of Killarney Lakes; a story. (M. Young) Nat'l M. (Bost.) **12**: 185.
Spiritual Content of Life, Eucken on the Struggle for. (F. Kennedy) Psychol. R. **6**: 92.
Spiritual Exercises. Spec. **80**: 11.
Spiritual Law through the Natural World. (S. H. Ferguson) N. Church R. **6**: 424.
Spiritual Physiology. (E. A. Whiston) N. Church R. **6**: 321.
Spiritual Power and Honesty. (G. P. Morris) Nation, **70**: 257.
Spiritual vs. Material Substance. (H. Vrooman) N. Church R. **7**: 66.
Spiritualism and Catholicism. (H. C. Corrance) Dub. R. **124**: 107.
— and Materialism. (C. Saint-Saens) Music, **19**: 254.
— and Theosophy. (T. F. Wright) N. Church R. **4**: 435.
— Claims of, upon Christianity. (T. E. Allen) Arena, **17**: 800.
— "From India to the Planet Mars." (J. H. Hyslop) No. Am. **171**: 734.
— Lily Dale, the Haunt of Spiritualists. (E. L. Earle) Cath. World, **68**: 507.
— Modern. (W. H. Hinkley) N. Church R. **6**: 526. — (W. E. Parson) Luth. Q. **28**: 1.
— of To-day. (C. L. V. Richmond) Arena, **21**: 359.
— On Some Fresh Facts indicating Man's Survival of Death. (F. W. H. Myers) National, **32**: 230.
— On the Threshold; a Psychic Experience. (G. T. Clark) Arena, **17**: 512.
— Mrs. Piper's Trances. Spec. **80**: 403.
— Recent Mediumistic Phenomena. (J. H. Hyslop) Forum, **25**: 736.
Spiritualist Camp in New England. (A. Blackwood) Macmil. **82**: 29.
Spiritualists, An Evening with the. (W. H. Gardner) Open Court, **15**: 721.
Spitalfields Brocades. (L. Liberty) Studio (Lond.) **1**: 20.
Spitta, Phillipp, Musical Professor, with portrait. Music, **15**: 450.
Spittle, Norman and Ernest, Metal Workers. Artist (N. Y.) **25**: 182.
Spitzbergen as a Summer Resort. (W. M. Conway) Liv. Age, **213**: 768.
— Exploration of Interior of, 1896. (W. M. Conway) Pall Mall M. **14**: 97.
— First Crossing of. (W. M. Conway) Geog. J. **9**: 353.
— — Conway's. Acad. **51**: 563. — Sat. R. **83**: 547.
— Glaciers of. Nature, **57**: 472. — (W. M. Conway) Geog. J. **12**: 137.
Spitzbergen Manuscripts, Some Unpublished. (W. M. Conway) Geog. J. **15**: 628.
Spofford, A. R. Book for all Readers. (W. D. Johnston) Critic, **38**: 459.
Spoilt Triumph, A; a story. (M. Quiller-Couch) Argosy, **73**: 323. Same art. Liv. Age, **229**: 488.

Stars, Variable, Some Suspected. (J. E. Gore) Knowl. 22: 176, 200, 233.

—— Study of. (P. S. Yendell) Pop. Astron. 4: 536. 5: 16, 84, 172, 302.

Starting the Burntwood Breeze; a story. (H. Carruth) Nat'l M. (Bost.) 7: 40-328.

State, The, and its Subjects. (G. W. Mansfield) Westm. 150: 404.

— Bosanquet on Philosophical Theory of. Church Q. 49: 42. — (S. W. Dyde) Philos. R. 9: 198.

— Development in Idea of. (A. Smith) Westm. 149: 204.

— Ethics of. (D. B. Purinton) Am. J. Theol. 1: 965.

— Fictions in regard to. (F. Smith) Conserv. R. 5: 84.

— Hegel's Theory of. (B. Bosanquet) Mind, 23: 1.

— its Right to be. (W. W. Willoughby) Int. J. Ethics, 9: 467.

— Recognition of a New : is it a Legislative Function ? (W. L. Penfield) Am. Law R. 32: 390.

— Suits against a. (J. Wheless) Am. Law R. 34: 689.

— vs. the Man. (W. J. Baylis) Westm. 155: 40.

State against Ellsworth, The ; a story. (W. R. Lighton) McClure, 13: 291.

State Boards of Control, with Special Reference to Wisconsin. (S. E. Sparling) Ann. Am. Acad. Pol. Sci. 17: 74.

State Control of Trade, Stickney's. (A. G. Sedgwick) Nation, 65: 520.

State Deficits, A Year of. (W. C. Ford) Am. Statis. Assoc. 6: 219.

State Employees and Factory Acts. (S. W. Belderson) Westm. 154: 177.

State Guards, Nationalization of the. (T. M. Anderson) Forum, 30: 653.

State History, Functions of a. Sewanee, 9: 204.

State Interference, Moral Limitations of. (E. F. B. Fell) Econ. R. 7: 57, 195.

State-papers, Annual Lists of. (F. B. F. Campbell) Library 4: 175.

State Reports, Digests, and Statutes. (G. E. Wire) Lib. J. 25: supp. 57.

State Sovereignty. The Hundred Years' Campaign. (F. N. Thorpe) Harper, 94: 956.

State Taxes, Equalizing the. (D. MacG. Means) Nation, 70: 160.

State Troops, The War Department and the. (O. G. Villard) Nation, 73: 353.

State University, Influence of, on the Public Schools. (R. H. Jesse) School R. 8: 466.

Statecraft. (H. S. Bird) Indep. 52: 2798.

States, Administration in, Recent Tendencies in. (L. A. Blue) Ann. Am. Acad. Pol. Sci. 18: 434.

— New, Admission of. (G. H. Alden) Ann. Am. Acad. Pol. Sci. 18: 469.

Statesmanship and Literature. Spec. 81: 827.

— in England and the U. S. (G. F. Hoar) Forum, 23: 709.

— Un-American. (G. Gunton) Gunton's M. 20: 243.

Statesmen, Favorite Books of. (F. G. Carpenter) Lippinc. 61: 715.

— Literary. Spec. 78: 197. — (Earl of Rosebery) Liv. Age, 220: 75. Same art. Ecl M. 132: 275.

— Morality of. Spec. 80: 435.

— Wanted —. Fortn. 73: 407.

Station, The, in Nancy Maguire's ; a story. (S. MacManus) Harper, 100: 209.

Statistical Blunders. (H. Gannett) Forum, 31: 683.

Statistical Ideas, General, Importance of. (Sir R. Giffen) Pop. Sci. Mo. 60: 106.

Statistical Institute, International, Meeting at St. Petersburg, 1897, Matters discussed at. (P. G. Craigie) J. Statis. Soc. 60: 735.

Statistical Method, Some Oddities of. (H. L. Bliss) J. Pol. Econ. 6: 100.

Statistics, Demographic, of the United Kingdom. (E. Cannan) J. Statis. Soc. 61: 49.

— Developments of Research and Methods. (J. M. Biddulph) J. Statis. Soc. 59: 579.

— Eccentric Official. (H. L. Bliss) Am. J. Sociol. 2: 515. 3: 79. 4: 79. 6: 105.

— Elements of, Bowley's. (C. P. Sanger) Econ. J. 11: 193. — (W. C. Ford) J. Pol. Econ. 9: 443. — (E. Cannan) Econ. R. 11: 371.

— Graphical Presentation of. (L. M. Haupt) J. Frankl. Inst. 148: 384.

— Importance of. (R. Giffen) J. Statis. Soc. 64: 444.

— Importance of Correctness in. (P. C. Craigie) J. Statis. Soc. 63: 459.

— Obstacles to Accurate. (J. H. Blodgett) Am. Statis. Assoc. 6: 1.

— of Continuous Variation, Use of Auxiliary Curves in. (W. F. Sheppard) J. Statis. Soc. 63: 433.

— of Population, Error in the Use of. (H. L. Bliss) J. Pol. Econ. 8: 94.

— Official. (W. M. Stuart) Am. J. Sociol. 3: 622.

— The Plague of. (E. R. White) Atlan. 88: 842.

— Representation by Mathematical Formulæ. (F. Y. Edgeworth) J. Statis. Soc. 62: 125, 373, 524. 63: 72.

Statocracy. Is it Possible ? Spec. 83: 485.

Statt, Wm., of Oldham. M. of Art, 26: 81.

Statuary and Architecture, On Coloring. (J. La Farge) Scrib. M. 27: 765.

— in the Ny Carlsberg Glyptotheca. (O. Tryde) Art J. 49: 156.

Statues and Pedestals. (S. Beale) Am. Arch. 70: 38.

Status, Science of. (H. Seal) Westm. 155: 171.

Staves, Episcopal. (F. G. Lee) Archæol. 51: 351.

Stead, W. T., a Journalist with 20th Century Ideals. (B. O. Flower) Arena, 25: 613.

— and Spiritual Exercises. Spec. 80: 11.

Stealing of the Buddha Pearl ; a story. (W. A. Fraser) Canad. M. 12: 530.

Steam and Labor in Isolated Plants. (P. R. Moses) Engin. M. 16: 99.

— District Distribution of Energy. (C. E. Emery) Engin. M. 14: 94.

— Exhaust, Economical Utilization of. (B. Donkin) Engin. M. 14: 930.

— Fuel Combustion and Generation of. (W. W. Christie) Engin. M. 20: 1013.

— Generation of, Actual Efficiency in. (A. Bement) Engin. M. 21: 370.

— High-pressure, Potency of. (R. H. Thurston) Science, 5: 573.

— in Non-condensing Engines. (J. B. Stanwood) Engin. M. 15: 213, 603.

— Regnault's Caloric and our Knowledge of the Specific Volumes of Steam. (G. P. Starkweather) Am. Jl Sci. 157: 13.

— Superheated, Economy of. (R. S. Hale) Engin. M. 17: 903.

— — Production and Utilization of. (R. S. Hale) Engin. M. 18: 722.

— Thermodynamic Relations for. (G. P. Starkweather) Am. J. Sci. 157: 129.

Steam Boilers at the Paris Exhibition. (W. D. Wansbrough) Cassier, 20: 43.

— Capacity Test of the Boiler Plant. (G. K. Hooper) Engin. M. 21: 684.

— Chemistry of Deposits in. (W. E. Ridenour) J. Frankl. Inst. 152: 113.

Steam Boilers and Furnaces, Efficiencies of. (R. S. Hale) Engin. M. 17: 622.

Stevenson, Robert Louis, and Sidney Colvin. (I. Strong) Critic, **35**: 886.
— as a Humorist. Acad. **53**: 667.
— as a Letter Writer and a Reviewer. Acad. **56**: 193, 219.
— at Anstruther. Acad. **57**: 314.
— at Play. (Lloyd Osbourne) Scrib. M. **24**: 709.
— Balfour's Life of. Ath. '01, 2: 549. — Blackw. **170**: 613. — (W. P. Trent) Bk. Buyer, **23**: 389. — (J. R. Smith) Dial (Ch.) **31**: 356.
— Canonization of. (M. Schuyler) Cent. **36**: 478.
— Characteristics. (J. A. Macculloch) Westm. **149**: 631. Same art. Ecl. M. **131**: 182. Same art. Liv. age, **218**: 532.
— The Country of "Kidnapped." (J. Buchan and others) Acad. **53**: 502–612.
— Davos-Platz Booklets of. (W. Roberts) Ath. '99, 1: 498.
— Deacon Brodie. (F. Brock) Gent. M. n. s. **65**: 349.
— Dr. Jekyll and Mr. Hyde, The Manuscript of. (E. Limedorfer) Bookman, **12**: 52.
— Essayist, Novelist, and Poet. (H. P. Baildon) Ecl. M. **133**: 123. Same art. Liv. Age, **221**: 671.
— Fables. Acad. **53**: 328.
— Face to the Front. Outl. **67**: 617.
— First Books of. (L. S. Livingston) Bookman, **10**: 437.
— from a New Point of View. Atlan. **85**: 429.
— W. E. Henley's Opinion of. Acad. **61**: 487–596.
— Hills of Home. (Eve B. Simpson) Chamb. J. **78**: 155. Same art. Liv. Age, **229**: 255. Same art. Ecl. M. **136**: 749.
— His Rank as a Writer. (V. Brown) Acad. **58**: 295, (A. Nutt) 337.
— His Relations with Children. (E. Gosse) Chamb. J. **76**: 449.
— In Memoriam ; a poem. (A. Dobson) Ecl. M. **137**: 89.
— in Samoa. (I. O. Strong) Cent. **36**: 476.
— in San Francisco. (W. M. Clemens) Nat'l M. (Bost.) **12**: 296. — (H. W. Bell) Pall Mall M. **24**: 267.
— — Alleged Newspaper Work of. Acad. **61**: 3.
— Inland Voyage, "Cigarette" and "Arethusa" of, with new portrait. Bookman, **7**: 472.
— Kipling, and Anglo-Saxon Imperialism. (E. H. Mullin) Bk. Buyer, **18**: 85.
— Letters ; ed. by S. Colvin. Scrib. M. **25**: 29 — 26: 570. — Bk. Buyer, **19**: 359. — (I. Strong) Critic, **35**: 1133. — (A. Birrell) Contemp. **77**: 50. Same art. Ecl. M. **134**: 429. Same art. Liv. Age, **224**: 337. — (J. C. Bailey) Fortn. **73**: 91. — (H. James) No. Am. **170**: 61. — Macmil. **81**: 182. — (J. B. Kenyon) Meth. R. **60**: 533.
— — New ; comment. (H. Townsend) Harper, **104**: 123.
— — to his Family and Friends. (R. Le Gallienne) Idler, **16**: 656.
— Memorial Committee in Canada. Canad. M. **10**: 277.
— Memorial Fountain at San Francisco. Lit. W. (Bost.) **28**: 458. — Critic, **31**: 205. — Overland, n. s. **30**: 529.
— Mother of. Chamb. J. **74**: 449.
— Notes on the Art of. (G. W. T. Omond) No. Am. **171**: 348.
— "One who Loved his Fellow-men." (J. MacArthur) Bookman, **10**: 466.
— Personality of. Quar. **191**: 176.
— A poem. (G. E. Montgomery) Pall Mall M. **14**: 202.
— Portrait of, from a Photograph by Notman. Bk. Buyer, **16**: 207.
— Posthumous Works of. (S. Gwynn) Fortn. **69**: 561. Same art. Liv. Age, **217**: 807.
— The Real. Atlan. **85**: 702. — (C. Kernahan) Lond. Q. **93**: 25.

Stevenson, Robert Louis, St. Ives, and Quiller-Couch. Acad. **51**: 547.
— Second Visit to America. (W. H. Duncan, jr.) Bookman, **10**: 455.
— Treasure Island. Acad. **58**: 189, 209, 237.
— A Unique Stevenson Collection. (F. J. Gregg) Bk. Buyer, **18**: 200.
— Works of. Ath. '97, 2: 213, 245. Same art. Liv. Age, **214**: 811–870.
Stevenson, Mrs. Robert Louis. Critic, **36**: 194.
— An Interview with. (G. Burgess) Bookman, 8: 23.
Stevenson, Sara Y., with portrait. Bk. News, **18**: 188.
Stewart, Donald Martin. Geog. J. **15**: 653. — Blackw. **167**: 709.
Steyn, Marthinas Theunis, President of the Orange Free State. (P. Bigelow) Harper, **94**: 452.
Stichospira Paradoxa. (V. Sterki) Am. Natural. **31**: 535.
Stichostemma, Habits and Natural History of. (C. M. Child) Am. Natural. **35**: 975.
Stickit Minister, A. (Donald Macleod) Good Words, **41**: 178.
Stickit Minister's Love Story, The. (S. R. Crockett) Outl. **65**: 38.
Stikine River in 1898. (Eliza R. Scidmore) Nat. Geog. M. **10**: 1.
Stileman, Elias. (E. S. Stearns) N. E. Reg. **51**: 346.
Stiles, George Kean. Writer, **14**: 90.
Stiles, Wm. A. (C. S. Sargent) Garden & F. **10**: 399.
Stillé, Dr. Charles J. Pennsyl. M. **23**: 390.
— Proceedings of Pennsyl. Hist. Soc. on the Death of. Pennsyl. M. **14**: i.
Stillman, William J., Autobiography of. Atlan. **85**: 1–811. — Bk. Buyer, **22**: 399. — (J. B. Gilder) Critic, **39**: 57. — (E. G. Johnson) Dial (Ch.) **30**: 225. — Sat. R. **91**: 775.
— An Earlier American. (W. D. Howells) No. Am. **172**: 934.
Stilts, Races on. (W. G. Fitzgerald) Strand, **15**: 15.
Stimson, Frederic J., with portrait. Bk. News, **15**: 607.
Stimson, John Ward, an Artist with 20th Century Ideals. (B. O. Flower) Arena, **26**: 67.
Stimulus, Relation to Sensation. (C. L. Morgan) Nature, **62**: 278.
Sting of Conscience, A ; a story. (H. L. Arden) Sund. M. **28**: 438.
Sting of the Wasp, The ; a yarn for the marines. (Park Benjamin) Eng. Illust. **22**: 97.
Stipules, Nature and Origin of, Tyler's. (L. F. Ward) Science, 6: 100.
Stock, Joseph. Diary of the Bishop of Killalla. (St. G. Stock) Fortn. **70**: 984.
Stock Broker, Day's Work of. (A. Goodrich) World's Work, 1: 1000.
Stock Companies ; Blackmail and Promoting. Contemp. **74**: 198.
Stock Exchange, Mechanism of the. Cornh. **76**: 490.
— N. Y., and its Members. Chamb. J. **76**: 193.
Stock Exchange Act, New German. (W. Lexis) Econ. J. 7: 368.
Stock Exchange Boom, Prospects of. (W. F. Ford) Econ. R. **11**: 218.
Stock Exchange Values. Bank. M. (Lond.) **63**: 71. **71**: 94.
Stock Gambling, Mr. Bryan on. Nation, **72**: 408.
Stock Speculation ; A Question of Ethics. Cosmopol. **25**: 226.
Stock-yards, Chicago. (E. S. Hoch) Nat'l M. (Bost.) 5: 350.
— — Social Aspects of. (C. J. Bushnell) Am. J. Sociol. 7: 145.

Stockbridge, Massachusetts, Evolution of. (Mrs. H. M. Plunkett) New Eng. M. n. s. **25**: 205.

Stockbridge Indians, during the American Revolution. (I. J. Greenwood) N. E. Reg. **54**: 162.

Stockholm, Women of. (E. F. Wheeler) Chaut. **26**: 653.

Stockings Full of Money. (M. K. Dallas) Lippinc. **59**: 3.

Stocking Lore. Chamb. J. **77**: 31.

Stockport Conference, The. Month, **94**: 337.

Stockton, Frank R., at Home. (J. H. Morse) Critic, **32**: 259.

— Novels and Stories of. (W. D. Howells) Bk. Buyer, **20**: 19.

— Where he wrote his Stories. (T. F. Wolfe) Lippinc. **64**: 367.

Stockton, John Potter, with portrait. Green Bag, **10**: 229.

Stoddard, Richard Henry, at Seventy-five. (J. B. Gilder) Critic, **37**: 215.

— Authors' Club Dinner to. Critic, **30**: 225. — (J. D. Barry) Lit. W. (Bost.) **28**: 104.

Stoddert, Mrs. Benjamin, Letters of. (K. M. Rowland) Lippinc. **62**: 804.

Stoic Attitude in Life. Spec. **83**: 46.

Stoke Pogis. (H. C. Shelley) New Eng. M. n. s. **18**: 665.

— and Gray's Elegy. (H. C. Shelley) Canad. M. **12**: 305.

Stokers, Mechanical. (W. R. Roney) Cassier, **13**: 311.

Stokes, Mr. and Mrs. Adrian Scott. Paintings. (Wilfrid Meynell) Art J. **52**: 193.

Stokes, Sir George Gabriel, Jubilee of. Nature, **60**: 109, 125. — (R. T. Glazebrook) Good Words, **42**: 312.

Stokes, Margaret. (J. P. Mahaffy) Ath. '00, **2**: 417.

Stokes, Marianne [Mrs. Adrian], Artist. (H. Ford) Studio (Internat.) **10**: 149. — (A. Meynell) M. of Art, **25**: 241.

Stoking, Mechanical, Advantages of. (A. E. Outerbridge) Engin. M. **12**: 807.

Stolen Story, The. (J. L. Williams) Scrib. M. **22**: 232.

Stolen Transport, The, a Story of the Boer War. (G. Hudworth) Idler, **17**: 205.

Stone, Benjamin F. Autobiography. New Eng. M. n. s. **16**: 210.

Stone, Edw. J. Nature, **56**: 57. — Ath. '97, **1**: 653.

Stone, Frederick D., Works of. Pennsyl. M. **21**: xxviii.

Stone, Marcus, with portraits. Strand, **18**: 123.

Stone, Dea. Simon, and his Descendants. (D. H. Brown) N. E. Reg. **53**: 345.

Stone in American Architecture. (R. Sturgis) Archit. R. **9**: 174.

— Return to. (W. S. Adams) Archit. R. **9**: 203.

Stone of Vortipore, The. (M. E. James) Month, **89**: 409.

Stone Age, Architecture in. (S. D. Peet) Am. Antiq. **22**: 367.

— Early, in Northern Europe. Church Q. **46**: 141.

— in Egypt. (J. De Morgan) Pop. Sci. Mo. **54**: 202.

— Monuments of, Age and Distribution of. (S. D. Peet) Am. Antiq. **23**: 291.

— Relics of. (J. Wickersham) Am. Antiq. **22**: 141.

Stone Axe found at Dove Dale. Reliquary, **39**: 126.

Stone Circles, British. (A. L. Lewis) Am. Antiq. **21**: 69, 204.

— in Europe and America. (S. D. Peet) Am. Antiq. **23**: 371.

— of Scotland. (A. L. Lewis) Am. Antiq. **23**: 199.

Stone Fleet of 1861. (F. P. McKibben) New Eng. M. n. s. **18**: 484.

Stone Graves of Tennessee. (A. H. Thompson) Am. Antiq. **23**: 411.

Stone Implements, Caves, and Shell-mounds of South Africa. (G. Leith) Anthrop. J. **28**: 258.

— found in a Cave in Griqualand-East, Cape Colony. (M. E. Frames) Anthrop. J. **28**: 251.

— from Asia Minor. Reliquary, **41**: 120.

— from Swaziland, South Africa. (T. R. Jones) Anthrop. J. **28**: 48.

— on the Gold Coast. (L. W. Bristowe and H. P. F. Marriott) Knowl. **23**: 241.

Stoneham, Mass., Church Records at. N. E. Reg. **54**: 392. **55**: 142.

Stonehenge and other Stone Circles. Nature, **63**: 575.

— Orientation and Date of. (N. Lockyer) Nature, **65**: 55.

— Preservation of. Am. Arch. **71**: 87.

— A Reasonable Price for. Spec. **83**: 279.

— Stone Circle at. (A. L. Lewis) Am. Antiq. **21**: 69.

Stones, American Ornamental. (G. P. Merrill) Am. Arch. **62**: 88.

— Building. (A. A. Julien) J. Frankl. Inst. **147**: 257, 378, 430.

— Large, Sinking, through the Action of Worms. (C. Davison) Knowl. **24**: 241.

— Sermons in. (C. H. Crandall) New Eng. M. n. s. **24**: 606.

Stones in the Head. (A. Cartaz) Pop. Sci. Mo. **51**: 514.

Stoning to Death of Teodoro Attardo. (Princess Palæologæ-Nicephoræ-Comnenæ) Belgra. **92**: 152.

Stonington, Connecticut. (H. R. Palmer) New Eng. M. n. s. **20**: 225.

Stony Pathway to the Woods. (O. T. Miller) Atlan. **80**: 121.

Stop-gap, The; a story. Argosy, **64**: 678.

Stoppani, Antonio. (W. D. McCrackan) Am. J. Soc. Sci. **35**: 112.

Storage Batteries and Electric Railways. (H. Lloyd) Cassier, **16**: 507.

— vs. Isolated Electric Plants. (A. D. Adams) Cassier, **16**: 659.

Storage Battery of Twenty Thousand Cells, Some Results obtained with a. (J. Trowbridge) Nature, **62**: 325.

Store Front, Problem of the. (J. R. Coolidge) Archit. R. **8**: 77.

Stores, Seats for Clerks in, Movement for. (M. H. Irwin) Fortn. **72**: 123.

Storey's Gate, Westminster. (H. Hutchinson) Cornh. **77**: 635.

Stories, Continued. (Emile Bergerat) Liv. Age, **222**: 261.

— from Afield. Overland, n. s. **38**: 307.

— Getting Plots for. (E. P. Stanton) Writer, **13**: 83.

— of British Battles. (J. D. Symon) Eng. Illust. **17**: 211.

— of Prison Life. (L. Meadows) Argosy, **63**: 104–758.

— of the Sanctuary Club. (L. T. Meade and R. Eustace) Strand, **18**: 3–665.

— of the Stone Age. (H. G. Wells) Idler, **11**: 418, 587, 736. **12**: 4, 430.

— To Let. Spec. **78**: 237.

Storm at Sea. (H. P. Whitmarsh) Cent. **34**: 929.

— The Great November, of 1898. (S. Baxter) Scrib. M. **26**: 515.

— Great, of 1703. (H. Harries) Cornh. **76**: 579.

Storm in the Calm; a story. (C. Battersby) Sund. M. **27**: 836.

Storm in Harvest, A; a poem. (I. F. Mayo) Argosy, **63**: 597.

Storm Song of the Norsemen. (M. I. McNeal) Cent. **39**: 342.

Storms. Coming of the Sou'wester. (J. M. Bacon) Argosy, **73**: 227.

— Gulf of Mexico, and U. S. Weather Bureau. (W. L. Moore) Nat'l M. (Bost.) **13**: 542.

Storrs, Richard S. (W. H. Ward) Indep. 52: 1417.— Outl. 65: 383.

Story, Emma Eames. (A. Leach) Munsey, 16: 522.

Story, Joseph, with portrait. Green Bag, 9: 49.

Story, Julian. (A. Leach) Munsey, 16: 522.

Story, The Short. (F. Wedmore) 19th Cent. 43: 406. Same art. Liv. Age, 217: 392. Same art. Ecl. M. 130: 546.

—— Rise of the. (Bret Harte) Cornh. 80: 1.

— Story of a. (E. E. Hale) Writer, 10: 80.

Story, The ; a story. (G. A. Hibbard) Harper, 97: 301.

Story about Gunnel. (P. Molin) Poet-Lore, 12: 1.

Story of Ann Powel. (A. E. Tynan) Cent. 38: 335.

Story of Annabel Lea. (F. W. Wharton) Cosmopol. 29: 170, 277, 384, 529.

Story of an Arizona Blizzard. (Will C. Barnes) Overland, n. s. 31: 301.

Story of the Beetle-hunter. (A. C. Doyle) Strand, 15: 603.

Story of the Big Timber. (Irving Bacheller) Cosmopol. 31: 396.

Story of the Black Doctor. (A. C. Doyle) Strand, 16: 372.

Story of Bleecker Street. (J. A. Riis) Cent. 39: 920.

Story of the Brazilian Cat. (A. C. Doyle) Strand, 16: 603.

Story of a Chapter, The. (Mary T. Van Denburgh) Overland, n. s. 36: 329.

Story of the Club-footed Grocer. (A. C. Doyle) Strand, 16: 483.

Story of Doña Concepcion. (J. Brooke) Outing, 30: 74.

Story of the Dry Leaves. (F. Remington) Harper, 99: 95.

Story of an East Side Family. (L. W. Betts) Outl. 69: 978, 1033, 1079.

Story of Elizabeth. (A. Dennis) Sund. M. 29: 759.

Story of a Failure. (F. K. Earl) Midland, 10: 248.

Story of the Fire Patrol, A. (R. S. Baker) McClure, 12: 19.

Story of a Heart. (Amélie Rives) Cosmopol. 23: 331.

Story of a Helpful Queen. (C. Sylva) No. Am. 169: 707.

Story of his First Battle ; a story. (C. B. Lewis) Cosmopol. 25: 216.

Story of Idwal Lake. (Edith G. Wheelwright) Gent. M. n. s. 62: 584.

Story of Im. (H. Farrant) Canad. M. 17: 551.

Story of Jerene, The. (E. B. Stapp) Nat'l M. (Bost.) 9: 125.

Story of John Corwell. (Louis Becke) Chamb. J. 78: 561-618.

Story of a King Fish. (M. Pollough-Pogue) Outing, 39: 183.

Story of a Little Siwash. (S. O'B. Porter) Midland, 10: 437.

Story of the Lost Special. (A. C. Doyle) Strand, 16: 153.

Story of the Man with the Matches. (A. C. Doyle) Strand, 16: 33.

Story of Margery Dill. (Lucia W. Wilson) Midland, 9: 341.

Story of a Mountain Feud. (J. R. Spears) Munsey, 24: 494.

Story of Naskatu, Priest of Ptah and Prince of Egypt. (John Le Breton) Pall Mall M. 11: 44.

Story of New Year's Eve. (Minnie R. Smith) Midland, 9: 80.

Story of an Orchid, The. (F. Boyle) Chamb. J. 76: 686-698.

Story of a Play, The. (W. D. Howells) Scrib. M. 21: 290 — 22: 99.

Story of a Portrait. (K. S. Macquoid) Eng. Illust. 19: 563.

Story of San Juan Capistrano, A. (H. R. P. Forbes) Overland, n. s. 37: 681.

Story of the Sea, A. (P. W. Hart) Chaut. 26: 530.

Story of the Sealed Room. (A. C. Doyle) Strand, 16: 243.

Story of the Second Lieutenant. (G. S. Ellis) Macmil. 80: 459.

Story of a Second Mate. (J. R. Spears) Scrib. M. 21: 85.

Story of Seti, the King. (D. Beddoe) Idler, 16: 346.

Story of a Sky-scraper. (P. W. Hart) Lippinc. 65: 149.

Story of a Sonnet. (W. Baptiste Scoones) Pall Mall M. 12: 569.

Story of a Story. (E. Pugh) Pall Mall M. 19: 387.

Story of a Strange Will. (S. M. C. Boevey) Sund. M. 27: 523.

Story of a Tin Soldier. (R. R. Gilson) Scrib. M. 27: 682.

Story of Tu-Phu. (George d'Espartés) Liv. Age, 226: 577.

Story of an Untold Love. (P. L. Ford) Atlan. 79: 1-803.

Story of a Waggoner. (N. W. Williams) Idler, 12: 32.

Story of a Witch and Some Bewitched. (O'Neill Latham) Cosmopol. 25: 690.

Story Torrance did not Tell. (H. Campbell) New Eng. M. n. s. 21: 153.

Story with a Happy Ending. (G. H. Page) New Eng. M. n. s. 20: 404.

Story-reading and Story-writing. (Mrs. Molesworth) Chamb. J. 75: 772.

Story-telling, Bad. (F. M. Bird) Lippinc. 60: 533.

Story-writing ; Rudimentary suggestions for beginners. (E. F. Andrews) Cosmopol. 22: 446.

Stott, Edward, Painter. (L. Housman) M. of Art, 24: 529.

— and his Work. (A. C. R. Carter) Art J. 51: 294.

— Work of. (J. S. Little) Studio (Lond.) 6: 71.

Stott, William, of Oldham. (R. A. M. Stevenson) Studio (Lond.) 4: 3.

Stout Miss Hopkins's Bicycle ; a story. (O. Thanet) Harper, 94: 409.

Stow, John. Acad. 55: 521.

Stow, Mass., First Settlers in, and their Fate. (A. G. R. Hale) N. E. Reg. 51: 294.

Stowe, Harriet Beecher. (G. S. Lee) Critic, 30: 281. —(W. A. Guerry) Sewanee, 6: 335.—Acad. 53: 169.

— Life and Letters of. Lond. Q. 90: 326.

— Reminiscences of. (Mrs. Annie Fields) Chamb. J. 216: 145.

— Uncle Tom's Cabin, Forty Years after. (F. A. Shoup) Sewanee, 2: 88.

Stowe Palace, near Buckingham, England. (J. O. Hartes) Pall Mall M. 24: 342.

Stradanus ; Landseer of the XVIth Century. (W. A. Baillie-Grohman) Eng. Illust. 16: 617.

Strafford, Thomas Wentworth, 1st Earl of. (A. D'Alcho) New Eng. M. n. s. 19: 271.

Strang, James. The King of Beaver Island. (H. E. Legler) Chaut. 31: 133.

Strang, Wm., Art Work of. Sat. R. 87: 396.

Strange Adventure of Father Baldwin. (B. Camm) Month, 92: 164.

Strange Adventure of John Archer ; a story. (Geraldine Bonner) Pall Mall M. 11: 510.

Strange Business, A ; a story. (M. A. Dickens) Pall Mall M. 19: 269.

Strange Ending of a Charade ; a story. (M. Crommelin) Argosy, 63: 41.

Strange Experience, A. (M. Forester) Argosy, 67: 228.

Strange Experiences in a Flat. (M. Forester) Argosy, 66: 680.

Strange Experiences of Alkali Dick; a story. (B. Harte) Strand, **14**: 25.

Strange Experiment and What came of it. Macmil. **79**: 182, 296, 367.

Strange Story of the "Emily Brand" Brigantine. (A. H. Allen) McClure, **8**: 483.

Strange Tale of Gheel, A; a story. (H. Butterworth) Harper, **95**: 780.

Strange Visit, A; a tale. (M. Anderson) Argosy, **67**: 116.

Stranger at the Dolphin, A. Macmil. **75**: 321. Same art. Liv. Age, **213**: 588.

Stranger, The, within their Gates. (Eleanor Stuart) Scrib. M. **30**: 750.

Stranger's Left-handed Race-horse; a story. (Hayden Carruth) Cosmopol. **31**: 55.

Strassburg, Convent of St. Margaret and St. Agnes at. (J. M. Stone) Dub. R. **124**: 36.

— Royal Univ. Observatory. (H. C. Wilson) Pop. Astron. **5**: 171.

Strategic Devastation. (T. M. Maguire) Un. Serv. M. **22**: 365.

Strategical Study, A. (H. H. Sargent) J. Mil. Serv. Inst. **21**: 27.

Strategist, The Stay-at-home. (H. Wyndham) Un. Serv. M. **24**: 199.

Strategos. (C. A. L. Totten) J. Mil. Serv. Inst. **1**: 185.

Strategy, Prince Kraft zu Hohenlohe-Ingelfingen on. (W. Fish) Dial (Ch.) **25**: 70.

— Tactics, and Policy. (J. C. Bush) J. Mil. Serv. Inst. **12**: 42.

Stratford-on-Avon. (W. J. Rolfe) Poet-Lore, **11**: 446.

— to London. (A. L. Moque) Outing, **29**: 460.

Stratford's Love Story. (S. C. Grier) Argosy, **65**: 599, 727.

Strathcona's Horse. (J. A. Cooper) Canad. M. **14**: 529.

— Embarkation of. (E. P. Weaver) Canad. M. **14**: 538.

Strathspey. (B. Taylor) Chamb. J. **74**: 454.

Strathtay, Scotland. (H. Macmillan) Art J. **52**: 50, 139.

Stratton, Parish of, Churchwarden's Accounts of. (E. Peacock) Archæol. **46**: 195.

Strauss, David F. (Countess von Krockow) Atlan. **80**: 139. — (G. Krüger) Am. J. Theol. **4**: 514.

— Eck on. (G. Milligan) Crit. R. **11**: 134.

Strauss, Johann. Music, **17**: 88.

— How he composed. Music, **16**: 312.

Straw Hat Industry, Tuscan. J. Soc. Arts, **45**: 735.

Straw Industry, The. Chamb. J. **75**: 792.

Strawberry, Evolution of a. (L. H. Bailey) Indep. **51**: 256.

Stream-music. (C. H. Crandall) Outing, **37**: 294.

Street, George Slythe. Acad. **52**: 495.

Street Architecture; Art Gallery of the New York streets. (R. Sturgis) Archit. R. **10**: 93.

Street-car Equipments, Electrical Inspection of. (A. H. Herrick) J. Frankl. Inst. **147**: 360.

Street-cleaning and Good Paving. (G. E. Waring) Engin. M. **12**: 781.

— by Contract — a Sidelight from Chicago. (G. E. Hooker) R. of Rs. (N. Y.) **15**: 437.

— in European Cities. (G. E. Waring, jr.) Munic. Aff. **2**: supp.

— in New York. (G. E. Waring, jr.) McClure, **9**: 911.
— (G. E. Waring, jr.) Munic. Aff. **2**: supp.

— — Work of Colonel Waring. (J. B. Walker) Cosmopol. **26**: 234.

— Paris and Berlin. (R. Grimshaw) Engin. M. **13**: 99.

Street Cries in Boston. (A. Bates) New Eng. M. n. s. **21**: 407.

Street Fighting and Defence of Villages. (C. B. Brackenbury) J. Mil. Serv. Inst. **11**: 794.

Street Music in London. (H. H. Statham) National, **31**: 734.

Street Railway Cars, Development of. (J. A. Brill) Cassier, **16**: 389.

Street Railway Consolidation. Outl. **64**: 712.

Street Railway Franchises in Berlin. (E. J. James) J. Pol. Econ. **9**: 260.

— Philadelphia. (C. R. Woodruff) Am. J. Sociol. **7**: 216.

— Taxes on. (W. S. Allen) Forum, **32**: 355.

Street Railway Problem, The. (P. Willis) Nation, **72**: 250.

— in Milwaukee. (J. A. Butler) Munic. Aff. **4**: 212.

Street Railway System of Philadelphia; its History and Present Condition. (F. W. Speirs) J. H. Univ. Stud. **15**: 94.

Street Railways and their Relation to the Public. (C. E. Curtis) Yale R. **6**: 17.

— Development of, in Great Britain. (J. C. Robinson) Cassier, **17**: 279.

— Franchise of, in Indianapolis. Ann. Am. Acad. Pol. Sci. **14**: 145.

— in Berlin. (E. J. James) Ann. Am. Acad. Pol. Sci. **15**: 437.

— in British Towns. (R. Donald) Munic. Aff. **4**: 31.

— in Columbus, O.; Attempt to secure 3-cent Fares. (E. W. Bemis) Ann. Am. Acad. Pol. Sci. **18**: 479.

— in Italy. (F. Benedetti) Chaut. **25**: 176.

— in U.S. (W. Hill) J. Pol. Econ. **5**: 403.

— Monopoly in England. (Robert Donald) Contemp. **76**: 174.

— Municipal Ownership of. (H. S. Pingree) Munsey, **22**: 220. — (F. Parsons) Arena, **25**: 198.

— — in Detroit. (C. Moore) Q. J. Econ. **13**: 453. **14**: 121. — Ann. Am. Acad. Pol. Sci. **14**: 262. — (E. W. Bemis) Munic. Aff. **3**: 473.

— — in the United Kingdom. (B. Taylor) Cassier, **16**: 381.

— — Practical. Outl. **61**: 949.

— Municipal Rapid Transit; a Gripman's View. Outl. **61**: 398.

— Municipal vs. Private Control. (E. E. Higgins) Munic. Aff. **1**: 458.

— New York: Should Greater New York operate them? Yes! (J. DeW. Warner) Munic. Aff. **1**: 421.

— Relation of Cities and Towns to. (L. S. Rowe) Ann. Am. Acad. Pol. Sci. **12**: 103.

— Situation in Chicago. (J. H. Gray) Q. J. Econ. **12**: 83.

— Taxation of. (C. E. Curtis) Yale R. **8**: 173. — (D. MacG. Means) Nation, **72**: 467.

Street Signs and Fixtures. (N. S. Spencer) Munic. Aff. **5**: 726.

Streets, Names of. (W. W. Crane) Lippinc. **60**: 264.

— Value of Quiet and Beautiful. (J. W. Howard) Engin. M. **12**: 924.

Streight's Raiders, Pursuit and Capture of. (J. A. Wyeth) Harper, **99**: 435.

Strength; Pain and Strength Measurements of School Children. (Ada Carman) Am. J. Psychol. **10**: 392.

— Some Endeavors to attain and retain it. Chamb. J. **75**: 423.

— Waste and Repair of. Spec. **79**: 377.

Strength of an Hour, The; a story. (A. H. Begbie) Temp. Bar, **112**: 44.

Strength of Gideon. (P. L. Dunbar) Lippinc. **64**: 617.

Strength that failed, A; a story. (N. W. Williams) Gent. M. n. s. **61**: 1.

Strengthfield, Lydia, Ancestry of. (H. A. Pitman) N. E. Reg. **54**: 309.

Stretensk to Lake Baikal. (G. F. Wright) Nation, 71: 225.

Strickland, Catherine, and her Sisters. (L. J. Burpee) Sewanee, 8: 207.

Striegel, Frances, Pianist. (Mrs. E. D. Adams) Midland, 9: 144.

Strike at Hull, England, 1893. (P. C. Standing) Idler, 12: 222.

— Clerical, at Beverley Minster in the 14th Century. (A. F. Leach) Archæol. 55: 1.

— Coal, of Eastern Pennsylvania, 1900. (F. J. Warne) Ann. Am. Acad. Pol. Sci. 17: 15. — (E. L. Bogart) Bib. Sac. 58: 136. — (T. Williams) Atlan. 87: 447. — Outl. 66: 250. — (J. Carroll) Indep. 52: 2508. — (J. Mitchell) Indep. 52: 2613. — Gunton's M. 19: 316. — (G. O. Virtue) J. Pol. Econ. 9: 1.

— — End of. (H. White) Nation, 71: 341.

— — Families of the Miners. (L. W. Betts) Outl. 66: 412.

— — Wages of Miners. (A. Pardee & Co.) Outl. 66: 416.

— Engineering, 1897-98. (E. Aves) Econ. J. 8: 115. — (B. C. Browne) National, 30: 937. Same art. Ecl. M. 130: 511. — (J. S. Jeans) Engin. M. 13: 851. — Sat. R. 84: 253, 336. — (L. Cassier) Cassier, 17: 487.

— — and the Archbishops. Spec. 80: 42.

— — and the British Navy. (A. S. Hurd) 19th Cent. 43: 366.

— — Great Industrial Danger. Spec. 80: 107.

— — Plevna of Labor. Contemp. 73: 142.

— — Policy of the Engineers. (F. W. Hirst) Econ. J. 8: 124.

— Evolution of the. (H. P. Willis) Nation, 73: 218.

— The First, recorded in History. (E. Eckstein) Liv. Age, 221: 589.

— in Municipal Gas Works at Glasgow. (A. C. Laughlin) Econ. R. 10: 237.

— in the Norwich (Eng.) Boot and Shoe Industry. (G. N. Herbert) Econ. R. 8: 101.

— in San Francisco. (H. P. Willis) Nation, 73: 275.

— — An Industrial Object Lesson. (S. N. D. North) Pop. Sci. Mo. 52: 721.

— Machinists', 1900. (E. L. Bogart) Yale R. 9: 302. — (C. B. Going) Engin. M. 19: 165.

— — Settlement of. Engin. M. 19: 518.

— Newspaper, in Chicago. Spec. 81: 107.

— Northeastern, End of. Spec. 78: 330.

— of the Bohemian Coal-miners. (E. Philippovich) Econ. J. 10: 261.

— of Colliers in South Wales. Westm. 150: 297.

— Psychology of the. (A. B. Cristy) Indep. 51: 2606.

— Pullman, Significance of. (A. P. Winston) J. Pol. Econ. 9: 540.

— Steel, 1901. (H. White) Nation, 73: 6, 44, 104. — (R. Ogden) Nation, 73: 124. — Engin. M. 21: 586. — (E. L. Bogart) Yale R. 10: 249. — (T. Williams) R. of Rs. (N. Y.) 24: 328.

— — Candid View of. (G. Gunton) Gunton's M. 21: 118.

— — A Lesson of. Outl. 69: 355.

— — Lesson on. (G. Gunton) Gunton's M. 21: 331.

— — More Light on. (G. Gunton) Gunton's M. 21: 232.

— — Politics and. (H. White) Nation, 73: 64.

— — Strikers and their Constitution. Nation, 73: 144.

Strike at Barton's. (W. T. Nichols) Lippinc. 60: 545.

Strike in the Sierras, A. Chamb. J. 74: 488.

Strike Epidemic, The. (D. MacG. Means) Nation, 79: 353.

Striker's Story, The ; a story. (F. H. Spearman) McClure, 17: 287.

Strikes, An American View of. (H. E. Highton) Overland, n. s. 38: 346.

Strikes and the Coal Miners. (S. Gompers) Forum, 24: 27.

— and Injunctions in the United States. Sat. R. 84: 335.

— and the Philosophy of the Strikers. (F. K. Foster) Internat. Mo. 4: 429.

— Are they ever Lost ? (D. A. Hayes) Indep. 53: 2506.

— as a Factor in Progress. (M. E. J. Kelley) No. Am. 164: 24.

— Buck-jumping of Labor. (W. H. Mallock) 19th Cent. 42: 337. Same art. Liv. Age, 215: 177.

— Colliery, in England, 1892-93. (S. Fothergill) Westm. 149: 82.

— — in 1897. (J. E. George) Q. J. Econ. 12: 186.

— in Europe. Spec. 81: 515.

— in North Carolina. (J. Dowd) Gunton's M. 20: 136.

— a Mill Town in Strike Time. (M. G. Cunniff) World's Work, 2: 1326.

— New Zealand, a Country without. (J. A. Ryan) Cath. World, 72: 145.

— The Other Side of. Gunton's M. 17: 275.

— Personal Liberty and. (J. Ireland) No. Am. 173: 445.

— Practical Remedy for. Gunton's M. 13: 88.

— Recent Street-railroad. Gunton's M. 17: 89.

— Trusts, Boycotts, and Black-lists. (F. D. Tandy) Arena, 23: 194.

— Unjustifiable. Am. Arch. 72: 94.

— vs. Conciliation. (H. White) Nation, 70: 450.

Strindberg, August. (F. S. Sharpe) Critic, 32: 103. — Acad. 57: 115.

String Alternator. (K. Honda and S. Shimizu) Am. J. Sci. 160: 64.

String of Pearls, A. (Gertrude Stanton) Overland, n. s. 36: 300.

Stringer, Arthur J. (H. A. Bruce) Canad. M. 15: 143.

Stringtown on the Pike ; a story. (J. U. Lloyd) Bookman, 11: 62-569. 12: 69-406.

Strong, Caleb, Letters to, 1786, 1800. Am. Hist. R. 4: 328.

Strong, Wm. L., Mayor of New York City. (A. C. Wheeler) Chaut. 25: 257.

"Strong and Weak" in their Economic Connection. (M. Pantaleoni) Econ. J. 8: 183.

Strong Weakness of Oiney Kittach. (S. MacManus) Cent. 36: 955.

Stronger Power, The ; a story. (L. C. Morant) Belgra. 97: 316.

Strozzi Palace, Florence, Lanterns of. (C. G. Leland) Am. Arch. 55: 30.

Structures, Statics of. (O. F. Semsch) Am. Arch. 55: 19 — 58: 39. 59: 43, 99. 60: 75. 61: 67.

Struthers, Sir John. Obituary. Nature, 59: 468.

Strutt, A. W. Humor in Animal Painting. (A. L. Baldry) M. of Art, 22: 309.

Stuart, Alexander Hugh Holmes. (Sallie E. M. Hardy) Green Bag, 10: 118.

Stuart, Lady Arabella. (E. Levi) Ath. '97, 2: 352.

Stuart, Charles, Admiral. "Old Ironsides." (E. S. Ellis) Chaut. 27: 411.

Stuart, Lady Elizabeth, Jewels of, Lawsuit concerning. (W. J. Hardy) Archæol. 56: 127.

Stuart, Gilbert, Portraits of Women. (C. H. Hart) Cent. v. 33-37.

Stuart, James, the Pretender, Portrait of. (F. Lord) Art J. 49: 275.

Stuart, Lady Louisa. (L. B. Lang) Longm. 35: 24. — (Stephen Gwynn) Macmil. 80: 348. — Spec. 83: 224.

— Letters of, to Miss Clinton. (C. L. H. Dempster) Longm. 39: 154.

Stuarts, Charm of the. Spec. 81: 238.

Suicide and the Law. (L. Irwell) Green Bag, 10: 141.
— and the Weather. (E. G. Dexter) Pop. Sci. Mo. 58: 604.
— Durkheim on. The Delusions of Durkheim's Sociological Objectivism: a reply. (G. Tosti) Am. J. Sociol. 4: 171.
— is it Worth while? (C. B. Newcomb) Arena, 18: 557.
— Modest Defence of. Green Bag, 11: 39.
— Statistics of. (R. A. Skelton) 19th Cent. 48: 465.
Suite. (C. Trollope) Gent. M. n. s. 62: 393. Same art. Ecl. M. 133: 40. Same art. Liv. Age, 221: 514.
Sullivan, Sir Arthur. (A. H. Lawrence) Strand, 14: 649. — (J. A. F. Maitland) Cornh. 83: 300. — (V. Blackburn and J. C. Carr) Fortn. 75: 81. Same art. Liv. Age, 228: 460. — With portrait. (L. M. Isaacs) Bookman, 12: 494. — With portraits. (G. Grossmith) Pall Mall M. 23: 250. — (Horace Ellis) Music, 19: 301. — Ath. '00, 2: 690. — (H. T. Finck) Indep. 52: 2921. — Spec. 85: 969.
— as a Boy, with portraits. (E. Swayne) Music, 18: 219.
— as an Old Friend knew Him. Argosy, 73: 161.
Sullivan, James, with portrait. Green Bag, 12: 609.
Sullivan, General John, 1740–95. (F. B. Sanborn) New Eng. M. n. s. 23: 323.
— Expedition of, 1779. (W. E. Griffis) New Eng. M. n. s. 23: 355.
Sullivan's Bargain; a story. (B. M. Croker) Cornh. 76: 59.
Sully, Mounet. (Y. Blaze de Bury) Fortn. 68: 905.
Sulphides, Sulphates, Sulphites, and Thiosulphates, Detection of, in the Presence of each other. (P. E. Browning and E. Howe) Am. J. Sci. 156: 317.
Sulphocyanides of Copper and Silver in Gravimetric Analysis. (R. G. Van Name) Am. J. Sci. 160: 451.
Sulphohalite, On the Chemical Composition of. (S. L. Penfield) Am. J. Sci. 159: 425.
Sulphur Mining in the North Pacific. (W. H. Crawford, jr.) Cassier, 19: 311.
Sulpitians at Baltimore. (R. R. Elliott) Am. Cath. Q. 24, no. 4: 99.
Sultan, the, Apotheosis of. Spec. 78: 685.
— and the Czar. Spec. 78: 720.
— and his Subjects, Davey on. Spec. 78: 701.
— at Home, The. (S. Whitman) Harper, 98: 276.
— Jubilee of, 1899. Liv. Age, 227: 132.
Sultan's Cakes, The; a poem. (Sir Edwin Arnold) Indep. 53: 3066.
Sultanas, Famous. (L. M. J. Garnett) Scot. R. 34: 110.
Sulu Archipelago, The. (P. Whitmarsh) Outl. 66: 578. 67: 221.
— American Rule in. (O. J. Sweet) Indep. 53: 2329.
— Our Agreement with the Sultan of. (M. Wilcox) Forum, 30: 238.
— Our Mohammedan Wards in. (Anna N. Benjamin) Outl. 63: 675.
— Slavery and Polygamy in. (E. M. Andre) Indep. 51: 3220. — Outl. 63: 765.
Sumatra, Island of. (E. H. Parker) Asia. R. 29: 127.
— West Coast of. (D. G. Fairchild) Nat. Geog. M. 9: 449.
Summary Procedure; a story. (N. Martley) Longm. 30: 60. Same art. Ecl. M. 129: 111.
Summer, Advent of. (A. F. Rees) Temp. Bar, 123: 79. Same art. Liv. Age, 229: 632.
Summer died Last Night; a poem. (M. C. Perry) Atlan. 82: 750.
Summer in Old Kentucky; a poem. (T. P. Terry) Outing, 32: 514.
Summer in Sabots, A. (Mary A. Peixotto) Scrib. M. 29: 608.
Summer on the Sands. Munsey, 17: 651.
Summer Camps for Boys. (L. Rouillion) R. of Rs. (N. Y.) 21: 697.

Summer Christmas; a story. (M. Maartens) Eng. Illust. 20: 261.
Summer Cobwebs. (E. Schobert) Argosy, 74: 337.
Summer Cold of 1898 in England. Spec. 80: 856.
Summer Dawn; a poem. (A. Furber) Outing, 34: 189.
Summer Hours and Work in a Library. (M. E. Hazeltine) Pub. Lib. 5: 234.
Summer Philanthropy. Charities, 7: 279.
Summer School in Philanthropic Work, The. (P. W. Ayres) Charities, 6: 186.
Summer Schools for Bible Study. Bib. World, 18: 3.
— of Methods. Music, 12: 621.
Summer Study in 1897. School R. 5: 311.
Summer's Dream, A; a story. Macmil. 80: 50. Same art. Liv. Age, 222: 124.
Summer's End on the Itchen. (W. H. Hudson) Longm. 38: 17. Same art. Ecl. M. 137: 445. Same art. Liv. Age, 230: 387.
Summum Bonum, Doctrine of the. (H. Sturt) Mind, 25: 372.
Summum Bonum; a poem. (E. Rogers) Argosy, 74: 116.
Summum Bonum; a sonnet. (P. McArthur) Atlan. 87: 864.
Sumner, Charles, Storey's Life of. Am. Hist. R. 6: 157. — (F. Bancroft) Atlan. 86: 277.
Sumner, George Henry, with portraits. Strand, 15: 572.
Sumner, Heywood, Decorator. (G. White) Studio (Internat.) 4: 153.
Sumptuary Laws, The Old. (G. H. Westley) Green Bag, 9: 291.
Sumter, Fort, Confederate Stories of Bombardment of. Nat'l M. (Bost.) 9: 266.
— The Drama of the April Dawn. (J. A. B. Scherer) Chaut. 31: 244.
Sun, The, and its Powers. (H. C. Hay) N. Church R. 7: 161.
— and Moon, Terrors of, in Biblical Times. (R. Winterbotham) Expos. 8: 355.
— Babylonian Representation of the Solar Disk. (W. H. Ward) Am. J. Theol. 2: 115.
— Constituents of. (A. Fowler) Knowl. 23: 11.
— Corona of. (E. W. Maunder) Knowl. 20: 9. — (I. E. Christian) Pop. Astron. 7: 28. — (R. W. Wood) Nature, 63: 230.
— — Dark Markings in. (H. W. Wesley) Knowl. 23: 225.
— — Magnetic Theory of. (F. H. Bigelow) Am. J. Sci. 161: 253.
— — Nature of. (R. W. Wood) Science, n. s. 13: 179.
— — Photographing the. (W. B. Featherstone) Pop. Astron. 8: 250.
— — — Burckhalter's Apparatus for. Pop. Astron. 8: 493.
— — — in 1900. (W. W. Payne) Pop. Astron. 7: 516.
— Destination of. (H. Jacoby) Pop. Sci. Mo. 57: 191.
— Distance of, Determination of. (W. W. Campbell) Science, n. s. 13: 176. — Blackw. 169: 629.
— — from Observations of Eros. (W. W. Campbell) Pop. Astron. 9: 88.
— Equatorial Acceleration of, and the Sun Spot Period, Causes of the. (E. J. Wilczynski) Pop. Astron. 6: 209.
— Energy of, Problem of Harnessing the. (N. Tesla) Cent. 38: 175.
— — Sustentation of. (J. Whitehead) N. Church R. 4: 536.
— — Utilizing the. (R. H. Thurston) Cassier, 20: 283. — (F. B. Millard) World's Work, 1: 599.
— Enlargement of, near Horizon, Ptolemy's Theorem on. (T. J. J. See) Pop. Astron. 8: 362.
— Faculæ on; artificial faculæ. (A. East) Knowl. 21: 183.

Sun, the, Heat of. (A. S. Young) Pop. Astron. 6: 145.
— — Extension of Helmholtz's Theory. (T. J. J. See) Science, n. s. 9: 740.
— Influence of, upon the Formation of the Earth's Surface. (N. S. Shaler) Internat. Mo. 1: 41.
— its Place in Nature, Lockyer's. Ath. '98, 2: 134.
— Non-eclipse of, May 3, 1899. (E. Miller) Pop. Astron. 8: 80.
— Observations of, Jan.-Aug., '99, Brief Review of. (D. E. Hadden) Pop. Astron. 7: 408.
— Origin of. (R. S. Baker) McClure, 13: 80.
— Parallax of, Feasibility of obtaining, from Simultaneous Micrometer Observations of Eros. (S. J. Brown) Pop. Astron. 8: 353.
— Periodic Changes of Solar Activity and the Earth's Motion, Relation between. (J. Halm) Nature, 61: 445.
— Radiation of. (J. Y. Buchanan) Nature, 64: 456.
— — Measurements of. (R. T. Glazebrooke) Nature, 64: 352.
— Size of, Apparent. (C. H. Chandler) Pop. Astron. 7: 342.
— Spot on, Great, of Sept. 1898, and the Aurora. (E. W. Maunder) Knowl. 21: 228.
— Spots on, and Rainfall. (Sir Norman Lockyer and W. J. S. Lockyer) Science, n. s. 12: 915. — (N. Lockyer) No. Am. 172: 827.
— — and Life. (A. B. MacDowall) Knowl. 21: 234.
— — and Magnetism. (W. Ellis) Nature, 58: 78.
— — and the Weather Forecast. (W. Fawcett) New Eng. M. n. s. 25: 94.
— — Artificial. (A. East) Knowl. 20: 288.
— — Discovery of. (M. A. Lancaster) Pop. Sci. Mo. 51: 681.
— — The Level of. (A. East) Knowl. 21: 89.
— — London Summers near Minima of. (A. B. MacDowall) Knowl. 22: 209.
— — Long-period Variation. (W. J. S. Lockyer) Nature, 64: 196.
— — Proctor on. (J. H. Jenkinson) Knowl. 21: 181.
— — Types of Disturbances. (A. L. Cortie) Knowl. 24: 104.
— Worship of, among the Moqui Indians. (J. W. Fewkes) Nature, 58: 295.
"Sun of my Soul, Thou Saviour Dear ; " Latin Version. (W. R. Kennedy) Ecl. M. 132: 40.
Sun's Journey through Space. (J. Ellard Gore) Gent. M. n. s. 62: 607.
Sun-dial, How to make a. (H. Jacoby) Cosmopol. 28: 652.
— of Ahaz. (S. A. Saunder) Pop. Astron. 7: 206. — (B. S. Easton) Pop. Astron. 7: 242. — (J. Morrison) Pop. Astron. 6: 537. 7: 368.
— Portable, of Gilt Brass, made by Cardinal Wolsey. (L. Evans) Archæol. 57: 331.
Sun-dials. Acad. 59: 379.
— Metal, of the Three Last Centuries. (F. Peacock) Reliquary, 40: 101.
— on our Old Churches. (Sarah Wilson) Chamb. J. 78: 83.
Sunbeam, Work of a. (T. Bird) Good Words, 42: 107.
Sun-down's Higher Self ; a story. (F. Remington) Harper, 97: 846.
Sun-down Leflare's Money ; a story. (F. Remington) Harper, 97: 195.
Sunrise ; a poem. (M. McNeal) Outing, 31: 270.
— a poem. (S. Sterne) Atlan. 86: 809.
— In the Woods at. (F. Whishaw) Longm. 38: 168.
— on the Crescent Moon. (E. W. Maunder) Good Words, 41: 685.
Sun-scald and its Prevention. (E. S. Goff) Garden & F. 10: 371.

Sunset, Mechanism of. (A. H. Bell) Knowl. 24: 235. Same art. Liv. Age, 231: 518.
Sunset at Lugano, A ; a story. (M. S. Hancock) Belgra. 97: 54.
Sundari. (R. W. Frazer) New R. 16: 1.
Sunday, The British. (H. H. Henson) National, 33: 758. Same art. Ecl. M. 133: 558. Same art. Liv. Age, 222: 452.
— in the Middle Ages. (H. Thurston) 19th Cent. 46: 36.
— Is it a Common Holiday ? (M. Dods) Sund. M. 27: 433.
— its Past, Present, and Future. (T. F. Wright) N. Church R. 7: 94.
— Man's Best Use of. (J. Reed) N. Church R. 8: 65.
— New Church Law of Observance of. (J. Reed) N. Church R. 5: 361.
— Observance of. Quar. 185: 36. — Macmil. 76: 30.
— — Bill for, and opening of Art Exhibitions on Sunday by Private Enterprise. (J. P. Thompson) Westm. 147: 630.
— — Legislation for. (M. H. Judge) Westm. 148: 72.
— Occupations for Children on. (Ida M. Gardner) Outl. 60: 673.
— Problem of. Outl. 61: 580. — (F. W. Farrar) Forum, 28: 140.
— — London County Council and the Lord's Day Act of 1781. (C. Hill) Westm. 151: 218.
— — Present Aspect of. (S. H. Laing) Westm. 151: 65.
— Sunday Goods Traffic. (L. Phillips) Econ. R. 11: 245.
— Travel on. (J. Pendleton) Sund. M. 28: 299.
— Zahn upon. (S. T. Lowrie) Presb. & Ref. R. 9: 101, 384.
Sunday Eclogue, A. (M. Thompson) Lippinc. 64: 425.
Sunday Journalism, How it was killed in London. (R. Donald) Outl. 63: 262. — (H. S. Lunn) R. of Rs. (N. Y.) 20: 181.
Sunday Legislation. (B. J. Ramage) Sewanee, 4: 116.
Sunday Opening Movement, Injury inflicted on the Toiling Classes by. (C. Hill) Westm. 151: 451.
Sunday-school and the Home. (W. H. Alden) N. Church R. 5: 568.
— Adapting Instruction in, to all Pupils. Bib. World, 12: 65.
— Authoritative Teaching in. Bib. World, 12: 225.
— Curriculum of. Bib. World, 11: 145.
— — Suggestion toward a Rational. (G. W. Pease) Bib. World, 16: 98.
— Examinations in. Bib. World, 14: 326.
— Genesis and Evolution of. (J. H. Harris) Lond. Q. 93: 251.
— High-school Pupils in. (P. S. Moxom) Bib. World, 14: 47.
— History of. (J. H. Harris) Sund. M. 28: 636.
— How to excite Interest in the Lesson. Bib. World, 13: 225.
— International Lesson Committee, Report of. Bib. World, 13: 426.
— International Lessons, July-Dec., 1899. (H. L. Willett) Bib. World, 14: 58.
— Kindergarten Methods in. (F. Beard) Bib. World, 18: 114.
— Main Purpose of ; a symposium. Bib. World, 15: 256.
— Mission, as a Social and Ethical Lever. (H. F. Perry) Bib. Sac. 56: 481.
— New Teaching in. (C. Lathbury) N. Church R. 4: 406.
— Nurseries of the Church. (C. Middleton) Sund. M. 26: 100.
— Problem of. Outl. 61: 910.

Surprise, in War. (S. Wilkinson) Cornh. 81: 318.

—— from a Military and a National Point of View. (T. M. Maguire) National, 31: 361.

Surprise at the Hydro, A; a story. (Mary L. Pendered) Idler, 13: 635.

Surprise of Mr. Milberry; a story. (J. K. Jerome) Eng. Illust. 20: 209.

Surprise Party, A. (Mrs. Newman) Strand, 18: 760.

Surrender at Discretion, A; a story. (K. Warfield) Outing, 34: 387.

Surrender of Joshua, The; a story. (A. L. Harris) Belgra. 97: 41.

Surrender of Sister Philomene; a story. (E. G. Jordan) Harper, 103: 570.

Surrey; the Fold Country. (W. Canton) Good Words, 42: 573.

— Pines and Pools of. Spec. 84: 918.

Surrey Garden, A. (S. R. Hole) 19th Cent. 43: 637. Same art. Liv. Age, 217: 542.

Sursum Corda; a poem. (R. G. A. S. Prudhomme) Argosy, 68: 119.

Survey, Methods of, employed by the Chilean Boundary Commission in the Cordillera of the Andes. (A. Bertrand) Geog. J. 16: 329.

Surveys, Historic and Economic, Ashley's. (L. L. Price) Econ. J. 11: 43. — (C. H. Hull) Am. Hist. R. 6: 793.

Survival, A; a story. (A. Werner) Temp. Bar, 122: 84. Same art. Liv. Age, 228: 504.

Susa, Explorations at. (W. St.C. Boscawen) Asia. R. 32: 330. — Am. Arch. 67: 62.

Susan; a story. (J. Orchardson) Idler, 17: 354.

Suspected Lodger, A; a story. (J. W. Sherer) Gent. M. n. s. 66: 521.

Suspension Bridge, Old and New Forms. (G. Lindenthal) Engin. M. 16: 359.

Suspension Railway, A German. (R. L. Pearse) Cassier, 20: 498.

Susquehanna Indians, Fate of. (J. S. Clark) Am. Antiq. 20: 14.

Sussex, Dawn of Christianity in. (V. L. Whitechurch) Good Words, 42: 820.

Sussex Auburns, A Brace of. (W. C. Sydney) Gent. M. n. s. 64: 579.

Sussex Farmhouses, Old, and Furniture. (J. L. André) Antiq. n. s. 34: 106, 135, 172.

Sussex Folk, Concerning. (C. B. Knox) Argosy, 72: 182.

Sutcliffe, L., Charcoal Drawings of. (A. H. Hinton) Artist (N. Y.) 24: 30.

Sutlej Campaign, Reminiscences of. (S. D. White) Un. Serv. M. 15: 584.

Sutton, H. S. The Saviour's Triple Crown. N. Church R. 6: 305.

Sutton Place, Guildford. Acad. 57: 307.

Suzerainty. Macmil. 81: 22.

Svendsen, Svend, Artist. Brush & P. 6: 28.

Swale, The, and its Waterfalls. (H. Brierley) Gent. M. n. s. 59: 189.

Swaledale. Temp. Bar, 110: 217.

Swallow; a story. (H. R. Haggard) Munsey, 19: 362 — 20: 943.

Swallowfield and its Owners, Lady Russell on. Ath. '01, 2: 52.

Swamis, The, in America. (A. J. Ingersoll) Arena, 22: 482.

Swammerdam, Jan, Malpighi, and Leeuwenhoek. (W. A. Locy) Pop. Sci. Mo. 58: 561.

Swamp Adventure in Mississippi. Midland, 11: 215.

Swamp Notes. (H. W. Morrow) Outing, 38: 293.

Swamps of Missouri. (W. Trelease) Garden & F. 10: 370.

— of Oswego County, N. Y., and their Flora. (W. W. Rowlee) Am. Natural. 31: 690, 792, 864.

Swan, J. M., Artist. (A. L. Baldry) Studio (Internat.) 2: 236. — (A. L. Baldry) Studio (Internat.) 13: 75, 151.

Swan, The Wild, of Australia. Chamb. J. 76: 593.

Swans, Our. (E. Kay Robinson) Good Words, 39: 811.

Swansea Porcelain. (C. Monkhouse) M. of Art, 22: 257.

Swasey, Ambrose, with portrait. (J. A. Brashear) Pop. Astron. 7: 345. — (J. A. Brashear) Cassier, 11: 399.

Swastika, The. (L. Viajero) Am. Arch. 59: 70.

— and the Cross. (J. F. Hewitt) Westm. 149: 248–688. 150: 73–435.

— and other Marks among Algonquin Indians. (W. W. Tooker) Am. Antiq. 20: 339.

— Origin and Meaning of. (R. P. Greg) Archæol. 48: 293.

— Wilson's Investigation of. (H. C. Mercer) Am. Natural. 31: 255.

Swatis and Afridis. (T. H. Holdich) Anthrop. J. 29: 2.

Sway-backed House, The; a story. (C. W. Chesnutt) Outl. 66: 588.

Sweating System. (F. J. C. Moran) No. Am. 166: 757.

Sweatshops, New York Law, Effects of. (H. White) Gunton's M. 18: 345.

— Some Phases of, in Garment Trades of Chicago. (Nellie M. Austen) Am. J. Sociol. 6: 602.

Sweden, Fishing in. (E. Francfort) Outing, 34: 46.

— Iron Industry of. (D. A. Louis) Engin. M. 17: 426.

— Mining and Metallurgical Industries, at Stockholm Exhibition, 1898. (B. H. Brough) J. Soc. Arts, 46: 61.

Swedenborg, E., and Coleridge. (C. Higham) N. Church R. 4: 273.

— and Kant on Cognition. (F. Sewall) N. Church R. 5: 481.

—— Philosophy of. (A. J. Edmunds) N. Church R. 4: 257.

— and Modern Thought. N. Church R. 6: 438.

— and the Nebular Hypothesis. (M. Nyrèn) Translated from German by F. Sewall. N. Church R. 4: 371.

— Character and Philosophy of. (G. Hawkes) N. Church R. 4: 481.

— Doctrine of " Remains." (W. E. Brickman) N. Church R. 5: 579.

— Many-sidedness of. (J. Reed) N. Church R. 7: 106.

— The Oneness of his Writings. (J. R. Swanton) N. Church R. 4: 616.

— Physiological Hypothesis of. (L. P. Mercer) N. Church R. 6: 86.

— Dr. A. T. Pierson in Error concerning. N. Church R. 4: 275.

— Science of Correspondences and its Demonstration. (J. E. Werren) N. Church R. 4: 208.

— Scientific Writings of. (J. B. Keene) N. Church R. 5: 120. — (J. R. Swanton) N. Church R. 6: 208.

— Teachings of, formulated. (Gilbert Hawkes) N. Church R. 5: 66.

Swedenborg Scientific Association. (J. K. Smyth) N. Church R. 5: 450.

Swedenborgian Belief Different from Others. (J. Reed) N. Church R. 7: 268.

Swedenborgian Church, and its Relations to Other Denominations. N. Church R. 5: 597.

— and the Scriptures. (T. F. Wright) N. Church R. 5: 606.

— and the World. N. Church R. 5: 407.

— in Great Britain. (T. F. Wright) N. Church R. 4: 595.

— its Distinctive Work. (J. Reed) N. Church R. 7: 321.

Symons, Arthur. Acad. **53**: 377.
— Poetry of. Acad. **61**: 627.
Symons, Geo. J. Nature, **61**: 475.
Sympathy. (W. A. Sutton) Cath. World, **69**: 61.
— Mechanism of. (H. F. Rulison) Open Court, **11**: 99.
Symphonies and their Meaning, Goepp on. Music, **13**: 814.
Symphony. (J. F. Runciman) Sat. R. **88**: 420.
—and Symphonic Poem. (M. Aronson) Music, **12**: 590.
— in the 19th Century. (W. S. B. Mathews) Music, **17**: 599.
— since Beethoven. (H. Imbert) Music, **19**: 55, 89, 355.
— (F. Weingartner) Contemp. **75**: 271, 418.
Symphony Crank, The; a story. (Amelie von Ende) Music, **11**: 518.
Symphony Hall, Boston, with illustrations. (W. S. B. Mathews) Music, **19**: 164.
Synæsthesia, Two Cases of. (G. M. Whipple) Am. J. Psychol. **11**: 377.
Synagogue, Jewish, and the Relation of Jesus to it. (E. K. Mitchell) Bib. World, **16**: 10.
— Why I do not go to. (A. G. Henriques) Jew. Q. **13**: 63.
Synagogues, Art in. (D. Kaufmann) Jew. Q. **9**: 254.
— of the Dispersion and Early Christianity. (W. M. Tippy) Meth. R. **60**: 446.
Synchronograph, Tests of. (A. C. Crehore and G. O. Squier) J. Frankl. Inst. **145**: 161-471.
Synod, The Great. (S. Krauss) Jew. Q. **10**: 347.
Synod Hall, Edinburgh, Sunday Evening at. (G. T. Brown) Sund. M. **26**: 705.
Syntax and Psychology. (G. Darling) Educa. **18**: 346.
Synthesists, Four; cross-sections from Comte, Spencer, Lilienfeld, and Schaeffle. (B. H. Meyer) Am. J. Sociol. **6**: 20.
Synthetic Experiment, The. (I. M. Bentley) Am. J. Psychol. **11**: 405.
Syracuse, N. Y., Water Supply of. (J. H. Hamilton) Munic. Aff. **4**: 60.
Syracuse University, Music in. (Pauline Jennings) Music, **11**: 557.
Syria, Germany in. Outl. **65**: 112.
— Note on a Skull from. (W. L. H. Duckworth) Anthrop. J. **29**: 145.
— Sources of History of. (A. Büchler) Jew. Q. **9**: 311.
Syriac Gospels, Earlier Home of the Sinaitic Palimpsest. (A. S. Lewis) Expos. **7**: 415.
Syriac Lectionaries of the Bible, Palestinian. (A. S. Lewis) Lond. Q. **91**: 75.
Syriac Manuscript of the New Testament. (F. F. Irving) Reliquary, **39**: 22.
Syriac "Testament of our Lord." (W. H. Kent) Dub. R. **126**: 245.
Syrian Canon of the New Testament. (J. A. Bewer) Am. J. Theol. **4**: 64, 345.
Syrian Fossils, Conrad's Types of. (C. E. Beecher) Am. J. Sci. **159**: 176.
Szczepanik, Jan, the Austrian Edison, keeping School again. (S. L. Clemens) Cent. **34**: 630.
Sze-Chuan, Journey in Western. (Isabella Bishop) Geog. J. **10**: 19.

Tabb, John B. Poems. (Sarah B. Elliott) Sewanee, **3**: 431.
— Poet for the Winter Evening. (E. B. Goodwin) Cath. World, **73**: 208.
Tabernacle, The; was it Oriental? (T. F. Wright) J. Bib. Lit. **18**: 195.
"Table of Green Fields," Mrs. Quickly's. (D. R. Fotheringham) Knowl. **24**: 31.
Table Service, Notes on Ornamental. (C. R. Ashbee) Art J. **50**: 336.

Table Sundries. (C. D. Wilson) Lippinc. **62**: 848.
Table Talk, a Lost Art. (Oliphant Smeaton) Scot. R. **36**: 292.
Tableaux, Some Society. (M. E. W. Sherwood) Cosmopol. **24**: 235.
Tablets, Waxed, said to have been found at Cambridge. (T. H. Hughes) Archæol. **55**: 257.
Tachometry. (J. A. Fleming) Cassier, **21**: 37.
Tachygraphy, Old Greek. (F. W. G. Foat) J. Hel. Stud. **21**: 238.
Tacitus, Rome of. (B. K. Hudson) New Eng. M. n. s. **22**: 21.
Tacoma, Past, Present, and Future. (S. E. Rothery) Overland, n. s. **31**: 244.
Tactical Evolution, Twenty Years of. (Mandes) J. Mil. Serv. Inst. **17**: 592.
Tactics, Battle. (F. H. Edmunds) J. Mil. Serv. Inst. **12**: 1202.
— Minor, Practical Instruction in. (J. P. Wisser) J. Mil. Serv. Inst. **8**: 130.
— Modern Coast Defence. (J. Stanley) J. Mil. Serv. Inst. **20**: 388.
— Offensive, of Infantry, (G. F. R. Henderson) J. Mil. Serv. Inst. **15**: 1014.
— Some Points of. (J. H. Patterson) J. Mil. Serv. Inst. **29**: 161.
Tactual Threshold for the Perception of Two Points. (G. A. Tawney) Am. Natural. **31**: 820.
Tadema, Miss Laurence Alma, Poems of. Acad. **52**: 518.
Tadpole, The, of an Archangel. (W. P. Drury) Un. Serv. M. **16**: 42.
Taffles; a story. (Q. Gordon) Gent. M. n. s. **60**: 417.
Taft, William Howard. Outl. **64**: 532. — (T. Roosevelt) Outl. **69**: 166.
— and our Philippine Policy, with portrait. (R. Patterson) R. of Rs. (N. Y.) **24**: 179.
Tahiti. (T. B. Severson) Overland, n. s. **37**: 1076.
— Passages from a Diary in the Pacific. (J. La Farge) Scrib. M. **30**: 69.
— Voyage to, and Return, 1901. (S. P. Langley) Nat. Geog. M. **12**: 413.
"Tai-Hoku," Wreck of the. (W. E. Ellis) Strand, **15**: 50.
Taine, Hippolyte Adolphe. Quar. **186**: 183.
— Provincial Notebooks. (A. Laugel) Nation, **64**: 27, 65.
Tai-ping Rebellion. (S. W. Williams) Open Court, **15**: 674, 740.
— Episodes of the. (L. A. Beardslee) Harper, **99**: 430.
Tait, Sir M., with portrait. (R. D. McGibbon) Green Bag, **9**: 417.
Tait, Peter Guthrie. (G. Chrystal) Nature, **64**: 305.
Taking of Ballynagle Tower; a story. (A. Merry) Belgra. **96**: 347.
Taku Forts, Capture of the. (Lieut. Myakishev) J. Mil. Serv. Inst. **29**: 274.
Tale of the American Volunteer; a Cuban story. (N. W. Williams) Strand, **17**: 409.
Tale of Anne; a story. (Katharine Silvester) Gent. M. n. s. **63**: 209.
Tale of Arion, A. (Elizabeth Taylor) Poet-Lore, **10**: 8.
Tale of the Doubtful Grandfather. (W. A. Curtis) Lippinc. **63**: 256.
Tale of '52, A; a story. (Lettie E. Shepherd) Midland, **11**: 57.
Tale of the Great Famine, A. (H. Fielding) Macmil. **79**: 460. Same art. Ecl. M. **133**: 25. Same art. Liv. Age, **221**: 506.
Tale of a Grecian Boy, The; a story. (Neil Wynn Williams) Gent. M. n. s. **59**: 1. Same art. Liv. Age, **214**: 671.
Tale of a Judy Show. (R. E. Vernède) Strand, **18**: 449.

Tale of King Constans the Emperor ; a story. (R. Le Gallienne) Cosmopol. **32**: 52. — (W. Morris) Poet-Lore, **11**: 465.

Tale of the Pasquia Post, A. (Herman Whitaker) Overland, n. s. **36**: 123.

Tale of the Sea, A. (A. H. Markham) Good Words, **39**: 549.

Tale of Sons, A. (E. Stuart-Langford) Sund. M. **29**: 39.

Tale of the South Shore. (P. H. Coggins) New Eng. M. n. s. **22**: 461.

Tale of a Tub, A ; a prison story. (T. Hopkins) McClure, **14**: 520.

Tale of a Tub, A. (H. A. Hinkson) Idler, **17**: 3.

Tale of a Tune, The. (G. B. McCutcheon) Nat'l M. (Bost.) **5**: 479.

Tale of a Tusker. Macmil. **82**: 354.

Tale of Two Horses. (H. M. Skinner) Arena, **17**: 1052.

Talk, A Theory of. Cornh. **77**: 809. Same art. Liv. Age, **218**: 330.

Talking Ships, The ; a story. (A. T. Quiller-Couch) Pall Mall M. **25**: 181.

"Tallahassee," Confederate Steamer, Dash into N. Y. Waters. (J. T. Wood) Cent. **34**: 408.

Talented Miss Hope, The ; a sketch. (J. K. Bangs) McClure, **9**: 904.

Tallien, J. E., The Last Days of. (A. Laugel) Nation, **69**: 257.

Tallies. (S. Baring-Gould) Chamb. J. **74**: 285.

— Beer, and Labor. (E. Lovett) Reliquary, **38**: 38.

— French Bakers'. Reliquary, **37**: 160.

— Hop. (E. Lovett) Reliquary, **37**: 37.

— used by Savages. (R. Quick) Reliquary, **38**: 189.

Tallow Cave, North Dorset, Vt. (E. S. Balch) J. Frankl. Inst. **151**: 179.

Talmage, T. DeWitt. (L. W. Lillingston) Sund. M. **29**: 603.

Talmud in History, The. (A. S. Isaacs) Jew. Q. **13**: 438.

Talmudic Books, Burning of, in Venice in 1553. (D. Kaufmann) Jew. Q. **13**: 533.

Tamalpais, Mount. (M. Manson) Pop. Sci. Mo. **57**: 69.

— and its Railroad. (Mabel C. Craft) Nat'l M. (Bost.) **6**: 258.

— Fog Studies on. (A. McAdie) Pop. Sci. Mo. **59**: 535.

Tamar River, Wanderings of. (Annie G. Hurd) M. of Art, **20**: 310.

Tamil Lands, The Poets of. (G. U. Pope) Asia. R. **24**: 99. **25**: 126. **27**: 115.

Taming of Jezrul, The ; a devil tale. (V. F. Boyle) Harper, **100**: 389.

Tamiobatis Vetustus ; a new form of Fossil Skate. (C. R. Eastman) Am. J. Sci. **154**: 85.

Tammany Commandment, The. (J. Flynt) McClure, **17**: 543.

Tammany Hall. (S. Brooks) Monthly R. **5**, no. **2**: 86. — (F. A. McKenzie) 19th Cent. **42**: 907. Same art. Ecl. M. **130**: 128.

— and the Courts. (E. P. Clark) Nation, **73**: 316.

— and the Dorr Rebellion. (A. M. Mowry) Am. Hist. R. **3**: 292.

— and "Respectability." Nation, **73**: 274.

— Credulity about. (R. Ogden) Nation, **73**: 296.

— Croker's Defence of. Spec. **79**: 547.

— in History. (D. MacG. Means) Nation, **72**: 106.

— Most Perfect Political Organization in the World. (H. Davis) Munsey, **24**: 55.

— Myers's History of. (W. L. Hawley) Bk. Buyer, **23**: 107.

— Past and Present. (E. Cary) Forum, **26**: 200.

— the People's Enemy. (J. A. Riis) Outl. **69**: 487.

— Plain Description of. (A. Goodrich) World's Work, **3**: 1368.

Tammany Hall, Secrets of Success of. (G. Myers) Forum, **31**: 488.

— Strength and Weakness of. (W. L. Hawley) No. Am. **173**: 481.

— Victory of, 1897. Spec. **79**: 637.

Tammany's Legal Education. (J. B. Bishop) Nation, **69**: 481.

Tamnau Mineralogical Endowment. (H. A. Miers) Nature, **63**: 453.

Tampa, Florida. (E. R. Hutchins) Midland, **11**: 245.

Tanagra Terra-cottas. (M. B. Huish) Studio (Internat.) **5**: 97. — (Thos. Sulman) Good Words, **39**: 405. — Liv. Age, **218**: 211.

Tandem Adventure in Montana. (A. R. Eggleston) Midland, **8**: 80.

Tandem Racing for High Stakes; a story. (A. R. Eggleston) Midland, **10**: 433.

Taney, Roger B., and the Maryland Catholics. (J. F. McLaughlin) Cath. World, **67**: 396.

Tanganyika, Lake, and the Countries North of it. (J. E. S. Moore) Geog. J. **17**: 1.

— Marine Fauna in. (J. E. S. Moore) Nature, **58**: 404.

Tanganyika Railway. (L. Decle) Fortn. **71**: 25.

Tangier, Morocco, as a Key to the Mediterranean. Sat. R. **84**: 332.

— as Sketching Ground. (N. Garstin) Studio (Internat.) **2**: 177.

Tangut of Marco Polo. (E. H. Parker) Asia. R. **31**: 128, 363. **32**: 156.

Tanner, Henry Ossawa, Negro Artist. (E. F. Baldwin) Outl. **64**: 793. — With portrait. (H. Cole) Brush & P. **6**: 97.

Tantalus Loving-cup. (W. G. V. T. Sutphen) Harper, **97**: 489.

Tante Fritzchen's Last Hour. (H. Hoffmann) Open Court, **14**: 22.

Tante Lotje ; a story. Blackw. **165**: 287.

Tao-Kwang, Emperor, and the Opium War. (M. M. Callery ; Yvan) Open Court, **15**: 556.

Tao Teh King, Authenticity of the. (P. Carus ; T. Suzuki) Monist, **11**: 574, 612.

Taoism. (G. G. Alexander) Asia. R. **4**: 387. — (F. M. Müller) 19th Cent. **48**: 569.

Taormina, Italy. (W. Sharp) Art J. **53**: 225.

Tapadas ; the Hidden Treasures of Peru. Chamb. J. **77**: 513.

Tapestries, Arras, at Stanmore Hall. Studio (Internat.) **6**: 98.

— of Altrand. (C. G. C. Graham) Chamb. J. **74**: 145-168.

Tapestry, American. Artist (N. Y.) **23**: xii.

— Museum of, at Florence. (A. Melani) Art J. **52**: 305.

— Royal, at Windsor. (E. M. Jessop) Pall Mall M. **22**: 436. — (F. S. Robinson) M. of Art, **22**: 89.

— Woven vs. Painted. Studio (Internat.) **6**: 1.

Tapestry-weaving, Revival of ; Interview with William Morris. (A. Vallance) Studio (Lond.) **3**: 99.

Tapir Hunt, A. (G. E. Mitchell) Outing, **33**: 558.

Tappen, Frederick D. (W. J. Boies) World's Work, **2**: 1167.

Tapper, Thomas. The Children's Music World. Music, **13**: 396.

Taps ; a poem. (L. W. Reese) Atlan. **84**: 858.

Tapu of Banderah, The. (L. Becke and W. Jeffery) Chamb. J. **76**: 417-472.

Tar and Ammonia from Blast Furnace Gases. (A. Gillespie) Cassier, **13**: 354.

Tar-baby Story, The. (A. Werner) Folk-Lore, **10**: 282.

Tarakanof's Idyll ; a story. (G. L. Calderon) Cornh. **77**: 358. Same art. Liv. Age, **217**: 182.

Tarasque, The. (A. Watson) Antiq. n. s. **37**: 234.

Tarawera, New Zealand, A Visit to. (F. C. T. Mann) Westm. **149**: 180.

Tarbell, Edmund C., Artist, with portrait. (D. M. Morrell) Brush & P. **3**: 193.

Tarbell, Ida M., with portrait. McClure, **10**: 427.

Tarde, Gabriel, Sociological Theories of. (G. Tosti) Pol. Sci. Q. **12**: 490. — (A. W. Small) Am. J. Sociol. **4**: 395.

Target Practice. (S. Pratt) J. Mil. Serv. Inst. **4**: 67. — (J. E. Brett) J. Mil. Serv. Inst. **14**: 573.

— Artillery. (S. M. Foote) J. Mil. Serv. Inst. **11**: 74.

— in Armies of Europe. (C. S. Roberts) J. Mil. Serv. Inst. **18**: 576.

— Light Artillery. (H. C. Davis) J. Mil. Serv. Inst. **18**: 102.

Targum MS. in British Museum. (H. Barnstein) Jew. Q. **11**: 167.

Targum of the Prophets, Notes on the Critique of the Text of. (W. Bacher) Jew. Q. **11**: 651.

Tariff, Act of 1897, Dingley's. (F. W. Taussig) Quar. J. Econ. **12**: 42. — Critic, **30**: 282. — (R. P. Porter) No. Am. **164**: 576. — (F. W. Taussig) Econ. J. **7**: 592.

— — Anatomy of the New Tariff. (C. A. Conant) R. of Rs. (N. Y.) **16**: 167.

— — and After. Spec. **79**: 102.

— — The Protective Features of "Section 22." (Joseph Nimmo, jr.) Forum, **24**: 159.

— — Why it Offends. (R. Ogden) Nation, **64**: 297.

— American Policy now shutting the Open Door. (W. L. Saunders) Engin. M. **21**: 15.

— and Prosperity. (G. L. Bolen) Gunton's M. **18**: 323.

— and Trusts. Gunton's M. **17**: 81. — (S. E. Payne) Internat. Mo. **4**: 742. — Nation, **72**: 427.

— — Byron W. Holt on. Gunton's M. **21**: 33.

— British Policy of Unfettered Commerce. (E. Atkinson) Engin. M. **21**: 1.

— Comparisons of, Official. (W. C. Ford) Pol. Sci. Q. **13**: 273.

— Discussion of, Need of Integrity in. Gunton's M. **12**: 223.

— German Project of. (H. White) Nation, **73**: 86.

— — Whom will it Affect? (J. Schoenhof) Forum, **32**: 105.

— Great Debate on, 1833. (C. C. Pinckney) Lippinc. **63**: 107.

— Imperial, The President's War Power and an. (P. Belmont) No. Am. **170**: 433.

— Keystone of. (H. White) Nation, **64**: 372.

— a Live Issue. (A. J. Hopkins) Forum, **28**: 531.

— Manufactures and. (E. P. Oberholtzer) Indep. **53**: 1491.

— Middle Ground on. (O. D. Ashley) Forum, **22**: 526.

— Muddle of. (H. White) Nation, **64**: 120.

— on Musical Instruments. (W. S. B. Mathews) Music, **17**: 415.

— on Paintings, American. Art J. **49**: 318.

— on Sugar, True Meaning of. (H. W. Wiley) Forum, **24**: 689.

— Our Islands and. (W. H. Johnson) Nation, **69**: 466.

— Real Cost of. (H. J. Davenport) J. Pol. Econ. **5**: 506.

— Senate Bill, April, 1897. Pub. Opin. **22**: 579, 611, 677.

Tariffs, Battle of. (W. L. Wilson) Munsey, **17**: 554.

— British, History of, Pittar's. (E. E. Williams) Sat. R. **85**: 707.

Tariff Agitation, Mania for. (G. Gunton) Gunton's M. **21**: 22.

Tariff Crutch, Falling over the. (R. Ogden) Nation, **72**: 168.

Tariff History, An Unwritten Chapter in Recent. (J. Schoenhof) Forum, **29**: 423.

Tariff Information, is it sufficiently disseminated by Her Majesty's Board of Trade? (A. Warren) Westm. **154**: 484.

Tariff Safety-valve, The. (R. Ogden) Nation, **73**: 430.

Tarkington, Booth, with portrait. Bk. News, **18**: 325.

Tarnished Flower, The; a story. (L. F. Burbank) Nat'l M. (Bost.) **6**: 136.

Tarpon, Pass Fishing for. (H. V. Warrender) 19th Cent. **42**: 317. Same art. Ecl. M. **130**: 416.

— Striking a. (J. D. Peabody) Outing, **29**: 469.

Tarpon-fishing. (W. H. Grenfell) National, **34**: 258. — (C. F. W. Mielatz) Outing, **38**: 3.

— at Aransas Pass. (N. D. S. Graham) Outing, **35**: 473.

— in Florida. (O. P. Hay) Outing, **31**: 378.

Tarragona, Spain. (A. Symons) Sat. R. **87**: 9.

Tarrytown, N. Y. (H. E. Miller) New Eng. M. n. s. **23**: 449.

Tarsius, Affinities of. (C. Earle) Am. Natural. **31**: 569, 680.

Tarsney Act. Am. Arch. **73**: 7. — (W. A. Boring) Am. Arch. **74**: 45.

— Effectiveness of. Am. Arch. **74**: 51.

Tartar who was not caught, The; a Shanghai story. (R. Wilsted) Scrib. M. **28**: 542.

Tartarin de Tarascon, The Trail of. (A. B. Maurice) Bookman, **14**: 128.

Tartary, Great, Ancient Church in. (G. Hawkes) N. Church R. **5**: 249.

Tashkend. (G. F. Wright) Nation, **71**: 441.

Tasman, Abel J., Voyages of. (E. Heawood) Geog. J. **13**: 277. — J. Soc. Arts, **45**: 127.

Tasmania, Aboriginal of, Last Living. (H. L. Roth) Anthrop. J. **27**: 451.

— A Glimpse of. (E. A. Richings) Belgra. **99**: 666.

Tasso, Torquato. Rival Poet in Shakespeare's Sonnets. (G. A. Leigh) Westm. **147**: 173.

Taste, Artistic, etc. Sat. R. **88**: 292.

— Can it be taught? Spec. **83**: 688.

— A Plea for Bad. (A. B. Miall) Acad. **57**: 188.

Tate, Sir Henry, and his Gift of the Tate Gallery. Sat. R. **84**: 110. **88**: 704. — Art J. **52**: 59. — Acad. **52**: 153, 185.

Tatham, William Penn. In Memoriam. J. Frankl. Inst. **149**: 218.

Tatian. Rearrangement of the Fourth Gospel. (B. W. Bacon) Am. J. Theol. **4**: 770.

Tattler, The. (M. Gradwohl) Overland, n. s. **37**: 840.

Tattnall, J. Blood is Thicker than Water. (J. P. Bocock) Munsey, **22**: 85.

Tattooing. (G. Bolton) Strand, **13**: 425.

— and its History. (O. Smeaton) Westm. **149**: 320. Same art. Ecl. M. **130**: 573.

Tau Ophiuchi, Orbit of. (S. W. Burnham) Pop. Astron. **4**: 347.

Tauchnitz, B., and the Tauchnitz Edition. (T. Hopkins) Pall Mall M. **25**: 197. Same art. Critic, **39**: 331.

Tavender's Last Term. (G. H. Powell) Cornh. **76**: 76.

Taverns and Tea Gardens, Old London. (C. W. Heckethorn) Gent. M. n. s. **63**: 223.

— on the Boston Road. (A. E. Herrick) New Eng. M. n. s. **16**: 88.

Tax, Franchise, Law in New York. (E. R. A. Seligman) Q. J. Econ. **13**: 445.

— of 1861 in California. (B. Moses) Q. J. Econ. **11**: 311.

— Property, A New. (G. H. Blunden) Econ. J. **7**: 607.

— Single, and the Trust. (L. F. Post; J. H. Ralston; B. Hall) Arena, **26**: 362.

— — applied to Cities. (B. W. Holt) Munic. Aff. **3**: 328.

— — as a Happy Medium. (W. A. Hawley) Arena, **26**: 292.

— — in Operation. (H. H. Lusk) Arena, **18**: 79.

— — What and why. (T. G. Shearman) Am. J. Sociol. **4**: 742.

Tax on Moustaches, The; a story. (H. J. W. Dam) Strand, **17**: 769.

Tax Commissions, State, in the United States. (J. W. Chapman) J. H. Univ. Stud. **15**: 461.

Taxation and the Philosophy of the State. (V. S. Yarros) Am. J. Sociol. **4**: 758.

— and Rate-making, Discussion on. Econ. Stud. **3**, supp. no. **1**: 80.

— and Taxes in the United States under the Internal Revenue System, Howe's. (A. C. Miller) Am. Hist. R. **2**: 743.

— Arbitrary. (D. MacG. Means) Nation, **70**: 296.

— Best Methods of. (D. A. Wells) Pop. Sci. Mo. **54**: 736. **55**: 524, 778.

— British, Royal Commission on. (J. King) Q. J. Econ. **14**: 277.

— Coöperative Benefits through. (R. Ward) Arena, **23**: 58.

— Direct, and the Federal Constitution. (C. J. Bullock) Yale R. **9**: 439. **10**: 6, 144.

— — Problem of. (G. T. Milton) Sewanee, **1**: 458.

— Distribution of Property Taxes between City and Country. (M. West) Pol. Sci. Q. **14**: 305, 470.

— Equity and Economy in. (E. Cannan) Econ. J. **11**: 469.

— Excessive, A State Official on. (F. Smith) Pop. Sci. Mo. **56**: 645.

— General Property Tax in California. (C. C. Plehn) Econ. Stud. **2**: 119.

— How We pay for the War. (T. G. Shearman) Outl. **59**: 19.

— in England, Local. Sat. R. **91**: 793.

— — Report of Commission on. (C. P. Sanger) Econ. J. **11**: 321.

— — Revolution in the Incidence of. (J. Ackland) Contemp. **79**: 738.

— — System of; is it fair? (C. P. Sanger) Econ. J. **9**: 10.

— in Germany, Local. (J. Row-Fogo) Econ. J. **11**: 354.

— in Hungary, Strike against. Spec. **80**: 8.

— in Michigan, Changes in. (H. C. Adams) Q. J. Econ. **16**: 116.

— in Ohio. (F. C. Howe) Ann. Am. Acad. Pol. Sci. **14**: 157.

— in the United Kingdom, The Incidence of. (C. P. Sanger) Yale R. **6**: 342.

— Incidence of Urban Rates. (F. Y. Edgeworth) Econ. J. **10**: 172, 340, 487.

— Inheritance Tax Decision. (W. C. Mitchell) J. Pol. Econ. **8**: 387.

— Intelligent. Gunton's M. **16**: 144.

— Its Sum, Justification, and Methods. (P. Belmont) Forum, **23**: 1.

— Land, and the General Election. (T. Burke) Forum, **29**: 523.

— — Some Inequalities in. (L. G. Powers) Am. J. Sociol. **4**: 489.

— Local, Growth of, in Scotland. (A. D. Russell) Jurid. R. **9**: 308.

— Local Option in. (L. Tuttle) Munic. Aff. **2**: 395.

— Modern. (B. J. Ramage) Sewanee, **4**: 312.

— of the Clergy. (H. H. Jebb) 19th Cent. **42**: 527.

— of College Property. (W. MacDonald) Nation, **70**: 334. — (S. Hoar) Harv. Grad. M. **6**: 499. — (D. MacG. Means) Nation, **67**: 45. — (C. F. Thwing) Educa. R. **17**: 124.

— of Franchises in Massachusetts. (J. R. Carret) Munic. Aff. **4**: 506.

— of Ground Values. (E. Sassoon) 19th Cent. **44**: 303. — (J. E. Graham) Scot. R. **35**: 105.

— of Mortgages in California. (C. C. Plehn) Yale R. **8**: 31.

Taxation of Personal Property. (L. Purdy) Munic. Aff. **3**: 299. — (H. White) Nation, **66**: 220.

— of Public Franchises. (J. Ford) No. Am. **168**: 730.

— — Ford Bill for. (J. D. Warner) Munic. Aff. **3**: 269.

— of Securities in the U. S. (F. W. Taussig) Pol. Sci. Q. **14**: 102.

— of Tea, 1767-73. (M. Farrand) Am. Hist. R. **3**: 266.

— Ohio Tax Inquisitor Law. (T. N. Carver) Econ. Stud. **3**: 167.

— Origin, Purpose, and Effect of the Direct-tax Clause of the Federal Constitution. (C. J. Bullock) Pol. Sci. Q. **15**: 217, 452.

— Place of the Service Tax in Modern Finance. (J. H. Hamilton) J. Pol. Econ. **8**: 303.

— Principles of. (D. A. Wells) Pop. Sci. Mo. **50**: 289-603. **51**: 44-765. **52**: 1-354. **53**: 64-433. **54**: 319, 490.

— Problem of, in Chicago. (E. W. Bemis) Bib. Sac. **54**: 746.

— Progressive, Legality of. (M. West) No. Am. **165**: 753.

— — Theory of. (G. Cassel) Econ. J. **11**: 481.

— Progressive Inheritance Tax. (J. A. Roberts) Forum, **23**: 257.

— Pure Theory of. (F. Y. Edgeworth) Econ. J. **7**: 46, 226, 500.

— Railroad, in Ohio. Outl. **69**: 255.

— Recent Books on. (E. R. A. Seligman) Q. J. Econ. **11**: 201.

— Reform Movement in. (M. M. Miller) Arena, **25**: 499.

— — Recent Discussion of. (E. R. A. Seligman) Pol. Sci. Q. **15**: 629.

— Reforms in. (R. T. Ely) Cosmopol. **30**: 307.

— Right Basis of. Spec. **79**: 6. Same art. Ecl. M. **129**: 634.

— Scientific Assessment and. (A. C. Smith) Arena, **23**: 485.

— Single Tax, as a Happy Medium. (W. A. Hawley) Arena, **26**: 292.

— Some Possible Reform in State and Local. (F. C. Howe) Am. Law R. **33**: 685.

— State, Studies in. (J. H. Hollander) J. H. Univ. Stud. **18**: 1.

— The Tax Inquisitor System in Ohio. (E. A. Angell) Yale R. **5**: 350.

— Theory of, with reference to Nationality, Residence, and Property. (J. Westlake) Econ. J. **9**: 365.

Taxes and Interest. (D. MacG. Means) Nation, **69**: 46.

— Direct and Indirect, in Economic Literature. (C. J. Bullock) Pol. Sci. Q. **13**: 442.

— Distribution and Incidence of Rates. (G. H. Blunden) J. Statis. Soc. **59**: 644.

— Distribution of. (E. Atkinson) Pop. Sci. Mo. **58**: 54.

— in Chicago, Assessment of. (R. H. Whitten) J. Pol. Econ. **5**: 175.

— Our New War-. (M. West) R. of Rs. (N. Y.) **18**: 48. — Gunton's M. **15**: 100.

— — Reduction of. Nation, **70**: 275.

Taxidermy as an Art. (F. Miller) Studio (Lond.) **2**: 160.

— for Sportsmen. (E. W. Sandys) Outing, **32**: 33.

"Taxil, Léo," Anti-masonic Mystifications of. (H. C. Lea) Lippinc. **66**: 948.

— A Survival of Mediæval Credulity. (E. P. Evans) Pop. Sci. Mo. **56**: 577.

Taxing Power, Abuse of the. (D. MacG. Means) Nation, **65**: 25.

Taxpayer, Justice for the. (H. Chisholm) Fortn. **67**: 399.

Tay River, Landscape of. (H. Macmillan) Art J. **51**: 151–260.

Taylor, Bayard, and Sidney Lanier. Correspondence. (H. W. Lanier) Atlan. **83**: 791. **84**: 127.

— The Haunts of. (T. Dreiser) Munsey, **18**: 594.

Taylor, Isaac, Canon. Ath. '01, **2**: 558.

Taylor, Jeremy. Acad. **57**: 185.

Taylor, John, Author of Monsieur Tonson. (A. Dobson) Longm. **31**: 246. Same art. Liv. Age, **216**: 458.

Taylor, Thomas, the Platonist. (W. E. A. Axon) Library, **2**: 245, 292.

Tazewell, Littleton Waller, with portrait. (Sallie E. M. Hardy) Green Bag, **10**: 65.

Tchaikovsky, Peter Iljitsch. Acad. **59**: 29.

Tchelkache. (M. Gorki) Fortn. **76**: 1083.

Tchelopeck Woods, The. (Ivan Vozoff) Liv. Age, **226**: 672.

Tea. (E. V. Lucas) Cornh. **75**: 72. Same art. Ecl. M. **128**: 264. Same art. Liv. Age, **212**: 345.

— Chemistry of. (D. Crole) J. Soc. Arts, **45**: 210.

Teas of the World, The. (G. C. Nuttall) Good Words, **41**: 183.

Tea-box Woods, Ceylon. (F. Lewis) J. Soc. Arts, **46**: 666.

Teacup Times. (F. M. Butler) Lippinc. **69**: 851.

Tea-drinking in Japan and China. Illus. (L. B. Starr) Chaut. **29**: 466.

— in Many Lands. Illus. (L. B. Starr) Cosmopol. **27**: 289.

Tea-gardens, American, Actual and Possible. (L. B. Ellis) R. of Rs. (N. Y.) **23**: 315.

Tea-growing, Successful, in America. (LaF. I. Parks) Cosmopol. **24**: 584.

Tea Industry in the South. (J. A. Stewart) Chaut. **29**: 529.

Tea-table in the 18th Century. Temp. Bar, **113**: 594.

Teacher, The, and his Duties. (M. P. E. Groszmann) Forum, **28**: 66.

— and Pupil, Mental Attitude of. (R. Medini) Music, **18**: 447.

— as a Moral Force ; a protest. (F. W. Osborn) Educa. R. **22**: 304.

— as Providence. (Foster Watson) Gent. M. n. s. **59**: 151.

— The Heart of a. Atlan. **84**: 716.

— High School, Sympathy in the. (B. B. Sciurus) Educa. **20**: 99.

— How can he become a Master ? (G. H. Martin) Educa. **18**: 131.

— Is he a Proletarian ? (Mrs. W. D. Cabell) Educa. **20**: 35.

— Licensing. (E. L. Cowdrick) Educa. **19**: 299.

— New England. (W. Scott) Educa. **20**: 28.

— Reforming the. (W. McAndrew) Outl. **66**: 217.

— The Trained. (E. E. Cates) School R. **7**: 24.

Teachers, Advanced Professional Training of. (J. E. Russell) Am. J. Soc. Sci. **38**: 79.

— and Social Rank. Outl. **63**: 150.

— A College for. Dial (Ch.) **25**: 249.

— The Economy in High Wages for. (J. Davidson) Educa. R. **15**: 155.

— Ethics of getting Teachers and of getting Positions. (A. S. Draper) Educa. R. **20**: 30.

— Examinations of, in Massachusetts. (E. W. Young) Educa. **22**: 240.

— Great. (T. W. Hunt) No. Am. **167**: 377.

— Hindrances to Efficient Service. (E. D. Daniels) Educa. **21**: 301.

— Influence of, Study of. (S. Bell) Pedagog. Sem. **7**: 492.

— Meditations of an Ex-school-committee Woman. (M. B. Dunn) Atlan. **86**: 36.

Teachers, Organizations of, More Business Purpose in. (W. M. Davis) School R. **5**: 40.

— Pensions for. Gunton's M. **14**: 393.

— Principals' Reports on. (F. L. Soldan) Educa. R. **20**: 252.

— Professional Spirit of. (C. B. Gilbert) Educa. **20**: 396.

— Professional Training of, in Germany, for Higher Schools. (J. E. Russell) Educa. R. **14**: 17.

— Registration of. (T. F. Willis) Dub. R. **129**: 1.

— — of Women Teachers. Blackw. **161**: 83.

— Retirement Fund for, Proposed for Boston. (Alfr. Bunker) Educa. **20**: 414.

— Societies of, in England. Citizen, **3**: 85.

— Status in some Foreign Countries. Educa. **19**: 642.

— Supply of. (H. Hodge) Fortn. **71**: 853.

— Technical, Training of. (S. H. Wells) J. Soc. Arts, **45**: 765.

— Training of. (T. J. Kirk) Overland, n. s. **33**: 442. — (F. Burk) Atlan. **80**: 547. — (W. H. Payne) Educa. R. **16**: 469.

— — Function of the University in. (M. V. O'Shea) School R. **8**: 157.

— — in France. (L. M. Salmon) Educa. R. **20**: 383.

— — Need of Special. Sat. R. **89**: 771.

— — One-sided. (N. C. Schaeffer) Forum, **32**: 456.

— Uncertainty of their Position. (E. L. Cowdrick) Educa. **18**: 338, 423.

— Why they have no Professional Standing. (J. M. Rice) Forum, **27**: 452.

Teacher's Office, Tenure of the. (E. L. Cowdrick) No. Am. **165**: 507.

Teachers' Agencies, Inquisitiveness of. Educa. **19**: 639.

Teachers' Conventions used too much for Sight-seeing. Educa. **20**: 245.

Teachers' Meetings and the Superintendent. (M. A. Tucker) Educa. **21**: 402.

Teachers' School of Science. (F. Zirngiebel) Pop. Sci. Mo. **55**: 451, 640.

Teaching as a Fine Art. (E. J. Hardy) Chamb. J. **74**: 646. — (E. E. Brown) Educa. R. **16**: 328.

— as a Profession — a Protest. (C. Shipman) Educa. R. **24**: 414.

— Decline of. (W. MacDonald) Nation, **70**: 180.

— Earnestness in. (R. G. Huling) Educa. **17**: 586.

— Economy of Time in. (J. M. Rice) Forum, **22**: 706.

— Ethics in the Profession of. (H. K. Wolfe) Educa. **19**: 455.

— Freedom of. (E. E. Brown) Educa. R. **19**: 209. — (E. W. Bemis) Indep. **51**: 2195.

— in High Schools as a Life Occupation for Men. (E. E. Hill) Forum, **29**: 437.

— Profession of. (W. A. Wilbur) Conserv. R. **4**: 331.

— — Some Aspects of. (W. H. Burnham) Forum, **25**: 481.

— Professional Improvement. (A. W. Edson) Educa. **20**: 129.

— Salmon on the Art of. Ath. '98, **2**: 711.

— Some Social Aspects of School Teaching. (M. V. O'Shea) No. Am. **166**: 378.

— Standard Type in. (R. G. Boone) Educa. **21**: 335.

— Sympathy in the School-room. (R. G. Huling) Educa. **20**: 11.

Teaching Instinct, The. (D. E. Phillips) Pedagog. Sem. **6**: 188.

Teak Forests, Burma. J. Soc. Arts, **45**: 129.

Teak Industry, Siam. Am. Arch. **72**: 78.

Teall, James Eastoe. Asia. R. **25**: 189.

Teallach, Iachach, Ancient Barony of. (J. B. McGovern) Antiq. n. s. **37**: 297, 334.

Temperance, Sensible. Outl. 65: 675.

Temperance Campaign, A; a story. (G. K. Turner) McClure, 16: 20.

Temperance Instruction in School. Educa. 21: 184.

— Scientific. (H. Sabin) Educa. 20: 531.

Temperance Legislation, Practical. (Lady Henry Somerset) Contemp. 76: 512.

— Recent. (A. Morgan) Pop. Sci. Mo. 55: 438, 610.

Temperance Problem in the Light of Christian Sociology. (W. Rupp) Ref. Ch. R. 46: 497.

— Women and. (M. E. J. Kelley) Cath. World, 69: 678.

Temperance Question, American, Study of. (A. P. Doyle) Cath. World, 66: 786.

— Present Phase of. (E. L. Hicks) Contemp. 76: 51.

— Various Views. Outl. 67: 369.

Temperance Reform, English, Failures in. (J. Dowman) Arena, 24: 118.

— Ethics of. Outl. 63: 530.

— Thirty Years of. (F. Murphy) Nat'l M. (Bost.) 10: 385.

— True. Outl. 67: 480.

— What blocks the Way? (T. C. Fry) Econ. R. 11: 153.

Temperance Reforms, Practicable. Econ. R. 10: 490.

Temperance Text-books, The; an Official Reply. Outl. 66: 996.

Temperance Workers, Salaried, in Cambridge and Gloucester, Mass. (W. H. Allen) Ann. Am. Acad. Pol. Sci. 16: 494.

Temperature, Measuring Extreme. (H. L. Callendar) Nature, 59: 494–519.

Temperature-entropy Diagram by Boulvin. (J. Perry) Nature, 60: 3.

Temperatures, High, Method of producing. Am. Arch. 70: 37.

— of Reptiles, Monotremes, and Marsupials. (A. Sutherland) Nature, 57: 66.

Tempest, Marie, Portrait of. Theatre, 38: 34.

— Portraits of. Strand, 13: 67.

Temple, Frederick, Archbp. of Canterbury. Sund. M. 28: 47.

Temple at Jerusalem, Statements of a Contemporary of the Emperor Julian on the Rebuilding of. (W. Bacher) Jew. Q. 10: 168.

— in Ezekiel. (T. G. Soares) Bib. World, 14: 93.

— in Worship. (H. C. Alleman) Luth. Q. 28: 89.

— Solomon's. (E. Schmidt) Bib. World, 14: 164.

Temple, London, Literary Associations of. Green Bag, 9: 382. Same art. Chamb. J. 74: 186.

Temple of Fate; a fable. (Grant Allen) Cosmopol. 31: 386.

Temple of Solomon, A; a story. (M. S. Briscoe) Cent. 35: 692.

Tempora Mutantur; a story. Idler, 16: 685.

Temptation, Spiritual. (W. H. Wynn) Luth. Q. 29: 301.

Temptation of Anthony, The. (G. Meyrick) Overland, n. s. 34: 244.

Temptation of Mr. Bulstrode; Study of the Subconscious Self. (J. H. Gulliver) New World, 9: 503.

Temptation of John McNairn; a story. (H. J. O'Higgins) Canad. M. 9: 283.

Temptations, Self-made, Prayer with Reference to. (A. F. Burbridge) Expos. 7: 122.

Tempting of MacAllister, The. (H. Bindloss) Good Words, 41: 691. Same art. Liv. Age, 227: 442.

Temptress, The; a story. (J. H. Rosny) Poet-Lore, 10: 26.

Ten American Painters; Exhibition, 1899. Artist (N. Y.) 25: vi.

Ten Beautiful Years; a story. (M. K. Potter) Atlan. 82: 822.

Ten Inches from the Tape; a story. (A. Ruhl) Outing, 38: 298.

Ten Shilling Tragedy, A. (J. Reid) Good Words, 37: 5 (Xmas no.). Same art. Liv. Age, 212: 371.

Tenancy Law in Northwestern India. (F. H. Brown) Westm. 156: 61.

Tenants, Dispossessed, in New York City. (F. H. McLean) Ann. Am. Acad. Pol. Sci. 11: 124.

Tendencies, Irresistible. (C. K. Adams) Atlan. 84: 289.

Tender Grace of a Day that is Dead; a poem. (A. H. Thompson) Canad. M. 9: 45.

Tenderfoot, Recollections of a. (J. R. E. Sumner) Longm. 38: 317. 39: 62.

Tenement, The, and Tuberculosis. (J. H. Pryor) Char. R. 10: 440.

Tenement Homes for American Cities. (G. A. Weber) Munic. Aff. 1: 745.

Tenement-house Commission, New York. (J. A. Riis) R. of Rs. (N. Y.) 21: 689.

— Exhibit of. (L. W. Betts) Outl. 64: 589. — (L. Veiller) Char. R. 10: 19.

Tenement-house Law, New York City. (P. C. Stuart) Am. Arch. 72: 75.

Tenement-house Legislation in New York, 1852–1900. Ann. Am. Acad. Pol. Sci. 17: 160.

Tenement-house Life and Recreation. (L. W. Betts) Outl. 61: 364.

Tenement-house Problem, The. Charities, 6: 191. — (J. A. Riis) Atlan. 83: 760. 84: 18–637.

Tenement-house Reform. New Eng. M. n. s. 22: 245.

— (L. Veiller) Ann. Am. Acad. Pol. Sci. 15: 138.

— in New York, 1834–1900. Ann. Am. Acad. Pol. Sci. 16: 164. — (S. P. Cadman) Chaut. 25: 587.

— Its Practical Results in the "Battle Row" District, New York. (F. R. Cope, jr.) Am. J. Sociol. 7: 331.

Tenement Houses. (E. L. Potter) Am. Arch. 70: 59.

— Construction of. Am. Arch. 67: 77.

— Model, Plans for. (P. Griffin and others) Munic. Aff. 3: 125.

— — Profit in. Am. Arch. 56: 46.

Teneriffe, A Day in. (M. Cholmondeley) Chaut. 33: 501.

Tennessee, History of, by Tennesseans. (J. B. Henneman) Sewanee, 4: 439.

— in Colonial Days. (G. F. Milton) Sewanee, 3: 290, 410.

— Place of, in History. (B. J. Ramage) Sewanee, 5: 171.

— State Military Pension System. (W. H. Glasson) Ann. Am. Acad. Pol. Sci. 18: 485.

Tennessee Centennial Exposition. (E. V. Seeler) Archit. R. 5: 15.

Tennessee River, Afloat on. (A. Hendricks) Lippinc. 66: 581.

Tenniel, Sir John. (R. R. Wilson) Critic, 38: 141.

— Fifty Years on "Punch," with portrait. R. of Rs. (N. Y.) 23: 31.

Tennis. (J. J. Jusserand) 19th Cent. 50: 506.

— American, New Era in. (J. P. Paret) Outing, 38: 320.

— and Racquets, American and English. (E. H. Miles) Outing, 36: 7.

— Comparison and Suggestions in. (J. P. Paret) Outing, 34: 273.

— in Continental Europe. (C. Hobart) Outing, 38: 685.

— in Great Britain. (J. P. Paret) Outing, 33: 71.

— International, 1897. (J. P. Paret) Outing, 31: 72.

— of 1898. (J. P. Paret) Outing, 33: 180.

— of 1899. (J. P. Paret) Outing, 35: 165.

— on the European Continent. (J. P. Paret) Outing, 34: 465.

Tennis, Present Status of, in England. (N. L. Jackson) Outing, 38: 187.
— Progress of. (J. P. Paret) Outing, 36: 517.
Tennis Experts, A Summer with. (J. P. Paret) Outing, 32: 483.
Tennyson, Alfred. Acad. 53: 34. — (J. E. Graham) Scot. R. 31: 23. — (A. Lang) Longm. 31: 27. Same art. Ecl. M. 129: 810. — (W. Knight) Blackw. 162: 264. Same art. Liv. Age, 214: 737. — Blackw. 162: 615. — With portrait. (F. Thompson) Acad. 51: 428. — (G. R. Parkin) Canad. M. 10: 167. — (S. Gwynn) Macmil. 77: 57. — Spec. 79: 522, 556. — (A. G. Weld) Contemp. 72: 689. Same art. Liv. Age, 215: 791. — (F. Thompson) New R. 17: 536.
— and the Birds. Sat. R. 87: 393. Same art. Ecl. M. 133: 103. Same art. Liv. Age, 221: 527.
— and Catullus. (W. P. Mustard) Nation, 66: 362.
— and his Commentators. Longm. 38: 474. Same art. Liv. Age, 231: 781.
— and his Friends at Freshwater. (V. C. S. O'Connor) Cent. 33: 240.
— and his Teachings. (J. Mudge) Meth. R. 59: 874.
— and Homer. (W. P. Mustard) Am. J. Philol. 21: 143. — (E. H. Haight) Poet-Lore, 12: 541.
— and Horace. (R. B. Richardson) Nation, 66: 438.
— and Musset, with portrait. (W. P. Trent) Bookman, 7: 108.
— and Virgil. Quar. 193: 99. — Spec. 86: 197. — (W. P. Mustard) Am. J. Philol. 20: 186.
— as acted Playwright. (H. Elliott) Theatre, 39: 223.
— as a Dramatist. Acad. 52: 134.
— as Pictured by his Son. Overland, n. s. 31: 255.
— as a Thinker. Spec. 85: 402. Same art. Liv. Age, 227: 455.
— Bibliography. (T. J. Wise) Ath. '97, 1: 417, 479, 681. 2: 388, 419.
— The Birds of. (E. Valdes) Temp. Bar, 110: 495.
— Collins's Critical Edition. (W. Archer) Critic, 37: 508.
— Crossing the Bar. (W. Clark) Canad. M. 8: 420.
— — Circumstances of its Composition. Acad. 59: 473, 497.
— Early Poems of. (W. Canton) Ecl. M. 135: 778. Same art. Liv. Age, 227: 187. — (A. E. Jack) Dial (Ch.) 30: 192.
— Faith of. (C. W. Barnes) Meth. R. 60: 582.
— Handbooks to. Lit. W. (Bost.) 31: 136.
— Idylls of the King. (Augusta Boedeker) Educa. 18: 355, 403, 476. — (T. W. Hunt) Bib. Sac. 55: 444.
— — Evolution of. (M. Luce) Acad. 53: 640.
— in the Isle of Wight. (W. H. Rideing) No. Am. 165: 701.
— in Ireland. (A. P. Graves) Cornh. 76: 594.
— In Memoriam. (H. E. Shepherd) Sewanee, 1: 402. — (T. W. Hunt) Bib. Sac. 54: 249.
— — Metre of. (C. A. Smith) Dial (Ch.) 22: 351.
— — Suggestions for Study. Poet-Lore, 13: 284.
— — The Three Christmases in. (C. W. Hodell) Poet-Lore, 11: 451. — (W. J. Rolfe) Poet-Lore, 13: 151.
— in New Aspects. (J. B. Kenyon) Meth. R. 58: 434.
— Lang's Life of. Ath. '01, 2: 551. — (F. Greenslet) Nation, 73: 443.
— Laureate of Lincolnshire. Blackw. 164: 670.
— A Letter from. Cent. 37: 956.
— Life of. (W. H. McKellar) Sewanee, 6: 94. — (H. W. Mabie) Atlan. 80: 577. — (W. Canton) Good Words, 38: 785. — (H. van Dyke) Bk. Buyer, 15: 433. — (E. Gosse) No. Am. 165: 513. — Quar. 186: 492. — Ed. R. 186: 275. — [Lond. Times] Liv. Age, 215: 295. — Critic, 31: 213, 217. — Acad. 52: 275. — Ath. '97, 2: 481, 521. — (E. Parsons) Chaut. 26: 641. — Church Q. 45: 331. — Lond. Q. 89: 206.

Tennyson, Alfred, the Man. (C. Fisher) Gent. M. n. s. 61: 265. Same art. Ecl. M. 131: 744.
— Mission of. (W. S. Lilly) Fortn. 67: 239. Same art. Ecl. M. 128: 617. Same art. Liv. Age, 213: 227.
— Monument in the Arctic Regions, named by Dr. Kane. (C. W. Shields) Cent. 34: 483.
— Mysticism in. (E. Mims) Meth. R. 61: 62.
— Ornithology of. Spec. 85: 203. Same art. Liv. Age, 226: 836.
— Poet and Man. (H. W. Mabie) Outl. 57: 577.
— Poetry of, Affectation in. (Mary M. Currier) Writer, 14: 51.
— Portrait of, by Watts. M. of Art, 20: 205.
— Ruling Passion of. Spec. 79: 207.
— Rustic Friends of, One of. (A. Whymper) Sund. M. 27: 221.
— A Study in Poetic Workmanship. (H. Spender) Fortn. 68: 778.
— The True Poet of Imperialism. Macmil. 80: 192. Same art. Ecl. M. 133: 625. Same art. Liv. Age, 222: 583.
— Withheld Poems of. Acad. 52: 326.
Tennyson, Frederick. (E. Parsons) Critic, 32: 184. — Sat. R. 85: 321. Same art. Liv. Age, 217: 468.
— and his Poetry. (W. Winthrop) Poet-Lore, 10: 258.
Tennyson, Horatio. Acad. 57: 436.
Tennysoniana, New. Acad. 57: 237.
Tennysons, The. (A. B. McGill) Bk. Buyer, 21: 30.
— First Books of. (L. S. Livingston) Bookman, 10: 123.
Tenochtitlan; its site identified. (A. H. Noll) Am. J. Archæol. 12: 515.
Tent Life in the Himalayas. (W. H. Workman) Outing, 38: 68.
Tentacoste, Domenico; a modern Italian sculptor. (Helen Zimmern) M. of Art, 23: 399.
"Tenting on the Old Camp Ground," and its Composer. (G. H. Gerould) New Eng. M. n. s. 20: 723.
Tents of a Night. (Mrs. N. Roach) Cent. 38: 129.
Tenure by Knight-service in Scotland. (G. Neilson) Jurid. R. 11: 71, 173.
— Military, before the Conquest. (J. H. Round) Eng. Hist. R. 12: 492.
-τεο, Greek Verbal in. (C. E. Bishop) Am. J. Philol. 20: 1, 121, 241.
Teonge, Henry, Diary of, 1675-79. (E. C. Godley) Longm. 34: 76.
Ter Borch, or Terburg, Gerard, Life, Works, and Bibliography, with portrait. Mast. in Art, 2: Pt. 20.
Terence, Codex Dunelmensis of. (C. Hoeing) Am. J. Archæol. 2d s. 4: 310.
Teresa, Santa, and San Juan de la Cruz: Spanish poets. (A. Symons) Contemp. 75: 542.
Termite Mounds of Australia. (W. Saville-Kent) Nature, 57: 81.
Termites, Social System of. (W. F. H. Blandford) Nature, 56: 517. See Ants, White.
Terns and the High Tide. Spec. 78: 913.
Terra Incognita; a story. (V. T. Sutphen) Harper, 103: 909.
Terra Soliata, a Phrase in the Court Rolls of Certain Norfolk Manors. (F. G. Davenport) Eng. Hist. R. 14: 507.
Terracotta Work in British Museum, Murray on. Ath. '98, 2: 166.
Terracottas, Forged. (E. Robinson) Nation, 71: 384.
Terrain, The. (C. W. Castle) J. Mil. Serv. Inst. 25: 1.
— in its Relations to Military Operations. (H. A. Reed) J. Mil. Serv. Inst. 13: 1. — (J. C. Gresham) J. Mil. Serv. Inst. 18: 113. — (J. S. Pettit) J. Mil. Serv. Inst. 13: 851.
Terrible Night, A; a story. Belgra. 97: 283.

Terrier, Airedale. (W. H. Huntington) Outing, **31**: 481.

Terriss, William. (G. B. Shaw) Sat. R. **84**: 742.

Territorial Expansion. Distant Possessions — the Parting of the Ways. (A. Carnegie) No. Am. **167**: 239.

— The Philippines; the Oriental problem. (N. P. Chipman) Overland, n. s. **35**: 23.

— Seward's Ideas of. (F. Bancroft) No. Am. **167**: 79.

Territorial Possessions, The Constitution and. (F. H. Cox) Sewanee, **8**: 317.

Territorial Problems; what the founders of the Union thought. (A. B. Hart) Harper, **100**: 311.

Territorial Sovereignty. (J. W. Stillman) Green Bag, **11**: 25.

Territories, Congressional Government of. (J. P. Buster) Am. Law R. **34**: 366.

Territory, Acquiring, by Act of Congress. (J. W. Stillman) Green Bag, **10**: 373.

— Acquisition and Government of. (H. W. Rogers) Am. J. Soc. Sci. **37**: 173.

— and District. (M. Farrand) Am. Hist. R. **5**: 676.

Terror, Red, St. Malo in Days of. Macmil. **80**: 443. Same art. Liv. Age, **223**: 710.

Terror, Reign of, Biré on. Spec. **78**: 22.

Terry, Ellen. (A. Brereton) Eng. Illust. **18**: 229.

— Art of. (Bram Stoker) Cosmopol. **31**: 241.

— in Madame Sans-Gêne. (G. B. Shaw) Sat. R. **83**: 410.

— — Portrait of. Theatre, **39**: 5.

Terry, Peter. Ath. '00, **1**: 435.

Terssen, General, of the Belgian Artillery. Un. Serv. M. **14**: 426.

Tertiary Horizons, New: Punta Arenas, Magellanes, Chili. (A. E. Ortmann) Am. J. Sci. **156**: 478.

Tesla, Nikola. (C. Barnard) Chaut. **25**: 380.

Tessellated Floor, Roman, at Leicester. (W. T. Tucker) Reliquary, **39**: 26.

Test, The; a poem. (G. N. Lovejoy) Chaut. **31**: 507.

Test, River, Fishing on. (G. A. B. Dewar) Longm. **35**: 149.

Testament of Our Lord. Church Q. **49**: 273. **50**: 1. *See also* Syriac.

Testaments of the XII. Patriarchs. (F. C. Conybeare) Jew. Q. **13**: 258.

Testators, Eccentric. Chamb. J. **77**: 539. Same art. Liv. Age, **227**: 94.

Testimonial, The; a rural comedy. (G. Burgess) Cent. **41**: 280.

Testimony and Authority. (A. F. Ravenshear) Mind, **24**: 63.

Testudinate Humerus, Some Observations on Certain Well-marked Stages in the Evolution of. (G. R. Wieland) Am. J. Sci. **159**: 413.

Tetragrammaton, The. (G. H. Skipwith) Jew. Q. **10**: 662.

— Origin of. (T. Tyler) Jew. Q. **13**: 581.

Teutonic Knights, Haunts of. (C. De Kay) Archit. R. **9**: 1.

Tewkesbury, Battle of. (H. E. Malden) Un. Serv. M. **21**: 163.

Texas, Admission of, and the Mexican War. (C. W. Hall) Nat'l M. (Bost.) **12**: 72.

— Greater. (Joaquin Miller) Overland, n. s. **37**: 999.

— Hill and Vaughan's Geology of the Edwards Plateau & Rio Grande Plain. (F. W. Simonds) Science, n. s. **9**: 481.

— Mineral Survey in. (F. W. Simonds) Science, n. s. **13**: 671.

— Oil Fields of. (A. Clark) Nat'l M. (Bost.) **14**: 381. **15**: 324.

— Out-of-doors in. (E. S. Nadal) Cent. **36**: 309.

— Past and Present. (R. T. Hill) Forum, **29**: 734.

— Sale of, to Spain. (H. S. Boutell) Forum, **31**: 530.

Texas, Two Points in the Early History of. (C. F. Lummis) Nation, **69**: 312.

— University of, State of Education at. (W. S. Sutton) Educa. R. **17**: 80.

— Wooten's History of. (W. F. McCaleb) Dial (Ch.) **29**: 122.

Texas Rangers. (E. Mayo) Idler, **20**: 387.

Text-books, Elementary, Defects of. (J. H. Blodgett) Educa. R. **21**: 64.

— for Schools, Renting. (E. J. Vert) Educa. **21**: 27.

— on the Strength of Materials. Nature, **61**: 197.

Textile Designs, by Photography. (Beaumont) Am. Arch. **70**: 6.

Textile Education, What is being done in. (J. A. Stewart) Chaut. **31**: 480.

Textile Exhibition, Recent Irish. (A. B. Maguire) M. of Art, **22**: 161.

Textile Impressions on an Early Clay Vessel. (J. L. Myres) Anthrop. J. **27**: 178.

Textile Industries, Evolution of the. (J. R. Allen) Reliquary, **37**: 165.

— of the United States. (H. G. Kittredge) Chaut. **28**: 538.

— since 1890. (H. G. Kittredge) Forum, **27**: 350.

Textile Processes, Recent Developments. (A. Hamburger) J. Frankl. Inst. **145**: 453.

Textile School at Lowell. (J. Lee) Am. J. Soc. Sci. **35**: 56.

Textile Schools, New Developments in. (J. A. Stewart) R. of Rs. (N. Y.) **22**: 67.

Textile Trade, Combination in the. Bank. M. (Lond.) **72**: 456.

Textiles, Ornamentation of. Mme. Errera's Collection at Brussels. (O. Mans) Studio (Internat.) **10**: 255.

Texts, Misapplied. (W. C. Preston) Sund. M. **27**: 35.

Texture, Pleasures of. (Oscar Eve) Cornh. **83**: 213. Same art. Ecl. M. **136**: 682. Same art. Liv. Age, **228**: 785.

Tezcatlipuca, To, an Aztec prayer; verse. (J. V. Cheney) Chaut. **31**: 519.

Tha-Anne River, Hudson Bay, A Trip on. (J. Lofthouse) Geog. J. **13**: 274.

Thackeray, William M., with portrait. Acad. **51**: 614. — Ed. R. **188**: 378. Same art. Liv. Age, **219**: 818, 883. Same art. Ecl. M. **132**: 206. — (W. C. Brownell) Scrib. M. **25**: 236. — (L. W. Payne, jr.) Sewanee, **8**: 437. — Church Q. **50**: 78.

— and the Cornhill Magazine. (Sir G. M. Smith) Critic, **38**: 154.

— and "Pendennis." (Anne T. Ritchie) Liv. Age, **217**: 768.

— as a Graphic Humorist. (Geo. Somes Layard) M. of Art, **23**: 256.

— at Charterhouse. Critic, **34**: 148.

— Biographical Edition of. Spec. **80**: 625. — (J. L. Gilder) Critic, **32**: 266.

— Contributions to Punch. (F. S. Dickson) Critic, **34**: 406-500. **35**: 600.

— First Books of. (L. S. Livingston) Bookman, **11**: 26.

— Foreigners of. Temp. Bar, **114**: 83. Same art. Liv. Age, **217**: 888.

— Glimpses of. (A. Leach) Munsey, **17**: 409.

— King Glumpus, and The Exquisites. (L. S. Livingston) Bookman, **8**: 567.

— — A Reprint of. Bookman, **8**: 342.

— Haunts and Homes of. (E. Crowe) Scrib. M. **21**: 68.

— Homes of, Crowe's. (Alice Brown) Bk. Buyer, **14**: 492.

— in the U. S. (J. G. Wilson) Cornh. **84**: 721. Same art. Cent. **41**: 221.

— in Weimar. (W. Vulpius) Cent. **31**: 920.

— The Law and Lawyers of. Green Bag, **11**: 453.

Thackeray, William M., Melville's Life of. Acad. 57: 447. — Sat. R. 80: 554.
— Memorial in Westminster Abbey. (Carolyn Shipman) Bk. Buyer, 22: 289.
— New Portrait of. Bk. Buyer, 15: 297.
— On Some Caricature Portraits of, by Pen and Pencil. Illus. (Geo. S. Layard) Good Words, 38: 702.
— One Aspect of. Temp. Bar, 124: 73.
— Pantomime of Humpty Dumpty. (B. Dobell) Ath. '00, 2: 548.
— Pessimism of. (M. Franke) Bk. Buyer, 20: 22.
— Philosophy of. Macmil. 75: 343. Same art. Liv. Age, 213: 335.
— Reputation of. Acad. 53: 463.
— Sentiment of. Quar. 191: 138. Same art. Ecl. M. 134: 619. Same art. Liv. Age, 224: 745.
— Some Aspects of. (H. D. Sedgwick, jr.) Atlan. 82: 707.
— Stray Papers. (M. H. Spielmann) Bookman, 13: 239.
— Vanity Fair and Mrs. Fiske. (J. L. Gilder) Critic, 35: 899.
— — Becky Sharp of. Bookman, 10: 239.
— Women of. (E. Manson) Gent. M. n. s. 66: 30.
— Writing of Pendennis. (J. L. Gilder) Critic, 32: 363.
Thackerays, The, in India. Liv. Age, 212: 699.
Thais. (K. M. C. Meredith) Harper, 104: 133.
Thakur Pertáb Singh ; a tale of an Indian famine. (C. H. T. Crosthwaite) Blackw. 162: 28. Same art. Liv. Age, 214: 445-529.
Thalatta. (Blanche W. Howard) Scrib. M. 22: 206.
Thallium, as the Acid and Neutral Sulphates, On the Estimation of. (P. E. Browning) Am. J. Sci. 159: 137.
— Estimation of, as the Chromate. (P. E. Browning and G. P. Hutchins) Am. J. Sci. 158: 460.
Thames River above Oxford. (E. C. Cook) Pall Mall M. 18: 507.
— and its Commerce. (A. M. Young) Idler, 13: 219, 349.
— from London to Windsor. Idler, 19: 560.
— as a National Trust. Spec. 82: 411.
— as a Salmon River. (R. B. Marston) 19th Cent. 45: 579.
— from Wapping to Blackwall. (W. Besant) Cent. 38: 746.
— in London. Sat. R. 87: 360.
— Shores of, by Night. (C. W. Wood) Argosy, 65: 434, 567.
— Steamboat Service. (A. F. Hills) J. Soc. Arts, 49: 454.
Thames Tunnel. (J. M. Bulloch) Eng. Illust. 16: 440.
Thane of Cawdor, Castle of the. (E. P. Cunningham) Cosmopol. 24: 16.
Thanet, The Isle ; a quaint corner of England. (H. W. Lucy) Chamb. J. 78: 465.
Thanksgiving on Herring Hill ; a story. (J. M. Tenney) Chaut. 26: 193.
Thanksgiving Shooting Trip, A. (W. R. Armstrong) Outing, 33: 121.
Thanlow, Fritz, Artist, with portrait. (G. Mourey) Studio (Internat.) 2: 3.
That! a story of South Devon. (E. M. Whishaw) Longm. 38: 36. Same art. Liv. Age, 229: 636.
That and This ; a story. (George Gamble) Eng. Illust. 22: 185.
That Amazing Middy. Temp. Bar, 119: 106.
That Awkward Boy. Macmil. 75: 365. Same art. Liv. Age, 213: 242.
That Figure-head. (A. H. Roe) Temp. Bar, 124: 517.

That Great Debt. (E. Stuart-Langford) Sund. M. 29: 399.
That Impossible She ; a story. (L. L. Lang) Temp. Bar, 110: 422.
That is quite Another Thing ; a poem. (S. Maber) Canad. M. 12: 75.
That Newspaper Man ; a story. Belgra. 94: 226.
That Russian Princess ; a story. (P. A. Nix) Eng. Illust. 20: 134.
That Terrible Quidnunc ; a cricket story. (A. Cochrane) Cornh. 80: 76. Same art. Liv. Age, 222: 573.
"That will be ere Set of Sun ; " a story. (E. de Balzac) Idler, 17: 13.
Thaxter, Celia. (J. Albee) New Eng. M. n. s. 24: 166.
— Home of. Lit. W. (Bost.) 30: 265.
Thayer, Abbott H. American Painter. (Mrs. A. Bell) Studio (Internat.) 6: 247.
Thayer, Alexander Wheelock. (J. S. Shedlock) Acad. 52: 117. — Ath. '97, 2: 170.
Theatre, American Invasion of the London. (E. R. Pennell) Nation, 69: 388.
— Ancient, at Orange. (Gaston Boissier) Liv. Age, 222: 498-564.
— and the Critics. (J. R. Towse) Nation, 73: 106.
— and Public Morals, The. (J. R. Towse) Nation, 68: 104.
— Applause in, Undue. (G. B. Shaw) Sat. R. 83: 243.
— Business of a. (W. J. Henderson) Scrib. M. 25: 297.
— Censorship of Plays in France. (M. Daumart) Gent. M. n. s. 67: 593.
— Christian ; Is it possible ? (C. M. Sheldon) Indep. 53: 616.
— Electricity in. (G. H. Guy) Chaut. 26: 287.
— Elevation of the. Outl. 68: 432.
— Endowed. (R. Stodart) Indep. 52: 2629. — Dial (Ch.) 26: 295.
— — Difficulties in the Way. (G. B. Shaw) Sat. R. 85: 204.
— Folk-. (Brander Matthews) Cosmopol. 30: 535.
— Humors of. (R. M. Sillard) Cornh. 77: 818. Same art. Ecl. M. 131: 372.
— in England, Position of. (F. Wedmore) 19th Cent. 44: 224.
— in its Relation to the State. (H. Irving) Fortn. 70: 88. Same art. Liv. Age, 218: 283.
— in Japan. Acad. 60: 181.
— Limits of. (John La Farge) Scrib. M. 25: 509.
— Moral Tendency of. (G. B. Shaw) Sat. R. 84: 741.
— My Art. (Adelaide Ristori) Macmil. 83: 182.
— National. (F. R. Benson) 19th Cent. 49: 772.
— — Appeal to the London County Council. (J. Coleman) 19th Cent. 50: 991.
— — Towards a. (H. H. Fyfe) Fortn. 75: 912.
— Need of Morning Performances of Plays. (Max Beerbohm) Sat. R. 92: 428.
— of London, 1896. Theatre, 38: 1.
— People's. (M. Pottecher) Indep. 52: 585.
— — in Berlin. (E. Sellers) Contemp. 77: 870.
— — Luxury and. Liv. Age, 215: 320.
— Public Morality and. (J. R. Towse) Nation, 72: 468.
— Puritanism and. (W. Archer) Critic, 37: 57.
— Recent English. (G. B. Shaw) Sat. R. 83: 632.
— Should Sacred Subjects be banished ? (M. Beerbohm) Sat. R. 92: 647.
— Staging of Plays, 300 Years ago. (E. R. Buckley) Gent. M. n. s. 67: 288.
— Subsidized. (J. F. Nisbet) Theatre, 38: 313. — (Sir E. Russell) Theatre, 39: 10.
— Upbuilding of. (N. Hapgood) Atlan. 83: 419.
— Victorian Stage. Quar. 197: 75. Same art. Liv. Age, 228: 665. Same art. Ecl. M. 136: 561.

Theatre Hat, St. Paul and the. (W. Weber) Open Court, **13**: 247.

Théâtre Français. (W. H. Pollock) Sat. R. **89**: 325.

— The House of Molière. (W. E. G. Fisher) Fortn. **73**: 557.

Theatre Programs, French Illustrated. (G. Mourey) Studio (Internat.) **1**: 236.

Theatres, At the New York, Nov., 1898. (J. G. Speed) Forum, **26**: 748.

— Bowery; How the Other Half laughs. (J. Corbin) Harper, **98**: 30.

— Organized Disturbance in. (A. W. à Beckett) Theatre, **38**: 74.

— Safety of, from Fire. (W. P. Gerhard) Am. Arch. **66**: 19, 27.

— Sanitation of, Needed Improvements in. (W. P. Gerhard) Pop. Sci. Mo. **56**: 84.

Theatrical Advance Agent. (Kirke La Shelle) Cosmopol. **28**: 325.

Theatrical Commercialism. Dial (Ch.) **28**: 5.

Theatrical Criticism. Midland, **11**: 489. — (R. M. Sillard) Westm. **150**: 634.

Theatrical Make-up, Art of. (Edith Davids) Cosmopol. **31**: 348.

Theatrical Prices. (E. Kuhe) Theatre, **38**: 155.

Theatrical Public, What is the? (W. D. Adams) Theatre, **38**: 198.

Theatrical Record, London, for 1896. Theatre, **38**: 1.

Theatrical Riots, Some Famous. (N. Williams) Argosy, **72**: 224.

Theatrical Syndicate. (N. Hapgood) Internat. Mo. **1**: 99.

Theatrical Touring, Should it be abolished? (L. Wagner) Theatre, **39**: 130.

Thebes; her Ruins and her Memories. (D. Hunter) Cosmopol. **30**: 3.

— Papyrus of Nesi-Amsu, Scribe in Temple of Amen-Rāat, B. C. 305. Archæol. **52**: 393.

Theed, William. Art J. **51**: 40.

Θειότης — Θεότης, Rom. i. 20; Col. ii. 9. (H. S. Nash) J. Bib. Lit. **18**: 1.

Their Destinies; a story. (H. C. Acheson) Pall Mall M. **18**: 412.

Their First Experience; a story. (M. Van Vorst) Pall Mall M. **22**: 314.

Their Golden Wedding; a story. (E. Rod) Acad. **57**: 208.

Their Great Crisis. (N. Stephenson) Lippinc. **62**: 128.

Their Last Trek, a Tale of the Veld. (H. A. Bryden) Lippinc. **65**: 615.

Their Prison House; a story. (Phillips Oppenheim) Eng. Illust. **21**: 158.

Their Second Marriage; a story. (M. S. Cutting) McClure, **14**: 183.

Their Secondary Christmas. (H. M. Hoke) New Eng. M. n. s. **21**: 412.

Their Silver Wedding Journey; a novel. (W. D. Howells) Harper, **98**: 193-922. **99**: 101-926.

Their Wedding Day. (A. M. Cameron) Good Words, **38**: 345. Same art. Liv. Age, **214**: 273.

Theism and Knowledge, Theory of. (G. A. Coe) Meth. R. **58**: 68.

— English, in 19th Century. (B. L. Hobson) Presb. & Ref. R. **12**: 509.

— Iverach on. (A. Macalister) Crit. R. **10**: 229.

— A New Form of. (J. E. Russell) New World, **7**: 289.

— Philosophy of, Fraser on. (J. Seth) Philos. R. **6**: 176. — (G. S. Patton) Presb. & Ref. R. **8**: 297, 770. — Ath. '97, **1**: 408. — Church Q. **43**: 419.

— — and Recent Gifford Lectures. (J. Seth) New World, **9**: 401.

— Psychological Evidence for. (G. M. Stratton) New World, **8**: 326.

Theism, Some Implicates of. (J. M. Whiton) Am. J. Theol. **5**: 316.

— Venture of. Quar. **187**: 61.

Theistic Speculations, New. Lond. Q. **87**: 270.

Themes, Daily, Literary Use of. (E. B. Brown) Educa. R. **16**: 86.

Then and Now; 1798-1898. Chamb. J. **75**: 693.

Theocracy, Roman. Spec. **86**: 689.

Theocritus. (H. W. Mabie) Outl. **55**: 458. — Acad. **60**: 182. — (J. W. Mackail) Macmil. **78**: 108.

Theodore of Canterbury. (B. W. Wells) Sewanee, **1**: 26.

Theodosian Code, The. Green Bag, **10**: 309.

Theological Changes of View in England. (F. W. Farrar) Outl. **66**: 64.

Theological Colleges. (J. O. Johnston) Contemp. **76**: 405.

Theological Curriculum, Modifications in the. (G. Harris and others) Am. J. Theol. **3**: 324.

— Shall it be Modified, and how? (W. R. Harper) Am. J. Theol. **3**: 45.

Theological Education for the Times. (G. B. Foster) Bib. World, **9**: 23.

— Question of. Ref. Ch. R. **47**: 248.

— Reconstruction in. (W. F. Slocum) Forum, **28**: 571.

— Reform in. (W. DeW. Hyde) Atlan. **85**: 16.

— Some Present-day Conditions affecting. (G. B. Stevens) New World, **9**: 674.

Theological Encyclopædia, Kuyper's. (H. C. Minton) Presb. & Ref. R. **10**: 677.

Theological Phraseology, Specious. (D. H. Bauslin) Luth. Q. **28**: 42.

Theological Professor Instructed. (J. C. Bowman) Ref. Ch. R. **47**: 153.

Theological Seminaries. Outl. **63**: 436.

— and their Critics. (T. F. Day) Presb. & Ref. R. **11**: 298.

— A Criticism on. Outl. **63**: 732.

— Ideals of, and the Needs of the Churches. (F. C. Porter) New World, **9**: 25.

— Place of Social Science in. (W. Rupp) Ref. Ch. R. **48**: 558.

— Preparation for. (W. B. Greene, jr.) Presb. & Ref. R. **11**: 66.

— Presidency of. (J. K. McLean) Bib. Sac. **58**: 314.

— Security of their Trust Funds. Ref. Q. **44**: 252.

Theological Students, Decrease in the Number of. Bib. World, **17**: 243.

Theological Terms Misapplied. (P. McA. Cole) Writer, **11**: 129.

Theological Thought of To-day, Hopeful Tendencies in. Bib. World, **17**: 323.

— Phases of. (J. Rickaby) Month, **93**: 364.

— Present Trend of. (J. I. Swander) Ref. Q. **44**: 157.

— Recent Tendencies in. (A. B. Strong) Am. J. Theol. **1**: 137.

Theological Views of a Layman. (E. A. Jenks) Arena, **25**: 113.

Theology and Devotion, Relation of. (G. Tyrrell) Month, **94**: 461.

— and Idealism, F. d'Arcy on. (H. C. Minton) Presb. & Ref. R. **11**: 512.

— and the Inductive Method. (W. F. Anderson) Outl. **64**: 453.

— and Modern Thought. (W. H. Kent) Dub. R. **127**: 353.

— and Science, Some Parallels between. (E. Noble) Open Court, **12**: 207.

— Apologetic, Ballard's. (W. B. Greene, jr.) Presb. & Ref. R. **12**: 692.

— Bavinck's Dogmatic. (G. Vos) Presb. & Ref. R. **10**: 694.

— Biblical. (F. A. Gast) Ref. Ch. R. **45**: 236.

Theology, Christian, of the Future. (A. S. Weber) Ref. Ch. R. 48: 526.
— Comparative Method in. (N. Schmidt) Indep. 53: 191.
— Conservative Progress, the Law of History. (J. I. Swander) Ref. Ch. R. 46: 39, 190.
— Contemporary. (J. Lindsay) Bib. Sac. 58: 419.
— Dogmatic, and Civilization. (W. Alexander) Presb. & Ref. R. 8: 35.
— — Harnack's History of. Presb. & Ref. R. 11: 185.
— — Inaugural Address. (J. Denny) Expos. 2: 502.
— Essential Dogmatic Differences between the Liberal and Positive Schools of. (G. U. Wenner) Luth. Q. 37: 50.
— Evangelical Revival in its Relations to. (G. R. Crooks) Meth. R. 57: 177.
— Evolution of; Caird's Gifford Lectures. (J. Sandison) Open Court, 15: 176.
— in Terms of Personal Relation. (H. C. King) Bib. Sac. 57: 723.
— Influence of Modern Science upon. (J. Y. Simpson) Expos. 8: 162.
— Modern; the Dead Hand in the Church. (C. Lathbury) Arena, 18: 535.
— — in its relation to Personal Piety and Christian Work. (H. M. Scott) Bib. Sac. 57: 1.
— Natural, Fiske on. (H. C. Minton) Presb. & Ref. R. 11: 149.
— — Wallace on. (A. B. Bruce) Crit. R. 9: 137.
— New. (J. A. Biddle) Bib. Sac. 54: 96.
— — Characteristics of. (E. H. Dewart) Bib. Sac. 58: 632.
— — Cross of Christ in. (W. DeW. Hyde) Outl. 64: 678.
— — Need of a. (L. Abbott) Am. J. Theol. 1: 460.
— Non-resident School of. (J. H. Vincent) Meth. R. 57: 195.
— of an Evolutionist. (L. Abbott) Outl. 55: 46–978.
— Outlook in. (E. L. Curtis) Bib. Sac. 56: 1.
— Present Status of, in U. S., 1898. (A. E. Truxal) Ref. Ch. R. 45: 13.
— Reconstruction in. (H. C. King) Am. J. Theol. 3: 295. — (D. N. Beach) Bib. Sac. 54: 108.
— — Warfield on. Ref. Ch. R. 45: 261.
— Schmid's Dogmatic. (S. G. Hefelbower) Luth. Q. 30: 243.
— Science in. (C. H. Cornill) Open Court, 11: 35.
— Scientific Method in. (F. S. Hoffman) No. Am. 170: 575.
— Scope of, and its Place in the University. (C. A. Briggs) Am. J. Theol. 1: 38.
— Systematic, Beet's. (T. G. Darling) Presb. & Ref. R. 8: 584.
— Vital, and its Cognates. (C. W. Jacobs) Meth. R. 79: 937.
Theophanes, Chronology of, in the 8th Century. (T. Hodgkin) Eng. Hist. R. 13: 283.
Theophilanthropy, The Centenary of. (M. D. Conway) Open Court, 11: 65.
Theory and Practice. (T. C. Allbutt) Nature, 56: 332. — Dial (Ch.) 28: 425. — (J. B. Baillie) Int. J. Ethics, 8: 291.
Theosophy and Ethics. (E. T. Hargrove) No. Am. 165: 213.
— and Spiritualism. (T. F. Wright) N. Church R. 4: 435.
— and Theosophists. (H. S. Olcott) Overland, n. s. 37: 992.
— as a Philosophy. (S. D. Hillman) Meth. R. 60: 592.
— in America. (J. E. Bennett) Nat'l M. (Bost.) 6: 403.
— its Leaders and its Leadings. (A. A. McGinley) Cath. World, 66: 34.

Theosophy, New and Old. (W. Hopkins) Indep. 52: 1552.
— Romances of. (A. H. Tuttle) Meth. R. 59: 20.
— vs. New-church Teachings. (W. H. Hinkley) N. Church R. 6: 261.
Theotocopuli, Domenico. (A. Symons) Monthly R. 2, no. 3: 144.
There and Here; a story. (A. Brown) Harper, 95: 791.
There shall be no Misunderstanding; a story. (Hildegarde Hawthorne) Harper, 102: 768.
There was once a Woman. (M. S. Cutting) Atlan. 86: 705.
There's Many a Slip; a story. (A. B. Romney) Temp. Bar, 114: 429. Same art. Liv. Age, 218: 447.
Thermo-electric and Galvanic Actions compared. (C. J. Reed) J. Frankl. Inst. 146: 424.
Thermodynamic Function, Graphics of. (W. Fox) J. Frankl. Inst. 145: 214.
Thermodynamic Relations for Steam. (G. P. Starkweather) Am. J. Sci. 157: 129.
Thermodynamics, Applications of, to Chemistry, Duhem on. (G. H. Bryan) Nature, 61: 72.
— Graphics and Geometry of. (R. H. Thurston) J. Frankl. Inst. 151: 62, 124.
— Modern, Buckingham on. Nature, 63: 269.
Thermometer, Evolution of the. (H. C. Bolton) Science, n. s. 13: 146.
Thermometer Glass at Higher Temperatures. (W. McClellan) J. Frankl. Inst. 152: 63.
Thermometers, First. (P. Duhern) Pop. Sci. Mo. 52: 688.
Thermometry, Recent Work in. (C. Cree) Nature, 58: 304.
Thermopylæ, The Beaten Army at. (H. Martin) Un. Serv. M. 15: 576.
Thermostat, Electrical. (W. Duane and C. A. Lory) Am. J. Sci. 159: 179.
Theses, American, Annual List of. (W. W. Bishop) Lib. J. 26: supp. 50.
Thessaly, The Fate of. Spec. 78: 756.
— in 1898. (T. W. Legh) Pall Mall M. 15: 276.
— Journey in. (T. D. Goodell) Cent. 32: 493.
— War of 1897. (C. Williams) Fortn. 67: 959. Same art. Liv. Age, 214: 91.
— — Bigham on. Spec. 79: 184.
— — The Sultan's Success. Spec. 79: 36.
— — What happened in. (G. W. Steevens) Blackw. 162: 146.
  See Greece.
They bore a Hand; a story. (F. Remington) Harper, 100: 705.
"They that walk in Darkness;" a story. (I. Zangwill) Pall Mall M. 16: 437.
They who go down to the Sea. (T. M. Maltby) New Eng. M. n. s. 24: 561.
Thiard, General. (A. Laugel) Nation, 72: 272.
Thibet. See Tibet.
Thicker than Water; a story. (M. Chater) Harper, 102: 555.
Thicker than Water; a story. (W. N. Harben) Bk. News, 16: 99.
Thiers, Pres. Louis Adolph. (D. C. Munro) Chaut. 25: 239.
Thiersch, Carl; Memorial Address. (W. His) Pop. Sci. Mo. 52: 338.
Thimbles, History and Description of. (Mrs. D. B. Williamson) Midland, 8: 506.
"Thin-skun;" a story. (M. L. Pendered) Idler, 14: 589.
Thing, What constitutes a. (Hiram M. Stanley) Philos. R. 9: 411.
Thing Apart, A. (G. Hibbard) Cent. 37: 512.

Thinges Nedefull for this Present State, 1562. (J. Mountgomery) Archæol. **47**: 209.

Things surely Believed, The; a sermon. (L. Abbott) Outl. **64**: 728.

Thinker, Evolution of a. (G. A. Gordon) Chaut. **26**: 373.

Third, The. (K. S. Macquoid) Eng. Illust. **16**: 607.

Third Ovanoff, The; a story. (E. G. Henham) Eng. Illust. **21**: 71.

Third Wife, a Mormon Episode. (Mrs. J. K. Hudson) Lippinc. **65**: 95.

Third-rail Conductors for Electric Railways. (L. Daft) Cassier, **17**: 235.

Thirst; an incident of southwestern Texas. (A. B. Paine) Lippinc. **64**: 418.

Thirst in the Desert. (W. J. McGee) Atlan. **81**: 483.

Thirteenth Anniversary. (H. Hutchinson) Longm. **31**: 347. Same art. Ecl. M. **130**: 637.

" This Animal of a Buldy Jones ; " a story. (F. Norris) McClure, **12**: 438.

This World a Dream. (P. W. Roose) Argosy, **64**: 619.

Thoma, Hans, Painter. (Helen Zimmern) Art J. **50**: 233. — (H. W. Singer) Studio (Internat.) **1**: 79.

Thomas Aquinas, St., The Triumph of. (M.-M. Snell) Dub. R. **125**: 33.

Thomas, Augustus. (E. A. Dithmar) Bk. Buyer, **16**: 323.

Thomas, Edith M., on Staten Island. (S. R. Elliott) Critic, **32**: 395.

Thomas, Ernest Chester. Library, **4**: 73.

Thomas, Henry Wilton. Writer, **14**: 90.

Thomas, Isaiah, an American Publisher a Hundred Years ago. (L. S. Livingston) Bookman, **11**: 530. — (F. R. Batchelder) New Eng. M. n. s. **25**: 284.

Thomas, Serjeant Ralph, and J. E. Millais. (R. Thomas) Ath. '00, **1**: 184.

Thomas, Reuen. The Kinship of Souls. N. Church R. **6**: 631.

Thomas, Theodore, with portrait. Music, **20**: 96, 167. — his First Pacific Coast Tour. (W. S. B. Mathews) Music, **19**: 153.

Thomas, Wm. Luson. J. Soc. Arts, **48**: 864.

Thompson, Ernest Seton, Portrait of. Bk. Buyer, **18**: 4.

Thompson, Francis, New Poems. (G. White) Sewanee, **6**: 39. — Poetry of. (E. G. Gardner) Month, **91**: 131. — Acad. **51**: 537, 598.

Thompson, George. (J. C. Hadden) Scot. R. **30**: 117.

Thompson, J. Stuart. (D. T. McLaren) Canad. M. **14**: 360.

Thompson, Leonard, Sketch of the Life of. (W. R. Cutter) N. E. Reg. **53**: 385.

Thompson, Maurice. Alice of Old Vincennes. (J. L. Gilder) Critic, **37**: 406. — at Home, with portrait. (M. K. Krout) Indep. **53**: 416.

Thompson, Richard Wigginton; " Grand Old Man " of Indiana. (O. S. Borne) Nat'l M. (Bost.) **12**: 33. — With portrait. (C. G. Bowers) Green Bag, **12**: 269.

Thompson, William James. Bank. M. (Lond.) **66**: 743.

Thompson's Island, Farm School at. (M. B. Thrasher) New Eng. M. n. s. **22**: 193.

Thomson, Elihu. Cassier, **19**: 319.

Thomson, Geo., Friend of Burns. (G. H. Ely) Macmil. **78**: 62. — Hadden's Life of. Acad. **53**: 227.

Thomson, Harry, Artist in Stained Glass. (G. White) Studio (Internat.) **4**: 12.

Thomson, Hugh. Acad. **52**: 57.

Thomson, James, 1700-48. (G. Douglas) Bookman, **12**: 151. — Poetry of. Acad. **51**: 417, (H. Chisholm) 458. — (J. C. Collins) Sat. R. **84**: 117. — Seasons. Was it corrected by Pope? (Léon Morel) Sat. R. **86**: 507.

Thomson, James (B. V.). Acad. **55**: 383.

Thomson, Joseph, African Explorer, Biography of. Sat. R. **83**: 126.

Thomson, Leslie, as an Artist. (R. A. M. Stevenson) Art J. **50**: 53.

Thomson, Sir William, Lord Kelvin, with portrait. (H. C. Marillier) Pall Mall M. **25**: 237.

Thomson, William, Artist, Sketches by. Studio (Internat.) **7**: 101.

Thoreau, Henry D. (F. M. Smith) Critic, **37**: 60. — and Emerson. (F. B. Sanborn) Forum, **23**: 218. — and J. A. Froude. (H. S. Salt) Acad. **56**: 305. — and Walden Pond. (P. G. Hubert, jr.) Bk. Buyer, **14**: 549. — as a Humorist. (G. Beardsley) Dial (Ch.) **28**: 241. — Attitude toward Nature. (B. Torrey) Atlan. **84**: 706. — First Books of. (L. S. Livingston) Bookman, **8**: 40. — A Hermit's Notes on. (P. E. More) Atlan. **87**: 857.

Thoresby, Ralph, Library of. Library, **1**: 185.

Thorn of the Crown of Thorns, Identity of. (A. E. P. R. Dowling) Am. Cath. Q. **23**: 510.

Thorne, Sir Richard Thorne. Nature, **61**: 183.

Thornycroft, Hamo. Monument to William Owen Stanley of Penrhos. Art J **50**: 60.

Thoroughbred, A. (A. E. P. Searing) New Eng. M. n. s. **17**: 287.

" Thou shalt not make to thyself any Graven Image ; " a story. (Emmie A. Keddell) Idler, **12**: 470.

Thought and Imagery. (J. R. Angell) Philos. R. **6**: 646. — European, in the 19th Century, J. T. Merz on. (A. Macalister) Crit. R. **7**: 142. — Hegelian Conception of. (A. K. Rogers) Philos. R. **9**: 152. — Stages of Logical. (J. Dewey Philos. R. **9**: 465. — Stirling on. (E. H. Blakeney) Crit. R. **10**: 502.

Thought of the Little Brother ; a poem. (A. H. Branch) Atlan. **86**: 518.

Thoughts of Clara Goodall ; a soliloquy. (E. F. Maitland) Cornh. **76**: 634. — Origin of. (J. B. Keene) N. Church R. **5**: 382.

Thousand and Second Knight, The ; a story. (L. Cleveland) Arena, **21**: 60.

Thousand Islands, International Park of. (L. Hubbard, jr.) Outing, **38**: 711.

Three against One ; a story. (P. Hudson) Idler, **18**: 308.

Three Bad Hats and a Cocked One. (W. P. Drury) Un. Serv. M. **14**: 409.

Three Blind Mice ; a story. (D. Dale) Argosy, **64**: 74.

Three Chokeydars, The ; a story. (H. A. V.) Temp. Bar, **110**: 35.

Three Churches in Paris ; a poem. (C. Sheldon) Chaut. **31**: 592.

Three-cornered Election, A ; a story. (A. M. Barnes) Green Bag, **11**: 385.

Three Corporals ; a story. (Mrs. Henniker) Idler, **15**: 4.

Three Diggers ; a poem. (A. L. Cole) Critic, **36**: 265.

Three Expert Cyclists ; a tale. (R. Barr) Canad. M. **13**: 64.

Three Flights of a Thrush ; a story. (M. Van Vorst) Harper, **100**: 621.

" Three Friends " Case, The. (A. G. Sedgwick) Nation, **64**: 176.

Three Heron's Feathers ; a drama. (H. Sudermann) Poet-Lore, **12**: 161.

Tiger-hunting in India. (F. Scheibler) Chaut. 29: 50.

Tiger-lily, A; a story. (J. Coniston) Temp. Bar, 122: 239.

Tiger-shoot in India, A. Outing, 32: 1.

Tiger Shooting in the Deccan. (R. G. Burton) Westm. 147: 164. Same art. Ecl. M. 128: 643.

Tiger Stories, Some Real. (A. S. Ghosh) Cornh. 77: 174.

Tiger-Tail [Island], Three Dynasties on. (L. B. Ellis) Outing, 37: 697.

Tigers Fighting. (A. H. Waddle) Outing, 36: 273.

— Photographs of. (G. Bolton) Idler, 14: 315.

Tigress, An Adventure with a. (C. E. Ashburner) Outing, 29: 565.

Tigris-Mesopotamian Railway and India. (H. Rassam) Asia. R. 24: 11.

Tijou, Jean. New Book of Drawings. (J. H. Slater) Ath. '00, 2: 585.

Tilak, Bal G., Case of. (A. Webb) Nation, 65: 433.

Tilden, Douglas, Sculptor. (W. D. Armes) Overland, n. s. 31: 142.

Tilden Commission, Report of the. Munic. Aff. 3: 434.

Tiles. (J. Walker) Am. Arch. 55: 6.

Tilford Oak. Spec. 80: 16.

Tillamook Indians, Traditions of. (Franz Boas) J. Am. Folk-Lore, 11: 23.

Tillo, Gen. A. A. Geog. J. 15: 185. — Natur 51: 396.

Tilsit, A British Agent at. (J. H. Ross) Eng. Hist. R. 16: 712.

Tim Mahan's Torpedo; a story of the Cuban War. (W. Packard) Nat'l M. (Bost.) 10: 400.

Timber, Preserving and Fire-proofing. (S. Cowper-Coles) Am. Arch. 64: 78.

Timber Famine, is it Imminent? (H. Gannett) Forum, 30: 147.

Timber Supply, The Outlook of the World's. (W. Schlich) J. Soc. Arts, 49: 249.

Timber Tests, Government. (Alfred Stone) Am. Arch. 58: 82.

Timber Wealth of Pacific North America. (F. H. Lamb) Engin. M. 16: 441.

Timbuctoo. Lond. Q. 88: 1.

Time, and Space. (H. Seal) Westm. 152: 675.

— — Doctrine of. (G. S. Fullerton) Philos. R. 375, 488, 583.

— as a Datum of History. (A. H. Lloyd) Philos. R. 8: 40.

— as related to Causality and to Space. (M. W. Calkins) Mind, 24: 216.

— Civil. (John Milne) Geog. J. 13: 173.

— Existence of Past and Future. (B. Bosanquet; S. H. Hodgson; G. E. Moore) Mind, 22: 228.

— Kant's Conception of the Leibnitz Space and Time Doctrine. (M. W. Calkins) Philos. R. 6: 356.

— Loss of. (H. M. E. Coleridge) Monthly R. 1, no. 1: 165.

— Position in. (B. Russell) Mind, 26: 293.

— Rhythms and Geologic Time. (G. K. Gilbert) Pop. Sci. Mo. 57: 339.

— Standard, How obtained. (T. B. Willson) Pop. Sci. Mo. 51: 213.

Time Element in Political Campaigns. (L. G. McConachie) Am. J. Sociol. 5: 51.

Time-gauge in Letters. (S. R. Elliott) Dial (Ch.) 25: 123.

Time-marking System in Music. (T. C. Whitmer) Music, 18: 164. 19: 121.

Time Perception. (H. M. Stanley) Psychol. R. 7: 284.

Time Values of Provincial Carboniferous Terranes. (C. R. Keyes) Am. J. Sci. 162: 305.

Timgad, Excavations at. Am. Arch. 55: 101.

Timoleague, Abbey of. (H. Elrington) Reliquary, 39: 88.

Timrod, Henry. (P. Bruns) Conserv. R. 1: 263. — (H. Austin) Indep. 51: 1084. — (J. A. B. Scherer) Luth. Q. 29: 415. — With portrait. (H. Austin) Bookman, 9: 341. — (S. Axson) Chaut. 30: 573. — (L. F. Tooker) Cent. 33: 932.

— New Edition of. (C. H. Ross) Sewanee, 7: 414.

— Poetry of. (R. A. Bowen) Bk. Buyer, 22: 385.

— Southern Poet. Outl. 68: 107.

Tin. Products found at the Trethellan Tin Works, Truro, Cornwall. (W. P. Headden) Am. J. Sci. 155: 93.

Tin Deposits at Temescal, Southern California. (H. W. Fairbanks) Am. J. Sci. 154: 39.

Tin Mines in Singkep. (M. L. Todd) Nation, 72: 508.

Tin-peddler's Cart. (H. M. North) New Eng. M. n. s. 20: 711.

Tin Plate Combination. (F. L. McVey) Yale R. 8: 156. — Gunton's M. 16: 329.

Tin Plate Industry in the U. S. (I. Ayer) J. Frankl. Inst. 143: 424. — (F. L. McVey) Yale R. 7: 302.

— N. Y. Evening Post against. Gunton's M. 14: 12.

Tin-smelting, Chinese. (E. H. Parker) Chamb. J. 75: 343.

Tinguaite, from Essex County, Mass. (H. S. Washington) Am. J. Sci. 156: 176.

Tinkling Simlins. (M. T. Earle) Atlan. 82: 225.

Tinsley Brothers, The Founding of. (W. Tinsley) Ath. '00, 1: 721.

Tintagel, England. (J. Ranken) Art J. 51: 19.

Tinto, As seen from. Chamb. J. 74: 241.

Tintoretto, Religious Paintings of, with portrait. (M. F. Nixon) Cath. World, 69: 762.

" Tiny," Some Notes upon the Word. (W. W. Skeat) Ath. '00, 2: 88.

Tioba. (A. Colton) Cent. 39: 20.

Tioga Road, The Old. (C. H. Shinn) Overland, n. s. 34: 387.

Tipping; the Pourboire in Danger. (R. Ogden) Nation, 65: 163.

Tipster, The; a story. (E. Lefèvre) McClure, 18: 71.

Tirah. (T. H. Holdich) Geog. J. 12: 337.

— Campaign of. Fortn. 69: 390. — Macmil. 78: 70.

— Field Fortification in. (A. K. Slessor) Un. Serv. M. 19: 400.

Tired Boy, A; a poem. (C. W. Williams) Outing, 35: 588.

'T is Sixty Years Since. Month, 89: 563.

Tish's Triumph. Lippinc. 62: 543.

Tissot, James, Artist. (C. F. Browne) Brush & P. 3: 335.

— and his Paintings of the Life of Christ. (C. Moffett) McClure, 12: 387. — (C. H. Levy) Bib. World, 13: 69.

— and his Work. (C. H. Levy) Outl. 60: 954. — (C. H. Levy) R. of Rs. (N. Y.) 18: 661.

— Art of. (E. Knaufft) R. of Rs. (N. Y.) 18: 666.

— Artist's Conception of the Life of Christ, with portrait. (J. Jacques) Bookman, 8: 352.

Titchfield. (J. Vaughan) Temp. Bar, 110: 109.

Tithe and its Rating. (M. Barlow) Econ. J. 10: 32.

Tithes and Rates. Spec. 83: 5.

— vs. Apportionments. (J. G. Noss) Ref. Ch. R. 45: 226.

— New Testament Giving vs. Old Testament Tithing. (S. Ream) Ref. Ch. R. 48: 204.

Titian Vecelli. (E. Polko) Argosy, 65: 279. — With portrait, and bibliography. Mast. in Art, 1: Pt. 2.

— Later Work of. Illus. Artist (N. Y.) 23: 204.

— Perseus and Andromeda. (C. Phillips) 19th Cent. 47: 793.

— Phillips's Study of Life and Works. Ath. '98, 2: 721.

— Recovery of a Picture by. (A. Robertson) Argosy, 75: 352.

Titian's Dream Madonna. (Mary Bell) Overland, n. s. 33: 48.

Title of Honor, A; a story. (M. Brooke) Argosy, 70: 138.

Titles; Mr. Hooley and his Baronetcy. Spec. 81: 733.
— Jubilee. Sat. R. 83: 706.
— Many Noted Scientific Men without. Sat. R. 83: 626.
— Native, in the United States. (H. T. Peck) Cosmopol. 28: 685.
— New Year Honors. Spec. 80: 37.
— The Use of. (A. Fosdick) Writer, 10: 61.

Tito; the story of the Coyote that learned how. (E. S. Thompson) Scrib. M. 28: 131-316.

Tivoli-Rome Electric Plant. (A. O. Dubsky) Cassier, 15: 331.

Tizzard Castle. (W. LeC. Beard) Scrib. M. 23: 85.

Tlaxcala, Mexico. Cath. World, 69: 110.

Tlingit Villages about Dixon's Entrance. (G. A. Dorsey) Pop. Sci. Mo. 53: 160.

To the Breaks of Sandy. (John Fox, jr.) Scrib. M. 28: 340.

To Catch a Thief; more Adventures of the Amateur Cracksman. (E. W. Hornung) Scrib. M. 29: 591.

To the Delight of the Mandarin; a story. (M. Y. Wynne) Atlan. 81: 423.

To Die in Jerusalem; a story. (I. Zangwill) Cosmopol. 26: 44.

To Have and to Hold. (M. Johnston) Atlan. 83: 721. 84: 53-773. 85: 54-335.

To Heliodore; a poem. (A. Lang) Ecl. M. 133: 340.

To Her; a poem. (Robert Loveman) Cosmopol. 25: 656.

"To Him that hath." (A. N. Meyer) Lippinc. 69: 854.

To "Jim;" a poem. (E. S. Thompson) Outing, 36: 44.

To Lecture Committees only; a story. (Alice French) Nat'l M. (Bost.) 10: 176.

To a Live-oak; a poem. (M. P. Guild) Chaut. 32: 148.

To the Man on the Trail; a Klondike Christmas. (Jack London) Overland, n. s. 33: 36.

To Milton,— Blind; a poem. (S. Phillips) Bk. Buyer, 16: 33.

To Morfydd Dead; a poem. (L. Johnson) Ecl. M. 132: 241.

To My Mother; a poem. (H. Heine) Argosy, 68: 385.

To One who writes of Pleasant Things; a poem. (M. Vandegrift) Outing, 29: 459.

To Pity; a poem. (Mrs. Van R. Cruger) Cosmopol. 25: 208.

To a Pretty Girl; a poem. (I. Zangwill) Cosmopol. 2: 509.

To prove her Wrong. (E. H. Martin) Longm. 33: 268.

To R. A. M. S.; a poem. (W. E. Henley) Bk. Buyer, 16: 229.

To a Recording Angel; a poem. (P. F. Hall) Green Bag, 11: 434.

To a Sleeper at Rome; a poem. (T. W. Dunton) Bk. Buyer, 16: 30.

To spread her Conquests further; a story. (H. M. Stafford) Outing, 33: 162, 278.

To a Swallow; a poem. (R. G. A. S. Prudhomme) Argosy, 65: 636.

To Those who Know; a poem. (H. C. Wright) Atlan. 82: 362.

Toad, The Natterjack. Chamb. J. 76: 577.
— A Peculiar. (F. L. Washburn) Am. Natural. 33: 139.

Toads and Frogs. (St.G. Mivart) Acad. 56: 531.

Toara Ceremony of the Dippil Tribes of Queensland. (R. H. Mathews) Am. Anthrop. 2: 139.

Toaripi. (J. Chalmers) Anthrop. J. 27: 326.

Tobacco. Nature, 62: 576.
— and Literature. Acad. 61: 225.

Tobacco, Cultivation of, in the U. S. Nat'l M. (Bost.) 5: 469.
— The Effects of Nicotine. (J. W. Seaver) Arena, 17: 470.
— Flavor of. (G. C. Nuttall) Contemp. 75: 880.
— in Germany. J. Soc. Arts, 45: 1125.
— in Relation to Health. (E. V. Heward) 19th Cent. 41: 808.
— Mexican. J. Soc. Arts, 45: 556.
— New Disease of. (A. J. Pieters) Am. Natural. 31: 231.

Tobacco-culture in England during the 17th Century. (W. J. Hardy) Archæol. 51: 157.

Tobacco-fields of Central America. (R. W. Cater) Chamb. J. 78: 298.

Tobacco Industry in Virginia from 1860 to 1894, History of. (B. W. Arnold, jr.) J. H. Univ. Stud. 15: 10.

Tobin's Monument. (A. Colton) Scrib. M. 28: 186.

Tobit, Double Text of. (J. R. Harris) Am. J. Theol. 3: 541.

Tobogganing. (E. W. Sandys) Outing, 31: 484.
— Suburban. (A. Chittenden) Outing, 33: 463.

Tocqueville, Alexis de, and his Book on America. (D. C. Gilman) Cent. 34: 703.
— and Jared Sparks. (H. B. Adams) J. H. Univ. Stud. 16: 12.
— "Recollections" and Self-revelations. (K. Blind) Forum, 24: 744.

Toe, Decline and Fall of the Great. (E. M. Aaron) Overland, n. s. 30: 158.

Toft, Albert. (J. Hamer) M. of Art, 25: 393.

Toiling of Felix, The; a poem. (H. van Dyke) Scrib. M. 23: 422.

Token of Francis Drake, The; a tale. (G. Grant) Argosy, 64: 474.

Token Money of the Bank of England, 1797 to 1816, Phillips on. Ath. '01, 1: 58.

Tokens of Woe. (J. R. S. Sterrett) Nation, 65: 203, 240.
— and the Pelasgi. (W. J. Stillman) Nation, 65: 336.

Tokio, Art School, Competition at. (G. Lynch) M. of Art, 25: 534.
— In Darkest, Chamb. J. 75: 433. Same art. Liv. Age, 218: 685.

Told at Midnight; a story. (Mrs. J. F. B. Firth) Belgra. 98: 227.

Told while Gamming. (F. T. Bullen) Cornh. 80: 303.

Toledo, the Imperial City of Spain. (Stephen Bonsal) Cent. 34: 163. — (Hannah Lynch) Idler, 13: 251.

Toledo, Ohio. Draining a Political Swamp. (H. N. Casson) Arena, 21: 768.

Tolerance, Evolution of. (J. Fiske) Liv. Age, 223: 330.
— Literature and. Spec. 80: 819.

Toll, Baron E.; New Siberia and the Circumpolar Tertiary Flora. (P. Kropotkin) Geog. J. 16: 95.

Tollit's Misfortune; a story. (O. Crawford) Idler, 14: 793.

Tolman, Stacy, Artist. (R. Davol) Brush & P. 7: 163.

Tolman, William Howe. Writer, 14: 10.

Tolstoi, Leo. Acad. 54: 139. — Dial (Ch.) 25: 121. — With portrait. (N. H. Dole) Bk. Buyer, 17: 89. — (E. Rod) Ecl. M. 133: 585. Same art. Liv. Age, 222: 629. — Ed. R. 194: 49. — Nat'l M. (Bost.) 14: 579. — (G. C. Edwards) Sewanee, 9: 457. — (A. D. White) McClure, 16: 507. — (A. D. White) Idler, 19: 479. — (H. W. Massingham) Contemp. 78: 809.
— and the Czar. Outl. 61: 209.
— and his Problems, Maude's. (L. F. Hapgood) Nation, 73: 420.
— and the Russian Censors. Outl. 69: 694.

Trees and Parks in Cities, A Plea for. Forum, **29**: 337.

— and Shrubs of Abnormal Colors, Use of. (C. S. Sargent) Garden & F. **10**: 301.

— Autumn Work among. (C. S. Sargent) Garden & F. **10**: 429.

— Big, of California, How they grow. (H. W. Warren) Chaut. **33**: 362.

— Care of Weak Limbs of. (J. G. Jack) Garden & F. **10**: 274.

— Curious Trimming of. (H. Matthews) Strand, **15**: 80.

— Effects of Wind on. Garden & F. **10**: 292.

— First Account of some Western. (C. S. Sargent) Garden & F. **10**: 28, 38.

— Horizontal, in Oregon. Critic, **32**: 334.

— in City Streets. (C. B. Mitchell) Munic. Aff. **3**: 691.

— in Public Parks. (C. Eliot; C. S. Sargent) Garden & F. **10**: 37.

— Notable, about Boston. (A. F. Brown) New Eng. M. n. s. **22**: 503.

— Old Hampstead, and their Associations. (M. Y. Maxwell) Antiq. n. s. **35**: 267.

— Old, Rejuvenescence of. (C. S. Sargent) Garden & F. **10**: 311.

— Pruning of. (C. S. Sargent) Garden & F. **10**: 71.

— Remarkable, Veneration for. (C. S. Sargent) Garden & F. **10**: 459.

— Roadside. (C. S. Sargent) Garden & F. **10**: 111.

— Rotation of, under Forest Conditions. (L. C. Corbett) Garden & F. **10**: 118.

— Vegetation a Remedy for the Summer Heat of Cities. (S. Smith) Pop. Sci. Mo. **54**: 433.

Tree-ghosts, London. Chamb. J. **75**: 415.

Tree-planting, National. (G. C. Nuttall) Gent. M. n. s. **60**: 177.

Tregavis the Chemist. (J. Patey) Chamb. J. **76**: 705-725.

Treitschke, Heinrich von. (J. W. Headlam) Eng. Hist. R. **12**: 727.

Treizième, Le; a story. (R. Gornalle) Canad. M. **8**: 507.

Trelawny, Edward John. (R. Edgcumbe) Ath. '01, **2**: 814.

— at Usk. (M. B. Byrde) Ath. '97, **2**: 257.

Trenor, Thomas, Romantic Life of. (A. H. T. McAllister) Overland, n. s. **32**: 130.

Trent's Trust. (Bret Harte) Cent. **40**: 769, 892. **41**: 124.

Trenton, N. J., Relic-bearing Sand at. (R. D. Salisbury) Science, **6**: 977.

— Battle of, Surprise at. (E. C. Shedd) Chaut. **31**: 525.

Trenton and Princeton, Battles of, Stryker's. (H. B. Cameron) Am. Hist. R. **4**: 731.

Trenton Rocks at Ungava, Recent Discovery of. (J. F. Whiteaves) Am. J. Sci. **157**: 433.

Tréport, France, as a Sketching Ground. (F. L. Emanuel) Studio (Internat.) **14**: 96.

Tresca, Alfred. (R. H. T.) Science, **5**: 53.

Tresguerras, F. E. de. (Sylvester Baxter) Am. Arch. **55**: 51, 67, 75, 83.

Trespassers will be Prosecuted. Temp. Bar, **115**: 98.

Trevelyan, Sir George Macaulay, as a Historian. Blackw. **165**: 581. — Ecl. M. **132**: 562. — Acad. **58**: 64.

Trevithick, Richard. (A. Titley) Cassier, **19**: 51.

Trevor, Sir John. Disgrace in Parliament. (J. Sykes) Macmil. **78**: 444.

Trial by Jury of Roman Origin. (B. Winchester) Green Bag, **9**: 35. *See* Jury.

Trial of the "Watch Below." (J. H. Whitfield) Strand, **18**: 26.

Trial Path, The; an Indian Romance. (Zitkala-Ša) Harper, **103**: 741.

Trials, Criminal, Early. Green Bag, **13**: 429.

— Famous. (J. B. Atlay) Cornh. **75**: 80 — **76**: 182.

Trials of the Bantocks; a story. (G. S. Street) Idler, **13**: 500-788. **14**: 99-777. **15**: 89, 160, 361.

Trials of a Puppy Walker. (Y. Stewart) Eng. Illust. **17**: 155.

Triangular Dinner-party, The; a story. (H. M. Hoke) Cosmopol. **28**: 93.

Triangular Duet; a story. (H. M. Henne) Cornh. **76**: 336.

Triangular Lodge, Rushton, Eng. (L. Viajero) Am. Arch. **71**: 67.

Triboluminescence. (W. J. Pope) Nature, **59**: 618.

Tribulations of the Hygienic Man; poem. (J. F. Cowan) Educa. **20**: 370.

Tribulations of a Princess. (E. K. Dunton) Dial (Ch.) **31**: 77.

Tribunal Aurelium, The. (C. J. O'Connor) Am. J. Archæol. **48**: 303.

Tribute from Brefny, The; a story. (Nora Hopper) Gent. M. n. s. **58**: 300.

Tribute of Souls, A; a story. (R. Hichens; Frederic Hamilton) Pall Mall M. **12**: 447. **13**: 31.

Tribute to the Flag. (N. K. Blisset) Blackw. **167**: 507. Same art. Liv. Age, **225**: 841.

Tributers, The. (E. W. Parker) Overland, n. s. **35**: 237.

Triclinic Minerals, Examination of, by means of Etching Figures. (T. L. Walker) Am. J. Sci. **155**: 176.

Trietschke, Heinrich von. (M. Todhunter) Westm. **155**: 679.

Trifle and Tragedy; a sketch. (C. L. Shaw) Canad. M. **11**: 48.

Trifler, A; a story. (L. Keith) Argosy, **63**: 257.

Trilobites, Alleged Hypostominal Eyes in, Lindström on. (G. B. Howes) Nature, **63**: 535.

— Outline of a Natural Classification of. (C. E. Beecher) Am. J. Sci. **153**: 89, 181.

Trimble, Henry, 1853–98, Obituary Notice of. J. Frankl. Inst. **146**: 307.

Trincolox; a story. (D. Sladen) Temp. Bar, **113**: 137.

Trine, Ralph Waldo. Lit. W. (Bost.) **31**: 227.

— What all the World's a-seeking. N. Church R. **4**: 305.

Trinidad; Colonial Memories. (Lady M. A. Broome) Ecl. M. **134**: 33, 231.

Trinitarianism, History of. (T. F. Wright) N. Church R. **8**: 381.

Trinity, the, An Ancient Tract on. (J. R. Harris) Am. J. Theol. **5**: 75.

— at Trinity. (G. Tyrrell) Month, **97**: 127.

— Doctrine of the, and the Religious Life of the Christian. (W. C. Schaeffer) Ref. Ch. R. **46**: 28.

— in Experience. (L. Abbott) Outl. **64**: 713.

Trinity Church, New York, 200 Years of. (F. E. Winslow) Outl. **56**: 112.

Trinity Church, Boston, New Porches of, Thoughts suggested by. (H. R. Marshall) Scrib. M. **23**: 509.

Trinity College, Dublin, and Catholic Students. (E. S. Robertson) Sat. R. **84**: 159.

— and a Catholic University. (A. Traill) 19th Cent. **45**: 512.

Trinity College, Oxford. (I. G. Smith) Argosy, **71**: 334.

Trinity Idea, The. (P. Carus) Open Court, **11**: 85.

Trio of Easter Episodes; a story. (Louise C. Henderson) Nat'l M. (Bost.) **8**: 50.

Trip Deferred, A; a story. (M. G. Pope) McClure, **14**: 414.

Trip on the Footplate, A. (V. L. Whitechurch) Good Words, **40**: 91.

Triple Alliance after Eighteen Years. (Crispi) Liv. Age, **228**: 18.

Triple Alliance, Dual and. (F. Crispi) 19th Cent. 42: 673. Same art. Liv. Age, 215: 645.

— Italy and. (W. B. Duffield) Monthly R. 4, no. 3: 63.

— Will Italy renew the? (R. Whitehouse) Atlan. 88: 743.

Triple Entanglement. (Mrs. B. Harrison) Lippinc. 62: 587.

Triplets. (A. Thomas) Strand, 16: 346.

Tripod, Stone, at Oxford. (P. Gardner) J. Hel. Stud. 16: 275.

Tripoli Hill Range, The. (H. S. Cowper) Geog. J. 9: 620.

Trippe, Simon. (W. Roberts ; W. F. Prideaux) Ath. '00, 2: 153, 217.

Triques, Theogony of. (Ph. J. J. Valentini) J. Am. Folk-Lore, 12: 38.

Tristan d'Acunha. Spec. 79: 11.

Tristram of Blent. (A. Hope) Monthly R. 1, no. 2: 157 — 5, no. 1: 159.

Trituberculy. (H. F. Osborn) Am. Natural. 31: 993.

Triumphal Arches. (A. Fish) M. of Art, 24: 445.

Triumph of Seba, The. (J. G. Neihardt) Overland, n. s. 38: 282.

Triumph of Shed. (V. F. Boyle) Cent. 40: 902.

Triumph's Evidence, A. (W. A. White) Scrib. M. 30: 463.

Triumphs of Atropos, The. (B. R. Webb) Overland, n. s. 31: 413.

Trivial Round. (A. E. Trumbull) New Eng. M. n. s. 23: 374.

Trobridge, Geo. By a Way they Knew not. N. Church R. 4: 301.

Troghlichtys Rosæ. (C. H. Eigenmann) Science, n. s. 9: 280.

Troglodyte Dwellings in Cappadocia. (J. R. S. Sterrett) Cent. 38: 677.

Troilus and Cressida, of Chaucer and of Shakspere. (H. H. Herdman, jr.) Sewanee, 7: 161.

Troja, Cathedral of. (W. H. Goodyear) Archit. R. 8: 279.

Trolling. (H. C. Daniels) Outing, 34: 577.

Trollope, Anthony, with portrait. (H. T. Peck) Bookman, 13: 114. — (G. S. Street) Cornh. 83: 349. Same art. Liv. Age, 229: 128. — (L. Stephen) National, 38: 68. Same art. Liv. Age, 231: 366.

— Novels of. (W. F. Lord) 19th Cent. 49: 805. — Lit. W. (Bost.) 31: 72.

— — Best. Acad. 51: 19.

Trollopes, The ; a famous literary clan. (A. B. McGill) Bk. Buyer, 21: 195.

Trooper Galahad. (C. King) Lippinc. 61: 147.

Trooper's Diary, A. (E. H. Blatchford) Outl. 61: 356.

Troops in Civil Disorders, Use of. (P. Leary) J. Mil. Serv. Inst. 20: 83.

— State, and a National Reserve. (E. E. Britton) J. Mil. Serv. Inst. 24: 207.

— — Reorganization of our. (J. C. Gilchrist) J. Mil. Serv. Inst. 23: 418.

— Transportation of, by Sea. (W. E. Birkhimer) J. Mil. Serv. Inst. 23: 438.

Trophies, Famous. (A. F. Aldridge) Munsey, 24: 616.

— Sporting Cups and. Studio (Internat.) 12: 21.

Tropic Climb, A. (J. Hawthorne) Cent. 31: 593.

Tropical Agriculture, The Yankee in. (F. V. Coville) Indep. 51: 3011.

Tropical Climates, Soldier in. Un. Serv. M. 21: 152.

Tropical Colonies, European Experience with. (W. A. Ireland) Atlan. 82: 729.

Tropical Colonization, Ireland's. (W. MacDonald) Nation, 69: 298.

Tropical Diseases and Cures. (T. P. Porter) Chamb. J. 77: 437.

Tropical Islands, How the Dutch manage. (S. Baxter) R. of Rs. (N. Y.) 19: 179.

Tropical Renaissance, The. (S. Baxter) Harper, 103: 283.

Tropical Territories, Government of, and our Federal Constitution. (H. P. Judson) R. of Rs. (N. Y.) 19: 67.

Tropics, Acclimatization of Europeans in. (L. W. Sambon) Geog. J. 12: 589.

— Army in, Ideal Ration for an. (E. L. Munson) J. Mil. Serv. Inst. 26: 309.

— Conquest of. (G. G. Groff) Pop. Sci. Mo. 57: 540.

— Control of. (D. S. Jordan) Gunton's M. 18: 401.

— — Kidd on. Book R. 6: 193. — Bk. Buyer, 17: 321. —Spec. 81: 235.

— Some Previous Expeditions to, and the Question of Health. (A. W. Greely) Cosmopol. 25: 135.

— Troops in, from the Surgeon's Standpoint. (J. H. Stone) J. Mil. Serv. Inst. 26: 358.

— The United States and the Control of. (B. Kidd) Atlan. 82: 721.

— White Men in. (A. R. Wallace ; W. F. Blackman) Indep. 51: 667. — (T. Beale) Forum, 27: 534.

Trott, Nicholas, and the Carolina Pirates. (A. M. Barnes) Green Bag, 11: 516.

Troubadours at Home, J. H. Smith's. (F. M. Warren) Am. Hist. R. 5: 561. — Nation, 72: 35.

— Modern. Quar. 194: 474.

Trouble at Beaulieu. (A. E. W. Mason) Lippinc. 67: 119.

Trouble at St. Luke's Church, The ; an Easter story. (S. M. Peck) Outl. 61: 762.

Trouble at Washington Gulch, The. (E. L. Kellogg) Overland, n. s. 34: 252.

Trouble on the Torolito, The ; a story. (F. Lynde) Nat'l M. (Bost.) 8: 331 — 9: 333.

Trouble Brothers, The ; Bill and the Wolf : a sketch. (F. Remington) Harper, 99: 887.

Trouble Hunter, The ; a story. (W. M. Raine) Nat'l M. (Bost.) 14: 479.

Troubler of Israel. (S. R. Crockett) Lippinc. 65: 766.

Troubridge, Thomas, Admiral. (E. C. T. Troubridge) Un. Serv. M. 19: 553. — (W. J. Fletcher) Cornh. 82: 340.

Troughton, Charles Edward. Bank. M. (Lond.) 65: 72.

Trouin du Gué, Réné, A Corsair of Saint Malo. Blackw. 170: 41.

Trout, Brook, Culture of. (A. N. Cheney) Outing, 39: 16.

— — Story of. (J. D. Quackenbos) Outing, 38: 369.

— Charr Trouts of American Waters. (W. C. Harris) Outing, 36: 157.

— in Scotland, A Close Time for. (J. Forrest) Blackw. 161: 869.

— Marquis of Granby on. Ath. '98, 2: 188. — Spec. 81: 183.

— Salmon Trout and Charrs. (W. C. Harris) Outing, 36: 75.

— Sea, Fishing in Nova Scotia. (R. A. Tremain) Outing, 38: 569.

Trout of '99, The ; a poem. (R. H. Vose) Outing, 34: 394.

Trout-angling. (M. T. Townsend) Outing, 34: 125.

Trout Culture in Mendocino. (E. D. Ward) Overland, n. s. 35: 545.

Trout-fisheries, New. (J. Bickerdyke) Blackw. 167: 256.

Trout-fishing. (J. R. Benton) Outing, 32: 155.

— April. (C. P. Middlebrook) Outing, 30: 63.

— in California. (J. R. Moore) Outing, 33: 33.

— in Pennsylvania. (E. W. Sandys) Outing, 34: 333.

Trusts, in Politics. (E. F. Adams) Overland, n. s. 34: 120. — (W. A. Peffer) No. Am. 170: 244.

— Industrial and Railroad Consolidations. 1. A Grave Danger to the Community. (R. Sage.) 2. Their Advantages to the Community. (J. J. Hill.) 3. What may be expected in the Steel and Iron Industry. (C. M. Schwab.) 4. Industrial Combinations: what they have accomplished for Capital and Labor. (C. R. Flint.) 5. The Influence of Trusts upon Prices. (F. B. Thurber.) 6. Unintelligent Competition a Large Factor in making Industrial Consolidation a Necessity. (J. Logan) No. Am. 172: 641.

— Industrial Combinations. (G. T. Oliver) Forum, 23: 298.

— — in Europe. (J. W. Jenks) Internat. Mo. 4: 648.

— Industrial Commission's Report on. Ann. Am. Acad. Pol. Sci. 18: 575.

— Influence of, in Development of undertaking Genius. (S. Sherwood) Yale R. 8: 362.

— Investigations concerning, by U. S. Dept. of Labor. Q. J. Econ. 14: 122.

— Is a Contract in Restraint of Trade Sustainable as an Independent Contract. (T. H. Cooke) Am. Law R. 35: 836.

— Judicial Decisions on. (R. C. Davis) Q. J. Econ. 14: 416.

— Legal Aspect of. (J. S. Auerbach) No. Am. 169: 375.

— Legal Restraints on. (L. Norman) Am. Law R. 33: 499.

— Legislation and Adjudication on. (J. W. Jenks) Q. J. Econ. 12: 461.

— — Federal. (C. F. Randolph) Pol. Sci. Q. 12: 622.

— Lexow Commission's Report. Gunton's M. 12: 251.

— Literature of. (C. J. Bullock) Q. J. Econ. 15: 167.

— Nature and Significance of Monopolies and. (R. T. Ely) Internat. J. Ethics, 10: 273.

— New Light on the Problem of. (C. R. Flint) R. of Rs. (N. Y.) 22: 445.

— A New Voice on. Gunton's M. 14: 158.

— New, Powers and Perils of the. Gunton's M. 16: 443.

— New York Business Companies' Act, 1900. (M. H. Robinson) Yale R. 9: 79.

— Opinion on, growing Sound. Gunton's M. 13: 9.

— Over-capitalized Industrial Corporations. (E. G. Johns) Arena, 24: 1.

— Pingree on. (W. Rupp) Ref. Ch. R. 46: 251.

— Popular Illusions about. (A. Carnegie) Cent. 38: 143.

— Present and Future. (J. B. Clark) Indep. 51: 1076.

— Problem of. (B. Winchester) Am. Law R. 33: 514.

— — and its Solution. (W. A. Peffer) Forum, 27: 523.

— — Financial Aspects of. (E. S. Meade) Ann. Am. Acad. Pol. Sci. 16: 345.

— — Great Britain and. (T. Scanlon) Arena, 24: 313.

— — its Development in America. (C. G. Miller) Arena, 23: 40.

— — its Real Nature. (E. W. Bemis) Forum, 28: 412.

— — Latest Phase of. (J. B. Clark) Gunton's M. 19: 209.

— — a Proposed Solution. (C. A. Ficke) J. Pol. Econ. 8: 242.

— Publicity a Remedy for the Evils of. (J. W. Jenks) R. of Rs. (N. Y.) 21: 445.

— The Rationale of. (H. White) Nation, 68: 471.

— Recent Construction of the Anti-trust Act. (D. Willcox) Forum, 26: 452.

— The Rush to Industrial Monopoly. (B. W. Holt) R. of Rs. (N. Y.) 19: 675.

— 16th-Century. (A. P. Winston) Atlan. 88: 5.

— State Control of. (R. Kleberg) Arena, 22: 191.

— Strength and Weakness of. (J. D. Rockefeller and others) Engin. M. 20: 761. — (J. G. Brooks) Engin. M. 18: 351.

Trusts, A Suggestion concerning. (H. Teichmueller) Am. Law R. 34: 229.

— Suicidal Methods of. (H. N. Casson) Arena, 23: 54.

— F. B. Thurber on. Gunton's M. 12: 258.

— Tin-plate Combination. (F. L. McVey) Yale R. 8: 156.

— The Trust and the Working-man. (L. Bryce) No. Am. 164: 719.

— The Truth about. (R. P. Flower) Gunton's M. 13: 251.

— Unconstitutionality of Recent Anti-trust Legislation. (D. Willcox) Forum, 24: 107.

— vs. the Town. (C. D. Chamberlin) Gunton's M. 15: 173.

— Why they cannot control Prices. (G. E. Roberts) R. of Rs. (N. Y.) 20: 305.

Trust Abuses, Remedies for. (F. Parsons) Arena, 24: 569.

Trust Companies and Banks, Competition among. Bank. M. (N. Y.) 63: 15.

Trust Conference, Chicago, 1899. (R. I. Holaind) Ann. Am. Acad. Pol. Sci. 15: 69.

— Functions of. Bank. M. (N. Y.) 62: 698.

— is there Danger in the System? (A. D. Noyes) Pol. Sci. Q. 16: 248.

Trust Funds, Following, in Cases of Insolvency or Administration. (C. A. Dickson) Am. Law R. 34: 342.

Trust Issue at Stonetop, The; a story. (L. R. Meekins) Harper, 102: 591.

Trust Money, Liability of Trustees for Interest on. Bank. M. (Lond.) 63: 87.

Truth, Sojourner. (L. B. C. Wyman) New Eng. M. n. s. 24: 59.

Truth and Error, Criteria of. (H. Sidgwick) Mind, 25: 8.

— and how we know it. (C. F. Dole) New World, 7: 1.

— Doctrine of the Twofold. (F. C. French) Philos. R. 10: 477.

— On. Liv. Age, 230: 51.

— The Price of. Month, 89: 490.

— Stability of. (D. S. Jordan) Pop. Sci. Mo. 50: 642, 749.

— What is? Macmil. 84: 44. Same art. Liv. Age, 229: 759.

Truth-seeking in Matters of Religion. (E. Ritchie) Internat. J. Ethics, 11: 71.

Truxton, Capt. Thomas, and the "Constellation." (C. T. Brady) McClure, 14: 272.

Trying of Cuchullin, The; poetry. (P. P. Graves) Ath. '01, 2: 284.

Trying of Friend Folger. (S. E. Johnson) New Eng. M. n. s. 19: 769.

Tryon, Sir George, Life of, FitzGerald's. (P. H. Colomb) Sat. R. 83: 225. — Ath. '97, 1: 303. — Spec. 78: 305.

Tsangpo, The. (J. M. Hubbard) Nat. Geog. M. 12: 32.

Tsanoff, Stoyan, and the Playgrounds Movement. (A. Truslow) Outl. 58: 772.

Tsar and a Bear. (F. Whishaw) Longm. 32: 169.

Tsar's Gratitude, A. (F. Whishaw) Chamb. J. 74: 273-675.

Tschäikovski, Peter Ilyitch. (A. E. Keeton) Contemp. 78: 74.

— as a Musical Critic, with portrait. (Translated by E. E. Simpson) Music, 19: 460.

— The Essential. (E. Newman) Contemp. 79: 887. Same art. Liv. Age, 230: 288.

Tschechow, Anton. The Biter Bit: Sorrow. Temp. Bar, 111: 104, 108.

Ts'ets'áut, Traditions of the. (F. Boas) J. Am. Folk-Lore, 10: 35.

2620 Oxford Place. (K. H. Brown) Lippinc. 66: 293.

Twenty Thousand Pounds; a story. (L. Meadows) Argosy, 65: 87.

'Twere Folly to be Wise; a story. (E. R. Moore) Canad. M. 11: 413.

Twilight, In the. Fortn. 72: 63. Same art. Liv. Age, 222: 543.

Twilight along the Wyantenaug. (A. W. Colton) New Eng. M. n. s. 15: 668.

Twilight Angels; a poem. (M. T. Moxon) Argosy, 67: 484.

Twin Flowers on the Portage. (D. C. Scott) Atlan. 88: 137.

'Twixt Love and Honor. (T. McEwen) Good Words, 41: 52.

Two, The Word, in Semitic Languages. (D. Künstlinger) Jew. Q. 10: 462.

Two, and a Rose; a story. (A. Ollivant) Harper, 101: 255.

Two Barks, The; a tale of the high seas. (A. C. Doyle) McClure, 9: 769.

Two Bikes; a poem. (P. V. Mighels) Outing, 30: 487.

Two Bold Impostors; a story. (A. H. Shirres) Temp. Bar, 123: 257.

Two Boys and a Robin. (M. M. Hickson) Longm. 29: 347. Same art. Liv. Age, 212: 683.

Two Brothers; a story. (S. MacManus) Harper, 101: 793.

Two Christmas Eves; a story. (C. Adams) Argosy, 69: 473.

Two Cockneys and a Conspirator. (S. MacManus) Lippinc. 66: 270.

Two Converts; a story. (O. Watanna) Harper, 103: 585.

Two Cottages. (A. B. Poor) New Eng. M. n. s. 18: 158.

Two Cronies, The; a Mississippi story. Midland, 11: 440.

Two Cyclones. (L. Halévy) Liv. Age, 212: 758.

Two Daughters of One Race. (E. Fawcett) Lippinc. 60: 147.

Two Faces, The. (H. James) Cornh. 83: 767.

Two for Peace. (M. E. Wilkins) Lippinc. 68: 51.

Two Friends; a tale of 1702. Liv. Age, 216: 535.

Two Geordie Tramps. Chamb. J. 78: 396.

Two Glories, The. (P. A. de Alarcón) Liv. Age, 212: 406.

Two Jacks, The; a story. (K. Blackburn) Munsey, 18: 133.

Two Kentucky Thoroughbreds; a story. (F. J. Hagan) Outing, 35: 453.

Two Letters. (F. M. Butler) Lippinc. 60: 278.

Two Life Sketches. (J. Cassidy) Gent. M. n. s. 63: 269. 66: 493.

Two Little Tales. (S. L. Clemens) Cent. 41: 24.

Two Lives that touched. (Mrs. Garnett) Sund. M. 27: 319.

Two Mayors, The. (René Bazin) Liv. Age, 228: 520.

Two Men o' Mendip. (W. Raymond) Longm. 32: 189— 33: 97.

Two Miss Burnhams. (C. Ticknor) New Eng. M. n. s. 16: 275.

Two Mysteries, The; a poem. (Mrs. M. M. Dodge) Bk. Buyer, 16: 110.

Two Names; a poem. (I. F. Mayo) Argosy, 63: 198.

"Two Noble Kinsmen," Prologue to; a poem. (A. C. Swinburne) Ecl. M. 134: 489.

Two of a Kind; a story. (E. Kelley) McClure, 17: 251.

Two Old Hunters; a story. (Alice W. French) Nat'l M. (Bost.) 7: 321.

Two Old Soldiers. (V. L. Whitchurch) Good Words, 41: 102.

Two Outlooks; a poem. (A. Mackay) Argosy, 68: 332.

Two Points of View; a story. (N. McCormick) Argosy, 66: 216.

Two Points of View; a story. (H. Martley) Idler, 17: 107.

Two Priests in Konnoto, The. Macmil. 75: 284. Same art. Liv. Age, 212: 846.

Two Quick Devils of Totsuka. (C. B. Fernald) Cent. 33: 622.

Two Rings, The; a story. (J. K. Leys) Temp. Bar, 113: 389. Same art. Liv. Age, 217: 450.

Two Roads that meet in Salem. (A. W. Colton) New Eng. M. n. s. 16: 146.

Two Scholars. (Edward Thomas) Atlan. 86: 96.

Two Schools; poem. (H. van Dyke) Atlan. 87: 566.

Two Sides to a Question. Liv. Age, 221: 789.

Two Sides of a Story; a tale. (P. W. Hart) Canad. M. 13: 270.

Two Singers, The; a poem. (A. Lamont) Argosy, 63: 271.

Two Soldiers; a poem. (M. Kendall) Ecl. M. 129: 647.

Two Treatments, The; a story. (L. S. Porter) Munsey, 18: 171.

Two Twilights, The. (C. L. Antrobus) Temp. Bar, 117: 496. Same art. Liv. Age, 223: 46.

Two Waifs of the Rail; a story. (J. A. Hill) McClure, 13: 17.

Two Ways; a poem. (Elizabeth Marshall) Cosmopol. 22: 289.

Two Ways of Doubt; a story. (E. Cox) Temp. Bar, 112: 186.

Two Women; a story. (J. F. Fraser) Pall Mall M. 18: 36.

Two's Company. (H. M. Henne) Cornh. 82: 447.

Tyburn Tree. (F. Watt) New R. 15: 692. Same art. Ecl. M. 128: 189.

Tycho Brahe. (C. Sterne) Open Court, 14: 385.

Tyler, John, Gov. of Va. (Sallie E. M. Hardy) Green Bag, 10: 15.

Tyler, Moses Coit. (G. L. Burr) Critic, 38: 136. — (W. P. Trent) Forum, 31: 750. — Ath. '01, 1: 82. — Outl. 67: 6.

Tyler, William S., with portrait. R. of Rs. (N. Y.) 17: 53.

Type, Determination of, in Composite Genera of Animals and Plants. (D. S. Jordan) Science, n. s. 13: 498.

— in Natural History, What is it? (C. Schuchert) Science, 5: 636.

Type of Bloomfield. (H. A. Nash) New Eng. M. n. s. 20: 472.

Type Specimens, Value of. (O. C. Marsh) Am. J. Sci. 156: 401.

Type, Designing of. Sat. R. 88: 610.

Type-setting Machines. (H. M. Duncan) J. Frankl. Inst. 144: 241.

Typewriter in the Public Schools. (A. W. Bacheler) Educa. 19: 626.

— Williams. J. Frankl. Inst. 146: 72.

Typewriting Clerk. (E. A. Smith) Longm. 31: 431.

Typewriting Machine, Evolution of. (C. L. McC. Stevens) Strand, 13: 649.

Typhoid Fever, Flies and. (L. O. Howard) Pop. Sci. Mo. 58: 249.

— in South Africa. J. Mil. Serv. Inst. 26: 441.

— Practical Treatment of. (B. M. Taylor) J. Mil. Serv. Inst. 25: 426.

— Suicide by. (A. Shadwell) National, 30: 715.

Tympana, Sculptured Norman, in Cornwall. (A. G. Langdon) Reliquary, 38: 91. 40: 53.

Typical Tenderfoot; a Northwest story. Canad. M. 13: 443.

United States. Finances; Surplus Revenues and Future Financial Legislation. Bank. M. (N. Y.) **57**: 605, 764.

— — War Loan. (F. A. Vanderlip) Forum, **26**: 27.

— — Withdrawal of the Treasury Notes of 1890. (J. L. Laughlin) J. Pol. Econ. **6**: 248.

— Financial Affairs. (E. G. Johns) Arena, **23**: 578.

— Flaw in our Democracy. (J. N. Larned) Atlan. **84**: 529.

— Foreign Policy. Ann. Am. Acad. Pol. Sci. **13**: supp. — Sat. R. **88**: 333. — (B. O. Flower) Nat'l M. (Bost.) **8**: 430.

— — Development of our. (H. N. Fisher) Atlan. **82**: 552.

— — Effects of Asiatic Conditions upon. (A. T. Mahan) No. Am. **171**: 609.

— — Gains and Losses from our Recent. Yale R. **8**: 225.

— — Growth of. (R. Olney) Atlan. **85**: 289.

— — of the New Administration, 1897. (M. W. Hazeltine) No. Am. **164**: 479.

— — Parting of the Ways in. (F. Adler) Int. J. Ethics, **9**: 1.

— Future Policy of. (J. G. Carlisle) Harper, **97**: 720.

— Geographic Work of the General Government. (H. Garnett) Nat. Geog. M. **9**: 329.

— Geologic Atlas. Nat. Geog. M. **9**: 339. — (W. M. Davis) Science, n. s. **13**: 950.

— Geological Survey. Nature, **60**: 182.

— — Work of. (B. Willis) Science, n. s. **10**: 203.

— Germany, and England. (P. Bigelow) Contemp. **77**: 881. Same art. Ecl. M. **135**: 283. Same art. Liv. Age, **226**: 201.

— Government in War-time. (René Bache) Cosmopol. **25**: 255.

— — in War and Peace. (C. W. Eliot) Outl. **60**: 169.

— — of Newly-acquired Territory. (C. E. Boyd) Atlan. **82**: 735.

— — Shall we have Trained Officials? (C. S. Bernheimer) Outl. **60**: 527.

— — Sovereignty in. Spec. **80**: 700.

— — "Uncle Sam" as a Business Man. (R. J. Hinton) Chaut. **32**: 481.

— — What it costs. (C. D. Wright) Cent. **39**: 433.

— Government Buildings at Washington. (E. V. Seeler) Am. Arch. **70**: 99.

— Government Printing Office. (T. E. Doty) Nat'l M. (Bost.) **10**: 274.

— Government Publications, List of Serial, Technical, and Scientific. Lib. J. **22**: 16.

See below — Public Documents.

— Growth of. (F. W. Hewes) McClure, **12**: 269. — (W. J. McGee) Nat. Geog. M. **9**: 378.

— Growth of Caste in. (J. E. Chamberlin) 19th Cent. **42**: 43. Same art. Liv. Age, **214**: 433.

— History; American Colonies in the 18th Century. Quar. **190**: 221.

— — American Revolution. Scot. R. **33**: 328. — (H. L. Osgood) Pol. Sci. Q. **13**: 41.

— — — and Province of Quebec. (V. Coffin) Canad. M. **9**: 56.

— — — France in. (J. A. Woodburn) Chaut. **25**: 247.

— — — French Aid in. (R. H. Clark) Am. Cath. Q. **22**. 399.

— — — Lodge's Story of. (J. Bigelow) Am. Hist. R. **5**: 362.

— — — Neglected Aspects of. (C. K. Adams) Atlan. **82**: 174.

— — — New England Governors in. (E. B. Bates) New Eng. M. n. s. **20**: 131.

— — — Orders of Mercer, Sullivan, and Stirling, 1776. Am. Hist. R. **3**: 302.

— — — Significance of, To-day. (I. S. Dodd) Bookman, **9**: 446.

United States. History; American Revolution, **Trevelyan's**. (F. J. Turner) Am. Hist. R. **5**: 141. — Ed. R. **189**: 262.

— — — Tyler's Literature of. (P. L. Ford) Nation, **64**: 439.

— — Beginners of a Nation, Eggleston's. (H. L. Osgood) Am. Hist. R. **2**: 528. '— (W. P. Trent) Forum, **22**: 590. — (F. W. Shepardson) Dial (Ch.) **22**: 83.

— — Civil War, and Reconstruction. (A. B. Hart) Book R. **5**: 203.

— — — Artillery during. (H. W. Hubbell) J. Mil. Serv. Inst. **11**: 396. — (J. C. Tidball) J. Mil. Serv. Inst. **12**: 697–1211.

— — — Blockade in. (H. L. Wait) Cent. **34**: 914.

— — — by a Confederate. Nat'l M. (Bost.) **9**: 161.

— — — Causes of. Ed. R. **193**: 1.

— — — Cavalry during. (B. W. Crowninshield) J. Mil. Serv. Inst. **12**: 527.

— — — Confederate Distress. Nat'l M. (Bost.) **10**: 41.

— — — Confederate Prisoners in Boston. (A. Hunter) New Eng. M. n. s. **23**: 683.

— — — "Congress" and the "Merrimac." (F. S. Alger) New Eng. M. n. s. **19**: 687.

— — — Cox's Military Reminiscences of. (G. A. Thayer) Nation, **72**: 138. — (F. W. Shepardson) Dial (Ch.) **30**: 369.

— — — Disbanding the Armies. (I. M. Tarbell) McClure, **15**: 400, 526.

— — — from a Confederate Standpoint. Nat'l M. (Bost.) **9**: 371, 448.

— — — An Incident of. (J. T. Weatherly) Nat'l M. (Bost.) **6**: 68.

— — — The Last Battle of. (Ben C. Truman) Overland, n. s. **33**: 135.

— — — Last Days of Confederate Government. (S. R. Mallory) McClure, **16**: 99, 239.

— — — Literature and. (H. A. Beers) Atlan. **88**: 749.

— — — The Men in the Ranks. (P. Douglas) McClure, **8**: 537.

— — — Personal Experiences of. (M. Davis) McClure, **9**: 661.

— — — Recollections of. (W. H. Russell) No. Am. **166**: 234–740. **167**: 16. — (W. T. Fitch) Conserv. R. **5**: 240.

— — — The Regulars in. (R. F. Zogbaum) No. Am. **167**: 16.

— — — Reminiscences of Men and Events of. (C. A. Dana) McClure, **10**: 20 — **11**: 380.

— — — Service in a Bowery Regiment. (M. Davis) McClure, **8**: 245.

— — — Story of, J. C. Ropes's. (J. H. Wilson) Am. Hist. R. **5**: 592.

— — — Story of a Paroled Prisoner in. (Wm. F. Prosser) Overland, n. s. **35**: 435.

— — — Two Years with a Colored Regiment. (F. B. Perkins) New Eng. M. n. s. **17**: 533.

— — Colonies. Struggle of France and England for the Possession of North America. (C. B. Shaw) New Eng. M. n. s. **21**: 567.

— — — Women in. (L. B. Lang) Longm. **35**: 323.

— — from the Compromise of 1850, Rhodes's. (W. A. Dunning) Am. Hist. R. **5**: 371.

— — McLaughlin's. (W. M. West) Am. Hist. R. **5**: 351.

— — Middle Period, 1817–58, Burgess's. (C. H. Levermore) Am. Hist. R. **2**: 746. — (G. W. Julian) Dial (Ch.) **22**: 274. — (J. L. Stewart) Ann. Am. Acad. Pol. Sci. **11**: 89.

— New Text Books in. (C. A. Herrick) Citizen, **4**: 32.

— Pending Problems. (H. Taylor) No. Am. **167**: 609.

Up at the 'Lotments. (M. E. Francis) Cornh. 82: 307. Same art. Ecl. M. 135: 758. Same art. Liv. Age, 227: 161.

Up-country Maid ; a story. (G. Mortimer) Eng. Illust. 17: 175.

Up the Matterhorn in a Boat. (M. M. Pope) Cent. 32: 450-899.

Up the Mine Shaft ; a story. (W. F. Gibbons) Outl. 67: 170.

Up-to-date Cinderella, An ; a story. (M. G. Cundill) Outing, 35: 589.

Upon Impulse ; a story. (H. Garland) Bookman, 4: 428.

Upper Shelf, From the. Macmil. 80: 463.

Upright Vision. (J. H. Hyslop) Psychol. R. 4: 142.
— and Retinal Image. (G. M. Stratton) Psychol. R. 4: 182.

Upshur, Abel Parker. (Sallie E. M. Hardy) Green Bag, 10: 111.

Ur of the Chaldees, Expedition to. Outl. 66: 963.

Ural Mountains, Railways in. (L. Lodian) Cassier, 18: 188.

Urfé, Honoré d'. Astrée ; first French novel. (B. W. Wells) Sewanee, 8: 179.

Uribe, Gen. Rafael U., and Castro, Gen. Cipriano ; Two Men of Revolutions, with portraits. (B. S. Coler) Indep. 53: 2156.

Urmi, Lake, and its Region. (R. T. Gunther) Geog. J. 14: 504.

Urquhart, Sir Thomas. (C. Whibley) New R. 17: 21.
— Acad. 58: 102.

Ursuline Nuns and a Normal College. (I. Allardyce) Cath. World, 69: 674.
— of Quebec. (A. G. Doughty) Canad. M. 10: 362.

Ursuline Order, Annals of. (L. S. Flintham) Cath. World, 66: 319.
— Unification of. Cath. World, 72: 665.

Useful Men, A Plea for the Protection of. R. of Rs. (N. Y.) 15: 192.

Usher Genealogy, Notes on. (R. U. Tyler) N. E. Reg. 54: 76.

Usury. Bank. M. (Lond.) 64: 127.
— Modern. Outl. 61: 864.

Utah, Central and Southern. (P. B. Eagle) Gent. M. n. s. 61: 596.
— Woman's Life in. (R. Everett) Arena, 21: 183.

Utah Art Commission Bill. (Alice M. Horne) Brush & P. 4: 143.

Utah Love Story, A. (Fanny Dare) Overland, n. s. 33: 495.

Utamaro, Japanese Designer, Art of. (S. Bing) Studio (Lond.) 4: 137.

Ute Lover, The ; a poem. (H. Garland) Cent. 36: 218.

Ute Pass, Colo., Dikes of. (W. O. Crosby) Science, 5: 604.

Utilitarianism, Sidgwick's Proof of. (E. Albee) Philos. R. 10: 251.

Utilitarians, English, L. Stephen on. (W. Graham) Contemp. 79: 221. — Ed. R. 193: 396. — (J. Bryce ; A. V. Dicey) Nation, 72: 236, 257. — (J. W. Chadwick) Critic, 38: 125. — (P. Shorey) Dial (Ch.) 30: 396. — Sat. R. 91: 406. — Outl. 67: 173. — Ath. '00, 2: 749, 785.
— Philosophical Radicals. Quar. 194: 54.

Utility and Natural Beauty. Spec. 80: 686.

Utopias, Real, in the Arid West. (W. E. Smythe) Atlan. 79: 599.

Utrera, Spain, Notes of. (R. B. C. Graham) Sat. R. 91: 665.

Utukuluk ; a story. (C. Graves) Eng. Illust. 18: 291.

Vaal Krantz, Battle of. Blackw. 169: 741.

Vaal River Adventure, A. Chamb. J. 78: 820-837.

Vacancy at Fossington, The. (W. Richards) Temp. Bar, 123: 400.

Vacant Chair, A ; a story. (W. E. Grogan) Idler, 17: 371.

"Vacant Chair," the Hero and the Author of the Song. (N. L. Jillson) New Eng. M. n. s. 16: 131.

Vacant Country, The ; a story of days to come. (H. G. Wells) Pall Mall M. 18: 309.

Vacant-lot Cultivation for the Unemployed. (F. W. Speirs ; S. McC. Lindsay ; F. B. Kirkbridge) Char. R. 8: 74.
— Bibliography of. (F. H. McLean) Char. R. 8: 107.

Vacarius ; a correction. (F. Liebermann) Eng. Hist. R. 13: 297.
— Summa de Matrimonio. (F. W. Maitland) Law Q. 13: 133, 270.

Vacation with Wheel and Gun. Outing, 35: 63.

Vacation Book Talks. (C. M. Hewins) Pub. Lib. 5: 231.

Vacation Rambles of a Naturalist. (L. C. Miall) Lond. Q. 91: 30.

Vacation School, California's First ; an Oakland Experiment. (Eva V. Carlin) Overland, n. s. 35: 426. — (H. C. Putnam) Forum, 30: 492. — (F. L. Cardozo, jr.) Educa. 22: 141. — (C. M. Robinson) Educa. R. 17: 250.
— and Playgrounds. (S. T. Stewart) Outl. 62: 798.
— for French in France and Switzerland. (W. H. Bishop) Nation, 66: 85.
— in Chicago. (O. J. Milliken) Am. J. Sociol. 4: 289.
— in New York. Munic. Aff. 2: 432.
— in the United States. (K. A. Jones) R. of Rs. (N. Y.) 17: 710.
— The Movement for. (Sadie American) Am. J. Sociol. 4: 309.

Vacation Work for Children. Ann. Am. Acad. Pol. Sci. 13: 419.

Vaccination. J. Mil. Serv. Inst. 27: 354.
— Act of 1898, English. (M. G. Fawcett) Contemp. 75: 328.
— and Conscience. Sat. R. 92: 422, 496, 559.
— and Dr. Garrett-Anderson. (A. S. Hunter) Westm. 151: 699.
— and Smallpox Statistics, with reference to Age-incidence, Sex-incidence, and Sanitation. (A. Milnes) J. Statis. Soc. 60: 503, 552.
— Fallacies of the Inoculators. (E. Haughton) Westm. 152: 214, 417.
— Future of. Nature, 58: 469.
— History and Effects of. Ed. R. 189: 335.
— Prospects of. Spec. 83: 832.
— Question of. Westm. 147: 634.
— Scientific Study of, Copeman on. Nature, 59: 435.
— Theory and Practice of, Cory's. Sci. Prog. 7: xxxv.
— Use of Glycerinated Calf-lymph for. Nature, 57: 391.

Vagabondage, French Commission on, Report of. Ann. Am. Acad. Pol. Sci. 12: 126.

Vagabonding with the Tenth Horse. (Frederic Remington) Cosmopol. 22: 347.

Vagabond's Wooing, A. (B. Copplestone) Cornh. 84: 298. Same art. Ecl. M. 137: 784. Same art. Liv. Age, 231: 241.

Vagabonds, Concerning. (M. M. Turnbull) Gent. M. n. s. 65: 444. Same art. Liv. Age, 227: 719. Same art. Ecl. M. 136: 178.

Vagrant, The ; a story. (R. H. Davis) Harper, 99: 25.

Vagrant of Caser Mine, The. (Helen F. Clute) Midland, 8: 152, 251.

Vagrants. Spec. 80: 896. Same art. Liv. Age, 217: 894.
— and the Law. (G. H. Westley) Green Bag, 12: 330.
— in Winter. (T. W. Wilkinson) Good Words, 40: 31.

Vailima ; the Place of the Five Rivers. (A. R. Rose-Soley) Overland, n. s. **33**: 389.

Vaillantcœur. (H. van Dyke) Scrib. M. **26**: 152.

Vain Search for God, A. (H. Balz) Open Court, **12**: 28.

Vain Shadow, The. (D. C. Scott) Scrib. M. **28**: 72.

Val, Battle of the. (F. Dixon) Temp. Bar, **110**: 330. Same art. Ecl. M. **128**: 624.

Val d'Or, Village in. (Mrs. P. G. Hamerton) Blackw. **170**: 64.

Valadon, Jules, painter. (R. H. Sherard) Art J. **51**: 375.

Valda Hanem. Macmil. **79**: 241–401. **80**: 1–321.

Valdés, A. P. A Great Modern Spaniard. (S. Baxter) Atlan. **85**: 546.

"Valdivia," German Expedition of, Oceanographical and Meteorological Work of. (G. Schott) Geog. J. **15**: 518.

Vale Press, The. (H. C. Marillier) Pall Mall M. **22**: 179.
— Publications of ; a bibliography. (E. D. North) Bk. Buyer, **20**: 132.

Valeggio, The Action at, 30 May, 1796. (B. Beaulieu) Eng. Hist. R. **13**: 741.

Valence, Chemical, Venable on. Science, n. s. **9**: 688.

Valencia, Spain. (Arthur Symons) Sat. R. **87**: 41. Same art. Ecl. M. **132**: 616. Same art. Liv. Age, **220**: 524.

Valfrey, M. Jules Joseph. (W. Roberts) Ath. '00, **2**: 724.

Valhalla. *See* Walhalla.

Valladolid, St. Alban's Seminary, 1602–08. (J. H. Pollen) Month, **94**: 348.

Vallenger, Stephen. (H. R. Plomer) Library, n. s. **2**: 108.

Valley of Decision. (R. M. Wenley) Bib. Sac. **58**: 51.

Valley of the Lost People ; a tale of British Columbia. (C. C. Pangman) Canad. M. **10**: 210.

Valley Forge, 1777–78. (A. Waldo) Pennsyl. M. **21**: 299. — (W. H. Richardson) New Eng. M. n. s. **23**: 597.
— as a National Park. (E. W. Hocker) Outl. **67**: 787.

Vallgren, M., Artificer and Sculptor. (B. Karageorgevitch) M. of Art, **22**: 218.

Vallotton, Felix, Woodcuts of. (J. Schopfer) Bk. Buyer, **20**: 292.

Valmore, Marceline, A Woman Poet. (B. W. Cornish) Fortn. **68**: 66.

Valmy and Auerstädt, Campaign of. Ed. R. **187**: 1.

Valois, The Last of the. (Eleanor Lewis) Cosmopol. **24**: 343.

Valor, True Measure of. (N. S. Shaler) Harv. Grad. M. **7**: 192.

Value and Distribution, Macfarlane's. (F. Y. Edgeworth) Econ. J. **9**: 233.
— and its Measurement. (D. I. Green) Yale R. **7**: 383.
— and Price, Theory of. Gunton's M. **14**: 40.
— Gold, Labor, and Commodities as Standards of. (A. M. Hyde) J. Pol. Econ. **6**: 95.
— Gottl on ; a misguided philosopher. (W. G. L. Taylor) Ann. Am. Acad. Pol. Sci. **11**: 227.
— in its relation to Interest. (R. S. Padan) J. Pol. Econ. **10**: 50.
— Philosophy of. (G. Simmel) Am. J. Sociol. **5**: 577.
— Relativity and Universality of. (W. G. L. Taylor) Ann. Am. Acad. Pol. Sci. **9**: 70.
— Theory of, and its Place in the History of Ethics. (C. G. Shaw) Internat. J. Ethics, **11**: 306.
— — Social Elements in. (E. R. A. Seligman) Q. J. Econ. **15**: 321.
— Utility and Cost as Determinants of. (C. Stroever) Ann. Am. Acad. Pol. Sci. **10**: 334.

Vanadium in Rocks of the United States, Distribution and Quantitative Occurrence of. (W. F. Hillebrand) Am. J. Sci. **156**: 209.

Van Beers, Jan, Home of. Critic, **30**: 131.

Vanbrugh, Irene, Portrait of. Theatre, **39**: 94.

Van Brunt, Henry. Annual Address before Am. Inst. of Arch., 1899. Am. Arch. **66**: 60.

Vancouver, British Columbia. (J. Durham) Canad. M. **12**: 109.
— Central Crags of. (W. W. Bolton and J. W. Laing) Overland, n. s. **29**: 265.
— Under the Western Pines. (H. Bindloss) Gent. M. n. s. **65**: 597.

Vandeleur, Seymour, Lieut.-Colonel. Geog. J. **18**: 542.

Vander's Marget ; a story. Ecl. M. **128**: 238.

Vanderbilt, Cornelius, d. 1899. Gunton's M. **17**: 251. — Outl. **63**: 192.

Vanderbilts and the Vanderbilt Millions. (F. L. Ford) Munsey, **22**: 467.

Vanderbilt University. (E. Mims) Outl. **66**: 508.

Van der Dyn's Inspiration ; a story. (C. Edwardes) Eng. Illust. **21**: 587.

Vanderkemp, John. (Dr. Geo. Smith) Good Words, **38**: 611.

Vanderpoel, Green & Cuming, Noted Law Firm, with portraits. (A. O. Hall) Green Bag, **11**: 460.

Van der Stucken, Frank, Musical Conductor, with portrait. Music, **18**: 461.

Van de Velde, Henry, Designs by. Artist (N. Y.) **30**: 65.

Van Dyck, Ernest, Tenor Singer, with portrait. Music, **15**: 187.

Van Dyke, Henry, with portrait. Bk. News, **17**: 263.
— With portrait. Outl. **56**: 18. — With portrait. Bookman, **9**: 149. — With portrait. Bk. Buyer, **18**: 178.
— in the Pulpit. (A. R. Kimball) Critic, **32**: 334.
— on an Age of Doubt and a World of Sin. Church Q. **49**: 369.
— Ruling Passion. (H. W. Mabie) Bk. Buyer, **23**: 365.

Van Dyke, J. C. Nature for its own Sake. (C. M. Skinner) Bk. Buyer, **17**: 49.

Vanes, Adjusting. (B. F. Fells) Am. Arch. **59**: 28.

Van Horne, Sir William C. (F. Yeigh) Canad. M. **8**: 327.

Van Hove. Triptych of Three Cities. Artist (N. Y.) **25**: 76.

Van Hoytema, T., Artist. Studio (Internat.) **2**: 30.

Vanilla-gathering in Central America. (R. W. Cater) Chamb. J. **78**: 278.

Vanished ; a story. (I. Garvey) Argosy, **69**: 37.

Van Pelt, Madeline K. Writer, **14**: 91.

Van Rensselaer, Mrs. John King, The Goede Vrouw of Mana-ha-ta. Bk. Buyer, **17**: 229.

Van Santvoord, Alfred. Bank. M. (N. Y.) **60**: 49.

Van Vechten, Helen Brumeau, Press of. (Delia T. Davis) Critic, **37**: 222.

Vapor Pressures of Liquids. (Kelvin) Nature, **55**: 273.

Varallo and the Val Sesia. (E. L. Weeks) Harper, **96**: 905.

Vardon, Harry, Golf Player. (C. S. Cox) Outing, **36**: 88.

Variation. (W. S. B. Mathews) Music, **15**: 376.
— and some Phenomena connected with Reproduction and Sex. (Adam Sedgwick) Science, n. s. **11**: 881, 923.
— Case of Variation in the Number of Ambulacral Systems of Arbacia Punctulata. (H. L. Osborn) Am. Natural. **32**: 259.
— Cases of Saltatory. (C. H. Eigenmann ; L. O. Cox) Am. Natural. **35**: 33.
— Causes of. (H. M. Vernon) Sci. Prog. n. s. **1**: 229.
— Organic, Theory of. (H. S. Williams) Science, **6** : 73.
— Progress in the Study of. (W. Bateson) Sci. Prog. **7**: 53. n. s. **1**: 554.
— *vs.* Heredity. (H. S. Williams) Am. Natural. **32**:821.

Venezuelan Boundary Dispute. (M. Baker) Nat. Geog. M. 11: 129. — (G. Cleveland) Cent. 40: 283, 405.
— Arbitration of. Ed. R. 191: 123. — (G. C. Worth ; G. H. Knott) Am. Law R. 31: 481.
— Boundary Commission and its Work. (M. Baker) Nat. Geog. M. 8: 193.
— Boundary Question ; the Olney Doctrine. (S. Low) 19th Cent. 40: 849. Same art. Liv. Age, 212: 2.
,— — The Decision on. Outl. 63: 391. — (H. Whates) Fortn. 72: 793. — Sat. R. 88: 445.
— — Our Sobering. (R. Ogden) Nation, 69: 272.
— Search for the Boundary. (G. L. Burr) Am. Hist. R. 4: 470.
Venice. (Pompeo Molmenti) Art J. 52: 83. — (Alfredo Melani) Am. Arch. 71: 78.
— as Sketching Ground. (F. Richards) Studio (Lond.) 3: 170.
— Fish Market. M. of Art, 26: 18.
— For. (Mrs. L. Turnbull) Liv. Age, 229: 61.
— Gardens of. (L. Bacon) Cent. 40: 532.
— Glamour of. Sat. R. 88: 480. Same art. Liv. Age, 223: 527.
— A Gondola Ride through. (L. O. Kuhns) Chaut. 34: 156.
— Housekeeping in. (T. Purdy) Outing, 30: 12.
— Lagoon of, Impressions of the. (E. Gosse) Indep. 53: 3073.
— Modern Art in. (E. R. Pennell) Nation, 73: 261.
— On the Lagoons. (E. McAuliffe) Cath. World, 69: 737.
— Palaces of. (C. S. Mathews) Am. Arch. 62: 43, 103.
— Republic of, Hazlitt on. (C. H. Haskins) Dial (Ch.) 30: 370.
— Santa Maria dei Miracoli, and the Lombardi. (A. B. Bibb) Am. Arch. 64: 99. 65: 3-83. 66: 35-51.
— St. Mark's, Restoration of. Am. Arch. 71: 96.
— Soul of. (A. Symons) Sat. R. 92: 584.
— Sources of the Greatness of. (C. Lombroso) Forum, 26: 485.
— Spring Days in. (Edgar Fawcett) Cosmopol. 30: 613.
— Venetian Child-angel, A. (M. Bramston) Sund. M. 27: 650.
— Visit to. (M. M. Mears) Nat'l M. (Bost.) 11: 200.
Venoms of the Toad and Salamander. (R. T. Hewlett) Sci. Prog. n. s. 1: 397.
Ventilation by Aspiration. (Frederic Tudor) Am. Arch. 73: 27-99. 74: 13-22.
— of Tunnels and Buildings. (F. Fox) Cassier, 17: 240.
— Systematized. (E. T. Potter) Am. J. Soc. Sci. 38: 15.
— without Draughts. (A. Rigg) J. Soc. Arts, 48: 184.
Venukoff, M. I., General. Geog. J. 18: 542.
Venus and Mercury, Rotation of. (S. C. Chandler) Pop. Astron. 4: 393.
— — Transits of. (J. Morrison) Pop. Astron. 5: 536.
— in the Light of Recent Discoveries. (P. Lowell) Atlan. 79: 327.
— New Views as to. (C. Flammarion) Knowl. 20: 234, 258.
— Photographing by the Light of. (W. R. Brooks) Cent. 40: 529.
Venus and Adonis. (Thomas H. B. Graham) Gent. M. n. s. 58: 500.
Venus, A Newly Discovered. Scrib. M. 22: 522.
Venus de' Medici, Migrations of the. (L. Scott) M. of Art, 21: 17.
Venus of the Belvedere. Sat. R. 88: 43.
Venus of Melos. (W. J. Stillman) Nation, 64: 125, (E. Robinson) 161, (S. Reinach) 222.
— Arms of. Am. Arch. 55: 45.
Vera Cruz Expedition, Landing of. (W. C. Lott) J. Mil. Serv. Inst. 24: 422.

Veracity. (W. H. Hudson) Pop. Sci. Mo. 53: 196.
Veramin Meteorite. (H. A. Ward) Am. J. Sci. 162: 453.
Verbal Magic. (B. Torrey) Atlan. 79: 123. Same art. Liv. Age, 212: 140.
Verbeck, Guido Fridolin, Griffis's Life of. Critic, 38: 236.
Verdi, Giuseppe. Critic, 32: 14. — (J. C. Hadden) Fortn. 75: 476. — (J. A. Fuller-Maitland) Monthly R. 2, no. 3: 133. — (E. Grieg) 19th Cent. 49: 451. Same art. Ecl. M. 136: 678. Same art. Liv. Age, 229: 11. — (R. Lazzari) Outl. 67: 534. — (W. S. B. Mathews) Music, 19: 502. — (E. Gagliardi) Music, 19: 521. — With portrait. (M. De Nevers) Pall Mall M. 23: 553. — With portrait. (C. M. Cottrell) Nat'l M. (Bost.) 9: 387.
— Aïda. (J. F. Runciman) Sat. R. 90: 488.
— and his Successors. (G. Minkowsky) Munsey, 24: 852.
— and Italian Opera. (J. F. Runciman) Sat. R. 91: 138.
— Anecdotic Record of. (J. C. Hadden) Argosy, 73: 244.
— an Appreciation, with portrait. (L. M. Isaacs) Bookman, 13: 54.
— as a Letter-writer. (I. P. Stevenson) Indep. 53: 895.
— as a Patriot, with portrait. (S. Cortesi) Indep. 53: 428. — (J. W. Mario) Nation, 72: 231.
— Operas. Music, 16: 310.
— Requiem. (J. F. Runciman) Sat. R. 91: 768.
— Tribute to. (P. Mascagni) Internat. Mo. 3: 434.
Verdict in the Rutherford Case ; a story. (W. Barr) Cosmopol. 26: 523.
Verestchagin, Vasili. (Prince B. Karageorgevitch) M. of Art, 23: 176. — (P. G. Konody) Idler, 15: 145. — With portraits. (A. Mee) Strand, 17: 396. — Liv. Age, 220: 463. Same art. Ecl. M. 132: 623.
— Napoleon at Moscow portrayed by. Illus. Cosmopol. 26: 587.
Verge of Tears ; poem. (E. M. Thomas) Atlan. 79: 492.
Vergers, The ; a social study. (G. Halford) Temp. Bar, 117: 567.
Vergil, Polydore. De Inventoribus Rerum, English Translation of. Archæol. 51: 107.
Verlaine, Paul. (M. J. Kelly) Month, 90: 153. — (A. S. van Westrum) Critic, 32: 325. — (C. F. Keary) New R. 16: 617. — (S. C. de Soissons) Forum, 24: 246. — Acad. 51: 234.
— the Poet of Absinthe. (H. Lyndon) Bookman, 8: 440.
— Portraits of. (A. Symons) Sat. R. 85: 319.
Vermont, Emigration in, 1826. (M. B. Thrasher) New Eng. M. n. s. 16: 372.
Vernal Spirit, The ; a poem. (C. Scollard) Outl. 64: 576.
Verne, Jules, Visit to. (E. de Amicis) Chaut. 24: 701.
Vernet, Joseph, Carle, and Horace. (A. Dayot) Studio (Internat.) 5: 28.
Verney Memoirs. Acad. 56: 181. Same art. Ecl. M. 132: 783. Same art. Liv. Age, 220: 777.
Vernon, Edward, Admiral. (H. V. Kyrke ; A. V. Kyrke) Un. Serv. M. 20: 109.
Verona. (W. S. Perry) Lippinc. 62: 859.
Veronica, St., Ebony Pax bearing the Legend of. (G. Stephens) Archæol. 46: 266.
Veronica's Will ; a story. (G. Dix) Pall Mall M. 21: 306.
Verrocchio or Leonardo da Vinci, perhaps the Sculptor of Madonna and Child, ascribed to A. Rossellino. (Claude Phillips) Art J. 51: 33.
Versailles. (R. Chaplain) Argosy, 72: 456.
— Fountains at, Early. (P. de Nolhac) Studio (Internat.) 10: 21.

Verse under Prosaic Conditions. Atlan. 80: 271.

Verse-division of the New Testament. (J. R. Harris) J. Bib. Lit. 19: 114.

Verse Vulgarism — g final. Nation, 66: 129, (F. Tupper, jr.) 184.

Verses. (J. R. Lowell) Atlan. 86: 721.

Verstegan, Richard (alias Rowly). (J. Fitzmaurice-Kelly) New R. 17: 39.

Vertebral Column, Dr. Alex. Goette on Development of. (O. P. Hay) Am. Natural. 31: 397.

Vertebrata, Anatomy of, Gegenbaur's. (H. Gadow) Nature, 59: 169.

— Annulates of. (H. M. Bernard) Nat. Sci. 13: 17.

Vertebrate Paleontology in America. (H. F. Osborn) Science, n. s. 13: 45.

— Kingsley's. Am. Natural. 35: 58.

— Recent Papers relating to. Am. Natural. 31: 314.

Very, F. W., on Atmospheric Radiation. (W. Hallock) Am. J. Sci. 161: 230.

Very, Jones ; a Son of the Spirit. (G. M. Hammell) Meth. R. 61: 20.

Very Cold Truth ; a story. (W. L. Alden) Idler, 11: 252.

Very like a Whale ; on the Illustrations to Ortus Sanitatis. (H. S. C. Everard) Eng. Illust. 19: 263.

Very Rev. Canon Domenico Pucci, D. D., Domestic Prelate to His Holiness. (M. Wedmore) Temp. Bar, 117: 84. Same art. Ecl. M. 133: 260.

Vespers at Huelgoat ; a story. Macmil. 80: 55.

Vespucci, Amerigo. (E. M. Clerke) Dub. R. 124: 60.

— and the Italian Navigators, with portrait. (E. McAuliffe) Cath. World, 67: 603.

— Commemoration of. Nat. Sci. 12: 377.

— New Portrait of. (M. Cruttwell) Art J. 50: 150. — (H. P. Horne) Sat. R. 85: 248.

Vesta Marie. (Lucy Van Tress) Overland, n. s. 35: 299.

Vesta and the Regia, Temple and Atrium of. (J. H. Middleton) Archæol. 49: 391.

"Vesta," Saving of the. (M. Petrie) Good Words, 40: 274.

Vestal Precinct in the Forum, The. (G. D. Kellogg) Nation, 71: 308.

Veteran. (R. B. C. Graham) Sat. R. 89: 455.

Veterans, U. S. (A. O. Genung ; G. R. Scott ; J. C. Ridpath) Arena, 20: 404.

Vestigial Characters in Man, Certain. (W. Kidd) Nature, 55: 236.

Vesuvius. (H. J. W. Dam) McClure, 12: 3.

— Cable Railway up. (A. Faerber) Cassier, 15: 155.

— Up. (E. T. Wilkinson) Outing, 33: 128.

Via Crucis. (F. M. Crawford) Cent. 35: 62-943. 36: 39-832.

Via Lucis. (C. J. Clifford) Month, 93: 337.

Viall Family Record. (J. Potter) N. E. Reg. 55: 184.

Viaud, Julien, an Attractive Pessimist. (A. H. Diplock) Temp. Bar, 114: 563.

— Figures et Choses qui passaient. (E. Gosse) Sat. R. 85: 81.

— Ramuntcho. Acad. 51: 358.

— Reflets sur la Sombre Route. Acad. 57: 187.

Vibia, The Tomb of. (E. Maas) Open Court, 14: 321.

Vibrations, Stability of. (C. Barus) Science, n. s. 14: 403.

Vicaire, Gabriel. (W. Roberts) Ath. '00, 2: 443.

Vicar of Barrakilty ; a story. Temp. Bar, 114: 102.

Vicar's Sermon, The ; a story. (D. Monro) Idler, 14: 183.

Vicarious Atonement, A ; a story. (C. Mounteney) Belgra. 96: 493.

Vicarious Suffering the Order of Nature. (J. Cooper) Ref. Ch. R. 46: 202.

Vicarson, A. Vicar's Dilemma. (M. Beerbohm) Sat. R. 86: 73.

Vice, Campaign against. Will it last ? (J. A. Riis) Outl. 64: 911.

— Licensed, in the British Army, Apotheosis of. (A. E. Turner) Un. Serv. M. 15: 276. — (J. K. Maconachie) Un. Serv. M. 16: 30. — (A. G. Wynen) Un. Serv. M. 16: 290.

— Municipalities and. Munic. Aff. 4: 698.

— One Aspect of. (E. C. Moore) Am. J. Sociol. 6: -

— Suppression of, as a Function of Popular Government. (C. G. Tiedeman) Am. J. Soc. Sci. 38: 245.

Vice-consort, The. (Frank R. Stockton) Scrib. M. 28: 642.

Vicenza, Two Great Pictures at. (M. H. Witt) Macmil. 83: 190.

Vice-Presidency, The. (F. E. Leupp) Nation, 69: 346.

— (E. P. Clark) Nation, 70: 332.

Vicissitudes of Engine 107 ; a story. (C. Warman) McClure, 9: 717.

Vicksburg, A Woman's Experiences during the Siege of. (L. L. Reed) Cent. 39: 922.

Victim of Prosperity, A. (E. A. Smith) Good Words, 40: 845.

Victor Emmanuel III., King of Italy. Sat. R. 90: 230.

— (H. Zimmern) Fortn. 75: 492.

— How he was Educated. (S. Cortesi) Indep. 53: 1982.

Victor at Chung-ke, A ; a story. (C. E. Craddock) Harper, 100: 509.

Victoria, Queen. (M. O. W. Oliphant) Critic, 37: 152.

— (W. T. Stead) Cosmopol. 29: 207. — (Emily Crawford) Contemp. 79: 153. Same art. Ecl. M. 136: 503. Same art. Liv. Age, 228: 601. — Blackw. 169: 436. Same art. Liv. Age, 229: 54. — (G. Chesterton) Westm. 155: 237. — Macmil. 83: 321. — Outl. 67: 241. — Nat'l M. (Bost.) 13: 359. — With portraits. (H. E. Maxwell) Pall Mall M. 23: 401. — (C. Owen) Indep. 53: 245. — (Mrs. Oliphant) Good Words, 36: 380. — (T. F. Bayard) Cent. 32: 310. — Quar. 185: 295. — (E. Crawford) Contemp. 71: 761. — Fortn. 67: 825. — Spec. 83: 740.

— and the American People. Spec. 86: 192. Same art. Liv. Age, 228: 790.

— and the Arts. Am. Arch. 71: 53.

— and the Fine Arts. (M. H. Spielmann) M. of Art, 25: 193.

— and Germany. Fortn. 75: 408.

— and her Ministers. (E. Crawford) Contemp. 72: 35.

— and her Reign. (M. Jeune) No. Am. 172: 322. — (G. Gunton) Gunton's M. 20: 220.

— and the Victorian Age. (G. R. Parkin) Canad. M. 16: 395.

— as an Etcher. (C. Brinton) Critic, 37: 34.

— as a Farmer. Spec. 86: 167. Same art. Liv. Age, 228: 723.

— as a Moral Force. (W. E. H. Lecky) Pall Mall M. 23: 596.

— as a Mountaineer. (A. I. McConnochie) Strand, 15: 613.

— as a Statesman. (M. MacDonagh) Fortn. 75: 420. Same art. Liv. Age, 229: 137.

— A Boy's Reminiscences of. (Earl of Aberdeen) Outl. 67: 542.

— Character of. Quar. 193: 301. Same art. Ecl. M. 137: 1. Same art. Liv. Age, 229: 465-538.

— Childhood of. Canad. M. 9: 109. — (R. Wood-Samuel) Nat'l M. (Bost.) 7: 395.

— — and Marriage. (J. H. Ellice) Cornh. 75: 730. Same art. Liv. Age, 214: 119.

— Children of. (M. S. Warren) Eng. Illust. 17: 363.

— "Coronation Roll." (F. Hayward) Cent. 32: 163.

— Death of. (P. Bigelow) Indep. 53: 473. — (W. Clark) Canad. M. 16: 402. — Sat. R. 91: 100, 132, 135, 168. — N. Church R. 8: 274. — Sund. M. 30: 191.

Virgil ; Georgics in Blank Verse, Specimen Translation of. (Lord Burghclere) 19th Cent. **43**: 448.
— The Legendary. Acad. **58**: 119.
— Portraits of. (H. N. Fowler) School R. **6**: 598.
— Tennyson's Appreciation of. Acad. **57**: 88.
— Why he did not write the Æneid. Atlan. **81**: 574.
Virginia, Awheel thro'. (J. B. Carrington) Outing, **30**: 65.
— Baptists and Religious Freedom in. (W. T. Thom) J. H. Univ. Stud. **18**: 479.
— Brown's First Republic in America. (W. MacDonald) Nation, **66**: 501. — (B. A. Hinsdale) Dial (Ch.) **25**: 165.
— Changes of a Half-century in. (O. Langhorne) Am. J. Soc. Sci. **38**: 168.
— Democracy *vs.* Aristocracy in. (J. R. Brackett) Sewanee, **4**: 257.
— Economic History of, in the 17th Century, Bruce's. (J. C. Ballagh) Citizen, **3**: 67.
— Education in, Private. (W. Baird) Educa. R. **15**: 339.
— Farm Life in. (D. H. Wheeler) Chaut. **27**: 513.
— In Old. (T. N. Page) Liv. Age, **216**: 139.
— its Rise and Fall ; a Sporting Colony in Walter Raleigh's Old Domains. (Geraldine Vane) Chamb. J. **75**: 817.
— 9th Continental Line. Roster of Officers. Pennsyl. M. **22**: 122.
— Old, and her Neighbours, Fiske's. (I. M. Price) Dial (Ch.) **24**: 73.
— Political Temper of. (J. H. Babcock) Chaut. **27**: 664.
— School System of. Educa. **20**: 373.
— Secession Convention of 1861. (J. Goode) Conserv. R. **3**: 75.
— Suffrage in, History of. (J. A. C. Chandler) J. H. Univ. Stud. **19**: 271.
— Sunday in, An Old. (T. N. Page) Scrib. M. **30**: 727.
— University of. (H. W. Mabie) Outl. **65**: 785.
Virginia and Kentucky Resolutions, Contemporary Opinion of. (F. M. Anderson) Am. Hist. R. **5**: 45, 224.
Virginia Correspondence, An Old. Atlan. **84**: 535.
Virginia Historical Society. (Sally N. Robins) Nat'l M. (Bost.) **6**: 156.
Virginians, The Great. (E. D. Warfield) Indep. **51**: 460.
" Virginius," The Story of the. (R. H. Lovell) Overland, n. s. **32**: 47.
Virtue, Psychological Test of. (G. M. Stratton) Internat. J. Ethics, **11**. 200.
Virtues, Fashions in. Sat. R. **92**: 456.
Visayas, the, A Visit to. (P. Whitmarsh) Outl. **66**: 166.
Visceral Disease and Pain. (E. A. Pace) Psychol. R. **4**: 405.
Viscose and Viscoid. (C. Beadle) J. Frankl. Inst. **143**: 1.
Visible Judgment, A. (Arthur Colton) Scrib. M. **28**: 481.
Vision, Defective, of School-children. (W. B. Johnson) Educa. R. **18**: 15.
— — Tests for, in School-children. (F. Allport) Educa. R. **14**: 150.
— Limits of. (E. Holmes) Pop. Astron. **9**: 499.
— Mind's Part in. (J. Jastrow) Pop. Sci. Mo. **54**: 299.
— New Determination of the Minimum Visible and its Bearing on Localization and Binocular Depths. (G. M. Stratton) Psychol. R. **7**: 429.
— Oblique, On the Brightness of Pigments by. (F. P. Whitman) Science, n. s. **9**: 734.
— Time and Space in. (J. M. Cattell) Psychol. R. **7**: 325.

Vision without Inversion. (G. M. Stratton) Psychol. R. **4**: 341.
 See Eyesight.
Vision at the Menhir, The. (E. J. R. Surrage) Chamb. J. **76**: 851.
Vision of the Desert, A. (V. Thompson) Nat'l M. (Bost.) **11**: 270.
Vision of his Own, A. Temp. Bar, **122**: 249.
Vision of the Polonaise, The ; a story. (K. Cher) Music, **18**: 455.
Visit, The ; a poem. (M. A. M. Marks) Argosy, **68**: 466.
Visit to the Dentist, A. Macmil. **81**: 27.
Visiting of Mother Danbury. (P. L. Dunbar) Lippinc. **68**: 746.
Visiting-cards. Liv. Age, **212**: 910.
— Some Old. Strand, **13**: 401.
Visual Image in Literature. (J. B. Fletcher) Sewanee, **6**: 385.
Visual Impressions, Relation of Stimulus to Sensation in. (C. Lloyd Morgan) Psychol. R. **7**: 217. **8**: 468.
Visual Perception during Eye Movement. (R. Dodge) Psychol. R. **7**: 454.
Vital Statistics. (Benj. Taylor) Macmil. **83**: 300.
Vitalism. (J. Haldane) 19th Cent. **44**: 375. Same art. Ecl. M. **131**: 509. — (C. L. Morgan) Monist, **9**: 179.
— A Historical and Critical Review. (C. S. Myers) Mind, **25**: 218, 319.
Vitality, Can we explain Life by ? (L. C. Miall) Lond. Q. **92**: 34.
Viticulture, Cape. Chamb. J. **77**: 654.
Vitreous Enamels. (C. Davenport) J. Soc. Arts, **47**: 315.
Vitrified Quartz. (W. A. Shenstone) Nature, **64**: 65.
Vittoria, Battle of. (S. Crane) Lippinc. **66**: 140.
Vivaria, Kassandra. Via Lucis. Bk. Buyer, **17**: 59.
Vivi ; a story. (L. Keith) Temp. Bar, **112**: 123.
Vivisection and London Hospitals. (S. Coleridge) Contemp. **77**: 343. — Reply. (Sir R. Thompson) Contemp. **77**: 606.
— Anti-, Men of Science and. (H. C. Mercer) Science, n. s. **9**: 221.
— Anti-vivisection Movement, Immorality of. (P. Carus) Open Court, **11**: 370.
— Ethics of. Ed. R. **190**: 147.
— from Ethical Point of View. (A. Waters and others) Open Court, **11**: 686.
— The Higher Civilization *vs.* (R. G. Abbott) Arena, **19**: 127.
— Human. (G. M. Searle) Cath. World, **70**: 493.
— Limits of Experimentation. (J. Oldfield) Westm. **154**: 190.
— May a Layman discuss ? (J. Oldfield) Westm. **154**: 302.
— Open Letter to the Secretary of State for the Home Department. (S. Coleridge) Fortn. **75**: 88.
Vixen ; a story. (E. M. Lynch) Temp. Bar, **123**: 385.
Vizianagram Treaty, The Forgotten. (J. D. B. Gribble) Asia. R. **24**: 152.
Vizier of the Two-horned Alexander. (F. R. Stockton) Cent. **35**: 52, 179. **36**. 10-746.
Vocabulary of School-children, The. (E. M. Buckingham) Nation, **71**: 270.
— The School-boy's. (N. S. Hooper) Nation, **71**: 210.
Vocal Science. (H. S. Kirkland) Music, **15**: 358.
Vocations. (H. Lucas) Month, **96**: 256.
Vogeler, Heinrich, Etchings by. Artist (N. Y.) **26**: 1.
Vogt, Carl, with portrait. Pop. Sci. Mo. **52**: 116.
Vogüé, E. M. de. The Dead who speak. Blackw. **166**: 149.
Voice and Speech. Chamb. J. **75**: 801.
— as a Revealer of Personality. (R. H. Williams) Educa. **21**: 572.

Wagner, Richard. Dusk of the Gods, at Covent Garden. (J. F. Runciman) Sat. R. 89: 743. 90: 14.
— Early Life of. (E. Swayne) Music, 13: 423.
— from behind the Scenes. (G. Kobbé) Cent. 37: 63.
— his Peculiar Style of Counterpoint. (A. W. Spencers) Music, 13: 53.
— in America. (G. Kobbé) R. of Rs. (N. Y.) 20: 687.
— Lavignac on. (J. G. Huneker) Bk. Buyer, 17: 323. — Ath. '98, 2: 265.
— Life of, Glasenapp's. (J. F. Runciman) Sat. R. 91: 108.
-- Lohengrin. (C. Barnard) Chaut. 26: 519.
— — Dedication of, to Liszt. (H. G. Daniels) Idler, 12: 819.
— Music of. (L. Tolstoi) Music, 14: 345.
— — and Tolstoi. Music, 14: 396.
— — Tonality in. (J. C. Fillmore) Music, 13: 762.
— Musical Expression of Human Emotions. (H. Schneider) Music, 15: 609.
— Musical Festival at Bayreuth. (J. M. Chapple) Nat'l M. (Bost.) 7: 13.
— Nibelungen Ring. (W. F. S. Wallace) Idler, 13: 505, 679, 828. — (J. F. Runciman) Sat. R. 86: 42.
— — and its Philosophy. (E. Newman) Fortn. 69: 867. Same art. Liv. Age, 218: 382.
— — Pt. 1: The Rape of the Rhine-gold. (F. J. Stimson) Scrib. M. 24: 693.
— — Shaw's Comments on. (J. F. Runciman) Sat. R. 86: 779.
— Parsifal. Sat. R. 84: 219.
— Personal Reminiscences of. (S. E. Schure) Music, 17: 374.
— Personality of (G. Kobbé) Forum, 28: 632.
— Siegfried. Sat. R. 84: 10.
— — " Der Bärenhauter." (E. E. Simpson) Music, 15: 575.
— Some Interpreters of. (A. Webber) No. Am. 172: 122.
— Tetralogy, given under Mottl, 1898. Sat. R. 85: 814.
— Tristan and Isolda, Acting of. (J. F. Runciman) Sat. R. 87: 173.
— — Muck's Performance. (J. F. Runciman) Sat. R. 87: 621.
— Valkyrie, at Covent Garden, 1897. Sat. R. 83: 684.
— Vocal Music of. (J. F. Runciman) Sat. R. 90: 617.
— Wagner Mania. (J. C. Hadden) 19th Cent. 44: 125.
— Writings of. Ed. R. 189: 96.
Wagner, Mme. Music, 18: 491.
Wagner, Siegfried, Son of Richard. (L. French) Nat'l M. (Bost.) 8: 453.
Wagnerian Illusion, The. (C. Saint-Saens) Music, 17: 22.
Wagneriana, Some Recent. Music, 13: 93.
Wagon Master's Returns, 1782-83. (F. E. Blake) N. E. Reg. 51: 39.
Waifs of the Rail; a story. (J. A. Hill) Idler, 19: 59.
Waifs of the White City. (V. Woods) New Eng. M. n. s. 16: 285.
Wail of the Guide, The; a poem. (F. C. Clarke) Outing, 35: 374.
Waiting; a poem. (F. Whitmore) Atlan. 83: 37.
Waiting; a poem. (P. L. Dunbar) Cosmopol. 25: 312.
Waiting, Sorrows of. Ecl. M. 131: 380.
Waiting; a story. Temp. Bar, 116: 508. Same art. Liv. Age, 221: 457.
Waiting; a story. (B. Atkinson) Sund. M. 29: 204.
Waiting of Marian Dean, The. (T. St. E. Hake) Chamb. J. 78: supp. 42.
Wakefield, Edward Gibbon, Garnet's. Blackw. 164: 821. — Sat. R. 86: 856.
Wakf, Mohammedan Law of. (W. C. Petheram) Law Q. 13: 383.

Waking of the Birds. (R. C. Nightingale) Good Words, 39: 521.
Wakley, Thomas. Acad. 51: 588.
Walamo Story, The. Spec. 83: 338.
Walbrook, Canada. St. Stephens. (H. C. Shelley) Canad. M. 15: 227.
Walcheren Island, Two Days in. (P. Fitzgerald) Gent. M. n. s. 64: 62.
Walcott, Charles Doolittle, with portrait. Pop. Sci. Mo. 52: 547.
Walcott, Earle Ashley. Writer, 14: 42.
Wald, Abraham. (H. Hapgood) Critic, 36: 259.
Walden Pond. (P. G. Hubert, jr.) Bk. Buyer, 14: 549.
Waldenses, Origin and Early Teachings of, according to Catholic Writers of 13th Century. (H. C. Vedder) Am. J. Theol. 4: 465.
Waldersee, Count von, in 1870. (L. Hale) Contemp. 78: 590. — (W. von Bremen) Liv. Age, 227: 793.
Waldo Family, Four Generations of, in America. (W. Lincoln) N. E. Reg. 52: 213.
Waldoboro, Maine. (E. A. Sawyer) New Eng. M. n. s. 24: 594.
Waldorf-Astoria Hotel. (W. G. Mitchell) Am. Arch. 60: 3.
Wales, Celtic Church in. Church Q. 45: 130.
— Conquest of. (J. E. Morris) Eng. Hist. R. 14: 506.
— Cycling in. (J. Pennell) Contemp. 75: 522.
— Gallant Little. (J. Finnemore) Macmil. 83: 62. Same art. Liv. Age, 228: 252.
— Hill-top Funeral in. Temp. Bar, 120: 261. Same art. Ecl. M. 135: 479.
— Land in, Report of the Royal Commissioner on. (H. L. Stephen) Econ. J. 7: 137.
— North. Siege of Denbigh. (A. G. Bradley) Macmil. 78: 471.
— Red-letter Day in. (Lady H. Somerset) Sund. M. 28: 87.
— Religion of, Genius of. Sat. R. 87: 424.
— Scenery. On Lake Vyrnwy. (A. G. Bradley) Macmil. 77: 369.
Walford, E. Ath. '97, 2: 751.
Walhalla, Echoes of. (M. Beaumont) Sund. M. 26: 836.
Walita; a trooper's story. (S. A. Cloman) Cosmopol. 24: 325.
Walker, Dr. Arthur de Noe. Ath. '00, 2: 442.
Walker, Byron Edmund; a sketch. (T. E. Champion) Canad. M. 13: 158.
Walker, Francis Amasa. (L. L. Price) Econ. J. 7: 148. — (J. L. Laughlin) J. Pol. Econ. 5: 228. — (R. P. Falkner) Ann. Am. Acad. Pol. Sci. 9: 173. — Critic, 30: 41. — With bibliography. (C. D. Wright) Am. Statis. Assoc. 5: 245. — With portrait. (J. P. Munroe) Bk. Buyer, 14: 48. — (C. J. H. Woodbury) Cassier, 13: 358. — (L. Hayward) N. E. Reg. 52: 69.
— as a Public Man. (D. R. Dewey) R. of Rs. (N. Y.) 15: 166.
— Career of. (C. F. Dunbar) Q. J. Econ. 11: 436.
— Character Sketch. (J. J. Spencer) R. of Rs. (N. Y.) 15: 159.
— Contribution of, to Economics. Gunton's M. 12: 89.
— Contributions to Economic Theory. (A. T. Hadley) Pol. Sci. Q. 12: 295.
— The Educational Work of. (H. W. Tyler) Educa. R. 14: 55.
Walker, Frederick. (J. L. Gilder) Critic, 30: 212.
— Life and Letters of, Marks on. Ath. '97, 2: 424. — Spec. 78: 482.
Walker, John G. (J. Barnes) R. of Rs. (N. Y.) 16: 298.
Walker, Jonathan. (F. E. Kittredge) New Eng. M. n. s. 19: 365.

WASHINGTON 621 WATER

Washington, George, Wilson's Life of. (B. A. Hinsdale) Dial (Ch.) **22**: 178. — (W. W. Henry) Am. Hist. R. **2**: 539.

Washingtons, Dutch. (W. C. Ford) Nation, **72**: 252.
— Seat of the. (W. Farrer) Nation, **70**: 9.

Washington-Brodhurst Connection. (W. C. Ford) Nation, **68**: 332.

Washington, D. C. (F. Sewall) Am. Arch. **72**: 60. — (De Frieze) Am. Arch. **69**: 5.
— Artistic Development of. Am. Arch. **71**: 46.
— Beautifying the National Capital. (F. E. Leupp) Nation, **72**: 485.
— The Building of a Great Capital. World's Work, **1**: 191.
— Centenary of. Spec. **85**: 963. — (F. W. Fitzpatrick) Cosmopol. **30**: 109.
— City Government of. (C. Meriwether) Pol. Sci. Q. **12**: 407.
— The City of Leisure. (A. M. Low) Atlan. **86**: 767.
— Current Events at. (J. M. Chapple) Nat'l M. (Bost.) **13**: 105.
— during Reconstruction. (S. W. McCall) Atlan. **87**: 817.
— Every-day. (L. W. Betts) Outl. **65**: 868.
— Familiar Figures in. (L. A. Coolidge) Cosmopol. **28**: 365.
— Gossip from. (M. A. Dodge) Liv. Age, **230**: 653.
— Historic Homes of. (C. F. Cavanagh) Munsey, **20**: 921.
— Historical Development of the National Capital. (M. Baker) Nat. Geog. M. **9**: 323.
— Homes of New England Statesmen in. (F. R. Batchelder) New Eng. M. n. s. **23**: 382.
— Improving the Capital. (F. E. Leupp) World's Work, **1**: 528.
— in Early Times. (D. E. Roberts) Nat'l M. (Bost.) **13**: 371.
— Inaugural Balls of the Past. (J. S. Campbell) Nat'l M. (Bost.) **13**: 441.
— Life in. (W. E. Curtis) Chaut. **25**: 467, 579.
— Literary Women of. (E. R. Goodwin) Chaut. **27**: 579.
— a Predestined Capital. (A. H. Wharton) Lippinc. **67**: 77.
— Public Library Building. Lib. J. **24**: 676.
— Recent Architecture. (P. C. Stuart) Archit. R. **10**: 425.
— Reminiscences of. (A. R. Spofford) Atlan. **81**: 668, 749.
— Sacking of, by British in 1814. (T. G. Alvord) Nat'l M. (Bost.) **10**: 237.
— Society in. Un. Serv. (Phila.) **17**: 1.

Washington, Fort, Capture of, May, 1822. Pennsyl. M. **23**: 95.
— — Letter on. Pennsyl. M. **25**: 259.

Washington, State of. Chamb. J. **77**: 366. — (W. D. Lyman) Atlan. **87**: 505.
— Forest Conditions of. (H. Gannett) Nat. Geog. M. **9**: 410.
— Forest Life in. (E. Tuttle) Midland, **9**: 396.
— Some Impressions of. (A. B. Coffey) Overland, n. s. **30**: 363.
— The Wonderful Northwest. (H. A. Stanley) World's Work, **2**: 812.

Washington Memorial Institution. (N. M. Butler) R. of Rs. (N. Y.) **24**: 56. — Science, n. s. **13**: 921.

Washington Monument, The. (R. Bache) Cosmopol. **28**: 204.

Washington University, St. Louis. (W. S. Chaplin) Science, n. s. **13**: 258.

Wash-tub Davis; an Alaskan sketch. (M. Roberts) Eng. Illust. **17**: 32.

Wasley, Frank, Charcoal Drawings of. (F. Emanuel) Artist (N. Y.) **31**: 121.

Wasps. (J. W. Cole) Gent. M. n. s. **62**: 430.
— as Paper Makers. (Grant Allen) Strand, **15**: 57.
— Ingenuity of. (A. B. Comstock) Chaut. **26**: 590.
— Instincts of, as a Problem in Evolution. Nature, **59**: 466.
— Some Facts about. (R. W. Shufeldt) Pop. Sci. Mo. **51**: 315.

Waste, John; Fragments of two persecutions. (J. Hyde) Gent. M. n. s. **63**: 576.

Waste, Human, in a Great City. (W. L. Hawley) Gunton's M. **21**: 414.
— Restraint upon. (Brooks Adams) Am. Arch. **74**: 99.
— Utilization of. (P. T. Austen) Forum, **32**: 74. — (J. Birkinbine) Am. Arch. **65**: 44. Same art. Cassier, **16**: 610.

Waste Products; a story. (P. T. Battersby) Belgra. **98**: 162.

Wastes from Use of White Metals, Utilization of. (J. Richards) J. Frankl. Inst. **151**: 445. **152**: 59.

Watanna, Onoto, with portrait. Bk. News, **17**: 451.

Watch and Clock Making. (T. D. Wright) J. Soc. Arts, **45**: 843.

Watch Plates, Tools for Drilling Holes in. (H. Roland) Engin. M. **18**: 530.

Watch Work, English. (F. J. Britten) Good Words, **38**: 527.

Watcher, The; a poem. (M. G. Dickinson) Outl. **64**: 796.

Watcher by the Threshold. (J. Buchan) Atlan. **86**: 797. Same art. Blackw. **168**: 817.

Watches, Magnetized, Observations on. (W. T. Lewis) J. Frankl. Inst. **143**: 60.
— Waltham; a Horological Pilgrimage. (J. Barnes) Scrib. M. **23**: adv. in Feb. no.

Watchman, What of the Night? a poem. Argosy, **69**: 50.

Water, Ascent of, in Trees. (F. Darwin) Nature, **56**: 307.
— Biological Studies in Massachusetts. (G. C. Whipple) Am. Natural. **31**: 503, 576, 1016.
— Davenport's Rôle of Water in Growth. Am. Natural. **32**: 122.
— Drinking, Sanitation of. (F. J. Thornbury) Arena, **17**: 956.
— Fermentation of, Causes and Prevention of. (S. McElroy) Engin. M. **13**: 535.
— Filtration of, for Public Use. J. Mil. Serv. Inst. **27**: 441.
— Flow of. (H. S. Hele-Shaw) Nature, **58**: 34.
— Flowing, Measurement of. (S. Webber) Cassier, **12**: 26.
— found by Boring through Rock, Nordenskjold's Discovery. (C. R. Markham) Geog. J. **10**: 465.
— Ground, Movements of. (B. S. Lyman) J. Frankl. Inst. **150**: 285.
— Hot, and Soft Glass in their Thermodynamic Relations. (C. Barus) Am. J. Sci. **159**: 161.
— Microscopical Examination of. (G. C. Whipple) Science, **6**: 85.
— Physics of. (G. F. Stradling) J. Frankl. Inst. **152**: 257.
— Pollution and Purification of. (E. E. Hatch) J. Mil. Serv. Inst. **22**: 495.
— Purification of. (F. J. Thornbury) Chaut. **24**: 576.
— — by Metallic Iron. (C. W. Chancellor) Am. Arch. **56**: 77.
— — in U. S. (A. R. Leeds) Cassier, **11**: 304.
— Rideal on. (S. C. Hooker) Citizen, **3**: 164.
— Softening of. (W. N. Twelvetrees) Cassier, **15**: 465.
— Struggle for, in the West. (W. E. Smythe) Atlan. **86**: 646.

Water; Torrents of Switzerland. (E. R. Dawson) Pop. Sci. Mo. **54**: 46.

Water Analyses, Interpretation of Sanitary. (F. Davis) Engin. M. **15**: 68.

Water Analysis, Standard Methods of. Science, n. s. **12**: 906.

Water-bicycles. (E. P. Bunyea) Outing, **33**: 607.

Water-bottle, The Pettersson-Nansen Insulating. (H. R. Mill) Geog. J. **16**: 469.

Water Buffalo, Wanderings of. Spec. **87**: 278.

Water-color Pictures in Washington, D. C. (A. B. Bibb) Am. Arch. **70**: 85.

Water Colors, Amer. Society of, Exhibition, 1899. Artist (N. Y.) **24**: xlix.

— N. Y. Club Exhibition, 1898. Artist (N. Y.) **23**: xxx.

— — 9th Annual, 1899. Artist (N. Y.) **26**: lxix.

— Sir J. C. Robinson's Collection of. M. of Art, **21**: 32.

— Royal Society of Painters in, Exhibition of 1897. Art J. **49**: 61. — Ath. '97, **1**: 155, 621. **2**: 791.

— — Winter Exhibitions. Ath. '00, **2**: 764.

Water Cooling Towers. (J. A. Reavell) Cassier, **18**: 510.

Water-falls and the Work of the World. (F. Waters) World's Work, **1**: 739.

Water-finder, A Lady. Sund. M. **29**: 674.

Water Gas, Chemical Composition of. (E. H. Earnshaw) J. Frankl. Inst. **146**: 161, 303.

Water-hyacinth. (W. W. Bailey) Cosmopol. **24**: 107.

Water-lilies; a poem. (A. W. Colton) Cosmopol. **23**: 335.

Water-lily, A; a poem. (E. M. Thomas) Outing, **30**: 131.

Water-lily, The; a poem. (G. Lea) Outing, **30**: 332.

Water Meters, Venturi. (C. Herschel) Cassier, **15**: 411.

Water-power and Electricity. Chamb. J. **77**: 728.

— and the Future of Cities. (E. H. Mullin) Cassier, **13**: 27.

— and Steam Power, Comparative Cost of. (W. O. Webber) Engin. M. **15**: 922.

— Development of, in Connection with Electricity. (J. B. C. Kershaw) Chamb. J. **75**: 54. — (F. C. Finkle) Engin. M. **14**: 1011.

— Electric Transmission of. (W. Baxter, jr.) Pop. Sci. Mo. **52**: 730.

See Electric Transmission.

— from High Water Heads. (J. E. Bennett) Cassier, **12**: 3.

— Future of. Spec. **79**: 303.

— Hydraulic Transmission of Power. (E. B. Ellington) Engin. M. **17**: 233, 399.

— A New Transmission Plant. (C. L. Fitch) Cassier, **19**: 243.

Water-power Governing, Commercial Requirements of. (E. F. Cassell) Engin. M. **19**: 841.

Water-power Plants, Speed Government in. (M. A. Replogle) J. Frankl. Inst. **145**: 81. — (A. V. Garratt) Cassier, **20**: 21.

Water Sports, Curious. (F. G. Callcott) Strand, **17**: 528.

Water Supplies, Filtration of. (W. J. Holland) Am. J. Soc. Sci. **36**: 246.

— River, Purification of. (A. Hazen) Engin. M. **15**: 249.

Water Supply and Sewage, Local Government in relation to, in England. (W. O. E. Meade-King) J. Soc. Arts, **48**: 201.

— Department of. (W. F. King) Munic. Aff. **4**: 751.

— English Water Question. Spec. **81**: 397.

— for Birmingham. Pall Mall M. **24**: 181.

— Municipal, Sanitary Problems connected with. (W. P. Mason) J. Frankl. Inst. **143**: 337.

Water Supply of London. (G. S. Lefevre) 19th **Cent. 44**: 980. — (P. Frankland) J. Soc. Arts, **45**: 611. — (W. Hunter) J. Soc. Arts, **47**: 475.

— of Greater New York. (M. N. Baker) Munic. Aff. **4**: 486.

— of Philadelphia. (M. R. Maltbie) Munic. Aff. **3**: 193. — (A. A. Bird) Citizen, **2**: 372.

— — Report of Commission on Extension and Improvement of. J. Frankl. Inst. **148**: 390.

— Relations of Forestation to. (H. M. Wilson) Engin. M. **14**: 807.

— Shall San Francisco Municipalize? (A. S. Baldwin) Munic. Aff. **4**: 317.

— State Rights and City Rights. (R. H. Past) Outl. **64**: 929.

— Syracuse. (J. H. Hamilton) Munic. Aff. **4**: 60.

— Turneaure and Russell on. (M. Merriam) Science, n. s. **14**: 104.

Water-tight Compartments in Steam Vessels. (J. H. Morrison) Cassier, **12**: 711.

Water-tube Boiler, The Marine. (J. Platt) Engin. M. **21**: 913.

Water Way, Deep, from the Great Lakes to the Ocean. (D. C. Kingman) J. Mil. Serv. Inst. **16**: 276. — (W. L. Simpson) J. Mil. Serv. Inst. **15**: 1193.

Water Ways and Maritime Works, Recent Progress in. Nature, **64**: 639.

— from the Great Lakes to the Sea. (A. R. Davis) Engin. M. **13**: 380.

— Inland, Our Neglected and Prospective. (A. H. Ford) Forum, **31**: 181.

— of America. (A. H. Ford) Harper, **101**: 783.

Water Wheel, Cascade, Tests of. (J. H. Cooper) J. Frankl. Inst. **143**: 376.

Water-works, Municipal, in England. Ann. Am. Acad. Pol. Sci. **14**: 143.

— Public and Private Ownership of. (M. N. Baker) Outl. **59**: 76.

Water-works, The; a story. (E. Nesbit) Pall Mall M. **22**: 215. Same art. Liv. Age, **227**: 506.

Water-works Laboratories, Municipal. (G. C. Whipple) Pop. Sci. Mo. **58**: 172.

Watering-pots, Old English. (R. Quick) Reliquary, **40**: 198.

Waters, Still. (J. C. Van Dyke) Liv. Age, **218**: 492.

— Subterranean. (C. Morris) J. Frankl. Inst. **151**: 182.

Waterhouse, J. W., and his Work. (A. L. Baldry) Studio (Lond.) **4**: 103.

— Mermaid. Art J. **53**: 182.

Waterloo, Battle of. (J. J. O'Connell) J. Mil. Serv. Inst. **8**: 197.

— A Black Hussar at. (C. H. Nieman) Chaut. **33**: 631.

— Bonaparte and Byron. (H. G. Keene) Westm. **148**: 37.

— The Bravest Briton at. (E. Bruce Low) Chamb. J. **78**: 401.

— Campaigner of, and his Pupils. (J. M. Stone) Month, **89**: 154.

— A Contemporary Letter. (K. Arden) Cornh. **77**: 72. Same art. Liv. Age, **216**: 463. Same art. Ecl. M. **130**: 349.

— Dutch-Belgians at. (C. Oman) 19th Cent. **48**: 629. — (D. C. Boulger) Contemp. **77**: 677.

— Houssaye's. (A. Laugel) Nation, **68**: 293.

— Last French Charge at. (E. M. Lloyd) Un. Serv. M. **21**: 58.

— Letters of a Soldier. (W. Windsor) Cornh. **79**: 739.

— Military Anecdotes. (R. Staveley) Cornh. **79**: 751.

— A Myth of. (A. Forbes) Cent. **33**: 464.

— Our Allies at. (H. Maxwell) 19th Cent. **48**: 407.

— The Peninsula and. (E. F. DuCane) Cornh. **76**: 750.

Weiss, Bernard, and the New Testament. (C. R. Gregory) Am. J. Theol. 1: 16.

Weld, Arthur, Composer and Littérateur, with portrait. Music, 15: 314.

Weld, Habijah, of Attleboro, Mass. (D. Jillson) N. E. Reg. 54: 442.

Well of Wailing, The; a tale. (G. Yeo) Argosy, 70: 431.

Wellby, Capt. M. S. Geog. J. 16: 358.

Wellcome Research Laboratories. (R. J. Friswell) Nature, 62: 271.

Wellesley College, Outdoor Life at. (J. A. Marks) Outing, 32: 117.

— Undergraduate Life at. (Abbe C. Goodloe) Scrib. M. 23: 515.

Wellesleys, Surname of the. Ath. '00, 1: 177.

Wellhausen, Julius, and his Latest Critic, W. L. Baxter. (S. Holmes) Westm. 147: 389.

Wellington, Duke of. (Goldwin Smith) Atlan. 87: 771. — Quar. 191: 492. — Ed. R. 192: 91.

— and the Bridge of Boats of 1814, over River Ardour. (W. H. James) Pall Mall M. 11: 85.

— and his Comrades, Griffiths's. Sat. R. 86: 116.

— at Salamanca. (W. H. Fitchett) Cornh. 78: 1.

— Maxwell's. (W. O'C. Morris) Fortn. 73: 200.

— Sanity of. (D. Hannay) Macmil. 81: 364.

Wellington, Capital of New Zealand. (T. L. Mills) Pall Mall M. 22: 531. — (F. Dolman) Idler, 15: 166.

Wellman, Samuel T. Cassier, 19: 238.

Wellman Polar Expedition, 1898-99. (W. Wellman) McClure, 14: 318, 405, 555. — (W. Wellman) Cent. 35: 531. — (W. Wellman) Nat. Geog. M. 10: 481. — With portrait. (J. H. Gore) Nat. Geog. M. 10: 267, 348.

— Meteorological Observations of Second. (Evelyn B. Baldwin) Nat. Geog. M. 10: 512.

Wells, David Ames. J. Pol. Econ. 7: 93. — (D. MacG. Means) Nation, 67: 346. — (E. L. Godkin) Harv. Grad. M. 7: 351. — With portrait. Bk. Buyer, 17: 583.

Wells, Herbert G. Acad. 52: 491. — With portraits. Strand, 16: 675.

— as a Novelist. Acad. 58: 535. Same art. Liv. Age, 226: 395.

— The War of the Worlds. Acad. 53: 121.

— When the Sleeper Wakes. Acad. 56: 624.

Wells, Lionel De Lantour, Portraits of. Strand, 13: 66.

Wells, Chapter of, Rise and Growth of, from 1242 to 1333. Archæol. 54: 1.

Wells Cathedral Church. Illus. (C. M. Church) Good Words, 38: 677, 767.

— — Misericords and Prebendal Stalls in. (C. M. Church) Archæol. 55: 319.

Wells Fargo's Box; a tale. Argosy, 64: 505.

Wells of Peace, The. (Fiona Macleod) Good Words, 39: 595.

Wellsite, a New Mineral. (J. H. Pratt and H. W. Foote) Am. J. Sci. 153: 443.

Welsbach Light. J. Frankl. Inst. 150: 406. — Science, n. s. 12: 951. — Contemp. 78: 710.

Welsh Church Customs, Obsolete. (E. Owen) Reliquary, 37: 208.

Welsh Funeral, A Hill-top. Temp. Bar, 120: 261. Same art. Liv. Age, 226: 388.

Welsh Indians of Virginia, Rev. Morgan Jones and. (I. J. Greenwood) N. E. Reg. 52: 28.

Welsh Literature of the Victorian Era. Liv. Age, 231: 124.

Welsh People, Rhys's. (W. J. Ashley) Nation, 71: 214.

Welsh Poetry. (A. Symons) Sat. R. 85: 457. Same art. Liv. Age, 217: 615.

— in Chaucer's Day. Quar. 194: 396.

Wendell, Barrett. Literary History of America. (L. E. Gates) Critic, 38: 341. — (W. D. Howells) No. Am. 172: 623. See American Literature.

— Portrait of. Bk. Buyer, 21: 531.

Wendt, William, Landscapes by. (C. F. Browne) Brush & P. 6: 257.

Wenlock and its Saint. (M. Barrett) Month, 95: 155.

Wentworth, Lady Maria, Monument to. Reliquary, 41: 52.

Wentworth-Woodhouse. (A. D. Alcho) New Eng. M. n. s. 19: 271.

Wenzelbibel, The. (W. Kurrelmeyer) Am. J. Philol. 21: 62.

Wenzell, Albert Beck, Artist, with portrait. (C. F. Bourke) Brush & P. 2: 65.

Werewolves, The. (H. Beaugrand) Cent. 34: 814.

Werther, Mr., Musician, with portrait. Music, 18: 464.

Wesley, Charles, Children's Hymns by. (A. Whyte) Sund. M. 28: 324.

Wesley, John, and the Salzburgers. (A. G. Voigt) Luth. Q. 27: 370.

— Aspects of the 18th Century in England. (A. Birrell) Scrib. M. 26: 753.

— Christian Socialist. (W. H. Meredith) Meth. R. 61: 426.

— Journals of. (Dora M. Jones) Temp. Bar, 122: 514.

— Last of the Great Reformers. (J. W. Johnson) Munsey, 23: 757.

— Original American Journal of. (E. R. Hendrix) Meth. R. 61: 513.

— School of, at Kingswood. (T. Telford) Meth. R. 59: 410.

— Services to England. Spec. 83: 81. Same art. Ecl. M. 133: 570. Same art. Liv. Age, 222: 590.

Wesley, Mrs. Susannah. A Spartan Mother. Temp. Bar, 115: 506.

Wesleys, The, and the New Portraits. (W. H. Withrow) Outl. 69: 315.

Wessex, Beginnings of. (H. H. Howorth) Eng. Hist. R. 13: 667. — (W. H. Stevenson) Eng. Hist. R. 14: 32.

— Pilgrimage to. (C. Holland) Critic, 39: 136.

West, Sir Algernon. Recollections. Sat. R. 88: 770. — (C. T. Brady) Bk. Buyer, 21: 124.

West, Anna; was she a Daughter of Robert Saunderson? (J. E. Alden) N. E. Reg. 52: 23.

West, J. Walter. Many Waters cannot quench Love. Art J. 49: 125.

— Work of. (A. L. Baldry) Studio (Lond.). 6: 139.

West, The, and Certain Literary Discoveries. (E. Hough) Cent. 37: 506.

— and its Growth. (C. S. Nichols) Nat'l M. (Bost.) 14: 565.

— and the South, Business Alliance of. (C. M. Harger) No. Am. 165: 380.

— Boomers of the. (J. R. Spears) Munsey, 25: 850.

— Dominant Forces in Life of. (F. J. Turner) Atlan. 79: 433.

— Golden Harvest of. (C. M. Harger) Outl. 66: 25.

— Higher Life of. (C. M. Harger) Indep. 52: 1726.

— in the '40's. (J. B. Pond) Cent. 36: 929.

— Intellectual Movement in. (H. W. Mabie) Atlan. 82: 592.

— The Middle. (F. J. Turner) Internat. Mo. 4: 794.

— — New Era in. (C. M. Harger) Harper, 97: 276.

— Political Future of the Great. (J. M. Thurston) Munsey, 18: 650.

— Real Utopias in the Arid. (W. E. Smythe) Atlan. 79: 599.

— Settlement of; a Study in Transportation. (E. Hough) Cent. 41: 91, 201.

Westminster Abbey, Wall-painting discovered at, 1882, On a. Archæol. 47: 471.

Westminster Assembly, England of. (E. D. Warfield) Presb. & Ref. R. 9: 44.

— Place of, in Modern History. (J. De Witt) Presb. & Ref. R. 9: 369.

Westminster Chambers Bill, Boston, Argument against. Am. Arch. 71: 60.

Westminster Confession, The. Outl. 67: 613.

— Beattie on. (B. B. Warfield) Presb. & Ref. R. 8: 355.

— Character of. (J. Macpherson) Presb. & Ref. R. 9: 239.

— Making of. (B. B. Warfield) Presb. & Ref. R. 12: 226.

— Printing of. (B. B. Warfield) Presb. & Ref. R. 12: 606.

Westminster Hall, Masons' Marks at. (E. Freshfield) Archæol. 50: 1.

— West Side of. (S. Clarke) Archæol. 50: 9.

Westminster "Improvement" Scheme. (E. P. Warren) Fortn. 69: 479. — Spec. 80: 617.

Westminster Palace, Mural Decorations of. Am. Arch. 73: 95.

Westminster School, Sargeant's Annals of. Spec. 82: 416. Same art. Ecl. M. 132: 872. Same art. Liv. Age, 221: 386.

Westmoreland Story, A. (A. Fleming) Gent. M. n. s. 59: 521.

Westward Movement. The Colonies and the Republic West of the Alleghanies, 1763–98, Winsor on. (C. D. Roberts) Bk. Buyer, 16: 138. — (C. E. Boyd) Nation, 66: 170. — (B. A. Hinsdale) Dial (Ch.) 24: 9.

Wet, Christian de, General. (H. C. Hillegas) World's Work, 1: 538. — (T. F. Millard) Scrib. M. 29: 547. — (H. Robertson) Canad. M. 15: 458.

— and his Campaign. (Allen Sangree) Cosmopol. 31: 65.

— First and Worse Repulse of. (F. R. O'Neill) Chamb. J. 78: 563–588.

— Soldier and Man. (R. H. Davis) Indep. 53: 599.

— With. (P. Pienar) Contemp. 79: 326. Same art. Liv. Age, 229: 47.

Weyler, General, Campaign of. (C. Marriott) Arena, 18: 374. See Cuba.

Weymouth, Mass., Old-time Ministerial Contract in. (R. R. Kendall) New Eng. M. n. s. 24: 329.

Whale, Right, Migration of the. Illus. (T. Southwell) Nat. Sci. 12: 397.

Whale-fishery, End of the British. Spec. 80: 81.

— Incidents of. (F. T. Bullen) Cornh. 75: 642. Same art. Ecl. M. 129: 105.

Whaler, Life on a Greenland. (A. C. Doyle) Strand, 13: 16. Same art. McClure, 8: 460.

— South Sea, Life on a. (F. T. Bullen) Pop. Sci. Mo. 54: 818.

Whalers, Rescue of the, 1897. (E. P. Bertholf) Harper, 99: 3.

Whales, Armor-clad. Nature, 64: 652.

— at South Kensington. Spec. 80: 789.

— Loss of the First-born; a story. (F. T. Bullen) Spec. 80: 44.

— Models of, at the Natural History Museum, London. (R. Lydekker) Knowl. 21: 193.

— The Orphan. (F. T. Bullen) Cornh. 79: 615. Same art. Ecl. M. 133: 296. Same art. Liv. Age, 222: 92.

— White, in Confinement. (F. Mather) Pop. Sci. Mo. 55: 362.

Whaling in America in the Old Days. (M. L. Osborne) Nat'l M. (Bost.) 11: 395.

— Offshore, in the Bay of Monterey. (E. Berwick) Cosmopol. 29: 631.

Whaling, Perils of. (A. F. Coffin) Outing, 33: 353.

— Romance of. (Malcolm Rees) Gent. M. n. s. 62: 83.

Whaling Disaster of 1871. (F. P. McKibben) New Eng. M. n. s. 18: 490.

Wharf Improvements and Harbor Facilities. (F. Crowell) Engin. M. 14: 12, 205, 444.

Wharfedale Revisited. Gent. M. n. s. 64: 476.

Wharton, Edith, with portrait. Bk. Buyer, 18: 354.

— as a Writer. Acad. 61: 75.

— Greater Inclination. (A. Gorren) Critic, 37: 173.

— her Use of the Epigram. Bk. Buyer, 18: 395.

What Dorothy did. (Grace Luce) Overland, n. s. 30: 109.

What the Gypsy foretold. (P. Antonio de Alarçon) Liv. Age, 221: 821.

What happened after Mary McArthur cut her Finger. (S. R. Crockett) Lippinc. 68: 357.

What it cost; a story. (A. H. Drury) Argosy, 65: 416.

What Maisie knew. (H. James) New R. 16: 113–581. 17: 1.

What the Moon revealed. (R. Hoare) Belgra. 96: 235.

What stopped the Ship. (H. P. Whitmarsh) Cent. 32: 776.

What the Storm did for Mattie; a story. Argosy, 65: 186.

"Whatsoever is Terrene;" verse. (R. D. Smith) Green Bag, 10: 478.

Wheat and its Distribution. (Joseph Leiter) Cosmopol. 26: 114.

— Breeding New Wheats. (W. S. Harwood) World's Work, 1: 745.

— Coming Scarcity of. (R. Giffen) Nature, 61: 169.

— Corner in, An International. (J. D. Whelpley) Fortn. 74: 208.

— in California. (Horace Davis) Overland, n. s. 32: 60.

— The Inland Empire's Harvests. (S. A. Clarke) Outl. 66: 286.

— The Mighty River of. (R. E. Smith) Munsey, 25: 17.

— The Movement of. (R. S. Baker) McClure, 14: 124.

— Problem of. (B. W. Snow) Forum, 28: 94. — (E. Atkinson) Pop. Sci. Mo. 54: 759.

— — America and. (J. Hyde) No. Am. 168: 191.

— — for England. Sat. R. 87: 103.

— Production of, from a Farmer's Standpoint. (G. A. Parcell) No. Am. 168: 511.

— The Question of. (W. C. Ford) Pop. Sci. Mo. 52: 760. 53: 1, 351.

— The Rise in. Spec. 79: 267.

— Rust of, Recent Investigations on. (W. G. Smith) Nature, 62: 352.

— Scarcity of. (A. D. Noyes) Nation, 66: 356.

— World's Supply of; Crookes vs. Atkinson, Dodge, et al. (C. W. Davis) Forum, 27: 101.

Wheat Crop, Evolution of a. (H. Bindloss) Macmil. 83: 23. Same art. Ecl. M. 136: 259. Same art. Liv. Age, 228: 48.

— The Farmer and the. (A. D. Noyes) Nation, 66: 417.

— of 1899, British. Sat. R. 88: 286.

— Transportation of the World's. (G. E. Walsh) Arena, 24: 516.

Wheat Broking, Day in. (W. Payne) Cent. 36: 340.

Wheat Famine, The Predicted. (A. D. Noyes) Nation, 67: 237.

Wheat Farm, The Business of a. (W. A. White) Scrib. M. 22: 531.

Wheat-growing Capacity of the Northwest Territories. (C. W. Peterson) Canad. M. 14: 137.

— of the United States. (E. Atkinson) Pop. Sci. Mo. 54: 145.

Wheat Lands of Canada. (S. C. D. Roper) Pop. Sci. Mo. 55: 766.

Wheat Reserve, Urgent Need of a. (R. B. Marston) 19th Cent. 43: 879.

Wheaton Seminary, Norton, Massachusetts. (G. H. Hubbard) New Eng. M. n. s. 18: 102.

Wheel, Evolution of. (S. M. Barton) Sewanee, 5: 48.

Wheel of Time, The; a bicycle story. (Mary C. Lee) Scrib. M. 28: 549.

Wheelman's Faery Queen, The; a poem. (C. Turner) Outing, 30: 207.

Whelen, John Leman. Bank. M. (Lond.) 64: 475.

When Bass begin to bite; a poem. (N. Nettire) Outing, 34: 385.

"When Beauty fades . . . ;" a story. (M. Diver) Argosy, 74: 93.

When Blades are out and Love's afield. (C. T. Brady) Lippinc. 67: 1.

When the Brook Trout leaps; a poem. Outing, 34: 76.

When Cholera came; a sketch. (J. Barrett) McClure, 16: 140.

When the Cholera came to Santa Cruz. (H. Bindloss) Macmil. 84: 62.

When Christmas Bells ring; a story. (Louise C. Henderson) Nat'l M. (Bost.) 7: 274.

When the Clouds fell down; a story. (J. Ralph) Harper, 97: 465.

When Cotton was King. (Eva V. Carlin) Overland, n. s. 36: 13.

When the Door opened; a story. (Sarah Grand) Idler, 12: 708.

When Early March seems Middle May; a poem. (J. W. Riley) Bk. Buyer, 16: 337.

When Gitchigamme warned the Muscovite. (Sewell Ford) Scrib. M. 30: 51.

When the Grass grew long. (J. M. Oskison) Cent. 40: 247.

"When Greek meets Greek;" a story. (W. Sparrow) Idler, 18: 238.

When I was a Child; a poem. Atlan. 86: 709.

When I was Young. (A. S. Swan) Sund. M. 30: 19.

When the Light failed; a story. (G. Reno) McClure, 14: 461.

When Losing is Winning; a story. (L. C. Howe) Outing, 36: 406.

When Love shall come; a poem. (A. G. Hopkins) Argosy, 66: 608.

When a Man comes to Himself. (W. Wilson) Cent. 40: 268.

When Me an' Ed got Religion. (F. W. Shibley) New Eng. M. n. s. 25: 278.

When Mrs. Van Worcester dines; a story. (A. W. Sears) Harper, 99: 422.

When October comes along; a poem. (E. M. Crossley) Canad. M. 18: 32.

When Ole Marster passed away; a Negro character sketch. (W. A. Dromgoole) Arena, 26: 528.

When the Overland comes in. (R. J. Sterrett) Overland, n. s. 38: 27.

When Radiance ripens; a poem. (I. E. Jones) Outing, 34: 296.

When the Snows drift. (J. G. Neihardt) Overland, n. s. 38: 103.

Where Angels fear to Tread; a story. (M. Robertson) Atlan. 82: 206.

Where Glory waits us; a poem. (C. Bryan) Canad. M. 14: 140.

Where the Roses grew. (Sarah R. Heath) Overland, n. s. 36: 23.

Where they found her. (Josephine Clifford) Overland, n. s. 32: 27.

Where the Trail forks; a romance. (Jack London) Outing, 37: 276.

Where's Nora? (Sarah O. Jewett) Scrib. M. 24: 739.

Whereyouwantogoto; or, the Bouncible Ball. (E. Nesbit) Strand, 18: 585.

Whibley, Charles. Acad. 52: 492.

Whichcote, Benjamin, 1609–83. (E. A. George) Outl. 58: 65.

Whigs, The, as Anti-expansionists. (A. Watkins) Sewanee, 8: 56.

"While the Lamp holds out to burn;" a story. (G. Parker) Pall Mall M. 19: 35.

While the Automobile ran down. (C. B. Loomis) Cent. 39: 187.

"While the Evil Days come not;" a story. (W. A. White) McClure, 11: 344.

While the Jury was out; a story. (W. F. Dix) McClure, 17: 466.

While waiting in a Friend's Room. (A. West) 19th Cent. 46: 77. Same art. Ecl. M. 133: 590. Same art. Liv. Age, 222: 623.

Whilomville Stories. (S. Crane) Harper, 99: 358, 855. 100: 25–963. 101: 56–401.

Whip Hand, The; a story. (A. Devoore) McClure, 9: 906.

Whipping, Restoration of, as a Punishment for Crime. (S. E. Baldwin) Green Bag, 13: 65. — Reply. (D. Mowry) Green Bag, 13: 553.

Whipping-post, Delaware's Abolition of the. (B. A. Miller) Cosmopol. 22: 661.

Whipple, Bishop Henry B., Apostle to the Indians. (A. Clifford) Sund. M. 28: 509. — (H. C. Merwin) Atlan. 85: 705.

— and the Indian. (C. T. Brady) Bk. Buyer, 20: 114.

— Friend of the Indian. (W. W. Folwell) R. of Rs. (N. Y.) 24: 575.

— Lights and Shadows of a Long Episcopate. Church Q. 50: 429.

— A Memorable Man. Outl. 69: 208.

Whirlwind Wooing, The; a story. (C. T. Brady) Harper, 103: 88.

Whiskey-tax, Morals of the. (E. Wilson) Sewanee, 2: 115.

Whiskey Trade, Troubles on the. Bank. M. (Lond.) 67: 203.

Whisper of Pan; a story. (L. G. Ackroyd) Temp. Bar, 113: 515. Same art. Ecl. M. 130: 750.

Whisperer, The; a story of 1798. (K. Tynan) Temp. Bar, 114: 209.

Whispering-gallery, The. (R. Johnson) Overland, n. s. 31: 175–561. 32: 174–568. 33: 70–559. 34: 88–556.

Whist, Evolution of. (W. B. Hall, jr.) Sewanee, 3: 457.

— Growth of, in America. (N. D. Messenger) Outing, 38: 208.

— Supplanted by "Bridge." (H. Jones) Cornh. 78: 802.

Whist "Fads." (Cavendish) Scrib. M. 22: 121.

Whistler, James Abbott McNeill. Critic, 38: 32.

— and Old Sandy in the '50's. (W. L. B. Jenney) Am. Arch. 59: 4.

— as a Teacher. (L. W. Jackson) Brush & P. 6: 141.

— at West Point. (T. Wilson) Bk. Buyer, 17: 113.

— a Champion of Art. (J. Hawthorne) Indep. 51: 2954.

— Chat with. Studio (Lond.) 4: 116.

— Lithographs by. (T. R. Way) Studio (Lond.) 6: 219.

— Master of the Lithograph. (E. R. Pennell) Scrib. M. 21: 277.

— New Pictures. Art J. 49: 10.

— Notes on. (M. Beerbohm) Sat. R. 84: 546.

— Piano. Art J. 52: 198.

— Some Early Pictures by. Art J. 49: 289.

Whistling Dick's Christmas Stocking; a story. (O. Henry) McClure, 14: 138.

Whitman, Walt. Woman and Freedom in. (H. A. Michael) Poet-Lore, 9: 216.

— Whitman Craze in England. Meth. R. 79: 952.

— Whitmania. (J. B. Perry) Critic, 32: 137.

Whitney, Mrs. A. D. T. Odd or Even? N. Church R. 4: 313.

— The Open Mystery. N. Church R. 4: 632.

Whitney, Eli. Cassier, 17: 166.

— Correspondence on the Invention of the Cotton Gin [1793–1805]. (M. B. Hammond) Am. Hist. R. 3: 90.

Whitney, James L., with portrait. Lib. J. 25: 19.

Whitney, William C., Turf Career of. (W. H. Rowe) Outing, 38: 453.

Whittier, John Greenleaf. Acad. 56: 424. — (Mrs. J. T. Fields) Chaut. 30: 194. — (R. H. Stoddard) Lippinc. 63: 808. — With portraits. (M. A. DeW. Howe) Bookman, 7: 28.

— First Books of. (L. S. Livingston) Bookman, 8: 41.

— Humor of. (J. L. Rickard) Midland, 7: 466.

— New Hampshire of. (D. L. Maulsby) New Eng. M. n. s. 22: 631.

— Story of "Captain's Well," with portrait. (M. E. Desmond) Cath. World, 71: 595.

— Story of "the Countess." (M. E. Desmond) Cath. World, 72: 478.

— Visit to. (E. Gosse) Good Words, 40: 16. Same art. Bookman, 8: 459.

Whittingham Ledgers. (H. R. Plomer) Library, n. s. 2: 147.

Who made the Match; a story. (R. Underhill) Harper, 95: 925.

Who's Georgina? a story. (J. Coniston) Belgra. 96: 84.

Who's who. The Paths of Glory. (J. Jacobs) Fortn. 73: 59.

"Whom God hath joined;" a story. (A. Merry) Belgra. 98: 12.

Whom the Gods love; a poem. (G. Custis) Outing, 33: 609.

Whortleberry Land. Pall Mall M. 14: 380. — Liv. Age, 217: 97.

Why the Hot Sulphur Mail was Late; a story. (C. Thomas) McClure, 18: 48.

Why I did not become a Smuggler. (L. C. Bradford) Lippinc. 63: 130.

Why Lydia left; a story. (G. Ewart) Idler, 16: 721.

Why Ovide don't go shanty dis Fall; a ballad. (E. W. Thomson) Canad. M. 9: 30.

Why she married the Market Gardener; a story. (M. E. Christie) Temp. Bar, 124: 204.

Why Tumash Dhu walked; a story. (J. MacManus) Idler, 13: 53.

Wibbandun and Wimbledon. (J. W. Hales) Ath. '01, 2: 222.

Wichita Indians, Hand or Guessing Game among. (G. A. Dorsey) Am. Antiq. 23: 363.

— Quivira and the. (J. Mooney) Harper, 99: 126.

Wicked Stepmother, The. (A. G. Seklemian) J. Am. Folk-Lore, 10: 135.

Wickham, John. (Sallie E. M. Hardy) Green Bag, 10: 63.

Wiclif, John. Lond. Q. 95: 251.

— Preferments and Literary Degrees. (J. A. Twemlow) Eng. Hist. R. 15: 529.

— Prophet of Protestantism and Methodist Itinerancy. (J. F. Hurst) Meth. R. 59: 177.

Widder Vlint. Blackw. 160: 463. Same art. Liv. Age, 213: 271.

Widor, C. M. Organ Symphonies. (T. C. Whitmer) Music, 15: 501, 644. 16: 32, 152.

— Symphony Gothique. (T. C. Whitmer) Music, 16: 269.

Widow in the Wilderness, A; a story. (A. H. Freechette) Harper, 100: 159.

Widow, a Maid, and Two or Three Men; a story. (I. W. Hanson) Nat'l M. (Bost.) 13: 570.

Widow of Dun-Angus; a story. (A. L. Milligan) Harper, 102: 294.

Widow of Mums; a story. (E. Cromer) Canad. M. 13: 74, 329, 457.

Widowed Stranger; a sketch. (E. S. Atkinson) Canad. M. 9: 464.

Widower, The; a story. (W. E. Norris) Temp. Bar, 113: 1–465. 114: 1–598.

Widow's Clock, The; a story. (B. Capes) Pall Mall M. 21: 26.

Widows' Funds in Scotland. Bank. M. (Lond.) 66: 65.

Wieck, Friedrich, Musician. (Lina Kleine) Music, 20: 230.

Wieliczka, a City of Salt. (J. W. Smith) Strand, 16: 664.

Wiertz's Spectre; a tale. (L. M'Clintock) Argosy, 66: 357.

Wife, The Disloyal, in Literature. (C. Porter and H. A. Clarke) Poet-Lore, 9: 265.

— The Ideal. (Lavinia Hart) Cosmopol. 30: 638.

— in International Marriages, Status of. (C. S. Walton) Am. Law R. 31: 870.

Wife of the Governor, The; a story. (B. Edwards) Argosy, 75: 62.

Wife of his Youth; a story. (C. W. Chesnutt) Atlan. 82: 55.

Wife of a King, The. (Jack London) Overland, n. s. 34: 112.

Wife of the Sporting Editor; a story. (E. C. Waltz) Nat'l M. (Bost.) 12: 466.

Wiggin, Albert H. Bank. M. (N. Y.) 58: 871.

Wiggin, Kate Douglas. Penelope's Experiences. (L. Hutton) Bk. Buyer, 21: 371.

Wigtownshire, Ancient Burial Custom near a Round Tower in. Reliquary, 39: 120.

Wight, Isle of. (Mercia A. Keith) Nat'l M. (Bost.) 6: 450.

Wightman, Mrs., of Shrewsbury. (F. D. How) Sund. M. 30: 399.

Wilberforce, Basil. Sermons preached in Westminster Abbey. N. Church R. 5: 632.

Wilberforce, Ernest Roland, with portraits. Strand, 15: 319.

Wilberforce, Wm., Papers of, ed. by A. M. Wilberforce. Ath. '97, 2: 555.

— A Study of Freedom. (A. B. Hyde) Meth. R. 61: 46.

Wilcock, Arthur. Designs for Pattern. Artist (N. Y.) 29: 49.

Wilcox, Daniel, Two Letters from, in 1775 and 1776. (D. W. Fowler) N. E. Reg. 54: 440.

Wilcox, Ella Wheeler. Autobiography. Cosmopol. 31: 415.

Wilcox, J. C., Baritone Singer, with portrait. Music, 15: 558.

Wild, Harrison M., Music Conductor, and his Critics. Music, 19: 242.

Wild Asters; a poem. (D. Dandridge) Poet-Lore, 13: 357.

Wild Beasts in a Great City [Cross Emporium, Liverpool]. (A. G. Page) Eng. Illust. 18: 249.

Wild Cat, Tortoise-shell. (W. H. Ballou) Pop. Sci. Mo. 51: 507.

Wild-cat Hunting in West Virginia. (R. H. Martin) Outing, 35: 483.

Wild Cats of the Pampa. Chamb. J. 75: 406.

Wild Dogs; a story. (B. Capes) Blackw. 162: 220. Same art. Liv. Age, 215: 51.

Wild Flowers of Early August. (C. S. Sargent) Garden & F. 10: 319.

Wild Flowers sold by London Venders. (A. Every) Pall Mall M. 11: 539.

Wild Fowl in Hockham Marshes. Spec. 80: 539.

— of Scotland. (J. G. Millais) Nature, 63: 567.

Wild Fowl Hunt on Currituck Sound. (T. M. Barnes, jr.) Outing, 33: 545.

Wild Ghost Chase, A; a story. Argosy, 66: 482.

Wild Irishman's Exploit, A; a story. (J. K. Leys) Gent. M. n. s. 67: 209.

Wild Life about my Cabin. (J. Burroughs) Cent. 36: 500.

— in Man. (J. Lewis) Canad. M. 17: 218.

— Precautions of. Liv. Age, 227: 820.

Wild Man, The. (B. Thomson) New R. 16: 453.

Wild Motherhood; a story. (C. G. D. Roberts) Canad. M. 17: 134.

Wild Things in Winter. (J. H. Kennedy) Harper, 94: 710.

Wilde, Oscar, Notes on. (M. Beerbohm) Sat. R. 90: 719.

Wilde, William Charles Kingsbury. Acad. 56: 337.

Wildenbruch, Ernst von. (J. F. Coar) Atlan. 81: 71.

Wildman, Sarah E., Pianist and Organist. Music, 17: 414.

Wilfred Hallett, Empire-builder. (H. Lander) Pall Mall M. 21: 6, 148, 366.

Wilhelmina, Queen of the Netherlands. (J. G. Roberts) Indep. 53: 376. — Pall Mall M. 23: 213. — Sund. M. 27: 606. — With portraits. Strand, 15: 409. — (W. Bates) Nat'l M. (Bost.) 9: 12.

— and her Consort. (J. Bell) Sund. M. 30: 110. — (W. E. Griffis) Outl. 67: 547.

— and her Realm. (W. E. Griffis) Outl. 60: 277.

— Childhood and Girlhood of. (M. S. Warren) Eng. Illust. 18: 123.

— Coming of Age of. (E. Lecky) Longm. 33: 154.

— Coronation of. (Cromwell Childe) Cosmopol. 25: 65. — (W. E. Griffis) Nation, 67: 221. — (H. S. Nollen) Midland, 11: 3.

Wilkes, John. (W. B. Duffield) Cornh. 76: 723.

Wilkes's Land. (E. S. Balch) Nation, 70: 357.

Wilkins, Mary E., at Home. (J. E. Chamberlain) Critic, 32: 155.

— An Idealist in Masquerade. (C. M. Thompson) Atlan. 83: 665.

— Novels of. (Mary E. Wardwell) Citizen, 4: 27.

— Portion of Labor. (Alice French) Bk. Buyer, 23: 379.

Wilkinson, Florence. Writer, 14: 43.

— Strength of the Hills. (Flora M. Holly) Bookman, 14: 257.

Wilkinson, James John Garth, New Church Writer. (J. Reed) N. Church R. 7: 116.

Wilks, Col. Mark, and Napoleon. (J. S. Corbett) Monthly R. 2, no. 1: 63.

Will, Edwards's Doctrine of. (L. A. Fox) Luth. Q. 31: 149.

— Free, and the Credit for Good Actions. (G. S. Fullerton) Pop. Sci. Mo. 59: 526.

— Melancthon's Doctrine of. (J. F. Seebach) Luth. Q. 30: 190.

— Training the. (J. E. Bradley) Educa. 20: 65.

— Types of. (A. F. Shand) Mind, 22: 289.

Will Power, Beliefs concerning, in the Siouan Tribes. (A. C. Fletcher) Science, 5: 331.

Will, A 14th-Century Parson's. (J. J. Britton) Antiq. n. s. 35: 213.

Will-making, Whimsical. (C. Draycott) Temp. Bar, 110: 66.

Willans's Valve Gear. (J. Svenson) Cassier, 15: 209.

Willard, Frances E. (I. W. Parks) Meth. R. 58: 849. — (M. L. Dickinson) Arena, 19: 658. — (Lady H. Somerset) No. Am. 166: 429. — With portrait. (Lady H. Somerset) Outl. 58: 575. — Midland, 9: 316. — (C. J. Little) Chaut. 27: 73.

Willard, Josiah Flynt. (A. Symons) Sat. R. 90: 391.

Willett's Point, Life at. (A. S. Cox) Outl. 60: 305.

William, St., of Norwich. Acad. 51: 251.

— Life and Miracles of. Church Q. 46: 94.

William the Conqueror, Companions of. (J. H. Round) Monthly R. 3, no. 3: 91.

— Family of, and the Church of Chartres. (F. Liebermann) Eng. Hist. R. 16: 498.

— Footprints in Domesday. (F. Baring) Eng. Hist. R. 13: 17.

— Old English Charter. (J. H. Round and W. H. Stevenson) Eng. Hist. R. 12: 105.

William I. and William II. Spec. 78: 428.

William II., Emperor of Germany. (P. Lindenberg) Forum, 23: 327. — Spec. 78: 325. — (L. Klausner-Dawoc) Fortn. 74: 947. — Good Words, 41: 110. — (P. Bigelow) Munsey, 21: 418. — (R. S. Baker) McClure, 16: 222. — (C. Lowe) Pall Mall M. 25: 146. — (C. F. Dewey) Cosmopol. 25: 235. — Blackw. 163: 133. Same art. Liv. Age, 216: 666.

— and Palestine. Fortn. 70: 548.

— and the Reichstag. Spec. 79: 816.

— and the Porte. (A. Laugel) Nation, 64: 471.

— as Art Patron. (Henry Eckford) Cent. 34: 434.

— as a Huntsman. (Edward Brecke) Cosmopol. 24: 529.

— as the Lord Chief Justice of Europe. (W. T. Stead) Contemp. 71: 595.

— Foreign Politics of. Fortn. 68: 471.

— Germans, and their Emperor. (Germanicus) Contemp. 71: 801.

— Germany under a Strenuous Emperor. (S. Brooks) World's Work, 1: 396.

— Herkomer's Portrait of. (M. H. Spielmann) M. of Art, 25: 345.

— His Better Nature. (A. Osborne) Sat. R. 85: 200.

— Kaiser's Speeches and German History. (K. Blind) Forum, 31: 432.

— in the Holy Land. (S. I. Curtiss) Cosmopol. 26: 363.

— Religious Side of. Spec. 81: 641.

— Ten Years Old. (Poultney Bigelow) Cent. 34: 450.

— Visit to Palestine, Import of. (F. Greenwood) Pall Mall M. 17: 382.

William Augustus, Duke of Cumberland in 1745. (F. Middleton) Un. Serv. M. 15: 107.

William of Ockam, Marsiglio of Padua and. (J. Sullivan) Am. Hist. R. 2: 593.

William Rufus, King, Two Letters addressed to. (J. P. Gilson) Eng. Hist. R. 12: 290.

William the Silent, Harrison's. (A. V. Dicey) Nation, 66: 133.

— Portraits of. (Mrs. Lecky) Good Words, 38: 183.

William Marsdal's Awakening; a story. (H. S. Edwards) Atlan. 81: 523.

William Moon, Clerk; a story. (H. Davies) Gent. M. n. s. 60: 313.

William Tyrwhitt's "Copy." (B. Capes) Lippinc. 61: 536.

William's Spree. (L. Boynton) Lippinc. 60: 126.

Williams, Alex. (E. M. Bacon) Bookman, 6: 303. — (G. M. Adams) N. E. Reg. 55: 91.

Williams, Alyn, Miniature Painter. (T. R. Reeve) Artist (N. Y.) 26: 26.

Williams, Anna, Portraits of. Strand, 14: 417.

Williams, Evan, Singer, with Portrait. Music, 15: 194.

Williams, Francis Churchill. Writer, 14: 43. — With portrait. Bk. News, 20: 51.

Williams, George H., Attorney-General under Pres. Grant, with portrait. (J. A. Watrous) Nat'l M. (Bost.) 12: 232.

Williams, Gilly; a Glass of Fashion. (C. Edwardes) Temp. Bar, 119: 188.

Windsor Castle, Hidden Treasure of. Eng. Illust. 18: 97.
— The Queen's Furniture at. (E. M. Jessop) Pall Mall M. 17: 458.
— Queen's Private Apartments. (E. M. Jessop) Pall Mall M. 18: 436.
Windus, Wm. Lindsay. (E. R. Dibdin) M. of Art, 24: 49.
Wine in its relation to Health. (N. E. Yorke-Davies) Gent. M. n. s. 58: 604.
— Italian Vintage. (L. Housman) Argosy, 71: 261.
— Shall we drink ? J. Madden on. Outl. 65: 933.
Wine Production in France, Methods of. (H. Haynie) Nat'l M. (Bost.) 7: 110.
— A New Departure in. (G. C. Frankland) Chamb. J. 74: 223.
Wines for the Sedentary. Spec. 80: 268.
Wines of our Forefathers in England. Sat. R. 90: 264.
Wing Sing and the Doctrines. (E. K. Latham) Outl. 63: 163.
Wingate, Fort, How we live at. (Maria B. Kimball) Outl. 58: 372.
Wingfield, Antonie; True Discourse of the Portugal Voyage. (M. Oppenheim; A. Wingfellde) Ath. '00, 2: 29.
Wingless Seagull, The ; a poem. (Isa J. Postgate) Gent. M. n. s. 58: 203.
Winlock, Wm. C. (S. P. Langley) Pop. Astron. 4: 351.
Winning Charm, The ; a story. (G. Morley) Gent. M. n. s. 66: 209.
Winning Colors, The ; a story. (E. M. Rhodes) Nat'l M. (Bost.) 12: 125.
Winning of the Hole, The ; a poem. (E. E. L. Ling) Outing, 34: 464.
Winning of the Trans-continental, The ; a story. (W. M. Raine) McClure, 14: 573. Same art. Idler, 19: 19.
Winnipeg Lake, Camping on. (C. Hanbury-Williams) Blackw. 170: 731.
Winnower, The ; a poem. (J. T. Trowbridge) Atlan. 84: 431.
Winona Assembly and Summer School. (S. C. Dickey) Chaut. 31: 635.
— Social Science Club. Ann. Am. Acad. Pol. Sci. 11: 288.
"Winslow," The, at Cardenas. (J. B. Bernadou) Cent. 35: 698.
— Rescue of the. (E. E. Mead) Harper, 98: 123.
Winsor, Justin. (W. E. A. Axon) Library, 10: 1. — (E. Channing) Am. Hist. R. 3: 197. — (W. C. Lane ; W. H. Tillinghast) Lib. J. 23: 7. — (Sir C. R. Markham) Geog. J. 11: 77. — Ath. '97, 2: 634. — (C. A. Cutter) Nation, 65: 335. — (W. C. Lane ; W. H. Tillinghast) Harv. Grad. M. 6: 182. — (W. I. Fletcher) Critic, 31: 254. — With portrait. Lib. J. 22: 689.
Winter in the City. (L. Vandervort) Outing, 37: 623.
— in a Deer-forest. (H. Fraser) Gent. M. n. s. 61: 443.
— in a Great Wood. (G. A. B. Dewar) Temp. Bar, 121: 443.
— in Scottish Poetry. (Florence Maccunn) Good Words, 38: 162.
— Nature in. (J. Albee) New Eng. M. n. s. 21: 476.
— Poetry of. Sat. R. 91: 10.
— Wild Things in. (J. H. Kennedy) Harper, 94: 710.
Winter ; a poem. (C. H. Urner) Outing, 33: 340.
Winter in the West ; a poem. (M. Markwell) Canad. M. 12: 325.
Winter Camp, The ; a poem. (T. Roberts) Outing, 35: 184.
Winter Holiday ; a poem. (B. Carman) Atlan. 83: 412.
Winter Note-book, From a. (R. Kipling) Harper, 100: 859.

Winter Ramble, A. (S. Hartmann) Harper, 103: 989.
Winter Song ; a poem. (Clinton Scollard) Cosmopol. 28: 294.
Winter Trees, The ; a poem. (J. B. Carrington) Outing, 37: 439.
Winter Weather, Long Waves of. (A. McDowall) Knowl. 23: 44.
Winter's Soliloquies ; a poem. (C. H. Cooley) Outing, 33: 485.
Winter's Walk, A. Macmil. 75: 120. Same art. Liv. Age, 212: 50.
Winterhalter, François Xavier. Munsey, 18: 561.
Winthrop, Gov. John, Jr., of Connecticut, Sir Richard Saltonstall's Letter to. (L. H. Greenlaw) N. E. Reg. 51: 65.
Winthrop, Margaret. Quar. 186: 44.
— and Eliza Pinckney. Quar. 186: 44. Same art. Liv. Age, 215: 90.
Winthrop, Robert C., Winthrop's Life of. (T. W. Higginson) Nation, 65: 439.
Winwood's Luck. (Mrs. B. Harrison) Lippinc. 68: 336.
Wire-glass ; Recent Developments. (F. Schumann) J. Frankl. Inst. 145: 100.
Wire Nail Association of 1895-96. (C. E. Edgerton) Pol. Sci. Q. 12: 246.
Wireless Telegraphy. See Telegraphy, Wireless.
Wiresaw, Use of, for Quarrying. Nature, 65: 84.
Wirt, William. (Sallie E. M. Hardy) Green Bag, 10: 61. — With portrait. (H. M. Dowling) Green Bag, 10: 453.
Wisby. (W. Hyams) Outl. 57: 321.
Wiscasset, Maine. (C. E. Allen) New Eng. M. n. s. 24: 516.
Wisconsin, New England in. (E. B. Usher) New Eng. M. n. s. 22: 446.
— History of, Leading Events in, Legler's. (J. D. Butler) Am. Hist. R. 4: 381.
— State Library Association, Annual Meeting of, 1900. Pub. Lib. 5: 336.
— Supreme Court of. (E. E. Bryant) Green Bag, 9: 17, 63, 110, 169, 213.
— University of, School of Education of. (M. V. O'Shea) Educa. R. 14: 496.
Wisdom, Practical. Spec. 87: 794.
Wisdom of Dark Pathrick. (S. MacManus) Cent. 37: 41.
Wisdom of Fools, The ; a story. (M Deland) Harper, 94: 759.
Wisdom of the Serpent. (D. Osborne) Harper, 103: 236.
"Wisdom of Solomon." (M. D. Conway) Open Court, 13: 21.
Wisdom of the Trail. (Jack London) Overland, n. s. 34: 541.
Wise, Henry A., with portrait. (Sallie E. M. Hardy) Green Bag, 10: 152. — With portrait. (E. S. Spaulding) Green Bag, 12: 1.
— Wise's Life of. (J. R. Brackett) Am. Hist. R. 5: 150.
Wise Woman of Killester. (L. O. Cooper) Good Words, 42: 699.
Wiseman, Nicholas, Cardinal. (St. G. Mivart) Am. Cath. Q. 23: 358. — (G. Tyrrell) Month, 91: 142.
— and Pusey. Quar. 187: 299.
— as revealed in Fabiola. (Alban Goodier) Am. Cath. Q. 24, no. 3: 157.
— Life of, by W. Ward. Church Q. 47: 107. — (T. E. Bridgett) Dub. R. 122: 245. — (W. S. Lilly) Fortn. 69: 287. Same art. Liv. Age, 216: 642. — (C. A. L. Richards) Dial (Ch.) 24: 253. — (J. W. Chadwick) Nation, 66: 481. — (C. A. L. Morse) Cath. World, 67: 2. — Acad. 52: 563. — Month, 91: 1.
— Recollections of, with portrait. Cath. World, 67: 433.

Wispelaere, P. de, Bruges Wood-carver. Artist (N. Y.) 29: 103.

Wister, Owen, with portrait. Bk. News, 16: 534.

Wit and Humor. Sat. R. 91: 9. — Ecl. M. 132: 145.
— French, in the 18th Century. Liv. Age, 227: 743.

Wit of Lauchlan Macintyre, The. (M. Lindsay) Chamb. J. 77: 249-267.

Witch Doctor of the Ovimbundu of Portuguese S. W. Africa. (G. A. Dorsey) J. Am. Folk-Lore, 12: 183.

Witch Doctors, Irish. (W. B. Yeats) Fortn. 74: 440.

Witch-finding in Western Maryland. (E. C. Seip) J. Am. Folk-Lore, 14: 39.

Witch Scarers of New York State Indians. Strand, 13: 785.

Witchcraft and Christianity. (H. M. Doughty) Blackw. 163: 378.
— in Ancient India. (M. Winternitz) New World, 7: 523.
— in Bavaria. (E. P. Evans) Pop. Sci. Mo. 53: 30.
— in England. (W. Wood) Cornh. 78: 655.
— in Ireland, Last Trial for. (J. M. Sullivan) Green Bag, 13: 146.
— in Old Scots Criminal Law. Green Bag, 13: 511.
— in Naples. (J. B. Andrews) Folk-Lore, 8: 1.
— Persecutions for, Burr on. (A. F. Chamberlain) Citizen, 3: 261.

With all her Heart. (René Bazin) Liv. Age, 215: 637-864. 216: 27-716.

With all Powders of the Merchant. Pall Mall M. 16: 50, 168, 339.

With Bell, Book, and Candle; a story. (E. Phillpotts) Pall Mall M. 25: 475.

With the Eyes of the Soul. Liv. Age, 224: 307.

With his Back to the Wall; a political story. (J. M. Rogers) McClure, 18: 33.

With the Indian Bayard; a story. (I. S. A. Herford) Chamb. J. 76: 785.

With Mrs. Kenworthy's Assistance; a story. (P. H. Coggins) McClure, 17: 215.

With Music and White Light; a story. (A. S. Meguire) Harper, 96: 135.

With Never a Chance; a story. (Ethel A. Fenwick) Pall Mall M. 11: 336.

"With Pipe and Tabor;" a street sketch. (G. B. Stuart) Pall Mall M. 12: 198.

With Rod and Reel; a poem. (A. H. Hall) Outing, 34: 128.

With Whips and Scorns. (E. F. Cahill) Overland, n. s. 37: 670.

Within an Ace of the End of the World; a story. (R. Barr) McClure, 14: 545.

Within the Eye of Honor; a story. (G. Hibbard) Harper, 95: 34.

Within the Gates; a play. (E. S. Phelps Ward) McClure, 17: 35-236.

Within the Walls. (G. H. Scull) Atlan. 80: 198.

Without are Dogs; a story. (Mary Bradford-Whiting) Gent. M. n. s. 65: 521. Same art. Liv. Age, 228: 182.

Without Benefit of Clergy; a story. (B. Clark) Nat'l M. (Bost.) 6: 468.

Without a Country. (K. L. Bates) New Eng. M. n. s. 24: 209.

Without the Courts; a story. (S. B. Elliott) Harper, 98: 575.

Without Due Authority; a tale. (N. K. Blissett) Belgra. 93: 241.

Without Law or License. (Sewell Ford) Scrib. M. 30: 566.

Without Orders. (Louis C. Senger) Scrib. M. 29: 621.

Without Words; a story. (K. Tavaststjerna) Poet-Lore, 12: 12.

Witness to the Marriage. (W. E. Cule) Chamb. J 14.

Witness-box Wit. Green Bag, 11: 457.

Witnesses, Irish, Whimsicalities of. (J. DeMorgan) Green Bag, 12: 530.
— Protection of. Spec. 81: 203.

Witte, M., and the Russian Commercial Crisis. (E. J. Dillon) Contemp. 79: 472.

Witticisms. (S. Gwynn) Ecl. M. 130: 711.

Witty Retorts of Politicians. (E. J. Moyle) Chamb. J. 77: 801.

Witty Sayings I have heard. (Justin McCarthy) Chamb. J. 77: 564.

Witwatersrand, Mining the Gold Ores of. (H. H. Webb and P. Yeatman) Engin. M. 15: 39.

Wives, Deserted. (Ada Eliot) Char. R. 10: 346.
— of the Presidents of the U. S. (Mrs. Burton Harrison) Cosmopol. 30: 406.
— of Prominent Generals. (E. R. Goodwin) Chaut. 27: 339.

Wizard's Wife, The; a tale. (F. E. M. Notley) Argosy, 64: 26-599.

Woad as a Blue Dye. (C. B. Plowright) Nature, 64: 413.

Wodenethe. (C. S. Sargent) Garden & F. 10: 449.

Woelfflin, Edouard von, Jubilee of. (J. C. Rolfe) Bookman, 13: 545.

Woelfl, Joseph, compared with Beethoven. (E. A. Richardson) Music, 14: 557.

Wogan Family. Child of the 18th Century. (V. A. Simpson) Cornh. 83: 822.

Wolcott, Roger, with portrait. (W. Lawrence) Harv. Grad. M. 9: 313. — (F. Hurtubis, jr.) New Eng. M. n. s. 23: 678.

Wolcott Commission and its Results. (J. H. Eckels) Forum, 24: 396.

Wold Jimmy and Zairey. (O. Agnus) Cornh. 75: 676. Same art. Liv. Age, 214: 37.

Wolf, Carl; his "Tales from Tirol." (L. Villari) Liv. Age, 216: 269.

Wolf, Joseph, Studies and Sketches by. (A. Trevor-Battye) Artist (N. Y.) 25: 1.

Wolf and Deer; a strange Friendship. (F. W. Calkins) Outing, 39: 174.
— British. Spec. 86: 134.
— in Myth, Legend, and History. (L. T. Sprague) Outing, 39: 358.
— The Respectable. (W. Marsh) Cosmopol. 28: 487.

Wolf-Charlie; a story. Macmil. 79: 44.

Wolf Chase, A. (F. S. Stimson) Outing, 39: 360.

Wolf-children. (G. A. Stockwell) Lippinc. 61: 117.

Wolfhound, Irish. (H. W. Huntington) Outing, 35: 569.

Wolf! a Wolf! (F. Whishaw) Longm. 34: 254.

Wolf-hunting in France. (V. Thompson) Outing, 37: 305.

Wolfe, Charles, Rev. (W. P. Trent) Sewanee, 1: 129.

Wolfe, General James, and Gray's Elegy. (E. E. Morris) Eng. Hist. R. 15: 125.
— Birthplace of. (J. C. Webster) Canad. M. 9: 22.
— Death of. (J. Henderson) Eng. Hist. R. 12: 762.
— How he changed the History of the World. (A. R. Ropes) Eng. Illust. 18: 67.
— Letters. (E. C. Godley) National, 36: 231.
— Portraits of. (P. L. Ford) Cent. 33: 323.

Wolfers, P., Art Work of. (Mrs. J. E. Whitby) M. of Art, 25: 322.

Wolff, Joseph, an Apostle of the Jews. Temp. Bar, 115: 344.

Wolfrum, Dr. Phillipp, Musical Professor, with portrait. Music, 15: 455.

Wollaschek, Dr. Richard, Music Professor, with portrait. Music, 15: 457.

Wollaton Hall, England. (E. M. Middleton) Pall Mall M. **22**: 148.

Wolmer Forest. (W. H. Hudson) Longm. **30**: 342. Same art. Ecl. M. **129**: 539.

Wolseley, Lord, as Commander-in-chief. Contemp. **79**: 161.

Wolves, Hybrid, of "Goshen Hole." (N. Ednoc) Outing, **36**: 120.

— in Canadian Northwest. (J. Innes) Canad. M. **18**: 144.

— of Canada. (C. H. Bramble) Canad. M. **14**: 464.

Woman, The American. (H. Muensterberg) Internat. Mo. **3**: 607.

— and the Essay. (E. Dickson) Dial (Ch.) **31**: 309.

— and her Bonds, The; a story. (E. Lefèvre) McClure, **16**: 339.

— and her Son. (I. Clark) New Eng. M. n. s. **19**: 326.

— and the Industrial Problem. (E. Meredith) Arena, **23**: 438.

— as an Athlete. (A. Kenealy) 19th Cent. **45**: 636. Same art. Liv. Age, **221**: 363. Same art. Ecl. M. **132**: 875. — Reply. (L. O. Chant) 19th Cent. **45**: 745. Same art. Ecl. M. **133**: 161. Same art. Liv. Age, **221**: 799. — Rejoinder. (A. Kenealy) 19th Cent. **45**: 915. Same art. Ecl. M. **133**: 357. Same art. Liv. Age, **222**: 201.

— The Awakening of. Westm. **152**: 69.

— Brain of. (A. Sutherland) 19th Cent. **47**: 802. Same art. Liv. Age, **225**: 821.

— Decline of. (F. Boyle) New R. **17**: 195.

— Depreciation of, in Literature. Acad. **51**: 627.

— Disillusioned Daughters. (P. Unite) Fortn. **74**: 850.

— Duty of. (E. C. Hewitt) Westm. **152**: 83.

— Economic Place of. (C. P. Stetson) Cosmopol. **27**: 309.

— Encroachment of. (C. Whibley) 19th Cent. **41**: 531.

— Equality of, with Man, A Plea against. (R. Thorne) Idler, **18**: 24.

— The Eternal Feminine. (A. Repplier) Liv. Age, **215**: 144.

— Evolution of the Character of, in English Literature. (Alice Groff) Poet-Lore, **10**: 242.

— The Extra. (R. T. Lang) Westm. **150**: 305.

— Fin-de-siècle. Lond. Q. **89**: 99. Same art. Liv. Age, **215**: 743.

— for Nothing. (L. B. Edwards) Lippinc. **68**: 3.

— Future Position of, in the World. (L. M. Holmes) Arena, **20**: 333.

— The Glittering Generality. Atlan. **86**: 863.

— in the Ancient Hebrew Cult. (I. J. Peritz) J. Bib. Lit. **17**: 111.

— in the Ancient World. (E. S. Diack) Westm. **153**: 676.

— in Emotional Expression. (L. C. Bull) Harper, **103**: 1002.

— in Journalism. (M. A. White) Arena, **23**: 669.

— in the Light of the Cross. (Canon Barkett) Sund. M. **27**: 506.

— in Modern Bohemian Literature. (S. C. de Soissons) Sat. R. **91**: 796.

— in New Countries, Position of. Atlan. **86**: 574.

— in Politics. Blackw. **161**: 342.

— in Retrospect. (H. B. Swineford) Arena, **22**: 443.

— Influence in Islam. (Ameer Ali) 19th Cent. **455**: 755.

— Intellectual Powers of. (F. Franklin) No. Am. **166**: 40.

— "The Lesser Man." (G. G. Buckler) No. Am. **165**: 295.

— Man's Equal. (E. Uhlrich) Midland, **10**: 60.

— — not his Divinity. Sat. R. **91**: 597.

— Medical, in Fiction. Blackw. **164**: 94.

— The Modern. (H. Jamieson) Westm. **152**: 571.

Woman, New. (R. McNeill) Macmil. **80**: 425.

— — Catholicism and. (G. Tyrrell) Am. Cath. Q. **22**: 630.

— — a Christian Handicap. (E. Starr-Martin) Arena, **24**: 525.

— — in her Relation to the New Man. (E. C. Hewitt) Westm. **147**: 335.

— — Role of. (N. Arling) Westm. **150**: 576.

— The New England. (K. Stephens) Atlan. **88**: 60.

— not Man's Equal. (Annie L. Mearkle) Midland, **9**: 173.

— of Fascination, The. (H. T. Peck) Cosmopol. **26**: 71.

— of Fashion, The. (Mrs. B. Harrison) Munsey, **17**: 699.

— of the Future. (A. Dennehy) Westm. **152**: 99.

— of the North; a tale. (A. J. Stringer) Canad. M. **9**: 162.

— of To-day and of To-morrow. (H. T. Peck) Cosmopol. **27**: 148.

— A Phase of Modernity. (E. O. Kirk) Lippinc. **64**: 295.

— Place in Literature. (A. S. Green) 19th Cent. **41**: 964. Same art. Liv. Age, **214**: 300.

— The Poet's Ideal. (A. G. Bishop) Chaut. **24**: 597.

— Political Evolution of. (J. E. Foster) No. Am. **165**: 600.

— Protestant. (J. Britton) Month, **91**: 33.

— Psychology of Feminism. (H. E. M. Stutfield) Blackw. **161**: 104.

— Reign of, under Queen Victoria. Argosy, **73**: Memorial no.

— Relation of, to the Trades and Professions. (W. T. Harris) Educa. R. **20**: 217.

— Status of, Past, Present, and Future. (S. B. Anthony) Arena, **17**: 901.

— The Studious, by the Bishop of Orleans; a Forgotten Book. Month, **93**: 39.

— A Transcendental View of. Spec. **78**: 796.

— The Truly Artistic. (S. Jarvis) Arena, **18**: 813.

— under the English Law, Cleveland on. Ath. '97, **2**: 344.

— under Monasticism, Eckenstein on. (M. Bateson) Eng. Hist. R. **12**: 139.

— Well-dressed. (A. R. Ramsey) Cosmopol. **28**: 414.

Woman, A. (W. H. Shelton) Scrib. M. **21**: 178.

Woman; a story. (J. B. Foster) Cosmopol. **29**: 659.

Woman of Ashanti; a tale. (H. H. Bell) Argosy, **73**: 60.

Woman of Kronstadt, The. (M. Pemberton) Munsey, **18**: 513 — **19**: 441.

Woman of Straw, A; a story. (H. Gilbert) Argosy, **74**: 171.

Woman of To-day, A; a tale. (J. E. English) Argosy, **70**: 428.

Woman that Understood, The. (Octave Thanet) Scrib. M. **28**: 729.

Woman who Hesitated, A; a story. (W. Barr) McClure, **12**: 535.

Woman who lost her Principles; a story. (L. B. Edwards) Harper, **96**: 110.

Woman who Remained; a story. (W. P. Ridge) Pall Mall M. **20**: 501.

Woman with the Caterpillar Fringe; a story. (Juliette M. Babbitt) Midland, **8**: 177.

Woman Collegian, The. (Helen W. Moody) Scrib. M. **22**: 150.

Woman-haters. (G. Martin) Sat. R. **85**: 136.

Woman-liberalism. (F. Tyrrell-Gill) Westm. **155**: 130.

Woman Question. (O. Schreiner) Cosmopol. **28**: 45, 182.

— in Italy. (Dora Melegari) Contemp. **76**: 819.

Woman Student's Experience in German Universities, A. (A. M. Bowen) Nation, **65**: 9.

Womanhood, Anglo-Saxon. Macmil. 80: 275.
— Ideal. (H. T. Finck) Indep. 53: 1061.
— Ideals of, by Browning and Greek Dramatists. (C. Porter) Poet-Lore, 9: 385.
Woman's Christian Temperance Union, Origin of the World's. (F. E. Willard) R. of Rs. (N. Y.) 16: 430.
Woman's Clubs. *See* Women's Clubs.
Woman's College, Shall there be a, in California? (Jane S. Klink) Overland, n. s. 33: 461.
Woman's Hand; a story. (Grant Allen) Cosmopol. 26: 151.
Woman's Heart; a story. (M. Keegan) Canad. M. 14: 16.
Woman's Home, A. (Mrs. Talbot Coke) Chamb. J. 77: 230. Same art. Liv. Age, 225: 190.
Woman's Logic, A; a farce. (Jerome K. Jerome) Idler, 12: 415.
Woman's Municipal League in New York. (J. S. Lowell) Munic. Aff. 2: 465.
Woman's Share, The; a poem. Argosy, 69: 295.
"Woman's Vocation" and other Poems. (Carmen Sylva) No. Am. 170: 446.
Woman's Work. (D. Dale) Canad. M. 8: 537.
— One. Month, 98: 70-627.
Women. (H. Desart) National, 29: 711. Same art. Ecl. M. 129: 377. — (E. S. Martin) McClure, 17: 103.
— Age Limit for. (Clara E. Collet) Contemp. 76: 868. Same art. Ecl. M. 134: 344. Same art. Liv. Age, 224: 242.
— Agricultural Employment for. (E. Bradley) Fortn. 69: 334.
— American, and the Labor Problem. Pub. Opin. 22: 748.
— — Two Centuries of. (L. B. Lang) Ecl. M. 134: 605. Same art. Liv. Age, 224: 704.
— and Children, Chicago Protective Agency for. (D. S. B. Conover) Char. R. 8: 287.
— — Employment of. (H. L. Bliss) Am. J. Sociol. 3: 355.
— and Culture. Spec. 85: 838.
— and the Intellectual Virtues. (E. Ritchie) Internat. J. Ethics, 12: 69.
— and Music. (Amy Fay) Music, 18: 505.
— and Politics. Atlan. 87: 589.
— and Science. Spec. 82: 409. Same art. Ecl. M. 133: 144. Same art. Liv. Age, 221: 727.
— and the Wage System. (W. L. Bonney) Arena, 26: 172.
— Are Englishwomen growing Worse? Spec. 81: 41.
— Art Education for. (Candace Wheeler) Outl. 55: 81.
— as Astronomers. (H. S. Davis) Pop. Astron. 6: 129, 211.
— as Book-lovers. (P. H. Ditchfield) Gent. M. n. s. 58: 35, 160.
— as Catalogers. (C. A. Hayward) Pub. Lib. 3: 121.
— as Criminals. (H. Harrell) Arena, 24: 108. — (Frances A. Kelloe) Int. J. Ethics, 9: 74.
— as Home Workers. (Lady Louisa M. Knightley) 19th Cent. 50: 287.
— as Letter-writers. (E. Sichel) Cornh. 79: 53. Same art. Ecl. M. 132: 509. Same art. Liv. Age, 220: 513.
— as Librarians. Library, 4: 217. — (M. S. R. James) Library, 5: 270. — (E. C. Richardson) Library, 6: 137.
— as Musicians. (T. L. Krebs) Sewanee, 2: 76.
— as a Race. Spec. 78: 832.
— as School Officers. (D. Mowry) Arena, 24: 198.
— as Stock-keepers. Spec. 81: 111.
— as Teachers in the Public Schools. (J. C. Boykin) Educa. R. 18: 138.
— as Telegraphists. (C. H. Garland) Econ. J. 11: 251.

Women as Thieves. Spec. 78: 120.
— at Cards in the 18th Century. Temp. Bar, 117: 248.
— at the English Universities. (R. B. Mory) Chaut. 29: 1. — Quar. 186: 529. Same art. Liv. Age, 216: 219. — Liv. Age, 218: 30.
— Bachelor. (S. Gwynn) Contemp. 73: 866. Same art. Ecl. M. 131: 130. Same art. Liv. Age, 218: 304.
— Barbarian Status of. (T. Veblen) Am. J. Sociol. 4: 503.
— Capacity in Men and. (E. Johnson) Westm. 153: 567.
— Club and Salon. (A. G. Mason) Cent. 34: 122, 185.
— Clubs for. (E. Tolman) Lippinc. 60: 824.
— College, and Matrimony. (G. E. Gardner) Educa. 20: 285.
— — and Non-college, Statistics of. (Mary R. Smith) Am. Statis. Assoc. 7: 1.
— — New England Girl Graduates. (M. E. Blood) Arena, 24: 214.
— Composers. (R. Hughes) Cent. 33: 768.
— — and Musicians of U. S. (Gilson Willets) Midland, 10: 401.
— Criminal, Physical Measurements of. (F. A. Kellor) Arena, 25: 510.
— Criminality among. (F. A. Kellor) Arena, 23: 516.
— Degrees for, at Cambridge. (J. R. Tanner) Fortn. 67: 716. — (W. C. France) Nation, 64: 219. — Spec. 78: 535. — Ath. '97, 1: 314.
— Disparagement of, in Literature. (E. R. Chapman) Liv. Age, 214: 144.
— Dress of, On Reform in. (Princess Ysenburg) No. Am. 173: 413.
— Economic Status of, in the South. (L. S. McAdoo) Arena, 21: 741.
— Educated, Employment of. (Mrs. Louise Creighton) 19th Cent. 50: 806.
— Education of. (A. L. Markle) Arena, 24: 206. — (J. B. Perry) Critic, 30: 137. — Outl. 61: 581. — (K. G. Wells) Nat'l M. (Bost.) 10: 268.
— — Advisable Differences between, and that of Young Men. (J. F. Goucher and others) School R. 7: 577.
— — and the Universities. (A. H. F. Boughey) New R. 16: 502. Same art. Ecl. M. 129: 19. — (Oscar Browning) Forum, 24: 225. — (M. T. Blauvelt) R. of Rs. (N. Y.) 16: 450.
— — College Graduate and the Bachelor Maid. (M. A. Jordan) Indep. 51: 1937.
— — Collegiate. (T. F. Wright) N. Church R. 7: 112.
— — Early Education of Girls in Massachusetts. (G. H. Martin) Educa. 20: 323.
— — for Domestic Life. (M. R. Smith) Pop. Sci. Mo. 53: 521.
— — Higher, and Posterity. (W. Seton) Cath. World, 73: 147.
— — — Catholic Training College for. (T. F. Willis) Dub. R. 128: 114.
— — — in France. (A. T. Smith) Forum, 30: 503.
— — — in Germany. (Mrs. J. W. Lindsey) Educa. 18: 621.
— — — Should it differ from that of Men? (M. C. Thomas) Educa. R. 21: 1. — (C. S. Parrish) Educa. R. 22: 383. — (C. F. Thwing) Forum, 30: 728.
— — Ideal Education of an American Girl. (T. Davidson) Forum, 25: 471.
— — in England. (E. C. Hinsdale) Dial (Ch.) 24: 103.
— — in France. Educa. 21: 444.
— — in Russia. (Sophie Kropotkin) 19th Cent. 43: 117. Same art. Liv. Age, 216: 603.
— — Modern. (A. E. Goddard) N. Church R. 6: 101.
— — The Overtaught Woman. (H. T. Peck) Cosmopol. 26: 329.

Women, Rights of, and Science. (H. E. Harvey) Westm. 148: 205.

—— Sophia, the 18th Century Champion of. (H. Mc-Ilquham) Westm. 150: 533.

— Rôle of, in Society: 18th Cent. France; 19th Cent. England. (M. E. Ponsonby) 19th Cent. 48: 941. 49: 64.

— Single, Housing of. (H. Fayès) Munic. Aff. 3: 95.

— Some American, in Science. (M. B. Williamson) Chaut. 28: 361, 465.

— Some Clever. (A. Chisholm) Canad. M. 15: 453.

— Some Modern. (M. M. Hammond) Sund. M. 26: 542.

— Struggle for Liberty in Germany. (M. M. Patrick) Pop. Sci. Mo. 56: 328.

— Suffrage for. (T. Chapman) 19th Cent. 42: 169. — Westm. 148: 357. — Outl. 64: 573, 599. — (A. Bell) Gunton's M. 17: 474.

—— and Education. (H. K. Johnson) Pop. Sci. Mo. 51: 222.

—— and Municipal Politics in Colorado. (J. E. Le Rossignol) Ann. Am. Acad. Pol. Sci. 18: 552.

——— in Wyoming. (H. H. Roberts) Ann. Am. Acad. Pol. Sci. 18: 556.

—— and Registration Reform. Westm. 156: 68.

—— a Comparative View of the Movement. (F. M. Abbott) No. Am. 166: 142.

—— Effect of Equal Suffrage in Colorado. (V. G. Ellard) Lippinc. 64: 411.

—— Feminism in France. (V. M. Crawford) Fortn. 67: 524.

—— in America, Legal View of. (J. A. Webb) Am. Law R. 31: 404.

—— in England. (E. F. S. Dilke) No. Am. 164: 151. — Sat. R. 83: 136.

—— in New Zealand. (H. H. Lusk) Forum, 23: 173.

——— How the Franchise was secured. Sat. R. 87: 328.

—— in Time of War. (Agnes Grove) Cornh. 82: 210.

—— in the West. Outl. 65: 430.

—— Judicial Sex Bias. Westm. 149: 147, 279.

—— "Let us therewith be Content." (E. C. Elliott) Pop. Sci. Mo. 51: 341.

—— Some Scientific Aspects of. (M. K. Sedgwick) Gunton's M. 20: 333.

— Terms applied to. Acad. 56: 22.

— Training of, for Teachers. (D. Beale) Longm. 30: 333.

— Truth about the Bachelor Girl. (W. Sothern) Munsey, 25: 282.

— "Unclassed," in France and the Colonies. (Count d'Haussonville) Chaut. 28: 76.

— Unmarried, Redundancy of (T. P. W.) Scot. R. 36: 88. Same art. Ecl. M. 136: 77.

— The Unquiet Sex; Women and Reforms. (Helen W. Moody) Scrib. M. 23: 116, 234.

—— Moody on. (H. W. Mabie) Bk. Buyer, 16: 344.

— Wages of. Outl. 63: 533.

—— in Manual Work. (M. B. Hammond) Pol. Sci. Q. 15: 508.

— What are Women striving for? (S. T. Stevenson) Lippinc. 64: 111.

— What Men like in. (H. T. Peck) Cosmopol. 31: 609.

— What they have done for the Public Health. (E. P. Thomson) Forum, 24: 46.

— who have passed as Men. Illus. (M. West) Munsey, 25: 273.

— Womanly. (C. S. Parrish) Indep. 53: 775.

—— Are they doomed? (H. T. Finck) Indep. 53: 267.

— Work of, Unpaid. (J. M. Loes) Canad. M. 17: 78.

—— and Wages of. (E. Whiting) Lippinc. 61: 670.

— Working, Expenditure of Middle Class. (C. E. Collet) Econ. J. 8: 543.

Women, Working; how they live and how they wish to live. (E. Hobhouse) 19th Cent. 47: 471.

—— in Large Cities, Homes for. (Annie M. Maclean) Char. R. 9: 215.

Women are made like that; a story. (E. Hoyt) Harper, 103: 854.

Women, The; a monologue. (R. M. Stuart) Cent. 39: 595.

Women of St. Honoria's; a tale. (J. McCrae) Canad. M. 14: 472.

Women Artists, Paris Club of International. (C. G. Hartley) Art J. 52: 282.

Women Bookbinders, Guild of. (D. M. Sutherland) M. of Art, 23: 420.

Women Duellists. (G. W. Willock) Eng. Illust. 20: 238.

Women Illustrators, American. (R. Armstrong) Critic, 36: 417.

Women Musicians, American. (H. H. Burr) Cosmopol. 31: 357.

Women Poets. Quar. 189: 32. Same art. Liv. Age, 221: 26, 123.

Women Speakers in England. (Frederick Dolman) Cosmopol. 22: 676.

Women Students in Colleges and Universities, Government of. (L. S. B. Saunders) Educa. R. 20: 475.

Women Writers in America, Early. (C. A. Urann) Chaut. 30: 377.

Women's Amateur Musical Club. (Rose F. Thomas) Music, 16: 277.

Women's Club, Building of, in Boston, Proposed. Nat'l M. (Bost.) 7: 468.

— Case of the. (Martha E. D. White) Outl. 59: 479.

Women's Club Movement in London. (Mrs. S. Amos) R. of Rs. (N. Y.) 16: 440.

Women's Clubs. (E. Anstruther) 19th Cent. 45: 598. Same art. Ecl. M. 133: 91. Same art. Liv. Age, 221: 533. — (Amelia G. Mason) Liv. Age, 231: 656. — (M. D. Frazar) Nat'l M. (Bost.) 9: 185. — Scrib. M. 22: 486.

— and Education. (L. G. Crozier) Educa. R. 17: 182.

— and Social Reforms. Gunton's M. 17: 179.

— Bibliography. (C. H. Hastings) Chaut. 31: 14.

— Federation of Iowa. (Harriet C. Towner) Midland, 7: 548.

— General Federation of. (Ellen M. Henrotin) Outl. 55: 442.

—— at Denver, 1898. (Harriet C. Towner) Midland, 10: 161.

— in America. (M. P. Murry) 19th Cent. 47: 846. Same art. Ecl. M. 135: 121. Same art. Liv. Age, 225: 558.

— in Kansas. (Lilian W. Hale) Midland, 7: 422.

— in London. (A. Zimmern) Forum, 22: 684.

— Influence of. (J. M. A. Hawksley) Westm. 153: 455.

— Madam President and her Constituents. (H. C. Candee) Cent. 40: 851.

— Missouri Federation of. (Harriet C. Towner) Midland, 7: 372.

— News about. (Harriet C. Towner) Midland, 9: 82 — 10: 468.

— N. Dakota Federation of. (Mrs. C. E. Conant) Midland, 8: 362.

— of Washington State. (Jennie Simpson-Moore) Midland, 7: 259.

— State Federations of. (Ellen M. Henrotin) R. of Rs. (N. Y.) 16: 437.

— Tennessee Federation of. (Rose Cawood) Midland, 7: 132.

Women's Colleges, Ethical Purpose of. (E. D. Hanscom) Educa. R. 22: 307.

— Life in. (Lavinia Hart) Cosmopol. 31: 188.

— Women Deans of. (J. A. Stewart) Chaut. 33: 486.

Wooed without Words; a story. (J. M. Chapple) Nat'l M. (Bost.) **9**: 230.

Woof of Thin Red Threads; a story. (Stephen Crane) Cosmopol. **26**: 164.

Wooing, The Art of. Atlan. **84**: 287.

Wooing of Aminta, The; a story. (M. L. van Vorst) Pall Mall M. **17**: 217.

Wooing of Em'ly Jane, The. (Eleanor G. Hayden) Cornh. **82**: 649.

Wooing of Jane Harp; a story. (W. Bidwell) Nat'l M. (Bost.) **10**: 638.

Wooing of Malkatoon, The; a narrative poem. (L. Wallace) Harper, **96**: 3.

Wooing of Sara Lepell. (V. A. Simpson) Longm. **35**: 157. Same art. Liv. Age, **224**: 373. Same art. Ecl. M. **134**: 460.

Wooing of the Señorita, The. (M. Austin) Overland, n. s. **29**: 258.

Wool; a Free-wool Lesson from Germany. (W. C. Ford) Nation, **64**: 449.

Wool Exchange at Work, The. (Robt. Donald) Good Words, **39**: 814.

Woolbridge Manor. (S. Beale) Temp. Bar, **120**: 106.

Woolen Industry, The French. (W. C. Ford) Nation, **64**: 410.

Woolens, Homespun, in Ireland. Sat. R. **90**: 325.

Woolgatherers, The; a story. (E. P. Finnemore) Argosy, **73**: 254.

Woolman, John; Social Reformer of the 18th Century. (E. C. Wilson) Econ. R. **11**: 170.

Woolos, St. (S. Baring-Gould) Sund. M. **27**: 438.

Woolsey, Theodore Dwight, Notice of. (J. Cooper) Bib. Sac. **56**: 607.

Woolson, Abba Goold. (E. C. Brown) Nat'l M. (Bost.) **10**: 435.

Worcester, 2d Marquis of, and his " Century of Inventions." (E. Beresford) Argosy, **65**: 664.

Worcester, John, Minister of the New Church. (T. F. Wright) N. Church R. **7**: 436, (James Reed) 481.
— His Life and Work. N. Church R. **8**: 32.

Worcester, Mrs. Theodore, Pianist, with portrait. Music, **19**: 614.

Worcester Cathedral. (T. Teignmouth-Shore) Good Words, **40**: 629, 700.

Worcester, England, Music Festival at. (T. W. Surrette) Lippinc. **65**: 88.

Worcester, Massachusetts. (A. S. Roe) New Eng. M. n. s. **23**: 543.
— Musical Festival. New Eng. M. n. s. **23**: 3. — (H. D. Sleeper) Music, **18**: 583.
— Natural History Society. (H. D. Braman) Am. Natural. **33**: 705.

Worcester Porcelain, Royal. Illus. Artist (N. Y.) **23**: 104. — (P. F. Slater) Good Words, **40**: 663.

Word from Canada; a poem. (F. Sherman) Canad. M. **9**: 324.

Word of an Englishman. (E. Greck) Temp. Bar, **114**: 365. Same art. Liv. Age, **218**: 396.

Words and their Uses, Some. (F. King) Am. Cath. Q. **24**, no. 3: 172.
— Coinage of. (C. Boyle) Macmil. **83**: 327. Same art. Liv. Age. **230**: 298.
— — by Living American Authors. (L. Mead) Chaut. **30**: 131. **33**: 525.
— coined in Boston. (C. W. Ernst) Writer, **12**: 145.
— Index Expurgatorius of, W. C. Bryant's. Acad. **58**: 371. Same art. Liv. Age, **225**: 655.
— Long, Use of. (A. Fosdick) Writer, **14**: 2.
— Naturalization of. (B. Matthews) Liv. Age, **212**: 130.
— New, and Old. (B. Matthews) Harper, **97**: 307.
— of One Kind and Another. (B. Matthews) Bk. Buyer, **17**: 277.

Words, Over-nice Distinctions in. (Myra V. Morys) Writer, **14**: 1.
— A Pinch of Attic Salt. (M. E. Merington) Chaut. **32**: 369.
— Powerful, Misuse of. (C. S. Doolittle) Writer, **14**: 23.
— Precision in the Use of. (A. S. Bryan) Writer, **12**: 81.
— Some True and False Uses of. Acad. **61**: 387.
— Unusual. Acad. **56**: 453.
— Usage in, Questions of. (B. Matthews) Harper, **102**: 431.

Words, Mere Words; a poem. (D. Cave) Gent. M. n. s. **67**: 101.

Wordsworth, Charles, The Episcopate of; a review. Church Q. **48**: 440. — Sat. R. **88**: 303.
— Wordsworth's Life of. (B. B. Warfield) Presb. & Ref. R. **11**: 361.

Wordsworth, John, Bishop of Salisbury, with portraits. Strand, **16**: 534.

Wordsworth, William. (A. P. Peabody) Forum, **23**: 622.
— and the Coleridges, by E. Varnall. Poet-Lore, **11**: 425.
— as a Prose Writer. Acad. **51**: 394.
— Birds of. (J. Hogben) Gent. M. n. s. **60**: 532.
— Knight on. Citizen, **4**: 49.
— Knight's Edition of. Acad. **52**: 176.
— Legouis' Early Life of. Acad. **52**: 233. — (A. B. McMahan) Dial (Ch.) **24**: 179.
— Manuscripts in Possession of T. N. Longman. Sat. R. **83**: 665.
— Poems dedicated to National Independence and Liberty; ed. by Brooke. (J. C. Collins) Sat. R. **84**: 226.
— Poems of Children and Childhood. (F. W. Osborn) Educa. **19**: 93.
— Poetry of, Background of. (H. W. Mabie) Outl. **58**: 591.
— Youth of. (L. Stephen) National, **28**: 769. Same art. Ecl. M. **128**: 514. Same art. Liv. Age, **212**: 859.

Wordsworth's Ode. Liv. Age, **217**: 826.

Work, The Gospel of Intelligent. (T. Roosevelt) Chaut. **30**: 45.
— How to. (F. Max Müller) Fortn. **67**: 194.
— Training the Hands for. (W. C. Whitney) Chaut. **29**: 271.
— What it is. (C. P. Stetson) Cosmopol. **27**: 678.

Workers, The. (W. H. Wyckoff) Scrib. M. **22**: 197 — **24**: 561.
— Wyckoff on. (J. W. Jenks) Citizen, **3**: 262. — (L. F. Abbott) Bk. Buyer, **16**: 140. — Spec. **81**: 181.

Workers' Coöperative Association. (J. P. Putnam) Am. Arch. **70**: 103.

Workhouse, English Country. (S. G. Tallentyre) Macmil. **78**: 219. Same art. Liv. Age, **218**: 583.
— from the Inside. (Edith M. Shaw) Contemp. **76**: 564.
— An Old Folks' Retreat. (Edith Sellers) New R. **17**: 95.

Workhouse Inmates, A Plea for. (Duchess of Somerset) Good Words, **39**: 396.

Workhouses. (V. M. Crawford) Contemp. **75**: 831.

Working out his Salvation. (A. B. Stone) New Eng. M. n. s. **18**: 723.

Working-boys' Clubs and Hooliganism. (E. Morley) Westm. **155**: 560.

Working Class, Incorporation of. (H. McGregor) Forum, **24**: 579.
— Property of. Quar. **189**: 399.

Working Classes, American, How their Condition may be benefited. (F. K. Foster) Forum, **24**: 711.

Yacht Racing for 1901, International. Nat'l M. (Bost.) 16: 655.
— International Cup Races. (J. D. Spears) Outing, 38: 674.
— Old-time Matches. (W. J. Henderson) Outing, 38: 609.
— Why the Yankee Yacht has won. (H. Haff) New Eng. M. n. s. 25: 47.
Yacht-racing Wrinkles. (A. J. Kenealy) Outing, 32: 388.
Yachting. Outing, 36: 440. — (S. E. White) Outing, 36: 258.
— and Yacht Racing. (Clive Holland) Idler, 12: 13.
— British, Effect of America's Cup on. (J. D. Bell) Outing, 38: 658.
— Cookery for. (A. J. Kenealy) Outing, 38: 548.
— Costliest of Sports. (A. F. Aldrich) Munsey, 25: 505.
— Cup Defender, 1901. (C. G. Davis) Outing, 36: 529.
— Duty and Discipline Afloat. (A. J. Kenealy) Outing, 34: 61.
— Evolution of the Yacht Designer: American. (W. P. Stephens) Outing, 39: 223.
— — English. (W. P. Stephens) Outing, 34: 49.
— in England. (R. S. Palmer) Pall Mall M. 12: 379.
— in the Sunny South. (C. H. Glidden) Outing, 32: 136.
— Inland, its Growth and Future. (W. P. Stephens) Outing, 38: 521.
— its Charms and Cost. (A. G. Bagot) Pall Mall M. 22: 110.
— Larchmont Regatta Week. (A. J. Kenealy) Outing, 30: 559.
— New Measurement Rule and some Old Ones. (C. H. Crane) Outing, 38: 690.
— New York Yacht Club August Cruise. (A. J. Kenealy) Outing, 34: 497.
— on the Great Lakes. (J. B. Berryman) Outing, 36: 511.
— on Northwestern Lakes. (W. S. Milnor) Outing, 31: 122.
— Pleasure, Down South. (L. D. Sampsell) Outing, 35: 399, 463.
— Seawanhaka Knockabouts' First Cruise. Outing, 32: 547.
— Trend and Drift of. (A. J. Kenealy) Outing, 31: 233.
— Weather Wrinkles. (A. J. Kenealy) Outing, 36: 616.
— Yarn of the Yampa. (E. L. H. McGinnis) Outing, 32: 449, 561. 33: 25–393.
Yachting Circuit of Lake Erie. (G. F. Flannery) Outing, 30: 355.
Yachting Season of 1901 in Canada. (F. J. Campbell) Canad. M. 18: 44.
Yachts and Designers, Western. (A. J. Pegler) Outing, 30: 3.
— and Freaks of the Season. (A. J. Kenealy) Outing, 30: 468.
— and Yachtsmen. Illus. (Rob. MacIntyre) Good Words, 38: 540.
— Cruising Types for All Waters. (W. P. Stephens) Outing, 36: 379.
— Evolution of the Double-huller. (A. J. Kenealy) Outing, 33: 476.
— New, of 1899. (A. J. Kenealy) Outing, 34: 245.
— New Seventy-footers, 1900. (W. E. Robinson) Outing, 36: 412.
— New Twenty-footers, 1897. (R. B. Burchard) Outing, 30: 333.
— Overhauling. (A. J. Kenealy) Outing, 31: 587. 36: 59.
— Question of. (C. L. Norton) Lippinc. 64: 469.

Yachts, Racing. (R. S. Baker) McClure, 13: 543.
— Steam, Trend of Building. (S. W. Barnaby) Outing, 38: 667.
— What Type? (A. J. Kenealy) Outing, 33: 577.
Yafei and Fadhli Countries, Exploration in. (Mrs. T. Bent) Geog. J. 12: 41.
Yagan, the "Australian Wallace." Chamb. J. 76: 680.
Yahveh and Manitou. Illus. (P. Carus) Monist, 9: 382.
Yak, Wild, Hunting. (W. J. Reid) Outing, 35: 184.
Yale University. (E. Oviatt) New Eng. M. n. s. 25: 426. — (A. R. Kimball) Outl. 62: 771.
— Bicentenary of. (E. P. Clark) Nation, 73: 318. — (L. S. Welsh) Indep. 53: 2348. — (B. Perrin) Atlan. 88: 449. — (A. R. Kimball) Outl. 68: 789. 69: 531.
— Bicentennial Portraits; a poem. (D. N. Beach) Outl. 69: 496.
— Bicentennial Publications. Indep. 53: 2767.
— Curriculum of, 1701–1901. (J. C. Schwab) Educa. R. 22: 1.
— Future of. (J. C. Schwab) Indep. 52: 1849.
— Graduates who are Teachers of Philosophy. Educa. 21: 549, 618.
— Her Campus, Class-rooms, and Athletics, Welch and Camp's. (A. R. Kimball) Bk. Buyer, 18: 459.
— Life at, 1818–20. (A. L. Hill) New Eng. M. n. s. 15: 756.
— New. (H. A. Smith) World's Work, 1: 253.
— Relation of, to Letters and Science. (D. C. Gilman) Science, n. s. 14: 665.
— — to Medicine. (W. H. Welch) Science, n. s. 14: 825.
— The Spirit of. Outl. 69: 529.
— Undergraduate Life at. (H. E. Howland) Scrib. M. 22: 1.
Yale Habit. (R. Clapp) New Eng. M. n. s. 22: 181.
Yale Pedigree. (C. H. Townshend) N. E. Reg. 53: 83.
Yamhill Country, the Richest Section of the Pacific Coast. (R. L. Fulton) Overland, n. s. 29: 498.
Yancey, William Lowndes, the Orator of Secession. (W. G. Brown) Atlan. 83: 605.
Yangchow, Sack of, in 1644. (R. K. Douglas) 19th Cent. 45: 486.
Yang-tze-kiang, The. (W. R. Carles) Geog. J. 12: 225.
— Cruising up the. (E. R. Scidmore) Cent. 36: 668.
— New Rapid of. Geog. J. 10: 191.
— The River of Tea. (E. R. Scidmore) Cent. 36: 547.
— Upper, Crux of the. (A. Little) Geog. J. 18: 498.
Yang-tze-kiang Basin and the British Sphere in China. (A. Little) J. Soc. Arts, 47: 77.
Yang-tze Holocaust, A; a story. (C. W. Mason) Eng. Illust. 20: 377.
Yang-tze Valley and British Commerce. (A. Barton) Asia. R. 26: 62.
— and Beyond. (Mrs. J. F. Bishop) Nature, 61: 252.
— Mrs. Bishop's. (W. E. Griffis) Nation, 70: 403. — Ath. '99, 2: 713.
Yankee Farmer in Florida. (R. G. Robinson) Lippinc. 69: 858.
Yarn, A; a poem. (C. E. Meetkerke) Argosy, 64: 640.
Yarrow, Alfred Fernandez. Cassier, 13: 83.
"Yashima," the Japanese Battleship. (E. H. T. D'Eyncourt) Cassier, 13: 275.
Yatton Church Tower. Ath. '00, 2: 129.
Yaw, Ellen Beach, with portraits. (M. D. Griffith) Strand, 17: 730.
Year, Season of. (Grant Allen) Longm. 31: 447.
Year of Jubilee and its Past History. (H. Thurston) Month, 95: 48.
Year of Nobility, A; a story. (H. van Dyke) McClure, 17: 348.
Year Books, English, Manuscripts of. (L. O. Pike) Green Bag, 12: 533.

Yeast and Alcoholic Fermentation. (J. R. Green) Nature, 57: 591.

Yeatman, James E., a Great Citizen, with portrait. R. of Rs. (N. Y.) 24: 186.

Yeats, Wm. Butler. (W. N. Guthrie) Sewanee, 9: 328.

— Countess Cathleen. (M. Beerbohm) Sat. R. 87: 586.

— Poetry of. Acad. 56: 501. — (A. Symons) Sat. R. 87: 553.

— The Wind among the Reeds. Acad. 58: 63.

Yellow Burgee, a yarn of the Spanish War. (C. B. Fernald) Cent. 34: 866.

Yellow China Dog, The; a story. (M. C. Huntington) Outl. 61: 359.

Yellow Fever. Science, n. s. 13: 513.

— Etiology of. (E. Klein) Nature, 56: 249.

— Sanarelli's Work on. (E. O. Jordan) Science, 6: 981.

— Scientific Prevention of. (A. H. Doty) No. Am. 167: 681.

— Transmission of, by Mosquitoes. (G. M. Sternberg) Pop. Sci. Mo. 59: 225.

Yellow Fever Epidemic, Some Lessons of. (Walter Wyman) Forum, 24: 282.

Yellow Gold; a story. (W. Kendrick) Belgra. 95: 97.

Yellow Journalism, Responsibility for. (E. P. Clark) Nation, 73: 238.

Yellow Ned and his Freedom Papers. (E. Deveaux) New Eng. M. n. s. 16: 432.

Yellowstone, Trout Fishing in. (M. T. Townsend) Outing, 30: 163.

Yellowstone National Park. (W. D. Van Blaram) Nat'l M. (Bost.) 6: 541. — (J. Muir) Atlan. 81: 509.

— as a Summer Resort. (H. T. Finck) Nation, 71: 248.

— Camp and Cycle in. (W. W. Thayer) Outing, 32: 17.

— Driving and Fishing in. (F. B. King) Overland, n. s. 29: 594.

— in 1897. (H. T. Finck) Nation, 65: 276.

— Through, on Foot. (C. H. Henderson) Outing, 34: 161.

— Vegetation of Hot Springs of. (B. M. Davis) Science, 6: 145.

Yenisei, Up the. (G. F. Wright) Nation, 71: 285.

Yeomanry, The. (R. H. Carr-Ellison) Un. Serv. M. 24: 48.

— Future of. (F. Green) Un. Serv. M. 20: 607. 22: 288.

Yerkes Observatory. Dial (Ch.) 23: 237. — (Gertrude Bacon) Good Words, 42: 85. — (E. B. Frost) Science, 6: 721. — (W. W. Payne) Pop. Astron. 5: 115.

— Dedication of. (W. W. Payne) Pop. Astron. 5: 340. — (D. P. Todd) Nation, 65: 391.

Yermak, Ice-breaker. (Admiral Makaroff) Geog. J. 15: 32.

Yersin, Dr., and Plague Virus. (G. C. Frankland) Nature, 55: 378.

Yew-trees of Great Britain. Acad. 52: 66.

Yiddish Literature. Scot. R. 36: 44.

— in the 19th Century, Wiener's. Sat. R. 88: 175. — Acad. 57: 229.

Yo Espero; a story. (R. W. Chambers) Scrib. M. 21: 413.

Yoga Philosophy, Vivikânanda's. (C. H. Hinton) Citizen, 3: 62.

Yohn, F. C., Artist. (A. B. Paine) Brush & P. 2: 161.

Yonge, Charlotte Mary. (E. H. Cooper) Fortn. 75: 852. — Quar. 194: 520. — With portrait. (Mary K. Seeger) Bookman, 13: 218. — Liv. Age, 229: 320. — (C. R. Coleridge) Sund. M. 30: 335.

— as a Chronicler. (Edith Sichel) Monthly R. 3, no. 2: 88. Same art. Ecl. M. 137: 189. Same art. Liv. Age, 229: 783.

Yonge, Charlotte Mary. Heir of Redclyffe. Acad. 57: 87.

— Interview with. (F. D. How) Sund. M. 30: 437.

Yonkers, N. Y., Housing of Working-people in. (E. L. Bogart) Econ. Stud. 3: 273.

York, Duke of. See George Frederick, Prince of Wales.

York in the 16th and 17th Centuries. (M. Sellers) Eng. Hist. R. 12: 437.

York, Three Ancient Churches at. (D. A. Walter) Antiq. n. s. 33: 174, 205, 232.

Yorkshire, Emigration from, to West Jersey, 1677. Am. Hist. R. 2: 472.

— Picturesque. (J. Telford) Lond. Q. 94: 228.

Yorkshire Moor, A. (L. C. Miall) Nature, 58: 377.

Yosemite, Among the Animals of the. (J. Muir) Atlan. 82: 617.

— Among the Birds of the. (J. Muir) Atlan. 82: 751.

— in a Dry Year. (C. S. Greene) Overland, n. s. 32: 99.

Yosemite Legends; a poem. (C. A. Vivian) Overland, n. s. 37: 1068.

Yosemite National Park. (J. Muir) Atlan. 84: 145.

— Forests of. (J. Muir) Atlan. 85: 493.

— Fountains and Streams of. (J. Muir) Atlan. 87: 556.

— The Wild Gardens of. (J. Muir) Atlan. 86: 167.

Yosemites, Some New. (T. S. Solomons) Overland, n. s. 29: 68.

"You-all." (M. F. Steele) Nation, 68: 396. — Nation, 68: 436.

You leave no room to mourn; a poem. (H. Hawthorne) Atlan. 86: 843.

You Sing. (F. T. Bullen) Chamb. J. 77: 8–61.

"You-Uns." Nation, 68: 476.

Youghal on the Blackwater. (H. Elrington) Reliquary, 37: 151.

Youlgreave, Eng.; National History and a Village Log. (John Hyde) Gent. M. n. s. 59: 73.

Young, Rev. Alfred, with portrait. Cath. World, 71: 257.

Young, Arthur. Acad. 53: 167.

— at the Society of Arts. J. Soc. Arts, 48: 879.

— Autobiography, ed. by Edwards. Spec. 80: 201. — Sat. R. 85: 498. — Ath. '98, 1: 176.

Young, Paganism of the. Outl. 61: 672. — (F. Palmer) New World, 6: 695.

Young April; a story. (E. Castle) Temp. Bar, 115: 321. 116: 135–590. 117: 128–435.

Young, Bridget, First Wife of Gov. Wyllys, and her Family. N. E. Reg. 53: 217.

Young Homesteaders, The; a story of Dakota. (F. W. Calkins) Midland, 7: 68, 170, 238.

Young Man from the Country; a story. (Brander Matthews) Cosmopol. 25: 527.

Young-man-leading-a-cow and Weaving-girl. (Evelyn H. Browne) Overland, n. s. 36: 259.

Young Martinet; a story. (P. W. Hart) Canad. M. 17: 557.

Young Men; are their Chances Less? (H. H. Lewis) World's Work, 1: 170.

Y. M. C. A., Army and Navy. (A. Shaw) R. of Rs. (N. Y.) 18: 529.

— as an Essential Factor in American Education. (E. L. Shuey) Educa. 21: 557.

— Fifty Years of, in America. (J. H. Ross) New Eng. M. n. s. 24: 373.

— in Europe. (W. S. Harwood) Cent. 40: 273.

— Jubilee of. (L. L. Doggett) No. Am. 172: 882. — (J. M. Whiton) Outl. 68: 586.

— Public Libraries and. (G. B. Hodge) Lib. J. 25: 733.

Young Socialist, A. Temp. Bar, 117: 553.

Young Squire, The; a poem. (T. Roberts) Canad. M. 9: 330.

Youngest Son of his Father's House; a poem. (A. H. Branch) Atlan. 82: 110.

Youth, Gayety of. (H. Fouquier) Liv. Age, 229: 56.

— Persistence of. (G. S. Street) Cornh. 84: 514. Same art. Liv. Age, 231: 569.

— Respect Due to. (Charlotte P. Gilman) Liv. Age, 228: 594.

— vs. Age. Spec. 80: 402.

Youth; a narrative. (J. Conrad) Blackw. 164: 309.

Youth; a poem. (A. L. Salmon) Gent. M. n. s. 61: 412.

Ysaye, Eugene, as a Musical Conductor. (J. F. Runciman) Sat. R. 90: 549, 679.

Yukon, Basin of, Geography and Resources of. (W. Ogilvie) Geog. J. 12: 21.

— Gold Fields of. (M. R. Davies) Good Words, 39: 555. — Chamb. J. 74: 609. — (G. F. Wright) Nation, 65: 105. — (J. Brigham) Midland, 8: 260.

— — Discoverer of the. (W. R. Quinan) Overland, n. s. 30: 340.

— — Future of. (W. H. Dall) Nat. Geog. M. 9: 117.

— — Output of. (F. Crissey) Midland, 8: 545.

— — Route to. (Mrs. F. Schwatka) Midland, 8: 395.

— — Story of. (T. Evans) Overland, n. s. 30: 330.

— — A Voice from. (C. Middleton) Sund. M. 27: 180.

— Northwest Passes to. Illus. (Eliza R. Scidmore) Nat. Geog. M. 9: 105.

— Overland to. (C. E. Mitchell) Overland, n. s. 31: 206.

Yukon Country, The. (P. T. Rowe) Chaut. 28: 355.

Yukon River Murders. (H. J. Woodside) Canad. M. 18: 108.

Yukon Romance; a story. (C. L. Shaw) Canad. M. 10: 427.

Yukon Trail, Life on a. (Arthur P. Dennis) Nat. Geog. M. 10: 377.

Yule and Christmas, Tille's. (W. H. Carpenter) Nation, 70: 420.

Yuma Trail, The Old. (W. J. McGee) Nat. Geog. M. 12: 103, 129.

Yumoto and its Surroundings. (G. B. Wolseley) Temp. Bar, 112: 200.

Yuste, Convent of. (C. Edwardes) Macmil. 76: 370. Same art. Liv. Age, 215: 193.

Zacharias; Matt. xxiii. 35. (J. Macpherson) Bib. World, 9: 26.

Zack, pseud. See Keats, Gwendoline.

Zahn, Otto, and his Bindings, with Portrait. (W. G. Bowdoin) Artist (N. Y.) 30: 16. — (W. Malone) Bk. Buyer, 16: 122.

Zaitha, Egg-carrying Habit of. (F. W. Slater) Am. Natural. 33: 931.

— Genital Organs of. (T. H. Montgomery) Am. Natural. 35: 119.

Zamora, Spain. (Mrs. M. L. Woods) Cornh. 80: 289.

Zamore, Louis. (A. H. Diplock) Temp. Bar, 118: 403.

Zangwill, Israel. (A. Tierney) Lit. W. (Bost.) 28: 356. — With portrait. (I. Harris) Bookman, 7: 104. Same art. condensed. Acad. 53: 419. — (H. Garland) Conserv. R. 2: 404.

— Art of. Acad. 58: 99, 129.

— Children of the Ghetto. (A. Cahan) Forum, 28: 503. — (M. Beerbohm) Sat. R. 88: 763.

— Egoism of. Sat. R. 83: 238.

— The Mantle of Elijah. Acad. 59: 466. — Ed. R. 193: 158.

— Without Prejudice. Critic, 30: 141.

Zanze's Festival; a tale. (W. L. Alden) Belgra. 93: 369.

Zanzibar, Bombardment of. (R. D. Mohun) Cosmopol. 25: 157.

Zanzibar Slave: his Condition and Prospects. (S. D. Gordon) Belgra. 95: 125.

Zanzibar Slavery. (S. D. Gordon) Chamb. J. 74: 475. — Sat. R. 84: 5, 27.

Zarza, Samuel, Shullam's Report of the Burning of. (D. Kaufmann) Jew. Q. 11: 658.

Zebras, Wild and Tame. Spec. 86: 651.

Zechariah and Haggai, Religious Teachings of. (T. D. Anderson) Bib. World, 14: 195.

Zeeman Effect. (H. M. Reese) Science, n. s. 12: 293.

Zehden, Karl. Geog. J. 18: 223.

Zekenim, or Council of Elders. (D. W. Amram) J. Bib. Lit. 19: 34.

Zeno, Nicolo and Antonio, Lucas's. (B. F. DeCosta) Am. Hist. R. 4: 726. — (B. A. Hinsdale) Dial (Ch.) 26: 240. — (C. R. Beazley) Geog. J. 13: 166. — (G. P. Winship) Nation, 68: 70.

Zephaniah, Royal Ancestry of. (G. B. Gray) Expos. 8: 76.

Zero, Absolute; the Scientist's Ultima Thule. (W. C. Peckham) Cent. 35: 877.

Zeuner Diagram. (W. Fox) J. Frankl. Inst. 145: 387, 447.

Zeus, Birth-cave of. (D. G. Hogarth) Monthly R. 2: no. 1: 49.

— Statue of, at Olympia. (B. I. Wheeler) Cent. 34: 494.

Zike Mouldom; a story. (O. Angus) Cornh. 78: 695, 828.

Zimmermann, Dr. Robert A. T. Ath. '98, 2: 355.

Zinc Mines at Franklin, N. J., New Minerals from. (S. L. Penfield and C. H. Warren) Am. J. Sci. 158: 339.

Zinc-mining. Illus. (F. Eberle) Cosmopol. 27: 599.

— in the United States. (D. A. Willey) Cassier, 20: 331.

Zionism. (R. Gotthiel) Cent. 37: 299. — (I. Zangwill) Contemp. 76: 500. Same art. Lippinc. 64: 577. — (J. Lazarus) New World, 8: 228. — (G. Deutsch) New World, 8: 242. — (R. Gotthiel) No. Am. 169: 227. — (H. P. Mendes) No. Am. 167: 200. — (A. White) Contemp. 72: 733. — (E. Reich) 19th Cent. 42: 260.

— Philo-Zionists and Anti-Semites. (H. Bentwich) 19th Cent. 42: 623.

— Progress of. (H. Bentwich) Fortn. 70: 928.

— The Truth about. (M. Gaster) Forum, 29: 230.

Zionist Conference at Basle, 1897. (H. P. Mendes) No. Am. 167: 625. — Chr. Lit. 17: 446. — (T. Herzl) Contemp. 72: 587. — Pub. Opin 23: 369.

Zionist Movement and Return of Jews to Palestine. (M. Gaster) Asia. R. 24: 301.

Zionists, The. (C. R. Conder) Blackw. 163: 598.

Zircon, Twined Crystals of, from North Carolina. (W. E. Hidden and J. H. Pratt) Am. J. Sci. 156: 323.

Zirconium, Double Fluorides of, with Lithium, Sodium, and Thallium. (H. L. Wells and H. W. Foote) Am. J. Sci. 153: 466.

Zoch, Hermann E., Pianist, with portrait. Music, 19: 292.

Zodiac, Signs of, Origin of. (R. Brown) Archæol. 47: 337.

Zodiacal Coins of the Emperor Jahāngīr. (E. W. Maunder) Knowl. 22: 155.

Zodiacal Light. (E. E. Markwick) Knowl. 20: 51.

— Photographs of. (A. E. Douglass) Pop. Astron. 8: 174. 9: 190.

Zola, Emile. (F. B. de Bury) Scot. R. 35: 89. — (A. MacDonald) Open Court, 12: 467. — With portrait. (W. Littlefield) Book R. 5: 343.

Zola, Emile, and the Dreyfus Case. (T. T. Bouvé) Nat'l M. (Bost.) 9: 211.
— and Literary Naturalism. (B. W. Wells) Sewanee, 1: 385.
— as an Apostle of Temperance. (V. Wilker) Lippinc. 62: 122.
— as a Moralist. (Edouard Rod) Liv. Age, 222: 137. Same art. Ecl. M. 133: 341.
— Brunetière on. Lit. W. (Bost.) 28: 160.
— Dr. Pascal. (F. M. Colby) Bookman, 8: 239.
— Fécondité. Acad. 57: 542. — Sat. R. 88: 523.
— — vs. Tolstoi's Kreutzer Sonata. (H. Lynch) Fortn. 73: 69.
— In the Days of my Youth. Bookman, 14: 343.
— One of his Hiding-places. (H. C. Shelley) Eng. Illust. 22: 110.
— Paris. Acad. 53: 279, 297, 330. — (S. H. Swinny) Westm. 150: 47. — Spec. 80: 378.
— Social Psychology in Contemporary French Fiction. (L. Marillier) Fortn. 76: 520.
— Trial of. (E. Stocquart) Am. Law R. 32: 249.
— — and of Dreyfus. (J. T. Morse, jr.) Atlan. 81: 589.
— — and the Anti-Jewish Crusade in France. R. of Rs. (N. Y.) 17: 309.
— — and the French Republic. (F. W. Whitridge) Pol. Sci. Q. 13: 259.
— — Some Notes on. (D. C. Murray) Contemp. 73: 481. Same art. Ecl. M. 130: 698.
Zollverein in Central Europe. (G. de Molinari) Gunton's M. 12: 38.
"Zoo," Children and the. Spec. 80: 820.
— for New York. Spec. 80: 788.
— The National, at Washington. (E. Seton Thompson) Cent. 37: 649. 38: 1.
— on Wheels. (Y. Stewart) Eng. Illust. 16: 487.
Zoos, Private. (F. G. Aflalo) Pall Mall M. 25: 77.
Zoölogical Club, University of Chicago. (C. M. Child) Science, n. s. 13: 1026. 14: 28.
Zoölogical Congress, Fifth International. Science, n. s. 14: 405.
Zoölogical Field-work. Importance of establishing Place-modes. (C. D. Davenport) Science, n. s. 9: 415.
Zoölogical Gardens, London. (C. Monkhouse) Art J. 49: 225.
— Cramped Quarters for Animals. Sat. R. 91: 365, 397.
— Needed Comfort for Animals. Sat. R. 91: 433.
Zoölogical Nomenclature, Some Disputed Points in. (R. Lydekker) Nature, 63: 348.
Zoölogical Park, New York. (W. T. Hornaday) Cent. 39: 85.

Zoölogical Science at Oxford. (G. C. Brodrick) Sat. R. 89: 331.
Zoölogy and the Australian Museums. Nature, 61: 275.
— as a Higher Study. (E. R. Lankester) Nature, 58: 25.
— Beddard's Elementary. (C. W. Dodge) Science, n. s. 9: 329.
— Brooks's Foundations of. (D. S. Jordan) Science, n. s. 9: 529.
— Economic, False Premises in. (S. N. Rhoads) Am. Natural. 32: 571.
— Emery's Zoölogia. Am. Natural. 33: 890.
— for the High-school and College Curriculum, Differentiation of. (H. L. Osborn) School R. 9: 566.
— 4th Internat. Congress of, Cambridge, Eng., 1898. Knowl. 21: 226. — Nat. Sci. 13: 259.
— Half Century of Evolution with Special Reference to Effects of Geological Changes on Animal Life. (A. S. Packard) Am. Natural. 32: 623.
— in Secondary Schools. (G. R. Wieland) Educa. 18: 165.
— Kingsley's American Text-book of. (R. Lydekker) Nature, 63: 556.
— Literary Influence of Mediæval. (O. Kuhns) Poet-Lore, 11: 73.
— of the 20th Century. (C. B. Davenport) Science, n. s. 14: 315. Same art. Nature, 64: 566.
— Parker and Haswell's. Am. Natural. 32: 787. — Sci. Prog. 7: xiii.
— Recent Advances in. Nature, 63: 58.
— Schmeil's Text-book of. (R. Lydekker) Nature, 63: 321.
— Sedgwick's Text-book of. (E. R. Lankester) Nature, 58: 147. — Sci. Prog. 7: xxiv.
— Teaching. Advances in Methods. (E. G. Conklin) Science, n. s. 9: 81.
Zoroaster and the Logos. (L. H. Mills) Am. J. Philol. 22: 432.
— Prophet of Ancient Iran. (J. Beames) Asia. R. 29: 108.
Zuchtman, Prof. Friedrich; the American Music System. (W. S. B. Mathews) Music, 12: 260.
Zuleta, The. (C. B. Acheson) Overland, n. s. 38: 41.
Zulu War, 1879. (P. W. Barrow) Un. Serv. M. 16: 190.
— — Reminiscences. (C. E. Fripp) Pall Mall M. 20: 547.
Zulus of South Africa. Canad. M. 15: 551.
— Sunday among the. (A. Werner) Sund. M. 27: 577.
Zunser, Eliakim. (H. Hapgood) Critic, 36: 250.
Zurich Federal Polytechnic School. Nature, 55: 537.
Zwingli, Heuldreich. (C. Cleaver) Ref. Ch. R. 48: 30. — Sat. R. 87: 618.

UNIVERSITY OF WOLVERHAMPTON
LEARNING & INFORMATION SERVICES